THE USES OF SOCIOLOGY

THE
USES
OF
SOCIOLOGY

PAUL F. LAZARSFELD

WILLIAM H. SEWELL

HAROLD L. WILENSKY

editors

B A S I C   B O O K S, *Inc.*, *Publishers*
N E W   Y O R K

TO
ROBERT S. LYND
AUTHOR OF *Knowledge for What?*

The Authors

MARK ABRAMS is Chairman, Research Services Ltd., London

ROBERT C. ANGELL is Professor of Sociology, The University of Michigan, Ann Arbor

KURT W. BACK is Professor of Sociology, Duke University, Durham, N.C.

DAVID J. BORDUA is Associate Professor of Sociology, University of Illinois, Urbana

RAYMOND V. BOWERS is Professor and Chairman, Department of Sociology, University of Arizona, Fayetteville

MARVIN BRESSLER is Professor of Sociology, Princeton University

W. PHILLIPS DAVISON is Visiting Professor of Sociology and Coordinator of the Russell Sage Program in Journalism and the Behavioral Sciences at the Graduate School of Journalism, Columbia University, New York

YEHEZKEL DROR is Head, Public Administration Division, Department of Political Science, The Hebrew University, Jerusalem

AMITAI W. ETZIONI is Professor of Sociology, Columbia University, New York

JOSHUA A. FISHMAN is Professor of Psychology, Yeshiva University, New York

HERBERT J. GANS is Senior Research Sociologist, Center for Urban Education, and Adjunct Professor of Sociology and Education, Teachers College, Columbia University, New York

NATHAN GLAZER is Professor of Sociology, University of California, Berkeley

CHARLES Y. GLOCK is Professor of Sociology, University of California, Berkeley

NEAL GROSS is Professor of Education and Sociology, Graduate School of Education, Harvard University, Cambridge

PHILIP M. HAUSER is Professor of Sociology and Director, Population Research and Training Center and Chicago Community Inventory, The University of Chicago

HERBERT H. HYMAN is Professor of Sociology, Columbia University, New York

MARTIN D. HYMAN is Research Associate, Cornell Medical College, New York

ANNE JARDIM is Research Assistant, Graduate School of Business, Harvard University, Cambridge

ALFRED J. KAHN is Professor of Social Policy and Social Welfare, School of Social Work, Columbia University, New York

JUDITH R. KRAMER is Assistant Professor of Sociology, Brooklyn College

PAUL F. LAZARSFELD is Quételet Professor of Social Science at Columbia University

EUGENE LITWAK is Professor of Social Welfare Research, School of Social Work, The University of Michigan, Ann Arbor

CHARLES P. LOOMIS is Research Professor of Sociology, Michigan State University, East Lansing

ZONA KEMP LOOMIS is Research Associate, Department of Sociology, Michigan State University, East Lansing

ELMER LUCHTERHAND is Research Director, Community Progress, Inc., New Haven, Connecticut, and Research Associate, Department of Sociology, Yale University

HENRY J. MEYER is Professor of Social Work and of Sociology, The University of Michigan, Ann Arbor

WILBERT E. MOORE is a sociologist with the Russell Sage Foundation

FRANCESCO M. NICOSIA is Associate Professor of Business Administration and Research Associate, Survey Research Center, University of California, Berkeley

HAROLD L. ORBACH is Lecturer in Sociology, The University of Michigan, Flint, Michigan

THOMAS F. PETTIGREW is Associate Professor of Social Psychology, Harvard University, Cambridge

ALBERT J. REISS, JR., is Professor and Chairman of the Department of Sociology, The University of Michigan, Ann Arbor

JOHN W. RILEY, JR., is Vice President and Director of Social Research, The Equitable Life Assurance Society of the United States

ARNOLD M. ROSE is Professor of Sociology, University of Minnesota, Minneapolis

WILLIAM H. SEWELL is Chancellor of the University of Wisconsin, Madison

HAROLD L. SHEPPARD is Staff Social Scientist, W. E. Upjohn Institute for Employment Research, Washington, D.C.

NEIL J. SMELSER is Professor of Sociology, University of California, Berkeley

GORDON F. STREIB is Professor of Sociology, Cornell University, Ithaca

EDWIN J. THOMAS is Professor and Head of the Human Behavior and Social Environment Sequence, School of Social Work, and Professor, Department of Psychology, The University of Michigan, Ann Arbor

ROBERT D. VINTER is Associate Dean and Professor of Social Work, The University of Michigan, Ann Arbor

HAROLD L. WILENSKY is Professor in the Department of Sociology and Research Sociologist in the Institute of Industrial Relations, University of California, Berkeley

CHARLES R. WRIGHT is Professor of Sociology, University of California, Los Angeles

ABRAHAM ZALEZNIK is Professor of Organizational Behavior, Graduate School of Business Administration, Harvard University, Cambridge

HANS ZEISEL is Professor of Sociology, The University of Chicago

Introduction

PAUL F. LAZARSFELD

WILLIAM H. SEWELL

HAROLD L. WILENSKY

In 1962 the American Sociological Association devoted a major part of its annual convention to the topic "The Uses of Sociology." The then president of the Association, in communications to the session chairmen and in the printed program, explained the reason for this choice and at the same time tried to provide a workable definition of the term "uses":

> Doubt is often raised as to whether the rapidly mounting stream of empirical studies and the increasing number of publications on social theory have contributed to anything the educated citizen would find worthwhile. . . .
> The rapid expansion of sociology, both in number of sociologists and in the growth of research, makes its uses a matter of special concern. We do not want to create expectations which we cannot fulfill, nor do we want to be excluded from the present surge of interest in scientific activities in the country. . . .
> I hope that something like a spectrum of utility will develop that leads from the use of social theory in neighboring fields, such as history and economics, at the one end, to the utilization of particular empirical research by agencies wanting to pursue a concrete goal more effectively, at the other end.

After the convention, the A.S.A. appointed the editors of this volume as a committee to prepare a book on the theme, a kind of sequel to the product of the 1957 convention, *Sociology Today*.[1] The authors invited to contribute to the book received a detailed guide in which we emphasized the need to avoid fruitless controversies and to balance intraprofessional biases. Also we did not construe "uses" as "applied sociology" in its narrowest form, but instead framed the broader question: "Where and how have sociological perspectives and findings penetrated modern society and with what effect?" The first group of requirements for the papers stressed "the use of sociological theories and concepts"; only the second dealt with "the use of actual studies." Others underscore "the use of research techniques" and the possible importance of "the sociological mode of thought." The list of suggestions ended with a section on what we considered the most important issue, "the mutual relations of research and policy." The two central questions deserve emphasis:

What are the difficulties of translating practical issues into research problems?

What are the unavoidable intellectual gaps between research findings and advice for action?

Finally, we stressed the importance of concrete examples; one of our concerns was to discover how the behavior of sociologists who held public office was affected by their sociological training.

In retrospect the guide had one shortcoming. Our forty-one authors shared no more than a general perspective and were not bound by a formal scheme for analysis. Although they provided a rich store of material, they inevitably produced chapters that were only loosely comparable. In this introduction we draw on our authors' contributions to construct a paradigm for the understanding of the uses of sociology; we hope that it will help the reader select from the contributions those elements which are most appropriate for his purpose. The introduction proceeds in two steps: first we sketch out briefly the structure as it emerged; then we present a more detailed discussion which should help the reader utilize the following pages most efficiently—either as a teacher, as a consulting sociologist, or as a critic of the chapters in this volume.

On the one side is the person or the agency engaged in action, setting general policies, making day-to-day decisions. This person or agency can be designated as the "client." On the other side is the sociologist. *The collaboration or lack of collaboration between client and sociologist is the central focus of this volume.*

A number of *major themes* derive from this formulation. The sociologist can play a variety of *roles* in relation to the client: he can share whatever general wisdom he has acquired; he can do a special study; he can sensitize personnel to sociological orientations. Sometimes he will assume the stance of general social critic. The sociologist has at his disposal a variety of *resources*. He has developed concepts and empirical generalizations, and sometimes theories. His techniques and experience are needed for specific studies—custom-tailored to the problem at hand. Finally, like all experts, he has encountered other situations seemingly very different from those in which the client finds himself which provide unexpected analogies—a major way to broaden the range of alternatives policy-makers perceive.

The client (sponsor, agency, or whatever other name we give him) is confronted with various *types of problems*. He may hope to persuade people to do something for their good or for his own profit. He may have a complex plan the implications of which require sociological knowledge. Organizational clients who have operational deficiencies may either expect the sociologist to discover the source of their trouble or, if it is known, to find a remedy. Occasionally the client will even collaborate with the sociologist in the formulation of goals—so that the sociologist can help him anticipate the various consequences of alternative decisions. The client may also want, or should want, to evaluate the merits of some past decision in order to improve future ones.

Between client and sociologist essentially *two types of intellectual communications* are needed. First, the sociologist must understand the client's problem; in some way he must *translate a practical issue into a research problem*. Second, if relevant knowledge is available, it almost never leads to just one piece of advice or points unequivocally to one line of action; additional conjectures are needed to make the *leap over the gap from knowledge to decision*. The problems of translation and gap are correlative, and the study of their formal nature is perhaps the greatest difficulty facing a theory of utilization.

Collaboration between the client and the sociologist does not take place in a void. The parties meet each other in an *administrative setting* which itself structures their relationship. The organization that relies mainly on outside research groups will develop traditions different from those of an organization with its own social research department. A government agency that allocates money for the study of public health education will greatly influence the intellectual work of the sociologist merely by deciding whether a grant should be made for two years or for six. The sociological curriculum of a graduate school will be quite different according to whether the university has social research centers available for contracts, and, if so, how they are organized and financed.

Finally, there remains a set of problems which can be summarized by Merton's term *sociological ambivalence*. Unavoidable misunderstandings and *conflicts of interests* will develop between the sociologist and the client just because they belong to different occupational groups. *Tensions within the profession* develop because sociologists take very different positions in regard to utilization and its place in the education of novice sociologists. Also, there are *value problems* which always crop up when scientists relate their knowledge to practical pursuits.

The scheme relating these various elements can be summarized in the following graph.

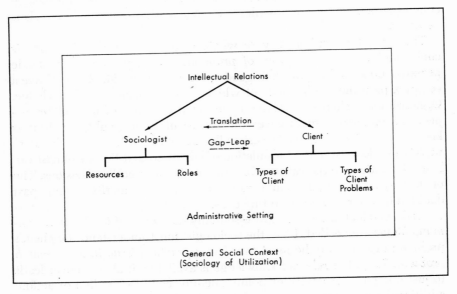

For each sector of this scheme we shall now discuss some of the issues which require special attention. One can debate under what category a concrete example belongs. But that does not matter so long as the reader regards the outline as a temporary organizing device.

Types of Problems Facing the Client

In principle, sociological contributions can be made at every phase of the decision process. Can the sociologist contribute to the initial phase, the setting of goals, or is he restricted to implementation? The question has moral overtones which can lead to acrimonious disputes. Actually, the very distinction creates logical difficulties. Means and ends are relative notions; what is the end in one context may be the means to reach a still broader end. Especially when social change is involved, targets are usually very broad: eliminate poverty at home, decrease the danger of war, help underdeveloped countries. If sociological ideas and studies can help to spell out alternatives or specify new ways to proceed, then it is reasonable to think of that as part of the *goal-setting* itself. Some of the contributions in this volume provide appropriate examples.

Gans (pp. 438–448) describes in detail how the tradition of social service to individuals or families was broadened to encompass the whole idea of community development. Not only were employment opportunities provided but an effort was made to encourage underprivileged individuals to take advantage of these opportunities. Sheppard (pp. 549–554, esp. 551–553) gives evidence of the ways in which policies regarding economically blighted areas have changed. Instead of relying on individual migration to more favorable regions, planners now more often consider the alternative of redeveloping the depressed areas themselves through financial assistance as well as through stimulation of local leadership. It is doubtful, however, that we yet know the full costs and benefits of community development relative to a policy of out-migration. Both Gans and Sheppard show that sociological ideas and studies have been very influential, although the authors are not explicit about the role of individual sociologists.

Between the problem of "what to do" and "how to do it" we can locate a situation where the client turns to the sociologist and asks, "Where am I?" Such clients are frequently organizational leaders who benefit from the kind of general sociological analysis that catalogues typical problems and weighs the consequences of various proposed solutions.

Thus Meyer *et al.* provide a careful analysis of social welfare organizations. Such agencies face three types of problems: the relation between client and social worker; the relation between the various components of the organization itself, the helping professions, the administrators, the donors; and the relation between the various welfare agencies within a community. Similar work is traditional in the field of business management. Zaleznik and Jardim give an up-to-date review of where the matter stands and bring out interesting ties to the sociological literature on leadership and, incidentally, to writings of political scientists. In the spirit of this volume one might talk here of *anticipatory utilization.* Probably the outstanding example, traced in the chapter by Pettigrew and Back, comes from the area of race relations.

Still, most of the chapters in this volume deal with the *implementation* of goals, which reflects, we think, the prevailing uses of sociology. The clients are more apt to be organizations rather than individuals. As such, they are concerned either with the efficiency of their operations (internal problems) or with their relation to the public, be it customers in the commercial sense or special groups they wish to serve (external problems). A surprising number of our contributors mention efforts to persuade or to evoke participation in an activity of the organization. At one time those activities would have been considered the domain of the psychologist. Today, more and more sociologists are called in for help because the collective aspect of attitude formation has become apparent and structural explanations of recalcitrance among subordinates or among rank-and-file members have become more widely known. Persuading farmers to accept innovations (Loomis and Loomis, pp. 661–668) and inducing low-income groups to utilize health facilities (Suchman, pp. 585–587, esp. 586) are typical instances. The identification of appropriate channels of communications is often a major part of this work. Litwak and Meyer analyze in detail the ways in which a school can reach a family; their scheme on page 538 deserves special attention.

Efforts to increase participation can take the relatively simple form of discovering what people want or need. The classic example, reported by Bowers (p. 252), is Stouffer's study of soldiers' postwar plans and their feelings about how demobilization should be handled; the Army used these findings to construct a point system of priorities for returning personnel from duty abroad. In other cases demographic data are quite sufficient. Loomis and Loomis (pp. 657–661) and Hauser (pp. 859–868) give examples from studies on the location of hospitals, churches, and similar centers. Sometimes more specific studies must be designed to identify needs: driving patterns (Loomis and Loomis, p. 658), trading patterns (Sheppard, pp. 556–557), or the specific problems of old people (Streib and Orbach, pp. 620–635). Efforts to predict the acceptance of new products by consumers also belong in this group (Glock and Nicosia, pp. 362–368). Students of mass communications suggest that these "needs and wants" studies may not be without noxious effects; the cultural dangers inherent in program ratings on the policy of television networks are well known.[2]

The distinction between external and internal-directed problems is fairly clear-cut, although sometimes the tools involved are quite similar. Thus, some public utilities use polling techniques to explore the public's "image" of the corporation and also to investigate the satisfactions and complaints of their own employees. If employee dissatisfaction is found, obviously the next questions concern causes and remedies. This would be a typical internal problem. Here the use of sociology is to analyze and if possible remove special difficulties and malfunctions in the organization. Why does it take so long for accident cases to come before a court? Is bail really necessary and useful to keep indicted criminals within jurisdiction of the court? (Zeisel, pp. 82–88.) Gross and Fishman (pp. 320–321) give an example in which difficulties in a school system turn out to be the result of mutual ignorance. School boards are misinformed about the grievances of the teachers and the teachers are not correctly informed about the boards' intentions. On a broader scale Sheppard (p. 548) mentions the simultaneous existence of unemployment and labor shortages in the same community. It is, incidentally, a challenge for further inquiry to compare the ways in which consulting engineers and organizational sociologists go about their jobs. A good example of the sociological approach is the Stanton-Schwartz study, which showed that periodic disturbances among mental patients could be traced to conflicts between doctors and nurses in the ward (M. Hyman, p. 143).

There is agreement that policy should be *evaluated,* and the social scientist is the proper man to provide the necessary information. Hyman and Wright's chapter contributes a description of the standard procedures, enriched by many concrete examples. But in many organizations, especially in government, there is no machinery or budget available for such work. On the other hand, in some commercial spheres, such as advertising, repetition is so frequent that the people involved feel it is more economical to gain cumulative impressionistic knowledge from daily experience.

The decision process is continuous. Initiation of issues, policy choices, decisions about means, and execution are all involved, and there is no reason why research should come only at the end. Evaluation should take place at many points. One might conceive of *concurrent evaluation,* even though it is not feasible to carry out a major project at every step along the way. What are some variations on the conventional technique?

A crucial step before any evaluation is the keeping of records every time a decision is reached: minutes of the discussion which preceded choosing; information on the discarded alternatives; explicit statements on the expectations which were held at the time. Once this basic material is preserved, one can be more parsimonious at later phases. A few qualitative interviews will reveal what surprised the participants in the actual development; these would point to factors neglected in the original decisions. Was a discarded alternative carried out elsewhere? If so, what happened? Did the participants overlook relevant information which was available at the time of the original decision? This kind of concurrent evaluation would permit modifications and improvements even while the whole enterprise was unfolding. Similarly, in depicting decision-making processes and particularly the relation of knowledge and policy, sociologists have made too little use of contemporary history, which swiftly spreads on the record detailed accounts of spectacular intelligence failures (e.g., the Bay of Pigs).

If a development is very new, even a straight narrative can have some evaluative function, as is evident in the chapter by Gans. The first part is identical with his presentation at the 1962 A.S.A. convention (a unique exception). Two years later, when this volume took shape, he summarized his own experiences in the Mobilization for Youth Movement and compared them with the opinions and expectations he had previously expressed. In a somewhat less explicit form the contributions by Gross and Fishman (pp. 312–317), Loomis and Loomis (pp. 669–678), and Sheppard (pp. 547–554) also contain descriptions of this kind.[3]

Types of Clients

Decision makers as clients vary considerably in their receptivity to social scientists other than economists. Labor unions are notoriously reluctant to use them except for an occasional public opinion survey.[4] Businessmen are willing to study their "victims"—consumers and workers—but have until recently been hesitant to let top management be analyzed. The radio industry supported research in its competition with printed media, but television networks are financially so successful that they have contributed little to the analysis of their own impact. Many foundations hesitate to support studies that might displease congressional committees that rule on tax exemptions. Such variations in receptivity to research have yet to be studied systematically.

There is an obvious difference between a private client who is likely to have a rather specific problem and a public client, e.g., the governor of a state who requires broad background intelligence for a legislative reform. Nowhere has sociological work yet been institutionalized in a form approaching the President's Council of Economic Advisors, although many federal and state programs would make such an innovation quite appropriate. Our foreign policy troubles would possibly be reduced, as our troubles in managing the economy have been reduced, if we set up a small top-level group of free-floating, highly trained, academically oriented, general advisers operating outside Defense or State, relatively free of bureaucratic rivalry, responsible to the President and the Senate Committee on Foreign Affairs, and assigned to tap social science and history for a comprehensive, long-run interpretation of problems and prospects abroad.

Mass-membership organizations—such as farm groups, veterans' organizations, labor unions—present a special case. There is some evidence that, in their strategy of competition and influence, they incline toward grass-roots campaigns and publicity and shy away from research. In contrast, organizations weak in grass-roots political resources, such as specialized trade associations, accent research. The mass-membership organization, whatever its objective need for studies of internal and external operations, is likely to resist sociology most.

Increasingly something one might call secondary clients appear. Agencies who themselves serve the community—testing organizations, hospitals, firms of consulting engineers—desire to broaden their scope or to understand better their social role by appointing sociologists to their staffs or by commissioning special studies. Practically all the contributors to this volume describe the clients most characteristic for their areas.

The Role of Sociologists

Some of the contributors deal explicitly with the role of the sociologist. Riley describes the sociologist as a staff member in nonacademic jobs. Rose reports his observations on the sociologist as an expert witness. We did not have the luck to obtain a firsthand description of what happens when a *sociologist* himself becomes a *decision-maker*. The few colleagues who occupy this dual role rarely have the luxury of self-examination. Nevertheless, more evidence on the sociologist as decision-maker could be gathered by asking for concrete incidents where the sociologist had a special point of view, how he defended it, and whether or not he was successful in affecting the vote or the opinion of others. If he is a member of a public body, it would be important to know whether he took on special assignments relevant to his background. If he has a top job in industry, we would like to know more about his relation to the social research activities of his organization. Special emphasis should be accorded to any change initiated when he took over.

Several contributors mentioned the role of the sociologist as teacher in specific professional situations. M. Hyman (pp. 131–134) shows developments in medical education which make the sociologist a partner in a comprehensive care program. Davison (pp. 394–395) reports that the foreign service becomes increasingly aware of the need for sensitizing its staff to the social structure of the countries in which they will serve. Gross and Fishman (p. 324) point out that conventionally trained teachers need additional instruction in the education of underprivileged children. Bordua and Reiss (pp. 294–299) stress the importance of sociological understanding for the patrolman's contact with ethnic minorities. Undoubtedly, as Bressler suggests (esp. pp. 54–60), these custom-tailored courses will not and should not subvert the role of sociology as a major ingredient of general education. Demystification of institutions which otherwise would be taken for granted, the fact that interpersonal relations are subject to general laws, the impact of social position on attitudes and behavior—these typical sociological ideas are standard fare in liberal arts curricula. The content of "training" courses deserve further studies because they would give substance to the often vague talk of the "*sociological mode of thought*" and its effects.

The sociologist can also be self-employed or can act as a free-wheeling intellectual from a university or other independent base. He can thus use his skills to improve situations without an explicit mandate. He might propose improvements of the city government very much to the discomfort of the mayor. Studies of substandard living conditions, of fertility control programs, of population problems, of changes in law and morality, have had considerable influence on legislation or at least in the change of public mores. The sociologist as *social critic* will often only point to general shortcomings rather than suggest specific remedies; after all, the term "sociology" itself was originally identified with the task of assessing the effect of industrialization on the destiny of mankind. Social criticism is discussed by Gans (p. 210), by Dror (p. 423), and most of all by Glazer. The complex interplay between reform and research is subtly caught in the chapter on race relations by Pettigrew and Back.

Hardly any of the contributors deal with jurisdictional disputes between sociology and the other social sciences—a sign of academic maturity. Obviously, if someone cannot decide whether he wants to be a Christian missionary among heathens or a stockbroker in New York he will rather consult a psychiatrist. Inversely, most city planning commissions are now adding sociologists to their staff of engineers, architects, and other professionals. For many fields, such as attitude measurement or sales forecasting, departmentalization has become outdated; more fluid teams of diverse specialists are typical. Still each discipline has its own traditions and its core problems. Smelser lucidly compares each of the social sciences along four dimensions: their most characteristic dependent and independent variables, the theoretical framework they emphasize, and the type of verification they consider adequate. By raising the question of what role sociology plays in modern economics, history, etc., he broadens the spectrum of "uses" with which this volume is concerned.

The type of clients with whom sociologists interact, the problem they work on, and the role they fill are intertwined. One of the editors has distinguished roles such as the "contact man," "the internal communications specialist," the "facts-and-figures man"; he described the situations in which each of these roles are likely to evolve. The examples given by our contributors do corroborate the value of such distinctions and should suggest additional ones.

Resources of the Sociologist

Specialized research techniques and awareness of sociological (in addition to economic) variables are an obvious part of the sociologist's equipment and need no further discussion. But how useful are his concepts? Some of our contributors have raised this question explicitly for their own field of specialization—e.g., Suchman (pp. 576–587), Pettigrew and Back (pp. 693–699), and Gross and Fishman (pp. 309–311). Other authors have made more casual references and they permitted an informal count of the notions which were mentioned most frequently. A more detailed analysis—covering additional sources—should permit interesting comparisons with the main textbook literature. In this volume the following notions stood out: stratification, primary social relations, reference groups, conflicts between different roles linked together in larger systems.

Stratification theory and research have diffused widely. Both Gans and Kahn show how the accumulated work on the sociological and psychological characteristics of the "poor" has shaped the development of anti-poverty programs. In the area of public health the differential sociology of ethnic minorities has been found useful (Suchman, pp. 585–586). Differential consumption patterns are stressed by Glock and Nicosia (pp. 377–380). Political campaigns are increasingly directed toward special groups identified by polls (Abrams, pp. 430–431). And the whole contribution by Hauser shows how contemporary social bookkeeping has been influenced by sociological concern with stratification variables.

The notion of *primary social relations* is equally ubiquitous. Teachers resist reforms which endanger their clique structure (Gross and Fishman, p. 322); farmhouses are built along roads rather than in the center of farms (which would be more practical) because of the farmer's desire for personal contact (Loomis and Loomis, p. 660); slum dwellers resist relocation to better dwellings if existing neighborhood ties are completely disregarded. Litwak and Meyer (pp. 528–532) analyze the differences between primary groups and bureaucracies, and isolate those functions that the family is uniquely qualified to perform in the education of the child.

Reference group ideas come up wherever persuasion and acquiescence are the aim of a plan of action. In market research (Glock and Nicosia, pp. 370–372), in the diffusion of agricultural innovation (Loomis and Loomis, pp. 664–665), and in the acceptance of medical services (Suchman, p. 585), the recurring theme is that it is easier to reach groups than individuals and that the search for "influentials" within groups is essential.

Role problems are mentioned in a variety of contexts. Difficulties between professionals and administrators flare up in welfare agencies (Meyer *et al.*, pp. 173–174), in correctional institutions (Kahn, p. 488), in business organizations (Zaleznik and Jardim, pp. 198–199), and probably in many other institutions not covered by the present volume. More idiosyncratic examples are the tax collector who makes concessions to a citizen with whom he has to maintain permanent relations (Dror, p. 420) and the foreign service officer who has selective relations in "his" country (Davison, p. 407). On a broader scale, role problems are implicitly referred to wherever a decision between a centralized and a locally dispersed policy has to be made, be it in the assistance to underdeveloped countries (Moore, pp. 651–652) or in the domestic poverty program.

Sociological concepts are usually notions that have stood the test of time and therefore are enshrined in textbooks. But many of them have started in the humbler status of what Herbert Blumer has called sensitizing concepts. These are ideas and terms which subsume a large number of observations under verbal "tags" which facilitate the intellectual or practical handling of social reality. The designation of the foreman or the noncommissioned officer as the "man in the middle," the "inside dopester" as a character of mass society, and the idea of "training for uncertainty" in professional education are typical examples. Sometimes such creations move up into the realm of solemn social theory; often they are soon forgotten or, if they are badly phrased, attacked as pseudo-scientific jargon.

One example will show how such "generalizing formulae" can be useful. It is in general very difficult for the top manager of an organization to know every operative detail within his domain. As a result, a kind of *half-knowledge* develops. People are vaguely aware of some aspects of their situation, just enough so that they can swiftly mobilize for action when it is needed. If everything goes well or if danger signals are arranged, this half-knowledge has great economic advantages. But if it is used as a screen to block out potentially unpleasant situations, it can become dysfunctional. Leaders of American television networks, for instance, were greatly disturbed by the quiz-program scandal, although they must have had half-knowledge of the deceit. The U. S. Space Administration was certainly embarrassed when it became known that long before the Apollo tragedy criticism of the main contractor's work had been expressed without the project leadership taking full cognizance of it. Doubtless auto industry executives knew something about cars "unsafe at any speed"; if they blocked out such knowledge and it therefore remained undeveloped, they saved money in the short run but risked much more stringent control of the industry in the long run. The sociologist as consultant can be very helpful to his client by keeping in the focus of attention the possibility of half-knowledge. And, of course, the sociologist as a social critic is habitually engaged in exposing the seamy side of society (see the chapter by Glazer).

If we had records of discussions between sociologists and their clients, or if we had inventories of studies which were considered most useful, it might well turn out that such intermediary sensitizing concepts are among the most important resources of the sociologist. This is one reason why they have been discussed here in some detail. Yet these creations have an additional force. They are the most promising link by which studies done for clients can, in the long run, contribute to the general fund of sociological knowledge—a topic treated below.

The Administrative Setting

The uses of sociology pose two kinds of contextual problems. The one derives from doubts about the very idea that social scientists should care whether their work is useful; this will be discussed in the next section. But many of our contributors report that problems exist even if the legitimacy of this relation is unquestioned.

These administrative issues fall essentially into four groups. The first has to do with the problem of the *continuity* of the relation between sociologist and client. As Luchterhand (p. 53) points out, a staff appointment has the advantage that the sociologist is thoroughly acquainted with the details of the subject matter as well as with the traditions and personalities of the organization. Can this continuity be approached with a consulting professor? Some business firms have established advisory committees which meet periodically. This makes for a two-way flow of information; if several social sciences are involved, each member of the group may stimulate the others. In the case of consulting work for the government, another device for continuity should be tried out. Task forces and advisory committees are usually dissolved after a formulation of opinions; the members do not know what happens thereafter. Provision could be made for such committees to reconvene later and to be told what action was finally taken and how it was influenced by the reaction of the various parties involved. The consultants would thus be better prepared for their next service; the procedure would also add valuable information on the uses of sociology, akin to what was called concurrent evaluation above. (Streib and Orbach (pp. 617–619) describe how a *sequence* of conferences helped to build up the new field of social gerontology.) More generally, there is need for systematic study of administrative devices for truth finding. The relative merits of reliance on technical experts, legislative investigations, public commissions, courts, and grievance commissioners (e.g. the Ombudsman) are little understood.[5]

Even those sociologists who are specially interested in contact with the world of decision-makers prefer most often the *rewards derived from an academic appointment*. It is difficult to pin these down. The pleasures of teaching? The peculiar mixture of anarchy and security characteristic of the academic world? A status difference between a teacher and a staff member? Several contributors allude to one or the other of these possibilities (Sheppard, p. 545; Gans, p. 438). But little is really known, although the problem will become increasingly acute.[6] An appropriate pilot study would be detailed case studies of sociologists who have confronted such choices at various phases of their career.

The *availability and use of outside funds* is a third administrative problem. Everyone knows that it is more difficult to get support for the study of sex or desegregation than, say, for a mental health project; the difficulty of financing long-term projects has practically blocked out knowledge on the effect of childhood experiences on adolescent development. Other taboos are discussed by Kramer (esp. p. 784).[7]

Among federal regulations the most debatable is the distinction between grants for demonstration projects and grants for so-called basic research. The distinction is often quite rigidly enforced in the judgment of applications; but it deprives many projects of their proper evaluation and introduces a misleading notion of "basic research" which will be questioned presently. Luchterhand (pp. 509–511) also deals with this topic.

Finally we are confronted with *difficulties within the university*. A Ph.D. in sociology does not really train one for any of the roles listed in the previous section, yet the number of available jobs which have to be filled is steadily increasing. What should we, as educators, do to satisfy this need? How do we combine professional training with the humanistic orientation so essential for sociological work? What role do the new types of university research bureaus, centers, and institutes play? Should the sociologists create professional schools of social research which would combine the foundations of various social sciences with clinical work, similar to the combination presented by the medical schools? The problems here raised are not too different from those existing in other areas where professional practice and the liberal arts tradition overlap.[8]

The Social Context

The relation between the sociologist and the client involves ambivalences which are due to differences in their occupational background, to value problems of the sociologist himself, and to intellectual differences he might have with his colleagues.

1. In their interaction, be it casual or sustained, the two partners work for similar goals but with different traditions and with expectations of gains which only partially overlap. The chapters in this volume are replete with observations on this point and, fortunately, they by and large center not on assigning blame but on locating unavoidable tensions which must somehow be worked out. The client wants a quick answer and the sociologist wants a thorough investigation (Riley, p. 791). Empirical findings might be crucial for the understanding of the situation but very difficult to act upon (M. Hyman, pp. 121–131). Advice given might be sound but following it would be too costly or would endanger legitimate interests of specific members in an organization (Luchterhand, pp. 512–513).

The difficulties most often mentioned are problems of communication in which both the client and the sociologist lack the training to listen or to talk to each other. Gross and Fishman have summarized the ensuing mishaps into a neat scheme (p. 343).

There is an undercurrent in many of these comments which deserves further exploration. Administrative leaders owe their success partly to their ability to make quick decisions, involving great risk or uncertainty. Such decisions are typically based on the intuitive assessments of somewhat opaque situations. It might well be that executives do not necessarily distrust or misunderstand the social scientist; rather they fear that an important property of theirs, a natural gift for decision making, might be impaired by too much concern with its rational aspect. The aversion of poets and other creative groups to literary and artistic criticism is often based on this kind of fear. Some of our contributors give pertinent examples: the clinician in a hospital who feels uneasy with the statistical approach of the sociologist (M. Hyman, pp. 124–126); the diplomat who feels that his style of work depends mainly on an undefinable "feel" (Davison, pp. 407–408)—which may be one reason why the intelligence resources of the U. S. State Department are so puny compared with those of Defense.

The sociologist can counter this hesitation by pointing to examples of occupational blindness in which the practitioner, to his detriment, has overlooked factors which quickly became obvious to the consultant. Detailed case studies of decisions made with and without the benefit of sociological—or any other—expertise will be needed before a balanced judgment can be arrived at. Maybe the type of study comparing the opinion of judges and of jurors in concrete legal cases which Zeisel (pp. 91–92) reports can be developed for this issue.

2. The basic paradigm also raises *value problems*. All occupational groups, even the most insulated ones, face issues of *professional ethics*. In contrast to medieval times we accept the dissection of cadavers; how about experimentation with living patients, however incurable? What are the rights of living statesmen in relation to contemporary historians? Empirical social research raises its own problems: invasion of privacy,[9] suppression of results injurious to a worthy social cause, classified research, etc. The American Sociological Association has for many years tried to develop a "code of ethics" and fortunately the background document by Robert Angell could be included in this volume for first publication.

But value ambivalence transcends basic professional ethics. It is well documented that the average American social scientist is *politically located* somewhat left of center. Many sociologists would prefer to study persuasion in the service of the civil rights movement or of labor unions rather than of business or military organizations. But, as one of the editors has shown, unions are more reluctant than almost any other complex organization to look for the services of sociologists. Should the sociologist forgo the opportunity for large-scale investigations because he is not in sympathy with the goals of the sponsors (Glock, pp. 382–383)? Inversely, at least one of the contributors feels that sociologists have often been too timid and passed up research opportunities which were actually not out of reach (Pettigrew and Back, p. 707).

Sometimes value problems can develop on *methodological grounds*. Etzioni advocates the merits of "sociological analysis": the grappling with large-scale problems, even if there are not yet any precise methods usable for this goal. He makes interesting procedural suggestions—for instance, the application on a macrosociological level of theorems which were developed on a smaller scale (pp. 814–819). But basically his position is that for the moment there is a conflict between the significance of a problem and our available research techniques: if in doubt, choose the former. (Glazer [pp. 70–72] sounds a note of skepticism: is sex a "small" problem, class conflict a "big" one?)

3. As a matter of fact, the issue itself is only a small part of the problems which are so well analyzed in Glazer's contribution on sociology and ideology. He makes a distinction between those who feel that microsociological studies are a social escape, those who wish sociologists were more concerned with revolutionary changes, and those who feel it is too early to be professionally concerned with macrosociological problems. Interestingly enough, he shows that no position is immune from the charge that it conceals unexplicated ideological premises, and points up the imperative for all to examine the relation between analysis and knowledge on the one hand and social action and change on the other, which is very much a central problem of the present volume. This whole area of *intraprofessional ambivalence* has been much in the minds of the editors and one specific aspect deserves more detailed comment.

Throughout the venture which ended with the writing of this introduction, one term has been carefully avoided: "applied sociology." The distinction between basic and applied research seems to us noxious because it confuses two very different dimensions. One is the origin of problems. Some of them are *"field-induced."* They stem from the need for action in a sector of social life. Work which is *not* field-induced can range from the desperation of the Ph.D. candidate seeking a dissertation topic to the unexpected insight of an ingenious social observer. We shall call all inquiries that are not field-induced *"autonomous."*

A second dimension refers to the *contribution made to the existing fund of sociological knowledge*. Such contribution may be significant or not quite, irrespective of where the problem itself originated. Experts will sometimes reach swift agreement on the significance of new work; often, time is required before an idea is recognized. But overall it certainly makes sense to talk of the gradual extension of basic knowledge. *Yet it is the ensuing knowledge that is basic and not the research or the purpose for which it was originally undertaken.*

The two dimensions lead, as usual, to four combinations according to the sources of the problem and the contribution its study makes to the arsenal of sociological knowledge.[10]

1. *Autonomous work without significance.* Alas, too many examples come to mind and no specific cases need to be cited. Yet an interesting sideline deserves attention. Generally, the professional journals put a premium on short articles reporting results of specific studies; discussions of

broader topics are relatively rare and are more likely to refer to older controversies. In this country supplementary information on current trends is obtained by personal contacts with colleagues, by participation in symposia, and of course by reading books. But for social scientists abroad American sociology is often known only through our journals and a false impression of the sociological tradition is created.

2. *Autonomous work with significant contributions to sociology.* Be it the historical studies of Max Weber or the statistical analysis of educational aspirations,[11] one might differ as to relative significance, but all would agree not only that this type exists but that it forms the core of sociological progress.

3. *Field-induced research without significant findings.* Again no specific examples are needed, just one reminder. There is often a confusion between service jobs and true field-induced research. In schools of education, for example, state laws often require a kind of social bookkeeping which is useful but better done by special agencies. It clogs up academic research bureaus and keeps them from doing the kind of truly field-induced work which is exemplified in the four cases reported by Gross and Fishman (pp. 313–317).

The critics of field-induced work have been misled by a confusion between it and service jobs. Rural and educational sociologists are now eager to clarify the situation by institutional separation of the two functions.

4. *Field-induced work with significant contributions to basic sociological knowledge.* On the analytical side, a good example would be Barnard's *The Functions of the Executive;* on the empirical side, studies of advertising have made many contributions to the knowledge of attitude change and the flow of information (Glock and Nicosia, pp. 360 ff., esp. 369–370). Field-induced research sometimes leads to a systematic result only after accumulation and synthesizing analysis of many studies. A well-known example is Stouffer's notion of relative deprivation which was extracted after the war from a series of studies done during the war for mere managerial purposes (Bowers, p. 254). The senior editor of this volume, while still at the University of Vienna, reported, in 1932, a number of market studies from which he derived the portrait of the "proletarian consumer." In a comparison with his middle-class counterpart, he was described as

. . . less psychologically mobile, less active, more inhibited in his behavior. The *radius of stores* he considers for possible purchases is smaller. He buys more often at the same store. His food *habits are more rigid* and less subject to seasonal variations. As part of his *reduction in effective scope*, the interest in other than the most essential details is lost; requirements in regard to quality, appearance, and other *discriminating* features of merchandise are the less frequent the more we deal with consumers from low social strata.

Notice that this is a summary of a large number of studies, no one of which, in its own right, is very interesting. But together they were the beginning for a general picture of low-income groups. These groups are handicapped by a low level of aspiration, a restricted sphere of social contacts, a small range of interests, etc. The reader of the contributions by Gans, Kahn, and Sheppard in the present volume will see how such ideas are now put to use in modern social action programs.

From the point of view that inaugurated the present volume, the field-induced studies or consultations which make contributions to generalized sociological knowledge are of special interest. Some contributors (Moore, pp. 648–649) mention specific examples. This volume might be used to explore the matter further through an examination of the theoretical fruits of studies of the problem of persuasion in agriculture (Loomis and Loomis), politics (Abrams), public health (Suchman), or marketing (Glock and Nicosia).

The interaction between sociologist and client, so characteristic for field-induced inquiries, raises an additional set of problems deriving from their intellectual relation. We have put this issue at the center of our paradigm, but we have delayed its discussion because it presents great difficulties. The formulation of the topic is easy: If you have a practical problem, how do you know what study is needed? If some factual and conceptual information is available, how do you derive from it what actually should be done in a concrete situation? These two questions, the translation of a practical issue into a research topic and the gap between knowledge and policy, are closely related and they should be the core of a "theory of uses." The examples provided by our contributors certainly help to highlight the challenge, but a really systematic answer is still to come. Here is what can be stated at the present stage.

"Translation" and "Gaps," the relation between decision making and sociological knowledge

The client presents the sociologist with a practical issue and expects *a translation into a research procedure.* The request can have different degrees of specificity. In certain situations only a restricted amount of information is needed and all the sociologist has to provide is the necessary technique. Thus, for instance, it will be difficult, conceptually as well as methodologically, to ascertain whether violence in television programs has a deleterious effect on young people; the research mission, however, is precise.

The broader the original assignment, the greater becomes the burden for translation. This happens in two typical situations. One occurs when the "cause of the difficulty" is to be explored. The civil courts are over-loaded with liability cases; a person injured in an accident case might have to wait years before an adjudication is completed. Zeisel (pp. 82–88) reports an analysis of every phase of the judicial process with the purpose of finding out at what point the "delay in court" could be alleviated. This study had to use data which were available from the regular bookkeeping procedures of the courts; it thus points to another characteristic aspect of the translation problem—the optimal use of available sources.

The second type of vagueness occurs when a goal is set and the sociologist is asked to find the best way to reach it. The problem of persuasion is the best example. Should one focus on the study of reluctant people? Are "arguments" the most promising objects of investigation? Should one concentrate on the influences which affected the acquiescent subjects? Loomis and Loomis (pp. 661–662) report that rural sociologists discovered the difference between "neighborhood" and "county" influentials which later was rediscovered when mass-media research distinguished between "local" and "cosmopolitan" influentials. How did the practical problem of diffusing innovations or selling merchandise end up in this research finding? [12]

Whatever study has been made, whatever fund of available knowledge has been drawn upon, there comes the moment when one has to make the *leap from knowledge to decision.* In a general way it is easy to see why no unique road leads from knowledge to action. Unpredictable events might occur; countermoves of competitors cannot be known in advance; reasonable moves in social policy might have quite unanticipated consequences. The client as decision-maker will have to make guesses and take risks beyond any contributions the sociologist can provide.

At least three types of such situations can be gleaned from the contributions in this volume.

1. *Choice of general strategy.* Should one adapt to a pattern revealed by the sociologist or should one try to change it? Immigrants shy away from the formal bureaucratized health services (M. Hyman, p. 129). Are speeches to their ethnic societies the best device or is it more efficient to introduce storefront techniques to hospitals with nurses at the entrance and no forms to be filled out? Retirement is one object of fear for aging people (Streib and Orbach, pp. 621–622). Should they be stimulated for new activities to delay the inevitable end or should they be prepared in time for "disengagement"?

2. *Choice of target populations and channels of communication.* Low-income women are less apt to vote, partly because in their subculture men derive self-respect by their voting monopoly in the family (Abrams, p. 429). If only limited funds for propaganda are available, should it be directed toward the women or toward the men? Farmers

trust supply dealers more than county agents (Loomis and Loomis, p. 667). Should the latter work through the former or strengthen their own channels of communications?

3. *Specification of general concepts.* Often a sociological idea applies to a policy problem but inventive imagination is needed to give it concrete realization in a specific situation. It is found that young delinquents lack role models for better conduct (Sheppard, pp. 560–562). How to provide them: social workers, reformed delinquents, family friends to substitute for a missing father, teachers especially trained for this role? Some studies in industrial sociology seem to show that the "right balance of people-oriented and production-oriented supervision" by foremen is desirable. What is this right balance? How can it be achieved?

It is no answer to say that "further research" would answer some of these questions. However far knowledge goes, there will always remain a gap which will have to be filled by additional assumptions and most of all by creative imagination which thinks of devices—institutional, technical, or symbolic—to turn factual knowledge into operational procedures. Whose responsibility is it to provide this imagination? As the role of the social sciences expands, a new profession might develop: a third force, a middleman who mediates between the sociologist and the client. He would be able to understand the social scientist and be well acquainted with the practical problems of the sponsor. But most of all he would have the talent and, hopefully, the training to take the knowledge which is delivered to him and to draw more conclusions from it than could either of the two partners upon whom we have concentrated so far. If his advice is carefully recorded and analyzed, then this itself would make contributions to the translation-gap problem, which, at the moment, is still the murkiest spot in the whole picture this volume tries to paint.

Using the "Uses"

The remaining observations are directed to academic colleagues who want to use this volume in teaching or to pursue problems it poses. Most helpful are the references at the end of the chapters; in all they comprise nearly 2,000 entries. The paradigm in our introduction was developed to organize the many facets of the central problem in a flexible and manageable way. Some of the contributors have briefly outlined alternative schemes (see especially Suchman, Gross and Fishman, Litwak and Meyer, Luchterhand). The detailed table of contents and index should enable the reader to quickly spot passages where contributions systematically approach the question: "Who uses what of sociology, to what purposes, with what effect?"

The plan of the book emphasizes what sociologists have to say (Part I), the contexts in which they say it (Parts II and III), selected social problems they tackle (Parts IV and V), and the difficulties they encounter in applying their knowledge—both the dangers and the promise of field-induced social research (Part VI). Part I, "Sociological Perspectives," discusses the most general diffusion of sociological ideas and research findings in the intellectual life of the United States—in other social science disciplines, in the liberal arts curriculum, and in ideological discourse. Because few serious studies are available, these essays are primarily speculative. Smelser emphasizes the academic uses of sociology—uses in economics, political science, anthropology, history, and psychology. Bressler deals with sociology as it affects curriculum content, pedagogical styles, and the intellectual orientation of college students. Glazer asks: "In what circumstances have sociologists performed the function of independent social criticism? What are the ideological roots of the major themes of contemporary sociology?"

Part II is confined to three professions that provide contrasting uses in professional schools. In social work we find extensive research, many positions for sociologists, moderate penetration in curriculum, some in practice. In medicine, there is extensive research, many positions, but limited uses in training and practice. In law, there is limited research, few positions, and little penetration in curriculum and practice. The focus of these chapters is not on workplaces and agencies but on occupational groups that cut across them—the uses of sociology by professions in recruitment and training, in the definition and organization of their work, and in the development of their functions in community and society.

Part III concentrates on the organizational consumer of sociology—enterprise, agency, voluntary association. The settings discussed range from the police and military to schools, political parties, and private businesses.

Part IV, "Social Problems and Formal Planning," deals with the more formal programs of public bodies accenting local community action. For the most part, these chapters analyze the possibilities and limits of programs designed to raise the cultural and economic level of less-privileged strata; together they present a sensitive depiction of the interplay of ideas and action in local community programs.

Under the heading "Rapid Social Change," Part V, we include situations in which established professions and agencies abound but in which massive problems are not and cannot be dealt with routinely. The general process of modernization, like the specific process of desegregation, has eluded control by established institutions. Prominent in all three chapters, as in the real life they describe, is the problem of local resistance to national plans administered by conventional agencies of change. Suggestions for overcoming such resistance are scattered throughout.

The chapters in concluding Part VI discuss problems—technical, organizational, political, and ethical—that recur in the uses of sociology generally. While they receive attention elsewhere in the volume in the context of specific areas of use, and take on different form in different settings, these problems cut across institutional spheres, types of clients, and types of decisions.

Given the descriptive detail of the volume as a whole, we hope that some readers will be tempted to play the game of comparison. Consider, for instance, Bordua and Reiss's analysis of police departments and Meyer *et al.*'s discussion of social welfare agencies. Both types of organizations are based on work done outside the central office by the patrolman and the social worker respectively. Both institutions try to increase their professional standing by bringing in social scientists and other experts, thus experiencing problems of administrative integration. Both develop complicated relations with other institutions, especially the courts. Policeman and social worker alike are supposed to help as well as to control individuals; their problems of "client" relations and public relations are therefore similar. In seminars, such comparisons should help to bring out what is specifically sociological in all this material. When M. Hyman talks about epidemiology and the Loomises about diffusion of innovation, they really talk about the same topic. When Pettigrew and Back describe predictions of which southern towns will desegregate first, they refer to a study whose design is similar to those used to identify students who will do well or poorly, described in the chapter by Gross and Fishman.

We regret that some topics are missing in this volume because no appropriate contributor was available; in the hope that our colleagues will see this as an opportunity to carry our efforts further, we here list our defeated efforts: mass communication, churches and religion, life-cycle phases other than old age, planning beyond the community level, and the diffusion of sociology into contemporary literature and literary criticism and into popular culture. Some of the contributors have also made suggestions for further inquiries in their own fields. See especially Glock and Nicosia (pp. 370–375), Davison (pp. 399–405), Kahn (pp. 484–491), and Streib and Orbach (pp. 620–635).

While ours is undoubtedly the largest undertaking, there have been several other valuable efforts to clarify the uses of sociology. In 1949 the journal *Philosophy of Science* published a symposium on applications of the social sciences centered on a memorandum written by Robert K. Merton.[13] The papers read in the educational section of the A.S.A.'s 1962 convention were subsequently published by its chairman.[14] Bressler's contribution to this volume forms a bridge between the two undertakings.

The Society for the Study of Social Problems is the center of organized interest in applied sociology; the pages of its journal, *Social Problems*, are an excellent source of current work on social issues. A volume edited by Alvin W. Gouldner and S. M. Miller constitutes an effort parallel to ours; it includes two programmatic papers by the editors.[15] The one by Miller fits very well into the spirit of this volume; the other, by Gouldner, is less congruent. Among papers published elsewhere we especially recommend Sutton's on the use of social research in developing countries[16] and Podell's on social research and welfare administration.[17] H. L. Zetterberg has selected a special case (efforts to increase attendance at a museum) to discuss social theory as a resource for the consulting sociologist.[18]

In the nature of our assignment our book contains only a few case studies. Additional material can be found in a recent collection edited by Shostak under the title *Sociology in Action*.[19]

Wilensky's treatment of the intelligence function in complex organizations draws on cases from international relations, economic life, politics, and welfare to analyze the structural and doctrinal roots of resistance to the use of social science in industry and government.[20]

Anthropologists have for a long time been concerned with their relation to colonial administration. The encyclopedic inventory *An Appraisal of Anthropology Today*[21] contains 150 pages of "problems of application." The Merton and Nisbet volume on a contemporary social problems is an obvious complement to the present volume.[22]

One can understand with hindsight, but it came as a surprise, to realize how difficult it is to find out how and where sociology is being used. The Loomises report that they wrote to several hundred rural sociologists about the uses of sociology; only those who were actively connected with some administrative enterprise could give concrete examples. In connection with M. Hyman's paper, a questionnaire was sent to the members of the A.S.A. section on medical sociology; the majority of the respondents had only vague ideas of what happened to their own work. Clients seem to be more likely to know of uses than the sociologists themselves. But not only are clients difficult to sample; they are often corporations, in which the officers who may have acted on the basis of a report are not easily traced.

A future theory of uses will require experimentation with various ways of gathering information. Here again the diverse approaches of our contributors provide instructive comparisons, and their joint efforts should enhance our understanding of the relation of social science to policy. We hope that the reader, like the editors, will be grateful for the energy and imagination that the authors have devoted to this task.[23]

REFERENCES

1. R. K. Merton, L. Broom, and L. S. Cottrell, eds., *Sociology Today: Problems and Prospects* (New York: Basic Books, 1959).

2. It is worth mentioning that the Norwegian governmental broadcasting system blocked funds for the study of people's program preferences by the newly created Oslo Institute of Social Research. The Ministry of Education knew that the public's taste was below the standards the ministry wanted to maintain. It did not want to be subject to pressures for change. The point, however, is that studies of audience preferences and tastes can be used by private and public agencies alike to broaden or narrow horizons and perceptions, elevate or depress cultural levels.

3. An impressive account of the life history and public impact of a sociological study of a major social issue was available just as this volume went to press. Sponsored by *Trans-action,* this book traces the political and intellectual controversies that developed in the wake of the Moynihan report, an analysis of the role of family life in the economic and cultural deprivation of the Negroes in the United States. See F. Lee Rainwater and William L. Yancey, eds., *The Moynihan Report and the Politics of Controversy* (Cambridge, Mass.: M.I.T. Press, 1967).

4. Wilensky discusses several roots of union reluctance to use professional staff generally. *Intellectuals in Labor Unions* (Glencoe, Ill.: The Free Press, 1956), pp. 260 ff.

5. For analysis of various organizational arrangements for tapping technical and political information, see H. L. Wilensky, *Organizational Intelligence: Knowledge and Policy in Government and Industry* (New York: Basic Books, 1967).

6. There is no adequate recent source of data on trends in employment of sociologists in academic and nonacademic settings. However, Matilda White Riley reports that between 1950 and 1959 "the proportion of members [of the American Sociological Association] in liberal arts affiliations has declined from 67 per cent in 1950 to 59 per cent at present [1959]. . . . Meanwhile, relatively more members have become associated with professional schools of medicine, business, and so on, as well as with hospitals, business firms, secondary schools, and other institutions in which sociology may be applied. Professional schools and such 'other' types of affiliation together claim one-third of the membership in 1959, as compared with one-quarter in 1950." Riley further indicates that younger members are more likely than older members to have non-liberal arts college affiliations and suggests a trend toward greater future opportunities for employment in nonacademic settings in which sociological knowledge may be used for the practical concerns of society. "Membership of the American Sociological Association, 1950–1959," *American Sociological Review,* XXV (December, 1960), 920–921. Recent emphasis on the uses of sociology by government agencies, commerce, and industry bear witness to this trend.

7. Incidentally, the very budgeting of a research project is an unsolved problem which calls for study by imaginative sociologists attuned to accounting practices. See Edmund deS. Brunner, "Social Research Dollars and Sense," *Public Opinion Quarterly,* XXVI (1962), 97–102.

8. P. F. Lazarsfeld and S. D. Sieber, *Organizing Educational Research* (Englewood Cliffs, N. J.: Prentice-Hall, 1964).

9. In view of the contemporary controversy it is striking to see that Williams James was aware of the problem in 1890: "Messrs. Darwin and Walton have set the example of circulars of questions sent out by the hundred to those supposed to be able to reply. The custom has spread, and it will be well for us in the next generation if such circulars be not ranked among the common pests of life." *The Principles of Psychology,* Vol. I. (reprint ed.; New York: Dover, 1950), p. 194

10. It should be stressed that we do *not* talk of the contribution an inquiry makes to the practical problems of the client, but to sociology as a field of knowledge.

11. See the recent critical review, W. H. Sewell and J. M. Armer, "Neighborhood

Context and College Plans," *American Sociological Review*, XXXI (1966), 159–168.

12. An interesting trap deserves attention. The client might formulate the problem in a way the sociologist really should challenge. The senior editor was involved in a characteristic situation of this kind. The president of The Fund for the Republic had made the statement that the McCarthy persecutions endangered American education because teachers became afraid to teach freely. He commissioned a study which used a great deal of technical skill to ascertain whether social science professors were affected this way. In retrospect it seems probable that the purpose of the sponsor—helping the cause of academic freedom—would have been better served by a systematic inquiry into the administrative mechanisms by which universities handled "incidents," accusations against teachers. (See P. F. Lazarsfeld and W. P. Thielens, *The Academic Mind* (Glencoe, Ill.: The Free Press, 1958).

13. Robert K. Merton, "The Role of Applied Social Science in the Formation of Policy," *Philosophy of Science*, XVI (1949), 161–181.

14. Charles H. Page, *Sociology and Contemporary Education* (New York: Random House, 1963).

15. Alvin W. Gouldner and S. M. Miller, eds., *Applied Sociology* (New York: The Free Press of Glencoe, 1965).

16. Francis X. Sutton, "The Uses of Social Research in the Developing Countries," in Bert F. Hoselitz and Wilbert E. Moore, eds., *Industrialization and Society* (Paris: UNESCO, 1963), pp. 393–409.

17. Lawrence Podell, "Social Research and Public Welfare," in American Public Welfare Association, *Mandate for Research* (Washington, D.C., 1965).

18. H. L. Zetterberg, *Social Theory and Social Practice* (New York: The Bedminster Press, 1962).

19. Arthur B. Shostak, ed., *Sociology in Action* (Homewood, Ill.: The Dorsey Press, 1966). Lewis M. Killian reports on his work with the Florida Desegregation Brief ("The Social Scientist's Role in the Preparation of the Florida Desegregation Brief," pp. 129–134), and Ray H. Elling describes how a health organization changed its policy by combining available knowledge on bureaucratic organization and the attitude structure of low-income people ("The Design and Evaluation of Planned Change in Health Organizations," pp. 292–302). Marshall B. Clinard's report on his experience in India is more explicit than many other such reports on the "mode of sociological thought" ("The Sociologist and Social Change in the Underdeveloped Countries," pp. 232–248) and also adds to the Loomises' corresponding section in the present volume. Donald J. Newman's summary of his studies of a large project on "Sociologists and the Administration of Criminal Justice" (pp. 177–187) is a useful complement to Zeisel's and to Bordua and Reiss's contributions to this book.

20. Wilensky, *Organizational Intelligence*.

21. Sol Tax *et al.*, *An Appraisal of Anthropology Today* (Chicago: University of Chicago Press, 1953).

22. Robert K. Merton and Robert A. Nisbet, eds., *Contemporary Social Problems* (New York: Harcourt, Brace and World, 1961).

23. The editors are greatly indebted to the efficiency and professional competence of our editorial assistant, Mr. Jeffrey G. Reitz. He catalogued every example in all the contributions and helped us greatly to put them at the appropriate places in this introduction.

Contents

Sociological
Perspectives

PART I

Sociology
and the Other
Social Sciences

NEIL J. SMELSER

chapter 1

An inquisitive layman will often ask a sociologist: "What is sociology, anyway?" The question is not an easy one. Moreover, after the sociologist replies—usually haltingly and in general terms—the layman may pose a second question, such as, "Well, how is that different from social psychology?" or "Isn't that what anthropologists do?" These, too, are likely to yield vague, unsatisfactory answers. Sociology seems to defy simple definition of itself and clear demarcation from related endeavors.

Somehow it seems more appropriate to ask the question of sociology than it does of some of her sister social sciences. *What Is Sociology?* seems a reasonable title for a recent introductory text.[1] The title *What Is Economics?* would appear more to signify a critical treatment of the foundations of economics than to introduce the field that has crystallized in the mid-twentieth century. *What Is History?* signifies more a foray into the philosophy of historical inquiry than an introduction to the field. In short, the query "What Is ——?" when applied to a discipline betokens an

3

effort to locate the distinctive focus of a field still in search of its identity, one which has only recently achieved solid institutional support.

In this chapter I aim to explore the distinctive character of sociology and its relations to the other social sciences. I shall proceed by opening four topics in sequence:

1. The criteria by which the various social-science disciplines can be described and related to one another.
2. The contours of sociology according to these criteria.
3. The contours of several neighboring fields according to the same criteria—the fields of economics, political science, anthropology, history, and psychology.[2] Some might object to the inclusion of the last two on grounds that history is in the humanities and psychology is scientific but not social, but I think that much can be learned by comparing sociology with these two fields.
4. Some possibilities of theoretical and empirical articulation between sociology and the other disciplines.

My emphasis will be conceptual. I am interested in the theoretical and empirical relations among the social sciences as they stand today. I shall not trace how these relations have developed in the history of thought. Nor shall I discuss, except by way of occasional illustration, the institutional relations among sociology and the other social sciences: for example, the consequences of the fact that sociology is departmentally linked here with anthropology, there with political science, and elsewhere with economics.

This chapter will differ considerably from others in this volume. The only sense in which I shall be concerned with the "uses" of sociology is the ways in which theory and research in different disciplines can be related to or used by one another. Thus I shall be concerned with the analytic rather than the applied uses of sociology. The uses of sociology in academic-professional departments such as business administration, education, social work, criminology, law, medicine, nursing, public administration, or home economics are considered elsewhere in this volume, as are the applications of sociology outside the academic setting—in social policy, industrial relations, race relations, penal reform, and so on.

Criteria for Describing and Comparing the Social Sciences

The simplest way to characterize a discipline is to depict its subject matter concretely. Economists may be said to study businessmen and organizations, as they produce and market commodities, and consumers as they buy and use these commodities. Other social sciences are not so specific in their focus. Upon being asked to define anthropology, Malinowski is reported to have replied that anthropology is "the study of man, embracing woman." Likewise, sociology is very diffuse, covering behavior in families, hospitals, educational institutions, street-corner gangs, experimental small groups, armies, and religious revivals, to name only a few settings. To describe a social science concretely, however, does not yield a very scientific account, since it usually refers to the list of topics that, over a long period, have interested those who call themselves economists or sociologists or whatever. Such a description is likely to change, moreover, as new problems make their appearance in society—problems such as imperfect competition, race relations, mental illness, and poverty.

A more analytic way of describing and comparing disciplines is to ask how knowledge is generated, organized, and verified in each. This, in turn, breaks down into a number of criteria:

First, it is necessary to specify what *about* the concrete subject matter preoccupies the investigator. Economists are not interested in every aspect of the behavior of businessmen; they wish to discover specifically why businessmen produce different quantities of commodities at different times, why they charge different prices at different times, why they hire more or fewer workers under different conditions, and so on. Sociologists are not interested in every aspect of the family; they focus on patterns of rights and obligations of family members, changes in the rates of family formation and dissolution, differences in fathers' and sons' career patterns, and so on. By asking such questions, we identify the distinctive *scientific problems, phenomena to be explained,* or *dependent variables* of a discipline.

Second, it is necessary to specify what each discipline treats as the distinctive causes (or determinants, or factors, or conditions) of variation in the dependent variables. In determining how much of a given commodity will be produced at a given price, the economist asks how much of the commodity the consumers are demanding, how much the businessman has to pay for raw materials and labor to produce the commodity, and how his competitors are behaving. In accounting for variations in divorce rates, the sociologist turns to the society's degree of urbanization and industrialization; its levels of interreligious, interethnic, and interclass marriage; and its laws affecting divorce. In this search for associated conditions, the social scientist attempts to identify distinctive *independent variables*.

The focus of a scientific discipline, then, can be specified by listing the dependent and independent variables that preoccupy its investigators. But these lists of variables do not tell the whole story. It is necessary, third, to specify the ways in which a discipline imposes a *logical ordering* on its variables. Indeed, merely by distinguishing between dependent and independent variables, we elicit one instance of logical ordering—that is, specifying which variables are to be viewed as causes and which as effects. On the basis of this ordering, various *hypotheses*—statements of the conditions under which dependent variables may be expected to vary in certain ways—can be formulated. A more complex kind of ordering results when a number of hypotheses are combined into an organized system (often called a *model*). Suppose, for example, the economist is equipped with three hypotheses: that private investment influences aggregate employment in specific ways, that government spending influences employment in other ways, and that foreign trade influences it in still other ways. A model is created when the economist states the interactions among these determinants, all in relation to employment, in a logically rigorous way (for example, in the form of simultaneous equations). An example of a cruder model is provided by psychoanalytic theory. Slips of the tongue are determined primarily by the strength of repressed instinctual conflicts. But in addition they occur more frequently when an individual is fatigued and thus inattentive. If it were possible to single out the precise strength of these two determinants—repressed conflict and fatigue—and combine them into a more complex form, a model would be at hand.

Logical ordering does not end with complex models. These models are embedded in a number of definitions, assumptions, and postulates. The hypothesis that investment creates a higher level of employment, for example, rests on the assumption that laborers are motivated to respond positively to wage offers made by employers. The hypothesis linking repressed conflict and slips of the tongue rests on a complex set of assumptions about instincts and their manifestations, the defensive operations of the repressing psychic agency, and the relations between psychic conflict and motor activity. Such definitions, assumptions, and postulates constitute the *theoretical framework* of a scientific discipline. Within this framework the specific hypotheses "make sense." To put it more strongly, the hypotheses and models should be *derived*, as rigorously as possible, from the theoretical framework.

Fourth, it is necessary to specify the *means employed to accept or reject statements* in the various scientific disciplines. These include the methods of scientific inquiry—such as the experimental—as well as specific techniques and instruments for collecting, measuring, and processing data. The several social sciences vary considerably in the research methods they can and do utilize.

In this chapter I shall use these four criteria—dependent variables, independent variables, logical ordering, and research methods—to describe, compare, contrast, and suggest ways of integrating the several social sciences. I shall digress momentarily, however, to comment on one additional way to characterize disciplines: to list their component "schools of thought."

Generally the term *school* refers to an indefinite number of scholars who stress a particular aspect of or approach to a discipline. The term also implies that its proponents are emotionally committed to their approach and are prepared to defend it from attack and to deprecate different or competing schools. A school, then, is simultaneously a subdivision of a field and a species of cult or sect.

Schools in the social sciences cluster around and can be classified according to the four criteria for describing a field:

1. What aspects of social life are to be studied? The "symbolic interactionist" school, for example, focuses on relatively microscopic units of social action and emphasizes various psychic processes that accompany acts; this contrasts, for example, with the "structuralist" approach, which studies institutional patterns without explicit reference to the social psychological aspects of discrete acts.

2. What are the determinants of social behavior? Schools clustering around independent variables may be quite specific in focus, as in the case of the "overconsumption" approach to the business cycle; or they may be quite general, as in the case of the schools of "geopolitics" or "economic determinism."

3. What are the most appropriate models or theoretical perspectives? The "organicist," and more recently the "functionalist," schools rest in part on a view of society as functioning like a biological organism; the "cultural relativist" school is based on scientific notions of how social units may be compared with one another as well as on moral notions of how legitimate it is to claim that one society is superior to another; the "phenomenological," "nominalist," and "realist" positions are based on different philosophical views regarding the nature of reality.

4. What are the methods by which propositions are accepted or rejected? One feature of the "positivist" school, for example, concerns the procedures necessary to consider a statement verified; this school contrasts with the "verstehen" and "intuitionist" approaches to inquiry. Sometimes schools are named after specific methodological procedures, as in the case of the "experimentalist," "statistical," or "survey" approaches to inquiry.

When a school is named after a man and his followers, this usually involves some distinctive combination of several criteria. For example, the Marxian approach is characterized by an emphasis on distinctive aspects of social life (economic and related institutional structures and processes), distinctive determinants ("economic determinism"), a distinctive theoretical and philosophical perspective ("dialectical materialism"), and a method of validating arguments (based mainly on logical demonstration and comparative historical analysis).

The presence of numerous "schools" in a discipline generally betokens a relative scientific immaturity (though certainly not an immaturity in all kinds of scholarship). As it achieves scientific maturity, it more nearly attains consensus on the scientific problems to be posed, the relevant independent variables, a theoretical and philosophical perspective, and appropriate research methods. Simultaneously it witnesses a decline of distinctive schools; a decline in the quantity of polemic about the "nature" of the field and the value of different "approaches" to the field; a decline in propaganda, proselytization, and defensiveness; and an increase in discussion of findings in relation to accepted criteria of validation. The existing disciplines may be ordered according to the degree to which they currently manifest these several concomitants of this aspect of scientific maturity. At one extreme are mathematics and physics, and at the other are humanistic disciplines such as literary and art criticism. The social sciences occupy an intermediate position, with sociology manifesting more signs of this kind of immaturity than economics, but perhaps fewer than political science.

Sociology[3]

Sociology, like many of its sister social sciences, is characterized by a proliferation of schools—such as functionalism, social behaviorism, symbolic interactionism, historicism, and so on[4]—and consequently great disagreement among sociologists about the fundamental problems, concepts, theories, and methods in the field. Moreover, the field displays an increasing number of subdivisions—sociology of the family, stratification, religion, medicine, leisure, law, deviance, collective behavior, for instance—each of which differs in one or more respects from the other. Because of this internal diversity, it is a difficult, even presumptuous, task to present a single view of the character of the field. Necessarily, then, my characterization of sociology will have to be approximate; it will overemphasize some and underemphasize other aspects of the field; and it will gloss over many disagreements concerning fundamental features of the field.

DEPENDENT VARIABLES

Sociological analysis begins with a problem. Posing a problem means identifying some variation in human behavior and framing a "why" question about this variation. Such variation becomes the dependent variable —that which is to be explained. This variation may involve a single event (Why did violence erupt in the Congo when it did?); it may involve presumed regularities in the occurrence of events (Why are colonial societies that are emerging from domination prone to outbursts of hostility?); or, at a higher level, it may involve questions of structural variation in large classes of events (Why do feudal land patterns arise and persist? Why do they break down, sometimes in one way and sometimes in another?).

After isolating a certain problem, the sociologist specifies concrete units that identify the dependent variable.[5] In the field of sociology these concrete units are most commonly found in the *units of social structure* and in *variation of human behavior oriented to social structure*.[6] This common focus obtains in spite of the facts that (1) the types of social groupings in which structure is observed vary greatly—small face-to-face groups, formal organizations, voluntary associations, and diffuse collectivities such as ethnic groups; (2) the types of institutional settings in which social structure is observed vary greatly—familial, political, religious, medical, and educational.

"Social structure" is a concept used to characterize recurrent and regularized interaction among two or more persons. The basic units of social structure are not persons as such, but selected aspects of interaction among persons, such as roles (for example, businessman, husband, church member) and social organization, which refers to structured clusters of roles (such as a bureaucracy, an informal clique, a family). The important defining feature of social structure is that interaction is selective, regularized, and regulated by various social controls.

In connection with these social controls, three basic concepts are particularly important:

1. *Values* legitimize the existence and importance of specific social structures and the kinds of behavior that transpire in social structure. The value of "free enterprise," for instance, endorses the existence of business firms organized around the institution of private property and engaged in the pursuit of private profit.

2. *Norms* are standards of conduct that regulate the interaction among individuals in social structures. The norms of contract and property law, for instance, set up obligations and prohibitions on the agents in economic transactions. As the examples show, at any given level of analysis norms are more specific than values in their control of interaction in social structures.

3. *Sanctions*—including both rewards and deprivations—involve the use of various social resources to control the behavior of personnel in social structures. Aspects of this control include the establishment of roles, the inducement of individuals to assume and perform in roles, and the control of deviance from expected role performance. Examples of sanctions are coercion, ridicule, appeal to duty, withdrawal of communication, and so on.

A concept which unifies the elements of social structure—including roles, collectivities, values, norms, and sanctions—is the concept of *institutionalization*. This refers to distinctive, enduring expectations whereby these elements are combined into a single complex. When we speak of the institutionalization of American business, for instance, we refer to a more or less enduring pattern of roles and collectivities (such as businessmen and firms), values (for instance, free enterprise), norms (laws of contract and property, informal business codes), and sanctions (profits, wages).

Many questions about dependent variables in sociology are stated as follows: Why are the elements of social structure patterned the way they are? Another class of dependent variables is specified in terms of systematic variations in human behavior oriented to social structure. Given some structure, when can conformity be expected? What are the consequences of conformity for the social structure? When can deviance from social structure be expected? What are the different forms of deviance, and why does one type of deviance rather than another arise? What are the consequences for the social structure of different kinds of deviance? Specifying the possible "consequences" of conformity or deviance involves identifying a further range of dependent variables—reactions to deviance (social control), changes in social structure, persistence of structural patterns, collective outbursts.

What are the major types of social structure? This question is usually answered by turning to some notion of the basic functions, or directional tendencies, of social systems. These functions concern the general orientations of social life. Or, as the question is often put: What are the exigencies that must be met in order for the social unit to continue functioning? Analysts who attempt to identify the basic directional tendencies of social units speak of "functional exigencies." Typical exigencies include:

1. Creation and maintenance of the cultural values of a system. For some systems, such as societies, this involves long periods of socialization and complex structures such as families, churches, schools, and training institutes.

2. Production, allocation, and consumption of scarce goods and services (sometimes called the economic function). Typical structures that specialize in this function are firms, banks, and other agencies of credit.

3. Creating, maintaining, and implementing norms governing interaction among units in the system (sometimes called the integrative function), such as the law and its enforcement agencies.

4. Co-ordination and control of the collective actions of the system or a collectivity within it, in modern societies by the state, political parties, and associated agencies (sometimes called the political function).

The usual basis for classifying social structures is to indicate the main functions they serve: political, economic, familial, religious, educational. The classification of social structures in this way involves assigning *primacy* of function only. Even though religious structure is a concept applied to a clustering of rites or an organized church, the social significance of this bundle of activities is not exhausted by this concept. Analytically, the concrete religious structure has a political aspect, an economic aspect, and so on. The notion of structure, then, is used to identify theoretically significant properties of concrete clusters of activities devoted primarily, but not exclusively, to meeting some social exigency.

This presentation of the central dependent variables in the field of sociology may convey the impression that there is uniform consensus as to these variables and the ways to describe and classify them. I do not mean to convey this impression. Much of contemporary sociological inquiry and debate does not involve systematic efforts to establish connections between these and other variables—in short, efforts to explain variations in dependent variables—but rather is a search for descriptive and classificatory languages for identifying various dependent variables, as well as continuing argumentation about what the dependent variables of the field *should* be. The latter are necessary ingredients of scientific inquiry, but they alone do not constitute scientific inquiry.

INDEPENDENT VARIABLES

The sociological concepts listed thus far—that is, those revolving around the notion of social structure—are used mainly to identify dependent variables and to frame scientific problems. As such they do not provide hypotheses to account for variation or to explain processes of social adjustment, maladjustment, and change. To generate these additional ingredients of sociological analysis, one must take account of several classes of independent variables.

For any given dependent variable in sociology, the number and kinds of conditions that potentially affect its variation are, at first sight, discouragingly great. An individual's ability to perform a simple task in a small-group setting is influenced most immediately by his intelligence, training, and motivation. These three immediate factors are further conditioned by his social-class background, his ordinal position in his family, the presence or absence of others in the same room when he is performing the task, the behavior of the person assigning him the task, and many other factors. When we turn to the search for conditions influencing social aggregates, such as changes in the divorce rate over the past century, the number and kinds of potentially operative conditions are even more complex. The initial picture, then, is one of a *multiplicity* of operating conditions, a *compounding* of their influences on the dependent variable, and an *indeterminacy* regarding the effect of any one condition or several conditions in combination. The corresponding problem facing the scientific investigator at this stage is to *reduce* the number of operating conditions, to *isolate* one condition from another, and thereby to *make precise* the role of each condition. How are these problems faced?

The general answer to the question is that the sociologist, by virtue of his disciplinary commitments, tends to opt for social-structural conditions as explanatory variables. But, in addition, the investigator must impose some sort of *organization* on the conditions. One of the simplest ways of organizing conditions is seen in the distinction between *independent* and *intervening* variables. A classic example will show the power of this distinction. Robert Michels, in his comparative study of political parties and trade-unions,[7] was preoccupied with the problem of why large-scale organizations, even those with liberal and socialist ideologies, tend universally to develop oligarchical authority systems. For Michels this problem constituted the dependent variable, or that which demanded explanation. According to Michels' account, three sets of independent variables produce oligarchy. The first are found in the technical and administrative characteristics of organizations themselves—the impossibility of direct communication and co-ordination of decisions by the many, with the consequence that responsibility falls into the hands of the few. The second are found in the psychological propensities of the masses to adulate and venerate leaders. The third are found in the superior oratorical, intellectual, and cultural skills of the leaders themselves.[8]

Oligarchy, once established, itself has consequences. In particular, Michels pointed out the tendency for leaders, once in power, to gain access to resource, to come to think of themselves as indispensable, and to regard their right to office as necessary and sacred. These by-products of oligarchical leadership, moreover, feed back and further consolidate the original tendencies for power to become centralized.[9] The several classes of variables identified by Michels thus constitute a set of independent, intervening, and dependent variables, as shown in Figure 1–1. The picture of the

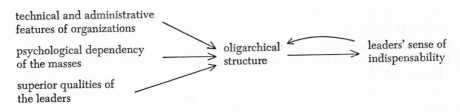

technical and administrative features of organizations

psychological dependency of the masses

superior qualities of the leaders

oligarchical structure

leaders' sense of indispensability

FIGURE 1–1.

variables, thus organized, is much simpler than a picture of the lengthy list of associations among every combined pair of variables.

The example also reveals that the distinction among independent, intervening, and dependent variables is a relative one and that the status of any given variable may change according to the analytic purposes at hand. For example, the variable "oligarchical structure" is dependent with respect to "technical and administrative features"; it is independent with respect to "leaders' sense of indispensability"; and it is intervening with respect to the relation between "technical and administrative features" and "leaders' sense of indispensability." Furthermore, "leaders' sense of indispensability" is both independent and dependent if we consider its feedback to the power structure. In sociological investigation, then, no given substantive variable can be considered as inherently independent, intervening, or dependent.

When we proceed from more or less static accounts of variation to the analysis of processes of adjustment and change, different sets of explanatory variables must be brought to bear. Among the most important of these variables in sociology are the concepts of strain, reactions to strain, and attempts to control reactions to strain.

1. Strain refers to various kinds of malintegration in the relations among elements of a social system. Among the many types of strain that arise in a social system are ambiguity in role expectations, role conflict, discrepancies between expectations and actual social experiences, and conflicts of values.

2. The initial responses to situations of strain tend to be disturbed reactions which are frequently, but not always, deviant and malintegrative from the standpoint of the social system. A variety of specific social problems arise from deviance: crime, alcoholism, hoboism, suicide, addiction, mental disorders, and social movements, to name a few.

3. Attempts to control reactions to strain may involve either structuring the initial situation so as to minimize strain or attempting to control reactions to strain, once they have arisen.

By arranging these three variables into different patterns, social investigators attempt to account for the persistence and change of behavior oriented to social structures. By way of qualification, however, it should be noted that these three sets of variables are not inherently independent variables, but may themselves be the subject of explanation; for example, the investigator of the social conditions underlying strain makes it the dependent variable and various social-structural categories the independent variables.

RELATIONS AMONG DIFFERENT CLASSES OF VARIABLES

In discussing the hypotheses relating independent and dependent variables, I have already opened the discussion of the relations among variables. Indeed, most research activity in sociology is directed either toward the discovery or establishment of empirical generalizations (which are not hypotheses as such, but rather data bearing on hypotheses)[10] or toward the establishment of quite specific and discrete relations between an independent variable and a dependent variable. The field still suffers from a shortage of full-scale explanatory models. Those models that do exist may be classified into three types:

1. Static models that organize a number of different variables to account for structural characteristics. The work of Michels is an example.

2. Process models, which refer to changes of variables *within* a social structure. Process models are used, for example, in analyzing rates of social mobility, voting rates, and certain types of social control (for instance, psychotherapy, which often "rehabilitates" persons considered to be "disturbed"). In these examples the social structure is assumed to remain unchanged.[11]

3. Change models, which refer to changes of the structure itself. For example, when attempts to control strain fail, new structural arrangements may result. The movement to the new structure may be *controlled* (as when a new law is passed by the constituted authorities to meet a pressing social problem) or *uncontrolled* (as when a revolutionary party overthrows the authority and sets up a new constitution and government). The new equilibrium, moreover, may be precarious; changes may necessitate further changes. Repeated failure of social control mechanisms may result in the disintegration of the system. All these examples involve changes in the social structure.[12]

Most sociological models are framed in nonmathematical language. Mathematical models, rare in sociology, are employed mainly in the analysis of population movements and small-group processes and occasionally in the analysis of voting behavior and social mobility.[13]

Sociology also displays a certain amount of systematic effort to formalize the various ingredients of scientific explanation—variables of several types and their organization into definite relationships—into comprehensive theoretical frameworks. These efforts are most conspicuously identified with the names of Talcott Parsons and his associates, who have attempted to specify the nature of systems of social action and state in very general terms the relations among the elements of these systems—relations which presumably form the basis for a great number of formal models.[14] Despite these efforts at formalization of theory, most models and theories in sociology rest on assumptions and postulates that are vaguely formulated and unexamined. For example, models of social mobility generally rest on a psychological postulate that individuals in a system of stratified positions and rewards are, other things equal, more or less uniformly motivated to move to as high a point as possible in the hierarchy. Such an assumption, while perhaps necessary for generating manageable models and specific hypotheses, is certainly open to doubt on empirical grounds and may contain hidden implications that would, if made explicit, lead investigators to modify their theoretical formulations. To choose another set of examples, theories of alienation, anomie, and conflict frequently rest on a variety of implicit assumptions about human nature, what sorts of experiences degrade the person, and how the person typically reacts to these experiences.[15] The field of sociology—as contrasted with economics, as we shall see presently—is notable for its extraordinary diversity of underlying assumptions concerning man's social and psychological existence. This phenomenon of diversity, more than any other single factor, probably leads to the frequently expressed view that sociology is not a unified field and to the frequent and not always well-informed disputes about fundamental principles in the field.

RESEARCH METHODS[16]

Sociology's diversity of dependent variables, independent variables, and theoretical frameworks is matched by a corresponding diversity in research methods. Before proceeding to illustrate this point, I shall introduce a distinction by which the various methods of drawing inferences in the social sciences can be compared with one another. This distinction is between determinants treated as *parameters* and determinants treated as *operative variables*. Parameters are determinants that are known or suspected to influence a dependent variable, but, in the investigation at hand, are made or assumed not to vary. Operative variables are conditions that are known or suspected to influence a dependent variable and, in the investigation, are made or allowed to vary in order to assess this influence. By making variables into parameters for purposes of analysis, most of the potentially operative conditions are made not to vary, so that the operation of one or a few conditions may be isolated and examined. The distinction between parameters and variables is, of course, a relative one. What may be treated as a parameter in one investigation may become a variable condition in another.

The field of sociology displays a plethora of research methods designed to accomplish the continuous and systematic transformation of conditions into parameters and variables in order to refine and generalize explanations. The *experimental method,* for example, which involves the direct manipulation of situations to create parameters and variables, finds widespread use in social-psychological and small-group experimentation. Most often experimentation is conducted by establishing two groups—the experimental and the control—that are identical in respect to many known or suspected sources of variation, such as age, sex, intelligence, educational level, socioeconomic background, and the like; these conditions that are shared by the two groups are established as parameters. Then, with regard to the operative condition under investigation, the experimental group is stimulated, the control group not; this condition not shared by the two groups is thereby established as the operative variable.

The *statistical method,* applying mathematical techniques to populations and samples of events containing large numbers, attempts to achieve the same manipulation of parameters and operative conditions as does the experimental method. The main difference between the two is that experimentation does so by situational manipulation, whereas statistical analysis does so by conceptual (mathematical) manipulation, which holds constant or cancels out sources of variation or shows them to be actually inoperative. An example of this type of analysis is found in the sociological analysis of intergenerational mobility. Over an intergenerational period, some social mobility (defined as differences in occupational status between father and son) is required simply by virtue of long-term structural changes in the occupational structure itself. If the tertiary sector is expanding, for example, more sons will necessarily move into service industries from other backgrounds. Investigators of mobility frequently wish to inquire into other determinants than changing industrial structure—determinants such as family size, ordinal position in family, or achievement motivation, for example. In order to isolate these other determinants, the investigator calculates some sort of mobility rate that is to be expected solely on the basis of structural changes alone, subtracts this rate from the gross mobility rate, and analyzes the difference in terms of the other suspected independent variables. In this way the effect of structural changes is held constant or made into a parameter for purposes of further analysis.[17]

Using this method to rule out spurious relations and thus isolating genuine ones is best illustrated in multivariate analysis as it is practiced in survey research. Suppose that in a national survey it is found that age is positively correlated with intolerance. Suppose also that level of education is found to be negatively correlated with intolerance. Since age and educational level are themselves correlated (above the age of completed education, young people are more educated than old people), it is impossible to know, on the basis of the two correlations taken alone, if either or both or neither is a determinant of intolerance. To gain this knowledge, a method of partial correlation is applied: Holding education constant, what is the apparent influence of age? And holding age constant, what is the apparent influence of education? By carrying out a succession of such operations, both on the two variables in question and on other variables that are associated with them, the investigator makes parameters out of a number of possibly and apparently operative conditions and arrives at a truer picture of the actually operative conditions.[18]

The method of statistical manipulation of historical data finds widespread use in sociology, both when the data are "given"—as in census reports—and when they are measured specifically for research purposes—as in attitude surveys. Sometimes, however, the number of cases is too small to permit manipulation by statistical methods; for example, when research involves the comparisons of large, complex nation-states. Under such conditions the sociologist has recourse to the *comparative method*. Because of the restricted number of cases, the investigator is forced to rely on the method of *systematic comparative illustration*. Despite this unique restrictive feature of the comparative method, its logic is identical to the methods just reviewed in that it attempts to yield scientific explanation by the systematic manipulation of parameters and operative variables. A classic example will show this identity. One of Durkheim's central findings in his study of suicide was that Protestants persistently display higher rates of suicide than Catholics.[19] The variable he employed to explain this finding was differential integration of the two religious groupings: Protestants, with their antiauthoritarian, individualistic traditions, are less integrated than Catholics and hence less protected against self-destruction. On examining the countries on which his religious data were available, however, Durkheim noticed that the Catholics were in the minority in every case. Could it not be, he asked, that minority status rather than religious tradition is the operative variable in the genesis of lower suicide rates among Catholics? To throw light on this question, he examined regions such as Austria and Bavaria, where Catholics are in the majority; in these regions he discovered some diminution of the religious differences between Protestants and Catholics, but Protestant rates were still higher. On the basis of this examination, he concluded that "Catholicism does not owe [its protective influence] solely to its minority status." [20] In this operation Durkheim used no statistical techniques; yet he was approximating their use through systematic comparative illustration. He was making minority status into a parameter in order to isolate the distinctive influence of the religious variable.

A fourth research method that finds wide application in sociology is the *case study,* in which a single social unit becomes the focus of intensive description and analysis with respect to certain variables. Examples of this kind of research are found in the classic study of the Bank Wiring Room in the Hawthorne studies;[21] the studies of behavior related to social class in a single local community;[22] and the studies of behavior and interaction in a single mental hospital.[23] The case study is methodologically inferior to the other methods just reviewed because, being based on a single case, it presents no basis for the systematic control of conditions by the manipulation of parameters and operative variables. Nevertheless, the case study has proved to be of great value in discovering and illustrating important new variables in sociological investigation. A further characteristic of the case method is that it is commonly—though by no means intrinsically—associated with participant observation and with using relatively few informants as sources of data.

A further method of transforming potentially operative variables into parameters is the crude but widely employed *method of heuristic assump-*

tion. For example, in an experimental small-group setting in which the influence of different leadership structures on morale is being investigated, the investigator makes use of a number of important but unexamined heuristic assumptions—that the subjects speak the same language, that they operate under many common cultural assumptions, that they are more or less uniformly motivated to participate in the experiment, and so on. All these variables, if treated as variables, would certainly influence the outcome of the experiment; but they are implicitly assumed not to be variables—that is, to be parameters—for purposes of the analysis. To choose another example, mentioned above, it is a convenient heuristic assumption that individuals in a stratification system are motivated to move upward.[24] Necessary as such assumptions are, and widely as they are employed, this method is inferior to the methods of experimentation, statistical analysis, and comparative analysis; the reason for this is that the method of heuristic assumption rests on no situational or conceptual manipulation other than making a simplifying or convenient assumption. Seldom if ever are serious attempts made to establish the empirical validity of the assumptions or to correct for the degree to which the assumption is not valid. The method of heuristic assumption accomplishes by making believe what the other methods accomplish by situational or conceptual manipulation in the light of some known or suspected empirical variation. Nevertheless, despite these shortcomings, the method of heuristic assumption provides the investigator a service that is logically the same as the experimental, statistical, and comparative methods: systematically to manipulate operative conditions and parameters to permit the isolated investigation of a limited number of selected independent variables.

In sociology no single method of research just reviewed can be said to predominate; sociology is relatively hybrid in this respect. As we shall see later, many of the other social sciences can be more readily characterized by a typical or favorite method of organizing data and drawing inferences.

Economics

The following "informative introductory description" of economics appears in the best-known text on the subject: "The study of how men and society *choose*, with or without the use of money, to employ *scarce* productive resources to produce various commodities over time and distribute them for consumption, now and in the future, among people and groups in society." [25] From this definition we may build a description of economics in terms of the ingredients of a scientific theory—dependent variables, independent variables, and relations among these variables in economics.

DEPENDENT VARIABLES

A first set of dependent variables is found in the term *commodities*. What is the level of the total production of goods and services in a society? What different kinds (shoes, guns, butter) are produced, and in what proportions? Economists thus attempt to account for variations in the level and composition of production.

A second set of dependent variables is found in the term *scarce productive resources*. Goods and services are produced by the application of the following factors of production: (1) land, or the state of the natural resources, cultural values, and technical knowledge; (2) labor, or the level of motivation and skill of human beings; (3) capital, or the level of resources available for future production rather than immediate consumption; and sometimes (4) organization, or the principles of combination and recombination of the other factors. Organization involves the operation of institutions such as property and contract as well as the activity of entrepreneurs. Economists are thus interested in explaining the levels and relative proportions of these resources in productive use and the techniques by which they are combined.

A third set of dependent variables is indicated by the term *distribute*. Which individuals and groups receive the goods and services generated in the productive process? Or, to put it in terms of payments, what is the distribution of income generated in the economic process?

The basic dependent variables in economics, then, are production, techniques of organizing resources, and distribution of wealth. In the Keynesian system, the basic dependent variables are the volume of employment (or the proportion of available labor in productive use at any given time) and the national income (or the total level of production).[26] Even in small subfields of economics the specific problems posed turn out to be instances of the basic dependent variables. In the study of wages in labor economics, for instance, the following elements generally need explaining:

(*a*) the general level of wages in the nation and its movements during past decades, (*b*) the wage spread between occupations and changes in the spread from time to time, (*c*) wage differentials between regions and areas and alterations in such differentials over the course of time, (*d*) interindustry differentials and shifts in them, (*e*) interfirm differentials in a locality and changes therein, and (*f*) differentials between persons working in the same occupation within a plant.[27]

INDEPENDENT VARIABLES

How are the level and composition of production, the allocation of resources, and the distribution of wealth determined? In the broad comparative sweep these may be determined by political regulation, custom,

religious decree, and so on. Formal economic analysis, however, has traditionally stressed supply and demand in the market as the immediate independent variables. For any given commodity, such as shoes, a person will
be willing to buy much if it costs little, little if it costs much. The producer
of this commodity will be willing to supply much if the price is high, little
if the price is low. The price of the commodity falls at that point where the
demand curve and the supply curve intersect.

This supply-demand principle is used to account for the behavior of all
the dependent variables. The level and composition of production depend
on the existing supply and demand conditions for products; the level and
composition of the factors of production depend on the same kinds of
condition for them; and finally, the proportions of income received by
different individuals and groups depend on the supply and demand conditions governing the relations among economic agents.

RELATIONS AMONG VARIABLES

By constructing various combinations of these dependent and independent variables, economists have created a whole variety of equilibrium
models to explain price levels, business cycles, economic growth, and other
economic phenomena. One of the most famous models in economics concerns the prediction of the quantity of a given commodity that an individual firm will produce under conditions of perfect competition. Given a
certain level of demand, the firm can expect to receive a given price (revenue) for each item it produces. But the firm itself has to pay for the factors
it utilizes in production. These costs determine the conditions of supplying
its commodity to consumers. By a series of constructions, economists have
built a model that predicts that the firm will produce that quantity of a
commodity at which the *cost* of producing the extra unit of the commodity
(marginal cost) equals the *revenue* that it will receive for that extra unit
(marginal revenue). Basically, this model says that the value of the dependent variable (quantity of the commodity produced by a firm) is a
function of the value of two sets of independent variables (demand and
supply).

Turning to the analysis of aggregates, the Keynesian model identifies
the independent variables—in the first instance—as the propensity to consume, the schedule of the marginal efficiency of capital, and the rate of
interest.[28] The propensity to consume is a demand category; the marginal
efficiency of capital rests on expectations about profits to be returned for
investments; and the rate of interest rests on the supply of money and the
demand for liquidity. By manipulating the values of these independent
variables, Keynes established a set of predictions leading to unemployment of a society's resources and reduction of its national product (dependent variables).

In these illustrative economic models the behavior of various dependent variables—prices, level of production, and so on—rests on the operation of the economic forces of supply and demand. But as a matter of empirical fact, many dozens of variables—economic, political, legal, religious—affect prices and production, and if a complete picture of economic life were to be given, many of these kinds of variable would have to be incorporated into the theoretical framework of economics. How do economists deal with these noneconomic variables? A common method is to realize that while they affect supply and demand conditions, it is necessary *for purposes of analysis* to assume that they do not change. This is the meaning of Samuelson's statement that economic analysis takes institutions and tastes as given;[29] by given he means that potential sources of influence are assumed to be constant.

To illustrate: In constructing his equilibrium system, Keynes considered several things as given: the existing skill of the labor force, the existing equipment, the existing technology, the existing degree of competition, the existing tastes of the consumer, the existing attitudes of people toward work, and the existing social structure.[30] All these, if they varied, would affect the independent variables (for example, the propensity to consume and the marginal efficiency of capital) and through them the dependent variables (employment and national income); but they are assumed not to vary.

One of the most important givens in traditional economic analysis is that of economic rationality: if an individual is presented with a situation of choice in an economic setting, he will behave so as to maximize his economic position. As an investigative device, however, economic rationality allows the economist to proceed *as if* the only independent variables were measurable changes in price and income. By employing givens such as those just reviewed, the economist simplifies the theoretical framework within which he operates. His world thus simplified, he is enabled to create theoretical solutions, often expressed in mathematical language, to economic problems.

RESEARCH METHODS

Several of the research methods that receive wide application in sociology find much more limited use in economics. The experimental method is seldom if ever employed by economists. The comparative method is limited mainly to its use by economic historians and those interested in the development of the emerging nations.[31] And finally, the case-study method is restricted to accounts of single firms, industries, banks, and so on.

The main research methods in economics, then, are the statistical method and the method of heuristic assumption. As an example of the former, let us say we wish to trace the influences on the long-term trend of potato prices. It is known that potato prices vary seasonally as well as year by year, but it is necessary to remove these influences. So the average seasonal variation for fifty years is calculated, and seasonal fluctuations for each individual year are canceled out by adding or subtracting the average seasonal variation from the actual prices. In this way one influence on prices is removed by statistical manipulation, and a truer picture of uncontaminated long-term price trends emerges. This sort of statistical analysis, as well as various tests of association, receives wide application in economics. The multivariate analysis of survey data, however, is found much less frequently in economics than in sociology, being limited, by and large, to surveys of consumers' and investors' attitudes.[32]

As indicated in the discussion of the economists' theoretical framework, the typical method in economics is the method of heuristic assumption. The most familiar version of this method is the famous explanatory strategy of *ceteris paribus*—other things equal. By assuming tastes and institutions to be given for purpose of analysis, and by assuming that certain factors do not change during a given time period, economists make parameters out of variables. By using this method to simplify sources of variation, economists have been able to reduce the number of operative variables to a manageable number and create relatively simple and elegant models of economic processes.

RELATIONS BETWEEN SOCIOLOGY AND ECONOMICS

From the accounts of the central concerns of sociology and economics reviewed thus far, it would appear that the two disciplines have little in common. Their concerns with dependent variables diverge: economics is concerned especially with variations in the level of production, techniques of production, and distribution of goods and services; sociology is concerned with variations in social structure and behavior oriented to this structure. Even when sociologists focus on economic behavior and institutions, as in the subfield of industrial sociology, they choose different aspects of these phenomena than do economists. Furthermore, there is little overlap in independent variables. And finally, the characteristic economic models are built on vastly different assumptions and logical ordering than are sociological models.

Despite these differences, the two disciplines can and should articulate at a number of critical points, to the profit of each. The most evident contribution that sociological analysis can make to economics is in the area of "givens." The various simplifying economic assumptions about human motivation and social structure are subject to widely divergent degrees of empirical accuracy; some persons "economize" much more than others, and some societies display much more economic rationality than others. The degree to which persons adhere to the postulate of economic rationality, moreover, is dependent on their social-structural moorings (for example, their religious doctrines and memberships, their position in the stratification system, and their past and present family involvements). Insofar as sociological theory and empirical research are sound in these areas, sociology can begin to provide more informed bases for the simplifying noneconomic assumptions that economists necessarily make in their discipline.[33] The need for systematic sociological supplementation of economic theory and research is especially evident in certain subbranches of economics: consumption theory, which is so obviously influenced by family and class memberships; labor economics, which is so clearly influenced by family and voluntary organization memberships; comparative economic structure, in which it becomes obviously unfeasible to assume tastes and institutional structure constant from one society to another; and economic development, in the analysis of which it becomes progressively less permissible to treat tastes and institutions as constant when the periods of time and magnitudes of change considered involve vast social and psychological reorganization.

In a number of areas economists have begun systematically to introduce noneconomic variables. To illustrate, organizational decision-making theorists have explicitly challenged the traditional economic assumptions that firms are free from internal conflict and that they possess full information about the market;[34] game theorists see organizations (such as firms, trade-unions, and government agencies) standing in political as well as economic relation to one another;[35] consumption theorists have begun systematically to introduce considerations of imitation, race, age, and marital status into their formal models;[36] and theorists of imperfect competition see firms standing in political relations to one another and to government agencies.

Likewise, sociological theories, insofar as they involve assumptions about economic life, can be systematically informed by economic theory and research. If, for example, an investigator of the family is interested in the impact of unemployment on a society's family system, he can inform himself of the magnitude of unemployment by reference to trade-cycle theory, investment theory, and theory of economic development. In general, however, the codification of sociologists' assumptions about economic behavior and institutions is neither simplified nor systematic enough to permit specification of the precise points of contribution from economics to sociology, as it is the other way around.

In addition to gaining substantively from economic theory and research, sociology stands to profit in a formal sense from economics. Of all the behavioral sciences, economics has reached the highest point of theoretical development, with the possible exception of certain branches of psychology, such as learning theory. It has done so by simplifying the number of variables via the method of heuristic assumption, combining these variables into simplified models, expressing these models in mathematical terms, and representing variables in quantifiable terms. Difficult as these operations are to perform in some branches of sociology, the field is in need of reducing the scatteration of variables and creating simpler, more concise models. Sociologists can profit from studying the formal aspects of economic theory in meeting this need, probably more than they can profit from the study of the formal aspects of psychology, biology, and the physical sciences, since economics, among all these possibilities, deals with social systems of one type, and social systems are the stuff of sociological analysis.[37]

Unfortunately, contemporary academic arrangements in universities are not the best for encouraging active collaboration between economists and sociologists. Departments of economics and sociology are infrequently conjoined, and few joint courses are given. Also, there is a subtle tendency for economists to view sociology as soft and for sociologists to be frightened away from using economics by the technical aspects of economic theory and research. The main points of contact between the two disciplines are in various professional schools and institutes, such as schools of business administration and institutions of industrial and labor relations; in addition, a number of promising points of active collaboration between economists and sociologists have appeared in the past two decades with the establishment of various interdisciplinary centers and institutes concerned with economic development.

Political Science

In principle, political science should be as amenable to formulation in as theoretically elegant terms as economics. Its focus on the creation, organization, distribution, and utilization of power parallels and is potentially as specific as economics' focus on the production, distribution, and consumption of wealth. Models concerning the principles by which the components of power—legitimacy, public support, administrative skill, financial resources, and so forth—are combined conceivably could parallel models of market equilibrium so typical of economics. In practice, however, theoretical formulation in scientific terms has not reached anything near the proportions in political science it has in economics. Only in recent decades can the study of political life—despite its traditional name of political science—be said to be becoming a social science at all, in the sense that it possesses the ingredients of a scientific framework as outlined earlier in this chapter. Therefore, while I shall use the same list of scientific ingredients I used in characterizing sociology and economics, I shall have to indicate those areas of activity in political science to which they do not apply.

DEPENDENT VARIABLES

I have already indicated the central substantive focus of political science: behavior and institutions that are concerned primarily with the creation and exercise of power. The ways in which political scientists define and describe this behavior and those institutions, however, vary greatly.

One tradition of political science is concerned with describing formal political institutions at different political-geographical levels. American Government, for example, customarily has been taught as an account of how American political institutions work, according to the Constitution, statutory law, and customary practice. The same could be said for traditional treatments of state government, federal-state relations, and county and municipal government. The same applies to the traditional approach to international relations, except that it has also been characterized in part by an emphasis on diplomatic history. In these traditional areas of political science, the literature also displays some concern with policy implications—for example, the pros and cons of various forms of city government, such as mayor, city council, and city manager. An offshoot of this historical-descriptive tradition in political science is one type of comparative government, preoccupied, by and large, with Western constitutional governments and large-scale political institutions such as legislatures, civil services, and judiciary systems.

In recent decades a new emphasis in political science has emerged: the behavioral approach. Given impetus by the conceptual frameworks and research methods of the other behavioral sciences, this approach has given quite a different definition to the subject matter of political science.[38] One contrast with the traditional approach[39] is that the behavioral emphasis concentrates more on the behavior of individuals in political situations and less on the formal structure of political institutions. The behavioral approach, moreover, is relatively more interested in explaining behavior in terms of social and psychological determinants and less in simply describing behavior. Moreover, the behavioral approach leans toward quantitative measurement and statistical manipulation and away from qualitative accounts of political phenomena. In addition, especially insofar as the behavioral approach has invaded comparative politics, it has not only concentrated more on the dynamics of political behavior rather than the structure of institutions but also enlarged the kinds of settings in which political behavior occurs to include tribes, clans, quasi-developed parties, and so on, as well as formal systems of representative government and bureaucracy.[40] Finally, the language associated with the behavioral approach, in both its noncomparative and comparative aspects, is considerably more abstract and analytic—employing terms like "political socialization" and "interest articulation"—than the language specific to the particular political institutions under study.

INDEPENDENT VARIABLES

Insofar as the traditional approach to empirical political science is descriptive of the history, workings, and effectiveness of various formal political institutions, it can be said that there is very little explicit interest in explanation via the use of independent variables. From time to time explanations are given—for instance, the paralysis of the political process in the French Fourth Republic may be attributed to the fragmentation of parties or to the French electoral system—but such explanations tend to be based on *ad hoc* and historically specific considerations, rather than on systematic specification of factors making for political effectiveness.

Investigators using the behavioral approach to politics are concerned explicitly with the determinants of political behavior. A list of these determinants, moreover, reads very much like a general catalogue of determinants in sociology and psychology. Voting behavior, for example, has been shown to be influenced by race, education, socioeconomic level, religion, and family, as well as by various psychological variables.[41] Indeed, it is somewhat arbitrary to assign this new tradition of research to either political science, sociology, or psychology, since variables from all three disciplines are liberally intermingled, and very similar research is conducted by those who call themselves sociologists, political scientists, and psychologists.

RELATIONS AMONG VARIABLES

Political science shows great diversity with respect to models and theories. In the essentially descriptive tradition of empirical political study, models and theories as I have characterized them can scarcely be said to exist, since the major thrust of the study is historical and descriptive, rather than formally explanatory. In addition, what has gone by the name of political theory in political science is usually not theory in the scientific sense of the word, but rather the study of the moral and political philosophy. This type of traditional political theory is more akin to the study of intellectual history or the study of ethics than it is to any of the social sciences.

The growth of scientific theory proper in political science is very recent and is also associated with the behavioral revolution in the field. To choose only a few illustrations, Harold Lasswell's early efforts at accounting for the distribution of power in a political system possess the embryonic ingredients of a formal theory;[42] Anthony Downs's endeavors to create a theory of democracy are considerably more formal—in fact, his model of political behavior imitates economic theory by postulating a version of political rationality and building a theory of political process on this and other simplifying assumptions;[43] David Easton, building mainly on the work of social-systems analysts in sociology, has developed a comprehensive and methodologically self-conscious theory of the political system;[44] and a number of analysts have attempted to systematize the structure and processes of international relations into a variety of theoretical frameworks.[45] In varying degrees of completeness, these models and theories contain the ingredients of formalized statements of relations among variables, explicit attention to guiding assumptions, and (to a lesser extent) derivation of testable hypotheses.

RESEARCH METHODS

In most of the traditional branches of political science, the research methods resemble those of the historian and philosopher more than those of the other social sciences. These methods include the examination and qualitative description of formal constitutional documents, laws, and historical events and an attempt to draw from these sources adequate characterizations of institutional political structures; also the examination and textual analysis of the writings of political philosophers in an effort to interpret, criticize, and synthesize their views on the broader philosophical aspects of politics and ethics. In the newer branches of political science that have been grouped loosely under the heading of the behavioral approach, the methods of research are, except for relative emphasis, almost indistinguishable from the methods of sociology and social psychology. Experimental research does find little use in political science,[46] but political scientists have employed a vast array of methods of data gathering, statistical manipulation, and comparative methods that are also commonly used in sociology.[47]

RELATIONS BETWEEN SOCIOLOGY AND POLITICAL SCIENCE

In reviewing the relations between sociology and economics, I emphasized the differences in dependent variables, independent variables, and theoretical models and frameworks.[48] Given these differences, the appropriate relations between the fields appeared to be *complementary articulation*. With respect to political science—and now I refer only to the behavioral approach—the story is different. Political sociologists and political scientists often study the same empirical phenomena: voting behavior, political attitudes, the structure of political parties, social mobility through political channels, social and political unrest, and so on. As we have seen, they explain these phenomena by using very similar types of independent variables. Research methods in the two fields also show striking resemblances. And insofar as political scientists have developed formal models of behavior, they tend often to resemble the theoretical frameworks employed by sociologists.[49] Correspondingly, the relations between the two fields have not been so much those of complementary articulation as those of *overlapping of common preoccupations.* Indeed, it strikes me that were it not for the historical fact that the behavioral approach to politics grew up in the context of existing academic departments of political science, there is little reason to believe that it would not be a special subdivision of sociology, similar to social stratification or the sociology of religion.

One exception to this general characterization of the two disciplines as overlapping should be noted. As formal theories of the political system continue to develop in political science, they will undoubtedly come to resemble formal economic theories, insofar as they will deal with the creation and exercise of power and will rest on a relatively formal series of assumptions regarding the givens within which political processes occur. As this type of analysis of specialized social processes advances, the need for mutual articulation will grow correspondingly, and the relations between sociology and political science will come to resemble more those that now obtain between sociology and economics.

In terms of academic arrangements, the linking of departments of sociology and political science is probably no more frequent than the linking of sociology and economics. The spirit of collaboration on both sides of the disciplinary boundaries, however, is more congenial than is the case with sociology and economics, and it seems safe to predict that the next few years will see the growth of joint courses and seminars and joint appointments in departments of sociology and political science. Other areas of interaction between the two fields are in survey research centers, area study programs (especially those dealing with nations with totalitarian governments), and various comparative study centers, such as the Center for the Study of Internal War at Princeton University and the Center for the Comparative Study of New Nations at the University of Chicago.

Anthropology

If we leave physical anthropology, archaeology, and the anthropological study of linguistic systems aside, we may be very brief in our treatment of anthropology. The reason for this is that the similarities between social and cultural anthropology on the one hand and sociology on the other vastly outweigh the differences; and the differences are frequently matters of shading.

By and large, sociology and anthropology are preoccupied with the same classes of dependent variables: social structure and behavior oriented toward social structure. Within this basic similarity, however, it is possible to discover some different emphases. Because of the important personality and culture subdivision in anthropology, it is probable that anthropologists focus more on socialization and personality than sociologists; but even this generalization is subject to question, particularly in the light of the growing interest in socialization and personality in the sociology of the family and the sociology of mental health and illness. It is also probable that the influence of Freudian psychology is more marked in anthropology than it is in sociology, but it is by no means absent in the latter. Again, anthropologists—particularly American anthropologists influenced by the work of scholars like Ruth Benedict and Clyde Kluckhohn —focus on cultural value and meaning systems more than do sociologists; but the existence of sociological interest in art, literature, religion, and mass culture qualifies this generalization. And finally, anthropological research has centered more on certain institutional sectors—especially kinship, magic, and religion—that have been thought to infuse the simpler societies they have studied; but these subjects are not without interest to sociologists, and, especially in modern times, anthropologists have interested themselves in economic structure, political structure, stratification, economic development, and other aspects of social life.

Anthropologists and sociologists traditionally have studied social life in different settings. Anthropologists have concentrated on small, simple, often nonliterate societies, whereas sociologists have chosen to study large, complex, literate civilizations. Particularly in the past two decades this distinction has been breaking down, as sociologists and anthropologists alike study caste in Indian villages, as anthropologists take up investigations of places like East London, and as sociologists generally widen their comparative scope.

Perhaps the most pervasive difference between the two fields resides in divergent styles of conceiving societies. Both anthropologists and sociologists do tend to think of societies as interrelated systems; the solid place of structural-functional thought in each discipline testifies to this commonality. Within this broadly similar framework, however, certain differences emerge. Anthropologists tend more to think in unique-pattern ways about society. Perhaps this tendency results from the historical fact that they have concentrated on small, relatively undifferentiated societies; perhaps it stems from the dominance of the relativistic viewpoint during the interwar period, in which "[emphasis] was placed . . . on the unique and the contextual. The search for internal coherence between institutions, or coherence between individual psychology and social form, or the coherence between belief and behavior all within a single and often arbitrarily defined unit was the fashion of the period." [50] This characterization must be qualified, however, by mentioning this considerable body of anthropological cross-cultural analysis that focuses on connections between a few sets of variables in a wide range of cultural settings.[51] By contrast with the anthropologists' predominantly unique-pattern approach, sociologists' preoccupation with the interrelatedness of social phenomena tends to be—

but is not always—characterized more by a search for aggregated connections between a limited number of variables and less by a focus on totality of patterns as such.

Related to these different styles of interpreting social interrelations are further differences in research methods and outlook. Anthropology tends to be characterized mainly by the case-study method, in which the investigator actually immerses himself in the single culture to be studied.[52] In many cases he becomes a participant observer and more often than not relies on informants for much of his data about the culture. One outgrowth of this kind of involvement is that the anthropological investigator comes to appreciate the richness and complexity of social life in the culture under study; he tends to focus more on the broader meaning-context of social behavior. At the same time and for the same reasons, he is likely to be unfriendly to objective methods of measurement that pull items of behavior from this meaning context. He therefore has a predilection to represent behavior in the same meaning context as that of the culture under study.[53] By contrast, the comparative sociologist (as well as the comparative economist and political scientist), being more concept- and variable-centered, tends to be more willing to apply objective comparative measures and to lift items of behavior from their unique cultural contexts.[54]

So much for some of the contrasts in substance, method, and style between anthropology and sociology. In all cases these contrasts appear to be subtle shadings, rather than clear-cut differences. We might conclude this brief section by suggesting the ways in which these two quite similar fields might interchange usefully with each other. Certainly the possibilities of mutual interchange of *empirical data* are great, since anthropologists and sociologists still tend to study different types of society and different institutional contexts within these societies. In particular, the comparative analysis of social structure and the study of social change can profit as sociologists inform themselves better on the character of social life in relatively undifferentiated societies and anthropologists on the character of social life in more complex societies. The opportunities for *complementary theoretical articulation*, however, are considerably less, simply because the variables and theoretical frameworks of the two disciplines are so fundamentally similar. The tendency, therefore, would seem to be one of consolidation of the theoretical frameworks of sociology and anthropology rather than complementary articulation of distinct frameworks, as is the case between sociology and economics. In fact, it is not unreasonable to suggest that as theoretical refinement and codification advance in the social sciences, the differences between anthropology and sociology will be the first to be absorbed into a common theoretical framework.

History

During the past century many opinions have been ventured on the general relations between history and sociology (or the social sciences in general). These notions range widely. At one extreme is the view of a number of German writers toward the end of the nineteenth century that sociology is a generalizing science in search of uniform laws of social life and that history is a particularizing study dealing with the unique occurrences of human life, and, as a consequence of this distinction, the two enterprises are completely separate from each other. At the other extreme is the recent view expressed by S. D. Clark that "nothing today would appear to set off [sociology and history] from one another other than the biases and prejudices inherited from the past. The . . . explanation of what occurs by comparing a particular occurrence with other occurrences is the task which the historian performs and it is a task which must be performed by the sociologist the moment he turns to examine the processes of change in society." [55] Writers on the philosophy of science and the sociological study of change take various positions between these two extremes.[56]

In treating history as a social science, it is possible, as with anthropology, to be quite brief, though for a different reason. History, more than any of the disciplines here considered in this chapter, lacks the ingredients of a formal scientific method,[57] so it would be inappropriate to attempt a point-by-point comparison with sociology in terms of these ingredients. Nevertheless, it is possible to compare the two disciplines from the standpoint of the data to be explained, the approach to causal explanation, the interpretative frameworks employed, and the research methods used.

History and sociology share a catholicism with respect to data that may legitimately be studied within their respective disciplines. It is literally true that there can be a history of anything: industrial capitalism, French doorknobs, or misspellings in New England cookbooks. And because the range of sociological variables is so great—including social structure and behavior oriented to social structure—it is virtually true that there can be a legitimate sociology of anything, so long as it can be encompassed by these broad categories. Certainly there could readily be a sociological treatment of industrial capitalism, French doorknobs, and even misspellings in New England cookbooks. Thus, in principle, historians and sociologists are immersed in a common mass of raw material. In practice, however, their attention is directed toward data that have been recorded at different points in time. Most historians choose data that have been recorded in the relatively distant past, whereas most sociologists choose data that have been recently or are being currently recorded. Not all historians and sociologists behave this way, however, and there is no inherent reason in either discipline why they should do so.

Despite their common comprehensiveness of data, history and sociology are subdivided in ways so different that ready comparisons between the two fields are quite difficult. As a rule, historians use three criteria to subdivide their field—chronological time, cultural or national tradition, and aspects of social life. The familiar phrases, "British social history of the late nineteenth century" and "Western European intellectual history during the eighteenth century," exemplify these criteria. Sociologists tend to divide their field by somewhat more abstract terms: types of social structure, types of behavior oriented to social structure, types of social groupings, and so on. It is true that some sociologists are regional or area specialists and thus focus on a distinctive cultural or national tradition. It is also true that the familiar institutional subdivisions of sociology—religion, law, military, and so forth—correspond with some of the subdivisions of history—religious, legal, or military history, for instance—but these correspondences are only very approximate.

In their methods of identifying problems for study, sociologists and historians also display different, though overlapping, emphases. A historical problem, generally speaking, is rooted in and emerges from the logic of events of a given place and period; for example, why did the French monarchy and aristocracy become so unresponsive to demands for social reform during the eighteenth century? By contrast, a sociological problem, generally speaking, tends to be rooted in and is generated by some conceptual apparatus; for example, what are the relations between blocked social mobility and social protest, as illustrated in the eighteenth-century French case? This is not to say that the approach of the historian is inductive and that of the sociologists deductive. Both necessarily rely on preconceived concepts, assumptions, and suspected associations among historical happenings. The relative differences are in degree of explicitness of preconceptions and in degree of abstraction from a particular historical context.

In their concern with explanations, a similar difference in emphasis between sociologists and historians emerges. By contrast with a field like economics, both tend to be comprehensive and eclectic in their concern with causes (or independent variables). This eclecticism, however, stems from different sources. For sociologists, it arises not from any commitment to diversity or complexity of causes—as a rule sociologists are as committed to determinate causal explanations as other social scientists—but rather because the field itself has not been able to specify these causes and hence displays a great proliferation of independent variables.[58] The eclecticism of historians stems from the fact that their historical problem is rooted in a particular place and historical period. A historical period itself, however, being quite indiscriminate in the way it unfolds, does very little by way of isolating, specifying, and organizing causes of events; it requires the machinations of human investigators—machinations that take the form of the experimental, statistical, and other methods of research—to manipulate causes and assess their general operation in a variety of different historical situations. The historian, attentive to a problem and period, interprets the causes of events as he finds them, as it were, and thus takes on the natural eclecticism of causation in an uncontrolled historical sequence of events. Thus, the historian is prepared to admit invasions, personality characteristics of kings, population increases, changes in landownership patterns, and social-protest movements as causes, if these appear to be important for his particular historical problem. The relatively more systematic social scientist, on the other hand, attempts to hold constant various of these events by diverse means of situational and conceptual manipulations, thus isolating, simplifying, and making less eclectic his concern with causes.

To summarize, a sociologist's approach to data, problems, and causes of events—in contrast to a historian's—tends to rest on a more formal explicit conceptual apparatus that is more self-consciously selective of facts. Insofar as the historian adopts such an apparatus, and insofar as he adopts the relatively systematic methods of manipulating data utilized by the sociologist, the difference between the two disciplines tends to disappear.

Given these contrasting emphases, what types of interchange might prove profitable between history and sociology? A first type stems from the fact that sociologists and historians emphasize present and past, respectively, in their studies of society.[59] Particularly in comparative analysis and in the study of social change, each discipline stands to profit from examining the data produced and analyzed in the other. A second type of exchange involves the use of historical investigations to formulate sociological problems and vice versa. A careful reading of a historical monograph—even one on a subject remote from the sociologist's substantive interests—indubitably will reveal empirical connections between events that can inform his sociological preoccupations. Similarly, a careful study of sociological theory and research will instruct historians in new connections, new kinds of data to be sought, and new kinds of historical questions to be asked. As indicated above, historical problems have tended to be rooted in specific empirical contexts, and sociological problems have tended to be generated from conceptual frameworks, though this generalization does not apply unequivocally to either discipline. Insofar as it is correct, however, both sociologists and historians will gain from studying each other's problems, since the origins of their respective problems complement each other.

A third type of exchange involves the respective methods of research and data assessment in history and sociology. Historians, like archaeologists, often confront isolated historical fragments in their work, from which they must, in the absence of more complete data, draw inferences about the historical period in question. Clearly it is impossible to use formal research methods such as statistical analysis in these circumstances. Instead, historians have developed an art of seeking out and piecing together isolated items to delineate a picture of society's past structure and activities. By and large the skills involved in this art have remained implicit; indeed, the art is almost an intuitive one. Certainly it would be of enormous service to both historians and sociologists if a historical investigator would set down a definitive methodology of historical inference from fragmented data. In particular, the sociologist could profit from such a methodology, since it would better enable him to turn to empirical situations that are relevant and important for his investigations, but meager in their supply of data. Historians, on their side, stand to gain from adopting —to a greater extent than they already have—the formal research techniques of sociologists, particularly in their analyses of historical data that can be represented quantitatively. These techniques are especially appropriate for the study of modern history, which is so much more abundant in formal, written records of human transactions.

Psychology[60]

Despite the differences I have noted, it is correct to say that sociology, economics, political science, and anthropology are *social* sciences.[61] The reason for this is that the overarching focus of these disciplines is on interpersonal relations that emerge when two or more persons interact with one another. The units of analysis are the relations among persons—or roles, or structures—and behavior oriented to these relations. In this respect, all four disciplines contrast with psychology, which studies the same mass of behavioral data, but has a different analytic focus. The analytic focus of psychology is the individual person as a system of needs, feelings, aptitudes, skills, defenses, and such, or on one or more processes, such as the learning of skills, considered in detail. In all cases the organizing conceptual unit is the person. The four social sciences differ in various ways in the kind of social structures and systems they study; psychology differs from all of these in that it lies at a separate analytic level altogether. This fundamental contrast not only epitomizes the differences between psychology and the social sciences but also suggests the distinctive ways they may contribute to one another.

Within its overarching analytic focus on the individual person, psychology studies a number of different kinds of variables.[62] Among the most important of these are the concept of need, which is a construct referring to the internal motivational forces that give direction, intensity, and persistence to behavior; the concept of capacities, including intelligence and skills by means of which the individual arrives at some resolution of tensions resulting from these motivational forces; the concept of personality structure, which refers to the combination of patterns of needs and capacities into relatively enduring modes of adaptation to his environment; and various more dynamic concepts, including stress and psychic conflict, responses to stress and conflict, attempts to control these responses, and resulting processes of personality change. In attempting to account for variations in these, psychologists tend to focus on the psychic system itself; but they frequently do make use of social units as independent variables: for example, size of family, order of birth in family, socioeconomic status, ethnic and religious group memberships, and so on.

In this chapter I shall not review the various ways in which psychologists organize their variables into models and systems, except to note in passing a contrast within psychology that parallels one of the contrasts between anthropology and sociology. I refer to the contrast between the clinical or unique-pattern approach versus the aggregated-variable approach.[63] Within psychology the clinical psychologist tends to focus on the single individual, interpreting his behavior in the meaning context of his personality pattern, whereas many experimental and social psychologists focus on a more limited number of personality variables and attempt to discover connections among these variables—connections manifested by an aggregate of individuals with different unique personality constellations—by using the formal research methods of experimental control and statistical analysis. It would be an instructive exercise in intellectual history to compare and contrast the tensions between anthropologists and sociologists, on the one hand, with the tensions between the clinical and experimental social psychologists, on the other.

In the light of this briefest of characterizations of psychology as a science, what can be said about the possibilities for exchange between it and sociology?[64] These possibilities are both formal and substantive; the substantive exchanges, in turn, break down into empirical and theoretical ones. With respect to formal interchanges, it is evident that many psychological variables are cognate with sociological variables at a different analytic level. For example, the concept of need parallels the concept of functional exigency of a social system in many ways; the concept of individual capacities parallels the concept of social resources; the concept of personality structure parallels the concept of social structure; the concept of ego control parallels the concept of social control; and so on.[65] Furthermore, various models of personality adjustment, growth, and disorganization parallel models of social change.[66] Careful study of psychological models by sociologists, and vice versa, is likely to produce new issues for both, since the analytic levels in which each have been generated are quite different.[67]

This formal interchange between variables and models at different levels should not be confused with psychological or social reductionism, which marks an attempt to translate, without loss, all statements at one analytic level into statements regarding the operations of variables at another level. An example of a reductionist statement would be: "Society is no more than the sum total of the psychological states of its members." The general consequence of reductionist reasoning, if pushed far enough, is to deny the independent conceptual status of one analytic level. In this respect reductionist reasoning is the opposite of reasoning by analogy. Analogy involves *no* claim of causal influence between two analytically independent levels, but only a claim of formal similarities between the levels; reductionism involves a claim of *total* determination of processes at one level by reference to variables at another level. The status of the reduced process is that of an epiphenomenal by-product with no causal feedback.

With respect to substantive exchanges, it is evident that social and psychological perspectives can be fruitfully combined into explanatory frameworks. For any given empirical problem—for example, the study of suicide rates in different settings—different social variables, such as religion, family structure, and ethnic group membership, can each account for some variation. If combined into a more complex interactive model of determinants, the explanatory power of these social determinants is even greater. After a certain point the continuous refinement of social variables becomes subject to diminishing returns. The investigator must ask how the various social influences are processed intrapsychically if he is to account for more variation and if he is to discover why some individuals do and others do not commit suicide under identical social conditions. Similarly, psychologists interested in the importance of early childhood experiences on personality development are able to enhance the adequacy of their explanations if they can be informed as to the influence of, say, family structure and social-class level on the probability of occurrence of diverse kinds of childhood traumas.

To appreciate the possibilities of substantive exchange between sociology and psychology at the theoretical level, we may refer to the problem of givens once more. As we have seen, sociological concepts, hypotheses, and theoretical frameworks always rest on a number of assumptions about human motivations, skills, and so on.[68] And psychological explanations inevitably rest on certain presuppositions regarding the kinds of social framework within which these explanations apply. Too often these underlying assumptions are vague, implicit, and unexamined appendages to the theory in question. Some of the most promising avenues of collaboration between sociologists and psychologists are through mutual enlightenment as to the psychological and sociological underpinnings of their respective theories, mutual instruction as to the questionable assertions these underpinnings may conceal, and mutual exchange of findings so that these assertions may be made more adequate theoretically.

I shall conclude this section with one observation on research methods in psychology. One distinguishing feature of psychology is that it makes much more extensive use of the experimental method than the other disciplines here considered. Another is that, because of its historical connection with psychotherapeutic and psychiatric practice, it makes very extensive use of the method of clinical case study. So pronounced is each of these features that research strategies in the field tend often to be thought of as either clinical approaches to depth variables or socioexperimental approaches to surface variables such as attitudes or overt behavior. I suggest that psychologists would benefit greatly by giving careful study to the uses of the comparative method in sociology,[69] which stands between these two extreme alternatives in the sense that it does not deal with enough cases to permit elaborate statistical control but does deal with enough to permit approximations to such control even with depth variables. Adaptation of this method to intraindividual comparisons would do much, in my opinion, to permit more systematic investigation of variables now considered inextricable from the richness and complexity of a single clinical case and to reduce conflicts among psychological investigators, who now tend to opt exclusively for either the clinical or the socioexperimental approach.

Summary and Conclusion: Integration and Collaboration among the Social Sciences

To pull together the various strands developed in this chapter, let me summarize the interchanges that may be expected among the various social sciences. This summary should provide the reader with an indication of the several analytic uses of sociology for the other social sciences, but I shall present the summary as it should be presented—not in terms of a one-way flow of "uses," but as two-way interchanges.

1. Insofar as sociology and other social sciences take an interest in common data, each discipline should be able to provide a partial account of empirical variations in these data. With reference to sexual behavior and attitudes, for instance, sociological research can provide insight as to the types of class background and family structure associated with distinctive patterns of sexual behavior; psychological research can provide evidence as to how social and other variables are processed intrapsychically, thus contributing more microscopic kinds of insight; and historical and anthropological research can shed light on how these social and psychological determinants have worked out in diverse cultural contexts. These relations among the various disciplines, it must be stressed, are not competitive, but essentially complementary.

2. Insofar as every discipline necessarily restricts its range of inquiry and makes simplifying assumptions about—that is, treats as given—those

areas outside this range, each discipline stands to be informed as to the adequacy of these assumptions by referring to the empirical research and theoretical formulations of neighboring disciplines. These more general relations among the disciplines are also of a complementary character.

3. Insofar as common formal problems are faced by theorists in different disciplines, they stand to profit from studying formal solutions generated in neighboring disciplines. Equilibrium theory as formulated in biology and economics, for example, has proved of value in formulating principles of equilibrium in sociology and psychology. Great care must be taken, however, to avoid wholesale importation of theoretical models from other disciplines, and the social scientist should always temper analogous formulations with qualifications appropriate to new empirical and theoretical settings.

4. Insofar as the various disciplines face common problems of drawing inferences from data, they stand to gain from studying the diverse research methods employed in neighboring disciplines. Sociologists, for example, when they meet a problem that demands tracing the course of quantitative indices over time, would do well to turn to the well-developed techniques of analyzing time series in economics. And, as indicated, psychologists can profit by developing research methods similar to the comparative method in sociology and anthropology.

These various types of interchange raise the more general problem of the integration of knowledge in the social sciences. This problem is a perennial one. Ever since the social sciences began to develop, scholars have repeatedly expressed apprehension about the increasing fragmentation of knowledge through specialization. Correspondingly, they have sounded the call for greater integration—even unification—of scientific knowledge. Justified as these demands are, they are not without their utopian elements; indeed, the hopes expressed for the unification of scientific knowledge often resemble the hopes for the unification of the world religions. The utopian element lies in the overemphasis on ends and the underemphasis on means.

During the past twenty years, scholars have expressed much misty-eyed enthusiasm about a number of words, all of which refer in one way or another to the end of unification: words such as codification, integration, cross-fertilization, interdisciplinary research, and the multidisciplinary approach. As is often the case, this proliferation of inexact synonyms signifies a search for something, the exact nature of which we are not aware. Moreover, a vague romanticism often seems to govern thinking about the means of attaining the end of unification. It appears to me that many of the numerous interdisciplinary arrangements of the past two decades—institutes, centers, regional study groups, seminars, conferences, and panels —have rested on the belief, even hope, that if only scholars from different specialties are placed in one another's presence, some process of integration will occur spontaneously. Unfortunately, the endeavors based on this hope are usually quite barren, yielding mainly general talk *about* integration rather than results *of* integration. Just as it is true that people of different nations will not reach sympathetic understanding of one another by virtue of being placed together in an international exchange program or seminar, so it is true that scholars will not integrate their specialized branches of knowledge merely by talking with one another about their subjects or even reading one another's books.

If spontaneous combustion is not the path to integration of scientific knowledge, what is? I hope I have indicated some guidelines in this essay. A major requirement of integration is that some common language be developed so that the elements of the different social sciences can be systematically compared and contrasted with one another. The language I have employed is the language of the ingredients of science: dependent variables, independent variables, theoretical frameworks, and research methods. Having developed this language, we may better see what kinds of integration are possible and what kinds are not. And in examining the relations between sociology and the other social sciences in terms of the scientific ingredients of each, we turned up a variety of types of integration. In the relations between sociology and anthropology, for example, we discovered an essential identity of scientific enterprise; in the relations between sociology and economics, we discovered possibilities of complementary theoretical articulation at the social level of analysis; in the relations between sociology and psychology, we discovered possibilities of complementary theoretical articulation at different analytic levels; in the relations between sociology and history, we saw possibilities of exchange mainly in terms of problems, data, and research methods; and in some cases—for example, in the relations between scientific sociology and traditional political theory—we discovered such a difference in approach and methods that the question of integration is probably irrelevant. In short, by employing this common language to compare and contrast the various social sciences, we have seen that integration of scientific knowledge is a complex and diversified, not a simple and unitary, thing.

This enterprise of comparing and contrasting the social sciences within a common language is a very laborious and disciplined one. So, also, is the process by which social scientists may actually profit from the theory and research of a neighboring social science. Unfortunately, it is not possible for a sociologist (or any other kind of social scientist), upon reaching a blind alley in his analysis, to ask, "How can (say) economics help me here?" and come up with a simple, satisfactory answer by reading a text in economics. In order to call upon the assistance of a sister discipline, he must become in some degree disciplined in that discipline, so that he may appreciate the context and significance of its contribution, rather than lift it from its disciplinary moorings and thus distort it. To insist upon this kind of continuing education as a precondition for successful interdisciplinary exchange is to insist upon a great deal of work for social scientists. But in the end this work is necessary, if interchanges between the disciplines are to be profound and rewarding, rather than superficial and disappointing.

REFERENCES

1. Alex Inkeles, *What Is Sociology? An Introduction to the Discipline and Profession* (Englewood Cliffs, N.J.: Prentice-Hall, 1964).
2. These five fields, plus sociology, are those which Bernard Berelson also classifies as "social sciences." "Introduction to the Behavioral Sciences," in Bernard Berelson, ed., *The Behaviorial Sciences Today* (New York: Basic Books, 1963), p. 1.
3. Part of this section, as well as the following section on economics, is an elaboration of material originally presented in my book *The Sociology of Economic Life* (Englewood Cliffs, N.J.: Prentice-Hall, 1963), pp. 24–31.
4. There are numerous ways to classify these schools, differing according to the descriptive criteria chosen. For two different efforts to classify schools, see Don Martindale, *The Nature and Types of Sociological Theory* (Boston: Houghton Mifflin, 1960), and Helmut R. Wagner, "Types of Sociological Theory: Toward a System of Classification," *American Sociological Review,* XXVIII (1963), 735–742.
5. In practice the operation of posing problems and the operation of specifying concrete units proceed simultaneously and interact with each other.
6. To characterize the field in this manner excludes, at first glance, several of its subfields: (1) those subfields at the "cultural" boundary of social behavior—the sociology of literature, art, music, ideology, and mass culture—which cannot be classified as units of social structure proper; (2) those subfields at the "physical" and "biological" boundaries of social behavior—specifically demography, ecology, and some parts of urban and rural sociology—where the units of behavior are not social-structural but rather events and situations classified in terms of biological processes and spatial location; (3) those subfields at the "personality" boundary of social behavior—for example, socialization, some aspects of deviance and collective behavior, and the catchall field of social psychology. Despite this difference from other fields that focus on social structure itself, the reason for including them in sociology is that the analysis of these kinds of behavior social structure appears as an important independent variable. For example, in the sociology of knowledge, the major focus is on those kinds of social structures that give rise to distinctive cultural productions; in some parts of demography, the focus is on those kinds of structure (family systems, the rural-urban balance, stratification) that give rise to, say, differential fertility rates; and in the analysis of the differential occurrence of attitudes and opinions, explanatory variables are frequently social-structural in character (age, sex, socioeconomic position, and religious affiliation).
7. *Political Parties: A Sociological Study of the Oligarchical Tendencies of Modern Democracy,* translated by Eden and Cedar Paul (New York: Dover Publications, 1959).
8. *Ibid.,* Part I.
9. *Ibid.,* Part II, Chapters 1 and 2.

10. An example of this kind of research is the preoccupation with the factual question of whether social mobility is increasing, decreasing, or remaining constant in recent American history. For a summary of recent research on this question, see Elton F. Jackson and Harry J. Crockett, Jr., "Occupational Mobility in the United States: A Point Estimate and Trend Comparison," *American Sociological Review*, XXIX (1964), 5–15.

11. An example of a model applied to voting behavior is the discussion of panel analysis in Patricia L. Kendall and Paul F. Lazarsfeld, "Problems of Survey Analysis," in Robert K. Merton and Paul F. Lazarsfeld, eds., *Continuities in Social Research* (Glencoe, Ill.: The Free Press, 1950).

12. Models of this kind may be found in Neil J. Smelser, *Theory of Collective Behavior* (New York: The Free Press of Glencoe, 1963).

13. For an example of the application of mathematical models to the explanation of structural variation, see Harrison C. White, *An Anatomy of Kinship: Mathematical Models for Structures of Cumulated Roles* (Englewood Cliffs, N.J.: Prentice-Hall, 1963); for an example of the application of mathematical models to non-experimental processes of collective behavior, see William N. McPhee, *Formal Theories of Mass Behavior* (New York: The Free Press of Glencoe, 1963).

14. See especially Talcott Parsons, Robert F. Bales, and Edward Shils, eds., *Working Papers in the Theory of Action* (Glencoe, Ill.: The Free Press, 1953), and Marion J. Levy, Jr., *The Structure of Society* (Princeton: Princeton University Press, 1952).

15. For an examination of some of the implications of the "Marxian" and "Durkheimian" views of the human condition as manifested in research in industrial sociology, see Louis Schneider and Sverre Lysgaard, " 'Deficiency' and 'Conflict' in Industrial Sociology," *American Journal of Economics and Sociology*, XII (1952–1953), 49–61.

16. In this section I shall be concerned with only one aspect of research methodology: the ways in which data are manipulated to permit the investigator to draw relatively valid inferences. These ways include the experimental, statistical, comparative, and clinical methods, as well as the method of heuristic assumption. I shall not be able to discuss particular methods of measurement, such as content analysis or attitude surveys; nor will I discuss particular statistical techniques, such as the analysis of variance.

17. For an example of a research on social mobility using this kind of statistical manipulation, see Natalie Rogoff Ramsøy, "Changing Rates of Mobility," in Neil J. Smelser and Seymour Martin Lipset, eds., *Social Structure and Mobility in Economic Development* (Chicago: Aldine Press, 1966).

18. For an extended exercise that used the variables of age, education, and various measures of intolerance, cf. Samuel A. Stouffer, *Communism, Conformity, and Civil Liberties: A Cross-section of the Nation Speaks Its Mind* (Garden City, N.Y.: Doubleday, 1955), pp. 89–108. Stouffer actually found both age and education correlated with intolerance, even after correcting for the influence of each on the other. For a brief general discussion of this method as applied to the wartime researches on the American soldier, cf. Kendall and Lazarsfeld, *op. cit.*

19. Emile Durkheim, *Suicide*, translated by John A. Spaulding and George Simpson (Glencoe, Ill.: The Free Press, 1951), pp. 152–156.

20. *Ibid.*, p. 157.

21. F. J. Roethlisberger and William J. Dickson, *Management and the Worker* (Cambridge: Harvard University Press, 1947), 2nd ed., Part IV.

22. W. Lloyd Warner and Associates, *Democracy in Jonesville* (New York: Harper, 1949).

23. Erving Goffman, *Asylums* (New York: Doubleday Anchor, 1961).

24. Above, page 14.
25. Paul A. Samuelson, *Economics: An Introductory Analysis* (New York: McGraw-Hill, 1961), 5th ed., p. 6.
26. J. M. Keynes, *The General Theory of Employment, Interest and Money* (New York: Harcourt, Brace, 1936), p. 245.
27. Richard A. Lester, *Labor and Industrial Relations: A General Analysis* (New York: Macmillan, 1951), p. 53.
28. *Ibid.*, p. 245.
29. Samuelson, *op. cit.*, 2nd ed., 1951, p. 15.
30. Keynes, *op. cit.*, p. 245.
31. For an example of the quite systematic use of the comparative method by an economic historian, see H. J. Habakkuk, *American and British Technology in the Nineteenth Century: The Search for Labour-Saving Inventions* (Cambridge: The University Press, 1962).
32. For assessments of some of the problems of using the survey method in economics, see George Katona and Eva Mueller, *Consumer Expectations, 1953–1956* (Ann Arbor: Survey Research Center, Institute for Social Research, University of Michigan, n.d.), pp. 7–11.
33. See Talcott Parsons and Neil J. Smelser, *Economy and Society* (Glencoe, Ill.: The Free Press, 1956), Chapter 4.
34. James G. March, "Some Recent Substantive and Methodological Developments in the Theory of Organizational Decision-Making," in Austin Ranney, ed., *Essays on the Behavioral Study of Politics* (Urbana: University of Illinois Press, 1962), pp. 191–208.
35. Martin Shubik, *Strategy and Market Structure* (New York: Wiley, 1959).
36. James Duesenberry, *Income, Savings, and the Theory of Consumer Behavior* (Cambridge: Harvard University Press, 1949); Milton Friedman, *A Theory of the Consumption Function* (Princeton: Princeton University Press, 1957); Guy H. Orcutt, Martin Greenberger, John Korbel, and Alice M. Rivlin, *Microanalysis of Socioeconomic Systems: A Simulation Study* (New York: Harper, 1961).
37. Parsons and Smelser, *op. cit.*, Chapter 2.
38. See, for example, Evron M. Kirkpatrick, "The Impact of the Behavioral Approach on Traditional Political Science," in Ranney, *op. cit.*, pp. 1–29.
39. I do not wish to convey the impression in my necessarily abbreviated account that the distinction between "traditional" empirical political science and the "behavioral" approach to political life is cleanly set off in two distinct divisions or that there is no internal diversity within each approach.
40. See Gabriel Almond and James S. Coleman, eds., *The Politics of the Developing Areas* (Princeton: Princeton University Press, 1960); Harry Eckstein and David E. Apter, eds., *Comparative Politics: A Reader* (New York: The Free Press of Glencoe, 1963).
41. For reviews of this literature, see Heinz Eulau, *Recent Developments in the Behavior Study of Politics* (Stanford: Stanford University Press, 1961), and Herbert Hyman, *Political Socialization* (Glencoe, Ill.: The Free Press, 1959).
42. Harold D. Lasswell, *Politics: Who Gets What, When, How* (New York: McGraw-Hill, 1936).
43. Anthony Downs, *An Economic Theory of Democracy* (New York: Harper, 1957).
44. David Easton, *The Political System* (New York: Knopf, 1953); *A Framework for Political Analysis* (Englewood Cliffs, N.J.: Prentice-Hall, 1965); *A Systems Analysis of Political Life* (New York: Wiley, 1965).
45. Morton Kaplan, *System and Process in International Relations* (New York: Wiley, 1957); Thomas C. Schelling, *The Strategy of Conflict* (Cambridge: Harvard University Press, 1960).

46. The relevance of small-group research for political science has, however, been examined by Sidney Verba in *Small Groups and Political Behavior* (Princeton: Princeton University Press, 1960).
47. For a brief sketch of common approaches and techniques, see Seymour Martin Lipset, "Sociology and Political Science: A Bibliographical Note," *American Sociological Review*, XXIX (1964), 730–734.
48. Above, pages 22–24.
49. Despite a considerable number of different emphases, the over-all formal similarities between the social-system models of Parsons and Easton are notable. See Easton, *A Systems Analysis*, and Parsons and Smelser, *op. cit.*
50. Cora DuBois, "Anthropology: Its Present Interests," in Berelson, *op. cit.*, p. 31.
51. A notable work in the tradition of cross-cultural analysis is George P. Murdock, *Social Structure* (New Haven: Yale University Press, 1948).
52. Again this statement must be qualified by reference to the considerable amount of systematic comparative analysis conducted by anthropologists.
53. Marcel Mauss stated this predilection very directly in characterizing his own comparative methodology: "*Since we are concerned with words and their meanings*, we choose only areas where we have access to the *minds of the societies* through documentation and philological research. This further limits our field of comparison. Each particular study has a bearing on the systems we set out to describe and is presented in its logical place. In this way we avoid that *method of haphazard comparison in which institutions lose their local colour and documents their value.*" *The Gift: Forms and Functions of Exchange in Archaic Societies* (Glencoe, Ill.: The Free Press, 1954), pp. 2–3. Emphasis added.
54. As we shall see, this difference between the clinical and the aggregated-variable emphases is paralleled in psychology. Above, page 35.
55. S. D. Clark, "Sociology, History, and the Problem of Social Change," *Canadian Journal of Economics and Political Science*, XXV (1959), 400.
56. For a variety of views on the relations between history and scientific explanation, see Patrick Gardiner, ed., *Theories of History* (Glencoe, Ill.: The Free Press, 1959).
57. I venture this statement, as well as all others in this section, with great caution. So great are the varieties of activities that today go under the name "sociological analysis" and "historical analysis" that any attempt to relate the two completely and accurately to each other would have to be couched in numerous qualifications.
58. Above, pages 14–15.
59. This difference of emphasis is formally similar to the difference between anthropologists, who tend to concentrate on simple societies, and sociologists, who tend to concentrate on complex ones. Above, page 29.
60. Part of this section is an elaboration of material originally presented in the Introduction to the book edited by William T. Smelser and me, *Personality and Social Systems* (New York: Wiley, 1963).
61. The same cannot be said of history, both because it does not focus so directly on systems of social interaction and because it does not rest on the use of scientific methods to as great a degree as the other disciplines.
62. I am not here considering physiological psychology, animal experimentation, and cognition and learning, since these do not always rely on conceptions of the individual personality. My remarks apply more to personality psychology and social psychology.
63. Above, pages 29–30.
64. Though I shall speak only of the relations with sociology, my remarks will apply equally well to economics, political science, and anthropology.

65. For an elaboration of these and other analogies, see Smelser and Smelser, *op. cit.*, pp. 5–12.

66. For an effort to work out the parallels between personality development and social processes of structural differentiation, see Talcott Parsons, Robert F. Bales, *et al., Family, Socialization, and Interaction Process* (Glencoe, Ill.: The Free Press, 1955).

67. See the brief discussion of the possibilities of formal interchange between economics and sociology, above, pages 22–24.

68. Above, pages 8–9, 14–15.

69. Above, page 17.

Sociology

and Collegiate

General Education

MARVIN BRESSLER

chapter 2

Sociologists have traditionally recognized the academy as their natural habitat. Lester F. Ward, the "Father of American Sociology," did not join the faculty at Brown University until his retirement as a career public servant; but such early masters as William Graham Sumner, Franklin H. Giddings, Charles Horton Cooley, and W. I. Thomas were already professors of other disciplines when they discovered sociology. The infiltration of the new science into the collegiate curriculum near the turn of the century was abetted by the participation of sociologists in the great debate on classical liberalism, then the most salient social and intellectual issue. They spoke with the authority of scholarship and borrowed prestige; the first generation did not hesitate to buttress its analysis of social "statics" and "dynamics" by invoking its disciplinary identification with Herbert Spencer, who was experiencing his American vogue. Sumner and Ward drew vastly different implications from the theory of social evolution, but each appealed to the canons of a generalizing science. Sociologists were, moreover, the beneficiaries of an ascribed expertise in the ethical realm. John Dewey's version of pragmatism, proclaiming all the while that it had triumphed over the Absolute, installed sociology as the final arbiter of social morality.

We may surmise that the founders were not merely children of circumstance. Taken collectively, their intellectual gifts and productivity were truly impressive, and their number included several who owed their influence on the campus to charismatic performances from the podium. "It is pretty generally conceded," writes William L. Kolb, "that E. A. Ross was the most dramatic and effective classroom teacher in American sociology." [1] A counterclaim filed by Harry Elmer Barnes on behalf of Sumner declares that he was "the most inspiring and popular teacher that either Yale University or American social science has ever produced." [2] Even the shy and reticent Charles Horton Cooley has been described as a "great teacher" of mature students. [3]

The routinization of charisma was significantly advanced by the efforts of Albion W. Small, who may truly be called the "St. Paul of American sociology." Small, a derivative thinker, but an inspired organization man, carried much of the burden of the newly formed American Sociological Society, founded and served as editor of the *American Journal of Sociology*, and assembled the celebrated department at Chicago that furnished intellectual capital and competent faculty to universities throughout the United States. By so doing he helped create the indispensable institutional mechanisms that transformed an enthusiastic sect into an established church. Today, sociology is a staple in the general education curriculum of every major university and nearly all liberal arts and junior colleges. [4]

The performance of sociologists as educators of students (and students of education) is in principle subject to evaluation by the ordinary criteria of utility. An applied intellectual activity is "useful" when the means chosen (instruction in sociology) demonstrably serve the ends sought (the goals of general education) and both are consistent with a valid philosophy of welfare. In applying this standard, an inquiry into the influence, if any, of general education on specified outcomes at various points in time is logically prior to speculations on the proportion of variance in such putative effects attributable to sociological instruction.

The Social Functions of Education

Education in the United States responds to tradition and novelty in the wider social universe, but it has never been a passive hostage to history. It has exerted a strong influence on events both as a major resource in the industrialization process and as an instrument for preserving the continuity of political and social institutions. As such its influence has been simultaneously revolutionary and conservative.

A reasonably high level of economic development is the *sine qua non* for passage from a traditional order to any of the forms of social development that sociologists have variously described as "*Gesellschaft*," "secondary," "industrial," "secular," "urban," "complex," or "advanced." A considerable body of accumulating evidence suggests that education may be a decisive element in accelerating economic growth. Harbison and Myers, for example, are able to show significant positive correlations between a composite index of "human resources" based mainly on educational criteria and GNP per capita for seventy-five countries at various growth levels.[5] It would be too great a logical and temporal leap to apply these data directly to pre-twentieth-century America, but they do speak for the view that historically education has been a capital good as well as an item of consumption.

Longitudinal studies of recent economic growth in the United States are consistent with the findings of comparative analysis. Edward F. Denison, for example, estimates that between 1929 and 1957 the rising education of the labor force in the United States was responsible for 21 per cent of the growth in real national income as compared to 14 per cent attributable to increased physical investment in plant and equipment.[6] T. W. Schultz concludes that the educational factor may account for as high as 70 per cent of "the otherwise unexplained increase in earnings per laborer."[7]

As a key element in the economic transformation of society education is of course partially responsible for the multiple perplexities of an industrial civilization: war, technological change, business cycles, urban concentration, migration, demographic heterogeneity, group conflict, moral ambiguity, and personal malaise. The most remarkable feature of American society has been the astonishing stability of its institutions in the face of the provocations that have been visited upon twentieth-century man. Education that is a source of social tensions is also one of the devices by which they can be managed. It has performed the latent function of dissipating revolutionary energy by furnishing an arena for the resolution of group conflicts and by opening careers to talent.

Rush Welter's authoritative account of the idea of education in America testifies that both the defenders of the *status quo* and their militant opposition have traditionally relied on the school as the guarantor of their most cherished group interests.[8] The rich and powerful, often acting out of naked motives of class interest and personal safety, relied on the school to pacify the working class. The liberal opposition promoted education as the most promising means of rectifying social injustice. As Welter points out, for nearly a century after the age of Jackson political theorists "treated popular education as the one sure cure for contemporary social and political evils."[9] Men so persuaded do not take to the barricades or engineer *coups d'état*.

Orthodox sociological analysis as first expounded by Lester F. Ward has been explicitly aware of these functions of education. Ward held that knowledge is the source of individual achievement and social power and that differential access to education was the fundamental source of the privileges of the few and the privations of the many. Universal compulsory education helps reduce these inequities by extending the benefits of civilization—its thoughtways, ethics, and material possessions—to a much larger segment of the population. A brotherhood of educated men sharing similar life styles and common intellectual experiences might then elect to do battle together against the ubiquitous vices of social existence.

Ward's proposals were designed to avoid rather than induce structural change. His was the liberal's retort to socialism, the promise of continuous progress and benign alternatives to class conflict and revolution. He did not seriously question the legitimacy of existing property arrangements, the stratification system, or any other basic feature of American society. Social meliorism did not, and does not, long for the destruction of the established social order; it proposes merely to increase the number of its beneficiaries.

This philosophy has found tangible expression in the accessibility of schooling, including tax-supported university training. The most talented and resourceful members of deprived groups may dream of emancipation from class and birth through personal escape rather than collective action. The militance of protest movements is heightened when, as in the case of Negroes and Puerto Ricans, entire populations are convinced that there is no realistic prospect of choosing between these options. Equality of educational opportunity is thus both a principle of social ethics and a guardian of national serenity.

Of late, sociologists have acted as scorekeepers on the actual operation of the system.[10] By now a substantial body of evidence has identified two general classes of restraints on educational opportunity: deliberate discrimination, and disqualification through the "normal" impact of the social system on nominal equals. With a consistency that is rare in social investigation, numerous American studies agree that (1) socio-economic status is strongly associated with measured intelligence and that both are positively related to educational opportunity; (2) the relationship between SES and years of school completed persists when ability level is held constant; and (3) comparable proportions of the least talented rich and the most talented poor seek higher education and actually enter college. Negroes have been especially disadvantaged as evidenced by the fact that as of 1960 only about one-half as many non-whites between sixteen and twenty-four were attending college as their white counterparts.[11] Such findings on the relationship between race, class, and educational opportunity have been demonstrably useful in revealing the discrepancy between the actual and the ideal in the American system of higher education.

The Macrocosmic Effects of General Education

The concepts "liberal" and "general" education may ordinarily be inter‑ changed without undue loss of analytical power. Each refers to "that part of a student's whole education which looks first of all to his life as a re‑ sponsible human being and citizen." [12] "General" education is now pre‑ ferred usage because it is comparatively unburdened by imputations of genteel ostentation, identification with the anachronistic *trivium* and *quadrivium,* exclusive association with higher learning, or intimations of intra‑academic rivalries.

Sociology is ordinarily taught in general education programs that are sustained by one or more structural patterns: distribution requirements, cognate offerings, and integrated programs. The first, and by far most common, specifies the distribution of required and elective credits that must be earned in courses in the humanities and the natural and social sciences. This procedure encourages the development of scholarly breadth, but it makes no systematic provision for converting untidy shreds and patches into an orderly intellectual universe. The "cognate" and "inte‑ grated" curriculums are designed to remedy this deficiency. Each aspires to help the student advance beyond fragmentation to unity, beyond analy‑ sis to synthesis, beyond the parochialism of specific time and place to his‑ tory and cross‑cultural perspective.

The cognate approach proceeds cautiously by viewing the same intel‑ lectual sector from a number of discrete vantage points. Each course in a cluster ("Sociology of Religion," "The Bible as Literature," "Erasmus, Lu‑ ther, and Calvin," "The Cathedral and Other Church Architecture") has as its counterpart a related offering in another department. The logical extrapolation of this tactic is the abolition of the department as the princi‑ pal unit of instruction. Instead, the "integrated" or "core" curriculum relies on the erudition of "generalists" or the corporative wisdom of interdiscipli‑ nary teams to introduce *simultaneously* all relevant products of human experience, thought, and passion. The content of these offerings varies from general surveys of contemporary existence to curriculums dominated by Robert M. Hutchins' conviction that the Thomist synthesis very nearly exhausts durable knowledge.

There is no consistent association between any of these curriculum phi‑ losophies and a specific array of classroom practices. These arise out of the interplay of pedagogic creed and institutional constraints and differ ac‑ cording to the following major dimensions: *structure* (e.g., size, lecture or seminar); *range* (e.g., exclusive reliance on course and campus or the "community as laboratory"); *austerity* (e.g., rigor of examinations, length and type of reading assignments); *climate* (e.g., "authoritarian" or "demo‑ cratic"); *autonomy* (e.g., directed or independent study); and characteris‑

tics of *professors* and *students* (e.g., their motivation, talent, and knowledge).

Collegiate general education in one of its numerous forms promotes the purposes of education at the macrocosmic level in three general ways:

1. The liberal arts school acts as a staging area for direct assignment or for further education to those who will occupy elite positions and second-level leadership in government, corporation, and community. It furnishes the skilled manpower that maintains the dynamism of an industrial society and binds its clientele to the social system by offering the promise of differential rewards.

2. Liberal education includes ethical and moral indoctrination that legitimizes existing power and economic arrangements, and reinforces appropriate attitudes for the sustenance of democratic institutions and the peaceful coexistence of diverse population groups.

3. General education is a constituent element in all scientific, professional, and managerial training and as such is presumably directly instrumental in enhancing occupational competencies. In one sense general education is the most efficient form of occupational training. Rapid change is hostile to narrow expertise and a curriculum that emphasizes breadth and flexibility may better equip students to meet unpredictable vocational demands. The numerous corporation-sponsored institutes of humanistic studies for executives are conspicuous illustrations of unsentimental wagers on the cash value of the liberal arts.

As an integral part of general education sociology has traditionally furnished much of the course content for undergraduate programs in teaching and social work, and it has recently extended its influence to include pre-professional curriculums in architecture, engineering, journalism, law, and medicine. These professions have welcomed such collaboration for diverse reasons that reflect internal developments within their respective disciplines. For example, the demise of purely "scholastic" approaches to the law has been accompanied in legal education by increasing attention to the actual operation of the system of distributive justice. Similarly, a contemporary architecture which now speaks of transforming the quality of existence in city and countryside becomes an authentic social discipline which is receptive to whatever assistance is available from theory and research on human communities.

Sociology is particularly cherished by the helping professions—education, nursing, casework—because it stresses the orderly relationship between social structure and personality and minimizes the role of human perversity as a source of behavior pathology. This emphasis simultaneously serves the scientific goal of intellectual economy and the latent ideological function of creating compassion for social deviants. Thus, the fact that Negroes and the poor are disproportionately represented among the physically and mentally ill, criminals, addicts, and dropouts may be interpreted as evidence of a "sick society" rather than as proof of personal guilt. The conversion of individual blame into collective responsibility transforms offenders into victims and renders them eligible for public sympathy and support.

It would be an error to conclude that sociology has labored exclusively on behalf of the disinherited and dispossessed. Indeed, one of its most notable and controversial achievements has been the dissemination, in business curriculums, of a managerial ideology to the industrial elite. The fundamental theorem of what has come to be known as the "human relations" approach is that employee dissatisfaction and conflict between various levels of an organizational hierarchy is the result of an outmoded theory of control that emphasizes ordering and forbidding and places exclusive reliance on economic motivation. Instead, management should recognize that employees function best when their work situation contributes to their sense of self-worth and is otherwise psychologically supportive. Such favorable environments are most likely to appear when workers are organized into small groups. These miniature social systems, each complete with its own distinctive values and norms, are presumably able to counteract the alienation that is induced by the size and complexity of the modern factory.

An enlightened management that is eager to insure the emergence of group standards that are consistent with its own organizational purposes must devise social mechanisms that stimulate vertical loyalty and emphasize the essential community of interests of all persons involved in the total industrial enterprise. Hence, the emphasis on "open" channels of communication, physical amenities, euphemistic titles, and the ingenious device of the psychodrama which is designed to supplement more orthodox methods of interaction. Role playing is essentially artificially structured stimulation of empathy in which manager and worker take the role of the other and presumably increase the depth of their insights into each other's problems.

The "human relations" school has been criticized on the grounds that its research problems have been defined by management and that it has concentrated its attention on those aspects of morale such as productivity, employee turnover, and absenteeism that relate to profit and other adaptive goals of the organization. Thus it is said that managerial sociology is a form of soft sell that serves as a subtle substitute for the more obvious forms of coercion. Its critics allege that the real objective of "human relations" is to deflect the loyalty of employees from their unions. Yet there is little doubt that whatever are the latent functions of managerial sociology its exertions have left American organizations, both public and private, more habitable.

College and the Student

The reluctance of academic social scientists to cultivate their own gardens is a much-noted paradox. However, a considerable literature now exists on the effects of a college education. A review of existing materials reveals many striking gaps in our knowledge; there has not been a single systematic effort to measure something so obvious as the retention of course content by college alumni. Much of it is methodologically flawed. For example, none of the studies sufficiently controls for input factors and none employs the elementary logic of before-after comparisons on an experimental group of college students and a control group of their noncollege age peers. Most employ pseudo-longitudinal designs involving comparisons of different groups at various levels of education. Very few reports are based on the observations of the same group at different points in time. The chief findings may be summarized as follows:

1. College students acquire considerable information and develop cognitive skills in the course of their education, but it is not known how much they retain.[13]
2. There is little evidence indicating that the personalities and the values of students are significantly altered by their collegiate experiences. There is "in general change in the direction of greater liberalism and sophistication in political, social, and religious outlook," [14] but the magnitude of the change is slight.
3. The values and outlook of students "do not vary greatly whether they have pursued a conventional liberal arts program, an integrated general education curriculum, or one of the strictly professional vocational options." [15]
4. Liberal arts students tend to be more "neurotic," "anxious," "disturbed," and so forth and they are somewhat more liberal on social and political issues. However, the relationships are weak. There is no consistent association between these and other values and undergraduate field of concentration. There have been no satisfactory studies of sociology majors.[16]
5. The typical finding in the area of classroom practices is "no significant differences." The existing literature fails to provide any clearcut evidence of superiority for small vs. large classes, homogeneous vs. heterogeneous grouping, discussion vs. lectures, live vs. television presentation, non-directive vs. teacher-centered classes, or independent vs. directed learning.[17]
6. The relationships between (a) teacher personality and teaching effectiveness and (b) student personality and student learning are inconclusive.[18]

These findings will disappoint, but should not greatly astonish, those who hope that empirical research will confirm that collegiate instruction in any of its numerous forms does more than convey information and develop cognitive skills. The university is, after all, primarily dedicated to the purposes of the mind and invests comparatively little energy in systematic efforts to reconstruct character and values. Moreover, it operates under external restraints that inhibit radical thought and experimentation; the reconstruction of attitude and personality through organized programs is a formidable technical task; and the students' malleability is limited by anticipatory socialization to their future careers.

There are, nevertheless, good reasons to reserve gloomy judgments about the reported effects of a college education.

1. Knowledge and competence are their own excuse for being. The disparagement of intellect rests on simplistic extrapolations of Freud, Marx, and Dewey—the theses that thought is merely a mask for emotion, that ideas are always superimposed on power, that books are only pale substitutes for experience. As against this, the university rightly maintains that the urge to know, to understand, to indulge the frivolous and holy motive of curiosity is as imperious as any among basic human impulses. The perception of fact and pattern, the cultivation of tastes and sensibilities, the development of competence and dexterity are manifestly private joys and public treasure.

2. A significant change in a small number of strategic people may exert an influence beyond their number. The decisions that shape men's lives are increasingly made in secret chambers and are informed by specialized knowledge that is hidden from ordinary comprehension. Our survival and public happiness rest *inter alia* on the innocent hope that the exercise of power will be responsible and that it will be restrained by civilized values and traditions first learned in the academy. Surely, President Kennedy's exposure to Harvard had consequences for his convictions and our history.

3. Greater methodological and theoretical refinement, the extension of research into uncharted areas, a more complex matrix of variables, may in time clarify ambiguous issues and complete gaps in knowledge. Given the fact of subtle outcomes and fallible techniques, it is dangerous to dismiss the possibility of diffuse change because we have been unable to detect it. This caution seems especially warranted since existing findings appear to contradict collective experience. It would be premature to discount the stubborn conviction among many graduates that college had a significant effect on every aspect of their lives.

Nevitt Sanford is correct when he observes "that there is a remarkable discrepancy between the wide public acceptance of a college education and the paucity of demonstrated knowledge that it does some good";[19] but neither have we yet demonstrated the contrary.

The Effects of Sociology on the Student

Evidence from intellectual history suggests that the intrusion of the presuppositions, findings, and implications of the sciences on prior belief may have direct personal consequences. They may, for instance, be perceived as psychologically benign or threatening. Thus, the fundamental postulate that the physical universe exhibits discernible order is almost wholly reassuring. Nature loses its terror, but not its grandeur, and so long as science does not presume to explain final causes none need be deprived of the consolations of faith.

At the same time, even idea systems that are invented to deal with distant galaxies and events remote in time may shatter universal certainties and discomfit private convictions. It is enough to recall that men resisted the heliocentric hypothesis because Copernicus removed them from the center of the cosmos, and the theory of biological evolution because they preferred to think of themselves as a little lower than the angels rather than a little higher than the apes. In our time, the uses of pure science for the impure purposes of Hiroshima have converted many to a neo-Calvinistic sobriety and restored the concept of evil to social philosophy.

The social sciences have a more obvious capacity to act as balm or abrasive. It is reasonable to suppose that a serious undergraduate who is exposed to sociology can hardly escape the shock of recognition; the lecturer is, so to speak, talking about him. The salience of the exposition may be temporarily concealed by the language of scholarship, but the classroom will ultimately connect with experience, and the student may well develop a heightened sense of self-consciousness and personal involvement.

The elements of sociology capable of influencing an educational outcome include (1) assertions about the social system, (2) methods that produce them including concepts, theories, and procedures for establishing relationships, and (3) an ambiance consisting of style, implicit orientations, and broader intellectual alliances. Outcomes may be defined as a change in (1) knowledge and competencies, (2) personal and social values, (3) personality, and (4) overt behavior. Such changes are most likely to occur when exposure to sociological knowledge is in some fashion salient for the student, i.e., when it is (1) psychologically rewarding or punitive or when it (2) guides choices in the crucial sectors of his life—work, play, friendship, love, parenthood, and community participation.

As indicated earlier, there is no satisfactory empirical evidence, nor even much published speculation, indicating that sociology actually does have any more influence on educational outcomes than any other component of the curriculum. It may be useful, therefore, to consider under what circumstances such effects might be discerned if they exist.

In approaching this task it is important to distinguish between (1) distinctive and shared interdisciplinary and intradisciplinary orientations, (2) sociology as a branch of learning and classroom enterprise, and (3) exported, imported, and cooperatively owned intellectual goods. It will be helpful in developing the significance of these distinctions to refer extensively to a summary paragraph and several other excerpts of an eloquent essay by Robert Bierstedt, the best work now extant on the role of sociology in general education.

> In the first place, like history in particular, the study of sociology liberates the student from the provincialisms of time, place, and circumstance and frees him from the constrictions of his natal culture. Secondly, it introduces him to the role of logic and of scientific method in the acquisition of knowledge and thus contributes, thirdly, to his sense of order and to his methodological sophistication. In the fourth place, sociology is a discipline that spans two cultures, the scientific and the humanistic, using as it does the method of science to explore the concerns and affairs of humanity. In the next instance, the fifth, I suggested that sociology initiates and keeps at the front of student awareness the ancient problem of the relationship between society and the individual. As a sixth point, I referred to another ancient problem, the meaning of history, and declared that the philosophy of history, when it becomes positivistic, is indistinguishable from sociology and that it is the responsibility of sociology ultimately to find an answer to this age-long quest. Finally, in opposition to those who accuse sociologists of stylistic inadequacies, I maintained that the literary quality of their work is not one whit inferior to that which can be found in other learned disciplines.[20]

The burden of Bierstedt's message is that sociology liberates the mind and renders it more efficient. This is a beguiling thesis, but it fails to establish any *special* role of sociology in the general education curriculum. The author makes only one claim for the distinctiveness of sociology, its capacity to unite the "two cultures." Elsewhere in the essay he refers to this function as "almost uniquely" a sociological contribution.[21] Most of the virtues that Bierstedt ascribes to sociology inhere in other disciplines and are sometimes more appropriately identified with them. Students who are denied the delights of sociological prose will suffer no irremediable insult to their aesthetic sensibilities. Similarly, if, "like history in particular," sociology is antagonistic to parochialism, this antidote would presumably survive even in the absence of sociological instruction.

These *shared* disciplinary orientations may be viewed from the vantage point of sociology as *imported* (e.g., "the role of logic and of scientific method in the acquisition of knowledge"); *cooperatively owned* (the "ancient problem of the relationship between society and the individual");

and *exported* intellectual goods ("the philosophy of history when it becomes positivistic is indistinguishable from sociology"). Distinctive sociological orientations are presumably taught only in sociology courses; shared perspectives are diffused throughout the curriculum. Paradoxically, as sociology extends its influence it further surrenders principal curricular jurisdiction over its original domain. Such notions as the "power elite," "alienation," "the Protestant ethic," "status striving," "urban anonymity" are already staples in more than one course in the social sciences and humanities. On the distant day that all historians agree with Bierstedt's implication that history *is* sociology with an added time dimension, students will absorb fundamental sociological insights in courses offered by either department.

The problem of identifying the effects of sociology is further confused by schismatic tendencies within the discipline. Elsewhere, we have argued that sociologists tend to think of themselves variously as natural scientists, engineers, or European intellectuals and that those self-images define their goals, value and theoretical perspectives, methodological strategies, and the criteria for evaluating the adequacy of their research.[22] S. M. Lipset has perceived the divisions in the field in kindred terms:

> Most sociology departments, in fact, are sharply divided intellectually between those who believe in system theory and methodological formalization, and those who see in sociology a field which should basically be content with generalizing about historical trends. On still another level, this is a controversy between exponents of a functionalist and equilibrium concept of sociology and those who prefer to view society in dialectical terms as ever changing and in a state of permanent conflict. Or, one may regard this partially as a debate between those who view sociology as a neutral, apolitical discipline, and those who believe that it must necessarily take political positions, and that as an innovating social science it is inherently dangerous to the *status quo* . . .[23]

The divisions within the field bespeak against a monolithic unity in actual instruction. Some of the characteristics that Bierstedt imputes to sociology are in point of fact a preoccupation of only one of its schools. For example, he writes:

> Behind all of our research and all of our theory there lies the desire, often subliminal, to find a meaning in the ebb and flow of human affairs, in the systole and diastole of human history. This may well be the most profound and difficult of all questions. But there is no doubt that it is a sociological question, the question in fact that motivated Auguste Comte to found our science and give it a name.[24]

Professor Bierstedt's own erudition leads him to an excessive generosity. He confuses an important tradition in sociology and its translation into current instruction. The overwhelming number of courses in sociology actually proceed as if the United States exhausts space and the present is the beginning of time. The philosophy of history tends to be a subliminal interest on both sides of the desk.

The uncertain flow of interdisciplinary and intradisciplinary influence enormously complicates prospective research on the effects of sociology. It is clearly more convenient to employ study designs that assume that differential exposure to sociology courses satisfactorily reflects differential exposure to sociology. The implication of the preceding discussion is that this assumption is tenable only when the sociology represented by departmental offerings is (1) "distinctive," (2) transcends "school" affiliations, and (3) is actually included in every course.

The shared methods and intellectual ambiance of sociology have the greatest potential for satisfying all of these criteria. Particular substantive items may be distinctive and salient, but, in the nature of the case, they will not always come to the attention of the student. Marital prediction scales may furnish clues for mate selection, studies of recidivism may cast doubts on public policy that favors committing juvenile offenders to correctional institutions, and research on the age structure may have a direct influence on investments in perambulators or wheel chairs. But only those sociology students who elect appropriate courses will have the opportunity to exhibit these hypothetical effects.

However, all sociologists by virtue of their membership in the same craft are committed to the following epistemological emphases: (1) objectivity, (2) skepticism, (3) categorization, (4) abstraction, (5) probability, (6) relativism, (7) context, and (8) paradox. These are, of course, the thoughtways of science, and sociology is not their sole guardian. Nevertheless, its insistence that these shall discipline the study of man, that they shall prevail even when the student becomes the object of his own scrutiny, endows them with a peculiar salience that is lacking when they are applied to physics or chemistry. Moreover, the scientific mode has vastly different meanings for sociology than for any of the other social sciences. Unlike history, sociology deals with the ominous present; in contrast to the segmental focus of economics or politics, its interests are thoroughly catholic; as distinguished from much psychology which is idiographic, sociology emphasizes statistical rather than individual lawfulness, group membership rather than personal biography, "role" rather than "personality."

The result is that a general thought system when adopted for sociological usage develops distinctive emergent properties. And since major generalizations that are well confirmed are admittedly few in sociology, the student is less likely to be influenced by its specific content than by a series of residual orientations toward self and fellows. Method and intellectual ambiance may thus be elevated to the level of a social philosophy with consequences that may turn out to be neither trivial nor obvious.

Observe, for example, how such seemingly neutral attributes as "skepticism," "categorization," and "complexity" in their sociological form may favor that political quietism among students that was once deplored and is now remembered nostalgically by commencement speakers. The first leads to the denial of the possibility of social knowledge; the second deflates the importance of self as an independent agent; and the last emphasizes the difficulty of social reconstruction.

The introductory lecture which warns the student about the laymen's naïveté and the fallibility of common sense exposes him to methodological skepticism. The distinction between emotion and reason will be forcibly thrust on his attention and he will be urged not to confuse authoritarian dicta with proof. The experience of his senses will be discredited on sampling grounds, and he will be reminded of the duplicity of small numbers and isolated cases. Exhortations against "simplistic" explanations and "monism" will be coupled with caveats against extending generalizations to inappropriate settings. In due course he will be introduced to the classic paradoxes—the Hawthorne studies, the high morale of the military police, the low rates of divorce among the native population of Nevada. He will learn in short that professors of sociology may seem, like Descartes, to seek their ultimate vindication in the principle *Dubito ergo sum*.

The portrait of the sociologist as cognitive nihilist is overdrawn, but it is not pure caricature. If the student absorbs the message too well, he may resemble one of Mary McCarthy's characters who

> could not get the idea of proof out of his noodle. Science and philosophy had deranged his common sense. "How do you know that?" he kept challenging when you let drop the most casual observation. And since he could not understand the only two fields in which proof was possible—logic and mathematics —he had fallen back, despondently, on the notion that everything was false.[25]

If all knowledge is problematic and all beliefs hazardous, then exertions on behalf of any doctrine of welfare may appear to be folly.

Sociology may further encourage passivity by subtly transforming the student's self-image. The ultimate agents of social behavior are individual men acting alone or in concert. Accordingly every theory of society is also implicitly a theory of personality. The indispensable process of categorization itself involves unstated psychological assumptions. In general, the utility of all orthodox sociological categories—e.g., age, sex, race, religion, social class—tend to be confirmed to the extent that idiosyncratic characteristics do not contaminate the principle of the classification. Similarly, sociological determinism as an epistemological presupposition is most persuasive if it can assert that sociological generalizations cannot be subverted by the capacity of the human personality to surprise. Indeed, the image of psychological man that best serves sociology's disciplinary purposes views him as *simple* in that he has few psychological dimensions and these are accessible to common sense; *utilitarian* in that he seeks to maximize his pleasure and minimize his pains; *rational* in that he is capable of selecting appropriate means to achieve desired ends; *malleable* in that he has few constitutional or socially derived characteristics that are not amenable to change; *morally neutral* in that he is neither inherently virtuous nor depraved; and *stable* in that he is not given to caprice or idiosyncrasy.

When such a man does not exist sociologists are obliged to invent him. The alternatives would be to abandon him to other disciplines or to acknowledge that psychological variables are indispensable for understanding social behavior. It is possible to escape the "reductionist fallacy" precisely because a personality with so few internal resources and so little complexity is consistent with the hidden assumption that sociological concepts and generalizations are parsimonious expressions of psychological phenomena. We are, for example, prepared to analyze some interactions between officers and enlisted men solely on the basis of role theory and to include "submissiveness" as part of the soldier's actual role only because of our conviction that in particular situations social definition also defines personality. Our confidence in "role" as a powerful analytic device would be considerably diminished if we suspected that the soldier was responsive to dark subterranean impulses, indifferent as to the comparative joys of weekend leave and the pains of the guardhouse, incapable of knowing his interests, or in any appreciable way markedly different from his fellows.

The image of man as predictable and comprehensible through his social classifications clashes with the conception of life as drama. In challenging the student's sense that he is unique, the sociological approach may well remove some of the burden of loneliness that is the affliction of late adolescence. Togetherness has long been rumored to have its own compensations. At the same time students are seldom wholly reconciled to a perspective which as in the customary sociological treatment of romantic love seems to demean their most significant experiences. The good-natured demolition of the "myth that there is only one man for every woman," the view of courtship as a market mechanism, the statistics on assortative mating all seem to affirm the truths of the actuary and scoff at the songs of the poet.

Some students may make the precocious discovery that there are many truths and many ways to celebrate them. Others will assert the imperious I in mindless protest against pattern. One suspects that the majority will adopt that amused irony toward self which serves to make knowledge bearable. Silent laughter is an effective defense against the banality of one's own life, but it is also the enemy of evangelical energy.

Sociology's recognition of the complexity of any social system is also incompatible with the mood of militant action. Its analytical scheme includes such polarities as functions and dysfunctions, manifest and latent functions, intended and unintended consequences, formal and informal structures, overt and covert behavior—all of which distinguish between the partial and complete, the apparent and real, the visible and hidden.

Saul Alinsky, himself a redoubtable actionist, has written that such restrictions make it difficult to participate in the daily world of decision and strife.

> In the sociology department it was a cardinal sin to make a categoric statement. You qualified everything you said; then you qualified the qualifiers and added some footnotes so that the final conclusion had more escape hatches in it than a loan shark's mortgage contract. Today the University of Chicago sociology department is just a tribe of head counters.
>
> Well, when I started working with people I found them asking, "Is it yes or no? Do we go this way or that?" So I had a lot of unlearning to do when I got out of college—including the fancy vocabulary I'd picked up.[26]

The doctrines of "who can tell," "why so hot little man," and "it is not so simple as all that" appear to be an integral and perhaps necessary part of sociology's *Weltanschauung*. This is not an outlook that prods a man to dispute the *status quo,* to embrace the radical right or left, to picket an embassy, or organize a mass meeting. The strength of a graduate's determination to remain disengaged should vary directly with (1) the number of sociology courses he has taken, (2) his mastery, and (3) his acceptance of its basic thoughtways. It would be premature to argue whether these or other hypothetical outcomes were "useful" effects of sociological instruction; as of now questions of value must await confirmation of fact.

We have confined ourselves to a very few illustrations of outcomes that might emerge from exposure to idea systems that are presumably transmitted only in sociology courses and by all sociologists. These ruminations represent the barest beginnings of what might be the larger benefits of self-consciousness. The inclusion of higher education as part of the sociology of knowledge would enrich both fields and might help us to devise a strategy of instruction that was not wholly dependent on group introspection. It is odd that in a craft that holds that ideas have consequences so few are interested in what ways and to what extent ours are consequential.

REFERENCES

1. William L. Kolb, "The Sociological Theories of Edward Alsworth Ross," in Harry Elmer Barnes, ed., *An Introduction to the History of Sociology* (Chicago: University of Chicago Press, 1948), p. 819.
2. Harry Elmer Barnes, "William Graham Sumner: Spencerianism in American Dress," in Barnes, *op. cit.*, p. 155.
3. Read Bain, "Cooley, a Great Teacher," *Social Forces*, IX (December, 1930), 160–163. Perhaps the most charming bit of apocrypha that has circulated about the early masters refers to a course at Harvard offered by W. I. Thomas. According to legend, a young instructor sympathetically relayed to a staff meeting a common student complaint that Thomas' anecdotal lectures could not be readily translated into systematic notes. He was thereupon reminded by a distinguished senior colleague that "once before in history a man walked this earth who delivered his message in parables."
4. See Abbott L. Ferriss, "Sociological Manpower," *American Sociological Review*, XXIX, No. 1 (February, 1964), 103–114.
5. Frederick Harbison and Charles A. Myers, *Education, Manpower, and Economic Growth* (New York: McGraw-Hill, 1964); see Chapter 3.
6. Edward F. Denison, *The Sources of Economic Growth in the United States and the Alternatives before Us*, Supplementary Paper No. 13, C.E.D. (New York: Committee for Economic Development, 1962).
7. T. W. Schultz, "Education and Economic Growth," in Nelson B. Henry, ed., *Social Forces Influencing American Education* (Chicago: National Society for the Study of Education, distributed by the University of Chicago Press, 1961), p. 82.
8. Rush Welter, *Popular Education and Democratic Thought in America* (New York: Columbia University Press, 1962).
9. *Ibid.*
10. For numerous references relating to educational opportunity in higher education see William H. Sewell, A. O. Haller, and M. A. Straus, "Social Status and Educational and Occupational Aspirations," *American Sociological Review*, XXII, No. 1 (February, 1957), 67–73.
11. U.S. Bureau of the Census, *Current Population Reports*, Population Characteristics, Series P–20, No. 110 (July 24, 1961), Table 10, p. 15.
12. *General Education in a Free Society: Report of the Harvard Committee* (Cambridge: Harvard University Press, 1945), p. 50.
13. See Nevitt Sanford, ed., *The American College* (New York: Wiley, 1962), p. 106 *et passim*.
14. *Ibid.*, p. 806.
15. Philip E. Jacob, *Changing Values in College* (New York: Harper, 1957), p. 5.
16. See Carl Berelter and Mervin B. Freedman, "Fields of Study and the People in Them," in Sanford, *op. cit.*, pp. 563–593.
17. See W. J. McKeachie, "Research on Teaching at the College and University Level," in N. L. Gage, ed., *Handbook of Research on Teaching* (Chicago: Rand McNally, 1963), pp. 1118–1172.
18. See J. W. Getzels and P. W. Jackson, "The Teacher's Personality and Characteristics," in *ibid.*, pp. 506–582.
19. Sanford, *op. cit.*, p. 805.
20. Robert Bierstedt, "Sociology and General Education," in Charles H. Page, ed.,

Sociology and Contemporary Education (New York: Random House, 1964), pp. 54–55.

21. *Ibid.*, p. 49.
22. Marvin Bressler, "The Conventional Wisdom of Education and Sociology," in *ibid.*, p. 99.
23. S. M. Lipset, Review of Barrington Moore, "Political Power and Social Theory: Six Studies," *American Sociological Review*, XXV, No. 2 (April, 1960), 283–285.
24. Robert Bierstedt in Page, *op. cit.*, p. 51.
25. Mary McCarthy, *A Charmed Circle* (New York: Harcourt Brace, 1954), p. 45.
26. Saul Alinsky, "The Professional Radical," *Harper's*, 230, 1381, p. 39.

The Ideological Uses of Sociology

NATHAN GLAZER

chapter 3

Ideology is unquestionably one of those terms that, like *alienation*, might best be abandoned in serious discussion—if, that is, we did not need it so much, and if we could have any confidence that it would not return through the back door. Ultimately we might well decide that in serious criticism of the work of sociology and sociologists the term *ideology*, with the heavy incrustation of various meanings that have been deposited on it over the years, should be abandoned; but while it still has life, it may be useful to analyze its various uses in sociology and by sociologists and to try to give what meaning we can to the recurrent charge: "That is not sociology; that is ideology."

I shall discuss three major uses: the first is that in which *ideology* is counterposed to *science;* the second, the usage of Karl Marx and Karl Mannheim, is that in which ideology is seen as the screen of the status quo, the defense and veil of existing society (here taking perhaps the guise of science, and thus, in this usage too, counterposed to "real" science); the third, and quite opposite to the second, is that in which ideology is seen as that element in sociology or in all thought which mobilizes the forces of social change for the positive transformation of society: here ideology is used as Mannheim used utopia. Perhaps Daniel Bell, in his argument against the value of political myths in advanced industrial societies (the "end of ideology"), gave this usage its chief contemporary currency. In doing so, he became the target of attack of those who believed in Mannheim's "utopias" as valuable; but he nevertheless seems to have won the battle of terminology: his critics, regardless of their debt to Marx and Mannheim, have not hesitated to use the term in Bell's meaning, abandoning that of both Marx and Mannheim. In giving it a positive rather than a pejorative meaning, they have taken the position, against their masters, that ideology is a "good thing."

Our first usage, which cannot fully be disentangled from the second, is nevertheless to be distinguished from it because here the charge of ideology may be separated from strongly held *political* objectives. Unquestionably the great body of American sociologists see themselves as engaged in the building of a science. They believe that sociology should have operationally defined terms; it should have hypotheses and theories; it should have some predictive value; it should have practical application; its knowledge should accumulate; its theories, developed on the basis of or tested by bodies of empirical research in one historical setting, should be applicable in some measure to other settings; and it should develop the power and authority that physical and biological science have developed.

It is on the basis of such a conception that much sociological theory and research is criticized as "unscientific" and at least on occasion as "ideological." This is not to say that "ideology" is ever simply equivalent to "unscientific." The unscientific can be simply poor science, based on insufficient knowledge, on poor training, on inadequate analysis. It becomes in addition ideological when it is suspected that some unacknowledged interest operated which explains the scientific weakness.

Because the material with which sociologists regularly deal is so controversial, the argument over whether analysis or research is sufficiently "scientific" almost always raises at least the hint that some "ideology"— conservative, liberal, or radical; capitalist or socialist; American or anti-American—operated to help produce the degree of "nonscience" detected. Consider some of the major disputes in sociology over the past thirty years: the argument over W. Lloyd Warner's analysis of classes in American society; over the studies of the Elton Mayo school of factory life; over the functions of social stratification; over the amount and kinds of social mobility in American society; over the utility of functionalist theory, in almost any of its forms; over the structure of power in American communities. In each case the problem of science was mixed in with the problem of ideology. What was the best theory, the best research methodology, the correct selection of a research problem, the truth? It was possible in each case to develop the argument solely in terms of the demands and needs of science, and yet in each of these disputes, and in others, other interests—social and political—came into play on both sides, too.

Thus, for example, there was much to criticize scientifically in Warner's work on stratification, and many excellent articles did so—articles by C. Wright Mills, Reinhard Bendix and S. M. Lipset, Harold Pfautz and Otis Dudley Duncan, Ruth Rosner Kornhauser, and others.[1] These discussions advanced our understanding of class in American society. However, to my mind the issue implied more than science and brushed the first category of "ideology" as I have given it, because on both sides, on the side of Warner and on the side of his critics, there was an often unstated and somewhat muted question as to the political implications of the positions taken. The nub of the matter was: did Warner's emphasis on an undifferentiated prestige in dividing American society into classes conceal the power dimension of class; did it underestimate the contradiction between democratic ethos and the reality of class? The critics of Warner were not all taken with Marx's view of class, but for some of them the possibility of a major structural change in which democracy would no longer be measured by ease of access to superior social-class position, but would become some radically different social order, was a strong vector in determining the attitude they took.[2] Passion and urgency were given to the discussion by more than the scientific questions involved. Can we call this additional component "ideology"? I believe we can, because I would hazard that for both Warner and his critics more was involved than issues of science—more even than issues of specific values. "Ideology" served at least as a lining to the scientific discussion.

In some of the later discussions, this ideological component is much sharper. This is true of the discussion of the degree of social mobility in the United States, which ranges from such a work as Reinhard Bendix and S. M. Lipset's *Social Mobility in Industrial Society*,[3] emphasizing the substantiality of social mobility, to Gabriel Kolko's *Wealth and Power in America*,[4] emphasizing how little change has occurred in the United States in the distribution of the major social goods of income, wealth, and power. Once again, for both sides in the controversy, the issue is not only a scientific one; the issue becomes: what measures of social change are required to realize democracy? And once again, science and value are not neatly differentiated: the social commitment affects one's treatment of the problem, and the charge of "ideology" is raised on both sides.

The ideological component is perhaps largest in the controversy around the structure of power in American society. On one side stand Robert Dahl, Nelson Polsby, Aaron Wildavsky, Edward C. Banfield[5] (who themselves take issue with earlier analysts of power in American society, such as Robert S. Lynd, Floyd Hunter, and C. Wright Mills); on the other side we may find arrayed at this point a host of critics in and outside the universities who insist that the United States, which has never looked *more* democratic to the Dahl-Polsby-Wildavsky group, is characterized by a centralized "power structure" or "power elite" which makes a mockery of democracy. At this point, we leave the relatively placid field of academic controversy quite behind: the most numerous critics of "pluralism" are now to be found in that middle area where sociology and politics tend to run together, the papers and journals of graduate students who seem poised between both worlds; and these sometimes become quite specifically "ideological." [6]

A number of different stances have been and can be taken on this question of disentangling sociology as science from sociology as ideology. One extreme position, which has been most sharply developed by George Lundberg and Stuart Dodd, demands a precision that most social scientists believe is at present unattainable, if one is to address oneself to interesting and significant problems and say interesting and significant things about them. Since most social scientists enter the field because of their interest in social problems, they have found this orientation too arid. Thus, from a very strict scientific perspective, almost all sociology can be denounced as ideology; and from this perspective, the unacknowledged part of the enterprise that makes it ideological is that mild or strong liberal or meliorist persuasion that seems to characterize most sociologists. From the point of view of the critics who base themselves on insistence on precision, science is abandoned in favor of doing something that might in some way help better race relations, improve class relations in the factory, aid the process of social modernization in undeveloped countries, help the underprivileged get more out of school, or what not.

The liberal-meliorist majority have not stood supinely by and allowed the imputation of unscientific and even ideological behavior to rest on them without counterattack. They have argued that the pure scientists are so busy with methodological and technical complexities that they cannot offer much overt guidance on pressing social questions. They retort, "Is science itself not an ideology?" or, following the more typical usage, is "scientism"—an attachment to the methods and orientations of science in an inappropriate context—itself not an ideology? In other words, what determines an insistence on precision, on quantification: a demand that all terms be made operational? If insistence on science (as in the insistence of the pure scientific sociologist that sociology must limit itself to science) is attacked as an ideology, then what is the element—essential in all critical uses of the term *ideology*—that is unacknowledged; what is being screened? From the point of view of critics of the pure scientific view, what is being screened is the reality that there can be no science of society, that large social and political commitments must be intimately tied up with the study of society—with the very selection of problems, methods, and data. Thus, to claim that a science of society can be developed is to raise sociology itself to an ideology, in which the necessity of the need for value choices, for decisions made on nonscientific grounds, is concealed. To claim that sociology is a science or can be is to claim more for it than the structure of society and knowledge permits—thus to make an untrue claim and an ideological claim. The unacknowledged motivation is to enhance the status of sociologists.

The criticism of sociology as pure science is sometimes pushed even further: the concealed motive is not only to enhance the status of the sociologist, so that he becomes scientist instead of statistician or humanist critic, but also to enhance the *power* of the sociologist. The sociologist is to become social technician, a social engineer; and thus the pure scientist does have values other than the simple scientific advancement of knowledge after all, the values of manipulation, control, order.

This is the way the arguments over pure science in sociology generally run. I make no attempt here to settle these ancient and yet also contemporary controversies or even to contribute to them in any helpful way, but only to characterize them. The most extreme formulations—those of Dodd and Lundberg—are attacked by almost everyone else. On the other hand, the majority view—that of Paul Lazarsfeld, Robert Merton, Samuel Stouffer (which also sees sociology as part of the history of science, but does not demand a precision as great as that of Dodd and Lundberg)— also finds itself under attack from the left, from those who, accepting Marx, refuse to distinguish value and science. When we review these controversies, we must conclude that any effort to set off a part of sociology that is beyond suspicion, that is not ideology, and accepted as such by the great body of sociologists, must fall to the ground. Even the most scientific parts of sociology—its most abstruse methodology, its most abstract theory—can be and are regularly brought under attack by some sociologists as ideology, as serving some social and political end by obscuring the social reality of society. This end may only be greater status for sociologists, or more seriously, greater power for sociologists, or—as we shall discuss shortly—the defense of the status quo through the subtle and ingenious technique of diverting those who might be exposing the ills of society and its true structure of power into channels that are inoffensive to the status quo.

Alas, poor sociology! Here one man's science is another man's ideology. And even worse than that: from one major sociological perspective, the more scientific, the more suspect of ideology.

And yet if one uses the *charge* of ideology, not *all* can be ideology: the charge of ideology can only be made from the perspective that there is a real science as against a false science or ideology, from the perspective of a real truth as against some false truth. This brings us to the second major usage of ideology we must consider, the core meaning of ideology in sociology, Marx's meaning: ideology conceals the reality of society in the interests of the ruling class; it is a false account of how society works. Ideology is that which claims that soldiers are patriots, factory owners are concerned with the interests of their workers, priests relate man to the eternal verities, the government reflects the will of the people and seeks the public interest, the worker's fatherland is the nation. And Mannheim in effect gives it the same meaning: ideology justifies and rationalizes the status quo.

If we limit ourselves to this usage of the term *ideology*, which is given authority by such respected names in the history of sociology, then we should examine those parts of sociology that do rationalize or justify the status quo. Obviously we would have no simple task, as we may see from the discussions over the analysis of class, social mobility, and power in American society. One man's critic is another man's liberal apologist; the careful scientist in one perspective is the ideologist in another.

From the point of view of the radical critic of society, numerous among sociologists, the mere accurate description of society (assuming it is accurate) can be seen as an effort to justify it; the account of how it works can also be seen as a rationalization that there is no other way it could work; indeed, scientific language itself can be seen as ideological: does it not conceal the true horror of society? Thus, C. Wright Mills attacks the writers of the "end of ideology" school in the following words: "The disclosure of fact . . . is the rule. The facts are duly weighed, carefully balanced, always hedged. Their power to outrage, their power to truly enlighten in a political way, their power to aid decision, their power to clarify some situation—all that is blunted and destroyed." [7] And if this is what C. Wright Mills had to say about the language of Daniel Bell, we should not be surprised at his horror as he confronted the gray, elephantine prose of Talcott Parsons.

If we then ask where does sociology rationalize, veil, justify, the status quo, we further have to determine *what* rationalizes, veils, and justifies the status quo? From a truly radical perspective, it would be almost everything in sociology that, as C. Wright Mills says, does not "outrage," for only the "outrageous" will in a corrupt society "truly enlighten" and "clarify" and lead to the necessary action. This point of view has a long history. As Marx said, our task is to change the world, not merely to understand it. And if that is our task, the organizing and social-action potential of language, of analysis, then even of science, must be taken into account. There are, of course, some terribly serious problems with this approach: one is that there may be an independent realm of truth, of science, of understanding, with no direct or only ambiguous implications for action; a second is that to improve our ability to understand or even to change society may require some concentration on the tools of scientific understanding, and even—for the scientist—a suspension of direct concern for action; a third is that the sociological analysis of a given social arrangement may indeed demonstrate its virtues and may hinder action. From understanding the world to changing it may not be a straight line, but quite the contrary; understanding it may inhibit our desire to change it.

These considerations have not reduced the popularity, especially among young sociologists, of Mills's version of the Marx-Mannheim conception of ideology.

In this rather extreme formulation, ideology is expanded accordion-fashion to encompass most of existing sociology, certainly not sparing its more rigorous efforts to be scientific; for whether it is the work of Paul Lazarsfeld, Robert K. Merton, or Talcott Parsons, we can criticize it all as ideological, if only in the sense that by paying too much attention to the reality and density and complexity of existing society it gives the society too much credit and fails to reveal its essential inhumanity and absurdity.

Does sociology then serve as an ideological cover for the status quo; does it rationalize society; does it prevent change? Here we can say that sociology plays a remarkably limited role in what most men would consider a defense of the status quo. This was not true in the past. In the nineteen-twenties, for example, William Sumner defended free enterprise, individualism, and the popular mores; Henry Pratt Fairchild argued against free immigration; E. A. Ross made invidious distinctions between immigrant groups. (At the same time, we must recall, sociology also included such liberals as Robert E. Park, W. I. Thomas, and other analysts of the problems of social conflict and social disorganization.) But who today argues in sociology that the Negro is inferior, that government (some government, even if not that of Lyndon Johnson) should not guide the economy, that social welfare will corrupt men? Sociologists are for the most part liberal Democrats, with a substantial minority further to the left. We may find Republican political scientists and economists; but if there are Republican sociologists, they are not the leaders of the field, and they are rather quiet.

We may argue whether the work of W. Lloyd Warner concealed the realities of class and power in American society or whether the work of Elton Mayo and his followers was a defense of the capitalist's right to manipulate his employees. But if these bodies of work could be so interpreted, they certainly did not lack sociological critics; and those critics now form part of the establishment in American sociology. Nor have the conservatives of the twenties and thirties found their successors among young sociologists.

But from the point of view of the radical critic of sociology as ideology, there are more ways of defending the status quo than Warner and Mayo ever dreamed of. Certainly to argue that the social basis of democracy is to be found in a variety of powerful, independent social groups (and imply that the United States is a democracy) is one. To analyze the concrete social and economic role of the Negro (and to suggest he is improving his social and economic position) is another. To study a variety of means of social change (and to imply that violence is not the author of all social change) is yet another. To consider social limitations on economic development (and to suggest revolution is not the all-sufficient precondition) is still another. Thus, while to emphasize theory and methodology is to be ideological (for where is the concentration on social problems?), to concentrate on social problems is also ideological—for does it not conceal the need for cataclysmic, revolutionary, violent change? Thus we come to the most ingenious of the arguments that sociology is ideology: that argument which claims "the problem is too small." In other words, sociology fails to truly understand society—indeed, conceals the real social forces—by concentration on the small scale, or the social problematic, rather than the social *systemic* (but not certainly in Parsons' sense, rather in the sense of a truly big and satisfactory change). There is nothing so bemusing and amusing as to trace the use of the criticism, "The problem is too small."

We may find a number of examples for an initial foray into the problem of "the problem is too small" in *Sociology on Trial*, edited by Maurice Stein and Arthur Vidich.

Thus Barrington Moore quotes from a study of "Male Sex Aggression on a University Campus," from which we learn that "of the 291 responding girls, 55.7 per cent reported themselves offended at least once during the academic year at some level of erotic intimacy . . . 20.9 per cent were offended by forceful attempts at intercourse." Professor Moore comments censoriously: "The professional journals are full of similar articles where careful methodology is used on trivial problems. . . . If the demonstration of uniformities like these were all that social science had to offer, it would constitute no more than an enormous diversion from more important problems." More important to whom? It strikes me that this is a subject of considerable importance to girls, boys, their parents, deans, and others. Professor Moore goes on to explain what an important problem is: "Uniformities in social behavior become important for us only when they concern important problems, such as freedom and compulsion." This is rather mystifying, for a study of "forceful attempts at intercourse" has just been dismissed as having nothing to do with important problems; that is, freedom and compulsion. But those of us skilled in this discourse know that Professor Moore means freedom and compulsion insofar as they are affected by "large structural changes." [8]

Perhaps many sociologists would agree that the sexual behavior of American college students is a small question in the range of possible questions (I am not so sure). But from the point of view of the critic of the scope of sociological investigations, rather larger questions are also "too small." Thus, in the same volume Hans Gerth and Saul Landau criticize American sociologists for having given up large questions, "all thought and theory that dealt with world or total structure. To be sure, there was still work to be done, but it was no more than a scattering of problems that remained to be solved, involving industrial efficiency and the rational adjustment of certain immigrant-alien milieus to the American system." Thus industrial efficiency and immigrant adjustment are also "too small." We search further for evidence as to what is big enough:

> Without a view of the total structure, from a historical bridge, only narrow currents can be analyzed, and much of their content will necessarily remain unknown. . . . The far-reaching results of the long Slavonic migration to Prussian Junker labor barracks, or of immigrants arriving in boatloads from Poland and heading to the mines, mills, and factories, cannot be grasped through the close-up camera, or attitude studies of changes in Old World patriarchalism. While such studies by Thomas and Znaniecki and other milieu sociologists greatly enriched the tool kit of the profession, the more basic issues were neglected: the analysis of *structures* which *cause* milieu changes, was forsaken for more "empirical" investigations.
>   Thus, compartmentalization and the confinement of precision work to milieu and industrial sociology have threatened to smother the original so-ciologist's ethos.[9]

And so on. Presumably labor migration, population movements, and the breakup of traditionalism are also "too small."

As our final contribution to the question "What is too small?" here is a passage from an interesting essay by Karl Mannheim on American sociol-ogy, also reprinted in Stein and Vidich:

> American sociology lacks a certain courage in outlining broad theories, or rather shrinks from inquiring into the structural aspects of social life as a whole. . . . Our claims on social science are not satisfied by typical Ameri-can contributions . . . [because] typical American studies start from ques-tions in nowise connected with those problems that arouse our passions in everyday political and social struggle.
>   In one respect American sociology is nearer to reality than German—namely, as regards the solution of everyday problems. The American scholar is no bookish person: he maintains contacts with criminal courts and social welfare institutions, lives in gangs, in slums and ghettos.[10]

Undoubtedly, in the Germany of 1932, when Mannheim's essay was writ-ten, such questions as were raised by criminal courts, gangs, slums, and ghettos were certainly not important. But to more contemporary contribu-tors to *Sociology on Trial*, who are not witnessing the victory of fascism and the end of democracy, these subjects are also considered "not impor-tant enough."

What, then, is important enough? Changes in the social system, in the social structure. This is not often defined; it is nothing so simple these days as a change in the ownership of the means of production; but we know that it is big, it is revolutionary, it is probably violent, and it is the kind of thing sociologists are not studying enough. In Mills's view, one should not only be studying how this should come about: in one's style and language one should be helping it come about. Those who criticize the scale of problems chosen for investigation do not often go this far; but Moore and Gerth and Landau (though not Mannheim) are at least willing to go far enough to say that the reason the larger questions are not taken up is that the sociologist is dependent on big organized research or does not want to rock the boat of the status quo. Thus the interesting recurrent theme, "The problem is too small," is often an index to the point of view that sociology is covering for modern society—and is in that sense ideological.

The most confusing twist in the history of the use of the term *ideology* in sociology is the most recent. Here the definitions of Marx and Mannheim are abandoned, and ideology is now used to refer in a positive way to the nonscientific element in sociology, insofar as it is directed to the transformation of existing society in the interest of power and deprived groups. This is what Daniel Bell had in mind when he spoke of the "end of ideology." His argument was that the large political slogans and myths around which conflict was organized in advanced industrial societies for many years had lost their power to move men. Men would no longer die to maintain capitalism or institute socialism. Neither "the socialization of the means of the production" nor "the maintenance of free enterprise" was seen to have any concrete meaning. Concrete meaning had shifted to the political and social programs, becoming more and more alike in all advanced industrial societies, by which production was increased, the income of the poorest raised, the goods of society—wealth, education, medical care, leisure—were more lavish and more equitably distributed. In this sense, ideology was coming to an end and social technology was taking its place.

Against the idea that the major divisions of interests and of social forces of the past hundred and fifty years were coming to an end in an age of affluence and of consensus, radicals rose up. The aim of such a theory as Bell's, they argued, was simply to conceal the fact that the great division of interests in society originally propounded with such force by Marx still existed. There would be—there must be, they claimed—an Armageddon, in which the capitalists (or imperialists or Americans) would be dispossessed of their wealth and power and a juster and more equalitarian society would come into existence.

But if one was to argue against the "end of ideology," what was one to argue for? One could pick up Mannheim's term, "utopia"—which is close to what Bell had in mind with his "ideology." The problem there is that those who believe in the necessity of "fundamental social transformation" have been rather prejudiced against the term *utopia* by Marx and Engels' violent attack on the utopian socialists. Nor could one simply defend "scientific socialism": no one of any modicum of intellectual seriousness believed that Marx's socialism had been "scientific" or that the official system of thought propounded under that name in the Soviet Union was scientific. Whatever the situation in mid-nineteenth-century Europe, where physics could still be referred to as natural philosophy, the term *science* in the twentieth century had been pre-empted by a certain form of scholarly activity, and it was impossible to retain, for what Marx and Engels had called "scientific socialism," Mannheim *"utopia,"* and Bell *"ideology,"* the first term in the series.

And at the same time, some Marxists, in particular those who called themselves Marxists in the Communist countries, had restored the term *ideology,* despite the usage of the master, to mean simply those large ideas that can move men to action; thus, "ideological warfare," "ideological defenses," as in Soviet Russia and Communist China.

In sum: those sociologists who did see the need for what they called massive social change were on the whole ready to take up the term again, regardless of Marx's meaning, and say, yes, sociology, and society too, need "ideology"; they need the big ideas that move men to act and introduce these social changes. Science in the social sphere had, for the most part, they felt, given up the effort to determine ends; it served only those who had the power to buy the scientists and set the problems for their analysis. Utopia, following Marx, seemed too utopian; that is to say, too mild and namby-pamby. But ideology—it offered the promise of utopia with the hardness of contemporary reality. It was utopia armed, so to speak. The "sociological imagination" means big ideas that can move men. And big ideas that can move men—well, if this is called ideology, some sociologists will not shy away.

But there is perhaps one additional point to be made in explaining why "utopia" has not become popular among radicals. Utopia means specific mechanisms: how a society will work. Three awful possibilities then raise themselves before the eyes of the cataclysmic radical. The first is that when he develops these mechanisms as to how a better society will work— a society which maximizes freedom, equality, human development—he has to assume relationships between kinds of specific social organization, specific human actions as they tend to be encouraged or discouraged by this organization, and a resultant in the form of some degree of human happiness. In other words, the concrete effort to define the better society inevitably means reintroducing some order of manipulation. For if man lives in society, and if those social mechanisms that make it up produce better or worse results, then one is engaged in trying to engineer those better mechanisms and doing so on the assumption that it will be better for men in general. Oddly enough, despite the commitment to massive social change (or because of it), specific new positive mechanisms and the discussion of their consequences for men seem to shrivel the soul of the radical. He consequently prefers to denounce the evils of an existent society and try to summon forth a reaction of rage and despair. But he refuses, in the spirit of Marx himself, to define the mechanisms that *will* exist in the new society. Thus, those modern sociologists and social critics that have placed themselves most wholeheartedly in the tradition of Marx— C. Wright Mills and Herbert Marcuse—denounce an existing society in all its forms, but hesitate to define what mechanisms will eliminate the evils they presently see. It is as if they were to say there need be no relation between social arrangements and men; whatever is decided on in a true moment of revolutionary ecstasy will work. It can have no negative consequences, if the heart of the revolutionary is pure. Or, not only history but also sociology will truly come to an end, as Marx foretold.

A second reason why the radical sociologist shies away from the work of utopia is that he suspects he may come to the conclusion that the arrangements he proposes in some parts of the new society will be not very different from arrangements already existing in societies that have not yet been seared by a cleansing revolutionary flame. He may propose a medical-care system that looks like Finland's, a housing and planning program that looks like England's, welfare and family programs similar to France's, an educational system not very different from that of California, and a work-training and placement program not very different from that in Western Germany. At that point the ultimate horror of utopian thought for the radical emerges: utopia may not *need* the cataclysmic, ultimate battle with evil on which his life is based.

The third reason why utopia arouses no enthusiasm among radical sociologists, I suspect, is that, since it *does* make us look at the consequences of different kinds of social mechanisms, it again brings us back to the problem that is "too small," and it brings us even further back, to "science." It brings us to the kind of domestic sociology that is practiced in England, where, without wasting much time on big notions of large systemic social change, sociologists study such questions as the effects of different kinds of housing arrangements on the life of low-income groups or the impact of different types of care on the aged. In other words, if one were to take utopia seriously, one would have to contemplate the possibility that the scientific study of the sexual behavior of students in college may not be so unimportant after all; for, as we all know, sex does seem to affect the happiness and unhappiness of young (and even somewhat older) people, and even after the revolution there will be boys, girls, and educational institutions, whose social and physical arrangements may have certain effects on their welfare and happiness.

So while the radical critic of established sociology as a defense of the status quo has a choice between summoning sociology to include a larger portion of utopia or a larger portion of ideology, on the whole he has opted for ideology, and David Riesman and Martin Meyerson, who have voted for more utopia, have found few followers. We might conclude by saying it seems to be more fun to attack society and its arrangements than to figure out how they might be improved. The target is the liberal equivocators, who, having been unimpressed with the effects of such large systemic social changes as massacring the upper classes, now devote themselves to problems that are "too small" and even wonder whether the various contributions of scientific methodology may help them to better arrangements on these problems.

What then can we say, after all this, of the ideological uses of sociology? First, of course, we should have to select a reasonable definition of ideology; and I would select as a sound definition, and one akin to one large common use, illusion. One would have to add to that, illusion in the form of large, systemic, and even "scientific" thought.

Does sociology have ideological functions? Indeed it does. For many of its practitioners, sociology strengthens one or another illusion. I would say it is *least* effective in fostering the illusion that present-day society is perfect and requires no changes to advance human happiness. Its whole bias, despite the criticisms of functional analysis which have bombarded us from all sides in recent years, is toward change. Sociology, for one thing, is the newest and least secure of the social sciences and the one least connected with the traditional upper classes. Political science, economics, history, and even anthropology all do better: young Rockefellers may become anthropologists, but hardly sociologists. Sociology attracts students from marginal groups: Jews today, Negroes tomorrow. Its teachers are liberal and skeptical in tone. Even if they are exposing nothing more exciting than the fact that America is *not* a classless society, they present it to their students as a big thing, which at least means that many young men who come into sociology want to expose something, though they may be at a loss as to just what it is they want to expose.

The chief illusion, then, that is fostered among sociologists—the chief ideological function of sociology, I suspect—is that there are more illusions around than there actually are. Thus, people *do* know that there are classes, do know that patriotism is abetted by profit, do know that factory owners have different interests from workers, and so on. The social groups from which sociologists are recruited are new groups, aspiring groups—or if we may indulge in that harsh illusion-stripping language sociologists like to use, parvenu and *nouveau riche* groups—and it is understandable that sociologists want to see where things are not what they claim to be. Thus when we say the sociology of religion, we mean the part that is *not* religion. When we say the sociology of industry, we mean the part that shows how people gum up productivity in the factory. When we say the sociology of health, we mean the part that shows that doctors and nurses are moved by prestige and status rather than simply the needs of patients. The sociology of politics deals with the nonpolitical reasons why people act the way they do in political life. And the sociology of social science will emphasize all the less pleasant reasons why people become social scientists. Since, as a matter of fact, people are moved by status, prestige, face, wealth, power, sociologists have something to say and are often enlightening to the practitioners in all these fields.

If this is what sociology is, in its concrete manifestations, if this is what sociologists *do,* there is not much chance that sociology and sociologists will prop up the façade of society; they are devoted to undermining it. Under these circumstances, the illusions that sociology is most heir to are not the illusions of the established and the establishment, but the illusions that life is a fraud, that men never mean what they say, and that institutions are never devoted to their ostensible ends. Now, while all this is true to some extent, to maximize such views is to shape an ideology.

In the course of this activity, as sociologists are fond of pointing out, they do undermine received faiths and beliefs, they do antagonize conservatives and defenders of received and existing institutions, and they will even get some liberals angry. But there is another side to this perverse tendency of sociologists to introduce a new perspective and to show that things are not fully what they are. In doing so they also prop up all sorts of institutions that the respectable elements in society would like to see weakened or eliminated. Thus, despite the presumed bias of the dominant "functionalist" school in sociology, functionalists—to the confusion of those who attack them—will also explain the "functions" of political machines, of organized crime, of drug addiction, of political apathy, and of slums (and presumably, then, slum-lords). Thus sociologists outrage the respectable on two scores: by attacking that which should be upheld and defended and by explaining and thus in some sense justifying that which should be attacked and suppressed.

I would then argue that sociology's functions are primarily those of complicating and undermining received opinions on social life. This helps to explain some of the ways in which sociology fails. One of the chief, of course, is the exposure that is no exposure; for example, the study of suburban life that either exaggerates its distinctiveness or insists on the originality of what everyone knows. As I suggested earlier, sociology specializes in unveiling the illusion that has deceived no one.

To say simply that sociology is the science of society is to ignore the question of those disciplines of society that devote themselves to the central elements for understanding how society works: political science and economics. As against these, sociology devotes itself to the unacknowledged elements, often unknown to the actors, that indeed do contribute to explaining what happens in society, but generally in an ancillary and secondary way. On the other hand, since sociology takes all of society within its scope, it becomes, at one limit, the science of all society, the philosophy of society or the philosophy of history, and here the way is open for those large perspectives on society which do suggest and propose major action, change, revolution. One might say these two aspects of sociology are in conflict: its exposures of illusions—all illusions—inhibit the action that some of its large philosophic orientations would encourage.

Sociology serves as a refuge for the academic action seeker, whether the action is on the level of the life of the underbelly of society or on the level of grand revolutionary change. But its specific perspectives and methodologies unveil the world and, properly carried out, unveil even the illusions of the action seekers, whether bohemian or revolutionary. At this point, some of the action seekers inhibit their true sociological imagination: they stop before unveiling some of the illusions—whether of the virtue of the proletariat, the happiness of the irresponsible, the altruism of the revolutionary. Insofar as they then call what they have done "sociology," sociology serves an ideological function.

REFERENCES

1. Specifically: C. Wright Mills, review of *The Social Life of a Modern Community, American Sociological Review,* VII (1942), 263–271, reprinted in Mills, *Power, Politics, and People* (New York: Ballantine Books, n.d.), pp. 53–76; Harold W. Pfautz and Otis Dudley Duncan, "A Critical Evaluation of Warner's Work in Community Stratification," *American Sociological Review,* XV, No. 2 (1950), 205–215; Seymour Martin Lipset and Richard Bendix, "Social Status and Social Structure," *British Journal of Sociology,* II (1951), 150–168, 230–254; Ruth Rosner Kornhauser, "The Warner Approach to Social Stratification," in R. Bendix and S. M. Lipset, eds., *Class, Status and Power,* 1st ed. (Glencoe, Ill.: The Free Press, 1953), pp. 224–255, 675–678.
2. For an article which makes these points most sharply, see Walter R. Goldschmidt, "America's Social Classes," *Commentary,* X (1950), 175–181.
3. Berkeley: University of California Press, 1959.
4. New York: Praeger, 1962.
5. Edward C. Banfield, *Political Influence* (Glencoe, Ill.: The Free Press, 1961); Robert A. Dahl, *Who Governs?* (New Haven: Yale University Press, 1961); Nelson W. Polsby, *Community Power and Political Theory* (New Haven: Yale University Press, 1963); Aaron Wildavsky, *Leadership in a Small Town* (Totowa, N.J.: Bedminster Press, 1964); and others.
6. See, for example, the issues of *Catalyst,* "a biennial publication of the Sociology Club of the State University of New York at Buffalo," Summer, 1965, and Summer, 1966. Of course the pluralist position can also be criticized from a more scientific, or less ideological, position, even in journals published by graduate students in sociology. See David Jessup, "Potential Power," *Berkeley Journal of Sociology,* XI (1966), 66–81.
7. Quoted in Stephen W. Rousseas and James Farganis, "American Politics and the End of Ideology," *British Journal of Sociology,* XIV (1963), 347–362.
8. Maurice Stein and Arthur Vidich, eds., *Sociology on Trial* (Englewood Cliffs, N.J.: Prentice-Hall, 1963), p. 77.
9. *Ibid.,* pp. 29–31.
10. *Ibid.,* p. 8.

The Uses of
Sociology in
the Professions

PART **II**

The Law

HANS ZEISEL

chapter 4

The law from one view is a continuous process
of synthesizing facts and rules, with new facts at times engendering new
rules. The process takes place wherever law is made: in the legislatures, in
the administrative agencies, and in the courts.

The facts reach these lawmakers in a variety of forms. The primary
source is still the witness who reports on his own private experience. Occasionally, however, facts are presented as cumulative knowledge, systematically gathered through surveys and most recently also through experiments, methods that are part of the tool chest of the social sciences.

The survey as a source of facts for the law predates modern social science by centuries and constitutes in fact one of its major historical roots.[1]
But it is only in recent years that the law has begun to use research operations conducted with technical rigor. The uses the law has made of such
systematic investigations differ widely, from simple citation in a brief or
opinion to being the decisive ground for a judgment or a legal reform.[2]
The great majority of the studies that come before the law raise only private issues, assisting courts and agencies in individual litigation. They may
be surveys of the quality of contracted goods, of the geographic range
from which a drive-in theater draws its clientele, of the commercial effects
of a merger, or of the socioeconomic structure of the jurors in a certain
community. But although such studies are at times gems of technical perfection and ingenuity, they will not be discussed here. Their variety is too
great, and they seldom reach the higher courts, hence they seldom affect

legal rule making; and they have been sufficiently discussed elsewhere.[3]

The studies we shall discuss here deal with more general problems: with substantive rules of law, with procedural rules, or with institutions that are a mixture of both. Some of these studies are broad surveys of a legal institution without more specific focus; they enter the stream of legal resolution only slowly, as but one of the many sources that shape the law. Other studies, in contrast, are designed to illuminate if not to resolve one narrow, crucial issue; these investigations—sometimes they are controlled experiments—are bound to affect the law more directly.

But all the studies on which this chapter will report have one thing in common: they were made for the purpose of being used by the law and in many instances have affected its course.[4]

We shall report these studies in the order of the spectrum that ranges from the narrowly but sharply focused controlled experiment to the broad, diffuse survey.

Controlled Experiment

There is no more powerful tool for assessing a legal innovation, or any innovaton for that matter, than the controlled experiment. But since its essence is to apply a rule of law to one group of cases and to withhold it from another, such purposeful discrimination would seem at first to violate the equal-protection guaranty of the Constitution.[5] Indeed, there are substantive limits to legal experimentation; there can be none that involves withholding of a right, guaranteed under all circumstances. It would be impossible, for instance, to insist that some criminal defendants be tried without counsel in order to find out what effect counsel has. But there are several reasons why, outside this rigidly protected sphere, the law should permit experimentation. First, the experimental discrimination is by definition temporary; second, the discrimination is applied impartially, by lot; third it is the very purpose of the experiment to learn what, if any, effect the discriminating rule would have: hence, at the outset, one cannot even be certain that there is discrimination; and fourth, the ultimate aim of the experiment is to eliminate the rule if it should be found to discriminate unfairly.

Controlled legal experiments, not surprisingly, have largely been confined to rules that convey privileges rather than rights.

The first controlled experiments within the precincts of the law were probably conducted by the Adult Prison Authority of the State of California, whch tried to assess the effectiveness of a variety of prisoner treatments. The most daring of these experiments was an effort to determine what happened if prisoners were released nine months before their appointed time; specifically, whether such a premature release was likely to increase the rate of recidivism.[6]

Not much came of these experiments, partly perhaps because the recidivism rate is too brittle a measure of effectiveness since, in order to be counted as a recidivist, it is not sufficient to have committed another crime; it is also necessary to be caught and reconvicted. And since the odds of being caught, as revealed by the published statistics, are on the average about one in five, this ratio might well have a great variance and hence be a very unstable measure.[7]

A controlled experiment that allowed of precise measurement and had an immediate effect on the law was conducted in the state courts of New Jersey.

In most of our courts some or all of the civil suits, before they come to trial, are scheduled for what has become known as pretrial. There, counsel for both sides, occasionally with their clients, meet with the judge to present briefly the issues under dispute and air the possibilities of settlement. Tradition has it that these pretrials, aside from preparing and facilitating the subsequent trial, increase the rate of settlements prior to trial. The institution has, therefore, been considered a most desirable means of reducing the trial load and thereby the intolerable congestion of our metropolitan courts. Since many cases, the trial of which would have lasted two days on the average, are settled during a half-hour pretrial conference, this notion seemed well supported.

But analysis of available statistics made the point doubtful; there were indications that the cases settled at pretrial would have been settled even without it and that the court time spent on pretrying cases might be wasted. The precise answer, it was suggested, could come only from a controlled experiment which pretried a random sample of cases and omitted pretrial in a comparable control group.[8]

At that time the New Jersey courts had a rule that made pretrial obligatory, and the state's distinguished Chief Justice and its Court Administrator, becoming sympathetic to both the query and the proposal, commissioned Professor Rosenberg, then Director of the Project for Effective Justice at Columbia University, to conduct the experiment.[9] The design called for random assignment of cases by the clerks of the respective courts to two alternative procedures: to obligatory pretrial in one group of cases, and to optional pretrial in the control group, where it would be held only if one or both of the litigants requested it.[10] Accordingly, 2,954 cases were assigned at random alternatingly to the two groups, for which the settlement ratios shown in Table 4–1 emerged. There was no difference. In addition, the experiment failed to confirm a subsidiary hypothesis, namely, that the pretried, and hence prepared, cases required a shorter trial time. Thus the conclusion emerged simple and clean: contrary to a widely held belief, obligatory pretrial did not save court time, but in fact wasted it.

TABLE 4-1.

	CONTROL GROUP: OBLIGATORY PRETRIAL	EXPERIMENTAL GROUP: OPTIONAL PRETRIAL
Suits settled before they reached the trial stage	76%	78%

Persuaded by the experiment, the State of New Jersey forthwith changed its rule and made pretrial optional.[11]

But the legal experiment that had the most profound and sweeping effect on the law was conducted in the criminal courts of Manhattan. It revolutionized one of the most solid traditions in the criminal law: the practice of setting bail for defendants arraigned in our criminal courts. Bail is set, as a matter of constitutional right, for nearly all defendants; if they can post it, they are set free; if not, they must remain in jail. Whether or not they *can* post it depends as a rule on the bondsman, who, against a premium of some 10 per cent, will or will not take the risk of providing the demanded bail. Only rarely is a defendant allowed to go free without posting bail.

The system has been heavily criticized because it favors the well-to-do, surrenders the actual decision to the bondsman, and keeps an inordinate proportion of defendants in jail, some of whom are subsequently acquitted. The system, nevertheless, withstood all criticism until the Vera Foundation made known its findings from a unique experiment which it conducted in 1961. With the co-operation of the New York judiciary and the New York University Law School, all defendants arraigned in the felony court of Manhattan were interviewed so as to assess the risk of their failing to appear at their trial, if the court were to free them without requiring bail. On the basis of these interviews the defendants were classified into two groups: those for whom a release without bail could be reasonably recommended to the court and those for whom such a recommendation could not be made. The recommendable group was then divided into two random halves: the experimental group, for which the recommendation to release the defendant without bail was actually transmitted to the arraignment judge, and the control group, with respect to which the judge was told nothing and thereby left to his own traditional mode of making the bail decision. In this latter group only 14 per cent of all defendants were freed without bail, as against 60 per cent in the recommended half. The hypothesis was that at the time of trial, from the group of which 60 per cent had been freed without bail, more would fail to appear in court than from the group where only 14 per cent were free without bail, and the question was: how many more? When trial time came, only 1 per cent of *all* defendants released without bail, whether recommended or not, purposely failed to appear in court. The experiment thereby proved that the number of defendants released without bail could be quadrupled without reducing their availability at the time of trial.[12]

The results of the experiment were stunning. The City of New York took over the interviewing from the foundation and established it as a permanent service. The Attorney-General of the United States convoked a conference on the topic, and today almost all major cities and many rural areas have adopted the Vera procedure, and with it the liberalized practice of release without bail. And the Department of Justice left no doubt as to where the credit belonged: "Of particular significance is the fact that these changes have flowed not out of a crisis . . . but rather from education, through empirical research and demonstration." [13]

The secret of the success of this experiment was twofold. First, except for the bail bondsmen, everybody stood to gain from the liberalization: the municipal jails saved money; the defendants themselves were spared unnecessary hardships; and last, but not least, the ends of justice were advanced. Secondly, the numerical result of the experiment was so clear that no probability calculus was needed for its appreciation.[14]

The Natural Experiment

Sometimes administrative routine will present the investigator with a natural experiment, that is, with an experimental and a control group that were not purposely designed by him.

The study of differential sentencing provides a classic example. The law has very little control over the sentence of a convicted defendant. It merely sets the range, usually wide, and thus leaves much discretion to the judge.[15] Since many courts assign cases at random to the different judges, the cases before each judge form a natural experimental unit. Thus, a study of the New York City Magistrate Court revealed that, among the thirteen judges, one discharged 73 per cent of the defendants before him on a charge of intoxication, while one of his colleagues discharged only 1 per cent.[16] Later studies, especially those of Gaudet, confirmed the problem.[17] Today the disparity of sentences for comparable crimes has become a major concern of the judiciary. Federal judges have instituted procedures designed to minimize these fluctuations.

A slightly different, natural experimental situation is provided by collegiate judicial tribunals, inasmuch as the judges there are confronted by the identical court record in each case, yet often come to different decisions. These studies often employ rather sophisticated analytical techniques, such as scale and factor analysis. But in some cases the data are so stunningly lopsided that they can stand in the raw. Thus it was found that in the Michigan Supreme Court's decisions on claims under the Workmen's Compensation law the judges simply split along party lines.[18]

Pritchett was the first to analyze collegiate court decisions in his studies of the United States Supreme Court.[19] In recent years studies of this type have proliferated.[20] The reason why they are not given more prominence in this essay is that they have yet proved of little "use" in the meaning of this book.

Following we report on a study of a different type. It too made use of variations among judges. But, in contrast to the studies cited above, it was a study which the court itself initiated to provide guidance for its procedural rules.

Under traditional trial procedure, the plaintiff in a civil case first presents his case both as to liability and size of damages and is followed in turn by the defendant, who presents his side of the case. After both have had their say, the jury retires and decides whether the defendant is at all liable for damages and, if so, how large these damages should be. The question of damages thus becomes relevant only if liability is found. The suggestion was made to split the trial and to limit evidence and argument in the first part of the trial to the liability issue, asking the jury to decide whether the defendant owes anything at all. Only if this decision is affirmative does the trial proceed with the evidence and subsequent verdict on the *size* of the damages.[21] Since liability is affirmed in only a little more than half of all cases, this mode of trial was expected to save something like half of the trial time normally spent on damages. The Federal District Court for Northern Illinois was sufficiently intrigued by this split-trial idea to try it out and to ask the University of Chicago Law School to help in assessing the effect of the split-trial rule, as it has come to be called.[22]

The court had adopted the rule in a form that left it to the discretion of the individual judges whether they wanted to apply it in the particular case. It was from this discretion that, seemingly, the difficulties, but eventually the salvation of the experimental design, arose. If each judge could apply the rule in some cases and not in others, and if he were to select—as in fact he often did—only those cases for split trial which, in his view, promised some gain in time from the application, the cases tried in the regular mode and those tried under the split-trial rule could not be compared. Whatever difference in trial length might be found between the two could not be attributed to the new rule, because the cases were admittedly different to begin with.

At first glance this lack of random assignment would seem fatal. Yet, while it made the analysis more complicated and less powerful, it did in fact make the experiment possible. Since the original assignment of cases to the individual judges was made randomly, the inference was allowed that the cases coming before Judge A did not differ from the cases coming before Judge B. And then something fortunate happened. The discretion of the judges resulted in an effective spread of the experimental stimulus: some used the rule in almost all their cases, some in hardly any, and some in varying proportions between.

If, then, it were true that the application of the split-trial rule saved time, the judges who applied the rule more often should require on the average less trial time than those who applied it less often. This turned out to be true, as Table 4–2 shows.

TABLE 4–2. *Proportion of Split Trials and Average Trial Time in Personal Injury Trials*

JUDGE	PROPORTION OF CASES TRIED UNDER SPLIT-RULE (PER CENT)	AVERAGE LENGTH OF ALL TRIALS BEFORE THIS JUDGE (DAYS)	NUMBER OF TRIALS BEFORE THIS JUDGE*
A	89	3.2	(26)
B	51	3.3	(41)
C	38	3.5	(26)
D	14	3.8	(22)
E	7	3.9	(27)
F	7	4.3	(14)

* Only judges with more than 10 trials are included.

The regression line based on these data indicated that at the point where a judge conducted all trials under the split-trial rule, his average trial time was about 20 per cent below the point where none of the trials were split. This, then, was the magnitude of the time that could be saved through application of the rule.

But since the variation in the stimulus was not random, but self-selected, it was desirable to provide supporting evidence. It was clear that whatever savings there were must come from the elimination of the damage trial. The frequency of damage trials was, therefore, determined both for the regular and for the split trials. (See Table 4–3.)

The dispositions of the two groups of cases were drastically different: 76 per cent of all regular cases went through a complete trial, against only 15 per cent of the separate trials. As for the latter group, 58 per cent were spared trial of the damage issue because of the intermediate verdict denying liability. In 43 per cent of the cases the trial simply ended when liability was denied, and in another 13 per cent of the cases there was no trial of the damages because they were settled after the jury had affirmed liability.

The split trial is a radical innovation in American law, brought to the fore by the pressures of court congestion. When the study was first pub-

TABLE 4-3. *Disposition of Case in Regular and Separated Trials*

	REGULAR TRIALS (PER CENT)	SEPARATE TRIALS (PER CENT)
Complete trial on liability and damages	76	15
Trial ended after liability verdict	—	58
because verdict was for defendant	—	43
because damages were settled after verdict affirming liability	—	15
Other dispositions (settlement during trial, directed verdicts)	24	27
	100%	100%

lished, the Joint Committee on Effective Administration of Justice, on suggestion of its chairman, United States Supreme Court Justice Clark, had copies sent to all trial judges in the United States; as of this writing, several state and federal courts have moved to authorize their judges to use the split-trial procedure, and the institution is likely to gain more ground.[23]

Experiment under Seminatural Conditions

If an issue falls into the constitutionally protected area, not even a natural experiment is likely to occur, and a simulated one must suffice. But even then, as many natural components as possible must be retained, as for instance in the following series of experiments concerning the defense of insanity. They were designed to test jury reaction to certain variations in the law. The natural element in these experiments was the jurors, summoned by a real trial judge from the jury pool of his court with the request to partake in the experiment and to deliberate on the case as if it were a real one.[24]

In Anglo-American law the defense of insanity has been embodied for more than a century in the so-called M'Naghten rule, which calls for an acquittal if the defendant either did not know what he was doing or did not know that what he was doing was wrong. Recently, the rule has come under criticism, primarily from psychiatrists. In 1954 the Federal Court in the District of Columbia established a new rule in a case in which one Durham was indicted, and subsequently acquitted, on a charge of burglary. The Durham rule considers the defense as established if the criminal act can be shown to be the "product of a mental disease or a mental defect." It became thus a point of major interest for the criminal law to find out what if any difference it made to the outcome of a trial whether insanity was defined under the M'Naghten or under the Durham rule.

The "law" in a criminal jury trial becomes operative primarily through the judge's instruction to the jury before it begins deliberation. In that instruction the judge spells out the circumstances under which the jury may find the defendant insane. In a way, then, the question as to what difference the law makes means what difference it makes to the jury whether it is instructed according to the rule in M'Naghten or in Durham.

To compare the insanity cases in the District of Columbia with cases from a court that operates under the M'Naghten doctrine could provide only unsatisfactory findings, since not only the rule of law but also the cases, the juries, and the judges are likely to be different. And it is obviously impossible to decide the issue through a controlled experiment under completely natural conditions. Therefore, an experiment had to be designed that combined natural with laboratory conditions, sufficiently realistic to justify confidence in its validity.

Two trial records were composed: one, a case of housebreaking, a simplified version of the original Durham trial; the other, an incest case, also an abbreviated version of an actual trial. In both trials the accused's only defense was insanity. The trial evidence was acted out and with the other elements of the trial put on recording tape. Of each case, three main variants were produced.[25] The tapes were identical but for that part of the judge's instruction that dealt with the defense of insanity and for the concomitant psychiatric testimony. In one version the instruction and psychiatric testimony were according to M'Naghten; in the second, according to Durham; and in the third, the instruction left it in fact to the jurors own judgment as to whether the evidence in the case supported a defense of insanity, forcing the jury to establish its own law of insanity.

Each of the three versions was then taken into two metropolitan courts and presented in turn to more than a hundred juries. A judge called these jurors into his courtroom and asked them to co-operate in the experiment; by so doing, he advised them, they would oblige the court and also discharge their present turn of jury duty. The jurors then listened to the taped trial and afterward deliberated and arrived at a verdict. Table 4–4 shows the outcome of the experiment in terms of the jurors' vote on their first ballot, prior to the beginning of the deliberation.[26]

In both trials, the Durham rule elicited a higher percentage of acquittals by reason of insanity than the M'Naghten rule. That the percentages

TABLE 4–4. *Per Cent of Jurors Voting "Not Guilty—Insane"*
on First Ballot

	M'NAGHTEN	DURHAM	NO RULE
Incest	24	36	34
case	(240)	(312)	(264)
Housebreaking	57	65	76
case	(120)	(120)	(120)

under Durham are very close to those obtained under the "No Rule" instruction suggests, furthermore, as indeed it has been argued,[27] that Durham comes close to being no rule.

The figures show that the incest case allowed a sharper differentiation between M'Naghten and Durham than the housebreaking case. This difference is instructive beyond the specific issue. The defendant in the incest case was an officer in a city's fire department, with an excellent record, who, except for the crime in question, had never shown any signs of abnormality. The defendant in the burglary case, on the other hand, much like the original Durham, had been in and out of mental institutions and hence had shown, by whatever legal or common-sense rule, signs of insanity. The fireman could be found insane only if the jury was instructed (as Durham allows) to consider the criminal act itself as a symptom of insanity.

The experiment raised two questions of general significance. One applies to the realism of simulation; the other, to the degree of generalizing from experimental findings.

In this experiment there were two simulated elements: the experimental stimulus was greatly reduced (a two-day trial condensed into an hour), and jury deliberation was clearly a mock procedure without consequences in the real world. As to the second point, there was considerable reassurance: these were real jurors called to duty by a real judge; they discharged their responsibilities with such obvious zeal and honesty that deliberations lasted up to ten hours, often engendering high-pitched battles among the jurors who, at times, ended in a "hung jury."

The other point raises a more serious problem. A tape recording of a trial, condensed to about an hour's length, may be something quite different from a full-blown trial, in which the jury not only hears but also sees over a period of many hours real people with all the significant details of their reactions. Without additional research, the point allows of no precise answer.

As to the consequences of the insanity experiments, one can at this stage only venture a guess. On the whole, the experiment should strengthen the hand of those who oppose the Durham rule, simply because its message to the jury is ambiguous. Whatever the shortcomings of the traditional right-wrong test, its criteria are clear and can be applied by the jury.

The Survey Experiment

The jury, in spite of its deep constitutional roots, has been the topic of perennial debate, with little precise knowledge to support it.

Some years ago, the University of Chicago Law School began a large-scale study of the jury system, and one of its key questions was: What difference would it make if all jury cases were tried only by a judge sitting without a jury?

The question would seem to demand a controlled experiment—every case to be tried twice, once with and once without a jury—an obviously impossible solution. Equally impossible it would be to assign cases at random to jury and judge, since this is a choice no defendant must be deprived of. Nor would the simple comparison of actual jury verdicts with actual judge verdicts help, even if limited to trials of the same type of crime, because we know that the cases in which the defendant waives a jury are quite different from those where he wants one.

Curiously enough, the design eventually adopted for the study came close to the ideal design, the controlled experiment. A nationwide sample of trial judges reported for a specified time period on all the jury trials over which they presided. Each judge told us how the jury decided the case and how he, the judge, would have decided it, had he sat without a jury. The design thus made use of the fact that every case is tried twice, albeit simultaneously: once before the jury and once before the presiding judge, who, if there were no jury in the case, would have to render the judgment.

This research design is but a natural controlled experiment of a special order. Experimental stimulus (the jury) and control (the judge) are present in every case, but unlike a planned experiment, there is, except for the judge who may preside over several trials, no replication. The jury changes from trial to trial; and most important, the case, too, of course, is never the same. The statistical precision of such an experiment is relatively low. But this lack of precision is the price for an unusually broad focus: the study surveys the whole spectrum of cases that come before the American jury. In this sense, the research design may fittingly be called a survey experiment.

From these data it was possible to determine how often judge and jury agree or disagree, when they disagree, and one could trace and count the reasons for their disagreement since through some fifty-odd questions most detailed information became available on every case.

The first part of this study on the role of the jury in criminal trials has just been published.[28] Table 4–5 reproduces one of its basic findings.

TABLE 4–5. *Agreement and Disagreement between Jury and Judge in Criminal Trials*

		Jury		
		Acquits	Convicts	Hangs
Judge	Acquits	13	2	1
	Convicts	17	63	4

TOTAL 100%
NUMBER OF TRIALS (3,576)

☐ = Agreement

Judge and jury agree in (13 + 63 =) 76 per cent of all cases; and of the 24 per cent disagreement cases, the jury is found on the defendant's side in (17 + 4 =) 21 per cent and on the prosecutor's side in (1 + 2 =) 3 per cent of these cases.

The evaluation of the jury as an institution hinges, of course, not only on the *extent* of its disagreement with the judge but on the reasons that produce these disagreements, and it is the presentation and analysis of these reasons that form the main body of the study. They range from different sentiments on the law which the jury entertains (in spite of what law the judge may give them) through sentiments concerning the particular defendant, different views on the weight of the evidence, and occasionally to an imbalance between the performance of the prosecutor and defense counsel in the trial; a few times it will even happen that the disagreement arises from a discrepancy between what jury and judge know about the case.

These are the five somewhat abstract categories into which the specific causes of the various individual disagreements were ultimately summarized.

At this early point it is not possible to assay the practical consequences of this study. At a minimum, it will lend focus and precision to an important debate in which both sides so far have never been able to draw on more than anecdotal support.[29]

Secondary Analysis

Two studies of contemporary legal problems are distinguished by their being primarily reanalyses of data collected in normal administrative routine: one concerned the alleged deterrent effect of capital punishment, the other the problem of court congestion and delay.

In the debate over the merits of capital punishment, the abolitionists had for a long time no good answer to the claim that the death penalty helped to deter would-be murderers. The change came after Thorsten Sellin investigated the problem.[30] He compared homicide rates before and after abolition in some jurisdictions; before and after reintroduction in others; and in jurisdictions that have the death penalty with adjacent jurisdictions that have abolished it. His data made one point clear: whatever other merits the death penalty may have, it has no traceable deterrent effect.

Sellin's data have been quoted wherever the issue is being argued. To what extent they have been an effective cause of abolition is nevertheless difficult to say. Probably they have not been a major cause; growing revulsion from deliberate killing and the actual or near execution of an innocently convicted man have nearly always provided the major impetus. But Sellin's data have helped to silence, if not to convince, a special opposition.

The study of court congestion opened insights into a problem that is less dramatic but in the long run perhaps more persistent. It is one of the puzzling aspects of our judicial system that the adjudication of civil claims in most of our metropolitan courts is scandalously delayed. In Chicago, for instance, it takes on the average five and a half years from the date a claim is filed until it can be tried before a jury.

In 1957, the University of Chicago Law School published a study of this congestion problem[31] which had this methodological distinction: its more than three hundred pages of measurement and analysis were based almost entirely on data that had become available in the course of routine housekeeping by the courts in their normal administrative business. From these data a number of measurements and parameters were developed that were to acquire some currency in the administration of the courts: a basic formula for measuring delay was developed;[32] a variety of remedies was evaluated, and, as the case may be, rejected, recommended, or suggested for further investigation. Among the latter were the pretrial and the split trial discussed above.

With the ever mounting costs of securing primary data, this harvest from secondary analysis holds a promise for social research generally.

Surveys

Although, as we have seen, the border line between experiment and survey is not a sharp one, it is useful to distinguish the two, especially since, in contrast to the experiment, the primary function of the survey is to provide description. Out of the rapidly growing number of surveys undertaken to give guidance to the lawmakers, only two will be mentioned here. Both deal with most acute legal problems; one with the enforcement of civil-rights legislation, the other with the costs of automobile accidents.

In 1962 Blumrosen and Zeitz began to investigate the operation of New Jersey's antidiscrimination laws and its Civil Rights Commission. Blumrosen examined all cases filed with the commission during the fiscal years 1962–1963, and Zeitz made a survey among Negroes on their attitudes toward enforcement of these laws.[33] The main finding of their study was that "the laws of New Jersey against discrimination were not meaningfully and effectively enforced," partly because the Negroes themselves shied away from individual enforcement and partly because of shortcomings in the commission itself. The study had a number of traceable effects: the legislature substantially increased the commission's budget; the commission itself sharpened some of its policies and much of its mode of operations; and the state's attorney-general would speak of his civil-rights division as having been "a shield" so far but now to become "a sword."[34]

The survey on the costs of automobile accidents is the latest on an issue of long-standing concern to the law and has a distinguished research history. The first major study was published in 1932 under the auspices of the Columbia University Committee for Research in the Social Sciences.[35] Like the latest, the Michigan study, it too was a joint effort of lawyers and social scientists. It surveyed broadly, if somewhat haphazardly, the reparation problem caused by automobile accidents. The evidence was drawn from a variety of sources, but even where survey data were used, no claim was made to precision and completeness. Nevertheless, as in many first approaches, the outlines of the problem and the areas of research emerged with great clarity and thus marked an important beginning. The next step came in 1953 when Professor Adams of the Business School at Temple University studied the financial and legal history of a random sample of one hundred automobile accidents in the City of Philadelphia and thus established the pattern for later efforts.[36] The Philadelphia survey displayed all the glories and some of the inadequacies of an inspired, pioneering, shoestring operation. The present study, undertaken jointly by lawyers and social scientists at the University of Michigan, is the apex of this development.[37]

It covers all individuals killed or injured in automobile accidents that occurred in the State of Michigan during one calendar year and ingeniously combines two samples to represent this universe: one taken from the files of the police, the other from the files of the courts where personal-injury claims are litigated. The difficulty of the yet unfinished court case was elegantly solved by substituting the results reached in a comparable group of earlier long-delayed cases. The major research instrument was a mail questionnaire to the parties concerned or to their heirs, thoughtfully supplemented at critical points with personal interviews, especially with the plaintiffs' lawyers in the cases.

We now have reliable, precise, quantitative information on almost every aspect of the injury-reparation process and hence a sound factual basis for the many debates which are currently raging over that problem area. To be sure, we have this knowledge only for one year and only for the State of Michigan. But, the United States being what it is, one should not be in danger if one generalizes from these findings. If there are doubts, they can be removed by duplication of the study elsewhere.

The survey provides, as any good survey should, information on both details and broad outlines. Roughly one of every hundred Michigan residents suffered some loss in an automobile accident during a year. For over 60 per cent of the persons involved in accidents, the loss was below $500; another 30 per cent suffered losses between $500 and $3,000; and the remaining 2 or 3 per cent suffered losses beyond $70,000.

In terms of all victims or their heirs, 23 per cent received no compensation from any source, 37 per cent received some tort liability settlement, and about half of the victims received some compensation from loss, collision, medical care or life insurance. But in terms of the total dollar amount paid to all victims, almost half of the total damages remained uncompensated. The sources of total compensation were tort liability, 55 per cent; loss liability, 38 per cent; workmen's compensation and social security, 7 per cent. The surprising finding is the great role played by loss insurance.

Finally, there is a group of qualitative surveys with hardly a number in them that nevertheless fulfill an important function. They all aim at illuminating the dark corners of the criminal law process. In theory this process is governed only by the law and the courts, but in practice the great bulk of it is decided by the informal practices of the police and the prosecutor's office. The major effort is the American Bar Foundation's Survey of Criminal Justice, of which Professor Remington is the editor.[38] The first volume in this series is a study of arrest procedures.[39] Its raw material are some two thousand field reports of on-the-scene reports. The unending variety of arrest decisions are presented in a meaningful framework, with just the right amount of detail to be both vivid and allow their classification. A systematic inventory is obtained of the variety of procedures, and thus the essential groundwork is laid for a later quantitative survey.[40]

The Trend

The sharp increase in recent years in the number and quality of social-science investigations of legal institutions was spawned by a number of convergent developments. There was first a jurisprudential movement, the Realists, who, beginning in the twenties, asked that the law in action be explored in contrast to the law on the books. Strangely enough, their aim remained for a long time no more than a battle cry. Only now, a generation later, does it assume substance.[41] The second source was the rapid development of research techniques and a concomitant growth of sociological research in general.[42]

It now appears that we are at the threshold of an era in which the lawmakers will find increasing use for empirical social-science research in the sound expectation that it is bound to alleviate their difficult task: to make good law.

REFERENCES

1. In modern times, William Petty's survey of Ireland, made at the time of the Cromwellian conquest, is perhaps one of the first systematic surveys conducted for the lawmaker. British, and to a much lesser extent also American, legislation has a tradition of relying on systematically collected facts whenever broad legislative issues are at debate. Royal Commissions, Select Committees, and Ad Hoc Committees in the British Empire and Commonwealth, Congressional and other legislative and administrative committees in the United States, have made in their time major contributions to the law and incidentally also the body of social science. See Marie Jahoda, Paul F. Lazarsfeld, Hans Zeisel, *Marienthal: Zur Geschichte der Soziographie,* new ed. (Allensbach: Verlag für Demoskopie, 1960), Appendix.

2. Ironically, the most famous of these social-science footnotes, in the celebrated decision of the United States Supreme Court in *Brown* v. *Board of Education,* the school desegregation case, refers probably to a not very relevant piece of research. It concerned an experiment designed to prove the evil of segregation. The legal scholars seem to be agreed that it did not influence the Court, which was clearly moved by larger, moral considerations; see, for instance, Edmond Cahn, "Jurisprudence," *New York University Law Review,* XXX (1955), 150. There was even considerable debate about the evidential value of that research. See Kenneth B. Clark, "The Desegregation Cases: Criticism of the Social Scientist's Role," *Villanova Law Review,* V (1960), 224, 236; Ernest van den Haag, "Social Science Testimony in the Desegregation Cases—A Reply to Professor Kenneth Clark," *Villanova Law Review,* VI (1960), 69; A. J. Gregor, "The Law, Social Science, and School Segregation: An Assessment," *Western Reserve Law Review,* XIV (1963), 621–636; Ovid C. Lewis, "Parry and Riposte to Gregor's *The Law, Social Scientist, and School Segregation,*" *ibid.,* 637.

3. See Hans Zeisel, "The Uniqueness of Survey Evidence," *Cornell Law Quarterly,* XLV (1960), 322.

4. By way of apology: it is impossible to list all such studies; any offered selection is bound to remain arbitrary.

5. The argument that follows has been developed in more detail in Hans Zeisel, "The New York Expert Testimony Project: Some Reflections on Legal Experiments," *Stanford Law Review,* VIII (1956), 730–749, and in Hans Zeisel, Harry Kalven, Jr., and Bernard Buchholz, *Delay in the Courts* (Boston: Little, Brown, 1959), Chapter 21: "The Case for the Official Experiment."

6. California Board of Correction Monographs, Sacramento.

7. See Daniel Glaser, *The Effectiveness of a Prison and Parole System* (Indianapolis: Bobbs-Merrill, 1964), p. 34.

8. Cf. Zeisel, Kalven, and Buchholz, *op. cit.,* note 5, pp. 143 ff.

9. Maurice Rosenberg, *The Pretrial Conference and Effective Justice* (Columbia University Press, New York and London, 1964).

10. The control group was allowed to have optional pretrial, because it was thought that to simply deprive these litigants of their right to pretrial might engender constitutional difficulties.

11. One may ask why the state did not abolish pretrial altogether. One answer is that the particular experiment answered the issue conclusively only with respect to the option alternative. Moreover, pretrial had deep roots in the state's tradition, and the limited design of the experiment probably offered a welcome pretext for a compromise.

12. The pioneering study was Arthur Beeley, *The Bail System in Chicago* (Chicago: University of Chicago Press, 1927). A survey of the literature can be found in Daniel Freed and Patricia Wald, *Bail in the United States* (Washington, D.C., 1964), pp. 9–21. The attack that brought the reform movement to fruition began with a distinguished study by Professor Caleb Foote of the University of Pennsylvania Law School. On the latest developments see C. E. Ares, A. Rankin, and H. Sturz, "The Manhattan Bail Project: An Interim Report on the Use of Pre-Trial Parole," *New York University Law Review,* XXXVIII (1963), 67. On the long-range implication, see also Caleb Foote, "The Coming Constitutional Crisis in Bail," *University of Pennsylvania Law Review,* CXIII (1965), 959.

13. National Conference on Bail and Criminal Justice, *Interim Report* (Washington, D.C.: 1965), p. xxv.

14. Normally, it is considered essential that in a controlled experiment the experimenter be in direct control of the experimental variable: if two types of fertilizer are to be tested, he must be able to control their assignment to the various plots of land. But in the realm of the law such direct control is rarely feasible. Even in the two experiments discussed so far, the ultimate experimental variable was not under the control of the experimenter: in the bail-bond experiment, the final decision whether or not to release the defendant without bail was up to the judge; and the decision whether or not a pretrial was to be held was, in fact, left to the litigants. Yet because of the prior randomization of the experimental and the control group, these decisions did not invalidate the controlled character of the experiments. For general exposition of this approach, see Irwin Towers, Leo Goodman, and Hans Zeisel, "A Method of Measuring the Effects of Television through Controlled Field Experiments," *Studies in Communication,* IV (1962), 87.

15. In some states, such as California, the court pronounces only the sentence range as provided by the statute; the prison authority makes the final decision.

16. Everson, "The Human Element in Justice," *Journal of Criminal Law and Criminology,* X (1919), 90.

17. Gaudet, "Individual Differences in the Sentencing Tendencies of Judges," *Archives*

of Psychology, XXXII (1938), 5. Edward Green, *Judicial Attitudes in Sentencing* (New York: St. Martin's Press, 1961), based on data from Criminal Court in Pennsylvania, is the only study that claims to have found no such differences, but its statistical analysis is open to criticism.

18. S. Sidney Ulmer, "The Political Variable in the Michigan Supreme Court," *Journal of Public Law*, XI (1962), 352.

19. C. Herman Pritchett, "Divisions of Opinion among Justices of the U. S. Supreme Court," *American Political Science Review*, XXXV (1941), 890; later, *The Roosevelt Court: A Study in Politics and Values, 1937–1947* (New York: Macmillan, 1948).

20. Glendon Schubert has been the prime contributor to the field. He has also edited to valuable anthologies which provide a systematic survey of these studies: *Judicial Decision-Making*, (Glencoe, Ill.: The Free Press, 1963) and *Judicial Behavior* (Chicago: Rand McNally, 1964).

21. This suggestion too was made in Zeisel, Kalven, and Buchholz, *op. cit.*, note 5, p. 99.

22. See Hans Zeisel and Thomas Callahan, "Split Trial and Time-Saving: A Statistical Analysis," *Harvard Law Review*, LXXVI (1963), 1606–1625.

23. One of these many court decisions had a direct reference to the Zeisel-Callahan paper: *Driver v. Phillips et al.*, U.S. District Court E.D. Pa., December 14, 1964, 36 FRD 261 (1964).

24. See Rita James Simon, *The American Jury—The Defense of Insanity* (Boston: Little, Brown, 1967).

25. There were also two minor variations built into the experiment pertaining to the quality of the psychiatric expert testimony and to the informing of the jury as to the consequences of a finding of insanity.

26. Simon, *op. cit.* note 18, Chapter 4.

27. Symposium, "Insanity and the Criminal Law—A Critique of Durham v. United States," *University of Chicago Law Review*, XXII (1955), 317.

28. Harry Kalven, Jr., and Hans Zeisel, *The American Jury* (Boston: Little, Brown, 1966).

29. It is, however, possible to cite one early application of findings from the jury study, albeit to a proposed reform of the English jury. The British government has proposed legislation that would allow majority verdicts of 10:2 and 11:1 votes and remove thereby the requirement of unanimity. It was possible to provide the British Home Office with a set of relevant predictions as to what to expect from such a law, because one of the American states, Oregon, allows the majority verdicts Great Britain plans to introduce. The first prediction was that the number of hung juries (juries in which a mistrial is declared because unanimity cannot be reached) would decrease by about 40 per cent. Since about 5 per cent of all trials end in hung juries, this means a change for two out of every hundred trials. The second piece of relevant information was that the presiding judge is by no means always critical of these juries who remain hung at a 10:2 or 11:1 vote; about one-third of these hung juries are characterized as a result at "which a judge too might have come to." Thus, not all of these hung juries are without merit. Third, the Oregon experience suggested that England must henceforth expect some dissent in about one-fourth of all jury verdicts, an experience that might well be shocking in view of the serious sentence that usually follows a verdict of guilty.

30. Thorsten Sellin, in Royal Commission on Capital Punishment, *Minutes of Evidence* (London: H. M. Stat. Off., 1951), p. 647.

31. Zeisel, Kalven, and Buchholz, *op. cit.* note 5.

32. *Ibid.*, pp. 6 and 43. It has now been adopted as a standard measurement by the Administrative Office of the Illinois Courts.
33. A. B. Blumrosen, "Antidiscrimination Laws in Action in New Jersey; A Law-Sociology Study," with a supplement: L. Zeitz, "Survey of Negro Attitudes toward Law," *Rutgers Law Review*, XIX (1965), 189, 288.
34. From a press release by the Office of the Attorney-General (May 12, 1965).
35. Committee to Study Compensation for Automobile Accidents, *Report* (New York: Columbia University Committee for Research in the Social Sciences, 1932).
36. J. Adams, "Economic Financial Consequences of Personal Injuries Sustained in 1953 Philadelphia Automobile Accidents," Temple University *Economics and Business Bulletin*, VII (1955).
37. Alfred F. Conard *et al.*, *Automobile Accident Costs and Payments: Studies in the Economics of Injury Reparation* (Ann Arbor: University of Michigan Press, 1964).
38. Compare, however, also J. Goldstein, "Police Discretion Not to Invoke the Criminal Process: Low Visibility Decisions in the Administration of Justice," *Yale Law Journal*, LXIX (1960), 543, and J. H. Skolnick, *Justice without Trial* (New York: Wiley, 1966).
39. La Fave, *Arrest: The Decision to Take a Suspect into Custody* (Boston: Little, Brown, 1965).
40. Other volumes in this series: D. J. Newman, *Conviction: The Determination of Guilt or Innocence without Trial* (Boston: Little, Brown, 1966); Miller, *Prosecution* (in preparation); Dawson and Ball, *Sentencing* (in preparation).
41. The two most distinguished names in that group were Karl N. Llewellyn, until his recent death professor at the University of Chicago Law School, and Jerome Frank, judge and author.
42. See Hans Zeisel, "Social Research on the Law: The Ideal and the Practical," in William M. Evan, ed., *Law and Sociology* (Glencoe, Ill.: The Free Press, 1962), p. 124.

The Social Scientist
as an Expert Witness
in Court Cases

ARNOLD M. ROSE

chapter 5

      There is a possibility that social scientists will be used increasingly in the future as expert witnesses in court cases of several kinds, and therefore some exploration is needed as to the varieties of service they can provide and as to their limitations as expert witnesses. Louisell [1] has made a most constructive start on this discussion in relation to the work of psychologists. Cahn,[2] also a lawyer, has analyzed the social-science testimony in the school segregation cases, and, while his article is most thoughtful, he has made a number of statements which represent to the social scientists a serious misunderstanding of their work. This chapter, written by a sociologist, will seek to contribute to the discussion by (1) analyzing the characteristics of the social sciences insofar as they are pertinent to providing expert testimony; (2) suggesting the limitations of social-science testimony; (3) indicating at least some of the areas of legal cases in which social-science testimony has already been used and other areas in which it might well be used; (4) specifying how the methodology of social science differs from the traditional methodology of lawyers and judges and indicating how the former may be used to supplement the latter; (5) suggesting some attitudes which lawyers and judges should have toward social scientists when they provide expert testimony in order to get the most value from their services. Since a thorough treatment of all these subjects cannot be achieved in a single chapter, this essay should be regarded as part of a continuing effort to discover the optimal relationship between law and the social sciences, rather than as a definitive study. The field is too nebulous to permit a definitive study, and when the latter can be accomplished it will not be done by a sociologist working by himself. This writer's particular qualifications for contributing to the discussion consist of four experiences as an expert witness, participation in preparing some of the briefs in the school segregation cases, and a long interest in the relation of law to the social sciences.[3]

Herein "social sciences" means those theoretical disciplines which seek to understand and predict human behavior in terms of general principles empirically tested. This includes, in aim if not in achievement, most of sociology, psychology, anthropology, political science, economics, and parts of psychiatry, history, and law itself. It does not include the study of particular cases for the purpose of handling them in some way; hence most of psychiatry, clinical psychology, accounting, and other business-school subjects, social work, and law are excluded. It also does not include the study of particular cases for the purposes of understanding them as special events in their own right; hence much of history and law is excluded. Of the fields mentioned, psychiatry,[4] social work, accounting, law (of course), and perhaps history (in cases where the "intent of the legislature" is in question) have been used extensively in providing expert testimony. But these are not social sciences in our definition and hence may have led to some misunderstanding as to the role the social sciences can play in court cases. Of the social sciences proper, only economics seems to have been used extensively and therefore will not be dealt with further except to cite a case in which it was pertinent, so as to provide an illustration of its similarity to other possible social-science testimony.

In *Morton Salt Co. v. Suppinger*,[5] the patentee was licensing a salt-vending machine which required the purchase of the salt tablets at the same time. The courts have held this illegal on the ground that the patentee is attempting to extend his monopoly beyond the area which has been granted to him. Economists pointed out that the only monopoly power the patentee has before and after the tie-in is based on the monopoly power of the patent (that is, on the machine, not the salt). If the monopoly power of the patentee is strong enough to compel the purchase of salt by the licensee, it is also strong enough to compel the licensee to pay more for the license to use the salt-vending machine. Thus there are no economic consequences for the patentee or the licensee or the consumer because of the tie-in requirement, although other wholesalers of salt

are hurt. The testimony of economists in cases involving antitrust legislation, licensing, taxation, labor law, corporations, and trade regulations
seems to be widely used and accepted in the courts.[6] While the general
nature of economists' testimony is relevant here, main consideration will
be given to case material from the testimony of sociologists, psychologists,
and other social scientists where there seems to be questioning among
lawyers regarding its pertinence and reliability.

The relevance of social-science findings to court cases will have to be
ascertained, case by case, by perspicacious lawyers. As yet, according to
Louisell, "there seem to be few cases and little recent discussion directly
concerned with the psychologist (or any social scientist) functioning as an
expert witness himself. . . . We search in vain for any substantial analysis
. . . of the psychologist functioning as an expert witness." [7] Louisell,
who has scoured the literature, mentions only two reports of cases[8] of
psychologists presenting expert testimony other than of a clinical kind,
and one of these is a case which he reports *in extenso* himself. Both cases
cited by Louisell involve public-opinion surveys done by competent psychologists: one regarding the meaning of a commercial advertisement to
an average reader and the other involving the question whether the patrons of a certain theater regarded it as a "neighborhood theater" or as one
which attracted them as would a downtown theater.[9]

The latter case[10] may be used to illustrate how an opinion survey (to do
which psychologists and sociologists have developed special techniques of
research) differs from the usual methods of the lawyer. The theater was
suing the distributor for treating it as a neighborhood theater rather than
as a city-wide theater in the distribution of films. The theater was located
outside the downtown area. A university psychologist was hired to make a
survey of the patrons to determine two things: (1) the geographic distribution of the patrons to ascertain if they were from the immediate neighborhood or from all over the city; (2) the attitudes of the patrons as to
whether they would be willing to pay "downtown prices" for first-run films
usually shown only at downtown theaters. The psychologist and his assistants asked a representative sample of the theater's patrons for their
address and their opinion about paying downtown prices. The facts of
widespread distribution of their residences and their willingness to pay
downtown prices were presented in court to support the theater's claim to
be treated as a city-wide theater by the distributor. Apparently in previous
cases of this sort lawyers had relied on the location of the theater and had
as witnesses a few patrons who lived a great distance from the theater and
would be willing to pay downtown prices, but never a representative sample of patrons. Thus, the selection of a representative sample of patrons
for the beliefs and for facts about themselves is a technique which the
public-opinion specialist can contribute to certain court cases.

Kendler[11] reports a case in which experimental social-psychological evidence was incorporated into a lawyer's brief *amicus curiae*. In 1943 the Territory of Hawaii passed a law prohibiting schools from teaching foreign languages to children under the age of ten or who had not completed the fourth grade or who were under the age of fifteen and were below average in English courses. Its purpose was to discourage ethnic enclaves, but the law's stated purpose was indicated by the clause holding that two languages early in life "may and do, in many cases, cause serious emotional disturbances, conflicts and maladjustments." The constitutionality of this act was challenged in the United States Supreme Court, and the American Jewish Congress submitted a brief *amicus curiae* which rested on three contentions:

1. The teaching of certain languages, such as Hebrew and Latin, is a religious obligation, and no law could constitutionally abridge religious freedom.

2. It has not been established that bilingualism has the negative effects attributed to it by the law; evidence from psychological tests showed no greater proportion of emotional disturbances or maladjustment.

3. The law was not an effective instrument for accomplishing its stated purpose, since sociological study showed that it was the home rather than the school which induced bilingualism.

Before the Court considered this brief, it threw the case out on technical grounds, and shortly thereafter the Hawaiian legislature substantially modified the act, so that the psychological and sociological evidence never received judicial notice.

During World War II, the political scientist Harold D. Lasswell and some of his assistants appeared in court to testify in government cases seeking to show that certain "native fascist" organizations were in communication with the German government.[12] They demonstrated that the propaganda put out for American consumption by these organizations was in many cases identical with that prepared by the German propaganda ministry. The sociologist Robert Sorensen has analyzed the possibilities of using the same technique (called "content analysis") as evidence in literary infringement cases, although he and his lawyer-collaborator cite no cases where the technique was actually employed.[13] A rough approximation of the technique has been used in the form of making a systematic summary of parallel statements in the two published sources when one is claimed as a copyright infringement on the other.[14]

Clearly, if there are other cases involving the use of nonclinical social-science testimony, it would be valuable to have them reported; therefore summaries of three cases in which the author presented expert testimony follow.

The first case involved the disposition of a three-year-old child whose mother the court had previously declared incompetent on grounds of immorality. The county welfare office was now seeking to have the child taken from the father, who lived apart from his wife, and placed with foster parents, but the father was strongly contesting this action. No allegation was made that the father did not provide the proper moral surroundings for the child; the social worker in charge of the case specifically testified that the father gave the child proper physical care and the affection expected from a parent. The county welfare office's contentions were three:

1. The father was sixty years old—too old to be a proper father for a young child (although he was in perfect physical health for his age).
2. There was no mother in the home (although the father agreed to hire a competent full-time housekeeper, and he had the income to do so).
3. The father was a mulatto identified with the Negro community, whereas the child was white in appearance (the mother was white in all known racial antecedents).

There was an implication that the father of the child was not the biological father (the biological father was alleged to be one of the white paramours of the mother), although no evidence was presented to this effect (except a questioning oral statement made by the father to the social worker a year previously), and the mother denied it under oath. There was no question that the father was the social father of the child, as it had been reared by him since its birth.

The attorney for the father had reason to believe that the third contention was most important in the minds of the social workers at the county welfare office. They seemed to believe that a white-appearing child could gain better opportunities in life by being raised by a white couple than by a mulatto father. Whether or not they were disturbed by the idea of a white child being raised as a Negro could not be said. As a sociologist who has studied the Negro community and race relations, this author was asked to serve as an expert witness for the father. After taking the witness stand and establishing position and field of competences, the following relevant facts were testified to:

1. While Negroes in Minneapolis had historically been subject to certain occupational and educational discriminations, these were rapidly declining and at the present rate of change could be expected to be inconsequential in a few years. The sources were decennial reports on the occupational, employment, and educational status of Negroes and whites from the United States Census; also a few miscellaneous reports from the United States Office of Education and the United States Employment Service.

2. Neighborhoods in Minneapolis were increasingly characterized by mixed occupancy; only a small minority of neighborhoods could be characterized as entirely Negro or entirely white at the time of the 1950 census (and even fewer by 1954, the time of this case). The sources were the block statistics of the United States Census and a special sample survey made in 1954.

3. A small number of persons identified socially as Negroes were not distinguishable in physical appearance from whites; there had been such persons in Negro communities for generations; and Negroes generally accorded high status to such persons. The sources were a number of community studies made by sociologists over twenty-five years.

4. Whites generally either were unaware that Negroes who appeared to be whites were socially Negroes or tended to treat them better than they did Negroes who physically appeared to be Negroes. In other words, a white-appearing Negro child would not be subjected to more discriminations than a Negro-appearing Negro child, and possibly fewer. The sources were studies of the differential status and "passing" habits of Negroes of different shades of skin color.

At several points in this testimony the writer brought out the fact that he knew nothing of the individual circumstances of this case, but was testifying solely on the basis of his own and other sociologists' published studies of the Negro community and race relations. The lawyer for the county welfare board, in cross-examination, did not contest any of the statements, but confined himself to asking two questions:

1. Whether the author's long study of the Negro question had not biased his point of view and observations (my reply was that social scientists were very much aware of the possibilities of bias and tried to hold it in check, but that bias was still possible).

2. Whether there were not special discriminations faced by a person known to be a Negro which were not faced by a person known to be white (to which the witness assented, but pointed out that such discriminations were decreasing).

The judge seemed to be greatly interested in this testimony and asked a number of questions. Apparently he had never before been offered such a wide array of census reports and specific sociological studies; in such cases lawyers usually present a more limited body of reports and "common knowledge."

One question asked by the judge raised the issue of conflicting expert testimony. A competent geneticist had testified on a previous occasion that, on the basis of his observation of the physical and behavioral characteristics of the father and the child, "It is hardly necessary to list such differences, as it is apparent that Mr. W could not have been the biological father of this boy. A blood test of the mother, Mr. W and Gregory (the child) would demonstrate conclusively that Mr. W could not possibly have been the biological father of Gregory W." Following this, the lawyer for the father had a competent technician (a doctor of medicine) take a blood test of mother, father, and child, and on the basis of this the technician concluded that "on the basis of the above listed blood factors, in my opinion, G. W. cannot be excluded as the father of the child Gregory W." The judge asked the writer's opinion of the testimony of the geneticist. My answer was that an inspection of the physical and behavioral characteristics of two persons could not exclude the possibility of their relationship, that the blood test and any other known objective test could exclude certain categories of persons from relationship to another but could not possibly exclude all nonrelatives, and that the only adequate test of relationship in this case was an honest statement by the mother. The judge was thus faced with conflicting testimony given by an expert geneticist and an expert sociologist on a question more closely related to genetics than to sociology.

There were other facets (although everything pertinent to the points raised in my testimony has been reported), and the case was carried on for several days. Eventually the judge ordered that the child be allowed to remain with the father, although it is not known whether my testimony aided him in arriving at this decision.

The second case was that of a young Negro woman who was being sent back to her home state of Florida by a social worker because, it was alleged, she was destined to become a public charge and she was not yet a resident of Minnesota (that is, she had lived there less than a year). The case was initiated by the attorney for the young woman to enjoin the public welfare agency from taking this action. The social worker in charge defended her action before the court with the following facts:

1. The young woman had applied to the public welfare agency for financial aid for an illegitimate pregnancy, for which she was not eligible as a nonresident.

2. The pregnancy, conceived with a married man, was an indication of the young woman's mental incompetence.

3. An intelligence test had been administered to the young woman, showing her to be feeble-minded.

By claiming the young woman to be mentally incompetent, the social worker could declare that she was destined to become a public charge, and hence—in accord with a Minnesota statute—should be shipped out of the state before living in Minnesota one year and becoming a resident.

The attorney for the young woman countered the first point by having the young woman withdraw her request for public aid (she was living with a married brother who was employed and could afford to pay for his sister's confinement). To counter the second and third points, he brought in the expert witness, a sociologist. He further established before the court the following facts:

1. The intelligence test was administered to the young woman without informing her what it was and that the results could be used to deport her from the state. She claimed that she did not take the questioning seriously and hesitated to answer the psychologist's questions because she thought they were a continuation of the social worker's obnoxious probe into her private life.

2. The young woman had been employed successfully as waitress and cashier at a lunch counter, which was evidence of mental competence and ability to support herself.

3. The young woman's paramour had sued for divorce from his wife and was planning to marry the young woman who was about to bear his child.

The crucial question in the case was thus the subject's mental competence and hence her capacity to maintain herself without becoming a public charge, that is, a candidate for the public institution for the feeble-minded. The expert witness, after being sworn in and establishing his qualifications, insisted on the fact that he had not examined the subject and could not testify that she was competent. He could only testify that the social worker had not established the fact of the subject's incompetence. He presented the following facts:

1. Becoming pregnant outside of marriage was not evidence of feeble-mindedness. The expert witness cited the vital statistics of the State of Florida for the preceding year, which showed that 20 per cent of all Negro births were illegitimate. Citing further sociological studies of the lower-class southern Negro family, he asserted that sex relations outside of marriage and resulting bearing of illegitimate children was a subcultural pattern. That is, he established this behavior as one which could be caused sufficiently by subcultural folkways and therefore did not necessarily result from feeble-mindedness.

2. Low intelligence-test scores, especially under certain conditions of test administration, were not necessarily evidence of mental incompetence. The expert witness stated that high scores could be evidence of high intelligence, but low scores were not necessarily evidence of low intelligence. He cited a number of specific studies showing that I.Q. test performance varied with such environmental variables as the race of the psychologist, the physical conditions under which the test was administered, and the

educational and cultural level of the subjects. He cited the Klineberg study showing that the same Negro individuals tested higher after migration to the North than they had in their previous residence in the South. He averred that the mood and attitude of the subject could be expected to influence test performance. He cited other studies showing a lack of relationship, among certain individuals, between I.Q. test scores and subsequent performance. He gave as his opinion that performance in ongoing social functions, such as serving as waitress and cashier at a lunch counter, would be better evidence of ability for self-maintenance than would an I.Q. test score.

On cross-examination, the attorney for the public welfare agency attempted to discredit the scientific validity of the various studies cited by the expert witness. But he did not succeed in shaking the expert witness' conclusion that the public welfare agency had not proved the subject's incapacity for self-maintenance. The judge also had before him the constitutional provision that no citizen might be deprived of his right to migrate freely within the United States, without due process of law. His decision was that the public welfare agency had no right to deport the young woman out of the State of Minnesota. Again it is not known whether my testimony aided the judge to arrive at this decision. It might also be recorded that the young woman was not subsequently sent to the state institution for the feeble-minded, although she became a public charge insofar as she sought public aid for bearing further illegitimate children.

The third case did not proceed to the point where the sociologist's expert testimony was brought into court, but he was prepared to do so on request of the plaintiff's attorney. The case involved the constitutionality of a suburban municipality's Sunday closing ordinance. The plaintiff was a discount house which did its largest volume of business on Sunday, when downtown department stores elected to remain closed. The case was a complicated one, with many issues completely outside the competence of the sociologist expert witness. But when the plaintiff's attorney asked the expert witness what testimony the latter could give, the following facts were agreed on as pertinent:

1. A large and growing proportion of housewives are gainfully employed Monday to Friday and thus have only the week end for shopping.

2. Sunday-afternoon shopping is largely a family affair in the suburbs, with husbands, wives, and children going to the shopping center together, whereas weekday shopping is usually done by the housewife alone or by the working person during the short time he can spare from his job. Family shopping tends to strengthen the family.

3. Sunday-afternoon shopping by gainfully employed persons is carried on at a more leisurely pace than is weekday shopping. Therefore it has

something of the character of recreation, and sometimes it can be carried on more wisely from an economic standpoint. It thus contributes a constructive element to our society's search for wholesome uses of leisure time.

4. While these advantages of Sunday shopping are equally applicable to Saturday shopping, it is becoming a custom in the suburbs for husbands to work around the house on Saturdays and avoid dressing up until the evening. This trend arises partly from the recent abandonment of work in most industries on Saturday. On Sundays, men dress up for church in the morning and are thus ready to go out in the afternoons.

5. Since Sunday-afternoon shopping is indulged in only occasionally by families, it does not prevent other uses of Sunday afternoons, such as driving in the country, visiting relatives or friends, and so on.

6. The above-mentioned functions of Sunday shopping are reflected in the actual increase in such shopping and in its popularity and general approval expressed in public-opinion polls.

There are many value implications in the points above, but they are closely related to empirical trends and sociological knowledge. It is unfortunate that their utility could not have been tested in an actual court case dealing with the controversial social issue of Sunday closing. They can be tied to other aspects of the controversy, such as the right of citizens and merchants to carry on economic activities not harmful to the social welfare whenever they choose and the conflicting economic interests of downtown department stores and suburban shopping centers.

The expert social-science testimony in the school segregation cases is part of the record and is probably familiar by now to most interested lawyers and sociologists.[15] In briefest summary, the issue of all these cases was whether segregation involved discrimination. Discrimination, when practiced by an arm of the state, has consistently been declared unconstitutional under the Fourteenth Amendment. If state facilities were "separate but equal" they were considered legal following the 1896 Supreme Court decision of *Plessy v. Ferguson*.[16] In a series of decisions beginning in 1938,[17] the Supreme Court narrowed the interpretation of what it considered to be equal. The material discrimination declared illegal related to such matters as the size of classes, the salaries of teachers, the physical condition of the school plant, and the distance required to travel to school. By 1950, in the case of *McLaurin v. Oklahoma State Regents*,[18] the Court had gone so far as to declare that professional school students were being discriminated against if they did not have the possibility—because of state action—of interacting with their future professional colleagues, even in college cafeterias and libraries. But the decision in the *McLaurin* case did not challenge segregation head on, and the *Plessy* doctrine presumably stood as law. In the South Carolina case of *Briggs v. Elliott*,[19] the state acknowledged the facts of material discrimination and asked that the decision be based solely on the question of segregation (the attorney-general promised that material discrimination would be eliminated in five years). Thus, by 1953 both sides were willing to argue on the single issue as to whether racial segregation itself inevitably involves discrimination. This is a question of social fact, not a matter either of law or of ethics, and both sides brought in social scientists as expert witnesses. The social scientists began to present evidence as early as 1946 in the first case of *Sweatt v. Painter*.[20] By 1952, they were offering new kinds of studies that directly linked segregation with discrimination: Negro children in segregated schools were found to have a sense of inferiority and a lowered morale; it was alleged that these hampered the learning process. Less evidence, but some, was adduced to the effect that segregated schools encouraged a sense of racial superiority in white children. Clark summarizes succinctly the types of evidence offered by social scientists in the various school cases:

1. That racial classification for the purposes of educational segregation is arbitrary and irrelevant since the available scientific evidence indicates that there are no innate racial differences in intelligence or other psychological characteristics. . . . This line of testimony was consistently unchallenged by the attorneys for the states.

2. That contemporary social-science interpretations of the nature of racial segregation indicate that it blocks communication and increases mutual hostility and suspicion; it reinforces prejudices and facilitates, rather than inhibits, outbreaks of racial violence.

3. That segregation has detrimental personality effects on Negro children which impair their ability to profit from the available educational facilities. Segregation also has certain complex detrimental effects on the personality and moral development of white children.

4. That the consequences of desegregation are in the direction of the improvement of interracial relations and an increase in social stability, rather than an increase in violence or social chaos.

5. That if nonsegregation can work on the graduate and professional level, it can work equally well on the elementary and high-school level, since children at this stage of development are more flexible in their attitudes and behavior.[21]

Whether the Supreme Court relied heavily on this evidence is a moot point,[22] but in its 1954 decision it did refer to this testimony in a footnote, and it did ask for further information regarding the probable effects of different procedures of desegregation—information which social scientists were obviously in the best position to provide. The social scientists involved in the school segregation cases presented studies of the behavior and attitudes of children—studies that are typically made not by lawyers but by psychologists and sociologists. According to Cahn, these social scientists provided weak or unreliable evidence to support what everyone knows unequivocally by intuition; or, to use a cliché, they "proved the obvious." Regarding the school segregation issue, he states that "one speaks in terms of the most familiar and universally accepted standards of right and wrong when one remarks (1) that racial segregation under government auspices inevitably inflicts humiliation, and (2) that official humiliation of innocent, law-abiding citizens is psychologically injurious and morally evil." In stating this, Cahn points up the distinction between the lawyer's approach and the social scientist's empirical approach based on tests, attitude surveys, and systematic observation. It is obvious that Cahn is not aware that the overwhelming majority of white Americans in 1896 believed that segregation was right and just and that practically all the relevant literature also took this position. Mr. Justice Harlan is one of the very few exceptions, but Cahn apparently thinks his splendid opinion was universal. Any survey of the literature would bear out the fact that, in recent years, it has been the studies of social scientists which have been building the case "separate cannot be equal" in contradiction to the *Plessy* dictum of "separate but equal." It is true that not all the evidence presented by the social scientists had a high reliability, but Cahn misses the point widely when he concentrates his fire on the Clark study, since the evidence he criticizes is merely a minor supplement to a more basic study published some years ago. He is correct, however, in stating that the social scientist should not present weak evidence without indicating its weakness.

We shall not know to what extent judges are significantly influenced by social-science testimony until they tell us, and this is not customary, expedient, nor even wise from the standpoint of their relation to the public and to the losing party. It seems to the writer, however, that in the few cases cited the social-science evidence was contributory to the decision in that the judges allowed the testimony and responded to it by questioning and asking for more. This does not mean, of course, that more traditional lines of argument were not also important in these cases or that social-science testimony would be relevant in most cases. But there probably are a considerable number of cases coming before the courts every month in which some facts, now available to social scientists and not presently known to lawyers, are just as materially relevant to the judgment that has to be made as in the cases cited here. The pertinence of social-science evidence will have to be decided by the judges in each case.

It is very important to note that in the cases cited here, the social scientist was in no way substituting for the lawyer; the social scientist cannot be an advocate in his role as scientist. It is equally important to recognize that the social scientist is not proposing a new rule to replace the law. He is not suggesting that principles of ethics or humanitarianism or majority rule (as determined by public-opinion polls) replace the law, as some have suggested. What the social scientist can do in the courtroom is to present certain social facts that serve as conditions affecting the outcome of the case; that is, there are certain cases in which the judge must *assume* certain social facts to be true before he can arrive at any decision. He may or may not be aware that he is assuming certain beliefs to be social facts; there may or may not be evidence available to the social scientists that the beliefs are or are not true; the lawyers and the judge are most often not aware that social scientists could ascertain the validity of their beliefs even when they are aware that these beliefs are being used as necessary assumptions. Yet these are the situations in which social scientists could serve as expert witnesses in court cases and possibly affect the outcome of decisions. Clever lawyers probably will be increasingly aware of the possibility of hiring social scientists to serve as expert witnesses for their side; and if this happens, conscientious judges will either have to acquaint themselves with the possibilities and limitations of social science to decide when the social-science evidence is reliable or else rely on court-appointed social scientists who are presumably neutral.

Social-science findings, like all scientific conclusions, have only a certain degree of reliability; this varies from one finding to another and can often itself be measured. The findings of sociology and psychology are almost always considerably less reliable than those in physical science, but far from always less reliable than those in certain of the biological sciences. The reliability of conclusions of sociological and psychological research is generally higher than diagnoses made by psychiatrists, which have long been accepted as expert testimony by the courts.

Another characteristic of social-science findings is that they apply, "on the average," to a category of cases, not to every single case in the category. When a finding is made, for example, that a foster home is better for the development of a child's personality—in terms of certain stated criteria —than an institutional home, this does not mean that every child will respond better to placement in a foster home than in an institution. The judge who has to decide on placement may find the social-science finding useful, but still take into consideration the qualities of the particular foster home and institutions and of the personality of the child in relation to them.[23]

While social scientists are human beings and humans are fallible, social scientists are trained to recognize the limitations of their researches—perhaps better trained in this regard than even the physical scientists, because the methods of the latter are ordinarily beset with fewer limitations. The judge who wishes to make the best use of social-science knowledge and yet be aware of the limitations of this knowledge can usually directly examine the social-scientist witness as to the applicability and limitations of his testimony. The judge must know the pertinent questions to ask; for example, about the representativeness of the sample, the validity and reliability of a test, the reproductibility of a scale, the confidence limits of the finding, and so on.

Some lawyers apparently think that social-science evidence can be used to support any point of view or both sides of a given issue equally well. Cahn, for example, states, "Shrewd, resourceful lawyers can put a Brandeis brief together in support of almost any conceivable exercise of legislative judgment. . . . In the last two decades, many Brandeis briefs have been conspicuously vulnerable in respect of statistical method, rationality of inferences from assembled data, adequacy of sampling, and failure to allow for—or to disclose—negative instances." [24] If this is what the Brandeis brief is, lawyers have been readers of the book *How to Lie with Statistics*,[25] but know nothing of legitimate social science. In science, there are rigorous rules of proof and disproof, and while social scientists not infrequently find themselves hampered in the application of these rules by the nature of the data, they are aware as to when they are or are not using the rules.

Cahn can also be cited as an example of a lawyer unaware of the difference between a social science and a social ideology. He states: "Recognizing as we do how sagacious Mr. Justice Holmes was to insist that the Constitution be not tied to the wheels of any economic system whatsoever, we ought to keep it similarly uncommitted in relation to the other social sciences." [26] A system is not a science, and if an economist advocates a given system he does so either as any other member of society or as an economist who clearly specifies his value premises, which are a matter of personal or group choice. Perhaps unfortunately, sociologists and psychologists are generally less given to advocacy in terms of certain specified values than are economists. But in any case, it is the lawyer's task, in a courtroom, to distinguish the value premises from the facts, the scientist from the advocate.

Levi puts his finger on another difficulty that will plague the lawyer who wishes to get the best use out of social science:

I have no doubt that where the social science materials are both relevant and available, they will be used by lawyers in litigation. The competence of the trained lawyer engaged in controversy insures this. The difficulty, of course, is that for the greatest part, the material is only somewhat relevant in its present form and is mostly unavailable. Perfection of the material and its use are then likely to be beyond the resources of the individual lawyer or law firm.[27]

The problem, of course, is one of the lawyer's communicating the legal issue to a competent social scientist; the social scientist's scouring the literature to ascertain if any relevant studies exist; if not, the social scientist's indicating the expense and time necessary to do an adequate study; the social scientist's communicating the scientific findings to the lawyer; the lawyer's deciding the best way of bringing this evidence into court. Each of these steps can be very difficult; but they are not insuperable.

Louisell, as a teacher of law interested in the use of social science, has presented an excellent list of injunctions to the social scientist preparing to give expert testimony.[28] This writer, a teacher of sociology, who believes its findings to have high relevance to the law, would like to offer a few suggestions for lawyers who might wish to bring in a social scientist to present expert testimony or might be confronted with a social scientist presenting testimony on the other side.

1. Don't accuse the social scientist of being biased *because* he has studied a matter for a long time; this argument can readily be turned against a conscientious lawyer or judge and seems to make a plea for ignorance.

2. Don't assume that he knows everything about a given subject or that his reliable findings apply in all cases.

3. Don't assume that he can adduce an equally good argument on both sides of an issue.

4. Don't assume that he is unfamiliar with the logical rules of evidence or that he cannot distinguish facts from values.

5. Do ask him what reliable findings he can bring to bear on relevant legal questions and what the limitations of these findings are.

6. Do distinguish his role as scientist from his role of advocate, if he brings the latter into the controversy.

7. Don't be overly impressed by his special terminology, but require him to translate obscure terms into straightforward English; the social scientist does the same thing the lawyer does in using special terminology to exclude the intelligent layman from understanding his subject matter.

The above list of do's and don'ts suggests the specific blocks in the mind of the attorney when he might contemplate asking a social scientist to serve as an expert witness in a specific case. But they do not account for the extreme infrequency with which the average attorney ever contemplates this possibility. We can only speculate on the reasons why this is so. The Brandeis brief—a statement of social facts pertinent to a case—has been familiar in the courtroom for several generations. The lawyer serves as his own social scientist in the preparation of this brief, without access to all the techniques of research and scholarship available to the social scientist and without much access to the latter's accumulated body of knowledge and theory. Why is this so?

The Brandeis brief is not yet wholly accepted among lawyers; many prefer to stress the approach to a case through the law itself and to restrict the presentation of facts to those immediately involved in the individual case. The law schools encourage this approach, since it is what law professors can teach; the latter can indicate briefly to their students the general nature of a Brandeis brief, but they can do little to explain in detail the full techniques of its preparation. Referring to the two elements involved in every law case—the "law" and the "facts"—law schools give almost exclusive attention to the law, even to the extent of minimizing the trial court, where the facts are presented, and concentrating on the appeals court, where the law alone is at issue. Jerome Frank[29] devoted a lifetime to criticizing his colleagues on this point, but cannot be said to have had much impact on them. Most lawyers adhere to traditions which have long opposed what they call the "sociological approach" as against the "legal approach."

Still, many practicing lawyers find it valuable for their clients to introduce general social facts into their cases and so use the medium of the Brandeis brief, which they prepare themselves. Not even the wealthiest law firm, to my knowledge, employs a sociologist to aid its legal research assistants, much less contracts with an independent sociologist to serve as expert witness. The only exception I am aware of is the attorneys for the National Association for the Advancement of Colored People, and it can be said that this group is the only one which has systematically introduced social-science knowledge into court cases, dealing exclusively with civil rights. Judging from the outcomes of the NAACP cases, the use of the social scientists has been successful. But many attorneys have criticized the NAACP, and the courts before which they have appeared, for this very use of social scientists. Their strictures provide some clues as to why social scientists are not more frequently used.

Lawyers are not convinced of the reliability and validity of most social-science studies; they are usually willing to accept a census datum, but not the results of a public-opinion poll or a community study, much less a more subjectively grounded observation. They have not studied the topic of scientific method, and they correctly observe that many published studies have defects of a methodological character. Their approach to the social sciences tends to be that of the historian of the Idealist school: social facts are specific events, never generalizations or abstract "findings." Thus, their attitude toward the social scientist may be summarized in the remark, "You do not really do scientific research, but even if you did, I would not accept your work." They have been reinforced in this attitude by their experience with psychiatrists, on whom they must rely frequently for expert testimony in criminal cases. They have found that they can buy almost any testimony they wish to have from the psychiatrists by approaching the one whose theoretical views on criminality meet their current needs. The lawyers do not distinguish the clinical approach of the psychiatrist from the scientific approach of the sociologist, but they correctly assess the biasing role of theory in the approach of even the most scientific sociologist: they believe, probably correctly, that if the sociologist is to be asked to provide more than census-type facts, the sociologist can be found who has a theoretical orientation which is relatively favorable to the position the given lawyer is seeking to sustain. Lawyers can gather census-type facts themselves.

The relatively few lawyers who have broken the barrier of their ignorance regarding social science, and of their traditions opposed to it, sometimes find an equal but opposite lack of understanding on the part of the social scientists. Sociologists, particularly, tend to be opposed to the law and what they call "the legalistic approach." American sociologists are inclined to accept Sumner's conception that a law was either an articulated folkway or only so much meaningless print and hence that the scientific sociologist could study only the folkways. American sociologists are not inclined to accept Durkheim's conception that laws provide the structure and forms into which institutions and behaviors are molded. Even those sociologists closest to the law—the criminologists—often argue that criminal cases ought to be decided on the basis of the facts in the case, not on the basis of rules governing admissible testimony, the "rights" of the accused, and punishments arbitrarily enacted several decades ago. Lawyers are just as much shocked by these views of sociologists as sociologists are shocked by the "legalistic" views of lawyers. The problem here is that the sociologist deals with the law as an element in his study, in a way that a biologist or a geologist does not; and since the sociologist's approach to the law is so different from that of the lawyer, the latter finds it much easier to use the biologist or the geologist as an expert witness than he does the sociologist. There is a fundamental *theoretical* tension between most lawyers and most sociologists. For this tension to be overcome, the sociologist will have to learn about legal procedure, the adversary approach, and the lawyer's conception of the law as a means of resolving disputes without recourse to personal violence.

Our conclusion is that social science, particularly sociology, has tremendous potential utility for the lawyer, but the barriers between the two disciplines are not likely to be overcome soon. For the present, only rarely will a lawyer seek a sociologist to present expert testimony, and then only sometimes will he find one who is prepared to present that testimony in a manner suitable for a court.

REFERENCES

NOTE: *This chapter was prepared while the author was engaged on a Rockefeller Foundation research grant. Appreciation is expressed to the Foundation and to Professors David Louisell and Monrad Paulsen, formerly of the University of Minne-*

sota Law School, for an advance reading of an earlier version of this essay, which appeared in the Minnesota Law Review, *XL, No. 3 (1956), 205–218.*

1. David W. Louisell, "The Psychologist in Today's Legal World," *Minnesota Law Review,* LIX (February, 1955), 235–272.
2. Edmund Cahn, "Jurisprudence," *New York University Law Review,* XXX (1955), 150–169.
3. The writer is also author of "Problems in the Sociology of Law and Law Enforcement," *Journal of Legal Education,* VI, No. 6 (1953), 191–202; "Voluntary Associations in France," in *Theory and Method in the Social Sciences* (Minneapolis: University of Minnesota Press, 1954); "Does the Punishment Fit the Crime? A Study in Social Valuation," *American Journal of Sociology,* LXI (November, 1955), 247; "The Use of Law to Induce Social Change," *Transactions of the Third World Congress of Sociology,* VI (Amsterdam, 1956), 52–63; "Sociological Factors in the Effectiveness of Projected Legislative Remedies," *Journal of Legal Education,* XI, No. 4 (1959), 470–481; "On Individualism and Social Responsibility," *European Journal of Sociology,* II (Summer, 1961), 163–169; "Some Suggestions for Research in the Sociology of Law," *Social Problems,* IX (Winter, 1962), 281–283.
4. For a good recent summary of the problems in the relationship between psychiatry and the law, see M. S. Guttmacher and H. Weihofen, *Psychiatry and the Law* (New York: Norton, 1952). For a consideration of the implications of the even more recent Durham case, see the proceedings of the conference on "Insanity and the Law" held at the University of Chicago, February 28, 1955, and B. C. Shiele and M. G. Paulsen, "Psychiatric Evidence in Legal Tests of Insanity," *Bulletin of the University of Minnesota Hospitals and Minnesota Medical Foundation,* XXVI (January 28, 1955), 325–332.
5. 314 U.S. 488 (1942). This case was brought to my attention by Edward H. Levi, *Four Talks on Legal Education* (Chicago: University of Chicago Law School, 1952), p. 34.
6. Levi, *op. cit.,* pp. 7, 47.
7. Louisell, *op. cit.,* pp. 236, 238.
8. *United States v. 38 Dozen Bottles,* 114 F. Supp. 461 (D. Minn. 1953); *Robbinsdale Amusement Co. v. Warner Bros. Pictures Distributing Corp.,* Civil No. 4584 (4th Div., Minneapolis).
9. *Op. cit.,* 249–250. Discussion of other uses of public-opinion surveys may be found in Lester E. Waterbury, "Opinion Surveys in Civil Litigation," *Public Opinion Quarterly,* XVII (Spring, 1953), 71–90; Frank R. Kennedy, "Law and the Courts," in N. C. Heier and H. W. Saunders, *The Polls and Public Opinion* (New York: Henry Holt, 1949), pp. 92–108; Eugene P. Sylvester, "Consumer Polls as Evidenced in Unfair Trade Cases," *George Washington Law Review,* XX (December, 1951), 211.
10. *Robbinsdale Amusement Co. v. Warner Bros. Pictures Distributing Corp.,* Civil No. 4584 (4th Div., Minneapolis).
11. Tracy S. Kendler, "Contributions of the Psychologist to Constitutional Law," *American Psychologist,* V (October, 1950), 505–510.
12. Harold D. Lasswell, "Applications: Detection; Propaganda Detection and the Courts," H. D. Lasswell, N. Leites and Associates, *Language of Politics* (New York: G. W. Stewart, 1949).
13. Robert C. Sorensen and Theodore C. Sorensen, "A Proposal for the Use of Content Analysis Evidence in Literary Infringement Cases," *Social Forces,* XXXIII (March, 1955), 262–267.

14. See *Morse v. Fields,* U.S. District Court, S.D. New York, December 16, 1954. 127 F. Supp. 63.
15. One of the main briefs in the Supreme Court cases leading to the decision of May 17, 1954, "The Effects of Segregation and the Consequences of Desegregation: A Social Science Statement," is reprinted in the *Minnesota Law Review,* XXXVII (1953), 427–439. The social scientists' brief in the case that was decided on May 31, 1955, was partly incorporated in the regular lawyers' brief by the NAACP ("Brief in the Supreme Court of the United States, October term, 1954, numbers 1, 2, 3 and 5"). The leading social scientist in the preparation of these briefs for the NAACP was Professor Kenneth B. Clark of City College, New York. Lawyers may find his summary for social scientists interesting: "Desegregation: An Appraisal of the Evidence," *Journal of Social Issues,* IX, No. 4 (1953), whole issue.

   Social scientists have served as expert witnesses in many civil-rights cases to document the facts of discrimination against minorities. To avoid repetition of similar materials, I shall refer here only to their work in the most celebrated of civil-rights cases—that of *Brown v. Board of Education.*
16. 163 U.S. 537 (1896).
17. *Missouri ex rel. Gaines v. Canada,* 305 U.S. 337 (1938).
18. 339 U.S. 637 (1950).
19. 98 F. Supp. 529 (1951).
20. 339 U.S. 629 (1950).
21. Kenneth B. Clark, "The Social Scientist as an Expert Witness in Civil Rights Litigation," *Social Problems,* I (June, 1953), 7.
22. The issue has been raised by Cahn (*op. cit.*). Neither the active advocates nor opponents of desegregation have questioned the crucial role of the social-science evidence. See, for example, the speech of Honorable James O. Eastland of Mississippi in the Senate of the United States, May 26, 1955 ("The Supreme Court's 'Modern Scientific Authorities' in the Segregation Cases"), and the speech of Will Maslow of the American Jewish Congress, "The Uses of Law in the Struggle for Equality," December, 1954.
23. Professor Monrad Paulsen has suggested that a valuable social-science study could be done for presentation in divorce cases where custody of children is at issue: is it better for the child to be raised by one parent or to be ordered to spend, say, nine months with one parent and three months with the other parent?
24. *Op. cit.,* p. 154.
25. Darrell Huff, *How to Lie with Statistics* (New York: Norton, 1954).
26. Cahn, *op. cit.,* p. 167.
27. Levi, *op. cit.,* p. 47.
28. Louisell, *op. cit.,* pp. 257–258.
29. See especially his *Courts on Trial* (Princeton: Princeton University Press, 1949).

Medicine

MARTIN D. HYMAN

chapter 6

Introduction

A large number of American sociologists are in some way professionally involved in the medical area. The American Sociological Association's Medical Sociology Section, a group consisting of sociologists and related specialists with an interest in medical phenomena, now numbers around 650, or about 7 per cent of the total membership of the Association. The Section is now the second largest specialty group within the Association. Furthermore, sociological interests in medicine has grown considerably in recent years. In 1957, Anderson and Seacat, on the basis of research inventories and personal contacts, were able to identify only 216 sociologists, anthropologists, and social psychologists engaged in research in the health field.[1] A 1961 survey of members of the Section on Medical Sociology showed that about one-half had been employed in the health field for five years or less.[2]

A 1957 study found that 34 of its 110 respondents were located at schools of medicine, nursing, or public health, with an equal number in sociology or related academic departments. Government agencies housed 18, 11 were with private research groups, and smaller numbers were affiliated with foundations, hospitals, and voluntary health agencies.[3] The 1957 Anderson and Seacat survey, which included anthropologists and social psychologists as well as sociologists, showed a much smaller proportion, 15 per cent, affiliated with schools of medicine, nursing, or public health and a somewhat larger proportion, 39 per cent, located in academic departments.[4] These differences may reflect variation either in the constitution

119

of the two samples or in the procedures used to classify respondents who had multiple institutional affiliations.

To look at the matter from a slightly different perspective, a considerable number of medical organizations employ sociologists. Buck, in 1961, surveyed the 80 medical schools then in operation in the United States and found sociologists working at 39 of the 70 schools from which he received replies.[5]

Among the functions performed by sociologists in medicine, research has received far more emphasis than teaching, consultation, or administration. A 1961 survey of members of the Section on Medical Sociology found 82 per cent engaged in some research activity, while 44 per cent were doing some teaching in either an academic or medical department and about 25 per cent were carrying out some administrative activity of a medical or nonmedical nature.[6] Furthermore, research was the primary or sole activity of about two-thirds, while teaching so characterized only 16 per cent and "comparatively few" were mainly or wholly occupied with administrative or consultative duties.[7] The 1961 survey of medical-school staff members corroborates this evidence; 90 per cent of the responding sociologists were performing some kind of research, while 46 per cent delivered at least some formal classroom lectures, 31 per cent participated in seminars on patient care, 16 per cent were involved in ward rounds, and 34 per cent were engaged in some other kind of teaching activity, such as participation in faculty seminars.[8] Of the 110 medical sociologists in a 1957 sample, 108 were conducting research, 57 were teaching some kind of medical sociology, and 16 had some administrative responsibility.[9]

And yet considerable numbers of medical sociologists do teach and, more important for our purposes, do so at schools of medicine and public health. A recent study identified 218 teachers of social science with formal appointments in such institutions.[10] It was also found that there has been a great increase in recent years in the number of such appointments. The positions held by about half of the respondents in this study *did not exist prior to 1962, while almost none of these positions were in existence prior to 1956.* In 1957, Straus was able to locate only 34 sociologists who were employed in *any* capacity by schools of medicine or public health, while Buck, in 1961, identified 96 in medical schools alone.[11]

We shall consider next a number of factors which determine the extent to which sociological outputs are utilized in medical decisions and actions. First we shall take up features of the intellectual and ideological orientations of medicine and medical sociology which bear on the kind of relationship that has been established between medicine and sociological research. There will follow an analysis of the role of sociologists as medical teachers. Next, an inventory of actual and potential uses of sociology in medicine will be presented. We shall conclude with the results of a recent survey of medical sociologists which attempted to elicit their experiences and attitudes concerning the application of their work to medicine.

Sociologists' Preferences Concerning the Subject Matter of Research in Medical Sociology

There is not complete agreement among medical and sociological spokesmen as to how a juncture of medicine and sociological research should be achieved. Nor are these differences due wholly to a medical-sociological schism, for there is considerable variation *within* each field.

The following crude dichotomy may shed some light on the range of sociological attitudes. There are those sociologists who regard medical settings as convenient "strategic" places for the testing of general sociological theory.[12] By contrast, others are dedicated to the principle of "sociology in the service of medicine," and their professional goal is to apply sociological theory and research to the solution of medical problems. For purposes of clarity and verbal parsimony let us refer to the first type of orientation as "deductive," while we call its opposite "inductive." [13]

The deductive orientation is well illustrated in the following comments by Oswald Hall, a pioneer medical sociologist:

> When the sociologist studies medicine he is studying work. Medicine has no unique interest for sociology. . . . The sociologist's interest, therefore, is first in the institutions in which the work goes on—in this paper in the hospital and in the doctor's office. Secondly, the sociologist is interested in medicine as part of the occupational division of labor in society. Finally, sociologists are interested in the social psychology of work, that is, in the relation of work to personality organization. . . . [The hospital is] an accessible area for studying the relations between and the congruence of status systems and specialized functions. . . . To summarize at this point, the study of hospitals offers a strategic opportunity for understanding complex institutional structures.[14]

A study exemplifying the deductive approach is Anderson and Warkov's use of veterans' hospital data to investigate the effect of organizational size and complexity on the proportion of employees doing administrative work.[15] In this instance the legal and operational factors which make it necessary for hospitals to maintain certain records make possible an empirical test of hypotheses with which social theorists have been concerned for several decades. The deductive approach is seen also in Kaplan and Bloom's description of physiological indicators of sociological concepts which are hard to measure in traditional ways.[16] For example, they point to the possibility that speech muscle tension can be used as a measure of response to social sanctions and hence also as an indicator of sensitivity to pressures from various reference groups. It is difficult to measure these characteristics in group observation studies because of their frequent lack of overt manifestation.

Examples of the inductive approach are provided by the studies of Freeman and Simmons and of Mercer, which demonstrate the extent to which various noninstitutional environments can accommodate those who have been hospitalized because of mental illness or mental retardation.[17] The service to medicine implicit in these studies consists, according to Freidson, in employing sociological resources to demonstrate "how deviants, some of whom may be truly psychotic, are nonetheless socially manageable and acceptable in some settings and not others." [18]

The distinction between deductive and inductive orientations bears on the probability that the results of sociological research will receive medical use. The findings of inductive studies are the more apt to be utilized. This follows from the possibility that many inductive studies are actually instigated by medical personnel and from the likelihood that the deductively oriented sociologist is less motivated than is his inductive counterpart to communicate his findings to medical personnel. Since, as we have seen, few sociologists possess medical administrative authority, a lack of involvement of medical personnel with deductive studies makes it improbable that the findings of such studies will actually be implemented in medical practice.

However, it is *not* argued that deductive studies are not *potentially* useful to medicine. Indeed, it is apparent that Kaplan and Bloom's article could be turned around and viewed as an analysis of social determinants of physiological responses—certainly an area of medical import. Similarly, the Anderson and Warkov data could be helpful to hospital administrators in assessing the consequences for their administrative budgets of expanding or increasing the complexity of their organizations.

There may be, of course, many studies that are neither purely inductive nor solely deductive, and it is even less likely that there are many medical sociologists who consistently fall into one or the other category. For example, the *Student Physician* studies were undertaken both in response to a medical problem, the effect of a new type of medical-school curriculum on the professional development of medical students, and in order to advance sociological knowledge of the process whereby individuals acquire a professional outlook.[19] Consider a comment by Davis, who, like Oswald Hall, is one of the forerunners of modern medical sociology.[20]

In current vital statistics and in the data available from hospitals and other medical institutions, we have a large mass of quantitative data which, if properly analyzed in relationship with social and economic data, should yield important results not only in connection with social medicine but in illuminating general problems of urban and rural life.[21]

The Preferences of Medical Personnel Concerning the Subject Matter of Research in Medical Sociology

There is, to begin with, a school of thought in medicine that would like additional sociological variables contributed to analyses of the epidemiology of disease.[22] For example, sociologists have been called upon to provide concepts for classifying social environments so as to explain intergroup variations in morbidity rates.[23] The growing relative prevalence of long-term chronic, as contrasted with short-term acute, disease has caused some in medicine to turn to sociology for an understanding of the changes in patients' social relationships that are likely to result from a continuing state of illness.[24] With regard to treatment, some medical writers regard the task of medicine as including the restoration of the patient to his preillness array of social roles insofar as possible. This interest in the question of role occupancy has naturally led to requests for sociological knowledge on which to base effective rehabilitation programs.[25] One writer in the medical field has suggested that social analysis is necessary too for efficient clinical diagnosis.[26] Finally, several medical representatives have pointed to the need for sociological assistance in planning and evaluating medical organizational structures and programs.[27]

Thus medicine has given sociology encouragement to delve into several areas of prime medical concern. However, a question should be raised here: how *heavy* a commitment of sociological resources is being requested by medicine? That is to say, are medical spokesmen calling for the medical application of sociological *techniques,* sociological *methodology,* sociological theory, or some combination of these? In distinguishing techniques from methodology we use the former to denote specific, discrete research skills such as questionnaire construction, interviewing, and data-processing knowledge, each of which can be learned and put into practice without the understanding of scientific method and its sociological applications. "Methodology," on the other hand, refers to the sociological application of scientific method, and "theory" is used here to indicate sociological concepts and theorems. Medical personnel vary considerably in weighting the sociological intervention which they request. On the one hand the published literature includes several complaints by medical sociologists that some medical colleagues view them mainly as technicians;[28] on the other hand it is clear that a number of medical spokesmen do call upon sociologists to be something more than technicians. For example, those who suggest a sociological contribution to effective social rehabilitation are really asking something of sociological theories concerning determinants of commitment to and performance of roles, and, when others in medicine see a role for sociology to play in assessing the effectiveness of health institutions and programs, they point directly at sociological expertise in the methodology of evaluation studies. However, the following differences in outlook between the medical and sociological cultures present some obstacles to collaboration.

The Clinical-Statistical Controversy

Earlier, the physician and historian Sigerist was quoted as calling for the application of sociology to problems in clinical medicine.[29] However, it may be that the clinical use of sociological research is hindered by certain differences in scientific values between it and medicine. To begin with, sociology is traditionally concerned with generalization to reasonably large populations, while clinical medicine aims at the understanding of individual patient-cases.[30] Furthermore, the views of some medical clinicians concerning characteristics of the individual patient tend to cluster around two polar positions, both in sharp opposition to a fundamental assumption of the behavioral sciences. That is, some medical personnel treat each patient as a thoroughly unique case, while others feel that all patients are alike with respect to their attitudes and behavior in a medical setting.[31] The sociological viewpoint lies between these positions and assumes the possibility of developing valid statements about the behavior of classes or categories of patients.

An example of this conflict is provided by French.[32] He describes a dispute between a medical social worker and sociologist, both members of a medical-school faculty, concerning the best method of presenting a lecture to medical students on the relationship between social class and responses to frustration. The sociologist wanted to review the empirical literature on this subject and base the lecture on generalizations abstracted from this literature. The social worker preferred that the lecture consist of a detailed description and analysis of individual cases. She reasoned that in this manner the relationship between social class and response to frustration would be viewed by the students in a manner appropriate to future practitioners: as only one part of the total and unique picture of factors to be taken into account in dealing with an individual patient.[33]

Probably as a result of this difference in perspective most medical sociologists do not participate in clinical analysis. As noted earlier, a survey of behavioral scientists affiliated with medical schools found that only 31 per cent of the sociologists at these institutions participate in patient seminars, while a mere 16 per cent teach ward rounds.[34] Moreover, these figures contrast unfavorably with comparable data for medical-college psychologists and anthropologists. The patient seminar participation percentages are 50 per cent for psychologists and 43 per cent for anthropologists, while 29 per cent of the former and 16 per cent of the latter teach ward rounds.[35] Undoubtedly the relatively heavy involvement of psychologists in medical clinical analysis reflects the presence of substantial numbers of clinical psychologists. One might also argue that the anthropological tradition of intensive analysis of single societal cases has facilitated a similar approach to individual human ones. Rosengren asked a sample of medical sociologist respondents to place themselves in one of five ordinal categories representing the degree of clinical decision-making power they felt they possessed.[36] Fifty-five per cent placed themselves in the lowest category, which, the respondents were told, was supposed to represent total absence of clinical power. However, the distribution was bimodal, with 33 per cent locating themselves in the two top categories.

In any event, at least some sociologists do participate in clinical analyses. Examples of such participation are provided by Wirth and by Simon.[37] Wirth, writing in 1931 on the subject of "clinical sociology," shows that some of the obstacles to the clinical application of sociology are by no means new. He comments:

That the sociologist has, perhaps, an understanding about the family, boys' gangs, community life, social institutions, and other phases of group life is quite generally admitted. What some psychiatrists are not so ready to grant is that the sociologist may have a contribution to make to the study of personality and individual behavior problems which is not already represented by other members of the clinic staff.[38]

This implies that there may be some other member of the clinic team, such as the medical social worker, who can convey a sociological perspective to clinical medicine. Wirth notes that most child-guidance clinics of his day did not employ sociologists and instead relied on social workers as a source of sociological knowledge.[39] However, he is dubious about the efficacy of this arrangement, claiming that the combination of a predominantly psychiatric orientation and a heavy case load prevents social workers from being sociological middlemen in clinical settings. Other, more recent writers have also called attention to the dominance of psychological over sociological perspective among social workers; but there is also some evidence that the social-work school curriculum is becoming more sociological in content and that medical social work is incorporating sociological principles.[40]

On the other side of the ledger stands a recent experience of the author. During an address to a group of about twenty medical social workers representing as many American hospitals the term "sick role" was used. The chairman of the meeting, who was well acquainted with the other social workers in the group, immediately asked the speaker to explain what he meant by this term. It is known that the chairman understood the speaker, but she felt that at least some of her colleagues would not. If she was correct, and we have no means of knowing this, it might indicate a lack of sociological perspective among medical social workers great enough to prevent them, whatever other important contribution they make, from filling the role of clinical sociologist.[41]

Medical and Sociological Time Perspectives

The conflict between the applied researcher, who is cognizant of the time required for careful, complete research, and the research user who expects results much sooner may be endemic to applied research.[42] This discrepancy in time perspectives has been observed in the relationship between medicine and sociological research.[43] The issue may be joined more sharply in medicine than in other applied research areas because of the life-and-death nature of many medical problems. The user may become impatient and proceed to take action without the benefit of research findings. Or he may decide to proceed on the basis of incomplete data. The danger here is that the action based on inadequate data will fail to advance the user's goals, the researchers will be blamed for the action's failure, and future prospects for research use will be jeopardized. The discrepancy in time perspectives may also hinder research use by demoralizing the researcher, who may come to feel that in view of the difficulty in producing results that are sufficiently timely from the user's standpoint he had best not even attempt to conduct applied research.

Values Concerning Patient Care

Rehabilitation researchers have noted that when patients are classified according to various social, psychological, and physical characteristics not all benefit equally from rehabilitation.[44] However, the administrators of rehabilitation programs believe that a maximum rehabilitation *effort* ought to be made for *all* patients regardless of the probability of success, and hence they tend not to act on findings which show how finite rehabilitation resources can be put to optimal use.[45] A recent article recommending that rehabilitation services be concentrated on patients whom research has shown can be benefited most was sharply challenged by the associate medical director of a major rehabilitation center.[46]

Medical norms concerning the *locus of responsibility* for patient care may also hinder the application of sociology. Goss's interviews with physicians demonstrated a widely shared belief that the individual physician should have final responsibility for making all decisions concerning the medical care of his patients.[47] This is not to say that these physicians showed an unwillingness to receive advice. However, they overwhelmingly felt that it was the prerogative of the patient's own physician to decide whether to follow consultative advice on patient care and that in any event such advice was welcome only if it came from colleagues of at least equal medical competence and rank. Although her data do not bear directly on this point, Goss's study alerts us to the possibility that the application of sociology to medicine, or for that matter the use of any science in any applied field, can take place only to the extent that the practitioners' norms permit them to act on advice. We have no direct evidence indicating the receptivity of medical practitioners to advice from sociologists. However, Goss's further finding that these physicians were quite willing to accept advice or even orders concerning administrative, as opposed to patient-care, matters suggests that some facets of medical practice may be more accessible to sociological intervention than others. Another implication of these findings is that sociological suggestions in many medical areas may be adopted through a process of diffusion if somehow the senior physicians can first be persuaded of their merits.

Social Science as Help or Threat

Practitioners in general, not merely the medical variety, will resist the application of research findings if this threatens their reputations or any other valued feature of the status quo. Thus Warren, drawing on his experience as a social research consultant to a health and welfare agency, admits, "One can appreciate the reticence that is likely to greet the behavioral scientist who comes into a social agency and says, in effect: 'Well, here I am, and the first thing I want to do is to make a series of studies to see if you practitioners are really doing anything effective.'" [48]

Some Implications of the Differences between Medical and Sociological Orientations Discussed Thus Far

How can the ideological and intellectual gap between medicine and sociology be bridged?

One possibility is the exposure of sociologists and medical personnel to increased training in the other's discipline. As sociology is increasingly taught in medical professional schools and the number of medical personnel who have been subjected to an undergraduate curriculum in the liberal arts rises, the total proportion of those in medicine who have had some formal training in sociology is likely to be higher in the years to come. There is no reason, however, for similar optimism regarding formal training in medical areas among medical sociologists. More crucial, however, may be the extent to which sociologists are informed in some fashion, before their entry into a medical setting, of its distinctive *social* and *cultural* features. As Cottrell and Sheldon have pointed out:

> The atmosphere of a hospital or social welfare agency or a professional school is very different from the university department of sociology or a social-research laboratory. Some initial recognition of the fact of differences and early briefing in the manners and customs of the "adopted country" will make for smoother and easier working relations. Neglect of these seemingly unimportant aspects may cause the newcomer sometimes to appear gauche, naïve, and alien and this unnecessarily handicaps him in establishing productive contacts.[49]

Of course, some mutual indoctrination of sociologists and medical personnel does occur through informal day-to-day contact.[50]

Young has advanced the intriguing notion that effective collaboration between sociologists and practicing professionals would be enhanced if only the former acted more like sociologists in their dealings with the latter.

> The key to effective collaboration between sociologists and members of the practicing professions lies in detailed study of the professional subcultures involved. As social scientists, and as a special category of social scientists, sociologists should be peculiarly sensitive to the fact that they have values, ways of working and other idiosyncrasies which are not wholly shared either by the subjects of their applied interest or by collaborators in other professions. All sociologists recognize the importance of such difference in their relations with Vermont farmers, Indiana steel workers, the Mexicans in Texas, the Puerto Ricans in New York, and countless other groups. Yet there seems to be little recognition of the importance of similar if less conspicuous differences between themselves and members of other professions with whom they have occasion to work. Difficulties and failures in cooperation with practitioners tend to be attributed to arrogance, narrow-mindedness, trade school education, authoritarianism, professional insecurity, plain stupidity, and what not. Frustration, anger, a sense of futility, discouragement and withdrawal are likely to be the reactions. It is not easy to explain why so many sociologists should respond so irrationally to subcultural variations at the professional level and yet behave understandingly when faced with similar subcultural differences in non-professional subjects of study. Perhaps it is merely that without sufficient thought it is erroneously taken for granted that professional people as a whole have so much in common that communication and mutual understanding should be simple.[51]

Lest we exaggerate the magnitude of the difference in outlook between sociology and medicine, it should be pointed out that the two fields do share a commitment to the scientific method, and, since medical sociologists are not immune to extraprofessional facets of modern Western culture, most of them, no less than their medical colleagues, are likely to favor the improvement of levels of health.[52]

Capabilities of Sociological Research and Theory

Cultural differences between medicine and sociological research are not the only obstacles to the latter's use in medicine. A number of writers within sociology itself have pointed to characteristics of its theoretical underpinnings which work against the utilization of sociological research results in any applied field. Research results can serve as a basis for action only if they identify causal variables that the practitioner can manipulate to further his goals.[53] These critics allege that current sociological theory and hence applied sociological research embrace too few such variables. Whether or not a particular variable is manipulable is a consequence of the practitioner's power, normative constraints, economic resources, and ingenuity. For example, sociological research on the fluoridation question has been criticized for identifying variables beyond the manipulative power of administrators. Kegeles, noting a finding that alienation is a cause of opposition to fluoridation, comments, "If a person feels alienated from his community because his job is relatively meaningless, one can hardly change the nature of industrialization in America." [54]

However, Lazarsfeld has pointed out that even when research findings are stated in terms of unmanipulable causal variables all is not lost. Such findings can be sometimes *adjusted to* so as to advance the client's interests.[55] For example, Suchman found that the more parochial an ethnic group's social structure, the less "scientific" the group members' attitudes and behavior in the health area.[56] Now, a health official desirous of increasing the acceptance of "scientific" principles of health care in his community is not able to change the community's ethnic composition and is powerless to manipulate the social structure of existing ethnic groups. However, he could conceivably change the mode of "delivery" of health services so as to increase their utilization by relatively parochial ethnic groups. For example, it might prove useful to broach the question of changes in health behavior through the medium of ethnic clubs and societies, to make available at least some medical personnel of the ethnic backgrounds prevalent in the community, and to make it possible for all the members of an ethnic organization or kinship group to receive medical care at the same location.

It is conceivable that the usefulness of sociological theory and research in medicine is limited also by their omission of certain variables relevant to medical phenomena. Hawkins observed that behavioral oscillations, a characteristic of the chronically ill, has, as a general sociological problem, received little attention.[57] Similarly, Foster has suggested that behavioral science is more effective in dealing with some medical problems than with others.[58] Specifically, it seems better able to deal with problems involving individual behavior and small, homogeneous groups than those concerning larger and more complex social phenomena. An example is the greater usefulness of behavioral science in tuberculosis control, where individual and small-group behavior are at issue, than in air-pollution reduction, where complex social organizations and interorganizational relationships are involved.

Glock distinguishes "evaluative" research, designed to assess the effects of planned action, "diagnostic" research, intended to identify the causes of a problem, and "prescriptive" research, the purpose of which is to indicate how the client should proceed in dealing with a problem.[59] He feels that contemporary social research is most capable in the evaluative area and least able to perform "prescriptive" research. But the needs of most applied-research clients run in exactly the opposite priority order, thus making for a certain amount of tension between researcher and client.

Another source of difficulty is the format in which contemporary social research is presented. It may be that the lines of interconnection that lead from sociological research and theory to medical applications are not clearly enough drawn in existing sociological and medical-sociological writings.[60] Zetterberg has suggested a solution to this problem: a practitioner attempting to make use of sociology would be greatly aided by a handbook in which, for each practical problem likely to be encountered in his field, relevant deductions from sociological theory would be listed.[61] Thus, to take an example not mentioned by Zetterberg, a handbook for hospital administrators might contain a problem heading such as "preventing patient discharges against medical advice." Under this heading there would be brought together action recommendations derived from general sociological theory as well as from studies carried out in this specific area. The aspects of general sociological theory which could yield helpful recommendations to the administrator here would include those dealing with deviation from social norms, interpersonal influence, socialization to new roles, and conflict among an individual's roles.

In view of the doubts expressed by sociologists themselves it is not surprising that some practitioners also lack confidence in sociology's ability to help them. However, the arguments of some medical personnel range beyond the points raised above and go so far as to question the discipline's scientific status. Thus the Group for the Advancement of Psychiatry, reporting on its survey of chairmen of psychiatry departments at American and Canadian medical schools, found the following statement characteristic of a current of thought among their respondents: "We are not convinced as a group that there is a behavioral science to be taught by anyone to anyone as yet. Much of the talk about a basic science of behavior is still, I feel, partly wish and partly mumbo-jumbo." [62]

Even where the scientific status of sociology is not challenged, the attempt to apply it to medicine is resisted by some medical personnel who are unconvinced of its medical relevance.[63] One variation on this argument states that the human-relations aspect of medicine is an art in which expertise can be developed only through gradual clinical experience and which is not susceptible to understanding through scientific research.[64] However, it should also be noted that some in medicine are at the other extreme and hold unrealistically high expectations of the ability of sociology to solve their problems.[65]

Factors Bearing on the Use of Sociological Teaching in Medicine

The literature in this area, which pertains mostly to the education of physicians, indicates a number of obstacles to the transmission of sociological knowledge to medical personnel. To begin with, teaching time is a scarce resource for which many medical-school disciplines compete fiercely.[66] Thus sociology faces a formidable task in gaining entrance to the medical-school curriculum. Evidence of this difficulty is the practice at some medical schools of assigning to sociology a small block of lectures within a course in psychiatry or preventive medicine.[67] This handicaps sociologists both in gaining medical teaching assignments and in carrying them out with effectiveness. It has been suggested, moreover, that sociologists with full as opposed to part-time medical-school appointments, as a result of their immersion in the medical world, are better able to demonstrate the medical relevance of sociology.[68] Others have pointed to the temporal location of sociological teaching in the medical-school curriculum as a determinant of the extent to which medical *students* perceive sociology as relevant to their endeavors. Sociology is usually taught, if at all, in the preclinical years. However, at this time medical students are preoccupied with physiology and anatomy and, since they lack contact with patients, tend to be relatively unconcerned with behavioral aspects of medical care. Hence medical students are confronted with sociology at the time when they are least likely to appreciate its medical usefulness.[69]

The viewpoint has been advanced, however, that the introduction of sociology during the preclinical years is necessary to offset the excessively physiological and anatomical view of medicine that students would otherwise develop at this time.[70] Bloom adds the argument that the medical utility of sociology can be better communicated to medical students if they encounter the sociologist as a basic researcher than if they confront him as a clinician.[71] He believes that only in the former role can the sociologist enable medical students to understand the nature of sociological conceptualization and problem formation. Of course, in some medical schools sociology is taught in both the preclinical and the clinical periods.[72]

The sociologist's location in the departmental structure of the medical school has also been alleged to hamper the diffusion of sociology. Most sociologists on medical-school faculties are located in either a psychiatry or a preventive-medicine department. However, these fields seem to command relatively little prestige within medicine.[73] As a result, sociologists may find themselves ignored by medical colleagues in other departments who could make use of sociological knowledge.[74] They become victims of the social-psychological theorem that the lower the status of an information source the less its credibility.[75] In response to their status difficulties has come the suggestion that medical-school sociologists branch out into departments with more prestige than that enjoyed by psychiatry and preventive medicine.[76] In the medical-center culture, patient care and research are the most highly valued activities, and these are embodied to a very great extent in the department of medicine.[77] It is not known, however, how receptive most departments of medicine would be to the entrance of sociologists.

It may be, however, that the affiliation of the sociologist with any department other than one labeled "sociology" or at least "behavioral science" beclouds his identity. For example, Stainbrook and Wexler observe that medical students tend to define a behavioral scientist's role in light of his departmental affiliation and will discuss only psychopathology with those teaching in psychiatry departments.[78] Thus, it is not surprising that separate medical-school behavioral-science departments have been suggested and at least one such department actually established.[79] Another advantage of such a department is its contribution to the co-ordination of clinical and preclinical behavioral-science programs.[80] However, the objection has been raised that at most medical schools this department would enjoy even lower status than psychiatry and preventive medicine and hence its creation would aggravate the status problems currently faced by medical sociologists.[81] More experience in teaching behavioral science *in a medical setting* may be needed before separate departments can be successfully established.[82]

Should sociologists who teach in medical schools hold simultaneous appointments on academic sociology faculties? Some have favored joint appointments as a means of preventing the medical sociologist from losing his sociological identity and taking on his medical colleagues as a reference group.[83] The comparative isolation of medical-school sociologists from their sociological colleagues is suggested by data showing that of 39 American medical schools employing sociologists in a teaching or research capacity, 26 employed only one or two sociologists, and only 4 schools had 5 or more sociologists on their staff.[84] Moreover, according to one writer, social-science research in the health field has already suffered from the tendency of many medical social scientists to accept physicians' rather than sociologists' notions as to what are the important research problems.[85] This tendency is said to result in failure to undertake certain studies of potential importance to both medicine and sociology. Thus it is alleged:

> No one seems to consider it necessary to ask how the physician ever arrived at the decision that a group of patients should be in bed at least twenty-two hours a day, or should do not more than three hours of occupational therapy a day, or should not play cards for more than one hour in the afternoon and one hour in the evening. These latter decisions are defined as "medical decisions" and thereby placed outside the province of the social scientist.[86]

We might note that this is not a criticism of studies motivated by medical rather than sociological concerns, or, as labeled in our earlier discussion, "inductive" rather than "deductive" studies. Rather, it is an objection to letting physicians decide *which* medical problems shall be the subject of social-science research. It has been suggested also that the docility with which some social scientists accept the hegemony of physicians over the choice of research problems results in part from the difference in status between these two groups.[87]

However, it may be that joint appointments in medical schools and academic departments, while serving to buttress the sociological identity of the medical sociologist, also reduce his effectiveness in transmitting sociological knowledge. It will be recalled that Stainbrook and Wexler have argued that only through full-time affiliation with medical institutions can social scientists learn enough about medicine to see how their capabilities can be applied to medical problems.[88]

Let us consider one more obstacle facing sociological teachers of medical students. Some physicians feel that they alone are competent to provide appropriate role models for medical students and that therefore, no matter what the subject, the proper training of the student requires that a physician teach it.[89] Also, as indicated earlier, physicians feel strongly that patient-care matters should rest in their hands. Attempts to teach sociology in a clinical setting may encounter problems as a result of this latter belief. An alternative arrangement has been attempted in at least one medical school. Here sociologists on the medical-school staff engage in research on patient care in close collaboration with physicians. Formal responsibility for teaching behavioral-science aspects of medicine rests with these physicians, who in many cases develop considerable sociological sophistication as a result of their research participation. In addition, the sociologists participate from time to time in student seminars.[90] At another institution, however, a sociologist observing social-science seminars taught by physicians and social workers reports a rather inadequate treatment of the subject.[91] He found, for example, that culture was treated as "something other people have," was reserved for exotic phenomena, and was never applied to medical students, medical schools, or hospitals.

Despite the difficulties just catalogued, there are some reasons for optimism concerning the medical teaching role of the sociologist. Pathology, bacteriology, biochemistry, physiology, and pharmacology first established their *research* contributions to medicine and only afterward were added to the medical-school curriculum.[92] Also, even when these disciplines became part of the medical curriculum, they were at first taught exclusively by physicians, while this is not the case today.[93] Finally, it has been observed that when biological-science departments were first established in medical schools they had very low status.[94]

Degree of Specialization in the Role of Medical Sociologist

Some sociologists complain that lack of understanding on the part of medical personnel of the potential contribution of the sociologist qua *sociologist,* coupled with the pressures of the moment, may cause them to view the sociologist as a "handyman who has a bag of tricks or as one who can help out as a kind of clinical aide, administrator, public-relations agent, and what not." [95] On the other hand, it has been argued that the social scientist can best insure co-operation from health personnel in the long run if he is willing to assume almost any role requested of him in the short run. An anthropologist was asked, soon after joining the New York State Health Department, to help rid a highway of an optical illusion. He accepted this task, despite its irrelevance to his professional capabilities, in order to enhance his rapport with colleagues in the Health Department.[96] The obvious danger here is that too little of the behavioral scientist's time will be spent delivering to medicine the best that he has to offer, namely his professional training. Also, participation in such diffuse activities increases the danger that his professional self-image will become eroded, with the undesirable consequences discussed earlier.

The medical sociologist's role may become diffuse in another sense, with somewhat less risk to his professional identity. That is, he may assume responsibility for *identifying* needed sociological research, consulting, or teaching which he is capable of doing and may also take it upon himself to see that his work is put to medical use. Such an expanded role is documented by Warren.[97] While serving as a social research consultant to a health and welfare agency he developed proposals for research which he felt would meet the agency's needs and, more unusual in applied sociology, took care to develop, in the process of designing and executing studies, the kind of organizational network that would maximize utilization of findings.

Some Further Comments on the Status Problems of Medical Sociologists

There is additional empirical information available on the status of medical sociologists. A recent survey of sociologists affiliated with medical institutions found that of those holding an academic rank 56 per cent were below the level of assistant professor, 23 per cent were assistant professors, 13 per cent were associate professors, and 8 per cent full professors.[98] This distribution would appear more skewed toward the lower ranks than is the case for medical-school faculties as a whole, but at the moment no data of the latter variety are available for comparison. However, Buck found (although he does not present the figures) that sociologists at medical schools are less likely than are anthropologists or psychologists to hold the highest academic ranks.[99] The youth of medical sociologists may partly explain these data on formal rank and may additionally handicap them in acquiring the esteem necessary for a useful advisory relationship with medical colleagues. One recent survey found only 10 per cent of them to be fifty or over, while 60 per cent were under forty.[100] The data indicated that half had been in the health field five years or less, while only 12 per cent had been in this field more than ten years.[101] Another factor likely to produce low status is marginality. In one sample of medical sociologists only 40 per cent were employed full time in the health field.[102] Another study found a percentage of full-time workers in the health field close to this, 34 per cent, but once again showed sociologists to be at a comparative disadvantage relative to psychologists and anthropologists. Seventy per cent of the psychologists and 42 per cent of the anthropologists were working full time in the health field.[103]

Working to counteract these factors is the high proportion of medical sociologists holding the Ph.D. degree. Anderson and Seacat found in 1957 that 82 per cent of their medical behavioral-scientist respondents held this degree, while in 1965 Rosengren unearthed a Ph.D. percentage of 72.[104] In 1963 New found that 90 per cent of his respondents, all of whom taught and held formal appointments in schools of medicine or public health, held a Ph.D.[105]

Let us now draw together the implications of the medical sociologist's status difficulties for the use of sociology in medicine. To begin with, the use of sociological research and consultation and the absorption of sociological teaching are likely to suffer to the extent that there is a correlation between prestige and influence, and we know that such a correlation exists for some kinds of influence.[106] Second, as noted earlier, the relatively low status of sociologists within medicine may be causing some of them to discard their sociological conceptual framework in favor of a docile acceptance of physicians' definitions of medical research problems.[107] We have also seen how the amount of medically and sociologically useful research may have been reduced as a result.[108] Finally, the status deprivations of medical sociologists may militate against the medical use of sociology by alienating them. They may decide to concentrate on pure research and theory or to do applied work in settings where their worth is more accepted than it is in medicine. To cite just one such setting, there are few marketing executives who need to be convinced that someone with sociological training can be of use to them or who must be dissuaded from the belief that effective marketing requires intuitive art more than it does applied science.

Actual and Desirable Uses of Sociology in Medicine

Thus far we have considered some of the intellectual, ideological, role, and status factors that affect the use of sociology in medicine. Now let us examine some of these uses. We shall define "the uses of sociology in medicine" as all inputs into medical decisions or actions issuing from sociological theory, methodology, or technology. For our purposes it will not matter *how* these sociological inputs arrive at their medical destinations, whether via sociological teachings, research reports, or consultation. This inventory of uses can be divided into two categories: sociological inputs that *have been* used in medical decisions or actions and sociological elements that could be so employed.

SOCIOLOGICAL CONTRIBUTIONS TO THE PREVENTION AND DIAGNOSIS OF ILLNESS

Epidemiological research has identified social factors associated both with the prevalence of disease and with the seeking of preventive medical care. For example, there are a large number of epidemiological studies showing an inverse relationship between socioeconomic level and the risk of disease and showing a greater prevalence of disease among nonwhites than among whites in the United States. The results of these studies have undoubtedly constituted a stimulant to the efforts of recent years to establish increased health services in disadvantaged areas and to modify the living standards of those groups with the highest disease risks.

Interpretations of the relationships found between social factors and disease prevalence, such as those involving social class, appear to have evolved through three stages. First, the tendency was to ascribe the findings, particularly with respect to infectious disease, to the differential *physical* characteristics of social-class environments such as nutrition, housing, and so on. There followed speculation as to *psychosocial* differences among these environments with respect to the prevalence of stress and its consequences.[109] More recently, the inverse relationship between social class and rates of illness has been treated in terms of *cultural* variations in attitudes toward professional medical care and, specifically, in terms of cultural variations in the tendency to seek preventive and therapeutic care.[110] Each of these modes of interpretation suggests a different strategy for reducing disease levels. It seems fair to say that the first interpretation listed above has become embodied in public and private medical-care policy more than has the second, and the second has received such recognition more than the third has. Programs which enforce minimal housing standards, which make free or cheap medical care available in clinics, and which provide food to the hungry, while not completely adequate, certainly have been in clear evidence for some time. Recognition of the psychosocial disease-producing characteristics of certain social environments has occurred through various features of the "war on poverty." An example is the attempt to reduce stress by opening new avenues to the fulfillment of aspirations for social mobility. There is not much evidence, however, that action to improve health levels is being taken on the basis of knowledge about the differential willingness of various cultural groups to seek medical care. Perhaps it is simply less obvious here than for the other interpretations of the relationship between social class and disease just how to proceed. Cultural orientations toward medical care certainly seem more difficult to manipulate than do housing conditions, the availability of clinics, or job opportunities. However, as we noted earlier, findings showing a relationship between culture and attitudes toward medical care do suggest ways in which medical care can be *modified* so as to enhance its attractiveness to groups which have avoided it. For example, research on Navajo culture and the social structure of Navajo folk medicine was a factor in the decision of public-health officials to train some Navajos as subprofessional health workers. A major function of these individuals is to interpret the requirements of scientific medical care in terms comprehensible and appealing to Navajos.[111]

There is some evidence of the usefulness of a sociological perspective in making medical diagnoses. Since the patient's experiencing of pain is often a diagnostic clue, Zborowski's findings[112] that Jewish and Italian-American males complain about pain more than do "Old Americans" might aid physicians in determining the diagnostic import of these complaints. Also of potential diagnostic utility is the more subtle distinction that Italian males tend to complain of pain more in the hospital than at home. In the latter environment they seem to feel that such behavior is inconsistent with their family role as an adult male.[113] Awareness of cultural considerations can avert serious diagnostic error. Macgregor reports the case of a young Puerto Rican man, who, but for the physicians' eventual realization of the intense stigma attached to scars in the lower-class Puerto Rican culture, would have been diagnosed as mentally ill. This patient had displayed a seemingly obsessive insistence on plastic surgery to obscure a barely visible facial scar.[114]

SOCIOLOGICAL CONTRIBUTIONS TO TREATMENT AND REHABILITATION

A number of sociological studies offer potential assistance in obtaining the compliance of patients with medical regimens. For example, one empirical study of discharge from hospitals against medical advice identified several determinants of this behavior, such as the extent to which the patient has social and psychological problems and whether social-work consultation has occurred.[115] Another empirical study found a positive association between the extent to which the physician informed the patient about his illness and the degree to which the latter accepted the prescribed medical program.[116] The implications for medical action here are apparent.

Since a satisfied patient is more likely to be a compliant one, it is important for more than humanitarian reasons to make medical care satisfactory to patients. The example of the Puerto Rican youth cited above indicates how cultural factors affect the patient's treatment priorities, which must be recognized if he is to be satisfied with his medical care.

It has been suggested that a sociological perspective can contribute to the psychiatric treatment process by enabling the psychiatrist to view dispassionately several sets of social normative systems, some of which may be more compatible than others with the patient's needs.[117] With a sociological orientation the psychiatrist will not approach his patient's problems solely with the view that certain norms and behavior are inherently ethically "good" while others are "bad," but instead will consider also "which system (of values) is most likely to facilitate development of a philosophy of life acceptable to the patient and to the society at large." [118]

Closely related to this idea is the notion that medical personnel who have some understanding of structural-functional analysis as applied to systems of belief and behavior are the better equipped to care for their patients. This type of awareness alerts the medical practitioner to the possibility that situations which are undesirable from a strictly medical standpoint may be functional from the patient's point of view; also it sensitizes him to the possible psychological and social dysfunctions, for patients, of health procedures well accepted in the medical culture.[119] For example, Italian-American hospital patients tend to receive frequent and lengthy visits from numerous relatives, to an extent that often threatens a medical prescription for rest. Yet, in view of the major role played by the Italian kinship structure in satisfying emotional needs, the prohibition of such visits might have dangerous psychological repercussions for both the patient and his relatives. On the other hand, in ethnic groups where kinship does not play such a powerful role it is possible to limit visiting privileges to the very closest relatives without any great risk.

The following analysis by Margaret Mead offers strong testimony concerning the need for medical personnel to be alert to possible dysfunctions of standard medical routines:

In the first place we treat childbirth not as a natural event of great significance but as an illness. We place the expectant mother in a hospital, otherwise assigned to the care of the ill, induce weakness and dependency in her by the use of drugs, straps, and soon isolate her from her husband and other children just as we isolate the sick and the dying. Again, under our dogma that the most important elements in nursing care are quiet, rest, and safeguard against infection, we separate the newborn infant from his mother, break up the essential rhythm of the first hours after birth, and let the father and brothers and sisters over fourteen years (a magical age set by various irrelevancies) look at the baby only through a glass window. This classification of childbirth with illness has a great variety of repercussions all through our culture, some of which we are now attempting to correct with such new practices as "rooming in," "self-regulating feeding," and inclusion of the father in prenatal training and in the delivery.[120]

Possible dysfunctions of accepted medical practices are also indicated by Scheff, who points out that physicians consider it more harmful, in situations of diagnostic uncertainty, to classify a sick person as well than to commit the opposite type of error.[121] Scheff attributes this to various legal and normative factors and to some questionable assumptions about the course of disease. For example, it is assumed that individuals with symptoms of disease will usually become sicker if not treated and that a diagnosis of illness, even if erroneous, does the patient little harm. Scheff invokes the growing sociological literature on the disabling consequences of entrance into the sick role to refute the latter assumption.

Scheff's article and Margaret Mead's comment imply also that certain features of medical treatment result not from scientific knowledge but rather from extrascientific features of both the medical and other cultures which have influenced medical personnel. It would seem that the identification of such phenomena is a task that sociologists, who are professionally sensitized to the impact of cultural milieu on behavior, are well equipped to perform. The resulting awareness on the part of medical personnel of aspects of their professional behavior which are not derived from scientific considerations should make possible a more rational assessment of the desirability of various medical practices. According to Kingsley Davis, the Mental Hygiene Movement constitutes an example of a medical treatment philosophy which is based on ideological rather than scientific premises.[122] On the basis mainly of an analysis of literature published by the National Committee for Mental Hygiene, Davis concludes that the Movement's approach to mental health expresses an ideology which constitutes an American version of the "Protestant Ethic." Its beliefs include asceticism, worldliness, individualism, rationalism, utilitarianism, democracy, and the conviction that an open-class system exists in the United States. Davis observes that as a consequence of this ideological commitment the Mental Hygiene Movement tends to view lack of ambition as a symptom of maladjustment, place a premium on leisure activities which do not impair and hopefully enhance the individual's capability for worldly striving, and point solely to characteristics of the individual, rather than to social factors, as determinants of mental illness. He notes that this last tendency, namely the asociological bias of the Movement, seriously limits the role it can play in dealing with mental illness. Similarly, Roth has described the extrascientific, ritualistic regimens often prescribed for hospitalized patients.[123]

Sociology can contribute to the treatment of illness by documenting and implying corrective responses to situations where individuals seek treatment from nonmedical sources. For example, Felix and Clausen have recommended the use of survey research to indicate the extent to which clergymen are called upon to treat symptoms of mental illness.[124] If this is found to occur often, some program of co-ordination between pastoral counseling and professional psychiatric services is called for. A recent study implies the widespread use of clergy for such a purpose in showing that people with symptoms of mental illness are stigmatized less by pastoral assistance than by a visit to a psychiatrist.[125]

As mentioned earlier, sociological research has been carried out which offers guidance to those concerned with posthospital rehabilitation. Social environments differ in the extent to which mental patients discharged to them are able to establish satisfactory levels of occupational and social functioning. Patients released to parental families tend to function at lower levels than those discharged to conjugal families.[126] This difference is a likely result of the fact that the roles of husband and father require more activity than does the role of child. Thus if the goal is to maximize functioning, the likelihood for success is greater where the patient will be discharged to a conjugal family. Another study showed the greater acceptibility of the mentally retarded in lower-class than in middle-class families.[127] With regard to the physically disabled, one study found that the married, males with financial dependents, females with homemaking responsibilities, and those with a favorable attitude toward the hospital showed better physical functioning in their home settings than did those with opposite characteristics.[128] However, a similar study employing a heavily Jewish sample found that married patients had lower posthospital levels of functioning than did the nonmarried. This result was attributed to the disabling consequences of the protective tendencies of Jewish spouses.[129] Studies such as these provide some of the evidence required for rational decisions as to which patients shall be discharged and which retained under institutional care.

Beginning with Parsons' casting of illness into a social-role framework, theory and research dealing with the "sick role" have pointed to the effect on rehabilitation of the behavior of significant others in the environment, including the physician, who influence the patient's choice between the sick role and other roles.[130] This literature directs the physician's attention to a broad set of environmental influences which, viewed negatively, may cause the patient to occupy the sick role unnecessarily long or which, viewed optimistically, are potential leverage points for the exertion of pressures toward rehabilitation.

Sociology is contributing to rehabilitation also by identifying factors associated with the *need* for rehabilitation efforts. The author is collaborating in an effort to determine empirically which of the patient's social and psychological attributes as of the time chronic illness develops are associated with his future level of physical, psychological, and social functioning. If these attributes are identified, it will be possible, at an early stage in the illness process, to single out those likely to function most poorly and hence most in need of rehabilitation.

The most substantial application of sociology to the rehabilitation process seems to have occurred in mental hospitals. Whether this is due to the fact that the relevance of social factors to mental illness is inherently more obvious than is their bearing on physical symptoms or whether, as seems more likely, it results from the intellectual influence of sociology on psychiatry as a whole cannot be readily ascertained.[131]

The following describes the scope of social research's contribution to patient care at the Boston Psychopathic Hospital:

> Most of the advances in ward care were based upon systematic observations. Observations of interaction on the ward led to an appreciation of the general low level of human intercourse, the marked psychological and social distance between personnel and patient, the gratifying effectiveness of occupational and recreational therapists with their special skills, the necessity for continued changing of activities to prevent slumps. . . . Studies of factors in rapport led to an appreciation of how various traits in patients attract or repel personnel, and this knowledge led in turn to emphasis upon the forgotten patient and eventually to resolution of antipathies through group therapeutic sessions with personnel. Studies of ward society gave insight into patient leaders, satellites, and isolates, and the potential importance of "place" in that society. . . . Observations of patients and relatives in interaction during the visiting hour gave cause for considerable positive thinking about the role of relatives in treatment and smoothed the way for longer visiting hours.[132]

The ideal psychiatric procedure to accomplish the changes in values and personality required for the patient's adjustment to society consists of intensive treatment by a psychiatrist. However, because of the shortage of psychiatrists, mental-hospital administrators have been forced to search for alternative modes of treatment. One such alternative, which has been described as "social treatment" or "social recovery," involves an application of the basic sociological theorem that values and personality are affected by all kinds of social interaction and not merely by contact with psychiatrists. The strategy is thus to utilize day-to-day contacts between patients and semi- and nonprofessional staff to effect desired changes in patients' attitudes and behavior.[133]

The role played by sociology here has not been limited to its suggestion of this treatment method. Cumming, Clancey, and Cumming have shown how methods of implementing "social recovery" in one mental hospital were derived from sociological principles.[134] They note that earlier attempts to establish such a treatment program at this hospital had failed because the dominant custodial tone of ward culture had not been sufficiently changed to a therapeutic one. This in turn was apparently due to the fact that changes in hospital social structure were required in order to bring ward personnel into greater contact with the higher echelons, from which the therapeutic philosophy was being dispensed. A related obstacle to the earlier effort had been the choice of nursing-staff members of low informal standing to be trained in, and in turn influence their colleagues toward, therapeutic social treatment.

To avoid these mistakes and produce the desired change in ward culture, the following steps, emanating from sociological considerations, were undertaken. The executive echelon of the nursing hierarchy was expanded to provide more therapeutically oriented leaders and so increase the amount of protherapeutic social interaction experienced by lower-echelon ward personnel. New formal lines of communication were established and strictly enforced to insure that patient care decisions had to pass through organizational nodes committed to a therapeutic orientation. In a further effort to bring all wards into the main stream of the new therapeutic program use was made of the sociological theorem that increasing the division of labor raises the level of social integration. For example, the possibility that one ward might persist as an isolated island of custodialism was avoided in the following way. Two wards were placed under the *administrative* authority of a single supervisor, but two additional staff members were charged with responsibility for the treatment program in the two wards. This arrangement forced communication between the wards and reduced the likelihood that one of them would remain isolated from the therapeutic program. Finally, applying the debatable sociological hypothesis that informal social rank is associated with the ability to transform group norms, the additional executive positions described above were filled from current staff on a seniority basis, on the assumption that these individuals could be imbued with a therapeutic orientation which they would then transmit to the lower echelon. In any event, this method of filling the new top positions avoided the status threats which had been experienced earlier when such jobs were filled without regard to seniority.

That these applications of sociological knowledge produced the desired results is suggested by data showing an increase in the proportion of patients participating in the hospital's activity program and by a decrease in the hospital's population. There is evidence that the influence of sociological concepts on the structuring of treatment programs in mental hospitals has been increasing in recent years.[135]

A number of other sociological writings suggest, explicitly or implicitly, application to the structuring of therapeutic organizations.[136] While peer-group therapy has long been familiar in psychiatric treatment, it has been suggested that recovery and rehabilitation can be thus enhanced in general hospitals too. Brown recommends, to counteract the socially disabling effects of stays in general hospitals, that patients be encouraged to assume active, utilitarian roles within the hospital.[137] She mentions as possibilities here serving as a language interpreter for other patients and teaching one's skills to other patients desirous of learning them. Brown concludes, "There are numerous ways whereby patients can engage in social interaction symbolic of normal living that may help to reduce boredom and strengthen their self-respect and returning sense of independence." [138]

SOCIOLOGICAL CONTRIBUTIONS TOWARD MORE SATISFACTORY INTERACTION BETWEEN PATIENTS AND MEDICAL PERSONNEL

Sociological training, formal or informal, can affect the orientations of medical personnel in a number of ways so as to improve the quality of their interaction with patients. In the first place, merely learning to view human behavior as an object of scientific concern can serve to produce intellectual in lieu of emotional reactions to patient behavior that deviates from the doctor's or nurse's values.[139] Since medical services are so often dispensed across social-class and ethnic boundaries the development of intellectual and the extinction of emotional responses to patient behavior should improve the latter's satisfaction with medical care and increase his utilization thereof. Macgregor, in describing her sociology course for nursing students, comments:

If, for example, she [the nurse] sees the woman who is a drug addict only as a "social parasite," the Mexican peasant who spits on the floor as "disgusting," the "swarm" of relatives who visit the Italian patient as a "nuisance," or the recently physically rehabilitated patient who does not want to return to work as "lazy," such conceptions are bound to get between her and her ability to give constructive care.[140]

Exposure to the concept of culture variation, and familiarity with the specific content of cultures prevalent in his patient population, should insulate the medical practitioner from the unpleasant experience of "culture shock" as a result of contact for which he has not been properly prepared with modes of thinking and acting which deviate sharply from his own.[141]

Sociological knowledge may contribute to the effectiveness of therapeutic relationships by indicating the combinations of therapist and patient characteristics that bode for successful therapeutic interaction. Simmons, drawing on empirical studies of psychiatric practice, suggests: "The degree to which . . . mutual trust . . . will be present in a given professional–patient relationship varies inversely with the amount of social distance. . . . The therapeutic relationship should function at its optimum where professional and patient are of the same class status." [142]

A closely related outgrowth of sociological awareness is the consideration, in assigning patients to medical institutions, of the compatibility between the patient's behavior and the institution's culture. Brown cites the case of a hysterectomy patient who, after successful surgery, began to decline, emotionally and physically, for no apparent reason.[143] The patient's surgeons called as a consultant a psychiatrist, who observed that the patient had been accustomed to receiving much more attention than had been given her in the hospital. When such attention was not forthcoming the patient became demanding, but this merely led the hospital staff to ignore her still more, thus further upsetting the patient and impeding her recovery. The psychiatrist noted that the hospital was of the "old American" variety, where emotional restraint was highly valued, and suggested that the patient would have been better off in the local Jewish hospital, which "was accustomed to care for patients who expressed their feelings readily and freely. In that institution it might be the quiet, restrained patients who would be overlooked and hence might receive inadequate attention." [144] Most important for our purposes is the psychiatrist's comment that at one time these observations would not have occurred to him, but that of late he had been in frequent contact with social scientists. These conversations had led him to consider, for the first time, he admitted, the relevance of cultural factors to the behavior of patients and hospital staff.

Sociological research and analysis can pinpoint sources of the hostility with which some laymen view medicine. To the extent that these sources are within the control of the medical profession they can be manipulated so as to reduce tension in the medical–layman relationship. Where these roots of conflict are not controllable, awareness of them on the part of medical personnel may be least produce more forbearance toward hostile patients.[145] It has also been suggested that public antipathy toward medicine results from public imposition upon medicine of unusually stringent and hard-to-fulfill ideals of scientific knowledge and devotion to the public interest.[146] A related hypothesis is that ambivalence toward physicians results from their being judged simultaneously high both in terms of social stratificational criteria and with respect to the criterion of public service.[147] With regard to this second point Gamson and Schuman comment:

> Thus, the observer must reconcile the picture of the dedicated and selfless healer devoted to the public welfare at considerable personal sacrifice with that of the wealthy and status-conscious sportscar owner organized in a trade association which helps to enforce "fair trade" through opposition to federally sponsored health programs. Both images have elements of truth, and ambivalence may well be the result.[148]

Knowledge of the obstinate social factors that impede recovery contributes to a realistic assessment on the doctor's part of the boundaries of currently possible care and thus improves his relationships with patients.[149]

SOCIOLOGICAL CONTRIBUTIONS TO DECISIONS CONCERNING THE
LOCATION OF HEALTH ORGANIZATIONS AND TO COMMUNITY
HEALTH PROGRAMS

Since information as to levels of health is a major factor in planning the location of health facilities, one contribution that sociology can make is to aid in the measurement of health levels. Adequate measurement requires that all dimensions of the phenomena at issue be taken into account. Since health does have a distinctive *social* component, which consists of the extent to which the individual is capable of performing his various social roles, it would seem that efforts at health measurement require sociological assistance.[150]

Weiner and his associates studied the need for rehabilitation services among members of the Amalgamated Clothing Workers Union.[151] It was found that very few of the chronically ill union members were receiving rehabilitation and that one reason was the belief held by many of them that rehabilitation could do them no good. Fellow workers, however, constituted an important norm-giving reference group for these individuals. Therefore it was recommended that health committees be organized in the various shops with the mission of identifying individuals in need of rehabilitation and encouraging them to seek such care. This study also identified a number of problems facing chronically ill members of the union which required the development of new social arrangements in the areas of housing, finances, transportation, and occupational roles. Thus relatively minor modifications in their duties could mean the difference between forced retirement and continued employment for a number of workers:

> For example, a cutter with a cardiac condition might be able to continue at work if he did not have to lift heavy bolts of cloth. Special adapters for sewing machines could enable some arthritis and stroke victims to continue working as operators. Such job modifications would minimize the impact of disability as well as improve the financial status of many of the chronically ill.[152]

APPLICATION OF SOCIOLOGICAL METHODS TO THE EVALUATION OF MEDICAL PROGRAMS

In recent years American medicine has engaged in considerable self-examination. Among the problems that have been uncovered are the segmentation and impersonality of medical care, as a consequence of its increasing specialization, and the failure of medicine to treat psychological and sociological aspects of disease with the effectiveness evidenced in dealing with its biological features. In response to these difficulties a number of medical schools have introduced the teaching of comprehensive care into their clinical training programs. This has consisted of a revamping of clinical training in an effort to give medical students more continuous and thorough contact with individual patients and to sensitize them to psychological and social aspects of illness.[153] Sociologists and psychologists have been called upon to apply their expertise in the evaluation of programs of planned social action to determine the impact of these educational innovations on the attitudes with which students approach medical practice, the quality of medical care received by the clinic patients whom these students treat, and the amount of technical medical knowledge learned by the students. One evaluation study revealed that the course in comprehensive care raised students' estimates of the amount of time a doctor should spend with each patient and increased students' concern for the patient's welfare.[154] Evaluation studies at two different medical schools found, for certain attitudes concerning comprehensive care, that the effect of the new program was to retard a deterioration that otherwise takes place over the four years.[155] These evaluation studies have rendered further assistance to medical education by showing what types of students are affected most by these new programs. For example, it was shown that emotional involvement with the family for whose medical care a student was responsible increased concern for the welfare of patients primarily among students who at first had the least such concern.[156]

Another recent evaluation study measured the effects of televised lectures on physicians' levels of medical information.[157] The results of this study implied the need for modification of the content of the lectures if their prime goal, namely informing the less well-trained physician, was to be realized. It was demonstrated that certain lectures produced an increase in knowledge only among the already better-informed doctors.

OTHER SOCIOLOGICAL CONTRIBUTIONS TO
MEDICAL PROFESSIONS

Sociology and anthropology have long been concerned with the processes whereby new ideas, inventions, and the like spread through a population. Sociological research on the diffusion of information within the medical profession can suggest procedures for increasing the number of practitioners who are aware of new medical developments. The empirical research by Coleman, Katz, and Menzel on physician adoption of a new drug documents the role played by professional and social ties among physicians in effecting adoptions during the first few months of the drug's availability.[158] The research points out that medical journals are actually a more powerful source of influence than one would assume merely on the basis of the proportion of physicians reading them, since these readers include a disproportionately great number of those who discuss professional matters with medical colleagues.

By analyzing the social characteristics of patients, sociologists can explore, along dimensions that medical personnel might ignore, the extent to which medical findings and treatment procedures are broadly applicable. For example, Hunt, drawing on studies of the relationship between social class and mental illness, notes the finding that lower-class individuals are underrepresented among patients undergoing psychoanalysis.[159] Thus, if psychoanalytic theory is based on experience in treating patients, it may not be valid with respect to lower-class behavior. A corollary observation is that treatment procedures derived from this theory may not be effective when administered to lower-class patients. The latter argument is supported by Hollingshead and Redlich's finding that even when payments were waived lower-class patients were disproportionately likely to break off psychotherapeutic treatment.[160]

To the extent that social factors underly public attitudes toward health programs, the sociologist, by identifying these factors, can suggest ways of increasing public support for such programs. Perhaps the greatest amount of research of this type has been carried out on the fluoridation issue. As pointed out earlier, however, much of this research has identified underlying factors such as alienation, which are not within the power of health administrators to manipulate. Nonetheless, sociological work in this area has provided some leads for those desirous of achieving public acceptance of fluoridation. For example, it has been found that when the public-health dentist assumes a political role and actively campaigns for fluoridation his scientific credibility suffers and the cause of fluoridation is set back.[161]

REFERENCES

NOTE: *The author has profited greatly from the personal guidance and the writings of Professor Patricia L. Kendall. He is indebted to Dr. George Reader for advice and a generous permission to use office time in the work for this chapter. Professor Paul Lazarsfeld gave considerable editorial help. During the preparation of this chapter, the author was supported by United States Public Health Service Grant No. 5T1GM1070.*

1. Odin W. Anderson and Milvoy S. Seacat, *The Behavioral Scientists and Research in the Health Field—A Questionnaire Survey* (New York: Health Information Foundation, 1957), pp. 1–2.
2. Odin W. Anderson and Milvoy S. Seacat, *An Analysis of Personnel in Medical Sociology* (New York: Health Information Foundation, 1962), p. 2.
3. Robert Straus, "The Nature and Status of Medical Sociology," *American Sociological Review*, XXII (April, 1957), 200.
4. Anderson and Seacat, *The Behavioral Scientists*, pp. 3–4.
5. Roger L. Buck, "Behavioral Scientists in Schools of Medicine," *Journal of Health and Human Behavior*, II (Spring, 1961), 60.
6. Anderson and Seacat, *An Analysis*, p. 3.
7. *Ibid.*
8. Buck, *op. cit.*, p. 61.
9. Straus, *op. cit.*, p. 201.
10. *Medical Sociology Newsletter* (a publication of the Section of Medical Sociology of the American Sociological Association), I (December, 1965), 5.
11. Straus, *op. cit.*, p. 201; Buck, *op. cit.*, p. 60.
12. For a discussion of the idea of "strategic research sites" see Robert K. Merton, "Problem-Finding in Sociology," in Robert K. Merton, Leonard Broom, and Leonard S. Cottrell, Jr., eds., *Sociology Today* (New York: Basic Books, 1959), pp. xxvi–xxix.
13. For related, although not identical, distinctions, see Straus, *op. cit.*, p. 203; Howard E. Freeman, Sol Levine, and Leo G. Reeder, "Present Status of Medical Sociology," in Howard E. Freeman, Sol Levine, and Leo G. Reeder, eds., *Handbook of Medical Sociology* (Englewood Cliffs, N.J.: Prentice-Hall, 1963), p. 476; Patricia L. Kendall, "Medical Sociology in the United States," *Social Science Information*, II (March, 1963), 1.
14. Oswald Hall, "Sociological Research in the Field of Medicine," *American Sociological Review*, XVI (October, 1951), 639.
15. Theodore R. Anderson and Seymour Warkov, "Organizational Size and Functional Complexity," *American Sociological Review*, XXVI (February, 1961), 23–28.
16. Howard B. Kaplan and Samuel W. Bloom, "The Use of Sociological and Social-Psychological Concepts in Physiological Research: A Review of Selected Experimental Studies," *Journal of Nervous and Mental Disease*, XIII (August, 1960), 128–134.
17. Howard E. Freeman and Ozzie G. Simmons, "Mental Patients in the Community," *American Sociological Review*, XXIII (April, 1958), 147–155; Howard E. Freeman and Ozzie G. Simmons, "Social Class and Posthospital Performance," *American Sociological Review*, XXIV (June, 1959), 345–351; Howard E. Freeman and Ozzie G. Simmons, *The Mental Patient Comes Home* (New York: Wiley, 1963); Jane R. Mercer, "Perspectives for Understanding the Mentally Retarded," *Social Problems*, XIII (Summer, 1965), 18–34.

18. Eliot Freidson, "The Sociology of Medicine," *Current Sociology*, X–XI (1961–1962), 127.
19. Robert K. Merton, George G. Reader, and Patricia L. Kendall, eds., *The Student Physician* (Cambridge: Harvard University Press, 1957).
20. Michael M. Davis, "Social Medicine as a Field for Social Research," *American Journal of Sociology*, XLIV (September, 1938), 274–279.
21. *Ibid.*, p. 279.
22. See, for example, J. A. Ryle, "Social Medicine: Its Meaning and Scope," *Milbank Memorial Fund Quarterly*, XXII (January, 1944), 58–71; Hugh R. Leavell, "Contributions of the Social Sciences to the Solution of Health Problems," *New England Journal of Medicine*, CCXLVII (1952), 885–897; Howard Reid Craig, The Introduction, in Iago Galdston, ed., *Social Medicine: Its Derivations and Objectives* (New York: Commonwealth Fund, 1949), pp. vii–xi; Iago Galdston, *The Meaning of Social Medicine* (Cambridge: Harvard University Press, 1954); Leo W. Simmons and Harold G. Wolff, *Social Science in Medicine* (New York: Russell Sage Foundation, 1954); Cecil G. Sheps and Eugene H. Taylor, *Needed Research in Health and Medical Care* (Chapel Hill: University of North Carolina Press, 1954).
23. Sheps and Taylor, *op. cit.*
24. Edward L. Bortz, "Social Components in Medicine," *Annals of Internal Medicine*, XIV (December, 1940), 1071.
25. *Ibid.*, pp. 1070–1071; Henry E. Sigerist, *The University at the Crossroads* (New York: Henry Schuman, 1946), pp. 128–131.
26. Sigerist, *op. cit.*
27. See, for example, Milton I. Roemer, "Social Science and Organized Health Services," *Human Organization*, XVIII (Summer, 1959), 75–77; Milton I. Roemer, "Health Service Organization as a Task in Applied Social Science," *Canadian Journal of Public Health*, XLV (April, 1954), 133–145; William R. Willard, "New Medical Schools: Some Preliminary Considerations," *Journal of Medical Education*, XXXV (February, 1960), 93–107. For a description of the extent to which sociologists have actually met these demands, see the discussion on actual uses of sociology below.
28. See Robert Straus and John A. Clausen, "Health, Society, and Social Science," *The Annals of the American Academy of Political and Social Science*, CCCXLVI (March, 1963), 4; Leonard S. Cottrell, Jr., and Eleanor Sheldon, "Problems of Collaboration between Social Scientists and the Practising Professions," *The Annals*, CCCXLVI (March, 1963), 129–130; Walter E. Boek and Herman E. Hilleboe, "Role of a Social Scientist in Public Health," *Human Organization*, XIV (Summer, 1955), 26–27; Frances Cooke Macgregor, *Social Science in Nursing* (New York: Russell Sage Foundation, 1960).
29. Sigerist, *op. cit.*, p. 114.
30. Esther Lucile Brown, *Newer Dimensions of Patient Care*, Part III (New York: Russell Sage Foundation, 1965), pp. 10–11; Donald Young, "Sociology and the Practicing Professions," *American Sociological Review*, XX (December, 1955), 647; Ozzie G. Simmons and James A. Davis, "Interdisciplinary Collaboration in Mental Illness Research," *American Journal of Sociology*, LXIII (November, 1957), 298–299; Alexander Robertson, "A Commentary on Sociology in the Medical School," *Canadian Medical Association Journal*, LXXXIV (April 1, 1961), 704.
31. Brown, *op. cit.*, pp. 10–11, 13, 46.
32. David G. French, "The Behavioral Sciences and the Professions," *Public Health Reports*, LXXI (May, 1956), 507.
33. For a description of tensions between sociologists and clinically oriented medical

personnel occurring in the context of a study of mental-patient rehabilitation, see Simmons and Davis, *loc. cit.*

34. Buck, *op. cit.,* p. 61.
35. *Ibid.*
36. William R. Rosengren, "The Organization Context of Social Research in Health and Mental Health," unpublished manuscript, Western Reserve University, 1965, p. 5.
37. Louis Wirth, "Clinical Sociology," *American Journal of Sociology,* XXXVII (July, 1931), 49–66; Abraham J. Simon, "Illness and the Psychodynamics of Stressful Life Situations as Seen in a Children's Clinic," *Journal of Health and Human Behavior,* I (Spring, 1960), 13–17.
38. *Ibid.,* pp. 61–62.
39. For a more recent reference to physicians' reliance on social workers for sociological knowledge see Samuel W. Bloom, "The Role of the Sociologist in Medical Education," *Journal of Medical Education,* XXXIV (July, 1959), 670–671.
40. Esther Lucile Brown, *op. cit.,* p. 21; Roger W. Little, "The Social Side of Casework," *Social Casework,* XXXI (April, 1950), 162–164; Alice Ullmann, "Social Work in a Home Care Program," *Journal of Chronic Diseases,* XV (December, 1962), 925–934.
41. For further evidence on this point see the concluding section of this chapter.
42. For examples of this in areas other than medical sociology, see Ronald Lippitt, "Case Studies of Utilization of the Behavioral Sciences," and Wilson, "The Communication and Utilization of the Results of Agricultural Research by American Farmers," in *Case Studies in Bringing Behavioral Science into Use* (Stanford: University Institute for Communication Research, 1961), pp. 33, 78–79.
43. See, for example, Boek and Hilleboe, *op. cit.,* p. 27; Roger L. Buck, "Training Social Scientists for Medical Research and Teaching," *Journal of Health and Human Behavior,* I (Spring, 1960), 53; French, *op. cit.,* p. 509; Macgregor, *op. cit.,* pp. 295–297; Julian Samora, "The Social Scientist as Researcher and Teacher in the Medical School," *Journal of Health and Human Behavior,* I (Spring, 1960), 45; Mary E. W. Goss and George G. Reader, "Collaboration between Sociologists and Physician," *Social Problems,* LV (July, 1956), 87.
44. Charles M. Wylie, "Administrative Research in the Rehabilitation of Stroke Patients," *Rehabilitation Literature,* XXV (January, 1954), 6–7.
45. *Ibid.*
46. Lawrence W. Friedmann, Letter to the Editor, *Archives of Physical Medicine and Rehabilitation,* XLIII (1962), 578.
47. Mary E. W. Goss, "Influence and Authority among Physicians," *American Sociological Review,* XXVI (February, 1961), 39–50.
48. Roland L. Warren, *Social Research Consultation* (New York: Russell Sage Foundation, 1963), p. 33.
49. Cottrell and Sheldon, *op. cit.,* p. 133.
50. Macgregor, *op. cit.,* p. 256; Goss and Reader, *op. cit.,* pp. 83–86.
51. Young, *op. cit.,* p. 647.
52. With respect to similarities between the medical and sociological subcultures see Cottrell and Sheldon, *op. cit.,* p. 130, and Jack H. Curtis, "Sociology and Medicine: Some Steps Toward Rapprochement," *American Catholic Sociological Review,* XXI (Spring, 1960), 14–15.
53. Alvin W. Gouldner, "Theoretical Requirements of the Applied Social Sciences," *American Sociological Review,* XXII (February, 1957), 96–98; Charles Y. Glock, "Applied Social Research: Some Conditions Affecting Its Utilization," in *Case Studies in Bringing Behavioral Science into Use,* p. 3; Stephen Kegeles, "Some Unanswered Questions and Action Implications of Social Research in Fluorida-

tion," *Journal of Social Issues,* XVII (1961), 76–77; Warren G. Bennis, "Theory and Method in Applying Behavioral Science to Planned Organizational Change," *Journal of Applied Behavioral Science,* I (October–November–December, 1965), 340.

54. *Ibid.* See also Gouldner, *op. cit.,* p. 96.
55. Personal communication.
56. Edward A. Suchman, "Socio-Medical Variations among Ethnic Groups," *American Journal of Sociology,* LXX (November, 1964), 319–331; Edward A. Suchman, "Social Patterns of Illness and Medical Care," *Journal of Health and Human Behavior,* VI (Spring, 1965), 2–16.
57. Norman G. Hawkins, *Medical Sociology* (Springfield, Ill.: Charles C Thomas, 1958), p. 125.
58. George Foster, "Public Health and Behavioral Science: The Problems of Teamwork," *American Journal of Public Health,* LI (September, 1961), 1290.
59. Glock, *op. cit.,* p. 3.
60. Donald Young, Foreword, in Simmons and Wolff, *op. cit.*
61. Hans L. Zetterberg, *Social Theory and Social Practice* (Totowa, N.J.: Bedminster Press, 1962), pp. 18–22.
62. "The Pre-Clinical Teaching of Psychiatry," *Group for the Advancement of Psychiatry Report No. 54* (October, 1962), p. 46.
63. Edward Stainbrook and Murray Wexler, "The Place of the Behavioral Sciences in the Medical School," *Psychiatry,* XIX (August, 1956), 263–269.
64. Macgregor, *op. cit.,* p. 26.
65. Goss and Reader, *loc. cit.;* Warren, *op. cit.,* p. 46.
66. Bloom, *op. cit.,* p. 672; Joseph W. Eaton, "The Social Science Content of a Medical Curriculum," *American Sociological Review,* XXI (October, 1956), 614; E. Gartly Jaco, "Problems and Prospects of the Social Sciences in Medical Education, *Journal of Health and Human Behavior,* I (Spring, 1960), 30–31.
67. Jaco, *loc. cit.;* Donald P. Hayes and Jean K. Jackson, "Teaching Social Science in the Medical School: A Case Study in Teamwork and Practice," *Journal of Health and Human Behavior,* I (Spring, 1960), 34–41; Robin F. Badgely, "Sociology in the Medical Curriculum," *Canadian Medical Association Journal,* LXXXIV (April 1, 1961), 705–709; Stainbrook and Wexler, *loc. cit.*
68. *Ibid.,* p. 265.
69. Jaco, *op. cit.,* p. 31.
70. "The Pre-Clinical Teaching of Psychiatry," p. 18; (Committee on Medical Education of the American Psychiatric Association), "An Ouline for a Curriculum for Teaching Psychiatry in Medical Schools," *Journal of Medical Education,* XXXI (February, 1956), 118–119.
71. Bloom, *op. cit.,* p. 673.
72. Bloom, *loc. cit.;* Badgely, *loc. cit.;* Stainbrook and Wexler, *loc. cit.*
73. See Robert K. Merton, Samuel Bloom, and Natalie Rogoff, "Studies in the Sociology of Medical Education," *Journal of Medical Education,* XXXI (August, 1956), 563–564; George G. Reader, "Development of Professional Attitudes and Capacities," in *The Ecology of the Medical Student* (Evanston, Ill.: Association of American Medical Colleges, 1958).
74. Cottrell and Sheldon, *op. cit.,* p. 129.
75. Hayes and Jackson, *op. cit.,* p. 41.
76. On the relative openness of psychiatry departments to sociologists see "The Pre-Clinical Teaching of Psychiatry," Jaco, *op. cit.,* p. 34; George Rosen, "The Why and How of Sociology in Medical Training," *Environmental Health,* IV (April, 1962), 640.
77. Rosen, *loc. cit.*

78. Stainbrook and Wexler, *op. cit.*, pp. 265–266.
79. This chapter will be followed by a description of such a department. See "Behavioral Science in a University Medical Center," below.
80. Stainbrook and Wexler, *op. cit.*, pp. 265–266.
81. Hayes and Jackson, *op. cit.*, p. 40; Bloom, *op. cit.*, p. 672.
82. "The Pre-Clinical Teaching of Psychiatry," pp. 45–46.
83. Hayes and Jackson, *op. cit.*, p. 37; French, *op. cit.*, p. 509.
84. Buck, *op. cit.*, p. 60.
85. Julius A. Roth, "Management Bias in Social Science Study of Medical Treatment," *Human Organization*, XXI (Spring, 1962), 47–50.
86. *Ibid.*, p. 48.
87. *Ibid.*, pp. 48–49.
88. Stainbrook and Wexler, *op. cit.*, p. 265; see also Robertson, *op. cit.*, p. 703.
89. "The Pre-Clinical Teaching of Psychiatry," pp. 45–46.
90. Bloom, *op. cit.*, p. 671. See also Doris Schwartz, Alice Ullmann, and George Reader, "The Nurse, Social Worker, and Medical Student in a Comprehensive Care Program," *Nursing Outlook*, VI (January, 1958).
91. Eaton, *loc. cit.*
92. Samora, *op. cit.*, p. 42.
93. Stainbrook and Wexler, *op. cit.*, p. 263.
94. Samuel W. Bloom, Albert F. Wessen, Robert Straus, George G. Reader, and Jerome K. Myers, "The Sociologist as Medical Educator: A Discussion," *American Sociological Review*, XXV (February, 1960), 97.
95. Cottrell and Sheldon, *op. cit.*, p. 133. See also Macgregor, *op. cit.*, p. 289.
96. Boek and Hilleboe, *op. cit.*, p. 27.
97. Warren, *op. cit.*
98. Rosengren, *op. cit.*, p. 22.
99. Buck, *op. cit.*, p. 64.
100. Anderson and Seacat, *An Analysis*, p. 2.
101. *Ibid.*
102. *Ibid.*
103. Buck, *op. cit.*, pp. 61–62.
104. Anderson and Seacat, *op. cit.*, p. 2; Rosengren, *op. cit.*, p. 22.
105. Medical Sociology Newsletter, *op. cit.*, p. 5.
106. See, for example, Elihu Katz and Paul F. Lazarsfeld, *Personal Influence* (Glencoe, Ill.: The Free Press, 1955); Helen Block Lewis, "An Experiment on the Operation of Prestige Suggestion," in Guy E. Swanson, Theodore M. Newcomb, and Eugene L. Hartley, eds., *Readings in Social Psychology* (New York: Henry Holt, 1952), pp. 18–27.
107. Roth, *op. cit.*, pp. 48–49. See also Freeman, Levine, and Reeder, *op. cit.*, p. 488.
108. Roth, *loc. cit.*
109. See, for example, Bernhard S. Stern, "Socio-Economic Aspects of Heart Disease," in E. Gartly Jaco, ed., *Patients, Physicians and Illness* (Glencoe, Ill.: The Free Press, 1958), p. 37; John M. Ellis, "Socio-Economic Differentials in Mortality from Chronic Diseases," in *ibid.*, p. 36.
110. See, for example, Suchman, "Social Patterns of Illness and Medical Care" and "Socio-Medical Variations among Ethnic Groups." See also Lyle Saunders, "Healing Ways in the Spanish Southwest," in Jaco, *Patients, Physicians and Illness*, pp. 189–206.
111. Kurt W. Deuschle and Hugh Fulmer, *Navajo-Cornell Field Health Research Projects* (New York: Cornell University Medical College, 1959), pp. 43–52.
112. Mark Zborowski, "Cultural Components in Responses to Pain," in Jaco, *Patients, Physicians and Illness*, pp. 256–268.

113. *Ibid.*

114. Macgregor, *op. cit.*, pp. 19–24.

115. Milton S. Davis and Robert Von Der Lippe, "Discharge from the Hospital against Medical Advice" (paper read at 1965 Meeting of the American Sociological Association).

116. Lois Pratt, Arthur Seligmann, and George G. Reader, "Physicians' Views on the Level of Medical Information among Patients," *American Journal of Public Health*, XLVII (October, 1957), 1282–1283.

117. Eugene V. Smith, "Sociology," in Peter F. Regan and Evan G. Pattishall, Jr., eds., "Behavioral Science Contributions to Psychiatry," *International Psychiatry Clinics*, II (April, 1965), 398–399.

118. *Ibid.*

119. See, for example, Brown, *op. cit.*, p. 45.

120. Macgregor, *op. cit.*, p. 80.

121. Thomas J. Scheff, "Decision Rules, Types of Error, and Their Consequences in Medical Diagnosis," *Behavioral Science*, VIII (April, 1963), 97–107.

122. Kingsley Davis, "Mental Hygiene and the Class Structure," in Patrick Mullahey, ed., *A Study of Interpersonal Relations* (New York: Hermitage, 1949), pp. 364–385.

123. Roth, *op. cit.*, p. 48. See also Julius A. Roth, "Ritual and Magic in the Control of Contagion," in Jaco, *Patients, Physicians and Illness*, pp. 229–234.

124. Robert H. Felix and John A. Clausen, "The Role of Surveys in Advancing Knowledge in the Field of Mental Health," *Public Opinion Quarterly*, XVII (Spring, 1953), 64.

125. Derek L. Phillips, "Rejection as a Consequence of Seeking Help for Mental Disorders," *American Sociological Review*, XXVIII (December, 1963), 963–972.

126. Freeman and Simmons, *The Mental Patient Comes Home.*

127. Mercer, *loc. cit.*

128. Edward Scull *et al.*, "A Follow-Up Study of Patients Discharged from a Community Rehabilitation Center," *Journal of Chronic Diseases*, XV (February, 1962), 207–213.

129. Joseph B. Rogoff, Donald V. Cooney, and Bernard Kutner, "Hemiplegia: A Study of Home Rehabilitation," *Journal of Chronic Diseases*, XVII (June, 1964), 539–550.

130. Talcott Parsons, *The Social System* (Glencoe, Ill.: The Free Press, 1951), pp. 428–479; see also Suchman, "Social Patterns of Illness and Medical Care"; Suchman, "Stages of Illness and Medical Care," *Journal of Health and Human Behavior*, VI (Fall, 1965), 114–128; Theodor Litman, "The Influence of Self Conceptions and Life Orientation Factors in the Rehabilitation of the Orthopedically Disabled," *Journal of Health and Human Behavior*, III (Winter, 1962), 249–256; Herbert S. Rabinowitz and Spirus B. Mitsos, "Rehabilitation as Planned Social Change: A Conceptual Framework," *Journal of Health and Human Behavior*, V (Spring, 1964), 2–14; G. Alan Roeher, "Significance of Public Attitudes in the Rehabilitation of the Disabled," *Rehabilitation Literature*, XXII (March, 1961), 66–72; Eliot Freidson, "Disability as Social Deviance," in Marvin B. Sussman, ed., *Sociology and Rehabilitation* (Washington: American Sociological Association, 1966), pp. 71–99.

131. It is apparent that a pioneer in the application of sociology to the treatment of mental patients, Harry Stack Sullivan, was influenced by a number of distinguished contemporaries in sociology. See Helen Swick Perry, Introduction, in Harry Stack Sullivan, *The Fusion of Psychiatry and Social Science* (New York: Norton, 1954), p. xix.

132. Milton Greenblatt, Richard H. York, Esther Lucile Brown, in collaboration

with Robert W. Hyde, *From Custodial to Therapeutic Patient Care in Mental Hospitals: Explorations in Social Treatment* (New York: Russell Sage Foundation, 1955), p. 215.

133. Greenblatt *et al., op. cit.;* Elaine Cumming, L. W. Clancey, and John Cumming, "Improving Patient Care through Organizational Changes in the Mental Hospital," *Psychiatry,* XIX (August, 1956), 249–261.

134. *Ibid.*

135. Alfred H. Stanton and Morris S. Schwartz, *The Mental Hospital* (New York: Basic Books, 1954), pp. 22–23.

136. For a critical review of some of these writings, which makes the point that they have tended to overemphasize the role of interpersonal communication and have largely overlooked the impact of social structural factors on the climate of the mental hospital, see Amitai Etzioni, "Interpersonal and Structural Factors in the Study of Mental Hospitals," *Psychiatry,* XXIII (1960), 13–22.

137. Brown, *op. cit.,* Part I, pp. 85–95; Hyman J. Weiner, "The Hospital, the Ward and the Patient as Clients: Use of the Group Method," *Social Work,* IV (October, 1959), 57–64.

138. *Ibid.,* p. 89.

139. Macgregor, *op. cit.,* p. 32.

140. *Ibid.,* p. 69.

141. Brown, *op. cit.,* p. 129.

142. Ozzie Simmons, "Implications of Social Class for Public Health," in Jaco, *Patients, Physicians and Illness,* pp. 109–110.

143. Brown, *op. cit.,* pp. 126–127.

144. *Ibid.*

145. Murray Wax, "On Public Dissatisfaction with the Medical Profession: Personal Observations," *Journal of Health and Human Behavior,* III (Summer, 1962), 155.

146. William A. Gamson and Howard Schuman, "Some Undercurrents in the Prestige of Physicians," *American Journal of Sociology,* LXVIII (January, 1963), 468.

147. See Werner Cohn, "Social Status and Ambivalence," *American Sociological Review,* XXV (August, 1960), 508–513.

148. Gamson and Schuman, *op. cit.,* p. 468.

149. This point is made by Macgregor, *op. cit.,* p. 159.

150. For a discussion of social components of health measurement see Aubrey Lewis, "Health as a Social Concept," *British Journal of Sociology,* IV (1953), 109–124.

151. Hyman J. Weiner, Shelley H. Akabas, and Bruce Grynbaum, *Demand for Rehabilitation in a Labor Union Population, Part One: Research Report* (New York: Sidney Hillman Health Center, 1964).

152. *Ibid.,* p. 96.

153. See Merton, Reader, and Kendall, *op. cit.;* Kenneth R. Hammond and Fred Kern, Jr., *Teaching Comprehensive Medical Care* (Cambridge, Mass.: Commonwealth Fund, 1959).

154. Patricia L. Kendall, "Evaluating an Experimental Program in Medical Education," in Matthew B. Miles ed., *Innovation in Education* (New York: Bureau of Publications, Teachers College, Columbia University, 1964), pp. 350–355.

155. *Ibid.,* pp. 355–356; Hammond and Kern, *op. cit.,* pp. 133–134.

156. Kendall, "Evaluating an Experimental Program," pp. 356–359.

157. Herbert Menzel and Raymond I. Maurice, *Medical Television,* unpublished manuscript (New York: Bureau of Applied Social Research, Columbia University, 1965).

158. Herbert Menzel and Elihu Katz, "Social Relations and Innovation in the Medical Profession: The Epidemiology of a New Drug," *Public Opinion Quarterly*, XIX (Winter, 1955–1956), 337–352; James Coleman, Elihu Katz, and Herbert Menzel, "The Diffusion of an Innovation among Physicians," *Sociometry*, XX (December, 1957), 253–270; see also Raymond Maurice, Herbert Menzel, and Rolf Meyersohn, "Physicians' Information Levels, as Affected by Milieu, Contact with Colleagues and Current Awareness Activities," Sixth World Congress of Sociology, September, 1966.

159. Raymond G. Hunt, "Social Class and Mental Illness: Some Implications for Clinical Theory and Practice," *American Journal of Psychiatry*, XVI (June, 1960), 1065–1069.

160. August B. Hollingshead and Fredrick C. Redlich, *Social Class and Mental Illness* (New York: Wiley, Science Editions, 1964), pp. 350–351.

161. Kegeles, *op. cit.*, p. 77.

Social Work
and Social Welfare

HENRY J. MEYER

EUGENE LITWAK

EDWIN J. THOMAS

ROBERT D. VINTER

chapter 7

Conceptions of practice are emerging in social work for which sociological analysis may be especially useful. This chapter identifies levels of practice suggested by current trends and presents in some detail three examples of possible contributions of sociological analysis.

Sociology and Social Work

Of all established professions, social work is probably most often associated with sociology. Around the turn of the century, social work and sociology were seeking to acquire separate identities, but they still shared overlapping interests in such social problems as poverty and dependency, immigration and assimilation, crime and deviant behavior, housing, and other conditions of an industrializing and urbanizing society. Both the discipline and the profession were concerned with causes and cures. Differentiation became more evident as sociology strove, particularly in the period between the two World Wars, to establish its claim to scientific status in the universities. Social work, concurrently, sought to establish its claim to professional status. During this period sociologists gave major attention to problems of research methodology while social workers, drawing heavily from psychoanalysis, turned their attention to perfecting casework as a distinctive social-work technique. The depression of the 1930's and the years of World War II shook both sociology and social work from such preoccupations. By 1950 sociology was securely established as a social science, and the interest of sociologists in social problems was no longer taken to indicate a lack of interest in building a scientific discipline. Social work, for its part, was sufficiently established as a profession to relax in some degree its fixation on an individual psychotherapeutic approach. The circumstances became congenial to mutual interaction between discipline and profession, albeit with many defensive revivals of earlier hostilities. As Donald Young put it,

> Both social science and social practice have made great advances in recent decades, but as they have progressed there has been costly failure by each to maintain sufficiently close liaison with the other. Research needs to be kept realistic by contact with the practitioners who use its results; the practitioners need to keep informed about the frontiers of research knowledge bearing on their techniques.[1]

Differing structures, norms, and ideologies hamper the interaction of sociology and social work and constitute in themselves subjects for investigation. Criteria for selecting from the existing body of scientific knowledge must be developed. Conceptualization of practice problems and theoretical issues must be made reasonably congruent. Much more research-tested theory must be developed to provide basic knowledge for both the discipline and the profession. What marks the current relationship between sociology and social work is that such work is proceeding.

Current effort to develop sociological knowledge useful for social work reflects the increasing employment of sociologists in social-work settings and the increasing interest of university sociologists in social problems. Such an interest rests on a belief that the development of sociology can be served by studying deviant behavior, institutional and community change, and the processes of deliberate influence and control. The analysis of established and experimental welfare and social-service programs has become one way to examine sociological theories. Examples may be found in delinquency (see Chapter 17 by Alfred J. Kahn in this volume), race relations (Chapter 25 by Thomas F. Pettigrew and Kurt W. Back), education (Chapter 11 by Neal Gross and Joshua A. Fishman), and population control (Chapter 31 by Philip M. Hauser). Sociological ideas about industrial society have been tested and elaborated by using them to analyze social-welfare institutions and professions.[2]

Precise data are unavailable, but some indication of the employment of sociologists in social-work education and research can be obtained from the directory of members of the American Sociological Association for 1963. Judging by their employment affiliation, approximately 6 per cent (331) of the 5,550 members listed may be formally identified with the field of social welfare.[3] Slightly more than one-third of these were affiliated with universities or colleges, primarily in faculty positions; two-thirds were affiliated with public or private agencies or research organizations. As might be expected, a higher proportion (45 per cent) of fellows and associate members was university-affiliated than was the case for student members (26 per cent university-affiliated). The number of members identified with social welfare was greater than the numbers identified with the fields of psychology (296, or 5 per cent) or health (177, or 3 per cent). Approximately one-half (52 per cent) of members identified with social welfare were students, a proportion also found among those in the fields of psychology and health. This is somewhat higher than the 44 per cent of all members of the ASA who were students. It suggests that social workers are attracted to graduate study in sociology, which is not surprising, since approximately one-third of the students admitted to schools of social work were undergraduate sociology majors.[4]

We do not have comparable information for earlier periods, but apparently a trend began about 1955 toward increasing utilization of sociologists in schools of social work and in research posts of social agencies. Most of the larger schools have sociologists or social psychologists, and sometimes both, on their faculties. Some of these schools have advanced programs heavily weighted with social-science studies.[5] Research institutes maintained by an increasing number of schools and agencies usually include sociologists on their staffs. In fact, there is a persistent, unsatisfied demand for sociologically trained research personnel, particularly with the growth of new community-oriented action and service programs in delinquency, poverty, and mental health.

Such programs have stimulated interest in social-science theories that had seemed less relevant in the earlier period when professional social work was to a large extent identified with casework and therapeutic interviews. Although ostensibly eclectic, casework in fact depended disproportionately on psychoanalytic theory. Like other psychotherapeutic approaches, casework emphasized insight gained from clinical practice more than scientific knowledge. Recently, however, the helping professions have given increased recognition to the social factors involved in individual behavior, utilizing concepts derived from theories of social role and interpersonal interaction in both diagnosis and treatment. Group treatment methods, such as family interviewing, have become acceptable (and, indeed, popular) in casework agencies.[6] Psychiatric social workers, formerly concerned almost exclusively with casework for the individual patient and his immediate family, have begun to think in terms of comprehensive community mental-health services.[7] Knowledge of the social factors involved in mental health has become necessary to develop programs of prevention and rehabilitation.

The involvement of social workers in planning and executing federally sponsored programs in other areas has also encouraged interest in sociological theories and research. Delinquency and youth projects have been conceived in terms of changing social conditions as well as individuals.[8] A major effort of the antipoverty program has been to stimulate the poor to participate in community action, and this effort draws on theories of representation and power.[9] The fact that social workers have been used in these programs to work with neighborhoods and community groups has affected the profession. For example, the number of students in schools of social work who specialize in group work and in community organization has increased at a more rapid rate than the number who specialize in casework, although the latter still predominate. Social workers also show a growing interest in practice in correctional and other institutions.[10] Although the tendency to characterize problems primarily in psychodynamic terms and to focus mainly on the individual client is still strong, the trends briefly mentioned here suggest that social work is accepting a more differentiated view of its practice.

Levels of Social-Work Practice and Theory

The four levels of practice and theory that seem to be emerging are not new conceptions to the profession. They are, rather, the extension of existing trends in practice and the reflection of theoretical developments in social science. We use the term *level* to suggest broad distinctions that may be made in the objectives of social-work practice—from helping the individual to changing features of the social system—as well as in the methods of achieving these objectives—from the use of interpersonal interaction to social legislation. The levels are, of course, interrelated. Our formulation is only a tentative attempt to locate where we believe major points of articulation between social work and social science are currently developing.

INTERPERSONAL LEVEL

The level of interpersonal interaction encompasses the central interest of social casework and social group work in ways of affecting the individual and the immediate group of which he is a part. If a line can be drawn anywhere between social casework and other psychotherapeutic modes of helping troubled persons, it is at the point where casework recognizes the interpersonal nature of its efforts.[11] The association of casework with psychoanalytic psychology has sometimes blurred this distinction and made it appear that caseworkers were interested only in intrapsychic conditions, but casework theories of helping have always included in principle the manipulation of the material environment and the social setting. The conception of the family as the client and the recent interest in family and other group interviewing techniques express this viewpoint. Group work, too, has been tending to emphasize changes in interpersonal behavior.[12] What marks this level is the use of interaction between the social worker and the client or clients—usually on a face-to-face basis—as the primary means of helping clients. More generally, it is the exercise of interpersonal influence by the professional helper to change individual behavior.

AGENCY LEVEL

A second level focuses on the social organization, or agency, as an instrument for intervention. In the past the agency was viewed primarily as a context for the interpersonal helping process and approached in terms of its effects on practice at the interpersonal level. An accent on organizational strategies has recently emerged as a by-product of the resurgence of the sociology of organizations—the studies of hospitals, prisons, schools, courts, and various institutions where social workers are employed. The scope of interest is broader than concern with the technical problems of administration in social-welfare agencies.[13] Some social workers have become sensitized to the possibility of manipulating organizations to alter the effects of the organizations on persons with whom they deal. They have been attracted to this possibility as an alternative to interpersonal helping methods which have had limited success in coping with such clients as delinquents, troublesome school children, and mental patients. The disappointing results of existing institutional efforts with such populations have stimulated social work and other helping professions to seek theories of organizational process and effect that promise more success. The role of the social worker in changing treatment organizations has not yet become clear, but there is a growing interest in this level of intervention.

COMMUNITY LEVEL

"Community organization" has long been a recognized part of social work, although it has at times been treated as peripheral by some professionals. Until recently it was identified with efforts to finance, plan, and co-ordinate services of private agencies in the local community, but its scope has become more comprehensive, leading to interest in problems such as decision making, community power structure, and community development.[14] Involvement of social workers in delinquency, poverty, and mental-health programs, as already mentioned, has broadened its perspective further. This has revived an earlier interest of social work in techniques of organization, in social movements and pressure groups, and in attacking social problems of the local community through working with a wide range of groups and organizations. The civil-rights movement has been an obvious stimulus to such developments. It may be noted that sociologists, too, have been stimulated to study community problems which had been relatively neglected in recent decades. A major objective of social-work practice at this level is to find effective methods of intervening in community processes and organization in order to deal with social problems.

SOCIETAL LEVEL

We use the term *societal level* to refer to the interest of social work in broad efforts to attack social problems through legislation and public policy. Some social workers, like some social scientists, have always been leaders in such efforts. The profession's concern with providing direct services to those needing help has often focused on expanding social security, for example, or instituting new state and federal programs to deal with conditions affecting children, criminals, the handicapped, and other disadvantaged groups. Work at this level has been only dimly recognized as a part of professional social work, and little attention has been given to technical, as distinguished from substantive, phases such as lobbying, mustering public pressure for legislation, and formulating legislation.[15] There appears to be, however, a growing sense that such activities should represent professional responsibilities and that some social workers should be trained to perform them. This will require, among other things, greater knowledge of the structure and dynamics of political systems, of law and social control, and of problems of implementing policy. There is a parallel growth of interest in political sociology, the sociology of law, and the study of social movements; the work of other social sciences is obviously also pertinent.

As these levels emerge in the professional interests of social work, the potential utility of social-science theory and research becomes more evident. Equally evident is the demand upon social scientists to investigate problems that their disciplines have neglected. There is less confusion than formerly between the respective requirements of a practicing profession and a scientific discipline.[16] There is more reason to believe that questions raised by social workers seeking a base of knowledge for practice at different levels will stimulate the development of scientific knowledge.

In the remainder of this chapter we shall illustrate how sociological perspectives illuminate significant issues of social-work practice at three of the levels. The first example highlights the fact that a wide range of experimental and theoretical work in social psychology can enhance understanding of the process of interpersonal helping and calls for a strategy to assess and assimilate existing material. We shall suggest a framework for viewing the interpersonal helping process that should make it more useful for social work.

Second, we shall apply some of the ideas developed in the sociology of organizations to a type of organization of special interest to social work: the treatment institution. We shall show one direction such analysis can take when a task of social work is visualized as the understanding and manipulation of treatment organizations to achieve desired changes in clients.

A final example will be taken from the community level. We shall deal with the organization of social services, concentrating on the question of co-ordination between organizations. Even though the research necessary to support the analysis has not yet been done, we shall suggest some variables relevant to the practitioner of community organization.

In these examples, our purpose is to illustrate how sociological conceptualizations may become useful to social work. The technical competence of social scientists is widely used in social work to plan and conduct research about clientele, social conditions, and program operations.[17] Particular concepts from sociology, such as social role, social class, role conflict, social deviancy, and the like, have also been found illuminating by social workers.[18] There has been less recognition that the application of more inclusive sociological perspectives and of substantive findings may now be fruitful.

Interpersonal Helping Processes: A Framework to Facilitate Utilization of Social-Science Materials[19]

At the interpersonal level, social work shares basic similarities with other therapeutic professions. It has depended primarily on the codification of practitioner experience and has generally explained personal problems by a psychodynamic theory of disease borrowed from psychiatry. It has been slow to adopt benefits from pertinent social-science developments. All the professions offering interpersonal help use interpersonal media as the principal means of change; that is, a professional helper, alone or with the aid of others, exerts social influence in a face-to-face relationship with one or more clients. Furthermore, the help is planned; that is, the change effort is conceived in relationship to problems of the client, possible means of intervention, and objectives of the profession offering help. These features apply to any of the helping professions, whether they work with voluntary or nonvoluntary clientele, whether the objectives are to prevent or to cure personal difficulties, whether change goals are short-term or long-term, whether the targets of change are principally cognitions, affect states, or motor behavior.

To use social-science knowledge fruitfully, the helping professions must accept two assumptions. The first is that the behavior to be affected is natural, lawful, and predictable. The second assumption is that the variables of interpersonal influence operate in contexts of interpersonal helping as they do in the rest of social life. This is not to say, however, that the range, magnitude, and particular combination of variables characteristic of the helping context would not differ from such factors in other situations. These assumptions make potentially relevant a very wide range of knowledge in psychology, social psychology, and sociology. Although we cannot assess this knowledge here, we shall suggest one way to think about interpersonal helping so that the questions asked point to various bodies of social-science knowledge.

GENERALIZING THE INTERPERSONAL HELPING PROCESS

The usual approach to providing interpersonal help in casework focuses on study, diagnosis, and treatment, giving secondary attention to the crucial activity of social influence itself.[20] We think that a more comprehensive framework of behavioral tasks is required to include all the major activities and the related decisions involved in the helping process. One useful scheme classifies these activities in three categories: (1) *obtaining information*, which includes getting facts, feelings, and evaluations relating to the client's problem; (2) *processing information*, which involves understanding the client's difficulty and planning what to do about it; and (3) *exerting social influence*, which involves setting the conditions of change, maintaining the interpersonal helping relationship, achieving and stabilizing change objectives, and terminating the relationship. Although these activities may not always be empirically separable, they are conceptually different, and we believe that the scheme makes the professional helper's work more understandable.

Using this framework, we may briefly note some of the relevant bodies of research and theory.[21] The specification of pertinent social-science areas will sometimes violate familiar conceptual boundaries and vested domains of various disciplines and helping professions. Such eclecticism, however, is necessary if we are to specify links between potentially useful scientific subject matter and the tasks of the helping process.

Obtaining Information To understand the client's problem in order to formulate a plan for change, the professional helper must obtain many types of information from and about the client. In addition to questions about the kinds of information that are needed—questions that depend essentially on the theories of behavior and of influence that are used—there are technical problems about obtaining information that have been carefully studied by social scientists. The direct verbal report of the client is usually required, and there are many studies of how to conduct interviews.[22] Information may also be obtained from test performance for which research on diagnostic and psychological testing may be relevant.[23] The professional helper may observe behavior in play and other "natural" situations, for which studies of participant and behavior observation would be pertinent.[24] He may observe role playing, about which there is a substantial literature.[25] He may use questionnaire responses and find applicable writings on questionnaire construction and interpretation.[26] Examples could be multiplied, but the point should be evident: the knowledge that social science has accumulated from its own interests might assist a helping profession to understand one of its activities.[27]

Processing Information   Having obtained information about the client's problem, it is necessary for the helper to use the information to understand the client better and decide what should be done. There are four typical problems in processing information for these purposes. First, there is diagnosis, an effort to understand the client's problem and its genesis. Both traditional and modern logic are important in this activity as are studies by social scientists of the inference-drawing behavior of clinicians.[28] Also relevant are research on thinking, especially as it is affected by motivational, perceptual, and cognitive processes, and the large literature on memory and forgetting, which has scarcely been related to diagnostic behavior.[29]

Second, predictions about future client behavior are often required. Logic, statistics, and probability theory are increasingly seen as sources of potentially useful guidelines for evolving predictive schemes for individuals with personal problems. The studies associated with the controversy of statistical vs. clinical prediction are pertinent.[30]

Third, the helper must formulate strategy and tactics of change. Research on thinking processes involved in formulating change plans is undeveloped, but there are various studies bearing indirectly on the component decisions of change plans. Thus decisions to accept or reject various types of clientele where clients vary in socioeconomic position, in ethnic or national origin, or in alleged amenability to treatment have been studied.[31]

Fourth, in processing information the helper must view himself as an instrument of change to be used more or less self-consciously. The studies of self-presentation and reflective processes in interaction and role taking are available here.[32]

Exerting Social Influence A first task in exerting social influence is to the conditions of change, often described as establishing the helping relationship. This requires decisions about the types of individuals who may be helped and the ways they are likely to change. Instructive here are researches on personality and persuasibility,[33] on the types of persons likely to improve with varying therapies,[34] on therapeutic continuance,[35] and on learning and susceptibility to conditioning.[36] Helper–client compatibility is one of the criteria often considered in matching clients to helpers, and there is a growing literature on personal compatibility derived from small-group and sociometric studies and from investigations of marital compatibility.[37] The problem arises of how large the therapeutic group should be. Research and theory on effects of group size can contribute to the solution of this problem.[38] Setting the conditions of change also involves determining the length and frequency of interviews for which studies of effects of frequency and amount of interaction,[39] of individual and group therapeutic processes,[40] and of social and sensory deprivation are germane.[41] To the early task of setting change goals, studies of level of aspiration,[42] goal clarity and ambiguity,[43] performance,[44] goal structure,[45] and sequencing of goals are pertinent. The social and organizational environment in which face-to-face contact is embedded is another factor in setting the conditions of change. Researches on social organizations in which interpersonal help is given—social agencies, treatment and correctional facilities—are pertinent.[46] Less obviously so are studies of brainwashing and thought control which offer insights into the interplay between environmental structuring and organizational ideology and how these facilitate or inhibit the achievement of change objectives.[47]

A second task in exerting social influence is to maintain the interpersonal relationship in order to achieve change objectives. Studies of factors affecting continuance in helping relationships are obviously applicable, as are researches on cohesion[48] and on the integration and equilibrium of groups.[49] Socialization of clientele is an early requisite of group maintenance, generally involving getting clients to talk about selected personal matters. Research on social learning in natural contexts could be relevant to this problem.

The other tasks in the exertion of social influence are to achieve and stabilize change and to terminate the helping relationship. Directly relevant are studies of individual and group therapeutic outcomes, including placebo phenomena, especially investigations of the effects of various therapies and therapeutic conditions and of the types of change which appear to be possible.[50] Studies of therapy processes and of group interaction processes through time offer promise of revealing initial, middle, and terminal phases of varying change efforts.[51] Research into social learning may well make increasing contributions to the theory and practice of interpersonal helping. Psychologists of various persuasions are increasingly seeing the importance for client learning of such factors as counterconditioning, extinction, discrimination learning, reinforcement, punishment, and social imitation.[52] Another promising group of inquiries relates to attitude, belief, and behavior change. Investigations of belief and attitude change,[53] factors in cognitive consistency,[54] mass communication,[55] small-group influence,[56] leadership,[57] role playing,[58] and authority and social power in different social contexts[59] may also be pertinent. Many of these studies are direct inquiries into social influence of various types and, like learning theory, should increasingly become sources of knowledge for constructing practice principles.

ASSESSING THE UTILITY OF AVAILABLE KNOWLEDGE

Examining the potentially useful social-science literature is obviously only a first step toward utilization of available knowledge. Application does not follow automatically from understanding the behavioral tasks of interpersonal helping indicated above. Only knowledge having promise for use in the *actions* of professional helpers in pursuit of their change objectives can be considered applicable. Such actions may be taken directly with clients, may be engaged in with intermediaries treated as indirect targets, or may be taken to alter the helper's behavior in other ways. A number of criteria for selecting such knowledge may be briefly mentioned here.[60]

First, the knowledge must have *content relevance*. Knowledge of interpersonal influence is most patently relevant to social work, as is knowledge of the influence processes at other levels of intervention in social work (for example, the organizational, community, and societal levels). The behavioral tasks of interpersonal helping just outlined—obtaining information, processing information, and exerting social influence—and the numerous bodies of research and theory referred to merely serve to explicate more finely the areas of pertinent content. Content in the interpersonal helping process has necessarily been most germane to this discussion of the interpersonal level of social-work intervention. There are other areas of relevant content applicable to the selection of social-science content for more general use in social work.[61]

In addition to meeting the criterion of content relevance, knowledge must also meet standards of power. Three features of the knowledge itself may be considered as defining its power. The first is that the propositions must be *valid*, this being determined mainly by the extent of empirical corroboration of the propositions. Generalizations based on poorly done studies, inconsistent findings, or limited empirical inquiry would generally not be valid. For example, the universality of the Oedipus complex, the stages of psychosexual development, and the existence of instincts have yet to be corroborated by reputable scientific methods.

A second feature of powerful knowledge is its *predictive potency,* which is a function of the formal structure of the theory. For example, a proposition embedded with many other propositions linked by logical relationships that make it possible to formulate genuine derivations contains vastly more predictive potency than a proposition that stands by itself or is among many other propositions not logically related such that when the propositions are combined, derivations may be made logically.

The third characteristic of powerful knowledge involves *potency of the variables* to which the knowledge pertains. A variable may be potent or weak, depending on how much of the variance it accounts for. For example, the variable of cognitive dissonance generally accounts for only a very small amount of the variance of the dependent variables to which it is related in empirical studies, whereas such variables as the amount and type of reinforcement and the schedules of reinforcement employed typically account for large portions of the variance of the behavior examined. Considering only the question of variable potency and these two areas of knowledge, one would therefore be constrained to employ knowledge from reinforcement theory rather than from theories of cognitive dissonance.

Although they are not always made explicit, the criteria of content relevance and knowledge power discussed above have generally been operative at least implicitly in most applications of scientific knowledge. It is becoming increasingly apparent, however, that applied fields such as social work, in which knowledge necessarily involves action, must make use of knowledge which makes possible such action. The knowledge must be engineerable, and, more specifically, the knowledge must have "engineerable referents." With few exceptions,[62] the empirical indicators, or referents, of the variables of potentially useful knowledge have simply been ignored in the applied behavioral sciences. The consequence has been that most consumers of knowledge for applied purposes end up employing essentially the same criteria for appraising the usefulness of knowledge that their nonapplied counterparts employ or, worse, they do not specify the additional requirements they demand of the knowledge they wish to apply.

The engineerable referent, as a variable indicator about which something concrete can be accomplished, has six component features. If all six are present, the referent is ideal in that it is fully engineerable.

The first requisite of the engineerable referent is that it be *identifiable.* Freud's libido and Jung's racial unconscious have no identifiable referents, to our knowledge at least, whereas such variables as group size and social class have readily identifiable referents. Clearly, if a referent is not identifiable, it cannot be accessible.

The second criterion is that of *referent accessibility,* which pertains to the extent to which any given referent may be approached by a professional helper. The importance of accessibility is that its presence enables one to manipulate a variable. Thus if the powerful members of a family are inaccessible to the professional helper, he cannot act directly through these members to alter the family, whereas if they are accessible, he may be able to achieve change.

When a referent is manipulable, that is, may be altered by a professional helper, the indicator meets the criterion of *referent manipulability*. Direct action is possible with manipulable referents. Thus the professional helper may not only have access to the influential members of a family; he may be able successfully to change their behavior so as to achieve treatment objectives. The size and composition of most groups are manipulable, as are many variables pertaining to reinforcement and punishment in face-to-face encounters. Knowledge about manipulable referents is understandably highly prized.

Ideally the referent should be not only manipulable but *operationally potent* as well. It is possible for variables that are potent in laboratory or field studies to be weak in a complex change context. Consider interpersonal attraction, a variable that has generally been found to be relatively potent in research inquiries. A client's attraction to a given helper may be insufficient to sustain the helping relationship simply because this variable may be counteracted by such factors as the client's limited time or the personal and economic costs entailed by the contacts.

A fifth referent criterion becomes relevant providing that a referent is manipulable and operationally potent. This is *manipulable cost*. Action necessarily entails costs of labor and money, and, clearly, many alternatives are not feasible simply because they cost too much. Thus one alternative to meet the problem of low income is to subsidize all the poor so as to bring their incomes up to some acceptable standard. This would indeed be a costly venture, and obviously it raises other problems as well.

A final criterion pertains to the *ethical suitability* of any proposed manipulation. The manipulation of a given referent may or may not be consistent with the profession's ethics and society's values. Bribes and sexual inducements are ethically unsuitable, although other positive reinforcers generally meet the standards of applicability previously outlined.

All these criteria of applicability may be employed as screening standards for selecting knowledge about the helping process and about other intervention areas as well. The use of the screening criteria hopefully encourages a more rational selection of scientific knowledge and a consequent adoption of the strongest knowledge for applied purposes. Furthermore, it is apparent that when knowledge is appraised against the applicability criteria, many distinct types of applicable knowledge may be identified.

Two extreme classes of knowledge are readily distinguishable. The first is *material immediately applicable for direct action*, defined by knowledge meeting all the screening criteria. Much of reinforcement theory is in this class, as is much of the research on the effects of group size and of group composition. The second is *inapplicable material,* defined by its failure to meet the criteria of content relevance, knowledge power, or the engineerable referents. Portions of knowledge on brainwashing and indoctrination fall here; many of the manipulations would not be ethically suitable, many of the claims regarding effectiveness of the procedure have been exaggerated, and the change situations have generally been so complex that it has been very difficult to isolate the operative variables.

But much knowledge from social science will not fall clearly into either of the two extreme classes, for the many screening criteria will be met in different combinations. For example, consider knowledge that meets the criteria of content relevance, knowledge power, referent identifiability, and operational potency, but is limited by virtue of variables having referents that are nonmanipulable, because inaccessible, or manipulable, but too costly or ethically unsuitable. Portions of research on the change-related personality characteristics of individuals fall here, for the personality characteristics, such as self-esteem, are not always accessible and manipulable. Knowledge of this type is useful, nonetheless, for despite the helper's general inability to alter the personality factors in question, he may alter his own behavior in working with individuals displaying the given personality characteristics. The knowledge is thus *immediately applicable for complementary or indirect action.* Such knowledge is also generally *hypothetically applicable for direct action,* providing that it is possible to discover ways to make the variable referents accessible to manipulation or, if the variables are manipulable, to find more economical or ethically suitable solutions to their use.

There are other intermediate types of applicable knowledge, but enough has been said to counter the misconception that almost all knowledge from social science is applicable to social work, or the opposite misconception that almost no knowledge from social science is applicable. The selection of scientific knowledge for use in interpersonal helping and social work in general is clearly not a simple process; rather, it calls for detailed, thoughtful appraisal of the relevance of content, the power of the knowledge, and the engineerability of the knowledge referents.

ADDITIONAL STEPS TOWARD UTILIZING SOCIAL-SCIENCE KNOWLEDGE

When social-science knowledge has been assessed for its utility, additional steps will have to be taken to complete the process of utilization. Both specific practice principles and more comprehensive practice theories will have to be developed. Science-based innovations will have to be introduced into practice, with necessary modification of agency and institutional structures. The training of practitioners will have to be altered. Although social scientists may contribute to each of these tasks, the burden will fall primarily on social-work practitioners. The main task of the social scientist will be to continue building the knowledge which the practitioner, using interpersonal helping and other intervention processes, can examine and assess.

Organizational Processes: The Treatment Organization from a Sociological Perspective[63]

The utility of sociological analysis to social work is nowhere more evident than at the organization level. When treatment institutions are viewed as social organizations, they can be subjected to the same types of analysis as other organizations studied by sociologists.[64] To illustrate how organizational theory is useful to social work, this section will describe the special features of treatment organizations and note some of the problems met with by social workers practicing at the organizational level.

In its early history social work was concerned with the reform of prisons, courts, mental hospitals, children's homes, and other institutions. This concern was motivated, however, more by humanitarian impulses than by a conception of institutions as potential instruments of treatment. At a later period, when social workers were brought onto the staffs of medical and psychiatric hospitals and public schools, they developed specializations corresponding to the "host setting." Such specializations constituted almost subprofessions,[65] and considerable attention was given to defining a distinctive role for social workers in each setting. Interest focused on how the setting limited or facilitated practice (usually of casework). Very little consideration was given to the organization itself and how it could be changed.

Stimulation for social workers to visualize organizations as instruments of treatment has come from experiments in group and milieu approaches to treating the mentally ill and delinquents. Further stimulation has come with the broadening of the sociology of organizations from studies of industry and government to studies of hospitals, correctional institutions, and schools. The empirical study of social-welfare organizations—public welfare agencies, probation offices and juvenile courts, child-guidance clinics, family-service agencies, and the like—has barely begun.[66] If there is to be social-work practice at the organizational level, it is useful to conceive of treatment organizations as a type and attempt sociological analysis that may guide research interests and suggest points at which practice theory can be developed.

SPECIAL FEATURES OF TREATMENT ORGANIZATIONS

Treatment organizations are characterized by their focus on producing changes in clientele, in contrast to organizations whose primary purpose is manufacturing goods or providing marketable services. Socialization organizations, such as schools and agencies that serve young people, also have as a major goal the changing of people, but such organizations may be differentiated from treatment organizations in terms of their conception of clients, the changes sought, and the public valuation of them. The broad and permanent changes in behavior or status sought by treatment and socialization organizations are defined by the larger society as necessary. Other types of organizations, to be sure, require participants to change, sometimes drastically, as in military organizations, but such changes are usually viewed as incidental to other goals. Treatment organizations may also have goals other than changing people (as, for example, the custodial purpose of the mental hospital), but these are viewed as secondary. It is obvious that goal emphases differ among treatment organizations and change through time.

Schools and other socialization organizations generally perceive their clientele as moving along normal developmental gradients and as motivated to change so that they respond to the learning opportunities provided to prepare them for new roles. In contrast, the clientele of treatment organizations are perceived as deviant or ill, as not moving along normal developmental gradients, and as insufficiently motivated to abandon socially disapproved roles and learn acceptable conventional ones. The conditions of their present or past are believed to impede efforts to change their disapproved behavior. Public attitudes toward treatment organizations reflect this valuation, often producing adverse sentiments and fears accompanied by the demand for punitive and repressive controls. Despite the rise of humanitarianism, treatment organizations still lack the favorable status of socialization organizations. Optimism about rehabilitation has, however, tempered some of the more extreme attitudes of the past. Public attitudes also vary according to the age, sex, and deviance of the clientele, but negative attitudes tend to prevail. The belief that deviance is intentional persists, and hence rehabilitative goals of treatment organizations are more precarious than custodial, punitive, and educational goals.[67]

TREATMENT STRATEGIES AND STAFF–CLIENT RELATIONS

Beliefs about clients and public valuations shape the strategies that treatment organizations develop for producing changes in clients and the ways they manage personnel—including professionals—engaged in the change effort. Some strategies stress manipulative persuasion; some, at the other extreme, stress coercive repression. But the deliberate structuring of staff–client relations is basic to all organizational strategies toward clients. If persuasion is emphasized, as in the typical mental-health clinic, affect and cognition are manipulated through staff–client communication. Staff are expected to view clients as "sick," essentially wanting to change, requiring individualized assessment and response, and responsive to warm and trustful relations. To follow this approach requires an esoteric, complex set of skills acquired through specialized training, usually in the educational system of a helping profession. The use of coercive approaches, in contrast, emphasizes containment and accommodation, rather than intrapersonal changes, as in the typical prison. Clients are viewed as opposed to change, rules and routines are fostered, and social distance is maintained between staff and clients. Skill in following this strategy is usually viewed as developed by experience rather than professional education. Which strategy is adopted will depend on belief systems accepted by, or imposed on, the organization. Generally, these tend to emphasize individual attributes of clients; only recently have conceptions of situational and social forces entered the ideologies of treatment organizations. The target for most treatment organizations continues to be the individual person— often abstracted and removed from his local environment—rather than the social conditions that may have generated or shaped his behavior.

Alternative strategies are evident in the way personnel treat clients. Staff–client relations vary along three dimensions. The first dimension is uniformity of procedures. All treatment organizations make distinctions among clients and adapt procedures accordingly. Sometimes the distinctions are crude: clients are assigned to categories, such as security units in prisons or "front" and "back" wards in mental hospitals, or to classifications, such as unmarried mothers or delinquents, and so forth. Clients within a category may be subjected to a common regimen and be expected to accommodate themselves appropriately. At the other extreme, the approach may be highly personalized, each client calling for a unique procedure. Some balance between these extremes is, of course, typical. The size and complexity of managerial requirements, particularly in residential institutions, probably affect the balance, but the treatment strategy adopted is in part independent of such factors. In short, the kind of staff–client relations found in a treatment organization is partly an expression of beliefs about how uniform or how differentiated treatment should be.[68]

The second dimension is the balance of gratification and deprivation. Punishment is stressed when the agency believes that the client is unable or unwilling to change; indulgence is encouraged when the client's motives are regarded as positive or when he can voluntarily terminate his affiliation with the organization. Here, again, while there are limiting conditions, the organization can exercise choice in the strategy it uses.

The third dimension on which staff–client relations vary is the complexity of change techniques utilized. Narrow approaches are more likely when the causation of client deviance is viewed in simplistic terms or the deviance is not regarded as severe. Varied techniques seem to reflect more complex theories of deviance and may represent highly esoteric and specialized activities which increase the need for co-ordination as well as for specialized personnel.

The relative effectiveness of various techniques is at present largely unknown. This affects the character of treatment organizations, increasing their dependence on professional personnel.[69]

THE HELPING PROFESSIONAL IN THE TREATMENT ORGANIZATION

The development of interpersonal helping professions—social workers, psychologists, psychiatrists, and various other counseling specialties—has coincided with the emergence of treatment organizations in health and social-welfare fields. Understanding the interdependence of professionals and organizations is a prerequisite to setting optimum conditions for their effectiveness.

Treatment organizations rely on helping professions for a number of reasons, the most obvious of which is the presumed technical competence of the helping professions. If the profession utilized is prestigious, as in the case of psychiatry, this serves to add legitimation and may enhance public acceptance, including command of resources. Such professionals also protect an organization by generalizing the certification that treatment has been properly done and clients "treated" or "rehabilitated." But the use of professionals also presents problems to the organization. When a treatment organization is dominated by a particular profession, it risks being limited by the perspective of that profession. Also, professionals may decide on operational arrangements according to what is convenient for professional practice rather than what is best for the achievement of the institution's goals. Some of the criticism of medical hospitals reflects these developments, and some social agencies, too, have been observed to be bound by limited casework perspectives.[70]

Treatment organizations vary in the extent to which they use the helping professions. For instance, prisons employ relatively few professionals, and child-guidance clinics many; public-assistance agencies use relatively few trained social workers, family service agencies many. In part, this is a reflection of the shortage of professional manpower, which allows social workers and others to choose locations congenial to their interests. In part, however, it does reflect organizational commitments to different strategies of changing clients for which professional competencies are deemed more or less useful.[71]

A special problem in treatment organizations arises from the principle of autonomy asserted by professionals, particularly in the primary areas of decisions about and transactions with clients. Such problems are complicated when there are several helping professions in the treatment agency, a circumstance likely to develop as treatment approaches become more complex. Control and co-ordination of professional behavior on behalf of organizational objectives presents a continuing problem. It is necessary to co-ordinate staff actions, particularly when organizational goals include custody, legal determinations, and similar nontherapeutic responsibilities. But it is also necessary to provide sufficient autonomy to allow the professionals to work according to their own requirements.

Mechanisms for resolving this problem include:

1. developing commitment to organizational goals;
2. increasing colleague controls through placing professionals in positions of authority, permitting collective decisions (for example, through committees and staff meetings), maintaining informal and equalitarian relations, and similar devices;
3. segregating tasks and roles so that crucial organizational decisions can be made by one hierarchy of authority while professionals can control decisions in a limited but clearly defined sector primarily affecting clients;
4. establishing the superordinate position of one among the professions in the organization: for example, making psychiatrists superior formally or informally within the organization.

Such mechanisms serve to accommodate the professional and bureaucratic requirements that characterize treatment organizations. The competencies of professionals are most likely to be developed through professional education, outside the control of the organizations, although the exercise of professional competencies will be affected by the demands of the organizations where they are practiced. The need to accommodate professionals is likely to be greater in treatment agencies than in most other types of bureaucratic organization. Further research in this area might uncover new and more fruitful arrangements, while clarifying general questions about the nature of professionalized bureaucracies.[72]

THE TREATMENT ORGANIZATION AND CLIENT MOTIVATION

Special problems for treatment organizations arise from the fact that their clientele—patients, prisoners, cases—must be simultaneously adapted to and changed. They are thus the raw material and the products of organizational activity, and the effectiveness of the organization can constantly be questioned by asking what happens to clients. The determination of optimum relations between staff and clients is made difficult by uncertainty about the organization's effectiveness in producing desired changes in its clients.

Since the clients of treatment organizations cannot usually be assumed to be motivated to change, the difficult problem is presented of coping with clients and motivating them simultaneously. Some agencies try to avoid this dilemma by accepting or selecting only those clients presumed already to be motivated to change. Most agencies, however, are obliged by other commitments to accept involuntary clients. This is the case, for example, with mental hospitals, correctional institutions, and public-assistance agencies, but so-called voluntary agencies are also often under pressures of various sorts to accept unmotivated clients. Such clients may wish to remain deviant, may be opposed to the official change objectives of the agency, and may define their participation in terms quite different from that of seeking help to change their behavior patterns. Clients may resist negative conceptions of them that have brought them to the agency and reject the disapproval by others of their condition or behavior.[73]

Initial experiences with the agency may increase the difficulty of motivating the client to change. Although the goals of the agency may be defined partly in terms of client well-being, the client must usually assume a status in the organization with minimal power, prestige, and reward. Acceptance of client status may require a major shift from the person's familiar situation. Nor can the client be motivated by the promise of promotion and advancement within the organization, as is often the case with the lower echelons of schools and other types of organizations. He cannot rise if he changes; he can only leave or be released.

The effects of such conditions may be offset to some extent by a treatment strategy that sufficiently rewards changes, but this is often vitiated by other organizational processes. Routinized and nonindividualized handling of clients, deprivations rather than rewards, denial of participation in decisions affecting themselves, and similar conditions often serve to crystallize both individual and—especially in residential agencies—collective opposition to the goals of treatment. Such developments may serve, indeed, to socialize clients in further deviant ways, as is often noted in prisons. Even when such conditions are recognized, the effort of the treatment organization to avoid them and to provide conditions that encourage change is hampered by the difficulty of evaluating the effectiveness of the organization.

PROBLEMS OF EVALUATING ORGANIZATIONAL SUCCESS

There are at least three reasons why treatment agencies find it difficult to judge their organizational success:

1. Their change goals are ambiguous or so general as to remain unclear. What is "mental health," "rehabilitation," or "better social functioning"? Defined criteria and objective measures of these goals do not exist.

2. The relation between treatment practices and outcomes is unclear.

The nature of "treatment" is largely indeterminate and of unknown validity.

3. Treatment organizations usually lack information about client performance after termination of client status.

Even when follow-up studies are pursued, the effects of the organization's interventions tend to be confounded by other influences in the life of the client after his discharge or release. All these difficulties can be reduced, but research on them is only beginning.

The limitations on objective assessment of effectiveness have several consequences for treatment organizations. They encourage emphasis on intraorganizational perspectives, press toward substitution of goals other than changing clients, and induce self-justifying doctrines in place of rational decision making. The first of these is evident in a tendency to judge organizational success by the client's adaptation to agency expectations and his relations to agency personnel, rather than in terms of his capability for performance in more general roles. "Good clients"—that is, those meeting such expectations—are presumed to have benefited without knowing anything about their extraorganizational behavior. The model patient or prisoner is one who conforms to the rules and routines; the model agency client is one who keeps his appointments and uses the language of therapy. Such organizationally valued changes may be not only irrelevant to community performance but even dysfunctional, as in the case of "institutionalization" of the mental patient. The organization needs external criteria by which to define successful client change.

Lacking such criteria, the organization may substitute excessive devotion to procedures and doctrines of treatment for outcome goals. The facilitation of professional practice may become an end in itself, or administrative efficiency and preservation of good order may become major goals. Belief systems become self-validating ritual, and the esoteric knowledge of "insiders" becomes the test of organizational success. While this serves in part as a protective device—particularly when supported by the growing prestige of the helping professions—it makes it harder for the organization to assure the public of its competence and effectiveness. This, in turn, often causes the treatment organization to elaborate its claims, rather than to seek objective evidence of its success.

The growing rationalism of the larger society and its increased reluctance to allocate resources without objective evidence of achievement[74] may, however, force the treatment organization to develop objective measures for determining effectiveness. In this process, as well as in development of alternative courses of action, sociological analysis will become increasingly important.

Interorganizational Relations: The Problem of Co-ordination between Community Agencies[75]

Social workers practicing community organization try to change social conditions through working with community groups and organizations. While continuing to work in health and welfare-planning agencies and in federated fund-raising bodies, community-organization workers are increasingly employed in urban-renewal, housing, and city-planning bodies, in interracial and intercultural agencies, in neighborhood-development programs, and in community-action efforts.[76] Sociological analysis is pertinent to a wide range of tasks of social-work practice at this level.

A problem often faced by the community-organization practitioner, which illustrates the potential utility of sociological analysis, is the problem of what determines the form of co-ordination between social agencies. The practitioner needs to know the possibilities and limitations of co-ordination, the forms which are feasible and useful under different conditions, and the factors which determine the effectiveness of different patterns of co-ordination. Sociological research and theory are not well developed on this problem,[77] but we shall suggest some relevant variables and indicate promising directions for analysis.

RELATIONS BETWEEN ORGANIZATIONS

Continuity of relationships and the extent to which they are formal or informal are two dimensions that differentiate forms of co-ordination between organizations. At one extreme, an organization may seek to relate its activities to another organization on an occasional, sporadic, *ad hoc* basis, as, for example, when a family social agency co-ordinates its service with a domestic-relations court in handling a case involving marital problems. At the other extreme, an organization may establish continuous relations with another organization, as when an agency serving unmarried mothers works out relatively permanent arrangements with an adoption agency. Under either of these circumstances, the relations may be formalized—for example, by laws or established rules—or left informal—for example, by personal contact between executives or staff of the agencies. Of course, intermediate positions are common, and several arrangements may characterize the relations between a given organization and all the other organizations it deals with.

Three determinants of continuity and formality seem to be central. Variation in these factors may be taken as a basis for estimating when different types of co-ordination are likely to occur and for judging their relative appropriateness. These factors are (1) agency awareness of dependence on other agencies, (2) the number of organizations engaged in the activity, and (3) the nature of the communications involved in the transactions between the agencies.

Agency Awareness of Dependence The extent to which a co-ordinating procedure will have a regular as opposed to an *ad hoc* basis depends in part on whether the agency, as a matter of agency policy, recognizes its dependence on other agencies. Official recognition—as distinguished from awareness of individual staff members, outsiders, or the actual degree of interdependence—is what is meant here by "agency awareness." For example, there may be many agencies dealing with one hard-core family: for example, the school, public-health clinic, courts, public-assistance agency, police, and several private social agencies.[78] These various agencies may have no explicit policy of co-ordination, despite the fact that the work of each affects that of others. Personnel from the several agencies may recognize the interdependence, but, without explicit agency policy, they can only work out personalized, informal arrangements. Even when interdependency is recognized at executive echelons, it may not be acknowledged officially. It seems a reasonable hypothesis that the more agency awareness there is, the more continuous and formal the co-ordination between agencies will be.

Number of Agencies As size affects a single organization, so the number of organizations aware of interdependencies may be expected to affect the formality and continuity of their relations. If only two or three agencies are involved, their contacts can readily be handled in more or less informal meetings of representatives. If there are many organizations—say, one hundred or more—communication between them becomes so difficult that some machinery for communication is necessary, especially when the organizations represent different fields and their personnel use different professional vocabularies. Fixed time schedules, agenda for meetings, and special co-ordinating personnel that might be merely burdensome for a small number of agencies become essential when there are a great many. When very large numbers are involved, their co-ordination may require the passage of laws or adoption of rules—often in the form of generalized guides and standards for agency action—as in the case of determining state-wide eligibility and benefit levels for public assistance. A special co-ordinating organization is apparently developed at some point between the extremes of size, but empirical data on this point are lacking. It is clear, however, that both formality and continuity vary with the number of organizations to be co-ordinated.

Standardization of Necessary Communications between Agencies The nature of the activities that require co-ordination is another variable that affects the continuity and formality of co-ordination. When the activities are relatively uniform and there is a generally understandable and pre-dictable way of communicating about them, routine co-ordination proc-esses are possible, and these, in turn, lend themselves to formal arrange-ments. To determine, for example, whether a client is known to other agencies requires only that his name be checked, and social-service ex-changes can easily handle such routine communications; the FBI operates a similar co-ordinating bureau for identifying suspected criminals by their fingerprints. Information about school marks can be centralized for a single school system and transmitted readily when needed by any particu-lar school. In contrast to such standardized information, some communica-tions necessary for co-ordinated action are relatively unstandardized and complex. The referral of a disturbed child from the school social worker to a child-guidance clinic, for example, requires detailed case-history, diag-nostic, and clinical information for which a referral summary is barely adequate and a case conference between professionals is often necessary. In general, the less standardized the messages and the activities to be affected by them, the more varied the contacts between personnel and the more personalized and informal the co-ordinating procedure needs to be.

Although the three factors just discussed are but roughly delineated, their consideration may suggest some guidelines for judging the appro-priate form of co-ordination under given conditions. The community-organization practitioner will also need to consider many other aspects of any given community, including the prestige hierarchy among agencies, their multiple goal commitments, their organizational resources and sta-bility, their latent functions for sponsors and supporters, the degree of autonomy they need to survive, and the history of prior interagency rela-tions. The professional judgment of the community organizer may be strengthened if he considers the extent of agency awareness of depend-ence, the number of agencies, and the nature of the communications in-volved.

For example, where there are a medium number of agencies (perhaps twenty to fifty), considerable agency awareness of dependency, and a moderate degree of standardization in information to be communicated and actions to be taken, a separate co-ordinating agency of some type might be indicated. Thus, the disbursement of funds for community-action programs of mental health or delinquency control—once the prin-ciple for their allocation has been determined—can be handled and super-vised by such a co-ordinating agency. Other examples are fund raising by community chests, a central referral agency for eligible clients, or a center for information about how to apply for funds under various federal pro-grams. On the other hand, if only a few agencies are involved and the information needed is complex, even though the agencies are highly aware of their dependencies, regular face-to-face conferences between agency staffs might be more suitable, as, for example, in the decision to transfer a case from vocational counseling to job training. If there are a great many organizations involved and the nature of co-ordinative activity is fairly standardized—as in the sharing of buildings and other physical facilities—a formal, general rule may be adopted; in the case of a small number of organizations, a simple formal understanding between the agencies can be arranged. When there is low official awareness of dependency between organizations that are relatively few in number, co-ordination may be achieved through personal and *ad hoc* contacts. This may be adequate when primarily complex communications are needed, but it is likely to be inefficient if standardized communications are called for. Under conditions of low agency awareness and a considerable number of agencies concerned with unstandardized problems—for example, criteria for the placement of children in foster homes—occasional conferences organized to discuss the problem in general terms may be useful.

It is evident that there are theoretically and empirically many possible co-ordinating procedures, ranging from the use of laws to personal friendships. Between these extremes are formal organizations whose special job is to co-ordinate agencies, interagency committees composed of staff members from different agencies, *ad hoc* conferences, and workshops of limited scope and duration. This variety of co-ordinating procedures can be visualized in a more orderly fashion by taking into account the factors discussed here.

CHANGING THE CONDITIONS AFFECTING CO-ORDINATION

It should not be assumed that the conditions affecting the form of co-ordination between agencies cannot be deliberately changed. The practitioner is often in a position to influence agencies and their modes of operation. Some considerations that might affect the factors previously discussed and hence the character of co-ordination between agencies are suggested below.

Changing Agency Awareness It is clear that organizations will benefit from official recognition of their interdependence when their goals are quite harmonious and when their personnel are not threatened by such recognition. There are many instances where a judgment that such a condition exists is sufficient to lead the practitioner to encourage formal interagency arrangements. In fact, there appears to be a tendency to assume mistakenly that it is always desirable that organizations increase their formal recognition of interdependency.

At least two circumstances may be suggested where increasing agency awareness of interdependency could be dysfunctional. In the first place, two organizations may have congruent goals, but conflicting means of working toward them. For instance, a youth agency using a street-worker approach to diverting gangs from delinquent behavior may rely in part on the gang's confidence that their actions will not be revealed to the police. The purpose of the agency and that of the police are congruent: to reduce delinquency. However, the police are expected to prosecute violations of law, not conceal them. Formal agency arrangements for co-operation with the police might well jeopardize agency effectiveness: the gang worker needs to be free from official interdependence with the police. Customary and legal protections of confidentiality protect the professional–client relationship, but they also reduce interdependency and hence affect interagency relationships. This is not to say that there is not, or should not be, any co-ordination between agencies with common goals and divergent means. Rather, the forms of co-ordination need to be informal and occasional.

A second condition which calls for maintenance of lower rather than higher levels of official awareness of interdependency occurs when differences in secondary goals, means, or values produce latent conflict. For instance, schools and local neighborhood associations may both be interested in afterschool adult-education programs. Secondary to its educational interest on the part of the school may be a concern for reducing racial tension by increasing interracial contact, and this may not be at all acceptable to the neighborhood group. It is obvious that full official assertion of interdependency, involving total agreement on arrangements for the program, might well bring into the open the potential conflict over racial policies. Accomplishment of the major purpose of both organizations is furthered by incomplete acknowledgment that each depends on the other.

Changing Level of Standardization of Communications Maximizing standardization of communications in order to facilitate interorganizational co-ordination is not always desirable. Premature formalization of procedures, diagnostic categories, and types of communication may seriously reduce flexibility where the technology of service is undeveloped. It may be spurious to formalize co-ordination, for example, between school social workers and child-guidance clinics by standardizing referrals on the basis of psychological tests whose validity for diagnostic purposes is quite uncertain.

If standardization is to be expanded, a number of different approaches are possible. Research may increase the certainty of procedures. If, for example, it is demonstrated that preschool programs improve subsequent school performance, formal arrangements for differential service to children so benefited might be made. Another approach is to encourage specialization. Thus, the specialists in assessing motivation for vocational training may develop effective understandings that cannot be formalized on a routine basis, but may nevertheless serve to bring agencies into co-ordinated action on behalf of particular clients. The agency itself may be made more specialized, with a similar result. In general, specialization increases interdependency in any system, and the more explicit the specialized activity is made, the easier it is for an organization to know when its own operations implicate those of another. Finally, sheer lack of knowledge about the activities of another agency may appear as unstandardized information that limits co-ordination. Therefore, in some instances increasing the knowledge of agencies about one another may serve to facilitate the transfer of information necessary for co-ordination.

Changing the Number of Organizations The practitioner is not often in a position to affect significantly the number of agencies involved in working on a particular social problem. This factor is not, however, impervious to change, although little attention has yet been given to analyzing the conditions that produce the merger of two or more agencies or the division of one agency into several. There may be compelling reasons for maintaining organizational autonomy as well as for encouraging combination. These reasons seem to be related to congruency or incongruency of organizational goals and established means, to functions served by agencies in a larger system, and to problems of organizational size and technological efficiency. The community-organization worker might well give attention to such variables in situations where economy is put forth as sufficient grounds to justify consolidation.

Conclusion

We have sketched some of the trends that support the conclusion that sociological analysis is becoming increasingly pertinent to social-work practice at its various levels of effort. We have illustrated some promising directions for research and have suggested a general strategy for tapping social-science knowledge, especially ideas and data concerning interpersonal helping processes. To indicate the possible contributions of the sociology of organizations, we have presented a generalized analysis of treatment organizations and an approach to the problem of interagency co-ordination. None of these examples are definitive, but they point to fruitful areas for the collaboration of social work and social science.

REFERENCES

NOTE: *This chapter is based on the papers presented at a session on "Sociology and Social Work: A Multi-level Approach," Fifty-seventh Annual Meeting, American Sociological Association, Washington, 1962. It does not purport to cover all aspects of social work and social welfare that sociologists have been interested in.*

1. *Annual Report* of the President of Russell Sage Foundation for 1948 (New York: Russell Sage Foundation, n.d.).

2. An example is the substantial work of Harold L. Wilensky and Charles N. Lebeaux, *Industrial Society and Social Welfare* (New York: Russell Sage Foundation, 1958), reissued in paperback with a new introduction by Wilensky entitled, "The Problems and Prospects of the Welfare State" (New York: The Free Press of Glencoe, 1965).

3. Roger Roffman, Graduate Assistant, School of Social Work, The University of Michigan, was responsible for tabulating these data. Affiliation was identified from the stated position and/or employment address.

4. Sidney Berengarten, *Admissions Prediction and Student Performance in Social Work Education* (New York: Council on Social Work Education, 1964), p. 39.

5. The schools of social work at Columbia University and The University of Michigan deliberately embarked on social-science training for social workers at the doctoral level under grants in 1956 from Russell Sage Foundation. With the addition of social scientists to their faculties and with fellowships made available to students, Columbia offered a special concentration in social science within its existing Doctor of Social Work program and Michigan established an interdepartmental Doctoral Program in Social Work and Social Science. The University of California at Berkeley soon thereafter embarked on an advanced program with similar emphasis. Although some schools included social scientists on their faculties before 1955, since then their use has been more evident and the promotion of social-science research more marked. The effect of social-science content on the training of social-work practitioners in the master's programs has been more controversial but is widely discussed by social workers among factors influencing professional education. For example, see Eileen Blackey, "Issues in Social Work Education—New and Changing Demands Made of the Profession," *Proceedings,* Twelfth Annual Program Meeting, Council on Social Work Education, 1964 (New York: Council on Social Work Education, 1964), pp. 75–89.

6. See *Group Treatment in Family Service Agencies* (New York: Family Service Association of America, 1964).

7. See Milton Wittman, "Significance of New Scientific Developments in the Mental Health Field for Social Work Education," *Social Service Review,* XXXI (June, 1957), 135–143; Luther E. Woodward, ed., *Psychiatric Social Workers and Mental Health* (New York: National Association of Social Workers, 1960). The trend has received further impetus from federal legislation in 1963 promoting comprehensive community mental-health centers and other programs.

8. For example, see the rationale offered for Mobilization for Youth, New York City, *A Proposal for the Prevention and Control of Delinquency by Expanding Opportunities:* A Demonstration Project Conceived and Developed by Mobilization for Youth, Inc. (New York: Mobilization for Youth, Inc., 1961); and the more general presentation of the theory of this project in Richard A. Cloward and Lloyd Ohlin, *Delinquency and Opportunity: A Theory of Delinquent Gangs* (New York: The Free Press of Glencoe, 1961).

9. An example is a project in Syracuse, New York, whose underlying theory is presented in Warren C. Haggstrom, "The Power of the Poor," in Louis A. Ferman, Joyce L. Kornbluh, and Alan Haber, eds., *Poverty in America* (Ann Arbor: University of Michigan Press, 1965), pp. 315–334.

10. See Elliot Studt, *Education for Social Workers in the Correctional Field,* Vol. 5 of *Social Work Curriculum Study* (New York: Council on Social Work Education, 1959).

11. See Helen H. Perlman, "Social Casework," in Harry L. Lurie, ed., *Encyclopedia*

of Social Work (New York: National Association of Social Workers, 1965), pp. 704–715.

12. See Gisela Konopka, *Social Group Work: A Helping Process* (Englewood Cliffs, N.J.: Prentice-Hall, 1963); Raymond Fisher, "Social Group Work Service Agencies," in *Social Work with Groups, 1959:* Selected Papers from the National Conference on Social Welfare (New York: National Association of Group Workers, 1960), pp. 18–29; Robert D. Vinter, "Social Group Work," in Lurie, *op. cit.*, pp. 715–724.

13. See David Fanshel, ed., *Research in Social Welfare Administration: Its Contributions and Problems* (New York: National Association of Social Workers, 1962).

14. Trends are reviewed in Lurie, *op. cit.*: Meyer Schwartz, "Community Organization," pp. 177–190; Charles E. Hendry, "Community Development," pp. 170–177.

15. See Eveline Burns, "Social Policy: The Stepchild of the Curriculum," *Proceedings*, Ninth Annual Program Meeting, Council on Social Work Education, Montreal, 1961 (New York: Council on Social Work Education, 1961).

16. Thoughtful analyses of Greenwood and of Gouldner have been especially clarifying. See Ernest Greenwood, "Social Science and Social Work, A Theory of Their Relationship," *Social Service Review*, XXX (March, 1955), 20–33; Ernest Greenwood, "The Practice of Science and the Science of Practice," in W. G. Bennis, K. D. Benne, and R. Chin, eds., *The Planning of Change* (New York: Holt, Rinehart, and Winston, 1961), pp. 73–82; Alvin W. Gouldner, "Theoretical Requirements of the Applied Social Sciences," *American Sociological Review*, XXII (February, 1957), 92–103.

17. The following suggest the scope of research in social work: David Fanshel, "Research in Child Welfare: A Critical Analysis," *Child Welfare*, XLI (December, 1962), 484–507; David Fanshel, "Administrative Research in Social Welfare: A Review of Current Trends," in Fanshel, ed., *Research in Social Welfare Administration, op. cit.*, pp. 11–21; Ann W. Shyne, "Social Work Research," in Lurie, *op. cit.*, pp. 763–773; Walter B. Johnson, ed., *Inventory of Research, 1962–63* (New York: National Association of Social Workers, 1964); *Listing of Research Projects in Local Communities* (New York: United Community Funds and Councils of America, annually); *Digest of Special Studies Relating to Public Assistance* (Washington: Bureau of Public Assistance, Department of Health, Education, and Welfare, annually). Research in social work is illustrated by examples used in a book on research methods for social workers, Norman A. Polansky, ed., *Social Work Research* (Chicago: University of Chicago Press, 1960).

18. One illustration is the widespread use in social-work courses of Herman D. Stein and Richard A. Cloward, eds., *Social Perspectives on Behavior* (Glencoe, Ill.: The Free Press, 1958). See also, for example, the two-part discussion of the concept of social role in casework by Helen H. Perlman, "The Role Concept and Social Casework: Some Explorations," *Social Service Review*, XXXV (December, 1961), 370–381, and *ibid.*, XXXVI (March, 1962), 17–31; Leonard S. Kogan, ed., *Social Science Theory and Social Work Research* (New York: National Association of Social Workers, 1960); Dorothy Schroeder, "Integrating Social Science Theory through Case Discussion," *Social Casework*, XXXIV (July, 1963), 379–384.

19. This section is based on a paper by Edwin J. Thomas presented at the Annual Meeting, American Sociological Association, Washington, 1962, and on the same author's "Selecting Knowledge from Behavioral Science," in *Building Social Work Knowledge: A Report of a Conference* (New York: National Association of Social Workers, 1964), pp. 38–48.

20. Representative of presentations of casework are two textbooks: Helen H. Perlman, *Social Casework: A Problem-Solving Approach* (Chicago: University of Chicago Press, 1957); Florence Hollis, *Casework: A Psychosocial Therapy* (New York: Random House, 1964).

21. References to the literature are not intended to be comprehensive, but to suggest areas where systematic review by social workers interested in interpersonal helping would be profitable. The task of reviewing the literature pertaining to interpersonal change is currently being undertaken by Edwin J. Thomas with the objective of developing a more comprehensive, empirical base for methods of interpersonal helping.

22. See Robert L. Kahn and Charles F. Cannell, *The Dynamics of Interviewing* (New York: Wiley, 1962); David Riesman and Mark Benny, "The Interview in Social Research," *American Journal of Sociology*, LXII (September, 1956), 137–195.

23. For example, see Anne Anastasi, *Psychological Testing* (New York: Macmillan, 1961); Paul H. Hoch and Joseph Zubin, *Relation of Psychological Tests to Psychiatry* (New York: Grune and Stratton, 1951).

24. For example, see Roger G. Barker, *One Boy's Day: A Specimen Record of Behavior* (New York: Harper, 1951); and Roger W. Heynes and Ronald Lippitt, "Systematic Observation Techniques," in Gardner Lindzey, ed., *Handbook of Social Psychology* (Cambridge, Mass.: Addison-Wesley, 1954), pp. 405–448.

25. For relevant reviews, see John H. Mann, "Experimental Evaluations of Role Playing," *Psychological Bulletin*, LIII (May, 1956), 227–234; Rosemary Lippitt and Anne Hubbell, "Role Playing for Personnel and Guidance Workers," *Group Psychotherapy*, IX (August, 1956), 89–114.

26. For example, see Claire Selltiz, Marie Jahoda, Morton Deutsch, and Stuart W. Cook, *Research Methods in Social Relations* (New York: Holt-Dryden, 1959), pp. 235–279, 385–441.

27. For a general conceptualization of uncertainty reduction, see Claude E. Shannon and W. Weaver, *The Mathematical Theory of Communication* (Urbana: University of Illinois Press, 1949).

28. The logical aspects of clinical inference are treated in part in Theodore R. Sarbin, Ronald Taft, and Daniel E. Bailey, *Clinical Inference and Cognitive Theory* (New York: Holt, Rinehart, and Winston, 1960), pp. 44–85.

29. *Ibid.*, pp. 106–267.

30. For example, see Paul E. Meehl, *Clinical versus Statistical Prediction* (Minneapolis: University of Minnesota Press, 1954); Robert E. Holt, "Clinical and Statistical Prediction: A Reformulation and Some New Data," *Journal of Abnormal and Social Psychology*, LVI (January, 1958), 1–13; Richard D. Mann, "A Critique of P. E. Meehl's *Clinical versus Statistical Prediction*," *Behavioral Science*, I (July, 1956), 224–231; Leo A. Goodman, "Generalizing the Problem of Prediction," in Paul F. Lazarsfeld and Morris Rosenberg, eds., *The Language of Social Research* (Glencoe, Ill.: The Free Press, 1955), pp. 277–282.

31. For the effects of social class, see, for example, August B. Hollingshead and Fredrick C. Redlich, *Social Class and Mental Illness: A Community Study* (New York: Wiley, 1958); and Betty Overall and Harriet Arenson, "Expectations of Psychotherapy in Patients of Lower Socioeconomic Class," *American Journal of Orthopsychiatry*, XXXIII (April, 1963), 421–430; a general review is offered in George Levinger, "Continuance in Casework and Other Helping Relationships: A Review of Current Research," *Social Work*, V (July, 1960), 40–52.

32. For example, see Erving Goffman, *The Presentation of Self in Everyday Life* (Garden City: Doubleday Anchor, 1959); Erving Goffman, *Encounters: Two*

Studies in the Sociology of Interaction (Indianapolis: Bobbs-Merrill, 1961); and Ralph H. Turner, "Role-Taking, Role Standpoint, and Reference-Group Behavior," *American Journal of Sociology*, LXI (January, 1956), 316–328.

33. Irving L. Janis *et al.*, *Personality and Persuasion* (New Haven: Yale University Press, 1959).

34. See *ibid.* for the role of self-esteem and change; also see Levinger, *op. cit.*, pp. 40–52.

35. *Ibid.*

36. For example, see Cyril M. Franks, "Individual Differences in Conditioning and Associated Techniques," in Joseph Wolpe, Andrew Salter, and L. J. Reyna, *The Conditioning Therapies: The Challenge in Psychotherapy* (New York: Holt, Rinehart, and Winston, 1964), pp. 149–164.

37. Robert F. Winch, *Mate-selection: A Study of Complementary Needs* (New York: Harper, 1958); Roland G. Tharp, "Psychological Patterning in Marriage," *Psychological Bulletin*, LX (March, 1963), 97–117; George Levinger, "Marital Cohesiveness and Dissolution: An Integrative Review," *Journal of Marriage and the Family*, XXVII (February, 1965), 19–28; and William C. Schutz, *FIRO: A Three-Dimensional Theory of Interpersonal Behavior* (New York: Holt, 1958).

38. Edwin J. Thomas and Clinton F. Fink, "Effects of Group Size," *Psychological Bulletin*, LX (July, 1963), 371–385.

39. For example, see Joseph D. Matarazzo and George Saslow, "Differences in Interview Interaction among Normal and Deviant Groups," in Irving A. Berg and Bernard M. Bass, eds., *Conformity and Deviation* (New York: Harper, 1961), pp. 286–328; and Harold L. Raush, Irwin Farbman, and L. G. Lynn, "Person, Setting, and Change in Social Interaction," *Human Relations*, XIII (November, 1960), 305–333.

40. For instance, see Henry L. Lennard and Arnold Bernstein, *The Anatomy of Psychotherapy: Systems of Communication and Expectation* (New York: Columbia University Press, 1960); Raymond J. Corsini and Bina Rosenberg, "Mechanisms of Group Psychotherapy: Processes and Dynamics," *Journal of Abnormal and Social Psychology*, LI (November, 1955), 406–412; Jerome B. Frank, "Some Determinants, Manifestations, and Effects of Cohesiveness in Therapy Groups," *International Journal of Group Psychotherapy*, VII (January, 1957), 53–63; Dorothy Fahs Beck, "The Dynamics of Group Therapy as Seen by a Sociologist, Part I: The Basic Process," *Sociometry*, XXI (June, 1958), 98–129; George Psathas, "Phase Movement and Equilibrium Tendencies in Interaction Process in Therapeutic Groups," *Sociometry*, XXIII (June, 1960), 177–195; and Arnold P. Goldstein, *Therapist–Patient Expectancies in Psychotherapy* (New York: Macmillan, 1962).

41. For example, see William C. Morse and David Wineman, "The Therapeutic Use of Social Isolation in a Camp for Ego-Disturbed Boys," *Journal of Social Issues*, XIII, No. 1 (1957), 32–40; Jacob L. Gewirtz and Donald M. Baer, "The Effect of Brief Social Deprivation on Behaviors for a Social Reinforcer," *Journal of Abnormal and Social Psychology*, LVI (January, 1958), 49–57; C. Wesley Jackson, Jr., and John C. Pollard, "Sensory Deprivation and Suggestion: A Theoretical Approach," *Behavioral Science*, VII (July, 1962), 332–343; and Philip E. Kubzansky, "The Effects of Reduced Environmental Stimulation in Human Behavior: A Review," in Albert D. Biderman and Herbert Zimmer, eds., *The Manipulation of Human Behavior* (New York: Wiley, 1961), pp. 51–96.

42. For a classical statement see Kurt Lewin, Tamara Dembo, Leon Festinger, and Paul Sears, "Level of Aspiration," in Joseph McV. Hunt, ed., *Handbook of Personality and Behavior Disorders* (New York: Ronald, 1944); an example of a recent research study is Alvin Zander, Thomas Natsoulas, and Edwin J. Thomas,

"Group Goals and the Group's Goals for the Member," *Human Relations*, XIII (November, 1960), 333–344.

43. For example, see Bertram H. Raven and Jan Rietsema, "The Effects of Varied Clarity of Group Goal and Group Path upon the Individual and His Relationship to His Group," *Human Relations*, X (February, 1957), 29–44.

44. A. Paul Hare, *Handbook of Small Group Research* (New York: The Free Press of Glencoe, 1962), pp. 339–395.

45. *Ibid.*, pp. 7–169.

46. For example, see Erving Goffman, *Asylums: Essays on the Social Situation of Mental Patients and Other Inmates* (Garden City, N.Y., Anchor Books, 1961); Lloyd W. McCorkle and Richard R. Korn, "Resocialization within Prison Walls," *Annals*, CCXCIII (May, 1954), 88–98; Peter M. Blau and W. Richard Scott, *Formal Organizations* (San Francisco: Chandler, 1962); Robert D. Vinter, "The Social Structure of Service," in Alfred J. Kahn, ed., *Issues in American Social Work* (New York: Columbia University Press, 1959), pp. 242–270; Raymond G. Hunt, Orville Gurrslin, and Jack L. Roach, "Social Status and Psychiatric Service in a Child Guidance Clinic," *American Sociological Review*, XXIII (February, 1958), 81–83; and Robert D. Vinter, "Analysis of Treatment Organizations," *Social Work*, VIII (July, 1963), 3–15.

47. For example, see Jerome D. Frank, *Persuasion and Healing* (Baltimore: Johns Hopkins, 1961); Edgar H. Schein, *Coercive Persuasion* (New York: Norton, 1961); and Albert D. Biderman, "Social Psychological Needs and 'Involuntary' Behavior as Illustrated by Compliance in Interrogation," *Sociometry*, XXIII (June, 1960), 120–148.

48. For example, see Albert J. and Bernice E. Lott, "Group Cohesion as Interpersonal Attraction: A Review of Relationships with Antecedent and Consequent Variables," *Psychological Bulletin*, LXIV (October, 1965), 259–309.

49. For example, see Robert F. Bales, "The Equilibrium Problem in Small Groups," in A. Paul Hare, Edgar F. Borgatta, and Robert F. Bales, eds., *Small Groups: Studies in Social Interaction*, rev. ed. (New York: Knopf, 1965), pp. 444–477.

50. For example, see Levinger, "Continuance in Casework and Other Helping Relationships," *op. cit.*, pp. 40–52; Carl R. Rogers and Rosalind F. Dymond, *Psychotherapy and Personality Change* (Chicago: University of Chicago Press, 1954); Herbert C. Kelman and Morris B. Parloff, "Interrelationships among Three Criteria of Improvement in Group Therapy: Comfort, Effectiveness, and Self-Awareness," *Journal of Abnormal and Social Psychology*, LIV (May, 1957), 281–288; Hans J. Eysenck, "The Effects of Psychotherapy: An Evaluation," *Journal of Consulting Psychology*, XVI (October, 1962), 319–324; George W. Fairweather *et al.*, "Relative Effectiveness of Psychotherapeutic Programs: Multi-Criteria Comparison of Four Programs for Three Different Patient Groups," *Psychological Monographs*, LXXIV, No. 5 (1960), 1–26; David Rosenthal and Jerome D. Frank, "Psychotherapy and the Placebo Effect," *Psychological Bulletin*, LIII (July, 1956), 294–303; and Henry J. Meyer, Edgar F. Borgatta, and Wyatt C. Jones, *Girls at Vocational High* (New York: Russell Sage Foundation, 1965).

51. For example, see Bruce W. Tuckman, "Developmental Sequence in Small Groups," *Psychological Bulletin*, VI (June, 1965), 384–400; also see Lennard and Bernstein, *op. cit.*; Psathas, *op. cit.*, pp. 177–195.

52. For some recent general expositions, see Albert Bandura, "Psychotherapy as a Learning Process," *Psychological Bulletin*, LVIII (March, 1961), 143–159; Ralph Metzner, "Learning Theory and a Therapy of Neurosis," *British Journal of Psychology, Monograph Supplements*, 33 (Cambridge at the University Press, 1961); Joseph Wolpe, *Psychotherapy by Reciprocal Inhibition* (Stanford: Stanford University Press, 1958); Arthur W. and Carolyn K. Staats, *Complex Human*

Behavior: A Systematic Extension of Learning Principles (New York: Holt, Rinehart, and Winston, 1964); Edwin J. Thomas and Esther Goodman, eds., *Socio-Behavioral Theory and Interpersonal Helping in Social Work—Lectures and Institute Proceedings* (Ann Arbor: Campus Publishers, 1965). Recent compilations of readings include Hans J. Eysenck, ed., *Behavior Therapy and the Neuroses* (New York: Pergamon Press, 1960); Wolpe, Salter, and Reyna, *op. cit.*; Leonard Ullmann and Leonard Krasner, *Case Studies in Behavior Modification* (New York: Holt, Rinehart, and Winston, 1965); and Cyril M. Franks, ed., *Conditioning Techniques in Clinical Practice and Research* (New York: Springer, 1964).

53. For reviews of this literature, see Donald T. Campbell, "Conformity in Psychology's Theories of Acquired Behavioral Dispositions," in Berg and Bass, *op. cit.*, pp. 101–143; and Robert B. Blake and Jane S. Monton, "The Experimental Investigation of Interpersonal Influence," in Biderman and Zimmer, *op. cit.*, pp. 216–277. More general theories are illustrated by the following: Herbert Kelman, "Processes of Opinion Change," *Public Opinion Quarterly,* XXV (Spring, 1961), 55–77; Daniel Katz, "The Functional Approach to the Study of Attitudes," *Public Opinion Quarterly,* XXIV (Summer, 1960), 163–205; Edward L. Walker and Roger W. Heyns, *An Anatomy of Conformity* (Englewood Cliffs, N.J.: Prentice-Hall, 1962).

54. For example, see Leon Festinger, *A Theory of Cognitive Dissonance* (New York: Row, Peterson, 1957); Jack W. Brehm and Arthur R. Cohen, *Explorations in Cognitive Dissonance* (New York: Wiley, 1962); Milton Rosenberg *et al., Attitude Organization and Change: An Analysis of Consistency among Attitude Components* (New Haven: Yale University Press, 1960); and Robert B. Zajine, "The Concepts of Balance, Congruity, and Dissonance," *Public Opinion Quarterly,* XXIV (Summer, 1960), 280–296.

55. For example, see Joseph T. Klapper, "What We Know about the Effects of Mass Communication: The Brink of Hope," *Public Opinion Quarterly,* XLI (Winter, 1957–1958), 453–474; and Eugene Litwak, "Some Policy Implications in Communications Theory with Emphasis on Group Factors," *Education for Social Work: Proceedings of the Seventh Annual Program Meeting* (New York: Council on Social Work Education, 1959), pp. 96–109, and Carl I. Hovland, "Effects of Mass Media of Communication," in Lindzey, *op. cit.*, pp. 1062–1104.

56. For a review see Hare, *Handbook of Small Group Research,* pp. 23–101.

57. For example, see *ibid.*, pp. 291–339; Cecil A. Gibb, "Leadership," in Lindzey, *op. cit.*, pp. 877–921; and Barry E. Collins and Harold Guetzkow, *A Social Psychology of Group Processes for Decision-Making* (New York: Wiley, 1964), pp. 210–223.

58. See John H. Mann, *op. cit.*, 227–234; John H. and Carola H. Mann, "The Effect of Role-Playing Experience on Role-Playing Ability," *Sociometry,* XXII (March, 1959), 64–74; and Irving L. Janis and Bert T. King, "The Influence of Role Playing on Opinion Change," *Journal of Abnormal and Social Psychology,* XLIX (April, 1954), 211–218.

59. A review of studies on social power is to be found in Collins and Guetzkow, *op. cit.*, pp. 120–166; for a compilation of studies, see Dorwin Cartwright, *Studies in Social Power* (Ann Arbor: Research Center for Group Dynamics, Institute for Social Research, University of Michigan, 1959).

60. The following discussion is adapted from Thomas, *op. cit.*

61. In addition to the helping process, content pertaining to normal behavior, abnormality and deviation, and to growth, maturation, and natural change is also relevant. Furthermore, subject matter in these areas of relevant content may be

considered for all levels of human aggregation dealt with in social work, namely, for individuals, groups, organizations, communities, and societies. For additional details see *ibid.*

62. An important case in point is Gouldner, *op. cit.* This treatment of engineerable referents was inspired partly by Gouldner's insightful discussion, and we have included his considerations of cost and ethics as these factors related to "engineerability."

63. This section summarizes, with some modification, a paper delivered by Robert D. Vinter at the annual meeting of the American Sociological Association and subsequently published as "Analysis of Treatment Organizations," *Social Work*, VIII (July, 1963), 3–15.

64. For two recent, general presentations of this field of sociology, see Amitai Etzioni, *Modern Organizations* (Englewood Cliffs, N.J.: Prentice-Hall, 1964), and James G. March, ed., *Handbook of Organizations* (Chicago: Rand McNally, 1965).

65. Until 1955, when the National Association of Social Workers was organized, there were separate professional associations of medical, school, and psychiatric social workers. See David G. French, "Professional Organization," in Lurie, *op. cit.*, pp. 574–579.

66. Note, however, the following: Peter M. Blau, *The Dynamics of Bureaucracy* (Chicago: University of Chicago Press, 1955); Donald R. Cressey, "Prison Organizations," in March, *op. cit.*; Blau and Scott, *op. cit.*; Roy G. Francis and Robert C. Stone, *Service and Procedure in Bureaucracy* (Minneapolis: University of Minnesota Press, 1956); Alfred J. Kahn, *A Court for Children* (New York: Columbia University Press, 1953); Howard Polsky, *Cottage Six* (New York: Russell Sage Foundation, 1962); David L. Sills, *The Volunteers* (Glencoe, Ill.: The Free Press, 1957); Mayer N. Zald and Patricia Denton, "From Evangelism to General Service: The Transformation of the YMCA," *Administrative Science Quarterly*, VIII (September, 1963), 214–234; Robert L. Peabody, *Organizational Authority: Superior–Subordinate Relationships in Three Public Service Organizations* (New York: Atherton, 1964); David Street, Robert D. Vinter, and Charles Perrow, *Organization for Treatment* (Glencoe, Ill.: The Free Press, 1966). For more general discussion of the social organization of social-welfare agencies, see Wilensky and Lebeaux, *op. cit.*, Chapter 10; and Vinter, "The Social Structure of Service," pp. 242–269.

67. The nature and varieties of deviance are discussed in Howard S. Becker, ed., *The Other Side: Perspectives on Deviance* (Glencoe, Ill.: The Free Press, 1964), and in Howard S. Becker, *Outsiders: Studies in the Sociology of Deviance* (Glencoe, Ill.: The Free Press, 1963). For an analysis of public attitudes toward deviance, see Elaine and John Cumming, *Closed Rank: An Experiment in Mental Health Education* (Cambridge: Harvard University Press, 1957), pp. 91–150.

68. Litwak observes that organization emphasis on impersonal relations and general rules is more likely to occur when events are uniform rather than nonuniform. However, *definitions* of the uniformity of human events vary among organizations and thus shape the procedures employed. Eugene Litwak, "Models of Bureaucracy Which Permit Conflict," *American Journal of Sociology*, LVII, No. 2 (September, 1961), 177–184.

69. Only recently have operational designs of treatment organizations been subjected to sociological analysis. See, for example, Ivan Belknap, *Human Problems of a State Mental Hospital* (New York: McGraw-Hill, 1956); Daniel Glaser, *The Effectiveness of a Prison and Parole System* (New York: Bobbs-Merrill,

1964); Meyer, Borgatta, and Jones, *op. cit.;* Robert N. Rapoport, *Community as Doctor* (Springfield, Ill.: Charles C Thomas, 1960); Street, Vinter, and Perrow, *op. cit.*

70. Goffman, *Asylums.* See especially "The Medical Model and Mental Hospitalization," pp. 321–386.

71. The skewed deployment of social workers is documented in U.S. Department of Labor, Bureau of Labor Statistics, *Salaries and Working Conditions of Social Welfare Manpower in 1960* (New York: National Social Welfare Assembly, 1961).

72. Problems of authority and co-ordination in this type of organization have received increasing attention. See, for example, Blau and Scott, *op. cit.,* Chapters 6 and 7; Rose L. Coser, "Authority and Decision-Making in a Hospital," *American Sociological Review,* XXIII (February, 1958), 56–64; Amitai Etzioni, "Authority Structure and Organizational Effectiveness," *Administrative Science Quarterly,* IV (June, 1959), 43–68; Lloyd E. Ohlin, "Conformity in American Society Today," *Social Work,* III (April, 1958), 58–66.

73. These issues have been critically discussed by McCorkle and Korn, *op. cit.;* and by Goffman, *Asylums,* "The Moral Career of the Mental Patient," pp. 125–170.

74. Study of these processes, within a comparative perspective, is presented in Street, Vinter, and Perrow, *op. cit.;* see especially Parts II and VI.

75. This section is based in part on Eugene Litwak and Lydia F. Hylton, "Interorganizational Analysis: A Hypothesis on Coordinating Agencies," *Administrative Science Quarterly,* VI (March, 1962), 395–420, and in part on materials for a manual for school-community social workers, in preparation under a grant from the President's Committee on Juvenile Delinquency and Youth Crime (Office of Juvenile Delinquency and Youth Development, Department of Health, Education, and Welfare, Project #7JD62218) by Eugene Litwak, Cheryl Mickelson, Henry J. Meyer, *et al., Theory and Practice of Local School–Community Relations* (Ann Arbor: School of Social Work, University of Michigan, mimeographed, 1964).

76. See Jack Rothman, "Community Organization as Applied Social Science," *Sociology and Social Research,* XLVIII (April, 1964), 315–323.

77. Note, however, Sol Levine and Paul E. White, "Exchange as a Conceptual Framework for the Study of Interorganizational Relationships," *Administrative Science Quarterly,* XXXVIII (March, 1961), 583–601; Sol Levine, Paul E. White, and Benjamin D. Paul, "Community Interorganizational Problems in Providing Medical Care and Social Services," *American Journal of Public Health,* LIII (August, 1963), 1183–1195; William Reid, "Interagency Coordination in Delinquency Prevention and Control," *Social Service Review,* XXXVIII (December, 1964), 418–428; Wilensky and Lebeaux, *op. cit.,* pp. 247–265; James D. Thompson and W. J. McEwen, "Organization Goals and Environment," *American Sociological Review,* XXIII (February, 1958), 23–31.

78. See Bradley Buell *et al., Community Planning for Human Services* (New York: Columbia University Press, 1952).

The Uses of
Sociology in
Establishments

PART III

Management

ABRAHAM ZALEZNIK

ANNE JARDIM

chapter 8

The sociology of management is concerned with the development and application of knowledge relevant to the actions of executives in all types of institutions.

Traditionally, sociologists have contributed to our understanding of management through three applications of sociological theory and methods. The first of these, industrial sociology, dates back to the pioneering studies conducted at the Western Electric Company[1] and is concerned with worker motivation and the social organization in which work experience is imbedded. The substantive problems of the early researches included job satisfaction, labor relations, productivity, group structure and function, and analyses of various forms of social-industrial pathology such as low morale, excessive absenteeism, and labor turnover.[2]

From these studies came a change in the emphasis of management theory and the development of a movement to alter management practice. Statements were made of what was *not* true: that employees were governed by responses to simple logics of management and that behavior was an outcome simply of the manifest contractual arrangements of work. The target of these statements, of course, was mainly the scientific management school, and Frederick Taylor, its main spokesman.[3]

A more positive outcome was the "human relations" school, normative in character, suggesting how managers *should* behave. The manager was

193

advised to diagnose and be aware of the interrelation of forces in the social system and to anticipate the effects of management action on the equilibrium of forces.[4] Borrowing from medicine and the functional schools of sociology, the manager was alerted to the dysfunctions in systems of control such as time standards and wage-incentive plans.[5] Managers were urged to encourage two-way communication with their employees as part of broad programs of participative management.

This normative position generated its own storm of controversy: as a counter to alleged authoritarianism in the typical structure of organizations, industrial counseling, using the concepts of catharsis and human communication, attempted to alter the psychological climate of work through the creation of a permissive atmosphere;[6] but the personnel counselor operated within a staff organization, had no supervisory responsibility, and was generally unable to control conditions of work. Counseling became isolated from the mainstream of activity and decision making and was finally abandoned by the Western Electric Company.[7]

There were two additional criticisms of the human relations approach: (1) that it aimed to create contented and apathetic workers who would be unwilling to join unions; (2) that because of this lack of militancy, collective power would not be used to correct the structural defects of industrial organizations. Critics sensed an implicit antiunion bias, a sense of patronage and "soft soap." "Cow sociology" and "aborigines and elites"[8] were typical assessments.

Interestingly enough, some of the strongest advocates of new organizational structures came from both labor and management. Golden and Ruttenberg, who fostered the ideals of a new industrial democracy, were leaders in the union movement.[9] William Given, a leading management figure of the American Brake Shoe Company, detailed his views of participative management in a book called *Bottom-up Management*.[10] The McCormick Company advanced similar concepts on techniques for bringing lower levels of management into the decision process.[11]

Despite many differences in their aims, it was the influence on these men of the studies of Mayo and others related to the field of industrial sociology that is important. The depression and sense of drift among business leaders[12] stimulated interest in broad ideological prescriptions, and these normative extensions of research in industrial sociology, reflecting issues which were already explicit or implicit in the literature, brought together the social scientist and the manager and laid the foundation for the development of social-science research applied to management.[13]

Research in occupations is a second field of traditional application in the sociology of management.[14] Closely related to industrial sociology, but with its own style and questions for inquiry, occupation sociology attempts to examine the structure, content, and value differences among professional and nonprofessional work fields, generally apart from the organizational settings in which work occurs. Work classifications are developed, and the characteristics of individuals who enter different fields are studied. These characteristics include social attributes such as education and family background, as well as psychological attributes such as personality traits, aptitudes, and intelligence. Trends into and out of occupations are related to problems of status mobility and the channels through which mobility is realized.[15]

Research in occupations is directed mainly to the description and analysis of dislocations in work adjustment. In general the aim is to formulate theories of work adjustment and mobility and to illuminate the nature of conflict and pathology in work. Professionals in personnel selection and guidance are more interested in practice and apply research in the field to counseling, predicting success and failure in job adjustment, and developing reliable and economical selection techniques.

Organization theory and research in complex organizations is the third branch of sociological applications to the study of management. Organization researches focus on the processes within and between defined work situations and thereby cut across occupational lines. Because individuals act within a specific organization, organizational analysis is of prime significance in the study of managerial behavior.

Weber rightfully holds the position of pioneer in organizational studies for his analyses of authority in bureaucratic systems.[16] His theories of what it is that leads men to accept authority and to contribute to purposes that go beyond narrow individual interests opened a wide area to research. For example, Barnard's classic theoretical work, *The Functions of the Executive*, attempted to formulate the ways in which executives sustain the organization as a system of co-operation.[17] More recently, empirical studies have led to modifications in the theory of authority.[18] Managerial transactions are far from the impersonal and rational processes described by Weber, and the many informal and seemingly deviant practices are shown to have an important mediative value in serving human needs and in correcting the negative effects of bureaucratic systems.

Allied to the literature on organizations are the studies on decision making and administration, notably those of Herbert Simon. His *Administrative Behavior*[19] is a devastating criticism of normative principles of management as typified by Fayol and Gulick.[20] These principles, intended as a guide to managers in the design of organization structures, were labeled "proverbs" by Simon. He emphasized their ambiguous and contradictory character, and both in this book and in a later study written with March[21] he proposed formulating criteria for decision making which take account of value and choice. The importance of Simon's work and that of other students of formal organization lies in their attempt to provide a framework for more adequate "situational analysis"[22]—a term that describes in brief what managers do in formulating decisions—and work in this area can thus serve both as a guide in descriptive research and as a normative approach to decision making.

The discussion so far has touched on broad fields of sociological study in management. Within each, different approaches are clearly discernible if the field is more narrowly viewed. Explanatory studies, for example, attempt to describe and analyze important phenomena, while normative studies try to formulate rules of action to indicate how an actor should behave to achieve certain desired objectives. In addition, how an organization relates to its environment and how it organizes itself to achieve its purposes are common bases for differentiation in research.

The relationships between the mode of investigation (normative or explanatory) and the research content (orientation toward the external environment or the internal organization) are represented in Table 8–1.

TABLE 8–1. *Orientations of Sociological Studies of Management*

	NORMATIVE	EXPLANATORY
The Environment (external)	A Policy formulation, Decision making	B Historical, comparative, or longitudinal analyses of corporate strategy and its outcomes
The Organization (internal)	C Exposition of principles of organization and management	D Organization analysis and theory

Lazarsfeld has elsewhere reviewed studies belonging in Cells A and B,[23] and although we shall cite studies which logically fall within Cell C, our primary concern in this chapter will be with Cell D: studies of organization structure, management, and the articulation and communication of organizational identity. This will allow us to focus on problems related to internal organization and executive responsibility. Specifically, we shall develop the discussion around five applied issues: (1) the design of formal organizations, (2) management control, (3) the management of change, (4) the analysis of role performance, and (5) executive leadership.

The Design of Formal Organizations

Sociological studies of management have tended to emphasize, in comparative analyses of formal organizations, the conscious, purposive aspects of organizational structure. Managers use the formal distribution of authority and the allocation of responsibility as important guidelines in choosing one or another form of structure: centralized versus decentralized, or functional versus divisional, and on this level, formal organizational design represents a consciously maintained system for the "quantitative" distribution of authority which is sanctioned by the highest management level within the structure.

A managerial decision, however, to distribute authority through the use of a flat or pyramidical structure, or a line-staff arrangement, carries with it an implicit decision as to the "qualitative" primacy of different types of authority. A centralized structure, for example, not only emphasizes limitations on the range of authority to be exercised as one moves down the hierarchy (a quantitative distribution of authority); it also tends to confine the exercise of individual competence to limited or specialized functions. As one moves up the hierarchy, the converse is implied: because of the need to co-ordinate specialist functions, authority at this level is expected to be wide-ranging, and knowledge and skill of a high order are taken for granted. In such a structure the emphasis is clearly on positional authority, and differences in individual competence are formally disregarded as legitimate bases for a wider or narrower exercise of authority.

The structural distribution of authority with its implicit legitimation of a type of authority system is, nonetheless, seldom accepted without question. Competing systems of authority emerge in the form of group norms, cliques, and interdepartmental rivalries, and they may also be introduced from outside with the entry into the organization of professional specialists. From this standpoint researchers must clearly account for the implicit meaning of the structure in terms of the authority systems it fosters in addition to analyses of the patterns of behavior which emerge in practice.

Weber's theoretical formulations on authority and bureaucracy outlined the types of authority systems which may exist within an organization.[24] He discussed three types of authority systems: traditional, legal, and charismatic.

The system of traditional authority, based on historically relevant rules, sanctions the right of a particular individual or group to exercise authority. Implicit in such systems is the extrarational basis on which acceptance of its rules depends. Legal authority is based on an acceptance of normative rules which prescribe the right of individuals who occupy positions in the structure to issue commands. Legal authority "legitimates" hierarchical authority, but it says little about horizontal relationships or channels of communication and influence among peers. The implicit meaning of this system is the assumption, referred to earlier, that as one descends the hierarchy he encounters a declining scale of individual competence, thus making subordinate dependence on a superior imperative and horizontal relationships of negligible importance. Charismatic authority is based on the emotional ties between leader and follower. In "Group Psychology and the Analysis of the Ego," Freud discussed the influence achieved by the charismatic leader, likening it to the primary emotional ties of parent and child.[25] In authority systems of this kind the symbolism attached to the authority figures is overridingly important.

While traditional and charismatic authority may reinforce the exercise of legal authority, individuals were seen by Weber as generally accepting the system of "legal" statuses and rules because of their implicit rationality in relating organizational means to clearly defined objectives.

Sociological research on formal organizations has since altered this aspect of Weber's qualitative analysis of authority. At the motivational level, legal authority systems do not by themselves provide for the universal requirement of men to establish relationships of equality as well as of authority.[26] The "informal" organization discussed in the literature on work groups is a deviation from bureaucratic rules,[27] and Blau has demonstrated the way in which variant behavior relates to individual problems of managing anxiety.[28]

Departures from the logic of formal authority relationships are increasingly the result of the complexity and resultant specialization of work roles in modern organizations. Selznick's TVA study emphasizes that specialist functions use knowledge and skill rather than hierarchical position as a basis for influence and tend in the process to develop their own subgoals as they become independent of other groups and of the dominant hierarchical system of authority.[29]

Gouldner described two organizational "cultures" to highlight the differences between investments in hierarchical and professional authority.[30] The influence of rewards and punishments in a hierarchical structure he termed "punishment-centered bureaucracy," and the more egalitarian and peerlike atmosphere among professionals he termed "representative bureaucracy." In these situations a shift takes place in the qualitative base of authority, and with it a corresponding shift in the quantitative distribution of authority occurs.

Some understanding of the structural problems encountered in accommodating both professional and hierarchical authority is suggested in Weiss's study of two sections of a government bureau.[31] While hierarchical authority relationships were widely accepted in the administrative section, differences in individual ability made it essential in the scientific section that primary emphasis be placed on professional competence and individual initiative as the basis for the allocation and co-ordination of activities. The "peerlike atmosphere," less a matter of personal preference than a vital functional requirement, was nonetheless widely disliked by the administrators.

The egalitarian culture generally fostered by those who invest in professional authority is built on a "flat" structure. The number of levels of authority between the top and bottom of the organization are fewer in the flat as compared with the pyramid structure. The emphasis is on lateral communication among peers, the use of committees, and *ad hoc* work groups. The legitimacy of any attempt at influence is based on the rationality of competence and skill that must be perceived in the transactions among individuals. In this sense, less emphasis is placed on positional authority, and in an absolute sense, there is less difference between the authority of the man at the top and the one at the bottom of the organization structure. Experimentation with flat organization structure, as we have indicated, is prevalent in science-based organizations with a heavy representation of individuals trained and committed initially to a professon.

An example of the interaction of authority systems in the transition from a hierarchical to an egalitarian structure is provided in a study of organizational change in a research and development center of a large company. Dalton, Barnes, and Zaleznik examined, through the use of a partially controlled field experiment, the rationale and outcome in the transition from a pyramid to a relatively flat formal structure.[32] This transition involved increased emphasis on lateral communication and autonomous work groups, but also included the elimination of key management jobs.

Their experiment, in addition, examined the interaction between hierarchical and professional authority, since the stated objective that led management to alter the formal structure was to give greater weight to the technical function.

A year and a half after the change, individuals whose authority had actually increased and who had experienced greater influence in their work were, notwithstanding this, inclined to be skeptical of a continuing emphasis on professional as compared with hierarchical authority. These individuals were typically in supervisory positions and increasingly committed to both positional and professional authority as bases for influence and control.

It seems relevant to suggest that contending authority systems operate like Gresham's Law of Money: "Bad money tends to drive out good money." We would convert this to mean (without taking the "good" or "bad" seriously) that in any organization, hierarchical authority ultimately becomes dominant, since as specialists achieve greater power and influence through the exercise of professional competence, they become increasingly attached to the organization and begin to exercise authority derived from position, which includes great proximity to top management.

The discussion so far has centered on both the qualitative and the quantitative aspects of distributing authority through commitment to a type of organization structure. The main theme that we have attempted to establish is that in exercising choice in the design of formal structure, managers are not only distributing authority but implicitly legitimating a specific type of authority which may or may not be completely relevant, given differences in activities, purposes, and the sophistication and competence of individuals.

Worthy's analysis of the Sears, Roebuck experiments in flat organization structure is of especial interest here because it indicates the subtle relationships among work activity, organization purpose, and need for co-ordination as variables affecting the design of the formal structure.[33] Sears dispensed with the need for the centralized co-ordination characteristic of functional organization structures by making store managers as self-sufficient as selection, training, and job rotation could make them and by capitalizing on the narrow opportunities for subgoal differentiation which the retail trade affords. In retailing, departmental objectives are the objectives of the store as a whole: to maximize the entry and movement of customers through the store and to maximize the amount spent by each customer. In the Sears experiment these objectives could be achieved independently by each department without recourse to the conflict characteristic of the zero-sum game, and as a result direct and frequent co-ordination of departmental activities was not required. The flat structure emphasized the quantitative distribution of authority at each management level, and the manager's training and experience, expressly designed to encourage autonomous action within broad policy limits, contributed to the legitimation of his positional authority in the minds of his subordinates.

When the requirements of the task and its related technology are such that specialization is essential, however, structural changes aimed at redistributing authority from higher to lower levels appear, at least initially, to be less successful.

In *The Changing Culture of a Factory*, Jaques describes a change intended to increase worker participation in management.[34] In putting the change into effect there was no explicit decision on the part of the company's management to flatten the structure; it was apparently expected that worker participation in the joint committees would simply provide for a less inhibited flow of information up through the hierarchy. Inherent in this, however, is the shift to an authority system that is no longer legitimated essentially by position. Jaques found that there was a strong tendency among members of top management to use the joint consultative machinery which brought them into direct contact with workers' representatives as a means of avoiding their immediate subordinates entirely. The changes resulted in a substantial loss of authority at the middle management level. Confusion over the role they were expected to play and noticeable interpersonal rivalry ensued.

Role confusion and rivalry are also a result of ambiguity in expected formal relationships; where decision making is impeded, remedial steps involving a change in formal organization structure usually occur.

Changes toward formalization and consensus in the distribution and exercise of authority are frequently coupled with efforts to decentralize responsibility through a new formal organization chart.

Weinshall studied the effects of a new organization chart in a company faced with expansion of business and an increase in the number of employees at all levels.[35] The immediate impetus for the change lay in the need to introduce a wider range of technological expertise to cope with the demands which expanding markets and product lines placed on the organization. Authority had been centralized around the figure of the chief executive, and formal relationships below his level were poorly defined. Decentralization involved a flatter structure, a redistribution of positional authority, and added weight attached to professional skills through the importance assigned to research and development.

Weinshall found that the effects of the changes were strongly felt only at the highest management level. At lower levels, there was a decrease in the clarity and reciprocity of both formal and informal relationships, suggesting that the introduction of a new authority system was not adequately tied into the structural change.

Informal attempts to introduce authority systems both parallel and compete with the formal system. Competition occurs when positional authority is exercised inadequately, for this represents a *de facto* structural change in which authority is sharply redistributed. Dalton's study *Men Who Manage* provides a striking example of this.[36]

Dalton distinguished three recurrent patterns of association which he classified on the basis of their relationships to the hierarchical authority system as: (1) vertical cliques, composed of employees at different levels, usually within a single department, in which the rewards to members included information and support for the superior and protection and advancement for the subordinates; (2) horizontal cliques of employees at roughly the same level in the organization which were usually formed to resist change or to advance it; and (3) random cliques of employees who were personal friends or who were rejected by the more functional cliques.

The dominant authority system lay in the hierarchy, but its sanctioning of the cliques simultaneously limited its effectiveness: comparatively low-status members of a clique dominated by a top-level manager exercised an autonomy that was almost inviolable by their own immediate hierarchical superiors. Except for one individual, who was widely believed to have the backing of the company's head office, staff personnel were dependent for advancement on the line and had no recourse to an authority system of their own. Wherever it was felt necessary, the power of clique members was used to stretch, misinterpret, or ignore the directives which staff members were officially expected to implement. Dalton attributed the emergence of such powerful informal structures to the discrepancy between "granted and exercised authority," which in and of itself does nothing more than describe the effects of cliques and informal relationships. The more important issue is to explain the shifts in authority relationships under conditions where the formal authority structure appears unchanged.

Dalton's analysis and others, such as Crozier's study of power and authority in bureaucratic settings,[37] suggest an underlying motivation on the part of individuals in organizations to regulate and control behavior. For top management, the desire is to control behavior in response to the relevance of over-all organizational objectives. As one proceeds down the hierarchy, there is an increasing tendency to control behavior in relation to the goals of subgroups, which include maintaining the identity and saliency of group structures and individual positions.

The issue of control goes back a long way in the history of organizational research to the arguments, for example, on the meaning of restriction of output in the factory work groups.[38] In a very fundamental sense the decision to establish a formal organization structure with its allocation of functions, responsibility, and authority is a decision to attempt to control individual and group performance. We do not wish to argue that control at one level (top management) is rational, while at another (low status) it is irrational. The question of control is always rational as long as means and ends are in harmony from the standpoint of the behavior under observation. Means and ends can be internally consistent at one level of the organization, but in conflict with those of another level.

The problem of control grows out of the basic motivations that lead people to participate in formal organizations. From the standpoint of the manager, control involves basic issues in the allocation of resources to achieve some desired and explicit objectives. To assist him in the process of control, he has available a new range of sophisticated techniques that are an integral part of the structure of authority in organizations. The nature of these techniques, their function in the exercise of authority, and the range of empirical research questions open to sociological inquiry will be considered next.

Management Control

One of the most important developments in managerial practice, still not fully articulated, is the concept of the organization structure as an action variable. This concept leads to efforts to fit organization structure to the conditions reflected in purposes, technologies, individual motivations, preferred work climates, and leadership style. Not only can forms be varied within a single over-all structure but forms may also be changed over time to reflect new conditions and problems in achieving organizational goals.

Recent developments in management control systems have contributed substantially to the treatment of organization structure as a variable, but their efforts have been largely overlooked in sociologists' studies. In exploring the literature, we could find few references to empirical studies of management control systems in relation to the dynamic aspects of management and organization.[39]

Managers assume responsibility for appraising the results of action and modifying performance to reach desired objectives. The cycle of appraisal, planning, and action can be as simple as a verbal exchange between a president and his sales manager, or it can be extremely complex. The complexity stems from several sources:

1. Large organizations require a breakdown of information to reflect the relatively autonomous performance of subunits.

2. Means of communication must be established which will give many people the information they need when they need it.

3. This in turn requires planning and decision as to who gets what information when, how, and at the least cost.

4. Information exchange, at any level, has motivational consequences which are crucial to continuing performance and must be controlled if behavior is to be directed toward desired objectives.

5. Executives need to regulate their own actions within the time-span demands of their area of responsibility.

The obvious way in which these complexities are being met is through the introduction of electronic data processing. This use of the computer merits study by sociologists in a context similar to that of the introduction of the assembly line in the factory. But of more basic concern are the conceptual changes underlying management control systems and their relevance to organization structure, decision making, and executive motivation and performance.

Information systems permit top managers to design formal organizations around "performance centers" [40]—units of organization under the responsibility of a manager with a purpose and a technology that permit the comparison of actual with expected performance. The comparison may be narrow or broad, depending on the level of authority of the performance center. The higher the level, the longer the time intervals between comparisons and the more the comparisons with units outside the boundaries of a particular organization. The concept of return on investment creates a universal comparison of organizations with different purposes and technologies.

The concept of the performance center permits wider choice of formal structure and style of executive behavior. For certain purposes, organizations can be flattened, with more heads of performance centers reporting to one executive as compared with pyramid structures that operate on the principle of span of control. But while flat organizations imply a high degree of delegation of responsibility, this may be more apparent than real. There may be wide latitude with respect to how the unit head maintains stability in his unit from day to day, but very little latitude in the technique of work and in capital expenditure. The techniques of work can be governed by staff personnel who develop new methods and program their use in routine operations. Similarly, capital expenditures can be regulated through top-level budget discussions and allocation of funds to be spent by units throughout the organization.

Formal budgeting as a management technique and process deserves careful study in a literal as well as symbolic sense. In the literal sense, the budget procedure brings executives to the point of decision and culminates in actions throughout an organization. In a symbolic sense, the budgeting process involves such issues as articulating the organization's identity, establishing the psychological bonds between superior and subordinate, clarifying problems of co-operation and competition among divisions of the organization, and other issues.

The issue of competition, as it comes into focus in budgeting, is a major problem in management control. The idea of establishing an organization with relatively autonomous performance centers is usually fostered by creating "arm's length" relationships among the major centers, requiring the establishment of an internal market and price structure through a system of "transfer pricing." If each center is to be evaluated on its performance, as reflected in measures such as profit percentage on sales and return on investment, then clearly conflicts of interest arise in the relationships among the centers, particularly where the product of one center is used by another.

The use of conflicts of interest and the regulation of internal competition depend on the development of information to measure performance and the actual distribution of rewards to correlate with performance. But despite the availability of information, competitive relationships can go beyond reasonable bounds. Subsidies and supports become necessary for the weaker bargaining units, including the right to appeal a conflict to higher authority. This in turn produces a structure for mediation and arbitration which is an important feature of authority relations within complex organizations.

Our intention here is to illustrate the value to sociologists of intensive study of management control systems as a springboard for organization analysis. The concept of the performance center as the significant structural unit within a complex organization rests on a very elaborate set of motivational premises, ranging from an expectation of compliance, supported by a system of rewards and punishments, to an expectation of initiative from the individual in the direction of his and others' performance.

The possibilities of correlating such premises with (1) the formal control system, (2) performance, and (3) the unanticipated effects on interpersonal relations are suggested in Blau's findings on the effects of statistical performance reports on individual and group behavior in a state government agency.[41]

This type of analysis offers the promise of much higher yields, were the area of study to be moved from the lower to the higher levels of organizations. As formal management control systems become even more sophisticated, they will open additional areas of experimentation in the structure of authority, in this way making the management of change, to which we shall now turn, an important area of executive responsibility.

The Management of Change

One of the earliest normative positions advanced by social scientists in the initiation of change in organizations grew out of the researches at the Western Electric Company.[42] The researches were designed initially as laboratory experiments to test various hypotheses on worker productivity, but the outcome of the researches and their elaboration resulted in a major statement of a normative theory of organization leadership. This normative theory has as its underlying objective the redistribution of power and authority from higher to lower status levels, or more generally the transformation of organization from hierarchical to egalitarian cultures. The leader gives up areas of control unique to his position in the hope of gaining greater involvement in work on the part of subordinates. Following the model of the nondirective counselor, the change in leadership practice is also aimed at shifting the balance between activity and passivity, in the behavior of both leaders and followers, to correspond to the transfer of power from the upper to the lower strata of the organization.

The method of introducing these changes in the balance of power and activity is largely *educative:* individual attitudes are changed through training programs and counseling, resulting in a culture closely resembling egalitarian ideals.

This theory is very much alive in current thinking and practice. It is fostered by Rogers and his students[43] and by the followers of Kurt Lewin;[44] it is much in evidence in current executive and supervisory training efforts and also in writings on management practice.

In *Executive Leadership,*[45] *Organization of a Bank,*[46] and *Personality and Organization,*[47] Argyris takes the position that there is an inevitable conflict between formal organization and the healthy individual. As an advocate of organizational change, he stresses the need to replace large-scale organization with individual-need-oriented groups which would weaken the element of subordinate dependency built into a hierarchy and would foster the growth of "democratic conditions."

In *Interpersonal Competence and Organization Effectiveness*,[48] Argyris discusses the initiation of change through alterations in the values and perceptions of members of an organization, but the empirical results of his work in using T-Group methods to change management values are far from clear. Subordinates found it difficult to accept the new permissive stance adopted by their superiors as a result of the training program: when they went in to discuss a problem with a superior they resented having it turned back to them for solution unaccompanied by the instructions or orders formerly issued. In the Jaques study cited earlier, similar difficulties on the part of subordinates emerged following the introduction of greater worker participation in management.

Douglas McGregor, in *The Human Side of Enterprise* and *Leadership and Motivation*,[49] also falls within the educative tradition. McGregor contrasts two types of leadership theory that he labels "theory X and theory Y," the X being older authoritarian assumptions and practices, based on the primary levels of motivation as distinguished by Maslow,[50] and the Y being the newer psychological practices aimed at meeting the increasingly intangible levels of need which are felt once physiological and safety needs are satisfied.

The normative theory developed by Kurt Lewin[51] and his followers, under the term *group dynamics,* is based on propositions relating individual, group, and cultural determinants of behavior. The individual is conceived of as acting within a field of forces, both internal and external, in the time and space of the here and now. Behavior is a result of forces within the individual's life space and is goal-directed. For behavior to change, the magnitude and direction of the forces must shift to yield a new balance, and the direction of the change must be supported by group or cultural norms; otherwise the individual is in conflict.

The theories of group dynamics as normative approaches to human relations also set guidelines for the behavior of leaders. The guidelines aim to establish democratic and participative group climates rather than autocratic and laissez-faire climates. The differences among the democratic, autocratic, and laissez-faire climates as a function of leadership style were specified in the famous experimental studies of White and Lippitt.[52] Groups of boys in leisure-time activities were exposed to the three climates, induced through the variable of leadership behavior. The democratic group climate produced more favorable responses in the boys in terms of reduced aggression, more enjoyment, the absence of scapegoating, more imaginative productivity, and like effects. The University of Michigan's Survey Research Center extended the examination of leadership and group climate to studies of productivity and satisfaction in industrial work groups. These studies suggested that "person-centered" leaders have more positive effects than "production-centered" leaders.[53]

A different normative approach views organizations as sociotechnical systems and focuses on technology as a major variable affecting interaction and activity. Researchers of this school suggest that as patterns of interaction change, patterns of behavior, and ultimately values, will also change. We include here Chapple and Sayles,[54] Walker and his colleagues,[55] Whyte,[56] Richardson,[57] and others.

The view that individual behavior is a dependent variable affected by the structure of the organization, especially by technology, has stimulated research into the relationship among activities, interactions, and sentiments and such organizational characteristics as the physical and spatial arrangements of work and the formal organization as it establishes the lines of communication and interaction. These researchers seek to develop methods of changing the technology and organization to influence interaction patterns and ultimately the quality of individual sentiments.

In a clear-cut example of this approach, Walker and Guest,[58] in studying the effects of technology on worker satisfaction, absenteeism, and turnover, found that assembly-line work, as compared with less standardized arrangements of work, prevents the development of readily definable work groups and reduces opportunities for building social cohesion among workers; as a result, satisfaction and other indicators of morale are low on mass-production jobs. The experimental work reported by the Tavistock researchers[59] seems to substantiate the validity of this approach to organizational and individual change through manipulation of the technology.

It should be emphasized that, while using technological change as a basis for broader organizational changes, the process of change itself is implemented through the use of consultation and participation at all levels in the organization. Studies of the arrangements of work in an organization viewed as a sociotechnical system result in planned changes not *necessarily* requiring leadership changes or participation. The group-dynamics theorists, on the other hand, see little hope for sustained change apart from creating supportive group climates and democratic-participative leadership patterns. However, insofar as sociotechnical systems theorists use consultation, presumably they are also hoping to alter the over-all culture of the organization toward egalitarian practices.

Our discussion so far has been concerned with two types of normative theories of change: one, associated with the human-relations school, attempts to alter the culture of organizations through educative practices; the second, the sociotechnical systems approach, aims at changing patterns of interaction and activity in the expectation that changes in sentiment will follow. On the whole, social-science literature is replete with material advocating one or another of the normative theories of change.

What is missing, in our view, are studies of change which explicate the nature and consequences of different types of organizational change at the managerial level.

As we suggested earlier, the authority structure and its related formal control system is a frequent object of change; yet, on the whole there have been few attempts to study such changes and their consequences for managerial action.

A study by Lawrence,[60] for example, describes changes in the behavior of three strategically placed district managers following a move to decentralization in a large chain of supermarkets. Where, from management's viewpoint, the results were positive in that the district manager acted more as consultant and teacher than as giver of orders and monitor of performance of the store managers he supervised, this was interpreted as stemming from compatibility between the new type of required behavior and the district manager's "self-concept." Similarly, resistance to change was attributed to self-concepts which inhibited individuals from acting in the required ways. However, the descriptive nature of the study does not lend itself to analysis centered on the changes in the authority structure; in fact, this aspect of the change is hardly considered.

There is, in fact, little analysis available of resistance to change, a phenomenon frequently reported in studies of worker behavior, in the literature on managerial change. There is no a priori reason to assume that resistances apparent at the worker level are not present at the managerial level simply because of the expectation that managers will tend to identify with the organization and accept whatever changes are promulgated by higher authority.

Cursory examination of efforts at change in bureaucratic structures shows ample evidence of resistance. One case reported on in part in Rogow's biography of James Forrestal [61] indicates dramatically how changes that alter the balance of authority (in this case establishing a superagency, the Department of Defense, over the existing military departments) will induce a wide range of sophisticated efforts to prevent the shift from occurring. In this instance, allegiances with particular groups in the Congress provided a means of flouting the changes through the handling of congressional appropriations.

Resistance to change among managers can be "rational" or "irrational." Rational resistance consists of efforts to block those changes resulting in an actual depletion in autonomy, status, and power in relation to other groups. The depletion is experienced as a deprivation, and the resistance is rational in the sense that no individual can be expected willingly to accept a deprivation without some offsetting compensation. Irrational resistance consists of acts countering change when there is no deprivation. The deprivation may be *felt*, but in relation to fantasied or assumed alterations in power.

Rationality or irrationality, acting in the ways defined here, does not belong exclusively to any particular status level in organizations. The problem is to trace through empirically instances of both kinds at the managerial level together with their antecedents and consequences.

One example of irrational resistance to change in the middle-class professional executive culture is available in Hodgson, Levinson, and Zaleznik's[62] study of the latent role structure of an executive group. The authors' approach to resistance to change is through the concept of "reification": *the conversion of an abstraction or mental construction into a supposed real thing.*[63]

Using Goffman's general notion of the staging of one's self, "the dramaturgical approach . . . to the study of organizations," [64] Hodgson, Levinson, and Zaleznik extended it to include its reciprocal: the response of the "audience."

In the course of research, the writers found that the reified personalities of the three top executives were so rigidly held to by their subordinates that the executives' attempts to institute changes were successful only when they appeared to be in consonance with the reified image. The holding of the reified image appears strong enough to transcend questions of self-interest, organizational gain, or achievement of purposes and therefore contains elements of irrational resistance to change.

A related problem occurs in instances of "organizational paralysis": when the need for change is accepted, but no person, instrument, or procedure to initiate change is available within the resources of the organization. Guest discusses this in *Organizational Change: The Effect of Successful Leadership*[65] and suggests that a point is reached when an organization is incapable of changing itself internally. In this study he held that new and constructive patterns of behavior could be introduced only from outside, since a cycle of superior-originated interactions, increased tension, and low performance had become established. The introduction of a new manager broke the cycle and led to an ability to change and to adjust that was free of earlier tension and conflict. For Guest, a central question was what would happen if the man who initiated the change process should leave the organization; the fact that when he did performance continued to improve was taken to mean that a rewarding and productive pattern of relationships had become institutionalized.

A central question, not considered in this study, would be why the state of paralysis under the first manager was ever reached, the issue of reification, and the implications of this for theories of change. Although Guest cites Fleishman, Burtt, and Harris[66] to support his thesis that a willingness to co-operate must "start at the top and permeate down through the entire organization in day-to-day relationships," [67] he ignores perhaps the most interesting findings of the Fleishman study: that leadership climate, itself a form of reification, molds patterns of expectation on the part of both supervisors and supervised. It is worth noting that in the Lawrence study cited earlier, the district manager who displayed the greatest resistance to the required behavioral changes supervised a store manager whose behavior reinforced his own. It appears that factors more intrinsic than patterns of interaction are helping to determine the effects of change.

The phenomenon of reification impedes the ability of subordinates to experience a superior's changed behavior as an actual behavioral change, because the new behavior more often seems to be a gimmick or, at best, behavior that is somehow not "in character." Mann found that "changes in subordinates' perceptions and attitudes which follow a change in supervisory personnel are frequently of much larger order than those generated by training, and other procedures for changing the attitudes or behavior of incumbents." [68] Clearly, individuals put their stamp on interaction to an extent that we can appreciate only if we consider this issue in some detail, as we shall now attempt to do.

The Analysis of Role Performance

The problem of analyzing managerial behavior in interpersonal situations can be approached in two ways: (1) as a problem in delineating the development of role structure in organizations; (2) as a problem in relating personality to performance. We suggest that both approaches warrant careful consideration in managerial studies.

Our aim in this section is to examine the structure of role performance, while in the concluding section we shall bring to bear concepts from the study of personality to explain the nature of different styles of leadership in executive role performance.

The term *role performance* in organizational studies applies to what individuals as members of an organizational hierarchy do in face-to-face encounters with other members of the organization. Role theory in sociology centers on others' expectations as to the behavior of the individual who occupies a given position.[69] These expectations are considered autonomous facts of culture[70] which sustain order and consistency in human interaction. These expectations are essentially normative prescriptions for behavior in relation to specific positions in the formal organization structure. A foreman, for example, occupies a position to which are attached certain expectations for his behavior toward others in the organization. The behavior of others toward him is equally a consequence of the expectations intrinsic to their positions. For a foreman to behave as he is expected to, others must be able to take the reciprocal role. Looked at in this way, role performance involves the mutual adaptation of individuals to one another in terms of the behavioral expectations prescribed for their respective positions. The total structure within which the expectations operate is the role set; and it includes vertical as well as lateral relationships.[71]

Elaborate role definitions are transmitted both formally and informally. They are inherent in the hierarchy in elaborate job descriptions but are also symbolically represented through dress, physical location, and other status attributes, including age and sex.[72] Foremost among the expectations that govern role performance in organizations are the deference patterns inherent in authority relationships.

Despite the necessity for accurate role prescriptions, it cannot be assumed that mutual role definitions are always well established. Interpersonal tension and conflict would not exist if this were always the case. Tension and conflict can arise from the failure of individuals to establish reciprocal role relationships: each may have clear but quite different expectations for the other's behavior. Gross and his colleagues explored this problem in a study of consensus in role definitions.[73] They defined consensus as the degree of agreement between role definers—in this case school superintendents and school-board members—on the expectations they held for incumbents of each others' positions. The researchers found that in allocating responsibilities between the two positions, school-board members assigned greater responsibility to themselves than to the superintendents, and vice versa. School-board members felt stronger obligations to the community than to the teaching staff, while the reverse was true for the superintendents. The conflict inherent in these disparate expectations was acutely felt in disputes over school curricula and finance—in particular the issue of teachers' salaries.

In contrast with this form of role conflict—essentially interrole conflict resulting from conflicting expectations within a role set—an individual may also be subject to intrarole conflict. This arises when members of a role set expect different and opposing kinds of behavior from a central figure in the set. A common source of this type of conflict in organizations lies in the demands made on supervisors to act both permissively and instrumentally—the conflict between the expectations from below that the superior will be a "nice guy" and the expectation from above that he will "get out the work." The individual caught in this kind of conflict is often uncertain how to act and may therefore behave quite inconsistently, eventually evoking conflict in the individual who must perform in the reciprocal role.

In Organizational Stress: Studies in Role Conflict and Ambiguity, Kahn and others[74] present and interpret data on the kinds of position most susceptible to intrarole conflict. They found that individuals who are the focus of conflicting demands are often the incumbents of "boundary positions." Salesmen, for example, are subject to pressure from outside the organization (from customers) as well as from inside (from production superintendents and schedulers). In general, they found evidence of intrarole conflict wherever an individual's position requires him to maintain contact with others outside his own department or outside the organization. A further source of intrarole conflict is the organizational need for innovation. To meet this need, an organization depends on individual creativity and acceptance of change, but both factors are constrained by the resistance the innovator must face from individuals who look on him as a threat to their own security. Still another source of conflict for the innovator is in the clash between the requirements of the innovating role and the more routine and rule-bound duties of administration.

Role conflicts create conditions which prevent orderliness in interaction while generating stress for members of the role set; an analogous condition is found in role ambiguity. In contrast to role conflict, where clear but opposing expectations are present, ambiguity exists where the role expectations have not crystallized or are otherwise vague. Such a condition frequently holds in staff jobs in organizations in which it is quite unclear where giving assistance is to be differentiated from giving orders or in any other way directly controlling the behavior of others.

In the Kahn study just cited, the authors found that role ambiguity exists under conditions which de-emphasize the general organization norms of orientation to rules, close supervision, and similar treatment for all. We would interpret this to mean that role ambiguity follows the movement away from positional authority to professional authority as the primary source of influence and from bureaucratic to individualized work cultures. A number of studies have shown the tendency for individuals high on authoritarian attributes to feel tension and dissatisfaction in loosely structured work situations.[75]

Yet another type of conflict which affects role performance arises from the fact that individuals play multiple roles at any given stage in the life cycle. A man, for example, is husband and father, has an occupation, and belongs to many formal and informal groups. Performance in any one role implies a capacity either to integrate the multiple role expectations or to select certain expectations to which he will respond while suppressing others in a fashion that is congruent with the situation at a given point in time. A man may "father" his son in the family setting with success, but the same behavior in relation to subordinates at work is apt to produce conflict, since it may imply a kind of subordination and dependency that others find inappropriate to the work setting.

How an individual integrates or selects and suppresses expectations for a given role performance is a function of personality structure and psychodynamic attributes, a problem we shall examine later in this section and in the one following. We shall consider now, as a further step in the analysis of role structure and performance, the theoretical formulations of Parsons and Bales.[76] Their theory and its related laboratory studies of problemsolving groups show how shifting role structures and performances are imbedded in the tensions inherent in work and interpersonal relations in organizations.[77]

Bales postulates that problem-solving activity in groups represents a moving equilibrium in which one observes the recurrence of disruptive modes followed by counterbalancing modes. Two main modes or cycles exist in problem solving. The first is task-oriented behavior when the acts are directed toward the solution of problems. During the course of task activity, the equilibrium is disrupted; work produces a build-up of tensions, since it essentially calls for a release of aggressive energy in the exchange and evaluation of ideas. Competition inevitably results, and as task-oriented behavior continues, the tension mounts. The cohesion of a group becomes threatened when the point is reached where the tension is intolerable (this point cannot be specified). To assure the survival and continuity of the group, a new mode or cycle must begin, directed toward draining the tension and restoring the cohesion within the group. This second modality requires catharsis, expression of warm feelings, and re-establishing the identity of the group in the minds of the members to assure their continued participation. At a certain point, however, acts directed toward cohesion become blocks toward work, and aggression is reintroduced in order to deal with problem-solving issues. Problem solving is thus a process of alternating modes or cycles in interpersonal relations.

Having identified and interpreted the equilibrium problem, Bales then describes how groups develop a structure of role relationships which is functionally related to the maintenance of group equilibrium. He notes that although groups without an assigned leader tend to have a more equal distribution of participation among members, there does tend to be a process of *quantitative* differentiation among members. When he ranked and aggregated participants in the laboratory study on the quantity of activity they produced, he found that the top man was the only one who addressed more comments to the group as a whole than he did to individual members, while all ranks distributed their comments to others in proportion to the amounts that the others spoke. Bales states that qualitative differentiation is associated with quantitative differentiation.[78] His findings, along with those of other investigators,[79] confirm the high degree of association between individuals' participation rates and their statuses as measured independently.

Bales's findings and interpretations lead to the conclusion that the dilemma of group problem solving lies in the apparent antithesis between work and affection. Affection is the cement that binds groups together. The aggressive activity which produces work tends to disintegrate groups. Yet in order for group work to be achieved, the group must hold itself together in some way. The processes by which cohesion and work are accomplished are similar in kind to the physiological processes which maintain organisms in a state of *internal* equilibrium while the organism as a whole maintains some form of stable adaptive equilibrium in its interactions with its environment.

Slater's study addresses the problem of role differentiation in small groups.[80] It asks essentially whether performances in a group are flexible and widely distributed among individuals or specialized with a resulting structure of complementary role performances. Using measures of participation and voting choices received on Ideas, Guidance, Liking, and Leadership, he finds that

> role differentiation in the High (consensus) groups seems to be bipartite, with an active "task specialist" and a best-liked man. In the low (consensus) groups it tends to be tripartite (as well as more extreme), with an active participator who is neither well-liked nor highly rated on task ability, a more passive task specialist who is not well-liked, and a popular individual who is neither active nor highly rated on task ability.[81]

He also finds that role specialization tends to *increase* over time. His groups each met four times. In each succeeding meeting, the likelihood that a man would be top choice on both ideas and liking decreased significantly.

When he compared the behavior patterns of idea men and best-liked men, Slater found that the idea men initiated more problem-solving attempts, disagreed more, and showed more antagonism, while the best-liked men initiated more positive social reactions, asked more questions, and showed more tension. He summarizes as follows:

> The general picture is thus one of specialization and complementarity, with the idea man concentrating on the task and playing a more aggressive role, while the best-liked man concentrates more on social-emotional problems, giving rewards and playing a more passive role.[82]

He also discusses evidence which shows that the idea men and the best-liked men tend to work in a complementary team relationship.

Confirming and elaborating on the apparent antithesis between task activity and social activity reported in Bales's work on equilibrium, Slater demonstrates how the roles tend to polarize in group processes. He found that role complementarity provides one way for groups to deal with the task-social dilemma while indicating that highly specialized role performance may be an indicator of rigidity in personality. Slater's ideas suggest that effective leaders in problem-solving groups attempt to overcome the situational forces which tend to force role specialization and are relatively free of strong personal predispositions to specialize in role performance.

The empirical findings presented seem to suggest a division of labor in a group along the instrumental-expressive axis. Further confirmation of this division of role performance is found in a more recent study by Moment and Zaleznik of interpersonal behavior in problem-solving situations.[83] The groups, consisting of mature executives and professional persons, met in an experimental setting. In the course of their participation they completed sociometric questionnaires similar to the type used by Bales in his studies. The resulting correlation matrix of performance ratings is represented in Table 8–2.

TABLE 8–2. *Degrees of Association among Components of Role Perceptions and Resultant Evaluations, Measured by Mutual Predictive Values*[84]

			GENERAL EVALUATIONS	
		LEADERSHIP	"LIKE TO WORK WITH"	"LIKE TO KNOW SOCIALLY"
	Ideas	.50	.26	.00
Specific comments	Guidance	.42	.05	.14
	Congeniality	.17	.00	.20

Clearly, there is a systematic relationship in the perception of task roles as a significant aspect of leadership and the social roles as an aspect of friendship patterns. This general proposition is also supported in the studies of friendship structures and may be summarized, following Homans, to mean that "love flees authority." [85] Individuals who exercise aggression (authority) through the expression of ideas may be viewed as leaders, but the desired relationship is one of distance and not intimacy.

While it appears true that role perceptions divide along the instrumental-expressive axis, it may not necessarily follow, however, that problem-solving activity involves a bipartite leadership structure. In the Moment and Zaleznik study just cited, the structure of roles was conceived in terms of a fourfold model. One role type consisted of the *fusion* of idea and congeniality components. A second and third consisted of the role specializations (task and social), following Bales. And a fourth conceived of an erratic pattern that is perceived as strong on neither task nor social components. This last role type was designated *underchosen*, representing impoverishment in role performance. The four role types proved a very valuable model empirically and showed distinct differences in performances and underlying motivational states.

Two questions emerge from Parsons' and Bales's formulations. The first deals with the adequacy of the model in its dichotomy between instrumental and expressive roles; in our view—and we shall shortly cite supporting evidence—no role performance exists without an affective component. In all likelihood the instrumental roles are charged with aggression, which accounts for their divisive potential; but aggression is no less expressive, from the viewpoint of the actors in a role set, than the warm and nurturant performances of the social leaders whose acts result in tension reduction.

The second question concerns the applicability of the model to large-scale organizations. The empirical data supporting the theory grew out of studies in the laboratory and observations of the family. Is extension to role structures in business, educational, and governmental organizations valid? Hodgson, Levinson, and Zaleznik in the *Executive Role Constellation* demonstrate the value of the Parsons and Bales model and offer modifications applicable to bureaucratic systems.[86]

Within the management structure of the mental hospital studied, the authors found a subsystem of three executives whose importance, although dependent in part on their high positions in the organization, was at the same time heavily reinforced by the ability of the three men to engage the task aspects of their jobs in ways which permitted a simultaneous "division of emotional labor."

The authors found that the primary function of each executive was not "the internalizing of existing organizational values, but the institutionalizing of values new to the organization, drawn from the executive's personal value system."[87] Each executive's role in the organization tended to become specialized around the performance of certain tasks and the expression of certain emotions. The authors' observations indicated the importance to each individual of actively developing situations which were satisfying to him for both personal and organizational reasons. His manner of doing so assumed a consistent pattern over time and created an image of him on the part of his subordinates which at times exerted a crucial influence on his ability to get on with his work as he wanted it done: as we noted in an earlier section, when he stepped out of the "personal role" he had established, acceptance by his subordinates was seriously impaired.

The literature on executive behavior is deficient in the study of the types of role structures found in different kinds of organizations. Studies of this kind are badly needed to provide an analytic model of action in which the objectives of action will relate at a manifest level to the strategy and tactics of purpose and at a latent level to the emotional and motivational spheres of individual existence. As we shall now try to show, the problem of action in executive leadership is one of demonstrating and explaining the outer and inner meaning of behavior and its consequences for organizational survival and development.

Executive Leadership

The problem of leadership is directly concerned with how individuals mobilize and use power as it is derived from position, competence, and personal charisma.

In Weber's ideal bureaucracy, only the man best qualified to hold an office might achieve it, and the authority of position or of office thus assumed paramount importance. In "classical" theories of organization, this connection between position and competence was lost sight of, and the office itself increasingly became the sole source of authority in analyses of organization structures. Orders from a superior were obeyed by subordinates because they emanated from a position of authority capable of meting out reward, punishment, or sanction. The formal authority delegated to a position was regarded as coterminous with the authority exercised by its holder and accepted by his subordinates: presumably, if the holder were authorized to lead, his subordinates would follow.

The discrepancy between classical theory and organizational processes inevitably led to revision of the theory. Barnard held that "authority is another name for the willingness and capacity of individuals to submit to the necessities of cooperative systems." [88] He distinguished two dimensions of authority: "authority of position" and "authority of leadership." Authority of position depended on centrality in the organization's communications system—it was determined by a structural decision—while authority of leadership was dependent on the superior ability of the leader. Barnard felt that, taken together, authority of position and of leadership determined the extent to which a superior's directives would be followed, and in this way he reintroduced the Weberian concept of expertise. Barnard differed from Weber, however, in according expertise the status of a variable; he did not view it as inherent in the system. To the extent that an executive lacked "authority of leadership," subordinates would tend to question whether an order was consistent with their understanding of organizational purpose or with their own personal interests; to the extent that he possessed it, his subordinates would function in a "zone of indifference" in which they felt no need to judge the order's merits, but simply accepted the prior judgment of their superior. Barnard felt that it was the task of the executive to widen the zone of indifference, to mobilize the authority of superior ability in order to encourage suspension of judgment on the part of his subordinates. At the same time, he expressly eliminated coercion from his analysis of authority: "authority lies always with him to whom it applies . . . force creates a contrary illusion but it destroys the authority postulated." [89] The inference here is that if authority exists, force is superfluous, and if force is used we are dealing, not with authority, but with something quite different. This effectively discounts the coercive power inherent in position.

Subsequent work has followed Barnard's line of reasoning, so that we find a distinction drawn by Gibb, among others, between "leadership" and "headship." [90] Leadership, in Gibb's view, is accorded by peers, not by subordinates. He states:

> The leader's authority is spontaneously accorded him by his fellow group members, the followers. The authority of the head derives from some extra-group power which he has over the members of the group, who cannot meaningfully be called his followers. They accept his domination on pain of punishment rather than follow. The business executive is an excellent example of a head exercising authority derived from his position in an organization through membership in which the workers, his subordinates, satisfy many strong needs. They obey his commands and accept his domination because this is part of their duty as organization members and to reject him would be to discontinue membership with all the punishments that would involve.[91]

Leadership, according to Gibb, is a variable, while headship is not. His definition of leadership clearly follows Barnard's, while his description of headship leans heavily on the classical theory of unilateral authority vested in position and backed by organizational sanctions.

For our purposes, distinctions such as these are meaningless, since the problem of leadership cannot be addressed by concentrating on, eliminating, or varying any *single* factor, whether it be authority of position or voluntary acceptance of authority by subordinates (itself a consequence of the use of authority inherent in competence and charisma). For us, the problem of leadership is essentially the problem of how and *for what purpose* an executive generates and mobilizes the power and authority vested in his position, in his level of competence, and in the charismatic appeal with which he may be endowed.

These concepts clearly owe much to Weberian analysis, but the fundamental difference in our use of them is that we view them, not as structural attributes normatively required, but as variables dependent for their functioning on the capacities of a man in action within a structure. We shall illustrate this view initially by reference to the work of political analysis whose accounts of Chief Executives in office provide the clearest indication of the extent to which individual predispositions and personality have shaped and reshaped an office. Political analysts point out that the positional power of the President of the United States is always there, but there are marked variations in the way different incumbents have used their powers; the variables are not simply the ways in which power is exercised, but whether the individual is sensitive to and aware of power processes.

As a guide in their comparisons of leaders exercising power, political analysts have used the concept of "style." We can define style, following the psychoanalytic concept of "character," as the patterned modes of behavior with which an individual relates himself to external reality and to his own internal dispositions. For the time being, we shall refrain from developing a more general conceptualization of what "reality" is in an executive situation; what, for instance, the functions are that must be served and what means are available for the purpose. We shall also leave until later the attempt to delineate the predispositional sets which affect the way in which a man perceives his functions and also affect, as a result, his ability to use the power available to him in their service. We shall concentrate initially on descriptions of Presidents in office and on the styles of leadership with which they respond to the functional demands of their positions. We shall thus attempt to move from what actually happens in the encounter between the individual and the situation to why it appears to happen in the way that it does.

In *Presidential Power* Neustadt gives a clear account of the functions a President must serve, of the means available to him for the purpose, and of the leadership styles of three very different Presidents as they used their power in the execution of policy.[92]

The President is, of course, acting within a structure, and Neustadt, while identifying the constitutional function that he must serve, also brings into relief one of the crucial dilemmas of power and position.

> In form, all Presidents are leaders nowadays. In fact, this guarantees no more than that they will be clerks. Everybody now expects the man in the White House to do something about everything. Laws and customs now reflect acceptance of him as the Great Initiator, an acceptance quite as widespread at the Capitol as at his end of Pennsylvania Avenue. But such acceptance does not signify that all the rest of the government is at his feet. *It merely signifies that other men have found it practically impossible to do their jobs without assurance of initiatives from him.* Service for themselves, not power for the President, has brought them to accept his leadership in form.[93]

The "constituents" of the President, who look to him for initiatives, come from five groups: executive officialdom, Congress, political partisans, citizens at large, and officials in foreign countries. Representatives of each of these constituent groups seek to develop claims on the Chief Executive in ways that enable them to perform, while the President himself must seek to establish claims on their decisions to act.

Presidential power, or the power to initiate successfully, according to Neustadt,

> is influence of an effective sort on the behavior of men actually involved in making public policy and carrying it out. Effective influence for the man in

the White House stems from three related sources: first are the bargaining advantages inherent in the job with which he persuades other men that what he wants of them is what their own responsibilities require them to do. Second are the expectations of those other men regarding his ability and will to use the various advantages they think he has. Third are those men's estimates of how his public views him and of how their public may view them if they do what he wants.[94]

The use of these powers, however, depends on an individual's conception of his role. Neustadt provides a striking example of this in his discussion of the leadership styles of Roosevelt and Eisenhower.

Eisenhower wanted to be President [although] what he wanted from it was a far cry from what F.D.R. had wanted. Roosevelt was a politician seeking personal power; Eisenhower was a hero seeking national unity. . . . He genuinely thought the President was or ought to be the source of unifying, moderating, influence above the struggle.[95]

Eisenhower's presidential style *was* that of a leader above the struggle. He established a staff system in the White House which

imparted more superficial symmetry and order to his flow of information than was ever done before. Therefore, he became typically the last man in his office to know tangible details and the last to come to grips with acts of choice. His one-time chief assistant in the White House, Sherman Adams, is reported to have told a close associate: "I count the day lost when I have not found some new way of lightening the President's load." [96]

Eisenhower did not want the details, as Roosevelt did, of every factor that could affect a decision. He wanted the details ready-weighed and only the final alternatives presented to him. These alternatives often reflected other men's interests more closely than his own, and Neustadt's description of the circumstances surrounding Eisenhower's 1957 budget points to this. The system limited Eisenhower's ability to exploit the power available to him, since he lacked information on how and where it should be applied.

Dahl stresses that a power base is inert or passive; it must be exploited in some way if the behavior of others is to be affected.[97] He defines the means of power as "a mediating activity by A between A's base and B's response," and he illustrates this by suggesting that

in the case of the President, the means would include the *promise* of patronage, the *threat* of veto, the *holding* of a conference, the *threat* of appeal to the electorate, the *exercise* of charm and charisma, etc.[98]

The bases of power in position, competence, and charisma are apparent, but in Eisenhower's case they went largely unused. Roosevelt, on the other hand, was a man bent on taking the initiative. The Roosevelt of the nineteen-thirties was intent on making new departures, and he exploited every base of power available to him to rally support for his decisions.

> The first task of an executive, as he evidently saw it, was to guarantee himself an effective flow of information and ideas. . . . Roosevelt's persistent effort therefore was to check and balance information acquired through official channels by information acquired through a myriad of private, informal, and unorthodox channels and espionage networks. At times he seemed almost to pit his personal sources against his public sources.[99]

In doing this, however, he not only checked and balanced the flow and validity of his information; at the same time he insured for himself a position of the utmost centrality at every stage of the decision-making process. He could assess who wanted what and why they wanted it. He could establish his priorities and make his choices guided by clear indications as to where and at whom his power should be directed in order to secure support. At the same time Roosevelt's style of leadership was not only that of an initiator; it involved the use of ambiguity in interpersonal relations. The use of ambiguity provided a means for maintaining a central position in the communications network and flexibility in negotiation and decision making.

A President can attempt to assume the initiative but with an interpersonal style which involves aloofness and distance. In *Woodrow Wilson and Colonel House*, the Georges make it clear that Wilson was dramatically aware of the Chief Executive's function as initiator.[100] In fact, whatever leadership position he attained, whether as President of Princeton University, Governor of New Jersey, or President of the United States, Wilson initiated reforms of a sweeping nature, but his style of initiation reflected an emotional attachment to abstract ideas and ideals such as justice and democracy, and his expression of these ideals involved a narcissistic bond between himself and the masses. This narcissistic transaction proceeded through the spoken word, the "giving" in verbal imagery of strong emotional currents which mobilized and sustained the idealism. The "getting" in this exchange involved the adoration of the masses to reinforce a self-image built on the theme of the warrior overcoming malevolent forces that impede man's struggle for justice and equality. Wilson was unable to function freely when action depended on negotiation and persuasion in close face-to-face relationships. In the earlier stages of his presidency he depended on Colonel House to deal with the hard realities of negotiation and in this sense established a pair relationship involving complementary role performances.

The point that we wish to underline here is that in all organizations executives face the problem of fusing a personal style with structural realities in asserting power. Executives may or may not be conscious of the functions that in reality they are called upon to serve. The structure does not necessarily make these functions clear and unequivocal. As a consequence, an individual may or may not be aware of the bases of power available to him, or, as in Wilson's case, he may overexploit a particular base while ignoring others that are equally available and in fact more appropriate as a means of achieving his objectives.

Little work has been done so far in the sociological study of leadership which attempts to deal systematically with the problem of the person-position encounter. A model for such analyses must provide concepts that relate to both personality and structural variables; a small attempt in this direction has been made by Zaleznik in his paper "Managerial Behavior and Interpersonal Competence."[101]

Zaleznik identifies three basic organizational functions: the homeostatic, the mediative, and the proactive. The homeostatic function is concerned with the maintenance of the organization—the assurance of its internal stability in the face of internal disruption. The mediative function, on the other hand, is fulfilled by processes which occur under the impact of environmental pressure: the executive attempts to influence individuals and groups within the organization to modify behavior and attitudes so that a different form of adaptation to the environment is secured. The proactive function, rather than being a reaction to environmental pressure, is concerned with inducing change in the environment to conform to the creative use of resources available within the organization.

In terms of the primacy of objectives, the homeostatic function stresses maintaining the stability of the system as the fundamental objective, sometimes to the point where it becomes a substitute for activity in the environment. Mediation involves activity in the environment in order to distinguish pressures to which the organization must respond by way of altered internal relationships. Proaction, on the other hand, is the mark differentiating the innovative entrepreneur and typically tends to induce resistance, aggression, and in some cases outright hostility within the organization; it may be disruptive of internal relations in the service of changing the environment.

Historically, organizations seem to move through phases in which emphasis is given to one of these three functional tasks. An example of this is available in a brief study of management succession in Sears, Roebuck by Perrin Stryker, in which he gives an account of the correlation between management succession and the changes in functional emphasis.[102]

The head of the company from 1893 to 1908 was the founder, Richard W. Sears. He started out in partnership with Roebuck, selling watches by direct mail. As the business grew, Sears introduced basic innovations in mail-order selling, not least among which was an insistence on keeping the quality of his goods up to the hyperbolic descriptions of his advertising copy, and this at a time when, as Stryker writes, "fleecing yokels was a standard business practice." Sears kept his prices low and his markup small and depended on high-pressure advertising to increase turnover. His advertising changed tastes and formed new ones. To compete with Sears's merchandising tactics, businessmen in the cities as well as those in small towns improved their sales and service policies and often copied his techniques outright. Sears, in fact, changed the environment which merchandisers up to then had taken for granted.

The man who followed him as head of the organization, however, had quite different views. Julius Rosenwald bought a half-interest in the company in 1895, and he found Sears's methods increasingly disruptive of what, in his view, was efficient management. Sears's advertising and promotion had spurred such a level of orders that in ten years the company's sales jumped from three-quarters of a million to nearly forty million dollars. The buying and shipping departments were overburdened and in confusion. When the sales fell in the 1907 depression, Sears argued strongly for even larger expenditures on advertising to combat the fall, but Rosenwald defeated him and began a drastic cost-cutting program. Sears resigned, and Rosenwald assumed control. He stressed the homeostatic function of maintaining internal stability. His most far-reaching innovation was the improvement of methods of quality control, but even these were later eliminated as part of an economy drive.

Rosenwald's eventual successor was Robert E. Wood. Wood, as Vice-President of Montgomery Ward, had begun to apply statistics to the mail-order market and had foreseen that the declining rural population was reducing the need for mail-order services, while at the same time increasing the need for retail stores in suburban towns. Realizing that competition from chain stores was intensifying, he became convinced that the future of mail-order houses lay in shifting the emphasis to retailing; after he joined Sears, Roebuck, he immediately began to move the company into the retail trade. In 1928 the number of company-owned stores rose from 27 to 192, and the chain grew to more than 630 over the next twenty years, accounting for approximately three-quarters of Sears's total sales. Wood's contribution to the company lay in the essentially mediative activity of adapting the business to an environment which had changed substantially. He foresaw trends and moved to meet them.

In 1954 Wood was succeeded by Theodore Houser. As chief merchandiser of Sears under Wood, Houser had devised an unusual strategy of "basic buying" which called for close co-operation with the company's suppliers in the design of products and in the calculation of materials, labor, overhead, and profit. Houser's aim was to develop low-cost suppliers capable of making a steady profit for themselves who were located so as to save distribution costs and, assisted by Sears, Roebuck's research and volume orders, to reduce their operating costs. Thus, Houser viewed Sears's suppliers as part of the company's structure, with Sears assisting each to become more efficient as a producer, rather than as sources of goods at the lowest possible price, the original mail-order buying concept.

This illustrates some of the difference between the adaptation of mediation and the innovation of proaction; a further innovation by Houser makes the distinction even clearer. Sears had long been criticized for the cash drain its mail-order sales imposed in many rural areas. Houser found, for example, that Sears was spending less than $500,000 a year in Mississippi, while selling $8 million to $9 million worth of goods in the state. He felt that Sears could change this situation if, instead of using one very large supplier, it encouraged the establishment of several small plants spread over a wider area. On this basis, Sears acquired suppliers across the country, bringing sales and purchases into balance; in the southeast alone Sears helped to establish nearly a hundred small factories, in this way increasing its purchases in the area to a point where they were approximately the same as the company's sales.

Stryker implicitly discusses the quality of the leadership shown by Wood and Houser in terms of the functions they served.

> Wood, for instance, dramatically expanded Sears into the retail-store business, and *changed its internal and external organization in line with the changes in population and marketing that he foresaw;* whereas Houser led by carefully *planning and developing the means for changing Sears into a new kind of industrial unit* that aims at linking the supplier, the distributor, and the customer—the linking to be not only for mutual benefit but for the benefit of the general economy.[103]

We would go back even further. Under its founder, Sears, Roebuck changed the mail-order environment; the organizational function which was discharged almost to the exclusion of any other was essentially proactive, and the internal disruption which ensued led to a homeostatic counterrevolution under Rosenwald. This was followed by Wood's successful attempts to adapt the company to an environment that had in the meantime changed appreciably. Houser in his turn reverted to an emphasis on proactivity.

If we consider that the fulfillment of these functions represents organizational reality for an executive, then it becomes necessary to discuss the means by which functional demands are met or avoided. The situation in which these demands are responded to is interpersonal, but the first stimulus is necessarily intrapersonal, and the question becomes one of whether, and how, the demands of organizational reality are first perceived by the individual.

In *Role Development and Interpersonal Competence,* cited earlier, the authors distinguished four predispositional sets to which we have already referred. Three of these sets concern us here. The sets represent essentially the direction of emotional energy, or the individual's energy cathexes. The objects toward which the cathexes are directed are of two main kinds: persons and ideas. In one internal set the individual may direct his emotional energy toward the task; technically we speak of his cathecting the idea aspects of the work. The interpersonal aspects are not cathected to the same degree and may even, in fact, be defended against. A second internal set consists of a strong orientation toward persons: the cathexis is directed toward human relationships. Tasks may assume relatively little significance in the individual's inner need and value structure, and in fact the cognitive-technical aspects of work may be defended against. The third predispositional set represents a fusion of cathexes. In this case, the individual in his inner world weighs both persons and ideas as important to him and blends them in his concern with situations in the real world.

In "Managerial Behavior and Interpersonal Competence," Zaleznik developed a matrix of the interrelationships between executive functions and predispositional sets which is reproduced as Figure 8–1. He noted:

> It would seem that the predispositional sets are conducive for performance within specialized functions. This idea is expressed by the shadings within each cell. While every individual can probably shift interpersonal modes to conform to the various functional requisites, each set would appear *to be selectively oriented toward a particular function.* The person-oriented individual would perform most easily in the range of interpersonal behavior associated with the homeostatic functions. We would assume that such an individual would, relatively speaking, avoid proactive functions. Under conditions where proaction was thrust upon him and avoidance became difficult, the defensive apparatus of the individual would be under stress. The idea-oriented individual, on the other hand, would perform most easily in the proactive functions, utilizing aggression and dominance as major components of his interpersonal style. Presumably the homeostatic functions are not well understood and may be strongly avoided; . . . organizational effectiveness would seem to require as a prerequisite some mix in the performance of executive functions to assure both the securing of purpose and the maintenance of the internal capacities of the organization.[104]

The concept of leadership style emerges from the selective orientation of an individual toward a particular function; the means by which style becomes apparent are the ways in which the individual makes use of the bases of his power. Implicit in Neustadt's analysis of the presidency, for example, is the degree to which its effectiveness, its "success," is dependent on proactivity; the system turns on presidential initiative. But for the President to win support for his initiatives, he must be able to use the power available to him, and this in turn depends on his awareness of the demands placed on him and on the way in which these coincide with the predispositions which he brings to the office.

FIGURE 8–1.   Executive Functions—Organizational Requisites

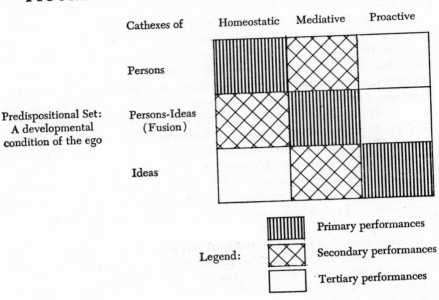

Thus, to speak of Roosevelt as "a politician seeking personal power" is to do him less than justice.[105] In him a predispositional idea-oriented set and the functional demands of his office effectively meshed. He was psychologically free to achieve his objectives through the use of all the bases of power available to him. He could *use* people.

> His favorite technique was to keep grants of authority incomplete, jurisdictions uncertain, charters overlapping. The results of this competitive theory of administration was often confusion and exasperation on the operating level; but no other method could so reliably insure that in a large bureaucracy filled with ambitious men eager for power, the decisions and the power to make them, would remain with the President.[106]

In this respect, he differed fundamentally from Wilson. Wilson's cathexis to ideas was fraught with inner conflict over the challenge to his authority that he felt in relationships with other men; in the presidency he dealt with this problem either by referring it to his close associate, House, or by avoiding it entirely and relying instead on positional and, to a much larger extent, charismatic power to achieve his objectives.

Neustadt's description of Eisenhower's style also suggests the contrasts with Roosevelt's:

> Eisenhower's use of men tended to smother, not enhance, the competition roused by overlapping jurisdictions. Apparently this was intentional; . . . Eisenhower seemingly preferred to let subordinates proceed upon the lowest common denominators of agreement than to have their quarrels—and issues and details—pushed up to him.[107]

Evidently Eisenhower defended against conflict and aggression, and his conscious attitude was one of altruism rather than the egoism of Franklin Roosevelt. Personal power—the means by which an idea orientation is transformed into a proactive style—held no attraction for Eisenhower. Doubting his own, he clung to the judgment of the people around him, and to this the conflict over his 1957 budget attests.

Another illustration of the meshing of functional demands with individual predispositions can be found in the *Executive Role Constellation*, cited earlier. In this study Hodgson, Levinson, and Zaleznik observed the work of three executives in an important teaching and research hospital. The three men, all doctors who had gained recognition in their field, were in the key positions of Superintendent, Clinical Director, and Director of Research. The Superintendent was an active, assertive, and dominating figure who specialized in external relations.

> [He] viewed himself very much as a builder, who could put things together and make them run. He talked of his many activities and commitments in terms of their instrumental place in building the future of psychiatry. His professional memberships as such were not only of interest or value in and of themselves. They too were part of [his] larger design to assist and to influence the unfolding cause of his profession.[108]

Yet in this hospital the homeostatic function had also to be met. The Superintendent contributed a sense of action and movement, but at the same time more than a few of his subordinates feared him for his very qualities of assertiveness. They avoided him and weakened his lines of communication throughout the organization. To a large extent this deficiency was met by the Clinical Director, a warm, quiet figure with close emotional ties to people in the organization and an intimate knowledge of what went on in their daily lives.

The researchers took the view that

> executive groups . . . usually consist of two or three (rarely more) central individuals, although some others may be peripherally involved. . . . We have used the word "constellation" rather than "group" to emphasize the

significance of the personal relations among members, the emotional climate of the group, and the psychological properties of the interactions that define the group. Constellations . . . involve (1) role specialization of executive members, (2) differentiation among individual roles, and (3) *complementary relations among them.* This would indicate that little in the way of group development could occur among individuals who had, for personal and tactical reasons, not specialized their organizational roles either *instrumentally* or *expressively.*[109]

Here the researchers are implicitly discussing the way in which power among executives is mobilized and redistributed in interpersonal structures to meet the functional demands of the organization. Assumption of particular function, whether it is homeostatic, mediative, or proactive, is closely related to personality structure and dynamics and, in its manifestation as a style of executive leadership, involves the mobilization and redistribution of power itself.

Executive constellations as structures for redistributing power can take a variety of forms, each with its own symbolic and instrumental meanings to the actors in the situation. Observation indicates that types of constellation include the *patriarchy* built around the dominant leader as the central figure; the *group,* an executive system of equals; and the *pair,* a structure often encountered in which one executive is concerned with external problems while the second deals with internal relations. The *triad,* discussed in the Hodgson, Levinson, and Zaleznik study, displays interesting features of instability in the internal status structure of the constellation. Research on types of constellations and their relation to leadership styles, interpersonal relations, and the strategy and tactics of organizational purpose promises ultimately to unfold new understanding of organizations as action systems.

Summary

We have attempted to move from consideration of organization structure to the study of individual action within a structure. In our view, the structure is necessarily a variable, dependent on the legitimation of authority systems within it. The legitimation of positional authority tends to create a pyramidal structure, while reliance on a professional authority system flattens the organization and redistributes positional authority. The problems that arise are essentially those of insuring the relevance of the authority system implicit in the structure to the achievement of organizational objectives. We have considered the effect of control systems on the definition of organizational objectives and through this their implications for the structure itself.

Underlying the views that we have put forward is our conviction that organization structures owe their variable character to the ways in which they are used by individuals in the service of their own individual needs, and we have illustrated this by reference to laboratory studies of role taking in groups. We have considered the process of organizational change from a similar point of view. The acceptance of organizational roles (and by this we do not refer to static behavior descriptions, but to the functional roles which keep an organization moving) is essentially a consequence of individual predispositions which, in actuality, take on a symbolic character both for the individual and for his subordinates, thus facilitating or impeding the process of change. Finally, we have attempted to bring these views together by considering men in action within a structure, on the face of it constrained by the functional demands imposed by the structure, but perceiving these demands and acting on them in very different ways.

The basic problem in social research on managerial behavior is to forge a strategy of investigation that will be equal to the task of *both* description and explanation. The unit of study is man in action in purposive organizations. The problem of explanation demands adequate conceptual tools for the interpretation of personality, action, and influence. To this end, the concepts of psychoanalytic psychology, linked with the theory of authority in sociology, provide exciting possibilities in the development of empirical studies of managerial behavior. If, in the end, managerial sociology becomes a social psychology of executive action, the profession of sociology will have strengthened its position in the applied social sciences.

REFERENCES

1. F. J. Roethlisberger and W. J. Dickson, *Management and the Worker* (Cambridge: Harvard University Press, 1939).
2. E. Mayo and G. F. F. Lombard, *Teamwork and Labor Turnover in the Aircraft Industry of Southern California* (Boston: Harvard University, Graduate School of Business Administration, Bureau of Business Research, 1944); J. B. Fox and J. R. Scott, *Absenteeism: Management's Problem* (Boston: Harvard University, Graduate School of Business Administration, Bureau of Business Research, 1943).
3. F. W. Taylor, *The Principles of Scientific Management* (New York: Harper, 1911).
4. F. J. Roethlisberger, *Management and Morale* (Cambridge: Harvard University Press, 1947).
5. Roethlisberger and Dickson, *op. cit.*
6. C. R. Rogers and F. J. Roethlisberger, "Barriers and Gateways to Communication," in *How Successful Executives Handle People: Twelve Studies on Communications and Management Skills* (Boston: Harvard University, Graduate School of Business Administration, *Harvard Business Review*, 1954).
7. H. A. Landsberger, *Hawthorne Revisited* (Ithaca: Cornell University Press, 1958).
8. C. Kerr and L. H. Fisher, "Plant Sociology: The Elite and the Aborigines," in

M. Komarovsky, ed., *Common Frontiers of the Social Sciences* (New York: The Free Press of Glencoe, 1957).

9. C. S. Golden and H. J. Ruttenberg, *The Dynamics of Industrial Democracy* (New York: Harper, 1942).

10. W. G. Given, *Bottom-up Management: People Working Together* (New York: Harper, 1949).

11. C. P. McCormick, *Multiple Management* (New York: Harper, 1938).

12. W. B. Donham, *Business Adrift* (New York: McGraw-Hill, 1931).

13. C. I. Barnard, *The Functions of the Executive* (Cambridge: Harvard University Press, 1948); W. B. D. Brown, *Exploration in Management* (New York: Wiley, 1960).

14. D. C. Miller and W. H. Form, *Industrial Sociology: The Sociology of Work Organizations* (New York: Harper and Row, 1964).

15. W. L. Warner and J. Abegglen, *Occupational Mobility in American Business, 1928–1952* (Minneapolis: University of Minnesota Press, 1955); Warner and Abegglen, *Big Business Leaders in America* (New York: Harper, 1955); P. Stryker and The Editors of Fortune, *The Executive Life* (Garden City, N.Y.: Doubleday, 1956).

16. M. Weber, *The Theory of Social and Economic Organization,* edited by T. Parsons, translated by A. M. Henderson and T. Parsons (New York: Oxford University Press, 1947).

17. Barnard, *op. cit.*

18. P. Selznick, *T.V.A. and the Grass Roots* (Berkeley: University of California Press, 1949); P. Selznick, *Leadership in Administration: A Sociological Interpretation* (Evanston, Ill.: Row, Peterson, 1957); A. W. Gouldner, *Patterns of Industrial Bureaucracy* (Glencoe, Ill.: The Free Press, 1954).

19. H. A. Simon, *Administrative Behavior* (New York: Macmillan, 1947).

20. H. Fayol, *General and Industrial Management,* translated by Constance Stours (London: Pitman, 1949); L. Gulick and L. Urwick, eds., *Papers on the Science of Administration* (New York: Columbia University, Institute of Public Administration, 1937).

21. J. G. March and H. A. Simon, *Organizations* (New York: Wiley, 1958).

22. H. Raiffa and R. Schlaifer, *Applied Statistical Decision Theory* (Boston: Harvard University, Graduate School of Business Administration, Division of Research, 1962); H. A. Simon, "A Behavioral Model of Rational Choice," *Quarterly Journal of Economics,* LXIX (1955), 99–118.

23. R. A. Dahl, M. Haire, and P. F. Lazarsfeld, eds., *Social Science Research on Business: Product and Potential* (New York: Columbia University Press, 1959).

24. Weber, *op. cit.*

25. S. Freud, "Group Psychology and the Analysis of the Ego," in J. Strachey, ed., *Standard Edition of the Complete Psychological Works,* Vol. XVIII (London: Hogarth, 1962).

26. G. C. Homans, *Social Behavior: Its Elementary Forms* (New York: Harcourt, Brace, 1961).

27. Roethlisberger and Dickson, *op. cit.;* G. F. F. Lombard, *Behavior in a Selling Group* (Boston: Harvard University, Graduate School of Business Administration, Division of Research, 1955); A. Zaleznik, *Worker Satisfaction and Development* (Boston: Harvard University, Graduate School of Business Administration, Division of Research, 1956).

28. P. M. Blau, *The Dynamics of Bureaucracy* (Chicago: University of Chicago Press, 1955).

29. Selznick, *T.V.A. and the Grass Roots.*

30. Gouldner, *op. cit.*

31. R. S. Weiss, *Processes of Organization* (Ann Arbor: University of Michigan, Survey Research Center, 1956).

32. G. Dalton, L. B. Barnes, and A. Zaleznik, *The Authority Structure as a Change Variable* (Paper presented at the 57th Annual Meeting of the American Sociological Association, August, 1962, in Washington, D.C.).

33. J. C. Worthy, "Organizational Structure and Employee Morale," *American Sociological Review*, XV (1950), 169–179.

34. E. Jaques, *The Changing Culture of a Factory* (London: Tavistock, 1951).

35. T. D. Weinshall, "The Effects of Management Changes on Organization Relationships and Attitudes," unpublished doctoral dissertation, Harvard University, Graduate School of Business Administration, 1960.

36. M. Dalton, *Men Who Manage* (New York: Wiley, 1959).

37. M. Crozier, *The Bureaucratic Phenomenon* (Chicago: University of Chicago Press, 1964).

38. Roethlisberger and Dickson, *op. cit.*

39. For an example of what we sought, see C. Argyris, *The Impact of Budgets on People* (New York: Controllership Foundation, 1952).

40. R. Anthony, *Planning and Control Systems* (Boston: Harvard University, Graduate School of Business Administration, Division of Research, 1965); E. P. Learned, C. R. Christensen, and K. R. Andrews, *Business Policy: Text and Cases* (Homewood, Ill.: Irwin, 1965); P. F. Drucker, *The Practice of Management* (New York: Harper, 1954).

41. Blau, *op. cit.*

42. Roethlisberger and Dickson, *op. cit.* See also E. Mayo, *The Political Problems of an Industrial Civilization* (Boston: Harvard University, Graduate School of Business Administration, Division of Research, 1947); E. Mayo, *The Human Problems of an Industrial Civilization* (London: Routledge and Kegan Paul, 1949).

43. C. R. Rogers, *Counselling and Psychotherapy* (Boston: Houghton Mifflin, 1942).

44. K. Lewin, *Field Theory in Social Science* (New York: Harper, 1951).

45. C. Argyris, *Executive Leadership* (New York: Harper, 1953).

46. C. Argyris, *Organization of a Bank* (New Haven: Yale University, Labor and Management Center, 1954).

47. C. Argyris, *Personality and Organization* (New York: Harper, 1957).

48. C. Argyris, *Interpersonal Competence and Organizational Effectiveness* (Homewood, Ill.: Irwin, 1962).

49. D. McGregor, *The Human Side of Enterprise* (New York: McGraw-Hill, 1960); D. McGregor, *Leadership and Motivation* (Cambridge: M.I.T. Press, 1966).

50. A. H. Maslow, *Motivation and Personality* (New York: Harper, 1954).

51. Lewin, *op. cit.*

52. R. White and R. Lippitt, "Leader Behavior and Membership Reaction in Three 'Social Climates,'" in D. Cartwright and A. Zander, eds., *Group Dynamics: Research and Theory* (Evanston, Ill.: Row, Peterson, 1953), pp. 585–611.

53. R. Likert, *New Patterns of Management* (New York: McGraw-Hill, 1961).

54. E. D. Chapple and L. R. Sayles, *Measure for Management* (New York: Macmillan, 1961).

55. C. R. Walker and R. H. Guest, *The Man on the Assembly Line* (Cambridge: Harvard University Press, 1952); C. R. Walker, R. H. Guest, and A. N. Turner, *The Foreman on the Assembly Line* (Cambridge: Harvard University Press, 1956).

56. W. F. Whyte, *Man and Organization, Three Problems in Human Relations in Industry* (Homewood, Ill.: Irwin, 1959).

57. F. L. W. Richardson, Jr., *Talk, Work and Action, Human Reactions to Organizational Change* (Ithaca: Cornell University, Society for Applied Anthropology, 1961).

58. Walker and Guest, *op. cit.*

59. G. L. Trist, "Socio-technical Systems" (Lecture given at University of Cambridge, November, 1959); G. L. Trist and K. W. Bamforth, "Some Social and Psychological Consequences of the Long-wall Method of Coal-getting," *Human Relations*, IV (1951), 3–38; A. K. Rice, *Productivity and Social Organization, the Ahmedabad Experiment* (London: Tavistock, 1958).

60. P. R. Lawrence, *The Changing of Organizational Behavior Pattern* (Boston: Harvard University, Graduate School of Business Administration, Division of Research, 1958).

61. A. A. Rogow, *James Forrestal: A Study of Personality, Politics, and Policy* (New York: Macmillan, 1963).

62. R. C. Hodgson, D. J. Levinson, and A. Zaleznik, *The Executive Role Constellation: An Analysis of Personality and Role Relations in Management* (Boston: Harvard University, Graduate School of Business Administration, Division of Research, 1965).

63. See *Webster's New Collegiate Dictionary*, 1956, p. 713.

64. E. Goffman, *The Presentation of Self in Everyday Life* (Garden City, N.Y.: Doubleday Anchor, 1959), p. 240.

65. R. H. Guest, *Organizational Change: The Effect of Successful Leadership* (Homewood, Ill.: Irwin, 1962).

66. E. A. Fleishman, W. E. Burtt, and E. F. Harris, *Leadership and Supervision in Industry: An Evaluation of a Supervisory Training Program* (Columbus, Ohio: Monograph No. 33, Bureau of Educational Research, 1955).

67. Guest, *op. cit.*, p. 96.

68. F. C. Mann, "Studying and Creating Change: A Means to Understanding Social Organization," in C. M. Arensberg, ed., *Research in Industrial Human Relations* (New York: Harper, 1957), pp. 146–167.

69. R. Linton, *Study of Man* (New York: Appleton Century, 1936).

70. E. Goffman, *Encounters* (New York: Bobbs-Merrill, 1961).

71. R. K. Merton, *Social Theory and Social Structure* (New York: The Free Press of Glencoe, 1964).

72. T. Parsons, "Age and Sex in the Social Structure of the United States," *American Sociological Review*, VII (1942), 604–616.

73. N. Gross, W. S. Mason, and A. W. McEachern, *Explorations in Role Analysis* (New York: Wiley, 1958).

74. R. L. Kahn, D. M. Wolfe, R. R. Quinn, and J. D. Snoek, *Organizational Stress: Studies in Role Conflict and Ambiguity* (New York: Wiley, 1964).

75. V. H. Vroom, *Some Personality Determinants of the Effects of Participation* (Englewood Cliffs, N.J.: Prentice-Hall, 1960); Barnes, Dalton, and Zaleznik, *op. cit.*

76. T. Parsons and R. F. Bales, *Family, Socialization, and Interaction Process* (Glencoe, Ill.: The Free Press, 1955); R. F. Bales, *Interaction Process Analysis* (Cambridge, Mass.: Addison-Wesley, 1951).

77. R. F. Bales, "The Equilibrium Problem in Small Groups," in T. Parsons, R. F. Bales, and E. A. Shils, eds., *Working Papers in the Theory of Action* (Glencoe, Ill.: The Free Press, 1953), pp. 111–161; abridged in A. P. Hare, E. F. Borgatta, and R. F. Bales, eds., *Small Groups* (New York: Knopf, 1955), pp. 424–456. See also P. E. Slater, "Role Differentiations in Small Groups," in *ibid.*, pp. 498–515.

78. Bales, "The Equilibrium Problem in Small Groups," p. 438.

79. Blau, *op. cit.*; A. Zaleznik, C. R. Christensen, and F. J. Roethlisberger, *The Motivation, Productivity, and Satisfaction of Workers: A Prediction Study* (Boston: Harvard University, Graduate School of Business Administration, Division of Research, 1958).

80. Slater, *op. cit.*

81. *Ibid.*, p. 504. Slater divided his groups into high-consensus and low-consensus groups on the basis of the degree of agreement among the members on their voting choices. Members of high-consensus groups tended to show more agreement in the way they ranked others than did the low-consensus group members.

82. *Ibid.*, p. 507.

83. D. Moment and A. Zaleznik, *Role Development and Interpersonal Competence* (Boston: Harvard University, Graduate School of Business Administration, Division of Research, 1963).

84. *Ibid.*, p. 34.

85. Homans, *op. cit.*

86. Hodgson, Levinson, and Zaleznik, *op. cit.*

87. *Ibid.*, p. 476.

88. Barnard, *op. cit.*, p. 184.

89. *Ibid.*, p. 183.

90. C. A. Gibb, "Leadership," in G. Lindzey, ed., *Handbook of Social Psychology* (Cambridge, Mass.: Addison-Wesley, 1954).

91. *Ibid.*, p. 882.

92. R. E. Neustadt, *Presidential Power: The Politics of Leadership* (New York: Wiley, 1964).

93. *Ibid.*, p. 6. Our italics.

94. *Ibid.*, p. 179.

95. *Ibid.*, pp. 165–166. Our italics.

96. *Ibid.*, pp. 158–159.

97. R. A. Dahl, "The Concept of Power," *Behavioral Science*, II (1957), 201–218.

98. *Ibid.*, p. 203.

99. A. M. Schlesinger, Jr., *The Age of Roosevelt*. Vol. 2: *The Coming of the New Deal* (Boston: Houghton Mifflin, 1959), pp. 522–523. Quoted in Neustadt, *op. cit.*, p. 156.

100. A. L. and J. L. George, *Woodrow Wilson and Colonel House: A Personality Study* (New York: Dover Publications, 1964).

101. A. Zaleznik, "Managerial Behavior and Interpersonal Competence," *Behavioral Science*, II (1964), 156–166.

102. P. Stryker, *The Character of the Executive* (New York: Harper and Row, 1961).

103. *Ibid.*, p. 210. Our italics.

104. Zaleznik, *op. cit.* "Managerial Behavior." (102).

105. Neustadt, *op. cit.*, p. 165.

106. Schlesinger, *op. cit.*, p. 528. Quoted in Neustadt, *op. cit.*, p. 157.

107. Neustadt, *op. cit.*, p. 161.

108. Hodgson, Levinson, and Zaleznik, *op. cit.*, p. 92.

109. *Ibid.*, p. 285.

The Military

Establishment

RAYMOND V. BOWERS

chapter 9

The Uniqueness of the Military Setting

The significance, at this time, of a survey of the uses to which sociology has been put in the armed forces stems not only from the growing importance of military affairs in this country, but from the presence of this trend throughout much of the world. Two world wars, the struggles involved in the creation of new nations, and the widespread campaigns of the cold war have combined to change the balance of institutional power in societies around the world.

In the United States, to which we shall confine our attention, the magnitude of this shift has been such that even the subject of "military takeover" has emerged as a matter for discussion and warning. From an insignificant set of garrison forces in 1940, poorly equipped with arms and prestige, our armed forces have become the most powerful military machine in history, allegedly capable of destroying the world as we know it. They wield by far the greatest economic power in the nation, with one-half the federal budget under their control, and constitute the largest employer of the nation's manpower, with some four million military and civilian personnel on their payrolls. They have beyond any doubt the most complex and diverse set of missions of any institution in our nation's history, ranging from supporting basic research in most fields of science at one end to deterring enemy aggression of many varieties at the other. And, in the course of accomplishing these tasks, they have all the organizational and management problems of a society, rather than of a single institution.

The Army, Navy, and Air Force must, for example, operate hundreds of their own communities, from small air-defense sites or ships to large air or naval bases and army posts, situated in all types of environments. They must also keep this network of communities integrated into a total system of military activity, each playing its part in any required military operation. Thus it is hardly any wonder that even an old soldier like former President Eisenhower has expressed concern over the possibility of such an institutional colossus radically changing the fabric of our national life. Nor should it be a wonder to sociologists that this institution, buffeted by waves of major technological change during and since World War II, should have experienced major sociological problems incident to such changes.

Another unique aspect of the American military establishment so far as the uses of science are concerned is that it is in many respects a single organization. Thus, whereas the chapters in such other areas of American life as education, law, business, public health, or the family are dealing with literally thousands of independent centers of decision making regarding the uses to which sociology might be put, this chapter is dealing with as few as one at times when matters are decided at the Secretary of Defense level.

A third unusual aspect of the military setting has been its sudden and somewhat forced partnership with science, dictated in part by our inadequate arsenal of weapons at the start of World War II. In 1941, the scientific community was hurriedly mobilized by White House directive, through the establishment of an independent Office of Scientific Research and Development (OSRD), to apply existing knowledge to military needs. Such critical developments as radar and sonar resulted, but, as reported in the histories of OSRD, considerable difficulty was often experienced in getting military acceptance of the new devices. Two lessons were learned: national security required constant concern over the adequacy of our armed forces, and this, in turn, necessitated a close working relationship between the scientific and military professions.

These lessons were supported vigorously after World War II by both the scientists and important segments of the military professionals and were written into law by Congress as an integral part of the National Security (Armed Forces Unification) Act of 1947. There, provision was made for the establishment of a Research and Development Board in the new Office of the Secretary of Defense to review, co-ordinate, and stimulate research and development programs in the Army, Navy, and newly created Air Force. The armed forces were, in effect, given a mandate to increase the use of science in their affairs. Of importance to sociology is the fact that the Research and Development Board, when organized, included the behavioral sciences as part of its mandate.

Committees of scientists were established in 1947 to execute the Board's work in the various scientific areas. A committee was established for the behavioral sciences, called by the neutral name Committee on Human Resources, and it proceeded to divide its responsibility into several areas: Psychophysiology and Human Engineering, Personnel and Training, Manpower, and Human Relations and Morale. This last area included all problems in interpersonal and group relations, from combat leadership to psychological warfare, and was the most relevant to sociologists, although Manpower embraced the field of demography. Panels of nationally recognized behavioral scientists were appointed to do the committee's spadework in each area.[1] The committee and its panels met periodically with representatives of the Army, Navy, and Air Force to review existing research programs and requirements and to construct a master plan for further research and development programs to meet these requirements. The services proceeded to establish staff groups at their headquarters level to insure support for the aspects of these programs of relevance to their requirements, and research organizations in the field to initiate the work.

The new Department of the Air Force responded strongly by establishing three in-service behavioral science research centers by 1949.[2] The responsibility for the programs in Manpower and in Human Relations and Morale was assigned for the most part to the Human Resources Research Institute (HRRI) at Air University. The Department of the Army chose to conduct its new programs primarily through major contract relations with universities in the Washington area.[3] The Department of the Navy's interests were handled through its existing organizations, such as the Office of Naval Research and the Bureau of Naval Personnel.[4] Thus, since the late 1940's there has been centralized machinery for the planning and review of psychological and social-science research in the Army, Navy, and Air Force and research organizations for accomplishing the research either on an in-service or contract basis.

This high-level recognition of these sciences—sociology among them—validated them to all levels of command and insured their inclusion in military plans and operations. However, since actual programmed support for any one field such as sociology depended on each service's definition of its priority requirements for "hardware" as well as "software," it is not surprising to find that the three services varied in their use of sociology and that the largest user, the Air Force, varied in its support from time to time. These variations will be mirrored throughout this chapter.

Uses for Military Intelligence, Strategic Planning, and Psychological Warfare: The Understanding and Influencing of Foreign Groups[5]

Knowledge about the external world (one's allies as well as one's enemies) has always been an important ingredient of military plans and operations. *Military intelligence* is the term used for the collection and interpretation of such knowledge: the determination of the types and priorities of information needed, as well as the techniques for their collection, evaluation, and analysis. The needs, speaking generally, are of two kinds: information useful for *strategic planning* on the one hand and for *military operations* on the other.

World War II, and particularly the Pacific campaign, convinced us that we needed not only more reliable knowledge about potential enemy nations but also a wider variety of knowledge about them. In addition to the traditional military, economic, and political types of information, we should know more about the social and psychological strengths and vulnerabilities of peoples, and the requirement for such information brought with it the demand for improved techniques to collect and process it.

This greater use of sociological and psychological forms of intelligence has been evident in strategic planning, as will be shown in the following pages. It has also been evident in various forms of warfare, especially those characterized by the use of nonviolent means to influence the attitudes and behavior of target groups in the direction of one's own military objectives. These so-called "psychological operations" require assessments of how individuals of various societies, classes, and categories will react to various communications and actions, and they are particularly important to such special types of tactical activities as counterinsurgency operations, unconventional warfare, military assistance programs, and military government.

USES FOR STRATEGIC PLANNING: ANALYSES OF ENEMY MORALE DURING WORLD WAR II

Two important examples of such operations involving sociologists were the programs of the Foreign Morale Analysis Division, Military Intelligence Service, and the Morale Divisions of the United States Strategic Bombing Surveys. Since descriptions of the usefulness of these programs are available through excellent published reports, the following account will be confined to one of them: the Japanese Morale survey.[6]

The United States Strategic Bombing Surveys were authorized by Presidents Roosevelt and Truman to assess the importance of the allied air offensives in the defeats of Germany and Japan, thus providing "a basis for evaluating the importance and potentialities of air power as an instrument of military strategy for planning the future development of the United States armed forces." [7] A Morale Division was included in each survey to assess the effects of the bombing on civilian morale. Sociologists played important parts in both studies.[8] The survey of Japanese civilian morale included chapters on Relations between Bombing Experiences and Morale, Morale of the Labor Force, Problems of Evacuation, Effects of the Atomic Bombs on Morale, The Apparatus of Morale Control, and The Role of Morale in Japan's Surrender. The 262-page final report was published as part of the *Strategic Bombing Survey Series* and was distributed to all offices in Washington concerned with future military planning.

The widespread accessibility of the report, and the great concern with strategic planning during the period since its publication, have insured extensive use of its material. It has appeared as a frequent footnote in military staff studies, has been redigested in such well-known books as Irving Janis' *Air War and Emotional Stress*,[9] and has been a major source for such special works as Fred Iklé's *The Social Impact of Bomb Destruction*.[10] In turn, these volumes by Janis and Iklé crop up in other studies done both inside the military services and on contract for them. One recent example of the latter is the report of Human Sciences Research, Inc., to the Air Force Office of Scientific Research entitled *Social Phenomena in a Post-Nuclear Attack Situation*.[11] This publication, again, will undoubtedly be quoted in the future by others, and so the use of the original study continues.

USES FOR STRATEGIC PLANNING:
ANALYSES OF FOREIGN SOCIAL SYSTEMS

The aftermath of World War II, with the rise of cold-war tensions and limited warfare focused attention on the deficiencies in our knowledge of those countries most likely to be aligned against us. Iron-curtain-type isolations required that something be done as quickly as possible to assess the social and psychological as well as the political and economic weaknesses and strengths of the major closed foreign social systems. Later this interest was extended to other countries as well. The establishment of programs to meet this broad and complex requirement provides an excellent example of the way the new research machinery of the Department of Defense was intended to operate.

The story begins in 1948. While intelligence agencies were doing their best to handle the day-to-day questions, the need for basic improvement in such knowledge was transmitted as general research requirements to the Committee on Human Resources of the Research and Development

Board. The committee proceeded to call upon its appropriate panel of military and civilian specialists to recommend the general types and magnitude of research effort that would be needed, and these recommendations were referred to the services for their guidance in meeting the requirements.

Knowledge of the Soviet Social System This was established as the number-one priority at that time, and a program of research to improve it was initiated in 1950 by the Air Force's Human Resources Research Institute through a major contract with the Russian Research Center at Harvard University specifying Clyde Kluckhohn as principal investigator. At least a dozen sociologists and sociological graduate students participated at one time or another in this four-year project.

Its objectives were to develop a method for (*a*) understanding how a relatively inaccessible foreign social system "looks from within" and (*b*) predicting how it would react to various strains and stresses placed on the pattern of interrelationships existing among its social institutions, administrative and political controls, and racial and socioeconomic groups. This was done by supplementing accessible materials with a unique body of data on the day-to-day experiences of Soviet citizens contained in approximately 700 intensive interviews and 12,000 lengthy questionnaires obtained in Europe during 1950–1951 from Soviet refugees, escapees, and *émigrés*.

The results of this project were made available in some eighteen special reports to the military services and approximately thirty-five journal articles to the social-science community. A final summary report, *How the Soviet System Works,* later published commercially, contained the project's assessment of the social and psychological strengths and weaknesses of Soviet society.[12] A later volume, *The Soviet Citizen,*[13] presented the main body of statistical data from the interviews and questionnaires and thus focused unique attention on the daily life of the Soviet people.

It is difficult to assess the total impact of a research effort of this sort in terms of either direct or indirect usefulness to the military services. Contrary to the overly optimistic expectations of some military administrators, no mathematical model of a social system, with weighted variables for computer predictions, was produced. But individual reports on various aspects of Soviet society provided Air Force and Joint Chiefs of Staff strategic planning offices with data and predictions theretofore unavailable. The members of the project staff were frequently called upon to contribute consultant services on classified strategic and psychological warfare planning studies. The project's final summary report was required reading at the Command and Staff and War Colleges of the Armed Services for a number of years. Sets of the interview protocols were bound in volumes and made available to the Intelligence community in Washington, at its request, to be used as data in the day-to-day studies they were responsible for preparing. A special "restricted" *Guide for Interviewing Soviet Escapees* was prepared from the team's experience for the use of the military intelligence operator.[14]

Finally, and not the least important by any means, the products of this contract (publications, raw data, and the experiences of the staff) were much used by other students of Soviet society, and references to the importance of this assistance are met frequently in the reports of the MIT Center for International Studies and other research groups serving the military establishment.[15]

Analyses of Other Social Systems   After 1950 the Army experienced increasing involvement with counterinsurgency operations, unconventional warfare, military aid, and civic action programs. These missions required the Army to be prepared for military interactions with a large number of foreign societies which required, in turn, sound studies on the ways of life of the peoples with whom the interactions might take place. Since such studies were not available in the breadth and depth desired, an agreement was reached in 1956 with Yale University's Human Relations Area Files (HRAF) to provide them.

By 1957 this and related programs were considered so significant to the Army's needs that a new research organization, the Special Operations Research Office (SORO) was created at American University, Washington, D.C., to devote full time to them. Altogether fifty "Foreign Area Studies' Handbooks," on a country-by-country basis, have been produced, each describing and interrelating data regarding that country's sociological, political, economic, and military institutions. The list includes countries from every continent, from the entire range of hostile to friendly nations, and from large nations (USSR, China, and India) to small ones (Laos, Guinea, Lebanon, Cuba, and Taiwan). They have found wide acceptance, not only in the Army but also in other governmental agencies whose operations involve foreign cultures. As a personal letter from Philip Sperling, SORO's Deputy Director, says: "These books are also used by the Foreign Service Institute of the State Department, by the Peace Corps, by USIA, AID and several other government agencies. . . . The printing is 2,000 (sometimes 4,000) so they get fairly wide distribution within the Army, Navy, and Air Force."

Sociologists played important parts in this program from the start: Leonard S. Cottrell, Jr., and John W. Riley, Jr., as key consultants to the Secretary of Defense at the time when the proposed plan required support at that level, and Clelland Ford, Milton Graham, Rex Hopper, and Maurice Price,[16] among others, as members of the HRAF or SORO staffs. The importance of sociology to the program is also evidenced by its prominent position under "Professional Skill Requirements" in SORO's recruiting brochure.

Other recent sociological research activities concerning foreign social systems have been sponsored by the Air Force Office of Scientific Research and relate to methodological problems in measuring attitude change cross-culturally. In one such study Alex Inkeles has been developing cross-national measures of attitude change under conditions of modernization. In another, Jiri Nehnevajsa is completing work on the development of an informational system capable of assessing and monitoring over time the changing judgments of foreign nationals as to the likelihood and desirability of certain future events or outcomes.

USES FOR STRATEGIC PLANNING: RECOVERY FROM NUCLEAR ATTACK

It became clear after World War II that military planning required increasingly dependable estimates of the capability of a nation, its socioeconomic regions and networks of urban centers, to survive atomic attack. It was also clear that this need could not be met by the existing state of the relevant sciences or of the military intelligence art. Some important types of information were available, if at all, in very unreliable forms. Techniques for improving their collection had to be developed or at least adapted to the purpose, as had analytical models capable of bringing these data to bear on the problem of "recovery."

The old military question, "What will it take to destroy the enemy's will to fight?", was being asked in the new context of total atomic war: how much, and what parts, of a city or region or nation would have to be destroyed to knock it out of the war? And the knowledge essential to answer this question would have to include information about the institutional structure of the cities and the community interrelationships of the regions—that is, knowledge of targets as ecological systems. Some imaginative starts to provide such knowledge were made in the early 1950's, and sociology was prominently represented in them, but a shift from contract to in-service research in 1953 terminated most of them before their real usefulness could be demonstrated. Nevertheless, brief references to some of them seem appropriate here.

A first effort was negotiated by the Air Force's Human Resources Research Institute in 1951 with Columbia University's Bureau of Applied Social Research, specifying Kingsley Davis as principal investigator, to develop a World Urban Resources Index consisting of files of basic information about each of the major cities of the world. These data would enable analysts to make comparative studies of urban and regional complexes and develop more dependable methods for the selection of air targets. This Index was well started, and reports to meet the current needs of Air Force intelligence had begun to appear, by the time the Air Force shifted its support to in-service work.[17] However, the enterprise was continued under other sponsorship and is presently located in Professor Davis' Institute for International Urban and Population Research on the Berkeley campus of the University of California.

A second urban research contract was written by HRRI with the University of Chicago's Community Inventory, designating Philip Hauser, and later, Albert Reiss, as principal investigator. The objective was to develop a model for describing and analyzing the distributive patterns of human and material resources in metropolitan areas which would be flexible, comprehensive, transferable, and oriented toward decision making. A prototype, based on the cost-utility method, was actually developed and was given some successful tests, mainly on Chicago, before the work was terminated in the 1953 shift of priorities. During the two years that the project was under way, its work was reported in a series of twenty detailed reports which had circulation among the Air Force's relevant using agencies. After the termination, Professor Hauser and his associates were urged to prepare a summary of the model for future use by military intelligence analysts.[18] Copies were distributed not only within the Air Force but to other government agencies through the Armed Services Technical Information Agency and were deposited in a number of libraries throughout the country.

Attempts to improve the data-collection processes were also undertaken in the early 1950's. A particularly intriguing one was directed by Norman E. Green, a sociologist and Air Force career officer who was prominent in HRRI's intelligence research program. His interest was in developing techniques for obtaining population and "social structural" information on urban centers through photographs taken from the air. The major question was one of determining which physical features identifiable in the photographic image were correlated with social information derived from ground data sources. Feasibility studies were completed on six United States cities, and intensive studies were done on Rochester, New York, and Birmingham, Alabama. As Green and Monier reported in 1959,

> All in all, the research program has developed quite convincing evidence that photographic interpretation is a possible approach to the problems of urban social analysis. In some situations it may be the only source for certain classes of data. It would seem desirable, in extending this work, to test the development on a larger sample of cities, and particularly to investigate its transferability to regions outside the United States.[19]

Although this extension of the project to foreign cities was never accomplished, a number of reports on the work appeared in professional as well as Air Force publications, and the services of Green and other sociologists involved in the project were frequently utilized in strategic and civil-defense planning.

The shift in Air Force research policy toward accomplishing population studies through in-service agencies led to a continuing program of population studies, contracted originally by HRRI with the Bureau of the Census. A Foreign Manpower Research Office was established in the Bureau to handle the contract under the over-all direction of Conrad Taeuber, the Bureau's assistant director, and the successive supervision of demographic sociologists Parker Mauldin, Norman Lawrence, and Paul Meyers. A series of fifty classified population and labor-force estimates for selected foreign areas and cities was produced. In addition, the controversial USSR Census of 1926 was given a special evaluation, and projections to future years as far as 1975 were accomplished. Studies on manpower utilization in specific industries in strategic foreign areas were also produced. All were in response to specific requirements of the using agencies, and the reports, together with consultant services of the research staff, were made available directly to the using strategic planning offices. At the same time, the high standards set by the Bureau of the Census staff resulted in some technical developments of note. In fact, the methodology of the studies became the subject of a separate monograph.[20]

USES FOR PSYCHOLOGICAL WARFARE:
WORLD WAR II AND THE KOREAN WAR

The so-called "psychological weapons" are various forms of *verbal or written communications* (leaflets, broadcasts, interrogations) and *nonlethal actions* (demonstrations, "shows of force," civic actions, symbolic gestures) employed by the military services to influence the opinions or behavior of foreign groups. Such forms of persuasion are applicable not only during hot war but in military occupations, limited-warfare, and cold-war situations as well.

The story of our psychological-warfare operations in World War II has been well documented by Daniel Lerner, Hans Speier, Morris Janowitz, and others, and the reader is referred to their writings for information on the uses of sociology in those operations.[21] These sources also contain highly regarded critical analyses of psychological-warfare policy, organization, personnel, media, and effectiveness of operations during that period, as well as significant contributions to the understanding of this "weapon system" and its more effective use.

During the Korean war, sociologists were involved in several studies of psychological operations. A grass-roots description of one such study— that conducted by a RAND Corporation team—appeared in the 1951 annual report of HRRI's Far East Research Group, which, having research offices in Tokyo and Pusan, provided some support for the RAND people. It says:

> During the year Alexander George, Ewald Schnitzer and Herbert Gold-hamer of the RAND Corporation have completed . . . approximately 1,000 interrogations of North Korean and Chinese POW's. This material is presently being processed by the RAND Corporation in Washington under the super-vision of Goldhamer and Schnitzer. Initial reports on the progress of the analysis should be in the hands of interested agencies some time during the first part of the coming year (1952).

> One interesting by-product of this research undertaking has been the utiliza-tion of Dr. Goldhamer as an observer-consultant at the Cease Fire Negotia-tions in Korea, based upon his experience and knowledge of the attitudes, morale, and thinking of the Chinese and Korean POW's. He has attended the discussions almost from the very start, from Kaesong to Panmunjom, and has not only been an observer-consultant to the Air Force representative at these meetings, but also to Admiral Joy, our chief negotiator.[22]

Studies of Korean and Chinese prisoners of war were also made by Wil-liam C. Bradbury and Samuel M. Meyers, of the Army's Human Resources Research Office (HumRRO), and Joseph D. Lohman advised the United Nations Command regarding the handling of prisoners of war who were declining repatriation at the close of the Korean war.

The Air University Human Resources Research Institute had its own sociologists on the Korean scene in 1950 making studies and extracting requirements for further research back home. Frederick W. Williams or-ganized an in-service team, supplemented by John W. Riley, Jr., and Wil-bur Schramm, to study the methods of Communist take-over. As described in an HRRI report:

> Detailed interviews were conducted with persons who had lived in North Korea for the last four of the five previous years. Besides, a thorough study was made in Seoul of the activities of the central ministries of the govern-ment during the three months of Communist control the previous summer. Interviews were also conducted with specialized informants and with numer-ous people with diversified backgrounds who had lived in Seoul during the Communist occupation. A study was also made of two villages which had been occupied by the Communists. And, finally, an extensive study was un-dertaken of motivations of refugees fleeing from Communist areas. . . . These materials were analyzed and reported in detail in a basic unclassified report entitled "A Preliminary Study of the Impact of Communism upon Korea." [23]

The report from which this quotation was taken is a summary of the findings and a statement of their implications for psychological warfare against a sovietized state such as Korea. Several open publications concerning these data were authorized, including a book by Riley and Schramm entitled *The Reds Take a City: The Communist Occupation of Seoul, with Eyewitness Accounts*.[24] These publications were widely used by the military services as one of the very first descriptions and analyses of a Chinese-type Communist take-over. *The Reds Take a City* has also been translated into some twelve languages and distributed throughout the world by the United States Information Service, and both authors have served in important psychological warfare advisory positions in the Office of the Secretary of Defense since the book was published.

The contributions of sociologists to the military government's program after World War II should also be included here and deserve more attention than space permits. Many, such as John Useem, served in uniform, and his 1945 article in the *American Journal of Sociology* appraises his experience in Micronesia and points to the urgent need to employ sociological principles in a governing process involving cross-cultural relations.[25] Others served in a civilian capacity: Arthur Raper made significant contributions as a rural sociologist to the reform of the land-tenure system in Japan; Herbert Passin, who occupied a key position in the Supreme Commander Allied Powers (SCAP) Information and Education Section, directed a program of research studies on various problems of importance to the occupation and assisted greatly in the training of Japanese social scientists in modern research methods; a team comprising Clyde Kluckhohn, Herbert Hyman, and Raymond Bowers was sent to Japan in 1946 to survey SCAP's needs for "sociological and public opionion studies" and to make recommendations to General MacArthur's staff regarding the organization and resources necessary to meet them.

USES FOR PSYCHOLOGICAL WARFARE:
THE PERIOD OF COLD AND LIMITED WARFARE

Although general war has so far been deterred, the period since 1945 has been burdened with cold-war problems, some of them sufficiently warm to be given the separate designation of limited warfare. This has required the military establishment to be prepared to engage in three types of operation: deterrence in support of cold-war objectives, counterinsurgency in support of limited-warfare objectives, and the nuclear offensive for general war itself. Psychological operations have been assigned parts to play in each.

The RAND Corporation's social science program, under the direction of Hans Speier, has included contributions to many types of military problems over the years, but none more persistently than psychological-operations problems. A recent communication, in response to a question regarding sociological emphasis, says:

Our people are well grounded not only in sociology, but also in political science, history, anthropology, and other pertinent disciplines. We almost of necessity have to be eclectic in selecting appropriate theoretical and other resources from whatever disciplines seem relevant when we are trying to cope with the implications of problems that are relevant to the wide-ranging fields of weapons systems, weapons procurement, weapons uses, arms control and disarmament, strategy, alliance problems, base problems, and the manifold other problems to which we devote our attention sometimes within our own set of disciplines, sometimes working interdepartmentally with practitioners trained in others. In the nature of the case, it is hard sometimes to tell which discipline provides the most salient or relevant assistance, if such an assessment is ever realistic.[26]

The unclassified bibliography of the Social Science Department includes a number of items by sociologists ranging from empirical case studies (for example, "The Berlin Blockade") to such general treatises as "Strategic Surrender" or "Sociological Aspects of the Information Process" and such methodological developments as "An Application of Markov Processes" or "Some Observations on Political Gaming." Some of the items are designed to meet a current psychological warfare concern, such as the 1956 paper "Soviet Atomic Blackmail and the North Atlantic Alliance," or Selznick's "Organizational Weapon." [27]

The RAND reports have had appropriately wide distribution in Defense planning circles and their authors have participated frequently over the years in Pentagon policy conferences. In addition, the reports have been available to other elements of the government and to Defense contractors through the Defense Documentation Center and to the public through forty-one libraries in this country and seven abroad. Some of the studies of wide interest have appeared in commercial editions. Thus the impact of RAND's influence on the military thinking of the country extends beyond the Pentagon and, indeed, beyond the federal government itself.

Other important contributions of sociology to psychological operations for limited warfare have been made through the programs of the Army's Special Operations Research Office (SORO) at American University. In addition to the fifty basic country studies previously described, this organization has produced classified *Psychological Operations Handbooks* for over twenty nations since 1958. As stated in SORO's *Bibliography of Publications,*

Each handbook provides appeals and symbols of tested persuasiveness for communicating messages to specific audiences in a given country. Each study further seeks to identify various groupings in the population—ethnic, geographic, economic, social, etc.—and their attitudes and probable behavior toward the U.S. The studies assess the susceptibility of the various audiences to persuasion and their effectiveness of influence in their own society. They also appraise their potential for furthering the interest of the United States under various conditions.[28]

Another SORO psychological-operations project is

concerned with a study of informal communications in selected countries to identify and describe potential word-of-mouth communicators of propaganda, and the infiltration and dissemination of information by means other than mass media. An attempt is made to provide the propagandist with a map of this informal communication network, so that he may be able to feed messages into it with some expectation that they will reach the desired audience. These studies are based, where possible, on field data collection.[29]

As stated in a letter from SORO's deputy director, all these psychological-operations reports had some input by sociologists.

Prior to SORO's establishment, the Army's Operations Research Office (ORO) supported a number of useful studies on psychological warfare in which sociologists played a significant role. Wilbur Schramm directed the work of preparing a manual on the nature of psychological warfare, and Morris Janowitz assisted William E. Daugherty in the preparation of the well-known and comprehensive psychological-warfare casebook.[30] The latter is a 900-page compendium containing sections on every important aspect and principle of psychological warfare, and is in the form of illustrative reports of specific operations and campaigns up to 1956. These volumes were undertaken to meet an expressed request of the Army's Chief of Psychological Warfare to provide training and reference books for psychological-warfare personnel. Seven hundred copies of the casebook were printed.

Psychological operations in support of strategic air power, whether engaged in deterrence or combat, were the chief focus of the Human Resources Research Institute's research in this area. The need to communicate with enemy troops or civilians from the air through leaflets, for example, suggested research on message diffusion as well as on social and psychological vulnerabilities which might be used to enhance the effect of the message on its receivers. So also the need to protect our own airmen against enemy propaganda or indoctrination suggested research on Communist psychological warfare and "brainwashing." These needs were quite real. Leaflets had to be stock-piled for possible use, and airmen had to be trained in "evasion and escape" techniques in the event of being shot down over enemy territory.

The requirement to learn more about message diffusion from leaflets was of interest to Stuart C. Dodd, Director of the University of Washington's Public Opinion Laboratory, and a major contract was negotiated with the university to get this work under way. The project became known as "Revere." Through a series of carefully controlled experiments, involving leaflet drops over American cities, the following questions about message diffusion and effectiveness were explored: effect of the number of leaflets per person, the spatial patterns of leaflet drops, leaflet-drop repetitions, motivational appeals, social structure, and population size. In addition intensive efforts were made to develop a mathematical description of the growth of knowers of leaflet messages in community situations. Over a hundred articles and reports were produced by the project, and several books have appeared or are still in preparation for publication.[31] Some of the early findings relative to optimum leaflet format, color, and quantity required for effective coverage came in time to be useful for psychological operations in Korea.

Research on Communist interrogation methods, including the so-called brainwashing of American military personnel during the Korean war, was begun under the direction of sociologists Frederick W. Williams, Herman J. Sander, and Albert D. Biderman at HRRI and has been carried on since 1958 by Biderman under the sponsorship of the Air Force Office of Scientific Research. This research effort has constituted a series of studies on prisoner-of-war captivity problems, based originally on the experience of the Air Force returnees from Korean prison camps. During the course of this research the findings about Communist exploitation of Air Force prisoners have been integrated with the findings of Army researchers regarding the experience of their prisoners, with the findings of other captivity studies, and with technical knowledge about the manipulation of human behavior.

These studies were much used in the Pentagon and contributed significantly to the fair administrative and judicial handling of the repatriated prisoners by the military services and to the formulation of the new Code of Conduct for the Armed Forces. It was, as a matter of fact, puzzlement over what to do with the returnees that caused the Air Force's Vice Chief of Staff in 1953 to request a thorough study of the situation. Biderman's report was in response to it and was used as key evidence in the decision-making process.[32] He was also called upon to report his findings to the United States Senate's Permanent Sub-Committee on Investigations of the Committee on Government Operations which was investigating the brainwashing and "softness of American youth" charges that grew out of the Korean war.[33]

In his most recent book Albert Biderman has addressed himself to the problem of why these sensational interpretations of Communist brainwashing and GI prison behavior were so popular. An extensive analysis was made of press and other reportage of these matters in an effort to account for the readiness with which the press, public, and officials adopted extreme positions. The story is well told for these audiences in his *March to Calumny: The Story of American POW's in the Korean War.*[34]

ROLES OF SOCIOLOGISTS AS CONSULTANTS

Mention has already been made of the roles of sociologists as consultants and advisers to the military services in the area of psychological operations. The restrictions of security and space do not permit us to do justice to this important topic. Practically every social scientist referred to in the above text or references has served in some consultant capacity at one time or another. Moreover, sociologists who are federal employees of the military or other government agencies confer and advise regularly with one another as part of their jobs.

Special note should, however, be made of the continuous and valuable services of Charles E. Hutchinson and Herman J. Sander in bringing the resources of the behavioral sciences, and sociology in particular, to bear on these military problems. Since 1950 they have been involved in the Air Force program at all levels from the laboratory to the Pentagon and have represented the Air Force at most Department of Defense research conferences related to it.

Special note should also be made of Leonard S. Cottrell's services as Chairman of the Advisory Committee on Psychological and Unconventional Warfare, Research and Development Board, Department of Defense, during the period 1952–1954. This was a critical period following the end of the Korean war when the major social-science programs supported by the military services in this subject area were in danger of being seriously retarded by shifts in priorities. It was due in no small measure to Cottrell's leadership that programs of research were maintained.

More recently a number of prominent sociologists have been involved in a major series of study task groups which have examined the needs of the military establishment for long-range effort in psychology and the social sciences. The basic general requirement was designated as a "technology of human behavior" in three areas: human performance, military organization, and persuasion and motivation. The task group on Basic Research in Persuasion and Motivation, relevant here, comprised Wilbur Schramm, W. P. Davison, Henry W. Riecken, and John W. Riley. Other sociologists were called in as consultants, including Bernard Berelson, Morris Janowitz, Daniel Lerner, Talcott Parsons, and Donald Young. The basic theme of their report,[35] as in the previously mentioned original 1948 Report of the Research and Development Board's Committee on Human Resources, is that *increased emphasis on and sustained support of basic research* in the areas of persuasion, motivation, and intercultural communication *is necessary now* if the capability of the military establishment in the field of psychological operations is to continue to match its responsibilities in future emergencies.

Uses for Personnel Management and Organizational Effectiveness: The Understanding and Utilization of Military Men and Institutions

Along with the military objective of knowing the enemy is the equally important one of "knowing thyself," and World War II was so vast and complex a human enterprise that social scientists of all varieties were enlisted in the effort to win it. For the first time in history sociologists were put to work, as sociologists, to help with problems of personnel management and organizational effectiveness, a collaboration which is now well into its third decade.

Prior to World War II there was little interest on the part of either party in the other. The military establishment had begun to use psychologists, as psychologists, only in World War I, and during the long military drought between the two world wars there was little use of science even in the "hardware" areas, let alone in such new areas as men and organizations. Similarly, the sociologists of the period ignored the military setting as a source of professional interest. As Morris Janowitz has recently put it, "In the United States the development of the social sciences is linked to the liberal tradition which, in general, has sought to handle the problem of military institutions by denial." [36] This is evidenced in the symposium on the status of sociology published in 1929, where there is no mention of military institutions even in the substantial chapter on "trends in applied sociology." [37] And in the *American Journal of Sociology* issue on "National Morale," published one month before Pearl Harbor, only four of the sixteen authors were sociologists, the article on "Military Morale," for example, coming from the pen of the Army's Adjutant General rather than that of a sociologist. [38]

SOME USES DURING WORLD WAR II

By coincidence, while the November 1941 issue of the *American Journal of Sociology* was still at the printers, the War Department issued its now famous directive establishing a Research Branch in the Information and Education Division "to provide the Army Command quickly and accurately with facts about the attitudes of soldiers, which, along with other facts and inferences, might be helpful in policy formation," [39] thus initiating the first official attempt to utilize sociology and sociologists with reference to military problems.

Troop Attitude Research Program [40]   The technical director was the late Samuel A. Stouffer, and during the next four wartime years more than 130 sociologists, including seven who have since become president of the American Sociological Association, and other social scientists served with him at one time or another, and over 200 questionnaires (some containing up to 100 questions) were distributed to more than a half-million soldiers. Other important sources of information, supplemental to the questionnaires, were informal sizing up of situations and official operational statistics.

As Stouffer described the operation,

> The Research Branch existed to do an engineering job, not a scientific one. . . . Many, if not most of the jobs seemed small indeed in the perspective of global war . . . as for example, to determine the factors that led men in the South Pacific not to use Atabrine as regularly as the Army thought they should . . . to learn about practices associated with trench foot . . . or what articles men most liked to read in Yank Magazine . . . to determine attitudes toward promotion, job assignments, etc. . . . The War Department files contain more than 300 reports on such topics, most of them of concern to local commanders overseas. . . . But some of the topics were of Army-wide significance, notably the determination of a point system for personnel demobilization after the war . . . which President Roosevelt explained to the American people was based on what the soldiers themselves wanted.[41]

In December 1942, a compendium of the troop-attitude studies that had been done up to that time by the Research Branch was published under the title *What the Soldier Thinks* for limited staff distribution. A second issue appeared in July 1943, which "led to an order by the Chief of Staff that a monthly periodical be prepared for distribution to officers throughout the Army in staff and command positions down to and including the regimental level. After three issues the distribution was extended to include the company level. Each issue was a "summary of current research findings as to attitudes of soldiers in various parts of the world on a wide variety of problems . . . with emphasis on problems that could be treated at the local command level." [42]

In addition, the Research Branch also published a monthly progress report for high-level staff distribution, as well as specially written memoranda to commanders and policy offices that had requested special studies. Thus the results of the research program were fed directly into the planning and operating agencies of the War Department.

Many of the studies dealt with morale and personal adjustment problems. Massive evidence was accumulated to show that various adjustment profiles to army life existed and that these in turn were related to a number of personal background characteristics of the soldier and to variations in army experience. Other studies dealt with such diverse topics as job assignment and job satisfaction; attitudes toward leadership and control; promotions and promotion policy; the special problems of the Negro soldier; motivations and attitudes of combat forces; adjustment problems of returnees from overseas; problems of the occupation of Germany; experimental investigations on the effectiveness of the printed word, lectures, radio, and films in imparting information and in changing attitudes; the opinions of soldiers as to the relative consideration to be given to various factors in determining demobilization priorities; and attitudes and plans of the soldiers regarding their civilian future.

These studies were of value in army planning and policy activities, but the last two deserve special mention because important administrative procedures and policies affecting millions of persons were based on them. In the case of the study of soldiers' postwar plans, the President and Congress used the results to make estimates of the costs of the various provisions of the pending GI bill. No doubt the plans and aspirations of the soldiers also influenced the nature of the many educational and other benefits which the bill finally provided. Moreover, it is interesting to note that the estimates of the numbers who would go back to college, if federal aid to veteran education were provided, were in close correspondence with actual postwar experience.

Perhaps the best known of the many projects of the Research Branch was the one which produced the point system for demobilization of the millions of men in military service at the close of the war. Representative samples of men throughout the world were queried about factors to be taken into account in demobilization. On the basis of their replies, the variables of length of service, overseas duty, combat duty, and parenthood were selected as most significant for determining priorities. Each of these variables was given a weight which had a close correspondence to the wishes of a maximum number of soldiers, and point totals were established for eligibility for demobilization, with the result that every serviceman not only understood the basis for demobilization but could compute his totals so he knew where he stood in relation to the required number of points needed at any given time. As Stouffer has said, "In view of the explosive tensions in the early demobilization period, it is possible that historians will find that the establishment of an objective system for order of demobilization whose justice was accepted by most men may have saved the country from what could have been a crisis seriously damaging to American prestige."

As Stouffer evaluated the job that the branch had done, he pointed out that its

> emphasis was on speed as well as accuracy . . . and although conclusions had frequently to be drawn from inadequate data . . . the Branch may have limited its usefulness too much rather than too little by the standards of accuracy it sought to meet. There were times when its findings were too slow, when they lacked the specificity which an administrator would have liked. In particular, there was hesitation to make explicit recommendations. . . . Fi-

nally, the channels of communication between the policy-makers and the actual study directors in the Branch were often very unsatisfactory. . . . Because of such problems, the potential effectiveness in policy making of some of the research was lost. Nevertheless, enough was accomplished to justify the Army in continuing in peacetime, on a reduced scale of course, a Research operation which provided perhaps the first example in military history of the engineering utility deriving from systematic study of the attitudes of soldiers.[43]

A tribute to the usefulness of the work of the Research Branch was its increased use by overseas as well as domestic commands from 1942 to 1945. In the fall of 1942 General Eisenhower cabled Washington requesting a unit for his theater, and by early 1944 units had also been established in the Mediterranean theater, the Central Pacific, India-Burma, and the Southwest Pacific. After the publication of the four-volume American Soldier series in 1949–1950, General George C. Marshall, the wartime Chief of Staff of the Army, had this to say in a letter to General Osborn, who had been the wartime chief of the Information and Education Division:

In the recent War the Research Branch of the Information and Education Division made available, for the first time in any Army, a current picture of what was in the soldier's mind. Through special monthly reports, this knowledge provided an important supplement to the information which formed the basis for many staff decisions. . . . The volumes of the American Soldier give a unique picture of what the American soldier was thinking and feeling at home and abroad before, during and after combat. These are so far as I know the first quantitative studies of the impact of war on the mental and emotional life of the soldier. They add enormously to our knowledge of the factors which affect soldier morale. Every serious student of military leadership will find in these volumes important criteria by which to judge the validity of previously established theories of morale and the circumstances which modify such theories.[44]

However, despite the magnitude and success of this rapprochement between the military and sociology, it was a somewhat narrowly defined one, primarily centered on studies of the attitudes of individuals. This meant that the focus was, as Hans Speier has put it, on the soldier rather than on the Army[45] and that the conceptual and methodological tools most generally used were from the social-psychological end of the sociological spectrum, as the title of the four-volume monographic series indicates. As Stouffer himself summarized the situation in historical perspective: "Just as World War I gave new emphasis to the study of human aptitudes, so World War II has given new impetus to the study of attitudes." [46]

Nevertheless, even though there was no direct observation of groups in action and only occasional indirect observations of group performance, problems of military social organization were not ignored. As Speier says, the studies contain "a great deal of material which is indispensable for assessing the human implications of the U.S. Army as a social organization," [47] and this evaluation is well supported in his, Edward Shils's, and Robert Merton and Alice Kitts's chapters in *Continuities in Social Research*. Their secondary analyses reveal how much evidence there is in the volumes of *The American Soldier* of significance to an understanding of the "primary group," "reference groups," and "military organization."

But there were others who saw the restricted "attitude" focus as an important limitation on the use of sociology for military purposes. As stated by Morris Janowitz,

> The limitation of attitude research is not that the strategy and tactics of war cannot be based on the preferences of soldiers. This is obvious to all. But, in fact, attitude research fails to describe the underlying social system—the realities of bureaucratic organization—of the Armed Forces. Morale is much too limited a concept to understand the coercive forces of bureaucratic organization, especially of military formations as they operate in combat. The findings of the American Soldier studies themselves serve to underline and reaffirm this sociological observation.[48]

In addition to contributions to military policies and operations and to sociological theory, the Research Branch made great contributions to the methodology of attitude research. In particular the branch became concerned with the problem of scale construction and a technique for demonstrating the unidimensionality of scales based on a small number of items. The work began in 1942 under Louis Guttman, whose name became attached to the technique which Stouffer called the most important single methodological contribution of the branch. This Guttman scalogram method has had wide use since the war, and further study of its properties by Paul F. Lazarsfeld led to latent content analysis as a more general model of which scalogram analysis turned out to be a special case.

Manpower Statistics Program National Headquarters, Selective Service System, was the seat of another major contribution of sociologists to military affairs during and after World War II. The system's Research and Statistics Division was activated in 1941 to design and keep accurate records on the military manpower pool of some thirty million militarily liable registrants in order to meet the manpower needs of the armed forces as equitably as possible and to provide analyses and forecasts of the manpower pool as required.[49]

The data for the division's program came from records of the decisions made by the 6,441 Selective Service Local Boards and the various Armed Forces Induction Centers. Tabulations summarizing the manpower status of each of the local boards and states were prepared monthly and served as the basis for determining the monthly manpower quotas.

The analytical part of the program concerned manpower estimates of great variety due to the constant changes introduced into the manpower procurement system. A congressional committee would request an estimate of the number of farmers and farm hands who would be inducted between such-and-such dates under current manpower policies; the War Department would want an estimate of how many persons in the medically rejected pool were there because of some particular disability such as hernia or illiteracy; the White House would want to know what would be the effect on the armed forces if married men with children were deferred.

After the war Kenneth H. McGill, who was chief of the division from the beginning, played a prominent part in editing the wartime history of the system. McGill has continued as head of the program throughout the postwar years, thus setting a record for continuous service as a sociologist in the same militarily important job.

In addition to these programmatic examples of the use of sociology during World War II, there were many sociologists in operational or staff assignments who contributed as individuals and wrote about their military experiences after returning home. The *American Journal of Sociology*, whose November 1941 issue on "National Morale" was so thinly represented by sociologists, published a special issue in March 1946 on "Human Behavior in Military Society" filled with sociologists' contributions. These analyses covered a wide range of topics, from the "nature of military society" at one extreme to the soldier's language at the other. Joseph Eaton, Daniel Glaser, A. B. Hollingshead, Alfred Lindesmith, Edward McDonagh, and Arnold Rose were among the contributors, and they were joined in other journals by George Homans, Ralph Turner, Morris Janowitz and Edward Shils, Lloyd McCorkle, Robert Stone, Theodore Caplow, and Leslie Zeleny, among others.[50] Some, such as Morroe Berger, called for a continuation of this interest in military affairs, saying that sociologists should try to understand the co-operative life the Army imposes on its men, how such a huge organization manages its business, and how so large a group of Americans have been living under this separate sovereignty existing alongside the civilian government.[51]

SOME USES SINCE WORLD WAR II

The realization of this hope was, of course, greatly facilitated by the impetus to the use of science in all aspects of military life following the organization of the Department of Defense in 1947. The Research and Development Board's stimulus to the use of sociology in support of strategic planning, military intelligence, and psychological warfare was also a stimulus to its use for purposes of military personnel planning and improving the effectiveness of men and organizations. As outlined by the Board's Committee on Human Resources in 1947–1949, the research requirements in this area were grouped into three categories. Two concerned personnel management problems: more dependable analyses of military manpower requirements and resources, and improved techniques for personnel selection, classification, training, and performance evaluation. The third concerned problems of organizational effectiveness: motivation and morale, leadership, command and staff relations, communication, organizational change, and the criteria of unit effectiveness. The following materials will be organized around these three foci of military interest.

Military Manpower Problems   The first focus is exemplified by the program of demographic-actuarial studies directed by C. A. McMahan at the Air University's Human Resources Research Institute, later at the Air Force Personnel and Training Research Center.[52]

In general, Air University's manpower requirements concerned studies that would assist in planning its educational programs, such as "the educational status of the Air Force officer population and eligibility to attend Air University courses"; "population projections for United States Air Force squadron grade officers"; and "the characteristics of active duty officers, including those entering and leaving active duty status." Appropriate studies were prepared on each and fed back to the Air University users.

During this same period Air Force Headquarters was concerned over a number of manpower problems which led to studies of such matters as the participation in reserve activities of Air Force reserve officers and the manpower potential available in the population of retired officers for possible use in the event of full-scale mobilization.[53]

However, the most fundamental and difficult requirement concerned how well the current manning structure of the Air Force was suited to the requirements of the Air Force mission. The research designed to meet this was one of the earliest ventures into the development of a mathematical manpower model. The model, using life-table methodology, would provide a standard against which to assess personnel policies. Two reports have so far been published, the senior author being John W. Merck, who has carried major responsibility since 1957 for the construction of the model.[54]

While research reports constituted the main products of this manpower program, other support services were frequently rendered. Acting in advisory roles, staff members of the Manpower Research Branch conferred frequently with Air University officials and served with them on committees concerned with personnel and manpower problems. Also on numerous occasions the branch furnished data to Air University students making special studies involving manpower considerations.

Personnel and Training Problems[55]   The second major focus of behavioral-science research on the military's personnel management problems includes such important matters as personnel selection, classification, assignment, training, and performance evaluation and are a set of problems to which sociologists have contributed comparatively little. However, the impact of sociology has been increasing over the past decade, particularly in connection with military training (including education) problems, and there is every indication that the participation will increase.

"System training," or "team training in a man-machine system," is a case in point. The major agency for the development of such training has been the Systems Development Corporation, Santa Monica, California, an offshoot of the RAND Corporation established primarily to service military requirements in this field.[56] Its program grew out of a series of small-group studies, conducted by the RAND Corporation in the early 1950's, using an Air Defense Direction Center as a model of an information-processing system involving men and machines. The success of these studies in improving system performance led the Air Defense Command to request the establishment of a system training program for the entire command, and in 1957 this program was extended to the computer-based SAGE (Semi-Automated Ground Environment) air-defense system.[57]

As SDC became responsible for the design and development of other large-scale computer-based systems, sociologists on the staff became involved in studies of operational requirements, human-actions requirements, and the organizational implications of automation. Some of these activities have been described by Michael Eckstein, James Singleton, and Marvin Feuers.[58]

The various uses of simulation technology have been one of the major concerns of sociologists at SDC. This interest includes both laboratory and computer-based simulation studies as applied to theory building and concept formulation, system design, and system training.[59]

The Army's use of behavioral science in support of troop-training programs has been accomplished primarily through its Human Resources Research Office (HumRRO) at George Washington University, which has a number of field research units at Army training posts such as the Infantry School at Fort Benning, Georgia. As at SDC, the HumRRO program has been directed and manned primarily by psychologists.

In the middle 1950's HumRRO instituted a long-range research task known as "Offtrain," whose very important objective was to evolve training methods and materials that would improve leadership skills prior to a junior officer's first assignment to troop duty. The research, participated in by Fred J. Shanley and Morris Showel, was carried out by HumRRO's Army Leadership Human Research Unit located at Presidio of Monterey, California, and a Leadership Training package was developed from these research materials, designed to permit its administration by instructors without special training for the assignment. This course was tried out on platoon leaders in Overseas Unit Replacement battle groups and received such favorable response that it has been incorporated into some Army programs on a package basis. In addition Army training films based on the Offtrain concept of leadership training through problem solving have been produced for Army-wide use in leadership training.[60]

The program in the Air Force comparable to HumRRO was instituted by the Air Training Command in 1949 through the establishment of the Human Resources Research Center (HRRC), which operated through laboratories in various parts of the country. The influence of sociology and sociologists in the original HRRC program was quite limited, being confined almost entirely to the program of the Crew Research Laboratory at Randolph Air Force Base, Texas. Of particular significance was the research accomplished by Robert L. Hall on the role of the aircraft commander in crew effectiveness.[61]

When attention is directed from training to education, the inputs of sociology are somewhat more numerous. Sociology is represented in the course offerings of the United States Armed Forces Institute (USAFI) and in perhaps most of the off-campus programs conducted by universities for military personnel here and overseas. In addition, programs for sending selected officers to civilian colleges have included quotas for sociological training, and some officers, such as above mentioned Norman E. Green, have actually taken graduate degrees in sociology. Furthermore, sociology is present in one way or another in all contemporary service schools as books in their libraries, as supplementary readings in courses, as separate courses, as the major professional identification of guest lecturers or faculty.

Problems of Organizational Effectiveness   This third major focus of interest in the military's internal human resources is the one with which sociologists have most concerned themselves since World War II and the one to which sociology as a discipline has made the greatest contribution. Moreover, in reviewing the record of these years, it is clear that the participating sociologists and their military sponsors, while still concerned with "attitude and morale" problems as in the World War II program, were showing greater interest in the problems of the military establishment as a social system. This has been demonstrated not only in increased attention to such parts of the system as leadership, command and communication channels, role structure and conflict, and group effectiveness and intergroup relations, but also to the functioning of the system as a whole.

By far the most comprehensive program in this broad area was that directed by Abbott L. Ferriss for the Air Force from 1950 to 1957. It was established at the Air University Human Resources Research Institute to cover this wide range of problems, was staffed predominantly with sociologists, and was assisted by other sociologists as consultants and contractors.

A bibliography of the program's published reports up to January, 1957, contains 139 items,[62] and others have appeared since then. The seven years of effort also included countless informal reports and briefings and much work in the field with Air Force officers. And, as an extra, probably thirty young sociologists, many of whom are now among the leaders of the profession, wrote their dissertations in connection with the contracts sponsored by the program.

Leadership was studied early and persistently. The first efforts were through contracts with Samuel A. Stouffer, Director of the Harvard University Laboratory of Social Relations, and Floyd L. Ruch, Director of the University of Southern California's Psychological Research Center. Both of these contracts were supported on basic research funds and were designed primarily to add to our knowledge rather than solve immediate practical problems.

The Harvard studies on officer leadership were proposed in 1950 by Stouffer, who served as their principal investigator and made the studies a major project of the Laboratory of Social Relations for the following three years. The research plan called for four types of studies, all mutually supporting and running concurrently. Three concerned substantive aspects of the leadership situation: Studies in Role Conflict; Studies in Social Perception, Affect and Communication; and Studies in Small Group Behavior. The fourth concerned Methodological Studies, to provide improved techniques for accomplishing the other three.

The research designs of the various substantive tasks called for both field surveys and laboratory experiments, and each involved the development of instruments containing numerous scales to measure the relevant variables. Thus *a major methodological task* involved improvements in attitude scaling. This led to the development of a new method for building cumulative scales with increased precision, the so-called H-technique; to simplification of techniques for handling nonscale response patterns (the restricted latent distance models); and to such basic considerations as the relationship of scaling to other types of analysis and to the content of the data themselves.[63]

The substantive tasks centered around the leader's management of informal social controls and role conflicts. The research plan called for (1) extensive investigation of the nature and variety of these situations from the experiences of Air Force staff and command officers in various Air Force units differing in organizational structure (questionnaires were administered to 2,430 officers at seventeen air bases in the United States and Europe); (2) intensive investigation of the underlying social and psychological dynamics through the experimental creation of role-conflict situations; and (3) a number of miscellaneous tasks relevant to the project such as studies of the communication of hostility between leader and follower, of the differential placement of information in interaction hierarchies, and of the development of a set of variables for rating one category of leader (the noncommissioned officer in charge) for which data were collected from 1,040 such leaders at five air bases.

Reports were prepared on most of these basic research tasks and submitted to HRRI. Some were technical, describing the development of instruments; some were devoted to substantive findings; and some were "peel-offs," thought to be of immediate interest to the Air Force.[64] Two of the latter came from the development of the variables for rating noncommissioned officers and were distributed by HRRI to many Air Force agencies. In another case, two of the members, Andrew Henry and Henry Riecken, were added temporarily to a team assembled to meet an urgent requirement to study troop behavior in the European theater.[65]

Ruch's contract concerned officer leadership behavior under combat conditions, and his interdisciplinary team not only delved into the records of World War II but also conducted an on-the-spot study of leadership behavior in combat during the Korean war. The objective was to increase knowledge of officer leadership in air-combat operations and to develop criteria of leadership which could contribute to the development of combat officers. A research team of five interviewers was sent to the Far East to collect critical incidents describing effective and ineffective leadership in combat situations. The incidents were then analyzed and used to construct a critical behavior check list for determining officer effectiveness.

This was such a unique body of information on the behavior of Air Force officers in combat that Air University requested that a selection of them be published (after eliminating all references to individuals) in order that Air Force instructors and lecturers, and writers of Air Force manuals, would have a source book of illustrations of air-combat leadership behavior with which to work.[66] Since then these materials have been widely used in the Air University schools and in the Air Force ROTC program, and were reprinted in 1962 by the United States Air Force Academy for cadet use as supplementary text materials for one of the Behavioral Sciences courses.[67]

The opportunity provided by the Korean conflict to study other factors in organizational effectiveness under combat conditions was seized upon early, and the field research units established by HRRI in Japan and Korea provided technical and logistic support for teams sent over from the United States. As one example, a rather formal survey covering a range of topics was conducted at a sample of air bases at the height of the conflict, and a number of confidential reports were prepared for Air Force use. These included D. L. Camp's "Acceptance of the Aims of the Korean Campaign by Air Force Personnel"; J. K. Folger's "Attitudes of Regular and Reserve Officers toward the Campaign"; and F. J. DiVesta's "Evaluation of the Presence of Air Force Dependents in Japan on the Morale of Air Force

Personnel." A summary of findings were prepared for Air Force use as early as December, 1951.

The impact of social factors on air-base efficiency, including the relations between an air base and its surrounding civilian world, was the complex subject of some large and unique research contracts. The peculiar nature of the air base as a social system was the focus of sponsored research at the University of North Carolina directed by Gordon Blackwell, E. William Noland, and Nicholas Demerath during the 1951–1954 period. Out of this work came reports on a variety of key factors in air-base efficiency: Raymond Mack's on social stratification; Richard Simpson's on friendship cliques; Frederick Bates's on co-ordination of maintenance activities; J. L. Dyer and W. E. Lambert's on the co-ordination of flying activities; J. D. Thompson's on the organization of executive action; and E. K. Karcher's analysis of the role of the first sergeant in the air-base social system. Twenty-four such technical reports were prepared under the contract and distributed by HRRI to the Air Force, and their findings were compiled in a 1954 final report entitled *The Organization and Performance of Bomb Wings: Studies of Complex Social Systems in Action.*[68]

The relations of an air base to its surrounding civilian community have been a problem of periodic concern from time to time since World War II. The North Carolina team included this topic in its design, and Floyd Hunter reported his study of an American example in *Host Community and Air Force Base.* However, the main interest of the Air Force was in the overseas situation, and a contract was written by HRRI with International Research Associates, Inc., to study the relations between the air depot and the community at Chateauroux, France. The reports covered such aspects of the situation as political, economic, and social organization of Chateauroux; attitudes of the French to the presence of the American air base; economic impact of the air base; contacts between Americans and French; and some factors associated with American airmen's morale.

Social factors in the efficiency of the isolated and smaller air-defense site was another early research target. The sudden threat of the cold war in the late 1940's had necessitated a most serious and hurried effort on our part to build an adequate air-defense system. Early-warning networks were strung hastily on land and sea and in the air, and upgrading them to equal the task was pushed with all speed. As stated in the official requirement for such research,

these installations, manned by relatively few personnel and located in isolated areas, pose rather unique human relations problems along the lines of motivation, team-work and sustained job satisfaction under stressful non-combat conditions. Hence research toward their most effective unit operation is highly indicated. This research is supported by letter from the Commanding General, Air Defense Command.[69]

Since a cluster of such sites was within reach of the University of Washington, arrangements were made with Dr. Delbert C. Miller in March 1951 to direct a major project to meet this requirement. The effort was known as the Air Site Project, and the products were to be reports on the human-relations problems, with particular reference to morale and leadership, and manuals on ways to alleviate them. Twenty-nine reports and manuals were delivered to the Air Force during the project's three and a half years of existence, and some twelve publications have appeared in the published literature since then.[70]

The exploratory phase constituted an experimental design involving seven sites: two very isolated, three moderately so, and two nonisolated. Members of the team lived on the sites during the survey, conducting focused interviews on samples of the men (fifteen to twenty per site), seeking information about their problems and morale, and observing what went on day by day. Analyses of the carefully kept interview and observation records resulted in the first reports of the project to HRRI on the problems as identified by the men themselves. These findings were also presented in monthly briefings to the commander and staff of the Air Defense Division whose sites were surveyed.

On the basis of this initial survey the research team was requested to extend the study to all sites of the division, which provided the opportunity to firm up the research design. Guttman scales were constructed for five dimensions of morale. A measure of site efficiency was produced in collaboration with the division's Inspector General (which was later adopted for use throughout the division and was also considered for national use). An inventory of personnel problems was constructed, and questionnaires were developed for special studies of personal-history factors, job adjustment, leadership, and family adjustment. Again the team members lived for periods of time at the sites while collecting the new data. Reports on each aspect of this larger survey were provided to HRRI and the Air Defense divisional commander. Also provided were the new *Squadron Efficiency Rating System Manual* and a report entitled *Suggestions for Improvement of Air Defense Sites Based on Research Findings*.

The favorable attention earned by the project for this first year's work led to requests from the commander of the parent Air Defense Command to conduct similar surveys in Japan and throughout the United States. Full analysis of these new materials was fed back to the Air Defense officials and, as previously stated, resulted in their interest in supporting the final experimental phase of the project.

That this important and interesting experimental phase was not accomplished is regrettable from the standpoint of the research group and the field commanders who wanted to carry it through. However, the Pentagon had higher priorities at the time and did not approve the required funds. Nevertheless, the knowledge gained from these studies was brought together in a report entitled *Abstracts: Research Reports from Projects on the Air Defense Command,* prepared by Ferriss, George Baker, William Noland, and Glenn McCann, and was distributed to the command for its use.

In-Service Studies In the above contracted projects in-service personnel collaborated with the contractors' teams both technically and administratively. However, other studies were conducted entirely in-service at HRRI as well as at its successor organization, The Office for Social Science Programs, Randolph AFB, Texas.[71] Among these were studies of organizational effectiveness in the research business itself as illustrated by the following case.

The mid-1950's were years of particularly acute growing pains for the Air Force's new Air Research and Development Command, under which was placed most of the laboratories and research activity carried on by the Air Force. Everything was happening at once—pressures to develop adequate air-defense systems, to maintain a manned aircraft superiority, to keep up or catch up with the Russians in the missile field, to maintain sound relations with the civilian scientific world which actually accomplishes most of the Air Force's research and engineering, and to convince the increasing numbers of officers assigned to research and development activities that their careers were not in jeopardy.

The senior officers of the Air Research and Development Command's headquarters met weekly to discuss these issues and more frequently than not ended up by talking about personnel problems. This led to a request to AFPTRC for "a study of the factors underlying the personnel and organizational effectiveness of ARDC, beginning with the headquarters." The team assigned to the project worked closely with a "Study Advisory Group" of senior officers appointed by General Thomas Power, the ARDC Commander, to assist in accomplishing the job. This was a most happy arrangement, and weekly meetings were held to discuss progress, problems, and findings.

The findings indicated that those factors in the work situation related to the organization's mission, or to the people with whom or under whom the respondents worked, were approved by military and civilian subsamples alike, whereas those related in any way to "the system" under which they had to work (manuals of instruction, authority to get the job done, personnel policies, knowing what they were supposed to be doing, communication channels, manning policies) were as widely disapproved. A summary of the findings was presented in briefings and a preliminary report to General Power and his senior staff within a month after the interviewing was terminated, and a full report, with technical appendixes, was available two months later.[72] A part of the report concerned "Implications of the Findings for Administrative Action," based on the respondents' suggestions, and many of the recommendations were implemented.

The problems of managing ARDC's research centers were also knotty, and recurrent demands on the Air Force civilian personnel offices for help in such matters as holding onto scientists already on the center's payrolls led to a conference on the "Management of Civilian Scientists in Air Force Laboratories," held in Washington, D.C., on August 6–8, 1963, attended by line and staff representatives of Air Force research activities, from both headquarters and laboratory levels, and by behavioral scientists who had been conducting research on the management of research activities and related topics. The presentations and discussions indicated that it would be desirable to have one or more social scientists at research headquarters and laboratory levels to conduct special studies and help interpret and apply findings from existing studies to current management problems. This suggestion was welcomed by General Ostrander, Commander of the Office of Aerospace Research that cosponsored the conference, and Howard M. Vollmer agreed to act in this capacity for a one-year period.

This project has provided a very useful link between the social scientist and the Air Force research manager. It has also provided a feedback of information on the applications of social-science research in certain specific organizational contexts that will be useful in the refinement of relevant organization and management theory. Moreover, the project has provided more information about the role of a sociologist as an "applications agent." Vollmer's account of the year's work is not only exciting reading, but also a model for this kind of reporting.[73]

An interesting feature of this conference and its aftermath was its continuity, in a sense, with previous Air Research and Development Command concern over research management problems. Bowers was asked, for example, to report on the above-described Hq ARDC survey, as well as on a later survey he did of an ARDC research center, and General Ostrander, the conference cohost, had been an active member of the ARDC Study Advisory Group that had worked closely with the research team during the earlier survey.

The work of Dr. Morris Janowitz in fostering the use of sociology in the military establishment has been previously mentioned in connection with psychological warfare programs. However, his best known contribution concerns his analysis of the internal structure and human resources of the institution. His 1960 monograph on *The Professional Soldier* uses sociological analysis to cast light on the past history and present status of the military profession, and to look into its future.[74]

Janowitz foresees that the armed forces of the future might more appropriately become *constabulary* than *military* forces, "continuously prepared to act, committed to the minimum use of force and seeking viable international relations rather than victory."[75] The implications of this for the professional soldier and the country are described in his final chapter.

The book has been widely reviewed by military journals and has enjoyed phenomenal sales in military circles, especially now that it is in a paper-back edition. Furthermore, it has become an essential part of the educational curricula of a great variety of military educational institutions. Both at the United States Military Academy and the United States Air Force Academy it has led to the establishment of specific courses on military sociology. At the Command and Staff College of Air University a detailed critique of it has been made a requirement of each class. Thus the military services have incorporated an explicit analysis of their professional structure into their training and indoctrination.

In addition, the ideas and concepts of the book have been integrated into many types of military planning and staff work, particularly in the areas of recruitment, professional training, and retirement policy. A specific current case involves the role of military honor as analyzed in the book, an analysis which figures prominently in the discussions and investigation of deviant behavior in examinations at the Air Force Academy.

Finally, the book has led to a considerable amount of research in depth, both by the military services and by civilian universities.

Thus it is indeed fitting that this section on the uses of sociology for military personnel management and organizational effectiveness, which began with an account of the application of sociological research technology to the problems of managing the American soldier in World War II, should end with an account of the application of sociological analysis to the military managers themselves.

Summary and Conclusions

Sociology, as a separate discipline, was less than a half-century old when its practitioners were called upon during World War II to help the War Department understand and manage its human resources. Only a decade later, sociologists were involved in the much wider variety of military problems cited in this chapter. Concurrently, social recognition was bestowed on this work through the appearance of sections on "military sociology" at annual meetings of the American Sociological Association, of chapters on military sociology in such compilations as the UNESCO volume on *Sociology in the United States of America*,[76] and, indeed, of a separate volume on *Sociology and the Military Establishment*[77] sponsored by the American Sociological Association and the Russell Sage Foundation.

The record shows that well over two hundred professional sociologists have contributed to this postwar use of sociology by the military establishment, and the list approximates a *Who's Who* of current American sociologists. Added to those mentioned in these pages are many who could have been included with equal justification.

The ups and downs of military support for such sociological services during this period have been widely commented on, and such shifts were, of course, regrettable from the standpoints of both the sociologists involved and the science itself. But these should be viewed in the perspectives of the period, of what was happening in the military research picture generally, and of where sociology and sociologists stand in military research circles today as compared with the late 1940's when research and development were first established as essential functions of the military establishment.

Disagreements over priorities and levels of support were not unusual, even in the "hardware" sciences, as military concepts changed or performance estimates hardened, and some of these shifts were so bitterly fought within the Pentagon that they became objects of congressional hearings and action. The story of the nuclear submarine is a notable example of this, as is the current conflict over manned bombers. In fact, the course of hardware development in the 1950's was not essentially dissimilar in many respects to that of behavioral-science research, as it, likewise, had its share of anguish incident to contract cutbacks and cancellations.

But today the level of military support for the behavioral sciences is much greater than that of the late 1940's. On a sheer money basis it has grown from an estimated annual total of $2,000,000 to some $20,000,000. On an organizational basis, the years have seen behavioral-science divisions established in the Office of the Secretary of Defense and in the headquarters of the three military services; behavioral scientists appointed to scientific advisory boards in these headquarters;[78] behavioral-science divisions organized in such basic research agencies as the Office of Naval Research and the Air Force Office of Scientific Research; behavioral-science laboratories created on both an in-service and a contract basis throughout the country; hundreds of behavioral-science research grantees working on military problems, likewise throughout the country; behavioral scientists employed in personnel, intelligence, and other segments of the services, and many involved in military activities of various kinds as members of the reserve forces. On an information basis, reports of these research efforts have become widely available through publication in the professional journals and through in-service publications, including annual volumes of abstracts.[79] And although the bulk of this behavioral-science activity today still involves psychology and psychologists, there is proportionately more participation by sociology and sociologists.

That this is so is due in part to the pioneering work of the sociologists cited in these pages and of the others who contributed their skills and zeal to military problems during this period. But it is also in part due to the increasing breadth of training and background of military leaders themselves and to the changing nature of our society and war. The farther the conflict is from nuclear war the more it is a sociological conflict, and the contributions of sociologists have been found useful in understanding both the external context of the variety of conflicts facing us today and the internal context of men and institutions that must wage them.

There seems little reason to doubt that this upward trend in the military use of sociology is here to stay, although the slope of the trend will depend on the extent to which jobs are established for applied sociologists and sociologists are willing and qualified to fill them. A certain amount of sociological diffusion will, of course, continue to occur without the active participation of full-time sociological catalysts. Libraries and the mails will continue to funnel sociological literature into the system, and informed officers and civilian professionals will continue to act as informal diffusion agents. But there comes a time when the level of technical sophistication necessary for full and proper utilization of any discipline calls for specialists, and that time has come for sociology, as stated repeatedly during the past decade by various advisory panels of behavioral scientists.

The implementation of this advice through the provision of positions within the military establishment has not been encouraging so far. However, the alternative procedure of providing such services through contractual rather than employee relationships has been successfully introduced through such organizations as the RAND and Systems Development Corporations and through contracts with industry and the universities, as described frequently above. Nevertheless, some in-service utilization specialists are also required if such outside assistance is to be properly planned, co-ordinated, followed up, and evaluated, and the lack of positions for them in the manning tables of the services is a limiting factor on the current utilization of sociology. Since much groundwork has been laid for the justification of such positions, there is no reason to believe they will not soon be sponsored in some segments of the establishment.

REFERENCES

NOTE: *The story of the military uses of sociology exists in only a small part in readily accessible public documents. Much more of it is found in in-service reports, staff memoranda, and briefing documents, copies of which do not ordinarily survive in official files beyond a certain records-management cut-off date, and hence are available, if at all, in personal files. Many examples are referenced below. Still more of the story, and perhaps the major part, resides only in the participants' memories. The writer's experience with these military uses after World War II began at the Secretary of Defense level and thus is based on some acquaintance with the programs and personnel of all three services. Nevertheless, to compensate for his greater contact over the years with the Air Force story, he called on two Army knowledgeables (E. Kenneth Karcher, Jr., and Charles H. Coates) to prepare papers covering major areas of utilization and attempted through correspondence to obtain information regarding other examples. That the examples selected for inclusion could not have come more evenly from the three services is regretted, but this imbalance, although based in part on the differential availability of information about cases, mirrors in* good measure the differential acceptance of the discipline by the three services during this period. At least the examples are believed to be representative of the more important uses made of sociology and sociologists since 1940, and probably also of the more important problems incident to applying new frames of reference and technologies to old and persistent problems.

1. Donald G. Marquis was the committee's first chairman. Other members were Samuel A. Stouffer, Carroll Shartle, Walter S. Hunter, and William Menninger. The Manpower Panel was first chaired by Philip Hauser, and the Human Relations and Morale Panel by Charles Dollard. Other sociologists involved in the early stages of the panel's work were: Leland DeVinney, William H. Sewell, Hans Speier, and Irene Taeuber. Raymond V. Bowers served first as the committee's Deputy Executive Director and then as its Executive Director during the first two years, 1947–1949. He did the staff work for both the Human Relations and Morale and the Manpower Panels.

2. The Human Resources Research Center (HRRC) of the Air Training Command, Lackland Air Force Base, Texas; The Human Resources Research Institute (HRRI) of Air University, Maxwell Air Force Base, Alabama; and The Human Resources Research Laboratory (HRRL) of the Headquarters Command, Bolling Air Force Base, D.C. In addition, the RAND Corporation, Santa Monica, California, which was established to serve the Air Force, had a Social Science Department. Sociologists were appointed to head two of these agencies: Raymond V. Bowers at HRRI and Hans Speier at RAND. Charles E. Hutchinson was in the main research office at Air Force Headquarters and in 1955 became the first Chief of the Behavioral Sciences Division, Air Force Office of Scientific Research.

3. The Human Resources Research Office (HumRRO) at George Washington University, the Operations Research Office (ORO) at Johns Hopkins University, and, later on, the Special Operations Research Office (SORO) at American University. Although no sociologist has directed these agencies, a number have participated in their programs, several of whom will be mentioned in the pages to follow. In addition, Dr. E. Kenneth Karcher, Jr., has served for many years in the Army Research Office at Army Headquarters.

4. The Navy's behavioral science programs have been heavily oriented to the uses of the various psychological specialties, physiological to clinical.

5. I am greatly indebted to Dr. Herman J. Sander for basic materials on which this section is based.

6. Alexander H. Leighton, *Human Relations in a Changing World* (New York: Dutton, 1949); U.S. Strategic Bombing Survey, *The Effects of Strategic Bombing on German Morale*, 2 vols. (Washington, D.C., Government Printing Office, 1946–1947), and *The Effects of Strategic Bombing on Japanese Morale* (Washington, D.C., Government Printing Office, 1947). A tribute to the program of the Foreign Morale Analysis Division is contained in *The Effective Use of Social Science Research in the Federal Services* (New York: Russell Sage Foundation, 1950), pp. 17 ff.

7. U.S. Strategic Bombing Survey (Japan), Foreword, III.

8. Burton Fisher directed the Japanese survey. Others participating in the surveys included Clifford Kirkpatrick, William H. Sewell, and Raymond V. Bowers.

9. Irving L. Janis, *Air War and Emotional Stress: Psychological Studies of Bombing and Civilian Defense* (New York: McGraw-Hill, 1951). A RAND Corporation Research Study.

10. Fred C. Iklé, *The Social Impact of Bomb Destruction* (Norman: University of Oklahoma Press, 1958).

11. Peter G. Nordlie and Robert D. Popper, *Social Phenomena in a Post-Nuclear Attack Situation*, AFOSR Technical Note 60–1495, ASTIA AD No. 263211, August, 1961.

12. Raymond A. Bauer, Alex Inkeles, and Clyde Kluckhohn, *How the Soviet System Works* (Cambridge: Harvard University Press, 1956).

13. Alex Inkeles and Raymond A. Bauer, *The Soviet Citizen: Daily Life in a Totalitarian State* (Cambridge: Harvard University Press, 1959). Several special reports and journal articles were written by such other sociologists as Mark Field, Ivan London, Peter Rossi, Kent Geiger, Robert Feldmesser, and Barrington Moore, Jr.

14. Alice H. Bauer, *A Guide for Interviewing Soviet Escapees* (Maxwell AFB: Human Resources Research Institute, 1953).

15. For example, in the Foreword to his widely read paperback *The Dynamics of Soviet Society* (1953), Walter W. Rostow says, "A considerable proportion of whatever value this essay may have derives from the outstanding support of the Russian Research Center at Harvard and from the wise advice of its director, Clyde Kluckhohn."

16. The late Maurice T. Price's career exemplifies the fact that much more utilization of sociology has gone on than any survey can properly appraise. After careers in China and academic life, he taught in the Army's specialized training program in World War II, served the Air Force as a research specialist on China during the 1950's, before going as consultant to SORO.

17. Fred C. Iklé's *The Social Effects of Bombing* was one response to such interest, as was a report on *Korean Urbanization: Past Development and Future Potentials*. Both were distributed in 1953 as HRRI Technical Research Reports.

18. Philip M. Hauser, Dudley Duncan, and Beverly Duncan, *Methods of Urban Analysis, A Summary Report*, AFPTRC Research Report TN-56–1 (Maxwell AFB: Officer Education Research Laboratory, Air Force Personnel and Training Research Center, 1956).

19. Norman E. Green and Robert B. Monier, "Aerial Photographic Interpretation and the Human Ecology of the City," *Photographic Engineering* (December, 1959), 773.

20. Foreign Manpower Research Office, Bureau of the Census (Unclassified title), *Methodology of USSR City Population and Labor Force Studies* (Secret), (Randolph AFB: Office for Social Science Programs, Air Force Personnel and Training Research Center, 1957).

21. Daniel Lerner, *Sykewar: Psychological Warfare Against Germany, D-Day to VE-Day* (New York: G. W. Stewart, 1949); Hans Speier, "Psychological Warfare Reconsidered," in D. Lerner and H. D. Lasswell, eds., *The Policy Sciences* (Stanford: Stanford University Press, 1951); William E. Daugherty and Morris Janowitz, *A Psychological Warfare Casebook* (Washington, D.C.: Operations Research Office, The Johns Hopkins University, 1958).

22. From a personal copy of this report in the files of Raymond V. Bowers, to whom the report was addressed in his capacity as Director of HRRI. The officer in charge of the Far East Research Group was Colonel John W. Quayle, a psychologist by training, who was a dedicated supporter of social science research in the Air Force during his tour of duty at HRRI and later as Deputy Commander of the Combined AFPTRC. Dr. Glaister Elmer and Major E. H. Conklin were sociologists in the Group.

23. *Implications and Summary of a Psychological Warfare Study in South Korea* (Maxwell AFB: Air University Human Resources Research Institute, 1951), p. II.

24. John W. Riley, Jr., and Wilbur Schramm, *The Reds Take a City: The Commu-*

nist Occupation of Seoul, with Eyewitness Accounts (New Brunswick: Rutgers University Press, 1951).

25. John Useem, "The American Pattern of Military Government in Micronesia," *American Journal of Sociology,* LI (1945), 93–102.

26. Letter from Charles A. H. Thomson to Raymond V. Bowers, dated March 23, 1964.

27. I. C. C. Graham and B. S. Lieb, *Publications of the Social Science Department, The RAND Corporation, 1948–1964* (Santa Monica: The RAND Corporation, 1964). Sociologists represented by the publications include Herbert Goldhamer, Fred Iklé, and Philip Selznick in addition to Hans Speier.

28. *Bibliography of Publications* (Washington, D.C.: Special Operations Research Office, The American University, November, 1963), p. 6.

29. *Ibid.,* p. 8.

30. Daugherty and Janowitz, *op. cit.* Contributors to this Casebook were such other sociologists as Howard Becker, Joel Berreman, Leonard Cottrell, Alex Inkeles, Leo Lowenthal, and John W. Riley, Jr.

31. A final report by Stuart C. Dodd, *Revere Studies in Interaction: On the Laws of Diffusion,* is in preparation. Sociologists who worked with Dodd included Charles Bowerman, Melvin de Fleur, Otto Larsen, and Jiri Nehnevajsa.

32. Albert D. Biderman, *Effects of Communist Indoctrination Attempts,* AFPTRC-TN-57-119 (Lackland AFB: Air Force Personnel and Training Research Center, 1957).

33. U.S. Senate's Permanent Sub-Committee on Investigations of the Committee on Government Operations, *Hearings June 26, 1956* (Washington, D.C.: Government Printing Office, 1956).

34. Albert D. Biderman, *March to Calumny: The Story of American POW's in the Korean War* (New York: Macmillan, 1962).

35. Charles W. Bray, "Toward a Technology of Human Behavior for Defense," *American Psychologist,* XVII (1962). This is a summary of the recommendations in the three areas.

36. Morris Janowitz, *Sociology and the Military Establishment* (New York: Russell Sage Foundation, 1959), p. 15.

37. George A. Lundberg, Read Bain, and Nels Anderson, eds., *Trends in American Sociology* (New York: Harper, 1929).

38. *American Journal of Sociology,* XLVII, No. 3 (November, 1941), 478 ff.

39. Samuel A. Stouffer *et al., The American Soldier: Adjustment during Army Life.* Vol. I of *Studies in Social Psychology in World War II* (Princeton: Princeton University Press, 1949), p. 5. The other volumes in the series are: Vol. II, *The American Soldier: Combat and Its Aftermath;* Vol. III, *Experiments on Mass Communication;* Vol. IV, *Measurement and Prediction.*

40. This program deserves much more detailed attention than can be given to it here, but its story is chronicled in the four volumes of *Studies in Social Psychology in World War II* cited in the previous note and widely available in libraries throughout the country.

41. *Ibid.,* Vol. I, pp. 5 ff.

42. *Ibid.,* Vol. I, pp. 10–11.

43. *Ibid.,* Vol. I, pp. 11 ff.

44. Reported in Daniel Lerner, "The American Soldier and the Public," in Robert K. Merton and Paul F. Lazarsfeld, eds., *Continuities in Social Research* (Glencoe, Ill.: The Free Press, 1950), p. 234.

45. Hans Speier, "The Sociology of Military Organization," in *ibid.,* p. 107.

46. Stouffer *et al., op. cit.,* Vol. I, p. 5.

47. Speier, "The Sociology of Military Organization," *op. cit.*, p. 107.

48. Janowitz, *op. cit.*, p. 12.

49. Kenneth H. McGill, "The Development and Operation of a Statistical Program for the Selective Service System," *American Sociological Review*, IX (October, 1944), 513 ff. Other sociologists in the program at various times were C. Arnold Anderson, Raymond V. Bowers, O. Harold Folk, Robert N. Ford, William H. Sewell, and J. Mapheus Smith.

50. George C. Homans, "The Small Warship," *American Sociological Review*, II (June, 1946), 294 ff.; Ralph H. Turner, "The Navy Disbursing Officer as a Bureaucrat," *American Sociological Review*, XII (June, 1947), 342 ff.; Edward A. Shils and Morris Janowitz, "Cohesion and Disintegration in the Wehrmacht in World War II," *Public Opinion Quarterly*, XII (1948), 280 ff.; Robert C. Stone, "Status and Leadership in a Combat Fighter Squadron," *American Journal of Sociology*, LI (March, 1946), 388 ff.; Theodore Caplow, "Rumors in War," *Social Forces*, XXV (March, 1947), 298 ff.; Joseph Abrahams and Lloyd W. McCorkle, "Group Psychotherapy of Military Offenders," *American Journal of Sociology*, LI (March, 1946), 455 ff.; Leslie D. Zeleny, "Selection of Compatible Flying Partners," *American Journal of Sociology*, LII (March, 1947), 424 ff.

51. Morroe Berger, "Law and Custom in the Army," *Social Forces*, XXV (1946–1947), 82 ff.

52. The following description of this program is taken in part from Stephen W. Fotis' *Program Development of the Manpower Research Branch 1951–1955, A Working Paper* (Maxwell AFB: Officer Education Research Laboratory, August, 1955), 50 pp. Other sociologists associated with McMahan were Jerry W. Combs, Jr., John K. Folger, Thomas R. Ford, John W. Merck, and Charles B. Nam.

53. Thomas R. Ford, Charles B. Nam, and C. A. McMahan, *Officer Affiliation with the Air Force Reserve Training Program in Continental Air Command, 1953*, OERL Technical Memorandum OERL-TM-54-3 (Maxwell AFB: Officer Education Research Laboratory, November, 1954), 39 pp.; C. A. McMahan, John K. Folger, and Stephen W. Fotis, "Retirement and Length of Life," *Social Forces*, XXXIV (March, 1956), 234 ff.

54. John W. Merck and F. B. Ford, *Feasibility of a Method for Estimating Short-Term and Long-Term Effects of Policy Decisions on the Airman Personnel System*, Report No. WADC-TR-59-38, ASTIA Document AD-217 079 (Lackland AFB: Personnel Research Laboratory, June, 1959); John W. Merck, *Retention of First Enlistment Airmen: Analysis of Results of a Mathematical Simulation*, Report No. PRL-TDR-62-17 (OTS) (Lackland AFB: Personnel Research Laboratory, August, 1962), 10 pp.

55. I am greatly indebted to Dr. E. Kenneth Karcher for basic materials on which this topic is based.

56. This description of the major activities of sociologists at SDC is taken from a letter by Dr. Ellis L. Scott. The letter, dated March 23, 1964, was written in response to a request for such information.

57. Robert Boguslaw and E. H. Porter, Jr., "Team Function and Training," in R. M. Gagne, ed., *Psychological Principles in System Design* (New York: Holt, Rinehart, and Winston, 1962), pp. 387 ff.; R. Boguslaw, "Situation Analysis and the Problem of Action," *Journal of Social Problems*, VIII, No. 3 (Winter, 1961), 212 ff.

58. M. E. Eckstein, *Sociological Perspective in the Analysis and Design of Large-Scale Man-Machine Systems*, Systems Development Corporation, Santa Monica, SP-1576; J. W. Singleton, *The Role of the Human Operator in Command-Control Systems*, Systems Development Corporation, Santa Monica, SP-179 (1960); M. N.

Feuers, "Scheduling and Phase of Management Decisions in an Automated Data Processing Cycle," *Institute in Electronics Data Processing*, Reprints of Presentations (January, 1963), 23 ff.

59. Earl Bogdanoff *et al.*, *Simulation: An Introduction to a New Technology*, Systems Development Corporation, Santa Monica, TM-499 (1960); Maria Davidson and Ellis L. Scott, *Simulation Techniques and Their Application*, Systems Development Corporation, Santa Monica, SP-1133 (1963); Jeanne E. and John T. Gullahorn, "A Computer Model of Elementary Social Behavior," *Behavioral Science*, VIII, No. 4 (October, 1963), 354 ff.

60. Carl J. Lange, Vincent Campbell, Robert V. Katter, and Fred J. Shanley, *A Study of Leadership in Army Infantry Platoons*, HumRRO Research Report 1, (Presidio of Monterey, Calif.: U.S. Army Leadership Human Research Unit, November, 1958).

61. Robert L. Hall, *Predicting Bomber Crew Performance from the Aircraft Commander's Role*, Research Report AFPTRC-TN-56-28 (Lackland AFB: Air Force Personnel and Training Research Center, February, 1956).

62. *Reports of the Organizational Effectiveness Research Program, December 1951– January 1957* (Randolph AFB: Air Force Personnel and Training Research Center, January, 1957).

63. Samuel A. Stouffer, Edgar F. Borgatta, David G. Hays, and Andrew F. Henry, "A Technique for Improving Cumulative Scales," *Public Opinion Quarterly*, XVI, No. 2 (1952), 273 ff.; Andrew F. Henry, "A Method of Classifying Non-Scale Response Patterns in a Guttman Scale," *Public Opinion Quarterly*, XVI, No. 1 1952), 94 ff.; Edgar Borgatta and David Hays, "Some Limitations on the Classification of Non-Scale Response Patterns in a Guttman Scale," *Public Opinion Quarterly*, XVI, No. 3 (1952), 410 ff.; David G. Hays and Edgar F. Borgatta, "An Empirical Comparison of Restricted and General Latent Distance Analysis," *Psychometrika*, XIX, No. 4 (December, 1954), 271 ff. Although most of the Stouffer team is mentioned in this and the following five notes, others who deserve similar recognition are Jackson Toby, Freed Bales, John Gullahorn, and Theodore Mills.

64. Andrew F. Henry, Edgar F. Borgatta, and Samuel A. Stouffer, "Role Conflict as a Factor in Organizational Effectiveness," in Raymond V. Bowers, ed., *Studies in Organizational Effectiveness—Contributions to Military Sociology* (Washington, D.C.: Air Force Office of Scientific Research, 1962), a volume of previously unpublished studies from the HRRI program; John W. Thibaut and Henry W. Riecken, "Authoritarianism, Status, and the Communication of Aggression," *Human Relations*, VIII, No. 2 (May, 1955), 95 ff.; Edgar F. Borgatta, *What Non-Commissioned Officers Think of Promotion and Reward Practices in the United States Air Force*, Research Memorandum No. 4 (Maxwell AFB: Human Resources Research Institute, December, 1952); Andrew F. Henry and Edgar F. Borgatta, *A Report on Attitudes Toward Desertion of Air Force Personnel*, Research Memorandum No. 8 (Maxwell AFB: Human Resources Research Institute, May, 1953).

65. N. Maccoby, A. F. Henry, H. W. Riecken, *et al.*, *Behavior Standards in USAFE Personnel*, HRRI Report No. HR-18 (Maxwell AFB: Human Resources Research Institute, August, 1952).

66. F. L. Ruch and R. Reveal, Jr., *Incidents of Leadership in Combat*, Vols. I–VI, HRRI Technical Memorandum No. 3 (Maxwell AFB: Human Resources Research Institute, Feb.-April, 1953). Bruce M. Pringle played a significant part in the over-all project.

67. F. L. Ruch and R. Reveal, Jr., *Incidents of Leadership in Combat* (Department of Behavioral Sciences, U.S. Air Force Academy, 1962), 153 pp.

68. This final, unedited report was one of the unpublished documents in the files of the Air Force Personnel and Training Research Center when its role as a major center for psychology and social science research was terminated in 1958. An edited version of the Karcher report was included as Chapter 2 in Bowers, ed., *op. cit.*, as an example of the contract's work.

69. Department of Defense, Research and Development Board Project Number 505–036–0001, "Human Relations Problems in Isolated Air Defense Sites" (Report date May 7, 1952).

70. An edited version of the team's final report appears in Bowers, ed., *op. cit.*, as Chapter 3, "Morale and Human Relations Leadership as Factors in Organizational Effectiveness," by Delbert C. Miller, Nahum Z. Medalia, Glenn C. McCann, *et al.*; all the published articles are cited in Edward Gross and Delbert C. Miller's "The Impact of Isolation on Worker Adjustment in Military Installations of the U.S. and Japan," *Estudios de Sociologia* (Buenos Aires), I, No. 1 (Fall, 1961), 70–86. The other sociologists covered by the *et al.* are Orvis Collins, F. James Davis, Edward Gross, Charles D. McGlamery, David Bushnell, David Garrity, Robert Hagedorn, Herman Loether, Duane Strinden, and David Yaukey.

71. Among the many publications resulting from these studies are: George W. Baker *et. al.*, *Attitudes and Judgments of Some Lieutenants Related to Their Present Active-duty Intentions*, HRRI Technical Report No. 14 (May, 1953); G. W. Baker, *Recruitment, Assignment and Utilization of New Research and Development Air Force Officers: A Study of Needs as Perceived by Two Status Groups*, Crew Research Lab. Technical Memorandum 54-1 (November, 1954); Abbott L. Ferriss, "Studies in the Organization of Maintenance: Authority Patterns in High and Low Performance Wings," (A report to the Office of the Asst. Secretary of Defense, August, 1955); Daniel L. Camp and G. C. McCann, *Follow-up Study of Personnel Who Received Pre-embarkation Orientation for Overseas Duty in France*, CRL Staff Research Memorandum (July, 1954); John K. Folger, *Attitudes of Regular and Reserve Officers toward the Korean Campaign*, HRRI Report No. HR-6 (1952); Daniel L. Camp, *Acceptance of the Aims of the Korean Campaign*, HRRI Report No. HR-5 (1952); Abbott L. Ferriss, *The Allocation of Material Control Functions in Six Maintenance Squadrons of the Strategic Air Command*, Office of Social Science Programs Technical Memorandum 56-3 (November, 1956); Alan C. Kerckhoff, *A Review of Current AFPTRC Attitude and Motivation Research*, OSSP-TM-56-1 (November, 1956); Raymond V. Bowers, *ARDC Studies in Personnel and Organizational Effectiveness: A Survey of the Opinions of AFPTRC Personnel after the Deactivation of the Center* (A report to the Headquarters, ARDC, August, 1958).

72. Raymond V. Bowers *et al.*, *ARDC Studies in Personnel and Organizational Effectiveness: An Exploratory Study of ARDC Headquarters*, Technical Memorandum, HQ-TM-56-1 (Lackland AFB: Air Force Personnel and Training Research Center, February, 1956). Other sociologists associated with the project were George Baker, Alan Kerckhoff, Raymond Mack, and Glenn McCann.

73. Howard M. Vollmer, *Application of the Behavioral Sciences to Research Management: An Initial Study in the Office of Aerospace Research* (Menlo Park, Calif.: Stanford Research Institute, November, 1964).

74. Morris Janowitz, *The Professional Soldier* (Glencoe, Ill.: The Free Press, 1960).

75. *Ibid.*, p. 418.

76. Robert L. Hall, "Military Sociology 1945–1955," in Hans L. Zetterberg, ed., *Sociology in the United States of America* (Netherlands: UNESCO, 1956), 59 ff.; Paul Walter, Jr., "Military Sociology," in Joseph S. Roucek, ed., *Contemporary Sociology* (New York: Philosophical Library, 1958), pp. 655 ff.

77. Janowitz, *Sociology and the Military Establishment*.

78. Dr. Launor Carter, a social psychologist, served for a year as Chief Scientist of the Air Force, a position occupied at all other times by "hard" scientists.

79. For example: *Abstracts of USAPRO Research Publications* (Washington, D.C.: U.S. Army Personnel Research Office); *Abstracts of Personnel Research Reports* (Lackland AFB: Personnel Research Laboratory), Vols. I–V.

Law Enforcement

DAVID J. BORDUA

ALBERT J. REISS, JR.

chapter 10

Until recently, sociologists paid little attention to police organization and behavior as an object of research. Within the last decade, however, a body of systematic studies has appeared. With what at first sight seems a peculiar perversity, the application of sociology to crime control began at the end of the crime-control process—with corrections—rather than at the beginning—with law enforcement and the police. There are several reasons for this relative neglect. Police until recently have been relatively inaccessible to social science investigation. Sociology itself was identified with the "good government" forces whose purpose was not to study and help the police, but to "expose" them. Moreover, sociologists until recently have been quite uncomfortable in the presence of coercion. They have made their way in the correctional field primarily by providing a "scientific" underpinning to the humanitarian rhetoric that has been so prominent in the correctional reform field.[1]

The professionalization movement in police administration gave sociologists a social base for investigation in much the same way that the high status prison reform groups did in corrections. The professional administrators by the very fact that they want to professionalize the police emphasize education and the transition from a closed to an open occupation. Moreover, they are increasingly coming to recognize that

275

sociological understanding of organization and behavior is a useful adjunct to the public administration training that most public professionals have gained.

The police can be viewed from a variety of sociological perspectives. Those that have informed recent studies of the police have arisen less from the traditional interest in criminology than from more general sociological perspectives. One of these arises from the institutional analysis of the law in the sociology of law. The work of Skolnick, especially, falls in this category. His primary aim was to investigate how value conflicts in a democratic society create conditions that affect the capacity of the police to respond to the rule of law.[2] A second major perspective on the police derives from the study of occupations and social roles. The police are seen as a special occupation group in an occupational organization, the department. The authors of this chapter have emphasized a third perspective, which stresses the transactions between organization and environment.[3] In the case of the police in the United States, both organization and environment are highly complex for any given police organization, and the variations in both are considerable. Moreover, both have been changing over time, so that understanding of current organization requires that attention be given to the historical development of the organization and its transactions with the environment.

Given the generally ahistorical character of American sociology, it is not surprising that sociologists have given little attention to the historical development of law enforcement systems. The writings of Selden D. Bacon and more recently that of Allan Silver[4] are the major sociological explanations of the emergence of municipal police systems respectively in the United States and England. No attempt has been made to explain their development in the modern period.

Early Developments in Municipal Police Organization

Law enforcement was problematic throughout the history of cities. Yet the modern police department, in the sense of an organization with city-wide jurisdiction, twenty-four-hour responsibility for much of law enforcement, and a regular, salaried, full-time, career police charged with general rather than specific police functions, did not develop until the nineteenth century. The establishment of the London Metropolitan Police in 1829 and that of New York City in 1844 are the earliest examples of municipal police organization. The underlying social processes that contributed to their establishment were increasing economic specialization, increasing social differentiation, and a growing segregation and density of the urban population.[5]

Increasing economic specialization led to greater citizen dependence on the economic performance of specialists whose performance no longer could be guaranteed by folk control or by market forces. Local governments responded by creating specialized offices of independent inspectors whose duty it was to insure that the populace was not cheated in the market or exploited by their neighbors. As an example, the necessity in New Amsterdam to rely on specialized suppliers of firewood led as early as 1658 to the employment of firewood inspectors. Regulation of butchers, bakers, and hack drivers showed the same consequences of the inability of the citizen to rely on his own resources in a period of increasing specialization. By the time of the emergence of municipal police systems, the list of special regulatory or inspectorial officials had become quite vast.[6] At the time of their formation, some of these inspectors were incorporated into the police department; others were organized in a centralized bureau of inspectors. Although the title of inspector remains in many police departments, most of these inspection services have since been removed to more specialized municipal agencies.

Increasing social differentiation, heterogeneity, and stratification of the population led to lowered consensus on major values and the necessity to develop formal controls if a heterogeneous community was to have at least a minimum of order. Bacon's interpretation covers the ground nicely.

Another method of curbing any overt manifestation of class differences and trying to make compromises or substitute plans of action so that hostility and consequent loss of security will not occur is to set down the acceptable modes of behavior and then place agents at those places and in those times where conflict is likely to arise, to see that the accepted modes of behavior are not infringed upon and to curb at the outset any activity which tends in that direction; this is an expensive adjustment, but not as expensive as the evil it avoids. Like specialization, class stratification may have its values, but it also has its disadvantages and it is costly to overcome these last and enjoy the benefits.[7]

The "class stratification" to which Bacon refers in the quotation corresponds to differences in "race, nationality, language, major economic function, education, religion, and so forth." [8] Within the rapidly growing American cities, the stage was set for conflict, and conflict there was: struggle over Sunday observance in Boston, near civil war between old inhabitants and immigrants in Philadelphia and between Yankee and Creole in New Orleans, disorders in New York culminating in the Doctors' Riot of 1788, and everywhere problems in the relations between the races. Even slavery under urban conditions became a menace to public order.[9] Matters did not change in the early nineteenth century. The depression years of the 1830's brought riots in three major American cities: a Negro riot in Philadelphia, flour riots in New York City, and riots between fire-fighting brigades in Boston.

Increasing population density heightened the need to regulate social activity in a variety of ways. It became impossible to continue using the streets as storage facilities, refuse dumps, pastures, or race tracks. Wooden chimneys under congested conditions became a public menace. It became necessary to regulate dogs, kite flying, refuse disposal, handling and storage of explosives, to name but a few. The need for regulation was felt unevenly, and regulation was not always successful. A particularly interesting example of resistance can be found in the swine problem faced by New York City.

Edict after edict and officer after officer appeared to control this urban problem but their success was limited. The swine were dirty, they dug up the streets, weakened the underpinnings of buildings, attacked small children, were obstructions in the the streets and appeared to many people as one of the most obnoxious sights in the city. On the other hand they were a cheap and important supply of food to the poorer people and also acted as a municipal streetcleaning and refuse-disposal department at no cost to the taxpayers.

Various limitations were imposed upon swine: they were ringed; they were forbidden to appear in this or that part of town. Various methods were attempted to enforce the regulations: informers were allowed large fees; the poorhouse officers were allowed to pick up all the hogs they could find and keep the profits for the benefit of their institutions; the constables were ordered to enforce the law; special informers were appointed; any citizen was allowed to claim any swine he might find running loose; hogreeves were appointed.[10]

The problem persisted however for 150 years and finally disappeared due to increasing land values and the attendant lack of vacant lots and to the development of street-paving and sanitation services. That the problem persisted whatever the efforts at enforcement illustrated the difficulty of regulation in the face of deep-rooted need and marked division in public opinion. This episode was a preview of enforcement problems in contemporary cities.

City administrations did not respond directly to these underlying processes of specialization, differentiation, and density, however, but rather to the various specific ills which they produced.[11] The rhythms of people, time, and place of city life then as now constituted the basic police reality. Crucial times were nighttimes and holidays; the arrival of many strangers; the advent of war, epidemic, or conflagration. Crucial places were where people of diverse backgrounds and interests were gathered in a limited area—street, marketplace, transport terminal, or theater. Significant objects included animals, weapons, liquor, explosives, and hanging signs.

Especially important people were the civic and social "outsiders"—transients (vagabonds), sailors in port, young immigrants, free or slave Negroes.[12]

> Situations comprising several of these symptoms were particularly likely to cause trouble. Negroes were dangerous; Negroes with weapons were so dangerous that they were forbidden to have even walking sticks; a drunken Negro with a weapon on a Saturday night at a theater was likely to result in a felony.[13]

The cities studied by Bacon—Boston, New York, Philadelphia, Charleston, and New Orleans—were all important port cities and early in their histories began to display characteristics of many modern American cities, one of the most significant of these being the existence of large populations who were functionally but not normatively integrated into the city. Whole districts became specialized as relatively "lawless," i.e., they housed and catered to the illegal desires of populations especially likely to be disorderly and violent. The "underworld" in early American cities like that in the cities of old consisted of special areas of the city where the "lawless" dwelled, not a dispersed minority of criminals organized as a syndicate.

Such "lawless" populations still loom large in the routine problems of policing cities; their ecological concentration helps account for the distribution of police within and among cities. A recent study by Shafter sought to discover why in two small cities of similar populations located sixty miles apart in a Midwestern state there was such a difference in the size of their police departments.[14] "Carbon" with a population of 9,004 in 1960 had five policemen. "Delta" with a population of 9,348 had eighteen policemen. Carbon is a market town that serves a rural hinterland. Delta is a river port and a center for traveling salesmen and seasonal hunters. Moreover one-third of Delta's population in 1960 was Negro and, except for residence, segregation is complete. Delta could be said to specialize in illegal services and the provision of opportunity for disorder, i.e., in liquor, gambling, prostitution. It is a crime-dependent community, and its economy and social structure require a large police establishment.

Emergence of a Career Police

Public response to the problem of order generated by urban change was piecemeal. Not until the establishment of modern police in the middle of the nineteenth century were enforcement officers with general powers and functions to appear. Bacon describes the development of "the night police, the market police, street police, animal police, liquor police, the vagabond and stranger police, vehicle police, fire police, election police, Sunday police and so on." [15] Similarly, we noted that a special inspector office was created each time a new activity had to be regulated. Only slowly did regulation for the public good and the maintenance of order become themselves specializations and the full-time career police develop. The process was however extremely slow. In New York it was not until 1741 that a regularly paid night watch was established. These men held full-time jobs in addition and were on duty every third night. It took approximately a century from this point before all the police were organized into a special department of the city.

One of the reasons for the slowness of development was the fiscal problem. Policing is expensive. Financing it on the general tax roles was politically unpopular. Fiscal difficulties helped account for the widespread reliance on informers to be paid out of fines. The financial lure here of course was the thought that law enforcement could be partially self-supporting. Also relevant was the idea that paying informers would motivate the citizenry to perform its functions in something like the rural folk pattern.

Paid *Gemeinschaft*, especially on piece rates, had its disadvantages however. Special classes of "professional" informers arose who could use the widespread illegal conduct as a means of livelihood. As would be expected, they themselves tended to be recruited from the less stable and civically integrated segments of the community, and, further, they tended to exploit even weaker and more estranged segments. The very threat to inform became a powerful weapon. Informers were under no organizational discipline whatever.

The most egregious abuse of the informer system in New York was in connection with the control of the behavior of slaves. As early as 1681 the control of slaves "abroad" on the streets became a serious problem. Fees for informers were increased to be paid out of fines levied on the masters who would pay because they disliked seeing their slaves whipped and thereby incapacitated. It was also to the advantage of the city to hold masters responsible for the conduct of slaves. The slave master as a link to the civic outsider seems therefore to have preceded by some years the detached worker in a similar role. Slaves were especially lucrative targets for informers because they as civic nonpersons could not testify in court and challenge the informer's testimony.

The informer system was an attempt to solve several problems that plague policing of cities—how to motivate citizens, how to secure information on crime and evidence for court, how to do so without a politically unsupportable drain on the public purse. The decline of the informer as a paid freelancer still leaves the problem of information and evidence largely unsolved despite the rise of the specialized detective role. Indeed it makes the matter even more complex since the informer was not ordinarily subject to the restrictions on the penetration of private systems which have been increasingly applied to the police in American society.[16]

The motivation of citizen participation in policing was also a live issue. Broadly speaking, in the United States and in England also there has been an evolution from "folk" enforcement based on the solidarities of kin and locality units to an essentially market mechanism based heavily on paid informants (and also piece-rate officers and justices) to a combination of a formally bureaucratized police and the citizen complainant. There is still, however, a widespread use of what are now called informants in police work, especially in offenses where there is no self-defined victim.

The modern informant, however, is "paid" either in foregone prosecutions or in money channeled through police units on a somewhat surreptitious basis. Also of central importance is the fact that informants are not sources of evidence and that indeed testimony of paid informants not only has no special legal standing, but is easily assailed by the defense. Modern informants provide tips, not testimony. Indeed it is possible to describe much modern detective work as the process whereby information satisfactory to the police—tips—is translated into information satisfactory to the courts—evidence.[17]

Formal organization of the police while a response to the underlying processes and symptoms to which Bacon directs our attention was also a response to weaknesses and abuses displayed in the informer system. Ideally formal organization—or bureaucratization—means the interposition between the victim, or complainant, and the offender of a disciplined and disinterested body of men whose decisions are affected by canons of law and formalized bureaucratic discipline rather than by thoughts either of private vengeance or of private gain. Police in a democratic society are to enforce the law and maintain order under the rule of law.

The sequence folk to market to bureaucratic organization may be general in modern societies; it can be seen in the development of armies, of educational systems, and in many other areas where society became too complex for functions to be performed on a folk basis, but where the market mechanism proved unsatisfactory precisely because it made no provision for either reliable execution of collective tasks or for principled conduct and restraint. It is reasonable to suggest that even today the police struggle against the modern versions of these two tendencies—on the one hand for law enforcement to become overwhelmed by private self-help or vigilantism and on the other for protection to be "sold" like a market commodity. Both of these constitute illicit "private" usurpation of "public" functions; they define as central not the relationship of citizen to state, but neighbor to neighbor and buyer to seller. Such "private arrangements" are commonly discussed as a feature of civil law, but of course it is quite appropriate to see them as of much more generic significance.[18]

The early form of police bureaucracy was that of paramilitary organization, a form of organization that continues to characterize the police and to render its professionalization not unlike that of the military.[19] The paramilitary form of early police bureaucracy was a response not only, or even primarily, to crime per se, but to the possibility of riotous disorder. Not crime and danger but the "criminal" and "dangerous classes" as part of the urban social structure led to the formation of uniformed and militarily organized police. Such organizations intervened between the propertied elites and the propertyless masses who were regarded as politically dangerous as a class.

In a recent paper, Allan Silver describes the development of the London Metropolitan Police in these terms and points out that a significant difference between England and the United States lies in the tradition of politically articulate riot among the poor in England.[20] The development of the modern police was part of a larger process of expanding normative consensus while solving the political problem by political means, e.g., the eventual reform of the franchise. The "outsiders" of the industrial city were incorporated in the civic body by a combination of legal process and political change.

Police above all link daily life to central authority; moral consensus is extended through the police as an instrument of legitimate coercion. At the same time, the police in performing this function often deflect the hostility of the mass from the class targets to the police themselves. Police in modern societies therefore often serve the dubious function of becoming substitute targets of hostility for problems of moral consensus. Much of the difficulty in the relations between Negroes and police in American cities today stems from the fact that the appropriate spheres of legal and political process have been confused. Attempts to provide adequate police protection for the Negro populace while at the same time protecting them from police violation of due process constitute a significant step in the progressive inclusion of this group of civic "outsiders." Nevertheless, no amount of sophistication by police and courts will overcome by itself the effects of housing, employment discrimination, or other problems of urban ghettos. Indeed it is no exaggeration to say that the police in many American cities are far *ahead* of other segments of civil society in their race relations practices.[21] American Negroes will get due process and protection from "whitey's" police long before they get due fellowship from "whitey's" churches.

The problem of civic inclusion of outsiders in Britain was made much simpler by the fact that lines of division were mainly class and not a combination of class, ethnic origin, religion, and race as in the United States. The main "minorities" in the British Isles—the Scots and the

Welsh—were integrated into the larger polity party partly by allowing local autonomy in legal administration and in the case of Scotland even a semi-autonomous *corpus juris.*[22]

Bureaucratization and Civic Accountability of Police

Bureaucratization of the police and the attendant control from the top largely solves one crucial problem which confronts societies with organized police—the problem of the political neutrality of the police as a body. Bureaucratization is a device whereby commitment to the occupational organization, to the occupational community, and to its norms of subordination and service takes precedence over extra-occupational commitments. In modern societies the political neutrality and legal reliability of the police is a matter less of the social sources of recruitment than it is a matter of the nature of internal organization, training, and control. Thus the insulation of police from populace which is so often cited as a "problem" in law enforcement is not only a requisite for principled conduct in daily law enforcement, but also a requisite for the removal of police from "high politics" however much they be involved in the "low politics" of patronage and local discretion.

The English solution to the problem of the political reliability of the police was to disarm them and make them directly responsible to the central government. This made it possible for England to have the "best of all possible worlds"—a highly effective police that would not be an internal military threat and therefore not have to be politically balanced by a large standing army. In the nineteenth century the London Metropolitan Police were a local police from the law enforcement standpoint, but a national police from the national political standpoint. In countries centered on a metropolis the way England is centered on London, the high politics of municipal police is of clear significance.[23] Thus, in England the bureaucratic professionalization of the police and the demand that they be able to police the population without firearms were responses not only to the requirements of urban law enforcement, but also to the requirements of high politics.

In the United States, on the other hand, the federal constitution combined with the nonmetropolitan character of most seats of national and state government meant that the problem of political neutrality of the police was never one of "high" politics, but only of "low." Correlatively the demand for rigid internal control of police by administrative elites directly responsible to the executive was less strongly pressed. These conditions when coupled with the general underdevelopment of government services, the successful translation of immigrant votes into municipal patronage, and the restriction of recruitment to local sources meant that, while the purpose of the organized police may have been to suppress the "dangerous classes," the outcome of the development was to staff the police largely with persons drawn from the "dangerous classes" themselves. The mechanisms of staffing the police then were one of the principal devices whereby excluded classes were integrated into the structure of government. "No Irish need apply" definitely did *not* apply to the police.

The inevitable consequence of this situation was police organization of a markedly less "bureaucratic" cast and a strong tendency for immigrant and machine influenced police to act not as insulated enforcers of abstract law, but rather as intermediaries between the legally and symbolically dominant white Anglo-Saxon Protestant culture and diverse immigrant groups. Through machine politics and ethnic patronage, immigrant groups in the United States were able to some degree to govern the speed of coerced assimilation.[24]

A major organizational dimension of police systems is their accountability to political authority. In modern democratic societies a crucial feature of the accountability of police organizations is the forms of political authority that protect the rights of citizens vis-à-vis the police organization. The mass is in a paradoxical situation in relation to governmental police systems. On the one hand, they are vulnerable to state tyranny enforced through the police organization, i.e., a "police state." On the other hand, they are vulnerable to police tyranny when state authority is unable to directly control the public police organization or hold it accountable.

The organizational form of the accountability system in modern societies bears an important relationship to this paradox. The vulnerability of the citizens to state tyranny has led in some societies to the development of local government police organizational systems that are directly accountable to *local* authority. Local police systems such as in the United States are relatively inaccessible to centralized state control unless their allegiance or compliance can be obtained by other means. These organizational safeguards against state tyranny lead, however, to greater vulnerability of the citizen to local police tyranny, since the state's right and opportunity to intervene generally is limited.

There is an interesting question as to whether the obverse cases obtain: Is the citizen less subject to local police tyranny in centrally organized and controlled police systems? Such systems (at least in the more populated democratic societies) are large-scale bureaucracies. Bureaucratization, of course, is a major way for governments to neutralize civic power. For the police, bureaucratization increases their legal reliability. The neutralization of civic power through bureaucracy makes the citizen less vulnerable to local police tyranny due to local interests, but it opens the way to local bureaucratic tyranny, particularly where the central bureaucracy cannot insure local accountability. To be sure, the central features of bureaucratic "tyranny" apply whether the bureaucracy is local or state controlled, but in a police bureaucracy one need only assure the allegiance of the central commanders to the political elites to insure reasonably effective control of the local organization.

There are a number of important consequences that follow from the organizational form of control and accountability in police systems. In democratic societies, the police bear an important relationship to the resolution of value conflicts in the society, particularly in situations where there is direct civic protest. Some of the important differences in the form and consequences of protest are related to whether the police system is centrally or locally organized and controlled. When there is civic protest involving basic values and the police are centrally organized and controlled, the state is more immediately involved as an organizational actor. The protest is more likely to be defined as an action against the state; if sanctions are applied, they tend to be made across the system. On the other hand, where the police are more locally organized and controlled such situations are more likely to be defined as protests against local authority; then both sanctions and action taken as a consequence of local protest are defined as local rather than society-wide. Indeed, one might hypothesize that political revolutions and revolutionary situations are more likely to arise in societies with highly centralized bureaucratic police systems. It would follow, then, that where citizens are vulnerable to state tyranny, the state is more vulnerable to revolutionary protest.

One of the major problems in holding the police accountable in all democratic societies is to insure police neutrality in their relations with local elites and interest groups. The criteria governing the legality of police-civil relations in a democratic society are universalistic. A centralized bureaucracy probably is more effective in insuring the legal neutrality of the police from local interests and elites than is a local one.

Yet, this very neutralization of local interests in a centralized system can substantially affect their opportunity to change the police bureaucracy. The problems of civil rights and minority groups in the United States serve as a case in point. The organization of most policing on a local basis has meant that the American Negro minority has had less equity in the legal system, particularly in its Southern states. National control of the police undoubtedly would result in a more equitable distribution of justice. At the same time, precisely because of patterns of local control, the Negro minority where effectively organized politically in American cities has changed the quality of police-civil relations and their organizations, changes that have benefited the white majority citizen as well as the Negro minority.

Quite clearly, local organization of the police leads to greater variability among police organizations in the society, both in form and in practice, than does centralized control. Such variability is conductive to innovation as well as to differential application of universalistic norms. It is not surprising, therefore, that police organization in the United States shows both more innovation toward modern police systems and more variability in police-citizen relations than do more centralized systems in other countries.

The organization of police on a local versus a centralized basis also is related to the nature of corruption of the police system when it occurs. In a local system, corruption is highly neutralized because of its linkage to local government and its insulation from the state: The state can neither corrupt or be corrupted by the police. The situation in a centralized system is quite different. While local bureaucratic corruption occurs, it becomes possible for the police to be corrupted by the state, as well as vice versa.

In the United States, with its local system of policing, one finds again and again instances of "police scandal" involving local government officials and the police or involving local political elites and the police. But it is misleading to conclude that corruption among the police and government officials is widespread in the United States. By the very nature of the local organization of the police, the corruption of both the state political system and of the police is restricted. The recent "Ben Barka" case in France illustrates the contrasting case. With a more centralized police system, the state may corrupt the police or, alternatively, be corrupted by it.

Thus the problems of crime and public order, of the patterns and varieties of bureaucratization, and of their relationship to the government and organization of cities along with problems of the divergence between formal law and subcultural organization set the stage for the analysis of the police in modern democratic societies.

Police Professionalization and Applied Sociology

Sociologists pay little attention to budgets. As Bacon pointed out in his discussion of the development of modern police, however, policing is expensive. We can gain some understanding of the significance of more recent police history and of the professionalization movement in the police by examining briefly the expenditure on police. From 1902 to 1960 annual expenditures for local police in the United States increased from 50 to 1,612 millions of dollars—an increase of 3,124 per cent. When account is taken of inflation, population growth, urban concentration, increases in motor vehicles, and increases in the per hour cost of police salaries, the net in funds available to the police is about 20 per cent. Although the study from which these data are drawn is still incomplete and considering the extreme difficulty of drawing unequivocal conclusions from trend data, it seems accurate nevertheless to conclude that during the first six decades of the twentieth century, there has been no appreciable real increase in funds available to the local police for crime control use. [25]

Small wonder then that the main thrust of the professionalization movement in the United States has been in the direction of improving operating efficiency, in communications systems and administrative competence, and in the search for ways of conserving and more effectively controlling scarce police manpower. From the beginning of the century to the present we can only conclude that there must have been a dramatic increase in police productivity as a consequence of the technological and managerial rationalization which has accompanied professionalization. Managerial rationalization and increased productivity have not been the only results of the professionalization movement. There can be little doubt that in some cities at least there have been significant gains in the degree to which the police conform to due process. Such conformity is difficult, however, even in the most professionalized departments both because the translation of elite professional perspectives to the rank and file is difficult and because the demands of some enforcement jobs create severe conflict between the requirments for effective enforcement and the demands of due process as enunciated by the courts.[26]

For the first time in American history the emergence of a self-consciously professional police elite coupled with its increasing (though far from complete) success in tightening internal control over department operations provides the organizational conditions whereby not only public demands for efficiency and productivity, but also judicial demands for legality can be translated into operations.[27] Developing professionalization of the police also provides the necessary base for the application of sociology to law enforcement concerns. Perhaps even more appropriately put, it provides the base for carrying out the necessary sociological research which in the near future will be translatable into application.

Areas of Application

Applied sociology cannot prosper in the absence of some criteria of effectiveness of personnel and of organization. The police professionalization movement has provided sociologists with a social base and a body of consumers of its material, but it has not provided solid criteria of effectiveness to guide research contributions. Unlike early industrial sociology, which could get along on simple criteria such as increased production or decreased turnover, the problem of criteria in the effectiveness of law enforcement and of policing is extremely complex.

Because of its emphasis on education, the professionalization movement has opened the way for what is probably the most significant "application" of sociology to date. While no definitive data are available the exposure of police students to sociology in police academies or at the college, junior college, and graduate levels is increasing very rapidly, though in absolute numbers the exposure is probably still small. While the immediate effect on police performance of exposure to academic sociology may be minimal or at best undemonstrable, the probable long-run effect of helping define policing as an open profession which participates in the general academic dialogue should be of great significance.

Beyond general education of police officers and the explanations of crime and criminality, applications of sociology to law enforcement and police organization can be divided into those touching upon internal organizational structure and process and those dealing with transactions between police organization and the surrounding environment. In both of these broad areas, in the immediate future the application of sociology is more likely to be a matter of providing more sophisticated information and analysis than a matter of operations research.

Internal Organization of Police Departments

Changes in internal organization of police departments have resulted in a considerable tightening of internal discipline and centralization of control.[28] At the same time, the police seek to attract more intelligent and better educated personnel. The potential conflict between these objectives of professionalization and centralization of command has been remarked on in the police literature.[29] The sociological analysis of professions and their practice in bureaucratic settings is applicable to the professionalization of the police.

It is common even among sociologists to think of a profession as a special kind of occupation where the job of the professional is technical, the technical knowledge generally having been acquired through long prescribed training, and the knowledge itself being systematic in nature. Furthermore, it is assumed that the professional person follows a set of professional norms that may include a code of ethics that binds the professional to behave ethically toward his clients. Both the training and norms generally fall under legal or professional organizational control, specifying who can practice.

All of these things usually characterize persons who are called professionals. But they miss a central feature that characterizes any profession.[30] At the core of any profession as distinct from a scholarly discipline is a relationship with clients. Professions are based on practice, and a major element in all practice is the relationship with clients. What is crucial in defining the professional is the nature of this relationship with clients. We can say that it is technical in nature where the specialized knowledge is utilized in practice, as when the physician calls on his specialized knowledge to diagnose illness. We can say that it is moral or ethical, as when the lawyer treats information from his client as privileged or confidential. Yet a core feature of the relationship with clients is a *decision* about the client—a decision in which the professional person decides something about the client that *relates to his future*. In some professions this decision is given largely in the form of advice. The client presumably is free to ignore or follow the advice. But in other professions and in certain roles within other professions, it is a decision over which the client can exercise little if any choice. We speak of this as a coerced decision, an evaluation, judgment, or a determination. The teacher decides whether the pupil shall pass or fail. The social worker decides whether the applicant is eligible for welfare benefits. The judge decides whether the defendant is guilty and what disposition shall be made for the case. Jurors, by the way, are not professionals, and some of the conflict in the criminal trial procedure today arises over the very question of competence of jurors to decide what have come to be called technical questions. Police are empowered with a decision that involves the fate of their clients—a decision to arrest, a discretionary decision. Police, therefore, are among the few occupations seeking professionalization that share the core feature of a decision that affects the fate of the client.

Studies of the "professionalization" of the police conclude that changes within modernizing police departments have led to professionalization of the department through bureaucratization and centralization of command. These changes work against professionalization of the line officer, particularly the patrol officer where contact is initially made with the public. Three main changes within the organization of police departments militate against professionalization of the line officer.[31]

First, there is the increasing centralization of both command and control in departments—a centralization of decision making. Some police departments have been reorganized so that most of the command and control functions are essentially removed from the precinct level of organization. The precinct functions then primarily to allocate men to assignments and supervise them in their work roles. The core of many modern police departments is the centralized communications center where allocative decisions are made under centralized command. The line officer on patrol is commanded from a central headquarters and reports directly to them by radio, with reports in some cases being made directly to central headquarters by radio or telephone. Furthermore, the bounds of decision making by the line are officially narrowed so that the officer is left without functions of investigation or, at most, a preliminary report. Although such moves toward a centralized bureaucratic system have not necessarily limited the discretionary decision in practice, they structurally limit professionalization of decision making by the line. A bureaucratic system where decision making is decentralized would be more consistent with professionalization of the line.

Second, most modern police departments centralize the investigative function in a "more technical" elite of the department—the detective bureau. Much overrated in its capacity to investigate and certainly to "solve" most crimes, it nonetheless increasingly bears the "professional" label. Though there is much evidence of increasing bureaucratization of the investigative functions within police departments leading to a large number of special investigation units over and above that of the detective division, there is much less evidence that the requirements of technical knowledge and training are consistent with professionalization of personnel in these units. It is in this sense that we speak of the professionalization of the organizational system, leaving the corollary development of specialization of professional roles relatively untouched.

Finally, there is a growing tendency to make decisions at the staff rather than the operating levels of the department. This is partly due to the fact that increased bureaucratization and introduction of a complex technology necessitate the utilization of other professions within the police system. But such professionals are generally introduced at the staff level or as special consultants inserted for a special reason into operating units. Thus a department employs medical internists and psychiatrists to perform certain applicant or promotion screening functions. The planning or analysis sections may include professional specialists. These professional specialists are generally referred to as "civilians" within the department, separating them not only from the line, but in many cases from the "sworn" staff as well.

The tendency to make decisions at staff rather than operating levels is readily apparent when one examines the staff units of a department. There is considerable evidence that the handling of "human relations" within police departments is largely a staff function. Despite a spate of human relations training for the line, it is the staff units that are regarded as "professional" in human relations work. The training division and the human relations unit of the department are more "professionalized." There is almost no provision for actual implementation of "human relations" in the line except by "central order" and some training of the line in the classroom of the Academy. Without explicit provision for implementation in the line, there is little opportunity for professional treatment of clients. That this characterization of professionalization is not unique to the more recently developed specialized staff functions such as "human relations" cannot be demonstrated here, but a careful examination of almost all new functional units in modernizing police departments serves to bear this out.

A metropolitan police organizational system faces considerable penetration of its organizational environment from organizations and interest groups that lie outside its boundaries. This is so for a number of reasons. Legally charged with responsibility for law enforcement, it nonetheless faces problems of overlapping jurisdiction with county, state, and national enforcement agencies. Law enforcement likewise is intricately linked with a larger organizational system of criminal justice such that its output is an input into the criminal justice system where it is evaluated. Furthermore, it is directly linked to a municipal, county, or state organizational system that controls at least its budget, and it also maintains a host of transactions with other municipal and community organizations in providing "police service." A police system thus engages in transactions not only with its clients who are *citizens* demanding a service and with victims and their violators, but with a multiplicity of organizations where problems of service, its assessment, resource allocation, and jurisdiction are paramount.

How these relationships tend on the whole to militate against the professionalization of the line and how they militate against the professionalization of the staff as well can only be illustrated here. The recent decisions of criminal and appellate courts defining the limits of interrogation, search of the person and property and the seizure of evidence, and of the use of force have been defined by the police and the courts as limits on discretionary decision making. The liberal and minority publics and the appellate courts view the police as exercising too much discretion in their relationships with the public. They generally hold that decision as to method is to be defined on legal professional rather than police professional grounds. In short, one prevailing view is that the police must be controlled by more legitimate authority—authority that is vested in either the law, the public prosecutor, and the courts or in a civil review procedure.

The controversy over the discretionary authority of the police is a classic case of disputes over professional jurisdiction. A group of professionals—in this case largely made up of lawyers and jurists—seeks to restrict the powers of "would-be-professionals"—in this case the police. This conflict is not unlike that between medical doctors and nurses or that between prosecutors and judges. In addition to the usual questions of jurisdiction, there is an equally important consideration: professional disputes over jurisdiction generally arise where one group of professionals controls the fate of another group of professionals (or aspirants to professional status) in an intricately balanced organizational system. Much of the conflict between the courts and the police is in this sense inevitable, given the American system of law enforcement and criminal justice. For in that system we have on the one hand institutionalized the introduction of clients into the larger system in the hands of the police, since operationally at least it is the police who exercise the power of arrest. Yet on the other hand we have institutionalized the power of assessing outcome of arrest of the client and assessment of police procedure in the prosecutor and the court. When the ultimate fate of clients rests in another group of clients—and particularly when they are removed from the situation that precipitated the client relationship—conflict is endemic.

Civil review boards pose some barrier to professionalization of the police because they restrict the latitude an occupation or an organization based on an occupation has to "police" itself. That the police have not been altogether ineffective in preventing the creation of civil review boards in the United States is apparent. Much of their success probably is due to the political organization of line officers backed by legitimation of their claims from the police chief. Locally organized they bring local pressures. Yet lacking effective organization on "professional grounds" across local departments, their long-run influence may be more restricted. Unlike trade unions that increased their bargaining power through extralocal organization, the only extra-local police organization of consequence is the International Association of Chiefs of Police. The line, therefore, is without national power.

The issue for professionalization of the police is whether civic accountability will take the form of an inquiry into an individual's work within an organization, whether it will take the form of accountability of an occupational organization of police, or whether accountability rests with a local police organizational system headed by a chief as the "accountable officer." Traditionally, line organizations of police have "protected" the rights of the officer in charges involving the local organization. Traditionally, the local police organization has been held accountable through control by the mayor, the occasional appointment of "civilian" chiefs, and the sporadic investigations of the department under charges of scandal by "blue-ribbon" committees. Traditionally, the organization of the line has failed to develop standards for control of practice by members of the occupation. The dilemma for the line, then, is that the police occupation exists within a local formally organized police department that controls practice rather than with a professional organization of the police. To shift the balance of review and control to an external review system, however, creates problems both for the operating departmental organization and the occupational association. This is particularly the case when there is external review of an individual's performance within an organization. For this form of accountability interferes with both institutional and organized forms of professional control in the United States. Public school teachers faced the same kind of dilemma. Historically they were under review from both a school organization and a civil review agency—respectively, the school administration and the school board. Increasingly the professional organization of teachers has resisted such review on "professional grounds," thereby coercing the relationship of public school teachers to organizations, employers, and clients more along the lines of traditional professional organizations. It is obvious that police now lack the increasingly effective extra-local organization developed among public school teachers.

Administrative centralization within police departments is partly a consequence of the fact that professionalization often arrives in a department in the form of crisis-produced reform. One area of research and application of great potential benefit to the police involves sociologists in studying the nature and consequences of patterns of supervision and control with a view to the design of systems which maintain the gains of professionalization without the loss of more desirable personnel.

A recent study of police reform indicates that the process of reform-centralization-professionalization heightens the significance of the organization rather than the public as a source of police self-esteem. It implies also that the reform process has increased member attachment—a necessary requisite to any eventual decentralization.[32] Another study of a department in the throes of change indicates that traditional techniques of control coupled with professionalization creates a punishment-centered bureaucracy with high levels of uncertainty among young officers and a consequent emphasis on personal ingratiation with superiors. In this department the formal rules seem more a set of opportunities for punishing officers than a set of bureaucratic imperatives.[33] These results also indicate that reform-based centralization may be necessary to produce sufficient trust and due process within the police department in order that more decentralized decision making may eventually be possible.

Methods of internal control in a police department have great relevance not only to police decision making, but also to problems of recruitment, training, and selection for promotion as the study by McNamara shows. Beyond the use of written civil service tests, which function more as instruments of equity than of effective selection, there is little sophistication of a social science sort in police selection procedures. Psychiatric screening to spot "bad apples" among potential recruits has appeared in some departments, but there has been little or no contribution by sociologists or sociology. One study in New York City attempts to use a modification of job analysis and the critical incident technique to develop selection instruments at the recruit evaluation level.[34] The study draws on sociological ideas and techniques. It does not, however, display the necessary sensitivity to the organizational position of the policeman which the previously cited study by McNamara indicates to be crucial.[35] Relations between training and role perception and performance are also central to a recently published study of a state police unit.[36]

Transactions between Police and Public

Studies of the external performance of the police are even more rare than studies of intra-organizational events. The early work by Westley, and the more recent work by Piliavin and Briar, Bittner, the Cummings, Skolnick, and Black and Reiss are among the few sociological studies of the external behavior of the police in relation to the police.[37] Apart from the work by Black and Reiss, these studies generally lack criteria of effectiveness of police performance.

Most of these studies focus on the relationship between the demeanor of the citizen and the actions and attitudes of the police. Westley was concerned with the transfer of violence by the police from a legal to a personal resource where violence becomes acceptable to the police as a generalized means. His most significant finding was that at least 37 per cent of the police officers he interviewed believed it legitimate to use violence to coerce respect, suggesting that policemen use violence to coerce their audience to respect their occupational status.[38] Piliavin and Briar's studies of police encounters with juveniles likewise emphasize the importance of client demeanor in police behavior. Other than prior record of delinquency, they conclude that the youth's demeanor was the most important factor in apprehension of juveniles by police officers. If the youth was "unco-operative," he was highly unlikely to receive either informal reprimands or admonishment and release; if he co-operated with the officer, they were likely outcomes.[39] Skolnick's study of the processing of traffic violators, narcotics users and peddlers, and prostitutes raises some doubts about personal prejudices and client demeanor in police practice. While he found that the police wanted to implicate the traffic offender more seriously in the criminal process when the violator abused the officer in some way, was an habitual violator who refused to "cop out," or when there were continuing and exacerbated relationships between the officer and the offender, he also found that in police relationships with prostitutes, the behavior of the policeman is less likely to involve how he personally feels about the suspect. With prostitutes, their relationship to other police goals, such as their informant status, may be more important.[40]

Among the more controversial areas of police behavior in the United States are those pertaining to police conduct in searches, in interrogation, and in confession. Seriously lacking in both public and judicial consideration of these issues has been reliable information about police conduct in these situations. The mass observation studies of Black and Reiss report data on the relative frequency of personal and property searches and interrogations, some of the conditions under which they occur, the response of persons to these practices in settings where they take place, and what the police learn in such situations.[41] They observed that officers very rarely ask for permission to conduct a search or an interrogation; most suspects do not object. The probability that the police will find a dangerous weapon or other evidence in property and personal searches is quite high for the high crime rate areas where the observations took place; about one in five frisks, for example, produced a dangerous weapon while almost one-half of all property searches produced something that the suspect did not wish the police to find. Contrary to expectations, at least a third of all field interrogations involved the interrogation of more than one person concomitantly. In only one in ten situations was there an objection to the interrogation. When objections occurred they were far more likely to be objections to how information was obtained than to the fact that they were questioned. For confessions, it was found that 7 in 10 of the confessions were obtained at the beginning of the police-citizen encounter; in fact, about one-half confessed before any interrogation on the part of the officer. Other than questioning, little or no pressure was applied in 70 per cent of the interrogations. Quite clearly, this research shows that much of this police behavior occurs in field settings and outside of the interrogation room or police station where it generally is presumed to occur. Furthermore, given the fact that the research was conducted in the period following the Miranda decision by the United States Supreme Court, compliance with court decisions on informing citizens of their rights was generally quite low, emphasizing again that decision making without organizational implementation generally brings low compliance, if not patterned evasion.

Despite generations of criminological research it is doubtful that sociology can in the near future contribute to the social technology available for apprehending criminals. It has nevertheless contributed to police sophistication and success in maintaining order in potentially riotous situations and especially in dealing with potentally dangerous racial tensions.[42] Some recent efforts at crime analysis show the indirect effect of sociological perspectives such as the attempt to develop a typology of sex offenses that would be useful for *modus operandi* files.[43] In general the police have provided more information on crime to sociologists than the reverse. The new computerized information systems provide an opportunity for sociologists to help construct more rationalized information-gathering strategies as work by Wolfgang demonstrates.[44] Sociologists will have to do much more research on the patterning and determinants of criminal conduct in the field rather than in the prison, and they will have to face up to the hard fact that offenders must be caught before they can be humanely rehabilitated if their research is to be relevant to police organization and policy.

In Western democratic societies the emergence of a police system distinct from the militia and "voluntary service" in a watch system led to the development of a tradition-oriented rather than a rationally efficient bureaucratic system. Primary-group loyalties, often based on a cohort effect of common movement through the ranks, and devotion to duty and honor bound the men in the organization together and brought the commanders close to the men in the line, particularly in those countries that did not recruit a distinct elite corps of staff and command. These traditional loyalties gave way before technical innovation and deliberate organizational strategies in the more rational bureaucratic departments. Their disintegration, however, has created a new set of problems of how the command can insure control—how it could make its orders stick— with less reliance on traditional forms of allegiance to the command.

A related dilemma arises at the staff and command level as well—the dilemma of the "professional managers" vs. the "hero leaders" noted by Janowitz.[45] His characterization for the military profession can be applied to the police. The professional police managers emerge with the highly centralized command based on information technology. A "professional police" must recruit and retrain men for its elite who are skilled in police management. At the same time, a department must recruit officers who can command the allegiance of the men in the line. This problem of leadership is particularly acute in departments that do not recruit solely into the line. While some professional managers command allegiance, many do not.

In rational organizations, symbolic appeals to courage, devotion to duty, and honor often do not ring true. Yet they are essential elements in a police system. The modern trends in police departments make it difficult to perpetuate these elements. The "new" cohorts of officers in the more modern American police department display less enthusiasm for symbolic appeals than their predecessors. Furthermore, an increasing emphasis on civic control of the police in the United States serves further to weaken such appeals—one does a "professional" job, not his duty. How far the police can go in dispensing with symbolism remains an open question. Potentially they should be able to go much further than the military, since, in contrast to the military, their success depends much more on the necessity for and willingness of a population to be policed and on the demand for police service. Because the police are not essentially in a conflict relationship with the public they need not display the elements of heroic leadership appropriate to combat.

That no bureaucracy conforms to a model of rational organization is well established. While the modern police department places heavy organizational emphasis on modern techniques of personnel selection and training, on technology and technical efficiency, and on rational planning and management, it perhaps cannot altogether dispense with charisma in its leaders and a commitment to duty and honor, particularly in democratic societies, such as the United States, that are fundamentally inhospitable to the police.[46]

A paramilitary organization such as the police displays, and perhaps must continue to display, elements of traditional and rational bureaucracies. In modern democratic societies, however, there are increasing demands that they be human-relations–centered bureaucracies.

Ideally the police should be able to secure compliance with lawful commands while incurring a minimum of citizen hostility. The ability to do so in a heterogeneous society requires formal training in human management rather than merely participation in a common culture. McNamara's study of the training and performance of recruits indicates that neither selection nor training nor post-academy probationary experience provides the necessary sensitivity to differences in values and interpersonal expectations. As a consequence the police tend to become over-authoritative in socially ambiguous situations—securing compliance at the cost of unnecessary levels of hostility.[47] Formal human-relations training is an increasingly common feature of police training and at least some semisociological ideas have been important in the development of training materials.[48]

There is considerable evidence that the American populace, particularly in its larger cities, is no longer content with either the traditional or the rational bureaucratic solutions to police-citizen relations. As noted earlier, the tradition-oriented departments in American society were peculiarly adapted to the accommodation of immigrant interests. More recently, the rational bureaucratic department has moved somewhat to guarantee equity both as to discretionary decisions in application of the law and the legality of means in law enforcement. Yet more is demanded of the officer. He must not only be civil in a rational bureaucratic sense, but he must be "human" or "personal" in his relations with citizens. He must not only be civil in a professional sense, but must also be "client-centered." He must not only be a responsible civil servant, but responsive as well.

Recent studies of the behavior of officers and citizens in police-citizen transactions show that in about three-fourths of police-citizen transactions the officers behaved in a rational bureaucratic manner.[49] Their conduct could be characterized as routinized, impersonal, or businesslike. Only in 16 per cent of the encounters could they be characterized as human-relations oriented where humor, interest in the citizen, or similar interpersonal tactics characterized their behavior. For only 6 per cent of the encounters did the officers behave in a negative or hostile fashion toward the citizen. Human relations was more characteristic of relations with white than Negro citizens, however. Correlatively, the behavior of citizens toward the police was characterized in three-fourths of the cases as civil with 11 per cent behaving deferentially and the remainder with some form of hostility.

The typical encounter between the citizen and a police officer then is one characterized by civility. The officer regards the citizen in a rational bureaucratic framework of civility while the citizen treats the officer with civil conduct. Yet paradoxically, the citizen who is civil toward the officer often regards civility in the officer as a sign of disrespect and a failure to regard him in human or personal terms. And the officer perceives civility in the citizen as a failure to command respect. Rational bureaucratic treatment is insufficient for many citizens in their encounters with the police.

Encounters between police and populace with which human-relations training deals have an even broader significance in police work. The populace is, after all, the source of suspects. Moreover segments of the populace may not only individually but collectively adopt a stance of principled opposition to the police. Where this occurs police practices of field inquiry, i.e., the systematic search for suspects to match known offenses, may simultaneously result in a challenge to police authority and a further alienation of the suspect group. Nowhere is this problem more apparent than in dealing with slum gangs. In a recent paper Werthman and Piliavin describe encounters between patrol police and Negro gang boys and indicate that the outcome of these encounters may increase hostility, strengthen gang solidarity, threaten police authority, and even help increase social tensions to the point of contributing to violent disorder—all without producing any great payoff to law enforcement.[50] This study also indicates the very real differences in the role of patrol police as compared to that of juvenile officers, who are more a combination of detectives and magistrates.

Yet it remains unclear how much and to what extent the relationship between the police and citizens accounts for the failure of citizens to mobilize the police and to co-operate with them in investigation. Recent studies for the National Crime Commission show that most police officers believe that minority group persons are unco-operative when they attempt to gain information from them.[51] Studies of citizen experiences with crime and the police, however, fail to support the contention that it is police behavior that accounts for citizen failure to mobilize the police or to co-operate with them. Biderman found that of the forty-two respondents who had witnessed a crime and failed to report it to the police, only three of them gave as a reason for their failure to report a negative expectation about dealing with the police.[52] Furthermore, although about four in ten experiences by 104 victims were not reported to the police, citizens rarely gave as their reason for nonreporting a negative expectation about encounters with the police. Rather they emphasized such things as that they saw no useful purpose in doing so as there was nothing that could be done about it or that they wished to avoid the trouble associated with getting involved, such as being a witness later in court. A few feared reprisals from offenders. But two citizens gave a response that they feared the police would give them trouble. Such studies suggest that citizen-police relations are determined more by the general orientation of citizens in American society and the structure of the legal system than by specific experiences with the police or negative images of potential encounters. Clearly further research is necessary to determine how police-citizen encounters influence police-citizen relationships.

One of the few sociological studies that tries to measure the effects of varying techniques among policemen is the attempt by Wattenberg and Bufe to study the effectiveness of juvenile officers.[53] The authors conclude that differences in interpersonal style among officers are related to the probability of later recidivism. If this finding should replicate, it promises to have considerable significance as a guide to juvenile officer training and supervision. Specialized juvenile officers playing quasi-judicial roles are an increasingly significant part of American municipal police systems and a considerable amount of research has been done or is under way on their interactions with juveniles and on the factors involved in police decisions with juveniles.[54]

This review of actual and potential applications of sociology to police and law enforcement can appropriately conclude by pointing out that its central theme—the importance of formal organization—can be applied to the clients of the police as well as to the police themselves. In an increasingly bureaucratized society police decisions may be affected by interorganizational relations. In a recent study Skolnick and Woodworth show that statutory rape complaints may originate in a public welfare agency, and the police morals detail studied was involved not only in the difficult and morale lowering business of interrogating for statutory rape, but also in a complex interagency information-sharing system.[55] Future developments in centralized information systems and interagency cooperation will raise the whole new issues not only of police expertise, but of the balance between organizational goals and personal liberties.

Epilogue: Some Issues of Sociological Research on Law Enforcement

We began by noting that sociological studies of law enforcement and the police were neglected until recently, partly because of the discomfort sociologists experience in the presence of coercion. One might add further that studies of law enforcement and the police create discomfiture because they inevitably raise certain ethical issues, particularly if, as has been the case, much of the data must be gathered by observational techniques.

Skolnick has made a beginning in the discussion of these ethical issues. There are important questions of the invasion of privacy, the effect of an observer's presence on a defendant's fate or constitutional rights, and the deception of his role both for officer and for citizen.[56] Inevitably there are other issues as well, issues that relate to disclosure of information and to an observer's legal obligations as a citizen. Though such issues arise in many social observation studies, they are of particular importance where one is enmeshed in studying the legal system and where legal sanctions on the investigator may be more germane. Quite clearly, continued work on the sociology of law enforcement, to the degree that it partakes of social observation, must cope with the ethical and legal issues generated by the research process.

Sociologists in the field of corrections increasingly have entered prominent roles as administrators and as counsel in the formation of public policy. Within the field of law enforcement, such a role has not as yet clearly emerged. Despite the fact that sociologists were involved in the work of the President's Commission on Law Enforcement and the Administration of Justice, no social scientist was a member of the Commission. The Commission's report itself, while clearly reflecting the research investigations of sociologists, displays less clearly their effectiveness in molding policy recommendations.[57] The entry of sociologists as policy scientists in the field of law enforcement poses problems of relationships not only with the "professionals" in police administration, but with the "professionals" in the law as well.

REFERENCES

1. Joseph P. Eaton, *Stone Walls Not a Prison Make* (Springfield, Ill.: Charles C Thomas, 1962).
2. Jerome H. Skolnick, *Justice without Trial: Law Enforcement in Democratic Society* (New York: John Wiley & Sons, 1966).
3. Albert J. Reiss, Jr., and David J. Bordua, "Organization and Environment: A Perspective on the Police" in David J. Bordua, ed., *The Police: Six Sociological Essays* (New York: John Wiley & Sons, 1967), pp. 25–55.
4. Allan Silver, "The Demand for Order in Civil Society: A Review of Some Themes in the History of Urban Crime, Police, and Riot in England," in Bordua, ed., *op. cit.*, pp. 1–24.
5. Selden D. Bacon, "The Early Development of American Municipal Police: A Study of the Evolution of Formal Control in a Changing Society," Unpublished Ph.D. dissertation, Yale University, New Haven, 1939, Vol. II, Ch. 10.
6. *Ibid.*, p. 767.
7. *Ibid.*, pp. 768–769.
8. *Ibid.*, p. 767.

9. *Ibid.*, pp. 769–773.
10. *Ibid.*, pp. 777–778.
11. *Ibid.*, p. 780.
12. *Ibid.*, see Digest, n. p.
13. *Ibid.*, p. 780.
14. Albert J. Shafter, "Numerical Strength of Small Police Departments," *Journal of Criminal Law, Criminology, and Police Science*, LII (1961), 344–346.
15. Bacon, *op. cit.*, p. 781.
16. Arthur Stinchcombe, "Institutions of Privacy in the Determination of Police Administrative Practice," *American Journal of Sociology*, LXIX (September, 1963), 150–160.
17. See Skolnick, *op. cit.*, Ch. 6, and Reiss and Bordua, *op. cit.*, pp. 41–45.
18. Reiss and Bordua, *op. cit.*, pp. 28–32.
19. Albert J. Reiss, Jr., "Reflections on Police Bureaucracies in Modern Societies," A Paper for the 6th World Congress of Sociology, Evian, France, September, 1966; also, University of Michigan, Center for Research on Social Organization, Paper No. 20.
20. Silver, *op. cit.*, pp. 1–24.
21. Just as they sometimes are in the problem of relations with adolescents. Trained and specialized juvenile officers probably are better at their jobs than are most schoolteachers, especially those teaching in slum schools.
22. Michael Banton, *The Policeman in the Community* (New York: Basic Books, 1964), Ch. 4.
23. David J. Bordua, "The Police," *International Encyclopedia of the Social Sciences* (New York: Crowell Collier, 1967).
24. The classic source is, of course, William Foote Whyte, *Street Corner Society: The Social Structure of an Italian Slum* (Chicago: University of Chicago Press, 1964).
25. This material on police expenditure is taken from a study currently being made by David J. Bordua and Edward Haurek, University of Illinois.
26. See Skolnick, *op. cit.* Also see Wayne R. Lafave, *Arrest: The Decision to Take a Suspect into Custody* (Boston: Little, Brown, 1965); Donald J. Newman, *Conviction: The Determination of Guilt or Innocence without Trial* (Boston: Little, Brown, 1966), esp. Ch. 14.
27. David J. Bordua and Albert J. Reiss, Jr., "Command, Control and Charisma: Reflections on Police Bureaucracy," *American Journal of Sociology*, LXXII (July, 1966), 68–76.
28. *Ibid.*
29. See, for example, Richard A. Myren, "A Crisis in Police Management," *Journal of Criminal Law, Criminology and Police Science*, L (1960), 600–604; Vernon L. Hoy, "A Study of Specialization and Decentralization of Municipal Police Departments with Emphasis on the Specialist in District Stations," unpublished M.S. thesis, University of Southern California, 1958; Ching Pei Tsu, "Police Administration in St. Louis," unpublished M.A. thesis, University of Missouri, 1936.
30. Cf., for example, Harold Wilensky, "The Professionalization of Everyone?," *The American Journal of Sociology*, LXX (September, 1964), 138.
31. Albert J. Reiss, Jr., "The Role of the Police in a Changing Society," Center for Research on Social Organization, University of Michigan, Paper No. 14, March, 1966, pp. 1–36.
32. James Q. Wilson, "Police Morale, Reform, and Citizen Respect: The Chicago Case," in Bordua, ed., *op. cit.*, pp. 137–162.
33. John H. McNamara, "Uncertainties in Police Work: The Relevance of Police Recruits' Backgrounds and Training," in Bordua, ed., *op. cit.*, pp. 163–252.

34. Leo R. Eilbert, John H. McNamara, Vernon L. Hanson, *Research on Selection and Training for Police Recruits* (Pittsburgh: American Institute for Research, 1961).

35. Cf. John H. McNamara, *op. cit.*

36. Jack J. Preiss and Howard J. Ehrlich, *An Examination of Role Theory: The Case of the State Police* (Lincoln: The University of Nebraska Press, 1966).

37. Egon Bittner, "Police Discretion in Emergency Apprehension of Mentally Ill Persons," *Social Problems*, XIV (1967), 278–292; Donald J. Black and Albert J. Reiss, Jr., "Coercive Authority and Citizen Rights in Field Patrol Settings"; "Some Aspects of Citizen Behavior in Routine Police Encounters"; "Personal and Property Searches Conducted in Radio-Dispatched Police Work"; "Police-Suspect Transactions in Field Settings According to the Race and Social Class of Suspects"; "Police and Citizen Behavior in Routine Field Encounters: Some Comparisons According to the Race and Social Class Status of Citizens"; "Transactions with Suspects in On-View Police Work," respectively Report Nos. 2, 4, 5, 6, 7, and 8, United States Department of Justice: Office of Law Enforcement Assistance, Grant No. 006, Reports Submitted to the President's Commission on Law Enforcement and the Administration of Criminal Justice, 1966; Elaine Cumming and Ian Cummings, "Policeman as Philosopher, Guide and Friend," *Social Problems*, XII (1965); Irving Piliavin and Scott Briar, "Police Encounters with Juveniles," *The American Journal of Sociology*, LXX (1964), 206–214; Skolnick, *op. cit.*; William A. Westley, "Violence and the Police," *The American Journal of Sociology*, LIX (July, 1953), 34–41.

38. Westley, *ibid.*, p. 39.

39. Piliavin and Briar, *op. cit.*

40. Skolnick, *op. cit.*, Ch. 5.

41. Black and Reiss, Jr., *op. cit.*

42. Joseph D. Lohman, *The Police and Minority Groups* (Chicago Park District Police, 1947).

43. William W. Hermann, "Acacia: A System for Automating Content and Critical Incident Analysis," Los Angeles: University of Southern California School of Public Administration, 1962.

44. Marvin E. Wolfgang and Harvey A. Smith, "Mathematical Methods in Criminology," *International Social Science Journal*, VIII (1966), 200–223.

45. Morris Janowitz, *The Professional Soldier: A Social and Political Portrait* (Glencoe, Ill.: The Free Press, 1960), esp., pp. 31–36.

46. See Bordua and Reiss, "Command, Control and Charisma: Reflections on Police Bureaucracy," *op. cit.*, pp. 73–76.

47. John H. McNamara, *op. cit.*

48. See, for example, Arthur I. Siegel, Philip J. Federman and Douglas G. Schultz, *Professional Police—Human Relations Training* (Springfield, Ill.: Charles C Thomas, 1963).

49. Black and Reiss, *op. cit.*, Report Nos. 6 and 7.

50. Carl Werthman and Irving Piliavin, "Gang Members and the Police," in Bordua, ed., *op. cit.*, pp. 56–98.

51. Albert J. Reiss, Jr., "Police Officer Attitudes toward Their Work and Job," United States Department of Justice: Office of Law Enforcement Assistance, Grant No. 006, A Report to the President's Commission on Law Enforcement and the Administration of Criminal Justice, 1966.

52. Albert D. Biderman *et al.*, "Salient Findings on Crime and Attitudes toward Law Enforcement in the District of Columbia," Washington, D.C., Bureau of Social

Science Research Project 382; United States Department of Justice: Office of Law Enforcement Assistance, May, 1966, Chapter III.

53. William W. Wattenberg and Noel Bufe, "The Effectiveness of Police Youth Bureau Officers," *Journal of Criminal Law, Criminology and Police Science*, LIV (December, 1963), 470–475.

54. Much of this research is summarized in David J. Bordua, "Recent Trends: Deviant Behavior and Social Control," *The Annals*, CCCLXIX (January, 1967), 149–163.

55. Jerome H. Skolnick and J. Richard Woodworth, "Bureaucracy, Information, and Social Control: A Study of a Morals Detail," in Bordua, *op. cit.*, pp. 99–136.

56. Skolnick, *op. cit.*, pp. 37–41.

57. *The Challenge of Crime in a Free Society*, A Report by President's Commission on Law Enforcement and the Administration of Criminal Justice (Washington, D.C.: United States Government Printing Office, February, 1967); also see *Report of the President's Commission on Crime in the District of Columbia* (Washington, D.C.: U. S. Government Printing Office, 1966).

The Management of Educational Establishments

NEAL GROSS

JOSHUA A. FISHMAN

chapter 11

Two polar positions are frequently encountered about the use of sociology in the management of educational establishments. The first, one of optimism, is usually premised on the idea that sociological ideas and studies have immediate and direct application to the tasks of educational administrators. It is illustrated by Lazarsfeld's comments.

I have elaborated on a number of social science concepts to show how these relate to problems with which administrators are faced. This was done so as to show how applicable the concern of the social sciences is to the study and practice of administration. . . . As I mentioned before, I am optimistic about the future of the relationship between the social sciences and the study of administration.[1]

304

Lazarsfeld then speculates that sociology and other social sciences will probably make their greatest contribution to the study and practice of administration in the future through their research inquiries.[2]

The other extreme, one of pessimism, is reflected in the observations that the president of a major university and a superintendent of a large city school system made to one of the authors. The university president stated: "I have examined the writings of several sociologists about the management and the operation of universities. I found them interesting and amusing, but not especially relevant or useful in coping with the complex problems I encounter in running the University."[3] The superintendent of schools stated:

> We agreed to allow several sociologists and their graduate students to do research in our schools, but we did not find the experience rewarding. We thought they might come up with some new ideas about how we could cope with certain of our basic problems, but instead, their findings were of little practical value and in fact told us what we had known for years. . . . To be brutally frank, we not only did not learn anything of importance from the labors of your sociological colleagues, but we also did not especially enjoy having them around. It was not only that they were naïve about the realities of running a school system and the problems we face. What was worse, they had an attitude that seemed to imply that they were experts on problems that, from our point of view, they never really understood.[4]

We hasten to add that as a consequence of many informal conversations with sociologists and the adminstrators of educational institutions about their experiences in, or feelings about, encounters of this kind, we have found both incorrigible optimists and prophets of gloom among *both* groups.

That such widely divergent views are held about the contributions that sociology is in a position to make to executives of educational establishments suggests one reason for the importance of a critical examination of this issue.[5] Another is the growing tendency for sociologists to become involved in deliberations and decisions about the development of policies and programs for education. In recent years an increasing number of sociologists have been asked to serve as consultants or to conduct research on matters bearing on strategies to improve public and private education and to cope with the operational problems that perplex educational decision makers at the federal and state levels of government.[6] Sociologists also have served in similar capacities with respect to questions of considerable concern to officials of institutions of lower and higher learning and those dealing with educational matters in foundations.[7] A number of sociologists have recently made pronouncements about shortcomings or the limited perspectives of educational decision makers[8] and steps that need to be taken to overcome them. The motivation of efforts of this kind in most instances is undoubtedly one of public service and is based on the premise that the insights, knowledge, and findings of sociological inquiry have direct relevance to critical educational problems—for example, designing more effective programs to meet the problem of school dropouts, developing programs to overcome the learning difficulties of the "culturally deprived" child, coping with the problem of the alienation of a growing number of high school and college students, and speeding up and maximizing the assumed benefits of the process of desegregation. In addition, a growing body of sociologists in the past decade have become aware that educational institutions provide excellent laboratories for the analysis of central problems of their discipline; for example, the study of the structure and functioning of complex organizations, the process of socialization, the study of small groups, interorganizational relationships, and issues in social stratification and social mobility. And many of them have felt that their research findings have direct implications for resolving pressing educational problems.[9] In addition, many school officials and professors of education who have been exposed to the research and ideas of sociologists on such topics as the Negro family, social class and education, the analysis of educational leadership, and social forces influencing learning have drawn sweeping conclusions for educational policy or practice from what they have read or heard. Furthermore, most of the leading centers for the preparation of school administrators in the United States have in recent years added sociologists and other kinds of social scientists to their faculties on the assumption that their knowledge and skills would materially improve these training programs. A similar development occurred in Australia and other countries and is now under way in England and Wales.

Although we shall contend that sociologists have and can contribute to the formulation and implementation of educational policy, we shall also argue that the result of their intervention is not always beneficial. There is a distinction between the terms "use" and "utility." Serious questions can be raised about the legitimacy and soundness of certain recommendations and assertions that social scientists have made with respect to issues of public educational policy. There is also reason to believe that some of them have failed to distinguish between their role as citizens and their obligations as social scientists. In the case of training programs for educational practitioners, speculative pronouncements of a decade ago about the contributions of social scientists have been put to the test of reality, and the results have not always been impressive and in some instances have been downright discouraging. In nearly all these programs unanticipated problems and serious complications have arisen.[10] Finally, as indicated at the outset, it appears that when sociologists have become involved in relationships with educational administrators, these encounters have not necessarily resulted in productive or gratifying outcomes for one or both parties in the relationship.

Two other preliminary matters: The first is that several other chapters in this volume deal directly or indirectly with the possible application of sociology to educational problems of concern to school and university executives: for example, collegiate general education (Chapter 2), urban poverty and social planning (Chapter 16), the treatment of delinquency (Chapter 17), interrelations between the school and the family (Chapter 19), sociology in the desegregation process (Chapter 25), and social accounting (Chapter 31). In view of this circumstance, we have attempted to draw our illustrations of the uses of sociology in education as much as possible from areas not treated in other chapters, although some overlap, because of the scope of our problem, is bound to occur. The second is that, although we would contend that our observations about the relevance of sociology today and in the future apply to decision makers in nearly all kinds of educational organizations, we have found it necessary, because of limitations of space, to restrict our discussion primarily to its use for administrators of public-school systems in the United States and thus will devote little attention to the now appreciable and expanding sociological literature on higher education and to schools and institutions of higher learning abroad.[11]

The Administrators of Educational Establishments

Our first task is to specify the *major* potential recipients or possible buyers of the products or services of sociologists in the field of educational administration. Educational establishments may be thought of as social systems designed to accomplish goals, and, like business corporations and hospitals, they must be managed. Boards of education require a complex bureaucratic apparatus to advise them, to implement their decisions, and to cope with the internal and external problems of school systems; hence they employ superintendents of school systems, deputy, associate, and assistant superintendents, and the principals of individual schools. The governing boards of colleges and universities appoint presidents, vice-presidents, provosts, deans, and many other administrative personnel who are held accountable for the over-all management of institutions of higher learning or their subunits. There is another set of officials who, although not directly involved in the administration of schools, colleges, or universities, influence, and undoubtedly will continue in the future to exert a greater impact on, the specification of their goals and their operation—those who serve as decision makers and educational advisers for establishments such as the United States Office of Education, state departments or boards of education, and private and governmental foundations. Their recommendations and decisions bear on strategic issues of public policy in education, and the priorities they assign to problems, the strategies they use to cope with them, and the fiscal resources they allocate to them are matters of great importance and concern to individuals responsible for the operation of educational organizations as well as to the leadership in other areas of our society.

The administrators of institutions of lower and higher education have many complex responsibilities. They are expected to delineate the goals of their organizations and redefine them when changing conditions require their revision. They are expected to mobilize, organize, and maximize the human, physical, and fiscal resources under their jurisdiction in order to achieve educational objectives. They are charged with the responsibility of motivating, evaluating, and co-ordinating the efforts of personnel engaged in diverse tasks that are tied together by a complex division of labor and a system of authority. They are expected to appraise the weaknesses of their organizations and to propose and carry out changes and innovations to eliminate them. They must cope with those stresses and strains, organizational and personal, that appear to be indigenous to rationally designed schemes that require the formalizing of interpersonal relationships. They must also deal with many problems connected with transactions of their institutions with the external environment, for example, obtaining fiscal support and recruiting personnel, dealing with pressures, and maintaining lines of communication with individuals and groups whose actions can materially influence the operation of educational establishments.[12] The specific nature of the tasks and problems of educational officials is undoubtedly a function of many conditions, including the characteristics of their clients, the size and tasks of their organization, the way they and others define their roles and that of their establishments, their own competence and the qualifications of their superordinates and subordinates, the social, economic, and political influences to which they are exposed, and the types and intensity of pressures that confront them. It is through their decisions, planning, strategies, and ability to influence others, and in their social relationships, that officials of educational establishments attempt to define and achieve organizational goals and to come to terms with the basic problems confronting them and their establishments.

In what ways might sociologists be of service to an educational decision maker? Sociologists can offer him intellectual tools that may lead him to perceive his organization and to analyze its operations in a more realistic and incisive manner and that can sensitize him to easily overlooked circumstances, conditions, and ideas that can be of considerable value in his planning and decisions. Members of this social-science discipline can also provide and interpret information about schools, communities, other institutional areas, and social forces that are of direct relevance to his deliberations and his efforts to cope with both immediate and long-range problems. Sociologists can also make an educational administrator aware of the state of knowledge on numerous issues involved in the vexing questions that it is his responsiblility to decide. They can offer him clues and propose strategies for moving his organization forward and can facilitate his adoption of a picture of reality, not myth, about the complex organization he manages.

Sociology and Its Intellectual Wares

We now turn to the producers, and possibly sellers, in the intellectual market place we are examining, and this requires a brief consideration of the question, "What is sociology?" Inkeles, in his short but excellent monograph on this subject,[13] has shown that this is a complex issue that can be approached from numerous points of view and that it is difficult, if not impossible, to offer a conceptual definition that sharply distinguishes sociology from other social-science disciplines and that would be acceptable to all social scientists who claim this identity. We concur with Smith in his observation that probably the most adequate way to define each social-science discipline "is to point to its history and to the current activities of the people who agree on identifying one another as members."[14] It is not appropriate to treat the historical development of sociology here, but it is necessary to comment on the meaning and scope of "sociology" as we conceive of this social-science discipline.

We conceive of sociology as a scientific discipline that is concerned with developing a body of theoretically significant and empirically verifiable propositions about the structure, processes, and functioning of social systems and the influence of these systems on man's social behavior. By a social system we mean a plurality of human beings united in some form of regular interaction or interdependence. The social systems that sociologists study vary in character from small intimate groups such as families and friendship groups to large and complex collectivities such as factories, cities, and nation-states. Since social systems, regardless of size, type, or complexity, constitute the domain of sociological inquiry, it is not surprising that a variety of subfields of this discipline have developed that focus on different ways of categorizing social systems, their dimensions, and their problems. Thus, some sociologists specialize in the study of small groups, others in the analysis of large-scale organizations, and still others analyze urban and rural social systems. Some sociologists give primary consideration to particular institutional areas resulting in specialized bodies of literature such as the sociology of religion, education, the family, medicine, industry, and political behavior. And there are still other areas of specialization: race and ethnic relations, population, social stratification, occupations, social disorganization and deviant behavior, social psychology, mass communications, and so on. More than thirty special subfields of sociology can be isolated.[15]

It is relevant to note here a point we shall consider in greater detail later: most officials of school systems, universities, and foundations with whom we have had contacts in our consulting and research activities had little awareness of the complexity of the sociological enterprise; their image of the discipline was apparently largely a consequence of the small segment of the literature that they had read or the particular sociologists whom they had known. If administrators want the help or advice of a sociologist, they need to know, and it is our obligation to inform them, that sociologists are typically not interchangeable units and that, for example, an expert in urban sociology may be quite inexpert in the analysis of the internal stresses and strains in organizations or in social factors that influence learning.

Most sociologists, but few educational administrators, are also aware of the following characteristic of our discipline: there are many competing and conflicting points of view about the "mission" of sociology and its central tasks. Furthermore, there are disagreements about the meaning, relevence, and use of theory.[16] Thus, some sociologists place great weight on the need for "master conceptual schemes"; others argue that primacy should be given to theories of the middle range;[17] and still others feel that sociology is not ripe for theory of any kind or display little interest in it. There are also differences of opinion, frequently sharp ones, over issues of methodology and about strategies for conducting research, for example, the merits of case studies and historical analysis versus survey procedures.[18] One way to summarize the heterogeneous and complex nature of the sociological enterprise is to conceive of it as a series of games at which sociologists work. Although some sociologists shift occasionally from one game to another, most tend to identify themselves with, and play by the rules of, a particular game. This characteristic of the discipline also underscores the difficulties of sociologists who attempt to deal with a topic such as the use of sociology for educational administration. Our work has been restricted to particular problem areas of sociology, and the games in which we are involved and the rules we tend to follow are linked to our own theoretical and methodological biases. What we say, therefore, needs to be viewed as the observations and judgments of only two sociologists who, incidentally, recognize that they, themselves, do not agree on certain issues. Others might very well take different points of view than those we shall express in part because of the games they play. In short, no sociologist can speak for his entire profession.

However, regardless of their special interests or biases most, although not all, sociologists accept two assumptions. The first is that the behavior of human beings is in part a function of their present, past, and anticipated participations in social systems. Sociologists do not minimize the importance of psychological, biological, or cultural variables as influences on human behavior. But at the same time they assume that efforts to account for social behavior that do not take into consideration man's group affiliations, interactions, and identities leave out crucial variables for understanding and explaining his beliefs, attitudes, and behavior. The second assumption is that the social systems in which men participate operate with some degree of order and disorder. We believe that most sociologists would agree that as a scientific discipline the salient tasks of sociology are to discover the nature, complexities, and patterns of this order and disorder.[19]

What intellectual wares does the discipline of sociology have that might be of possible use or service to educational administrators? From our perspective, we would classify the goods and potential services of the "sociological package" in the following way. One part consists of perspectives, theoretical ideas, and concepts. A second part includes empirical research findings, only some of which are linked to theoretical formulations. A third segment is its research methods. The final part consists of the intellectual wares and the research skills that different members of the disciplines possess and can bring to bear on problems confronting educational executives. We now turn to an examination of how the different parts of this "package" have been used in the field of educational administration.

The Sociologist as a Consultant to Educational Establishments on Specific Problems

A small but growing contingent of sociologists has served in the roles of consultants on specific problems to school boards, school superintendents, and other educational officers. Those sociologists who to our knowledge have assumed this position report that their services have been requested for so many different reasons that these reasons themselves must be considered as client characteristics. The desire to engage an expert who "knows the answers" may be particularly characteristic of a crisis context or a power struggle. The desire to engage an expert who can "find the answers" may be characteristic of more sophisticated and more affluent clients with the necessary perspective and peace of mind (not to mention objective control) to invest in long-range, rational planning as a normal operating procedure. Nevertheless, this latter approach may also have been employed in order to avoid action or decision, whereas the former may have been the culmination of a long-term relationship with a consultant hitherto engaged primarily for "fact-finding purposes."

In either case a surprisingly diversified list of problems has been put before sociologists whom we know who have served as consultants. Most of them may be categorized as problems dealing with how to cope with pressing educational issues or obtaining information bearing on them. In view of the lack of hard data about the value of the services of sociologists as consultants from the perspective of their educational clients, we shall report our *impressions* of the way we believe our services have been of utility to them in several cases where we have served in this capacity. First, however, we present examples of the two general kinds of problems on which sociologists appear to have most frequently advised educational organizations.[20]

"HOW TO . . ." REQUESTS

These include: How to improve the reputation of the schools in the community? How to convince voters to approve a new school bond issue or an increase in the school tax? How to improve relations between policy-making boards and their educational executives? How to improve relations between the administration and the faculty? How to improve teacher morale? How to reorganize school administration in order to make it a *facilitating* and stimulating rather than a *policing* structure? How to encourage greater interest in new educational ideas? How to deal with school integration pressures and counterpressures? How to change the total educational environment to facilitate personality and intellectual growth? How to revise the social-studies curriculum so as to provide greater recognition for modern topics and approaches? How to provide minority-group children with enriched educational experiences? How to train or retrain teachers so that they can work more effectively with these children?

"INFORMATION PROVIDING" REQUESTS

Sociologists have been asked to provide data bearing on the following questions: What changes can be anticipated in the quantity and composition of school enrollments?[21] How many schools should be built and where should they be located? How can school district lines be redrawn to achieve a specified "mix" of pupils?[22] What can be anticipated if a merit salary plan is adopted? What has been the educational outcome of a curricular or pedagogical chance?[23] What are the attitudes or opinions of parents, pupils, teachers, board members, community influentials, and the press about educational quality, processes, goals, programs, costs, and so on?[24] How will, or how do, parents and pupils react to plans or programs to desegregate schools?[25] What trends can be anticipated with respect to budgets, salaries, and the influence of teachers' unions?[26]

Although the lists are not exhaustive, they illustrate common characteristics of such requests. Much "how to" consultation is requested in response to pressures exerted on education from outside groups or due to large-scale social problems. Often, advice is sought on how to deal with critics or how to escape from pressures related to community-wide conflict, rather than on how to modify education per se. When "how to" consultation is requested with respect to internal educational problems, the structural-organizational differentiations within the educational system (such as voters versus board versus administration versus teachers versus pupils versus parents) loom large in the minds of clients—but, again, frequently in a "coping" rather than a "restructuring" sense. Finally many requests are surrounded by unstated restrictions or qualifications which derive from both of the foregoing observations. Thus, a request for consultation on "how to deal with school integration pressures and counterpressures" may actually contain the following unstated restrictions: so as to satisfy all major segments of the community, involve no major budgetary increases, improve the education of Negro children without diluting that of white children, and elicit co-operation (rather than increased resignations or transfer requests) among teachers. Informational requests are also frequently characterized by unstated (and frequently unformulated) restrictions, although at a lesser level of urgency or immediacy. Both kinds of consultative requests are very likely to be couched in nonsociological terms and, indeed, to deal with some matters that either are commonly outside the scope of sociological analysis or extend considerably beyond the commonly recognized boundaries of sociology alone. We shall consider in greater detail problems of the client-consultant relationship in a later section of this chapter.

What types of goods and services do sociologists attempt to provide when they serve as consultants on specific problems of educational establishments? The most meaningful way to examine this question is to consider concrete instances in which sociologists have served as educational consultants. We turn, therefore, to four assignments[27] in which we were involved and the outcomes that we believe emerged from them.

The first problem to be examined was initially defined by the chairman of a school board in a wealthy suburban New England community in the following terms: "We believe our superintendent has done an excellent job in upgrading the quality of our school curricula, but the board is acutely concerned about the strong negative attitudes toward him on the part of the community and the staff. The board is faced with the decision during the next six months of whether to place him on tenure or fire him. We would like you to tell us what to do."

The consultant informed the school board that he would not accept the consulting assignment as defined since he viewed it as the responsibility of the board, not the consultant, to decide whether to retain the superintendent. He did indicate, however, that he would agree to undertake a study to ascertain if the board's information about the feelings of the community and attitudes of teachers toward the superintendent were myth or reality. He also indicated that he would be willing, on the basis of his findings, to suggest courses of action that the board might wish to consider to alleviate any problems he uncovered in the course of his study. The board agreed to this definition of his assignment and to the specifications of the study design he proposed, including the anonymity of respondents.

The results of the study, completed within a five-month period, may be summarized as follows: (1) Only a minority of the teachers in the school system (largely the old-timers) had negative feelings about the superintendent. The great majority of the teachers had an extremely positive assessment of his performance. (2) Three of the most influential members of the power structure in the community (who were also friends of teachers with negative views of the superintendent) represented the core of the small body of citizenry who were opposed to the superintendent. (3) Nearly all the reasons given by those who had strong negative feelings about the superintendent were based on rumors that had no foundation in fact. One of these was that the superintendent was "loading the schools" with members of a minority group; a second was that he had treated certain teachers unjustly; and a third was that he was spending a great deal of his time on noneducational matters. (4) The superintendent and the school board seldom discussed "delicate" issues involving their own relationships. (5) Few channels for obtaining reliable information about the schools existed in the community.

As a consequence of the consultation, the school board recognized that its "intelligence" about school affairs was sorely deficient, and, on the basis of the findings of the study, it decided to place the superintendent on tenure. A number of the recommendations of the sociological consultant were subsequently adopted and implemented. These included the development of a set of ground rules covering major problems that had been encountered in the relationship between the superintendent and the board; the holding of occasional informal meetings at which they could consider issues of concern to them, but which they felt were inappropriate to raise at public school-board meetings; the establishment of a school-community communications program designed to provide more information about the schools to citizens; the creation of a faculty-administrator council to discuss professional and organizational problems of the school system; and the employment of an assistant for the superintendent so that he could be relieved of many of his routine administrative duties and devote more time to his professional responsibilities, including public relations.

The second consultation was with a school system in a medium-sized city in the East that had experienced a great deal of conflict in the relationship between the school administration and its teachers. The school board, the higher administration, the principals, and the teachers' organization recognized that outside help was needed. After the consultant had held several exploratory sessions with representatives of the school board, the administration, and the teachers' organization, it was agreed that his tasks would be to isolate the circumstances that accounted for the difficulties that had developed between the administration and the teachers and to recommend steps that might be taken to eliminate them.

The initial phase of the consultation involved lengthy open-ended interviews with school-board members, the superintendent, the central-office staff, the principals, and a sample of the teachers in an effort to isolate the basic conditions that had created the serious interpersonal frictions that had disrupted the school system. The interviews with the teachers revealed that the major grievances of a majority of them against the central office and the principals focused on three issues: (1) their administrators had attempted to introduce new curricular materials into the schools without benefit of the professional judgment of the faculty; (2) the administrators showed little interest in the economic and social welfare of the faculty; and (3) the teachers' organization was constantly rebuffed in its efforts to get a hearing for its grievances.

Most, but not all, of the administrators expressed the following serious concern about the behavior of teachers: (1) a large proportion of them were opposed to the introduction of educational innovations; (2) most teachers showed little respect for the central administrative staff; and (3) the teachers' organization had attempted to pressure the higher administration to make changes in the school program that were directed at the teachers', not the students', welfare.

The second phase of the consultation focused on gathering data that would reveal how the teachers and higher administrators perceived *each other's* grievances. These interviews revealed, among other things, that most teachers were *not* opposed to educational innovations, but to the methods used by the central office to introduce them. They revealed that a substantial portion of the teachers did in fact have little respect for the central-office staff largely because they felt that their higher administrators offered them little professional leadership. Interviews with leaders of the teachers' organization showed that they felt that the reforms their association was supporting would be of benefit to *both* the students and the faculty and that only by using pressure tactics could they influence the higher administration. In addition, interviews with the school superintendent and board members revealed that the superintendent had previously attempted, without success, to obtain a number of changes in the personnel policies of the school system that were highly similar to those desired by the teachers' organization.

The consultant's findings indicated that the major sources of organizational and personal stress could be attributed to ambiguity over role definitions, the professionalism-autonomy dilemma, and failures in communications. The consultant's report pinpointed those conditions and how they had resulted in misperceptions and misunderstandings. He suggested that a committee be created, composed of members of the school board, the higher administration, principals, and representatives of the teachers' organization, to consider the consultant's ideas and his proposals to resolve the major issues of contentions between the higher administrators and the teachers. This proposed strategy was accepted, and seven of his eight recommendations, with minor revisions, were unanimously agreed on by the committee and later adopted as policies by the board. When the consultant contacted members of the committee one year after the completion of his assignment, they reported that the interpersonal relationships between the higher administration and the teachers had markedly improved.

The third consultation dealt with the inability of a school system to win a bond-issue election for building new schools. In two previous elections a majority of the citizens, but not the two-thirds required, had supported the bond issue. The problem was to develop a strategy that would result in a two-thirds affirmative vote. An analysis of the election results indicated that a large block of negative votes were cast in a section of the community composed primarily of first-generation Italian families of low socioeconomic status. As a consequence of the information obtained from a set of exploratory interviews with the formal and informal leadership in the community, the consultant suggested that the school administration might focus its efforts on two strategies: first, to convince the opinion leaders of the Italian section of the community of the positive educational consequences for children of low socioeconomic backgrounds that would result from the proposed school building program; and, second, to solicit the support of the local labor leadership in convincing its membership of the necessity for new schools. These suggestions were followed, and the success of the third attempt to pass the bond issue is largely attributed by school officials to the use of these two strategies.

The fourth consultation involved an assignment with a foundation to consult on problems related to the development and strengthening of research and training programs in a specialized field of education at American universities. In defining the consultant's role, it was agreed that he would explore any issue that he judged relevant to it. The first phase of the consultation required an overview of the present state of affairs in the field under examination. A series of conferences was held with key individuals in the area as well as with social scientists and other faculty members at a number of major universities who had an interest in, or might have useful ideas about, further development of the field. As a consequence of these conferences, an examination of the literature and programs in this educational area, and a number of related activities that turned out to be more demanding and time-consuming than originally anticipated, the consultant initially developed a "profile" of the field.

In sociological perspective, it consisted of answers to the following kinds of issue: the role problems and strains of personnel in the area; the norms and values of its academic personnel; their desire for social change and the introduction of innovations; functional and dysfunctional aspects of its organizational arrangements; its relationships to other subsystems in universities; criteria used in assessing outstanding role performance; its division of labor with respect to the production and dissemination of knowledge and training activities; its relative status as compared to other disciplines; the way universities selected, socialized, and allocated students; and so on.

This assignment illustrates well a frequent circumstance that we and other sociologists have frequently encountered in our consulting activities: numerous difficulties arise for the consultant until he explicitly recognizes the possibility that a critical problem of the assignment may be the *redefinition of the problem.* That is, in this instance the consultant had uncritically accepted the assignment as defined by the client, and it turned out that the heart of the client's problem was the "improper" way it had been initially defined. Only after considerable deliberations about the meaning and possible interpretations of the several kinds of data the consultant had obtained did it occur to him that rational decisions about ways to further develop this field required coming to grips with the issue of whether the then current view of the area of study as an intellectual discipline was based on a set of reasonable assumptions. A critical appraisal of these assumptions revealed that they were tenuous. Once this issue was resolved, the rest of the assignment could be treated as a problem in systems or operational analysis: what steps, in what order, what feedback mechanisms, and what checks and balances were required to maximize allocation of resources to develop further quite different conceptions of the field? In short, as in so many other areas of human affairs, including sociological research, the key problem was the definition of the problem. Our impression was that the foundation found the consultation useful since its decisions about allocating resources to the field appeared to be influenced by the adviser's report.[28]

The Sociologist's Contributions to Programs for Training Educational Administrators and His Role as a "General" Consultant

A number of sociologists during the past decade, along with other social scientists, such as economists and political scientists, have actively participated in preservice and in-service training programs for educational administrators at the institutions of higher education. Of the several capacities in which sociologists may offer their services to educational administrators, they have been most frequently involved in the teaching role. At present a number of sociologists hold full- or part-time appointments in colleges or schools of education and offer or participate in courses and interdisciplinary seminars for educational administrators as well as for a variety of other psychoeducational specialists. These sociologists are sometimes also called on to participate in workshops and other types of in-service programs in school systems. Some of them have even attempted to teach key ideas of their discipline to professors of educational administration.

In addition, sociologists have served in what might be called "a general consulting" role with officials of educational establishments; that is, they have accepted assignments, typically lasting one to three days, in which they offer advice or suggest ideas that may be useful to administrators in their efforts to cope with sociological aspects of long-range or immediate problems of their institutions. Such assignments typically do not entail research activities, as did those considered in the previous section. Since the tasks of the sociologist in this role are similar to those he performs in training programs for educational administrators, we shall consider simultaneously the types of contributions they attempt to offer in both of these capacities.

No systematic study exists of the value those educational administrators who have been exposed to sociologists in their training or as general consultants to them or their staffs attribute to these experiences. However, a large number of informal discussions with school executives who have participated in such activities during the past decade lead us to believe that sociologists have been especially useful to them in the following respects: (1) sensitized them to organizational and interpersonal forces that influence the functioning of schools; (2) provided them with a greater sense of reality about the actual conditions that exist in schools and their external environments; (3) offered them clues to cope with some of their basic problems; and (4) provided them with knowledge about research techniques that may be useful to them in their administrative assignments.

In addition to examining how the perspectives, concepts, findings, and research methods of the sociologist have been or may be useful to educational administrators, we shall also consider at the close of this section several additional ideas that arise from a sociological perspective to educational institutions that in our judgment are of special significance for these administrators, but of which relatively few appear to have any awareness.

SENSITIZES ADMINISTRATORS TO THE IMPORTANCE OF ORGANIZATIONAL AND INTERPERSONAL FACTORS

Nearly all administrators-in-training have held previous teaching or minor managerial positions in school systems. They therefore come to university programs preparing them for more responsible positions with a great deal of detailed knowledge about the operation of school systems in which they have been employed and with a number of frequently incisive ideas about sources of their malfunctioning. However, the limited perspectives and common-sense orientations they bring to the analysis of an educational system typically are inadequate to alert them to many of its elements that may constitute basic sources of organizational instability. A sociological perspective toward structural features of school systems brings some of these circumstances into sharp focus.

The starting point for most sociological analyses of school systems is to view them as organizations or goal-directed social systems composed of positions linked together by a division of labor and a system of authority. This way of conceptualizing school systems is of value to school administrators because it focuses their attention on certain of their assumptions about school systems which in fact may be tenuous.

Most administrators-in-training typically treat the goals of school systems and their structure of roles as nonproblematic. They assume that administrators, teachers, and the community are in basic agreement about the objectives of schools. They also usually take it for granted that the respective rights and obligations of teachers, principals, and other personnel are matters on which there is basic consensus. In exploring conditions that may have dysfunctional effects for the operation of their schools or constitute levers for social change, they therefore typically overlook the possibility that two sources of organizational disequilibrium may be found in disagreements over goals and definitions of roles.

Exposure to a sociological orientation to schools focuses their attention on their goals, and they are made aware that in contrast to other types of organizations, such as business firms, the objectives of public schools are extremely vague and can be subject to varying interpretations. Many administrators-in-training recognize for the first time that the statement "The purpose of schools is to educate children" is largely meaningless until the phrase "for [what]" is added. They also learn that efforts to specify educational goals involve value issues such as what should be the respective responsibilities of the home and the school and what is the meaning of a "good education."

As a consequence of their exposure to sociological studies on the values of educators,[29] they become aware that principals and teachers frequently disagree in their beliefs with respect to the following kinds of issues: Should the schools give greater primacy to the intellectual, social, or emotional development of the child? Is it their responsibility to impart moral values? Should the schools attempt to solve race-relations problems of their society? Should they encourage or discourage the questioning of the status quo? Should schools engage in driver education and physical education and offer courses in home economics and family living? Their examination of the findings of other sociological investigations makes them recognize that striking disagreements may exist between superintendents and their school boards in their educational values and that one of the major sources of pressures that confront school administrators lies in conflicting viewpoints in their communities about school objectives and programs.[30]

A second frequently held assumption of administrators-in-training is that there is agreement on the role definition for educational positions. Sociological studies, however, sensitize them to the possibility that lack of agreement on the rights and obligations associated with educational positions may constitute another major dysfunctional element in educational organizations or serve as a leverage for change. Instead of assuming that they and their staffs are in basic agreement about the roles of the teacher, principal, and guidance worker, the sociologist alerts them to the possibility that they and their subordinates may not share similar views about the rights and obligations associated with their positions.

Should teachers be expected to attend P.T.A. meetings regularly? Does the teacher's job include the counseling function? What are the teacher's obligations to the especially bright or especially dull child? Or the problem child? What are the respective obligations of teachers and principals in handling discipline problems? Should teachers be required to participate in in-service training programs? Does the teacher have the right to expect that the principal will invariably support her when parents complain about her behavior? On these and many other phases of a teacher's job, contrary to the assumptions held by many educators, the evidence from sociological inquiries shows that frequently there is considerable disagreement between principals and teachers as well as among teachers themselves.[31] In addition to bringing these facts about disagreements over role expectations to the attention of school administrators, the sociologist can also show on the basis of findings of empirical studies that most school principals are exposed to conflicting expectations from their superintendent and their teachers over many issues; for example, the supervision of classroom instruction and the handling of discipline problems. In addition, he can also point to studies that reveal that teachers in the same school frequently hold conflicting expectations for their principal's performance[32] and that parents and teachers also frequently hold contradictory expectations for his behavior in many areas, such as student promotion and discipline.

As a consequence of studies conducted by sociologists, students preparing to become administrators learn that the school superintendent is the official who is probably exposed most often to severe role conflicts.[33] A major part of these conflicting expectations arises from the differential views held by his school board and his staff for his behavior on issues such as the size of the school budget or on promotion policies. Superintendents, like school principals, must also frequently deal with differential expectations among the teaching staff. And their most difficult problems may emerge from conflicting expectations for their performance held by members of their school board.[34]

To sum up: the conceptual tools and research findings of the sociologists sensitize educational administrators to those sources of organizational disequilibrium that they might otherwise ignore. Whether there is agreement or disagreement on organizational goals and role definition or the extent of dissension in the particular school system in which administrators-in-training will be later employed is, of course, an empirical question. The incorporation of a sociological perspective in their kit of intellectual tools alerts them to the importance of raising and exploring such questions and sensitizes them to the possibility that such organizational characteristics need to be considered in their analysis of sources of personal and organizational stress, strategies for educational change, and in their exercise of leadership.

A sociological orientation also alerts administrators to certain other features of schools which they typically overlook and which may constitute sources of serious disturbances in their operation. One of these is that the school is staffed by personnel who claim the prerogatives of a professional staff, but whose policy makers are laymen. Another is that administrators such as secondary-school principals have greater authority but usually less expertise than their subordinates. Still a third possible source of friction is the potential collision between the professional status of teachers and the authority structure of schools. Like any organization, a school needs functionaries to cope with problems of co-ordination and supervision of its personnel who carry out the technical tasks in its division of labor. The school principal, for example, must allocate teaching assignments, see that they are accomplished, and attempt to integrate the socialization experiences of pupils in a meaningful way. His responsibilities require him to have some degree of control over what goes on in classrooms. The work of his teachers is, therefore, of central concern to him. The authority structure may readily collide with another characteristic of the school as an organization, namely that its staff has a claim to professional status. As professionals, they can be expected to desire a high degree of autonomy over their own activities and considerable freedom in their decisions. This potential source of stress appears to be indigenous to professional bureaucracies such as schools and can be presumed to account in part for both organizational and personal strain. To be aware of these and other incompatible features of schools as organizations is not only useful to administrators in providing them with an understanding of the organizational-linked sources of many problems they will encounter; it also leads them to explore the kinds of strategies that will minimize their dysfunctional consequences or permit them to utilize these sources of instability as bases for effecting organizational change.[35]

Sociologists who have participated in training programs for educational administrators frequently comment on the strong psychological bias these students bring to their analysis of behavior. This is not surprising in view of the heavy emphasis in the teacher-training programs in which they previously were enrolled that stressed individual differences and exposed them to heavy doses of theories of learning and motivation. The idea that the behavior of an individual can also be presumed to be in part a function of *inter*personal and social forces is, surprisingly enough, familiar to relatively few of them or one that they frequently tend to forget.

This basic sociological perspective is useful to them in many ways. Consider, for example, a problem frequently encountered by school superintendents and principals: the resistance of their teachers to the acceptance of new educational ideas or programs.[36] The notion that interpersonal forces influence behavior suggests the importance of determining whether they may in part account for the resistance of school staffs to innovations and of exploring means whereby these influences can be used to facilitate their acceptance. The administrators' awareness that a school system consists of a set of informal as well as formal relationships alerts them to the possible impact on teachers of the beliefs and opinions of their informal leaders and to the fact that they may represent important gate keepers for the acceptance or rejection of innovations. It suggests the strategy of attempting to convince the informal opinion leaders in their schools of the necessity or benefits of a proposed change prior to presenting it to all the teachers. It makes them aware that proposed innovations such as team teaching and the ungraded school may disrupt existing clique and power relationships in schools and that such disruptions, unless anticipated and coped with prior to the introduction of new arrangements, can undermine rationally contrived schemes for improving the educational program.

In addition, the general idea that group forces influence behavior sensitizes an administrator to the importance of keeping in mind when he interacts with his subordinates that they have multiple group memberships[37] and reference groups[38] and that the expectations, rewards, and sanctions that flow from these interpersonal forces may constitute significant elements in the way they will react to him and his ideas. It also alerts him to the possibility that informal sanctions of peer-group members may constitute more effective mechanisms of social control than formalized rules.[39]

These key perspectives of the sociologist also can be suggestive for the design of strategies to cope with many central instructional problems of schools, for example, how to upgrade the performance of pupils in slum schools. Recognition of the variety of interpersonal influences to which the student is exposed, such as peer groups, the family, teachers, and the principal, leads to an exploration of not only how these forces may be depressing his academic performance but also how they, or other group forces, may be utilized to improve it.[40] The fact that learning outcomes may be in part a function of interpersonal, as well as intrapersonal, influences is a novel and provocative notion to many school administrators.[41]

There are a number of other sensitizing ideas derived from sociological analyses of organizations and social behavior that they also find especially useful. One of these is that elements of educational organizations, such as the school board, may have latent as well as manifest functions; sociological studies have revealed that the primary motivation of a substantial proportion of school-board members for seeking their office is of a "political" nature.[42] A second is that a proposed change in one part of the structure of a school system needs to be reviewed in terms of its consequences for other facets of the school's operation; a third is that leadership at times may be more profitably viewed as a property of a group than of an individual;[43] and a fourth is that there are a variety of mechanisms whereby management can achieve a high degree of informal control over their staffs.[44]

These perspectives and concepts of the sociologist are useful to administrators-in-training and those in practice because they provide them with a set of intellectual tools that alert them to organizational and interpersonal circumstances and conditions that they can readily overlook in diagnosing problems of educational systems and in developing plans to cope with them.

PROVIDES A REALITY ORIENTATION TO SCHOOLS AND THEIR EXTERNAL ENVIRONMENTS

Textbooks in educational administration have typically been hortative in nature, stressing the biases of their writers about how educational administrators *should* behave. They have been relatively silent, until recently, about the organizational and community facts of life to which they will be exposed. The findings of sociological studies have been incorporated into recently published textbooks and have been extremely useful in providing a more realistic view of the world of work of school administrators.[45] We shall consider later the implications of two of these studies for coping with the pressing problems that confront school administrators. Here we simply want to indicate their utility in providing a sense of realism about the problems to which administrators-in-training will be exposed.

We have earlier considered several kinds of studies conducted by sociologists that serve to sensitize educational administrators to organizational and interpersonal variables that influence the operation of their organization: inquiries that have isolated common sources of stress and strain in the relationship between superintendents and their school boards and the major occupational problems that confront superintendents and principals; inquiries that have delineated the major types of role conflicts to which superintendents, principals, and teachers are exposed; and investigations that have documented differences in the educational values of school-board members, their administrators, and parents. These studies also provide future administrators with a sense of reality about the problems of administrative positions.

Other kinds of sociological inquiry of considerable value in providing a reality perspective for educational administrators are those that describe the educational consequences of the social and ecological structure of different types of communities. The social-class studies of Warner,[46] Hollingshead,[47] Sexton,[48] and others[49] have been important in this respect, as have the community power studies conducted by sociologists.[50] In addition, sociological analyses of the racial composition of schools and of the changing composition of the population of large cities and suburbs have given educational administrators a greater understanding of the way demographic trends influence the quantity and composition of school populations.[51] Findings of these studies have led to a greater awareness of the need to devise educational programs based on a realistic assessment of the background characteristics and attitudes of students and parents.[52]

Rossi,[53] Haak,[54] and other sociologists[55] have conducted studies on community attitudes and beliefs about local school systems. Their findings make school administrators aware that large sections of the public in the communities where they will or do work probably have little interest in the schools or their problems and that a realistic appraisal of the community requires segmenting it into different publics whose activity and interest in school affairs vary in many important respects.

The work of sociologists such as Gordon,[56] Coleman,[57] and Stinchcombe[58] alert school principals and other administrators to the necessity of examining the normative climates of schools and their possible impact on learning outcomes. Their studies suggest that the norms held by many students and their teachers may be at variance and that student resistance to new programs may be a function of variations in the adolescent subcultures of schools.

Many other types of sociological studies have facilitated the development of current programs in educational administration that are based on a more reality-oriented posture to the schools and their major problems. Some examples are the studies of Becker[59] and of Herriott and St. John[60] on the mobility of teachers within school systems and of the problems of authority and teacher resistance to change that confront administrators; the studies of the role problems and conflicts of principals conducted at Harvard University;[61] Mason's study of the job and career satisfaction and career plans of teachers;[62] and the studies of Clark on critical organizational problems of adult education and the junior college.[63] Although some of these studies and many others that could be cited were conducted with sociological rather than educational problems in mind, they, according to the testimony of some practicing administrators, have made a substantial contribution to their recognition and understanding of the complex and interrelated set of forces and circumstances that are involved in the operation of educational institutions and that bear on their salient problems.[64]

PROVIDES CLUES TO COPING WITH SOME BASIC ORGANIZATIONAL PROBLEMS

To this point we have stressed two contributions of sociology to the management of educational establishments: (1) its perspectives, concepts, and empirical findings can be useful in the diagnosis of many internal and external problems of their organizations and (2) its research studies provide them with a greater sense of reality about actual problems and conditions. Now we turn to a third possible use of sociology for school superintendents, principals, and other types of educational administrators: sociological perspectives, concepts, and research findings *suggest* possible strategies or circumstances that deserve consideration in their efforts to deal with basic organizational problems. To illustrate this usage of sociology, we shall focus on two issues of considerable concern.[65]

A problem of long-standing and considerable national importance is reflected in the following finding of a study conducted by the Educational Testing Service: 20 per cent of the twelfth-grade students in the United States in 1955 who had mental-ability scores in the top three deciles indicated that they did not plan to attend college.[66] A number of other studies[67] have reported similar data. Sociologists concerned with problems of social mobility in American society have conducted a number of inquiries that shed light on social factors associated with student level of educational aspiration, and their findings suggest several strategies that can be explored by school systems in their efforts to cope with this problem.

The central finding of most sociological studies of student level of educational aspiration—that social class is positively related to it—is of little value to administrators, for school administrators are in no position to change the class structure of their communities. What they are interested in is findings that specify variables related to level of educational aspiration that the schools might be able to manipulate or influence. It is studies of this type that we shall now consider.

One of the first is Kahl's inquiry, initiated as a consequence of an intriguing finding of the Harvard Mobility Project[68] that examined the educational and occupational aspirations of nearly four thousand boys in public high schools in the Boston Metropolitan area:

Of particular interest was the fact that if a boy had high intelligence and came from the most populous part of the status range—its lower middle section—one could not well predict his aspiration. Thus a boy from the top quintile of intelligence whose father was a minor white collar worker or a skilled laborer had almost a fifty-fifty chance of aiming at a college career.[69]

To explore what might account for the differential level of aspirations of these high-I.Q. boys from "upper-lower" class families, Kahl interviewed twenty-four of them as well as their parents. Half of the boys definitely planned to go to college after high school and were in the college preparatory course, while the other half did not plan to go to college and were not in the college preparatory course. Kahl isolated the importance of parents' attitudes as an independent variable. In his words, "Some parents were satisfied with their own lot and did not attempt to push their sons up the status ladder, whereas other parents really encouraged their sons to strive for a 'better life.' " [70] Whereas eight of the twelve boys who were planning college were experiencing parental pressure to continue their formal education, only one of the twelve boys who did not plan to attend college was exposed to it.[71]

Cohen corroborated these findings.[72] She selected fifty matched pairs of high-school boys from socioeconomic backgrounds similar to the one studied by Kahl. One boy in each pair had decided to go to college. Approximately the same number of boys from various ethnic and religious backgrounds were in the two groups. Cohen developed a "pressure index" from parental interview responses and found noticeable differences between the two types of students. Two other sets of data provide further empirical support. In a study of the educational plans of approximately two thousand public and parochial secondary-school students in a Massachusetts community, Stouffer and Shea found striking differences among high-ability students who were and were not planning to attend college when they were cross-classified on the variable, parental urging.[73] Similar findings emerged from a national sample of students in grades six through nine.[74]

Such studies led the late Professor Stouffer to develop one of the few sociological instruments currently being widely used in the schools, *Your Educational Plans*.[75] It is a tool that, among other things, allows counselors to sort out the able yet unmotivated child and to help parents to understand their child's potentialities and difficulties. This instrument also contains a good deal of compactly organized information about the family as reported by the pupils.

Herriott[76] assumed that the primary determinants of educational plans were not the status characteristics of adolescents, but rather social forces which intervene between these characteristics and educational aspirations. With data obtained from nearly 1,500 adolescents in a New England high school, he found that level of aspiration is a function of level of self-assessment relative to others and level of expectations perceived from others. Of the educational expectation variables studied, those perceived from father, mother, older sibling or relative, friend of same age, and high-school counselor made the greatest independent contribution to variance in educational aspirations. The two factors most highly correlated with plans to attend college were expectations perceived from the adolescent's best friend and from the senior-high counselor. These findings indicate additional forces in the role set of students that may depress or increase their educational aspirations. The instrument used in this study, as Herriott suggests, can also be used by guidance counselors to sort out able students with little interest in going on to higher education who may be in need of special counseling. His findings about the impact of the student's perception of the expectations of the guidance counselor with respect to his attendance at college also suggest that educational administrators may need to reassess the adequacy of the counseling programs in their schools.[77]

Wilson's[78] research on high-school students in the San Francisco Bay area revealed that the "dominant social class character" of a school influences the level of educational aspiration of students from different social strata: 33 per cent of sons of manual workers had college aspirations in low-status schools, in comparison to 59 per cent in high-status schools. And 93 per cent of the sons of professionals in high-status schools, in comparison to 64 per cent in low-status schools, aspired to go to college. Wilson's study *suggests* that these differences may be attributed to varying normative forces operating on students enrolled in schools with varying dominant social-class characteristics. He has reported similar findings with respect to reading achievement-test scores for sixth-grade pupils in fourteen elementary schools in Berkeley, California.[79] The studies we have considered, plus those of sociologists such as Sewell,[80] Haller,[81] McDill and Coleman,[82] Rogoff,[83] and others,[84] are of great potential value to educational administrators because they shed light on social forces influencing educational aspirations and lead them to explore ways in which negative forces in the student's role set can be overcome and how those forces that could increase educational aspirations may be activated.[85]

A quite different kind of problem area confronting superintendents of schools is the performance of their principals. These officials manage individual units of their organization. For many years principals have been exhorted to maximize the potentialities for educational leadership inherent in their positions. However, critics of the professional leadership conception of the principal's role argue that his duties should be restricted to providing administrative services to his staff, a question of considerable controversy in educational circles and one of great practical concern to superintendents and their principals.

In sociological perspective the problem can be viewed as one of the effects on organizations of the role performance of their formal leaders. This orientation was used in a study[86] that obtained a measure of efforts of principals to offer professional leadership to their teachers in a national sample of elementary schools and examined the relationship of such efforts to organizational variables such as the teachers' morale, their professional performance, and pupils' learning. The findings revealed that there were positive relationships between the professional leadership efforts of the principal and these three types of organizational performance and therefore indicate that abandoning the professional leadership component of the principal's role may lead to negative educational effects.

In addition, the study attempted to isolate circumstances that account in part for the variation in the professional leadership of principals. On the basis of a theoretical formulation that specified organizational obstacles to an executive's efforts to offer leadership to a staff with professional status, several hypotheses were tested about determinants of the principal's leadership. The study found some support for the spillover hypothesis: that the stronger the professional leadership offered by the principal's immediate superior, the greater his own leadership efforts. Principals whose higher administrations allowed them to participate in the evaluation of applicants for positions as teachers in their schools tended to offer a greater degree of professional leadership than those who did not. Those principals who perceived their higher administrators as endorsing their efforts to improve teaching methods exhibited somewhat greater professional leadership than those who did not. Such findings suggest that higher administrators would be well advised to explore how their own performance, policies, and attitudes may influence the behavior of their principals. They alert individuals who will serve as school superintendents to the easily overlooked possibility that efforts to increase the principal's leadership may require changes in the behavior of higher administrators.

In addition, the study isolated many characteristics of principals and of their relationships with teachers that appear to have a bearing on their performance. Some of the circumstances positively associated with the principal's professional leadership were: his involvement of his teachers in his decision making, his egalitarian relationships with his staff, the social and administrative support he offers his teachers, his support of teachers in cases of conflict between teacher and pupil, his self-evaluation of his ability to provide professional leadership to his staff, and his interpersonal skills. Many variables that school boards and superintendents typically assume to be correlates of professional leadership of principals were in fact not related to it; for example, the amount of teaching or previous administrative experience. Some of these findings suggest the types of issues that need consideration in in-service training programs for principals. Others suggest criteria that may deserve greater consideration in the selection of school principals.

Some school superintendents have informed us that their exposure to sociological studies of school systems or the perspectives of the sociologists has been especially valuable in suggesting courses of action that they later employed in coping with problems encountered in their relationships with their school board and their staffs. For example, several established the practice of holding orientation meetings with new school-board members in order to achieve greater consensus on the respective rights and obligations of the superintendent and school-board members. Another superintendent indicated that he and several other school administrators had taken the leadership in persuading the state associations of school superintendents and school-board members jointly to sponsor seminars that focused on strains and tensions in the superintendent–school-board relationship and methods to alleviate them. He indicated that the major reason for the acceptance of this idea could be attributed to the findings of sociological studies on common sources of stress in the school-board–superintendent relationship. He also indicated that the code of ethics for board members that resulted from these seminars had materially reduced his problems with his own school board. Another superintendent reported that as a consequence of his exposure to the sociological treatment of the authority-professionalism dilemma in schools, he had candidly discussed this problem with both his teachers' association and his principals and then, in collaboration with them, had developed a set of ground rules to cover areas that constituted sources of long-standing stress and strain in their relationships.

Limitations of space, or because they are treated elsewhere in this volume, preclude our examination of the possible usefulness of many other sociological studies for educational administrators in their efforts to cope with some of their salient problems; for example, improving the academic achievement of Negro children in slum schools,[87] upgrading the performance of underachievers,[88] securing acceptance of innovations,[89] improving school-press relationships,[90] improving the guidance program,[91] dealing with problems of adolescents,[92] the use of tests,[93] and obtaining greater financial support from their communities.[94] As in the case of the two problem areas we have extensively considered, most of these studies suggest that sociological factors in and out of the schools need to be taken into account in diagnosing educational problems and offer clues to possible courses of action that might be explored or experimented with in efforts to circumvent or surmount them.

MAKES EDUCATIONAL ADMINISTRATORS AWARE
OF THE UTILITY OF SOCIOLOGICAL
RESEARCH TECHNIQUES FOR COPING WITH
THEIR PROBLEMS

Sociological research techniques may be used to secure data that will be of help to education administrators in their planning and decision making. A suburban school system in Michigan used the survey technique to obtain information about the attitudes of the residents of its community to proposed changes in the educational curriculum, to an increase in school taxes, and to the performance of its schools.[95] The success of a vote to increase school taxes was attributed by the school administration primarily to the availability of the data to guide its planning and strategy. As a consequence of the data obtained from the study, the school administration was able to allocate its energies and time more efficiently by focusing its attention on sections of the community that were ill informed about school problems and by clarifying educational issues on which there was considerable misunderstanding in the school district.

THE SOCIOLOGICAL PERSPECTIVE:
SOME ESPECIALLY STRATEGIC IDEAS

Our research and consulting activities have brought us in contact with numerous educational officials who are attempting to cope with many complex problems. In these encounters we have become acutely aware that if the cognitive structures[96] of more officials at the several levels of government, in the foundations, and in educational institutions had included certain ideas that arise from a sociological and social psychological, in addition to other, perspectives—for example, operations analysis or simple economic or psychological models—in their diagnosis of educational problems and in the development of plans and programs to solve or minimize them, their deliberations and decisions would have been more realistic and the chances of their successful implementation would have been materially increased. The benefits from the expenditure of hundreds of millions of dollars of governmental funds in recent years designed to improve the curriculums and practices in both urban and rural schools and in other types of educational establishments have in many instances been embarrassingly small.

There are undoubtedly many reasons for this apparent inefficient use of resources, including the shortage of competent personnel, the haste and lack of careful planning that have characterized so many projects initiated in Washington, D.C., and at state and local levels, and the lack of experimental and developmental studies to test out schemes that appear practical on a common-sense basis. But it is our judgment, after observing a number of these widely heralded innovations come to naught and talking with personnel involved in them, that other, and perhaps more basic, circumstances may be involved. They are suggested by a sociological or social-psychological perspective on these varied educational programs.

First, few officials take seriously the notion that nearly all new educational plans and programs must be implemented by individuals who occupy positions in networks of social relationships in organizational settings. These personnel hold conceptions of the objectives of educational institutions and of their roles in them. A sociological perspective suggests that the way they react to new ideas and programs and the effort they make to implement them will in large measure be attributable to the degree to which they are compatible with their role definitions and their view of the mission of their organization. Most major educational innovations—for example, team teaching, the nongraded school, programs based on the Higher Horizons approach—require a redefinition of the teacher's and principal's role if they are to have a chance to succeed. Many teachers may need to be resocialized—that is, to view themselves as members of a total organization and as part of a total socialization process—if schools serving disadvantaged children are to achieve their educational objectives. But we see small evidence of planning and strategies directed to this simple but fundamental idea.

Second, there appears to be little awareness of one of the central findings of the sociological literature on the diffusion and acceptance of innovations: the *way* innovations are introduced may be as significant as *what* is introduced.[97] Third, there are many other agencies of socialization; for example, the family, the church, and peer groups may be as important as, or more important than, school personnel in motivating children.[98] The major thrust of educational programs and the allocation of resources, as Moynihan suggests,[99] may be misdirected. Fourth, few officials appear to recognize that the introduction of educational innovations into a school sets in motion a complex social process and that the response to innovations by members of an organization will probably be influenced by a number of social-system and interpersonal forces. Fifth, many educational planners forget or overlook the large-scale bureaucratic characteristics of school systems, and hence some of the major obstacles to change may be located in an aspect of their managerial apparatus that can be readily overlooked: the sector including officials such as deputy, associate, and assistant superintendents, who serve as the intermediate links between the school superintendent and individual schools. Sixth, educational officials in their plans to solve certain school problems, such as de facto segregation, ignore the implications of the operation of ecological processes that result in population concentration and dispersion and reveal the necessity of thinking in terms of the social, in contrast to the legal, community.

Some Improper Uses of the Findings of Sociological Inquiry

Before considering additional ways that sociologists can be of service to individuals responsible for the formulation and implementation of educational objectives and policies and the benefits that sociologists and their discipline may derive from their investment of time and energy in such endeavors, we think it important to examine dysfunctional consequences and difficulties that have arisen from these exchanges. There is no doubt that when many educational administrators and some sociologists have attempted to apply *the research findings* of sociology, they have ignored or failed to recognize the hazards and dangers involved. In addition, one or both parties in transactions of this kind have sometimes been jarred by the experience and have been exposed to considerable stress in these encounters.

We now consider a number of ways in which the findings of sociological studies have been inappropriately applied to problems confronting educational administrators; in the next section, we draw attention to some of the major types and sources of stress and strain that have arisen in relationships between sociologists and their educational clients. These matters demand consideration in a treatment of the use of sociology for educational practitioners because it is our belief that failure to recognize them has materially reduced the value both parties have derived from encounters of this kind in the past.

Among the many improper uses of the findings of sociological studies, in our judgment seven are especially serious. The first stems from a failure to recognize fundamental differences in the analytic frameworks typically employed by educational executives and social scientists. Sociologists, especially those who develop theories and test hypotheses, generally focus on selected aspects of the empirical phenomena with which they are concerned, and therefore they usually test propositions that involve only a small set of variables. The theoretical framework or concepts they use specify the types of phenomena to be studied and the particular ways in which they will be viewed. That is, most sociological analyses, like all scientific analyses, are both *abstract* and *selective*. In contrast to the social scientist, who deliberately restricts the number of variables he examines and views them in an abstract manner, the administrator always works in a concrete setting and needs to take into account many variables which the sociologist may ignore in his analysis. These multidimensional forces in the administrator's work milieu also contain elements that are unique, at least in their combination or importance, to his situation. He needs to consider all possibly relevant variables that he judges might have any significant impact on the particular problem he is attempting to solve. In addition, most administrators are unaware that the sociologist's basic research strategy is typically to focus his analysis on the relationship between a few independent variables and a single dependent one and to attempt to control, if at all possible, other variables that may confound the relationship he is examining. But these third variables, in some instances, could be critical factors for the education problem that the administrator wants to solve. In designing and attempting to solve organizational problems, the educational executive first must attempt to isolate the complex of relevant circumstances and conditions, including social, psychological, economic, and other types of forces operating within his organization or outside of it; then he has to assign weights to those variables he assesses as of greatest importance; and finally he must make a decision based on his calculations and frequently his hunches. He needs to see the problem confronting him in its full complexity. Thus, the administrator who believes that he can directly apply the findings of most sociological inquiries to his own situation is usually operating on a spurious assumption: that a limited and deliberately restricted perspective toward the analysis of social behavior constitutes an adequate view for an administrator's diagnosis of the complexities of his situation.

A second misapplication of the findings of sociological studies derives from the failure to realize that they typically apply only to specified conditions or in particular contexts. They may not hold under other sets of conditions, and this is a circumstance that many educational administrators, and some sociologists who advise them, unfortunately overlook. Conclusions derived from data ascertained to isolate determinants of leadership in industrial organizations may or may not be applicable to educational settings. Findings about conditions associated with learning outcomes in suburban school systems may not hold for schools in slum areas. Whether or not research results obtained from the study of small decision-making groups in laboratory settings are applicable to classrooms is a moot question: a decision-making group is not necessarily the same as a group of individuals engaged in a process of socialization.

A third abuse is the result of misinterpreting correlations between variables as necessary indicators of causal relationships. The findings of most sociological studies that reveal relationships between variables can typically be interpreted only as showing that some form of association exists between them, and the association may be symmetrical or asymmetrical. Cause-and-effect relationships are extremely difficult to demonstrate in sociological inquiry, even in panel studies or in those that use laboratory settings. This red flag must be constantly kept in view in interpreting and applying the findings of sociological studies.

Fourth is the failure to realize that sociological hypotheses that receive empirical support refer to classes of events, not to individual cases. An illustration of this misuse of sociological studies that we have frequently encountered is the way many educators interpret the large body of data that support hypotheses about the relationship between social class and variables such as the academic achievement, social participation, or educational aspirations of students.[100] They ignore the fact that although the evidence indicates that each of these student characteristics is related to social class, research findings also consistently reveal variance in each of these dependent variables among children from the same social class. For example, a substantial proportion of lower-class youth have high educational aspirations, and a minority of students from upper-class families do not.

A fifth misinterpretation of sociological studies stems from the following circumstance: lack of understanding of the rationale underlying the conservative stance taken by many sociologists when they use tests of statistical significance in interpretating their sample findings. Unless a finding is significant statistically at below the .05 level, most social scientists still do not claim support for a hypothesis. However, in many cases, for certain types of decisions the practitioner needs to make, such a criterion may be too rigid; conversely, results significant statistically at the .001 level may still have little or no practical significance in respect to practical applications.

Another abuse of a more general nature deserves emphasis. We have encountered educational administrators who too easily overbuy the findings of social-science inquiries and some sociologists who apparently have attempted to oversell them. Most administrators of school systems and some in the institutions of higher learning are not aware that sociology emerged as an analytical science centrally involved with the structure and functioning of social systems only at the beginning of the twentieth century. And prior to World War I only a small group of sociologists showed any interest in developing theories capable of empirical verification. Merton's observations about the current state of affairs in sociology in the 1950's is still essentially applicable today:

> One must admit that a large part of what is now called sociological theory consists of *general orientations toward data, suggesting types of variables which need somehow to be taken into account, rather than clear, verifiable statements of relationships between specified variables.* We have many concepts but few confirmed theories; many points of view, but few theorems; many "approaches," but few arrivals.[101]

The final misuse of sociological inquiries is one that we believe deserves special stress. The danger is that sociologists may too quickly assume that when in their research studies that bear on questions of public policy they demonstrate an association between an independent and dependent variable for which the evidence suggests a causal relationship, they then also have found the answer to questions about the way to prevent or solve a practical problem. Most social scientists who have fallen into this illogic would undoubtedly admit that there is a difference between isolating the cause of dental cavities and finding ways to eliminate them. They would also probably accept the distinction between isolating the cause of polio-myelitis and finding vaccines to prevent it. Yet, in their studies that bear on issues of public policy, some social scientists, including sociologists, have overlooked these critical distinctions. This tendency, in our judg-ment, is especially alarming in such fields as public housing, welfare, and education. Numerous programs have been adopted on the recommenda-tions of social scientists as a consequence of the implications they have drawn from purely correlational studies. In many cases, the issue of causa-tion is never even raised; even if causal relationships are demonstrated, we would contend, that because an individual knows the cause of a problem he does not necessarily know how to solve it or prevent its occurrence in the future. Psychiatrists can testify to this point eloquently.

Although we could cite many cases of this type of fallacy in the litera-ture (pick at random almost any recent book reporting findings on "deter-minants" of juvenile delinquency, the dropout rate, academic achieve-ment, student subcultures, and so on and examine the final chapter on "implications" of the findings or the section on recommendations), we see little point in doing so. At times we have become disturbed by the conclu-sions educators sometimes draw about our observations in regard to *"pos-sible* implications for practice" of our own research findings. As has been the case for other sociologists who have carried out studies that bear on educational problems, we too have been quite frequently exposed to the expectation that, since we have done research on a particular problem, we have an obligation to offer an *unequivocal* answer to some pressing practi-cal problem of the schools. The problem we have raised is a complicated one and involves a host of subissues, but limitations of space preclude our discussing them here.

But there is one hazard for sociologists involved in the matter under consideration that demands treatment at this point. It is that unless sociol-ogists who conduct studies on educational phenomena are not careful, they may join that group of persons who may be described as the "medi-cine men" of education. We are referring to individuals, many of whom are talented persons with distinguished reputations in education or other fields, who sell their ideas to professional educators about "needed" inno-vations in schools even though there is no empirical evidence to support their claims for their ideas or wares. A great deal of money and energy has been expended and is currently being spent in introducing, instituting, and attempting to gain acceptance of large-scale innovations, the merits of which are problematic at best.

What does this imply for sociologists whose research deals with issues of importance to education? Not only does it imply that they need to be acutely aware of the limitations as well as the possible uses of their work for educational practice; in addition, it suggests the need for a type of research that has been infrequently done in the sociology of education and in other subfields of sociology. We have in mind experimental and evaluation studies whose designs are suggested by inquiries that attempt to isolate possible determinants or effects of sociological and educationally relevant variables. If, for example, as we already know, parents' attitudes toward education have a bearing on student learning, we could design experiments to test the utility of different proposed strategies for increasing positive attitudes on the part of parents toward learning by measuring their educational effects. A few studies of this experimental or evaluative kind have been carried out by sociologists. Brookover and his associates,[102] for example, have performed experiments designed to heighten self-concept and then have ascertained their educational effects. Lippitt[103] has conducted experiments in an effort to isolate the most effective methods to cope with the problems of "deviant" children in elementary-school classrooms. The studies of Sherif *et al.*,[104] Hyman *et al.*,[105] and Meyer *et al.*,[106] constitute noteworthy examples in our judgment of efforts to evaluate or test the utility of proposed solutions to problems of relevance to educators. Not only would additional studies of this type be of considerable value to educators, but when based on carefully developed theoretical formulations they could also add in important respects to our limited storehouse of sociological knowledge.

To sum up: not only must we be cautious in drawing conclusions for men of practical affairs from our correlational studies. In addition, sociologists who conduct such investigations and who desire on occasion to utilize their skills in efforts to improve educational practice or to be of service to educational executives need to take the next step: they need to carry out experimental and evaluative inquiries, a type of research that, as we shall indicate later, could have significant effects for theory as well as for practice.

Problems Encountered in the Relationship between Sociologists and Their Educational Clients

SOME PROBLEMS OF THE CLIENT

We and other sociologists have noted that officials in school systems, the government, and institutions of higher education, including professors in departments of educational administration, have at times experienced major difficulties in working with sociologists because they had little or no awareness of the possible unanticipated consequences of these relationships. This lack of awareness was attributable in some cases to the inexperience of educational "clients" with respect to objective research as a means of arriving at informed decisions. In other cases, it resulted from the fact that the services of sociologists were sought largely because it had become fashionable to involve social scientists in educational training programs or because a school system hoped to use a sociologist as a means to escape from external or internal pressures. In addition, some clients have engaged sociologists without fully realizing that such efforts may well call for the reallocation of scarce commodities such as time, money, personnel, and space or a challenge to some of their basic premises. Thus, the very process of consultation, even when delimited to the less "sensitive" information-providing domain, has in some instances raised new problems, exacerbated conflict, and aroused opposition. This has apparently occurred most frequently when sensitive issues are involved, as in value conflicts between a superintendent and his school board or when the very appointment of a sociologist has itself been a matter on which strong differences of opinion have been voiced.

Some clients also have found that the *outcome or product* of the services sociologists have provided have at times raised new and unexpected problems. They have belatedly recognized that the knowledge or advice tendered by the sociologist has in some cases been controversial, impractical to apply, or completely unanticipated. Their views or recommendations have upset some clients (or certain subcategories of clients) and left them not only with the original problem but with the additional one of what to do with the tendered advice or information. When, for example, a sociological consultant discovered that the basic problem of a school system was the lack of confidence teachers had in their school board, the superintendent and the board were at a loss about how to deal with it: they considered at great length whether it should be presented to the general public or only to a restricted audience or whether it should be quietly filed away so that it could "do no damage."

Since educational clients frequently want sociological advice or information so as to escape from public-relations problems, they typically do not want the advice or information provided by the consultant used to increase these problems. As a result, some sociologists have observed that educational clients are more receptive to sociological advice and information when they deal with the less powerful constituents or the less central aspects of the educational process (such as extracurricular activities or resident or service arrangements) than when advice or information deals with components of the power or authority structure of the school system or the community.

Educational clients, as noted, frequently turn to sociological consultants in a context of educational conflict. Such conflict may involve lifelong habits, strong prejudices, primordial loyalties, and thinly disguised personal or group advantage. Is it any wonder, then, that the sociological consultant, who defines his role as a spokesman for objective, data-oriented rationality, may be viewed with considerable ambivalence? Some naïvely expect him to reveal the royal road to salvation, that is, to provide advice or information that will point the way to risk-free reforms. The sociologist as a consultant or as a participant in preparation programs for educational administrators is quite likely to shock and lose his initial supporters either by pointing out that the problems they recognize are surface problems which must be viewed quite differently if the underlying factors are to be grasped or by pointing out that the circumstances involved are extremely complex and that sociological knowledge about them is insufficient to provide specific recommendations.

PROBLEMS OF THE SOCIOLOGIST

Some sociologists who have accepted assignments in programs for training educational administrators have experienced "cultural shock." They find themselves in an unfamiliar part of the university terrain that operates with different standards and holds a somewhat different conception of the academic role from the one to which they had become accustomed. The experiences they encounter appear to be highly similar to those reported by social scientists who work in the fields of public health and nursing.[107]

One difficulty is the different set of expectations a sociologist and his colleagues in educational administration apply to his performance. Above everything else his associates usually expect him to make "practical" contributions to their programs. They want him to accept their judgment as to what constitutes a contribution to their activities. They may downgrade basic research and theoretical approaches to problems. They desire answers to on-the-job problems of practitioners, and he is seldom able to supply them. Furthermore, he is frequently expected to work as a member of a team that includes educational administrators, an economist, a political scientist, and other kinds of social scientists. Differences in their values and their biases about the use of theory and the criteria to be employed in evaluating research serve to block communication and create barriers to accomplishment. It is not surprising, then, that a number of these collaborative ventures have been characterized by tension and conflict.

Sociologists in these programs are frequently exposed to unrealistic role expectations. School officials and professors of educational administration typically have little realization of the complexity of the sociological enterprise and that the sociologists in their midst is competent in only one or a few areas. Those sociologists who, in their zeal to demonstrate the utility of sociology, attempt to meet these unrealistic expectations not surprisingly experience considerable frustration and stress.

Some sociologists involved in training programs for educational administrators report that they were overwhelmed by the variety of tasks in which they were asked to engage. Their previous academic experience had typically been restricted to teaching and research activities. In these programs, however, they are normally expected to carry out segments of field studies directed by other members of the staff, prepare reports in nontechnical language on their findings, participate in the innumerable staff conferences that characterize these programs, meet frequently with students to discuss their problems, address conferences of practicing administrators, and attend a whole series of state, regional, and national meetings of educational administrators. Fulfilling these expectations leaves them little or no time to conduct their own sociological studies, with the result that they worry about their professional reputation in sociological circles.

Suchman[108] has noted that one of the most important problems confronting sociologists in public health is that of role identification. A similar condition exists for the sociologist involved in training programs for educational administrators. Heavy demands on his time may result in infrequent contact with colleagues in the sociology department, and he is likely to be the single sociologist in his work unit. Further, since he is usually a member of a small staff dominated by educational administrators, there are strong group pressures on him to identify with the values and norms of their subculture, one that, as noted, varies greatly from that to which he has formerly been accustomed. Since his background and training are quite different from those of his educational colleagues, he does not always find it easy to identify with them. For some sociologists this clearly represents an identity crisis, one most easily resolved by removing themselves from the situation. This may account in part for the relatively heavy turnover rate among sociologists in programs of this kind.

To this point we have focused on sociologists who have been involved in training programs for educational administrators. Now we turn to problems encountered by consultants to school systems. One is similar to a difficulty they can experience when they have attempted to offer their wares to administrators-in-training: many school-board members and professional schoolmen do not recognize the difference between sociological and nonsociological problems; at times, they do not differentiate between research and social bookkeeping. They approach the sociologist on the basis of his "recognized interest in education" rather than on the basis of any great appropriateness of fit between the problem they have in mind and the sociologist's interests and qualifications. This circumstance frequently results in the consultant's attempting to find a sociological problem for the educational client rather than working on the one that is proffered. The problem defined by the sociologist may actually be a "better" problem (a more important, more basic, more clean-cut, or more novel problem) than the one the client initially had in mind. The client himself may agree that this is so. Nevertheless, the initial problem may crop up unexpectedly on various occasions, particularly toward the end of a consultant's services, and most particularly if these services have not relieved the client from pressures initially exerted on him or if they have exposed him to new ones.

Advice and findings are especially subject to being viewed as unilluminating (if not downright unintelligible) because of a basic difference between education and sociology. Education, as an operation, is most frequently concerned with finding the best compromise solution for system-wide (or unit-wide) operation. Sociology, as a discipline, is accustomed to differentiating *within* systems or structures or aggregates so as to determine the particular contexts or conditions under which particular circumstances apply to one subset rather than to another. Thus, when a sociologist caters to clients' needs for over-all system-wide advice or information he can usually provide only a generally sensitizing perspective or "way of viewing." Although the sociological perspective may not be familiar to the client (and therefore a possible addition to the clients' intellectual repertoire) it is nevertheless unlikely to provide complete solutions oriented to the specifics of any given context. On the other hand, when a sociological consultant provides more detailed contextual analyses (assuming that he can do so in understandable language) he is likely to crisscross the organizational-structural levels established and recognized by educators. As a result he is inclined to point to needs or approaches that cannot be met or implemented unless the basic structure is changed or altered. Many charges of "gobbledegook" are due to such differences between educational and sociological lines of analysis and action.

Value differences between the sociologist and his clients constitute an additional source of his role problems. They have both expected and unexpected consequences. Among the former are varying views concerning the confidentiality of data and the nature of line-staff relationships. Board members and administrators of educational systems sometimes develop a proprietary or paternalistic attitude toward the system and its personnel. The sociologist, on the other hand, is accustomed to think of himself as an unencumbered scientist whose impartiality and independence are not affected by the consultant-client relationship. Nevertheless, this very self-image may well lead the sociologist who is exposed to new pressures to ask himself, "For whom am I really working: for the administrator, for the staff, for the community, for science?"

A more subtle consequence is the conviction of some professional educators that the sociologist cannot be counted on "when the heat is on." Education, like diplomacy, is frequently an "art of the possible." In the pursuit of this art its practitioners develop a form of phatic communion based on similar experiences, similar expectations, and similar understandings. When a consultant is needed "in order to help bring about changes the desirability of which is already known" it is simpler and safer to pick a consultant who also *knows* that the changes in question are desirable, who is aware how difficult it is to bring about changes in the world of education, who realizes the full complexity of internal and external pressures exerted on the system, and whose basic assumptions and values can be counted on to provide the justification and authoritative backing needed by those on the educational firing line. In comparison with many professors in the more traditional specialty fields of schools of education, the sociologist is likely to be deficient in all these respects. As a result, the appointment of a sociological consultant may be considered a threat or a risk rather than an aid by many professional educational leaders. There may be much truth to this view, particularly when a lay board has engaged the consultant. This attitude apparently accounts for the negative reception accorded the findings or advice of certain sociological consultants. It may also account for the relatively briefer relationships of school systems with sociological consultants than with consultants from other backgrounds. Long-term relationships between sociologists and educational clients, in which reservoirs of mutual understanding and experiences are built up, are still quite rare.

Although the distinction between "sociological adviser" and "sociological fact finder" is frequently made, sociologists sometimes find it difficult to separate these roles. They appear to be more comfortable in the fact-finding role, and their consultation is usually requested in order to discharge responsibilities within this capacity. Nevertheless, most sociological fact finders are also pressed to go beyond the role that they have accepted. Many find this distressing. They are uncomfortable when they are asked "what to do" rather than "how to understand."

Sociologists frequently request that educational leaders, lay and professional, clearly and fully define their goals and purposes, for without such definitions evaluations and recommendations are impossible. However, education has immediate and long-range goals, tangible and intangible ones, cognitive and noncognitive goals and subgoals that are subscribed to in varying degrees of consciousness and articulateness. Neither the goals, the priorities attached to them, nor their proponents are likely to remain unaltered during the time it takes to conduct a study or evaluate a program.

However, by far the greater share of ambivalence toward sociological rationality is manifested by educators who have become quite experienced and sophisticated with respect to "staying alive" in the world of education. In working with such individuals, sociologists report great cynicism toward research and expert opinion. On the one hand, the *Zeitgeist* is viewed as favoring expert opinion, objective "hard" data, and support for research (even pure research) under educational auspices. On the other hand, some of these "old-timers" already know the answers they want or do not want and are involved in "practical steps" that will lead to the point of view or decisions they favor. Furthermore, many professors of educational administration and school superintendents recognize that educational decision making is frequently a resultant of "power politics" and "behind-the-scenes" compromises. As a result they at times tend to be cynical or pessimistic concerning the research or expert opinion of the sociologist. Thus, the sociologist must learn to labor in the midst of clients many of whom are convinced that his activities are (1) "political" in nature or being used to delay decisions, (2) unlikely to come up with anything new, (3) unlikely to provide anything useful, or (4) unlikely to make any difference, since "the system" responds primarily to public pressure and entrenched interest. Such views are reported most frequently by sociologists who have served in one consultative capacity or another for large city school systems or work in training programs with professors of educational administration who have cherished views based on "common-sense" interpretations of their own restricted experiences. It is in large urban school systems (where, by the way, "research divisions" are most frequently encountered in boards of education) that research and consultation are most frequently viewed as bureaucratic mechanisms that large-scale organizations simply must endure in order to introduce changes whose wisdom has already been established or to obstruct innovations that could shift power relationships.

Finally, surrounding the complex of goals is the ubiquitous factor of morality. A good deal of what takes place in American education is designed not only to make man wise, not only to provide him with skills, but to make him good, kind, just, ethical, healthy, mature, and democratic. If the advice-giving role makes many sociologists uncomfortable, the moral issues surrounding education make them even more so. Awareness of cultural relativity, awareness of the distance between values and behavior, scientific objectivity, and penchant for intellectualization all combine to make most sociologists wary of contributing directly to the definition and attainment of educational goals at the level of a particular system at a particular time and place. This wariness is likely to disappoint one or another segment of the educational clientele searching for allies in the struggle for better education and a better life. This disappointment contributes to criticism of the sociological consultant as being vague, impractical, inconclusive, and so on. Such criticism may be fully justified to the extent that our lack of concern for educational-societal goals leads the sociologist to prolong the well-nigh exclusive use of more superficial criteria of "educational success" such as test scores, grade averages, rate of tax support, teacher salaries, and the like.[109]

In summary, a small number of communication problem "types" or "clusters" are recognizable. Communication problems may arise either due to poor "output" (the sociologist uses "jargon" in his findings; the educators cannot clearly explain what they want from the consultant) or due to poor "input" (the sociologist considers the educators naïve and does not really listen to them; the educators consider the sociologist impractical and misinterpret what he says). Given these two sources of errors and the two different parties to the relationship, the typology presented in Table 11–1 indicates four kinds of communication problems illustrated in previous sections of this chapter.

TABLE 11–1. *Types of Recurring Communication Problems between Sociologists and Educational Administrators*

| | | AGENT | |
		SOCIOLOGIST	SCHOOL ADMINISTRATOR
Source of Error	Output	1	2
	Input	3	4

Sociologists are most likely to recognize problems of types 2 and 4, in which the educational administrator is the active or passive "cause." Educational administrators are most likely to recognize problems of types 1 and 3, in which the sociologist is to "blame." However, if already existing difficulties in cross-cultural communication are not to be further complicated by simplex views of reality, it is also necessary to recognize that in any Goffmanesque occasion either one or *both* agents may be simultaneously contributing to *both* sources of error. Thus, rather than assume a typology of discrete communication problems, we must recognize that we are faced by a set of very broad co-occurrence events in which the presence of one type of error merely increases the likelihood of another error of the same or of a different type.

Improving Collaborative Relationships

While personality conflicts undoubtedly account for some of the problems that have arisen, we submit that the root of many of the difficulties may be traced to circumstances such as *dissensus* on values, ambiguity in role definition, and the different perspectives and assumptions of the parties to the relationship. Much more than good will is required if they are to be overcome. What is needed is an understanding of the sources of potential stress at the outset of the collaboration and systematic procedures to discuss and develop ground rules to cope with these problems at the earliest possible time.[110] We conclude this discussion with six sets of tentative propositions that we and our colleagues in our consulting activities have found useful and that may be of some value to other sociologists interested in working with clients in the field of education.

1. Recognize the adversary nature of many educational endeavors; differentiate between the expectations of subgroups of the clientele; attempt to find out precisely *what* is wanted from the sociological consultant and *why* it is wanted; and decide whether you can and whether you want to provide what the various (contending) subgroups desire.

2. Consider whether it is necessary to redefine the client's conception of his problems if your services are to be of value to him.

3. Try to educate educational clients with respect to the limits and potentialities of the logic and techniques of social inquiry. However, recognize the dangers in leading educational clients away from the topics and concerns uppermost in their minds.

4. Express your findings, interpretations, and recommendations briefly and simply, so as to be understandable to nonspecialists. Remember that sociology may have little validated knowledge with respect to certain educational operations and that it may be premature to apply even the most conceptually coherent views in specific contexts without appropriate contextual analysis.

5. Consider carefully what sensitizing concepts, substantive information, and types of variables in addition to those previously considered by the client could shed light on his problems and attempt, if at all possible, to relate these to local circumstances rather than to education in general. Stimulate active discussion of your findings or suggestions with respect to their interrelationships, causes, and consequences.

6. Determine how you will handle pressures to enter into direct educational planning, decision making, or goal setting. If you are opposed to such a role, or feel ill equipped to play it, determine whether you can still substantially fulfill the expectations of your clients.

Other Contributions of Sociology to Educational Administration

We have earlier examined the major roles, those of a consultant and a teacher, that sociologists have assumed in their efforts to be of service to educational administrators and the intellectual goods and services they have offered in these capacities, and we have just completed our consideration of some of the major kinds of problems that have arisen for them and their clients in these relationships. Now we turn to another role in which a sociologist could be of service to educational administrators and additional services he might make available to them.

It can be maintained that as full-time staff specialists, sociologists can make their greatest contribution to the administration of school systems.

Although the number of sociologists so employed has undoubtedly increased manifold during the past few years, the total number who work in this capacity is still extremely small.[111] One such individual known to us has occupied such a position for a number of years as the director of a Bureau of Human Relations in a large city school system. Before spelling out our conception of the role of sociologists who might serve in this capacity, it is of interest to see what services this particular official provides to his school system.

One of his central tasks was to anticipate potentially explosive situations for the schools and take steps to minimize the possibility of their occurrence. For example, the school board had adopted a policy that permitted children from crowded schools to attend underused schools in the city. The school administration and the sociologist anticipated serious problems in carrying it out in several sections of the community that were opposed to Negro students' attending schools in their neighborhood. The sociologist identified the key individuals in these areas who were opposed to the plan of the board of education and was able to neutralize their opposition by having local power figures such as the police captain, the alderman, the school principal, the district superintendent, and a representative from the Mayor's Commission on Human Relations call on these individuals and make them aware of the implications of actions that attempted to forestall attendance by Negro children at schools in their area. In short, the sociologist used his knowledge about the nature of a community, its informal opinion leaders, and social control to prevent a potential community crisis by neutralizing the opposition to a policy of the school board.

A second task was to identify informal neighborhood leaders in certain low socioeconomic areas of the community and then to give them training in leadership skills. He was attempting to aid the school administration in coping with its problem of finding communication links with parents of children in underprivileged areas of the community.

A third activity dealt with efforts to improve the climate of "human relations" in the schools. Through workshops for teachers and visits to hundreds of classrooms, an effort was made to isolate basic types of interpersonal problems that confront teachers in their classes. A course focused on these problems has been given over sixty times through the local teachers' college and the "television college" of the school system. The teachers' assessment of the course is reported to be quite positive.

Are there other ways sociologists who might serve as full-time staff specialists can be useful to the administration of school systems? We think that there are and would suggest that a new role, school-system sociologist, be established to maximize the knowledge and skills of sociologists for the benefit of operation of educational systems.

School systems, particularly those of large cities, need expert help in viewing themselves as *systems* and in recognizing their *relatedness to other systems*. Public education is being increasingly influenced by changes in industry, commerce, demography, housing, government, and higher education. The steady decline in unskilled jobs due to automation, the in-migration of hitherto rural and small-town white and Negro residents, the out-migration of the middle class to suburban areas, urban redevelopment, the pressure on education to "do something" about nearly every major social problem (even when neither the problems nor their solutions are substantially within the school's control)—all these add up to a growing need for school systems to employ social scientists who can interpret social change and examine its implications for public education. In addition, school personnel need to be made aware that many educational problems—for example, school dropouts, desegregation, vandalism, education of the child in the slum school, and increasing the level of educational aspiration of talented students—can be realistically dealt with only in collaboration and co-operation with other community institutions and agencies. Furthermore, educational administrators require individuals who can help them analyze dysfunctional aspects of present organizational arrangements of their school systems in efforts to make them more efficient and effective. Sociologists serving as staff specialists to the school administration might well be made responsible for the analysis of these intra-system and intersystem problems and could serve in key capacities in attempts to resolve them.

It is disconcerting to see many educational institutions attempting to cope with extremely complex social-system problems with models derived primarily from the psychology of individual differences, individual psychodynamics, and individual conflict resolution. The recognition given these models a quarter-century or more ago brought a new panoply of full-time auxiliary workers to the field of education: school psychologists, guidance counselors, psychoeducational researchers, and others. As noted, there is a growing awareness among educational officials that the analysis of many of the basic problems of their organzations requires other perspectives. This recognition will almost certainly usher in a greater utilization of sociologists and other social scientists in American public education during the coming decade. We shall thus be able to test our belief that sociologists, as full-time staff associates of school administrators, are in a position to be of considerable service to them in coping with their complex managerial responsibilities.

Sociologists also can help in the resolution of salient problems confronting the schools by applying their perspectives, concepts, analytic skills, and research techniques to the analysis of the *assumptions* underlying local, state, and federal programs designed to improve public education. A number of these programs assume that the major forces influencing learning are the personal characteristics of students. They ignore many interpersonal influences and social structural and normative conditions in schools that may influence learning outcomes. Sociologists need to make those individuals who formulate educational policies and programs aware that two schools with pupils from similar socioeconomic backgrounds may vary greatly in their "academic productivity" and thus that social-system variables, as well as personal ones, may influence academic achievement.[112] They need to emphasize that educational programs are carried out by people in social settings and that the images they have of their own roles, the mission of schools, and the social influences operating on pupils may constitute important variables in determining the success of school programs. They need to make educational policy makers and individuals who implement them aware that children are exposed to *multiple* socialization agencies and that programs that ignore the possible countervailing influences of peer groups, the family, and other agencies of socialization may be largely doomed from the outset. They need to make them aware that in addition to allocating resources to the planning of new programs, there is also an urgent need to plan, develop, and test the effectiveness of different strategies for the introduction and acceptance by faculties of "proven" innovations. We are also of the opinion that the insights and perspectives of the sociologist could have important effects on the development of more efficient and effective educational programs. To have maximum impact, they need to be buttressed by systematic and rigorous studies, primarily of an experimental nature, that demonstrate the educational consequences of proposed innovations and of the effectiveness of different strategies to facilitate the process of educational change. A strong case could be developed in support of the proposition that the greatest contribution of sociologists to the educational administrator will derive from their analysis of the validity of the basic assumptions underlying the teaching, learning, and social arrangements that presently take place in the schools, their critical appraisal of proposed programs to improve them, and their sustained research efforts designed to examine the utility of alternative schemes for maximizing student learning that are based on sociological as well as on other types of assumptions.

One final point. It has been our experience that our consulting activities and our participation in programs designed to prepare executives for their occupational roles have yielded some of our most valued learning experiences as sociologists. We have found, as a consequence of such activities, that many of our theoretical ideas had to be discarded or modified and that certain assumptions we had long held about social systems and social relationships were tenuous. Educational establishments are social systems, and the relationships between a teacher and a pupil and between a president and his deans are social relationships; and if our basic assumptions and theories have any validity, they should facilitate, not block, our ability to shed light on these social phenomena. We have on several occasions found that the concepts, theoretical notions, and even our ideas about research methods were of little value in attempting to diagnose problems that were clearly sociological in nature. For example, in attempting to determine why the higher administration of a school system was experiencing so much difficulty in introducing new educational programs into the schools, one of us found that existing theories of social change offered little of value in obtaining leverage on this problem. The problems we encountered also forced us to re-examine the assumptions underlying these formulations and to develop a quite different theoretical model to deal with it. Furthermore, if the empirical findings indicate that the theoretical analysis we were forced to develop in our efforts to diagnose this problem is heuristic, we then propose to conduct experimental studies to test the utility of several different strategies to speed up the acceptance of educational innovations that are suggested by this same theoretical scheme. This example suggests that many commonly held assumptions about the distinction between pure and applied sociology deserve critical reappraisal.[113] It also implies that a concern for the "practical" problems of social systems may lead to important theoretical advances in our discipline; for example, the development of more heuristic theories of social and cultural change.

REFERENCES

1. Paul F. Lazarsfeld, "The Social Sciences and Educational Administration," in Lawrence W. Downey and Frederick Enns, eds., *The Social Sciences and Educational Administration* (Edmonton: Division of Educational Administration, University of Alberta, 1963).
2. *Ibid.*, p. 12.
3. From a private conversation with a president of a large university in the eastern region of the United States.
4. From an interview with the superintendent of schools of a big city school system in the East. The respondent was guaranteed anonymity.
5. For valuable contributions to this general problem area, see Alvin W. Gouldner and S. M. Miller, eds., *Applied Sociology: Opportunities and Problems* (New York: The Free Press of Glencoe, 1965); Warren G. Bennis, "Theory and Method in Applying Behavioral Science to Planned Organizational Change," *Journal of Applied Behavioral Science*, I (1965), 337–360; and Hans L. Zetterberg, *Social Theory and Social Practice* (Totowa, N.J.: Bedminster Press, 1962).
6. Sociologists have served as consultants to Commissioners of Education or State Boards of Education in New York, Michigan, Pennsylvania, California, and many other states and to regional boards of higher education in all parts of the United States.
7. Several of the state universities in the Midwest and in the East have made more or less regular use of sociologists as consultants on internal and external problems confronting their institutions. In addition, both large and small foundations have used the consulting services of sociologists in efforts to cope with organizational problems as well as decisions bearing on the allocation of their resources.
8. For discussions of this kind, see Albert J. Reiss, Jr., ed., *Schools in a Changing Society* (New York: The Free Press of Glencoe, 1965).

9. In the following books, for example, the authors attempt to draw possible implications of their findings for educational practice: James S. Coleman, *The Adolescent Society* (New York: The Free Press of Glencoe, 1961); Neal Gross and Robert E. Herriott, *Staff Leadership in Public Schools* (New York: Wiley, 1965); David A. Goslin, *The Search for Ability: Standardized Testing in Social Perspective* (New York: Russell Sage Foundation, 1963).

10. For a very thoughtful consideration of the relationship to, and impact of the social sciences on, educational administration see Laurence D. Haskew, "A Projective Appraisal," in Daniel E. Griffiths, ed., *Behavioral Science and Educational Administration*, The Sixty-third Yearbook of the National Society for the Study of Education, Part II (Chicago: National Society for the Study of Education, 1964), pp. 333–348. Also, see Roald F. Campbell and James M. Lipham, eds., *Administrative Theory as a Guide to Action* (Chicago: Midwest Administration Center, University of Chicago, 1960).

11. Among the many references dealing with the sociology of higher education, the following will serve as useful introductions to this topic: Allen H. Barton, *Studying the Effects of College Education* (New Haven, Conn.: Edward W. Hazen Foundation, 1959). Burton R. Clark, "The 'Cooling-out' Function in Higher Education," *American Journal of Sociology*, LXV (1960), 569–576; also *The Open Door College* (New York: McGraw-Hill, 1960). Joshua A. Fishman, ed., "The Social Psychology of School to College Transition," *Journal of Educational Sociology*, XXXIII (1960), No. 6 (entire issue); also "Social-psychological Theory for Selecting and Guiding College Students," *American Journal of Sociology*, LXVI (1961), 472–484. Neal Gross, "Organizational Lag in American Universities," *Harvard Educational Review*, XXXIII (1963), 58–73. Theodore M. Newcomb, *Personality and Social Change* (New York: Dryden, 1963). C. Robert Pace and George C. Stern, *A Criterion Study of College Environment* (Syracuse: Psychological Research Center, 1958). David Riesman, *Constraint and Variety in American Education* (New York: Doubleday Anchor, 1958). Natalie Rogoff-Ramsøy, *Social Structure and College Recruitment* (New York: Bureau of Applied Social Research, Columbia University, 1962). Nevitt Sanford, *The American College* (New York: Wiley, 1962). George C. Stern, "Congruence and Dissonance in the Ecology of College Students," *Student Medicine*, VIII (1960), 304–339; also G. Stern, M. I. Stein, and B. S. Bloom, *Methods in Personality Assessment* (Glencoe, Ill.: The Free Press, 1956). Martin Trow, "Student Cultures and Administrative Action," in R. L. Sutherland *et al.*, eds., *Personality Factors on the College Campus* (Austin: Hogg Foundation for Mental Health, University of Texas, 1963), pp. 203–225. Theodore M. Newcomb and Everett K. Wilson, eds., *College Peer Groups* (Chicago: Aldine Press, 1966). The reader is particularly directed to the many research reports of the Center for the Study of Higher Education, University of California (Berkeley). In addition, there is also a sizable sociological literature on professional education covering such fields as the training of teachers, physicians, nurses, psychologists, sociologists, and so on; see, for example, the series of papers in Nelson B. Henry, ed., *Education for the Professions*, The Sixty-first Yearbook of the National Society for the Study of Education, Part II (Chicago: National Society for the Study of Education, 1962).

12. Educational Policies Commission, *The Unique Role of the Superintendent of Schools* (Washington: National Education Association, 1965). Also see *Professional Administrators for America's Schools*, Thirty-eighth Yearbook of the American Association of School Administrators (Washington: American Association of School Administrators, 1960); Roald F. Campbell, Luvern L. Cunning-

ham, and Roderick F. McPhee, *The Organization and Control of American Schools* (Columbus: Charles E. Merrill, 1965); Herold C. Hunt and Paul R. Pierce, *The Practice of School Administration: A Cooperative Professional Enterprise* (Boston: Houghton Mifflin, 1958); and Arthur B. Moehlman, *School Administration: Its Development, Principles, and Function in the United States,* 2nd ed. (Boston: Houghton Mifflin, 1951). For a consideration of problems of school principals, see Lloyd E. McCleary and Stephen P. Hencley, *Secondary School Administration: Theoretical Bases of Professional Practice* (New York: Dodd, Mead, 1965); Donald H. Ross, ed., *Administration for Adaptability* (New York: Metropolitan School Study Council, 1958); and Charles R. Spain, Harold D. Drummond, and John I. Goodlad, *Educational Leadership and the Elementary School Principal* (New York: Rinehart, 1956). For treatments of issues confronting presidents of institutions of higher learning, see Clark Kerr, *The Uses of the University* (Cambridge: Harvard University Press, 1963); James A. Perkins, *The University in Transition* (Princeton: Princeton University Press, 1966); and Harold W. Dodds, *The Academic President: Educator or Caretaker* (New York: McGraw-Hill, 1962).

13. Alex Inkeles, *What Is Sociology?: An Introduction to the Discipline and Profession* (Englewood Cliffs, N.J.: Prentice-Hall, 1964).

14. M. Brewster Smith, "Anthropology and Psychology," in John Gillin, ed., *For a Science of Social Man* (New York: Macmillan, 1954), p. 40.

15. See Robert K. Merton, Leonard Broom, and Leonard S. Cottrell, Jr., eds., *Sociology Today: Problems and Prospects* (New York: Basic Books, 1959).

16. See George C. Homans, "Contemporary Theory in Sociology," in Robert E. L. Faris, ed., *Handbook of Modern Sociology* (Chicago: Rand McNally, 1964), pp. 951–977.

17. See Robert K. Merton, *Social Theory and Social Structure,* rev. ed. (Glencoe, Ill.: The Free Press, 1957); and Homans, *op. cit.*

18. See Matilda White Riley, *Sociological Research: I. A Case Approach* (New York: Harcourt, Brace, and World, 1963); and Bernard S. Phillips, *Social Research: Strategy and Tactics* (New York: Macmillan, 1966).

19. See Faris, *op. cit.,* for a series of assessments of the present state of knowledge in different areas.

20. The examples of problems on which sociologists have consulted presented in the following section are based on information primarily derived from conversations and correspondence with eight sociologists whom we could identify as having had experience as consultants for public-school systems. Each problem mentioned is based on one or more of their advisory activities. In view of the absence of formally documented reports or published empirical studies concerning the experiences of sociologists as consultants to educators, we would propose that this lack be remedied by initiating a nation-wide study of consulting efforts and experiences. From such a study, it should be possible to cull particularly interesting, typical, or unusual cases for intensive clinical analysis. The growing concern for the education of the "disadvantaged" child will undoubtedly increase the participation of sociologists in educational systems and related ventures. Bench-mark studies at this time would also enable us to recognize changes in the consultant's role as the number of consultants increases and their novelty wears off.

21. For excellent illustrations of this type of service that sociologists can offer, see Eleanor B. Sheldon, James R. Hudson, and Raymond A. Glazier, "Administrative Implications of Integration Plans for Schools," in Reiss, *op. cit.,* pp. 160–188; Eleanor B. Sheldon and Raymond A. Glazier, *Pupils and Schools in New York*

City: A Fact Book (New York: Russell Sage Foundation, 1965); Philip M. Hauser, "Demographic Factors in the Integration of the Negro," *Daedalus,* XCIV (1965), 847–878; Donald Bogue, *Components of Population Change, 1940–1950* (Oxford, Ohio: Scripps Foundation Studies in Population Distribution, No. 12, 1957); and Karl E. and Alma F. Taeuber, *Negroes in Cities: Residential Segregation and Neighborhood Change* (Chicago: Aldine Press, 1965).

22. The redrawing of the school district lines in Chicago in the early nineteen-fifties was based largely on the recommendations of the late Louis Wirth and other members of the faculty in the Sociology Department of the University of Chicago. In the past few years the recommendations of sociologists such as Robert J. Havighurst and Philip M. Hauser about the need to redraw school boundaries have been given serious consideration by the Chicago Board of Education. See Robert J. Havighurst, *The Public Schools of Chicago: A Survey for the Board of Education of the City of Chicago* (Chicago: Board of Education of the City of Chicago, 1964). Other sociologists such as Robert A. Dentler and Neal Gross have advised school superintendents in the East about problems of this kind.

23. Studies of this kind are now being carried out by the project of the American Sociological Association, Sociological Resources for Secondary Schools, under the general direction of Robert C. Angell, executive director of the project. A team of sociologists at Harvard University is also currently conducting studies on the effects of curricular change. In addition, see Everett M. Rogers, *Diffusion of Innovations* (New York: The Free Press of Glencoe, 1962), pp. 39–43, for a brief report of the work of Barton, Eichholz, and other sociologists on curricular change. Also, see Henry J. Meyer, Edgar F. Borgatta, and Wyatt C. Jones, *Girls at Vocational High* (New York: Russell Sage Foundation, 1965); and Herbert H. Hyman, Charles R. Wright, and Terence K. Hopkins, *Applications of Methods of Evaluation: Four Studies of the Encampment for Citizenship* (Berkeley: University of California Press, 1962).

24. See, for example, R. V. Smith, Stan Flory, Rashid Bashur, and Walter Piel, *The Community Reports: A Study of Citizen Reaction to the Birmingham Public Schools* (Ypsilanti: Institute for Community Research, 1963); and Neal Gross, *The Schools and the Press: A Study of the Relationships between Newspapermen and School Administrators* (Cambridge: New England School Development Council, 1956).

25. For an illustration of this usage of the sociologist, see Robin M. Williams, Jr., and Margaret W. Ryan, eds., *Schools in Transition* (Chapel Hill: University of North Carolina Press, 1954); and Richard Robbins, "Local Voluntarism in Race Relations Strategy: The Illinois Experience with Community Human Relations Groups," in Gouldner and Miller, *op. cit.,* pp. 147–162. Also see Melvin M. Tumin, *Desegregation: Resistance and Readiness* (Princeton: Princeton University Press, 1958).

26. We have encountered several requests of this kind from school administrators in our consulting activities.

27. Space limitations preclude our consideration of consulting activities in which we have been involved with institutions of higher education. We emphasize this point because the conditions we have encountered in activities of this kind have been different in certain important respects from those we have experienced in working with school officials and officers of foundations.

28. Another consequence of this consultation should be noted: officials of two universities indicated that the involvement of their institutions in the study led them to revamp the objectives and content of their programs.

29. For example, see Neal Gross, *Who Runs Our Schools?* (New York: Wiley, 1958), pp. 113–125; and M. G. Abbott, "Values and Value-Perceptions in Superintendent–School Board Relationships," *Administrator's Notebook*, IX (1960), 1–4. For a summary of studies of the value orientations of teachers, see W. W. Charters, Jr., "The Social Background of Teaching," in N. L. Gage, ed., *Handbook of Research on Teaching* (Chicago: Rand McNally, 1963), pp. 715–813.

30. Gross, *Who Runs Our Schools?*, Chapters 5 and 6; Wilbur B. Brookover and David Gottlieb, *A Sociology of Education*, rev. ed. (New York: American Book Co., 1964), pp. 339–352; and Orville G. Brim, Jr., *Sociology and the Field of Education* (New York: Russell Sage Foundation, 1958).

31. See, for example, D. H. Jenkins and Ronald Lippitt, *Interpersonal Perceptions of Teachers, Students, and Parents* (Washington: National Education Association, Division of Adult Education Service, 1951); Charters, *op. cit.*, pp. 764–780; Bruce J. Biddle, H. A. Rosencranz, and E. F. Rankin, *Studies in the Role of the Public School Teacher* (Columbia: Social Psychological Laboratory, University of Missouri, 1961).

32. Peter C. Dodd, "Role Conflicts in the School Principalship," unpublished Ph.D. dissertation, Harvard University, 1962.

33. Melvin Seeman, *Social Status and Leadership: The Case of the School Executive* (Columbus: Bureau of Educational Research and Service, Ohio State University, 1960), pp. 39–59; and Neal Gross, Ward S. Mason, and Alexander W. McEachern, *Explorations in Role Analysis: Studies of the School Superintendency Role* (New York: Wiley, 1958).

34. *Ibid.*, pp. 254–274; Seeman, *op. cit.;* and T. R. Bowman, "Participation of Superintendents in School Board Decision-Making," *Administrator's Notebook*, XI (1963), 1–4. For a summary of several of these studies and a related body of literature see Charles E. Bidwell, "The School as a Formal Organization," in James G. March, ed., *Handbook of Organizations* (Chicago: Rand McNally, 1965), pp. 992–998.

35. Peter Blau and W. Richard Scott, *Formal Organizations* (San Francisco: Chandler, 1962), Chapter 7; Amitai Etzioni, "Organizational Control Structure," in March, *op. cit.*, pp. 650–657; and W. G. Bennis, K. D. Benne, and R. Chin, *The Planning of Change* (New York: Henry Holt, 1961).

36. Matthew B. Miles (ed.), *Innovation in Education* (New York: Bureau of Publications, Teachers College, Columbia University, 1964).

37. Theodore M. Newcomb, *Social Psychology* (New York: Dryden, 1950).

38. Robert K. Merton and Alice S. Kitt, "Contributions to the Theory of Reference Group Behavior," in Robert K. Merton and Paul F. Lazarsfeld, eds., *Continuities in Social Research: Studies in the Scope and Methods of "The American Soldier"* (Glencoe, Ill.: The Free Press, 1950), pp. 40–105.

39. George C. Homans, *Social Behavior: Its Elementary Forms* (New York: Harcourt, Brace, and World, 1961).

40. See, for example, H. Otto Dahlke, *Values in Culture and Classroom* (New York: Harper, 1958); Norman E. Gronlund, "The Accuracy of Teacher's Judgments Concerning the Sociometric Status of Sixth Grade Pupils," *Sociometry*, XIII (1959), 197–225; and Coleman, *op. cit.*

41. For a description of many of these interpersonal forces see A. Paul Hare, "Interpersonal Relations in the Small Group," and Burton R. Clark, "Sociology of Education," in Faris, *op. cit.*, pp. 217–271 and 734–769; also Brim, *op. cit.;* Neal Gross, "The Sociology of Education," in Merton, Broom, and Cottrell, *op. cit.*, pp. 128–152; and A. H. Halsey, Jean Floud, and C. A. Anderson, eds.,

Education, Economy, and Society: A Reader in the Sociology of Education (New York: The Free Press of Glencoe, 1961).

42. Gross, *Who Runs Our Schools?*, pp. 70–87.

43. See Hanan C. Selvin, *The Effects of Leadership* (Glencoe, Ill.: The Free Press, 1960), pp. 27–42.

44. See, for example, Blau and Scott, *op. cit.*

45. For some recently published textbooks of this kind, see Campbell, Cunningham, and McPhee, *op. cit.*; Jack A. Culbertson, Paul B. Jacobson, and Theodore I. Reller, eds., *Administrative Relationships: A Casebook* (Englewood Cliffs, N.J.: Prentice-Hall, 1960); and Van Miller and Willard B. Spalding, *The Public Administration of American Schools*, rev. ed. (Yonkers-on-Hudson: World Book Co., 1958). Also see Roald F. Campbell and Russell T. Gregg, eds., *Administrative Behavior in Education* (New York: Harper, 1957).

46. W. Lloyd Warner, Robert J. Havighurst, and Martin B. Loeb, *Who Shall Be Educated?* (New York: Harper, 1944).

47. August B. Hollingshead, *Elmtown's Youth* (New York: Wiley, 1949).

48. Patricia Sexton, *Education and Income* (New York: Viking, 1961).

49. Allison Davis, *Social-Class Influences upon Learning* (Cambridge: Harvard University Press, 1948); Robert J. Havighurst, "Social Class Influences on American Education," in Nelson B. Henry, ed., *Social Forces Influencing American Education*, The Sixtieth Yearbook of the National Society for the Study of Education, Part II (Chicago: National Society for the Study of Education, 1961), pp. 120–143; Basil Bernstein, "Social Class and Linguistic Development: A Theory of Social Learning," in Halsey, Floud, and Anderson, *op. cit.*, pp. 288–314; for a summary of the social-class and education literature, see Brookover and Gottlieb, *op. cit.*, pp. 153–192; and Ronald G. Corwin, *A Sociology of Education* (New York: Appleton-Century-Crofts, 1965), pp. 155–216.

50. For a review of a number of these studies, see Ralph Kimbrough, *Political Power and Educational Decision Making* (New York: Rand McNally, 1963); and Corwin, *op. cit.*, pp. 343–417.

51. Bogue, *op. cit.*; Otis D. Duncan and Albert J. Reiss, Jr., *Social Characteristics of Urban and Rural Communities, 1950* (New York: Wiley, 1956); Morton Grodzins, *The Metropolitan Area as a Racial Problem* (Pittsburgh: University of Pittsburgh Press, 1958); Conrad Taeuber, "Some Recent Population Changes in the United States," *Journal of Intergroup Relations*, I (1960), 113–122; and Karl E. and Alma F. Taeuber, "White Migration and Socio-Economic Differences between Cities and Suburbs," *American Sociological Review*, XXIX (1964), 718–729; also see Robert E. Herriott and Nancy Hoyt St. John, *Social Class and the Urban School* (New York: Wiley, 1966).

52. Otis D. Duncan and Beverly Duncan, "Residential Distribution and Occupational Stratification," *American Journal of Sociology*, LX (1955), 493–503; Otis D. Duncan and Stanley Lieberson, "Ethnic Segregation and Assimilation," *American Journal of Sociology*, LXIV (1959), 364–374; Philip M. Hauser, "The Changing Population Pattern of the Modern City," in Paul K. Hatt and Albert J. Reiss, Jr., eds., *Cities and Society* (Glencoe, Ill.: The Free Press, 1959); Bobby J. Chandler, "Forces Influencing Urban Schools," in Bobby J. Chandler, Lindley J. Stiles, and John I. Kitsuse, *Education in Urban Society* (New York: Dodd, Mead, 1962); and Robert J. Havighurst, "Urban Development and the Educational System," in A. Harry Passow, ed., *Education in Depressed Areas* (New York: Bureau of Publications, Teachers College, Columbia University, 1963), pp. 24–45. For the most recent and comprehensive findings on equality of educational opportunity and two interpretations of their possible implications

for educational practice, see James S. Coleman *et al., Equality of Educational Opportunity* (Washington: U.S. Government Printing Office, 1966); James S. Coleman, "Educational Dilemmas: Equal Schools or Equal Students," *Public Interest,* No. 4 (Summer, 1966), pp. 70–75; and Christopher Jencks, "Education: The Racial Gap," *New Republic,* October 1, 1966, pp. 21–26.

53. Peter H. Rossi, *The Publics of Local Schools* (Cambridge: Graduate School of Education, Harvard University, Staff Research Memorandum No. 2, September, 1954), pp. 109 ff.

54. Leo A. Haak, "The General Public and the Public Schools," *Administrator's Notebook,* IV (April, 1956), No. 8.

55. Arthur Vidich and Joseph Bensman, *Small Town in Mass Society* (New York: Doubleday, 1960), Chapter 7; R. R. Alford, "School District Reorganization and Community Integration," *Harvard Educational Review,* XXX (1960), 350–371; R. F. Carter and J. Suthoff, *Communities and Their Schools* (Stanford: Stanford University, School of Education, 1960); Bidwell, *op. cit.,* pp. 1009–1012.

56. C. Wayne Gordon, *The Social System of the High School: A Study in the Sociology of Adolescence* (Glencoe, Ill.: The Free Press, 1957).

57. Coleman, *The Adolescent Society.*

58. Arthur L. Stinchcombe, *Rebellion in a High School* (Chicago: Quadrangle Books, 1964).

59. Howard S. Becker, "The Career of the Chicago Public School Teacher," *American Journal of Sociology,* LVII (1952), 470–477.

60. Herriott and St. John, *op. cit.*

61. Gross and Herriott, *op. cit.;* Neal Gross and Anne E. Trask, *The Sex Factor and the Administration of Schools* (New York: Wiley, forthcoming, title tentative); Robert Dreeben and Neal Gross, *The Role Behavior of School Principals,* Final Report No. 3, Cooperative Research Project No. 853 (Cambridge: Graduate School of Education, Harvard University, 1965); and Peter C. Dodd, *Role Conflicts of School Principals,* Final Report No. 4, Cooperative Research Project No. 853 (Cambridge: Graduate School of Education, Harvard University, 1965).

62. Ward S. Mason, *The Beginning School Teacher: Status and Career Orientations* (Washington: U.S. Government Printing Office, 1961), OE-23009, Circular No. 644.

63. Burton R. Clark, *Adult Education in Transition* (Berkeley: University of California Press, 1958); and Clark, *The Open Door College: A Case Study.*

64. This observation is made on the basis of informal conversations with a small group of administrators who had finished a training program for educational administrators at a major American university in the past five years.

65. See Chapters 2, 16, 17, 19, 25 and 31 for a consideration of other issues of great concern to school officials and for possible implications of studies on these problems that may have relevance for efforts to cope with them.

66. Educational Testing Service, *Background Factors Relating to College Plans and College Enrollment among Public High School Students* (Princeton: Educational Testing Service, 1957).

67. Examples of studies from the large body of literature that show social-status correlates of the level of student educational aspirations include William H. Sewell, Archie O. Haller, and Murray A. Straus, "Social Status and Educational and Occupational Aspirations," *American Sociological Review,* XXII (1957), 67–73; R. Gould, "Some Sociological Determinants of Goal Strivings," *Journal of Social Psychology,* XIII (1941), 461–473; Ralph Berdie, *After High School—*

What? (Minneapolis: University of Minnesota Press, 1954); and Howard F. Hjelm, *Factors Related to College Attendance,* Cooperative Research Monograph No. 8, U.S. Department of Health, Education, and Welfare (Washington: U.S. Government Printing Office, 1961).

68. The Harvard Mobility Project was under the direction of Florence R. Kluckhohn, Talcott Parsons, and Samuel A. Stouffer. See Talcott Parsons, "The Social Class as a Social System in American Society," *Harvard Educational Review,* XXIX (1959), 297–318.

69. Joseph A. Kahl, "Educational and Occupational Aspirations of 'Common-Man' Boys," *Harvard Educational Review,* XXIII (1953), 188.

70. *Ibid.,* p. 189.

71. *Ibid.*

72. Elizabeth G. Cohen, "Parental Factors in Educational Mobility," unpublished doctoral dissertation, Radcliffe College, 1958, and "Parental Factors in Educational Mobility," *Harvard Educational Review,* XXXVIII (1965), 404–425.

73. Samuel A. Stouffer and Paul Shea, "Report on College Plans of Public and Parochial School Students of Leominster, Massachusetts," unpublished report.

74. Paul Shea, "Parental Influence on College Planning by Boys and Girls of High Ability during the Sixth to Ninth Grades," unpublished Ed.D. thesis, Graduate School of Education, Harvard University, 1964.

75. Samuel A. Stouffer, *Your Educational Plans* (Chicago: Science Research Associates, 1958).

76. Robert E. Herriott, "Some Social Determinants of Educational Aspiration," *Harvard Education Review,* XXXIII (1963), 157–177.

77. The crucial importance of counselors in decisions about the future education of high-school students is revealed in Aaron V. Cicourel and John I. Kitsuse, *The Educational Decision Makers* (Indianapolis and New York: Bobbs-Merrill, 1963); also see Bud B. Khleif, "A Socio-cultural Framework for Studying Guidance in Public Schools," in Edward Landy and Arthur M. Kroll, eds., *Guidance in American Education III: Needs and Influencing Forces* (Cambridge: Harvard University Press, 1966).

78. Alan B. Wilson, "Residential Segregation of Social Classes and Aspirations of High School Boys," *American Sociological Review,* XXIV (1959), 836–845.

79. Alan B. Wilson, "Social Stratification and Academic Achievement," in Passow, *op. cit.,* pp. 223–224. See also John A. Michael, "High School Climates and Plans for Entering College," *Public Opinion Quarterly,* XXV (1961), 585–595.

80. William H. Sewell, "Community of Residence and College Plans," *American Sociological Review,* XXIX (1963), 24–38; and William H. Sewell and J. Michael Armer, "Neighborhood Context and College Plans," *American Sociological Review,* XXXI (1966), 159–168.

81. A. O. Haller and W. H. Sewell, "Farm Residence and Levels of Educational and Occupational Aspiration," *American Journal of Sociology,* LXII (1957), 407–411.

82. Edward L. McDill and James Coleman, "High School Social Status, College Plans, and Interest in Academic Achievement," *American Sociological Review,* XXVIII (1963), 905–918; and Edward L. McDill and James Coleman, "Family and Peer Influences in College Plans of High School Students," *Sociology of Education,* XXXVIII (1965), 112–126.

83. Natalie Rogoff, "Social Structure and Educational Selection," in Halsey, Floud, and Anderson, *op. cit.,* pp. 241–251.

84. We have considered only a small portion of the literature that deals with sociological correlates of level of educational and occupational aspiration. Other

studies that educational administrators may find of especial interest are: Phillip Cutright, "Students' Decisions to Attend College," *Journal of Educational Sociology,* XXXIII (1960), 292–299; Murray A. Straus, "Personality Characteristics and Functional Needs in the Choice of Farming as an Occupation," *Rural Sociology,* XXI (1956), 257–266; Fred L. Strodtbeck, "Family Interaction, Values, and Achievement," in David C. McClelland *et al., Talent and Society* (New York: D. Van Nostrand, 1958), pp. 135–194; Raymond W. Mack, Raymond J. Murphy, and Seymour Yellin, "The Protestant Ethic, Level of Aspiration, and Social Mobility: An Empirical Test," *American Sociological Review,* XXI (1956), 295–300; Marvin Bressler and Charles F. Westoff, "Catholic Education, Economic Values, and Achievement," *American Journal of Sociology,* LIX (1963), 225–233; David C. McClelland, *The Achieving Society* (Princeton: D. Van Nostrand, 1961); James A. Duncan and Burton W. Kreitlow, "Selected Cultural Characteristics and the Acceptance of Education Programs," *Rural Sociology,* XIX (1954), 349–357; Bernard C. Rosen, "Family Structure and Achievement Motivation," *American Sociological Review,* XXVI (1961), 574–585; Bernard C. Rosen, "Race, Ethnicity, and the Achievement Syndrome," *American Sociological Review,* XXIV (1959), 47–60; Robert G. Holloway and Joel V. Berreman, "The Educational and Occupational Aspirations and Plans of Negro and White Male Elementary School Students," *Pacific Sociological Review,* XXII (1957), 204–212; Albert J. Reiss, Jr., and Albert L. Rhodes, "Are Educational Norms and Goals of Conforming, Truant and Delinquent Adolescents Influenced by Group Positions in American Society?", *Journal of Negro Education,* XXVIII (1959), 252–267; and Mary H. Lystad, "Family Patterns, Achievements, and Aspirations of Urban Negroes," *Sociology and Social Research,* XLV (1961), 281–288. Also see Glen H. Elder, Jr., *Adolescent Achievement and Mobility Aspirations* (Chapel Hill: Institution for Research in Social Science, University of North Carolina, 1962).

85. See, for example, Wilson, "Residential Segregation of Social Classes and Aspirations of High School Boys."

86. Gross and Herriott, *op. cit.*

87. For a series of papers that present a number of the findings of studies on the disadvantaged child, see Passow, *op. cit.;* for a lengthy bibliography of books, monographs, and papers on this problem, see Joe L. Frost and Glenn R. Hawkes, eds., *The Disadvantaged Child: Issues and Innovations* (Boston: Houghton Mifflin, 1966).

88. See, for example, Wilbur B. Brookover, Thomas Shailer, and Ann Paterson, "Self-concept of Ability and School Achievement," *Sociology of Education,* XXXVII (1964), 271–280; and Brookover and Gottlieb, *op. cit.,* pp. 468–481.

89. Miles, *op. cit.*

90. Gross, *The Schools and the Press.*

91. Cicourel and Kitsuse, *op. cit.;* and Khleif, *op. cit.*

92. David Gottlieb and Jon Reeves, *Adolescent Behavior in Urban Areas* (New York: The Free Press of Glencoe, 1963).

93. Goslin, *op. cit.*

94. See, for example, F. T. Rope, *Opinion Conflict and School Support,* Teachers College Contributions to Education, No. 838 (New York: Columbia University, 1941); John Foskett, "Differential Discussion of School Affairs," *Phi Delta Kappan,* XXXVII (1956), 311–315; Donald McNassor, "Barriers and Gateways in School–Community Relationships," *Journal of Educational Sociology,* XXVI (1954), 1–10; Gresham Sykes, "PTA and Parent–Teacher Conflict," *Harvard*

Educational Review, XXIII (1953), 86–92; Vynce A. Hines and Robert L. Curran, "The Schools and Community Forces," *Review of Educational Research,* XXV (1955), 48–60. Also see Eugene Litwak and Henry J. Meyer, "Administration Styles and Community Linkages of Public Schools: Some Theoretical Considerations," in Reiss, *op. cit.,* pp. 49–98.

95. Smith, Flory, Bashbur, and Piel, *op. cit.* Another important use of the research tools of the sociologist for educational administrators deserves mention: the application of survey methods, including questionnaires and interviews, to the analysis of the internal and external problems of educational research organizations. Under the direction of Paul F. Lazarsfeld and Sam Sieber, the Bureau of Applied Research has carried out a number of studies of this kind. See Paul F. Lazarsfeld and Sam D. Sieber, *Organizing Educational Research: An Exploration* (Englewood Cliffs, N.J.: Prentice-Hall, 1964). Also, sociologists at the University of Pittsburgh have been conducting an organizational analysis of the Learning Research and Development Center at their institution since its inception.

96. W. W. Charters, Jr., "Anthropology and the Study of Administration—Response," in Downey and Enns, *op. cit.,* pp. 85–94; and Neal Gross, "The Use and Abuse of Sociological Inquiry in Training Programs for Educational Administrators," in Downey and Enns, *op. cit.,* pp. 23–38.

97. Rogers, *op. cit.*

98. Ronald Lippitt, "The Youth Culture, The School System, and the Socialization Agency," in Reiss, *op. cit.,* pp. 99–120.

99. *The Negro Family: The Case for National Action* (Washington: Office of Planning and Research, U.S. Department of Labor, March, 1965).

100. For a review of these studies see Brookover and Gottlieb, *op. cit.,* pp. 153–194; and Corwin, *op. cit.,* pp. 155–216.

101. Merton, *Social Theory and Social Structure,* p. 9.

102. Wilbur B. Brookover, Jean M. LePere, Edsel L. Erickson, and Thomas Shailer, *Definitions of Others, Self-Concept, and Academic Achievement: A Longitudinal Study,* unpublished paper presented at the American Sociological Association meetings, August 30, 1965, in Chicago, Illinois.

103. The studies of Ronald Lippitt and his associates suggest that the manipulation of group forces tends to be more effective than the traditional psychological approaches to working with these children.

104. Muzafer Sherif, O. J. Harvey, B. J. White, W. R. Hood, and Carolyn Sherif, *Intergroup Conflict and Cooperation: The Robbers Cave Experiment* (Norman, Okla.: University Book Exchange, 1961).

105. Hyman, Wright, and Hopkins, *op. cit.*

106. Meyer and Borgatta and Jones, *op. cit.*

107. Edward A. Suchman, *Sociology and the Field of Public Health* (New York: Russell Sage Foundation, 1963); and Frances C. Macgregor, *Social Science in Nursing* (New York: Russell Sage Foundation, 1960).

108. Suchman, *op. cit.,* pp. 160–161.

109. See Brim, *op. cit.,* Chapter 2; and Allen H. Barton, *Organizational Measurement and Its Bearing on the Study of College Environments* (Princeton: College Entrance Examination Board, 1961).

110. See Macgregor, *op. cit.,* pp. 285–309.

111. Our efforts to identify sociologists who were full-time staff members of large city school systems in 1964 uncovered only one sociologist who was serving in this capacity.

112. It deserves stress, however, that at this stage of our knowledge sociologists are

equipped primarily to sensitize administrators to the importance of taking into account how social factors may influence learning. For an assessment of our limited knowledge about social factors influencing learning, see Sarane S. Boocock, "Toward a Sociology of Learning: A Selective Review of Existing Research," *Sociology of Education*, XXXIX (1966), 41–45.

113. See Gouldner and Miller, *op. cit.*

The

Consumer

CHARLES Y. GLOCK

FRANCESCO M. NICOSIA

chapter **12**

In the last few decades we have witnessed a growth in social-science research on the consumer which has no precedent. The proliferation of work—much of it highly detailed, circumscribed in conception, and often atheoretical—has made the sheer task of keeping up with past and current investigation a formidable one in itself. More than this, conceptualizing the field so that past work may be appropriately assessed and future work intelligently charted has become a problem that is growing increasingly more acute.

The task of cataloguing research on the consumer has been attempted in a number of recent papers.[1] No concentrated attention has been given, however, to the task of conceptualizing consumer research. We have elected, therefore, to make this the focus of our inquiry.

Social scientists have adopted two fundamental approaches in their study of the consumer. One of these approaches concentrates on understanding the behavior of individual consumers or consuming units (micro-behavior). The second deals with the behavior of the mass of consumers (macro-behavior). We shall call the first approach the study of consumer behavior; the second the study of consumption behavior.

The study of consumer behavior encompasses the efforts expended to describe and explain the consumer's act of choice either at a given point in time or through time. It may focus on his investment of money and personal labor in goods and services or on his investment of time and money in leisure pursuits. It may concentrate on his decisions with respect to saving and assets or on his "purchase" of ideas. The behavior under consideration may be that of the individual or of a consuming unit (the family or some other consuming unit). However, the center of inquiry is always on the decisions of the individual or individual unit.

In contrast, the study of consumption behavior is concerned with describing and explaining the behavior of aggregates of consumers or consuming units, again at a given point in time or through time. The subject matter parallels at the aggregate level that of consumer behavior at the individual level. It includes the aggregate investment of money and personal labor in goods and services, aggregate investments of time and money in leisure pursuits, aggregate savings and assets, the aggregate "purchase" of ideas, and so on.

The two approaches, as we shall see, rely on distinct bodies of theory and distinct methodologies. At the same time, the results of research done at the one level can have bearing on research done at the other. For example, information on the factors influencing the saving habits of individuals over time may help to account for shifts in aggregate saving. In turn, knowledge of shifts in aggregate saving can provoke specific questions about the behavior of individual savers.

Sociology becomes relevant to the study of both kinds of behavior: to consumer behavior insofar as the individual's social context influences his decision processes[2] and to consumption behavior insofar as the society's system of beliefs, values, and norms and its institutional structure help to shape the behavior of the mass.

Sociology and the Study of Consumer Behavior

Over the course of its history, the study of consumer behavior has been dominated in different degrees by three research traditions. The first may be called the "descriptive" (or distributive, taxonomic) tradition.[3] Descriptive studies are those which state, for example, how many units of a certain brand are sold, how much of a certain class of products is sold by what type of retailing units,[4] and so on to more differentiated descriptions such as those indicating who buys what, where, when, at what price, in what quantities.[5] This tradition provides basic information necessary to production, distribution, and other decisions and consequently is very widely employed. Although some of the research methods of sociology, especially survey research, have contributed to it, this tradition is essentially atheoretical. Accordingly, we shall not consider the great many studies that belong to it.

The second tradition, which we shall call "prescriptive," has been largely inspired by a concern with problems of everyday policy and conduct of public and private firms. While for the most part it has by-passed sociology and the social sciences in general, we shall present a brief account of it in order to set the third tradition in proper perspective.

The third—the explanatory tradition—has been motivated by a more basic interest in understanding what makes the consumer tick: how he comes to make the decisions he does. Here the role of the social sciences (psychology, economics, sociology, and anthropology) has been of great significance, and understandably this tradition will be our major concern.

THE PRESCRIPTIVE TRADITION IN CONSUMER-BEHAVIOR RESEARCH

To a considerable extent, research on consumer behavior in this country has been paid for, and conducted on behalf of, marketers, advertising agencies, and mass media. Consequently, its character and direction have been shaped by the interests of these sponsors and the conditions under which they feel they must operate. The primary interest of the marketer, and of the advertising agencies and mass media who aid him, is to control as much of the market as is feasible and economically profitable. The achievement of this control rests ultimately on the ability to manipulate not only price(s) and volume of output but also the character and packaging of the products and brands, their promotion, advertising, and display. The sponsors' interest in research, therefore, has been mainly to inform themselves as to how they may best manipulate these variables so as to optimize their immediate and long-range goals.

This orientation has produced a tradition of studies designed to assess consumer responses to specific stimuli, predominantly those which can be manipulated. Product tests, research on product and package design, distribution, price and income, readership, and measurement of recall and effectiveness of advertising—all generally form part of this tradition.[6]

This approach does not explicitly postulate the existence of a consumer-decision process beyond the simple association (statistical) between a stimulus and a response. It operates on the notion that, all other things being equal, the taste and appearance of a product, the shape of its container, the way it is advertised, and so forth can exercise leverage on the consumer's decision to act. The research task, then, is to assess the capacity of one or another of these stimuli to produce a desired response.

Over the years, the techniques used in conducting these studies have been considerably refined. Great attention is now given to sampling problems, to controlling for possible biases depending on the way a stimulus is presented, to pretesting research instruments, and so on.[7] Furthermore, studies are now done in the field more often than in constructed laboratory situations.[8] By and large, however, the basic logic of this research is not fundamentally different from what it was thirty to forty years ago.

It is obviously useful to know that, other things being equal, people prefer the taste of version A of a product over version B, or that a square box will produce more sales than a round one, or that using four colors, rather than black and white, in an advertisement will result in more sales per advertising dollar. The ability of stimulus-response research to perform this task quickly and relatively cheaply has a great deal to do with its viability. However, the knowledge, if any, which it generates does not provide a basis for understanding the broader problems of consumer decision making: the configuration of factors which enter into the purchase decision.[9] The tradition virtually ignores the interplay between different stimuli and its effect on consumer action. And it overlooks the subject's economic, social, and psychological characteristics as mediating influences on his response to specific stimuli. In sum, the tradition does not attempt to investigate the cognitive mechanism or mechanisms which transform a stimulus into a response, nor does it specify the contextual conditions which make one mechanism rather than another operative.

Such matters began to interest social scientists in the thirties, and during that decade, theoretical and empirical work on the process of consumer decision making began to develop.

THE EXPLANATORY TRADITION IN CONSUMER-BEHAVIOR RESEARCH

The explanatory tradition derives from an image of the consumer as acting in response not to a single stimulus, but rather to a great network of them interacting over time. In this conception, stimuli are not simply the variables manipulated by marketers but encompass all the factors external and internal to the actor which bear on his action. The research task, therefore, is to specify both the stimuli relevant to the act of choice and the process of their interaction which leads to the choice. While not negating the relevance of the stimuli germane to the prescriptive tradition, the explanatory tradition goes further in suggesting that other attributes of the social environment and of the subject himself must be taken into account if even the operation of the marketer's stimuli is to be understood.

The ultimate goal implicit in this conception of consumer behavior is a process paradigm which would comprehensively delineate the morphology and the operation of the consumer decision process. Given present knowledge, it is evident that this goal is far from realization. Nevertheless, the prospect of such a paradigm has influenced social-science research on consumer behavior.

This conception of consumer behavior calls for an interdisciplinary approach; clearly, the act of choice cannot be understood from within an exclusively sociological, psychological, or economic frame of reference. At the same time, there are few social scientists who are competent in all these fields. Consequently, we find that the attempts to build what are now referred to as "paradigms of action" [10] tend to be influenced primarily by the discipline of the investigator, but inevitably spill over into the other disciplines as well. To assess the uses of sociology in research on consumer behavior, it is necessary to consider not only the paradigms which have been formulated by sociologists but also those constructed by economists and psychologists.

In sociology, or perhaps more appropriately social psychology, the closest approximation to a paradigm of consumer action has been proposed by Lazarsfeld and elaborated by his colleagues and students. In economics (and psychology) the work of Katona is most relevant to our purposes. There is no single paradigm which has gained prominence in psychology, specifically clinical psychology, although the presence of a basic scheme of social action is implicit in much current research. Our subsequent discussion focuses on the perspectives of these three disciplines and on their implications for future study of consumer behavior. While we shall be particularly sensitive to the role of sociology in past and future investigation, the nature of the subject requires that we not be too parochially oriented.

The Lazarsfeld Paradigm   The first attempt to move beyond the prescriptive tradition and to develop an all-encompassing paradigm of consumer action was made by Lazarsfeld in the mid-thirties. In a paper entitled "The Art of Asking Why" [11] he postulated that any act of choice involves an interplay among three broad sets of variables, which he called predispositions, influences, and product attributes. This trilogy gave major impetus to subsequent work directed toward the study in depth of the morphology of these classes of variables and the dynamic relationships among them.

Predispositions, in Lazarsfeld's conception, refer to all the characteristics an individual brings with him when he is exposed to a stimulus, when he executes an act of choice, and when he experiences the consequences of this choice. Predisposition, then, would include the individual's personality. It would also include all the beliefs, values, and norms to which he has been socialized since childhood and which, in themselves, are largely influenced by his changing position in the social structure. The effect of these social variables on consumer action has been the subject of a number of studies produced both within and outside the Lazarsfeld school.[12]

Uniformly, these studies show that social variables significantly influence a wide range of consumer acts. For example, the individual's social milieu and the values and norms it supports have been found to be relevant to the beverages he drinks,[13] his shopping behavior,[14] his adoption of new products,[15] his pattern of saving[16] and installment buying,[17] his brand motivations in the purchase of major household appliances,[18] his residential mobility,[19] his image of a car,[20] and so on. In effect, these studies demonstrate that social variables, once internalized, become psychologically relevant to the individual's decision process.[21]

Product attributes and influences, then, are in essence "external" variables which interact with what may be termed "internal" variables—that is, predispositions—thereby determining consumer action. Product attributes refer to the characteristics of the means available to the subject. They consist of the chemical and physical properties of the product; that is, how it tastes, its design, the way it is packaged. However, as an increasing number of studies have shown, there is a tendency to superimpose social and psychological characteristics upon the physical and chemical qualities of the product.[22] Thus, a particular style of furniture is to be characterized not only with regard to its cost, its material composition, and so on but also with respect to the kinds of people—poor, rich; modern, old-fashioned; upwardly, downwardly mobile—who are likely to own it. It has been suggested that not all products, and brands within products, have the same propensity to absorb social and psychological characteristics.[23] Such a propensity is probably operative where differences in physical characteristics cannot be readily identified *and* where the possession of the brand and product is visible to others.[24] Thus, brands of automobile are likely to take on social and psychological meaning, whereas brands of table salt may not.

Influences include the remaining "external" variables—all the stimuli, both personal (for example, the salesman) and impersonal (such as the mass media)—which become internalized in the individual's subjective field. Much of Lazarsfeld's personal attention, as well as that of his colleagues, has been directed toward locating and tracing the effect of "influence" variables in the decision making process. Their research has shown that different influences interact, both among themselves within one class and also with the other two classes of variables, to produce consumer action.

The details of research on influences have been effectively summarized by Katz and by Rogers,[25] and we need not dwell on them here. Briefly, however, it has been demonstrated that stimuli flowing through mass media are mediated by the individual's interpersonal relations and that the two influences, mass media and interpersonal, interact in complex patterns to guide behavior. In this process, opinion leaders are identified as playing a special role. They act not only as channels of information but also as a source of social pressure toward a particular choice and as a source of social support to reinforce that choice once it has been made. The individual's place in the social structure establishes the conditions under which he may act as an opinion leader and also controls the content areas in which leadership may be exercised. The sociologist's interest in the interaction between mass and interpersonal channels of communication has clarified several management problems and thrown new light on previous empirical knowledge. To illustrate this last point, a study focused specifically and exclusively on the role of the detail man (drug salesman) in the physician's decision to adopt new pharmaceutical products found the salesman to have considerable influence.[26] A subsequent study, however, based on a broader conceptualization of communication processes and on a careful consideration of doctors' positions in their social milieu, showed that the detail man has a primary and direct influence on the drug decisions of physicians isolated in the medical community, but can perform only a reinforcing function for doctors integrated in that community.[27]

The work produced by the Lazarsfeld school has amply demonstrated the significance of social variables in consumer decision making and in this sense has persuasively illustrated the direct relevance of sociology to its study. While it has not produced, or sought to produce, a comprehensive process scheme of consumer behavior, it has established the requirements for such a scheme and suggested the way in which its subparts might work.[28] It has been particularly successful in locating the potential role of "influence" variables in the scheme.

The Katona Paradigm The work of George Katona and the members of the Economic Behavior Program of the University of Michigan's Institute of Social Research also forms part of the explanatory tradition.[29] Katona's paradigm, like that of Lazarsfeld, postulates three broad sets of variables which bear on consumer behavior: (1) enabling conditions; (2) precipitating circumstances; and (3) attitudes.[30] Enabling conditions would be exemplified by income, assets, ability to borrow. Their relative size and availability set limits on the consumer's purchasing capability. Precipitating circumstances, also external variables, either produce a problem resolvable by means of a purchase—such as the breakdown of a car—or trigger the resolution of an existing problem (need)—for instance, learning of a new product. Attitudes are intervening variables through which the first two sets of variables must filter before they can influence the act of choice.

It is apparent that attitudes are a subset of the subject's attributes, while precipitating circumstances and enabling conditions are two subsets of the attributes of his environment. Thus, the paradigms of both Katona and Lazarsfeld share the general point of view of social psychology: specifically, that behavior is the result of the interplay between a subject and his environment. As delineated by the work of Katona and his associates, the action orientation (attitudes) of a consumer is affected by his possibilities for action as determined by enabling conditions and by the presence or absence of precipitating circumstances.

In the most recent presentation of his paradigm, Katona postulates the variables that enter into the purchase decision and hypothesizes a general map of their relationships.[31] Because of its emphasis on enabling conditions, the paradigm draws attention to economic variables that are not made equally explicit by Lazarsfeld. Although appearing to overlook the role of social variables, the paradigm considers them implicitly in the class of variables called attitudes. In fact, Katona's empirical work shows that attitudes are shaped by the political, economic, and social factors of the past and present; once internalized, these factors become part of the individual's social psychological field and thus exert influence on his behavior.[32] To illustrate further, Katona has observed that it is customary to assume in macro-economics that expectations of rising prices will bring increases in consumption expenditures.[33] However one of his studies suggests the possibility that expectations of rising prices may be psychologically transformed into expectations of future diminishing purchasing power on the market place and thus lead to increased saving rather than increased expenditures.[34] Finally, since Katona and his colleagues have been primarily concerned with classes of products, rather than specific products and brands, such variables as advertising and other stimuli manipulated by the marketer are not explicitly considered. Nevertheless, they may function in his paradigm as precipitating circumstances.

The empirical application of this paradigm has not yet produced the promised map of the relations existing between the postulated variables. The procedure followed has been to collect data on the three classes of variables and on actual purchases and to analyze the data primarily by testing the effect of a particular variable, with other variables held constant. Consequently, the interplay among the three primary classes of variables is never completely explicated. Katona does, however, suggest how subparts of the attitudinal variable are interrelated. For example, he shows that the attitude "intention to buy" has an effect on actual purchases and that intention to buy is, in part, a function of other attitude sets (such as feeling of optimism about the economy).[35]

In sum, the relevance of Katona's work to our inquiry lies more in the theory of his scheme than in the way the scheme has been realized. Katona helps to identify the variables pertinent to consumer action and demonstrates the significance of social variables by establishing their influence on attitude formation and buying behavior. In addition, his findings have uncovered some of the ways by which consumer decisions exert an influence on the behavior of other sectors of the economy.[36]

Clinical Paradigms A third effort to transcend the stimulus-response model in consumer research draws its inspiration from clinical psychology and has become popularly known as motivation research. Practitioners of motivation research share an underlying assumption that human behavior can be largely interpreted in psychological terms, but they differ rather sharply in their specific attempts at interpretation. Consequently, we cannot identify a single clinical paradigm akin to Lazarsfeld's or Katona's which would comprehend the varied conceptualizations sometimes explicit, but more often implicit, in motivation research. (One observer has commented that there are as many conceptions of human nature in motivation research as there are motivation researchers.) However, we wish to make at least some general observations about clinical work since, at first glance, it would appear to obviate any consideration of social variables in consumer decision making.

The key to understanding consumer action, according to the clinicians, lies in the needs, drives, motives, cognitive structures of the human personality. Thus, they differ from the two preceding theorists in their almost exclusive concentration on the study of the subject's attributes. They also differ methodologically in their greater reliance on so-called "qualitative" observations, on projective techniques, unstructured interviews, and other clinical procedures; consequently collecting qualitative information in depth from small samples is emphasized, rather than collecting standardized information from larger ones.

Despite, however, the implicit assertion that psychological factors are singularly important in consumer action, motivation research and the clinical theories from which it borrows almost always include the environment as a basic determinant of motivation and cognition.[37] This is most evident in the formulations of Fromm, Sullivan, Kardiner, and May, which explicitly emphasize social and cultural factors. For example, in postulating the market-oriented personality, Fromm attributes its evolution to fundamental changes in the economic importance of the market in modern social systems. Freud, too, recognized that the prevailing values of the society give important direction to the way basic biological drives are channeled. His addition of the "super-ego" concept to form the trichotomy "id, ego, super-ego" was the result of his inability to explain human behavior by means of the first two concepts alone.

The results of motivation research reflect this understanding originally gained from clinical research, but tend not to make it explicit. For example, a number of motivational studies have indicated that housewives initially reject such new products as prepared cake mixes and instant coffee, apparently out of fear that the use of these labor-saving products creates an image of laziness. This feeling, it would seem, is an exemplification of the respect for work in the value system of the society. This societal value, once internalized, becomes part of the psychological make-up of the housewife. Motivation researchers, however, tend to explain her behavior simply as a psychological reaction to guilt feelings (shirking her job), without specifying the interaction and conflict of the several variables which underlie her final action.

More generally, motivation and clinical researchers, because of their reliance on small samples and a depth approach, often tend to infer that motives, whether they are socially or biologically determined, are generally operative in all individuals. This may be true, of course, for some biological drives, presuming they could be effectively isolated.[38] It is not true for socially determined drives. The failure to make this explicit frequently constitutes a flaw in clinical paradigms of consumer action. This, in turn, is one additional argument for the relevance of sociology to the study of consumer behavior.

All in all, then, clinical paradigms, as well as the two considered earlier, do not provide an integrated conception of consumer action. However, they point once again to the requirements for developing such conceptualization and make particularly salient the need to consider the way that social variables become internalized and part of the individual's cognitive structure, thus becoming important variables in the determination of the morphology and the dynamic mechanism of his decision process.

THE USES OF THESE TRADITIONS

While implicit in the descriptive and prescriptive traditions and in both Katona's and clinical paradigms, sociology is the explicit informing discipline in only the Lazarsfeld paradigm. Relatively, this paradigm has probably been the least frequently used by marketing managers of any that have been discussed. Measured simply in terms of frequency of use, marketers are still most closely wedded to the descriptive and prescriptive traditions. And, of the three explanatory paradigms, the clinical ones have probably had the greatest popularity, certainly more so than Lazarsfeld's, and probably more so than the Katona scheme.

One reason for the continued dominance of the prescriptive tradition has already been alluded to; namely, its focus on variables over which the marketer can exercise direct control. Also contributing to the tradition's wide use is that it demands relatively little sophistication on the part of its users. The average marketer is not well versed in the intricacies of social science. Consequently, the simplicity and unambiguity of research done in the prescriptive tradition has a particular appeal.

Clinical paradigms, while more complex conceptually, nevertheless tend to produce results whose implications for action appear to be reasonably clear-cut and straightforward, usually in the form of concrete recommendations for advertising and campaign themes. This is not an inherent characteristic of research done in this genre. However, because motivation researchers tend to be commercially rather than academically oriented, they are understandably prone to respond to clients' demands for research which will clearly inform everyday decisions. Since the clinical approach is particularly well suited to discovering latent motivations which may be tapped by advertising, this is the primary purpose to which it has been put, and since it performs this task with apparently considerable success, it enjoys wide popularity.

Like clinical paradigms, both the Katona and Lazarsfeld paradigms are conceptually intricate and difficult for the layman to understand. Unlike clinical paradigms, however, they have stimulated research whose results are not so directly subject to the marketer's control. This is because the end in view is to understand consumer decision processes in broad compass, rather than to focus narrowly on those factors over which the marketer may exercise leverage. This has meant that the research which has been done has made more of a contribution to general understanding than to immediate practice. The importance of this contribution is not to be underestimated, of course, since knowledge of the general process by which consumers make decisions is important to establishing the limits of the marketer's power and to informing him how he might best use the power he has. Not many marketers, however, are this sophisticated, and relatively, explanatory consumer research done in the Katona and Lazarsfeld modes has had somewhat limited use. Moreover, the uses to which it has been put have tended to be strategic, rather than tactical, and therefore difficult to pin down in a concrete way.

Generally speaking, research done by Katona and his associates has been particularly useful to agencies of the federal government, banks, consumer credit companies, manufacturers of automobiles and other durable goods, in providing them basic insights into the state of consumers' predispositions to buy and in aiding them, therefore, in establishing controls on credit and in planning production schedules. Government and business planners have also benefited from specialized studies done on the impact of growing private pension plans on individual saving and the effect of tax cuts on consumer expenditures.

Contributions of the Lazarsfeld school to marketing strategy have come from studies introducing and elaborating on such concepts as the two-step flow of communication, opinion leadership, reference groups, cross pressures, and social contexts, as these have been found to bear on consumer purchasing decisions. All these concepts have pointed to the inadequacy of conceiving of mass-media effects in simple stimulus-response terms and to the need for developing channels of communication, formal and informal, to reach different publics rather than the public as a mass. In practical terms, marketers have sought to use these concepts through special campaigns to reach and influence opinion leaders, through attempting to identify their products with reference groups found to be salient to prospective customers, through mixing the use of media to maximize impact on special publics, and through giving attention to generating favorable social images of their products.

All in all, the sheer amount of attention which sociologists have given to research on consumer behavior is not great. (We shall want later to consider what some of the barriers have been.) The research which has been done, however, has served generally to change the fundamental character of marketing strategy. The influences are perhaps more latent than manifest, but there can be no doubt that in formulating and executing marketing plans, the contemporary marketer can no longer afford to ignore what sociology and other behavioral sciences have learned about consumer decision making.

THE TASK AHEAD

Our review of the concepts which have, up to the present, informed research on consumer behavior has demonstrated the greater potentiality of explanatory concepts over prescriptive ones as means to comprehend consumer action. While showing existing paradigms to be incomplete, the review has directed attention to the requirements for a more comprehensive process scheme. In this respect, it has suggested that the morphology of the variables relevant to consumer behavior be further specified and that their interaction leading to a response be more effectively described. What our review has not done, however, is to suggest clearly a research strategy to allow orderly progress toward the goal of working out a more comprehensive scheme. Presumably, in the natural course of events, evidence would slowly accumulate and would provide increasingly refined specifications of the variables affecting different kinds of consumer choices. And, along the way, we would learn more and more about how the decision process itself operates; that is, how these variables interact. But this will take time: must we then merely wait, or are there ways to accelerate progress? We would suggest three research strategies toward the latter end.

Studies of Strategic Populations[39]   In the current situation of consumer behavior research, the advancement of a considerable number of imaginative ideas is frustrated by the absence of an operative research strategy. Such central concepts as the two-step flow,[40] opinion leaders,[41] taste makers,[42] reference groups,[43] to mention only a few,[44] are all more or less begging for refinement, elaboration, and further empirical test. A central problem is to devise a method of studying them which would at once uncover their interrelationships in the decision making process and also provide a means for defining the kinds of decision to which they apply.[45]

A solution obviously requires that consumers be observed as they are in the midst of making, not one, but a wide variety of choices. It is also necessary that the observed individuals be confronted with the same decision problems. These requirements are not met in the ordinary market situation. It is possible to find people who are all in the process of deciding whether or not to buy a new car. But it is unlikely that these same people will share at the same time other decision making problems; for example, deciding on the purchase of a durable good, on how to invest savings, and so on.

There are occasions, however, where these conditions are approximately met in everyday life. One such occasion would be represented by the newly married couple, another by the birth of a first child, another by a change of residence, and still another by an increase in income. Taking newly married couples as a case in point, they all confront decisions as to how to distribute their new combined income, where to live, how to furnish their new home, how to spend their leisure time, what durable goods to buy, and indeed what kind of toothpaste they will use.

In operational terms, the study of newly married couples would involve first contacting them while they are still only engaged. Interviews at this time would be focused on their predispositions, attitudes, buying habits, and intentions and on the formal and informal influences to which they have been exposed. Parallel interviews might also be held with significant reference figures in their milieu, such as parents, relatives, friends, to assess their aspirations for the prospective couple. Reinterviews would then be conducted following the marriage to discover what buying decisions have, in fact, been made and how these are related to variables in the subjects' external and internal environment. In order to trace the effects of these initial decisions on subsequent behavior—to see, for example, whether or not and how patterns established early in marriage become traditionalized —the sample might be formed into a panel to be reinterviewed over an extended period of time.

The advantage of research of this kind is that it could help to resolve simultaneously a number of outstanding questions about consumer decision making. It would be a start toward learning whether the same or different variables are operative for different kinds of decisions. By identifying the ways in which the marriage partners come to resolve past differences in their value and behavior patterns, new knowledge would be gained about how attitudes are formed and about how they are internalized to become psychologically relevant for action.[46] Concomitantly, knowledge of how people react under cross pressures would be extended, as would the understanding of the reference figures and groups against which they "compare" their own present behavior and plan for their future.[47] There would also be an opportunity to test current postulations about the operation of the "two-step flow of influence" [48] and to explore the relative role of opinion leaders and reference groups in the communication flow.[49] In this way, further understanding would be gained of the role of the mass media in decision making.[50] Although these examples bear primarily on the social, rather than on the economic and psychological components of decision processes, these components could, of course, be studied within the same framework.

In sum, bearing in mind the goal of a process paradigm of consumer behavior, research on strategic populations appears to be a good way to build more quickly toward that end.

Studies of Innovation and Diffusion   Implicit in the preceding discussion is the idea that decision processes may be different when people are deciding for the first time from when they are merely repeating a previous decision. Thus, buying the first television set is a different experience for the newly married couple from buying a replacement some years later. Part of our rationale for suggesting that the study of strategic publics be carried on over an extended period of time was to see how the morphology and the mechanism of the decision process evolve with experience.

There is an additional kind of decision situation not represented in these examples which would seem to justify separate study. This is the situation of innovation—where new goods and services appear on the market for the first time. Here, the individual has neither had experience with the product himself nor can he refer to the experience of others in making his decision. This presents an opportunity to study how new attitudes and behavior patterns are formed.

There is already a tradition (now more than thirty years old, in fact) of research on the innovation of new farm practices. This research has been primarily concerned with the practical problem of persuading farmers to accept and adopt new improvements in farming methods. Naturally enough, considerable attention has been given to the effectiveness of publicity, advertising, and personal communication (through the county agent) in getting farmers to change old ways and adopt new ones. This has resulted in a significant finding that such influences are mediated in important ways by the farmer's position in the rural social structure.

Media tend to influence early innovators to act. However, these innovators are usually "maverick" farmers whose reference groups are outside the farm community and whose status in the community is not high. Consequently, their act does not trigger a wave of adoptions on the part of other farmers. In fact, after the early innovators have acted, the propensity is for a hiatus period to set in during which very few new adoptions occur. During this period, the high-status farmers observe the experience of the innovators and give careful attention to professional information about the innovation before deciding to act. If they do decide to adopt the innovation, this sparks widespread adoption on the part of the majority of farmers, for whom they function as opinion leaders. With some variation, Coleman, Katz, and Menzel have found the same general pattern to exist with respect to physicians' adoption of new drugs.[51]

The number of innovations and the rather special populations which have been studied do not warrant generalizations about all kinds of innovation behavior. We suspect it will be found that the nature of the innovation—whether it represents a sharp or limited break with past practice, for example—will strongly affect whether or not social structural variables, now thought to be paramount, will in fact be primary in the diffusion process. However, the work already done demonstrates the leverage toward the understanding of decision making processes which research on innovation can exercise. What we are proposing here is that a more general effort be made to use the occasion of innovation as subject matter for consumer behavior research.

Innovations may range, of course, all the way from relatively minor changes in the design or packaging of a product to the introduction of entirely new inventions. In the long run, it would appear to be desirable that research on innovation cover the entire range. More immediate attention, however, should probably be given to "more significant" innovations.

How this is to be done, particularly if the diffusion of innovations throughout an entire population is to be studied, is not at once evident. In the above-cited studies of farmers and physicians, it was possible to observe all the members of the communities investigated and consequently to examine the relationships between their behaviors. Obviously, it becomes impractical to study all members of the population at large.

The research strategy to adopt probably depends on how long the diffusion process takes. Where a substantial proportion of the population adopts the new product or service within a year's period or less, it would be both practical and desirable to make all members of some circumscribed population—for instance, a neighborhood—the subjects for investigation and to study this entire population as the diffusion process evolves. This would not be practical where the diffusion process extends over a considerably longer period of time, as has been the case, for example, with color television. Here, the appropriate research strategy might be to make those who adopt the innovation the primary subjects for study and arrange to have them interviewed as soon after adoption as possible. This is not the place to consider all possible ramifications in research design; we merely intended to show that useful designs can be developed.

We would urge more concentrated work on the diffusion process, then, so as to provide another vantage point for studying the interaction of external and internal variables in consumer decision processes. Its more singular contribution would be to help us learn how the past attitudes and behavior patterns of consumers are reshaped when they confront new situations and react to them.

Mathematical Models of Consumer-Decision Processes Finally, some effort to express current conceptualizations of consumer decision making in mathematical form would appear to be justified. Such models could add precision to theory construction in the field and provide both for testing the adequacy of existing theoretical statements and for specifying the properties of such statements.

Admittedly, applications of sociology and other disciplines to consumer research have not yet generated the whole body of empirical evidence nor the integration of their theoretical views necessary to construct fully developed mathematical models. As for the collection of the empirical data, we suggest the priority of the following areas:

1. Investigation of the role of and interaction among the so-called social, psychological, and economic variables. Although with mixed results, work in this direction has already started.[52]

2. Investigation of the interaction among the attributes of the subject; that is, more detailed blueprints of thinking processes. Here, the student of consumer behavior can learn a great deal from basic research—from the classical literature in opinion and attitude formation and change through the present work on simulation of thinking processes. Among the most promising current concepts are the following: the notion of discrepancy between level of aspiration and level of satisfaction.[53] Bauer uses Festinger's notion of cognitive dissonance to explain how a consumer may reduce risk.[54] The previously cited studies by Clawson and Bilkey extend and apply Lewin's notion of valence. More recently, Nicosia has developed the above suggestion of March and Simon and has incorporated it into an over-all model of consumer-decision processes,[55] part of which relies on the Lazarsfeld classification of components of action and dimensions of dispositions (scope, time, directedness).[56]

3. Investigation of the interdependences of a subject's decisions in different areas: work, politics, religion, consumption, and so on.[57]

4. Finally, investigation of the interactions among the decision processes of two or more people.[58]

Concerning the necessary efforts toward integration of theoretical views developed in the social sciences and translations of them into formal models, a recent study has reviewed the notion of consumer behavior in marketing, economics, and the behavioral sciences, developed some models of the processes underlying this behavior, and derived some new hypotheses from the analysis of such models which point to new directions of research.[59] The view of consumer behavior obtained in this integration sees the decision process as a mechanism that repeats itself and evolves over time; that is, consumer behavior is viewed as a *decision process*, rather than as the result of a decision process. Thus, the "final" acts of purchase and consumption are treated as only additional variables, rather than as explicitly the dependent variable; this idea, it will be recalled, was exemplified empirically in our earlier discussion of studies of strategic populations. Several implications for sociological work follow from this perspective. First of all, the usual classifications of variables—external, internal; independent, intervening, dependent; rational, irrational; conscious, unconscious; psychological, social, economic, anthropological; and so forth—lose a great deal of their operational meaning. The researcher's task is simply that of postulating the variables of the decision process and their functional relations; these postulates are the necessary and sufficient conditions for designing a blueprint for research. This is probably the only way to effect the much-discussed notion of interdisciplinary studies. Sociology can contribute to this development and, we hope, lead the formulation of new theories and research methods.

In conclusion, our over-all view of the state of, and prospects for, research on consumer behavior is an optimistic one. To be sure, the subject matter has not been given systematic attention in the social sciences, and sociological interest in it has been limited indeed. Nevertheless, the work which has been done has spawned conceptualizations of considerable sophistication, both on general and on intermediate levels. In turn, these conceptualizations have stimulated a small but still significant body of empirical research, whose use in guiding general policy, if not explicit action, is growing.

Past sociological work in consumer behavior gives rise to challenges and prospects for the future understanding of basic decision processes. However, there exists the danger that such prospects may be frustrated by the conditions which appear to govern the commissioning and financing of consumer research. Because these same conditions also apply to future work on consumption behavior, we shall postpone discussing them until after that topic has been considered.

Sociology and the Study of Consumption Behavior

In studying consumption behavior, the focus of attention shifts from the individual to the aggregate, changing not only the subject matter of the inquiry but the research methodology which may be employed as well.

There are almost infinite kinds of aggregate consumption behavior. One could study, for instance, the sales of a product or brand, the popularity of a particular style of clothes, the ratio of saving to spending, investments in the stock market, the distribution of income, total consumer expenditures, and so forth. Although studies of these topics may be done statically (for example, the ratio of spending to saving may be observed at one point in time and some attempt made to explain it), for the most part they are investigated dynamically; that is, the interest centers on a shift in some aggregate behavior over time.

Analysis of such macro-phenomena is usually made by economists; the procedures, consequently, may be unfamiliar to sociologists. We shall be in a better position to examine the place of sociology in the study of consumption behavior if we first briefly consider what these procedures are. The analytical steps will vary somewhat, depending on the subject studied, but generally speaking the economist proceeds about as follows.

To begin, data are collected on the aggregate observed over time. The resultant time series is then analyzed statistically to establish the character of its oscillations: a long-term trend, a cyclical trend, a seasonal trend, random oscillations, or some combination of these. To this point the primary objective is to describe what amounts to the dependent variable in all its ramifications. While economists most often perform these operations, they draw upon statistical theory and method, rather than theory and method of economics. In other words, this initial procedure is essentially atheoretical from the viewpoint of the social sciences.[60]

There follows a series of operations which, explicitly or implicitly, is directed toward explaining the oscillations described in the time series. The essential technique is the comparison of the oscillations with those plotted from time series of other aggregate behaviors. Thus, the car manufacturer will compare time series on his own sales with similar data on the sales of other brands of car, with sales for the entire automobile industry, with sales of related industries (such as steel), with total consumer expenditures, with the Gross National Product, and so on. Or he may break down his own data along with data from other car manufacturers (where available) to compare shifts in sales by different price lines, styles, colors, and so on. The aim is to see how his own aggregate behavior is related to these other aggregate behaviors.[61]

This comparative time series analysis of different aggregate behaviors may or may not be directed by theoretical considerations. It is conceivable that an investigator, searching for data that correlate, may introduce comparative material almost at random. Usually, however, the time series to be compared are chosen on theoretical grounds drawn primarily, if not exclusively, from economic theory. Thus, he may introduce data on income on the hypothesis that his own sales are a function of fluctuations in total income. Or, less theoretically, he may compare his own investment in advertising with the investments made by his competitors.

Obviously, different time series variables will be pertinent to different problems. The economist, for example, who works for a financial institution and is interested in shifts in the ratio of saving to spending will draw upon variables other than those of the economist working for the car manufacturer. Nevertheless, the fundamental procedures in the two cases are essentially the same.

At this point the analysis is refined to examine the relationship between variables, with time, in effect, controlled. The goal is to discover whether a given relationship is the same or different within different time intervals. Thus, it becomes possible to make statements of the order that within a defined time interval aggregate purchases of a given product vary in describable ways with level of income, or assets, or whatever other economic factor is introduced. The result of these procedures establishes the degree and character of the association between one or more independent variables and the dependent variable; for example, the suggestion that expenditures rise with increasing income, but do not decline with falling income.[62]

Carried to this point, economic analysis provides a basis for predicting aggregate behavior; at best, it only partially explains it. The interpretation of the relationship between economic variables, if pursued, invariably requires the introduction of sociological and psychological considerations.

By and large, however, sociologists (and psychologists) have not been concerned with the study of consumption behavior. Our discussion, therefore, of the uses of sociology in this subject area will necessarily deal more with prospects than with accomplishments. Along the way we shall have occasion to say something about how economists have tried to fill the gap in sociological work by turning sociologists themselves.

We have organized our discussion around three topics: the interplay between social and economic theory, sources of data in macro-analysis, and the study of marketing processes.

INTERPLAY BETWEEN SOCIAL AND ECONOMIC THEORY

A first and minimal kind of contribution which sociologists can make is to bring sociological theory to bear on prevailing economic theory and research in the field. This means, in effect, trying, where appropriate, to interpret in sociological terms the relationships which economists have found to persist between economic variables.

As Parsons and Smelser point out,[63] there have been some efforts toward a rapprochement between social and economic theory at the general-systems level.[64] Much of the work of Marshall, of Weber, and of Pareto may be viewed in these terms, and the Parsons and Smelser volume itself is, of course, an attempt to synthesize theory in the two fields.

Such effort toward the general integration of social and economic theory has not been paralleled, however, by attempts on the part of sociologists to apply sociological insight to the everyday problems dealt with by economists in the study of consumption behavior. In the face of the apparent indifference of sociologists to this task, economists have tried increasingly to suggest interpretations themselves. In the economic literature, consequently, it is not unusual to find that sociological notions are frequently introduced to explain a particular relationship. For example, in an attempt to reconcile the aforementioned different statistical associations between consumption expenditures and disposable income, Duesenberry has suggested that our society makes it mandatory for consumers to "emulate their neighbors" ("keep up with the Joneses"),[65] thus explaining why expenditures increase with increasing income. This same social pressure also makes them reluctant to return to a lower standard of living, thus explaining why expenditures tend to remain stable with declining income.[66]

Speculative interpretations of the social factors underlying the relationships among economic variables is obviously only a beginning toward understanding consumption behavior. However, such speculations can provide a core set of hypotheses to be tested through research.

SOURCES OF DATA IN MACRO-ANALYSIS

The problem, however, cannot be resolved by simply asking sociologists to theorize about the nature of consumption behavior. Theory must necessarily be tested by research. In this respect, the sociologist is at a serious disadvantage relative to the economist. The government, business and industry, the mass media, and so on are all busily engaged in compiling data to document shifts in aggregate economic variables. For many economic indices, data have been collected for many years providing the fund of knowledge and information which makes economic analysis of consumption behavior possible. There is no comparable body of material to document shifts and changes in the social fabric of society. The census, of course, regularly collects basic information on the social composition of the population—on sex, age, education, and the like. However, information is not collected on a regular basis to assess and document changes in the values, norms, habits, and customs of the population. Consequently, the fundamental data for studying the bearing of social factors on consumption behavior are seldom, if ever, available.

Sociologists can probably fill the gap by collecting the data themselves where the problem being studied is of a short-term character and relatively circumscribed. It is the absence of regularly collected data over extended periods of time which constitutes the lack. One can think of a myriad of consumption problems which are closed to sociological analysis because necessary data are not available. It can be assumed, for example, that an important factor affecting consumption behavior is the amount of leisure time available to the population and the ways in which it is spent.[67] In such problems, the possession of current information would scarcely be as valuable as data accumulated at regular intervals, say, over the last fifty years.

It is easy, of course, to suggest that it would be useful to have fuller information about changes in the social structure and in the society's values over time. However, it would obviously require considerable thought and experimentation to decide what kinds of social data ought to be collected on a regular basis. Furthermore, their value would have to be amply documented to gain co-operation from the appropriate official agencies. Despite the obstacles, these are matters, we would suggest, which might profitably be the concern of sociologists.

As a first step in this direction, sociologists could seriously consider the ways in which changes in the social structure and in the value system might affect consumption behavior. A large number of sociological concepts imply that these factors have an impact on consumption behavior. For some of these concepts, research and applications have begun; for example, the early ideas on life cycle have guided part of the design of the *Life* magazine study cited previously; the concept of social class guides the work of several consulting firms;[68] the notion of compensatory conspicuous consumption has led to reformulations of programs of welfare agencies.[69] And yet this is only a beginning, in the sense that the implications and applications of these concepts have been scarcely tapped. Further, concepts such as social mobility, cultural lag, social integration, conformity, achievement orientations, and life styles immediately come to mind as having direct relevance, although their potential to explain consumption behavior has been essentially overlooked. To have such concepts inform the nation's data-collection apparatus, they would obviously have to be translated into more precise propositions as to how they bear on the aggregate behavior of consumers. Once this is done, the indicators on which data might be collected could be specified.

The prospects for implementing these ideas in the near future are undoubtedly rather slim; once adopted, a considerable time will still have to be spent in accumulating data before they can become analytically useful. However, if sociology is to make a meaningful contribution to the study of consumption behavior and, indeed, mass behavior in general, this seems the basic path which must be followed.

THE STUDY OF MARKETING PROCESSES

Thus far in our discussion of consumption behavior, the focus of our attention has been on the aggregate behavior of consumers, implying that this behavior can be understood solely as the result of other forces impinging upon it. However, the aggregate behavior of consumers is only a part of a larger process of interaction among consumers *and* manufacturers, middlemen, retailers, advertising agencies, mass media, and so on, who are all functionally related to one another. Research on consumption behavior is incomplete without some effort to understand the nature of these functional relationships.

We have found no discussion in the literature of the general nature of these functional relationships. However, some attention has been given to specifying the processes by case studies of particular consumption behaviors.

One study was concerned with understanding the process as it operated in the development of the "rhythm and blues" fad in popular music.[70] The fad is pictured as resulting from the interaction among the Negro market, the concomitant development of independent record companies, the disk jockey, the major record companies, and the white radio audience. The essential point made is that each of these "aggregates" was functioning both as originator and as recipient of stimuli out of which, then, the fad emerged. In somewhat similar fashion, McPhee has investigated the processes underlying the survival of television programs and the popularity rankings of magazines.[71]

Paralleling such empirical studies, there has been an attempt on theoretical levels to explain the religious revival of the last decade also as the result of the functional interaction between different aggregates.[72] Here the process seems to begin with the publication, by the National Council of Churches, of statistics showing a slight increase in church membership. This statistical evidence is then picked up by the mass media, who interpret it as a religious revival. This, in turn, generates a commercial interest in producing and promoting religious books and literature, songs and plays with a religious motif, and commodities having a religious connotation. The mass media are thus encouraged to give further coverage to religious events. All of this activity has the consequence of accelerating awareness of and interest in religion on the part of the general public, which is manifested in larger church attendance, increased concentration on religious material by the media, and the purchase of religious books and commodities. This feeds back to the churches, the mass media, and producers, who are encouraged to further activity.

Neither this account of the revival nor the study of the "rhythm and blues" fad suggests how the process comes to a close, but both document the need to consider the process in consumption behavior research. These examples share a concern with short-term changes in consumption behavior: that is, fads and styles to which this kind of analysis is particularly appropriate. Longer variations of such studies in consumption behavior will probably have to await the collection of the kind of data discussed above.

The burden of our discussion, then, is that sociology has tended to relinquish to economics its stake in the study of consumption behavior. Economists have been willing to take up the challenge and to use sociological theory and method wherever they consider it germane to their problems. The prospects for work in this area, in our judgment, would be enhanced if a genuine concern could be generated among sociologists. We hope that our remarks, general as they have been, may stimulate such effort.

Barriers to Sociological Research on the Consumer

Relatively speaking, sociology has given substantially less attention to consumer and consumption behavior than have psychology and economics. In fact, the literature in the field is virtually dominated by the other two disciplines.[73] This is not because sociology is irrelevant to the subject matter; everything we have been saying points to the contrary. Then how is this to be explained? In a paper aimed at encouraging sociological research on the consumer, it seems appropriate to attempt an answer. An understanding of the obstacles is a necessary prerequisite to their being overcome.

The obstacles arise, we suspect, out of a combination of factors, of which four appear to be crucial: (1) historical factors which have made psychology and economics more visible than sociology to the business community;[74] (2) the prevailing perception in the business community of its needs for research on the consumer; (3) differences in how the three disciplines relate to these perceived needs; and (4) differences in prevailing attitudes among sociologists, economists, and psychologists about engaging in consumer research.

Psychology and economics were the first to translate tentative speculations into precise and often verifiable statements about human phenomena and, in this respect, had something to contribute to management before sociology did. Early use of personality and aptitude tests in personnel management had the effect of making psychology more visible to businessmen, and as interest developed in applying research to marketing problems, psychology seemed a natural source of help. As for economics, the subject matter itself is, of course, closely related to business problems, and this relationship was reflected very early in the great emphasis given to training in economics in business schools.[75] Thus, many trained businessmen had a personal familiarity with economics which they did not have with sociology, a subject only recently introduced into business school curricula. To begin with, then, the setting favored an involvement of economics and psychology in marketing and consumer problems.[76]

This was reinforced by a tendency of management to approach marketing problems with bread-and-butter questions to which they wanted unambiguous answers.[77] A tradition has never developed in marketing, as it has in the technological and productive aspects of business, for support of basic research alongside applied research. The bread-and-butter questions tended, naturally, to focus on those aspects of the marketing processes over which management was capable of exercising some control. Almost from the beginning, therefore, interest was centered on the influence of such factors as price, product and package design, and advertising on the consumer's acts of choice.

Here again psychology and economics were favored, since these variables lent themselves to experimentation and to economic analysis. The more recent popularity of motivation research, which relies so heavily on clinical psychology, fits the pattern, too, because its results tend to produce (or profess to produce) relatively unambiguous recommendations for policy.[78]

When sociologists began to enter the field in the late thirties and the forties, the findings of their research were received at first with considerable enthusiasm by management. For a time, for example, such ideas as opinion leadership, the two-step flow of influence, and reference groups were major topics of conversation along Madison Avenue. But the difficulty of practically applying these ideas tended to dissipate quickly the interest aroused. Because its results pointed to the complexity and ambiguity of the marketing processes, sociological research on the consumer came to be viewed, implicitly at least, as a luxury which few business firms could afford. The absence of alternative sources of support (foundations have shown a notable reluctance to give grants in this field [79]) has had the consequence of making sociological research on the consumer almost fallow.

To these conditions must be added the fact that sociologists generally have not shown much interest in working in this field. The sociological research on which we have reported earlier has been contributed really by only a handful of sociologists. To some extent, this is explained by an attitude of "looking down" on applied research, particularly where it is evidently to be used for manipulative purposes. But this is an attitude which psychologists and economists share with sociologists, and it would not explain the special propensity of sociologists to avoid the subject matter.

We suspect that another factor at work is that sociologists, more than economists or psychologists, are inclined to view the business world with a certain degree of suspicion and to be particularly concerned about the way it exercises its power. The fact that an industrial sociology has developed, but not a sociology of the consumer, reflects perhaps the sociologists' sympathy for the worker, rather than for management. The additional fact that sociologists have shown a willingness to do applied research in education, politics, government, and religion, where the results are clearly manipulative, raises questions about the claim that consumer research is avoided for that reason.

An unfortunate by-product of this attitude is that sociologists have tended to avoid all research on the consumer, basic as well as applied. Thus, the society at large is deprived of the insights which sociology might bring to understanding the place of consumption and of consumer activities in functioning social systems.

That these conditions have arisen and continue to exist does not mean that they cannot be changed, though from our point of view this will be difficult. What is needed, we would suggest, is a greater recognition on the part of the business community of their responsibility and, indeed, their personal stake in supporting more basic programs of research on the consumer. In turn, sociologists need to be persuaded that their present attitudes, presuming we have assessed them correctly, are a disservice to their commitment to the advancement of knowledge as well as to the general interests of the community at large.

If the circle is to be broken, it is probably the business community which will have to take the lead by supplying the funds needed for basic research. The establishment of the Marketing Science Institute in Philadelphia by the Scott Paper Company and other large firms perhaps indicates it may be ready to do so. Once initiated, it is possible (as happened in production and agriculture) that government, the foundations, and the universities may well be persuaded to come along. In the long run, however, the potentialities for basic research on the consumer will depend on the social sciences, and among them, most particularly on sociology.

REFERENCES

1. L. Guest, "Consumer Analysis," *Annual Review of Psychology*, XIII (1962), and R. Ferber, "Research on Household Behavior," *American Economic Review*, March, 1962.
2. That is, sociology becomes relevant insofar as social variables may help to account for the act of choice under investigation (cf., e.g., A. Inkeles, "Personality and Social Structure," in R. K. Merton, L. Broom, and L. S. Cottrell, Jr., eds., *Sociology Today: Problems and Prospects* (New York: Basic Books, 1959) and D. McGregor, "Motives as a Tool of Market Research," *Harvard Business Review*, Autumn 1940.
3. P. F. Lazarsfeld, "Sociological Reflections on Business; Consumers and Managers," in R. A. Dahl, M. Haire, and P. F. Lazarsfeld, *Social Reflections on Business: Product and Potential* (New York: Columbia University Press, 1959).
4. See, for example, the Census of Business, Retailing and Wholesaling Volumes.
5. See, for example, *Life* magazine, "Life Study of Consumer Expenditures" (New York: Time, Inc., 1957).
6. It is interesting to observe that in everyday practice a large part of this research evaluates the effectiveness of a stimulus on the basis of indicators other than sales. For example, in recall studies the response observed is recall, and not sales. Perhaps the assumption underlying this research is that recall may lead

to shifts of attitudes, then of product image, and finally of purchasing behavior.

7. See S. Banks, *Experimentation in Marketing* (New York: McGraw-Hill, 1965).

8. Among other refinements, one must mention the growing series of studies concerned with the differential impact of the structural components of a stimulus; for example, see the studies about the impact on readership by the size of the advertisement, its color(s), the subject of its headline, its copy theme, the size and subject of its illustration, etc., as reported in "Effective Business Publication Advertising," a McGraw-Hill Report, s.d.

9. It should be emphasized that stimulus-response research may have the ability to prescribe an optimal course of action only under the assumption "all other things—that is, factors—being equal." Therefore, its "practical" superiority to other research models (inexpensive, quick, and so on) exists, at best, only in the short run. More generally, stimulus-response research is analogous to medical practice, which may locate a remedy (stimulus) for a disease (response) without understanding the nature of the disease. Knowing that a stimulus produces a certain response "under certain conditions" may provide a prescription, but it does not explain why the stimulus has its effect, and, above all, it does not provide a basis for determining what changes of the stimulus must be if those "certain conditions" change.

10. See P. F. Lazarsfeld and M. Rosenberg, eds., *The Language of Social Research* (Glencoe, Ill.: The Free Press, 1955), Section V; see also the notion of "accounting scheme" in H. Zeisel, *Say It with Figures* (New York: Harper, 1957), Ch. VI.

11. P. F. Lazarsfeld, "The Art of Asking Why in Marketing Research," *National Marketing Review*, I (Summer, 1935); cf. also A. Kornhauser and P. F. Lazarsfeld, "The Techniques of Market Research from the Standpoint of a Psychologist," *Institute of Management Series* (American Management Association, Inc.), 1935.

12. For example, see W. H. Whyte, Jr., "The Web of Word of Mouth," *Fortune* (November, 1954); P. Martineau, "Social Class and Spending Behavior," *Journal of Marketing* (October, 1958); Opinion Research Corporation, *America's Tastemakers*, Vol. I and II (Princeton, N.J., April and June, 1959); and Opinion Research Corporation, *The Initiators* (Princeton, N.J., December, 1960); J. C. Maloney, "Attitude Measurement and Formation," *Test Market Design and Measurement Workshop*, American Marketing Association (Chicago, Ill., April, 1966).

13. Bureau of Applied Social Research, *A Socio-Psychological Study of Wine Drinking* (New York: Columbia University, 1944).

14. Bureau of Applied Social Research, *Should Abraham and Straus Remain Open One Night a Week?* (New York: Columbia University, 1949).

15. Bureau of Applied Social Research, *On the Flow of Scientific Information in the Medical Profession* (New York: Columbia University, 1954).

16. Bureau of Applied Social Research, *The Role of Dividends in Savings Behavior* (New York: Columbia University, 1956).

17. Bureau of Applied Social Research, *The Social Psychology of Installment Buying* (New York: Columbia University, 1949).

18. Bureau of Applied Social Research, *Brand Motivations in the Purchase of Major Household Appliances* (New York: Columbia University, 1950).

19. Peter H. Rossi, *Why Families Move* (Glencoe, Ill.: The Free Press, 1955).

20. Bureau of Applied Social Research, *Owner Loyalty to Make of Automobile* (New York: Columbia University, 1957).

21. For example, in a study by the Bureau of Applied Social Research, *They*

Changed to Tea: A Study in the Dynamics of Consumer Behavior (New York: Columbia University, 1954), of why certain consumers had stopped drinking coffee, the researchers investigated why they had chosen tea, rather than other beverages, as a substitute. In a large number of cases it was found that an early moment of their socialization process had already predisposed them toward the choice of tea; indeed, they had been raised in families who were tea drinkers. In other cases, the social process was different: some of them had married and taken up the tea-drinking "preference" of their mates, while some had moved into situations where the "others" drank tea.

22. Among studies outside the Lazarsfeld school, see for instance W. A. Woods, "Psychological Dimensions of Consumer Decisions," *Journal of Marketing* (January, 1960); and I. S. White, "The Functions of Advertising in Our Culture," *Journal of Marketing* (July, 1959).

23. F. S. Bourne, "Group Influence in Marketing and Public Relations," in R. Likert and S. P. Hayes, Jr., eds., *Some Applications of Behavioral Research* (Paris: UNESCO, 1957).

24. F. S. Bourne, *ibid.*, p. 218.

25. E. Katz, "The Two-Step Flow of Communication: An Up-to-Date Report on an Hypothesis," *The Public Opinion Quarterly* (Spring, 1957); and E. M. Rogers, *Diffusion of Innovations* (New York: Free Press, 1962).

26. T. Caplow and J. Raymond, "Factors Influencing the Selection of Pharmaceutical Products," *Journal of Marketing* (July, 1954).

27. J. Coleman, E. Katz, and H. Menzel, *Medical Innovation: A Diffusion Study* (New York: Bobbs-Merrill, 1966).

28. In this last regard, most valuable suggestions on the morphology of attitudes have been presented in P. F. Lazarsfeld, *op. cit.*, n 3.

29. Here, however, the quest for understanding consumer behavior is somewhat more narrowly pursued than in the Lazarsfeld paradigm. The focus of attention is primarily on the purchase of products which are durable and infrequently bought and involve relatively large expenditures. See, for example, the publications by the Federal Reserve Board, "Reports on the Surveys of Consumer Finances," *Federal Reserve Bulletin* (1949–59), and the subsequent yearly publications by the Institute for Social Research, *Survey of Consumer Finances* (Ann Arbor, Mich.; 1960 and following years). For some exceptions, see G. Katona, *The Powerful Consumer* (New York: McGraw-Hill, 1960), Ch. 10 *passim.*

30. From a summary by G. Morrissett, "Psychological Surveys in Business Forecasting," in R. Likert, and S. R. Hayes, Jr., eds., *Some Applications of Behavioral Sciences* (Paris, France: UNESCO, 1957). For a more detailed presentation, see the paradigm's major tenets proposed in G. Katona, *Psychological Analysis of Economic Behavior* (New York: McGraw-Hill, 1951), and, after a decade of intensive and systematic research, the clarifications and refinements in G. Katona, *op. cit.* The relation of Katona's view to stimulus-response research is most effectively worded when he states that his paradigm "does not posit a fixed, one-to-one relation between stimuli and responses. Stimuli elicit responses; they represent occasions for responses rather than fully determining them. It is not possible to predict the response by knowing the stimulus alone" (G. Katona, *ibid.*, p. 54).

31. G. Katona, *ibid.*

32. See, for example, how Katona's discussion of the psychology of prosperity, of inflation, and of recession identifies the "psychological" meaning and thus the impact of "social" events on consumer decisions (G. Katona, *ibid.*, Part IV).

33. "Public Poised to Open Purse," *Business Week*, April 2, 1960, pp. 116–120.

34. For more detailed comments on the psychological meaning of external variables such as price and price changes, see G. Katona, *op. cit.*, Ch. 12.

35. Katona's findings show unequivocally the necessity of further research on the cognitive processes underlying a consumer reaction to his environment, his selective perception and internalization of environmental stimuli, the ensuing thinking and overt activities, and so forth, all gradually specified in a buying intention which eventually will be realized in the consummation of an act of overt choice. In our opinion it is most unfortunate that the "controversy" about the relative role of attitudes and intentions to buy has been resolved in some quarters on the basis of a prescriptive, stimulus-response approach to the study of consumer behavior, rather than along the lines suggested by theories and findings emerging from basic research.

36. Katona's findings and interpretations on the impact of consumer decisions on the economy have been recently stressed by R. Ferber, *op. cit.*, who agrees with him about the limitations of the economist's view of consumer decision making. For example, Ferber has obtained results which confirm Katona's argument, G. Katona, *op. cit.*, pp. 14 ff., against the notion that consumers simply save what they do not spend and vice versa. Summarizing his findings, Ferber states that "the experience of more recent recessions suggests that one of the basic [economic] tenets in consumer behavior in the business cycle may be violated, namely, the positive relationship between the saving rate and economic activity. At least in moderate recessions it appears that consumers may be treating various categories of expenditures rather than saving as residual variables." And he then concludes, "Whether this is because of an overriding desire for security, or because debts accumulated during prosperity years are being paid off during recession, or for other reasons, remains to be established." R. Ferber, "Making Less Money and Saving More," *Illinois Business Review* (September, 1961). See also, G. Katona, *op. cit.*, Part IV, especially Ch. 13; Katona, *The Mass Consumption Society* (New York: McGraw-Hill, 1964).

37. The recent popularity of group interviews shows, at the methodological level, a concern with at least some of the attributes of the subject's environment. See, for example, E. Dichter, *The Strategy of Desire* (Garden City, New York: Doubleday, 1960), Ch. 7.

38. We doubt that in today's society of abundance any final act of choice can be usefully explained in biological terms. For example, although drinking may be explained in terms of a biological need (thirst), the consumption of soft drinks rather than liquors, and the choice of soft drink A over B, cannot. In fact, there are times when drinking itself may not be at all related to a biological need, but rather to needs such as meeting a person, being a member of a group, and so forth. (How many times do we go to a cocktail party because we are thirsty?)

39. The authors acknowledge their indebtedness for the ideas presented here to E. Katz, P. Ennis, and W. McPhee, all of whom contributed to their evolution in a seminar held at the Bureau of Applied Social Research some years ago.

40. E. Katz, *op. cit.*

41. E. Katz and Paul F. Lazarsfeld, *Personal Influence* (Glencoe, Ill.: The Free Press, 1955).

42. Opinion Research Corporation, *America's Tastemakers, op. cit.*

43. Charles Glock in F. S. Bourne, *op. cit.*, p. 218; R. A. Bauer, "The Communicator and the Audience," *Journal of Conflict Resolution*, II (1958), and E. M. Rogers and G. M. Beal, *Reference Group Influence in the Adoption of Agricultural*

Technology (Iowa Agricultural and Home Economics Experiment Station, Project No. 1236, 1958).

44. See, for example, W. Gruen, "Preference for New Products and Its Relationship to Different Measures of Conformity," *Journal of Applied Psychology*, XLIV (1960), concerning the relation of nonconformity and other-directedness to preference for new products; G. Bush and P. London, "On the Disappearance of Knickers: Hypothesis for the Functional Analysis of Clothing," *Journal of Social Psychology*, LI (1960), concerning the relation of social roles and self-concepts to the variability in clothing styles; and J. Clawson, "Lewin's Vector Psychology and the Analysis of Motives in Marketing," in R. Cox and W. Alderson, eds., *Theory in Marketing* (Chicago, Ill.: Irwin, 1950), W. J. Bilkey, "The Vector Hypothesis of Consumer Behavior," *Journal of Marketing*, XVI (1951), W. J. Bilkey, "A Psychological Approach to Consumer Behavior Analysis, *Journal of Marketing* (July 1953), and W. J. Bilkey, "Consistency Test of Psychic Tension Rating Involved in Consumer Purchasing Behavior," *Journal of Social Psychology* (February 1957), concerning applications of Lewin's social psychology.

45. For example, is the opinion-leader variable operating in decisions other than those concerning breakfast cereals, movies, fashion, farm equipment and practice, and new drugs? Working in this direction, we have found evidence, in a secondary analysis, that opinion leaders may be also operative in the area of auto insurance. See H. D. Roberts, *The Opinion Leader and Insurance*, A Report for the Degree of Master of Business Administration, University of California, Berkeley, May 1962, and F. M. Nicosia, "Opinion Leadership and the Flow of Communication: Some Problems and Prospects," in L. G. Smith, ed., *Reflections on Progress in Marketing*, Proceedings, American Marketing Association, Winter Conference (December 1964).

46. We must stress that the newly married couple case is most pertinent because it would not only allow the observation of the individual decision processes as they undergo a moment of strong perturbances and adjustments but also because it would permit observation of the interaction between the decision processes of the two parties. On the problem of interaction among two or more decision processes, see below, section on mathematical models of decision making.

47. Although the reference-group variable has gained increasing attention in many research areas—see H. H. Hyman, "Reflections on Reference Groups," *Public Opinion Quarterly* (Fall, 1960)—it has not been popular in either basic or applied consumer behavior research. Furthermore, the few studies on the role of this variable in consumer decision making have investigated only what appears to be its "normative" function (influence in the formation of attitudes) and have excluded its "comparative function" (that is, as the subject's measure of self-appraisal). The work of Bauer is an example of current studies; see R. A. Bauer, "Consumer Behavior as Risk Taking," in R. S. Hancock, ed., *Dynamic Marketing for a Changing World* (Chicago, Ill.: American Marketing Association, 1960). Following a suggestion by P. F. Lazarsfeld, "Sociological Reflections on Business," *op. cit.*, that group influence will be stronger where the wisdom of one's decision is difficult to assess, Bauer points out that "in many instances the function of group influence is to reduce perceived risk by confirming the wisdom of the choice" (*op. cit.*, p. 394). It is interesting to notice that, although introduced only as an *ad hoc* explanation of empirical data, reference groups in their comparative role have been implicitly used in some major economic studies; see, for instance, J. S. Duesenberry, *Income, Saving and the Theory of Consumer Be-*

havior (Cambridge, Mass.: Harvard University Press, 1949). The data presented by Glock and mentioned above suggest that reference groups may assume a comparative role in the decision to buy goods which are socially conspicuous (such as cars, cigarettes).

48. For example, no research on the two-step flow has been done under conditions of mass-media saturation such as those of the 1960 presidential campaign. One may thus question whether the two-step flow applies in situations of extreme saturation where selective exposure, and perhaps other factors making for selective cognition, are to a great extent eliminated. A preliminary study of this question has not provided conclusive evidence, but it has strongly demonstrated the complexity of the problem and the need for new research designs. See J. R. Goeke, "The Two-Step Flow of Mass Communication—The Theory Re-examined," Proceedings of AAPOR 16th meeting, *Public Opinion Quarterly*, Vol. XXV, No. 3 (Fall, 1961).

49. For example, we notice that Bauer attributes a risk-reduction function to both opinion leaders and reference groups (R. A. Bauer, "Consumer Behavior as Risk Taking," *op. cit.*). More generally, and in connection with the process of communication and influence, the opinion-leader studies show that this process is also "horizontal." But we know also that non-face-to-face reference groups and reference individuals (that is, the "reference idol" in H. H. Hyman, *op. cit.*) are sources of influence which may have a status higher than the person influenced. By investigating the relative role of both variables, we may succeed in mapping out the flow of information and influence both vertically and horizontally.

Other relationships could and should be also investigated. For example, a relation between the concepts of opinion leaders, reference groups, perception of self, and role perception emerges in a study by H. Trier, H. C. Smith, and J. Shaffer, "Differences in Food-buying Attitudes of Housewives," *Journal of Marketing* (July, 1960). In studying differences in food-buying attitudes of housewives, the researchers found that the influence of friends, parents, and husband varies with the wife's perception of her role and of her self.

50. The questions we must now answer are: What patterns of interaction among different channels of communication and influence exist for what kinds of purchasing behavior? Or: Do there also exist temporal patterns of interactions among different channels? These questions illustrate the need for a reorientation of much of current research assessing the effectiveness of various channels in any information campaign. Although progress in data processing now enables us to compute optimal allocations of a budget among various media, some of the basic prerequisites for these computations are not yet satisfied. Not only, in fact, can one not accept indicators such as readership and the like as measurements of each medium's effectiveness in producing a certain target behavior, but we must include in these computations provisions accounting for interactions among media. For an early and, to the best of our knowledge, still unique attempt to explore this problem of media interaction, see Bureau of Applied Social Research, *An Evaluation of Oil Progress Week* (New York: Columbia University, 1952–1954).

51. J. Coleman, E. Katz, and H. Menzel, *op. cit.*

52. For example, F. B. Evans, "Psychological and Objective Factors in the Prediction of Brand Choice: Ford Versus Chevrolet," *The Journal of Business* (October, 1959), on the role of personality and "objective" factors in predicting brand choice, and the discussion in the *Journal of Business* (January, 1961); see also

R. Westfall, "Psychological Factors in Predicting Product Choice," *Journal of Marketing* (April, 1962).

53. J. G. March and H. A. Simon, *Organizations* (New York: Wiley, 1958).

54. R. A. Bauer, "Consumer Behavior as Risk Taking," *op. cit.*

55. F. M. Nicosia, *Consumer Decision Processes, Marketing and Advertising Implications* (Englewood Cliffs, N.J.: Prentice-Hall, 1966).

56. Paul F. Lazarsfeld, "Sociological Reflections on Business," *op. cit.*

57. For an interesting study relating labor activity to family income and consumption, see J. Mincer, "Labor Supply, Family Income and Consumption," *American Economic Review*, Proceedings (May 1960).

58. For a very early speculation on household decisions, see Lewin's notion of "gate-keeper." Other suggestions on household decision processes are presented in W. Alderson, *Marketing Behavior and Executive Action* (Homewood, Ill.: Irwin, 1957), and W. Alderson, "Advertising Strategy and Theories of Motivation," in R. Ferber and H. Wales, eds., *Motivation and Market Behavior* (Homewood, Ill.: Irwin, 1958). For a summary of the major current ideas on this subject, see N. N. Foote, ed., *Household Decision-Making* (New York: New York University Press, 1961); the most classic empirical study is still G. Katona and E. Mueller, "A Study of Purchase Decisions," in L. Clark, ed., *Consumer Behavior, The Dynamics of Consumer Reaction* (New York: New York University Press, 1954). For simulation work in this area see the model developed for the prediction of the 1960 Wisconsin presidential primary elections; see particularly the role of the "discussion process" in the model's flow chart, W. McPhee, "Note on a Campaign Simulator," *Public Opinion Quarterly* (Summer, 1961), p. 185, Fig. 1. See also Clarkson's model for simulating investment decisions of a bank trust officer, G. P. E. Clarkson, "A Model of the Trust Investment Process," in E. A. Feigenbaum and J. Feldman, eds., *Computers and Thoughts* (New York: McGraw-Hill, 1963); the work by H. J. Claycamp and A. E. Amstutz, "Behavioral Simulation in Evaluating Alternative Marketing Strategies," *Proceedings, The Applications of Sciences in Marketing Management* (Lafayette, Indiana: Purdue University, 1966); and F. M. Nicosia, "Consumer Decision Processes, *op. cit.*, Ch. VI.

59. F. M. Nicosia, *ibid.*, esp. Ch. VII.

60. For an elementary description of a phenomenon over time and a "statistical" interpretation of the resulting curve, followed by a sociological interpretation, see The Foundation for Research on Human Behavior, *The Adoption of New Products: Process and Influence* (Ann Arbor, Mich.: 1959), pp. 1–4.

61. C. M. Crawford, *Sales Forecasting: Methods of Selected Firms* (Urbana, Ill.: Bureau of Economic and Business Research, University of Illinois, 1955).

62. Duesenberry, *op. cit.*

63. T. Parsons and N. J. Smelser, *Economy and Society* (Glencoe, Ill.: The Free Press, 1956).

64. See also N. J. Smelser, *New Directions in Sociology: Theory of Collective Behavior* (New York: Free Press, 1963); E. E. Hagen, *On the Theory of Social Change* (Homewood, Ill.: Dorsey Press, 1962); K. E. Boulding, *Conflict and Defense* (New York: Harper & Row, 1962); and C. Menger, *Problems of Economics and Sociology* (Urbana, Ill.: University of Illinois Press, 1963).

65. Duesenberry, *op. cit.*

66. For other examples see R. Ferber, "Research on Household Behavior," *op. cit.*, *passim*.

67. For more or less direct evidence, see A. C. Clarke, "The Use of Leisure and Its

Relation to Levels of Occupational Prestige," *American Sociological Review*, June 1956; E. Larrabee and R. Meyersohn, eds., *Mass Leisure* (New York: Free Press, 1958); and N. Anderson, *Work and Leisure* (New York: Free Press, 1961).

68. P. Martineau, *op. cit.*
69. D. Caplovitz, *The Poor Pay More* (New York: Free Press, 1963).
70. Bureau of Applied Social Research, *The "Rhythm and Blues" Fad* (New York: Columbia University, 1955).
71. W. N. McPhee, *Formal Theories of Mass Behavior* (New York: Free Press, 1963).
72. C. Y. Glock, "The Religious Revival in America," in J. C. Zahn, ed., *Religion and the Face of America* (Berkeley, Calif.: University of California, 1958).
73. For example, see the literature cited in the article-review by L. Guest, *op. cit.*, and R. Ferber, "Research on Household Behavior," *op. cit.* The great influence of psychology and economics in marketing and advertising literature is striking (see, for example, any textbook in these two fields; see also R. Ferber and H. G. Wales, *op. cit.*). We have looked at the articles on consumer research which have appeared in the *Journal of Marketing* over the last few years to count the number of authors who had had their academic training in sociology, psychology, and economics. Again, we found sociologists conspicuous by their absence. In a brief evaluation of the relationship between sociology and marketing studies of the consumer, C. T. Jonassen, "Contributions of Sociology to Marketing," *Journal of Marketing* (October, 1959), notes that significant marketing findings have been produced by sociologists in population, collective behavior, stratification, methodology, measurement, human ecology, and the family. But Jonassen summarizes his review by stating, "Much of this [sociological] knowledge, of course, remains a potential rather than a realized source of information."
74. We shall not consider in these remarks the influence that public agencies have had in the development of consumer research. Actually, their impact, in our judgment, has not been very great. These agencies' lack of concern with the social sciences, and with sociology in particular, reaches its maximum at the various Consumer Councils at the state and federal level. Notable exceptions are the Federal Reserve Board, the U.S. Department of Commerce, the U.S. Department of Agriculture, and intermittently the Bureau of Labor Statistics.
75. R. Bartels, *The Development of Marketing Thought* (Homewood, Ill.: Irwin, 1962).
76. Another factor making psychology more visible to management may be its widespread treatment in popular literature.
77. This lack of tolerance for ambiguity is illustrated in the propensity to be satisfied that an association of, say, .68 between a stimulus and response is a sufficient basis for action. The question of why the stimulus was not associated with responses in the remaining cases is almost never raised, nor is the question of whether those who fail to respond may represent a more suitable market for a product than those who do.
78. In point of fact, of course, motivation research never produces a completely unambiguous result, since there will always be exceptions to the general tendency. However, the exceptions tend to be overlooked in recommendations for policy.
79. We are referring here specifically to sociological research. Foundations have been a major source of support of economic research on consumption and consumer behavior.

Foreign Policy

W. PHILLIPS DAVISON

chapter 13

By the exercise of diligence, one can accumulate an impressive number of instances in which research on individual and group behavior has contributed to the planning or implementation of United States foreign policy. Such an inventory, by itself, could easily lead to the false conclusion that the behavioral sciences[1] play an important part in the conduct of our international relations. In fact, their role has been relatively minor. While a detailed examination of the ways in which the techniques and theory of the behavioral sciences have hitherto been utilized in United States foreign policy would be both interesting and pertinent, it is perhaps more important to ask why their role has been so limited, what their potential contribution is, and under what conditions they might contribute more. This essay will accordingly touch only lightly on present utilization and will devote more attention to potentialities, problems, and prescriptions.

Patterns of Use and Nonuse

Three principal modes of utilization can be observed. Behavioral-science research techniques have been employed to gather data that can be used in carrying out or evaluating foreign policy measures that have already been decided on; research studies have occasionally been undertaken to assist in policy decisions on specific problems or problem areas; and the literature of the behavioral sciences has frequently played a part in the training or orientation of foreign policy personnel.

In the case of data-gathering activities, heavy reliance has been placed on the sample survey, although depth interviews, content analysis, and other techniques have also been employed. The United States Information Agency and its predecessor agencies have maintained survey units ever since the days of World War II. These have focused mainly on audience attitudes and characteristics and on the extent to which information materials have been reaching those for whom they were intended. In the fiscal year 1966, the USIA spent approximately $500,000 for data gathering in various parts of the world—an amount that is substantial without being impressive.[2] The Agency for International Development has also used surveys, mainly to gather information on the extent to which technical training given in the United States has actually been put to work in the developing countries. The State Department has sponsored studies of foreigners who have visited the United States under government exchange programs in order to determine the usefulness of these visits to the exchangees, the attitude changes that have occurred among them, and the extent to which they have disseminated ideas about the United States after their return home. Various agencies of the armed services have undertaken surveys and other studies to gather social and psychological data about areas where United States forces are stationed or about present and potential adversaries. Because of the nonspecificity of budgets, particularly in AID and the Defense Department, and the fact that many studies are confidential, the total amount of money spent for surveys and other data-gathering enterprises that use behavioral-science techniques cannot be estimated with any accuracy.

More interesting, but also more difficult to find, are cases in which the behavioral sciences have directly affected the planning or execution of foreign policies. The United States attitude toward the Emperor of Japan during the final stages of World War II was influenced by analyses made largely by social anthropologists in the Office of War Information, who recommended that the United States should not attack the Emperor, but should leave his fate to be decided by the Japanese themselves after the war; and behavioral studies of the German armed forces helped Allied psychological-warfare personnel in Europe to take into account both the individual psychology of the German soldier and the social structure of which he was a part and thus to frame more effective surrender appeals.[3] Clandestine opinion surveys in North Africa prior to the landing of United States forces there apparently played a role in strategic decisions. These surveys found, for example, that an invasion force composed only of American troops was likely to encounter less resistance than one that included British personnel as well.[4] Analyses of the negotiating patterns of the Soviets and other Communist powers seem to have assisted American negotiators at the Korean truce talks in Panmunjom and at disarmament conferences at Geneva in anticipating how their North Korean or Soviet opposite numbers would behave.[5] In at least a few instances, political gaming techniques have been used by advisers to the White House or individual government departments to study alternative courses of action on foreign policy problems.

The Policy Planning Council of the State Department, in connection with long-range area planning, has shown an interest in theories of modernization and has occasionally invited behavioral scientists in the Department to contribute to the long-range planning process. In addition, the Department's Bureau of Intelligence and Research regularly produces political, economic, and sociological analyses of foreign developments that are injected into the foreign policy process on an almost daily basis. Some of these analyses explore the probable consequences of alternative courses of action; others put forward check lists of possible actions for consideration by policy makers.[6] The behavioral science component of this research is, however, usually very modest.

Data-gathering activities of the USIA, the Defense Department, and the educational exchange staff of the State Department have occasionally contributed directly to the formulation of specific policies, as well as to record keeping and background information. Surveys of the world reaction to the first Soviet satellite, for instance, played a role in recommendations that the United States space effort be accelerated.

While some fairly clear examples of behavioral-science utilization in foreign policy formulation can be found, in most cases it is difficult to determine how large a role it has played in any given decision. The number and diversity of considerations involved in the foreign policy process is so great that social research or theory may be a minor or insignificant factor, even when it points in the direction of the action that eventually is taken. For instance, a study of popular morale in West Berlin during the blockade of 1948 concluded that one of the reasons Berliners were able to resist Soviet pressure so successfully was that they felt the eyes of the world focused on them.[7] This conclusion suggested that one requirement for maintaining good morale in Berlin through subsequent crises was to assure the people of the city that they were still an object of world attention. The United States acted accordingly, sending one prominent personality after another to visit Berlin and making Berlin an issue in its world-wide information program. Nevertheless, it might very well have taken these actions for reasons other than the ones suggested by behavioral analysis.

Perhaps this is as it should be. In a 1960 symposium on research for public policy at the Brookings Institution, several speakers warned against a tendency to substitute research for policy making. Philip E. Mosely noted that social-science studies could serve as only one of the tools available to governmental leaders. Robert R. Bowie advised academicians to resist the urge to play the role of the Secretary of State. Pendleton Herring suggested that the measure of the contribution of social scientists to public policy was not the number of "solutions" proposed, but rather the influence of their thinking on the general tone of political discourse.[8] Certainly one must expect the relationship between the behavioral sciences and foreign policy to be a complex one, even when utilization can be demonstrated.

On the administrative side, several foreign policy agencies have experimented with the use of testing devices for the selection, placement, and assessment of personnel, as well as for evaluation of training programs. The Peace Corps has done this most systematically, although the State Department, USIA, AID, and military agencies have also shown an interest. The Air Force has used sociological and psychological research to determine the composition of air crews that will work most effectively as a team, and the other armed services have made analogous applications.

It is in the realm of education and orientation of officials concerned with international relations that the behavioral sciences probably make their most important contribution to foreign policy. Few of the senior personnel now employed by the State Department or other agencies involved in international relations have escaped exposure during their education to sociology, psychology, or anthropology, either directly or as a result of the infiltration of thinking from these disciplines into political science and history. Those most centrally concerned, including foreign service officers and some others, are likely to receive additional exposure through the Foreign Service Institute of the State Department or through a variety of special training programs in which they are given area orientation before proceeding to overseas posts. The War Colleges of the armed services and the National War College customarily include some material on individual and group behavior in their courses of study.

Inspection of either the Foreign Service Institute's excellent library or the outlines of its area and country study programs suggests the important part that the behavioral sciences play in its curriculum. Area study courses emphasize such concepts as comparative national character, comparative status and role analysis, social stratification, and cross-cultural communication. Readings for these and other courses at the Institute include Hall's

Silent Language, Herskovits' *The Human Factor in Changing Africa,* Almond and Coleman's *The Politics of the Developing Areas,* Goldhamer and Speier's pioneer article on political gaming, and Special Warfare Area Handbooks on numerous countries.[9] These handbooks, which are based in large part on material from the Human Relations Area Files, contain voluminous data on ethnic groups, social stratification, the family, social values, and related subjects.

How many foreign policy personnel retain and put to work the social theory and data to which they are exposed at their own universities and at the Foreign Service Institute or other government institutions has not been investigated. A State Department official has reported that at least one foreign service officer has regularly followed sociological categories in reporting information about the areas in which he has been stationed, although before sending in his reports he has carefully removed all traces of technical terminology. Others have found a background in the behavioral sciences to be useful in suggesting pertinent questions and ordering observations about foreign societies. It is helpful, for instance, to see commercial organizations, or courts and other legal structures, as institutions whose practical utility can be appreciated only in the local social and cultural context.

The extent to which the behavioral disciplines have been ignored in the conduct of our foreign relations is, however, much more impressive than the degree to which they have been used. Cases of utilization that can be cited tend to be isolated or tenuous; the main stream of foreign policy is affected only sporadically and tangentially by sociological or psychological theory, or by systematic research on individuals and groups. When questioned about their personal experiences, most foreign service officers find it difficult to cite instances where behavioral research or theory have affected their activities. The Country Desks and Geographic Bureaus of the State Department, where the spadework of foreign policy planning and administration is performed, are influenced at most only marginally by behavioral studies. At United States embassies overseas one can usually find several economists practicing their trade, but discovery of an active sociologist, psychologist, or anthropologist is a rare event.[10] USIA research officers, of which there were about 15 at overseas posts in 1966, are often the sole representatives of the behavioral sciences. Examination of the files of the *Foreign Service Journal* and of *Foreign Affairs,* probably the most widely read of the professional periodicals reaching foreign policy personnel, discloses very little attention to the concepts or methods of the behavioral disciplines, except insofar as these are occasionally referred to in articles by political scientists and area specialists.

By contrast to the situation among officials who are centrally located in the foreign policy process, relatively greater utilization is found among those in peripheral agencies and in newer agencies. The Defense Department has been notable for both its sponsorship and its use of social research, in these respects overshadowing all other federal agencies.[11] A congressional committee has pointed out that the bulk of research in foreign affairs is controlled by military agencies, rather than by the people who are directly in charge of the conduct of United States foreign policy. The Department of the Army, for instance, spent $600,000 in 1963 on a single foreign area study, while the entire contract research program of the State Department's Bureau of Intelligence and Research limped along on a scant $84,000.[12] During the following two years, behavioral-research programs sponsored by the Defense Department cost approximately $20 million per year, and the State Department commitment for similar studies rose to about $200,000.

Of the civilian bodies concerned with foreign policy, the Arms Control and Disarmament Agency may have made the most systematic efforts to use behavioral research for policy purposes, possibly because the newness and difficulty of this agency's task has forced it to extend its search for ideas into nontraditional areas. Starting in approximately 1961, the Agency for International Development substantially increased its efforts to employ social studies in planning and evaluating development projects, but the extent of actual utilization is still very modest. It is the exception, rather than the rule, when cultural and social factors are systematically taken into account in AID activities.

Examples of the utilization of the behavioral sciences can be found more frequently in time of war than in time of peace. Some of the most telling examples still stem from World War II; others from the Korean War. The increase in the tempo of hostilities in Vietnam from 1963 to 1966 led to a substantial growth in the number of research projects in Southeast Asia involving behavioral scientists. Even in wartime, however, the central foreign policy agencies have remained dependent almost exclusively on their traditional sources of information and traditional modes of analysis, and it has been the military and communication agencies that have turned to sociology, psychology, or anthropology.

The important role of the Defense Department in the sponsorship and utilization of behavioral research has yielded considerable benefits, but has also led to serious problems. On the one hand, the resources for the conduct of our foreign policy, and social science as a whole, would be poorer if military agencies had not stepped in and provided funds and encouragement that were not forthcoming from civilian departments. Much of the research of the RAND Corporation, the former Operations Research Office of John Hopkins University, and the former Human Resources Research Institute of the Air University, all of which have (or had) strong behavioral-science components, has been applicable far beyond the strictly military sphere. On the other hand, the necessity for justifying research under military budgets has led to emphases and nomenclature that have sometimes been experienced as embarrassing or counter-productive by foreign policy officials. The "Special Warfare Area Handbooks," so named because they were produced under military auspices, seem out of place on the bookshelves of State Department officials overseas, even though the contents of these volumes are for the most part useful, scholarly, and inoffensive. Long before Project Camelot was heard of, diplomats wondered how they could explain to friendly governments why American scholars in their countries were conducting projects labeled "psychological warfare" or "counterinsurgency," even though these studies often were concerned primarily with comparative value systems or varying types of group structure.

A Digression on "Camelot"

In the summer of 1965, an Army-supported behavioral-research project with the exotic title "Camelot" aroused unfavorable attention in Chile. This led to diplomatic complications, to a Presidential letter directing the Secretary of State to insure that government-sponsored social-science research in foreign areas did not adversely affect United States foreign relations, to some sharp criticism of behavioral studies in the United States Senate, and to a situation where, in the judgment of one Latin American specialist, not a single survey research study could be done in Chile and quantitative studies were halted or impeded throughout Latin America.[13]

Camelot was described in Army documents as a "basic social science research project on preconditions of internal conflict, and on effects of indigenous government actions—easing, exacerbating or resolving—on those preconditions." Its task was to find "methods for predicting and influencing social change and internal war potential."[14] Stated in less technical language, the project's purpose was to study the conditions that might lead to armed insurrections in a variety of developing countries so as to enable United States authorities to help friendly governments eliminate the causes of such insurrections or to deal with them should they occur. Camelot was to be conducted by the Special Operations Research Office of American University, with a four-year budget of $6 million.

The proposed research never progressed beyond a preliminary stage, and available accounts differ slightly as to exactly what happened.[15] Apparently, one of Camelot's consultants, who was traveling in Latin America primarily on another mission, started to discuss the project with Chilean behavioral scientists just prior to the time when American intervention in the Dominican Republic occurred. News of the Dominican affair led to the not unnatural interpretation in Chile that the research project was somehow connected with a United States policy of opposing any revolutionary movement in Latin America—an interpretation that was also advanced by Senate Foreign Relations Committee Chairman William Fulbright. Camelot received unflattering attention in the Chilean press, which pointed out among other things that its representative had been less than candid in revealing its military sponsorship. The Chilean government protested to the American Ambassador, who had not been advised about the undertaking in advance; the Ambassador lodged a protest in Washington, and Camelot was canceled. According to those responsible for the project, there had in any case been no plans to conduct research specifically in Chile.

Even following cancellation there were continued repercussions in Washington as well as throughout Latin America. In accordance with Presidential instructions, the State Department started working out a procedure for reviewing government-sponsored social-science research in foreign areas to insure that it did not affect United States foreign relations adversely. This led to apprehension on the part of some American social scientists that freedom to pursue foreign area studies under government sponsorship would be sharply curtailed, or that State Department clearance would be so difficult and time-consuming to obtain that research of this nature would be stifled.

These fears were at least partially quieted by the announcement of clearance procedures by the State Department in October, 1965. The review function was to be performed by a Foreign Affairs Research Council, chaired by the Department's Director of Intelligence and Research, who stated that the purpose of the body would be to encourage rather than to stifle inquiry. The Research Council would not try to decide whether individual studies were or were not important, nor would it attempt to dictate how they were to be carried out; the review would be solely for the purpose of safeguarding United States foreign relations from "predictable harm." Furthermore, formal clearance procedures were to apply only to research supported by foreign affairs, defense, and intelligence agencies and were expected to take about two weeks.[16] Optimists in the Washington social-science community commented that assignment of this responsibility to the Department of State would at least compel that agency to pay more attention to social and psychological research than it had in the past.

In spite of the furor aroused by Camelot, *Science* magazine reported a high measure of agreement, in and out of government, that research of this nature was necessary.[17] Indeed, it is difficult to argue against the proposition that additional knowledge about social change in developing areas would be a valuable asset not only to the conduct of United States foreign relations but also to the developing nations themselves. As a behavioral scientist who served as a consultant to Camelot has pointed out, such knowledge can indeed be used either to foment or to repress revolutions, but it is also necessary if one is to find peaceful ways of satisfying the aspirations of those whose old social systems are falling apart.[18]

There is a wider division of opinion as to whether such studies should be supported by military agencies. Camelot has underlined the fact that military sponsorship can make the task of the researcher much more difficult under some conditions. (Under other conditions—for example, when he is dealing with foreign military officials—it may facilitate his work.) Nevertheless, until civilian agencies or private sources are willing and able to support behavioral studies abroad on a larger scale, those who believe that such studies are increasingly vital will frequently have to choose between military sponsorship and inaction. Thus far, the State Department has made few determined efforts to secure funds for behavioral studies in foreign areas, and congressional appropriations committees have proved inhospitable to those attempts that have been made.

One subject that has received very little attention in connection with the debate about Camelot is whether, if the project had been completed as planned, its results would have appreciably affected United States foreign policy. This is very doubtful. If past experience is any guide, it would have contributed to our knowledge about developing societies, it would have enriched the literature, but its effects on this country's international relations would probably have been tangential and indirect.

Expected Potentialities

While only sporadic use has been made of the behavioral sciences in the conduct of foreign affairs, some government officials and numerous social scientists have indicated by word and deed that they have high expectations as to the potential utility of these disciplines. The Subcommittee on International Organizations and Movements of the House Foreign Affairs Committee has repeatedly called for increased contributions to the psychological and ideological dimensions of foreign policy by the behaviorial sciences.[19] In 1962, the Behavioral Science Subpanel of the President's Science Advisory Committee and Vice-President (then Senator) Hubert Humphrey both advocated an increased role for the social sciences in foreign affairs, as well as in other fields.[20] During the past decade repeated attempts have been made to establish a National Academy or Foundation that would serve as a channel for social science advice to policy makers. A number of proposals along these lines have received congressional attention, but none had been enacted as of 1966.

Several federal agencies have indicated even more concretely, by allocating research funds and by establishing mechanisms for keeping track of both government and private studies, that they think behavioral research can be useful to foreign policy officials. The amounts that are spent by the government for behavioral research in the foreign policy area are substantial, although they cannot be estimated accurately, since it is difficult to disentangle funds devoted to economic, historical, and other studies from those used to support research in the behavioral sciences. An estimate in 1964 was that the total cost of government-sponsored social research in the foreign policy field ran to about $64 million annually, although this included $25 million presumably devoted by the Central Intelligence Agency to data collection from open sources.[21] In 1965, State Department sources estimated that about 750 research contracts dealing with foreign policy and international affairs were signed annually by federal agencies and that the total government expenditure for this research was at least $31 million per year.[22] These estimates probably do not include United States contributions to UNESCO and other international organizations that conduct some behavioral research, but probably do include some activities that could be classified as social-science research only under an extremely generous definition of the term.

Another evidence of federal interest in behavioral research on matters of potential relevance to foreign policy is the establishment in Washington of a Foreign Area Research Coordination Group, which held its first meeting in April, 1964. The group includes representation from the Departments of State, Defense, Agriculture, and Health, Education, and Welfare, as well as from the Agency for International Development, the Arms Control Agency, the Central Intelligence Agency, the United States Information Agency, the National Science Foundation, and several other governmental units. The External Research Staff of the State Department serves as Executive Secretariat for the group and keeps members informed about studies completed and in progress under both government and private sponsorship. It also maintains a Foreign Area Research Documentation Center. Started in September, 1964, the Center filled 300 requests for information in the first month of its existence and over 500 in the second month.[23] Some of the lists and indices compiled by the External Research Staff are available to private scholars as well as to other government offices. These include bibliographies of research on various regions of the world, directories of area research centers at American universities, and surveys of research studies in nongeographic categories that bear on international relations.

Somewhat similar but more specialized functions are performed by a number of military or quasi-military agencies and governmental libraries. The Defense Documentation Center at Alexandria, Virginia, includes social-science materials among the 750,000 documents that are registered in the memory of its Univac computer and fills about 6,000 requests a day. A Counterinsurgency Information Analysis Center, serving the defense community and other authorized users, is maintained by the Center for Research in Social Systems of American University under contract with the Department of the Army. Several divisions of the Library of Congress keep track of social-science materials that bear on certain aspects of foreign affairs, as do a number of departmental and agency libraries.

It would be possible to cite government statements of interest, expenditures of funds, and cataloguing activities as evidence that behavioral research is being used in the formulation and implementation of our foreign policy, but such an interpretation would be true to only a limited extent. Some of the information that is laboriously collected and analyzed does indeed penetrate the barriers that separate the "Indians" from the "chiefs" in Washington, and it enters into the policy process. Much more, however, revolves at a lower level among those who are themselves researchers or research administrators, never percolating "upstairs" to influence what the United States says and does in the world arena. As far as foreign policy is concerned, government support of behavioral research is largely an expression of confidence and hope on the part of a relatively small number of officials that the behavioral sciences can and should contribute more to foreign policy formulation and implementation in the future; it is not proof that social research or theory is being used extensively or effectively now.

Academicians have expressed similar expectations by both deeds and words. In particular, the rapidly increasing numbers of language and area study programs, most of which include a behavioral-science component, seem to reflect policy as well as educational interests. The State Department's External Research Staff found that the number of these programs increased from 62 in 1954 to 153 by 1964. In the latter year, 48 programs were devoted to Asia, 34 to Russia and Eastern Europe, 30 to Latin America, 18 to the Near East, 16 to Africa, and the rest to Western Europe.[24]

Statements by academicians about the potential utility of the behavioral sciences in international relations range from expression of a generalized hope that the destructive forces at work in society can be brought under control through use of the scientific method, to specific advice as to how theory or research techniques could be employed in particular areas.[25] Gardner Murphy has outlined ten ways that behavioral science might contribute to a more peaceful world. These include using attitude and opinion research methods to assess American readiness to accept changes associated with disarmament, discovery of "choice points" at which social movements can be channeled into a peaceful rather than a warlike direction, intensive studies of specific social and political leaders, and developing more effective ways of communicating between the Communist and non-Communist worlds.[26] Morton A. Kaplan has suggested that game theory can be applied to statecraft, at least insofar as it narrows the range within which solutions can reasonably be sought and makes the factors involved more explicit.[27] Karl Deutsch has expressed the hope that a theory of politics can be developed which will "link the *is* and the *ought*" and thus help us to find policies that will be more effective in realizing our principal values.[28] An extensive bibliography of writings by social scientists on the role of social-science research in American international and military policy has been compiled by the Bureau of Social Science Research, and Herbert C. Kelman has noted the increasing tendency of psychologists and those in related disciplines to bring their specialized knowledge or analytic approach to bear on policy issues.[29] All this does not mean, however, that the proffered advice is being accepted.

It is perhaps indicative of the dominant strain of thinking among behavioral scientists that the three papers on utilization of sociology in foreign relations that were presented at the American Sociological Association's meeting in 1962 gave more attention to ways that social research could or should be used than to current uses.[30] Robert T. Bower, in discussing the evaluation of foreign policy, cited a substantial number of studies that had been made for purposes of evaluation, but he also pointed out their limitations and emphasized the greater role that research has the capacity to play in specifying critical variables, sensitizing policy makers to them, and extracting more useful information from traditional sources such as the mass media and informed observers. David Rodnick advocated increased attention to the aspirations and frustrations of both those who formulate foreign policies and those who accept them. Feliks Gross suggested a typology of international tensions that could be used in deciding what kinds of action might be taken to relieve these tensions. He noted, for instance, that friction between Italian- and German-speaking ethnic groups in Alto Adige might be ameliorated by the application of some of the methods developed to relieve intergroup tensions in the United States.

The conviction of many social scientists that behavioral studies can help to solve problems in international relations has led to an increasing number of books and articles on the problem of preserving peace. Some of these have focused on the body of theory and knowledge that might be used by the policy maker working to lessen the danger of war; others have offered specific policy prescriptions. Otto Klineberg's *Human Dimension in International Relations*[31] and *Psychiatric Aspects of the Prevention of Nuclear War* by the Group for the Advancement of Psychiatry[32] both summarize a large volume of behavioral data that the authors believe could be relevant to the avoidance or solution of conflict. Klineberg points out, for instance, that research has disclosed nothing in human nature that makes war inevitable, that myths about race have bequeathed a needless legacy of hatred to the world, and that national stereotypes may be used to justify warlike policies toward other peoples. The Group for the Advancement of Psychiatry, in an effort to contribute to a "new manner of thinking" about international conflict, discusses such topics as the effects of fear, the employment of dehumanization as a psychological defense mechanism, distortions of perception in relation to war, and a variety of measures for managing conflict in interpersonal relations that might be applied on the international level.

Among the more specific policy recommendations by behavioral scientists that have been published in book form during the past few years are Charles E. Osgood's *Alternative to War or Surrender*,[33] Amitai Etzioni's *The Hard Way to Peace*,[34] and Vincent P. Rock's *A Strategy of Interdependence*.[35] Osgood advocates a policy of Graduated Reciprocation in Tension-Reduction, which he describes as a formula for waging the arms race in reverse, with built-in safeguards. Under this policy, the United States would embark on a series of carefully phased unilateral measures to reduce tension with the Communist powers. These measures in numerous areas, including economic and cultural exchanges as well as disarmament, would be taken in such a way as to maximize the probability that the Communist powers would respond with tension-reduction measures of their own. Communist responses, in turn, would facilitate renewed peaceful efforts by the United States. Etzioni, writing from the standpoint of a political sociologist, recommends a strategy aimed at reducing nonrational barriers that now obstruct successful interbloc communication and negotiation. In his view, unilateral tension-reducing steps by the United States, both symbolic and substantive, could pave the way for fruitful multilateral negotiations. Rock's prescription, which involves weaving a web of cooperative relationships between the United States and the Soviet Union, is in the tradition of suggestions proposed by a number of writers, including Morton Deutsch and Robert C. Angell.[36] Articles in which behavioral scientists offer either background information or policy suggestions on the problem of peace can be found in profusion in American and foreign professional journals, especially in such specialized periodicals as the *Journal of Conflict Resolution*, the *Journal of Peace Research* (Oslo), and the *Bulletin of the Atomic Scientists*. These and many other sources are listed and annotated in the quarterly bibliography *Arms Control and Disarmament* prepared by the Library of Congress.

In addition to those publications that are concerned primarily with questions of peace and war, there is a vast library of writings containing observations and insights about individual and group behavior relating to other aspects of international relations. Notable among the categories of this literature are studies of political development, of which the Social Science Research Council series on political development and the publications of the Center of International Studies at Princeton offer a number of outstanding examples.[37] Development administration alone is the subject of 340 periodical references that have been annotated by Allan A. Spitz and Edward W. Weidner in their bibliography on the subject.[38] A selective bibliography prepared by the State Department in 1965 suggests that the literature on cross-cultural education is even more voluminous.[39]

Some of the conclusions reached by behavioral scientists in their studies of the international scene have been so clear in their policy implications that it is surprising that so little notice has been taken of them by government agencies. For example, David C. McClelland's finding that ideas shape institutions, which in turn change the material environment (thus contradicting the assumption that the environment is primary and that individuals and social institutions merely adapt to it), points to the need for paying more attention to values and motivation in developing countries. Yet there is no indication that a serious attempt has been made to do this in our foreign-aid program. To quote McClelland: "Isn't it time we stopped rediscovering the importance of values for economic development and began to act as if we believed what we know?" [40] Perhaps more attention has been given to Herbert C. Kelman's injunction that exchange-of-persons programs are more likely to achieve their objectives if the foreign visitors are given an opportunity to become involved in an ongoing enterprise[41] and to the observation of Gabriel A. Almond and Sidney Verba that "it is possible to communicate through education the explicit norms of democratic participation and responsibility." [42]

One can also cite examples of perceptive analyses of specific situations by social scientists, which suggest that behavioral techniques and theory can usefully supplement traditional styles of political reporting. By studying birthday greetings to Stalin, Nathan Leites and his collaborators identified the triumvirate that succeeded to power immediately after the Soviet dictator's death.[43] Harold D. Lasswell, using content-analysis methods, found that the pattern of attention in the Nazi press changed suddenly just prior to the Molotov-Ribbentrop pact in 1939. A precipitous decline in references to the Soviet Union indicated that Germany was clearing the path for a change in diplomatic orientation.[44] David Rodnick, employing the techniques of cultural anthropology, related the frustrations that widespread circles in post-war France experienced in their daily lives to an equally widespread desire for a strong national leader. His analysis foreshadowed not only the return of de Gaulle to power but also the approximate political form that Gaullist France would assume.[45] Lloyd A. Free, on the basis of surveys conducted in Cuba well before the Bay of Pigs invasion, concluded that Castro enjoyed immense popularity in the Cuban countryside and that a small but growing opposition was limited largely to the city of Havana. Following the invasion, a White House official expressed regret that these surveys had not been taken into account in top-level policy decisions regarding Cuba, although they had in fact been made available to the government. Free's conclusions after a study of the Dominican Republic in 1962 were even more unequivocal: "An extremely serious situation of popular discontent and frustration, fraught with a dangerous potential for upheaval, exists in the Dominican Republic." [46] These fears were amply borne out in 1965.

It is obviously unfair to assemble such examples after the fact, without also searching for cases in which political predictions or analyses by social scientists have gone awry. Be that as it may, behavioral research has never seriously threatened the dominance of anecdotal methods and hunch in political reporting and analysis by the central foreign policy agencies.

Barriers to Greater Utilization

"The planner does not face a choice between long-run and short-run interests," wrote State Department planning chief Walt W. Rostow in 1964; "he must combine them. . . . In foreign policy, as in economics, the long-run consists of the accumulation of what we do in the short run." [47] Rostow goes on to say that the planner thus has to concern himself not only with goals but also with how to get from here to there; in other words, he must understand thoroughly the present operational environment in which any recommendation or concept is to be applied.

These observations point to one of the most important difficulties standing in the way of greater utilization of the behavioral sciences by those who are most centrally concerned with foreign policy planning and implementation. The problems that present themselves most urgently to foreign policy personnel are nearly always short-run problems, even though they may be part of a series having long-run implications. Actions and decisions must be taken in the here and now in the real world of international relations. Any advice that can easily be used, therefore, has to be applicable to the immediate situation.

Advice received from behavioral scientists rarely satisfies this criterion of immediate applicability. It is frequently couched in language that is impenetrable as far as foreign policy personnel are concerned;[48] it often deals in generalities or with subjects that are not actionable at the time; and it usually ignores the historical and political contexts in which decisions have to be made or actions taken. In addition, those who are charged with making foreign policy decisions frequently complain that behavioral scientists are reluctant to provide advice when it is needed; their insistence on thorough and time-consuming analysis means that their reports are received long after decisions have been made.

The tendency to ignore historical testimony, and even the political realities of the present, is especially strong. In general, behavioral scientists have not taken to heart Harold D. Lasswell's injunction that experience in the practical realm should be considered relevant data.[49] As a result, many of their observations are dismissed as unhelpful by those closer to day-to-day international politics, who feel that the gap between the proffered advice and the needs of the present moment is too wide. Typical of this reaction are the remarks of a foreign service officer to the effect that a recent book on international relations by a sociologist was "optimistic, attractive, intellectually stimulating, but quite unrealistic." [50] In reviewing a volume on the potential contributions of psychology to foreign policy, a political scientist reacted in somewhat the same way when he expressed discouragement about "the attempt to apply psychological generalizations in the abstract." [51] More specific policy proposals, also, no matter how thoroughly they are grounded in psychological or sociological theory, are likely to be viewed with suspicion by foreign policy personnel if they do not take the historical record into account: What has been the experience of nations that have tried to use concessions as a means of reducing tensions? Did Chamberlain's willingness to negotiate with Mussolini encourage the latter to proceed with his military adventures in Albania and Ethiopia? Questions such as these, often arising out of a diplomat's own experience, tend to stand between him and suggestions arising out of the systematic study of individual and group behavior.

Criticisms to the effect that the observations of behavioral scientists are of little value because they slight the historical dimension of international relations, or fail to take current political realities into account, are not entirely justified. A one-sided contribution may be valuable; and even though some elements of political reality are visible only to those with access to confidential information or daily cables, it does not follow that other kinds of knowledge should be excluded from the decision process. Nevertheless, whether justified or not, criticisms that fall into this category are important in explaining the limited extent to which the work of behavioral scientists is utilized in the planning and implementation of foreign policy.

A closely related criticism is that the advice of social scientists is frequently too general or too theoretical. A theory of enormous significance may still have little applicability if the steps leading from the general to the particular are not spelled out. Cross-cultural communication, for instance, is a concept of unquestioned utility in the practice of foreign relations, but handing a treatise on the subject to a diplomat faced with a specific problem is a little like giving a volume on electrical engineering to a man who wants to find out why his desk lamp isn't working. As a writer in the London *Economist* observed, although not with specific reference to foreign affairs, "the relationship between the front line of theoretical sociology and the detailed research on which social policy is built is surprisingly weak." [52] The number of cases in which a body of social theory or research has been systematically culled for information of utility in foreign policy, which has then been presented in a form comprehensible to operational personnel, is rather small. One outstanding case of putting research to work in a specific area is Wilbur Schramm's *Mass Media and National Development*.[53] Schramm painstakingly spells out ways that governments of developing countries might apply knowledge about communication and economic development, even suggesting a model for a basic mass-communication inventory. Another possible candidate in a very different area is *How Nations Negotiate,* by Fred Charles Iklé.[54] In his work, Iklé breaks down international negotiations into their component parts and discusses the relationships among these. It is, in effect, a handbook for negotiators. These volumes, however, are exceptions to the general rule.

In addition to objecting that the contributions of social science are too general or are presented in an unusable form, foreign policy personnel frequently complain that behavioral scientists tend to focus on the wrong subjects. One foreign service officer observed that when you consult an anthropologist about Latin America he can usually tell you a great deal about Indian tribes, but very little about the people you are trying to deal with. Another practitioner deplored the influence of "academic giants" whose interests are likely to determine the interests of their students, with the result that a dozen studies may be produced on one specialized subject, while other subjects of equal political significance are ignored. The problem of researchability and the favor shown to areas of potential theoretical significance also help to rule out from consideration numerous subjects that may, at one time or another, prove to be of burning political interest.

For these reasons, and probably others, striking gaps in the coverage of American scholars (both behavioral scientists and those in related areas) have become evident. At the time Castro came to power, no American academician had made contemporary Cuba a major focus of his interest.[55] State Department officials were unable to discover anyone who had specialized in Vietnamese Buddhism when Buddhist-led demonstrations erupted in South Vietnam. Students of South African society, which gives promise of being a nexus of international tension during the next decade, are still in extremely short supply.

Other reasons why the behavioral sciences do not make a greater contribution to international affairs are to be found in the attitudes of foreign policy personnel and in the current governmental structure. Although most academicians may not be aware of it, since they come in contact mainly with government officials who are not unfavorably disposed toward them, there is still a deep suspicion of social science among many foreign affairs practitioners, especially those of the older generation. There are also strong prejudices against the use of the word "science" in connection with behavioral studies, and the objection is frequently heard that the results of social research are trivial, incomprehensible, or obvious to anyone who cares to use common sense, in spite of the demolition of the argument of "obviousness" by Paul F. Lazarsfeld almost twenty years ago.[56] This complex of attitudes was reflected in a House of Representatives Appropriations Committee report that commented on behavioral research proposed by the Defense Department in the spring of 1965: "Some of the areas being pursued in behavioral sciences appear not to offer any real promise of providing useful information. Other studies appear to be concerned with trivial matters on which intelligent people should not require studies in order to be informed." [57]

A part of the prejudice against students of human behavior stems from the belief that foreign policy is an area that should be dealt with by generalists. The Foreign Service, somewhat like the military establishment, has traditionally insisted that any officer should be able to perform any job. He should not be a geographical or functional specialist, but should have a well-rounded appreciation of all the major factors entering into international relations. Specialists can be tolerated in the lower ranks of the service, but the higher one goes the more important a broad and diversified career becomes. This attitude is now starting to break down, in part because of the distinction with which economists have filled some high diplomatic posts that were previously reserved for generalists; but the antispecialist prejudice still causes resistance to the idea that behavioral studies can add significantly to the usable knowledge of an experienced foreign service officer.

An even more important attitudinal factor that limits the utilization of behavioral science and scientists is the basic difference between the world view of the scientist and that of the traditional diplomat. This difference has been noted especially by some of the natural scientists who have served as attachés at American embassies abroad. The diplomat, they report, usually looks at major developments and trends as phenomena to which the United States should adjust. Perhaps some advantage can be taken of these developments and trends by skillful diplomatic maneuvering, but basically they cannot be affected. They are part of the inexorable march of history. The scientist, on the other hand, usually responds to a situation with such questions as: What causes it? What can be done about it? How can it be controlled? This difference in outlook adds to the difficulties that scientific and diplomatic personnel have in communicating with each other.

The laissez-faire view of social and political events entertained by most traditional diplomatists contrasts sharply with their attitudes in the economic sphere, where it is generally accepted that foreign economic policy can influence and even direct economic development. The carry-over of this thinking to noneconomic fields seems thus far to have been severely limited, however, and in the political and social sphere foreign policy personnel tend to take refuge behind such slogans as "Each nation must work out its own future by itself." Such an attitude contrasts sharply with that of the Communist powers, which, through mass indoctrination and the formation of cadres, have made concerted efforts to create new social and political environments in several parts of the world.

A complex of attitudes opposed to behavioral research is found most frequently in the central foreign policy agencies. One result is that these agencies have never made a major and sustained effort to secure substantial funds for research on social and psychological questions of critical importance to them. In the State Department, the available funds have been sufficient to catalogue research done elsewhere and to commission a few studies drawing mainly on work originally performed with other ends in view, but they have not allowed the Department to embark on major behavioral research programs of operational utility in dealing with principal foreign policy issues.

Overriding importance should not, however, be ascribed to attitudes opposed to behavioral science. Even though these predominate and tend to prevent the channeling of research funds into areas where they could be useful, there are still an adequate number of doors in the State Department open to anyone who has something important to say. The proportion of foreign affairs personnel who are favorably disposed—possibly because they have at one time received assistance from a USIA research officer or an academic social scientist—grows from year to year. In addition, those engaged in the planning and administration of foreign policy not infrequently raise questions that behavioral scientists might help to answer. For instance, the writer recently heard an ambassador say that he wished more could be done to identify emerging leaders in developing countries. He was disturbed, he added, at the frequency with which members of new governments were totally unknown to the United States mission prior to their rise to cabinet level. A former State Department Office Director expressed dissatisfaction with the political reporting received from overseas posts and asked whether some way could be found to designate more clearly those categories of social and economic information that were likely to be politically significant. A United States military adviser complained that he found the foreign officers with whom he was working to be "inscrutable" and wondered how a more fruitful exchange of ideas with them could be established. Questions such as these suggest a hospitality to behavioral research, even though those who raise the questions rarely think of turning to social scientists for the answers.

Even officials who are favorably disposed toward the use of behavioral studies are, however, hampered by the staffing patterns and business tempo in most foreign policy agencies. The pressure of short-term assignments on nearly all ranking personnel means that they are barely able to keep up with the most pressing duties, and the task of reading anything that is not both brief and directly applicable to a current problem is almost insuperable. In the Policy Planning Council, the ivory tower of the State Department, principal foreign policy officials rarely have time to digest and apply research that might be relevant to their work; nor do they have the staffs that might do this for them. The intelligence and research personnel in the State Department find themselves buried under a deluge of current information, and when they are able to prepare longer-range analyses they find it difficult to secure the attention of those engaged directly in operations. One State Department analyst observed that at the most one could secure high-level attention to "quickie" background papers on subjects of current burning interest. The Defense Department and armed services are partial exceptions to these observations, in that their more generously proportioned staffs and budgets allow more opportunities for reviewing research and working out applications.

The same pressures make it difficult for foreign policy personnel to initiate social research on the relatively rare occasions when they wish to do so and have funds available. It takes time to select the questions that are likely to be amenable to investigation by behavioral scientists and to formulate these questions in such a manner that they can be attacked with available research techniques. If systematic research is to be used for evaluation purposes, for example, aims must be stated in a form that allows the investigator to employ objective criteria in gauging the degree of their achievement.[58] Furthermore, formulating research tasks often requires the assistance of specialized personnel, who are usually not easily available for the purpose. Those agencies (in most cases military ones) that have made the most extensive use of behavioral science have often invited outside scholars to work with them in designing research programs, or they have entrusted the task to behavioral scientists on their staffs. If they are to lead to easily applicable results, research designs must ordinarily reflect a knowledge both of research techniques and of the day-to-day operating procedures of the using officials. Under present circumstances, this combination is difficult to achieve in the central foreign policy agencies.

Compounding all the attitudinal and structural difficulties that stand in the way of greater utilization of behavioral science is the screen of government security and the difficulty of studying some of the most critical aspects of foreign policy operations. The functioning of the National Security Council, the relationship between the State Department and the foreign affairs specialists in the White House, and the operating procedures of the Joint Chiefs of Staff are all inaccessible to the systematic observational techniques that have been used in studying other social institutions. The degree of inaccessibility increases when the instrumentalities of foreign governments are concerned. Classified information may be made available to behavioral scientists working within the government or directly for it; but the cumbersome precautions involved in handling these data, and the fact that reports making use of them are ordinarily not subject to the criticism of the broader academic community, limit the benefits that can be derived from access to classified sources.

Is Greater Utilization Possible?

There is no guaranty that sweeping away these barriers to greater utilization would automatically lead to a larger contribution by behavioral scientists to foreign policy, since several uncomfortable questions remain. Of what would this contribution consist, and how would it be made? Is it possible that the skeptics are correct and that the potentialities of behavioral science to assist in the planning and administration of United States foreign policy are at most marginal? Perhaps the fact that sociology, psychology, and anthropology have proved most useful in wartime and to agencies on the fringes of foreign policy indicates, not that behavioral research should be utilized more by central policy agencies, but that a peripheral role is the correct one. Indeed, it is possible that greater utilization is not desirable.

The only way in which these questions can be answered satisfactorily is by creating conditions under which a greater contribution is possible and then testing various modes of application over a period of time. Even to create such conditions is a difficult task and would require adjustments on the part of both government and academicians.

In the governmental sphere, three conditions should ideally be satisfied: there should be a greater willingness to apply the results of behavioral studies; behavioral scientists should be employed in positions where they can serve as a communication channel between central foreign policy organs and the academic community; and one or more organizations should be established to undertake or contract out research that is designed to be operationally useful to the central foreign policy agencies.

At present, it is improbable that any of these conditions could be met on the government side. Attitudes of resistance to behavioral studies will change slowly and only as more and more demonstrations of the successful application of behavioral research to foreign policy can be provided. An adequate supply of personnel who are trained to serve as liaison channels between the world of foreign policy and that of the behavioral sciences is not available; and even if such persons were at hand, the process of establishing positions for them within the government would take a generous period of time. Judging from its past record, Congress is unlikely to appropriate funds for an extensive applied research effort in the sphere of international relations, except in the case of the Defense Department. One can expect only gradual progress on all three fronts.

More could be done in the private and academic spheres. Indeed, the rate of increase in the utilization of behavioral science in foreign policy will probably depend largely on the vigor with which behavioral scientists approach the problem of equipping themselves for a constructive advisory role. This will involve new emphases in academic training, a research approach that is more oriented toward specific foreign policy issues, and a more sympathetic attitude toward government personnel engaged in the practice of international relations. If researchers are able to provide a greater flow of behavioral studies that can be applied to current problems, the barriers to increased utilization will tend to fall and additional government funds will become available for work on questions with longer-range significance. As Robert K. Merton has observed, the repute of applied social science is in part a product of its accomplishments. "Not only does utilization affect esteem but esteem also affects utilization." [59]

Insofar as academic training is concerned, a major advance would be recorded if more students in the behavioral sciences could be given a grounding in history and current international relations. A broader interdisciplinary approach within social science would also be useful, especially in connection with area studies. A 1964 survey of research on Latin America, for instance, concluded that it was difficult to point to any major piece of research that could be considered a product of true interdisciplinary scholarship, one important exception being *Education and the Social Meaning of Development,* by K. H. Silvert (political science) and Frank Bonilla (sociology).[60] More students should be encouraged to make a long-range commitment to specified geographic and functional areas.

Also desirable would be an approach to the selection of research problems and to research design that would place more emphasis on the study of questions with which foreign policy personnel are concerned or are likely to become concerned in the future. Behavioral scientists who take an interest in foreign policy issues frequently start by asking themselves whether existing theory or research could be used to illuminate these questions or contribute to their solution. They therefore sift the data and findings of research that has been undertaken with no policy purposes in mind in order to discover those nuggets that may have operational significance. In such cases, practical usefulness is a by-product of prior explorations devoted primarily to enlarging scientific knowledge and building theory. This is certainly a valid approach and derives considerable authority from the success of the natural sciences in basing applications on theoretical advances.

It is, however, not the only approach and deserves to be supplemented by a broad range of studies that start with practical problems and treat theoretical advances as by-products. The experience of those who have followed this "project approach," particularly in connection with questions of interest to the military establishment, have found that these theoretical by-products may be impressive indeed. The social-psychological studies of the American soldier carried out by Samuel A. Stouffer and his collaborators during World War II offer an outstanding case in point.[61] In addition, those researchers who design their investigations to throw light on policy questions are more likely to produce results that can be utilized, since the gap between theory and application is then not so wide and difficult to close.

While the project approach has been followed in studies conducted on behalf of the armed services, and to some extent by researchers working under contract with the Agency for International Development, the Arms Control Agency, and the United States Information Agency, it has never been given a fair trial in the case of problems faced by those who are most centrally concerned with foreign policy planning and administration. Nor is it likely to be tried on the initiative of the State Department until more impressive demonstrations of its utility can be provided, in view of the attitudinal, structural, and financial limitations discussed above. At the present time, therefore, it would be desirable for behavioral scientists working with private support to familiarize themselves in as much detail as possible with specific operational problems of foreign policy, select a number that appears to be amenable to behavioral research, and pursue these with a view to providing results that can be used by foreign policy personnel. This appears to be the most likely way of breaking the vicious circle whereby behavioral studies are not supported by the central foreign policy agencies because there is little evidence of their usefulness, while little evidence of usefulness can be accumulated because of the lack of support.

But more than usable results are necessary. They should, in addition, be presented in such a manner that they can be used. This implies a sympathetic understanding on the part of the researcher of the situation in which government foreign policy officials find themselves. The researcher should be aware of the enormous pressures on those who work in large bureaucratic structures and of the terrifying complexities involved in piloting a policy recommendation through the governmental machinery. He should take these factors into account in presenting his results. That they should also be presented in nontechnical language and in a minimum of space goes without saying. Furthermore, researchers should try to anticipate the major objections that will be raised by innumerable officials who have the power to stop any action and should offer as much comfort as possible to those who are willing to take the ball and run with it. It may not be necessary for a behavioral scientist to know how to write a government staff paper, but at least he should appreciate the problems of those who do write them.

In sum, there is at present a widely felt sense that there is a disparity between the potentiality or promise of the behavioral sciences to contribute to foreign policy and their actual utilization. This disparity is sensed by many academicians and by some government officials. The extent to which the promise can be converted into reality will be ascertained only when more focused behavioral studies are available and when greater efforts have been made to apply them to foreign policy problems.

REFERENCES

NOTE: *I am indebted to several social scientists and foreign policy officials with whom I have discussed this topic. Particular thanks are due to Glen H. Fisher of the Foreign Service Institute and Elisabeth T. Crawford of the Bureau of Social Science Research, Washington, D.C.*

1. The term *behavioral science,* as used here, refers primarily to sociology, social psychology, and anthropology. It also includes that part of the work of political scientists which is devoted to the study of regularities in individual and group behavior. To resort to a tautology, political scientists are considered behavioral scientists when they act like them, as increasing numbers do. The term *social science* is used to include the work of behavioral scientists, as well as that of the balance of political scientists, economists, and some historians.
2. Because of the way the USIA budget is divided between Washington and field units, this figure is an approximation covering contract surveys. It does not include the salary or other personnel costs of USIA employees.
3. Alexander H. Leighton, *Human Relations in a Changing World: Observations on the Use of Social Sciences* (New York: Dutton, 1949), pp. 55–56; Leonard W. Doob, "The Utilization of Social Scientists in the Overseas Branch of the Office of War Information," *American Political Science Review,* XLI (August, 1947); Murray I. Gurfein and Morris Janowitz, "Trends in Wehrmacht Mirale," *Public Opinion Quarterly,* X (Spring, 1946); Edward A. Shils and Morris Janowitz, "Cohesion and Disintegration in the Wehrmacht in World War II," *Public Opinion Quarterly,* XII (Summer, 1948).
4. Hadley Cantril, "Evaluating the Probable Reactions to the Landing in North Africa in 1942: A Case Study," *Public Opinion Quarterly,* XXIX (Fall, 1965). For an account of other foreign-policy–oriented research studies by Cantril and his associates, see *The Human Dimension: Experiences in Policy Research* (New Brunswick, N. J.: Rutgers University Press, 1967).
5. Admiral Joy, United States negotiator during the first stages of the Korean truce talks, was quoted in press reports as having found *The Operational Code of the Politburo* by Nathan Leites (New York: McGraw-Hill, 1951) to be useful in predicting the behavior of the Communist negotiating team. Arthur H. Dean, Chairman of the United States delegation at disarmament negotiations in Geneva during 1961 and 1962, has also made reference to the utility of studies of Soviet negotiating behavior. See *Test Ban and Disarmament: The Path of Negotiation* (New York: Harper and Row, for the Council on Foreign Relations, 1966), pp. 43 ff.
6. Allan Evans, "Research in Action: The Department of State's Bureau of Intelligence and Research," *Department of State Bulletin,* August 30, 1965.
7. W. Phillips Davison, *The Berlin Blockade: A Study in Cold War Politics* (Princeton: Princeton University Press, 1958).
8. Pendleton Herring, Philip E. Mosely, and Charles J. Hitch, *Research for Public Policy* (Washington: The Brookings Institution, 1961).
9. Herbert Goldhamer and Hans Speier, "Some Observations on Political Gaming," *World Politics* (October, 1959). The Special Warfare Area Handbooks were prepared by the Special Operations Research Office of the American University, Washington, D.C., under a contract with the Department of the Army.
10. A survey in 1962 found 11 sociologists in the Department of State, 16 in the Department of Defense, and 6 in the United States Information Agency. Nearly

all of these reported that their sociological background was useful in their work. Nahum Z. Medalia and Ward S. Mason, "Sociologists in Federal Employment," *American Sociological Review*, XXVIII (April, 1963).

11. See Herman J. Sander, "The Uses of Sociology for Military Intelligence, Strategic Planning and Psychological Warfare," paper read at the meetings of the American Sociological Association, 1962.

12. *Ideological Operations and Foreign Policy*, Report No. 2 of the Subcommittee on International Organizations and Movements, Committee on Foreign Affairs, House of Representatives (Washington: Government Printing Office, April 27, 1964), p. 8.

13. Kalman H. Silvert, "American Academic Ethics and Social Research Abroad— The Lesson of Project Camelot," American University Field Staff Reports Service, July, 1965.

14. *Congressional Record*, Senate, August 25, 1965, p. 20906.

15. The account given here is drawn principally from Silvert, *op. cit.*, and from the Hearings of the Subcommittee on International Organizations and Movements, Committee on Foreign Affairs, U.S. House of Representatives, Part IX (Washington: Government Printing Office, December 6, 1965), pp. 16 ff. Project Camelot led to widespread discussion in the academic community and numerous subsequent expressions of opinion. Of these, two of the most comprehensive are Irving Louis Horowitz, "The Life and Death of Project Camelot," *Trans-Action*, III, November–December 1965, and Robert A. Nisbet, "Project Camelot: An Autopsy," *The Public Interest*. No. 5, Fall 1966.

16. Department of State Press Release No. 250, October 21, 1965. Address by the Honorable Thomas L. Hughes, Director of Intelligence and Research, Department of State, at Hamilton College, October 21.

17. John Walsh, "Social Science: Cancellation of Camelot after Row in Chile Brings Research under Scrutiny," *Science* (September 10, 1965).

18. Jessie Bernard, in a letter to the editor, *American Sociologist* (November, 1965), p. 25.

19. *Behavioral Sciences and the National Security*, Report No. 4 of the Subcommittee on International Organizations and Movements (Washington: Government Printing Office, December 6, 1965).

20. "Strengthening the Behavioral Sciences," a report of the Behavioral Science Subpanel of the President's Science Advisory Committee, reprinted in *Science*, CXXXVI (April 20, 1962); Hubert H. Humphrey, "A Magna Carta for the Social Sciences," *American Behavioral Scientist*, V (February, 1962).

21. William W. Ellis, "The Federal Government in Behavioral Science: Fields, Methods, and Funds," *American Behavioral Scientist*, VII (May, 1964).

22. "INR Leads in Research Coordination," *Department of State Newsletter*, January, 1965; *First Annual Report*, Foreign Area Research Coordination Group (Washington: Department of State, mimeographed, June, 1965).

23. *Foreign Area Research Notes*, External Research Staff (Washington: Department of State, mimeographed, November 10, 1964).

24. *Ibid.*, September 14, 1964.

25. See, for example, Barbara Wootton, *Testament for Social Science* (New York: Norton, 1951); James T. Tedeschi and E. T. Malagodi, "Psychology and International Relations," *American Behavioral Scientist*, VIII (October, 1964).

26. Gardner Murphy, "Science and World Order," *Background: Journal of the International Studies Association*, VI, Nos. 1–3 (Fall, 1962).

27. Morton A. Kaplan, *System and Process in International Politics* (New York: Wiley, 1957), p. 239.

28. Karl W. Deutsch, *The Nerves of Government: Models of Political Communication and Control* (New York: Free Press of Glencoe, 1963), preface.

29. Elisabeth T. Crawford, *The Social Sciences in International and Military Policy* (Washington: Bureau of Social Science Research, Inc., October, 1965). See also Herbert C. Kelman, ed., *International Behavior* (New York: Holt, Rinehart and Winston, 1965), pp. 18 ff.

30. Robert T. Bower, "Evaluating the Effect of Foreign Policy"; David Rodnick, "Foreign Policies as Phases of National Culture"; Feliks Gross, "Methods of Tension Area Analysis."

31. New York: Holt, Rinehart, and Winston, 1964.

32. Report No. 57 (New York: Group for the Advancement of Psychiatry, 1964).

33. Urbana: University of Illinois Press, 1962.

34. New York: Collier, 1962.

35. New York: Scribner, 1964.

36. Morton Deutsch, "A Psychological Basis for Peace," in Quincy Wright, William M. Evan, and Morton Deutsch, eds., *Preventing World War III: Some Proposals* (New York: Simon and Schuster, 1962); Robert C. Angell, "International Communications and the World Society," in Quincy Wright, ed., *The World Community* (Chicago: University of Chicago Press, 1948).

37. SSRC Studies in Political Development include: Lucian W. Pye, ed., *Communications and Political Development* (Princeton: Princeton University Press, 1963); Joseph Lapolombara, ed., *Bureaucracy and Political Development* (Princeton: Princeton University Press, 1964); Robert E. Ward and Dankwart A. Rustow, ed., *Political Modernization in Japan and Turkey* (Princeton: Princeton University Press, 1964); James S. Coleman, ed., *Education and Political Development* (Princeton: Princeton University Press, 1965); Lucian Pye and Sidney Verba, eds., *Political Culture and Political Development* (Princeton: Princeton University Press, 1965); Joseph Lapolombara and Myron Wiener, eds., *Political Parties and Political Development* (Princeton: Princeton University Press, 1966).

38. *Development Administration: An Annotated Bibliography* (Honolulu: East-West Center Press, 1963).

39. *Cross-Cultural Education, 1946–1964: A Selective Bibliography* (Washington: External Research Staff, Department of State, mimeographed, March, 1965).

40. David C. McClelland, "Motivational Patterns in Southeast Asia with Special Reference to the Chinese Case," *Journal of Social Issues*, XIX (January, 1963). See also McClelland's *The Achieving Society* (Princeton: Van Nostrand, 1961).

41. "Changing Attitudes through International Activities," *Journal of Social Issues*, XVIII (January, 1962).

42. *The Civic Culture* (Princeton: Princeton University Press, 1963), p. 502.

43. Nathan Leites, Elsa Bernaut, and Raymond L. Garthoff, "Politburo Images of Stalin," *World Politics*, III (April, 1951).

44. Harold D. Lasswell, "The World Attention Survey," *Public Opinion Quarterly*, V (Fall, 1941), 457–458.

45. In a personal communication to the writer in 1954.

46. Lloyd A. Free, *Attitudes of the Cuban People toward the Castro Regime* (Princeton: Institute for International Social Research, 1960); Lloyd A. Free, *Attitudes, Hopes and Fears of the Dominican People* (Princeton: Institute for International Social Research, June 25, 1962).

47. Walt W. Rostow, "The Planning of Foreign Policy," *Department of State Newsletter*, July, 1964.

48. A former foreign service officer recently showed the writer a letter he had received from a behavioral scientist at a leading American university. It re-

quested his co-operation in a research project that, in the language of the letter, proposed to compare the judgments of several populations of experts with the results of simulation procedures on selected foreign policy issues. The foreign service man was baffled by the proposal. What, he asked, were "populations of experts"; and what was meant by "simulation"? When the letter was translated into terms more familiar to him, he decided to co-operate.

49. Harold D. Lasswell, "The Policy Orientation," in Daniel Lerner and H. D. Lasswell, eds., *The Policy Sciences* (Stanford: Stanford University Press, 1951).

50. M.F.H., reviewing Etzioni's *Winning without War, Foreign Service Journal* (April, 1965).

51. Morton A. Kaplan, reviewing Klineberg's *Human Dimension in International Relations, American Political Science Review* (September, 1964).

52. "Social Deviance: Social Policy, Action and Research," *Economist*, November 7, 1964.

53. Stanford: Stanford University Press, 1964.

54. New York: Harper and Row, 1964.

55. Ronald Hilton, in preface to Ronald H. Chilcote, "The Press in Latin America, Spain and Portugal" (special issue of *Hispanic American Report*), Stanford University, 1963.

56. Lazarsfeld pointed out that fallacious findings, if presented in a plausible manner, may be just as "obvious" as correct findings. "Since every kind of human reaction is conceivable, it is of great importance to know which reactions actually occur most frequently and under what conditions." In "The American Soldier: An Expository Review," *Public Opinion Quarterly*, XIII, No. 3 (Fall, 1949), 360.

57. Quoted by Walsh, *op. cit.*, p. 1211.

58. In his paper at the 1962 ASA meetings, Robert T. Bower pointed out that foreign policy programs often seek to achieve simultaneously a multiplicity of goals, thus making evaluation particularly difficult. The foreign-aid program, for instance, is expected to help create stability and raise the standard of living in developing societies, promote good will toward the United States, assist in containing Communism, increase the market for American products, and contribute to a variety of other more specific aims in individual countries.

59. Robert K. Merton, "The Role of Applied Science in the Formation of Policy," *Philosophy of Science*, XVI (July, 1949), 164.

60. Merle Kling, "Area Studies and Comparative Politics," *American Behavioral Scientist* (September, 1964).

61. Studies in Social Psychology in World War II; Samuel A. Stouffer *et al.*, *The American Soldier: Adjustment during Army Life* (Vol. I); *The American Soldier: Combat and Its Aftermath* (Vol. II); *Measurement and Prediction* (Vol. IV); Carl I. Hovland *et al.*, *Experiments on Mass Communication* (Vol. III) (Princeton: Princeton University Press, 1949).

Public Administration: Four Cases from Israel and the Netherlands

YEHEZKEL DROR

chapter 14

Two approaches to the problem of how to make optimum use of sociologists in public administration are most fruitful: (1) systems analysis; (2) empirical case studies. Systems analysis involves deductive construction of an optimal model of the utilization of sociologists in public administration, based on organization theory and management sciences, on one hand, and analysis of sociological knowledge, on the other hand; analysis and evaluation of the actual situation in public administrative agencies in terms of the optimal model; identification of the main barriers hindering approximation of optimality; and suggestions designed to overcome those barriers—so as to move reality toward the optimal model.[1] Empirical case studies begin with real cases of sociologists in public administration; derive insights from the cases into the variables shaping the role of sociologists; and, if possible, proceed to statistically reliable generalizations, preferably in the form of a quantitative behavioral model.

Using the second approach, I shall outline four cases of sociologists in action in public administration, two from the Netherlands and two from Israel. The cases are based on interviews with participants. Each is accompanied by a short interpretation, an attempt to derive insights from the facts. The chapter concludes with some tentative hypotheses. My limited purpose is to illustrate some problems facing sociologists and other social scientists in public administration.

Case No. 1. The Community Health Center[2]

FACTS

In 1952 the Israeli Ministry of Health considered establishing a community health center in an Arab village in the coastal plain of Israel. A preliminary decision was taken to build the center in Taiba, and a social anthropologist was invited to prepare an anthropological and social study of relevant habits and attitudes of the local population. His study, paid for by United States aid funds, dealt mainly with the local power structure and with local health habits. The main recommendation was that steps should be taken to mobilize the support of the local power elite for the proposed center.

The report was distributed in writing to the members of a ministerial committee in charge of planning the health center. The anthropologist never appeared in person before that committee. For reasons of military security and geography, the center was finally built in another, similar village. The study was totally ignored in the work of the committee. When interviewed, most members of the committee did not even remember having heard about it.

After the center was built, serious difficulties in running it were encountered, mainly because of lack of support by the local power elite and differences between local health habits and the medical treatment patterns followed in the center.

INTERPRETATION

In this case, the social scientist was not a member of the organization, but an outsider. He was given a rather ill-defined task, not clearly related to the problems as perceived by the main decision makers and not paid by them. He did not participate in the ongoing decision-making process, and no effective communication channels existed between him and the decision makers. His survey did include relevant data, but he was unable to educate the decision makers to appreciate those data and to see their significance for their problems.

Case No. 2. The Sociological Adviser of an Israeli Revenue-Collecting Agency

FACTS

In 1962 the director of an Israeli revenue-collecting agency decided to appoint a sociologist as a member of his personal staff. After some search, a highly qualified sociologist who had studied in Israel and the United States was engaged.

Neither the director nor the sociologist had any clear role expectations. Both agreed to let things work themselves out on an experimental basis. The director was, at the beginning, mainly eager to utilize the sociologist for improving relations with the clientele; then he asked the sociologist to examine some problems of internal administration and staff training. In general, the sociologist was left to his own resources. He participated in the regular meetings of the director with his senior staff advisers, commenting on the subjects under discussion.

The sociologist did a number of small field studies. For instance, he investigated the reasons for delays in tax payments due to one of the divisions of the agency; his main finding was that officials were often unwilling to impair their continuous working relations with the clientele by imposing a monetary penalty for overdue tax payments, though entitled by law to do so. As a result of this study, administrative instructions were issued to be more strict in imposition of sanctions for delays in tax payments.

The various divisions of the agency, which enjoyed considerable autonomy, resented the intrusions of the sociologist, who was regarded as an agent of the director. The director became increasingly disappointed in that his rather undefined expectations were not being met. The sociologist became progressively frustrated and uneasy and looked around for an academic position.

In 1964, when an opening at one of the higher institutes of education occurred, the sociologist left the agency. The director made little effort to prevent his resignation. Shortly thereafter a new director was appointed, who had served before as head of one of the divisions and had had in that capacity some contact with the sociologist. The new director decided to delay appointment of another sociological adviser.

During the interviews, the former director admitted that the sociologist had made some useful contributions. Especially interesting was the admission by a senior subdirector that the sociologist had perhaps been right in an important public-relations strategy recommendation which at that time had been rejected. Being very anxious to improve its public image and to increase co-operation by the clientele in assessing and collecting the respective taxes, the agency adopted an active public-relations policy directed at convincing the clientele that the taxes were urgently needed for important national activities. The sociological adviser opposed that policy, expressing the opinion that it is natural for people to dislike paying taxes; he thought that the less people heard about the tax and the agency, the better would relations with the public be, and therefore the agency should avoid visibility rather than attract attention through public-relations activities.

But in general all interviewed officials professed disappointment. The sociologist also regarded his term of office in some respects as a failure, claiming that he was expected to do undefined things and blamed for not doing them. The director and his interviewed staff agreed with that formulation and blamed themselves for not arriving at a clearer job definition, but claimed that the sociologist did not show enough initiative and did not "sell" himself.

INTERPRETATION

The sociological adviser entered an agency which had no experience with such positions; therefore the situation was nonstructured and his role definition very loose. He did not succeed in building up a realistic image of his position, either for himself or for the organization. Perhaps he engaged prematurely in hostility-generating specific studies without adequate prior educational activities. He apparently did not show sufficient initiative and salesmanship. There are some indications, however, that had he stayed on, many of the difficulties would have resolved themselves.

Case No. 3. The Research Division of a Physical Planning Unit in the Netherlands

FACTS

The Physical Planning unit studied in the Netherlands is in charge of preparing physical planning studies and physical planning policies. It has a research division staffed by three sociologists and a number of social geographers. This research division tackles a variety of problems defined by the physical planners and designers in charge of the service. A typical study dealing with recreation patterns found that people do not travel far on Sundays. As a result of this finding, the policy was adopted to locate recreation areas near the population centers.

Highly regarded in the service, well staffed, and supplied with an adequate budget, the research division makes both detailed intelligence contributions and general educational contributions to the agency. The head of the research division participates in all senior staff meetings and has full opportunity to participate in decision making as a member of the higher management team.

Despite these favorable conditions, the interviews uncovered some mutual disappointments of the sociologists and the physical planners and some substantial frustrations. The main difficulties mentioned in the interviews were:

1. Differences in outlook between the sociologists and the physical planners and physical designers. The sociologists tend to stick to facts, while the physical planners and designers—in the opinion of the interviewed sociologists—are trained to use imagination and prize creativity.

2. Trained in physical planning disciplines, the physical planners demand from the sociologists definite, quantitative answers to clear questions; with respect to their concrete and detailed planning work (in contrast to the more imaginative aspects), they have a very low tolerance of ambiguity. Thus, the sociologists were asked to predict the number of sailing boats the population will own in 1980 and to determine the amount of land which should be allocated for gardens in a town of a given size. The sociologists explained that they were unable to provide such data and could only give general answers, such as that the number of sailing boats tends to increase and that a town with inhabitants having an agricultural background needs more land for gardens than a town with inhabitants having an urban background. These answers did not meet the needs of the planners, who had to prepare a detailed master plan and as a consequence were irritated with the sociologists.

3. Another difficulty mentioned was the problem of lead time. The soci-

ologists demanded a substantial lead time before answering queries, in order to be able to do the necessary studies. The physical planners often wanted an answer from one day to another, blaming the sociologists for seeking scientific certainty instead of making, when necessary, a good guess. The sociologists reported that they developed a strategy of stockpiling answers by trying to anticipate the probable questions and doing the necessary studies in advance. But this did not always work out.

Although these conflicts were mentioned, both sides plainly regarded the partnership as a permanent one and evaluated the benefits highly.

INTERPRETATION

The interviews in this case show a rather sophisticated awareness of the problems, thus making detailed interpretation redundant. By all signs, we have here an instance of quite successful symbiosis between sociologists and physical planners and designers within an organizational setting. There is some conflict, but working relationships appear to be smooth on the personal level. In this instance sociological knowledge achieved visible and recognized impact on administrative operations.

Case No. 4. The Sociological Adviser in a Social Affairs Department in the Netherlands

FACTS

The department has a senior sociological adviser, who is in charge of a group of sociologists who are dispersed throughout the organization. The head of the department is himself a trained sociologist, but achieved his position because of personal qualities and not his specific academic training.

The senior sociological adviser serves as a policy analyst. All major proposals and memoranda pass his office for comments, and he participates in the policy-making senior staff meetings. He enjoys the personal confidence of the head of the department and is apparently highly regarded personally throughout the department. His contributions include educational effects, strategy recommendations, and specific data. In particular, he emphasizes the social dimensions of the various problems dealt with by the department, regarding himself, to use his phrase, as a "social critic" of departmental operations. For example, he emphasized the need to preserve a role for small shops when planning a new community center.

In the interviews, the adviser clearly distinguished between three distinct sociological roles in the organizational setup: the director of the department, the sociological adviser (himself), and the research sociologists (the other sociologists). The adviser described his role as including two mutually reinforcing functions: (1) a policy analyst, contributing a specific point of view and type of knowledge to decision making; (2) a liaison officer between the executives and the research sociologists. He felt frustration at not engaging himself in research and expressed a desire to do so.

The head of the department held very favorable opinions of the sociological adviser and his contributions to departmental operations. In respect to the other sociologists, he complained about lack of political sophistication, oscillation between overdetailed comments and meaningless generalities, high turnover (50 per cent, or 4 out of 8, in one year), ignorance of organizational behavior, and neglect in their thinking of the cost element. Incidentally, the sociological adviser expressed essentially similar views about the research sociologists, but more fully recognized their difficulties in working without sufficient basic data on which to base their recommendations.

INTERPRETATION

This case is distinguished by the bifurcation between the sociological adviser and the research sociologists. The sociological academic training of the senior executive is unusual. It is a pity that circumstances prevented interviewing some of the research sociologists, although the view from the top provides some insight. When they heard about my interest in sociologists in public administration a number of persons in other departments in the Netherlands told me to study this department because, in their opinion, here sociologists achieved unusual influence on the policy level. Interviews in the agency confirm that view.

Some Tentative Hypotheses

Inferences from these cases must be taken as shaky. The cases have been presented in bare outline, the number of cases is insignificant, and critical environmental variables are ignored (such as the relatively high propensity in the Netherlands to rely on experts and the tendency in Israel toward a lower estimate of the usefulness of social sciences in public administration).

For instance, it would be incorrect to conclude that sociological advisers always succeed in the Netherlands and fail in Israel: there are other cases of clear failure of sociological advisers and resistance to their introduction in the Netherlands (for instance, in the Central Economic Planning Office, which is staffed by professional economists and statisticians) and of their success in Israel (for instance, the highly developed sociological advisory service in the Settlement Department of the Jewish Agency, which has some real influence on agricultural settlement planning and development).

With these reservations, I conclude by presenting a number of preliminary and tentative hypotheses formulated on the basis of the four cases:

1. Sociologists can make significant contributions to the operations of public administration. These possible contributions can be of three main types: (a) general educational contributions, sensitizing the decision makers to social aspects of their operations; (b) strategy contributions, by helping the decision makers in choosing major guidelines for operations; (c) tactics contributions, by providing specific intelligence and ideas applicable to concrete and detailed issues.

These different levels of contribution are interdependent and reinforce one another: general educational activities seem essential for gaining acceptability for strategy and tactics contributions; specific contributions having an obvious pay-off for agency operations seem necessary for legitimizing the position of sociologists in administrative agencies and creating the favorable climate needed for educational impact.

2. In order to make significant contributions to the operations of public administration, some conditions are necessary and helpful. Necessary conditions seem to include: (a) availability of sociological knowledge directly applicable to the substantive activities of the agency; (b) close communication between the sociologists and the main executives; (c) capacity by the sociologists as persons to operate in a nonacademic organization, to adjust themselves to an "action-oriented" environment, and to "sell" themselves and their professional knowledge; (d) some involvement and interest by the executives in the activities of the sociological advisers (at least by paying for them from the agency's budget).

Helpful conditions seem to include: (a) familiarity by the senior executives with sociology; (b) a minimum "critical number" of sociologists, who support one another, strengthen their morale, and can engage in research which provides significant findings relevant for agency operations. A single sociologist can—if highly qualified professionally and very strong personally—make significant educational and strategic contributions as a policy analyst. But availability of several sociologists in an administrative agency seems helpful for all types of contributions and is, perhaps, essential for tactical contributions.

3. The role of sociologists in public organizations involves a number of role conflicts. Especially acute are the pressures for identification with the organization and adjustment of patterns of work to organizational needs

on one hand, and professional norms and scientific criteria, on the other hand. A partial solution of this role conflict is to differentiate between sociological policy analyst and research sociologist.

4. Sociologists in public organizations come into conflict with administrators and other groups. These conflicts are the result, *inter alia*, of different time perspectives, different tolerances of ambiguity, different professional self-images and norms, and different locations in the organizational structure ("line" versus "staff").

5. Introduction of a sociological adviser as a new role into an established organization involves many difficulties, mainly because of the unstructured role definition and the noncomplementary expectations. Even under optimal conditions, time is needed for these problems to be worked out. (During that time, especially much depends on the personality of the sociological adviser and his human-relations capacities.) Therefore, study and evaluation of the actual contributions of sociology to the operations of an administrative agency is significant only if allowance is made for a considerable lead time, needed for mutual adjustment and situation structuring.

These and similar hypotheses deserve more thorough study, through systematic comparison of a large sample of organizations.

REFERENCES

1. I apply this method to optimization of public policy making in my book *Policymaking* (San Francisco: Chandler, 1967).
2. This description is based on a case study prepared by Rachel Elboim-Dror and published in Hebrew.

Political Parties
and the Polls

MARK ABRAMS

chapter 15

From the very nature of their work, it is not surprising that, almost from the start of modern political systems, imaginative and intelligent (but not necessarily successful) politicians have shown a sociological understanding of party politics without the benefit of any help from professional sociologists or polling organizations. For example, approximately a century before any academic discussion of "consensus politics," Disraeli, from his everyday experience in a two-party British Parliament and his observation of an urbanized and industrial society enjoying a rising standard of living, enunciated his doctrine that "the Tory Party is a national party or it is nothing," that the Conservative Party could not win a General Election unless in addition to its ideological supporters it attracted votes from all sections of the community. In 1959 Hugh Gaitskell, then leader of the British Labour Party, in analyzing the reasons for his party's third successive defeat at a General Election, arrived at very much the same conclusion. He was particularly concerned that "somehow, we let the Tories get away with the monstrous falsehood that *we* are a Class Party and they are *not*. We must surely now attend to this." [1]

Again, the unsuccessful Parliamentary candidate, Walter Bagehot, anticipating Professors McKenzie and Silver[2] by almost one hundred years, identified the working-class deferential voter who, contrary to what others saw as his own self-interest, preferred to place his political trust in politicians who were obviously rich and well born.[3]

At the beginning of this century there can be little doubt that Graham Wallas' experience of London electioneering was reflected in his writings —particularly *Human Nature in Politics,* in which he developed from an analogy with commercial advertising the concept of a party image and described its foundations, its advantages, and limitations.[4]

One final example can be drawn from the work of J. A. Hobson. Although he never ran for elective office, Hobson was vigorously engaged in public affairs and at various times worked closely with men who in Britain held office as Prime Minister (Ramsay MacDonald) and Cabinet Minister (C. F. G. Masterman). In 1910 he read a paper before the Sociological Society in London entitled "The General Election: A Sociological Interpretation." [5] Using a statistical analysis of constituency voting returns, he pointed out, half a century before the debate among sociologists about "the end of ideology," that the great mass of ordinary working-class electors had not been moved by ideological politics. In interpreting the election results he concluded that "no doubt larger, vaguer aspirations are present, [but] definite problems of poverty and injustice have been stirring the minds [and deciding the voting behavior] of the working and poorer classes. . . . A curbing of landlordism, public assistance against the risks and injuries of proletarian life . . . are the strongest strains" in their political thinking.

These and similar instances should be kept in mind as a protection against the belief that the political use of sociology started in 1936 and the assumption that where sociological insights are concerned the politicians have always been pupils and never teachers. Nevertheless, it remains true that the systematic use of sample surveys in party politics was launched when, in the mid-1930's, three Americans (George Gallup, Elmo Roper, and Archibald Crossley), utilizing their experience in consumer research, predicted accurately the outcome of the 1936 Presidential election. The methods used in election forecasting were (and remain) very simple: well-drawn, but small (e.g., 800 to 3,000) samples of the electorate were interviewed in their homes and in the streets and asked two or three simple questions on voting intentions.

The success of the pioneers helped to launch in 1937 a new periodical, *The Public Opinion Quarterly,* and to found almost simultaneously similar polling organizations in Britain and France.

It also apparently legitimized the use of the same techniques as a means of measuring public opinion over a wide range of issues, political and nonpolitical, trivial and substantial. Through syndicated features the newspaper reader was given poll findings on such questions as "Do you approve or disapprove of the way Roosevelt is handling his job as President today?" "Would you rather ride in a car driven by a man or a woman?" "Do you think some form of socialism would be a good thing or a bad thing for the country as a whole?" "Do you think that Spain under its present government should or should not be recognized?" With much less publicity a handful of Congressional candidates or would-be candidates commissioned private polls as a guide to their chances of election.

More importantly, starting with the classic 1940 study, *The People's Choice*,[6] academics were stimulated to examine voting behavior by the use of survey techniques. Similar studies in the United States, Great Britain, and Germany followed, but there is little overt and specific evidence that their findings impinged upon the awareness and behavior of party leaders anywhere until R. A. Butler (now Lord Butler), deputy Prime Minister in the then British Conservative Government, spelled out the implications for "active political workers" in his Foreword to *Marginal Seat 1955*.[7]

From the mid-1950's onward, the polling organizations in dealing with political matters substantially widened their approach so as to embrace what they had learned from political sociology and from more sophisticated commercial consumer research. This was particularly marked in the work they did for political parties rather than for the mass media.

Thus, a survey carried out in 1956 by the present author for the British Labour Party used a questionnaire designed: (1) to identify floating voters, to locate the issues most likely to convert them into voters and the policies most likely to swing them either to the Left or the Right; (2) to classify the supporters of each party by age, sex, occupation, self-ascribed social class; (3) to ascertain the relationship, if any, between social mobility and party preferences; (4) to discover the extent of participation by uncommitted electors in nonpolitical groups and voluntary organizations; (5) to measure the attitudes of various sections of the electorate toward general policies and issues—distinguishing between ideological policies and secular ones; (6) to assess differences in party images. The wide-ranging scope of the survey was probably due, in part, to the researcher's own awareness of relevant sociological research and, in part, to the party leader's own experience as a university teacher in the social sciences.

More often the pollster's brief was not so explicit as this; at worst it might be no more than a desperate and urgent request to "do a survey"; at best it reached the level of the specifications set out for one State-wide survey executed in early 1963:

To determine the issues of major concern to Pennsylvania voters.
To measure John F. Kennedy's popularity as President, and test his strength against Rockefeller, Scranton, and Goldwater.
To determine voter reaction toward various programs of the Kennedy Administration.

To determine how well the public knows and recognizes certain political figures in Pennsylvania.

To measure the strength and popularity of the client and his main opponent.

To determine if certain racial, ethnic, educational, or sociological characteristics would cause voters to vote against certain candidates for the office of United States Senator.

To determine the matters of most concern to Pennsylvania voters at this moment, whether they be political, personal, or economic.

But almost irrespective of the brief and of the electorate being studied all receptive party politicians operating in a Western-style country where national politics are dominated by two parties—one of the Left and one of the Right—learn from the polls certain basic facts about political behavior.[8] The main findings are:

1. Although it is true that most working-class electors vote Left and most middle class electors vote Right,[9] yet there is no simple and complete alignment of social class and political faith. A substantial minority of the working class votes Right, and a smaller, but still politically important, minority of the middle class votes Left. The former deviants are, for the most part, working-class people who have prospered and who feel, either because of their material prosperity, or because of the educational success of their children, that their style of life is no longer working class. They see themselves as merging with the middle class, and by voting Right they hope to consolidate their new class aspirations. This is most likely to happen where upwardly mobile workers come from parents who did not themselves vote Left. Where they did then the upwardly mobile are prone to be solidly Left in their party loyalties. Middle-class deviants (i.e., those who vote Left) tend to be those who have experienced lateral mobility within the middle class—they are employed in the professions, whereas their parents were in the business section of the middle class.

The lesson learned by the politician is that the class identity of his party must be soft-pedaled. Thus, in preparing for the 1967 Greater London Council elections the British Labour Party's first press release did no more than call attention to the classlessness of its panel of candidates—21 business executives, 15 skilled manual workers, 16 teachers, 7 transport workers, etc. Again, in the 1964 General Election the Labour Party ostentatiously placed some of its initial advertising in the newspapers mainly read by middle-class people. (For their special benefit the advertising copy and layout was changed to convey, it was hoped, a party of dignity and reason—lots of white space and no illustration.)

2. Another lesson learned from surveys by the politician is that each of the two major parties can rely upon the unwavering support of approximately one-third of the electorate. Their devotion is unaffected by any shortcomings in party leadership, party program, constituency candidate,

or party organization. Most of them have acquired their voting habits by inheritance, i.e., they follow in the political footsteps of their parents. The remaining uncommitted one-third of the electorate do not form a homogeneous group. Its members are drawn from both sexes, all social classes and all age groups. All that the politician can be certain of is that no more than half of them will vote and that those who do vote will do so usually on the basis of fear or direct personal dissatisfaction. It is the task of the politician to identify these fears and dissatisfactions—war, "ethnic pollution," housing shortages, etc. As the British Conservatives discovered in 1959, with the direct aid of surveys, this section of the electorate responded very effectively to the open-ended slogan "Don't Let Labour Ruin It."

At the same time the politician learns not to squander his ammunition on the committed voters. Certainly those who are not on his side can be ignored; up to a point those already on his side must be encouraged by morale building gestures. (It was on these grounds that in the 1964 General Election the Labour Party used part of its limited publicity funds to place advertisements—at regular commercial rates—in the two newspapers read almost exclusively by committed Labour supporters.) But in the battle for votes the attack is concentrated on the one-third of the electorate regarded as uncommitted to the two main parties.

Moreover, since these "targets" lack social and demographic homogeneity, and since their interest in party politics is usually only marginal three action steps follow. First, the propaganda directed at them is fragmented in content: some is directed at parents of school children, some at old people, some at people with poor housing accommodation, some at motorists, etc. Second, since housing, education, roads, economic growth are for them the central issues of the political battle the party must "prove" that it alone has the skill, brains, competence, and talent to carry out the programs effectively. Accordingly, the party tries to mobilize around its propaganda as many names of elite experts as possible and publicizes the enthusiasm of "Doctors for X," "Physicists for X," "Businessmen for X," and so on. Third, because the uncommitted electors' interest in party politics is slight, the propagandist personifies the Party in the personality and appearance of the party leader; the elector is exhorted to vote primarily for a man and only secondarily for a party. And once a successful personification has been achieved it tends to be perpetuated. After Kennedy's victory in 1960 several European parties set out to establish local versions of the original.

3. Polls show the politician that the committed rank-and-file supporters of the two main parties are in substantial agreement on the relative value of many social and political ends. Left and Right supporters attach equally high importance to policies which will increase the rate of housebuilding, raise the rate of economic growth, provide better roads, protect the consumer from shoddy goods and misleading labeling, create better

schools, raise the nation's international prestige. Their differences are concentrated on two or three issues and even here the contrast is one of degree rather than kind. For example, Left supporters attach greater importance to the desirability and effectiveness of governmental action in solving economic and social problems, and they attach more value to policies that will reduce economic and social inequality. The task then for the politician is to demonstrate his opponent's incompetence in the area where there is general agreement and to attribute this incompetence to the other side's stubborn attachment to its out-of-date ideological bases. This usually means that before a politician makes too much of the differences between the two parties he must be reasonably sure that the electorate is convinced or about to be convinced that the opposing party is incompetent in its handling of mundane affairs. For example, in 1966, Mr. Heath, the British Conservative leader, waited until after the wage-freeze and the increase in unemployment before making the headlines with his policy of "The Great Divide" and before asserting that "to me the word 'consensus' suggests wishy-washy, cynical compromise." [10] The dramatic repudiation of consensus came after the Party had carried out several surveys and was at least stimulated by their findings.

In short, the potential use that political parties can make of private polls ranges over the fields of party propaganda, party organization, and party policy. The average polling organization with its main experience in consumer market research tends to translate these three into publicity, distribution, and product. This translation is understandable and highly relevant for an appreciation of party politics in an affluent society.

The demand for market research springs from a threefold separation between producer and consumer in a mass society; they are separated by space, time, and function. The typical large-scale manufacturer produces for consumers hundreds and even thousands of miles away from his plant; he undertakes and completes his production many months before the consumer decides to make a purchase, and he depends upon middlemen to complete his connection with the consumer. To overcome the risks inherent in this situation the manufacturer, before turning to market research, tries to collect inferential information about consumers' preferences, intentions, and attitudes by analyzing his sales figures and by mulling over reports from his salesmen and retailers. He soon realizes that these sources are inadequate and unreliable since they only tell him about the past, they are incomplete (they tell him about sales made but not about sales lost), and they are biased. The manufacturer's more effective solution is to brand his product and then use sample surveys among consumers. Armed with the findings he is able to appeal over the heads of retailers direct to consumers by using mass-media advertising to mold demand for his brand; he creates an image for his brand—sometimes by listing its functional attributes but more frequently by describing the people who consume the brand. Additionally, he uses his mass-media advertising to impress retailers and his research findings to hold more effective sales conferences. The whole process can be applied to mass politics simply by substituting "political party" for "manufacturer" and "elector" for "consumer."

Broadly, therefore, one would expect that poll findings would be most widely used in societies dominated by large-scale production of consumer goods. In part this is true. At the beginning of 1966 the chairman of the British Conservative Party spent a fortnight in the United States studying the electoral methods of the two political parties. He was primarily concerned with his party's arrangements for market research and techniques of analyzing research findings. "He came home satisfied that there was nothing essential they needed to adopt." [11]

Probably much the same conclusions would have been reached if representatives of the main German parties had made similar visits. But few other European parties are either so ready to commission polls or so sophisticated in their use of them.

For example, in the Fall of 1965 representatives from the research departments of the Social Democratic parties of most European countries met in Vienna to share their experiences in commissioning polls and using the results. It was clear that with one or two exceptions (e.g., the British Labour Party) little had been done and most participants were pessimistic about the possibilities of any expansion. They were acutely aware from personal experience of the obstructionist and obscurantist attitudes described by the present writer in *The Public Opinion Quarterly*.[12] Briefly, politicians of the Left opposed polls because they saw them as potential threats to the party's traditional doctrines.

Almost simultaneously people associated with the European Union of Christian Democrats met to consider the possibility of using survey research to work out for all member parties a common doctrinal basis that would override national boundaries. In spite of the fact that some European Christian Democratic parties are already systematic users of private polls (e.g., Italy and Germany) the suggestions for an international approach came to nothing—largely because, despite their common party name, the various parties range in their political outlook from well left of center to extreme Right; and those of the latter persuasion were fearful that the findings of public opinion surveys would strengthen the former.

In the last resort it is this fear—that surveys will create internal party dissension on policy—which is the main barrier inhibiting party politicians from a wider use of polls. The appearance of party unity is an important electoral asset and while party dissidents cannot be silenced there is nothing to be gained by allowing them to learn that significant minorities of the electorate support their rebelliousness.

The end result, therefore, is that for most of the time the use made of polls by party leaders is restricted to guidance on publicity and organization. And here the aid provided is remarkably uniform irrespective of party and irrespective of country. The *Democratic Congressional Campaign Manual for 1962* and the *British Labour Party's Campaign Guide for 1963* could be equally well used by their opponents at home, and, allowing for local legal and constitutional differences, both publications could be used by all political parties in the rest of the Western world.

REFERENCES

1. Report of the 58th Annual Conference of The Labour Party (London: The Labour Party, 1960), pp. 105–137.
2. R. T. McKenzie and Allan Silver, "Working Class Conservatism," in Anthony King, ed., *British Politics* (Boston: D. C. Heath & Co., 1966).
3. Walther Bagehot, *The English Constitution* (London: Oxford University Press, 1867).
4. Graham Wallas, *Human Nature in Politics* (London: Constable & Co., 1908), cf. chapter on "Political Entities."
5. *The Sociological Review* (Summer, 1910), 105–117.
6. P. F. Lazarsfeld, B. Berelson, and H. Gaudet, *The People's Choice* (New York: Columbia University Press, 1948).
7. R. S. Milne and H. C. Mackenzie, *Marginal Seat 1955* (London: Hansard Society, 1958).
8. This section is based on my paper, "Opinion Polls and Party Propaganda," *The Public Opinion Quarterly*, XXVIII (Spring, 1964).
9. In the United States, Left and Right would presumably equate with Democrats and Republicans.
10. *The Sunday Times,* London, October 23, 1966.
11. *The Times,* London, January 15, 1966.
12. "Public Opinion Polls and Political Parties," *The Public Opinion Quarterly* (Spring, 1963).

Social Problems
and
Formal Planning

PART **IV**

Urban Poverty

and

Social Planning

HERBERT J. GANS

chapter **16**

This chapter is a case study of the uses of sociology. It consists of two parts. The first is a revised version of a paper presented at the 1962 meetings of the American Sociological Association, which was written to acquaint sociologists with what were then called social-planning projects, being developed by city planners and other professionals in a number of cities. The paper was both a critique of these projects and an attempt to encourage sociologists to participate in them. The second part of the chapter is a review of the state of these projects in 1965, by then called antipoverty or community-action programs, and a brief analysis of the actual uses of sociology in them. In its entirety, the chapter thus illustrates the rapid development of a new type of social action and, less fortunately, of the all too minor role sociologists have been playing in it.

PART ONE

The Re-emergence of Social Planning

Around the turn of the century, a number of the pioneers of American sociology were deeply involved in the social-action issues of their day, especially those concerning the welfare of the city and its less fortunate residents.[1] They participated in such reform movements as city planning, public recreation, "good government," sanitation and public health, and they helped to establish settlement houses, philanthropic agencies, and a variety of other social-welfare programs and services. Sometimes they functioned purely as researchers, but in many cases they also played advisory or participant roles in policy formation and program development. Insofar as they were helping to shape community goals and to choose the methods to be used for achieving these goals, they were participating in what is today being called "social planning."

As these reform movements took hold, they became institutionalized as public agencies and municipal activities. Concurrently, lay leaders and volunteer workers, including the sociologists among them, were replaced by paid professionals. The departure of the sociologists can be explained by three factors. First, with the rapid growth of sociology as an academic discipline, sociologists began to spend most of their time as teachers. Second, the subsequent boom in sociological research and the attempt to create a scientific sociological method discouraged sociologists from participating in action programs and even from doing research on controversial issues. Third, the professionals who took over the new bureaucracies developed techniques of service and of caretaking, to use Erich Lindemann's apt phrase, which left little room for the sociologist. Thus, city planning was carried out by engineers and architecturally trained practitioners who believed that the goals of their calling—the good community and the good life—could be attained by architectural and site-planning methods and that the alteration of the physical environment was the main priority. Recreation officials sought to achieve the same goals by supplying supervised facilities, such as the playground, park, and community center, in the belief that these would attract users to interact with professionally trained leaders who would teach them "constructive" and "wholesome" forms of leisure behavior. Public-health officials turned to clinics, and social workers to settlement houses, as well as to case-work techniques. Only in some caretaking agencies, notably those dealing with delinquents and older lawbreakers, did sociologists continue to find a function. In the others, they participated only as occasional consultants or as sporadic, and usually uninvited, critics.[2]

In the last two decades, the barrier between the planning and caretaking professions and the sociologists has begun to break down. This has come about for two reasons. First, the more thoughtful members of these professions have been realizing that the traditional techniques were not working so well as was being claimed. For example, the caretakers' success among European immigrants and their children was not being duplicated with the Negro and Puerto Rican newcomers to the city, and some professionals went so far as to suspect that all along their techniques had been effective largely because of the existence of highly mobile and self-selected clients among the European immigrants. In short, these professions began to realize that they were not reaching their intended clients, and as Richard Cloward has put it, what they had mistaken for service was only the illusion of service. In the call for new approaches, they began to turn to the social sciences for help. Their decision to do so was also affected by the new prestige of the social sciences and by the availability of research and other funds for sociological help. Indeed, today it is fashionable for professional agencies of all kinds to hire sociologists.

Second, social scientists themselves have begun to take an interest in the work of these professions. Thanks to the activities of the federal government and private foundations, behavioral scientists from a number of disciplines are doing research and developing ways of applying social-science knowledge to their programs. This, too, has cut down the barriers between them.

PLANNING FOR GUIDED MOBILITY: THE PROPOSAL STAGE, 1962

Of all the welfare-oriented professions, perhaps none has grown faster in the postwar era than city planning. Although the modern city-planning movement emerged in the middle of the nineteenth century, much of its growth has come in the last fifteen to twenty years, stimulated by the federally supported programs of urban redevelopment (now called urban renewal), which began with the passage of the 1949 Housing Act. The planners and the "housers" were concerned mainly with eliminating slums and conserving the less blighted structures and neighborhoods, but in addition to these "physical" goals they also sought social ones. Thus, they hoped not only that slum clearance would provide the slum dwellers with better housing but that these people would adopt middle-class ways of life. After a decade of experience, however, it has become clear that tearing down the slums and moving their occupants elsewhere may have improved their housing conditions—although it did not even do this very often—but it did not reduce their poverty or radically change their ways of life.[3] Crime, delinquency, alcoholism, school failure, unemployment, mental illness, and other disabilities of the low-income population have not been reduced by alterations in the physical environment.[4]

As a reaction to the shortcomings of urban renewal, a new approach is being developed which has been given many names, including human renewal, community development, gray-area programs, and social planning.[5] Broadly speaking, the purpose of this approach is to find nonphysical ways of helping the low-income population and reducing deviant behavior. This goal is hardly novel, and in essence the new approach is only the most recent version of the never-ending attempt to help the deprived elements of society improve their living standards. What is new is the involvement of city planners in this effort and the fiscal scale of the programs that are being developed.

The term *social planning* has been used most often to describe these programs, if only to distinguish them from the physical planning methods used in urban renewal.[6] The term itself was borrowed from the social-welfare profession, which has long used it to refer to the co-ordination of the activities of the many individual agencies that provide social service in the city by councils of social agencies, community chests, or United Fund organizations.[7] The programs now being developed by city planners and others are not exactly plans in the usual sense of the word, and they are no more nor less social than any other form of human activity. From a sociological perspective, such programs might best be described as schemes for *guided mobility*, or, more correctly, for guided lower-class mobility, since they propose to induce mobility among people whom sociologists describe as lower-class (or in the Warnerian terminology, lower-lower-class).

It should be noted, however, that none of the agencies conceived or conceptualized their efforts in this way, and they did not see themselves as encouraging mobility, guided or unguided, for they did not think systematically about what changes they sought to encourage in their clients. Moreover, since the programs are aimed at helping those individuals who are attracted to them, rather than entire population groups, their actual mobility potential is low. Indeed, it seems likely that they will principally help people who are already upwardly mobile. Needless to say, there is no intent to change the class structure of American society, but only to help the people who are at the bottom of the hierarchy.

Guided-mobility plans have been springing up with considerable rapidity. As of 1962 they existed or were being readied in such cities as New York, Chicago, Los Angeles, Philadelphia, Boston, Pittsburgh, Washington, Oakland, and New Haven, to name only a few. Many of them are specifically geared to the prevention of juvenile delinquency and thus are primarily focused on services for young people; for example, the Mobilization for Youth project in New York City.[8] Others, especially those emanating from city-planning agencies, seek to deal with all age groups of the population, and it is these which I shall discuss in the remainder of the chapter.[9]

Although most of these projects have not proceeded beyond the drafting of prospectuses, the soliciting of financial support, and the recruitment of staff, some over-all similarities in their goals and programs are already apparent. It should be noted that any generalizations that can be made are highly preliminary, for the programs are likely to change as they move from the exhortatory language of the fund-raising brochure to actual implementation in the field.

By and large, the guided-mobility plans emphasize four major programmatic goals: to extend the amount and quality of present social services to the hard-to-reach lower-class population; to offer new methods of education, especially in the area of job training; to reduce unemployment by retraining and the creation of new jobs; and to encourage self-help both on an individual and group basis, notably through community participation and neighborhood organization. In addition, programs in recreation, public health, delinquency prevention, and housing are often included in the plan.

Generally speaking, the programs being proposed reflect the fact that guided-mobility plans are developing out of an alliance between city planners, the suppliers of social services, and experts in community organization. For one thing, they are organized to deal not with social structures and peoples, but with neighborhoods and their residents. Often the neighborhoods are chosen because of the physical renewal projects taking place in them. Conversely, some plans also include areas which are not occupied by lower-class people. Moreover, the proposals stress the use, not of whatever functional services are needed to solve problems, but of public— and physical—*facilities,* such as the school, the recreation center, or the clinic. These emphases are contributed by city planners and reflect traditional programmatic concepts of the planning profession.

Furthermore, the programs propose that the services offered by these facilities and by social-service agencies generally be increased beyond present levels and that they be co-ordinated. Instead of separate agencies each working individually with the same clients, the proposal is to have these agencies work in concert, or at least to know what the others are doing. This technique reflects a long-term goal of the suppliers of social services, and is a part of their concept of social planning. And, finally, the schemes call for new efforts to reach the previously unreached by using professional community organizers and other caretakers working in the neighborhood, much like the detached street or gang worker in delinquency prevention, and by finding nonprofessional "natural leaders" who will carry the message and the services of guided mobility to people who shy away from contact with public facilities and professional staffs. This is the contribution of community organization.

Some of the plans stress the increased use of present techniques, while others call for the development of new ones. Some proposals are highly sophisticated, but by and large and it is fair to say that most of them are from a sociologist's perspective quite unsophisticated and even naïve. This naïveté takes several forms.

First, many of the plans are based on the traditional goal of persuading the lower class to become middle class, both in behavior and values, and they hope to attain this goal by the traditional means of confronting this population with middle-class services and staffs. Although there are proposals to call on "natural" or "indigeneous" leaders who are not middle class, their function will be to bring the low-income population in touch with the middle-class staff and services. Moreover, the proposals are quite optimistic that the lower-class clients will assent to this confrontation and that rapport with them can be achieved. Beyond that, it is believed that once rapport is obtained, they are willing and able to resort to self-help and to formal organization to achieve the goals set for them.

Also, the programs proposed in these plans are determined less by the needs and present conditions among the intended clients than by the skills and services of the programmers. Indeed, variations in programs among the individual cities can be related to the characteristics of the sponsoring agencies in each. As a result, the plans frequently give as much attention to such essentially low-priority programs as improvements in leisure behavior, training in citizenship, and the stimulation of neighborhood consciousness as to such much higher priority needs as job opportunities, higher incomes, and solutions to basic social and psychological problems prevalent in the lower-class population.

Similarly, not only does the city planners' concern with neighborhood divert the programs to goals of neighborhood cohesion or stability, and so use guided mobility as a means to physical-renewal aims, but, more important, it overestimates the importance of the role that the neighborhood plays in the life of the lower-class population. Thus, the proposals run the danger that in prescribing for the neighborhood they may sidestep the real problems.

In some cases, the naïveté I have described stems from traditional program emphases among the sponsors. In other cases, it follows from the fact that the agencies running the guided-mobility programs cannot do much to change basic structural deficiencies of the society. They can do little to create more jobs for low-income people and to remove the practices of racial discrimination that prevent access to the available jobs and other opportunities. Even so, more often the naïveté is based on the absence of a conceptual and theoretical framework about the nature of lower-class life and accompanying processes of social deprivation and disorganization. For example, most of the proposals do not seem to be aware of the concepts of class, social stratification, or social mobility. A theoretical framework is required to allow the formulators of action programs to move from an understanding of present conditions and their causes to the setting of goals and to the development of programs that will achieve these goals. In a word, what the plans need, but now lack, is the sophistication and rationality that can be supplied by social-science theory and data. These alone will not produce miracles, but they may prevent some politically and financially costly failures.

Criticism is always easy, and my comments have failed to call attention to the pioneering thought and effort that have gone into these plans. Even so, I think that social scientists could do much to help improve them, and I believe that they should take part in them. In fact, the remainder of this chapter is primarily an appeal asking sociologists to do just that. In elaborating the appeal, I shall also indicate my conception of the direction that guided-mobility theory and planning programs ought to take.

THE ROLE OF SOCIOLOGY IN PLANNING AGAINST POVERTY

What can sociologists do? It goes without saying that they can do research *about* guided-mobility planning, studying the issues involved and the programs themselves in order to add to our theoretical knowledge in the fields of class, urban life, social disorganization, and deviant behavior. They can also conduct research *for* these programs, and they will undoubtedly be asked to do so in the coming years, either on a staff or consultant basis. But I believe that the sociologist ought to be more than a detached researcher and that he should participate more directly in social-action programs. The guided-mobility planners can use the sociologist in at least four ways: for the *development of a theoretical scheme to guide the planning,* for *goal determination,* for *means or program development,* and for *the evaluation of action programs.*

Although research about the nature and dynamics of lower-class life is still in its infancy, the main outlines of a theoretical scheme can be set out in brief.[10] The low-income population can be divided into the *working class* and the *lower class* (upper-lower and lower-lower in the Warnerian scheme). The former is distinguished by relatively stable semiskilled or skilled blue-collar employment and by a way of life that centers on the family circle, or extended family. The lower class is characterized by temporary, unstable employment in unskilled—and the most menial—blue-collar jobs and by a way of life equally marked by instability. S. M. Miller has aptly described it as crisis-life.[11] Largely as a result of the man's occupational instability, the lower-class family is often matrifocal or female-based. This is most marked among the Negro population, in which the woman has been the dominant figure since the days of slavery, but it can also be found in other groups suffering from male occupational instability. Although this type of family organization has some stable and positive features, especially for its female members, the hypothesis has been suggested that it raises boys who lack the self-image, the aspirations, and the motivational structure that would help them to develop the skills necessary to function in the modern job market.[12] Also it may prevent boys from participating in a "normal" family relationship in adulthood, thus perpetuating the pattern for another generation. These conditions are, of course, exacerbated by racial and class discrimination, low income, slum and overcrowded housing conditions, as well as illness and other deprivations which bring about frequent crises. Under these conditions, lower-class people are not motivated to develop mobility aspirations, but instead defend themselves against frustration by rejecting the rest of the world and by searching for what gratifications are available, including such forms of retreat as alcohol and narcotics.

The result is a vicious cycle of lack of opportunity and of aspiration. To begin with, the lower class suffers from lack of occupational opportunities and access to education and social institutions. These deprivations create social-structural and cultural patterns which inhibit many people from developing the values and skills needed to take advantage of the opportunities if they were available. If and when they do become available, these inhibitions thus prevent mobility from taking place. Without aspirations, available opportunities cannot be used; but without opportunities, few people in their right mind are motivated to develop aspirations that may be frustrated.

This vicious cycle can, however, be broken. Opportunities must precede aspirations, not only because many lower-class people do develop the requisite motivation to take advantage of opportunities, only holding it in abeyance until opportunities appear, but also because the remainder will not develop the needed aspirations without evidence that opportunities will be open to them. For example, a number of studies show that educationl aspirations are quite strong in the Negro community, but that a variety of factors and forces erode them as children become older and are socialized into the ever present lower-class culture.[13] If the proper educational opportunities were available, the aspirations would not need to erode so often.

This sketchy theoretical scheme has implications for action programs. To begin with, it suggests that the working-class population needs guided-mobility plans much less urgently than the lower class, especially given the scarcity of public funds and political "capital" for social change. Not only the working class has achieved a reasonable amount of economic stability, if not affluence, but its members also have skills to maneuver in the modern labor market. The lower class, on the other hand, suffers from much more intense deprivation and is capable of filling only jobs which are rapidly disappearing from the economy. Its need for help is infinitely greater.

The theoretical scheme also suggests two types of action programs for this population. First, it is necessary to increase opportunities for jobs as well as for educational skills—and equally important, credentials—that permit the holding of skilled blue- and white-collar jobs and to reduce discrimination based on ascribed aspects of race and class. Second, methods must be found to develop the aspirations, motivations, and skills needed for these opportunities. Insofar as their development may be hindered by the dynamics of the female-based family and other elements of lower-class life, changes in the social structure and culture of the lower class may be required before the psychological prerequisites can develop.

Although this theoretical scheme is preliminary and as yet unsupported by sufficient empirical verification, it is sufficient to allow me to consider the other three functions the sociologist can play in guided-mobility planning and to raise some of the questions which must be answered before such planning can be successful.

Perhaps the most important function is the determination of goals. The planners must begin by asking what problems are to be solved and what goals are to guide the problem-solving process. Is it the amelioration of antisocial and self-destructive behavior or, beyond that, the elimination of all lower-class behavior which is visible and displeasing to the dominant middle-class culture? Or is the aim the traditional one of making middle-class citizens out of the lower class?

These questions are framed from the point of view of the sponsors and suppliers of guided-mobility plans. The sociologist should, however, shift the focus of questions to the clients of these plans. Thus he must ask: What do lower-class people find desirable and undesirable in their way of life; also, which aspects of this life are pathological for them, regardless of their own attitudes, and which are likely to lead to pathological consequences for others in the society? Needless to say, the determination that a behavior pattern is pathological must be based on empirically valid and reliable evidence to prevent the facile labeling of deviant or only culturally different behavior as pathological. The sociologist must also ask: What is the goal of the lower-class individual? Is he content with social instability, wanting only economic stability for himself and his children? Or does he want middle-class ways for him and them? Or is his goal, at least in the foreseeable future, to become working class, to achieve the stability of employment, family life, and group membership that distinguishes it from his own ways? And if this is so, as seems quite likely, what are the dominant aspects of working-class life that he wants and how do they differ from both his present ways and the middle-class ones of the programmers of guided mobility?

These questions are only a sample of the ones that need to be asked. Once they are answered—even if only in the preliminary forms necessary to get action programs started—the sociologist can help to develop the means necessary to achieve the goals; that is, by participating in the development of programs of action. It is here that he can perhaps make his most useful contribution. As already noted, caretakers and city planners are often wedded to techniques that give the illusion of service rather than service, proposing inadequate or irrelevant means for the right goals. Moreover, the sociologist is trained to look for basic processes, functions, and causes, so that he can see fairly clearly what means do and do not achieve the goals for which they are intended. For example, he can demonstrate with little effort that improved playgrounds or new school buildings will not by themselves contribute much to cure the pathologies of lower-class life.

Means necessarily depend on the goals selected for action. If the primary goal is to help lower-class people achieve working-class status and culture, the methods to be chosen will seek to overcome the two types of obstacles that now stand in the way: lack of opportunities and absence of the proper aspirations, motivations, and skills. In order to deal with this question here, I limit the discussion to that portion of the lower-class population which can most easily respond to opportunities; that is, the people who can work and learn, who might be called the *adaptable poor*. It thus excludes the minority of lower-class people who are either too old or physically and otherwise disabled—the people whom Hylan Lewis has aptly called the *clinical poor*.[14] Among the adaptable group, it is useful to distinguish between those who are potentially middle or working class—who have the requisite emotional, intellectual, and other cultural attributes for responding to opportunities—from those who do not and are in that sense culturally more lower class.

As already indicated, both types need programs that increase job and other opportunities, higher incomes, the reduction of discrimination, and access to schools and a variety of social services. This is more easily said than done. The establishment of better schools and social services is comparatively simple to program if funds and staff are available. Of course, the services must be designed to attract the intended clients. Moreover, incentives may be necessary to induce people to use these services, especially on a long-term basis. For example, money payments to students may persuade lower-class parents who are skeptical about education to send them to school. Similarly, grants in lieu of wages might allow men with families, who dropped out of school in adolescence, to return in their twenties when they have realized the importance of education.

The provision of more jobs and the elimination of discrimination are much more difficult to accomplish. In a society in which the number of jobs cannot keep up with population growth, no one has yet come up with ways of determining, much less instituting, the needed structural changes that will create more jobs or, for that matter, of channeling them to a population that is least able to compete for them. These are challenges for economic and political planners, for people who can devise "social inventions" to overcome the opposition of vested interests, and for politicians willing to carry out the difficult process of creating change.

The potentially middle- or working-class segment will be able to respond to these opportunities with a relatively small amount of help, but the remainder of the lower-class population—and the proportion is unknown—must be aided by methods that will help individuals, families, and other groups to develop the emotional, intellectual, and social responses necessary to allow them to take hold of such opportunities.

This requires a catalogue of generalizations about the characteristics of the attitudes and skills that are lacking and the social and psychological causes of their absence. This, in turn, takes the inquiry into the nature of lower-class problems. Is it aspirations for mobility that are lacking, or the motivations to pursue these aspirations, or the emotional, intellectual, and social skills that are necessary to implement both? And what causes these to be absent? Is the female-based family at fault, and if so, in what ways does it inhibit people from responding to opportunity? Is it the matriarchal dominance which is said to emasculate boys and send them on the way to familial and other forms of marginality? Or is it the lack of male models in the child-rearing process? If so, could surrogate models be provided by guided-mobility programs? Or are there deeper, dynamic factors which require the presence of a stable father figure? He is not so easily supplied. Or does the problem lie less with the family structure than with parental lack of education, the thought processes taught by lower-class parents, and the skills required to succeed in lower-class surroundings which are learned from siblings and peers and differ sharply from the skills needed to do well in school? Is it the inability to concentrate, to use words as concepts rather than as tools in interpersonal struggles, or is it simply the absence of books and privacy for study at home, or perhaps the unskilled and culturally myopic teacher that causes the problems? Or is the source of the difficulties to be found in the high rate of mental illness among the lower-class population and the fact that the youngster is from his earliest days surrounded by many people who are mentally ill, including even his parents?

Once these questions are answered and basic causal processes are isolated from psychological symptoms, program planning must determine whether the needed attitudes and skills can be encouraged or whether adults and even adolescents who have grown up in a lower-class milieu have so hardened their defenses against deprivation that they can no longer change. In that case, perhaps only young children can be helped effectively, and much of the effort might best be spent on rescuing them from the negative elements in the lower-class milieu. After that, it must be determined to what extent these attitudes and skills can be taught either by formal or informal methods and to what extent they can come about only as a result of structural changes in lower-class life. If the latter is true, then preschool forms of education may be less effective than attempts to remove children from the lower-class milieu through day-care centers, summer camps, foster parents, and even boarding schools and "children's societies" modeled on those in the Israeli collectives.

Finally, there is the important and equally difficult problem of developing rapport with a population which has traditionally rejected contact with caretakers and is so despairing of being helped that it has often turned aside all aid in order to save what little dignity it is able to maintain.

I am not suggesting that the sociologist can answer these questions or that action programs can be developed to achieve the desired goals. Many of the questions have no answers at present, and action programs will have to be experimental until the right ones are found. All the sociologist can do is to work with other behavioral scientists to help programmers achieve the best methods, provided, of course, that he is invited to do so. Since guided mobility is a form of social mobility, the extensive sociological literature on this topic may provide useful leads for action programs.

The fourth function of the sociologist is that of evaluation: analyzing the action programs in terms of their consequences and finding out whether or not they have achieved the intended goals and without undesirable side effects. Because many of the programs will be experimental, the sociologist can help set them up so that they can be studied and evaluated most effectively. Evaluation research is already an accepted field of inquiry in sociology, and although its method and techniques are still primitive, and much more research must be done before it can become a mature branch of sociology, its relevance needs no more discussion here.

THE NEED FOR POLICY-ORIENTED SOCIOLOGY

The four functions I have proposed for the sociologist in guided mobility require considerable theoretical exploration and much more detailed theory building, but they do not require any radical theoretical innovation, for they are based on a theory of planning which has its roots in the social sciences and can be "plugged into" a number of sociological theories, including symbolic interactionism, action theory, and the structural-functional approach. They do, however, require some changes in the use of research, in the conceptualization of theory, and in professional self-definition.

Most of the questions which must be answered before planning can take place on a rational basis have not yet been sufficiently studied; yet the planners cannot wait for further research. Sociologists who participate in guided-mobility programs must be able to come to conclusions on the basis of past research, a modicum of impressionistic observation, and a large amount of freewheeling hypothesizing—that is, guessing. They must gamble further by being willing to build the products of this highly unscientific approach into experimental programs. There is no doubt that this type of sociological endeavor will lay the practitioner open to criticism from colleagues in the discipline as being unscientific or controversial, but it will be countered by appreciation—and the surrender of an ancient stereotype about the unwillingness of sociologists to come to conclusions—on the part of the planners.

Moreover, the sociologist must revamp the concepts that he uses so that they can answer the questions posed by the plan and in such a way that they will lead to ideas and techniques for action programs. Concepts framed for theory and for action differ considerably, and while not every sociologist has the skill and imagination for social invention, his concepts must be able to help those who do and who make up action programs. While it is important for these programs to have a theoretical understanding of lower-class behavior patterns and attitudes, it is much more important for them to know how lower-class people may be helped. For example, the guided-mobility planners who want to provide aid to lower-class Negro women must know what kinds of help these women need most urgently and how the always limited resources can be allocated with this priority in mind. Is their first need for a direct income grant, or for help in finding a job, or for job training, or for better housing, or for assistance in taking care of the children? Also, if the first priority were an income grant, what kind of grant would be least humiliating, least likely to create further dependency, and least likely to reduce even more the function of the father? If the first priority were for assistance in child care, what kind of assistance would be accepted by women without making them feel that they are inferior mothers or that they might be losing their children to strangers practicing a different culture? And perhaps most important, if jobs for Negro men are not yet available, what kinds of aid will maintain the positive functions of the female-based family but will also reduce the dysfunctions for its male members?

Answers to questions like these will also force the sociologist to make unaccustomed value judgments. A question about what aspects of lower-class life are undesirable differs sharply from the usual question of what lower-class life is like. For example, the sociologist must frame value judgments on the issue of Negro family structure. Coming from a culture in which the two-parent nuclear family is the norm, he must decide whether or not to suggest programs that would maintain the Negro female-based family. Part of the problem is, of course, empirical; he must have data to determine whether such a family is functional for the present social and economic position of its various members and how these members feel about the kind of family in which they are living. But even if such a family is a functional and wanted solution, the sociologist in an action program still has to decide for himself whether he can propose programs that will maintain this family type for yet another generation.

Many similar questions must be answered about other behavior patterns and attitudes that differ from the middle-class ones with which most sociologists identify. And whether he functions as a researcher or joins those who design action programs, the sociologist must make value judgments about behavior patterns, institutions, and attitudes which he has not made before. This is not so difficult as it might appear, for the basic value judgment—that society can and ought to be improved—already lurks in the hearts and minds of most contemporary sociologists. Even so, large ideological steps must be taken to get from the prevalent liberalism of the social-problems approach to the kind of radical social innovation that is needed to make guided-mobility programs successful, especially when these involve the redistribution of power, income, opportunities, and prerogatives. Moreover, what is needed is a pragmatic radicalism, oriented less to classical concepts of revolution than to techniques for changing social, economic, and political institutions which resist change.

What I have been describing here is applied or, more correctly, *policy-oriented* sociology. This type of analysis is not new; it was practiced among the early sociologists, if only in a primitive way, and it has become popular in our time among sociologists working in market research, medical sociology, and wherever else their efforts are used in policy formulation and decision making. Planning for guided mobility is just another, although much broader, topic for policy-oriented sociology. If sociologists become involved in it, their work may speed the development of a branch of sociology which is explicitly concerned with policy formation and should be equal, in resources, productivity, and intellectual standing to traditional theoretical-empirical sociology. Given similar developments in other disciplines, the social sciences may one day be more help in solving the pressing questions of our society than has heretofore been the case. Needless to say, I believe this to be a desirable goal.

PART TWO[15]

From Social Planning to Community-Action Programs, 1962–1965

Since 1962, the guided-mobility projects have moved into the action phase. This section will suggest in a preliminary fashion the uses of sociology in the various projects, applying my critique of the initial project formulations and describing the role of the sociologists in these programs.

Much has happened to the guided-mobility projects between 1962 and 1965, and many of my critical comments are now out of date. To begin with, new names have developed for the projects. Although city planners still call them social-planning, human-renewal, or gray-area projects, since the creation of the federal antipoverty program, they are now often described as antipoverty projects as well. However, this term refers to the entire war on poverty, including the Job Corps, VISTA, and others, so that it would be more correct to call the projects by the name used in Title II of the Economic Opportunity Act of 1964, "community action programs." According to this Act, "the term 'community action program' means a program which mobilizes and utilizes, in an attack on poverty, public and private resources of any urban or rural or combined urban and rural geographical area (referred to in this title as 'community') . . . to give promise of progress toward elimination of poverty through developing employment opportunities, improving human performance, motivation and productivity and bettering the conditions under which people live, learn and work." [16]

Since 1962, the projects described in the first part of the chapter have gone into the action phase, and with the passage of the Economic Opportunity Act and the appropriation in 1964 of $340 million for community-action programs, many additional projects have been started. Over 150 cities in the country are now mounting a program, although many of the new ones are at present writing still in the planning stage. Consequently, my observations will be based principally on the projects that already existed in 1962.

Between 1962 and 1965, these projects have begun to move away from counteracting the negative effects of urban renewal, from improving the physical condition of neighborhoods, and from the cultural uplifting of their residents. As they have gone into the action phase, some have become increasingly concerned with improving educational, occupational, legal, and political opportunities—and in about that order of priority. Indeed, probably most of the projects' effort and money has gone into education, ranging from "Headstart" schools for children of prekindergarten age to occupational retraining for adults. As before, the attempt is to provide guidance for mobility, although, again as before, not always in a deliberate manner. Also, whether the end product of mobility is to be working-class or middle-class ways of living is not clear, although the transformation of poor people into middle-class citizens is still a major aim of many of the projects. Similarly, most of the projects still focus on people in specific neighborhoods, and, as before, they are oriented to helping individuals more than whole groups or entire neighborhoods.

The major reasons for the changes in programmatic emphasis are three: the contact with low-income people as the projects moved into the field; the planning and experience of Mobilization for Youth which influenced later efforts; and the funding activities and program requirements of the foundations and federal agencies which sponsored the projects.

One important cause of change was simply the natural progress of the projects from the proposal to the action stage. As staffs were hired and went into action, it was quickly realized that some of the initial proposals were either not so important or premature; that the principal needs of the low-income population were not for recreation and culture, but for jobs, income, help in obtaining education and educational skill, and the elimination of racial barriers. Even before that, however, the program planners had been influenced by Mobilization for Youth, the New York program for delinquency prevention, which was already under way when the programs initiated by city planners were just starting out.

Mobilization for Youth began with a systematically developed and stated program, based on the "opportunity theory" of Richard Cloward and Lloyd Ohlin, which argued that much delinquency was a reaction to the lack of opportunities in achieving normal American working-class and middle-class goals.[17] Drawing on Merton's theory of anomie, Cloward, Ohlin, and their staff developed an action program which sought to increase these opportunities. Noting that obstacles to the opportunities stemmed not only from the lack of skills of low-income peoples but also from the political and bureaucratic barriers arrayed against them by private and city agencies, Mobilization for Youth set up a community-organization program which sought to make lower-class people a political force with sufficient power to break down these barriers. In addition, Mobilization for Youth created what might be called "advocate programs," in which professionals and technicians became advocates for lower-class people at city hall and in court. For example, a legal-services program was set up to provide lawyers to area residents so that they could bring suits against landlords, merchants, and even city officials. Neighborhood service centers were also instituted to enable citizens to lodge complaints and voice problems and to obtain help in demanding aid from the relevant public and private agencies. Finally, Mobilization for Youth community-organization specialists rendered technical assistance to residents mounting a rent strike against slum landlords.

Because the emerging action programs of the city planners were largely financed by the Ford Foundation and the President's Committee on Juvenile Delinquency and Youth Crime, which had also funded Mobilization for Youth, they were put into contact with the Mobilization staff. Moreover, Lloyd Ohlin, one of the founders of Mobilization for Youth, went to work for the President's Committee and helped to bring many other projects into being.[18] Later, many of the ideas developed by the President's Committee were adopted by the Office of Economic Opportunity, which administers the federal war on poverty. In fact, a number of the people initially responsible for developing local and federal action programs eventually joined the staff of OEO.

The diffusion of some of Mobilization's ideas and programs was encouraged also by the fact that these had been developed as part of a relatively systematic theory. Consequently, as the city planners were moving away from programs centered on urban renewal and neighborhood improvement and were uncertain over what direction their efforts should take, the experiences of Mobilization for Youth, diffused through the foundations and the federal funding agencies, offered them guidance.

The final and perhaps most important cause of the programmatic changes was the funding activities and requirements of the sponsors. Since most of the first funds came from the Ford Foundation, the initial program formulations reflected its interest in human renewal. Later, when the President's Committee on Juvenile Delinquency and Youth Crime made funds available for delinquency prevention and the Office of Manpower, Automation, and Training gave grants for job training and retraining, their interests were added to the projects, and subsequently programs supported by the Office of Economic Opportunity were also included.

As a result of the close relationships between the initial projects and the funding agencies and the subsequent incorporation of early experience into federal manuals to guide local community-action agencies, the projects are becoming increasingly similar in their approach and in the variety of programs they are developing. Even so, their specific activities are not likely to be uniform the nation over. Every city has a somewhat different set of programs, depending partly on the amount of money available; the quality and size of staff that could be hired; the amount of interest and cooperation on the part of existing agencies serving poor people, both private and public; the political relationship between the action agency and city hall; and, of course, the characteristics of the low-income clients.

So far, however, many cities have reported quite similar experiences and difficulties in implementing the four programmatic goals described above in Part One: extending social services to the hard-to-reach; offering new methods of education; reducing unemployment; and encouraging community participation on the part of poor people. A similar set of problems has also developed in connection with the new category of advocate programs.

Many of the cities reported initial difficulties in the extension of social services due to opposition from established welfare agencies. A new agency's ability to hire the best staff, to infuse funds into the established agencies for new programs, or to co-opt them by other means has, however, reduced this difficulty somewhat. The most notable improvement in providing services to the hard to reach has been through the use of subprofessionals, neighbors of the intended clients, who have received some training in giving service. Being of similar background, they have been able to overcome the traditional reluctance of many low-income clients to accept offers of aid (other than money) from middle-class social workers.[19]

One of the major advantages of the trained neighborhood resident is what Riessman calls "lower-class knowhow." [20] In describing Mobilization's "home-maker" program, which uses neighboorhood mothers to help others with homemaking and family problems, he quotes a middle-class social worker who is comparing the skills of the middle-class professional with the so-called indigenous worker:

> Indigenous people could teach professional staff a great deal if the latter were willing to learn. . . . They don't perceive people as problems, or at least disagree with professionals about what constitutes a problem. . . . Somehow, Mrs. Smith was less forbidding to the homemaker than the caseworker who was frightened of her. She was well-meaning, easily misunderstood, and temperamental. But she wasn't "paranoid, rejecting, abusive." Mrs. Casey was "a fine person who cared for her children" and that was the main thing even if she had four illegitimate offspring. To the social worker, she was depressed, practically egoless, "so self-destructive." [21]

Writing about her own contact with the clients, this social worker continues:

> The lack of felt, in contrast to actual, social distance between homemaker and client is evident and results from several factors. I sometimes feel like an inhibiting influence when I go along to introduce a homemaker to a client. When I leave, they break out into their own language and vernacular. . . . Empathy rather sympathy sometimes comes more naturally to the homemaker than the professional worker. [22]

Of course, reducing the class difference between staff and client is not enough, for some services can be provided only by technically or professionally trained staff members who are likely to be middle class. For example, legal-aid services must be provided by lawyers. Experience gathered so far indicates, however, that when it comes to formally defined services or relationships like the legal one, the class barrier is not so important as it is for informal ones, like those of social work and counseling, where the staff member is impinging on the culture and family structure of the client. [23] Even so, a lawyer who is uninterested in the legal problems of poor clients or impatient with their inability to understand legal and bureaucratic language and behavior is not likely to be of much help as an advocate.

The initial success in the use of trained subprofessionals has led to proposals for and experiments in employing such workers in all kinds of caretaking institutions, as aids in schools, hospitals, libraries, recreation centers, mental-health clinics, and the like. Their employment would not only improve the relevance of service to the clients but open up a whole new series of jobs for people who are being put out of work by technology. Frank Riessman has estimated that four to six million subprofessionals could be put to work in this fashion, and the proposal is now being implemented by a number of local agencies, aided by federal grants throughout the country.[24]

Despite the success of the trained subprofessionals, many action programs are finding that the most deprived people, as well as the addicts, the serious delinquents, the mentally ill, and the totally despairing, are still hard to reach by public programs and that without extreme care, every program can easily "cream," that is, attract the cream of the client population, who are easiest to reach but also need help less urgently than their less fortunate neighbors.

Attempts to develop new educational programs for low-income children are proceeding, although here, too, progress is slow. Some impetus is currently being created by Operation Headstart, a federal program of prekindergarten schooling, and by local tutoring programs, in which college students, adults, and even older youngsters from the same school or neighborhood help poorly performing children of all ages. But these programs also tend to cream, and their positive effects are likely to evaporate quickly if the child who has gone through a Headstart program must then go on to the same inadequate slum school. Because research on why some lower-class children are poor learners is only just beginning, there is as yet no consensus on effective methods for new teaching programs. A number of experiments are being undertaken, including the use of new texts and curriculums, teaching machines, teacher aids, remedial-reading programs, and smaller classes, as well as the search for teachers more able to communicate with lower-class students. Unfortunately, many school systems are resistant to innovation, and some action programs have found that cooperation with them is harder to obtain than with other city agencies. Moreover, teachers who can effectively communicate with lower-class youngsters are quite scarce, and proposals to use trained subprofessionals in the schoolroom have not yet been implemented in large enough numbers to evaluate their usefulness.

Changes in educational programs are also being held back by a fundamental ideological conflict over the explanation of poor school performance by children from low-income homes. One point of view argues that the primary cause is *cultural deprivation,* that is, the failure of the home to provide the kind of preschool culture and training which middle-class children receive from their parents, providing anticipatory socialization for the student role. From this perspective, the fault lies in the lower-class family, home, and culture.[25] The opposing point of view holds that the primary cause is *educational deprivation* or inadequacy, that is, the failure of the schools to teach youngsters from low-income homes. Although the former point of view is defended by educators and the educational profession, the latter one is strongly supported by available research. For example, Kenneth Clark's data show that the longer Negro children in Harlem remain in school, the poorer their performance in class and on intelligence tests, and that Negro children equal to white ones in the first grade begin to do considerably poorer work from the third grade on.[26] These data indicate that whatever the effects of the home, the school is creating additional deprivation, partly because of its inexperience in teaching non-middle-class students, partly because slum schools are staffed either by inexperienced teachers fresh out of college or by substitutes, and partly because they are racially segregated.

Some of the critics who have stressed educational inadequacy take the argument one step further, pointing out that school performance is poor because society gives the lower-class child, and especially the nonwhite boy, no reason for succeeding in school. In his neighborhood, many of the adult men are unemployed, and without some guarantee that his fate will not be similar to theirs, he has little incentive to learn, especially when success in school may result in immediate sanction from his peers. No such guarantee is now available, for a study by Robert Dentler and Ellen Warshauer shows that white dropouts have a much better chance of obtaining employment than Negro high-school graduates.[27] This point of view puts the emphasis on *societal inadequacy* and suggests that until the low-income nonwhite population is admitted to first-class citizenship, even the best school is powerless to help its youngsters significantly.

Despite the conflict between these explanations, there is some truth in all of them. Undoubtedly, poor home conditions hold back learning, and so do poor schools; but society must also promise the child a useful function after graduation if going to school is to make sense to him. If that function is available, a child is motivated to learn even in poor schools; if not, only the most ambitious and upwardly mobile one will do so. Thus, the first priority is to assure this function. Beyond that, the conflict between cultural and educational deprivation theories can be resolved by the fact that however difficult it is to change the schools, it is much easier than to change the culture of the home. Consequently, the second priority is to eliminate current forms of educational deprivation.

A revealing parallel may be drawn between the three explanations of poor school performance and the dispute over social services. The advocates of cultural deprivation and the established social-service agencies argue that present professional services are adequate and that these services are not accepted because of client inadequacies. The proponents of educational deprivation and at least some of the community-action agencies argue that existing services are inadequate and must be altered to help the lower-class population, while the advocates of societal inadequacy take the position of the client population, pointing out that improvements in social services and education are nearly useless until more basic economic and social opportunities are provided. For many lower-class people, the most basic need is for employment.

Unfortunately, the reduction of unemployment has probably been the least successful of the community-action programs. Some cities have reported success with on-the-site job retraining, because unlike off-site training, the former offers a job after the completion of training. However, in both types of training much of the success has so far resulted from the tendency to cream and to select the better-educated among the unemployed for these programs.[28]

Occupational training and retraining may be just as irrelevant as social services and education if they do not guarantee employment, however, and this guaranty is presently nonexistent. The action agencies can create only a few jobs, and many of those they have created are temporary, poorly paid, and often make-work ones.[29] The fact is that these agencies lack the economic power or resources to affect the job market. Until they or other community agencies obtain this power, unemployment, especially among adolescent school dropouts and young adults, is not going to be affected significantly, and, as a result, aspirations among lower-class youth to prepare themselves for work are likely to remain low. The need for governmental action to create new jobs is becoming ever more urgent, but this involves a radical transformation of the relationship between government and the economy.[30] Since the unemployed are at present too few and too ineffective politically, the required political pressures that must precede federal job-creation programs are building up only slowly.

The community-organization and advocate programs have been the most controversial action-agency projects. The community-organization efforts have been of two types. One was based on the assumption that a significant increase in economic and social opportunities could be obtained only through political means and that, in effect, the community-action agency ought to help the low-income population organize to voice its demands politically. As a result, there have been voter-registration campaigns, and in the case of Mobilization for Youth, rent strikes and demonstrations to protest conditions in the school, police brutality, and so on. The other, more prevalent, type has been to set up neighborhood organizations which would help and support the community-action agencies themselves.

Neither of these has been especially successful. Citizen groups to support the action agencies are often little more than company unions whose first priority is to defend "management." Since the action agencies have not yet provided much real help to low-income people, they are not easily defended in the poor neighborhoods, and the local people who try to do so are often condemned as having sold out to city hall. In some instances, this has happened, for leaders of protest groups have been offered jobs by the action agency and thus co-opted into its ranks.[31]

The attempt to organize low-income people politically has also been unsuccessful so far. For one thing, it is difficult to get them to meetings and demonstrations in numbers large enough to impress the politicians.

Moreover, low-income areas have little power in the city, and the action agencies themselves are also relatively powerless, so that even a good turnout is no guarantee of political success. This only reinforces the cynical conviction among low-income people that one cannot fight city hall.

Actually, the political-organization schemes were never adequately tested, for the demonstrations and protests that did take place were immediately opposed by the agencies against which they were lodged. These agencies had sufficient political influence to put pressure on the community-action agencies to eliminate or emasculate them. For example, in 1964, Mobilization for Youth came under heavy attack from the press and from city hall, allegedly for harboring Communists and mismanaging funds. The real reason for the attack was, however, the opposition that had developed among powerful city agencies. The school system was upset over demonstrations against local school officials; the welfare agency, over suits against the department; and the police, for Mobilization's protests against police brutality and its advocacy of a civilian review board to monitor police treatment of low-income people. The hostility of these and other agencies and interest groups whose position was threatened by the Mobilization for Youth program led to an investigation of the agency and subsequently to closer supervision of its activities by city hall. This, in turn, resulted in the virtual emasculation of the more militant organization programs. At this time, city hall also obtained closer control over the expenditure of agency funds, thus assuring it that the funds would be spent so as to help the party in power, or at least not aid its opponents. This, too, helped to reduce the vitality of the agency at that time.

A similar fate threatens to befall the advocate programs. Among them, the provision of legal aid has aroused particularly strong protest. In New York, for example, Mobilization for Youth helped its clients sue politically influential individuals and agencies, who then complained to city hall. Current attempts to set up legal services on a larger scale are being fought by Legal Aid, a national organization which has offered some free legal service to the indigent in the past, and by lawyers who are fearful that extensive free legal service would deprive them of fees. Nevertheless, the Office of Economic Opportunity has been attempting to develop a nationwide program of "neighborhood law firms" to provide legal services to the poor, and as this is being written, negotiations are under way to obtain the co-operation of Legal Aid and the American Bar Association.[32]

The opposition to community-organization and advocacy programs is easily explained. Through these programs, the action agencies have encouraged and helped their clients to fight city hall and the larger power structure and to demand changes in the allocation of public funds, the quality and distribution of public services, and the distribution of political power generally. By power structure, or what some action-agency officials call the Establishment, I mean the network of alliances between city hall, political parties, established welfare agencies, school-board and other municipal agencies, and interest groups such as the downtown business community, neighborhood merchant groups, realtors, landlords, and the like. In most cities, these groups do not form a permanent or organized power structure, but frequently some of them band together to defend their interests, or they do so individually by appeals to city hall.

When the action agencies began to take over traditional functions of established agencies, or set up substitutes for them, or otherwise threatened powerful interests, these fought back by putting pressure on the action agencies. Since city hall and individual elements in the power structure usually participated in setting up the action agencies in the first place and customarily dominate their boards of trustees, they had no real difficulty in demanding a halt to political activities or to any others that stepped on influential toes.[33]

Most often, the conflict has been between the action agencies and city hall, for the latter, being the broker among conflicting interest groups, represents those whose power is being threatened. The conflict has been escalated by the additional funds provided by OEO for antipoverty programs. These programs bring sizable amounts of federal money into the community, and it is to city hall's advantage to make sure that its allocation will benefit or not hurt it politically. Moreover, the federal legislation that brought OEO into being requires specifically that local antipoverty programs be conducted with "the maximum feasible participation of the residents of the areas [affected]."[34] As a result, OEO will not make grants until poor people are given places on the policy-making boards which control local antipoverty and community-action projects. In most cities, poor people have been appointed by city hall or the antipoverty agency, but in Philadelphia, an election was held in May, 1965, to select area representatives from poor neighborhoods.

Despite the fact that poor people are a minority on the policy-making board and are often not brought in until the programs have been set up, this clause of the antipoverty legislation has generated considerable protest from city halls the country over. For instance, at the 1965 meeting of the United States Conference of Mayors, OEO was accused of "fostering class struggle" and "creating tensions among the urban poor by insisting on participation by impoverished citizens in the antipoverty program." A conference resolution criticized OEO for failing "to recognize the legal and moral responsibilities of local officials who are accountable to the taxpayers for expenditures of local funds," and Vice-President Humphrey had to be called in to meet with the mayors and arrange a compromise that would satisfy them.[35] The mayors, including those of most of the large cities, minced no words in arguing that the balance of power ought not to be changed and that the antipoverty program should be shaped, not by the needs of the poor, but by those of city hall and the taxpayers, that is, the affluent citizens of the community.

The action agencies are squarely in the middle in this conflict, for they must choose whether their first allegiance is to their boards, to city hall and the power structure, or to their clients. The agencies are trying to avoid such a choice, for whichever one they make, they can only lose. If they side with city hall, they lose rapport with their clients, thus impairing the success of their programs; but if they side with the clients, they are subject to sanctions from the power structure. The local agencies have looked for support to Washington, but as the confrontation with the mayors suggest, OEO is also subject to political pressure from local power holders with influence in Washington. Since the clients are presently unorganized and powerless, and since they do not expect much from the antipoverty program in the first place, they are not likely to provide political support for the action agencies. Although one can argue that if poverty is to be reduced, the action agencies must nevertheless side with the clients and develop programs that will increase their economic and political role, the agencies cannot help but respond first to the sources of present power. Since most of the power is held by the "Establishment," moral imperatives and programmatic necessities are of lower priority.[36]

What will probably happen is that the action agencies will side with the poor when they can and when the issue is not of great political significance, but the rest of the time they will side with those who have power in the community, meanwhile making it look as if they were on the side of the poor. Thus community-organization programs may continue, but their leaders will take their direction from downtown, and local protest leaders in the neighborhood may be co-opted into the action agency. Similarly, the present tendency of city halls and incumbent political parties to exert control over the antipoverty and community-action agencies, even if they are nominally independent, is also likely to succeed, for as soon as public funds are involved, these agencies lack the power to prevent it. The poverty-stricken clients must thus obtain greater political power by their own efforts; and until they do so and can express this power in their own community and in Washington, the action programs will be forced to side with city hall and against them when a conflict of interest develops.

SUCCESSES AND FAILURES IN THE
COMMUNITY-ACTION PROGRAMS

The many obstacles placed in the path of the action agencies make it extremely doubtful that their present efforts will do much to reduce poverty or to achieve success in other programs. For one thing, there is as yet no agreement on how success is to be measured.[37] Martin Rein has suggested three criteria for evaluating the projects: institutional change within public agencies to offer more aid to low-income people; the amount of community participation on their part; and the reduction of antisocial behavior among them.[38] It is clear from the foregoing that there has been little positive change with respect to the first two, and the third has been de-emphasized as the programs reduced their concern with delinquency prevention.[39]

Actually, it may not be possible to measure success by overt criteria. Although most of the projects have evaluation sections, it was usually not possible to set up systematic measures of before-and-after performance, or control groups.[40] Besides, the evaluation research has lagged for a variety of reasons, one of which is the difficulty of one arm of an agency in evaluating the action of another. Finally, the projects are still in an early stage, and it may be a number of years before their impact can be evaluated even in an unsystematic way.

Yet even if a proper evaluation were possible, it is unrealistic to expect that the present programs would produce much of a pay-off for their clients. The funds allocated so far are much too small, and the resulting programs can affect the lives of only a few people. Moreover, many are educational ones that seek to change the low-income population, rather than its living conditions, and too little is being done to attack the basic causes of poverty. New jobs are not yet being created in significant numbers; nothing is being done to raise the income of the low-income population or to move it out of the slums, and no programs have yet been developed to make significant inroads on racial discrimination in jobs, housing, or even education.[41] Indeed, the principal beneficiaries of the programs will be the people who staff them (for salaries of social workers and other professionals rise when action agencies are established) and city hall, which will use the programs to consolidate its power in the poorer neighborhoods. The recent entry of private industry into the antipoverty program and the willingness of the federal government to hire defense firms to run Job Corps camps and other projects suggests that they, too, will benefit from the new federal activities.[42] In short, then, the principal beneficiaries of the antipoverty program may well be the affluent sector of American society, thus confirming once again Titmuss' thesis that the welfare state offers more help to the rich than to the poor.[43]

Even so, the projects have had some positive effects. They have created a greater public awareness of the existence of poverty, and they will help some poor people, especially upwardly mobile children, to escape from the lower class. Moreover, the inability of job-training and retraining programs to significantly reduce unemployment is generating some pressure for the deliberate creation of new jobs by governmental initiative. If nothing else, a precedent has been set for local and federal antipoverty efforts, and current failures may lead to more comprehensive and more effective programs to reduce urban poverty in the future. If this does not happen, it is possible that the rising expectations which have been induced among the poverty-stricken by the publicity about present programs, the general concern with poverty, and the relentless presence of affluence all around them may have some now unanticipated consequences. Specifically, the poverty-stricken populations of the city may realize that ultimately their condition will be improved only through the exertion of political power. While they are likely to lose the current power struggle with city hall, they are numerous enough in the big cities to exert considerable influence if they organize themselves and form coalitions with other groups who have similar interests in bringing about social and economic change.[44] In addition, they can—as they already have—resort to one very potent weapon, upsetting the social order through demonstrations and riots, which may result in concessions from city hall and its more affluent constituents, for whom order is a prime goal.

The Uses of Sociology in Community-Action Projects[45]

In Part One of this chapter I suggested four functions for the sociologist involved in planning programs for the elimination of urban poverty: the development of a theoretical scheme to guide the planning, the determination of action goals, the formulation of means or programs, and the evaluation of these programs.

Three years of experience in various action projects suggests that while sociologists have helped in performing these functions, in reality the use of sociology lags considerably behind the ideal, and the ideal itself is in need of some redefinition.[46] A number of sociologists are participating in these projects in various cities: some in the action phases, more of them in the evaluation schemes and as consultants on program development and research.

One of the principal contributions of sociology has been at the level of theory. As noted in Part One, many of the projects began with a naïve reformer's point of view, aiming toward social and cultural uplift. The theory underlying this uplift was partly moralistic, but primarily psychological, proposing that deficiencies among the lower-class population could be removed by education and programs oriented to attitude change, after which this population would accept middle-class values and adjust to the middle-class society.

As the projects began to enter the action phase, however, the underlying theory became somewhat more sociological. Many of the projects accepted the Cloward-Ohlin "opportunity theory" that guided the Mobilization for Youth project, and while they rarely went in for theoretical statements, and were certainly not conscious of adopting a sociological perspective, some of their programs have emphasized the provision of previously unavailable opportunities. This theoretical change of emphasis was accompanied by an equally unconscious acceptance of a sociological approach to class, that is, the realization of the existence of a class structure, of class differences, and the development of a pluralistic point of view that did not demand adjustment to middle-class values on the part of the lower class.

These changes resulted in part from the direct efforts of sociologists. Cloward and Ohlin, the formulators of the Mobilization program, are both sociologists, and as indicated earlier, their ideas influenced the development of subsequent projects in other cities. In addition, contact with lower-class clients probably helped to convince the action-project staffs that a sociological perspective, one which treated the clients as suffering from lack of opportunity and status, was more useful than either a psychological or a moralistic one, which considered them as impaired or undeserving.

Even so, many of the programs still reflect inadequate or undesirable theoretical assumptions. There is still too much attribution of deviant behavior to pathologies within the actor and not enough understanding of the extent to which deviance is encouraged by the nondeviant majority. Also, too little attention is being paid to the role of power and to the inevitability of conflict if programs are to help the lower class.

Since most of the sociological assumptions were not introduced deliberately and sociologists took only a minor role in the shaping of programs, they cannot either take credit for them or be given blame for remaining inadequacies. Indeed, a number of sociologists have become active critics of the projects and, as I shall note below, have pointed out their shortcomings.

While sociological formulations have played a role in the theory that underlies the projects, they have been less significant in determining their goals and activities. Again, the fault is less that of sociology and sociologists than of the political context in which the programs must operate. Like all public ventures, the community-action agency must demonstrate quickly that it can produce results. Beset by powerful enemies, surrounded by influential skeptics, and pressed for results by uneasy politicians who have helped bring the agency into being, its first priority is for activities that can generate fairly rapid and visible successes, even if these are illusory or aimed at symptoms. Such pressures can easily create programs that cream by providing help to those who need it least and activities that look good on paper, but do not attract many clients. In short, the action agencies begin by selecting goals and programs that can be implemented most easily, and if the political pressures do not let up, this pattern is likely to continue. As a result, action is guided less by opportunity theory or the needs of the clients than by opportunities for producing results or the bureaucratic needs of the agencies and the political ones of their sponsors.

For example, although many of the theoreticians and the directors of the action agencies realized that the prime need was for the increase in economic opportunities, notably in employment, they also learned quickly that they lacked the access to economic institutions to create new jobs, or the power to put pressure on public and private agencies to do so. Similarly, in many communities the action agencies found themselves unable to gain access to school boards and thus could not institute the proposed changes in the education of lower-class children. As a result, the action projects have stressed programs that could be established outside the giant bureaucracies. Indeed, the current emphasis on prekindergarten education stems partly from difficulties in persuading the schools to improve their teaching methods, even though Clark's findings, cited previously, suggest that the most urgent need for improvement is beyond the third grade.

Even in the more limited action programs, the role of sociology has been less significant than I had hoped for in 1962. To begin with, there has been no time for new sociological research on the nature of lower-class culture, on the aspirations of lower-class people, on their willingness to adapt to—and participate in—social change, or on their ability to accept new opportunities when these were available. Nor was enough research available for use in the initial formulations of action programs. Also, few sociologists were involved in the framing of such programs; and even if they had been asked to help, it is questionable whether they would have been willing or able to do the huge amount of guessing about the nature of lower-class populations necessary to develop action programs.

Moreover, the data requirements of the action program and of the "activists" who carry them out are not satisfied by available sociological research and, more important, by the concepts of present sociological theory. Since the action agencies have little power, they cannot do away with the fundamental causes of poverty or frame long-range plans to attack other basic problems. Instead, they have to improvise almost on a day-to-day basis, developing new tactics and strategies when the old ones prove useless. The kind of information they want is that which enables them to move ahead: data on the targets of an action program, that is, on the goals or grievances of the clients; strategic information that can predict the success of one approach as compared to another; and finally, data that are highly specific and directly relevant to the institutions within which they are working. They asked for and used quick studies about the goals, problems, and grievances among the lower-class population, and they could have used studies of how lower-class people would react to different kinds of organizational techniques; for example, how job trainees would react to different kinds of training programs, or under what conditions children would learn from different kinds of instructional material. Such studies are not yet available, however.

Conversely, the activists have not been interested in detailed sociological field studies, especially those which complicated the development of an action program. They have preferred to employ models of action which are simple, which maximize the role of the activist, and which do not consider differences among the clients, especially of the kind that would necessitate more and more complex action plans. As one social scientist describing activist colleagues in his agency put it:

> Our agency had done a study of voluntary associations before the action project began, but it was never used. By the time it was needed it was outdated, but even if it had still been relevant, the activists would not have sought it out. It is too confusing and complicated to apply knowledge from studies; it is clearer to make assumptions about reality and go on from there. A study involves qualification, and confuses program formulation.[47]

Similarly, the activists have been cool to sociological concepts that could not be operationalized because they did not offer a function for activists, such as theories of social change that call for large-scale structural change. For example, theories of stratification which ascribe undesirable lower-class behavior to poverty and imply that behavior cannot be altered until poverty is removed were rejected, for these did not provide sociological concepts that stressed the role of the activist or that allowed him to set up feasible programs. Conversely, the action agencies have also been drawn toward theories that help them cope with their own inability to act, for example, those which ascribe lower-class behavior to inadequacies among the clients.

THE ROLE OF SOCIOLOGISTS IN THE COMMUNITY-ACTION AGENCY

While existing sociological theory and research have not been overly useful, sociologists employed by action agencies and directly involved in action programs have been somewhat more effective. They seem to have performed at least two functions. Some sociologists have been able to offer strategic information, that is, information on specific strategies to be used in the day-to-day activities. By strategic information, I mean information on actions that should be taken to achieve success in the immediate venture at hand. It could be an idea for increasing greater program usage by clients, or a set of tactics for coping with opposition from the agency's competitors. Strategic information is not intrinsically sociological, of course; it is, rather, developed out of an orientation to political action.

Some people can think in strategic terms, but others cannot, and sociological training alone is not conducive to strategic thinking. Indeed, most sociological concepts are useful neither for strategy nor for action; they describe what is happening, rather than what should happen. Even when the concepts are action-oriented, they emphasize long-range and impersonally created forms of change. For example, my own conception of guided mobility falls into both categories. It refers to a long-term process, and it does not offer much help to an activist involved in day-to-day attempts at change.

In addition, sociologists have provided some "reality orientation" to activists. Using their detachment, ability to view action from different perspectives, and empathy with the ways of other subcultures, they have sometimes been able to provide estimates on how proposed action schemes would be received and post-mortem generalizations on why a scheme failed, or why the various participants in the action process behaved as they did. One sociologist working in a community-action agency describes these functions as follows:

> Sociologists can help provide, first, an accurate image of things, classes, ghettoes and slums; second, an accurate image of events, hearings in the midst of controversy, crowd behavior in meeting situations, the proliferation of ad hoc groups and of emergent social movements; and third, a sound assessment of prospects for structural change.
>
> The present day, liberal political actionist is conditioned and "trained" to manage the images held by voters, more than to fight and to implement great sociological changes. . . . When he confronts the massive resistance generated by structural change he may flinch . . . he moves confidently as long as he is dealing with what I call detail changes, but at the point where those grow over into structural changes, he sometimes panics and looks for a path of retreat, back to more modest efforts.
>
> The sociologist, if he will, can break this little circle of political actionist behavior. He can only do so, however, if he is interested and unafraid of an enlightened citizen role, and if he can make application, while performing this role, of tested knowledge in his field. He will then be able to provide an accurate image of things, of events and will be able to assess prospects for structural change. . . .
>
> The sociologist . . . must first recognize the rather common theoretical naivete of the actionist, and that it may serve at least one useful purpose . . . to walk in where he might be afraid to go if he had more theoretical sophistication. . . . But thereafter he may need an action-oriented sociologist, and for the following reasons:
>
> First, his political career orbit may have deprived him of many kinds of experience, for example, in deep community conflict. Second, his career objectives may prohibit direct participation in some events, . . . and his information may therefore be dependent on ill-informed press agents. Third, he is apt to be dependent on advisors to report events whose perception is

often distorted by their own, politically motivated caution, and a concern with protecting their own politically important relationships. . . . A contributing element in the inability to arrive at a correct image of events in a fast-moving community conflict is an initially incorrect image of conditions. Since his memberships and references are most often from the upper middle class, he overestimates the liberalism of the upper-middles . . . and also the illiberalism of the lower classes. The press "documents" his invalid image by citing the spectacular and somewhat raucous repressive crowd behavior of the lower classes . . . and thereafter he makes some tactical and strategic errors. . . .

The burden of this statement is that sociologists—if they participate in policy debates and are not afraid to trade punches with political actionists . . . can help a great deal to make some changes succeed and to make other things fail that deserve to fail.[48]

This statement speaks more to what the sociologist ought to do than to what he is doing and is perhaps more an expression of hope than of current reality. It does suggest, however, that the sociologist can contribute detached observations of the action and change process, as well as objective statements about why things happen as they do. Such statements are objective in the sense that they explain behavior in terms of class background, group characteristics, and group processes and discourage explanations of behavior as an outcome of moral weakness or failure on the part of opponents to the action program. When the activist is unsuccessful, he likes to explain events as resulting from evil motives held by opponents or by self-seeking political interference. Such explanations are of little help in improving action programs, for they do not enable the activist to see why his opponents—or for that matter, his clients—acted as they did and what must be done to encourage them to act differently.

Even so, if sociological explanations are to be useful—and to be used by activists—they must be framed in operational and strategic terms, so as to suggest new modes of action to be used the next time in order to prevent mistaken tactics from being applied again. Needless to say, the activist must be able to accept such information. If he prefers to think in moralistic terms about his opponents, he is unlikely to listen to information that views them from a sociological perspective.

The application of sociological insight is not always positive, however, for a detached view has some dangers, especially if the sociologist is not oriented to action or is not skillful in relating his own role to that of the activist. Indeed, if he makes frequent use of technical concepts and jargon, he may be rejected for being obtuse or for using technical knowledge to increase his status within the agency and downgrade that of the activist. He will probably also be rejected if he is careless in applications of functional analysis and uses it to justify the status quo. As one researcher working in an action-agency program observed:

> I don't think sociologists have such keen insight or judgment regarding the problems and limits of social change and conflict. They may, but they may also mislead by their exclusive focus on the function of current arrangements. One might charge them to examine the potentialities for change and the boundaries of conflict. . . . I wonder if (sociologists) can get by with "sociological understanding" or "perspective." I don't agree that it's necessarily such a valuable contribution; it also feeds the presumptuousness of a lot of them.[49]

My observations overstate the sociologist's current role in the action programs, for actually he has functioned principally as a researcher in their evaluation schemes. Sociologists have been active in setting up evaluation schemes and in doing studies that can be used in evaluating the action programs. Even here, however, their contribution has been less significant than I initially hoped, although once again this is not their fault. While an evaluation research program is comparatively easy to develop in theory, it is more difficult to set up in practice. As noted earlier, before-and-after situations and control groups are not available. More important, the activists lack both the time and the inclination to set up their action programs in ways that would permit easy evaluation. Not only do they have difficulty in framing the goals of action but because they work in ad hoc ways, it is difficult to formulate operational indices against which to measure the effectiveness of action programs. In addition, the activists lack the time or patience to record their activities, and unless they are constantly accompanied by a researcher, many of the on-the-spot action data are lost. Evaluators can, of course, do follow-up studies, but sometimes it is difficult to get access to the clients, and, of course, even when access is available, it is difficult to separate the impact of the action program from other impinging forces.

Moreover, some problems stem from the fact that the evaluation units are part of the action-project agency. If the action programs have not been very successful, the activists may be reluctant to permit access to researchers. Conversely, if the activists have a great degree of status in the agency, the researchers may feel hostile toward them and use research in order to find failure. Since the action projects rarely deal with the real problems and the basic causes of poverty, it is easy for researchers so inclined to prove that the action programs have been useless. But even when relations between activists and researchers are positive and peaceful, the two groups think differently about action and research, get their rewards from different reference groups, and thus run into some obstacles in cooperating. As a result, the evaluation programs that have been developed within the action agencies have so far not been very fruitful, and the funding agencies have taken steps to develop external evaluation programs under their own auspices.[50]

Even so, evaluation research has shown some results. When the action program has simple or easily measurable goals so that indices of success or failure can be set up, research can show whether or not the indices are being achieved, and if not, program changes can be suggested. For example, in one agency a delinquency-prevention experiment was altered when data showed that recidivism had not been decreased by it.

In addition, what little sociological and anthropological research exists on lower-class culture and social structure and on social change processes has provided background information for the projects. Although the action projects are also generating new research on these topics, the hectic and improvisational pace of the action programs indicates they will not be used in action now, but will provide new data to be integrated into the reservoir of background information for the future.[51] There is considerable need for much more research on the lower class, and if data were available on the kinds of questions suggested in Part One, it would be simpler to develop new programs as old ones fail or are superseded.

Unfortunately, despite a recent increase in the studies of working- and lower-class populations, there is still very little basic research on the life and problems of the poverty stricken.[52] Not only are academic research funds still limited but the action agencies or their sources of funds are still doubtful of the usefulness of sociological research and especially of basic research that provides an understanding of lower-class groups and cultures. Also, sociologists have been so long wedded to studies among middle-class respondents that they have little enthusiasm about venturing among a less affluent population and one that is less responsive to the survey interview than the college student or the middle-class housewife.

In summary, it should be obvious that the optimistic and overly rationalistic scheme which I proposed for the use of sociology and sociologists has not been adopted. Not enough sociologists have been asked to participate in the action projects, and too few have come forward to volunteer their services. Also, while some have made contributions to the action and evaluation programs, others have been too abstract or too much concerned with explaining what now exists, rather than specifying the conditions under which change can take place. Finally, the political restrictions on action and the bureaucratic limitations on evaluation have not encouraged the use of sociology. The sociologist, or at least the good one, is interested in what really happens, in the reality that underlies appearances, and in what goes on behind the scenes. When agencies are politically weak, however, and when many of their programs are not so effective as their publicity claims, they are not enthusiastic about having a sociologist in their midst.

THE SOCIOLOGICAL CRITIC

In fact, perhaps the most important function being played by sociologists is that of outside evaluator and critic. A number of sociologists, for example Ivar Berg, Richard Cloward, Robert Dentler, Peter Marris, S. M. Miller, and Martin Rein, have made critical analyses of the present programs, either as free-lance researchers or as consultants brought in by the funding agencies.[53] As such, they have made useful, although not always well-received, contributions to the action projects.[54] Indeed, the high quality of their work suggests that more sociologists should fill this function.

The sociologist is not accustomed to the role of outside critical analyst, but it is one which he can perform particularly well, provided that he has some independently arrived at knowledge and understanding of the community-action project and the agency, that his criticism is informed and responsible, and, most important, that it is sociological in nature.

By sociological criticism I mean simply that which incorporates sociological concepts and findings. For example, quite often the activities of the action projects result in conflict, bitterness, and hostility among the various participants. The sociological critic can make a useful contribution by explaining the causes of this bitterness and by showing how social processes, rather than the moral attributes of the participants caused the conflict that led to the ill feeling.

Nevertheless, the sociologist's criticism must be normative as well. If any blame can properly be placed on anyone, be it for violations of the moral or ethical code, lack of knowledge, or failure to plan properly, he should feel free to do so. His criticism can and should be harsh when conditions justify such a tone. But blame and harsh words must be directed to the agencies who deserve them, and, more important, should be guided by sociological insight. If an agency has done something the sociologist considers wrong, he should use his sociological perspective to be understanding, that is, to note the political or social forces that helped to bring about the wrong acts.

The same themes should be emphasized in suggestions for change. For example, utopian or radical proposals—such as those which call for immediate and massive change or those which require basic cultural, personality, and role transformations among the participants in action programs—are rarely useful, even if they are in accord with the noblest precepts of morality and social justice. Instead, the sociologist should think in terms of changes that relate to the institutional and cultural needs of the relevant participants in the action process, and wherever possible he should suggest proposals that include an incentive for change by the institution from whom change is demanded.

One of the sociologist-critic's most significant functions is to be sensitive to the values of the clients and of all participants in the action process who are unable to express their values or to obtain proper hearing for them. Participant-observation and interviewing techniques enable the sociologist to discover the values and needs of the hard-to-reach among the clients, and he ought to use his technical skills for this purpose, so that his data can represent these clients before the action agency when they cannot easily represent themselves.

Finally, the sociologist-critic should be aware of his own position and role in the action process and use these to develop helpful criticism. The freedom that is available to the outside critic and the status of the academic make it possible for the sociologist to propose changes that cannot so easily be suggested by participants in the action process, and if proposals are made with understanding and the application of strategic thinking, they may carry more weight than might be expected.

The sociologist is, of course, first and foremost a scientist. Even so, he is also a citizen; and if he functions as an employee in an action agency or as an outside critic, he has a right to participate in the processes of social change. In doing so, he must not only formulate his own values and understand the perspective from which they emerge but he must also relate them to the values of other participants in the action process and eliminate those which are not shared by them, are not relevant to them, or make impossible demands on them. Once he has gone through this process, he can then state those values which deserve to be built into his proposals and can combine them with his distinctive skills as a sociologist to contribute to the improvement of the action programs.

REFERENCES

NOTE: *I am grateful to Robert Dentler, Elmer Luchterhand, Peter Marris, and Frances Piven for comments on earlier drafts of this chapter.*

1. This is not to slight European sociologists, although their participation was more at the national than the local community level.
2. See, for example, the highly relevant—but rejected—critique of the settlement house by William F. Whyte, Jr., *Street Corner Society,* 2nd ed. (Chicago: University of Chicago Press, 1955), pp. 98–108, 275–276, 354–356. See also Herbert J. Gans, "Redefining the Settlement's Function for the War on Poverty," *Social Work,* IX (October, 1964), 3–12.
3. Marc Fried, "Grieving for a Lost Home," in Leonard J. Duhl, ed., *The Urban Condition* (New York: Basic Books, 1963), pp. 151–171; Chester Hartman, "The Housing of Relocated Families," *Journal of the American Institute of Planners,* XXX (November, 1964), 266–286; and Herbert J. Gans, "The Failure of Urban Renewal: A Critique and Some Proposals," *Commentary,* XXXIX (April, 1965), 29–37.
4. See, for example, Irving Rosow, "The Social Effects of the Physical Environment," *Journal of the American Institute of Planners,* XXVII (1961), 127–133;

and D. Wilner, R. Walkley, T. Pinkerton, and M. Tayback, *Housing Environment and Family Life* (Baltimore: John Hopkins Press, 1962).

5. More specifically, the approach developed first as an attempt to counteract the failure of relocation programs to help the slum dwellers. In some cities, it grew out of urban-renewal planning for skid-row districts and the fear that if the derelict population of such areas were simply relocated in the normal manner, skid row would spread to other residential areas. For this and other reasons, attempts are under way to "rehabilitate" this population as part of the relocation process. In yet other cities, and especially in projects financed by the Ford Foundation, the aim was to prevent the deterioration of so-called "gray areas" into slums.

   The term *gray area* was initially coined by researchers in the New York Metropolitan Region study to describe deteriorating working-class areas beyond the present slums which would decline further with the increasing suburbanization of residents and industry in the coming generation and would thus be gray in mood. The term may have originated from map-coloring habits, in which the slums are often colored black and the less deteriorating areas gray. There might also be a racial connotation, since the areas are now often occupied by whites, but are likely to become nonwhite in the future.

6. The term *social planning* has also been applied to plans which attempt to outline social goals for the entire society, an approach that might better be called *societal planning*. For example, the Central Planning Board of Puerto Rico has been working on a social plan for the island. This project developed as a reaction by the then incumbent governor, Muñoz Marín, to the emphasis on economic planning and grew out of his appeals for an "Operation Serenity" to slow down the urbanizing and industrializing influences of the "Operation Bootstrap" program which brought industry to Puerto Rico.

7. Davis McEntire, "Social Planning and Urban Renewal," in George S. Duggar, ed., *The New Renewal* (Berkeley: Bureau of Public Administration, University of California, 1961), pp. 117–126.

8. Mobilization for Youth, Inc., *A Proposal for the Prevention and Control of Delinquency by Expanding Opportunities* (New York: Mobilization for Youth, mimeographed, December, 1961).

9. Illustrative of such plans are: City of Oakland, *Proposal . . . for a Program of Community Development* (Oakland, California: City of Oakland, mimeographed, June, 1961, revised December, 1961); *Action Housing Inc., . . . Urban Extension . . . in the Pittsburgh Area* (Pittsburgh: Action Housing, mimeographed, September, 1961); Action for Boston Community Development, *A Proposal for a Community Development Program in Boston* (Boston: A.B.C.D., mimeographed, December, 1961); and Community Progress Inc., *Opening Opportunities: New Haven's Comprehensive Program for Community Progress* (New Haven: Community Progress, mimeographed, April, 1962). My comments about the plans below are based on these and on other published and unpublished documents which I have examined, as well as on discussions about existing and proposed plans in which I have participated in several cities. My description of these plans is an ideal type and does not fit exactly any one of the proposals now in existence.

10. A more detailed formulation is presented in Herbert J. Gans, *The Urban Villagers: Group and Class in the Life of Italian-Americans* (New York: Free Press of Glencoe, 1962), Chapters 11, 12. For a somewhat similar scheme, see Mobilization for Youth, *op. cit.*, Chapter 2. An excellent brief statement of the nature of lower-class life is contained in Walter B. Miller, "Lower Class Culture

as a Generating Milieu of Gang Delinquency," *Journal of Social Issues*, XIV (1958), 5–19.

11. S. M. Miller, "Definition of Lower Class: Some Notes for Discussion," unpublished Memorandum, p. 4. See also S. M. Miller and Frank Riessman, "The Working Class Subculture: A New View," *Social Problems*, IX (1961), 86–97.

12. See, for example, W. B. Miller, *op. cit.*

13. Harlem Youth Opportunities Unlimited, Inc., *Youth in the Ghetto* (New York: H.A.R.Y.O.U., 1964); Richard A. Cloward and J. A. Jones, "Social Class: Educational Attitudes and Participation," in A. H. Passow, ed., *Education in Depressed Areas* (New York: Bureau of Publications, Teachers College, Columbia University, 1963), pp. 190–264; and Hylan Lewis, "Culture, Class and the Behavior of Low Income Families," paper presented at the Conference on Low Income Culture, New York, June, 1963, mimeographed.

14. *Ibid.*

15. The idea for Part Two of this chapter came from Paul F. Lazarsfeld, who suggested that updating the first part would provide a graphic illustration of the uses of sociology in a rapidly changing action situation. The conclusions contained in Part Two are based on my readings of the literature on the projects, frequent although random discussion with colleagues active in some of the projects —especially in research and evaluation—and my own quite marginal participation as a consultant in these projects or in conferences emanating from them. The conclusions are quite impressionistic and highly preliminary. Moreover, they apply to the time of writing (June, 1965), and some may be outdated by the time they are published.

16. Economic Opportunity Act of 1964, Title II, Section 202 (a) (1–2).

17. Richard Cloward and Lloyd Ohlin, *Delinquency and Opportunity* (Glencoe, Ill.: The Free Press, 1960).

18. For a description of these programs, see President's Committee on Juvenile Delinquency and Youth Crime, *Counterattack on Delinquency* (Washington: The President's Committee, mimeographed, undated).

19. The experience and problems of using trained nonprofessionals are described in detail in Frank Riessman, *The Revolution in Social Work: The New Nonprofessional* (New York: Mobilization for Youth, mimeographed, October, 1963).

20. *Ibid.*, p. 24.

21. *Ibid.*, p. 26. Riessman is quoting from an unpublished memorandum by Gertrude Goldberg.

22. *Ibid.*, p. 35.

23. These observations would cast some doubt on Henry Cohen's critique of my 1962 paper that "the middle class values of the people who are doing the planning . . . is an old cliché. The middle class is traditionally the agent through which value and behavioral systems are spread to newcomers or lower class groups. . . . Why do we keep beating the poor guilt-ridden middle class straw man all the time?" Henry Cohen, *An Administrator Looks at the Sociologist in Planning*, comments made at the 1962 meetings of the American Sociological Association (New York: Office of the Deputy City Administrator, mimeographed, 1962).

Cohen is right, of course, in suggesting that the planners are middle class, but the experience of many of the community-action projects suggests that they cannot confront the lower class with middle-class values unless the clients have previously acquired the opportunities and background to act in middle-class ways. Until this happens, contact must be achieved through workers of a class level similar to that of the client—someone who, as Gertrude Goldberg puts it, "may have come up a bit or never been so low, but (with whom) there is common ground." Quoted in Riessman, *op. cit.,* p. 35.

24. *Ibid.,* p. 1. See also Frank Riessman, "The Revolution in Social Work," *Transaction,* II (November–December, 1964), 12–17; and Arthur Pearl and Frank Riessman, *New Careers for the Poor* (New York: Free Press of Glencoe, 1965).

25. Bernard Mackler and Morsley G. Giddings, "Cultural Deprivation: A Study in Mythology," *Teachers College Record,* LXVI (April, 1965), 608–613.

26. Harlem Youth Opportunities Unlimited, Inc., *op. cit.;* and Kenneth Clark, *The Dark Ghetto* (New York: Harper and Row, 1965). See also Patricia C. Sexton, *Education and Income: Inequalities in Our Public Schools* (New York: Viking, 1961).

27. Robert A. Dentler and Mary Ellen Warshauer, *Big City Dropouts and Illiterates* (New York: Center for Urban Education, 1965).

28. Richard A. Cloward and Robert Ontell, "Our Illusions about Training," *American Child,* XLVII (January, 1965), 6–10.

29. Robert Arnold, "Mobilization for Youth: Patchwork or Solution," *Dissent,* XI, No. 3 (Summer, 1964), 347–354.

30. A lively literature of publications and proposals for governmental action is developing on this topic. See, for example, Michael Harrington, *The Other America: Poverty in the United States* (New York: Macmillan, 1961); Gunnar Myrdal, *Challenge to Affluence* (New York: Pantheon, 1963); and Robert Theobald, *Free Man and Free Markets* (New York: Clarkson Potter, 1963).

31. Edgar S. and Jean C. Cahn, "The War on Poverty: A Civilian Perspective," *Yale Law Review,* LXXIII (July, 1964), 1318–1352.

32. This idea was originally proposed by the Cahns in the previously noted article. See also Jerome E. Carlin and Jan Howard, "Legal Representation and Class Justice," *U.C.L.A. Law Review,* XII (January, 1965), 381–437.

33. The relationship between the action agency and the power structure is discussed in a number of papers, most as yet unpublished. See Cahn and Cahn, *op. cit.;* Richard A. Cloward and Frances F. Piven, *Low Income People and Political Process* (New York: Training Institute, Columbia University School of Social Work and Mobilization for Youth, Inc., mimeographed, April, 1964); Martin Rein and S. M. Miller, *The Demonstration as a Strategy of Change* (New York: Training Institute, mimeographed, April, 1964); and Peter Marris, "Synopsis for an Analysis of Poverty Programs" (New York: The Ford Foundation, undated [1964]). See also Erwin Knoll and Jules Witcover, "Fighting Poverty—and City Hall," *The Reporter,* XXXII (June 3, 1965), 19–22; and James Ridgeway, "Poor Chicago," *New Republic,* CLVII (May 15, 1965), 17–20.

34. Economic Opportunity Act of 1964, Title II, Sec. 202 (a) (3).

35. "Mayors Challenge Anti-Poverty Plan," New York *Times,* June 1, 1965, and "Mayors Assured of Poverty Role: Humphrey Meets Group on 'Class Struggle Charges,'" *ibid.,* June 8, 1965.

36. For arguments for the need to side with the clients, see Cahn and Cahn, *op. cit.,* and Cloward and Piven, *op. cit.*

37. For some preliminary attempts at evaluation, see Arnold, *op. cit.,* Rein and Miller, *op. cit.,* and Marris, *op. cit.*

38. Unpublished remarks made at the Training Institute held by Columbia University School of Social Work and Mobilization for Youth, May, 1964.

39. Although the main reason for the de-emphasis of delinquency prevention was the new concern with antipoverty programs, prevention efforts were set back considerably by an evaluation of a large-scale and well-done delinquency-prevention program in Boston which showed almost no change in rates of delin-

quency as a result of the program. See Walter B. Miller, "The Impact of a 'Total Community' Delinquency Control Project," *Social Problems,* X (Fall, 1962), 168–190.

40. Peter Marris, "Experimenting in Social Reform," unpublished paper presented at the 1964 meeting of the American Orthopsychiatric Association (New York: The Ford Foundation, mimeographed, March 19, 1964).

41. S. M. Miller and Martin Rein, "Escalating the War on Poverty," *American Child,* XLVII (March, 1965), 12–18, and "The War on Poverty: Perspectives and Prospects," in Ben B. Seligman, ed., *Poverty as a Public Issue* (New York: Free Press of Glencoe, 1965), pp. 272–320.

42. Ivar Berg and Marcia Freedman, "The Job Corps: A Business Bonanza," *Christianity and Crisis,* XXV (May 31, 1965), 115–119; and John McHale, "The Big Business of Poverty," *Trans-action,* II (May–June, 1965), 3–9.

43. Richard T. Titmuss, *Essays on the Welfare State* (New Haven: Yale University Press, 1958). See also Adam Walinsky, "Keeping the Poor in Their Place," in Arthur B. Shostak and William Gomberg, eds., *New Perspectives on Poverty* (Englewood Cliffs, N.J.: Prentice-Hall Spectrum Book, 1965), pp. 159–167; and Irving Kristol, "The Poverty of Equality," *New Leader,* XLVIII (March 1, 1965), 15–16.

44. Bayard Rustin, "From Protest to Politics: The Future of the Civil Rights Movement," *Commentary,* XXXIX (February, 1965), 25–31.

45. The observations on the uses of sociology are even more impressionistic and speculative than the rest of the chapter and rest on slim data. They are based largely on discussions with several sociologists employed in action agencies and thus may reflect conditions in those agencies only.

46. Admittedly, Part One overstated the feasibility of the ideal—and of the four functions—in order to interest sociologists in the community-action projects.

47. Personal correspondence from a sociologist working in an action agency.

48. *Ibid.*

49. *Ibid.*

50. Thus, the Ford Foundation and the President's Committee on Juvenile Delinquency have undertaken independent evaluation studies of the projects which they are funding and have hired sociologists to travel from city to city to observe these projects. The Office of Economic Opportunity is also setting up evaluation studies.

51. Most of these studies have concerned the clients of action programs, although there are also some studies of the action process and even of the action agencies themselves. For an example of the latter, see Frances Piven, *Conceptual Themes in the Evolution of Mobilization for Youth* (New York: Training Institute, Columbia University School of Social Work and Mobilization for Youth, mimeographed, April, 1963).

52. Although journalists have written voluminously on poverty, anthropologists have done some studies among the urban low-income population of ethnic background (especially Puerto Ricans), and psychologists among the Negro population, there have been no recent large-scale systematic empirical studies by sociologists in book form. There have been no sociological community studies of the Negro slum since Cayton and Drake published *Black Metropolis* in 1945, and the only sociological study of Puerto Ricans is a brief book by Patricia Sexton, *Spanish Harlem* (New York: Harper and Row, 1965). Except for Harold Sheppard's work on unemployed auto workers in South Bend, not yet in book form, no sociologist seems to have published empirical studies of the effects of unemployment and poverty since Marie Jahoda, Paul Lazarsfeld, and Hans Zeisel

wrote *The Unemployed of Marienthal* in 1932, and this book has not yet been translated into English. Indeed, a recent compendium of research, Arthur Shostak and William Gomberg, eds., *Blue Collar World: Studies of the American Worker* (Englewood Cliffs, N.J.: Prentice-Hall, 1964), dealt principally with the working class and not the lower class, and many sociologists still do not even make the distinction between working and lower class in their essays and texts. The principal sociological research on the lower class continues to be studies of deviant behavior, notably juvenile delinquency and mental illness.

53. Berg and Freedman, *op. cit.;* Cloward and Ontell, *op. cit.;* Cloward and Piven, *op. cit.;* Robert Dentler, *Strategies for Innovation in Education: A View from the Top,* paper given at the Columbia University School of Social Work Public Policy Institute (mimeographed, October 15, 1964); Marris, "Experimenting in Social Reform"; S. M. Miller and Rein, *op cit.;* and Rein and Miller, *op. cit.*

54. See, for example, the angry response to Cloward and Ontell, *op. cit.,* by Melvin Herman, "Problems of Evaluation," *American Child,* XLVII (March, 1965), 5–10, and the reply by Cloward and Ontell, p. 11.

From Delinquency Treatment to Community Development

ALFRED J. KAHN

chapter **17**

The history of theory and practice in the fields of juvenile delinquency and adult corrections yields a rich series of case illustrations of problems in the use of sociology. This chapter aims to tell the story of a major intellectual transition among practitioners: from a view of the delinquency problem as requiring intrapsychic treatment to a much broader, sociologically inspired perspective. In this transition sociological efforts at precision have given way to a rather loose, common-sense interpretation of concepts. It is not yet clear just where this will lead or how sociologists will cope with the problem of optimizing their intellectual contribution while seeking to function in action programs. In the meantime, those in social work, probation, and the correctional field who have taken these new steps (in response to the demands of the social scene and to proposals of "experts") have moved from treatment to preventive and community-development approaches to social problems.

The Student of Delinquency in a Universe of Experts

The sociologist who attempted during the 1950's and 1960's systematically to develop or test delinquency theory faced popular competition difficult to overcome.

First, some basic data were generally available: 1,500,000–2,000,000 children reporting to the police each year; about 600,000 juvenile court cases annually (traffic matters excluded), involving about 518,000 children; a nationwide court referral rate of almost 2 per 100 children.

Data such as these provided a convenient platform for the lecturer or headline writer, whose themes were recurrent: this is a large problem, and the projections for the next decade are overwhelming, even given a stabilized rate. Most American children are not delinquents, and the troublesome group must be predicted, identified, isolated, and dealt with effectively. Parents must resume their responsibilities.

Nor were competing "explanations" difficult to come by. While there are styles and fads in theory, as there are in all other human arenas, a reasonable sampling of sermons, lectures, magazine articles, and TV panel shows of two decades yields many of the following, often as part of one presentation and not in any sense ranked or interrelated:

Juvenile delinquency begins in the home.
The problem is in the decline in moral and spiritual values.
Youth have too much free time and too few responsibilities.
Leisure time is not well guided.
TV programs teach violence and sadism.
Schools are failing in their primary responsibility of teaching citizenship.
Youth who are not motivated to learn are kept in school too long by the compulsory education laws.
Racial and ethnic tensions encourage gang wars.
Delinquency and crime is a normal way of life for those living in the lower-class culture.
True delinquency is a problem of basic personality disturbances of an identifiable type.

Practitioners and students of delinquency have sought to confront those offering overeasy answers with additional "facts." The first is that the data themselves are highly unreliable and of a low degree of validity because as one moves from jurisdiction to jurisdiction, city to city, and state to state, the definitions, procedures, and outcomes are affected by many local factors. These factors vary over time as well. Changes in the composition, leadership, or policies of a police force affect delinquency types and totals, as do differences in staffing and practices as between cities. The quality and mission of a court intake service may well result in a redefinition of delinquency in a community. The readiness of police and prosecutors to count on parents to handle problems and make adjustments in some cities or some sections of cities, but not in others, affects both reported delinquency rates and the characteristics of the case samples subsequently studied for theory making and program development. Moreover, statistical systems themselves may be poorly organized and incomplete.

Even the highly questionable statistics suggest that the data usually cited need some qualification or at least more complete interpretation: boys outnumber girls in court at the rate of 4 to 1; urban rates are 3 times rural rates; there are tendencies in recent years (but they are not firm) for suburban and rural rates to show unusual increases. There are some cities in which the rate is 3 to 4 court cases per 100 children, not the 2 per 100 of the national data. There are some neighborhoods or health areas in large cities in which the rate may be 10, 15, 20, or 30 per 100 or higher. Rates for some ethnic groups or racial groups are far above city-wide rates.

Intensive studies in several cities have sought to estimate the likelihood that a given child will be known to a juvenile court during the course of his adolescence.[1] Those studies yield the finding that approximately one boy in five will reach juvenile court during adolescence (the rate for girls is lower). However, in certain disorganized neighborhoods and for members of some minority groups, the rate is substantially higher. It is not unreasonable to speculate that one-third or one-half of the boys on some blocks in the core of large-city slum areas may reach court between the ages of ten and seventeen.

Since the statistics deal only with alleged delinquency which is reported, the complexities are even greater. One of the difficulties in theory building, however, has to do with the fact that one cannot, from the data themselves, distinguish between group, neighborhood, area, age, or sex differences which have to do with *actual* behavior, with *reported* behavior, or with local *evaluations* of behavior. Of this, more later.

While data to illustrate generalizations of the sort listed above are relatively easy for the platform speaker to come by, library shelves and the files of scientific journals also contain many sociological, social-psychological, and psychological studies which show that in some sense at least each is inadequate. For many delinquents attend church and apparently believe in religious doctrine; many delinquents have "normal" leisure-time habits: in fact, vandalism and gang fights have been known to occur en route from recreation centers and ball games. Some delinquents are psychiatrically disturbed, but many are not; the connection (if any) between the psychiatric disturbance in a child and his delinquency is often not clear. Some delinquents do seem to be "fighting" their schools, but their problems become even more acute when they leave school and prove unable to hold employment. TV programs obviously do not affect all children who watch them in the same way, or the copied violence would increase several thousandfold. Finally, a surprisingly large number of delinquents seem to come from law-abiding families which accept basic social mores, do not dispute traditional "virtues," and do not deliberately teach delinquency as a way of life.

Thus, students of the problem have been able to show that common-sense interpretations of statistics are in themselves not quite adequate, nor are the most popular theories alone fully able to interpret delinquency. One sophisticated group solves this problem by coming out for "multiple causation." Delinquency is the complex result of a convergence of many, or at least several, of these factors. The trouble is, as Wilkins has noted, that to affirm multiple causation is to affirm nothing. A theory should be a "concise, elegant summary of observations" which are sound and replicated. We test theories by noting whether deductions from them hold up under experimental testing or daily-life observations: "The value of a theory is directly related to its relevance to the particular problem under study and the consequences and operational definitions which can be deduced from it." Multiple causation as a theory "does not facilitate the deduction of any hypotheses or practical consequences that are of any help at all." There is no test whereby a theory of this sort may be nullified. It may be described as "anti-theory." [2]

This view of multiple causation does not mean, of course, that an adequate explanation must deal with only one variable. Rather, interrelations must be specified so that consequences may be predicted.

Let us then move from this level of looking at "simple" facts and ready generalizations to the efforts to apply more elaborate theoretical schemes. Here the influence of sociology has been considerable, and the problems confronted gradually emerge.

Theories

The history of theories of delinquency[3] is long and complex. For present purposes, attention to the dominant current views (and even a degree of oversimplification) serves to illustate changing influences in the approach to prevention and control strategy. The selection is from the vantage point of what has influenced the social-work profession and the fields of juvenile probation and parole. Through the 1940's and well into the 1950's these personnel took an essentially clinical view of delinquency. Whatever the social context, they tended to think, behavior must eventually be interpreted in psychological-motivational terms, and the roots of motivational dynamics were to be found in parent–child relationships as seen in the perspective of psychoanalytic theory. Some delinquency was seen as the product of psychosis, interpreted as either biologically or functionally determined; but much was in the realm of the primary behavior disorder or the neuroses. Conduct disorders in children were seen as "acting out" types of psychoneuroses.[4]

There are many variations on these themes and in the conceptions as to exactly how personality pathology is translated into delinquent conduct. Adelaide Johnson has stressed "superego lacunae." Fritz Redl has talked of "children who hate." Irving Kaufman has described neglectful home environments characterized by parents on "pregenital levels of frustration" whose inadequacy causes delinquency in their children. The Gluecks chose the parent–child relationship items from among the many factors distinguishing their delinquent from their nondelinquent sample for the construction of a prediction instrument.[5]

The resulting treatment prescriptions were logical enough. Delinquency must be treated intrapsychically, the exact form of treatment to vary with the age and diagnosis. Child-guidance clinics should involve both children and their parents. Institutions must offer casework and psychiatric therapy, while the parents are (or should be) "worked with" at home. Group therapy, where introduced, was guided by psychoanalytic conceptions of the problem and of processes of change.

Clinicians are able to cite enough positive accomplishment through these approaches to justify requests for expansion and to reinforce their faith in the method. They know that rigorous research validation is limited, but this may be said of almost any action program. Failures are attributed to inadequate training, heavy loads, and the incomplete development of treatment methods based on clinical knowledge.

Although clinical interpretations of delinquency and clinically based treatment dominated social work and probation for some decades, there was also a tradition of *interest* in social problems and in the concentration of delinquency in underprivileged areas, in poor housing and so on. The parallel work of criminologists and penologists from the 1930's to the 1960's was not unknown, but use was selective. Theories related to acculturation and its import for delinquency have affected settlement programs and neighborhood work. Relevant data have been used to support housing legislation, day care, and other social provisions. With important exceptions, the social level of interpretation has seemed most relevant to social policy, "prevention," group services, and social action. When they organized "treatment," social workers, juvenile-court judges, and probation personnel turned to clinical approaches. This was certainly the situation until a decade ago and generally still is.

To illustrate the exceptions, one might cite the interest in the work of Jenkins and his collaborators, who describe some delinquents as *unsocialized* in that they lack impulse control (psychopaths or sociopaths), some as *overinhibited* (neurotic compulsions cause the trouble), and some as *socialized* into the way of life of a community antisocial minority.[6] The Jenkins typology was in use at the New York State Training School at Warwick at a time when many others did not include a "social" category in their classifications. Similarly, the Training School at Hudson found that Jennings' sociometry guided groupings in such a way as to increase institutional impact.

Albert Cohen's book *Delinquent Boys* marked a turning point for workers in the field of delinquency, as it may have for sociological theory in this field.[7] Cohen stresses that the delinquent subculture is the source of a considerable amount of antisocial behavior and may be considered as a solution adopted by working-class boys who find that they can win neither success nor status in a society dominated by middle-class standards. Because the subculture is an attack on and a rationale against society's dominant codes, it is characterized by negativistic behavior, nonutilitarian stealing, hedonism, and malicious activity.

The Cohen theory is far from complete and rounded. He does not think that it explains all delinquency, and he tends to see middle-class delinquency in psychodynamic terms (problems of male identification in a female-dominated culture). Besides, one can rearrange his variable to suggest that it is gang participation which teaches antisocial behavior, consequently closing off middle-class opportunity and reinforcing an antisocial protest. Finally, there is research evidence from Sykes, Matza, and others that many delinquents actually know and identify with the norms of middle-class society.[8] Nonetheless, the Cohen work stressed the peer group, the values—codes—beliefs—routine activities which may be learned and which are considered delinquent, apart from one's personality problems. It gave social workers and others working with delinquents an alternate perspective. Some began to consider these dimensions more salient than the intrapsychic ones.

In the meantime, research in inmate culture, well known to social scientists, but previously considered only in the mental-hospital field, was introduced to social work by Cloward, Cressey, and Ohlin, among others, and offered a new understanding of institutional failures.[9] It reached administrators with a variety of backgrounds. If informal organization of inmates is a potent force contributing to adjustment in a living situation in which there is belief that the outside world is hostile and that one is powerless, small wonder that formal authority and an occasional casework interview does not change much. A similar analysis of institutional staff suggests the complexity of creating a truly therapeutic milieu. Now one could look at the cottage group in a new way and suggest problems of orientation to the institution, grouping, definition of the situation, and so on.[10] Moreover, the task of rehabilitation could be defined as one of facilitating community reintegration of a group to whom commitment may very well have been an act of exile. The assuring of continuity between institution and community services could be seen as urgent.

Some social scientists had begun to talk of delinquency as the normal adaptive behavior in lower-class culture; others saw it as a transitional adolescent phenomenon.[11] Social workers and other practitioners in the delinquency field were quick to realize that the new ideas helped. They were interested readers of Cloward and Ohlin's *Delinquency and Opportunity*, which took the next step. Noting that the sociological tradition includes two major groups of theories, these authors sought to pull them together into a unified explanatory model. Sutherland, Shaw, McKay, and others ("differential association," "delinquency areas," and so on) have dealt with the learning of delinquent norms and behavior in specific environments. Parsons, Merton, and others ("anomie") talk of the "dysfunction between culturally prescribed goals and socially organized access to them by legitimate means." But there is actually differential access to both legitimate and illegitimate means. If one joins these threads together, one may be able to explain why some young people go toward the rackets, some find their solutions in the conflict type of delinquent subculture, some withdraw to drugs, and others adjust in the normal stream of acceptable society.[12]

This oversimplified, thematic sketch of the emergence of "opportunity theory" leaves out the prophetic Wilensky and Lebeaux analysis and proposals of 1955 and such significant episodes as the Erikson-Merton dialogue at the United States Children's Bureau Conference in 1955.[13] It does not report the gang studies and adolescent-culture research which changed assumptions about subcultural values. It does not refer to the pioneering by Bixby and Elias with sociologically oriented therapies.[14] It does not indicate major critiques of the theory. It does serve, however, to set the stage for the work done by Lloyd Ohlin in Washington as the first director of the President's Committee on Delinquency and Youth Crime, from the beginning of the Kennedy administration, and the work of both Ohlin and Richard A. Cloward in the conceptualization of the action program for Mobilization for Youth; for the latter undertaking, designed originally as a delinquency-prevention effort in New York's lower East Side, was to become a youth-development and then community-development program as the opportunity concept was broadened and popularized.

Before this latter theme is followed in more detail, however, it may be useful to discuss the limitations of the applications to the delinquency field of anomie theory and the potential for an as yet untried application of the sociology of deviant behavior.

More Work Is Needed

The arrival of anomie theory and its enshrinement in the delinquency program in Washington impressed practitioners everywhere. Such theory inspired a diversity of projects throughout the country funded by the Ford Foundation. The literature on lower-class gang culture had attention of the sort never before experienced, and the dimensions of "opportunity" were seriously probed. Increasingly, delinquent rehabilitation and aftercare was mentioned as a problem in community reintegration.

But the practitioner, however influenced, could not be fully satisfied even though he did not encounter sociological debates about the development. None of the new theoreticians claims to account for all of delinquency, and the proponents of the "opportunity" theory do not hold that the delinquent subculture accounts for most delinquency. In fact, their writing theorizes about subcultures, not about individual actors. On the one hand, clinicians can now see more than ever before that one should not interpret behavior as though a family were isolated from the world in which it functions. They turn to the social scientists and ask for interpretations of differential impact of group and cultural experiences. On the other hand, they ask, does one not have to deal in psychodynamic dimensions to explain why, in neighborhoods where there is "legitimate" opportunity, some adapt and some fight it or withdraw? Similarly, are not individual psyches at stake where many join conflict gangs (or preracket groups), while others withdraw and become addicts—or find their way to college and to middle-class respectability?

Does one not have to establish that the lower-class youth being "explained" have the values, ambitions, drives, goals, postulated in the several social-dynamic theories? Environment, moreover, must be translated into differential motivation; and one is thereby soon back at the personality level.

In short, practitioners did not consider it a defense of the "old" to wonder about the explanatory validity of the sociological stress on differential learning through exposure to delinquent subcultures and their "solutions." Wilkins cites Glaser's lead: Why not consider differential association theory instead, emphasizing the roots of differential identification and the interaction of perceptual processes and personality differences? [15] The practitioner thus has found the sociological contribution of the 1950's and 1960's valuable: it has introduced a major corrective in focus. The need remains at the *service* and *intervention* level for an *integrating* behavioral theory. *By its very nature, sociology guides certain levels of intervention and has nothing to say about the other levels.*

There is, in fact, need for more adequate sociological examination of styles, faddism, and conflicts in theory about delinquency. A few introductory notes are here offered, but this is an area in which much work remains to be done.

There are actually two elements in the controversy about theories of delinquency: (1) the choice of a theory of human behavior; (2) the definition of the phenomena being described and accounted for.

Each of the social and behavioral sciences represents a somewhat unique perspective on the human condition, as does psychoanalysis. Each introduces a conceptual scheme which guides perception, defines salient behavioral units, and interrelates factors. Within the established framework, predictions may be made and outcomes assessed. If one does not demand perfect predictions and accepts relationships shown to have greater than chance occurrence, and if measuring devices are generally imprecise, a given unit of human experience can be partially explained by each of a variety of social-science disciplines and specialties. And if, as in the instance of psychoanalytic theory and a surprisingly large number of sociological, psychological, and anthropological subtheories, propositions are not stated in nullifiable form, the process is seldom seriously threatened.

Because of this, changes from theory to theory among practitioners result not so much from the research validation as from practical implications and from the developments in professional or scientific styles or "cultures." A degree of faddism tends to persist. Anthropology, psychoanalysis, sociology, rise and fall in popularity. Thus the recent attention given by delinquency practitioners to work by Cohen, Ohlin, Cloward, and others reflects not research validation (since the trend was rather a response to plausible preresearch formulations), but immediate recognition of practical utility in relation to accumulated experience.

From the practitioner's point of view, in fact, we need not choose among delinquency theories on the social-structural, cultural, interpersonal, or intrapsychic levels. For practitioners concerned with constructive intervention and planned change each of these levels is useful. Professional knowledge must be sought in relation to the circumstances requiring intervention on different levels. One would not wish to drop the clinical perspective in favor of the sociological or anthropological, but to continue with the improvement of each and to assure that it comes into play *as appropriate*.

Finally, data on delinquency rates by social and geographic location, sex, age, and emotional status tell us that delinquency is a matter of cultural and administrative definition. It is not a unitary diagnostic group, behavioral act, or social occurrence. Delinquency does not exist except in relation to social observation, social detection, and social stereotypes and in a society which is not a homogeneous entity. Delinquency is defined at a given time in the interaction among subgroups characterized by cultural, social-stratification, geographic, and racial dimensions.

Delinquency is a particularly complex administrative category, since it is described somewhat differently in the constitution or law of each state. (How much more shaky do attempts to talk of delinquency across national or continental lines become!)

In the light of all this, it may be useful to talk of the *delinquencies*, not of delinquency. The term suggests an over-all social umbrella under which several orientations to theory may be relevant, depending on what purpose the theory is to fill. For the treatment person it serves to underscore the need for a framework which will serve to differentiate: psychiatric problems relevant to one's delinquency and psychiatric problems not relevant; situations requiring intrapsychic treatment and those which may be coped with interpersonally in family or peer group; situations which are unapproachable except through neighborhood mobilization, raising the social horizons of subgroups, increase of educational and job opportunities, and so forth.

While no one theoretical perspective on delinquent *behavior* is useful for all purposes, a social-science perspective on this very phenomenon has value: how can one account for the tendency to group so many things together, to act as though they were one thing, to create competing theories and competing methods of intervention, to allow and to accept so many different and apparently discriminatory modes of definition, discovery, and action? The hypothesis may be suggested that the unity is of only one kind: a society's social-control (and related stratification) objectives at a given time. The various phenomena recognized, reported, and subsumed under "delinquency" constitute that deviance in children toward which a society applies relatively potent sanctions. This is the unifying social-control motive which brings into police complaint listings, juvenile courts, or clinics an admixture of acts of omission and commission, as well as situational problems:

The equivalent of crime (misdemeanor, felony, offense) in an adult, when committed by a child.

Deviant or defiant behavior in children which would not be a crime in adults, but which most adults in a society or a community want to stop.

The situations above, but only when they involve children of certain social-class, ethnic, or racial backgrounds.

The equivalent of the two categories above—that is, annoying anti-social behavior or the equivalent of crime—with the age cutoff point defined within a given state as somewhat different than the age cutoff point in another state.

Why does society develop an authoritative mode of intervention which unifies all of these? Ultimately one would have to answer in terms of the social changes which came about with industrialism and the decrease of primary-group controls. More immediately, society has reacted to certain circumstances or acts as endangering itself or its children and draws upon potent sanctions if necessary. The cutoff point of definition of delinquency may be determined to be that point at which actions are perceived as undermining social control at sensitive spots. This may account for some of the regional, social-class, and ethnic differences: society's control mechanisms take different views of the significance and hazard in deviant behavior, depending on where it is socially located. And behavior normal for a social subgroup may be seen as delinquent if it threatens the mores which prevail in the community power structure. Students of stratification have much to offer to this analysis.

The analysis of delinquency is complicated by the inclusion of acts and phenomena which on the surface seem to endanger nobody and are not necessarily thought to be predictive of future hazard. Courts are used as leverage for social intervention even though there is no physical danger, property danger, or property-relationship change involved, but rather learning difficulty, psychosis, illegitimacy, or parent–child problems. Only analysis of the challenge to mores of community social structure implied in these patterns clarifies why they, too, are grouped with more aggressive attacks on society or its members and demand court intervention. In effect, changes in socialization processes and in the competence of the primary group have been followed by public assumption of certain social responsibilities, and the courts are the assigned instrument. It may be expected that a similar process will be seen increasingly in the adult field.

The especially interesting thing about delinquency as a unifying concept is that it represents the willingness of twentieth-century society to develop a treatment rationale for broad control measures. Such rationale is used to justify the inclusion of the other forms of deviance mentioned, from learning problems and marital disturbance to parent–child problems.

Yet the many assumptions on which such cases are handled within a court network are never adequately explored and tested. Is it true that actions on the basis of which adjudications of delinquency are made endanger the self and others or undermine other aspects of social control? Is it true that actions considered symptomatic of emerging delinquency are really symptomatic? Is the intervention truly preventive: does the police, court, agency, clinic, or similar process negate an earlier, valid prediction about danger, damage, and social consequence? When the court intervenes in situations which are not the equivalent of adult crime, yet does not launch beneficial preventive and remedial action, does it not undermine individual rights?

In instances of alleged or emerging delinquency, positive action following case finding is a complex process involving the careful integration and co-ordination of schools, police, courts, detention, many social and medical agencies, clinics, institutions, hostels, child-care facilities, and so on. Many observers are agreed that in this sense a scientific, rehabilitative approach as a way to deal with this problem is as yet an "untried weapon." The "contract" under which the delinquency category is set up and implemented has not been kept.[16] There is a gap between humanitarian rationale and actual practice. Facilities are in short supply and poorly staffed and have partially developed programs. All the components of a necessary intervention network are seldom present in one place at one time or are not adequately co-ordinated. Whatever the philosophy and objectives of the juvenile court movement or of individual agencies and treatment facilities, for the parent and child brought into the network of delinquency services the impact is largely one of punishment, deprivation, and control. What is defined as social control through individual help and therapy emerges as control through threat, separation, and surveillance. It is not very effective because these latter mechanisms never block successfully and fully action flowing from very strong motives.

Incomplete implementation of announced intent and the simultaneous following of mutually contradictory courses reflect the fact that there are actually many publics involved and that they do not have the same objectives. The premises of delinquency statutes are not always accepted. Moreover, values and goals are in transition, so that one over-all policy is not dominant nationally. Some elements in society stress punitive approaches. Others affirm deterrence, moral reform, and treatment simultaneously. Still others are openly discriminatory in their enforcement of social and legal codes between groups. This situation may serve a variety of latent functions, such as the slowing of a social-change process and the absorption of its swift transitions, a subject which awaits more comprehensive sociological investigation.

From Clinical Resources to Opportunities

We have thus explored one line of sociological influence which involves broader understanding of the delinquency phenomenon and new approaches to intervention with those who do deviate. Even more striking has been the recent effect of "opportunity theory" on social-welfare planning and the strategy of planned change in deprived urban areas. In effect, what began as an effort to control and treat delinquency under the President's Committee on Delinquency and Youth Crime soon became an urban youth development effort. Its concepts were, in fact, ultimately to provide the underpinnings for the antipoverty war's community-action program—an American version of urban community development. More recently, one detects a further transition from community development to political action.

Let us briefly examine the relevant antidelinquency "planning" literature in the period 1961–1963, accenting the so-called "opportunity mobilizations" and updating it only with limited reference to new trends in 1965.[17] The Kennedy administration sought to bring a new approach to delinquency prevention and control by stressing the need to open opportunities to lower-class youth previously closed out. The Johnson administration expanded the effort. Cities were invited to undertake research and planning, after which some would be funded for long-term action. In addition to the President's Committee on Delinquency and Youth Crime, the National Institute for Mental Health and the Ford Foundation were the major national bodies which added funds and impetus to the efforts of local groups. With few exceptions, those supported in the local efforts represented much broader public-voluntary action coalitions than did the local community councils which had taken the lead previously. And because of the concern for research as preliminary to planning and the built-in bias of the funding groups in favor of "opportunity" programs, considerable numbers of social scientists and social-science–trained social workers were employed in strategic staff positions.

In 1957 or 1958 a local planner, asked what should be done about delinquency, would have talked about neighborhood saturation by social services and therapeutic resources and about devices for program co-ordination and case integration in the attack on multiproblem families.

The new efforts were characterized by a dramatic shift in their view of the task. In effect, the change may be symbolized by the sequence of transitions implied in the words "delinquency control and treatment" to "delinquency prevention," to "youth development," to "community development," and now to "eradication of poverty." Each of the opportunity mobilizations has taken its stance somewhere along this route—a stance defined to some degree by local factors, sponsorship, a moment in history—as well as by the intellectual outcome of the planning process.

By 1960, almost fifteen years of concern with rising adolescent crime rates and gang depredations in metropolitan areas had created a state of alarm, and it was inevitable that P.L. 87–274, creating the President's Committee on Delinquency and Youth Crime, should have been seen initially as aimed at delinquency control.

Thus, the authors of Boston's Youth Opportunities Project plan focus first on the objective of reducing the number of "illegal criminal-type acts," with emphasis on acts considered serious by the community. With some notable exceptions, the planning efforts of the 1950's would have tended at this point to emphasize the personal and familial characteristics of offenders and to seek solutions through early case finding and treatment, improved law enforcement by better-prepared officials, more effective rehabilitation of offenders. In the late 1950's there would have been added the concerns for family-oriented treatment measures, for continuity between correctional institutions and aftercare, and for general translation of improved clinical knowledge into staff competence.[18] The new ingredient may be symbolized by *Delinquency and Opportunity*, as reflected in Mobilization for Youth's request for funding: "Much delinquent behavior is engendered because opportunities for conformity are limited. Delinquency therefore represents not a lack of motivation to conform but quite the opposite: the desire to meet social expectations itself becomes the source of delinquent behavior if the possibility of doing so is limited or nonexistent."

Therefore, according to Mobilization,

> in order to reduce the incidence of delinquent behavior or to rehabilitate persons who are already enmeshed in delinquent patterns, *we must provide the social and psychological resources that make conformity possible*. . . . If the possibilities for a conventional adjustment are restricted or absent, the likelihood is that the offender, no matter how favorably motivated, will continue to engage in non-conforming behavior. Thus we must concern ourselves with expanding opportunities for conventional behavior.

Indeed, the first funding application for a comprehensive approach as presented to the President's Committee was entitled *A Proposal for the Prevention and Control of Delinquency by Expanding Opportunities*. Similar phrasing was to characterize many of the applications which followed and also was to appear in the official literature and public pronouncements from the federal agencies involved. Clearly the shift was toward social institutional and away from individualistic solutions to delinquency, although most projects sought to combine both dimensions to a degree.

The scientific status of the productive, but still unproved, opportunity hypothesis was not in focus. The ideas took hold quickly, and the logical deductions from them and from the research explorations which they engendered gave new emphasis to schools and to the world of work, major segments of the institutional structure which had somehow not generally been encompassed by social-welfare planners, particularly those based in local community welfare councils. Washington had its Department of Health, Education, and Welfare, but very few local communities had previously created health-education-welfare teams for planning or even for operational co-ordination purposes. Nor was it difficult to understand the long separation: for good historical reasons councils tended to co-ordinate or plan for voluntarily financed social services and for some segments of health, whereas schools were financed by taxes and controlled by citizen boards and employment services were generally under state auspices and not much concerned with youth. Now, given the new definition of the centrality of schools, job counseling, placement, and job training in the "opportunity structure" (a phrase which became increasingly important), one could no longer conceive of delinquency prevention or control programs which did not address these elements.

To introduce these concerns is to launch a process with a spiral effect. One cannot plan for the education, job training, placement, and counseling of deprived inner-city youth without new concentration on the public sector generally. What was often tokenism in welfare-council participation would not do for these endeavors. Furthermore, to accomplish innovation, expansion, or change in these sectors one must learn to deal with, involve, plan with, bring pressure upon, or even cause changes in local and state governmental bodies. Finally, even though the target might be the most deprived youth in high-delinquency areas, one could not think of planning in the worlds of education and work as affecting only a small segment of clients. New strategies, concepts, resources, would inevitably affect the whole. Some welfare planning had always been addressed to "all the children," and much of it to the deprived. The portion of the planning task undertaken which would have relevance to all families had begun to increase. A process had begun which would add even another element to the many forces in modern society which are compelling interest in social planning as it affects all members of the community, and not the disadvantaged alone.[19]

Thus, community after community, addressing the problem of offering true access to social participation to those who have been kept out through discrimination, incomplete acculturation or socialization, exploitation, ignorance, or neglect has developed a view of the planning task as encompassing, at the core, (1) education, (2) employment, placement, and counseling for youth, and (3) cultural opportunities which lead to development of social skills.

Somewhat more in the tradition of delinquency control, there are usually provisions for enforcement measures as well, buttressed by efforts to have the adult community reassert its responsibilities and to articulate its rejection of antisocial solutions. Along similar lines, most of the proposals (with Boston as a good example) point out that new educational, social-service, law-enforcement, and work programs attuned to the needs of inner-city youth will provide the adult-role models often sadly lacking in their primary-group environments. To several of the projects, the lack of such role models is the major defect of the social environment as experienced by youth. Others, like Cleveland, include role models among the many determinants of sound youth development, the enunciated goal.

The emphasis on work and school in the delinquency program puts these proposals in step with broader social forces which had launched experimentation in educational reform from the time of Sputnik and had increasingly added youth-employment concerns as well. All of this had been propelled by the push for equality for minority-group members. It was therefore not surprising that in a significant number of instances the "opportunity projects" joined locally with Ford Foundation-supported "gray area" educational innovations and with either local or state (and later federal) "youth and work" projects. A broader planning base was emerging out of a broadening of the task.

But there were additional ingredients in the new formulations. *Action for Appalachian Youth* stressed the need to achieve change in people, groups, and institutions through a community development approach which would sound quite familiar to those engaged in village development projects in many countries. Mobilization for Youth in New York, dealing with the urban area's problem, went further and suggested that "the task is to direct the expression of alienation against the social structure which is its cause and to discourage its expression in delinquent acts." Thus, a delinquency prevention and control proposal pointed in new directions in urging that "attempts to deal with the aspirations of delinquents and low-income youth generally should also include an orientation toward social change. *Opportunities for collective social action should be incorporated into any large-scale delinquency program.*" (Emphasis added.)

Mobilization for Youth proposed what appeared to be a modest and limited community-organization effort to encourage local participation in community social and political activity through the development of indigenous social organizations. It was a step beyond earlier formulations about involving the deprived in self-help largely for therapeutic reasons, and it was more attuned to complex urban political processes than rural village development. About two years later the Central Harlem "Haryou" plan was to define the attack on a local community's "powerlessness" as the central objective of its social planning (and later the 1965 discussion of poverty-war strategies was to concentrate on this as a central issue). Haryou sees the political and economic weaknesses of Harlem (which are in turn based on discrimination) as the base of most other problems, including defects in self-confidence, and therefore defines the basic solution as requiring the creation of political and economic strength through an elaborate community-action program. All the rest (educational reform, job training, cultural programs, case services) should support this effort and will be made possible by it. As a result, whereas most of the planning endeavors involve the vesting of power in existing structures, which themselves undergo some change, or in new structures involving new combinations of existing groups, the Haryou report sees need for a basic change in the controlling local power group.

The social planning reflected in the newer opportunity action proposals contains all of these ingredients in some degree: the concern with social control, the determination to address institutions which shape opportunity for the individual, and some commitment to support social-change efforts and to facilitate participation in social change by the most disadvantaged. Yet it should also be noted that *much of the related writing and planning tends to be quite imprecise about the very opportunity concept which is the core of the rationale.* In effect, theoretical formulations deriving from anomie theory had led to "opportunity," but the latter soon became a common-sense slogan, not a precise definition of the direction for needed action. Here sociology gave way to politics, social work, civil rights, and common sense.

The result is differing balances among the components and, in some instances, strategies which do not always address central questions. When we talk of opportunity, are we referring only to subjective perception or to hard, objective reality? Do we mean that we undertake only to *open up* that which is to deprived, disadvantaged, discriminated-against youth, or do we also mean to reform the schools and social agencies which have tended to close out certain segments of our poverty-stricken population? The latter, reply most of the programs. But then, we must ask, is it enough to address the schools and the employment-training-placement services? What of the realities of the job market and its ability to absorb those who are remotivated and helped to develop skills? (The planning efforts usually ignored this central question even though other social developments accented it by 1966.)

Similarly, is it realistic to launch all-out institutional-change measures independently of concurrently developing urban-renewal and housing strategies?

In other words, once we recognize that it will take a measure of institutional change to alter the experiences of disadvantaged youth and their families in urban areas, logic and hard facts carry us a bit further. Horizons of planners must truly be broadened if we really mean to alter life experiences in the inner city. The issue of what is locally possible must be faced and a broader frame placed around the entire effort.

This process is certainly under way. New Haven and Boston illustrate how the once narrowly conceived social-agency–co-ordinated planning of the welfare council has become aligned with broader measures in an urban community development movement. The Boston Youth Opportunities Project, an opportunity-type program, was developed in the context of Action for Boston Community Development (ABCD), an organization which emerged out of Boston's commitment to urban renewal and its increasing recognition that any renewal would be unsuccessful without simultaneous attention to social needs and problems. ABCD was set up to design new programs in education, employment, and social services, while it began an initial period of work to achieve citizen participation in urban-renewal planning. While a special youth program was developed in response to the initiative and support of the Ford Foundation and the President's Committee, it was shaped in the total ABCD context and was affected by it. Thus, the question was to arise even before the antipoverty program absorbed these local youth-development efforts as to whether the planning logic actually required a special "youth-opportunities" project or whether, given the option, one could not make the case for adequate funding to ABCD and a consequent freedom from the report's need to trace a "scientific" path from delinquency control to a program which has most of the ingredients listed above.

Similarly, in New Haven, the Youth Development program is placed in the context of a Comprehensive Program for Community Progress led by the mayor and addressed to the total physical and social environment. The planning process dealt with manpower, leisure, law enforcement, corrections, health, public welfare, legal services, and cultural arts and took place against a backdrop of five large-scale renewed projects, a housing and school building program, and an awareness of the need to address some issues on the level of the metropolitan community. In fact, youth-employment proposals were placed in the context of a long-range New Haven manpower training program as submitted to the Office of Manpower, Automation, and Training. Again, it would appear likely that funding patterns, not planning logic, explained much of the effort to separate out youth-development programs.

The Appalachian action report, while in many ways far less comprehensive in its relationship to basic opportunity-shaping institutions than the New England proposals, does describe its youth-employment program as part of an Office of Manpower, Automation, and Training proposal.

Subsequent to the completion of the planning reports here analyzed, the efforts to rally against poverty highlighted the fact that, if we intend more than short-range relief measures, local programs will need to develop in knowledge of broader national, regional, state, and metropolitan planning strategies involving (merely to illustrate) fiscal and tax policy, area redevelopment, city rebuilding, assurance of equal opportunities for all. Indeed, the arrival of the Community Action Programs under the Economic Opportunities Act of 1964, superseding the broad youth-development programs launched by the President's Committee (and relegating them again to a delinquency control and corrections task), symbolized the process. The meaning of "opportunity" is being worked out operationally. And the realities of the subsequent struggle, to which insight has been added by the civil-rights revolution, now highlights the issue of social power—a subject certainly inherent in the anomie formulation, but not put originally as a central issue by those who helped generate the opportunity approach.

Case Services in Context

Of especial interest is the placement of individual treatment and rehabilitation services in a larger community context; for, as already suggested, these, too, tend to be part of the newer planning packages. One finds interesting, if understandable, ambivalences and differing points of emphasis, in marked contrast to earlier products of community planning for social welfare in which case services were almost always the central concern.

The Appalachian report holds little that is new here, since its delinquency-control "field" theory calls for institutional and individual change to achieve sound balance. The other documents represent significant departure.

To move chronologically, once again, the planning report of Mobilization for Youth stresses education, work, and indigenous social organization as affecting the "opportunity structure" but also gives a significant part to what it calls "new frontiers in services" to individuals and groups, emphasizing the use of social casework as especially appropriate for those who are "enmeshed in self-defeating adaptations." Casework, it notes, has long concerned itself with the relationship between people and their social environment. Characterized by controlled use of worker–client interaction and by use of concrete social services, casework seems to the authors to be a most appropriate helping tool. Adaptations have to be made to take account of the special life patterns and needs of low-income families, and an emphasis is placed on information, informal education, enabling social resources, and help in negotiating the bureaucracy of official agencies. Where individual psychologically oriented therapeutic processes are needed, they should be undertaken only in relation to previous or parallel efforts to improve the individual's social conditions. (In his subsequent work, Cloward attacked social work's estrangement from the poor more vigorously, condemned what he called an "illusion of service," and urged considerable reform of the modes of service delivery.)[20]

The New Haven formulation follows logically: new jobs may be provided, but some people are unable or unwilling to apply; new housing projects may be built, only to be turned into slums; exciting educational opportunities may be conceived, but people may let them die for lack of participation. Therefore, one does not merely improve the world of work and education through program change and expansion; one also addresses the motivation, attitudes, and values of people of the city. In addition, one plans for restorative services since—despite the hoped-for long-term effects of reforms in education, employment, and leisure time—appreciable numbers will be in trouble or in need in the short run, and the response should be adequate. Effective rehabilitation services cut contagion, affect future generations, and increase positive social control.

In short, one begins to detect in the New Haven proposals a note of apology for therapeutic-rehabilitative programs, once the major concern of welfare planners.

Boston's plannning rationale "calls for intervening in the processes by which youth and adults learn and perform their roles" on the assumption that strengthening these processes will lead to more conforming behavior by youth with respect to the law. Case services are to be located in multiple-purpose service centers which are to be assigned a case-finding, evaluation, brief-service, referral role, concentrating on families unable to exercise initiative in seeking help and justified as necessary to remove the blockages in the way of adequate role performance. More than in traditional programs, emphasis is placed on the knowledge and skill component of adult-role performance, but personal psychological defect is not ignored.

Haryou displays the developing polarization more dramatically. Its position is not new, intellectually, but is significant in the context of a planning effort in which there has been considerable social-work involvement. The report notes, directly and early, that "delinquency and anti-social behavior are individual symptoms of a systematic social pathology. Attempts to obscure, solve or redirect the symptoms merely delay the needed therapy for the disease itself." School failure is not necessarily the result of family pathology and deprivation, but of the expectation of substandard performance by the school as a social institution. Haryou rejects any "service saturation" approach. Justifying its social-action emphasis in relation to the delinquency problem, it refers to the alleged vanishing of antisocial behavior in Montgomery, Alabama, when the Negro community mobilized for sustained action against prevailing social injustice. It reports that Harlem's social agencies are perceived locally as trying to do a good job, but it stresses shortages, service lacks, and failure to address "real problems of the community and people." The social agencies are challenged to modify "their approaches, procedures and programs quickly enough to be relevant to the contemporary complex of problems."

In the history of social reform, many social-action strategies, including those of Marxists, Fabians, and trade-unionists, have warned that case services may be (to borrow a relevant phrase) "the opium of the masses." On the level of specific planning, none fully sustains the position, however. This much may be said of the efforts here in focus as well. Whether because of (1) the demands of funding agencies, (2) the expectations of some of the supporters on the local level, (3) the difficulties of specifying broad social-"change" strategies in contrast to the experience with individually oriented services, (4) the need to produce budgets and spend significant sums, or (5) the basic perception of the need to make it possible for people to use the new opportunities and to overcome the obstacles in themselves, all the planning efforts do provide for case services, and some give them major importance. While stressing schools, work, the economy, and social action, even Haryou provides for "aggressive casework" for multiproblem families as a "secondary" program. It also proposes to offer large-scale remedial programs in all other areas, such as remedial educational centers, a reading mobilization year, remedial job exploratory training for the unmotivated, and even community-based halfway treatment houses for offenders. All the programs provide for information and individual help to cope with confusing and forbidding official agency machinery.

Any social-planning approach concerned with the deprived, the antisocial, the poor, the discriminated against which fails to deal both with institutional provision and change, on the one hand, and with case-therapeutic-rehabilitative services, on the other, is unreal and out of balance. The new mood in planning is turning us toward the fundamental social institutions and their adequacy to urban industrial life. The basic validity of this process need not be established through rejection of case measures, however. The Haryou formulation derives its way of thinking about case services in an over-all context because its basic goal is the creation of a social movement in its community. Yet, while it undertakes in many ways to affect the modes of service delivery and continues to warn against "case" approaches as evading basic issues, it does not find it possible operationally to move away from services to the deprived. In fact the various community mobilizations are not as different from one another as the slogans in their planning documents would seem to suggest. The balance in Haryou shifted even further, and case services became central when the original leadership lost control. Similarly, the office of Economic Opportunity was to stress institutional change initiated by the poor in its public pronouncement during the first year; yet the heart of the Community Action Program was in the field of individual remediation, help, retraining, counseling, and aid. A social-change strategy, thus, continues to require case and individual elements, and political realities may even render individual services primary despite ideological commitment.

Definition of Preferences

Most of those interested in planning theory make a distinction between the choice of policy direction and the technologies of implementation. Significant shifts are taking place in the new opportunity programs in their reference points for policy guidance.

The health and welfare council tradition involves co-ordination efforts and a degree of *ad hoc* planning by a leadership group representative of voluntary agency interests; a scattering of physicians, lawyers, and labor representatives; some public officials and some of the interested segments of the community power structure generally. The latter have tended to be a limited self-selective group, derived largely (1) from those in the admirable long tradition of voluntary service which has been so important to the American ethic and (2) from professional workers in the field. In recent years, and in some places, they have been augmented by (3) leadership implementing the community-responsibility concepts of locally located large industries.

Health and welfare council planning, however, has also been influenced by a variety of types of "need" studies which have in various ways affected the community leadership view of the issues and priorities. Case analyses, opinion studies, analyses of demographic trends, reviews of social breakdown statistics, studies of agency waiting lists, interviews with clients, efforts to gauge agency effectiveness, have all contributed in some degree to the perception of need and the formulation of the planning task. Since —except for some leisure-time services—the frame of reference was often that of the case service agency, there were predetermined limitations on the planning. The "filter" of council leadership and staff, focusing on limited aspects of the community social system, also tended to narrow the range of outcomes.

Social-work community organization has long been preoccupied with ways of assuring community involvement in setting and implementing goals. In fact, until recently, the community-organization method was conceptualized entirely in relation to the enabling role. Yet it seems reasonable to state that the enabling usually took the form of facilitating development of consensus among leaders or winning local assent to leadership-sanctioned direction and plans—not of true community-wide involvement in goal setting.

Those who would question this broad generalization will find it difficult to account for the small number of instances in which local grass-roots initiative changed the fundamental direction of welfare planning. In fact, the extent to which the preoccupations of national standard-setting organizations (family, child-welfare, mental-health, and group services) have tended to guide the concerns of local councils indicates that local processes have influenced priorities, scale, quality, and administration far more than they have shaped content and direction.

To some degree, in the context of the "opportunity" emphasis, some new ingredients have affected outcomes and have generated other possibilities for the future. If we think of a planning formula in which what people wish—or are assumed to wish—and what will motivate them are represented by the term *preference*, we may say that new elements are entering into the preferences affecting planning. That is why the task formulations have changed and continue to change.

First, there is the effort to understand "lower-class culture," a subject about which there has been much recent writing. Many investigations and crusading efforts by a number of sociologists, social workers, and civil-rights leaders have underscored the fact that some members of the population do not share certain middle-class life styles and norms and consequently do not rear children who can participate fully in social institutions governed by such styles and norms.[21] The result is only token participation by some in education, an inability to comply with role expectations of patients and clients in medical and health services, difficulties in taking advantage of governmental instrumentalities generally, and an attitude toward some illegitimate activity which complicates law-enforcement tasks.

Out of commitment to "reach the unreached," social workers and others have begun to plan neighborhood experiments which take account of lower-class culture and have sought to understand the implications for agency organization, social-work practice, and treatment modalities inherent in a more accurate social diagnosis of potential or actual clientele.

None of this is foreign to the tradition of planning in health and welfare councils, and, in fact, some of the first efforts along these lines had—and continue to have—important council backing. Concern with adaptation of service modes to lower-class culture is nonetheless a general mark of all the new mobilizations.

The investigations and experiments, however, have added another ingredient. Those who would open social institutions to the "culturally deprived" began to discover in lower-class culture ingredients and styles which, they felt, were useful alternatives and need not give way in an acculturation process. They began to speak (in what to some observers, at least, appears to be a somewhat romantic fashion) of spontaneity, physical as opposed to verbal expression, primary-group solidarity and child-rearing stability of the extended family, as these characterized some of the deprived. Thus, assuming a society of limited upward social mobility, they began to ask about accommodating institutions to these life styles.

Full analysis of this phenomenon would require that we review the many definitions and concepts of the "lower class," "working class," "poor," "culturally deprived," "anomic poor"—all terms which are introduced into the discussion. There is much inconsistency and confusion. The fact remains, nonetheless, that all of the discussion has had its effect. Many of the newer planning efforts take the members of the most deprived populations in the most disadvantaged districts as target populations. They ask whether the proposal advanced will make a significant difference to the basic problems of people in the "lower class." As noted, the planning aims to facilitate lower-class access to general community resources and to education and work opportunity. There is serious effort to change education and work induction to meet the situations of the deprived. There is also

some commitment to use the new local mobilizations to encourage participation by the deprived in local politics on behalf of themselves and their
children. Indeed, the requirement that the poor be represented on local
and neighborhood planning and policy bodies under the Community Action Program of the Economic Opportunities Act of 1964 was to unleash a
series of political disputes as yet unresolved at this writing.

The new opportunity mobilizations were characterized as "planning for
upward mobility." There was no general tendency to follow those who
extolled the virtues of lower-class culture by seeking to build fundamental
institutions around such culture. Concentration on preserving lower-
class patterns could block the acculturation inherent in mobility if the
organization of schools, work training, and social services concerned themselves with reaching the deprived, paid no attention to the continuing society, and were accepted as adequate by the poor. The tendency would be
to reinforce and freeze differences in knowledge, training, and social skills
and the very barriers to opportunity which have been blamed on such
differences. The fact is that our pluralistic society has shown itself capable
of teaching to everyone the cultural prerequisites of mobility in an urban
industrial world while simultaneously guarding the ethnic-generational-
religious-regional-class variables which enrich community life. The new
planning will need to attend to this issue. The sociologist will wish to note
whether the poor, themselves, now increasingly represented in the planning and policy development, opt for integration or preservation of their
"uniqueness."

There are other new elements entering into the definitions of preference. The new planning efforts began where the councils were, but soon
added concern with education and the world of work. The researchers
incorporated all of the usual fact finding, but added their facts about the
social-class dimensions and their concern for the distribution of power.
Interested in the question of opportunity, both citizen leadership and researchers gave attention as never before to the obstacles placed in the way
of those who would participate in community life or use services and to
the internalized handicaps to which such obstacles give rise.

While the community-leadership "filter" inevitably shapes these new ingredients, enough new has been added so that the products are different
from the services produced by the older planning processes. The major
funding sources in the federal government and foundations provide new
leverage for communities which will go even further. As put by a spokesman for the President's Committee on Delinquency and Youth Crime: the
planning process encouraged by the federal government addresses the
youth problem "as being rooted in the social system." The planning is to
focus on prevention; the "product of planning must be construed to produce appropriate change in all the conditions identified as contributing to
the social disorders." What is more, the solutions imposed should not

merely "secure conformity as publicly defined." The goal is rather to "improve the affected individual's ability to realize a socially healthy and productive life." [22] Or, in the words of an official policy guide, "These efforts aimed at individual rehabilitation will remain a major part of the national approach to the problem of delinquency. However . . . it becomes apparent that intervention aimed at the social situation of youth is more strategic." [23]

A reader of any sampling of the new planning reports will recognize that the national influence has been potent. These new nonlocal sources of preferences are in their orientations in contrast with the direct service-oriented national agencies which were the major prior outside influence. All the new efforts are now characterized by a commitment to "inducing change and adaptations," [24] where once the "more service" or "better staff" or "co-ordination" goals prevailed.

The question may be raised as to whether one should attribute more influence to the findings of the considerable "inner-city" and "youth" research generated by these programs in the planning phase. Much of the funding for the one-year planning grants which produced the reports here analyzed was, in fact, devoted to youth-problem and community-trend research. Is this not local influence? To some extent findings of research may have been a secondary factor in the choices from among local options within the given framework. To a considerable degree the research conceptualizations and conclusions were the vehicles for the shifts in the definition of the task. It is clear, however, that federal and foundation guidelines, based on a national view of trends, plus local political and organizational realities, were more important preference ingredients. The former are reflected in the repetition of core "expected" concepts in almost all the research formulations, in contrast to the variability in any similar volume of randomly selected social-science research. The latter are seen in a report-by-report analysis as to why specific solutions were developed in a given city's plan.

The Haryou planning process did introduce a new and quite interesting element: youth participation which went beyond the usual tokenism. In the course of the planning process, a youth group called Haryou Associates was established, and its responses became important to the adult leadership. Programs are suspect if these youth (whose representativeness is neither asserted nor validated) do not consider them to be "for real"—sincerely conceived and addressed to basic issues.

Interestingly, the planning process in projects funded by the President's Committee on Delinquency and Youth Crime was committed ideologically to decision making in the light of local preferences; yet such preferences could hardly become fully evident, given the centrally generated conceptual guides and obvious affinity for certain types of programs. The antipoverty Community Action Program does not require a similar research and formal planning process, but the potency of national staff is everywhere apparent.

While these facts may create concern in some quarters and could lead to abuse and lack of local creativity, they are not necessarily to be deplored. For, if the objective is to be area redevelopment, renewal, economic opportunity, a neighborhood cannot be the only planning unit; there is need for national, regional, and state participation and influence through our democratic political process and accountable administrative agencies. Yet our local, city, and regional differences, and our concern for pluralism as a major value, demand that we address the question of the appropriate sources of preference for different planning levels and purposes. Such exploration inevitably will take place as we develop vehicles for the needed decentralization of planning, a phrase which expresses a social value, but not necessarily an inconsistency. In fact, the neighborhood activities generated by the antipoverty effort will create local power groups which will assert themselves in new ways.

Conclusion

Sociologists and sociologically influenced foundation executives, officials, and social workers have wrought a major change in delinquency-treatment programs and have played a significant role in the shift in the prevention field to broad concern with poverty and urban community development. It seems clear, however, that their theory-oriented concepts ("opportunity structure") were quickly popularized and became vehicles for a variety of goals, derived out of other experiences and interests. Nonetheless, studies of youth gangs, delinquent subcultures, and the lives of the poor have influenced over-all goals, program philosophy, and action strategy.

While sociologists may deplore the ensuing imprecision and the conversion of concepts into slogans (one could write an essay about the reification of "community power structure"), a significant contribution has been made. To some observers American sociology has become *relevant* as never before. Others may regard all this as a departure from the responsibility to develop and test knowledge. Those who would make their contribution in this latter domain might now turn quite profitably to the as yet little addressed tasks of studying the choices which American society has been willing to make—and those which it has skirted—in noting, defining, and coping with deviance. They might also seize the opportunity now around us for the conceptualization and study of a massive effort at planned social change.

REFERENCES

NOTE: *Earlier versions of some of this chapter will be found in the following, by the author: "Social Work and the Control of Delinquency," Social Work, X, No. 2 (April, 1965), 3–13, and "Trends and Problems in Community Organization," in National Conference on Social Welfare, Social Work Practice 1964 (New York: Columbia University Press, 1964), pp. 3–27. Since the present chapter is a case study, no effort has been made to update it beyond its original cut-off date.*

1. Richard Perlman, "Delinquency Prevention: The Size of the Problem," *Annals of the American Academy of Political and Social Science,* CCCXXII (March, 1959), 3–4. Also Robert H. Hardt, *A Delinquency Profile of Syracuse and Onondaga County, New York, 1957–58* (Syracuse: Youth Development Center, 1960), pp. 11, 43; Thomas P. Monahan, "On the Incidence of Delinquency," *Social Forces,* XXXIX (October, 1960), 66–72.
2. Leslie T. Wilkins, "Crime, Cause and Treatment: Recent Research and Theory," an offprint from *Education Research* (Britain), IV, No. 1 (November, 1961), 22–23.
3. For a review of theories, see any test. For example, Paul W. Tappan, *Juvenile Delinquency* (New York: McGraw-Hill, 1949), or Herbert A. Bloch and Frank Flynn, *Delinquency: The Juvenile Offender in America Today* (New York: Random House, 1956). Also Harry Elmer Barnes and Negley K. Teeters, *New Horizons in Criminology* (New York: Prentice-Hall, 1943).
4. A widely read psychoanalytic text on delinquency is K. R. Eissler, *Searchlights on Delinquency* (New York: International Universities Press, 1949).
5. Adelaide Johnson, "Sanctions for Superego Lacunae of Adolescents," in *ibid.,* pp. 225–245. Also Fritz Redl and Ralph Wineman, *Children Who Hate* (Glencoe, Ill.: The Free Press, 1951); Sheldon and Eleanor Glueck, *Unraveling Juvenile Delinquency* (New York: The Commonwealth Fund, 1950); Beatrice Simcox Reiner and Irving Kaufman, *Character Disorders in Parents of Delinquents* (New York: Family Service Association of America, 1959).
6. Lester E. Hewitt and Richard L. Jenkins, *Fundamental Patterns of Maladjustment* (Springfield, Ill.: Charles C Thomas, 1947).
7. Albert Cohen, *Delinquent Boys: The Culture of the Gang* (Glencoe, Ill.: The Free Press, 1955).
8. Gresham M. Sykes and David Matza, "Techniques of Neutralization: A Theory of Delinquency," *American Sociological Review,* XXII (1957), 664–670.
9. Richard A. Cloward, Donald R. Cressey, *et al., Theoretical Studies in Social Organization of the Prison* (New York: Social Science Research Council, 1960); Helen L. Witmer and Ruth Kotinsky, eds., *New Perspectives for Research on Juvenile Delinquency,* Publication No. 356 (Washington: Government Printing Office, 1956).
10. Howard W. Polsky, "Changing Delinquent Subcultures: A Social-Psychological Approach," *Social Work,* IV, No. 4 (October, 1959), 3–15; and Lloyd E. Ohlin and William C. Lawrence, "Social Interaction among Clients as a Treatment Problem," *Social Work,* IV, No. 2 (April, 1959), 3–13.
11. Helen L. Witmer, *Delinquency and Adolescent Crisis,* Juvenile Delinquency Facts and Facets, No. 11 (Washington, D.C.: Government Printing Office, 1960); and W. C. Kvaracius and W. B. Miller, *Delinquent Behavior: Culture and the Individual* (Washington, D.C.: National Association, 1959).

12. Richard A. Cloward and Lloyd E. Ohlin, *Delinquency and Opportunity: A Theory of Delinquent Gangs* (Glencoe, Ill.: The Free Press, 1960).

13. The 1956 American position paper at the International Conference of Social Work was published in revised form as Harold L. Wilensky and Charles N. Lebeaux, *Industrial Society and Social Welfare* (New York: Russell Sage Foundation, 1958). Paperback revision now available; published by The Free Press, 1965. Also see, *New Perspectives for Research on Juvenile Delinquency.*

14. Lloyd W. McCorkle, Albert Elias, and F. Lovell Bixby, *The Highfields Story* (New York: Henry Holt, 1958).

15. Wilkins, *op. cit.*, 26.

16. Alfred J. Kahn, *Planning Community Services for Children in Trouble* (New York: Columbia University Press, 1963).

17. The following sampling of planning reports as submitted to the President's Committee on Delinquency and Youth Crime and other sources of funding represents the major basis for the discussion in this paper and the source of illustrations. We shall not attempt to trace the impact of operational experience on subsequent reformulations, since the task would then become unmanageable; our purpose is served by analysis of the reports alone.

    a. *Action for Appalachian Youth* (Charleston, W. Va.: The Charleston Youth Community, Inc., 1963).

    b. *A Proposal for the Prevention and Control of Delinquency by Expanding Opportunities* (New York: Mobilization for Youth, Inc., 1961).

    c. *Community Action for Youth* (Cleveland: Greater Cleveland Youth Services Planning Commission, 1963).

    d. *New Haven Youth Development Program*, 2 vols. (New Haven, Community Progress, Inc., 1963).

    e. *Opening Opportunities: New Haven's Comprehensive Program for Community Progress* (New Haven: The City, 1962).

    f. *The Boston Youth Opportunities Project* (Boston: Action for Boston Community Development, Inc., 1963).

    g. *Youth in the Ghetto: A Study of the Consequences of Powerlessness* (New York: Harlem Youth Opportunities Unlimited, 1964).

18. Kahn, *op. cit.*

19. Alfred J. Kahn, ed., *Issues in American Social Work* (New York: Columbia University Press, 1959), and "Therapy, Prevention and Developmental Provision: A Social Work Strategy," in *Public Health Concepts in Social Work Education* (New York: Council on Social Work Education, 1962). Also Kahn, "The Societal Context of Social Work Practice," *Social Work*, X, No. 4 (October, 1965).

20. Richard A. Cloward, *Social Problems, Social Definitions and Social Opportunities* (New York: National Council on Crime and Delinquency, mimeographed, 1963). Also, Richard A. Cloward and Irwin Epstein, "Private Social Welfare's Disengagement from the Poor," in Mayer N. Zald (ed.), *Social Welfare Institutions: A Sociological Reader* (New York: John Wiley and Sons, Inc., 1965), pp. 623–644.

21.   a. S. M. Miller, "The American Lower Classes," *Social Research* (Spring, 1964).

    b. Walter B. Miller, "Lower Class Culture as a Generating Milieu of Gang Delinquency," *Journal of Social Issues*, XIV, No. 3 (1958).

    c. Jerome Cohen, "Social Work and the Culture of Poverty," *Social Work*, IX (January, 1964), 3–11.

    d. Frank Riessman, *The Culturally Deprived Child* (New York: Harper, 1962).

22. Sanford Kravitz, *A New Strategy for the Prevention and Control of Juvenile*

Delinquency (Washington: President's Committee on Delinquency and Youth Crime, mimeographed, 1963).

23. *Policy Guides to the Presentation of Proposals for Funding under Public Law 87–234* (Washington: Office of Juvenile Delinquency and Youth Development, 1963).

24. Kravitz, *op. cit.*

Research and
the Dilemmas
in Developing
Social Programs

ELMER LUCHTERHAND

chapter 18

Introduction

Many of the best-known community-action programs and demonstration projects in the United States are being implemented by new, specially contrived agencies. This chapter outlines the circumstances out of which some of them have arisen and the directions and dilemmas of program development. On this background are sketched the life condition and problems of demonstration researchers and the uses of sociology in the new agencies.

In the national antipoverty campaigns the new community organizations serve as agents of change with regard to policies and practices of schools, social-work groups, housing administrations, and employment services. The section to follow indicates how elite origins may incline the new agencies toward elitist objectives, strategies, and tactics of change.

Origins

There is an unconscious tendency, if not a conscious preference, for staffs of the new agencies to define themselves as pioneer fighters against poverty. The absurdity of such a view is patent after a moment's reflection on all the utopias of man. The new staffs are only the most recent poverty fighters, the most richly equipped.

There is a need for agency histories to be written.[1] In most cities the community-action agencies are descended in a fairly direct line from urban-redevelopment efforts. The elitist approach to social problems in much redevelopment work has been the subject of considerable discussion.[2] Writing on New Haven, Dahl emphasizes that "redevelopment was not produced by a surge of popular demand for a new city."[3] He states further that "the direct influence of the electorate on the key decisions involving redevelopment has been negligible compared with the direct influence of a few leaders. In origins, conception, and execution, it is not too much to say that urban redevelopment has been the direct product of a small handful of leaders."[4] It should be added that, in contrast to the prevailing pattern elsewhere at the time, the local mayor stood at their head.[5]

Dahl characterizes New Haven's redevelopment efforts as follows: "With respect to the physical pattern of the city, the redevelopment leaders were radical; with respect to the socioeconomic structure they were— by comparison with proponents of the New Deal, for example—conservative."[6]

The redevelopers in New Haven and elsewhere have usually been interested in what Lewis Coser calls "detail reform."[7] Such change may affect convenience, esthetic qualities, or both, but does not directly alter social structure. Efforts to improve dismal neighborhoods and run-down central business districts are examples of detail change. "Structural reform"[8] involves a fundamental rearrangement of patterns of living.

Redevelopers have generally been keenly aware of differences in the receptivity of most people to these kinds of reform or change. Initially, the renewal program promises the city a new-car smell and more mileage; with time, more fundamental matters like deghettoization may come to the fore. Residents who welcome, or at least put up with, detail reforms may resist bitterly the structural ones.

As redevelopment progressed in New Haven, new problems arose:

The movement of the lower classes . . . promised to intensify the social and economic problems in other city neighborhoods; to heighten the pressures on existing housing and public institutions, such as the schools; to increase the likelihood of social friction between old and new residents, between the white and Negro populations; to hasten the deterioration of these neighborhoods and complicate further efforts to redevelop them. These considerations, sufficient in themselves to occasion official concern, were re-enforced by the personal predisposition of the redevelopers. As one local observer notes, they were planners with a social conscience.[9]

Out of the concern of the redevelopers over this transplanting of people and problems came a number of proposals to study the situation and to mobilize welfare agencies to serve the relocated families better. These first proposals were never satisfactorily implemented. A later one, which took hold after several delays, was a proposal for a new agency, with a new delivery system for providing social services to the needy. The proposal was written and rewritten in informal discussion with top leaders of local welfare agencies and the welfare planning council.[10]

New Haven's achievements reflect an earlier and better articulation of elites than has occurred in most other American cities.[11] The urban redevelopment and "human renewal" efforts went forward with a team of professional planners and prominent local people led by the political elite. This combination, in a city which now serves as a national model, is important for understanding the directions and dilemmas of program development.

The Political Context

Having been born in the pulling and hauling of politics, the new agencies must establish themselves in a context of fast-moving political contests between supporters and opponents of change. The nature of the interaction between politicians and their audiences or publics has been aptly described by Long in the following statement:

The politicians who might be expected to be protagonists of the general interest, may indeed be so, but the sphere of their activity and the glasses through which they see the problem will be determined in great part by the way they see the issue affecting their political game. The generality of this game is to a great extent that of the politician's calculus of votes and interests important to his and his side's success. To be sure, some of what Walter Lippmann has called "the public philosophy" affects both politicians and other game-players. This indicates the existence of roles and norms of a larger, vaguer game with a relevant audience that has some sense of cricket. This potentially mobilizable audience is not utterly without importance, but it provides no sure or adequate basis for support in the particular game that the politician or anyone else is playing. Instead of a set of norms to structure enduring role-playing, this audience provides a cross-pressure for momentary aberrancy from gamesmanship or constitutes just another hazard to be calculated in one's play.[12]

The newly emerging community-action agencies represent an audience segment which is mobilized and is able to mobilize other parts of the audience. In the usual case they are product and part of the liberal establishment. (As used here, the term *establishment* refers to a loose combination having power—including, in some instances, formal, public authority —or serious power capabilities.) Besides the new action agencies, the liberal establishment typically includes part or all of the trade-union movement, planning, urban-renewal, and social-welfare agencies, private foundations, and academic groups.

Demonstration Projects: Their Place in Agency Programs

One of the powerful instruments for social change which have been fashioned by the liberal establishment and serve to extend it is the demonstration project. It has been characterized as

> an innovative attack on social problems, developed by research-and-action staff. Further, it is a project which is systematically evaluated at points in the flow, for purposes of administrative corrective action, and to facilitate a final evaluation in terms of over-all and component effects. An essential aspect of demonstration research is that it be designed to enhance basic understanding of human behavior. Without this aspect, research which concentrates only on measuring net effects will lose an invaluable opportunity to contribute to the development of viable programs in a fast-moving world.[13]

The demonstration project has peculiar potency in that it offers the possibility to bring into productive co-operation the people in government, the service professions, and the social sciences. In addition it provides contact between the private foundation operating in social-problem areas and the government bureau. The administration of demonstration projects is one of the characteristic functions of the new action agencies.

Cloward and Piven speak of two major program means to effect change:

1. "By demonstration, especially in cooperation with the institutions themselves, of new and innovating patterns of service or new policies governing the giving of service;
2. "By allocating resources (staff, money, facilities, etc.) to low-income

groups to enhance their capacity to influence institutional practices and policies." [14]

Cloward and Piven refer to the demonstration project as an " 'elite' strategy" and to the other as a means to bring about a "low-income social movement." They see these two program approaches as coexisting in some agencies with a certain amount of strain and therefore as constituting a major organizational dilemma of the new action agencies.[15] They go on to deal with the organizational strains that result from the "conflicting strategies of social change" and with the formidable difficulties of resolving these strains. Besides their low political influence, low-income people tend to lack the organizational experience and educational requirements to assert effectively their particular interests. They are handicapped further by a belief system in which "a sense of political inefficacy" [16] is a major element.

Whatever the prospects of resolving the organizational dilemma noted by Cloward and Piven, sociologists can help solve the problems of involving low-income people. As a starting point it would seem necessary to conceptualize different levels of program involvement. Four such levels are suggested here, generally ordered according to present feasibility:

Most feasible now:

1. Exercising choice between proffered program alternatives;
2. Collective presentation of protests and demands to community organizations and individuals;

Least feasible now:

3. Direct participation in planning and designing social programs either in the new agencies or in new organizations built by low-income groups themselves;
4. The administration of social programs.

Only one example of deliberate program effort to attain one of these four levels of involvement (Level 1) will be given. In one new agency a housing demonstration was undertaken for large (seven or more members), low-income families who were part of the relocation work load of a redevelopment agency and were almost all Negro. It was reasoned that deprivation of alternatives in many areas of family life was a distinguishing feature of *large*, low-income families, the more so if they were Negro. It was conjectured that, for these families, to have even a limited choice of apartments would mean to realize forgotten hopes. On the basis of cognitive-dissonance theory[17] it was hypothesized that families given a choice of housing would reflect greater gains in family functioning and adjustment than families that were not given a choice.

In the program-design phase, the research staff emphasized the possibility of heightened program effects by providing choice. Professional housing managers were emphatic in noting the administrative advantages in permitting prospective tenants to see more than one unit, that is, to reject as well as accept. It was pointed out that offering choice might be interpreted as indicating good intentions and thereby reassure those family heads who were most alienated. In addition it was pointed out that a program design which provided choice would require the same number of hard-to-get housing units as a program which did not provide choice. It was agreed finally to administer choice to a random half of the relocation work load. In developing this program, use was made of experience with a highly successful, massive application of choice in employee placement in an industrial setting.[18]

This feature of the project broke down at the level of field administration. However, field workers regularly reported comments of family members which supported the wisdom of the original program design. The following remark by one woman, when she was shown the apartment selected for her family, is typical: "I have to take this, don't I? I don't have any choice, do I?"

An examination of the breakdown in this feature of the program resulted in these observations by the research team:

> To be effective, administrators have to have confidence in their own judgment, a confidence nurtured by making decisions. But to administer choice means to inhibit the impulse to decide for the family. The art of administering choice is to transfer something of administrative self-confidence to others, and to permit time to pass. It is often necessary to slow down the decision-making process so that the decider can interact with family members and non-family peers and pick up the maximum of cues needed for his decision. These requirements for administering choice were too much to handle for those who were responsible for the program in the field.

We suspect that the dilemmas noted are fairly common in administering choice; that wherever choice is important in the implementation of preventive and therapeutic social programs, this problem is apt to arise. It is an elitist ill. Administrators who attend carefully to democratic form may be appallingly adept at undermining democratic substance.

Some Agency and Program Dilemmas

We may now turn to the dilemmas that arise from agency involvement in the larger interaction between politicians and audiences. There is no attempt here to provide an exhaustive list of agency and program dilemmas, for it is impossible to define, expand, and exemplify them fully. It should be sufficient to indicate some areas in which dilemmas are important and obvious.

ORGANIZATION-ADMINISTRATION DILEMMAS

Should the agency have a large or small board of directors? Should it enlist "locals" or "outsiders"? Should it recruit mainly professionals or nonprofessionals to administer services? Should it build a flat organization or a peaked one?

DILEMMAS REGARDING STRATEGY OF INTERVENTION

These are related to the preceding ones of organization. Thus the decision on the size of the board may be predictive, or fatefully controlling, with regard to the decisions on moving fast or slowly. Should the agency try to involve broad community groups in designing programs, or work swiftly with its own staff and consultants? (By analogy from industry, should the design work be done on the shop floor, as in the Lincoln Electric Company,[19] or exclusively in the engineering division by formally qualified people?)

COMMUNICATION DILEMMAS

These relate to all the others. Should the agency dramatize the new program or be "cool"? (This involves a judgmental dilemma by agency heads on whether they can successfully meet the demands for service that may be generated by dramatic announcement, or whether they will be unable to meet the demands and then be blamed for failure.)

ACTION-AND-CONTROL DILEMMAS

Rarely is the liberal establishment a nicely coherent entity, with clear boundaries that permit it to function with easy confidence in the face of conservative power plays. Because it is involved in winning or retaining power, the liberal establishment attempts action with acute concern for tactical and strategic advantage. While liberals generally do more than conservatives to launch social programs, once in power, liberal and conservative regimes exhibit certain common characteristics. They want to hold political "territory," that is, they want to defend the boundaries of their establishment against other claimants and, whenever possible, to enlarge their influence. To defend, they need to set limits on some types of action which may jeopardize their power position. Protest action and demands for structural reform have a way of originating at the boundaries of the establishment. To maintain these boundaries requires strict control over action. This leads to what has been called the "odd and interesting conservatism" of the establishment, whether its origins are liberal or conservative. While the liberal orientation, in contrast to the conservative, tends toward social change, the establishment determines the limits on action by the "politician's calculus." In short, it acts like an establishment.[20]

The effort to keep protests within safe bounds was recently illustrated in one metropolitan center. A local action committee slowly emerged in a depressed and slumlike neighborhood. The committee acquired a great deal of experience in reducing school problems and traffic overloads, and it finally organized its forces to present a series of demands on city officials to improve conditions in the neighborhood. The *city-wide* action organization became aware of the impending protest. Its staff members assisted the *local* action committee in formulating its demands on the city and then turned to work with city officials to prepare them for the impending protest. This two-way effort might be called "the double rehearsal" technique of control.[21]

While in the past there have been much concern and criticism about the efforts of urban-renewal groups to manage consent, now one may find efforts to manage protest and control. Variants of this technique are in common use by program administrators in many metropolitan centers. They represent a cautious departure from "the trend to the smooth" of the 1950's. Administration efforts to restrain action have special importance where programs are predicated on neighborhood action. Obviously we have here a major dilemma, the importance of which is heightened by granting-agency requirements.

ADMINISTRATIVE DILEMMAS REGARDING RESEARCH

Administrative concern with control is not limited to questions of neighborhood action, but also relates to research. Sooner or later the following questions arise: Should research objectives be assigned by program administration, or be developed under the direction of research people, working closely with action staff? Should program administration handle all questions of communication about, and use of, research findings, or should this be done in a team relationship of research people working closely with action staff?

Occasionally the research staff may face the question of what to do about impossible administrative demands. One such demand is for a fictitious new product, "instant knowledge." [22] Researchers have occasionally helped to generate this demand by extravagant and unwarranted claims for research and for computer technology. Sometimes administration desires access to raw data. There may also be requests to do a variety of chores that are inappropriate to the research role. For those who know how to work and live in a bureaucracy, these things pass away, but they are annoying while they last; for the inexperienced, "free" intellectual in an agency such demands result in strains which may destroy the action-and-research relationship.

There is the administrative dilemma on whether to have an "inside" or an "outside" group do the demonstration research. What sort of organization is likely to be more objective: a team of *outside* research consultants or a unit *within* the community-action agency? There is a rather common notion that only outsiders are likely to provide objective research and boldly present any negative findings on program effects.[23]

Freeman presents a quite different view. He states that

the image of the researcher who remains outside the environment and evaluates what others are doing in no way squares with the reality of his engagement in these programs. It is clear that the researcher is involved in a situation in which he must lock himself into the environment, not only because he has a background that can be exploited by persons designing programs, but because otherwise he cannot accomplish his evaluation task. Unless he participates, indeed leads the dialogue and bargaining required for the identification of goals, for description of input-output variables, and for the elaboration of a rationale that specifies the relationship between input variables and goals, these tasks are likely to remain undone. Once formulated he must continue to remain within the environment, like a snarling watchdog ready to fight alterations in program and procedures that could render his evaluation efforts useless.[24]

To limit discussion to the objectivity of insiders versus outsiders is to grossly oversimplify the problems of demonstration research. Performing one's role responsibly is apt to be more a matter of professional identification than of organization membership. The outside consultant often conducts himself like an insider in the way he cultivates his account; the insider, experiencing more or less career deprivation in his work situation, may act like an outsider. (Agency researchers, having been socialized to the research profession by the same processes as members of academic departments, may feel concern because they do not acquire time toward tenure or sabbaticals and in some places have little or no opportunity to teach or to turn out career tangibles.) The insider-outsider dichotomy falsely states the issues. The real issue is whether or not there is genuine concern for the goals of the action agency *and* for the profession of research. Organizationally, the real question is: How can one build and develop a staff to do demonstration research?

The Position of Research

Consideration of the administrative dilemmas regarding research leads to the question: What is the position of research? To carry through a demonstration project, the establishment welcomes the researcher. It needs him. He can, if things turn out well, provide justification for public expenditures to reduce social problems.

The researcher-recruit to the demonstration team gets a proper welcome. Besides this, there is *apparent* relief from financial problems of research. Fund raising is typically handled by agency professionals, armed with political influence. Because the researcher may have strong allegiance to reform, he is apt to be drawn to the liberal establishment on intellectual grounds.

The agency, for all its contributions to preventive and therapeutic social programs, creates hazards for social research. The danger to be emphasized here is the loss of autonomy by researching individuals and groups. There is always the prospect that they may be assimilated to a degree that will be damaging to the research process and, in turn, to program development. The peculiar way in which this hazard emerges and the ways in which it can be counteracted are central to this part of the discussion.

The romantics in action agencies, who are engaged in contriving demonstration projects, speak wistfully of the research-and-action dialogue, unmindful of the limits on the resulting communication from the unequal status of action and research imposed by politics. The researcher, if he is not actually naïve about power, is apt to be ineffectual in nonacademic power contests. He carries into the demonstration team his previous vague "minority" feelings, where they are quickly reinforced by work styles of the dominant action people. Thus when the situation is considered by the activists to be propitious for some kind of program, there is not likely to be much patience with the planning and design problems of evaluation research. To research people this may sound like a too sympathetic statement of the position of the liberal establishment, and so it may be.

The concern with control by the establishment eventuates in a concern with *so-called* negative evidence from demonstration research. Research staffs may be asked: "Suppose that an important federal program was up for renewal by Congress, and suppose your research turned up negative findings; what would you do with them?" The following answer was offered on one occasion by a lawyer in rebutting the reply to this question by research personnel: "The defense attorney in the court has an obligation to his client to make the best possible case for him, even though it means withholding information that might be useful to the court."

How the research staff deals with such implied demands depends on how it defines and perceives the action-and-research relationship, the working of a political opposition, and the *complex process* of reporting findings from demonstration research. These factors, in turn, depend partly on the nature of research-staff involvement in program development and on the quality of the research itself.

Along with administrative concern with so-called negative findings goes a tendency to change goals in the middle of the program—a tendency which is highly upsetting to a research staff. The problem of goal displacement arises from poor relations between action and research and from administrative defensiveness about limited program outcomes. This is not the place to argue the point that it is by co-operation between action and research—by effective dialogue—that better programs are developed. Without such dialogue, the chances of failure are increased. The point to be emphasized here is that goal slippage is one result of poorly developed relationships in planning and conducting demonstrations.

Reference has already been made to the vague "minority" feelings of the researcher-recruit to the action agency. The essence of minority–majority relations is not arithmetic, but power. As a member of a community-action agency, however, he may easily become the victim of both the preponderant numbers and the decision-making influence of program staffs. One response to this situation is to withdraw to the university; another is to do narrow "evaluation." The latter course is fraught with the same psychological hazards for the researcher as abandonment by the minority member of his ethnic identity. When industrial sociology began to come to the attention of enlightened corporation management, sociologists found new roles studying work organization and administrative practices. In some cases they were invited to evaluate training in human relations and administrative practices. It was not long before those in general sociology began to look doubtfully at those in industrial sociology and to speak of "managerial sociology." [25]

The trend toward narrow evaluation[26] in the field of community-action programs is one variety of establishment research. This pejorative term may well conjure up greater offenses than are committed, but there can be no doubt that narrow program evaluation means losses, both to social science and to program development.

Administrators usually want firm, clear generalizations which can be applied with complete confidence to particular clients or situations. But research findings are stated in terms of probabilities which apply to specified populations only. This tends to alienate practitioners, who may think that findings which are so hedged about with restrictions are of doubtful worth, if not actually useless. Such feelings may then add force to the all-purpose myth that demonstration research must necessarily get in the way of action programs. It follows that the action-and-research relationship is delicate, if not precarious. It can be sustained and made to grow by the thoughtful concern of social scientists in the government, the foundation, and the university. Without such concern, the bright promise of the demonstration project may not be fulfilled.

Prospects

There are many reasons why the demonstration project, despite some limitations, merits a major place in the repertoire of change strategies:

1. Its appeal spans a wide range of community organizations, including a broad network of liberal elitist groups; it can help them to cohere.
2. It is readily interpretable in the popular terms of "research and development."
3. It is hard to assail on economy grounds.
4. The well-planned demonstration seems to be the most effective means to penetrate what Merton once called the "opaque faith" [27] that gains in the technology of service will lead to good.
5. With sociologically informed design of programs it can be a versatile means to involve low-income people.

The new agencies have entered a massive antipoverty campaign with few tested procedures for improving the life chances of low-income groups. The sociologist can strengthen the new agencies against possible disappointment by guiding them toward more varied strategies, such as demonstrations that include evaluation and basic research components.

With proper doubts about the adequacy of present theories of social change, the sociologist may help the agencies to resolve their dilemmas. How that is done will depend in part on what agency heads want. What is "wanted" will depend partly on their definition of "what has to be."

When large areas of cities become, by any reasonable criteria, uninhabitable, the society runs out of alternatives to transformation and turns to alternate ways to transform. The cities that were flattened by World War II have removed their rubble and now stand upright. The problems of inner-city neighborhoods in the great metropolitan centers that appeared insoluble in 1960 or even 1964 may undergo a grand-scale redefinition tomorrow or the day after.[28] One thinks immediately of the Borough of Manhattan, Washington, D.C., Chicago, Los Angeles, and other examples.

To solve the problems of life in our ghettos and slums, the contributions of sociology are essential. Sociological knowledge and skill are needed to define problems, to design action-and-research programs, to widen their base of support, and to administer them effectively. In these programs, sociological knowledge and skills are necessary ingredients, but not the only ones. Working along with urban planners, city administrators, economists, political scientists, and social workers, the sociologist meets new challenges to his professional expertness and patience and develops new, more realistic sociological perspectives.

REFERENCES

NOTE: *The opinions expressed in this chapter are solely those of the author, and cannot be assumed to represent the position of particular community-action agencies. The author is grateful to various members of the Advisory Council on Research, New Haven, for comments on an earlier draft.*

1. For a brief but useful approach to the history of one agency, see Frances F. Piven, *Conceptual Themes in the Evolution of Mobilization for Youth* (New York: Training Institute, Columbia University School of Social Work and Mobilization for Youth, Inc., mimeographed, April, 1964). Recognizing the need for research on project development, the President's Committee on Juvenile Delinquency and Youth Crime in 1964 allocated funds for a comparative study of youth programs being conducted in a number of cities. Norton E. Long has assumed direction of this work.
2. In particular, see Herbert J. Gans, *The Urban Villagers* (New York: The Free Press of Glencoe, 1962).
3. Robert A. Dahl, *Who Governs?* (New Haven: Yale University Press, 1961), p. 115.
4. *Ibid.*
5. The New Haven events stand in such sharp and favorable contrast to those elsewhere that some interpretation beyond a statement of the high leadership skills of Mayor R. C. Lee is necessary. Rossi observes that one "striking characteristic of the American community of today in contrast to that of the past is the status gap between the personnel of local government and the local elites of wealth, intellect and status." In consequence of this gap Rossi notes further that "in many communities the mayor and city council often appear to be dragging their heels while organized 'prominent' citizens exhort the community to push toward progress." (Peter H. Rossi, "The Organizational Structure of an American Community," in Amitai Etzioni, *Complex Organizations* [New York: Holt, Rinehart, and Winston, 1961], pp. 301–302.) In New Haven there has been better articulation of the political elite on the one hand and the "prominent citizens"—the intellectual and professional elites—on the other. Despite the memories and some persisting reality of town-grown conflict, the critical factor in this better articulation of elites seems to be the social symbiosis of intellectual and corporate uppers living the suburban life in close proximity and without a metropolis.

    This symbiotic relationship has brought about greater political restraint on social issues by the economic elite, has repeatedly prevented the emergence of a strong, unified organizing center of such reactionary elements as exist, and has helped to insure the continuity of energetic liberal city administration under a long-established two-party political system. This situation has encouraged risk taking by the liberal political elite and has served to add stature and worth to the office of mayor.

    It is not only at the top levels that symbiotic relations have helped to neutralize the bitterness of the opposition but also in the middle strata. The small businessmen, who were seriously disaffected by the bold redevelopment of the central business district, did not align themselves solidly with the opposition. One reason, though probably not the main one, seems to have been the influence within the business and professional group of many people in the high-status health professions who have formal or informal ties to Yale.

Opposing the view that Yale University has served a very important function is an argument offered by Dahl. "Although a few individual faculty members are involved in New Haven politics—the last three Democratic aldermen from the First Ward have been young Yale faculty members—most Yale people are much less interested in the politics of New Haven than in the politics of Yale, their professional associations, the nation, or the international arena. And more of Yale's faculty and other employees live outside New Haven than in the city. Finally, although the university is one of the largest property owners in New Haven, it also happens to be far and away the largest owner of taxfree property; hence Yale officials are highly sensitive to community hostility and fearful of any action that might embroil the university in local controversy." (Dahl, *op. cit.*, p. 138.) In the view offered here, the claim of low participation by Yale people in city affairs, whatever the facts, is not critical. Nor is it so important that a high proportion of the children in Yale families attend private rather than public schools. It could even be argued that this increases the contact of their families with the economic elite. What *is* important is the presence of a major university in a small city with a fairly diverse economic elite.

6. *Ibid.*, p. 138.
7. See Lewis A. Coser, *The Functions of Social Conflict* (Glencoe, Ill.: The Free Press, 1956, pp. 16–20.
8. *Ibid.*
9. From an unpublished memorandum by Russell Murphy written in 1964. Murphy was then a Research Associate of Community Progress, Inc.
10. For an early but comprehensive description of the organizational structure of Community Progress, Inc., see Mitchell Sviridoff, *CPI: Window Dressing or a Program with Meaning?* (New Haven: Community Progress, Inc., mimeographed, November, 1963). Sviridoff is the head of New York City's newly established Human Resources Administration. Previously he was Executive Director of Community Progress, Inc. Also see Howard Hallman, "What One City Can Do," in Robert E. Will and Harold G. Vatter, *Poverty in Affluence* (New York: Harcourt, Brace, and World, 1965), pp. 248–252.
11. The basis for this better articulation of elites is presented in footnote 5.
12. Norton E. Long, "The Local Community as an Ecology of Games," *American Journal of Sociology*, LXIV (November, 1958).
13. This definition by Elmer Luchterhand is included in the *New Haven Youth Development Program* (New Haven: Community Progress, Inc., 1963) (a proposal to the President's Committee on Juvenile Delinquency and Youth Crime and a report on the planning studies), Vol. III, p. 5.
14. Richard A. Cloward and Frances F. Piven, *Low Income People and Political Process* (New York: Training Institute, Columbia University School of Social Work and Mobilization for Youth, Inc., mimeographed April, 1964), pp. 1–2.
15. Cloward and Piven define an elite strategy as one that is "carried on by an organization which is an established, recognized and regular participant in the influence structure" (*ibid.*). There is no question that in the main, demonstration projects have more appeal to professional and political elites than a social movement, which may be regarded as threatening by a political elite which holds power. This follows from another observation by Cloward that "the controversy over the involvement of the poor is precisely one of power and its redistribution,

not alone in the broader society but also in the vast field of social welfare." (See his "Testimony before Senate Select Subcommittee on Poverty," June 29, 1965, mimeographed.) In the present national antipoverty campaign the involvement of low-income people in agency policy making and program planning is a formal requirement, but the efforts so far point to participation which is more symbolic than real.

16. Cloward and Piven, *op. cit.*, p. 22.

17. See Leon Festinger, *A Theory of Cognitive Dissonance* (Evanston, Ill.: Row, Peterson, 1957). Also see A. R. Cohen, "Attitudinal Consequences of Induced Discrepancies between Cognitions and Behavior," *Public Opinion Quarterly*, XXIV (1960), pp. 297–318.

18. This is a "mutual system of placement" which began in 1955 in a plant with over 7,000 workers in Quebec, Canada. Under the system, a choice of jobs is offered to employees with physical impairments due to aging, accident, and illness. The offering of genuine choice is made possible by the gathering, with employee participation, of data on the physical demands of all jobs and, in comparable units, data on individual physical capacities. Suitable jobs are made available to individuals with impaired capacity by normal openings and by the co-operation of the work force in arranging transfers on a strictly voluntary basis. In evaluating six years of operation it was found that over 2,500 placements were made under the system, half of them involving workers with reductions of physical capacity of some severity. From all of these placements only six grievances arose requiring formal handling. See Elmer Luchterhand and Daniel Sydiaha, *Choice in Human Affairs: An Application to Aging, Accident and Illness Problems* (New Haven: College and University Press, 1966).

19. See "The Lincoln Electric Company," in John Glover and Ralph Hower, eds., *The Administrator* (Homewood, Ill.: Irwin, 1953), pp. 553–584.

20. It is important to recognize, however, that once an agency gets its sea legs it can move with greater boldness in the contests between the proponents and opponents of change. Thus Sviridoff speaks of the need for "basic social changes —changes directed at the causes of poverty and the prevention of related social problems, rather than simply administering essential social services to the victims of poverty." (Sviridoff, *op. cit.*, p. 3.)

21. This illustration was contributed by Sviridoff, in a seminar devoted to the problems of community-action agencies.

22. From a comment by August Hollingshead in a meeting of the New Haven Advisory Council on Research, April, 1965.

23. H. J. Gans offers the questionable view that because researchers in inside units "may feel hostile" toward activists, who have higher status in the agency, the former may "use research in order to find failure." ("Urban Poverty and Social Planning," this volume.)

24. Howard E. Freeman, "Conceptual Approaches to Assessing Impacts of Large-Scale Intervention Programs," *1964 Social Statistics Proceedings*, American Statistical Association, pp. 193–194.

25. See Howard L. Sheppard, "The Treatment of Unionism in 'Managerial Sociology,'" *American Sociological Review*, XIV, No. 2 (April, 1949), 310–313.

26. The representatives of this trend advocate impressionistic assessment as the main approach to evaluation. Marris uses the term *speculative insight*. (Peter Marris, *On the Evaluation of the Grey Area Projects* [New York: The Ford Foundation, mimeographed, n.d.], p. 2.) In a lengthy paper on the demonstration, Rein and Miller devote a single page to research. They disparage the efforts to study inputs and outputs and argue for participant observation "to see what is happen-

ing, to study conflicts as they develop and dissolve, to report on what actually went on in a program which affected its success or failure. And, if our research tools are not adequate to measure outputs, then we need Marris' kind of 'speculative evaluation' where a greater variety of assessments are utilized, including the trained eye and ear." (Martin Rein and S. M. Miller, *The Demonstration as a Strategy of Change* [New York: Training Institute, mimeographed, April, 1964], p. 51.)

27. See Robert K. Merton's essay "The Machine, The Worker, and the Engineer," in his *Social Theory and Social Structure* (Glencoe, Ill.: The Free Press, 1957), p. 572.

28. Mrs. Constance Baker Motley, while she held the office of Borough President of Manhattan, proposed major efforts for the social rebuilding of Harlem.

The School and the Family: Linking Organizations and External Primary Groups

EUGENE LITWAK
HENRY J. MEYER

chapter 19

Practical problems for educators converge with theoretical problems for sociologists when questions such as the following are asked: "What should be the relationship between the school and the families of its children? If some type of relationship is desirable to enhance education, how can that relationship be achieved?" The posing of these questions calls upon the sociologist to re-examine his theories about the functions of the primary group and the bureaucratic organization as well as to consider mechanisms of co-ordination between them.

The Educator's Practical Problem

A brief account of a program to increase the educational motivation and achievement of "culturally deprived" children in Detroit will illustrate how a practical problem of relating school and family arose. Like other school systems in large cities, the Detroit public schools sought to respond to increasing public concern about educational accomplishments of children from low-income families concentrated in the so-called gray areas of the city. Evidence of educational shortcoming was as striking as that of deprivation in the situations of the children in these areas. High rates of dropout, reading retardation, low performance levels on achievement tests, irregular school attendance, apathetic attitudes toward learning, problems of discipline, and other difficulties documented the conclusion that the existing program was not meeting the educational objectives of the schools.[1] As the educators analyzed the problem, they identified a complex of factors: the content and form of the curriculum, the structure and style of classroom teaching, unacknowledged variability of individual children faced with standardized methods of teaching reading and arithmetic, physical and emotional problems of some children, demoralizing economic and social conditions of some homes, and a gap between school and home often so wide as to leave them at cross purposes.

A program to effect these factors was launched in 1959 in two central city schools and extended in 1960 to seven schools when a grant from the Ford Foundation was added to allocations from the regular budget to support a demonstration project that was given the name Great Cities School Improvement Project. Four elementary schools, two junior high schools, and one high school were included. A small staff to develop a program and to give central direction was assembled, consisting of a director, an "evaluator," and, somewhat later, a reading specialist. The decision was made to limit increased costs to 10 per cent of the regular budget, and this averaged about $35,000 per school. These funds were used to make available the time of additional coaching teachers in reading and arithmetic, to provide more school social workers, and to add to each school a person who was called a "school-community agent" (or "school-community co-ordinator"). Some of the funds were allocated for new curriculum materials and for workshops of teachers to consider new classroom and teaching approaches. There were some funds, too, for "cultural enrichment" through bus trips and excursions for the children. The added funds also allowed the schools to be kept open for afterschool uses by both children and adults.

The central thrust of the program was the belief that the school and its immediate community should be brought closer together. It was believed that the complex of remedial efforts directed at the children and the modifications of teaching and curriculum would be frustrated if the families were not somehow involved. It was to be the job of the school-community agents to do this, but there was little experience to guide them. Furthermore, the project directors were uncertain about the qualifications needed to perform such a function. They proceeded pragmatically and tentatively.

Recognizing that the school-community agent would have to work within an established structure in the schools, the first ones selected were teachers with apparent capacities to make contact with parents. It soon became evident, however, that such persons were likely to be "building-bound": they worked well with the principal and the teachers, but had difficulty extending their vision beyond the school building itself. As one principal put it, "My first school-community agent got along well inside but didn't know how to work with people outside." The first school-community agents were gradually replaced where possible by persons whose experience had been in community work, such as social workers from community centers and group-work agencies. These, in turn, had difficulties adapting to the routines and regulations of the school. "My second agent," said the same principal, "is good on the outside but doesn't get along so well in the building." Nevertheless, as the project proceeded it was concluded that a community-organization orientation was preferable to a teaching orientation for the role of school-community agent.

The school-community agents began to try various approaches. Taking advantage of the availability of the building, most of them sought to establish afterschool programs for parents, usually of a recreational or quasi-educational character. Some tried to increase the activities of the parent-teacher organizations and to develop clubs for room mothers. Several began to work with groups of youths and adults in the neighborhood. Most sought to publicize the program among the local organizations, such as churches, business and labor groups, and social agencies. Their approaches were empirical ones guided by the conviction that closer contact between school and school community was desirable. Only rudimentary theory was available on which to base the rationale for the program or to provide direction for specific activities.

Even these tentative efforts were beset with difficulties. Although principals and teachers had been made conscious from experience of the relative futility of trying to teach and maintain discipline in the face of out-of-school influences in the homes and neighborhoods, they were often skeptical of attempts to "reach" parents and neighborhood groups. Furthermore, neither the work schedules of the school-community agents nor the activities they tried to stimulate fitted into the familiar organization of the school. New demands on the administrators and teachers were sometimes viewed as distractions from their established responsibilities. They were more or less accustomed to the other features of the Great Cities program; they could refer more children to the social worker, and they could identify children who needed remedial work and arrange for them to go to special classes. But increasing contacts with parents and making arrangements for adult activities in the school building constituted different demands and responsibilities. The directors of the program met regularly with the principals and periodically with the teaching staffs to interpret what they were trying to do, but such meetings did not solve the day-to-day problems. There were difficulties enough just trying to run regular school programs expected of them by the school system.

The directors of the Great Cities Project also faced the difficult problem of evaluating their program, and it was this, rather than the problems described above, that brought them to ask for assistance from sociologists. It soon became apparent that the technical problems of evaluation could not even be addressed until some of the theoretical problems had been explicitly analyzed. It was sociological theory, rather than research methodology, that turned out to be of most use.

The Sociological Problem

From a sociological viewpoint, the Great Cities School Improvement Project was attempting to change the relationship between bureaucratic organizations—the schools—on the one hand and external primary groups—families and neighborhoods—on the other hand. The body of sociological theory that deals with the linkage between these two social forms seemed most relevant. This theory is, however, only stated in most general terms. It was necessary to elaborate it in more detail and to take into account both the objectives and the experiences of the action project if it were to be useful. The interplay of theoretical issues and practical experiences will be evident in the following discussion of the development of sociological theory that ensued.

Sociologists have generally been more concerned with incompatibilities between bureaucratic organizations and primary groups than they have with their complementarities. Max Weber, emphasizing the efficiency of rational formal organization for industrial society, suggested that industrialization might well be delayed where the family system was very strong.[2] Some students of the family have implied that the transfer of traditional functions from the family to formal organizations casts doubt on the viability of the modern family.[3] Less extreme views of contemporary theorists hold that certain necessary functions, such as early socialization of the child and management of tensions of both adults and children, are best performed in the family and constitute its central contribution.[4] They argue, however, that antithetical principles of bureaucratic and family organization require that the two forms be relatively isolated from each other. Thus they point out that a nuclear family structure with a sex-linked division of labor tends to limit the number of family members who will have to bridge the worlds of family and occupation and minimize the clash between their antithetical atmospheres.

The implications of these positions for a wider theory of relations between bureaucracies and primary groups have not been explored in much detail, even with reference to family and work, which had been given most attention. As a consequence, alternative linkages have not been considered nor have specific relations between schools and families been analyzed. If the more extreme position were adopted, the family would be viewed as limiting the school's effectiveness, and it would be consistent to propose that a total institution, such as the boarding school, would best achieve educational goals. If the less extreme position were adopted, the family would be seen as necessary in the educational process for its socialization and tension management functions, but contact between school and family should be kept to a bare minimum with the child as the main point of contact.

If we turn our attention to educational practitioners, we find an interesting parallel to this theoretical position. Not only in France and Germany but in the United States as well, many educators have adopted what we have called the "locked-door policy." [5] It takes its name from the fact that some school principals have their doors locked during school hours, symbolizing their more general view that the community is extraneous if not damaging to the education of the child. The family should be kept out of the school building. In its more modern form this view takes cognizance of the problem of motivation, but suggests that in most cases it can be handled by the teachers or, in extreme situations, by trained experts: school social workers, psychologists, counselors, nurses, and so forth. Such a view, consistent with the extreme theoretical position, would visualize something like the British public school as ideal. However, few educators go this far. More commonly their view resembles the less extreme theoretical position. The family has essential responsibilities that cannot be replaced by trained professionals, but families should be kept separated from the school with communication taking place between them through the child, often carrying written messages, or through formal authority such as truant officers.

An alternative viewpoint which seems to be gaining increasing support among educators is what we have called the "open-door policy." In essence, this position holds that maximum education will occur where the families and schools are brought closer together, where families are drawn into the schools and schools taken into the community. It is significant that the implicit sociological theory of this position—that maximum goal achievement in contemporary society occurs where bureaucratic organizations and families are intertwined—is rarely expressed in sociological analysis of industrial society. Educators holding this view argue that motivation is central in educating the child, and the best way to motivate him is by relating the teaching situation to his ongoing life experiences, which are always partially unique because dependent on his particular family situation. Therefore, it is necessary to take learning experiences into the community and to bring the community into the school if one is to achieve maximum motivation in the child.

Many recent experimental approaches to educating "culturally deprived" children have assumed this position. It is often implicit in the idea of the "community school" advocated by many educators.[6] One school has gone so far as to consider installing washing machines and cooking facilities which families may use, because they feel that locating such family activities in the school can have a bearing on the child's education. The Great Cities Project in Detroit does not go so far, but its underlying viewpoint is essentially that of the "open-door policy."

It is important to recognize that some schools are seeking closer contact with families precisely because they want to increase the efficiency of education. Furthermore, if we observe practitioners in other institutional areas—such as business, the army, fund raising, control of delinquency—we find their procedures reflecting a theory of linkage that closely parallels the "open-door policy" of the educator.[7] Moreover, sociologists who are working very closely with practitioners, as in studies of voting and consumer behavior, have reached a similar conclusion, although they usually do not generalize its implication for linkage theory.[8]

If one takes seriously such responses of practitioners to the empirical world, modification of the earlier theory of bureaucracy–primary-group relations is necessary. The "open door" viewpoint suggests that the earlier positions do not conform to experience. The primary group is thought to increase effectiveness in achievement of organizational goals and the family to perform more functions than basic socialization and tension management. Among those with practical organizational problems to solve there seems to be as great a tendency to bring primary group and bureaucracy together as there is to keep them apart.

Reconsideration of the Functions of Primary Groups and Bureaucracies

In the face of practitioner experience, it becomes necessary to reopen the theoretical inquiry into the alternative functions of primary groups and bureaucratic organizations.

One lead into the problem may be taken from students of voting and consumer behavior who have tried to account for findings that show the major influence of face-to-face contact. They suggest that its effectiveness is related to the flexibility and rapid reaction of face-to-face communication as compared to that directed through mass media from formal organizations.[9] But speed and flexibility do not seem to be intrinsic advantages that primary groups have over formal organizations. Thus a surgeon in a hospital has many more alternatives and is capable of speedier reaction to heart failure than the wife of the victim. And fire departments have wider options to deal with a burning house than neighbors do. More abstractly, Katz and Lazarsfeld have suggested that the potency of primary-group relations rests on their capacity to influence behavior through normative and instrumental pressures.[10] They do not, however, systematically compare these capacities with those of formal organizations. A police force and an army have instrumental power, and large-scale organizations are capable of creating and enforcing norms. Further analysis is required of the central issue raised here: under what conditions are primary groups more effective than bureaucratic organizations?

We would approach the issue by noting those dimensions of organization that define the respective structures. As an ideal type, primary-group structure has been described in terms of the following dimensions: face-to-face contact, diffuse, noninstrumental, and relatively permanent relations.[11] One ideal-type bureaucracy has been described in terms of these dimensions: hierarchy of authority, use of rules to guide behavior, impersonal social relations, a priori definition of duties and privileges, separation of policy and administrative decisions, use of specialists, and the appointment and advancement of personnel on the basis of merit, that is, their competence to accomplish the tasks of the organization.[12] We shall use this simplified formulation of Weber's analysis because it highlights the points at issue. More contemporary theories of bureaucracy are also consistent with the approach developed later in this chapter.

If the dimensions of such a Weberian bureaucracy are examined, its claim for efficiency rests primarily on the fact that the organization is designed to bring the maximum amount of knowledge and experience to bear on any task. Specialization and appointment on the basis of knowledge are the chief means for insuring maximum knowledge and experience. To protect against favoritism or the introduction of personal rather

than organizational goals, policy is separated from administrative decision, duties and privileges are defined in advance, and relations are deper-
sonalized. Finally, in order to insure that specialists and trained experts
are co-ordinated (necessary where there is a large organization), rules are
developed for standardized tasks and a hierarchy of authority is used to
decide when rules have not been set.

By contrast, the primary group provides no support for the trained expert. Admission to the primary group is not by merit, but by birth or by
personal affection, and as such is relatively permanent. The group is not
task-limited, but encompasses many interests of its membership (diffused
relations). It does not have sufficient size (with face-to-face contact) to
develop specialists within its boundaries, but defines roles only generally.

It seems quite clear that the structure of the bureaucratic organization
serves to support and encourage the trained expert, whereas the primary
group tends to do the opposite. Therefore to answer the question "Under
what circumstances are primary groups more effective than formal organizations?" we must seek to answer a prior question, "Under what circumstances are trained experts of little use in achievement of goals?" For it is
in exactly the areas where the trained expert is of little use that the primary groups may be more efficient in goal achievement than the bureaucratic organization.

There are at least three classes of tasks for which there is no substantial
advantage in using a trained expert. First, and most obvious, are those
tasks where the knowledge required is so simple that everyone is expert
enough to perform it. Thus, pulling a child out of the path of an automobile requires no special training beyond that which the average person can
readily learn. Dressing a child, feeding him, insuring that he is in bed at a
certain time, seeing that he is studying rather than at the show, having
him up in time for school, seeing that he has eaten, has dressed appropriately for the given weather, and so forth, are all tasks which the average
parent can learn to do satisfactorily without special training. Little would
be gained by having professional experts do these jobs.

A second class of tasks comprises those that fall at the opposite extreme:
problems for which we have very limited knowledge. The advantage in
having the advice of an expert is greatly diminished if in fact the state of
knowledge is such that his advice is not clearly superior to that of an
untrained person. There are many tasks and decisions to which the expert
cannot bring sufficiently definitive knowledge to guide action. For example, consider the following: how to carry out parental socialization functions that lead to the internalization of achievement orientation in children, the management of marital relations to ease tensions, the assessment
of which of two candidates would make the better president, the decision
to encourage nuclear disarmament, and so forth. These are not only in-
credibly complex problems involving many inadequately specified vari-

ables; they also represent problems in which expert opinions may conflict. Under such circumstances the function of the expert would seem to depend more on attribution of legitimacy to his role than on superior knowledge. Therefore, when faced with such problems, persons often seem satisfied to rely on the advice of trusted nonexperts. This is not to deny a function for experts in such areas—a function whose characteristics have been only partially explored [13]—but it is to suggest that experts do not have a clear and obvious utility for this class of tasks.

A third class of tasks which gain little from the use of trained experts consists of those involving essentially idiosyncratic events. Sometimes events are so unique to a given time or a given person that there is no opportunity to train an expert or it would be too expensive to train one. Thus, since earthquakes occur rarely and at unpredictable places, it is economically and socially prohibitive to train experts who specialize in taking care of consequences of earthquakes. Likewise, if an event may happen to a given individual, but it is difficult to say when it will happen, it becomes prohibitive to assign experts to that individual. In addition, there are aspects of the role behavior of participants in work, educational, leisure, religious, and all other social activities that are idiosyncratic; socialization into roles is never perfect. Although the more standardized forms of role behavior may benefit from expert assistance, the nonstandardized are unlikely to do so. In particular, since they are largely internalized, the motivational aspects of role behavior tend to have more idiosyncratic components and fewer known regularities about which expertness can be developed.

To refer to all three classes of tasks, or behavioral situations, where trained expertise may be of limited advantage (knowledge required too simple, knowledge too limited, or behavior idiosyncratic), we use the term *nonuniform events*. If our theoretical analysis is correct, the availability of the trained expert in the bureaucratic organization gives it no advantage over the primary group in dealing with nonuniform events.

Furthermore, there appear to be actual disadvantages for bureaucracies when faced with nonuniform events. Larger numbers of persons and long chains of communication become impediments in contrast to immediate, face-to-face communication among the smaller number of the primary group. We are not saying that the primary group can act faster or with more flexibility than the formal organization *in general*, but only that it can do so when dealing with nonuniform events. Moreover, there is some evidence that specialists tend to develop commitment to the procedures of their specialties, so that specialization may actually reduce flexibility.[14] As critics of Weber's view of bureaucratic efficiency have pointed out, the use of rules in idiosyncratic situations tends to inhibit the solution of organizational problems or leads to inappropriate decisions since a new rule must be developed for every such situation, or a decision on it must be obtained at higher levels of the hierarchy, or an existing but not applicable rule must be applied.[15] There is also some evidence that internalization of organizational goals that may direct even idiosyncratic behavior toward common ends occurs more readily among persons in reciprocal affective interaction.[16] The emphasis on impersonal relations and organizationally evaluated performance in bureaucratic organizations might well impede such internalization of goals. The possible difficulties we have been discussing are usually noted in analyses of the functions of primary groups, or "informal organization," *within* bureaucracies,[17] but they are equally evident when considering functions of external primary groups for organizational effectiveness with nonuniform events.

In sum, we suggest that nonuniform events present problems for which the expertise that especially characterizes the bureaucratic organization is not useful or is actually disadvantageous and that the characteristics of the primary group might provide a better organizational base for goal achievement under such conditions. This position is put forth as a theoretical conclusion; we do not argue that other factors may not play a part in determining which organizational form will be considered most efficient for some social objective. A high value might be placed on a given problem and trained experts in organizations called on to deal with it, even if their demonstrable effectiveness is little better than that of nonexpert primary-group members. Although the evidence suggests that the psychotherapist achieves little more success in treating the mentally ill than the untrained person, our society appears willing to support bureaucratic organizations for this margin of efficiency. Furthermore, long-run, rather than immediate, expectations may encourage society to believe that research or more intensive development of expertise will finally justify the use of bureaucratic forms. Or, lacking success in meeting a problem through primary-group forms, the society may treat the *effects* of nonuniform events as sufficiently standardized (as in the case of the disruptive effects of the mentally ill) to accept bureaucratic forms (mental hospitals, for instance) as more effective. We would note, however, that where such factors encourage the development of bureaucratic organizations to deal with nonuniform events, the necessity for primary-group influences will condition the form of the organization.[18] Thus some mental hospitals, correctional institutions, large research institutes, universities, and schools often appear to exhibit both bureaucratic and primary-group characteristics in their structures and have been distinguished from other formal organizations by a special designation.[19] We would suggest that some of the differences between contemporary organizational theory and that of Weber might be understood in the light of the discussion above.

If we accept the conclusion that primary groups are more effective in nonuniform areas and formal organizations more effective in uniform areas, can we distinguish in fact between nonuniform and uniform social tasks? We would answer that all social tasks have both uniform and non-uniform aspects. In the first place, insofar as science and technology can be brought to bear, behaviors become predictable and hence subject to treatment as uniform; nonuniformity appears to be reduced, although not eliminated. Second, social interaction and imperfect role socialization inevitably seem to yield some nonuniformity. Finally, technological innovations and demographic factors seem for our society to present continuing sources of unanticipated circumstances. For reasons such as these we argue that most areas of social endeavor must take account of both uniform and nonuniform tasks and therefore will be most effectively carried on when both bureaucratic and primary-group organizational forms are involved. This is not to say that at any time the balance between uniform and nonuniform aspects of a given social task may not change. It is only to say that in principle both aspects will be involved and both must, in the achievement of most social objectives, be considered.

The Policy Paradox

If the foregoing reasoning is used as a guide to a policy to govern a program of school-community relations, such as that of the Great Cities Project, it would seem to lead to contradictory implications:

1. Families and schools must work closely together to achieve educational goals.
2. Families and schools must be kept separated since their basic organizational principles are antithetical.

Nothing in our analysis has challenged the observation that primary groups and formal organizations have antithetical atmospheres. On the contrary, their very difference in form of social relations accounts for the differential efficiency of each when dealing with uniform and nonuniform tasks.

The paradox can be resolved if we accept both statements as simultaneously true: educational objectives will be relatively limited both by keeping schools too far apart from families and by bringing them too close together. The optimal solution is therefore some midpoint where limiting effects are minimized and complementary contributions of both organizational forms are maximized. We have given the name "balance theory of co-ordination" to this theoretical viewpoint. Such a linkage theory of relations between bureaucratic organizations and primary groups is proposed as an alternative to theories which view relations between these forms as conflicting.[20]

Mechanisms of Co-ordination between Bureaucratic Organizations and External Primary Groups: An Empirical Typology

This theoretical analysis has led us to a basis on which a program to alter school-community relations can be formulated. Such a program should seek a complementary balance. Therefore, it must look for linking mechanisms of two types: (1) those that can increase the "social distance" without destroying communication necessary for co-ordination and (2) those that can decrease the "social distance" without the destructive consequences of mutual interference. What procedures might be followed to bring families closer, but not too close, to the schools?

There has been little attention in sociological theory to types of linking mechanisms, but social practitioners have devised many types from the empirical necessities they have faced. The implicit theories underlying such mechanisms are, indeed, in advance of stated theories. From examination of practitioners' writings we have distinguished seven linking mechanisms that seem to account for most of the types in use. No claim can be made that these types are mutually exclusive or exhaustive. A brief description of each of these empirically observed types follows.

1. *Detached-worker approach.* In this procedure professionals from the bureaucratic organization go into the "home" of the primary group and develop an informal relationship with the family they seek to convert to organizational goals. Among practitioners the most successful use of this procedure has probably been the county agent of the agricultural extension services. Its most dramatic use in the urban environment has probably been by social workers who attach themselves to delinquent "street gangs." [21] A version of this approach has been used in the Detroit schools by some school-community agents working more often with families than with gangs.

2. *Opinion-leader approach.* In this approach the organization communicates with the community through the indigenous leaders. The conceptual elaboration of this approach has been most clearly stated in the fields of consumer and political behavior.[22] Earlier, Shaw and McKay used such a procedure as a key element in their delinquency-control programs.[23] In private fund raising this is frequently a prime technique. In Detroit, both school principals and school-community agents often make efforts to reach "key people" in their school districts.

3. *Settlement-house approach* is one where physical facilities and professional personnel are provided in geographical proximity to the potential clientele. The name is borrowed from social work, but we use it here in a

more restricted sense. Social agencies occasionally locate their services in "store-front centers." Branch libraries, neighborhood clinics of health departments, local political party offices, and so forth, which bring services directly into the neighborhood, are all making use of a settlement-house approach. Schoolmen sometimes use the term *lighted school* to designate a type of settlement-house program. A lighted school is one kept open after school hours so that adults and children in the community can make use of the physical facilities and special programs set up for their use.[24] This approach is a major part of the experimental programs of school systems in a number of cities, including Detroit.

4. *Auxiliary voluntary association approach.* An auxiliary voluntary association through which the organization communicates with the community may be established. Among schools, the P.T.A. and homeroom mothers' clubs are examples of this approach. Hospital service groups, volunteer fund-raising organizations for charitable agencies, alumni associations of universities, military officers' associations, act in this capacity as well. These are all associations attached to organizations, not independent voluntary associations.

5. *Common-messenger approach* takes advantage of individuals who are members of the bureaucratic organization and the family system at the same time. Because he occupies this dual position, the individual becomes a communication link between the two social systems. The child most obviously acts in this capacity for the school. The breadwinner linking family and occupational structure, as noted by Parsons, is a common messenger. Since all organizations are linked in this fashion to families, it is not surprising that this is a frequent channel of communication. It is surprising, however, that common messengers are not more often deliberately created by organizations. Parents brought into school to perform various services and teacher-aid tasks become available as common messengers.

6. *Mass-media approach* is one where the organization resorts to newspapers, printed notices, mass mailings, and so forth to communicate with families. Of all mechanisms, the problems and theories of mass media have been most thoroughly studied by sociologists and probably most widely used by practitioners. Some of the basic principles of communication that have emerged from the study of mass media take on new meaning when applied to other linking mechanisms.

7. *Formal-authority approach.* Some organizations have a legal or a strong normative basis for communication and often for enforcement of their purposes. The juvenile court can compel the presence of parents in a court procedure. Schools may use the formal authority of the truant officer to visit the home of a family and demand compliance with compulsory attendance laws. It is the capacity to communicate through this mechanism, rather than coercive power of the organization, that we wish to emphasize here.

These mechanisms have been described in terms of communication *from* the organization *to* the family or the neighborhood. Communications initiated from the primary group toward the bureaucratic organization may use some, but not all, of these mechanisms; other mechanisms may be identified as operative in this direction, but they will not be described here.[25]

Mechanisms of Co-ordination between Bureaucratic Organizations and External Primary Groups: A Tentative Theoretical Analysis

According to our earlier analysis, a balance at some point between isolation and intimacy would constitute the relation between school and family most likely to optimize educational objectives. Therefore, linking mechanisms must be assessed with reference to their capacities to effect this balance by increasing social distance when school and family are too close, decreasing it when they are too far apart, and maintaining it when they are in balance. Determination that an optimum balance has been achieved is a difficult theoretical and empirical problem that we shall not deal with here.[26] Lack of balance, however, has not been difficult to observe.

For example, some middle-class families with high educational or professional backgrounds in some school districts, often suburban, place such value on academic performance that their children are under constant pressure and exceptional demands are made on their schools. Such parents may even seek to influence what the school does with respect to grading, curriculum, type of academic assignments, and other functions which are presumably the responsibility of competent professional educators to whom the community has delegated the job of education. Oversensitized to the demands of such parents, teachers may make judgments in terms of parental pressures, rather than educationally appropriate standards. Although the children may do very well in school, the quality of their education may suffer by the confusion of family and school criteria. In our terms, family and school are too close for optimum educational goals to be achieved.

The opposite situation is more common, particularly in areas of low-income and transient families where parents may have little educational background. Whatever their verbalized opinions may be, some parents see little advantage in education, are suspicious of the school, fail to see a relation between home conditions and school success, and generally avoid contact with the school. They do not attend P.T.A. meetings and rarely see principal or teacher unless a problem with their child becomes severe enough for them to be sent for. This gap between school and family may be further increased because cultural values may differ from those of the teachers, who may add further distance by inadvertent middle-class bias.[27]

From the viewpoint of balance theory, the problem is to adopt mechanisms to increase distance in the first example and to decrease it in the second.

Sociologists working in the area of communication have particularly been concerned with bridging social distances, since the practical problems of political and consumer influence usually entail hostile or indifferent target groups. Four problems delineated by such students are particularly pertinent to our interests: (1) the problem of selective listening, (2) the problem of selective interpretation, (3) the problem of sufficient feedback when complex messages are communicated, and (4) the problem of scope, that is, extensiveness of numbers reached.[28] Although there are other problems in communication theory not here included, these seem to be especially relevant to school-family communication, and it was with them in mind that we developed the following general criteria for assessing the empirical linking mechanisms:

1. *Organizational initiative.* Communication studies have pointed out that an unsympathetic audience frequently cannot be reached because it will not listen to the message in the first place. Parents whose children are seen by the school to be most in need of help are frequently the least likely to come to P.T.A. meetings or to pay attention to school suggestions. In political campaigns it has been noted that people rarely listen to the opposition candidate.[29] In order to overcome this problem of selective listening, the communication procedures or linking mechanisms must permit the organization to take the initiative in reaching families who disagree with organizational goals, rather than leave the initiative to the family. If we examine the various linking procedures we see that they differ in the amount of initiative they permit the organization. Thus the detached-worker approach and the formal-authority approach permit the organization considerable initiative in confronting the family. By contrast, the mass-media and the voluntary-association approaches assume that the family will take the initiative. As a consequence the former are expected to be better procedures for communicating where there is a great social distance and selective listening is likely to muffle communication, whereas the latter should serve well for communicating across narrow social distances where selective listening and family initiative favor communication.

2. *Intensity.* Even where people can be reached, they may selectively absorb or selectively forget parts of the communication so that it has little effect on their views.[30] Thus the principal might bring a parent into the school under threat of formal authority and force him to listen, but the parent might nevertheless misinterpret the principal's statements or forget those parts of the message with which he disagrees. Katz and Lazarsfeld

suggest that where the individual is encased in a primary-group atmosphere which is hostile to the views of the communicator, it is virtually impossible to produce change.[31] We would argue that in order to reach very distant families—those organized in primary groups and holding views antithetical to education—it is necessary to establish a primary-group type of relation with them. Only after the communicator has been accepted as a trusted member of the group can the school's views make an impact on the family.

Of the mechanisms noted, the detached-worker, the opinion-leader, and the settlement-house approaches permit this type of relation to develop most fully. The opinion-leader approach carries the most intensity because it makes use of existing primary-group relations. The detached-worker and settlement-house approaches develop intensity because the professional roles involve a mandate to develop friendly face-to-face contact. By contrast, formal authority is thought by many to be antithetical to the development of primary-group intensity. The mass-media approach can be expected to achieve hardly any primary-group intensity. Mechanisms high in intensity should be more effective for closing social distance and those low in intensity for increasing or maintaining social distance.

3. *Focused expertise.* Messages, or contents of communications, can vary in complexity. In general, we would hypothesize that the more complex the message, the greater the need to provide feedback and flexible response if the message is to be communicated. Schools often need to communicate quite complex information, for example, about new approaches to mathematics or reading or about problems of adaptation for rural migrants to the urban community. Other messages are essentially simple, such as giving dates of meetings, school openings and closings, the child's specific academic standing, and so forth. Attempting to change values and perceptions of socially distant families is likely to involve complex communications. The detached-worker, settlement-house, and formal-authority approaches are clearly most likely to provide the informed, flexible responses to face-to-face feedback which we call "focused expertise." In general, we suggest that linking procedures permitting considerable focused expertise will be more useful than those with limited focused expertise for communicating when distance is great and for narrowing the distance.

4. *Scope.* Although it is not necessarily related directly to social distance between school and families, the capacity of a mechanism of co-ordination to reach many or few families with given resources will always have to be considered as a practical matter. Other things being equal, we should expect the procedure with the greatest scope to be preferred as a matter of economy. With its almost one-to-one relationship, the detached-worker approach is obviously very limited in scope, whereas the mass-media approach has very wide scope.

Recognizing this analysis of dimensions as both tentative and incomplete, it is useful nevertheless to summarize our assessment of the mechanisms of co-ordination empirically identified. Table 19–1 assigns an arbitrary position along each dimension for the seven mechanisms. These are

T A B L E   1 9 – 1.   *Dimensions of Communication*

MECHANISMS	INITIATIVE	INTENSITY	FOCUSED EXPERTISE	SCOPE
Detached worker	highest	high	highest	lowest
Opinion leader	low	highest	low	moderate
Settlement house	moderate to low	high to moderate	high	moderate
Voluntary association	lowest	moderate to low	moderate	high
Common messenger	moderate	moderate to low	lowest	highest
Mass media	moderate to low	lowest	lowest	highest
Formal authority	high	high to low	high to low	moderate

initial estimates of how each linking mechanism might fall on some strategic dimensions of communication. Other dimensions of communication may also be relevant, and aspects of linking mechanisms other than communication may need to be considered. This analysis is intended only to suggest a general strategy for approaching the problem of co-ordinating mechanisms between bureaucratic organizations and external primary groups.

Balance Theory and Linking Mechanisms: Some Practical and Theoretical Implications

When balance theory and analysis of co-ordinating mechanisms are combined, some practical problems for the educator engaged in a program of school-community relations are clarified. If initiative, intensity, and focused expertise are necessary to communicate in order to achieve congruent goals and perceptions and hence, in this sense, to close social distance, the detached-worker approach would appear to be most useful. Its chief limitation is with respect to scope. If communication is intended to increase or maintain distance, mechanisms moderate or low in initiative, intensity, and focused expertise but high in scope would be preferred, such as voluntary-association, common-messenger, or mass-media approaches.

Furthermore, the analysis suggests that mechanisms should be used in sequence. Thus, if the educator wants to move a family that is very distant closer to the school, he might well start with the detached-worker approach and, as this succeeds, follow with the settlement-house approach, finally making use of voluntary-association and common-messenger approaches to sustain the distance he deems desirable. Deliberate programming of school-community relations is often neglected in favor of indiscriminate efforts trying all approaches at once or intensive efforts through one approach, such as the P.T.A. But families change in their relations with the school; also, school populations change with residential succession of families. Many urban school districts contain mixed populations requiring different strategies for each group in a program of school-community relations.

Whatever underlying theory of school-community relations an administrator adopts, he has some basis for deciding among alternative approaches if the direction of the analysis here presented is valid. Considerable research will be required before the policy implications of balance theory and of co-ordinating mechanisms can be adequately tested. We cannot assert that a balance theory, rather than a "closed door" or an "open door" policy, will be most effective. At the present state of knowledge available to us, we believe a policy based on balance theory to be most promising, but as a sociological theory this belief must be shaped as a question rather than an assertion. Experimentation is called for to determine which theory of relationships between bureaucratic organizations and external groups is valid, as well as to test out the efficacy of various linking mechanisms.

The analysis we have presented offers initial suggestions to the school administrator, however, whatever his underlying policy conclusion. From a "locked door" position, he would do well to separate his school and its families by relying on minimal communication through mass-media and common-messenger approaches and the use of formal authority under special circumstances. If an "open door" position is taken, the use of detached-worker and settlement-house approaches, coupled with the use of opinion leaders when the community is essentially friendly, seems promising. The balance-theory position calls for differential use of all mechanisms of co-ordination, depending on assessments of the existing state of relations between school and families. All the suggestions made here constitute, from the viewpoint of the sociologist, alternative hypotheses about linkage systems and dependent variables such as educational achievement and satisfactory school behavior.

Because of limitations of space we have not explored many of the issues relevant to both policy maker and theorist. For the educator, each theory suggests that principals should have information enough to differentially assess neighborhood situations and family types so as to select and sequence linkage procedures accordingly. Just as important, the educational policy maker must be aware that the selective use of a program of linkages requires awareness of the administrative structures from which these linkages can operate. Thus a detached-worker approach is not very consistent with a Weberian, rationalistic bureaucracy, but it is consistent with a human-relations bureaucracy. On the other hand, formal authority might not be consistent with a human-relations structure, but might be consistent with the more rationalistic structure. The degree to which the administrative style of the principal is congenial with various linking mechanisms is a practical issue which also presents important theoretical problems.[32] Likewise, many practical and theoretical issues arise with respect to sequencing and patterning among the various mechanisms of co-ordination.[33]

Each practical and theoretical issue represents a problem for which much careful research is required. Nevertheless, the application and development of sociological theory of linking mechanisms between bureaucratic structures and external primary groups can introduce some clarification into the complex problem of school-community relations.

REFERENCES

1. Carl L. Marburger, "Considerations for Educational Planning," in A. Harry Passow, ed., *Education in Depressed Areas* (New York: Teachers College, Columbia University, 1964), pp. 303–321.
2. Max Weber, *The Theory of Social and Economic Organization,* translated by A. M. Henderson and Talcott Parsons (New York: Oxford University Press, 1947), pp. 354–358; Talcott Parsons, *The Structure of Social Action* (Glencoe, Ill.: The Free Press, 1949), pp. 542–552.
3. William F. Ogburn, "The Changing Functions of the Family," in Robert F. Winch and Robert McGinnis, eds., *Selected Readings in Marriage and the Family* (New York: Henry Holt, 1953), pp. 74–76; Joseph A. Schumpeter, *Capitalism, Socialism, and Democracy,* 2nd ed. (New York: Harper, 1947), p. 157; Louis Wirth, "Urbanism as a Way of Life," in Paul K. Hatt and Albert J. Reiss, Jr., eds., *Cities and Society: The Revised Reader in Urban Sociology* (Glencoe, Ill.: The Free Press, 1957), pp. 593–594.
4. Talcott Parsons, "The Social Structure of the Family," in Ruth N. Anshen, ed., *The Family: Its Function and Destiny,* rev. ed. (New York: Harper, 1959), pp. 260–263; George A. Theodorson, "Acceptance of Industrialization and Its Attendant Consequences for the Social Patterns of Non-Western Societies," *American Sociological Review,* XVIII (October, 1953), 480–481.
5. Eugene Litwak and Henry J. Meyer, "Administrative Styles and Community Linkages of Public Schools: Some Theoretical Consideration," in Albert J. Reiss, Jr., ed., *Schools in a Changing Society* (New York: The Free Press of Glencoe, 1965), pp. 49–56.
6. Henry Saltzman, "The Community School in the Urban Setting," in Passow, *op. cit.,* pp. 322–331.

7. With regard to the business world, there is evidence pro and con that large-scale bureaucratic companies are interested in local community and family linkages. The following are some articles supporting the view of strong linkages: Irving A. Fowler, "Local Industrial Structures, Economic Power, and Community Welfare," *Social Problems*, VI (Summer, 1958), 41–51; R. J. Pellegrin and C. H. Coates, "Absentee Owned Corporations and Community Power Structure," *American Journal of Sociology*, LXI (March, 1956), 413–419; William H. Whyte, Jr., *The Organization Man* (New York: Simon and Schuster, 1956), pp. 295–296. For a summary of literature and a systematic consideration of theoretical issues see Eugene Litwak, "Voluntary Associations and Neighborhood Cohesion," *American Sociological Review*, XXVI (April, 1961), 258–262. In the army, frequently cited as the model bureaucracy, there are very explicit ties to the families. During wartime, proper family relations are directly linked to fighting morale. It was pointed out by Edward Shils and Morris Janowitz, "Cohesion and Disintegration in the Wehrmacht in World War II," *Public Opinion Quarterly*, XII (1948), 280–315, that referrals to family danger were one of the few appeals that made the German soldier susceptible to surrender. In peacetime, the elaborate and costly expenditure which the army makes to keep the dependents close to the soldier is well known. In 1963, when the United States sought to redress an unfavorable flow of gold by ordering dependents back to the States, the government had to rescind the order because of its obvious impact on the recruitment of troops and the maintenance of troop morale.

One of the great advances in the area of private welfare fund raising has been the attempt to supplement professional fund raising by using the local community volunteer. Now funds in a given neighborhood are generally solicited by a neighbor or friend. Similarly, one of the major innovations in delinquency control in the last twenty years has been the emphasis on the milieu from which the delinquent comes. For many delinquents nothing lasting can be done if their gang, family, and local neighbors have not been altered as well. The development of the detached gang worker is the best idea of this movement as well as the agency's explicit link to the community.

8. The revival of local organizing efforts of political parties—"volunteers," neighborhood units, clubs, and so on—seems evident, expressing in this fashion what an early study of political behavior documented: that to understand how people vote it is necessary to take account of family and friends. See Paul F. Lazarsfeld, Bernard Berelson, and Hazel Gaudet, *The People's Choice* (New York: Duell, Sloan, and Pearce, 1944), pp. 153 ff. S. Martin Lipset, Martin Trow, and James Coleman, *Union Democracy* (Glencoe, Ill.: The Free Press, 1956), pp. 67–83, suggest more generally that governmental systems when under stress will seek to organize and control primary-type organizations, and they mention the Nazis' development of block clubs during World War II as a case in point.

9. Lazarsfeld, Berelson, and Gaudet, *op. cit.*, pp. 153 ff.; Carl I. Hovland, "Effects of the Mass Media of Communication," in Gardner Lindzey, ed., *Handbook of Social Psychology* (Cambridge, Mass.: Addison-Wesley, 1954), II, 1083–1084.

10. Elihu Katz and Paul F. Lazarsfeld, *Personal Influence* (Glencoe, Ill.: The Free Press, 1955), pp. 43–64.

11. Charles H. Cooley in Paul Hare, Edgar F. Borgatta, and Robert F. Bales, eds., *Small Groups* (New York: Knopf, 1955), pp. 15–20.

12. H. H. Gerth and C. Wright Mills, trans. and eds., *From Max Weber: Essays in Sociology* (New York: Oxford University Press, 1946), pp. 196–203.

13. The development of experts might be supported, even when they are no better than the nonexpert, on the grounds that in the long run they will be able to do

better. This hope is often fulfilled, as evidenced by the success of some research efforts. However, this should not obscure the issue that for any decision that has to be made at a given time the expert may not have the adequate answers. An excellent illustration of this point is given by Edward C. Banfield, *Political Influence* (Glencoe, Ill.: The Free Press, 1961), pp. 33–36. In attempting to decide where a hospital should be built, there were sharp disagreements by experts on whether new staff could be attracted to a given location and, if it could be attracted, what the quality of the staff would be. Furthermore, to gather the information necessary to answer these questions would be very expensive and unlikely to be conclusive because of insufficient knowledge with which to determine with exactitude what attracts doctors and nurses to a given hospital and what surrounding circumstances are necessary for excellence in practice. Harold L. Wilensky, *Intellectuals in Labor Unions* (Glencoe, Ill.: The Free Press, 1956), pp. 187 ff., has pointed out some of the circumstances when experts may be most profitably used.

14. Harold L. Wilensky and Charles N. Lebeaux, *Industrial Society and Social Welfare* (New York: Russell Sage Foundation, 1958), pp. 250–257, point out some further defects of premature specialization, such as the problem of communication between specialists and the development of gaps which are handled by no one at all because they do not fit within the prior job definitions.

15. Peter M. Blau, *Bureaucracy in Modern Society* (New York: Random House, 1956), pp. 58, 62; Robert K. Merton, "Bureaucratic Structure and Personality," in R. K. Merton, A. P. Gray, B. Hockey, and H. C. Selvin, eds., *Reader in Bureaucracy* (Glencoe, Ill.: The Free Press, 1952), p. 364; Philip Selznick, "A Theory of Organizational Commitment," in *ibid.*, pp. 194–202.

16. Donald I. Warren, "Modes of Conformity and the Character of Formal and Informal Organization Structure: A Comparative Study of Public Schools," unpublished Ph.D. dissertation for the University of Michigan, December, 1964, pp. 122–151.

17. Peter Blau and W. Richard Scott, *Formal Organizations* (San Francisco: Chandler, 1962), pp. 87–115.

18. Eugene Litwak, "Models of Bureaucracy Which Permit Conflict," *American Journal of Sociology*, LXVII, No. 2 (September, 1961), 177–184.

19. *Ibid.*, pp. 181–184.

20. This "balance theory of co-ordination" is elaborated in another paper by Litwak and Meyer, "A Balance Theory of Coordination between Bureaucratic Organizations and Community Primary Groups," *Administrative Science Quarterly*, XI, No. 1 (June, 1966), 31–58. Our use of the term "balance" should not be confused with the use of psychological theories of balance. These are restricted to cognitive states. One psychological theory of balance which ours possibly overlaps is J. Alan Winter's concept of strategic balance: *Cognitive Balance, Strategic Balance and Discomfort in a Competitive Situation* (Pre-print Center for Conflict Resolution, The University of Michigan, 1963). Most psychological theories of balance do not deal with the concept of balance where the individual might seek to maximize two or more equally desirable events.

21. For a description of such a program, see P. L. Crawford, D. I. Malamud, and J. R. Dumpson, *Working with Teenage Gangs* (New York: Welfare Council of New York City, 1950). A detailed consideration of this as well as the following linking mechanisms has been made in Eugene Litwak, Cheryl Mickelson, Henry J. Meyer, *et al.*, *Theory and Practice of Local School-Community Relations* (mimeographed, December, 1964).

22. Katz and Lazarsfeld, *op. cit.*, pp. 1–100.

23. S. Kobrin, "The Chicago Area Project: A Twenty-Five-Year Assessment," *Annals of the American Academy of Political and Social Sciences,* CCCXXII (1959), 19–37.

24. Another term which is commonly used to express the same settlement-house idea is "store-front" services. Thus store-front libraries, store-front welfare services, and so forth are generally embraced in our concept of settlement house.

25. We do not believe that the use of these mechanisms is the same when initiation is from the primary group rather than the formal organization. There are at least two major sources of difference. First, there is a matter of resources. Most formal organizations have resources to employ any or all of these linking mechanisms. By contrast, few primary groups can employ detached workers or settlement houses. Because of this differential we would suggest that when the primary group initiates linkage procedures, they must generally start with voluntary associations in order to provide a resource base for the other mechanisms.

    A second consideration is that formal organizations are more likely than primary groups to be sensitive to public pressure because, in general, they are more exposed and need public support to survive. As a consequence, they can frequently be reached by mechanisms with low initiative like the mass media. Efforts to change the community stance of formal organizations are likely to use different mechanisms, and in different sequences, than organizations seeking to change primary groups.

    Such considerations do not exhaust possible factors in the asymmetry of the linking mechanisms, but only point out some bases for it. For a more detailed discussion, see Litwak, Mickelson, Meyer, *et al., op. cit.,* Chapter 8.

26. We approach this problem theoretically by analyzing the extent of uniformity and nonuniformity characterizing specified "educational tasks" and hence seek to develop criteria for determining relative contributions of primary-group relations and of organizational expertise necessary for task accomplishment. An empirical approach would seek to determine correlates of some dependent variable (such as high educational achievement) with measures of "social distance" between school and family. An experimental approach would manipulate "social distance" to determine optimum balance by maximizing some dependent variable.

27. The possibility of inadvertent class bias among teachers was most forcefully made by W. Lloyd Warner, Robert J. Havighurst, and Martin B. Loeb, *Who Shall Be Educated?* (New York: Harper, 1944). Also see Albert K. Cohen, *Delinquent Boys: The Culture of the Gang* (Glencoe, Ill.: The Free Press, 1955), pp. 112–120.

28. Hovland, *op. cit.,* pp. 1062–1103; Eugene Litwak, "Some Policy Implications in Communications Theory with Emphasis on Group Factors," in *Education for Social Work, Proceedings, Seventh Annual Program Meeting* (New York: Council on Social Work Education, 1959), pp. 96–109; Herbert I. Abelson, *Persuasion: How Opinions and Attitudes Are Changed* (New York: Springer, 1959).

29. Herbert H. Hyman and Paul Sheatsley, "Some Reasons Why Information Campaigns Fail," *Public Opinion Quarterly,* XI (Fall, 1947), 412–423.

30. *Ibid.*

31. Katz and Lazarsfeld, *op. cit.,* pp. 48–66.

32. We have developed this issue in Litwak and Meyer, "Administrative Styles."

33. Initial explorations of these issues have been done in Litwak, Mickelson, Meyer, *et al., op. cit.*

Unemployment, Manpower, and Area Development

HAROLD L. SHEPPARD

chapter **20**

The uses of sociology in solving the problems of unemployment, manpower, and area development in the United States—especially through governmental action—have generally been most limited. Sociology in the minds of many policy makers and administrators means primarily a reference to the welfare *impact* and "problem" aspects of such phenomena as unemployment and poverty.[1] Rarely does sociology mean for them a set of ideas and programs directed at preventing and solving these problems. More frequently it means calling attention to the "human" aspects of severe unemployment, "depressed" areas, and related subjects.

The reasons for this limited use are many, but they include the following:

1. The dominance of program personnel trained primarily in the academic disciplines of economics and public administration, which give little attention to the social factors involved in economic development and in

544

the implementation of public programs devoted to economic development.

2. An antiplanning ideology that has pervaded the public mind in recent years, which is not receptive to sociology's emphasis on the interdependence and reciprocal cause-and-effect relationships of "separate" institutions.

3. A dominant viewpoint within the field of sociology itself that has minimized the importance of action programs and the practical solution of many of the problems studied in the field of social disorganization. Some observers might even claim that the study of social problems is an enterprise of declining prestige within the discipline.

Whatever the state of applied sociology, many government administrators and other program directors feel that sociologists tend to be hostile to applied sociology. That stereotype is reinforced when they compare sociologists with men of other disciplines. Discussing the unwillingness of sociologists to deal more directly with problem-solving programs, both overseas and in our own society, Marshall Clinard observes, "When the sociologist is asked to propose a practical solution for some issue falling within the supposed area of his personal competence, he usually asks for more research money." [2] Few, if any, sociologists ever feel secure enough about research conclusions already reached to recommend action. Clinard adds:

In spite of the problems of our age today, few sociologists are in a position in government to make or even draw up policy decisions. There is no sociological equivalent to the President's Council of Economic Advisers. While economists, historians, political scientists, and others are brought in to serve on advisory commissions in government, the sociologist continues to be left out. For them the phone from those in high places seldom rings. [3]

Some sociologists also fear that they may jeopardize their professional reputation by engaging in some form of social action. This is in sharp contrast to professional and academic economists and political scientists whose reputations are indeed often created out of their roles in governmental action programs. Few of the latter kinds of social scientists feel their careers complete without some experience in government agencies.

Few sociologists are prepared to engage in applied research and analysis or in action roles relating to the solution of problems such as unemployment and poverty, especially if the research is defined by lay institutions and organizations. Examples of some exceptions (in the early 1960's) will be cited in this chapter, but for the most part analyses by sociologists have been confined to certain kinds of diagnosis, and not to prescription. And often the diagnoses are not susceptible to translation into action or the design of programs.

In addition to this trained incapacity of most sociologists to contribute to "actionable" social research, the discipline also suffers from its historical desire not to be identified with the profession or art of social work. The scientific attitude for sociologists has come to mean detachment and freedom from value judgments which would have to be sacrificed through more direct participation. One practices medicine, law, or social work. One does not practice sociology, any more than others might practice physics.

On the positive side, there is some degree of recognition of the sociological *aspects* of programs dealing with unemployment, area redevelopment, manpower training, and poverty. This has come about primarily as a result of discovering the limitations in the use of traditional economic and public administration approaches in the process of designing, and especially implementating, programs directed at such problems. In many respects, this is similar to what has taken place in programs of overseas economic development, which have gradually come, in varying degrees, to "build in" sociological considerations at the outset of program design and implementation. Instead of merely thinking of sociology as encompassing only the *effects* of unemployment and area depression, there is some slight appreciation of social factors as being *causally* involved in the conditions making for or against employment increases and the economic development of given areas and thus as being important at the outset in action programs designed to solve and prevent problems.

We can cite (1) some selected related policy issues to illustrate how sociological perspectives are in process of being recognized and (2) those instances where such perspectives need recognition. The issues have to do with economic programs involving explanations and solutions of unemployment and poverty, depressed areas, and geographical mobility. One argument current in academic, private, and especially governmental circles has centered around the "inadequate aggregate demand" explanation of the high American unemployment rates since the mid-1950's, as contrasted to the "structural unemployment" explanation of this phenomenon.

The first approach emphasizes the importance of providing greater purchasing power among consumers and greater investment incentives among producers as a means of creating more demand for goods and services which would thus lead to a demand for more workers. Gross National Product, investment incentives, public expenditures, and market mechanisms are prominent among the major concepts in the analytical model associated with this perspective. The second approach calls attention to the imbalance of the skills of the labor force relative to the skill requirements of occupations recently emerging; discrimination against older workers and minority groups; the nonuniform distribution, geographically, of employment and economic opportunities; and a recognition of the relative difficulties in reliance on voluntary migration (mobility) as a major means of solving unemployment problems within areas and occupations. The structural approach would also take into consideration certain population dynamics such as family structure, and changes in the total size and component parts, especially as these dynamics affect and are affected by labor-market economics. For some time, many economists and policy makers have divided into two opposite camps: those stressing the "inadequate demand" problems and those stressing the problem of "structural" unemployment.

A sociological approach to the problems of unemployment and poverty has much in common with the structural approach among economists. At the same time, it has to be noted that the issue, which bears on the directions in which public programs will be pushed, could probably have been avoided or minimized if the various personalities and government agencies engaged in debating the issue had been trained in appreciating the importance of such notions as "necessary but not sufficient." Instead, in Washington the issue frequently became an "either-or" controversy, without adequate recognition of the mutual dependence of fiscal measures (such as tax reductions) and structural measures (such as manpower training) on each other as *dual* prerequisites for a growing, "full employment" economy. The emphasis in this chapter, however, is on the neglect of sociologically relevant approaches.

Manpower Development

Gunnar Myrdal [4] has persistently stressed the proposition that without an effective manpower development program, in particular the training of unemployed and underemployed persons, it is possible that an increased demand for goods and services—deriving from increased personal and corporate income resulting from a substantial tax cut such as the one of 1964—cannot be fully met. The assumption that unemployment will be solved, and the further one that the demand for goods and services will be satisfied, through a virtually exclusive dependence on fiscal measures, may prove to be inadequate if one or more conditions such as the following are allowed to prevail:

1. the lack of qualified manpower in adequate numbers;
2. the inability of small and "marginal" employers to afford private training programs, on a company-by-company basis, for additional workers needed to meet the demand (or for developing new skills among present employees);

3. concentration of industries in existing congested urban areas which have available trained labor supplies, in the face of geographical "pockets" of high unemployment and/or rural poverty;

4. the absence of effective measures to facilitate the movement of individuals and families to areas with growing employment opportunities;

5. the prevalence of job discrimination against minority groups and "older" workers;

6. resistances to, and lags in, redesigning job specifications and entry requirements so as to make eligible for employment numbers of currently "unqualified" job seekers.

The competition for manpower with appropriate qualifications, and for space in those areas having such manpower, could actually contribute to an inflationary trend, offsetting much of the increased purchasing power intended by the tax reduction. "Appropriate" qualifications often include not only the rationally functional prerequisites, such as the ability to perform effectively the job to be done, but also such "social" qualifications as the "proper" ethnic attributes or the possession of a high-school diploma.

The odd combination of strong demand and manpower deficiencies based on both economic and social criteria is illustrated by the New York City labor market of early 1964. According to the New York City Department of Labor there were at that time openings in the city for 50,000 office, white-collar jobs going unfilled because of a "labor shortage." [5] The 1964 tax cut did not produce the men and women needed to fill such vacancies. Indeed, it could be argued that an increased demand for goods and services may create *more* openings for clerks, typists, and other office employees. The paradox is that, at the same time and in the same labor-market area, there were approximately 77,000 persons aged sixteen to twenty-four who were unemployed, all, or nearly all, of whom were high-school dropouts and most of them Negroes and Puerto Ricans.

Conceivably, with the proper programs and techniques of motivation, recruitment, training, and job placement, many, if not most, of these youths could form the "labor reserve" for meeting the imbalance between occupational demands and labor supply. The failure to match this type of demand with the supply is a reflection of our inadequacies in economic and social planning. These inadequacies include the lack of a more rational labor-market policy and program (matching our educational system with the economic and technological systems); institutional obstacles (such as restrictive trade-union policies regarding apprenticeships); discrimination by employers against various ethnic and age groups; and primary reliance on market mechanisms as the means of solving area unemployment and poverty. The explanations for these inadequacies and the means required for improving them do not lie exclusively within the domain of the main currents of economic theory. They pose an interdisciplinary problem for which sociologists could provide some of the explanations and solutions.

Manpower development planning—a basic ingredient in social and economic planning, public or private—is not adequately recognized as a necessary condition for successful functioning of the economy and the technology. Generally speaking, training programs inaugurated since 1961 have instead been viewed essentially as minor advancements and improvements on our welfare approaches to unemployment, and not as major tools in economic growth. A usual comment about these recent training programs has been, "Why train people at a time when the economy is not expanding?" And, to complete such reasoning, it is frequently argued that the way to get the economy to expand (and thus decrease unemployment) is to introduce changes in fiscal and monetary policy.

Example upon example could be provided to illustrate this inadequate recognition of the importance of manpower development programs as vital to economic growth.[6] In general, these examples are mostly to be found in the "service" categories of occupations and industries, whether we are talking about the new "data retrieval and distribution" world, the health industry, tourism and recreation, or even the sphere of production and transport-machine maintenance. For example, in the latter category the average age of automobile repair and maintenance mechanics has been rising steadily: this means inadequate numbers of young entrants into the occupation, despite the growing shortage of such mechanics.

Area Redevelopment and Labor Mobility[7]

In 1961, after several years of abortive effort to enact programs directed at alleviating distress in areas of chronically high unemployment and rural poverty, the Area Redevelopment Act was passed by Congress and signed by President Kennedy (President Eisenhower had previously vetoed similar bills). In general, these areas were the ones adversely affected by changes in technology, supplies of natural resources, consumer tastes, lack of industrial diversification, and lags in the development of human resources. Areas that formerly provided substantial employment in coal mining, textiles and apparel, and railroading make up a large part of the total list. Rural areas with extremely low family incomes are also included.

Data on these areas, especially the urban ones, reveal a story of slow growth, low labor-force participation rates, high unemployment, and deteriorating services, public and private. While population in the "viable" areas of the United States—that is, those areas with relatively low rates of unemployment and rural areas with high family income—had increased by more than 22 per cent between 1950 and 1960, it had increased by only

8.4 per cent in the urban depressed areas and *decreased* by 3 per cent in the rural depressed areas. In contrast to the viable areas, the entry of youths into the labor market of the depressed areas is delayed longer, older persons leave the labor market earlier, and women participate in the labor force to a lesser degree. The over-all labor-force participation rate in the urban depressed areas (as of 1960) was only 50 per cent, as compared with 56 per cent for the viable areas. The lower participation rate suggests that the reported unemployment rates for the depressed areas *underestimate* the full extent of the problem, since many persons withdraw from or do not enter the labor force of those areas, but nevertheless continue to reside in them.

Furthermore, unemployment in almost every occupation in the urban depressed areas was higher than in the viable areas. In terms of occupational structure, the depressed areas had a smaller percentage of males in all the white-collar occupations than did the viable areas in 1950 and 1960. Educationally, the percentage of the population twenty-five years and older with high-school degrees is lower in the depressed areas than in the viable ones.

Two sets of characteristics show that the problems facing depressed areas constitute a vicious circle. One of these has to do with the areas' relatively low degree of increase of persons employed in the service and public administration "industries," with the 1950–1960 rate of increase in each of these industries being less than half that for the country as a whole. The other datum relates to local government finances and expenditures: the deteriorating private base as a source of public revenues impairs the ability of local governments to cope with school and welfare needs and with capital improvements so necessary for effective economic growth (for example, the attraction of private industry and commerce to areas with requisite community facilities).

In an effort to improve the economic and employment opportunities for such areas (about a thousand counties and labor-market areas), the Area Redevelopment Administration (now superseded by the Economic Development Administration) was created in 1961 as part of the United States Department of Commerce, but with co-ordinating responsibilities with the Departments of Labor, Interior, and Agriculture, the Small Business Administration, and the Housing and Home Finance Agency. The major provisions of this agency include relatively liberal loan terms for new job-creating commerce and industry locating or expanding in designated areas, loans and grants to local governments for community facilities needed to improve their economic base, technical assistance (for feasibility studies, management assistance, and other forms of filling "technical knowledge gaps"), and vocational training and retraining. All of these benefits generally require local economic development plans (Overall Economic Development Programs or "OEDP's") as a prerequisite for eligibility. The intent of the Act is that local citizens and officials draw up their own economic analyses and blueprints for action.

In the period in which proposals for such a program were being made and since the date of its actual creation in 1961, the policy implications of area redevelopment were an issue, and they remain so. Part of the opposition stems from the doctrine that economic activity should be allowed to develop only in its "natural" course. Measures aimed at diverting that natural course *away from* areas that need no organized, deliberate human intervention to reveal their "true" economic potential and *toward* depressed areas are labeled "artificial" and seen as creating a misallocation of resources. This doctrine assumes that all economic growth in given areas can take place only at the expense of growth in other areas; and it neglects those developments in economic history in America and elsewhere in which economic transformations—the modernization of industry, commerce, and agriculture—have been made possible by governmental actions. These actions have often been applied successfully in areas previously deemed incapable of change for the better.

In opposing "subsidized" economic development, the critics insist that the basic conditions of depressed areas cannot be changed, or they insist that such changes may be possible, but too costly. But this latter proposition has never been adequately tested. Area redevelopment programs, it is claimed by such critics, discourage job seekers from migrating to areas of economic opportunity. Hence migration becomes a major policy recommendation in this school of thought. Any measure that tends to keep people in areas of high unemployment and rural poverty is considered undesirable and uneconomical. People, therefore, should move. The normative content of such a doctrine should be clear, especially since the total costs of alternative policies (and trends) have never been calculated—that is, the costs of *not* having a program of area redevelopment aimed at "bringing jobs and industry to workers."

A major policy issue with regard to problems of unemployment in general, and of area redevelopment in particular, thus centers on the degree to which mobility, under *current* conditions of public and private policies, can be relied on as an adequate solution to the problems of unemployment. The advocacy of mobility as a significant or sufficient answer seems to rest on the belief that workers and businessmen will leave areas of low economic opportunity and move to those locations where economic and employment opportunities are the greatest. The neglect of a sociological perspective in diagnosing and prescribing in this matter means, among other things, first, that the individual becomes the key unit of analysis and prediction in the minds of the advocates of this particular policy and, second, that it is assumed that an individual acting in his own separate interests will seek out and be attracted to new sources of income when faced with a loss of income. In such a way it is expected that the economy and the society will arrive at a harmonious equilibrium, that the problem of area unemployment is solved. Briefly, the limitations of this viewpoint are:

1. the questionable validity of the individual as the key unit in such analysis;
2. the assumption that the unemployed worker or profit-losing business-man is fully aware of the wide range of employment and economic opportunities elsewhere;
3. the assumption that such individuals possess the necessary skills to perform either in the new job or in the new business enterprise;
4. the assumption that, even when fully informed, they possess the means of taking advantage of new opportunities, that is, the means of meeting travel and moving expenses (including the possible costs of selling the old and buying the new residence).

Needless to say, the model underlying the viewpoint is based on a highly rationalistic theory of human motivation. The model also omits any recognition of the bonds or ties that the unit of analysis—the individual—may have with his family and the community in which he lives. It further usually omits the indirect costs to the community from which migration takes place and to the community of destination. And, to date, few suggestions have been made by adherents to this model as to how individuals might effectively be induced to move.

There is thus a widespread belief that current social and economic processes, especially the magnetism of "high economic opportunities," will produce adequate mobility. Such a belief often includes, furthermore, a rejection of proposals and programs for the redevelopment of labor-market areas and regions with high unemployment and poverty. Empirical data are often used to support policies relating to geographical mobility as a mechanism to be depended on as a major solution to area unemployment. For example, it is frequently pointed out that 20 per cent of the American population is mobile during any one year. Even if we accept the 20 per cent figure, we must note that approximately 80 per cent of this mobility is within the same county or state.[8]

Migration rates and direction have, of course, been directly related to economic growth and employment opportunities in the areas of destination. It is also correct to assert in inverse relationship between (1) income and employment status and (2) geographical mobility.[9] The point at issue here, however, is the *adequacy* of migration as the major solution to problems of unemployment.

Furthermore, outmigration as a solution to the problems of geographic *areas* of chronic unemployment and low economic growth is not completely identical to outmigration as a solution to the problem of an *individual* unemployed worker. The recommendation that individuals in such areas migrate from them implies that, by such action, the area unemployment rate would decline and thus, by definition, the area would begin to enjoy a better, or at least a stable, economic growth.

Partly in an effort to "test" this popular theory, Sheppard, Maitland, and Atelsek examined the comparative demographic and economic characteristics and trends in sixteen depressed urban areas and in sixteen viable urban areas.[10] To be sure, this comparative analysis revealed that many individuals in the depressed areas apparently have responded to the high unemployment rates in those areas by outmigration. Comparisons of the 1940–1960 net migration rates indicate that for the eleven of the sixteen depressed areas for which data are available, nine of them in 1940–1950 and ten in 1950–1960 had net *decreases* (that is, outmigration in excess of inmigration), while for the eleven of the sixteen viable areas with available data, eleven of them in 1940–1950 and nine in 1950–1960 had net *increases* (inmigration in excess of outmigration). In the ten years after 1950, the size of the male labor force in the depressed areas decreased on the average by 5.2 per cent, while in the viable areas the male labor force increased on the average by 18 per cent.

While these two sets of figures, on net migration and size of labor force, tend to support the model of the economists that would predict that individuals in areas of high unemployment and low economic opportunity will leave more than individuals in viable areas, this is not the basic point here. Such behavior on the part of *individual* members of a labor force is not necessarily a solution for *area* problems. The critical set of data lies in the fact that even after a decade or more of apparent migration from the areas of chronically high unemployment, average unemployment in the male labor force of the sixteen depressed areas nevertheless remained about 8 per cent in 1960.

More dramatically, four Pennsylvania labor-market areas (Altoona, Johnstown, Scranton, and Wilkes-Barre-Hazelton) experienced the greatest decreases in their male labor forces, ranging from 11 to 23 per cent, between 1950 and 1960; and yet their average 1960 unemployment rate was *greater* than it was ten years earlier: more than 9 per cent versus slightly less than 7 per cent. Despite an apparently significant rate of individual worker migration from these areas over a decade or longer, area unemployment increased. These data suggest, again, that under existing conditions problems of area employment and development apparently cannot be adequately solved by reliance on the expectation of migration by individuals toward locations of economic opportunity.

Two further observations should be made:

1. there are no empirical data on the fate of those individuals who do migrate from areas of high unemployment (do they find employment at

their destinations? What is the impact of their migration on the communities of destination? and so forth);

2. without a highly complicated empirical analysis, we do not know whether heavy migration from areas of high, chronic unemployment may or may not indeed create further unemployment and declines in business activity in these areas.

It should be kept in mind that (1) the particular areas under consideration here range in population size from 138,000 to 3 million and (2) in nearly all of these areas unemployment rates remained well over 6 per cent for a decade or more, regardless of national ups and downs in over-all unemployment rates. This point is generally neglected in most discussions dealing with labor-market economics and unemployment phenomena. The degree of practicality and feasibility of any current policy or program based on the migration approach to the problems of area development and employment is obviously highly limited. It is difficult to conceive of the total evacuation of cities with large populations as a means of solving the problem of area unemployment and regional poverty. One inconvenient fact that should be confronted is that, during 1958–1961, total employment in sixty-one major labor-market areas with chronically high unemployment rates had *decreased* by 30,000, but then, in 1961–1963, total employment in these same areas *increased* by 200,000.[11] These areas apparently did not accept the proposition that economic conditions of depressed areas cannot be changed. As a nation, we are only slowly turning to the more strenuous challenge of discovering positive approaches to developing and redeveloping such regions, instead of merely relying on traditional mechanisms and worn-out clichés.[12]

Examples of the Application of Sociology

In carrying out recently enacted programs of area economic and manpower development, the participants, from the Washington administrators to the field staff, have come to recognize in varying degrees the role of those factors that one might call sociological. Indeed, there are instances in which "sociological inputs" have in fact been guides to action. I have already cited some of these inputs when I discussed the limits of mobility and migration as basic solutions to area unemployment. Attempts to use sociological knowledge in the current programs of area redevelopment and manpower training have taken the form of an emphasis on the following types of problems and programs.

THE IMPORTANCE OF THE NATURE AND COMPOSITION OF COMMUNITY LEADERSHIP

Under the provisions of the legislation creating the Area Redevelopment Administration, the overt initiation of actions leading to the utilization of assistance available through ARA had to be from the local community. Furthermore, this initiation required broad community support, whether in the form of submitting an Overall Economic Development Program[13] for approval from Washington as a prerequisite for material assistance or applying for an industrial or commercial loan, a community facility loan or grant, or technical assistance. Frequently, the local leadership structure is too apathetic to act, since it may share the low morale of the local citizenry induced by long years of economic stagnation. Often it may desire to act, but cannot rally the community behind it. And, in other instances, it serves as an obstacle to economic change and will not lend its support to other segments of the population that may wish to participate in the federal program. Resistance may be ideological—that is, the leadership rejects the idea of governmental action in the economic sphere or federal "intervention" in local matters; or it may be economic—that is, the leadership may not wish to have new or expanded industries in their community; or the leadership may view such new industries as increasing the chances for changes in the community prestige structure to its own status detriment.

When it comes to sponsorship of research into this type of phenomenon, very little has been done to date. It would be fruitful for the Economic Development Administration to determine the role played by assorted types of leadership in affecting different rates of economic area responses to the program. After more than five years of experience, there are sufficient cases to categorize these areas according to their degree of response and participation and then to examine the various community factors associated with these categories, including the factor of leadership.

COMMUNITY SIZE

The same type of inquiry could also be carried out in order to determine whether or not size of an area's population is associated with degree of response and participation (which really means degree of economic recovery, in large part). Size per se is not the crucial factor, but rather the question of whether the problems of communication, co-ordination, consensus, and decision making encountered in the agency's operations in the larger mass urban areas call for special approaches that are usually not required in the urban areas large enough to contain economic potentials and yet small enough to act decisively on economic redevelopment programs.

This in turn raises the question of size and "overspecialization": in tackling the problems of unemployment in large urban areas, the man of knowledge and the man who makes the decisions are much more frequently segregated from each other than their counterparts in the typical middle-size urban area.[14] A sense of "community" is frequently missing, too, in the larger areas, as compared to the greater identification of the power groups in smaller ones with the welfare of the area.

IGNORANCE OF ALTERNATIVES

While most students of the problems of economic development in non-Western societies have cited this element, scholars and practitioners confronting the American economy have often been oblivious to it. Yet in many areas of the United States, and not just in regions like the South or Appalachia, the scope of know-how in management, production, marketing, and so on, is quite narrow. Wilbert Moore's statement on this factor as it applies to the non-Western case of underdevelopment is just as significant for the American scene:

> While traditional modes of orientation are aided by the whole framework of social cohesion and the positive operation of the social codes and pressures for conformity, ignorance of alternatives is not alone sufficient to break down the traditional behavior, whatever may be their relative economic, that is, material, advantages. But their acceptance as genuine alternatives already indicates a weakening of traditional controls. An element of choice has been intruded into a more or less closed system.[15]

As an example of deliberately increasing awareness of alternatives, the Area Redevelopment Administration, through its technical-assistance program and in some instances through its public facility loan-grant program, financed university-based centers of economic development in selected depressed areas (in West Virginia, Michigan's northern Lower Peninsula, northeastern Pennsylvania, and New England). Their purpose was to carry out a type of "industrial extension" program to individual businesses and local communities; to improve the human resources of such areas which may possess the natural and financial resources for economic improvement, but lack the missing ingredient of knowledge and skills to exploit them.

STIMULATION OF "ENTREPRENEURSHIP"

The ignorance of alternatives also relates to the problem of injecting in a local economy behavioral patterns that can best be labeled "entrepreneurial." It is noteworthy that in urban depressed areas the absolute numbers of managers and proprietors declined by an average of nearly 10 per cent in the decade beginning with 1950, while in the viable ones the absolute numbers in these occupations increased by an average of more than 18 per cent.[16] A loss of entrepreneurial manpower is usually seen only as an *effect* of declining economic conditions; it is rarely viewed as a further *condition* for continuing decline in local economies of the United States. But in other contexts (for example, in southern Italy and in non-Western countries), the absence or scarcity of individuals with entrepreneurial know-how is often cited as a significant variable in retarded economic development. Very often, opportunities for economic change and progress may prevail in a given situation, but they will remain unexploited if individuals capable of recognizing these opportunities, and willing to act on them, are not available.

University-based "centers of economic development" constitute one form of action to overcome such deficiencies of managerial talent. Another variation consists of efforts of the Area Redevelopment Administration (and since 1964, the Office of Economic Opportunity and the Small Business Administration) to effect a small but sociologically significant increase in the number of Negro businessmen. With a substantial technical-assistance grant, for example, a local university's school of business administration, in co-operation with community leaders and organizations engaged in business and in human-relations activities, was enabled to recruit a small group of Negroes and train them for a number of months in the techniques of business operations. Once established in a small business, frequently with the aid of government small-business loans, these persons were to be counseled for another period of several months in order to see them through what is typically the "make-or-break" period for new businesses.[17] Advice, based on research, was also provided to determine the types of businesses most suitable in the local market area. Incidentally, this is one case where a sociologist in the decision-making echelon of a government agency was instrumental in the design and approval of a pilot program which later received wider application.

REGIONAL PLANNING VERSUS LOCAL PARTICIPATION

One of the basic criticisms of the activities of the Area Redevelopment Administration during its first two years was its neglect of regional or multicounty planning and its insistence on county-by-county, or labor-market area-by-area, Overall Economic Development Programs (OEDP's). This criticism properly points out the artificiality of such small, segmented, geographical-economic perspectives. ARA, however, was originally not intended by Congress to attempt another TVA-type program of massive regional planning. Its budget and authority were too limited to accomplish such a feat. While recognizing the value of regional orientations, the agency took the position that the initiation of action in the sphere of economic behavior is typically on the local level and that by requiring OEDP's to be worked out by committees composed of local citizens and officials, the chances for such initiation of action would be increased. As a case in point, one state agency for economic development submitted one single development plan for all the two dozen or so counties eligible for ARA designation, without involving the participation and consultation of key decision makers within each of the counties and labor-market areas. As a result, few concrete proposals for industrial and commercial projects were submitted. A key cause of failure was the lack of identification of local individuals and organizations with the master economic development plan submitted by the state government, stemming from their low level of participation in the planning process.

Either as a result of the agency's working within a value framework that puts a premium on "small-scale democracy" or as a result of its conceptual recognition of the practical importance of participation by local initiators of economic action, the ARA was faced with an apparent dilemma, for there is no doubt about the importance of multicounty and regional approaches to economic planning. Education through the experience of long-term local participation and perhaps the eventual recognition of the value of regional planning by local individuals (as a result of confronting problems at the local level that can only be solved through larger area approaches) are probably the most useful mechanisms for resolving this dilemma. The more recent legislation creating the Economic Development Administration did, however, aim at this broader regional approach. Nevertheless, regional plans (outside of those dealing with interstate highways and water-resource development, perhaps) cannot be imposed on local individuals and organizations, even though a good case could be made at the time required by the mechanisms of education and "eventual recognition" may be too long to meet the vital challenges of contemporary technological and economic change and of population growth. In some European countries with area redevelopment programs, the central governments play a more decisive role in the location of private industries, an ultimate target of all area development programs.

TRAINING PROGRAMS

The numbers of long-term unemployed workers as a percentage of all trainees participating in the newly established training programs (under ARA and the Manpower Development and Training Act) have been somewhat higher than the percentage they represent among all the unemployed—a fact which is encouraging because long-term unemployment (for example, six months or longer) means not only exhaustion of unemployment compensation benefits but also the possible erosion of skills, work habits, and personal morale. On the other hand, older unemployed workers and jobless workers with less than a high-school education have been underrepresented in the training programs. There is little appreciation of the reasons for this discrepancy and of the types of action needed to remedy it. The reasons include:

1. the role played by the various screening devices for accepting trainees which are biased against the undereducated, such as aptitude tests;
2. employer preferences for younger workers and the acceptance of this pattern by agencies administering training programs;
3. self-selection by unemployed workers themselves whose self-conceptions and levels of aspiration prevent them from even applying for training programs ("Nobody wants to hire a man like me, over forty-five"; "I'm too old to learn a new job").

Often it is a matter of faulty communication to the unemployed by training agencies, which typically assume that the traditional use of mass media is an adequate technique for reaching their audience. When the response is low, the agencies' usual interpretation is that "the unemployed don't want to be trained." Recent improvements in communication have resulted from a more conscious use of "natural leaders" and informal groups in neighborhoods to recruit trainees.

There is an increasing recognition, including explicit legislation to this effect, that certain unique kinds of training must precede what is ordinarily known as vocational education. This often includes a process of cultural assimilation: not only literacy training (with novel and modern teaching techniques) but also an orientation toward the world of work. As stated by a sociologist who was a codirector of a demonstration manpower program for hard-core unemployed Negroes, this orientation was at first new to the participants, including "the shape of and interactions in the job-market, the psychology of the foreman and manager, how loan sharks and credit unions operate, what a contract is in all the manifold senses of that term." [18]

Such projects have revealed for the first time to many policy makers, administrators, and political leaders the full extent to which such "obvious" knowledge as how to fill out job applications, how to dress and behave for job interviews, what an employment service is, and so on are virtually nonexistent among urban and rural unemployed and low-income Americans.

Experience with dropouts from such adult training programs is bringing some administrators to a recognition of numerous social factors that operate in the behavior and decision making of actual and potential trainees and that thus affect the success or failure of massive efforts to attack the problems of structural unemployment and poverty. For example, in one case a Negro woman was prohibited from entering a course by her husband who felt threatened by the change in status relationships between the two if she were to complete her instruction in a clerical occupation and then obtain employment higher than his own manual-labor job. In another example, an unemployed Negro auto worker, married to a schoolteacher, quit a one-year training course in refrigeration maintenance (an occupation which pays wages of at least $120 per week) within three weeks after starting to accept a readily available job in a filling station paying $55 per week. This man felt he had to show his wife that he did not have to be dependent on her and that he could succeed on his own. Both of these cases, it could be said, are symptoms of the Negro male's contemporary revolt against the generations-old pattern of female dominance and male dependency in American Negro families.[19] The successful implementation of vocational education programs among those groups most in need of upgrading obviously requires more than just the ordinary techniques of teaching and learning.

The problem of expectations and aspirations, of course, cannot be explained on an individualistic basis, without regard for the "structure of opportunity." One early clear-cut and encouraging example of the conscious use of sociology in problems of unemployment and training can be seen in the new programs designed to prevent and to combat juvenile delinquency in urban areas, with major financial support deriving from the President's Committee on Juvenile Delinquency, initiated under President Kennedy. The approach of that committee was substantially influenced by the participation at the national level by Lloyd Ohlin, whose major emphasis has been on the relationship between delinquency and opportunity. This emphasis, in turn, has led to the subordination of individualistic, personality explanations (and hence treatment) of delinquency. The projects sponsored by the committee form, in many cases, a nucleus for the more recent "war on poverty" program.

Specific programs approved by the committee (which uses a panel of outside as well as government experts consisting of such sociologists as Leonard Cottrell, Joseph Lohman, and Robert Sutherland) were also making active use of sociologists in the local community. For example, the St. Louis project has had as its executive director Nicholas Demerath of Washington University.[20] If nothing else, this particular project brought to the attention of a community's decision makers and other civic leaders a sociological perspective as one of the bases for acting on a social problem, especially an understanding of the structure of job opportunities for particular socioeconomic strata in the "inner city."

For example, the St. Louis proposal indicates that the causes of the employment problem, particularly as related to the problem of delinquency, are to be found in the following:

1. *Lack of job opportunities for unskilled and semi-skilled workers: automation.* . . . Existing industry has not expanded sufficiently nor is new industry coming into St. Louis . . . at a rapid enough pace to provide enough new unskilled and semi-skilled jobs for the new youth entries into the . . . labor market, let alone for the new *and* the existing unemployed youth.

2. *Lack of skills to compete for the job opportunities that do exist.*

3. *Discrimination.*

4. *Lack of knowledge of job opportunities.* One of the characteristics of Inner Cities is their isolation. This is especially true for the youth of the Inner City and their isolation affects particularly their awareness of the existence of job opportunities.

5. *Lack of motivation.* Not only do the youth of the Inner City know little about job opportunities; they know little about jobs: what they are really like, what is involved in work, in working for pay. And what they do know is often warped by the worker image they see among many of the adults who live in the Inner City. They see adults in menial low status jobs. They see failure, frustration, fear among adults—and they decide too often that the world of work is either unattainable or, if attained, a dead end.[21]

Given this definition of the situation, then, an action program dealing with the linkage between the job-opportunity structure and delinquency is clear:

1. Strengthen motivations to seek employment and/or higher levels of employment and use training programs to impart new skills.

2. Expand existing training facilities and resources and create new ones when necessary.

3. Create an awareness among unemployed and underemployed youth of existing job opportunities.

4. Make employers aware of their responsibilities in coping with the job problems of nonwhite and young job seekers.

5. Co-ordinate activities and programs related to these goals and develop effective community co-operation and support "so that the activities dealing with the employment factor will reinforce and be reinforced by other activities and programs addressed to other factors in juvenile delinquency."

Underlying these objectives is the recognition that training programs and job opportunities per se will not prevent or control delinquency or necessarily secure a permanent solution to the employment problem. However, the increase in the employability and the actual employment of certain youths will replace some of the frustration "by a sense of achievement and of belonging to the larger society about them." In addition, there is a recognition of the need to create direct, immediate access, on a local neighborhood basis (as opposed to the traditional bureaucratic and mass-media approaches), to the youths themselves and to the channels of influence, information, and services associated with their lives and behavior.

The St. Louis project proposal showed an explicit appreciation of the importance of socialization factors and of anomie in the vicious circle of poverty, unemployment, and delinquency in the population stratum to which the project is directed. Its strategy included the placing of youngsters as fellow experimenters in association with others acting as role models, providing engaging examples of legitimate roles in actual operation, including personal rewards for the models and inviting the fellow experimenters to try the same or preparatory roles. "In this strategy, the desirable role model is at once the instructor in skills, the exemplar of skill-linked controls, and the recipient of appealing rewards. The models will be sanctioned and legitimated by organizations of influential adults and older youths in the neighborhoods in which the youth-experimenters themselves reside." [22]

A more extensive discussion of the actual and potential uses of sociology in the problems of poverty, unemployment, manpower, and area development would consider (1) the value premises under which analyses and programs are conducted and (2) the experience of other countries facing similar problems.

Values sustained by interest groups have often prevented serious attention to the problems of population control, hours of work and related matters, and national planning as these affect poverty. Until very recently there has been an almost total neglect of differential birth rates and of birth-control policy as factors in the generation and solution of some of these problems. There is almost a taboo on new and serious thinking about the pros and cons of shorter working hours, including fewer hours worked per week, longer annual vacations, "sabbaticals" every nth year, delaying the age of entry into the labor force, or lowering the age of leaving the labor force. Nearly all analyses and proposals are kept within the limits of the conventional wisdoms about the link between job, income, living standards, and social status. Other "givens" include accepted bounds of federal, state, or local governmental actions in the economic sphere. The working papers of the presidential and similar task forces devoted to The Great Society may, implicitly or explicitly, lead to a break-out from these and other value boundaries.

A better sense of the limits of our cultural premises and more receptivity to sociological advice would come from close examination of the economic development programs of other countries. The "reconversion" programs of southern France and Italy, for example, have made extensive use of sociologists.[23] For many social scientists and policy makers, Sweden continues to be a source of "models" in manpower and area development programs. In contrast to current American activity, area and manpower development programs in Sweden are run from a genuinely national standpoint and involve tight co-ordination of private and public decisions in economic and social spheres. Federal government programs in the United States are not as yet effectively co-ordinated with one another, and public decisions are seldom integrated closely with private ones. In addition, Sweden more consciously and deliberately carries out its programs of training for the purpose of sustaining and stimulating its economy of full employment and high growth rates and in widespread recognition of the role of manpower development in the prevention of serious unemployment. Its approach includes a systematic advance warning, usually no less than two months, by employers who expect layoffs; the effective facilitating of worker migration to available work sites; direct and co-ordinated stimulation of needed investment at the first sign of economic downturn; and the encouragement of new industry in areas with high unemployment with more effective tools than are provided in the United States. Furthermore, all these policies and programs are part of the country's permanent machinery to combat and prevent unemployment, in contrast to the temporary nature of many of the United States programs.

If sociology is to make a more vital contribution to programs such as those discussed in this chapter, sociologists will have to take greater initiative in letting administrators and other decision makers (including elected officials) know just what it is that sociology can contribute. This is at least the opinion of thoughtful participants in programs dealing with problems of unemployment and area and manpower development. This initiative might also include the greater willingness of sociologists to work in agencies administering the programs.

The contributions would have to go beyond providing only perspectives to the men of action: they would have to include concrete policy and program suggestions that flow from the perspectives. To date, such suggestions are often only by-products and afterthoughts—postscripts to final reports of research projects designed primarily to produce contributions to a rather vague body of sociological theory, or "action implications" tacked on with little serious thought. The response of the solution seekers to such reports is frequently, "What can we do with it?", either in the present or in the long-term future. Many top administrators and political leaders have already adopted something of a sociological outlook. The problem for them is, how does one make use of it for given social and economic problems and public programs? In my opinion, few sociologists have devoted their energies to answering the question, for reasons discussed in part in the opening pages of this chapter.

Perhaps what is also required to enhance the uses of sociology in meeting problems of unemployment and area and manpower development is for sociologists themselves to grant more respectability to government employment among sociologists—in positions that go beyond merely serving as agency researchers and consultants. Such a proposal, to be sure, tends to conflict with the discipline's high premium placed on the ethic of neutrality; but we may look to the other social sciences, such as economics and political science, for examples of relative success in achieving professional self-respect and respect by peers despite or because of service in administrative, policy-making, and action positions with governmental agencies. What has been said here concerning government employment also applies to a great extent to employment in various private organizations devoted to meeting the problems discussed in this chapter.

Another prerequisite for increasing the uses of sociology may also be greater interdisciplinary "fertilization." It is difficult for a sociologist to make a contribution in a program with economic or political facets such as those discussed in these pages if he has no working knowledge, say, of labor economics, financing mechanisms, or political-governmental units. This suggestion perhaps moves in the direction of placing greater stress on sociology as an eclectic integration of the separate social sciences than is currently the case in most university departments.

The challenges to sociology as a useful body of knowledge will increase over the next three decades of this century. The unceasing growth of technology, dynamic changes in the nature and size of the labor force, the slow but definite trend toward public and private planning, the increasing urbanization of Negroes, the emergence of the megalopolis, and the expansion of science and higher education are among the conditions under which problems of unemployment, training, and area development will increasingly demand that sociology indicate concrete ways in which it might be of help to the society which it purports to study.

REFERENCES

NOTE: *This chapter is based primarily on the author's experiences and research prior to 1964, when the "war on poverty" was first enacted, and thus omits what may be the beginnings of a greater use of sociology in programs related to that effort.*

1. See the hearings and other publications of the U.S. Senate Special Committee on Unemployment Problems: for example, the Committee's Report, March 30, 1960, especially pp. 19–22, on the "Social Effects of Unemployment"; *Studies in Unemployment*, published by the same committee, as well as its 1,700-page *Readings in Unemployment*, which includes selections from the "classic" studies by Mirra Komarovksy, E. W. Bakke, and others, in addition to materials on "special problem groups" such as youths, Negroes, migratory workers, and so forth. The same committee also published a social-psychological study of a permanent plant shutdown: *Too Old to Work—Too Young to Retire*, by Harold L. Sheppard, Louis Ferman, and Seymour Faber, which was given prominence in a popular form by Michael Harrington in *The Other America* (New York: Macmillan, 1962). This latter book has done much to publicize and to gain general acceptance of unemployment, area distress, and poverty as national problems.

2. "The Sociologist and Social Change in Underdeveloped Countries," Presidential Address, Society for the Study of Social Problems, Washington, D.C., August 28, 1962, *Social Problems* (Winter, 1963).

3. *Ibid.*

4. *Challenge to Affluence* (New York: Pantheon, 1963), especially pp. 25 ff.

5. See "Job Activity in the New York City Labor Market," March, 1964, described in a *New York Times* article, March 2, 1964, entitled "50,000 White Collar Jobs Here Are Found to Be 'Going Begging.'"

6. A major exception to this lack of recognition might be said to be found among members of Congress who by their actions at least have shown appreciation of the nonwelfare function of such programs, not only through their enactment of the 1962 Manpower Development and Training Act (and the important 1963 amendments) but also—and perhaps more historically important—their enactment of the 1963 Vocational Education Act.

7. Parts of this section are based on data analyzed and reported by Sar A. Levitan, *Federal Aid to Depressed Areas* (Baltimore: Johns Hopkins Press, 1964), Chapter 3. See also Sar A. Levitan and Harold L. Sheppard, "Technological Change and the Community," in Gerald Somers, Edward L. Cushman, and Nat Weinberg, eds., *Adjusting to Technological Change* (New York: Harper and Row, 1963).

   Since the writing of this chapter, the Area Redevelopment Act was broadened and replaced by the Public Works and Economic Development Act of 1965.

8. See Table 4, "Annual Geographic Mobility, by Type, in the United States, April 1948–March 1961," in *Mobility and Worker Adaptation to Economic Change in the United States* (Washington, D.C.: U.S. Department of Labor, July, 1963), p. 22.

9. *Ibid.*, p. 21. For example, the rate of such mobility among males with 1960–1961 incomes between $1,000 and $2,000 was twice the rate among those with incomes of $10,000 and over. And nearly 30 per cent of unemployed males had moved in the year ending March, 1961, while only 20 per cent of employed males had moved. Unfortunately, the data from which these statistics were drawn are not adequately refined to derive any knowledge concerning distances and thus are subject to the same limitations as the ones cited earlier. Furthermore, they should also serve to demonstrate the inadequacy of reliance on migration as a fully effective adjustive mechanism for problems of area unemployment and underemployment (or poverty). That is, sufficient numbers of the unemployed or the impoverished apparently do not move.

   Some data, however, are available pertaining to distances moved from birth-

place, since birth, by heads of families, based on a study by the University of
Michigan Survey Research Center on geographical mobility of labor, carried
out in 1962 for the U.S. Departments of Commerce, Labor, and Health, Education, and Welfare. See John Lansing, Eva Mueller, *et al.*, *The Geographical
Mobility of Labor: A First Report* (Ann Arbor: Survey Research Center, April,
1963).

10. "Occupational Trends and Problems in America's Depressed Areas," paper delivered at 1963 meetings of the American Sociological Association, Los Angeles.

11. Unpublished study by the Area Redevelopment Administration, 1964.

12. In this connection, there is an uncritical acceptance of the sentiment that mobility among American workers is the highest in the world. There has been no serious
attempt to re-examine this belief, despite the recent rapid changes in rates of
economic growth in Europe, in contrast to that of North America, and the recent
build-up of deliberate governmental policies in European countries that recognize
the need for greater mobility and have instituted effective implementing programs
that materially facilitate the movement of workers over long distances.

13. The OEDP must include information about the local area's economic history,
the composition of the local economic development organization, a profile of its
labor force, natural resources, markets, financial resources, and so forth; obstacles
to economic improvements; and a program of action for creating new employment opportunities.

14. See Herbert E. Striner, "An Experiment in Communication and Civic Action,
1959–61," The Committee on Problems of the American Community, The Brookings Institution, August, 1961 (mimeographed).

15. *Industrialization and Labor: Social Aspects of Economic Development* (Ithaca:
Cornell University Press, 1951), p. 15.

16. Sheppard, Maitland, and Atelsek, *op. cit.*

17. See Kurt B. Mayer and Sidney Goldstein, *The First Two Years: Problems of
Small Firm Growth and Survival* (Washington, D.C.: Small Business Administration, 1961).

18. From discussions with Dr. John Blue, Department of Sociology, Norfolk State
College (now with the U.S. Department of Labor).

19. See Pauli Murray, Yale Law School, "The Negro Woman in the Quest for
Equality," a paper delivered at the National Council of Negro Women's Leadership Conference, Washington, D.C., November 4, 1963 (mimeographed), for a
discussion of the emergence of potential tensions in male–female relations among
Negroes.

20. "Gateways for Youth," St. Louis Human Development Corporation, 1964 (mimeographed).

21. *Ibid.*

22. *Ibid.*

23. For example, see Serge Moscovici, "La résistance à la mobilité géographique
dans les expériences de reconversion," *Sociologie du Travail* (October–December,
1959), pp. 24–36; the forthcoming series of reports under the direction of
Frederick Myers and Yves Delamotte (the latter from the Institut des Sciences
Sociales du Travail, Paris) on the area development programs of several European countries, sponsored by the U.S. Area Redevelopment Administration; and
the reports by the Manpower and Social Affairs Directorate, OECD, for example,
"Manpower and Social Aspects of Rural Redevelopment Programmes," by Solomon Barkin, October, 1963.

Public

Health

EDWARD A. SUCHMAN

chapter 21

"Public health," an eminent public health professional once observed, "is an applied technology resting on the joint pillars of natural science and social science. . . . Until both the pillars of natural and social science are strong, the arch of public health will not be firm." [1] In the decade and a half since this comment was made, the rapidly increasing utilization of sociological theory, knowledge, and methodology in public health work has underscored the basic nature of public health as "an applied social science." [2] The American Public Health Association in 1953 officially recognized the need for a sociological approach in public health by passing a resolution to "encourage collaboration between public health workers and social scientists."

But recognition of need and satisfaction of need are different matters, just as awareness of the significance of sociological principles for health action and even a knowledge of specific relevant social factors provide no guaranty that such awareness or knowledge will be put to productive use in actual program operation. While it is true that the field of public health has been repeatedly warned that "public health workers cannot ignore the social sciences, or if they do, it is at their peril," [3] a recent analysis of the "bad habits" of present-day public health workers listed the prevailing beliefs that "the social and political aspects need *not* be considered" and "the technical aspects of public health are more important than social and political." [4]

Historical Background

The history of public health goes back to antiquity. All societies have developed some means, reflecting their basic cultural forms, for meeting illness and death. However, the public health movement as we know it today is a late nineteenth-century development.[5] Following the Industrial Revolution and the rapid rise of modern urban centers, public health, like education and welfare, became a target for the powerful social reform movements of the last century. These movements were sparked by pioneers like Edwin Chadwick in England and Lemuel Shattuck in the United States and fed by extensive social surveys that documented the urban living conditions detrimental to the health of the worker.[6]

While anthropologists have had a long-standing interest in primitive medicine and the relationship of such phenomena as prayers and rituals to the prevention and treatment of illness,[7] sociologists have until recently largely neglected the area of health.[8] Economists in the 1920's and 1930's, concerned with rising costs and inadequate resources, brought the issue of medical care to the public's attention.[9] Even today in the United States controversy over "medical economics" rather than social need continues to dominate public debate about the medical care system.

Until recently, the field of public health did not take an active interest in the social problems involved in providing for the health and welfare of the public. The early concern with social reform gave way before the overwhelming promise of disease control offered by the newly propounded germ theory of disease. Public health entered a bacteriological era which was to witness some of its greatest successes and result in its firm establishment as an official public service.[10] The possibility of completely eradicating the major killers of the day—the communicable diseases of smallpox, diphtheria, tuberculosis, and malaria—did not depend on help from the social scientists. Formal authority and legal sanctions supported by incontrovertible evidence of the effectiveness of such measures as mass immunization and enforced quarantine provided public health with the organization and tools to do its job.

The job was done with awe-inspiring success, and slowly but surely the communicable diseases were brought under control in the Western world.[11] Federal, state, and local health departments, supported by a myriad of voluntary community health agencies, became firmly established; occupational categories such as sanitarian, public health nurse, and public health educator received academic and professional recognition; and it seemed that public health work would proceed in a routine fashion.

But as the communicable diseases declined in importance, other diseases rapidly took their place. The newly important diseases, such as cancer, heart disease, and mental illness, however, were basically different from their predecessors; they represented chronic, degenerative processes, incipient in their beginnings, long-term in their treatment, and largely irreversible in their progress.[12] The existing public health services, geared to dealing with the sudden, obvious, and acute onslaught of communicable diseases by proved methods of medical control and with legal authority to enforce these methods, foundered in a sea of unfamiliar problems: how to change behavioral patterns to prevent the development of chronic diseases; how to adjust victims and the public to long-term care with little prospect of cure; how to secure voluntary participation in such undramatic drives as mass chest X-rays or diabetes clinics; how to organize community support for such controversial measures as fluoridation; how to combat business interests and pressure groups whose economic survival depended on the public continuation of bad health habits; how to meet the objections of private medicine to public health's forced entry into treatment activities and medical care; and how to establish productive working relationships with each other and with the independently organized voluntary health agencies.[13] Social problems replaced medical problems as the target for public health activity, and this is why sociology entered the field of public health.[14]

Current Trends in Public Health

Some of the major changes in public health that are providing the stimulus for increased sociological activity are:

1. The shift in disease control from the acute, communicable diseases to the chronic, degenerative ones, with the consequent blurring of the distinction between prevention and treatment.

2. The greater emphasis on the social as opposed to the physical environment, representing the increased importance of a stressful environment and the decreased importance of an unsanitary one.

3. The change in public health objectives from lowering the incidence of illness and disease to "positive" health, or physical, mental, and social well-being.

4. The growing recognition that many social problems, such as alcoholism, narcotics addiction, and even poverty and juvenile delinquency, fall within the scope of public health.

5. The increased reliance on voluntary individual and community cooperation, as opposed to the use of legal sanctions.

6. The change in social expectations concerning health and medical care from that of personal privilege to a basic public right.

7. The greater concern of public health with medical care, especially long-term care among low-income groups and the aged.

8. The increased complexity and cost of medical care and mounting personnel shortages, requiring the development of new forms of public health organization and training.

Public health agencies faced with planning, operating, and evaluating new programs involving social as well as medical problems naturally turned to sociologists because of their knowledge of social forces and their training in research on human populations. Support for training and employing sociologists in public health work has been provided by the United States Public Health Service, by private foundations, and by universities.

The number of sociologists interested in health problems has increased tremendously in the past ten years. For example, the number of members of the American Sociological Association who gave "medical sociology" as their major field of competence increased 723 per cent between 1950 and 1959, and in 1962 the Section on Medical Sociology, with 878 members, was the largest single section. Social-science programs have been established in many national and local official and voluntary health agencies, in schools of public health, and in medical schools.[15] There can be little question that the utilization of sociology and sociologists by the field of public health will continue to increase rapidly in the coming years; there is a serious question, however, about how effective this utilization will be.

The Major Questions Concerning Utilization

A thorough analysis of the uses of sociology in public health work might attempt to answer the following four-part question: "*Who* in public health makes use of *what* in sociology, *for what purposes,* and *with what effects?*" Before turning to these questions, we should like to characterize briefly our principal terms of discourse.

SOCIOLOGY

We shall adopt a rather broad view of the discipline of sociology and include those aspects of psychology, anthropology, economics, and political science which bear either directly or indirectly on community, group, or individual behavior in relation to public health work. We firmly believe that such a multidisciplinary, generalist approach is necessary to deal realistically with a public service which cuts across disciplinary lines. We shall stress the sociological aspects of public health problems, but we shall include other behavioral sciences when appropriate.[16]

Similarly, we shall exercise a preference for the use of sociology by sociologists rather than by other behavioral scientists or even professional public health workers, but we shall emphasize the sociological principle or method being used and not who is using it. By and large, social anthropologists were active in public health several years before sociologists, and certainly public health educators and administrators had been "speaking sociological prose" long before they were told it was sociological. Furthermore, because a sociologist is working on a public health problem does not *ipso facto* mean that sociology is being utilized.

PUBLIC HEALTH

Public health is an area of applied medical science, certainly not an academic discipline (although closely linked to preventive medicine), and in only some respects a profession (as opposed to an occupation). Although the field has steadily increased its reliance on scientific research and professional training, its basic objective is still to provide concrete health services to the public. These services range from the highly professional work of the school health physician or the public health educator to the strictly engineering functions of the sanitarian or the police duties of the restaurant inspector.

It may be instructive for a sociological audience to outline the major elements underlying the practice of public health. According to Roney, a health officer and anthropologist, these include the prevention of illness or disability in any stage of the condition, within a community context, by control of agent, host and environmental factors, through activities of public health practitioners utilizing public funds with the support and cooperation of interested community groups and individuals.[17] From this definition it is obvious that public health work basically involves the application of knowledge derived from the medical sciences about the control of disease or the conditions that impair health by using knowledge about social organization and individual behavior derived from the social sciences.

USES

We shall define "use" quite broadly. Use may vary along a number of dimensions:

1. from the *direct* application of sociological techniques, such as procedures for group organization applied to the formation of an anticoronary club, to the *indirect* use of knowledge concerning social values, such as understanding religious objections to population control programs;
2. from the *immediately* utilizable, such as an analysis of community pressure groups opposed to fluoridation, to the *potentially* relevant finding that social stress is related to mental illness;
3. from the *descriptive* account of how a health clinic is organized to the *predictive* analysis of which individuals are most likely to participate in a tuberculosis mass screening campaign.[18]

Few sociological contributions to the field of public health are specific enough to be directly and immediately applicable. An unfortunate gap exists between what we know as sociologists and what we are actually applying to increase the effectiveness of public health programs. According to James, former Commissioner of Health of New York City, "We have the biological knowledge to make an impressive impact on a problem, but lack the social wisdom to apply it." [19]

Given our broad interpretation of use, we can conceive of three major channels by which sociologists can influence public health workers:

1. through a change in the *cognitive* processes of the practitioner, as, for example, in producing an increased knowledge and understanding, or even only greater perception and awareness, of the significance of social forces in public health;
2. through a change in the *affective* processes related to the beliefs, values, and motivation of the practitioner concerning the need to deal with social forces;
3. through a change in the *behavioral* processes of the practitioner so that he actually takes social forces into account in organizing and administering his public health programs.

From this point of view, we may analyze the contributions of sociology to public health as including increased knowledge concerning social factors in disease and its control, greater sensitivity to the importance of social factors, and increased attention to and control of social factors in program planning and operation. We may now proceed to a brief discussion of each of the major components of our basic question, "*Who* in public health makes use of *what* in sociology, *for what purposes,* and *with what effects?*"

Who in Public Health?

If we divide the field of public health workers into practitioners, teachers, and researchers, it becomes immediately clear that sociology has a different use for each of these groups. For the practitioner, the emphasis will be on program planning, development, operation, and evaluation. For the teacher, it will be on sociological knowledge, concepts, and theory applicable to a better understanding of public health problems. For the researcher, it will be on social research designs for testing hypotheses concerning the causes and control of disease and on methodological techniques for collecting and analyzing public health data.

There can be little question concerning the value of sociology to the public health teacher and researcher. Teaching such courses as public health practice, medical care administration, health education, or social epidemiology—all key courses in the public health curriculum—would be impossible without sociological knowledge. Similarly, research cannot be conducted on such public health problems as social factors in the etiology of disease, community resistance to health innovations, or the social organization of health agencies without employing survey or observation techniques developed by sociologists and utilizing research instruments that measure sociological variables.

It is the public health practitioner who seems to have the greatest difficulty utilizing sociology—a difficulty that increases as one moves down the organizational ladder from health commissioner to program director to field worker. Undoubtedly, this reflects an increasing emphasis on concrete practices, as compared to abstract principles. Sociologists can be fairly constructive in program planning and development, given a sympathetic and knowledgeable program director, but few sociologists are equipped by either training or disposition to assume the role of a field worker or even to give advice on actual program operation. Furthermore, the more removed the public health task is from social factors, the less help the sociologists can give. While he may be able to provide assistance to the public health educator in organizing community discussion groups, to the public health nurse in motivating a physically handicapped individual to seek rehabilitation, or to the public health physician, dentist, or social worker in establishing rapport with his clients, he has much less to offer the sanitarian concerned with problems of water supply or air pollution[20] or the laboratory technician conducting routine medical tests. Whether or not sociologists *should* function as public health workers, while often a topic of heated controversy, is at present an academic question, since there are so few sociologists interested in this use of their abilities.[21]

Public Health Administration

One of the most productive uses of sociology in the field of public health has been made by the *public health administrator* for purposes of policy making. For example, under special grants from the Russell Sage Foundation, New York City, Philadelphia, and Puerto Rico established social-science programs within the office of the Commissioner of Health. These programs supplemented already existing appointments of sociologists, social anthropologists, and social psychologists to health departments in such places as New York State, California, Vermont, and Pennsylvania and sparked a tremendous burst of interest in the employment of social scientists in official and voluntary health agencies.

A social scientist and a state health commissioner conclude that a sociologist could help an administrator "(1) Evaluate a program, such as classes for expectant parents; (2) investigate aspects of some pathological conditions, such as heart disease or cancer; or (3) discover principles of human organization that apply in getting water supplies fluoridated in a community." [22] The typical public health officer functions as a kind of doctor–administrator–community leader and must combine social with medical decisions. A study of health officers by Cohart and Hiscock found that the largest proportion of their time was spent on administrative work, community relations, and organization.[23] Another study concluded that the health officer was subject to many role conflicts as health administrator, public official, physician, and community leader.[24] It is significant that when public health administrators were asked to evaluate their professional training, they considered their greatest need was for instruction in such subjects as "interpersonal relations" and "knowledge of community." [25]

Many examples can be offered of the kinds of help sociologists can give and have given on the policy-making level. Increasingly, as we have noted, public health programs must turn to the community for voluntary support, and a sociologist who is aware of the state of local public opinion and the structure of community power can offer valuable advice on how to proceed. For example, the New York City Health Department had unsuccessfully sought to introduce fluoridation of the water supply for many years. The immediate policy question facing the health commissioner was whether to attempt to organize public opinion in favor of fluoridation and secure it by means of a referendum or to work through legislative action of the Board of Health and the City Council. A sociological analysis of the then existing political situation indicated that favorable City Council action was doubtful, while a number of sociological studies on public opinion indicated a high probability that any referendum would be defeated. The advice of the sociologist and the administrative decision were to postpone any action until a pending change in the composition of the City Council would permit a favorable decision. This change took place, and fluoridation was successfully legislated in 1963. It would be arrogant to assume that the sociological analysis did more than substantiate a politically keen commissioner's appraisal, but it did play a major role in assessing public opinion as confused and divided.

One of the major problems involved in giving advice on a policy-making level is that the recommendations often have a negative tone. Underlying much of the public resistance to such projects as a mass program for detection of cancer of the cervix in women, an antismoking campaign, or a rat-control drive are strongly entrenched political and economic interests and highly conditioned social and individual behavior patterns. Unfortunately, it does not help the administrator for the sociologist to document the existence of such barriers. But often there are no easy practical answers, and the sociologist should not be blamed for his inability to "halt the movement of the tide" any more than should the medical researcher or practitioner who points out the inevitability of degenerative processes in heart disease.

Sociology can often help policy making by questioning program objectives and the assumptions underlying them. This use is advocated by a health commissioner, who urges that social science research in an operating program constantly appraise the assumptions on which the operating program is based, examine the objectives of these programs, and evaluate the extent to which they actually contribute to the improvement of the health of the population.[26]

Public Health Education

We can briefly mention only one other major group of public health workers for whom sociological concepts have particular relevance—public health educators. In terms of training and work objectives, health educators come closest to being sociologists, as, in fact, a number of them are. Health educators are charged with such tasks as preparing materials dealing with disease prevention and control, including mass-media presentation, lectures to community groups, pamphlets, posters, and so on to be used in the community; organizing community groups in support of health programs; preparing course materials for health education in schools; and supervising the educational aspects of the other operating programs.[27]

From this brief description it is obvious that sociological knowledge concerning the relationship of information to attitude change and of attitude changes to behavior changes is essential to the work of the health educator. Similarly, sociological knowledge of community organization, leadership, and power structure is a prerequisite for attempts to involve community groups in public health programs. A comprehensive analysis of current problems in health education lists the following areas of sociological concern as most relevant to the work of the health educator: (1) dynamics of behavior (motivation); (2) attitudes; (3) decision making; (4) status and role; (5) small groups; and (6) community studies.[28] This review summarizes hundreds of research studies on the discovery and application of social-science knowledge relevant to public health education programs.

The quantity of activity in this area is overwhelming; unfortunately, the quality is not. The research studies are apt to be poorly designed, the execution haphazard, and the analysis oversimplified. The result is a vast array of disconnected, dubious findings. At present, health education activities in the community are likely to be superficial and ineffectual. Here, indeed, is an excellent opportunity for the sociologist to introduce better research studies and, even more important, more sophisticated community education campaigns based on an awareness of the greater importance of personal influence compared to formal media of communication and of the need to fit new information and behavior into existing beliefs and practices.[29] Of course, there are many outstanding health educators who are well aware of the shortcomings of their field and are diligently endeavoring to raise its standards.[30]

What in Sociology?

Sociology has to offer to public health, as to any applied field, content, methodology, and sociological skills and perspective. However, a great deal of existing sociological content is only indirectly applicable. On the whole, the public health aspects of our social system have not received the same degree of attention as, say, public education, religion, or government. The field of medical sociology, especially that aspect relating to public health, is in its infancy and contains few established facts, well-defined concepts, or clearly formulated hypotheses and certainly no systematic framework of organization.[31]

Almost all content areas of sociological fact and theory are relevant to the social aspects of public health. These range from a knowledge of *cultural* forces which determine the values and meaning of health and illness in a society, and which play a major part in defining what constitutes a significant health problem and what is an acceptable means of meeting the problem, to *social* forces which affect both the occurrences of health problems and the structure and function of community and group reactions to these problems, to *psychological* forces which influence the cognitive, affective, and behavioral components of the individual's response to his own and others' health and to efforts to improve his health and prolong his life, to *economic* forces which affect both the individual's health and the supply, demand, and costs of the community's health resources and facilities, and finally to *political* forces which strongly influence the strength and form of public health institutions.

Health Innovation

A tremendous amount of work has been done, mainly by social anthropologists, on the cultural components influencing the acceptance or rejection of health innovations, particularly in underdeveloped areas.[32] Paul offers an excellent discussion of the kinds of health problem tackled and the concepts employed to meet these problems. He points out that the directors of health programs need to understand the nature of certain gaps to the attainment of program objectives. One is the *cultural* gap related to differences in cultural values and in culturally conditioned assumptions about the cause of illness. A second is the *status* gap between the health worker and the public and between the community leaders and their people. A third is the *urban-adjustment* gap produced by the migration of rural inhabitants into the cities.[33]

Paul has edited a series of case studies which deal directly with the use of anthropological, sociological, and psychological principles and, perhaps more important, skills in public health action. Each case is presented by the social scientist who was directly involved and concerns a specific, concrete health problem; failures as well as successes are reported. The volume could serve as a detailed expansion of the present section.[34]

For illustrative purposes, we mention briefly some of the main findings from these case studies. One of the major problems in public health is how to re-educate the community to accept new health values and practices. Three specific attempts at re-education are reported in this series; although they dealt with widely divergent topics, they resulted in similar conclusions. "What appears from the outside as irrational belief and behavior becomes intelligible when viewed from within. Perceiving the connections between items of belief and behavior as the people themselves perceive them enables us to make better sense of the seemingly capricious pattern of acceptance and rejection of successful and unsuccessful educational efforts." [35] In New York City, for example, one of the major problems is getting Puerto Rican mothers to attend prenatal clinics. Benefiting from experience in dealing with cultural factors, these clinics, and other health services intended for ethnic subgroups, are increasingly being organized and operated in accord with the values and behavioral patterns of these groups. To aid this process, public health nurses are sent regularly to live with families in Puerto Rico in order to learn their cultural patterns at first hand.

Another series of case studies deals with the reaction-to-crisis situations produced by illness. Case studies in India, China, and Thailand document the fact that the behavior of an individual in the face of illness "is determined as much by cultural definition as by the intrinsic nature of the ailment. . . . But what seems natural in one social milieu often appears unnatural in another." [36] Here, too, is a sociological "fact" which helps explain the current underutilization of public health services by the ethnic minorities in our large cities and suggests that these services should be reorganized to fit public need instead of attempting to make the low-income client fit the established tradition of a largely middle-class professional service. For example, it cannot be assumed that referrals will automatically be followed up by the lower-class patients who lack the compulsive rationality of the middle- and upper-class groups. Such follow-ups must be built into the routine treatment process and not left to the initiative of the individual.

A third series of case studies deals with the increasingly serious public health problem of population control. Public health, by having reduced infant mortality and early death from the communicable diseases, is itself largely responsible for the existence of this problem. The contraceptive means for controlling the problem are at hand; yet social science forces us to recognize that "the controversial issue of birth control rests on conflicting basic values and is thus not subject to scientific adjudication." [37] And, as Stycos points out, local conceptions of virility, fidelity, and male authority have made a relative failure of the most carefully planned and executed public health programs in this area.

Social stratification produces lines of cleavage and conflict which strongly affect public health programs. Case studies in India, Alabama, and Boston show how efforts to introduce health programs or practices are seriously hampered by divided community interests—a problem which exists in every major community in the United States today. A final series of case studies deals directly with three organizational devices to secure community co-operation in health programs—the public health team, the community council, and the health co-operative. The first proved successful; the other two did not since "organizational devices that facilitate health action in one social setting may be obstructive in another." [38]

This latter generalization has proved to be the bane of existence for many sociologists in public health. How is one to know when it is safe to apply a social-science theorem to an urgent program needing immediate action? If one has time, one may check for contra-indications in the community; if one does not have time, one must probably gamble on the general rule. Still, sociologists have been successful in increasing the awareness of public health workers of the need to watch for "boomerang" effects, similar to negative side reactions in drug therapy, which indicate for whom and under what conditions certain public health procedures need to be modified.

Polgar points out four "fallacies" that tend to decrease the effectiveness of public health programs. First is the "fallacy of the empty vessel"—the tendency to act as if no health measures or popular health culture existed and to fail to build a new approach on the positive features of what already exists. Second is the "fallacy of the separate capsule"—the tendency to set the boundaries of health action in terms of one's own beliefs and practices. Third is the "fallacy of the single pyramid"—the tendency to assume homogeneity of groups, especially within the artificially created boundaries of one's administrative organization. Fourth is the "fallacy of the interchangeable faces"—the tendency to ignore individual differences and person-to-person relationships.[39] Each fallacy is documented with many illustrations showing that public health practitioners who disregarded it reduced the effectiveness of their program.

Many other reports and reviews by social anthropologists and sociologists attempting to introduce new public health programs in differing cultures support the sociological theorems implicit in the case studies cited above.[40] These reports provide part of the answer to the question: "*What does sociology have to offer of significance to the public health worker?*" But it is only realistic to ask how much a knowledge of basic principles actually helps the public health officer. Is it of practical use to present him with the following prerequisites to successful program operation: (1) recognizing the social group's health values; (2) making sure the recipients participate in the decision making; (3) designing services to be functional in existing social organizations; and (4) minimizing communication problems; or the following prerequisites to the successful introduction of a health program into a community: (1) demonstration of the program's value; (2) the support of local authority and leadership; and (3) participation of the target population?[41]

This is a difficult question to answer. We suspect that what the public health worker is really looking for is an easy, cheap, and quick answer to a difficult, costly, and long-term problem. If we point out so simple a change as employing Spanish-speaking personnel to deal with the Puerto Rican population, much less employing a Puerto Rican health visitor,[42] we are apt to be reminded immediately of the cost and time involved. However, the problem has been a long time developing, and it will take a long time to correct—indefinitely, if a start is never made.

Community Support and Participation

Of more direct relevance and immediate utility to the public health practitioner are those aspects of sociological knowledge that deal with factors directly affecting community support and individual participation in specific ongoing public health programs. Two primary objectives of public health work are to maximize the community's acceptance of a health program and the individual's utilization of available public health resources. The successful realization of these objectives requires a working knowledge of sociological principles in such areas as community organization and disorganization, social control and deviance, public opinion and apathy, special-interest groups, social group and interpersonal pressures, and individual perceptions, expectations, and behavior.

Many examples of the use of sociological principles in securing community support and individual participation in public health programs can be cited. On the most general level are community studies aimed specifically at the analysis of community processes related to health action.[43] These studies underscore the importance of a knowledge of community structure and function in planning and carrying out public health programs. They demonstrate the need to view the community as a social rather than an administrative entity whose effective boundaries and leadership are more likely to be informal than formal. Koos illustrates this with the example of a community in which a health officer who was cognizant of the community structure formed an advisory committee with representatives from each of the major community groups. Its members consisted of the town banker, a Slav bricklayer, a society matron, her Italian gardener, and so on. In no sense did this committee represent the "best people," but it did serve the community well. In another community, the public health officer also established a committee, composed of the "best" people in the community. This public health officer constantly faces a problem in having his programs accepted among the "dirty" people across the tracks.[44]

A novel approach to implementing findings regarding community organization and planning for health and welfare is given by a sociologist who describes the formation of a Community Health Seminar. This seminar is composed of public and private health and welfare agency administrators, medical college faculty, and interested citizens associated with the major religious, economic, and educational institutions in the community. In 1960, this seminar was in its fifth year and had successfully served the following functions: (1) as a forum for the interchange of ideas and information about the community; (2) as a means of communication between professional and lay personnel; (3) as a source of support for systematic research on community issues; and (4) as an informal body of consultants on community organization and planning.[45]

An excellent critique of the current status of sociological research and knowledge about community forces in public health is offered by Sanders.[46] He presents a three-dimensional view of the community as a place, a collection of people, and a social system; such a conception should help dispel much of the current controversy over what is meant by the community. Public health workers are apt to emphasize the first dimension, although it is really the latter two which exert the most influence on health programs. Viewing public health as a major social system in the community, Sanders discusses the organization or structure of public health agencies and services, the latent and manifest functions of the various components of the health system, the functionaries and their respective roles, the ideology and rationale of public health goals, the paraphernalia or tools of public health work, and linkages of public health with other systems. All these features are basic to public health as a community service field, and an awareness of their importance would do much to alleviate the narrow preoccupation of many public health workers with their own particular programs, often to the detriment of over-all public health service.

In conclusion, Sanders offers ten propositions which may be viewed as sociological theorems directly applicable to public health work. We summarize only three of these in further answer to the question of *what* sociology has to offer:

1. The need to distinguish between economic, political, and social power and to decide which combination of these is most important; for example, the support of businessmen may have little influence upon political decisions.

2. The contribution of key leaders is limited by the time they have available, the competition for their support, and the extent to which they feel they can influence their followers.

3. Support for a health program should come from many different levels of the power structure since the ordinary citizen exerts his influence in such varied ways as making financial contributions, being a client, serving as a volunteer worker, re-electing officials, or shifting his opinion about those responsible for the program.

These propositions are supported by an analysis of the reasons for the success and failure of a number of community health action programs. Particularly relevant for public health administration is the ability to predict when a proposed public health program will become a controversial issue. The Miller-Form theory of issue outcome is also highly relevant here,[47] as is Barth and Johnson's typology of social issues.[48] A great many public health problems are basically social problems; in fact it might be argued that a health condition does not become a public health problem until it is first recognized and defined as a social problem. It is not so much the existence of the disease itself but rather its social consequences that make it important as a health problem. Thus, mental illness[49] and mental retardation were not formerly considered the concern of health departments. In an excellent analysis of narcotics addiction, Chein and his associates present a well-documented argument for removing responsibility for the control of the narcotics problem from the legal authorities and making it a legitimate public health concern.[50]

Whether or not public health workers will make use of findings and recommendations such as Chein's will, however, depend largely on the alignment of political and social forces within the community. Other social–health problem areas subject to the same mixture of medical and social considerations include alcoholism,[51] suicide,[52] illegitimacy,[53] juvenile delinquency,[54] and, we predict, in due time, smoking.[55] It is essential to recognize the interrelatedness of these problems: many of them are behavioral disorders which have common roots in social disorganization and deviant behavior. Effective public health action will come about only when social factors are accorded the same type of recognition, research, and control that is now given the germ theory in relation to the communicable diseases. Lacking this concern with basic social causes, public health will continue to deal with these problems not on the level of prevention— which should be its basic concern—but on the haphazard, ineffective level of containment or maintenance. These are public health problems for which sociologists are perhaps more capable than physicians of being the "doctor."

One controversial community health issue that has received a great deal of sociological attention is fluoridation. In one of the first studies, Meltzer compared communities which accepted fluoridation and communities which did not and concluded that three conditions were necessary to the acceptance of fluoridation: (1) the action was perceived as leading to a desired goal; (2) the action was perceived as a clearly defined path to the goal; and (3) the action was perceived as leading to the satisfaction of other needs.[56] Since this study was completed, numerous other community studies have indicated that the issue is much more complex. The rather naïve, if heartfelt, plea of a city health commissioner, "This is where the social scientist comes in. We would like to have him help us change the values of the population in such a way that they will wish to accept the evidence from the epidemiological studies in this area, and instruct their legislatures to support a program of fluoridation," [57] fails to recognize the conflict of values that remains in many groups even after the scientific evidence becomes conclusive.[58] Some of the sociological lessons to be learned from social research on fluoridation include the following:

1. Referendums are usually unsuccessful; two-thirds of such campaigns lost.

2. Fluoridation provides an outlet for the ventilation of obsessions and frustrations among some people who have no real knowledge of this health problem.

3. Intervention of federal and state officials in local campaigns is not desirable.

4. Public health campaigns often resulted in uninformed technical debate and the raising of irrelevant philosophical and political issues.[59]

Public Opinion and Pressure Groups

Pressure groups and special interests exist in the field of public health as they do elsewhere. According to an editorial in the official journal of the American Public Health Association, significant power is wielded by organized interest groups whose activities can be important and even decisive elements in the acceptance or rejection of health policies or programs. The editorial points out that modern public health was born and has grown in the arena of political controversy, for example the efforts to develop effective official health agencies, the fight for pure food, the fluoridation of water supplies, or the control of communicable diseases. All of these involved political activity.[60]

Pressure groups may be religious (as in the case of birth control), economic (as in the case of air pollution), or educational (as in the case of venereal-disease education in the public schools). Powerful vested interests in tobacco, dairy products, cosmetics, vitamins, drugs, insecticides, and food additives are often opposed to desirable public health measures.[61] Private medicine, because of self-interest, may find itself opposed to public health plans especially in the area of medical care. Sociological analysis of public opinion in regard to these controversial issues is apt to be particularly productive and helpful to the public health administrator in locating focuses of support and opposition. For example, an analysis of successful opposition to a change in outdated milk inspection regulations revealed that the central source of resistance came from labor unions whose milk-truck drivers would be adversely affected economically by the change.

The study and management of public opinion concerning health problems constitutes a major area of sociological activity. While public health practice depends on constitutional law for the enactment of health codes and on administrative law for the power to inspect and license,[62] as Roemer points out, "The laws, of course, cannot be expected to evolve faster than public demand." [63] Public opinion in the health field has been found to be generally conservative, uninformed, and apathetic and not, as a rule, a dependable source of support. Only in cases of sudden emergencies such as a threatened smallpox epidemic can the public be counted on to demand action. A more or less accepted principle of public health administration is that the more one can proceed by legislative or community-wide environmental changes rather than by voluntary individual support, the more successful one will be.

Individual Motivation

In general, attempts to influence public information, attitudes, or behavior in regard to public health problems have not proved successful. In part this is because so many of these attempts have proceeded on a superficial level with a presentation of the "facts" only. However, it should also be recognized that health habits are apt to be deeply ingrained and not easily changed. Several studies of public participation in health campaigns have pointed to the same conclusion: the desired health behavior did not have enough salience for the individual to motivate him to change his previous behavior or to seek the offered service. Rosenstock lists three conditions conducive to individual action: "Other things being equal, a person will not take action to ward off a disease unless he believes, first, that he is susceptible to it; second, that its occurrence would be a serious matter; and third, that effective and acceptable means for preventing or controlling it exist and are available to him." [64] Hochbaum found a similar combination of factors related to participation in a tuberculosis mass screening program: A person will participate if he "(1) Accepts the possibility that he can contract tuberculosis. (2) Accepts the fact that he might not be aware of having contracted tuberculosis. (3) Believes that he would benefit from early diagnosis." [65]

These and many other studies[66] indicate that research and development in the area of "marketing" health programs would be a major sociological contribution. The public is no more rational in its choice of health products and activities than it is in its other purchases or acts. Preventive medicine ranks extremely low as a value for most segments of the population, especially for low-income groups most in need of preventive measures.[67] The medically deprived groups of the population have too many more pressing daily concerns to worry about than lengthening their life span,[68] and their narrower health horizons are another aspect of their generally lower levels of expectation and aspiration.[69] For them, medical disorganization is simply another facet of general social disorganization. The problem is further aggravated for ethnic minority groups where problems of economic deprivation are compounded by social alienation.[70]

Social Group Influence

Of particular interest to sociologists are a number of studies which have shown the importance of personal influence or social interaction in promoting participation in mass public health campaigns. A comprehensive evaluation of a poliomyelitis immunization drive in Florida found through a multiple variable analysis that by far the most important set of variables were those that dealt with the individual's group memberships and social contacts. For example, the belief that one's friends had taken the new vaccine was strongly related to the respondent's own vaccine status. This survey found that the most powerful predictors of vaccine acceptance and rejection were informal interpersonal factors, membership in social organizations, social class, and education.[71]

This study presents a very clear formulation of a basic proposition concerning personal influence in public health:

> The respondent's perceived friends are his reference group. The actions he believes they took become the basis for deciding what is "the way my kind of people are supposed to act." Thus, persons who believed their friends took the oral vaccine also believed that their friends would approve and praise them for taking the vaccine too. Similarly, where the persons important to the respondent were believed to have refused the vaccine, the respondent had the psychological experience [of] group support for his nonacceptance.[72]

This proposition is supported by the work of Clausen and his associates, who found that a mother's perception of what was expected of her by other mothers was a primary motivating force in getting her to bring her child in for poliomyelitis immunization.[73] Additional evidence comes from a study of health practices among a low-income group in Washington, D.C., which concludes that "it may not be necessary for people to be informed provided they can be motivated by other means. The mothers who took their children to be vaccinated, although ignorant about the disease, may have been motivated by the thought that this is what is expected of good mothers." [74]

The importance of determining when a desired health action is seen as "acceptable, appropriate, and desirable" by the social group as a whole is also indicated by the studies of Rosenstock[75] and Hochbaum. The latter concludes, in relation to a mass X-ray campaign for tuberculosis, "Even when this state of [psychological] readiness is absent or of very low intensity, people were found to come for X-rays *in response to external influences alone*. These may be influences exerted by other individuals or groups. In other words, people may come for X-rays not for any health-relevant reasons, but to please other people, to be accepted by their groups, and the like." [76]

Utilization of the above sociological approach can have tremendous implications for public health work. In place of the current emphasis on informational campaigns aimed at motivating the single individual through appealing to his fear of disease or through presenting preventive behavior as "rational," public health workers would seek to make participation in the desired health program a group activity. It is probably more feasible to try to change group norms, values, attitudes, and beliefs than it is to try to change individual motivation.

Individual variation in behavior is obviously important, but for policy making a knowledge of group characteristics is more practical, and sociological variables are particularly important. Such group attributes as amount of traditionalism, cohesiveness, generational continuity, intensity of shared values, content of group values, group sanctions, degree of shared experiences, degree of identity of situational, ethnic, and geographic backgrounds, and minority–majority status will presumably be especially productive variables to study. Although certain demographic differences may be associated with groups that vary on these and other criteria, our level of explanation would seek primarily to elucidate the way in which the individual's behavior is constrained by social-group structure, with the classificatory demographic variables remaining secondary. [77]

The greater significance of social-group factors is also stressed by Cassel, who in a comparison of the relative importance of situational factors— that is, convenience, cognitive knowledge (information about the disease or campaign), and social pressures—found social pressures most significant. Cassel infers from this that "the more individuals are involved in group life, particularly those groups whose norms are similar to those of the professional community, the more likely are they to accept such a program." [78]

This conclusion is strongly supported by a study of health behavior of a cross section of New York City residents which found that the greater social isolation and parochialism of the lower-income ethnic minorities resulted in a negative orientation toward the professional health system. The study stresses the need to organize public health and medical programs in ways that are more congenial to lower class social structure and modes of functioning. This would require a modification of the present organization of public health and medical care programs to make them more congruent with the needs and desires of the low income client and an attempt to raise the aspirations and expectations of the lower income groups so that they desire better health and medical care and realize what they must do in order to attain these. [79]

A study of a mass tuberculosis X-ray campaign in New York City found that the failure of the campaign to achieve its desired goal could be attributed largely to the absence of any effective community organization in low-income areas. Since most public health campaigns are predicated on the presence of a cohesive social group whose existing community organization can be applied to the problem at hand, the implications of this study are far-reaching. As pointed out by the authors, successful community organization depends upon the existence of communication and leadership patterns in the community, and sufficient social cohesion to produce community identification.[80] They recommend using "community mobilization," instead of relying on nonexistent organization.[81]

This recommendation has been embraced in other areas such as the "mobilization for youth" to fight juvenile delinquency and the mobilization of local neighborhood groups toward self-help projects emphasized in the community action programs of the "war on poverty." There can be little question that, sooner or later, if the public health problems of our large cities are to be met, a "mobilization for health" must also be mounted.

For What Purpose?

We now turn to an examination of the public health purposes or objectives for which sociological knowledge, methods, and skills have relevance. We shall continue to discuss the field in terms of research, teaching, and service. While there is, of course, a constant interchange between these three areas with, for example, research results forming the basis for what is taught and teaching in turn being geared to more effective job performance, there is a fairly well-defined administrative separation of these three areas, and sociologists may be found engaged in each. Reflecting both professional competence and predisposition and available support and opportunities, sociologists in public health are most likely to be engaged in research, next in teaching, and least often in service. This order is probably the reverse of what the public health professional would desire and has led one health officer to observe, "One gets the concept from the paper, and I fear too often it is the general attitude, that social scientists are essentially *studiers* of social groups; that they are somewhat apart from the everyday operational scene; that they watch groups behave after they have behaved; that they draw conclusions but that they are seldom actively involved in the changing of attitudes or behavior; that they are 'thinkers not doers.' " [82]

This accusation, if such it be, is for the most part justified. A survey by the Health Information Foundation of medical sociologists found an overwhelming majority, 82 per cent, engaged in research, less than half in some teaching, and only about one-fourth in any service activities. This distribution also reflected the expressed preferences of the group studied.[83]

Thus, the major purposes served at present by sociologists in the field of public health are: first, the study of social factors involved in public health problems; second, the teaching of sociological concepts related to public health work; and last, putting these concepts into operation.

Research

Before describing some of the major areas of sociological research in public health, let us examine for a moment the question of the utility of social research in public health. As in all public service areas, much controversy, most of it acrimonious and unproductive, exists concerning the value of basic versus applied research. In public health there is room and need for both; there is a continuum rather than a dichotomy between the two, and each has aspects of the other within it.

More to the point is the question of whether whatever research social scientists are doing in public health is useful. An analysis of 565 social-science research projects in the health field from 1954 to 1959 produced the following distribution of topics being studied:[84]

> I. *Social Factors in Disease and Health (291)*
>   a) Social factors in etiology, and distribution (125)
>   b) Response and adjustment to disease (50)
>   c) Attitudes related to disease (45)
>   d) The therapeutic process (43)
>   e) Health levels and health needs (16)
>   f) Relation of disease to various social problems (12)
> II. *Social Factors in the Organization of Medical Care (274)*
>   a) Services and facilities (93)
>   b) Personnel (91)
>   c) Social systems (90)

Group I might be referred to as research *in* public health, while Group II consists of research *on* or *of* public health. It is interesting to note that the two categories are about equally divided.

A fairly common classification system for research in the health field is based on the object being studied: (1) the disease or health problem; (2) the individuals or public affected; and (3) the organization or personnel providing the services. Wellin, for example, talks about (a) disease (or social pathology with health implications); (b) behavior and belief (responses to illness and to health programs); and (c) means, agencies, personnel (institutional patterns for the management of illness).[85] Kendall and Merton divide the field into four categories: (a) etiology and ecology; (b) variations in response to illness and maintenance of health; (c) organization of health facilities; and (d) professional education and training.[86]

In each of these areas sociology has proved useful as a valuable source of hypotheses concerning the etiology of disease, the behavior of people faced with a health problem, and the structure and functioning of the agency and personnel charged with meeting these problems. In addition, the methodology of social research has proved particularly appropriate for public health research. The population survey is, of course, the basic research approach of both fields, and public health research has shown perhaps even greater sophistication than social research in problems of research design, especially in the longitudinal or panel study and the predictive or evaluative use of sample surveys.[87] However, it lags behind social research in techniques of data gathering, especially questionnaire construction and interviewing, data analysis involving the construction of scales and indices for the definition and measurement of concepts, and multivariate correlational analysis models for the treatment of "causal" relationships among independent, intervening, and dependent variables.[88]

We can only discuss the major research contributions or uses of sociology for the field of public health briefly. We shall look at one major area within each of the three categories mentioned: in relation to disease— studies of social epidemiology; in relation to the public—studies of reactions to health problems; and in relation to the field of public health— studies of organizational structure and occupational roles. These examples by no means exhaust the wide range of basic and applied social research in the public health area.

SOCIAL EPIDEMIOLOGY

There is little question that some of the most productive work on the social epidemiology of mental illness, and less directly on social factors in the etiology of other diseases, has been the product of sociological research. Social epidemiology utilizes the social survey method, including retrospective and prospective designs, to determine the "causal" relationship between social factors as the independent variables and disease states as the dependent variable. Much work remains to be done in the development of models that explain how these social factors act as causative agents,[89] but there can be little doubt that social factors are significantly associated with the incidence of disease.

The basic objective of epidemiological research is to discover and account for the differential incidence of disease among different subgroups of the population. Classically, causative factors have been divided into *host* or human individual variables, *agent* or disease-carrying variables, and *environment* or the surrounding medium within which the host and agent interact. It is interesting to note the parallel between these three disease-causing factors and Lazarsfeld's classification in social causation of attributes (agent), tendencies (host), and influences (environment).[90]

With the shift away from the communicable diseases where clear-cut infectious agents could be viewed as single causes of disease to the chronic diseases where multiple causes predominate, epidemiology was forced to adopt a multivariate model of analysis in which host, agent, and environmental factors could no longer be easily separated. Social and psychological factors assumed increasing importance in this new ecological model, until now many epidemiologists would claim that almost all epidemiology is social epidemiology. As Gordon points out, epidemiology today is intrinsically concerned with "the social components of environment . . . that part which results from the association of man with his fellow man." [91]

A major controversy in social epidemiology concerns the process whereby social factors affect the occurrence of disease. Grotjahn lists the following four possibilities: "Social conditions (a) may create or favor a predisposition for a disease; (b) may themselves cause disease directly; (c) may transmit the causes of disease; and (d) may influence the course of disease." [92] Ackerknecht, a physician and anthropologist, carried out a classic study in which an observed difference in malaria between French and American settlements in similarly infected geographical areas was explained in terms of differences in cultural patterns of living between the two groups. [93] Major social epidemiological surveys have been conducted in relation to heart disease, cancer, mental illness, arthritis, accidents, and narcotics addiction, and social variables are included in almost all current epidemiological surveys. [94]

SOCIAL PATTERNS OF HEALTH BEHAVIOR

A second sociological area of public health research concerns social factors that affect the values and behavior of society and individuals regarding illness. As we have had occasion to observe, public health is becoming increasingly dependent on voluntary action by the community and the individual. Research on those factors which determine how and why individuals and social groups perceive and respond to threats to their health and well-being has important implications for the planning and operation of public health programs.

The conceptual basis for such research rests mainly on social anthropological knowledge of the cultural meaning of ill-health, [95] sociological knowledge of the so-called "sick" role, [96] and psychological knowledge of perception, learning, and motivation in regard to responses to illness stimuli. [97] Illness as a social phenomenon is defined largely in terms of its interference with normal social functioning, and public health preventive, therapeutic, and rehabilitative programs are apt to be perceived and responded to in terms of their social rather than their medical significance.

The utility of research in this area is not so pronounced as it might be. This is partly the result of a failure to develop any systematic framework for relating the various components of illness behavior to each other and partly to the low priority given to translating research findings into public health action. Unlike social epidemiology, research in this area is almost totally in the hands of social scientists who seem more concerned with its utility for testing and developing social theory than for planning public health activities. Concepts are apt to be highly technical, and descriptive and explanatory models are more common than predictive models.

Yet research in this area could help redirect public health activities away from outmoded programs concerned with communicable disease and sanitary engineering toward active leadership in designing programs to meet the major public health needs of today—early detection, referral, treatment, and rehabilitation of the chronic diseases.[98] Public health activities in the future will inevitably shift their emphasis from the physical to the social environment and from a concern with the control of disease-causing agents to an understanding of the social patterns of chronic disease behavior.[99]

ORGANIZATIONAL AND OCCUPATIONAL STUDIES

A major area of both basic and applied research in public health deals with the structure and function of health agencies and the selection, training, and performance of health workers. Most of these studies have been conducted by and for public health agencies on specific problems and therefore have had high applicability. One might even say that this area suffers somewhat from too much emphasis on the practical problems of administration, recruitment, training, and job performance and too little emphasis on a more general understanding of basic organizational forces and occupational roles. No systematic studies have yet been made of the internal structure and staff relationships of health agencies comparable to those made of hospitals or of educational and industrial organizations.[100] Similarly, no studies have been made of the socialization process of students attending schools of public health similar to those of Merton[101] or Becker[102] on medical students.

Elling points out that the field of public health, like other health areas, is faced with many serious organizational and occupational problems: "Health organizations and occupations have proliferated to the point where their costs, bureaucratic impersonality, and effectiveness are being seriously questioned." [103] The administration of a modern public health agency in a metropolitan area presents serious problems of staff organization and interrelationships, especially between the central office and field workers, of communication and co-operation, of personnel policies and budgetary practices, and of community and interagency relations. There are few systematic principles and no organized body of knowledge about public health administration and, while the situation is slowly changing, public health administrators have by and large received very little training in the principles and practice of public administration.

Levine and White analyzed 130 health and welfare agencies and their interaction in four northeastern communities and found the following four aspects most in need of sociological study: (1) the internal structure of the health agency; (2) the organization and its community environment; (3) vertical relationships with parent bodies; and (4) interagency relationships. They point out that "in the area of health and welfare organizations, the physician usually has little expert knowledge and if anyone can lay claim to this particular province, it is the sociologist." [104]

Some of the potentially productive areas for administrative research are listed by Demerath as follows: (1) analysis of programs of medical care; (2) co-ordination and intraorganization impacts of programs or units on each other; (3) costs and financing of medical care; (4) studies of the health professions; (5) utilization of medical facilities and services; (6) innovations and innovative techniques in medical care administration; and (7) methodological studies. [105]

Sociologists have conducted a number of studies on the choice of public health as a career by physicians and nurses. The extreme shortages and high turnover of personnel in these two critical occupations make these studies highly significant. Public health characteristically "borrows" professional help, often on a part-time basis. This is a result partly of its lower prestige, especially among physicians, and partly of budgetary and administrative difficulties. As public health work acquires greater professional stature through increased emphasis on professional training at schools of public health and as public health services become more closely allied with medical care, the general occupational standing of the field should rise. [106]

Back and his colleagues have studied the selection of public health as a career among medical students. [107] In general, their findings indicate that public health is an unpopular second choice among the medical specialties. Fowler found that the choice of public health as a specialty created serious professional role conflicts for the young physician. [108] Furthermore, a study of 1,129 public health workers in four state and local health departments found that only 17 per cent of the professional and semiprofessional public health workers started their careers directly in the public health field. [109]

Nursing has been a favorite target for research by occupational sociologists. [110] In part, this reflects the critical importance of this group (public health nurses comprise by far the largest single category of public health workers—14,384 out of 44,007 full-time employees of official health agencies, which is more than twice as many as the next professional group, the sanitarians), [111] and in part the tremendous concern among nurses with their professional role and image. [112] In general, nursing compares favorably with teaching and social work as a career choice among high-school girls.[113] The decision to become a nurse is usually made early in life and is motivated largely by humanitarian desires and, for many lower-class girls, by the opportunity for upward social mobility. This research has played an important part in the organization and conduct of recruitment drives and in the determination of working assignments and conditions.

Surveys of nurses on the job have indicated that they become disillusioned as direct personal care of the patient increasingly gives way to administrative and clerical tasks.[114] Dissatisfaction is also related to poor working conditions and low salary.[115] Attempts to introduce nonprofessional public health nursing assistants to ease personnel shortages and allow the nurse to spend more time on professional nursing care are generally resisted. Nursing established itself as a profession only after a long, hard fight and is unwilling to take a chance on losing status. At the present time, all aspects of public health nursing—recruitment, training, and work roles—are in a state of transition, and social research will play an important part in determining the final outcome.[116]

Compared to studies of organizational and occupational problems in other professional and business fields, social research in the public health field is inadequate. Despite the fact that a survey by the National Health Council of fifty health officials found problems of administration and personnel at the top of the list of their "most important" current concerns,[117] public health agencies, by and large, have not turned to sociologists for help in these areas. This may reflect a general process of development: social scientists are first brought into a professional area to help with substantive and operational problems, and only later, as sociologists enter a field and run into organizational and occupational problems, does this type of internal research occur. At the present time neither sociologists nor public health workers are devoting much attention to research on public health organizational or occupational problems.

Teaching and Training

The problems caused by using sociology (and sociologists) for teaching purposes in public health schools or for training functions in operating health agencies are similar to those found whenever attempts are made to introduce sociological content and method into a professional school or organization. We shall therefore limit our discussion of this contribution of sociologists to a few aspects of particular relevance to public health.

There are twelve graduate schools of public health in the United States, and as of 1960 these were utilizing the teaching services of about twenty-nine social scientists, not all of whom were sociologists.[118] Other sociologists are to be found teaching courses on the sociological aspects of public health in departments of preventive medicine in medical schools and in schools of nursing.[119] Most of these courses deal with the types of problems mentioned above—social epidemiology, cultural factors in health and disease, community forces involved in health action, and individual and group decision-making processes. With few exceptions, their approach is broad, involving all the behavioral sciences, and their objective is narrow, relating primarily to the application of theory and method to the problems of public health.

Supplementing formal instruction, and probably of greater immediate utility to public health work, is a wide range of in-service and continuation training programs. Only a small minority of public health workers have received professional training in public health; of the 1,129 public health workers surveyed by Cohart and Hiscock, only 10 per cent had graduate degrees in public health, while 67 per cent had only informal training or none at all.[120] The situation has undoubtedly improved in the ten years since this survey was made, but it is still probably true that if sociological training is to reach the mass of public health workers, it will have to be done on the job.

That there is a need for such sociological training would be hard to deny. Both Fowler's study of public health officers and Cohart and Hiscock's study of public health workers mentioned previously found these groups stressing that "interpersonal relations" and "knowledge of community forces" were inadequately covered in their course work. Despite this recognition of need, however, progress in introducing sociological teaching into the school curriculums and the training programs of operating agencies is extremely slow. It is the exception rather than the rule that such teaching is accorded either sufficient time or status.

Service

Program operation may be viewed as a form of social activity involving two major sets of interacting groups: (1) among service personnel within the program; and (2) between service personnel and the outside community. While medical science may provide the knowledge base for the type of program activity or service, social-science considerations predominate in the organization of the program and its presentation to and reception by the public. The effective application of existing medical knowledge through public health programs is a major challenge to social rather than medical science.

At a joint meeting of health officials and behavioral scientists, the health officials stressed the following specific uses of the social sciences in program operation: (1) to orient and sensitize the health official to the social aspects of departmental problems; (2) to help identify the sources of resistance and support in the community; and (3) to help devise specific measures to overcome sources of resistance and to take advantage of sources of support.[121] On a more specific level, the California State Department of Health lists the following uses of sociology for program operation:

1. Operating public health programs which deal with concomitant social problems.

2. Formulating policies and procedures which consider basic needs of children and adults as well as individual and group differences, including staff and community education.

3. Helping individuals and groups to use existing services which best meet their health, social, and emotional problems.

4. Modifying and extending services and programs including referrals and exchange of information with other agencies.[122]

These are the sociological activities which the public health professional is apt to consider of direct and immediate utility. Social research is likely to be judged as useless unless there is some observable feedback of the findings into program operations. The program director must provide many routine public services such as nursing, health education, sanitary inspections, and the recording of births and deaths. He has also to face the growing number of new health problems created by a changing social and physical environment. He must make decisions daily, and only rarely can he wait for the results of a social research project.

This is a difficult situation for most sociologists. Their training and orientation do not as a rule prepare them for quick judgments based on incomplete evidence or for specific recommendations of corrective measures. This problem has been analyzed by Foster in terms of the almost inevitable clash between theoretical research and goal-directed practice. Not only are basic values and objectives different between the two, but so also are the ego-satisfying criteria. The sociologist is apt to have a sense of accomplishment when he feels that he has made a contribution to knowledge, while the public health practitioner feels gratified when he can see an improvement in the health of the community.[123]

A great deal of attention has been devoted to this problem of collaboration between applied practitioners and social scientists, not only in the public health field but elsewhere, and it need not concern us here. Suffice it to say that role and status problems, differing cultural backgrounds strongly affecting perceptions, values, and goals, and conflicting definitions of the situation constitute serious barriers to the effective utilization of sociology in operating health programs.[124]

The existence of conflict does not, of course, mean that sociology is not being used in program planning, operation, and evaluation. Many of the illustrations presented in previous sections were taken from the work of sociologists connected with service programs. These range from the policy-making level of the health administrator to the standard operating procedures of the public health worker in the field. Let us look briefly at two of the major service activities of a public health agency in an attempt to illustrate where and how sociology can be and is being used.[125]

DISEASE CONTROL PROGRAMS

Public health control of disease involves three major aspects: (1) primary prevention, which may be defined as averting the actual occurrence of the disease; (2) secondary prevention, which refers to halting the progress of a disease and preventing complications; and (3) tertiary prevention, which means attempting to restore or rehabilitate the victim of the disease.[126] The major diseases involved are the communicable ones such as tuberculosis, poliomyelitis, and venereal disease; the chronic diseases such as cancer and heart disease; mental illness and behavioral disorders such as alcoholism and narcotics addiction; and other causes of morbidity and mortality, such as accidents.

We have already noted many examples of the use of sociology in mass screening programs and in mass immunization drives. The organization of community support for a tuberculosis mass X-ray campaign, for a diabetes detection program, or for a mental health clinic involves the application of knowledge concerning community structure, social organization, power distribution, and leadership and requires a knowledge of the social and psychological forces which affect the individual's motivation and decision-making processes. Attendance at a venereal-disease clinic and, indeed, exposure to venereal disease itself are strongly influenced by social factors, and control programs must take these factors into account.

Preventive measures aimed at reducing social stress and personality disturbance are basically social in nature. Therapeutic programs involving institutionalization and home care are strongly affected by the attitudes and behavior of the public toward mental patients. Rehabilitation in the community depends to a large extent on the efforts of the individual's family and social group to take him back again and on the community's provision of continuing care in such settings as halfway houses and sheltered workshops.[127] All three aspects of primary, secondary, and tertiary prevention in regard to such behavioral disorders as alcoholism and narcotics addiction are also strongly related to social factors both in the definition of the condition as a health problem and in the types of control measures which a community will consider acceptable and appropriate.[128]

CHILD AND MATERNAL HEALTH PROGRAMS

A wide range of services are aimed at the care of the mother and child before, during, and after birth. Such activities include prenatal clinics, maternity and newborn care, well-baby clinics, preschool health services, school health programs, adolescent health clinics, day care centers, family counseling, and special services for the handicapped child. As in the case of disease-control programs, participation in child and maternal health programs is largely voluntary, and several studies have shown that the group most in need of such programs is the least likely to take advantage of them.[129] A joint discussion of these programs by behavioral scientists and public health workers concluded that the following considerations are crucial to effective operation:

1. Are we dealing with scattered families, isolated from one another, or with families living close together and close to the clinic?
2. In the local population, who customarily takes care of the babies—mother, father, grandmother, aunt, baby-sitter?
3. In the local population, what is the prevailing pattern of use of medical services? Is there rejection of things locally defined as charity? Are medical men in private practice unfriendly to the kind of services we had intended to offer?
4. How do those serving as staff for the particular well-child conference communicate with one another? Is there a vacuum of authority, i.e., does neither the physician nor the nurse feel primary responsibility for encouraging mothers to bring in pre-school children for general checkups?
5. Are the clients well and respectfully treated by clinic personnel? Do the clients themselves feel that this is so—or are there courtesy conventions peculiar to the group and unknown to clinic personnel? [130]

A good illustration of the application of sociology to problems such as these is offered by Wellin. He asked why so few preschool children (as compared to infants) were seen at clinics? His findings showed that preschool children were being deflected from the clinics by parents who did not feel that the well preschool child needed such services or assumed that the well-child clinic was not the place to go. The study also found that the physician and nurse had conflicting expectations about their own and the other's role in the clinic.[131]

This report contains another example dealing with school health programs. Participating physicians in many traditional school health programs often function primarily as inspectors. A new program was offered which would alter the physician's role to the more diffuse but more strategic and effective one of consultant. Although there was little disagreement that the changed program would use the talents and time of physicians more efficiently and meet more of the schools' health needs, the proposed change created a great deal of controversy in the community. School principals and teachers became worried about what the health department was really up to in the schools; nurses and doctors felt uncertain as to how they would be used; counseling personnel in the schools believed that their bailiwicks were being invaded; private practitioners—even those convinced of the inadequacy of the old school health program—opposed the change because it seemed to alter the balance of medical care forces in the community.

Certainly, this sort of situation is understandable. Embodied in the old school health program were sets of ramified and interlocking relationships. People operating in different systems in the community had arrived at relatively stable, mutual expectations of their respective roles and behavior. A change in one part of the system may have reverberations and unanticipated consequences in other parts. In an effort to help the community, one may also threaten it.

With What Effect?

The last of our questions will attempt to evaluate the effectiveness of the use of sociology in public health, including an analysis of the major factors limiting such effectiveness. A crucial question is to assess the balance between the uses sociology *can* have and the uses it actually *does* have. Like the poet who remarked upon being installed as a member of the French Academy, "I know that poetry is essential. But I do not know what it is essential for," is the state health commissioner who stated with unspecific enthusiasm, "Our experience suggests that a very small behavioral science staff, given favorable administrative climate and what we have come to call 'a good deal of freedom' to design its own operations, can be expected to carry on a variety of activities that constitute an impressively useful program." [132]

An obvious but often neglected fact is that to a large extent the success of sociology *in* public health is tied up with the success of public health itself. Before sociology can be of practical use, public health itself must formulate its objectives clearly and correctly and have at hand reasonably workable and valid programs for achieving these objectives. In the absence of any clear picture of what public health is trying to do or of how it could accomplish whatever goals are defined, sociology can only share in a general sense of failure—it can neither help nor be held responsible, although it may take on the unpleasant task of pointing to basic weaknesses in both ends and means of public health as a subsystem in modern society.

While the success of public health was spectacular during the era of the communicable diseases,[133] when there was no organized discipline of sociology, it is ineffective in controlling the major public health problems of today, even in the presence of a mature science of sociology.[134] As James points out, "Of the 19 leading causes of death in New York, only two represent conditions that can be controlled effectively by existing health programs." [135]

The public health problems of today are difficult: they involve health conditions about which relatively little is known and which appear to require drastic changes not only in public health but in medicine as a whole. The field of public health is striving for a new role which would justify continued, or even increased, public support. While it may recognize that many of its basic difficulties can be traced to social causes,[136] identifying the problem as sociological does not mean that sociology has the answer, but only that sociology may be able to help. The answers sociology can offer in many cases appear useless and impractical since they often depend on a revolutionary change in the social structure of the medical and public health fields. Sociology stands in danger of being labeled a "dismal science" for many of the same reasons that economics was once called the dismal science: "because it set itself the unpleasant task of explaining to well-meaning people that the world was too poor a place to permit them to accomplish all of their well-meaning objectives."

On the whole, public health has recognized that it is facing a serious problem of failure, but does not know where to turn.[137] As stated by a health commissioner, "We are not quite certain whether our problem lies in apathy of the general population or particularly of affected individuals and their families, in limited facilities or personnel, in the influences of welfare or compensation considerations, in failure to get our message across, or possibly in a faulty or impractical product." [138] It is highly probable that all these factors contribute to current difficulties in public health. The public is largely apathetic about health conditions which are not an immediate threat, require continuous effort at prevention, and hold little promise of being cured when discovered, and such apathy is greatest among the most affected lower socioeconomic groups because of alienation and parochialism.[139] But sociological recommendations which challenge traditional values of middle-class public health and suggest approaching the public in the public's frame of reference rather than in the professional's are often dismissed as impractical.

If we define effectiveness in terms of efficiency and adequacy of performance, rather than solely in terms of effort, then sociology shares the generally low level of effectiveness assigned to most public health activities.[140] A great deal of sociological activity is taking place in public health today, but only occasionally have the *results* of such effort been effective—much less efficient or adequate to the problem at hand. Perhaps it is too early to apply such rigorous criteria to sociological efforts in public health, but sooner or later this must be done if a realistic evaluation is to be made.

We conclude by noting some of the barriers to the more effective use of sociology in public health, following a classification by Saunders.[141]

A. LIMITATIONS OF SOCIOLOGY AS A DISCIPLINE

1. The rather narrowly restricted training, interests, and skills of the sociologist which preclude the "generalist" approach required to deal with public health in all its cultural, social, psychological, and biological facets.

2. The general inability of sociologists to predict or control behavior of the individual.

3. The limited amount of proved knowledge and the relatively low level of methodological rigor.

4. The inherent difficulty of changing cultural and social patterns of organization and behavior.

B. LIMITATIONS IN THE PEOPLE

1. The sociologist's basic orientation is toward science and understanding; the public health worker's is toward practice and action.

2. The sociologist and public health worker lack training in and understanding of each other's field.

3. The sociologist and public health worker have different reference groups by whom they want their work to be judged.

C. LIMITATIONS IN THE NATURE OF THE COLLABORATIVE SITUATION

1. The relatively unstructured position and, at times, conflicting role definition of the sociologist who works in public health.

2. The difference in the sociologist's emphasis on research and the public health worker's emphasis on service.

3. The fact that public health people and programs themselves become the objects of study and evaluation by sociologists.

Other limitations and barriers to the more effective use of sociology in public health could be mentioned.[142] Most of these difficulties exist whenever sociologists, qua sociologists, are called upon to apply their knowledge, methods, and skills to applied programs. Despite these difficulties, there is an impressively high and ever increasing degree of collaboration between sociologists and public health workers. Obviously, then, there must be something of mutual advantage. For the public health worker, this probably comes from whatever greater inner security and more rational outward behavior can be provided by some knowledge about the social factors affecting the occurrence and management of disease, while the sociologist has the satisfaction of forging and testing his knowledge in the crucible of real-life experience and the gratification of a belief that "in our era, the road to holiness necessarily passes through the world of action." [143]

REFERENCES

1. Joseph W. Mountin, "Foreword," in Milton I. Roemer and Ethel A. Wilson, *Organized Health Service in a County of the United States,* U.S. Public Health Service, Publication 197 (Washington: Government Printing Office, 1951).
2. C.-E. A. Winslow, *The Changing Front of Health* (New York: Milbank Memorial Fund, 1940), p. 76.
3. C. E. A. Robinson, "Social Sciences and Mental Health," *Canadian Journal of Public Health,* LIV (1963), 157.
4. J. H. Romani, in keynote address to the Michigan Public Health Association, as reported in *American Journal of Public Health,* LIV (1964), 1612.
5. A brief account of the historical background and philosophy of public health, compiled by John J. Hanlon, Fred B. Rogers, and George Rosen, "A Bookshelf of the History and Philosophy of Public Health," appears in the *American Journal of Public Health,* L (1960), 445–458. For a more detailed history, see George Rosen, *A History of Public Health* (New York: M.D. Publications, 1958). Also George Rosen, "The Evolution of Social Medicine," in Howard Freeman, Sol Levine, and Leo G. Reeder, eds., *Handbook of Medical Sociology* (Englewood Cliffs, N.J.: Prentice-Hall, 1963), pp. 17–61.
6. For example, see Lemuel Shattuck, *Report of the Sanitary Commission of Massachusetts,* 1850 (reprinted at Cambridge: Harvard University Press, 1948). This report played a major role in the establishment of official public health agencies in the United States.
7. E. H. Ackerknecht, "Primitive Medicine and Culture Pattern," *Bulletin of the History of Medicine,* XII (1942), 545–574.
8. As described by Straus and Clausen—"Even though social scientists were interested in man's major social institutions such as the family, government, education, and religion, it is significant that they gave virtually no attention to health and medicine. Inconceivable as it may seem, until the 1940's most students of modern society completely overlooked the significance of health and medicine as a major focus of organized human behavior. A thorough examination of major social science writings prior to 1940 clearly reveals this void." Robert Straus and John A. Clausen, "Health, Society, and Social Science," *Annals of the American Academy of Political and Social Science,* CCCXLVI (1963), 6–7. This entire issue is devoted to articles dealing with medicine and society in the United States today.
9. I. S. Falk, C. R. Rorem, and M. D. Ring, *The Costs of Medical Care,* Committee on the Costs of Medical Care Publication No. 27 (Chicago: University of Chicago Press, 1933).
10. Anderson and Rosen describe five eras of disease over the past thousand years: (1) leprosy and plague; (2) louse-borne disease and syphilis; (3) gastrointestinal diseases; (4) tuberculosis and communicable diseases of childhood; and (5) cardiovascular-renal diseases, malignant neoplasms, and accidents. They predict a sixth era, now beginning, of psychosomatic illnesses. Odin W. Anderson and George Rosen, *An Examination of the Concept of Preventive Medicine,* Health Information Foundation Research Series 12 (New York: Health Information Foundation, 1960), pp. 4–6.
11. They are still not under control in the underdeveloped areas of the world, where the major task of public health remains one of securing public acceptance of and co-operation in communicable disease control programs.
12. As summarized by a public health professional, "The major health problems of

the community have changed from the control of the acute communicable diseases of the early years to the chronic degenerative diseases generally found in later life. Because of the nature of these chronic illnesses and our present knowledge of them, control technics have shifted from the legal and administrative mass procedures, relatively easily applied to the public, to the personal, supportive type of service requiring active participation by the individual and the group." Jesse B. Aronson, "Reactions and Summary," *American Journal of Public Health,* XLIX (1959), 311.

13. A sanitary engineer admits, "Fifty years ago the population could be largely protected against the communicable diseases by environmental measures which the people themselves seldom saw, or by inoculations which could be simply and routinely administered with no special or unusual effort on the part of the individual. Today's complex pattern of living confronts the individual with a whole new array of chronic ailments, against which he cannot be immunized, with environmental hazards that cannot be eradicated, and with the prospect that he must stand up against these forces for an extra ten or twenty years." Frank M. Stead, "Man and His Changing Environment—Engineering Viewpoint," *American Journal of Public Health,* LI (1961), 1022.

14. Edward A. Suchman, *Sociology and the Field of Public Health* (New York: Russell Sage Foundation, 1963), p. 180. This volume prepared for the American Sociological Association offers a comprehensive description and analysis of the current relationship of sociology to public health work.

15. Several reports deal with the current status of sociology in public health. See Edward Wellin and Milvoy S. Seacat, "Social Science in the Health Field: A Review of Research (1954–1959)," *American Journal of Public Health,* LII (1962), 1465–1472; Milton I. Roemer and Ray H. Elling, "Sociological Research on Medical Care," *Journal of Health and Human Behavior,* IV (Spring, 1963), 49–68; H. Freeman, S. Levine, and L. Reeder, "Present Status of Medical Sociology," in Freeman, Levine, and Reeder, eds., *Handbook of Medical Sociology,* pp. 473–491.

16. While attempts are being made today to delineate a special subject area of "social medicine" or "medical sociology," at present no such categorization seems valid. As evaluated by Freeman, Levine, and Reeder in their *Handbook of Medical Sociology,* "Medical sociology is an applied field, and is distinctive only in its subject matter" (p. 476). For an excellent introduction to social medicine utilizing a holistic approach, see M. W. Susser and W. Watson, *Sociology in Medicine* (London: Oxford University Press, 1962).

17. James G. Roney, Jr., "Social Sciences in the Teaching of Public Health," *Journal of Health and Human Behavior,* I (1960), 48. For a good introduction to the field of public health, the reader is referred to John J. Hanlon, *Principles of Public Health Administration,* 4th ed. (St. Louis: Mosby, 1960). This volume contains two chapters, pages 98–153, dealing specifically with the behavioral sciences and social pathology. A good description of the organization of public health services will be found in Joseph W. Mountin and Evelyn Flock, *Guide to Health Organization in the United States,* U.S. Public Health Service, Publication No. 196 (Washington: Government Printing Office, 1953).

18. Similar distinctions are proposed in George G. Reader, "Contributions of Sociology to Medicine," in Freeman, Levine, and Reeder, *Handbook of Medical Sociology,* pp. 4–5. For an insightful discussion of potentially relevant uses of basic research, see Robert K. Merton, "Basic Research and Potentials of Relevance," *American Behavioral Scientist,* VI (1963), 86–90.

19. George James, "The Present Status and Future Development of Community

Health Research—A Critique from the Viewpoint of Community Health Agencies," *Annals of the New York Academy of Sciences,* CVII (1963), 766.

20. Even in the case of sanitarians, Wellin points out the following sociological application: "Where the health agency has responsibilities in the hygiene of housing, sanitarians are often the "line" workers involved. In one local health department, most of the sanitarian group came of age during the depression of the 1930's. At that time, evictions of tenants for non-payment of rent were common, and the issue for people in the neighborhoods where the future sanitarians lived was *any* housing versus the threat of none rather than hygienic versus substandard housing. Not surprisingly, these sanitarians operate with strong tenant-oriented biases and with equally firm norms of their own about housing. How do they perform as enforcers of housing codes which are dispassionate as between tenant and landlord and which involve standards quite different from those which have taken-for-granted and strong personal meaning to sanitarians? Putting it in a more general way, what happens when people who hold one set of values are asked to promote policies which embody different, and sometimes conflicting, values?" American Public Health Association, *Possibilities and Problems in the Utilization of Behavioral Sciences in Official Health Agencies,* 1961, pp. 14–15.

21. In a survey of medical sociologists in 1961, the Health Information Foundation asked which activities in the health field were preferred. Consultation and administration were only rarely mentioned compared to teaching and research. Odin W. Anderson and Milvoy S. Seacat, *An Analysis of Personnel in Medical Sociology,* Research Series 21 (New York: Health Information Foundation, 1962).

22. Walter E. Boek and Herman E. Hilleboe, "Role of a Social Scientist in Public Health," *Human Organization,* XIV (1956), 25.

23. Edward M. Cohart and Ira V. Hiscock, "A Profile of the Public Health Worker," *American Journal of Public Health,* XLV (1955), 1525–1532. See also E. Cohart, W. Willard, and I. Hiscock, "The Yale Study in Public Health Administration," *Public Health Reports,* LXX (1955), 452.

24. Edward Wellin and Sol Levine, "The Role of the Health Officer: A Sociological Inquiry," paper presented to the Committee on Preventive Medicine and Social Science, Social Science Research Council, 1960. The study of occupational roles in public health is in itself a valuable contribution of sociology to the field of public health.

25. Cohart and Hiscock, *op. cit.,* p. 1526.

26. State Charities Aid Association, Proceedings of an Invitational Conference on Social Research in the Development of Health and Welfare Agency Programs, April, 1961, pp. 53–54.

27. G. W. Larimore, "The Elements of Health Education in Good Public Health Programs," *Public Health Reports,* LXXV (1960), 933–936.

28. "Review of Research Related to Health Education Practice," *Health Education Monographs,* Supplement No. 1, 1963.

29. Stanley H. King, "What We Can Learn from the Behavioral Sciences," *International Journal of Health Education,* I (1958), 194–200.

30. See summaries in *Health Education in Action,* Proceedings of International Conferences on Health and Health Education, 7 vols., 1962. Also *Health Education Journal,* "Social Anthropology and Health Education," XV (1957), entire issue.

31. Freeman, Levine, and Reeder maintain that "its [medical sociology] boundaries are phenotypic, and there are no reasons for the development of unique or special theories in medical sociology." *Handbook of Medical Sociology,* p. 476.

32. These contributions have been summarized and discussed in a number of ex-

cellent reviews. See, for example, two reviews by Steven Polgar, "Health and Human Behavior: Areas of Interest Common to the Social and Medical Sciences," *Current Anthropology*, III (1962), 159–205; and "Health Action in Cross-Cultural Perspectives," in Freeman, Levine, and Reeder, *Handbook of Medical Sociology*, pp. 397–419.

33. Benjamin D. Paul, "Anthropological Perspectives on Medicine and Public Health," *Annals of the American Academy of Political and Social Science*, CCCXLVI (1963), 34.

34. Benjamin Paul, ed., *Health, Culture, and Community: Case Studies of Reactions to Health Programs* (New York: Russell Sage Foundation, 1955).

35. *Ibid.*, p. 5.

36. *Ibid.*, p. 6.

37. *Ibid.*, p 7.

38. *Ibid.*, p. 10.

39. Polgar, *op. cit.*, pp. 411–414.

40. See, for example, Vera Rubin, ed., "Culture, Society, and Health," *Annals of the New York Academy of Science*, LXXXIV (December, 1960), 783–1060; Margaret Mead, *Social and Cultural Backgrounds for Planning Public Health Programs in Africa* (Brazzaville: World Health Organization, 1957); Lyle Saunders, *Cultural Difference and Medical Care* (New York: Russell Sage Foundation, 1954); George M. Foster, *Problems in Intercultural Health Programs*, Social Science Research Council, Pamphlet 12 (New York, 1958).

41. As derived from the Conference of Preventive Medicine and Social Science Research sponsored by the Social Science Research Council, Skytop, Pennsylvania, June, 1958.

42. A similar method is discussed in John Adair, "The Indian Health Worker in the Cornell Navajo Project," *Human Organization*, XIX (1960), 59–63.

43. See, for example, Solon T. Kimball and Marion Pearsall, *The Talladega Story: A Study in Community Process* (Tuscaloosa: University of Alabama Press, 1954); Floyd Hunter, R. C. Schaffer, and C. G. Sheps, *Community Organization: Action and Inaction* (Chapel Hill: University of North Carolina Press, 1956); Christopher Sower, *Community Involvement* (Glencoe, Ill.: The Free Press, 1957); Paul A. Miller, *Community Health Action* (East Lansing: Michigan State College Press, 1953).

44. Earl L. Koos, "Some Contributions of Anthropology and Sociology to Public Health," University of Rochester (mimeographed), p. 11.

45. State Charities Aid Association, *op. cit.*, p. 41. See also Charles V. Willie and Herbert Notkin, "Community Organization for Health: A Case Study," in E. G. Jaco, ed., *Patients, Physicians, and Illness* (New York: The Free Press of Glencoe, 1958), pp. 148–158.

46. Irwin T. Sanders, "Public Health in the Community," in Freeman, Levine, and Reeder, *Handbook of Medical Sociology*, pp. 369–396. See also Sanders, "The Community: Structure and Function," *Nursing Outlook*, XI (1963), 642–646.

47. Robert C. Hanson, "Predicting a Community Decision: A Test of the Miller-Form Theory," *American Sociological Review*, XXIV (1959), 662–663.

48. Ernest A. T. Barth and Stuart D. Johnson, "Community Power and a Typology of Social Issues," *Social Forces*, XXXVIII (1959), 29–32.

49. As Clausen states, "Any attempt to define the sociology of mental health and illness runs into the difficulty that the designation of behaviors as manifestations of mental health or illness seems to be largely peculiar to our own culture and speech. . . . Psychiatric knowledge and the mental health movement are social

products." John A. Clausen, "The Sociology of Mental Illness," in R. K. Merton, L. Brown, and L. Cottrell, eds., *Sociology Today* (New York: Basic Books, 1962), pp. 485–486.

50. Isidor Chein, Donald L. Gerard, Robert S. Lee, and Eva Rosenfeld, *The Road to H: Narcotics, Delinquency, and Social Policy* (New York: Basic Books, 1964).

51. D. J. Pittman and C. R. Snyder, eds., *Society, Culture, and Drinking Patterns* (New York: Wiley, 1962).

52. Guido M. Crocetti, "Suicide and Public Health: An Attempt at Reconceptualization," *American Journal of Public Health*, XLIX (1959), 881–887.

53. Jean Pakter *et al.*, "Out-of-Wedlock Births in New York City. I. Sociologic Aspects," *American Journal of Public Health*, LI (1961), 683–696.

54. Bellenden R. Hutcheson, Saul Cooper, and Elizabeth Kaiser, "A Public Mental Health Approach to Delinquency Control," *American Journal of Public Health*, LIII (1963), 418–424.

55. E. J. Salber and B. MacMahon, "Cigarette Smoking among High School Students Related to Social Class and Parental Smoking Habits," *American Journal of Public Health*, LI (1961), 1780–1789.

56. Nancy Starbuck Meltzer, "A Psychological Approach to Developing Principles of Community Organization," *American Journal of Public Health*, XLIII (1953), 198–203.

57. State Charities Aid Association, *op. cit.*, p. 51.

58. *Journal of Social Issues*, "Trigger for Community Conflict: The Case of Fluoridation," XVII (1961), entire issue. See also William A. Gamson and Peter H. Irons, "Community Characteristics and Fluoridation Outcome," *Journal of Social Issues*, XVII (1961), 66–74.

59. Conference on Preventive Medicine and Social Science Research, *op. cit.*

60. Editorial, "The Politics of Public Health," *American Journal of Public Health*, XLIX (1959), 364.

61. As described by Clausen, "In this area, then, we move to the largest canvas on which the relationships between health and society are painted, the dynamic interplay of values and interests. Although cigarette smoking has been highlighted as an example, it should be noted that some of the same considerations apply to health hazards associated with certain cosmetics, soft drinks, condiments, food additives, and alcohol. Values are clearly in conflict both at the individual level —health against pleasure—and at the organizational level—responsibility against profit." John A. Clausen, "Social Factors in Disease," *Annals of the American Academy of Political and Social Science*, CCCXLVI (1963), 147. This entire issue is devoted to "Medicine and Society."

62. George A. McKray, "Community Health and the Law," *Public Health Reports*, LXXIX (1964), 654–663.

63. Milton I. Roemer, "Current Problems in Medical Care," *Public Health Reports*, LXXIX (1964), 722.

64. Irwin M. Rosenstock, "Public Acceptance of Influenza Vaccination," *American Review of Respiratory Diseases* (1961), p. 172.

65. Godfrey M. Hochbaum, *Public Participation in Medical Screening Programs*, U.S. Public Health Service, Publication No. 572 (Washington: Government Printing Office, 1958).

66. See, for example, John Belcher, "Acceptance of the Salk Polio Vaccine," *Rural Sociology*, XXIII (June, 1958), 158–170; Warren Winkelstein and Saxon Graham, "Factors in Participation in the 1954 Poliomyelitis Vaccine Field Trials, Erie County, New York," *American Journal of Public Health*, XLIX (1959), 1454–

1466; Constantine A. Yeracaris, "Social Factors Associated with the Acceptance of Medical Innovations: A Pilot Study," *Journal of Health and Human Behavior,* III (1962), 193–198.

67. Paul B. Cornely and Stanley K. Bigman, "Cultural Considerations in Changing Health Attitudes," *Medical Annals of the District of Columbia,* XXX (1961), 191–199.

68. Daniel Rosenblatt and Edward A. Suchman, "Blue-Collar Attitudes and Information toward Health and Illness," in A. Shostak and W. Gomberg, eds., *Blue-Collar World* (Englewood Cliffs, N.J.: Prentice-Hall, 1964), pp. 324–333.

69. Wylda Cowles *et al.,* "Health and Communication in a Negro Census Tract," *Social Problems,* X (1963), 228–236.

70. Edward A. Suchman, "Socio-Medical Variations among Ethnic Groups," *American Journal of Sociology,* LXX (1964), 319–331.

71. Albert L. Johnson *et al., Epidemiology of Polio Vaccine Acceptance,* Florida State Board of Health, Monograph No. 3 (1962), p. 98.

72. *Ibid.,* p. 42.

73. John A. Clausen, Morton A. Seidenfeld, and Leila G. Deasy, "Parent Attitudes toward Participation of Their Children in Polio Vaccine Trials," *American Journal of Public Health,* XLIV (1954), 1526–1536.

74. Paul B. Cornely and Stanley K. Bigman, *Cultural Considerations in Changing Health Attitudes* (Washington: Howard University, mimeographed, 1961), p. 169.

75. Irwin M. Rosenstock *et al.,* "Why People Fail to Seek Poliomyelitis Vaccination," *Public Health Reports,* LXXIV (1959), 98–104. See also *The Impact of Asian Influenza on Community Life,* U.S. Public Health Service, Publication No. 766 (Washington: Government Printing Office, 1960).

76. Hochbaum, *op. cit.,* p. 21.

77. Edward A. Suchman, "Social Patterns of Illness and Medical Care," *Journal of Health and Human Behavior,* VI (1965), 2–16.

78. John Cassel, "Social and Cultural Considerations in Health Innovations," *Annals of the New York Academy of Medicine,* CVII (1963), 746.

79. Edward A. Suchman, "Social Factors in Medical Deprivation," *American Journal of Public Health,* LV (1965), 1725–1733.

80. Charles A. Metzner and Gerald Gurin, *Personal Response and Social Organization in a Health Campaign* (Ann Arbor: University of Michigan, Bureau of Public Health Economics, Research Series No. 9, 1960), pp. 1–2.

81. *Ibid.,* pp. 33–35.

82. American Public Health Association, *op. cit.,* p. 19.

83. Anderson and Seacat, *op. cit.*

84. Wellin and Seacat, *op. cit.*

85. Edward Wellin, "Socio-Cultural Factors in Public Health: A Discussion," *Annals of the New York Academy of Sciences,* LXXXIV (1960), 1044.

86. Patricia L. Kendall and Robert K. Merton, "Medical Education as a Social Process," in Jaco, *op. cit.,* pp. 321–350.

87. For example, see such excellent methodological critiques as Herbert Pollack and Dean E. Krueger, eds., "Epidemiology of Cardiovascular Diseases: Methodology," Supplement to *American Journal of Public Health,* L (1960), 1–124. This report of a Conference on Methodology in Epidemiological Studies of Cardiovascular Diseases provides a thorough analysis of the longitudinal method; Leonard M. Schuman, ed., "Research Methodology and Potential in Community Health and Preventive Medicine," *Annals of the New York Academy of Sciences,* CVII (1963), 471–808; Elizabeth Herzog, *Some Guide Lines for Evaluative Research,*

Children's Bureau (Washington: Government Printing Office, 1959). Also see the detailed and painstaking methodological appendices in the Commission on Chronic Illness series, especially *Chronic Illness in a Rural Area*, 3 (1959), and *Chronic Illness in a Large City*, 4 (1957) (Cambridge: Harvard University Press).

88. Jack Elinson, "Methods of Socio-Medical Research," in Freeman, Levine, and Reeder, *Handbook of Medical Sociology*, pp. 449–471.

89. John Cassel, Ralph Patrick, and David Jenkins, "Epidemiological Analysis of the Health Implications of Culture Change: A Conceptual Model," *Annals of the New York Academy of Sciences*, LXXXIV (1960), 938–949; William Caudill, *Effects of Social and Cultural Systems in Reactions to Stress*, Pamphlet 14 (New York: Social Science Research Council, 1958); Leo W. Simmons and Harold C. Wolff, *Social Science in Medicine* (New York: Russell Sage Foundation, 1954).

90. This parallel is developed further by Suchman in *Sociology and the Field of Public Health*, pp. 86–97.

91. John E. Gordon, "The Twentieth Century—Yesterday, Today, and Tomorrow (1920——)," in Franklin H. Top, ed., *The History of American Epidemiology* (St. Louis: Mosby, 1952), pp. 124–125. Contains a comprehensive bibliography and discussion of modern developments.

92. Alfred Grotjahn, *Soziale Pathologie*, 1915, as quoted in George Rosen, *"Approaches to a Concept of Social Medicine, A Historical Survey"* (New York: Milbank Memorial Fund, 1949), p. 18.

93. Erwin H. Ackerknecht, "Malaria in the Upper Mississippi Valley, 1760–1900," *Bulletin of the History of Medicine*, Supplement No. 4 (Baltimore: Johns Hopkins Press, 1945).

94. Adequate treatment of the uses of social epidemiological research in public health would require a volume in itself. We can only cite a few references for the interested student. A general discussion may be found in Stanley H. King, "Social Psychological Factors in Illness," in Freeman, Levine, and Reeder, *Handbook of Medical Sociology*, pp. 99–121. This chapter offers a summary of various theories concerning the relationship of social factors to disease. An excellent theoretical and methodological critique will be found in Paul H. Hoch and Joseph Zubin, eds., *Comparative Epidemiology of the Mental Disorders* (New York: Grune and Stratton, 1961). General analyses of the role of the behavioral sciences in epidemiology are offered in Walter I. Wardwell and Claus B. Bahnson, "Problems Encountered in Behavioral Science Research in Epidemiological Studies," *American Journal of Public Health*, LIV (1964), 972–981; and Andrew C. Fleck and Francis A. J. Janni, "Epidemiology and Anthropology: Some Suggested Affinities in Theory and Method," *Human Organization*, XVI (1958), 38–40. Specific examples of social epidemiological studies are the following: E. Gartly Jaco, *The Social Epidemiology of Mental Disorders* (New York: Russell Sage Foundation, 1960); Stanley H. King and Sidney Cobb, "Psychosocial Factors in the Epidemiology of Rheumatoid Arthritis," *Journal of Chronic Diseases*, VII (1958), 466–475; Alexander Leighton, *My Name Is Legion* (New York: Basic Books, 1959). Leighton presents a detailed theoretical framework of social stress as a factor in mental illness. See also other volumes in this series by Leighton and his colleagues Leo Srole *et al.*, *Mental Health in the Metropolis* (New York: McGraw-Hill, 1962). See also other volumes in this New York City series. Saxon Graham, "Social Factors in the Epidemiology of Cancer at Various Sites," *Annals of the New York Academy of Sciences*, LXXXIV (1960), 807–815.

Elliot G. Mishler and Norman A. Scotch, "Socio-Cultural Factors in the Epidemiology of Schizophrenia," *Psychiatry: Journal for the Study of Interpersonal Processes,* XXVI (1963), 315–351. Charles Y. Glock and H. Lennard, "Studies in Hypertension," *Journal of Chronic Diseases,* V (1956), 178–184.

95. Saunders, *op. cit.*

96. Talcott Parsons, *The Social System* (Glencoe, Ill.: The Free Press, 1951), Chapter 10. See also "Definitions of Health Illness in the Light of American Values and Social Structure," in Jaco, *Patients, Physicians, and Illness,* pp. 165–187.

97. Stanley King, *Perceptions of Illness and Medical Practices* (New York: Russell Sage Foundation, 1962). This book offers an excellent conceptual framework for integrating all the cultural, social, and psychological, as well as the physiological, components of the health system.

98. The public health literature today is full of exhortations to public health workers to recognize this dramatic shift in the basic nature of their problems. See, for example, Alan Gregg, "The Future Health Officer's Responsibility: Past, Present, and Future," *American Journal of Public Health,* XLVI (1956), 1384–1389.

99. Edward Stainbrook, "Health and Disease and the Changing Social and Cultural Environment of Man," *American Journal of Public Health,* LI (1961), 1011.

100. A very useful model for such research on public health organizations may be easily adapted from the following analysis by Barton of educational organizations:

A simple *substantive* classification of what is measured may be the best starting point. We may distinguish three "external characteristics" of organizations:

1. *Inputs:* the kind of personnel recruited, the economic resources available, the physical facilities.

2. *Outputs:* the physical production, effects on people, or other services and consequences of organizational activity.

3. *Environment:* the characteristics of the community to which the organization belongs, or its relations with other organizations.

We may also distinguish three main types of "internal characteristics," each of which has important subdivisions.

4. *Social structure:* formal and informal relationships within the organization, including:
    a. formal authority structure
    b. power structure
    c. communication and job contact structure
    d. informal social relationship
    e. division of labor and departmentalization
    f. size

5. *Attitudes:* broadly defined to include values, norms, perceptions, satisfaction, and similar individual states of mind.
    a. organizational goals and values
    b. norms concerning organizational roles
    c. perceptions of organizational characteristics
    d. satisfaction with role or with organization

6. *Activities*—including:
    a. individual role behavior
    b. collective activities
    c. administrative devices

Allen Barton, *The Measurement of Organizational Characteristics and Its Bearing on the Study of Colleges* (New York: Columbia University Press, 1960), pp. 1–2.

101. Robert K. Merton, George G. Reader, and Patricia L. Kendall, eds., *The Student Physician* (Cambridge: Harvard University Press, 1957).
102. Howard Becker *et al.*, *Boys in White: Student Culture in Medical School* (Chicago: University of Chicago Press, 1961).
103. Ray H. Elling, "Health Organizations and the Social Environment," paper presented at Annual Meeting of the American Sociological Association, Montreal, Canada, 1964, p. 38. This paper presents an excellent appraisal of the development and current status of organizational and occupational problems in the health field today.
104. Sol Levine and Paul E. White, "The Community of Health Organizations," in Freeman, Levine, and Reeder, *Handbook of Medical Sociology*, p. 343.
105. Nicholas J. Demerath, "The Place of the Sciences of Administration in Medical Care," paper presented at the Annual Meeting of the American Association for the Advancement of Science, Denver, Colorado, December 29, 1961.
106. Edward G. McGavran, "The Future of Schools of Public Health," unpublished paper presented at the School of Public Health Dedication Ceremony, University of North Carolina, Chapel Hill, North Carolina, April 6, 1963, pp. 1–2. McGavran observes, "If we are not a profession of public health distinct in purpose and function with a distinctive body of knowledge and competence, then the quicker we return to medical schools from which we sprung—to nursing schools, dental schools, veterinary schools, to engineering schools, to schools of education, etc., the better—to be trained as public health specialists in these professions."
107. Kurt W. Back *et al.*, "Public Health as a Career of Medicine: Secondary Choice within a Profession," *American Sociological Review*, XXIII (1958), 533–541. See also R. E. Coker *et al.*, "Public Health as Viewed by the Medical Student," *American Journal of Public Health*, XLIX (1959), 601–609.
108. Manet Fowler, *Evaluation of Public Health Physician Training*, New York State Department of Health, Progress Report (mimeographed, February, 1959).
109. Cohart and Hiscock, *op. cit.*, pp. 1525–1532. See also Cohart, Willard, and Hiscock, *op. cit.*, p. 452.
110. Ronald G. Corwin and Marvin J. Taves, "Nursing and Other Health Professions," in Freeman, Levine, and Reeder, *Handbook of Medical Sociology*, pp. 187–212.
111. Clifford H. Grove and Josephine R. Campbell, *Organization and Staffing for Local Health Services*, rev. ed., U.S. Public Health Service, Publication No. 682 (Washington: Government Printing Office, 1961).
112. Robert P. Bullock, *What Do Nurses Think of Their Profession?* (Columbus: Ohio State University Research Foundation, 1954), pp. 27–62.
113. Marvin J. Taves, Ronald G. Corwin, and J. Eugene Haas, *Role Conception and Vocational Success and Satisfaction* (Columbus, Ohio: Bureau of Business Research, 1964).
114. As Saunders points out, "The present function of the graduate nurse is not to nurse the patient but to see that he is nursed." Lyle Saunders, "The Changing Role of Nurses," *American Journal of Nursing*, LIV (1954), 1094–1098. See also Ronald G. Corwin, Marvin J. Taves, and J. Eugene Haas, "Professional Disillusionment," *Nursing Research*, X (1961), 141–144.
115. Everett C. Hughes, Helen M. Hughes, and Irwin Deutscher, *Twenty Thousand Nurses Tell Their Story* (Philadelphia: Lippincott, 1958).

116. Leonard Reissman and John H. Rohrer, eds., *Change and Dilemma in the Nursing Profession* (New York: Putnam, 1957).

117. Howard Ennes, ed., "A Critique of Community Public Health Services," *American Journal of Public Health*, XLVII (1957), Part 2, p. 40.

118. James L. Troupin, "Schools of Public Health in the United States and Canada: 1959–1960," *American Journal of Public Health*, L (1960), 1–22.

119. Rodger L. Buck, "Behavioral Scientists in Schools of Medicine," *Journal of Health and Human Behavior*, II (1961), 59–64.

120. Cohart and Hiscock, *op. cit.*, p. 1527.

121. Conference on Public Health and the Behavioral Sciences, Harrisburg, Pennsylvania, March, 1963.

122. California State Department of Health, "Identification of Social Components in Health Department Programs: A Guide Developed by the Social Service Staff," *American Journal of Public Health*, XLV (1955), 125.

123. George Foster, "Public Health and Behavioral Science: The Problem of Teamwork," *American Journal of Public Health*, LI (1961), 1288.

124. Leonard S. Cottrell, Jr., and Eleanor B. Sheldon, "Problems of Collaboration between Social Scientists and the Practicing Professions," *Annals of the American Academy of Political and Social Science*, CCCXLVI (1963), 126–137.

125. See Haven Emerson, "Essential Local Public Health Services," *Annals of the American Academy of Political and Social Science*, CCLXXIII (1951), 19–24; and Hanlon, *op. cit.*, for more detailed descriptions of public health programs. The following two articles deal with the relation of social science to the planning of these programs: Andie L. Knutson, "Human Behavior Factors in Program Planning," *Public Health Reports*, LXX (1954), 1129–1134; and George M. Foster, "Use of Anthropological Methods and Data in Planning and Operation," *Public Health Reports*, LXVIII (1953), 841–857.

126. Tertiary prevention, or rehabilitation, is particularly amenable to a sociological approach. Rabinowitz and Mitsos point out that rehabilitation is based on the following sociological assumptions: (1) therapeutic services are required only to the extent that they help to overcome "sociocultural dislocation"; (2) stages of rehabilitation are divided and characterized by a series of emotional and interpersonal crises; (3) the primary service of rehabilitation personnel is to promote role-reforming experiences (resocialization). Herbert S. Rabinowitz and Spiro B. Mitsos, "Rehabilitation as Planned Social Change: A Conceptual Framework," *Journal of Health and Human Behavior*, V (1964), 2–14. Also see Marvin B. Sussman, ed., *Sociology and Rehabilitation* (Washington, D.C.: American Sociological Association, 1965).

127. John A. Clausen, *Sociology and the Field of Mental Health* (New York: Russell Sage Foundation, 1956).

128. Edward A. Suchman, "The Addictive Diseases as Socio-Environmental Health Problems," in Freeman, Levine, and Reeder, *Handbook of Medical Sociology*, pp. 123–143.

129. See, for example, A. Yankauer *et al.*, "An Evaluation of Prenatal Care and Its Relationship to Social Class and Social Disorganization," *American Journal of Public Health*, XLIII (1953), 1001.

130. Conference on Public Health and the Behavioral Sciences, *op. cit.*, pp. 18–19.

131. "Possibilities and Problems in the Utilization of Behavioral Sciences in Official Health Agencies," *op. cit.*, pp. 6–7.

132. Charles L. Wilber, "Introduction," Conference on Public Health and the Behavioral Sciences, *op. cit.*, p. 3.

133. And continue to be successful today both in maintaining communicable disease

control and in mounting new programs such as immunization against poliomyelitis.

134. Prominent among these are such conditions as coronary heart disease, cancer,
accidents, diabetes, nephritis, arthritis, mental illness, air pollution, alcoholism,
and perinatal mortality. In regard to these conditions, James states, "It must
be recognized that none of these programs [current public health programs],
intriguing though they may be, has accomplished a major breakthrough against
the total community health problem posed by the given disease." George James,
"Planning and Evaluation of Health Programs," in *Administration of Community Health Services* (Chicago: The International City Managers' Association,
1961), p. 132.

135. George James, "Community Disease Detection Programs," *New York State
Journal of Medicine,* LXI (1961), 2757.

136. As described by Dwork, a state commissioner of health, "We talk today, all
of us, about the factors that go into this lack of success: basic inertia, lack of
understanding on the part of the public, the desire to retain local political prerogatives, the fear of losing out by vested interests—these are but some of the
obstacles that confront us." Ralph E. Dwork, "A Critique of Community Public
Health Services: Purpose and Nature," *American Journal of Public Health,*
XLVII (1957), Part 2, p. 4.

137. "If this need has been met in very few communities, official and voluntary
agencies at every level—national, state, and local must say their *mea culpas.*
None of us is guiltless. The fault may be a failure to recognize the social trends,
the new forces arising in community life and already giving impetus to the
application of new health knowledge. . . . The failure is ours." John D. Porter-
field, "Local Health Services . . . Now and in the Future," *American Journal
of Public Health,* XLVII (1957), Part 2, p. 30.

138. State Charities Aid Association, *op. cit.,* p. 16.

139. Edward A. Suchman, "Health Orientation and Medical Care," *American Journal
of Public Health,* LVI (1966), 97–105.

140. First National Conference on Evaluation in Public Health (University of Michigan, 1955), p. 17; State Charities Aid Association, *op. cit.,* p. 43.

141. Lyle Saunders, "The Contributions and Limitations of Behavioral Science in
Public Health," paper prepared for the Institute on Behavioral Sciences and
Public Health, Santa Monica, California, April 9–11, 1961.

142. For a fairly detailed discussion of these problems in collaboration between
sociologists and public health workers, see Edward A. Suchman, *Sociology and
the Field of Public Health,* pp. 155–174.

143. Dag Hammarskjöld, *Markings* (New York: Knopf, 1964), p. 122.

Aging

GORDON F. STREIB

HAROLD L. ORBACH

chapter 22

The Development of Social Gerontology and the Sociology of Aging

Social gerontology as a field has been molded and shaped by the concepts and ideas of sociology and social psychology. Its origin and development as a branch of the broader field of gerontology—the scientific study of aging in all its aspects—can be traced to the blending and merging of theoretical, research, and practical efforts on the part of sociologists, psychologists, physicians, psychiatrists, biologists, anthropologists, economists, and social workers in academic, governmental, and private settings in the past twenty-five years.

Despite the central role that sociological concepts and ideas and sociological thinking in general occupy in social gerontology, and despite the fact that sociologists have been primarily responsible for the emergence and development of the field as it exists today, it is curious that the initial impulses for its development did not come from sociologists. As a discipline, sociology was slow to recognize and adopt a strong interest and concern with gerontology and aging as a substantive field. In contrast to other portions of the life cycle, such as youth or childhood, and to other areas of social problems and social institutionalization, such as crime and delinquency, the study of aging and of the older population's impact on society have been relatively neglected or ignored. Similarly there has been little attention given to the study of age as a central aspect of social organization and social structure: age groups, age statuses, and age grading. Moreover, there has been little work on age as an important characteristic of societies and social systems, both in terms of their age structure and their process of aging over time, and of the interrelationship of the two facets as they affect the various institutional arrangements in society.[1]

Social gerontology and the sociology of aging are closely related fields, both relatively undeveloped and both emerging as a result of similar impulses and interest. Social gerontology is more than merely a sociology of old age, although the latter is its original central sociological core. Burgess, who historically has been the key figure in initiating much of the activity and research that led to the establishment of the field,[2] has offered this definition:

> Social gerontology is a new field of research and teaching which is not directly concerned with the biological aspects of aging but concentrates rather upon its economic, social psychological, sociological, and political aspects. Its object of research is not individual organisms but people as population aggregates, as members of society and its component groups, and as the creators and carriers of culture. Specifically social gerontology studies the status and roles of older persons, their cultural patterns, social organization, and collective behavior as they are affected by and as they affect social change.[3]

Tibbitts, the developer and popularizer of the term *social gerontology* and editor of the landmark *Handbook of Social Gerontology,* commenting on Burgess' definition, has argued that "social gerontology is . . . an organized field of knowledge concerned with the behavioral aspects of aging in the individual, with aging as a societal phenomenon, and with the interrelationships between the two."[4] Taking its primary concern from the period of the Middle Ages and after, social gerontology is seen by Tibbitts to involve a cross-disciplinary social-science approach.

The course of development of social gerontology as a field has seen the initial primary interest in old age expand to a consideration of the general problem of age roles and age grading in society. Furthermore, there is a realization that the problems of a sociology of old age cannot be approached properly without a consideration of the over-all character of age-infused and age-related phenomena.[5] Thus, in area after area, consideration of a given problem of old age has been extended because its meaning cannot otherwise be fathomed. The aged as a population group become a meaningful unit of study only in relation to other age groups, and this leads to the study of population composition. The impetus of studying the older segment has led to basic theoretical work on population composition itself.[6] Problems of age consciousness and self-conception of the aged lead directly to the general subject of age consciousness of all age groups, the relative self-conceptions of varying age groups and their conceptions of other age groups, and the importance of age statuses in different cultures and in different segments of any given society. Questions of ethnic, class, and sex differences immediately pose themselves. In the purely biological study of aging, the focus is not only the nature of old age but the entire process of aging itself, of the entire scope of growth and development; similarly, in the field of social gerontology, the focus on old age leads to a study of the aging process and the social nature and meaning of age and age changes.

As the growth of social gerontology as a discipline has moved from much of its initial ameliorative domination, it has contributed the basic fund of research and theoretical development from which a sociology of aging could be constructed. The historical circumstance of this intellectual development and its underlying causes in the accelerating attention and concern with the problems of older people in modern society has meant that the sociology of aging is so far essentially a part of social gerontology. Unlike the psychology of aging, which took a "natural" course of development from concern with early childhood to growth and development into adulthood and thence into old age, marked by the intellectual domination of developmental psychology, sociological concern with aging has moved from the older ages downward to a meeting with concerns for the earlier ages. In so doing, it has in various areas such as work, family, and socialization prodded the beginnings of thinking and research in the direction of more general consciousness of age-related phenomena. As a consequence the use of sociological perspectives in gerontology has had an important feedback effect on the perspectives of many basic areas of sociology.

Thus the proper understanding of the importance of sociological ideas in gerontology requires an awareness of the development of gerontology itself as a relatively new scientific field in which a combination of purely scientific, practical, and applied interests from a variety of scientific and practical fields has been blended into an identifiable area under the impact of the social phenomenon of population aging and its consequences.

Historical Perspective—The Emergence of a New Field

Concern with the length of human life, or more precisely with the prolongation of human life, has been a subject of interest to man for as far back as historical evidence is available. Parallel to this has been the quest for the prolongation of the attributes of youthful life, whether through the warding off of the effects of age or through rejuvenation. From the 4,000-year-old Smith Papyrus which begins with the exciting promise "The beginning of the book for transforming an old man into a youth"[7] to the latest, most modern methods of chemical and physiological treatments, the records of the concerns with long life and youthful life are abundant.[8] Through the ages the search for longevity and youthfulness has gone hand in hand with a distaste for the conditions of age and its infirmities and quite often for the aged themselves. While writers, poets, and playwrights, with an occasional assist from philosophers, were portraying the process and effects of aging, alchemists and doctors were busy attempting to do something about it. Scientific concern with gerontology—with the study of the nature and process of aging—may be dated as Comfort does with Francis Bacon's *History of Life and Death* (1645), but it was not until the twentieth century that systematic study of aging commenced, although there were many attempts in the nineteenth century.[9]

Quite naturally, the founders and leaders of research and study into the nature and problems of aging were physicians and medical researchers. Almost invariably the pioneers combined a purely scientific concern for knowledge with its application and uses. Just as sociology came of age with the designation of the discipline by Comte, so too the study of aging can be linked to the identification of a separate, specialized field of study by its name givers. The father of modern geriatric medical research and practice, Ignatz L. Nascher, coined the word "geriatrics" in 1909 and gave birth to a new medical field.[10] A pioneer in social medicine, Nascher concerned himself with social conditions of the aged as much as with pure medicine and even wrote on social conditions in general, publishing a volume entitled *The Wretches of Povertyville*, a study of the New York Bowery, the same year he christened geriatrics. Nascher's early concern with aging is reputed to have arisen from his observation of elderly patients in a municipal hospital in his native Vienna, and he retired from medical practice to run New York City's old-age colony.[11]

Concern with broader aspects of aging than the purely medical ones blossomed in the 1920's with the publication of G. Stanley Hall's *Senescence*[12] and the simultaneous development of psychological research in Russia under Pavlov and his school, in France, Germany, and central Europe, and in Japan.[13] Hall's very title and the nature of most psychological research in this period characterize the orientation of the field at this time. *Senescence* and *senility* are the key concepts, and it is the nature of *individual* deterioration and decline that is the focus of study. Just as biological and medical research in aging was oriented around growth and decline, so psychological research, arising out of developmental psychology, concentrated on age-related changes in psychomotor and functional capacities. Learning ability, intelligence, and motor-processes changes in the later years, along with the nature of senility as a psychological state, are the major topics of concern in early studies. The field was still called "aging," and apparently unnoticed was Rybnikov, the originator of the term *gerontology*, as well as his outlining of the nature of this new discipline: "The behavior of old age must become a special field, 'gerontology,' of the science of behavior. The aim of this science is the investigation of the conditioning causes of old age, as well as the study and careful description of the regular progress of the changes in behavior peculiar to age."[14]

Although research and publication of studies on various aspects of aging grew rapidly in the late 1920's and in the 1930's, the discipline of gerontology was not formally recognized, nor was the name used in any form until 1940. The pioneer work in the United States around which the new emerging field crystallized, Cowdry's *Problems of Ageing*, contains only one oblique reference to "gerontologists," and this refers to the need for "so-called gerontologists," physicians specializing in "geriatrics," the medical problems of the elderly.[15] Along with the ignoring of Rybnikov's new discipline of gerontology there was a similar lack of continuity of geriatrics, which made only the above-mentioned appearance in Cowdry, although it did appear as the title of a few articles in the 1920's and 1930's.[16] But neither term made any public impact until the 1940's, when both were simultaneously rediscovered. The study of aging then entered into its scientific maturity with the self-conscious articulation of gerontology as a scientific discipline and the formation of professional societies devoted to gerontology and geriatrics.

The rechristener of gerontology appears to have been the physician Edward J. Stieglitz, who in 1940 became the head of a newly established Unit on Gerontology in the National Institute of Health. The appearance of this first distinct organization devoted self-consciously to gerontology coincided with the sudden public use of the term, first in the new name of the unit itself, in articles by Stieglitz and then by others in both scientific and popular journals.[17] The history of the Unit on Gerontology has been traced by a number of gerontologists.[18] Its impact was to carry forward the developing special concern with aging as a separate discipline which had been galvanized by the publication of Cowdry's *Problems of Ageing* and the formation of the Club for Research in Ageing in 1939. Through the identification of aging and old age as a separate and unified field of study, the rechristening had the effect of stimulating research and the development of theory. The intervention of World War II delayed activity, but in 1945 the Gerontological Society, Inc., was organized, and in 1946 the *Journal of Gerontology* made its appearance. The first issue carried as its lead article an articulation of the new field.[19] The notable feature of this presentation was its conception of gerontology as a broad multidisciplinary field encompassing both natural and social sciences. Prior to this time, despite the increasing contributions of social scientists, gerontology had been dominated and guarded by biological and clinical scientists. It was viewed as essentially a biological-medical field with some concession to physiological psychology.[20]

This was true despite the fact that a great deal of research had already been undertaken on nonmedical and nonbiological aspects of aging and that the major basis for increasing interest and concern with problems of aging was due to the impact of a growing older population. The problem seems to have been that there was a good deal of concern with *social* aspects and *social* implications of an aging population, but that thinking about these subjects was not *sociological*. While a growing number of medical scientists were concerned with social medicine, many others were not. Social science was not entirely respectable in the 1930's and many natural scientists looked with disdain upon social science as merely pretentious social welfare. The social thinking of many nonsocial scientists was anything but sociological. It was ideological: couched in terms of emotional, financial, and welfare needs of the poor and guided by paternalistic and philanthropic motives.

The growing concern with aging had arisen out of the social and economic conditions of the 1920's and 1930's and the basic population facts of a growing number and proportion of older persons in the United States and other Western nations. The notion of population decline was current because of the falling birth rate, and with it population "decay" as an aging, thus intellectually and physically declining, population was foreseen for the future. With the depression of the 1930's making the aged more visible and vocal, the demand for old-age pensions reached its apex in the Townsend Movement. The passage of the Social Security Act had given rise to forecasts of economic disaster, for it was predicted that the aged would drain the struggling economy of its lifeblood because tax revenues would give them benefits and support them in idleness. It was further argued that the consequences of these actions would be physically and psychologically damaging to the individual, to his family, and to society.[21]

More enlightened influences existed, however, and pointed out the potential of the social-science contributions to gerontology. One of these was Lawrence K. Frank, who held a strategic position within the Josiah Macy, Jr., Foundation, which financially supported the Club for Research in Ageing. Other influences were the publication of Cowdry's volume (with social-science chapters by Wissler, Dubin, Hamilton, and Miles),[22] the establishment of the Unit on Gerontology in the National Institute of Health, and the founding of the Gerontological Society. All these led to the infusion of ideas of social science and social medicine into gerontology from as early as 1936.[23]

The character of this influence and its guiding ideas can probably be seen best from the earliest statement. In its first report, the Macy Foundation outlined its approach. Under the heading of "Growth, Development,

Maturation and Aging" is indicated the developmental viewpoint that guided its granting activity from behavioral development in infants to the problems of old age:

Scientific interest in these earlier stages of growth and development, both animal and human, has been rapidly increasing during the past few decades, but the problems of aging have only recently begun to receive attention. The Foundation's concern with the problem of aging arises from the belief that this rather neglected field of investigation demands increasing attention because of its implications for individual and social welfare. All competent students of population trends agree that the age distribution of the population of the United States is rapidly changing toward a predominantly older group. At the same time students of economics agree that the trend is toward the elimination of the older worker from employment, not only because the older worker cannot sustain the pressure of present day occupations, but also because of the availability of younger men and women for a limited and perhaps rapidly diminishing supply of jobs. . . .[24]

It is evident that under the best possible circumstances and with continued employment, individual men and women passing middle life must face serious readjustments for which we have little knowledge, insights, or releases. Furthermore, since each individual is inextricably caught in the web of life, involving his whole family, the failure of the older individual to achieve some measure of adjustment to his surroundings and within himself carries serious consequences for others. . . . The study of how the various organ systems age must be conceived in terms of the inevitable personality readjustments that go with advancing years. The individual man or woman is no more capable of dealing with these personality problems alone than with the more strictly somatic difficulties, or the larger social economic trends. In providing for the aging individual the health-care of the future is confronted with one of its largest opportunities and most severe challenges.[25]

The Macy Foundation also stressed the importance of medicine as a social institution, and it was the notion of social medicine that originally gave rise to the idea of social gerontology. The expression "social gerontology" was also used by Stieglitz. In the course of his articulation of gerontology and geriatrics and their relationship, Stieglitz as a geriatrician and proponent of social medicine apparently naturally fell into this terminology. His first use of the term came in a paper given in 1948, which later formed the basis for the initial chapter of his book on *Geriatric Medicine*, published in 1954.[26]

Dividing gerontology into three major areas, Stieglitz proposed them as (1) Geriatric Medicine, (2) The Biology of Senescence, and (3) Social Gerontology.[27] Under the latter he included all economic and cultural facets of aging such as employment, retirement, chronic illness, housing, education for senescence, marriage, family attitudes toward the aged, social attitudes, cultural maturation, and international aspects of maturing populations.[28] He stated summarily that "sociologic gerontology concerns man as a social organism, existing in a social environment and being affected by it as well as affecting it." [29] "Social medicine," he argued, "is essentially identical with medical sociology." [30] As a clinician, Stieglitz naturally did not contribute to any detailed articulation of social gerontology in terms of theoretical or research concepts, but he demonstrated an advanced awareness of its cross-disciplinary character, while revealing some of his personal ideological concerns at the same time.[31]

The initial conceptualization of social gerontology and its clear identification with sociology, then, came from a physician responsible for the identification of the field of gerontology proper. Stieglitz' idea, however, was not immediately picked up, as had been his earlier introduction of "gerontology." In fact, it was generally ignored and forgotten until it was revived and expanded through the efforts of Tibbitts and Donahue. The growing interest and attention of social scientists in the 1940's and 1950's to gerontology led to the creation of an Inter-University Training Institute in Social Gerontology in 1957. Arising out of a conference under the auspices of the Psychological and Social Science Division of the Gerontological Society, this institute, located at the University of Michigan under Donahue's direction, was the spark that repeated for social gerontology what Stieglitz' Unit on Gerontology had done earlier for gerontology.[32]

Tibbitts developed and conceptualized the field of social gerontology in a paper at the 1958 University of Michigan Conference on Aging, *Social Gerontology and Its Applications*. This became the basis for his introductory chapter in the sociologically oriented *Handbook of Social Gerontology*. The usage of social gerontology in the pioneering work of the institute by Donahue fixed the academic and popular conception of the field and finally crystallized its emergence as a new field. In this process sociological perspectives and sociological concepts and theories began to assume a dominant role in molding and shaping its content and in directing the character of the applied and practical aspects of its work.

This development can be seen in the contributions to the volumes in the *Handbooks of Social Gerontology* edited by Tibbitts and Burgess and in the research and publications in the field since their appearance.[33] The over-all characteristic of this infusion of sociological perspectives has been the shifting of the orientation of research and theory from the earlier concern with the individual and his adjustment as the focus of attention, often without any theoretical perspective other than a derived biological and developmental version of aging as a sort of development in reverse or period of declining individual organismic activity, to a more richly infused awareness of the essentially social meaning and definition of old age and aging on both the personal and societal levels.

Applications and Potential Uses of Sociology

The preceding historical analysis has pointed up the intellectual roots of the sociology of aging and suggests that its potential applications are very broad. However, we see that the sociology of aging is a relatively new subdiscipline, and hence the degree to which practitioners have applied sociological concepts and findings is limited.

In this section, we shall first consider some of the major research findings which sociologists have presented and point out that, given the present state of knowledge, there are important concepts and data which might be considered by the practitioner. Furthermore, we shall present a few examples where concepts and findings have already been utilized in practical situations. Five areas will be considered which are of crucial importance to practitioners in the field of aging: retirement, health, family, housing, and community.

RETIREMENT

One of the crucial problems related to aging in an industrialized society is retirement, for it involves a cessation of important social roles, a sharp reduction in income, and lessened opportunity for social contacts. In considering retirement, we should first examine some of the myths and stereotypes which have arisen and may be influencing the fields of application. When the growing body of systematic knowledge is more widely known, it is presumed that these myths and stereotypes will give way to more realistic and valid views of retirement and its characteristics.

Social scientists have made a basic contribution which enriches our understanding of retirement; namely, that it is not a simple phenomenon. It is highly complex and is interrelated with other social variables and processes. Research has clearly pointed out that in order to assess the effect of retirement, one needs to know more than the fact that a person has undergone a major status and role change.

One of the important findings which sociologists have uncovered concerning retirement is that persons of all occupational levels tend to view it negatively. This generalization is based on small and nonrepresentative samples, but the consistency with which the finding is reported permits us to accept it as valid.[34]

Another dimension of expectation that may influence a person's adjustment to retirement is the accuracy of his preconception of the retirement role. Thompson has shown that accuracy of preconception and a favorable preretirement attitude are major variables contributing to adjustment in retirement.[35] Moreover, a favorable retirement attitude is closely related to expected retirement income.

These findings suggest that the practitioner who is interested in facilitating adjustment to retirement must consider a program of creating more favorable preretirement attitudes. Given the present state of knowledge, we cannot state with great assurance what are the most effective ways of developing such attitudes. Some experimentation is being conducted with counseling programs and preretirement courses. Probably what is needed is a general shift in the attitudes of important segments of American society concerning retirement and leisure. With the present emphasis in our society on youth activities and work, there is a need for a change in attitudes and values supportive of the situation of the older person who has completed the more gainful and productive period of his life. Sociologists and others have sharpened our perspectives on leisure and the uses of time in the middle years and later phases of the life cycle. The volumes edited by Kleemeier[36] and Donahue *et al.*[37] are particularly valuable.

One stereotype which is commonly held concerning aging and retirement is that retirement has a deleterious mental and physical effect on the health of the retiree. Evidence from several studies indicates that this is not true.[38] Moreover, studies of mortality tables show that persons who are compulsorily retired do not have higher mortality rates than would be expected on the basis of actuarial experience. Research has shown that persons who retire voluntarily have higher death rates than expectation, but this is probably due to the fact that this group includes a large number who retire because of poor health. This finding suggests that it is necessary to consider retirees on a more individual basis than is presently the case. The use of arbitrary age categories to determine retirement results in sick persons' staying on until the formal retirement age in order to collect their benefits and healthy persons' being retired while they are still able to be productive members of the labor force. The development of flexible criteria for retirement is probably one of the most important applied areas worthy of further systematic inquiry.

Another misconception concerning the aged which sociological research has modified is the idea of the aged as a homogeneous population. It is true that there is a disproportionate number of sick and poor people among the aged; however, there is a full range of income levels and health conditions among them, too. Furthermore, all major strata, categories, and groupings are found among the aged. From the standpoint of the person concerned with applied programs, it is absolutely essential that the fundamental heterogeneity of these people be recognized and made a basic assumption in planning for them. Community leaders who establish Senior Citizens' Centers in the hope of attracting the interest of the great majority of the community's retired citizens are bound to be disappointed. Only a small percentage of the aged, like all other age categories, are participants in voluntary organizations.

Another major sociological concept which can be helpful in understanding the problems of the aged is that of role and role definition. The role of the retiree is probably one of the most ambiguous in our society. Part of this ambiguity is the result of the lack of a distinct reference group for the aged, and particularly the male retiree. Leonard Cottrell and others have shown the importance of clear-cut role definitions.[39] Cottrell says, "The degree of adjustment to roles which a society assigns to its age-sex categories varies directly with the clarity with which such roles are defined."[40]

Another proposition from role theory which may be used by practitioners in the field of aging is one related to the practical problem of whether it is desirable to retire persons gradually or suddenly. Cottrell says, "The degree of adjustment to a future role varies directly with the degree of importance attached to and the definiteness of the transitional procedures used by the society in designating the change in the role."[41]

In practical terms, this proposition suggests that if an employing organization adheres to a policy of gradual retirement, such as lengthening the vacation period from one month to two or three months over a period of years, the retiree will adapt more satisfactorily than if he is retired suddenly. Unfortunately, the empirical data concerning gradual versus sudden retirement are so limited that it is difficult to generalize about this matter.

Retirement, like many other social phenomena, is highly complex, and if one is to understand the adjustment people make in retirement, one must view it from the standpoint of role deficits. The low morale of some aged males has been shown to be related to a complex of at least three factors: not working (retirement), poor health, and low socioeconomic status. These three variables tend to act independently and create a cumulative effect on the adjustment of the retiree.[42] One other role deficit which undoubtedly affects the morale of the aged male is whether or not he is widowed. All these factors must be considered in analyzing the outlook, adjustment, and morale of crucial subgroups of the aged in industrialized societies.

It is, of course, premature to say how these findings will eventually be applied. However, we assume that with increased concern with problems of the aging and the aged, they will be useful to administrators and persons in applied fields who are looking for new insights and approaches to problems of application.

An example of how sociological research information has affected policy and eventually resulted in a change in practices is the way in which certain findings obtained in the Cornell Study of Occupational Retirement were employed to establish a preretirement preparation program and to initiate a selective retirement schedule in the Tennessee Valley Authority.

The Cornell Retirement study included about three hundred organizations, both private and governmental. After the data had been processed from the first wave of this longitudinal study, a progress report was sent to the participating organizations. The data were presented in chart form showing the way in which the employees in the various categories of organizations—clothing and textiles, machinery, education, federal government, among others—responded to the questions in the study. The researchers selected a series of questions which might be of interest to executives and administrators concerned with retirement and programs related to it. Charts were offered showing frequency distributions for each of the major industrial categories. In addition, for those organizations which had twenty-five or more employees in the study, the percentage of participating employees who responded to a particular item was shown on the charts. Thus the reader could see how the employees of his organization responded in comparison with those of others in the industrial categories.

Among the findings which impressed the TVA administrators were those which showed that older employees did not expect to retire until required to do so. The report also disclosed that a large majority of the employees had not made any plans for retirement, disliked the idea of retiring, and felt that retirement would have an unhealthy effect on them. These older employees also believed that they were more capable than younger employees because of their skills and experience and felt they had not declined in their ability to do their work. Moreover, they believed they should be permitted to work until they wished to retire.

The Cornell findings alerted the TVA management to the fact that although they had a retirement program and provided pensions for retirees, there were misconceptions and lack of information about the retirement plan. It was thought that as a consequence of these attitudes, opinions, and beliefs employees would not be so efficient or so happy as they might be during their last years of employment and during their retirement years. Thus there was a need to resocialize the older employees.

Another consequence of the Cornell research report was that the TVA management decided to conduct a survey of their own on the opinions of supervisors about older employees. The findings were reasonably consistent with those of the Cornell study.

As a result, the normal retirement age was reduced from seventy to sixty-five, with the provision that the management could permit some employees to work beyond that age if they considered it advisable. However, retirement was mandatory at seventy. Second, the employer's contribution to the pension of an employee was increased by a third. The latter change was instituted because management reasoned that employees would be more willing to retire voluntarily if they had a larger pension, and also it might make retirements by management more acceptable. In short, the TVA management decided that some form of selective retirement was desirable and that employees should be prepared for the eventuality in advance.

As part of this shift in policy and practice, the TVA brought in a team of five outside experts, including two sociologists, who conferred with management about the implementation of the plans. Two major tasks stood out as important: the development of specific procedures for selective retirement and the inauguration of a program which would prepare employees for retirement. Both of these programs were established and are in operation. The preretirement program was evaluated by TVA personnel [43] and by a social scientist about three years after it was established.[44] They agreed in their conclusions that the program was of real benefit to employees during retirement and had improved their efficiency during their last years of service.

Finally, it should be stressed that in terms of the uses of sociology the activities which resulted in the TVA probably would not have been initiated if the sociologists had not prepared a progress report which attempted to present the findings of the Cornell survey in a form which was meaningful to the administrators who might make use of them.

When one views the uses of sociology in retirement programs and in other fields, one must distinguish between applications initiated by the practitioner and those initiated by the sociologist. In the case of the TVA we have an example in which the administration concerned with the practical problems saw how research findings pointed up problems of which they had not been fully cognizant.

A second approach is one in which the sociologist conversant with his discipline and its research findings deliberately attempts to put into practice his sociological knowledge. An example of this use of sociology is the work of Margery Mack and Ernest W. Burgess in establishing preretirement counseling programs in a number of companies in the Middle West. Mack and Burgess realized that older workers had to be resocialized for the role of retiree. Therefore they advised that some preparation be made for the new role. Burgess and Mack and their associates at the Industrial Relations Center of the University of Chicago worked out materials and plans to be used in preretirement courses. A number of industrial and business firms were contacted, and they were convinced of the value of resocializing their employees for retirement. Several companies adopted the plans, some of which have been operating for a number of years.

HEALTH

Another important research area in which sociologists have worked and which relates very closely to problems of application is that of health. Their achievements in this field are dealt with in other sections of this book, but the specific implications of the health factor for problems and applications related to aging deserve special attention here. Once again it is premature to point to specific situations in which sociological findings have been utilized, but the applied significance of the work is beyond question, particularly since the field of health care for the aged is in the forefront of public concern and is involved in many political and social discussions. Hence the role of the sociologists in this area, as in others, is that of clarifier: throwing a clear light on subjects which are obscure or distorted because of limited information or because of a failure to recognize that the facts may contravene commonly accepted ideas and preconceptions.

The research of Shanas is particularly valuable in illustrating how sociologists can clarify obscurities and misconceptions. Her data are based on a nationwide area-probability sample in which almost two thousand older persons were interviewed. The work is thus of considerable value for actual applications because the findings are representative of the older non-institutional population in the United States. A common stereotype is that the elderly are indigent, infirm, and sick. Some do suffer from these difficulties, but the research evidence clearly shows that most of the aged are functioning well both mentally and physically. Only 14 per cent of the aged outside institutions can be classified as "very sick." [45] However, the specter of extended illness is the greatest worry of the elderly. Older people believe they are in good health, and this is probably the major reason they do not think they need medical care. Many may have physical complaints, but they define these aches and pains as the normal accompaniments of growing old. This basic attitude on the part of the aged toward illness and health undoubtedly explains in large measure why they do not seek medical care. Thus it appears that the reasons are social-psychological, rather than financial. In the Shanas study a careful series of questions was used in order to ascertain why the older persons were not using medical care. Only 8 per cent of the study population—about one person in twelve—stated that they were not using medical or dental care because of lack of money.

The notion of the aged as a highly dependent segment of the population living off the earnings of others is also not supported by the facts of the nationwide survey. Shanas reported: "About seven of every ten non-institutionalized older people who incurred costs for physician services in 1957 paid these costs themselves; and at least six of every ten older people who incurred hospitalization costs met them from their own resources: income, savings, or health and hospital insurance." [46]

Obviously, the aged are not homogeneous in terms of health, income, or style of life. Therefore, there is a need to consider the heterogeneity of the aged in terms of their health, for, as Shanas emphasizes, serious physical illness is a precipitating factor in the institutionalization of many old people.[47] It is important to point out that the percentage of older persons who are in institutions of all kinds has been estimated at only between 3 and 5 per cent of the aged population.[48] Thus, empirical facts are again very useful in counteracting the misconceptions of many people that a high number of the elderly are committed to institutions.

In terms of applications, we have pointed out that it is somewhat difficult to document a direct linkage between what the sociologist reports and the adoption of new practices or the modification of existing programs. However, it is pertinent to emphasize that after the findings of the Shanas nationwide health survey appeared, which pointed up the heterogeneity of the aged population, the Division of Program Research in the Social Security Administration no longer stated that *all* the aged are poverty-stricken or *all* the aged are sick.[49]

Sociological research may have a latent function in terms of application. This type of use is illustrated by an experimental study of geriatric rehabilitation directed by Harry Posman, a sociologist, formerly of the Community Service Society of New York and now Director of Social Research in the New York State Department of Social Welfare. In conducting this research, a questionnaire was devised to determine the physical capacities of the experimental subjects. The instrument assessed powers of locomotion, ability for self-care, degree of physical independence, and so on. After the study was over, the public-health nurses found that the instrument could be used as a practical diagnostic tool in evaluating the capacity of older patients. It is now employed by public-health nurses in New York City.[50]

FAMILY

In the field of aging, the family is one of the crucial sociological groupings that have been studied. Persons concerned with the uses of sociology in the later phases of the life cycle must give careful attention to the structure and function of the family and how it relates to other groups and institutions in urban, industrialized societies. Although the family has been the focus of study by many sociologists, there are gaps in our knowledge regarding the family situation of older people and the relationship of older families to younger families.[51]

In recent years there has been a revision of the conceptual map which sociologists use in studying the family. Earlier writers such as Talcott Parsons[52] tended to view the family in terms of polarities. From this point of view, the family in industrialized society is seen in its prototypical form as the isolated nuclear family. More recent thinking has altered this theoretical analysis of the family, and empirical research has shown that the older, Parsons approach had serious limitations. Eugene Litwak,[53] who has done some of the most original thinking about family structure, has suggested the concept of the modified extended family. Marvin Sussman has brought together the relevant data which indicate that the isolated family is mostly a fiction and that intergenerational ties are of far more significance for the urban family than earlier writers have claimed.[54] Litwak has clearly shown the way in which extended family groups can be involved in the achievement of social goals. He observes that many family-life programs tend to be deficient because they are organized in terms of psychological rather than sociological premises.[55]

William E. Knox has carried further the analyses initiated by Litwak and Sussman, and he has argued that what we find in industrial America is a "conjugal system with extended family features." [56] Going further, he asserts that this type of family system is the one that functions optimally for both individuals and secondary institutions. The major implications of Knox's conceptualization of generational relations is that the generations are in a kind of symbiotic relationship to one another. The parents help young adults when they are establishing their families, and the children help their parents when they are in need.

Another example of the way in which sociological concepts and research may sharpen one's perspective on a problem related to the aged and the family is seen in the work of Schneider. Employing concepts from role theory, he examined the implications of role analysis for working women and those in retirement. Role theorists suggest that married women who live with their husbands are more likely to have a clearly defined role as retirees than do the retired single women. Schneider found, however, that the single women, and not the married, are generally more favorable toward retirement. Moreover, his work points out that the single women are more likely to make a better adjustment in retirement.[57]

Another important stereotype which can be modified on the basis of sociological research concerns the degree to which the aged are socially isolated. Here again the commonly held notion is that the aged are lonely, neglected, and cut off from human contact—particularly from their children and other relatives. In Shanas' nationwide study of older people, she reports that eight out of every ten older people are living with a spouse or others. Only 19.9 per cent live alone, and of these, three-fourths are women. Shanas estimated that less than 6 per cent of all of the old people in the United States are socially isolated.[58]

When the findings of this survey were released, personnel in the Social Security Administration became concerned about the proximity of older people and their children, for the sociological data contradicted their preconceptions about the isolated aged. As a result, the 1963 Social Security Survey of the aged included questions from the earlier nationwide survey on the proximity of parents and children.[59]

A specific example of the way in which sociological concepts and research were used in establishing a governmental program concerning the family and older persons is a project initiated in the Office of Aging (now

Administration on Aging) and carried out with funds provided by the Office of Economic Opportunity. Marvin Taves, a sociologist, brought together in an imaginative way two sociological observations: first, that old people, particularly retired persons, have a vague and diffuse role in an industrialized society like the United States, and second, that it is important for the young child to have sustained affectionate contacts with an adult. This idea was formulated by Taves and his sociologist colleagues, Donald Kent and Clark Tibbitts, in the Office of Aging and resulted in a program which employs people sixty years of age and over whose income is low. They are paid a minimum of $1.25 an hour to work four hours a day, five days a week, in close association with children under five years of age who live in orphanages and similar institutions. The participants spend about two hours a day with each child.

The program gives the older person a definite social role in the community, because he is paid for doing an important, humane public service. Furthermore, the child receives the kind of love, warmth, and attention which has been shown to be essential by a large body of research on human growth and development. Although the initiators of the idea had some reservations as to whether old people would respond positively to this kind of parent surrogate role, there have been many more applicants for the program than could be accommodated.[60]

HOUSING

One of the areas of application which have received considerable attention from policy makers and practitioners at all levels of government is that of housing for the aged.

Housing presents a unique opportunity for the uses of sociology. Here one finds an area of practical concern and application in which the practitioners and policy makers may be overstressing an assumed difficulty, for only a very small proportion of older people mention housing as a problem. Where housing is perceived as a problem for them, it can be understood more clearly as essentially a matter of inadequate income. Therefore it would be more strategic to concentrate on solving the income problem of the aged than to be concerned with details of housing facilities.

Undoubtedly one of the reasons that housing receives so much attention in applied programs is that it is concerned with material objects which are tangible and visible. On the one hand, the construction of housing specifically designed for older people is tangible evidence that "something has been done for the aged." On the other hand, when one attempts to establish programs which deal with social, emotional, and psychological problems, one encounters greater difficulty—first, in proving that the problems exist, and second, in establishing ways of solving them. It is obviously easier to focus on accomplishing something in a tangible area such as housing than in these vaguer aspects of aging that are more difficult to evaluate.

If we accept the premise that the physical aspects of housing have been overestimated as an area of concern and are not a central problem for the aged, we can then turn our attention to the social aspects of housing and consider the relevance of some of the empirical data.

Research by sociologists in the field of housing points up the importance of *social* factors of housing which can be of interest to people working in applied fields. One significant research finding, reported by Rosow, is that the density of the aged population in a given area may have significant consequences for the residents.[61] A commonly accepted premise in the field of housing has been that heterogeneous areas and housing units are more likely to contribute to the social and psychological functioning of the aged. The Rosow data contradict this notion, for they indicate that dense social areas can provide major social functions for the aged: the opportunity to create and maintain friendships; the possibility of mutual aid and support, particularly for dependent individuals and groups; and finally the provision of role models which will aid in socializing people to an aged role. The findings of research indicate that these integrated functions are most likely to occur when the proportion of the aged in the given area reaches 50 per cent or more. Further, persons who have suffered role losses, as widows and retirees, are most likely to gain from residence in areas with a high proportion of older people. These data suggest the need to re-examine the establishment of heterogeneous housing units which include old and young families in dealing with the problems of the aged.

Rosow's research also indicates that there are segments of the aged population whose needs are not being met because for social or personal reasons they resist the idea of turning to agencies which might help them. Examples of this are middle-class people who are not accustomed to depending on social and professional agencies and also certain lower-class people, particularly ethnic groups who may not like to deal with strangers. Therefore practitioners must devise ways of reaching these segments of the population who may need help.

COMMUNITY

Another basic sociological concept which has been used by social gerontologists and practitioners is that of community. This concept, although it is vague and somewhat diffuse, has deep roots in the sociological tradition and—perhaps of particular interest in this context—is a kind of common-sense notion which is of use to the program planner or practitioner.

The community concept has been developed by Sanders[62] and in the field of aging has been utilized by social scientists interested in the uses of sociological research. Some investigators, like Havighurst and Albrecht,[63] have used the small community as their focus of reference, employing broad sociological categories like the family, the class system, the church, the work place, and so forth.

Other investigators, like Stone and Slocum, have used the county as the framework for their sociological endeavors; these writers have published a monograph, *A Look at Thurston County's Older People*.[64] In this publication they have discussed, for example, health, economic circumstances, housing, use of time, and social adjustment. What is of particular interest to the readers of this volume is that the authors have explicitly set aside a section of the report in which they consider the implications of their findings for Thurston County and presumably for other counties facing similar problems and desiring to take action about them. Stone and Slocum point out that very few of their respondents have difficulty in using their free time. Only one out of ten indicated any interest in special types of housing for the aged. It is striking, however, that the need for transportation was mentioned frequently by older people living in all areas of the county. The investigators suggest that this problem might be handled on an individual basis, that is, that young people might provide transportation for their older neighbors for shopping, visiting, and leisure activities. It might be argued, however, that a more realistic approach to the problem of transportation of older citizens would be the establishment of some kind of public transportation available to all. Obviously, because of the wide use of the automobile, public transportation would have to be subsidized, but such a procedure could be justified in the same way that subsidized housing is currently accepted for the aged and other less privileged members of the community.

From the standpoint of the uses of sociological research, the Stone and Slocum study points up the importance of considering the economic status of the aged. Many of the older residents interviewed reported that they were getting along reasonably well on limited incomes. Some were in economic distress and might be helped by suitable employment. The investigators suggested that there is also a need to adjust pensions and Old Age and Survivors Insurance benefits to the cost of living. Finally, it is interesting to note in retrospect, following the passage of Medicare legislation, that Stone and Slocum stressed the need for "a more adequate method for helping older people to meet the heavy cost of hospitalization and medical care." [65]

The Stone and Slocum research was carried out at the request of state agencies. A different approach to research and its application is illustrated by the study conducted by Leonard Breen, Professor of Sociology at Purdue University, and his associates. In this instance, the research was undertaken at the invitation of the county, and during the course of the study a variety of community groups helped to identify the problems which were thought to be appropriate for investigation. Moreover, unlike the Stone and Slocum study, in which professional interviewers were employed, the Breen study used volunteer interviewers who were recruited and trained by other members of the community.

The greater involvement of community personnel in the sociological research undoubtedly contributed to the specific action programs which were initiated. The investigators observe that it is difficult to ascertain whether there was a direct connection in every case between findings and the resultant action. Breen says: "In many cases, the findings themselves at least *support* actions and decisions taken by persons in the community and are used to justify that behavior. Where tentative steps are taken in response to community behavior shown as appropriate for re-examination, the findings themselves constitute a kind of encouragement to those who would seek to make changes." [66]

The five programs in which sociological information was utilized were:

1. The establishment of an organization providing part-time work for retired persons.

2. The erection of a Senior Citizens' Housing Project financed by local banks.

3. The establishment of a recreational program for older people organized in co-operation with the City Department of Recreation.

4. A preparation for retirement education program. It was expected that the public-school system would take over this program and operate it.

5. A health program in which (a) health practitioners were informed about the survey findings and (b) a home-care program was developed in cooperation with the county medical society and county hospital.

The Purdue study clearly shows the close relationship between a community-initiated survey and the application of the resulting sociological information. Breen states, "To be sure, persons may have felt these needs prior to the survey. If this was the case, the survey served to sharpen the understanding of these needs and to make it possible to bring to the attention of the public the appropriate facts." [67]

Another political unit often considered a form of community in this country is the state. This unit is frequently used by political scientists and economists, but is rarely employed by sociologists. Much political information and considerable economic data are gathered, processed, and analyzed with the state as the basic unit. In the field of aging, the category of the state has been used in gathering large bodies of social facts and has been the field in which practical programs have been established and implemented. The White House Conference on Aging in 1961 began in a sense by sponsoring activities at the state and local level. Indeed, the federal government has awarded grants-in-aid to the states to prepare for the nationwide conference. These state conferences on aging and attendant problems have resulted in a voluminous literature.[68] Some of these materials were presented in the form of other publications or were expanded and reanalyzed for a larger audience. Examples of this kind of publication are the books published on aging in the states of Minnesota, Tennessee, and Washington.[69]

The first volume cited was edited by Arnold M. Rose, Professor of Sociology at the University of Minnesota. One of the most useful parts of this volume is a survey analyzed by Marvin J. Taves and Gary B. Hansen.[70] Here again sociologists were fact finders for administrators, practitioners, and politicians. The Taves and Hansen survey of 1,700 older persons in Minnesota focused its attention on the needs of the aging as the primary themes for their research. They report that the major dimensions of life, according to the 1,700 respondents, were social and economic well-being, health, and work. Taves and Hansen report that many of the problems related to these dimensions stem from the nature of the American social structure. Elderly citizens think that they have difficulty realizing these goals, and thus some aged feel frustrated in attempting to satisfy their needs, which they share in common with persons of other age groups.

Another way to view the problem of the aged is from the standpoint of the nation. Here, again, sociologists and other social scientists have been called upon repeatedly to offer counsel and guidance as to how programs should be established, co-ordinated, and administered. Perhaps the outstanding example of this was the collaboration by academic sociologists, other social scientists, and the administrators of programs in the 1961 White House Conference of Aging.

One of the most important areas in which sociologists have had an opportunity to apply sociological concepts and findings related to aging is through the activities of the various branches of the federal government, particularly the Office of Aging, which was established in 1963 in the Department of Health, Education, and Welfare. The organization was formerly known as the Special Staff on Aging, created in 1956; it was originally located in the Office of the Secretary of the Department of Health, Education, and Welfare. Under the Older Americans Act signed by President Johnson in July, 1965, there will be created a new Administration on Aging which will be headed by a commissioner appointed by the President. It will be the seventh major operating agency of the Department of Health, Education, and Welfare, along with the Public Health Service, Social Security Administration, Office of Education, and others. The Administration on Aging will supersede and expand the work of the Office of Aging.

The Director of the Office of Aging from 1961 to August, 1965, was a prominent sociologist, Donald Kent, formerly of the University of Connecticut, and Special Consultant on Aging to the Governor of Connecticut from 1957 to 1961. He is now Head of the Department of Sociology and Anthropology at Pennsylvania State University. Kent also served for two years as chairman of the executive committee of the Federal Council on Aging, which is the top-level policy and advisory group in the federal government concerned with aging. Members of the council include the Secretary of Labor, the Secretary of Commerce, and the Secretary of Health, Education, and Welfare, among others.

The significance of the new Administration on Aging and its two predecessor organizations was pointed up very cogently by Cottrell when he analyzed the role of the Office of Aging. He wrote:

> The strategic position of this staff makes it very significant for the study of both political influence and *decision-making*. Through the examination of the literature which it publishes, the student will be able to discern which of the many lines of possible development is likely to be pressed, the progress being made at the grass roots, some points of blockage, and the results of research which reveal new light on the needs of the aged and the possibilities of serving them more adequately.[71]

The Deputy Director of the Office of Aging has been Clark Tibbitts, also a sociologist. Tibbitts, who was also a key member of the Special Staff on Aging, has been associated with the federal government in various agencies related to aging and the aged since 1950. He has also served as an adviser and consultant to diverse public and private organizations. In 1950 he was Director of the First National Conference on Aging called by President Truman, and he played an important role in the 1961 White House Conference on Aging. Those who are familiar with the emergence and growth of federal—and also state and local—programs concerned with the aged and aging must assign a great deal of strategic influence to the sociologist-administrator Clark Tibbitts. Thus, when sociologists have important administrative posts and are called upon by policy makers in governmental agencies, it seems reasonable to assume that sociological ideas and findings are adapted and used.

Another way in which sociologists have been influential in implementing the use of sociology in applied settings related to the aged and the aging is by means of the numerous conferences and committees which have been convened in the last fifteen years. Some of these meetings have been sponsored by federal agencies, others by state bodies, and still others by private organizations related to foundations, universities, and other nonprofit organizations. A fascinating long-range research project in itself would be to try to trace the way in which the reports and recommendations of these conferences compare with subsequent legislation and action programs.

An example of a recent federal conference is one jointly sponsored by the National Institute of Child Health and Human Development

(NICHD), the Housing and Home Finance Agency, the Office of Aging, and the Gerontology Branch, Bureau of State Services, Public Health Service, and held in Washington in March, 1965. Approximately fifty persons, including a number of sociologists, considered the subject of special housing for older people. Research results were presented on patterns of living and housing, discussions of new research which is needed, and consideration of how research results presently available might be used to guide public policy in the housing field.[72] At this writing it is difficult to predict precisely the influence of a conference of this kind. However, from personal observation of a number of these conferences, the authors can state that the staff members of both executive and legislative branches of the government are very interested in knowing what sociology and, of course, other disciplines have to offer in meeting the important practical and human problems of older citizens.

An example of the kind of conference convened by a nongovernmental agency is the series of meetings sponsored by the Division of Gerontology of the University of Michigan. Here again sociological findings have been presented and undoubtedly utilized, but in ways too complex to trace here. Over the years an impressive body of social-science knowledge has been presented to the participants of these conferences. Let us take as an example the Fourteenth Annual Conference on Aging, whose proceedings were published in book form as *Politics of Age*. In describing the conference, the editors of the conference proceedings state:

> To achieve this educational experience the University was joined in cosponsorship and planning of the conference by the United States Department of Labor, the Department of Health, Education, and Welfare, the Housing and Home Finance Agency, the Veterans' Administration, the United States Senate Committee on Aging, and the Federal Council on Aging. Also, co-sponsoring were eight Michigan State agencies—Departments of Social Welfare, Mental Health, Public Instruction, the Employment Security Commission, Division of Vocational Rehabilitation, Civil Service Commission, State Library, Commission on Aging—and six voluntary groups—Michigan Society of Gerontology, Older and Retired Workers Department of the United Automobile Workers International Union, AFL-CIO Committee on Older and Retired Workers of the United Steel Workers of America, Golden Age and Senior Citizens' Clubs of the United States, Senior Citizens of America, and Senior Citizens' Association of Los Angeles County, Inc. In addition, 198 voluntary organizations—122 national, 52 state, and 24 local—served as participating agencies and most sent representatives to take part in the discussion. Thus practically all interested groups were represented—business, welfare, labor, religion, government, professional, scientific, service, and community planning.[73]

If one is to understand how sociology is used in applied gerontological activities, he must be sensitive to the important role such conferences play in bringing practitioners and sociologists and other social scientists and researchers together. It is extremely difficult to trace the causal network between the papers read, the discussions heard, and the final decision to initiate a program or to modify an existing one. Students of sociology and political scientists have not given adequate attention to the important way in which conferences are mechanisms in the process of applying concepts and ideas in programs and activities of private and governmental organizations. Cottrell has correctly pointed out that these conferences and the activities which precede and follow them are "an important new kind of structure for carrying on democratic government." In terms of applied sociology his observation of these activities is very cogent: "The study of this group process, then, may yield more satisfactory results than the study of party politics, opinion surveys, voting analysis, or other means by which some political scientists and social psychologists have tried to predict trends." [74]

If one views social science, like other science, as international in its methods, theories, and applications, an interesting example of the uses of sociology in an international setting is found in the sociology of aging. Sociologists in Denmark, Great Britain, and the United States have been conducting cross-national studies in which similar research instruments have been used to investigate common problems concerning the aged in the three countries. After hearing about this research, officials seeking to solve certain problems of the aged in Israel and Poland became interested in learning how they might conduct surveys in their countries similar to those under way elsewhere. Funds for such surveys were available under Public Law 480, but the foreign officials did not know how to proceed. With the help of the personnel in the International Office of the Welfare Administration, Department of Health, Education, and Welfare, the foreign administrators and researchers were able to initiate their projects. Thus the sociological research undertaking itself was used in obtaining precise knowledge about problems concerning the aged, with the view of initiating programs. Thus we find an application of sociology in which the practitioners had a problem to solve and initiated a sociological survey in order to obtain information to guide them in planning a program.

The Outlook for Social Gerontology and the Sociology of Aging

In this chapter we have attempted to point out the intellectual developments in the history of the fields of sociology and gerontology. We have examined theory and research in these two fields as they relate to the uses of sociology—in retirement, health, family, housing, and community programs—and have presented specific examples.

In considering the future outlook of social gerontology and the sociology of aging, it seems likely, first, that there will be greater development of theoretical approaches to deal with the problems of human aging, and these will be more infused with sociological perspectives. Second, sociological instruction will become more and more a core of training for professional personnel engaged in carrying out practical programs and formulating policies in the field at all levels. Third, sociologists will continue to be involved at all levels with the development of academic training, research, and policy making. Finally, the development of a specific sociology of aging will be part of the broader development of social gerontology.

In conclusion, when one considers the question of the uses of sociology, one cannot escape the inevitable problem of the way in which value orientations, value premises, and value judgments of individuals, subgroups, and communities enter into the articulation of theory, research, and social action. This is a problem that faces all social scientists who have interest and concern for the uses of the knowledge of their fields. One of the few writers in sociology or in social gerontology who have incisively examined basic value premises is Irving Rosow. In a brilliant essay, "Old Age: One Moral Dilemma of an Affluent Society," Rosow says:

> By now it should be clear that the crucial people in the aging problem are not the old, but the younger age groups, for it is the rest of us who determine the status and position of the old person in the social order. What is at stake for the future is not only the alienation of the old from the young, but the alienation of the young from each other and of man from man. There is no real way out of this dilemma, for young or old, without a basic reordering of our national aspirations and values, of which the aging problem is but a token. Anything less than this will see us concentrating only on superficial symptoms, especially tangible ones like housing the aged, and nibbling at the tattered edges of our problems without penetrating to their heart. But, unfortunately, at this point in our history, without almost catastrophic crisis, such pervasive changes in our national life seem most improbable in the foreseeable future.[75]

REFERENCES

1. Leonard D. Cain, Jr., "The Sociology of Aging. A Trend Report and Bibliography," *Current Sociology*, VIII, No. 2 (1959), 57–133; and "Life Course and Social Structure," in Robert E. L. Faris, ed., *Handbook of Modern Sociology* (Chicago: Rand McNally, 1964), pp. 272–309.
2. Harold L. Orbach, "The Emergence of Gerontology: Historical Background to a New Discipline," unpublished manuscript, 1964; Donald Young, "Memorandum on Suggestions for Research in the Field of Social Adjustment," *American Journal of Sociology*, XLVI (1941), 873–886.
3. Ernest W. Burgess, "Preface," *Journal of Social Issues*, XIV, No. 2 (1958), 1–2.

4. Clark Tibbitts, "Origin, Scope, and Fields of Social Gerontology," in Clark Tibbitts, ed., *Handbook of Social Gerontology* (Chicago: University of Chicago Press, 1960), pp. 3–26.

5. *Ibid.*, pp. 22 f.; Bernice L. Neugarten, "The Changing Age-Status System," in W. Lloyd Warner, ed., *The Emergence of the Great Society*, in press; Irving Rosow, "Adjustment of the Normal Aged," in Richard H. Williams, Clark Tibbitts, and Wilma Donahue, eds., *Processes of Aging* (New York: Atherton Press, 1963), II, 195–223.

6. United Nations, Department of Economic and Social Affairs, *The Aging of Populations and Its Economic and Social Implications*, Population Studies, No. 26 (New York: United Nations, 1956).

7. *Edwin Smith Surgical Papyrus*, translated by John Breasted (Chicago: University of Chicago Press, 1930).

8. Alex Comfort, *The Process of Ageing* (New York: New American Library, 1964), presents a useful review.

9. Walter R. Miles, "Age and Human Society," in Carl Murchison, ed., *A Handbook of Social Psychology* (Worcester, Mass.: Clark University Press, 1935), pp. 596–682; Frederick D. Zeman, "Life's Later Years; Studies in the Medical History of Old Age, Part 1. Introduction," *Journal of Mount Sinai Hospital*, XI (1944), 45–52, "Part 2. The Nineteenth Century," *ibid.*, XIII (1947), 241–256; James E. Birren, "A Brief History of the Psychology of Aging," *Gerontologist*, I (1961), 69–77, 124–134; Wilma Donahue, "Aging: A Historical Perspective," in *Research Utilization in Aging* (Bethesda, Md.: National Institute of Health, Department of Health, Education, and Welfare, 1964), Public Health Service Publication No. 1211, pp. 7–15.

10. Joseph T. Freeman, "The First Fifty Years of Geriatrics (1909–1959)," *Geriatrics*, XV (1960), 216–217.

11. Joseph T. Freeman, "Nascher: Excerpts from His Life, Letters, and Works," *Gerontologist*, I (1961), 17–26.

12. G. Stanley Hall, *Senescence: The Last Half of Life* (New York: Appleton, 1923).

13. Birren, *op. cit.*

14. N. A. Rybnikov, "K Vopruso o Psikhologii Starosti (The Problem of the Psychology of Age)," *Zhurnal Psikhologii i Psikhotekniki*, II (1929), 16–32. [*Psychological Abstracts*, III (1929), No. 4175.]

15. Lewellyn F. Barker, "Ageing from the Point of View of the Clinician," in Eugene V. Cowdry, ed., *Problems of Ageing: Biological and Medical Aspects* (Baltimore: Williams and Wilkins, 1939), p. 741. It should be noted that the sociologist Ernest R. Groves made a similar reference in his family textbook five years earlier: *The American Family* (Philadelphia: Lippincott, 1934), p. 300, says: "Gerontologists are rare among physicians and there is little reliable medical advice for aging." Miles, *op. cit.*, p. 619, has a single passing reference to the medical "specialty known as gerontology."

16. Orbach, *op. cit.*

17. The tracing of the emergence of the conscious elaboration of the field is detailed in *ibid.*

18. Notably, Birren, *op. cit.*; Donahue, *op. cit.*

19. Lawrence K. Frank, "Gerontology," *Journal of Gerontology*, I (1946), 1–2.

20. The Club for Research in Ageing, founded in 1939, had been almost entirely composed of biologically oriented scientists. The Gerontological Society grew out of this club, and its early officers and executive council reflected this orientation. Walter R. Miles was the only social scientist on the first executive board. After his first year as a representative of the social sciences, the board was offi-

eially constituted of three groups: representatives of the two "professional" sections, biology and clinical medicine, and a third "general" membership section. The creation of separate professional sections from the "psychological and social sciences" and for "social welfare" did not take place until 1952. Marjorie Adler, "History of the Gerontological Society," *Journal of Gerontology*, XIII (1958), 94–102.

21. This picture of older people's needs and the fright caused by the Townsend Movement can be seen in a plethora of articles by physicians, economists, psychiatrists, and popular writers, as well as some social scientists in the nineteen-thirties and forties and even into the fifties. See the first volumes of *Geriatrics*, *Journal of Gerontology, Journal of the American Geriatrics Society* and various articles and editorials listed in Nathan Shock, *The Classified Bibliography of Gerontology and Geriatrics* (Stanford: Stanford University Press, 1959). Much of the same type of view can still be found expressed today in the course of the controversy over medical care for the aged under the Social Security Act.

22. Clark Wissler, "Human Cultural Levels," in Cowdry, *op. cit.*, pp. 83–99; Louis I. Dublin, "Longevity in Retrospect and in Prospect," *ibid.*, pp. 100–119; G. V. Hamilton, "Changes in Personality and Psychosexual Phenomena Associated with Age," *ibid.*, pp. 459–482; Walter R. Miles, "Psychological Aspects of Aging," *ibid.*, pp. 535–567. The second and third editions continued this tradition with the addition of chapters on population, social adjustment, the older worker in industry, and roles and status of older people. See Albert I. Lansing, ed., Cowdry's *Problems of Ageing: Biological and Medical Aspects*, 3rd ed. (Baltimore: Williams and Wilkins, 1952). Frank wrote a preface, and John Dewey, at Frank's invitation, an introduction to the first edition. Note the subtitle of the Cowdry volume nonetheless.

23. For discussions of his influence, see Birren, *op. cit.*, Donahue, *op. cit.*, Orbach, *op. cit.*, Tibbitts, *op. cit.*

24. Josiah Macy, Jr., Foundation, *A Review by the President of Activities for the Six Years Ended December 31, 1936* (New York: The Foundation, 1937), p. 37. Frank was assistant to the President of the Foundation.

25. *Ibid.*, pp. 41 f.

26. Edward J. Stieglitz, "The Orientation of Geriatrics, *Geriatrics*, IV (1949), 127–135; "Foundations of Geriatric Medicine," in Edward J. Stieglitz, ed., *Geriatric Medicine*, 3rd ed. (Philadelphia: Lippincott, 1954), pp. 3–26.

27. This initial ordering was changed in the 1954 volume to (1) The Biology of Aging, (2) Geriatric Medicine, and (3) Social Gerontology.

28. Stieglitz, "The Orientation of Geriatrics," pp. 130 f.

29. Stieglitz, *Geratric Medicine*, pp. 14 ff.

30. *Ibid.*

31. In the course of discussing the political and economic implications of gerontology and of aging he pointed out, "The political implications of the recent dramatic shifts in the age structure of the population are alarming. The clamor of the aged for economic security may be heard throughout the breadth of the land. It will become louder. Fantastic and obviously unsound schemes are advanced with fanatic vigor and dangerous political skill. . . . Socialistic schemes, pampering paternalism by the state and financial assistance for the elderly at the expense of younger age groups will not solve these problems." *Ibid.*

32. The history of this development has been detailed in Tibbitts, *op. cit.;* Donahue, *op. cit.;* Donahue, "Foreword," in Tibbitts, *op. cit.;* Robert W. Kleemeier, "Training Needs in Psycho-Social Gerontology and the Problems of Mental Health in the Elderly; Proceedings of a Conference held in Palm Beach, Florida, July

25–31, 1956," in U.S. Senate Committee on Labor and Public Welfare, *Studies of the Aged and Aging* (Washington: Government Printing Office, 1957), IX, 27–58; Orbach, *op. cit.*

33. Most of the contributors to Tibbitts, *op. cit.*, and Ernest W. Burgess, ed., *Aging in Western Societies* (Chicago: University of Chicago Press, 1960), are sociologists, and these volumes have shaped the course of developments, both theoretical and practical, since 1960.

34. Gordon F. Streib and Wayne E. Thompson, "Personal and Social Adjustment in Retirement," in Wilma Donahue and Clark Tibbitts, eds., *The New Frontiers of Aging* (Ann Arbor: University of Michigan Press, 1957), pp. 180–197.

35. Wayne E. Thompson, "Pre-Retirement Anticipation and Adjustment in Retirement," *Journal of Social Issues*, XIV (1958), 35–45.

36. Robert W. Kleemeier, *Aging and Leisure: A Research Perspective into the Meaningful Use of Time* (New York: Oxford University Press, 1961).

37. Wilma Donahue, Woodrow W. Hunter, Dorothy H. Coons, and Helen K. Maurice, *Free Time: Challenge to Later Maturity* (Ann Arbor: University of Michigan Press, 1958).

38. J. S. Tyhurst, L. Salk, and M. Kennedy, "Mortality, Morbidity and Retirement," *American Journal of Public Health*, XLVII (1957), 1434–1444. See also Wayne E. Thompson and Gordon F. Streib, "Situational Determinants: Health and Economic Deprivation in Retirement," *Journal of Social Issues*, XIV (1958), 18–34.

39. Leonard S. Cottrell, Jr., "The Adjustment of the Individual to His Age and Sex Roles," *American Sociological Review*, VII (1942), 617–620.

40. *Ibid.*, p. 618.

41. *Ibid.*, p. 619.

42. Gordon F. Streib, "Morale of the Retired," *Social Problems*, III (1956), 270–276.

43. E. B. Shultz, "Selective Retirement and Preretirement Counseling in the TVA," *Industrial and Labor Relations Review*, XII (1959), 206–213.

44. Roger Williams Walker, "An Evaluation of a Preretirement Planning Program— The TVA Experience," unpublished Ph.D. dissertation, Cornell University, 1959.

45. Ethel Shanas, *The Health of Older People* (Cambridge: Harvard University Press, 1962), p. 52.

46. *Ibid.*, p. 177.

47. Ethel Shanas, "The Older Person at Home—A Potential Isolate or Participant," in *Research Utilization in Aging*, U.S. Department of Health, Education, and Welfare, Public Health Service Publication No. 1211, 1964, pp. 81–86.

48. *Ibid.*, p. 82.

49. Personal communication from Dr. Ethel Shanas.

50. Personal communication from Dr. Harry Posman.

51. For a summary of literature as of 1960, see Gordon F. Streib and Wayne E. Thompson, "The Older Person in a Family Context," in Tibbitts, *op. cit.*, pp. 447–488.

52. Talcott Parsons, "The Social Structure of the Family," in Ruth N. Anshen, ed., *The Family: Its Function and Destiny* (New York: Harper, 1949), pp. 173–201. This essay is reprinted in the revised edition published in 1959.

53. Eugene Litwak, "Occupational Mobility and Extended Family Cohesion," *American Sociological Review*, XXV (1960), 9–21. See also Eugene Litwak, "Geographic Mobility and Extended Family Cohesion," *American Sociological Review*, XXV (1960), 385–394.

54. Marvin B. Sussman, "The Isolated Nuclear Family: Fact or Fiction," *Social Problems*, VI (1959), 333–340.

55. Eugene Litwak, "The Use of Extended Family Groups in the Achievement of Social Goals: Some Policy Implications," *Social Problems*, VII (1960), 177–187.
56. William E. Knox, "Filial Bonds: The Correlates of the Retired Father's Perception of Solidarity with His Adult Children," unpublished Ph.D. dissertation, Cornell University, 1965, p. 29.
57. Clement J. Schneider, "Adjustment of Employed Women to Retirement," unpublished Ph.D. dissertation, Cornell University, September, 1964.
58. Shanas, *The Health of Older People*, p. 117.
59. Personal communication from Dr. Ethel Shanas.
60. Personal communication from Clark Tibbitts.
61. Irving Rosow, *Housing and Social Integration of the Aged* (Cleveland, Ohio: Western Reserve University, 1964).
62. Irwin T. Sanders, *The Community: An Introduction to a Social System* (New York: Ronald, 1958).
63. Robert J. Havighurst and Ruth Albrecht, *Older People* (New York: Longmans, Green, 1953).
64. Carol Larson Stone and Walter L. Slocum, Bulletin 573, May, 1957, Washington Agricultural Experiment Station, State College of Washington.
65. *Ibid.*, p. 51.
66. Leonard Z. Breen, *Community Concepts of Aging: A Case of Problem Solution*, mimeographed: (West LaFayette, Indiana: Department of Sociology, Purdue University, 1962), p. 10. Paper read before the Fifty-seventh Annual Meeting of the American Sociological Association, Washington, D.C., August 30, 1962. Italics the author's.
67. *Ibid.*, p. 16.
68. Background Studies Prepared by State Committees for The White House Conference on Aging. A Report by the Subcommittee on Problems of the Aged and Aging to the Committee on Labor and Public Welfare, United States Senate. Parts I to XIV. 86th Congress, 2nd Session, United States Government Printing Office, 1960.
69. See Arnold M. Rose, ed., *Aging in Minnesota* (Minneapolis: University of Minnesota Press, 1963); Clarence W. Boebel, ed., *Tennessee's Aging* (Tennessee, Division of Finance and Administration, 1960); William S. Hopkins, ed., *Aging in the State of Washington* (Seattle: University of Washington Press, 1961).
70. Marvin J. Taves and Gary B. Hansen, "Seventeen Hundred Elderly Citizens," in Rose, *op. cit.*, pp. 73–181.
71. Fred Cottrell, "Governmental Functions and the Politics of Age," in Tibbitts, *op. cit.*, pp. 624–665. Quoted from p. 658; italics inserted.
72. We do point up on page 628 that housing is a tangible outcome and probably appeals to some administrators and others concerned with doing something for the aged.
73. Wilma Donahue and Clark Tibbitts, *Politics of Age* (Ann Arbor: University of Michigan, Division of Gerontology, 1962), p. XI.
74. Fred Cottrell, *op. cit.*, p. 661.
75. Irving Rosow, *The Gerontologist*, II (1962), 182–191. Quoted from page 191.

Rapid
Social
Change

PART V

Sociology in
Developing Areas

WILBERT E. MOORE

chapter *23*

The quest for rapid economic growth has become evident in virtually every part of the world—and not only in the programs of political leaders but also in the massive migration to the cities and demonstrations of restless discontent on the part of populations previously thought to be unalterably committed to traditional standards and methods of production.

The sweeping changes of the contemporary era were scarcely designed for the convenience of scholars. Yet many of the social transformations that have occurred since World War II have been especially helpful to the comparative sociologist. Formerly unknown areas are now accessible to him, and he has the opportunity to observe rapid transitions actually in process.

The growth in interest in the study of developing areas probably owes more to the course of events than to the evolution of sociological scholarship. There are scientific reasons for the undeniable appeal of the specialty, however, as well as the more pragmatic reasons that will be the principal subject of this essay. And the first of the scientific reasons is precisely the opportunity for comparative studies on an unprecedented scale. This interest tends to be self-accelerating: as more local studies are made, more opportunities are afforded for determining common characteristics of the developmental process and, conversely, for determining the differences that are dependent on time and place. Sociologists are thus presented with a kind of "lateral replication" that enables them to test the effects of these variable conditions and thus to determine their relevance and weight. Furthermore, with sufficient comparative data typologies can be constructed so that the theorist, when faced with a failure of generalization, is not driven back to particularities.

It is not just the richness of comparative data that is theoretically appealing but also the rapidity of change. Thus generalizations based on the historic course of economic development in countries now industrialized may be tested and refined in the current course of accelerated change. Both functional relationships—that is, the interdependent features of social systems—and causal relationships in sequential chains can be observed and ordered. An important side effect of this attention to sequences has been to give a new impetus to historical studies, especially to quantitative history which has been neglected by professional historians.

Developing areas are sometimes called "laboratories of social change." The metaphor is usually imprecise, although comparative analysis may use the logic of experimental design, and in rare instances quasi-controlled experimentation is practiced. The large-scale controlled experiment is rare for several reasons:

1. Contamination is difficult to control. The simultaneous use of alternative educational policies and curriculums, for example, would be likely to provoke political opposition as knowledge of the differences became known; that knowledge and opposition might crucially affect the several outcomes.

2. Where success has an extremely high valence, the "Arrowsmith problem" is encountered: that is, there is reluctance to withhold a possible remedy, even though its efficacy is untested.

3. The same sense of urgency is likely to favor a policy of trying everything at once. For example, the Soviet Union and subsequently other Communist countries probably have used the widest variety of labor incentives (positive and negative) in the modern world, but their simultaneous use prevents any appraisal of relative efficacy under standardized conditions.

For many sociologists the study of developing areas is appealing because it combines scientific purity and practical utility. Aid in the achievement of economic development seems, at least at first, to evade the value problem:—toward what ends is knowledge to be used? Goals of material well-being appear to be ubiquitous, as the economists have been saying all along.[1] Arguments over the morality of interference with traditional cultures, still common in the first decade after World War II,[2] now seem academic on two counts: (1) interference has gone on, and will do so, willy-nilly, and (2) change is actively sought by political power holders almost everywhere. The admonition "Leave them alone, they're happy" is generally belied by such phenomena as a massive rural exodus and widespread political restiveness.

An interesting question does arise, however, of both scientific and evaluative import: if world-wide cultural pluralism is still possible, in what form and to what degree? Sociologists are accustomed to a theoretical model of society that enables them to identify the uniform structural features of industrialized or economically advanced systems, and the use of this model may have led them to emphasize the "creation of a common culture." [3] When discussing developing areas reconsideration of both theory and empirical evidence suggests a less deterministic view of social integration and system requirements. Aesthetic forms, many aspects of supernatural religious beliefs and their attendant practices, and even some traditional elements of political practice are likely to survive the impact of economic modernization. Indeed, the preservation of some elements of the past may be actively supported to provide a thin line of continuity. In some cases, of course, forms that might have been retained are abandoned because they symbolize discredited regimes. Although no society can be expected to cling to large portions of its traditional forms of social organization, believers in cultural pluralism can be comforted with the thought that developmental efforts are unlikely to create endless human aggregates "just like us."

Value costs do inevitably arise. Economic development may be more highly prized as a goal than are the instrumental changes necessary to bring it about.[4] Many instrumental changes will in fact conflict with normatively prescribed practices that have been firmly rationalized in values having little apparent relation to material concerns. It is the intersecting or weblike character of social infrastructures that confirms the systemic qualities of social life and challenges the social practitioner. The opportunity to estimate these value costs and perhaps reduce them is another attraction of developing areas to the sociologist and an activity that calls upon his professional knowledge of social systems.

The value problem persists, however, for the costs and benefits of economic development are certain to be unequally distributed. The classic question "For whose benefit?" is not easily evaded. I think it is safe to say that in no case yet on record have the actual costs and benefits matched the professed values and principles of distributive justice of the country concerned or, indeed, of any other group. Thus decisions must be made about the amount of hardship that is justifiable for the ends in view and the length of time the hardship should be tolerated. These are technical questions in form, though the decisions are quite unlikely to be made on solely technical grounds.

The importance of social factors in economic development is widely conceded. The practical questions are being put by policy makers but unfortunately the answers are only partially at hand. In what follows, the potential range of applications of sociology in developing areas will be examined, with only brief reference to some examples from the literature.

The Range of Uses in Developing Areas

Since whole societies are potentially in transformation in developing areas, the entire range of sociology is in principle useful, but in practice the range is substantially narrower. Social structures, both antecedent and emergent, do differ, and so, therefore, do the problems to be solved. Market research and pre-election polls have little meaning in a totalitarian or even in a one-party "socialist" country. The uses of sociology in higher education, literary criticism, or the writing of history will have little or no relevance in countries with a meager scholarly establishment. And though sociologists may see long-range advantages in advising on the development of legal and medical curriculums, the shortage of teaching personnel and the acute need for minimally trained technicians may make notions of broadening professional education unrealistic.

There are many such limitations on the potential range of sociological uses. For example, useful quantitative forecasts depend on data on "current state" that do not exist and cannot be constituted without a national census or an impossibly expensive sample survey. Programs to alleviate various social problems depend in part on identifying their variety and magnitude, and such information on "incidence" is far from perfect anywhere. Even adequate descriptive (or at least nonquantitative) data are often lacking. Generalities are valuable, but application requires particularities also—a point to which I shall return. Not all the antecedent social structures have been recorded in the ethnographic literature; other records are out of date or otherwise poor. An even more serious problem is that many anthropological field reports describe ideal rather than actual situations. The current, sometimes frantic, quest to retrieve the precontact culture by seeking out the oldest living inhabitant as an informant can only exacerbate the tendency to idealization by adding nostalgic distortion. I believe that this emphasis on ideal patterns and the associated attempt at deliberate abstraction from visible evidence of adaptation to cultural contact help account for the exaggeration of resistances to change—an exaggeration that has made many anthropologists and sociologists rather poor forecasters.

Types of Uses in Practice

In selecting for discussion various uses of sociology in developing areas, it is convenient to distinguish between sociological applications in local developmental measures and the incorporation of sociological perspectives and techniques into more or less integrated national planning.

Through much of human history the local community comprised the compass of social life, and that situation remains true in extensive (but dwindling) areas of the world today. Given the incest taboo, the family cannot serve as the microcosm of society, as erroneously alleged in the older texts, and some interfamilial specialization in production and other social functions is probably the statistical rule, rather than the exception. The community, however, may represent effective social boundaries for exchange, mate selection, and the maintenance of order. In fact, the community may be the primary focus of loyalty, and in some situations one would look in vain for a more inclusive identity.

These circumstances have encouraged some organizations and individuals concerned with developmental plans to identify the community as at least the locus of change and perhaps its effective agency. Other circumstances have enhanced the appeal of community development: Community organization has been a principal specialty of rural sociology, but in highly industrialized countries, particularly in the United States, which has supported the vast majority of these specialists, the autonomous character of communities is decreasing and the distinctive qualities of rural life are disappearing. This has not made rural sociologists technologically unemployable in the United States, but it has increased their availability for technical-assistance missions in areas where the village still occupies an outstanding part of the social landscape.[5] Anthropologists have also participated in programs of community development.[6] They can be expected to have a greater knowledge of local customs and traditional structures than do the rural sociologists, but they too are threatened with loss of their primary specialty, the analysis of nonliterate societies. For them, the changing community offers a way of adapting their own specialty to the secular changes in developing areas.[7]

The appeal of community development also owes something, I believe, to value preferences of the practitioners. Anthropologists and rural sociologists clearly regret the passing of the traditional forms of social organization, and particularly the tendencies to centralization, standardization, and "massification" (an ugly but communicative term). If change must come—and they would not oppose all its elements—they would prefer that it arise from the grass roots, rather than be imposed by a centralized political power. In this preference they are often supported by technical assistants recruited from other professions, ranging from social workers and schoolteachers to dieticians and agronomists.

But a preference for local over national organization does not in fact insure popular participation in change. If communities are microcosms of societies, one must expect manifestations of hereditary strata, authoritarian rule, and superstitious beliefs. Indeed, if by communities are meant the relatively small agrarian and traditional villages and towns, they are likely to be centers of resistance to change rather than its effective agencies. This may heighten their strategic importance in large-scale developmental plans, but one may voice the suspicion that social scientists who prefer a community approach to change would also prefer that the change be small and slow. I shall return to this question in the terminal discussion of strategies.

Public-health measures and measures to foster fertility control are likely to be local in their implementation. Some types of control of infectious diseases—such as the spraying of malarial swamps or governmental sponsorship of the manufacture of antibiotics—are national or regional in scope, but these are likely to require little help from the social scientist. Health education, preventive medicine, and changes in dietary or sanitary practices, on the other hand, are likely to require skills in communication and involve attempts to change attitudes and daily patterns of activity (read "social structures"). No doubt experienced field workers in public health and preventive medicine can recite a long list of examples of resistances to, and unexpected *social* side effects of, their programs. Nevertheless, there has been a startling reduction in mortality in many developing areas. This result, however, owes more to the combination of modern technology with the universal preference for health and longevity than it does to the activities of social scientists.

The situation is quite otherwise with regard to fertility control. As Kingsley Davis and Frank Notestein[8] have remarked in their classic analyses of population problems, not only is death control a positive value everywhere but fertility is also a positive value nearly everywhere: To achieve death control, the problem is "merely" that of instrumentation. To achieve fertility control a change in values is necessary, though instrumentation is not wholly irrelevant, since economy, ease, and efficacy of contraception would at least reduce part of the set of barriers.[9]

Since human reproduction is normally a familial function, it is scarcely surprising that sociologists concerned with "the demographic problem" or the "population explosion" have turned primarily to studies of familial organization and social position.[10] Yet, as Blake and Davis have pointed out,[11] the determinants of fertility are not exclusively familial, and this suggests the possibility of working with other, hopefully more maneuverable, variables. The older doctrine that fertility inevitably declines under the impact of urbanization and industrialization has proved unsatisfactory for several reasons:

1. Unprecedented declines in the rate of mortality, especially in areas already densely settled, have yielded unprecedented rates of population growth that jeopardize plans for growth in income per capita.

2. The mechanism of change in the older doctrine was in any event too gross for either prediction or control. Just how did urbanization and industrialization effect changes in reproductive behavior? Davis has suggested that the crucial variable was in fact mobility aspirations,[12] an explanation that has the advantage of varying somewhat independently of occupation and residence and the disadvantage of requiring evidence on attitudes not readily available in the absence of survey data.

3. The supposed leadership of cities in fertility decline is questionable, except possibly as the locus of superior educational opportunities and school attendance.

Education, including communications in a broader sense, appears to be a critical variable in the voluntary control of fertility.[13] This tentative conclusion points clearly to the use of skills that are within the repertory of sociologists. In particular, the analysis of "informal" communication networks and of the school and its curriculum as agencies of change seems appropriate.

Another type of local development is that of city planning, which employs urban sociologists along with more strictly "professional" planners. The "urbanistas" of Latin America are most likely to be architects or engineers, and indeed the primacy of strictly physical planning is common everywhere. Nevertheless, instances can be found of a more comprehensive approach, including the sociological view of the city as a complex social system. Also, the extremely rapid rate of urbanization in most developing areas has pushed to the foreground the problem of assimilating urban newcomers and providing social services for them. Several conferences and corresponding symposia sponsored by UNESCO[14] indicate the prospects for utilizing sociological skills, while highlighting the paucity of elementary quantitative and descriptive data.

Industrial organization also affords a potential area of sociological use at the local level. Although a few studies have been made of the actual adaptation of administrative structures to local customs and available qualities of labor supply,[15] and some theoretical attention has been given the subject,[16] actual utilization of sociological advice is probably rare. Administrators are remarkably confident of their ability to manage, whether their origins are domestic or foreign. Indeed it appears that the standard model of a hierarchical administrative structure has been assumed to be the one best way, aside from such obvious (and hopefully temporary) concessions as greater instructional and disciplinary duties for supervisors dealing with an unskilled and possibly uncommitted work force. Neither systematic comparative analysis nor speculative theory has been brought to bear effectively on that assumption. There may yet turn out to be viable and efficient alternatives. Yet the simple advice to "adapt" may be shortsighted because it may assume and exaggerate resistance to change on the part of recruits and because concessions to poor qualities of personnel may become traditionalized.[17] Nothing approximating a cross-sectional typology of the relations between industrial organization and variable settings exists, and the attempts at sequential types are still rather sketchy.[18]

The national level of analysis and advice is often more appealing to general sociologists than the local, partly because of the preoccupation of many sociologists with "societies," partly because the interdependence of structures is seemingly more obvious and more significant in large and complex social aggregates.

Sociologists working at a national level may be employed by such ministries as social welfare, housing, and urban affairs or they may participate in integrated national planning.[19] In the latter situation economists are likely to be dominant, but either because of development theory or actual experience they are likely to have discovered the relevance of sociology to national planning. In the late 1950's, for example, Jorge Ahumada, a leading Latin American economist then attached to the United Nations Economic Commission for Latin America, issued a kind of intellectual challenge. He said, in effect, "We economists now know how to develop a country's economy, but we recognize both social resistances and social values. Tell us how, where, and when to introduce social factors into national plans." The challenge was issued through UNESCO and resulted in an interdisciplinary conference and published symposium.[20] The answers to Dr. Ahumada's questions were neither complete nor entirely practical, but perhaps it is fair to plead that planned social change is both more complex and less easily measurable than strictly economic change.

Sociologists at present are far better equipped to talk of eventual changes in social structure than they are to specify rates, routes, or timetables or, *a fortiori*, what deliberate changes are likely to be effective at what temporal junctures. An additional desideratum for increasing the utility of sociology would be a set of scales measuring "vulnerability," or proneness to change. Some current controversies might be thereby clarified. For example, by emphasizing the crucial role of early socialization in character formation, and by identifying the social segments likely to produce creativity, Hagen espouses a multigenerational view of motivational change.[21] By contrast, those who emphasize prospects for adult socialization think that Hagen has exaggerated the difficulty and rarity of adaptation and innovation and of the special structural conditions necessary for the appearance of groups suffering from status deprivation which Hagen argues are the eventual source of creative personalities.

Sociologists can clearly help national planners deal with problems of occupational structure and mobility, educational policy, demographic projections and possible controls, the selection of prospective urban migrants, prediction of changes in consumer demand and styles of life, and probable points and types of tension and their alleviation. All these social variables lend themselves to measurement of some kind. Thus both "current state" and, more importantly from a practical point of view, the effectiveness of policies are potentially subject to determination. But it would be pretentious to claim that these potentials have been realized yet.

Questions of Strategy

The first strategic problem in the use of sociology in developing areas is the problem of level of generalization. Although many sociological contributions to the theory of developing areas have resulted from intensive, localized investigations, other sociologists have quite properly attempted generalization and formalization of the structural and dynamic implications of economic modernization. This process of generalization is practical also, for only in this way is the wider applicability of scattered studies subject to examination. Yet as higher-level information is thus produced inductively, lower-level information is inevitably lost, and information lost through generalization may have to be partially restored in practical application. For example, it is clearly useful to have at hand the general principle that one early impact of industry is to undermine or destroy the network of social relationships that lie beyond the immediate family and short of national or cultural identity. If, however, policy makers seek advice on ways of ameliorating social atomization—say, through formation of new forms of social participation—it is essential to have rather detailed knowledge of prior arrangements, the segments of the population that are especially vulnerable, and so on. In fact, it is often necessary for the consulting sociologist to know the particular politicians or administrators in the local situation—knowledge that has little or no place in the intellectual equipment of the sociologist as social analyst.

A closely related strategic question arises with respect to what may be called the "level of change." As I have implied earlier, enthusiasts for community development tend to the view that every little bit helps. This provides for flexibility in identifying problems that can be readily solved. More theoretically oriented sociologists are likely to agree with those economists who are concerned with national income accounts and major structural sectors that the strategy of seeking the key variables is preferable.[22]

The dispute is likely to remain inconclusive because both strategies will receive support. Proponents of the grand strategy emphasize the interplay of changes and the importance of both structural and temporal priorities. Proponents of the local strategy emphasize existing attitudes of the ordinary citizen, local customs and leadership patterns, and the importance of showing visible results in daily life. It does appear to the uncommitted observer that the "practical people" are likely to be quite impractical if they do not widen their structural and temporal horizons and that the "desk generals" may be equally impractical if they do not learn the paths and pitfalls of implementation.

The alternative strategies are less distinct in totalitarian regimes, where the central authorities attempt to think of everything and change everything. But if the major strategies of change are determined by ideological dogma, as in Communist states, the doctrine may be made almost self-confirming by the imposition of coercive power. The only sociology permitted in such countries will be either wholly impractical (and uncritical) or strictly pragmatic at rather minor and instrumental levels. Thus industrial studies of worker attitudes may be permitted, but not an examination of the alternative forms of administrative co-ordination or accountability.

Part of the strategy of deliberate change that operates at both local and national levels is a recognition that not all structures or trends are equally amenable to control. Though dichotomies are rarely real, an approximation may be made by distinguishing teleology and teleonomy. Teleology involves the identification and implementation of future goals. Teleonomy involves the "inevitable" future and making preparatory adaptations to it. Obviously the assignment of a future state to one category or the other is subject to such variables as political and technological control. For example, economic planners in Latin America tend to assume and project population growth at the rapid rate of three per cent a year and then propose teleonomic adaptations of economic inputs to reach stipulated, teleological goals of growth in income per capita. Action-oriented demographers would question the inevitability of such rapid population growth and seek the sociomedical technology to reduce the rate. A totalitarian political regime might be sufficiently powerful simply to "liquidate" all excessive growth as determined by the expert planners.

This small excursion into the realm of terror underscores once more the ineluctable problem of values. The problem arises in a less stark form in the final question of strategy, which we may call the "urgency problem." Once a political commitment is made to rapid economic growth—and that is the nearly universal situation—instrumental decisions will be made, whether or not the evidence is in. The problem is exacerbated by the acute shortage of social scientists in developing areas. Those most competent to do more fundamental work are the ones most likely to be asked to give advice. This probability is further enhanced by the pattern of the part-time professor, especially notable in Latin America. University salaries are inadequate to sustain a professional level of living. The professor teaches, but he does not conduct research or construct theory; he serves in a ministry, consults with or administers business concerns, or practices law.

There is no quick or easy solution to this problem, but the universities generally do support some "useless" scholars, even in Latin America. Thus we encounter the irony that where fundamental research is most important for the long term, it is least possible because of present urgency. The expansion of intellectual resources in the social sciences also has some urgency, since needs for present advice can scarcely be denied, but neither can the meager base from which it must be given. All this gains added points from the inadequate state of developmental sociology anywhere. Were highly competent, indigenous sociologists to be given the opportunity to study rapid social change in process, the future prospects for utility would be greatly enhanced. And, as a beneficial side effect, the awkward domination of world sociology by North Americans would be curtailed. This, too, would be of use, but that is another story.

REFERENCES

1. See Wilbert E. Moore, "Social Aspects of Economic Development," in Robert E. L. Faris, ed., *Handbook of Modern Sociology* (Chicago: Rand McNally, 1964), Chapter 23; especially pp. 890–892.
2. For a review and criticism of such arguments, see Wilbert E. Moore, *Industrialization and Labor* (Ithaca: Cornell University Press, 1951).
3. Wilbert E. Moore, "Creation of a Common Culture," *Confluence*, IV (1955), 229–238.
4. See Arnold S. Feldman and Wilbert E. Moore, "Commitment of the Industrial Labor Force," in Moore and Feldman, eds., *Labor Commitment and Social Change in Developing Areas* (New York: Social Science Research Council, 1960).
5. See, for example, Charles P. Loomis *et al.*, eds., *Turrialba: Social Systems and the Introduction of Change* (Glencoe, Ill.: The Free Press, 1953); Loomis, *Social Systems* (Princeton: Van Nostrand, 1960), especially Essay 2, "The Division of Labor, The Community and Society."
6. See Ward H. Goodenough, *Cooperation in Change: An Anthropological Approach to Community Development* (New York: Russell Sage Foundation, 1963).
7. See, for example, Ralph L. Beals, "The Village in an Industrial World," *Scientific Monthly*, LXXVII (1953), 65–75.
8. Kingsley Davis, *Human Society* (New York: Macmillan, 1949), Chapter 21, "World Population in Transition"; Frank W. Notestein, "Problems of Policy in Relation to Areas of Heavy Population Pressure," in Milbank Memorial Fund, *Demographic Studies of Selected Areas of Rapid Growth* (New York: 1944).
9. See Judith Blake and Kingsley Davis, "Social Structure and Fertility: An Analytic Framework," *Economic Development and Cultural Change*, IV (1956), 211–235.
10. See, for example, Reuben Hill *et al.*, *The Family and Population Control: A Puerto Rican Experiment in Social Change* (Chapel Hill: University of North Carolina Press, 1959); Judith Blake *et al.*, *Family Structure in Jamaica: The*

Social Context of Reproduction (New York: The Free Press of Glencoe, 1960).

11. Blake and Davis, *op. cit.*

12. Kingsley Davis, "The Demographic Consequences of Changes in Productive Technology," in International Social Science Council, *Social, Economic, and Technological Change: A Theoretical Approach* (Paris: 1958).

13. See, for example, Hill *et al.*, *op. cit.*

14. Philip M. Hauser, ed., *Urbanization in Asia and the Far East* (Calcutta: UNESCO, 1957); Hauser, ed., *Urbanization in Latin America* (Paris: UNESCO, 1961); International African Institute, *Social Implications of Industrialization and Urbanization in Africa South of the Sahara* (Paris: UNESCO, 1956).

15. See Peter B. Hammond, "Management in Economic Transition," in Moore and Feldman, *op. cit.*

16. See Moore, *Industrialization and Labor*, pp. 31–34.

17. *Ibid.*

18. See George Friedmann, *Industrial Society* (Glencoe, Ill.: The Free Press, 1955); Wilbert E. Moore, "Technological Change and Industrial Organization," in International Social Science Council, *Social Implications of Technological Change* (Paris: 1962).

19. See Louis J. Walinsky, *The Planning and Execution of Economic Development* (New York: McGraw-Hill, 1963).

20. Egbert de Vries and José Medina Echavarría, *Social Aspects of Economic Development in Latin America*, Vol. I (Paris: UNESCO, 1963); see especially the essay by Jorge Ahumada, "Economic Development and Problems of Social Change in Latin America."

21. Everett E. Hagen, *On the Theory of Social Change: How Economic Growth Begins* (Homewood, Ill.: Dorsey, 1962).

22. See Wilbert E. Moore, "Problems of Timing, Balance, and Priorities in Development Measures," *Economic Development and Cultural Change*, II (1954), 239–248.

Rural

Sociology

CHARLES P. LOOMIS

ZONA KEMP LOOMIS

chapter 24

From the earliest days of their discipline, the demands of "pure" science have been distinguished from those of "applied" science by rural sociologists. For them, the world of the professional agriculturalist and farmer has been their arena of action at the same time that the world of the social scientist has continued to command their allegiance. A prominent sociologist, a specialist in diffusion of ideas and personal influence, notes in a lead article in the *American Journal of Sociology* that his own work bore a parallel to "the twenty-year-old tradition of research by rural sociologists on the acceptance of new farm practices . . . [while the two branches of inquiry] were hardly aware of each other's existence or of their possible relevance for each other." [1] The present chapter has been written in part to broaden the awarness of others to rural sociology—the first sociological specialty to be linked significantly to the practicing professions and occupations.

Historical Background of the Linkages of Rural Sociology[2]

The first of "annual informal gatherings, which eventually expanded into the rural section of the society and then into the Rural Sociological Society,"[3] was held in 1912. The occasion was the annual meeting of the American Sociological Society, whose theme that year was rural life. Just one year before this meeting, the Roosevelt Country Life Commission, which had questioned thousands of rural people about the shortcomings of rural life, had published its famous report. It is but one of 154 rural sociological studies mentioned by Brunner[4] as having preceded the Purnell Act of 1925 by which federal funds for rural sociological research in land-grant institutions were specified. Most of these early studies were done outside colleges of agriculture. The non-college-of-agriculture influence has continued to be strong, as have been the United States Department of Agriculture connections and experiment-station activities. The monumental *Systematic Source Book in Rural Sociology*,[5] published in the early thirties, came out of such a combination.

The setting for *using* sociology—for putting it to work in a rapidly changing rural society—is clearly indicated by these early linkages. The farmers' movement, the farmers' organizations, such organizations as the Roosevelt Country Life Commission, the American Country Life Association, the federal legislation concerning agriculture, and the federal bureaus and departments devoted to agricultural affairs constituted or reflected a nationwide rural-life movement to which rural sociology has been functionally related from the first. No balder statement about its useful intent can be made than that of William H. Sewell: "Most research in rural sociology is for the purpose of helping in the solution of practical problems of rural people and rural society."[6]

In reviewing rural sociology from its beginnings a half-century or more ago, the idea of "uses" becomes blurred. What of a classic such as Galpin's *Social Anatomy of an Agricultural Community?*[7] Is its contribution to ecology generally, and to the University of Chicago group particularly, to be considered a "use"?[8] And should rural sociology be credited with useful techniques such as the sociogram which it has so profitably employed, since a rural sociologist did not actually invent the technique, and since other specialties within sociology have also put it to advantageous use, although by some decades later than the rural sociologists? To answer such questions, and to get information about how rural sociology has been used, we turned to the rural sociologists of the United States. Some responses were very helpful in appraising the relative importance of groups of studies, but not so helpful on how such studies have been used. Others were extremely helpful in reporting uses which were almost surely made, but were impossible to document. It cannot be stated too emphatically that the present chapter makes no claim to being exhaustive. Some excellent studies will not be mentioned here if their use is in question. Real but intangible uses will not be mentioned here if they are not documentable. Even the most solid of uses usually are documentable, however, only because the investigator has been in personal contact with the user. Therefore much of the documentation will be confined to personal letters which are on file with the senior author.

To give some order to the wide range of uses indicated by the letters, we have followed the rough and sometimes overlapping categories suggested by the most frequently cited and most numerous uses. Three streams of sociological thought and procedures can be singled out as being rich in ultimate application, influential in delineating problems, and of consequence in their solution. One of these is ecological, or the specifications of the space dimensions of pluralities: the delineation of locality groupings such as the neighborhood, community, and region and the diverse uses to which both the findings and the procedures have been put. The second is a mélange of communication, influence, and social change which most often is called diffusion. The third is that area of investigation which is a response to the needs of government, both in policy formation and in legislation.

Locality Group Delineation

The spatial relations among and between social systems such as families, neighborhoods, communities, associations, and similar pluralities have changed radically in America during the last half-century and are similarly changing the world over, as rational organization, industrialization, and bureaucratization affect larger and larger portions of populations. Institutions rooted in a given historical territorial pattern are less than adequate when spatial relations change. To rural sociologists, Galpin's Wisconsin Experiment Station Bulletin *The Social Anatomy of an Agricultural Community*,[9] published in 1915, is the most important pioneering study of rural locality groupings. Galpin's basic observation was the "road turnings"; that is, the ruts vehicles wore into the ground as they turned from the farm home. The well-worn rut in the direction of trade center A, as contrasted with the little-worn rut in the direction of trade center B, would identify the farm family with trade center A. Of course, as the trade-center dimensions changed from the "team haul" of the horse-drawn wagon to the "tin Lizzie spin" of the early farm automobile days to the fast transportation of the modern four-lane highway, the "road turnings" have been supplanted by other cues which have been found to be useful in demarcating an area. Nevertheless, so simple, explicit, and persuasive were the Galpin-Sanderson methods of determining trade-center community boundaries that in New York for many years the State Board of Education would not approve consolidation of school districts unless these procedures were used for reorganization on a "natural trade center" community basis.[10] What happened in New York was paralleled, with various methods of delineation of locality-groupings, all across the country as the small school districts of a basically neighborhood-oriented, agricultural society yielded to the larger trade-center pluralities of an increasingly urban society.

A number of innovations in method of delineation[11] was climaxed by a related search for "optimum" configurations to serve various social and economic purposes. In effect, these latter studies sought to determine how big and inclusive an administrative unit must become in terms of number of people, taxable wealth, and accessibility to other resources to insure a stipulated minimum service and how small it must remain to be responsive to the needs of its constituents. The legion uses to which these studies have been put should not obscure the solid impact of accomplishments: of communities prepared to accommodate to a highway relocation because social factors as well as engineering factors have been available and used;[12] of schools which spring from and belong to the communities which they serve because considerations other than population factors were known to be important;[13] of the reduction of marginal memberships in such organizations as county libraries and regional health units because integration is based on something more solid than geographic proximity;[14] of vitalized neighborhoods working together on problems significant to all.[15] It is impossible to specify how many formulas for state aid have been based on sociologically determined "needy areas," but that pedestrian fact does not make less important the equalized opportunity resulting therefrom.

Various modifications of delineation method made it possible for laymen to devise fairly accurate approximations of area demarcations. For example, an "optimum efficiency index" was developed which was based on density of population, total population, economic base, and location of roads and highways. The governmental and administrative units of a southeastern state were modeled after this formula. In the same region a North Carolina rural sociologist devised a measure of the combination of graduated community ability and need on the one hand, and a graduated scale of hospital service on the other, which led to a probably unique system of hospitals, with one metropolitan county hospital and smaller rural hospital branches.[16] Two fundamental formulas and other planning devices, developed in Michigan and North Carolina by rural sociologists, have been used by many other states in determining the number and location of hospitals to be built under the Hill-Burton program. The two formulas are (1) bed–death ratio formula and (2) percentage formula as related to average daily requirements for hospitalization. The techniques developed there for delineating hospital service areas have also been widely used.[17] Sometimes it was discovered that a supposedly significant ecological factor was relatively minor. The location of health facilities in one state was altered when it was established by rural sociologists that age, education, level of living, and occupation contributed to the use of the health facility, but that distance from it played a relatively minor role.[18]

Nor have the uses been entirely governmental. On the one hand the churches limited the practice of "overchurching" as studies showed the affiliations of farm families with the larger centers.[19] A far-sweeping example may be found in the Rural Life Division of the Methodist Church of Oklahoma which "remapped the parish organization of the entire state, using Hagood's level-of-living indexes and rural sociology population studies as base."[20] At the same time market-research organizations reshaped their advertising campaigns and retooled their sales programs. The old Dodge Motor Company required local agents to do a rough community delineation in the manner of the then prevalent locality delineation methods. For the first time salesmen *knew* the social boundaries of their sales territories.[21] Especially during World War II, the various personnel of the Agricultural Extension Service—the county agricultural agents, the home demonstration agents, and the 4-H Club agents—who were linked with rural sociologists through the Agricultural Experiment Stations and by USDA connections sought, on the sociologists' advice, to find meeting places which were consonant with "natural groupings."[22] The American Medical Association was stimulated toward making studies of physician distribution after rural sociologists showed a high incidence of sickness in counties with the fewest physicians.[23]

Large migrations provide a dual need for the application of sociological-population facts—an application in the areas of both out-migration and in-migration. Especially in the case of slow, steady out-migration, the projection of school enrollments, of relief loads, of employment opportunities, and of markets is more than a simple extrapolation. It requires the judgment of rural sociologists on such factors as net migration, replacement ratios, and dependency ratios. If most of the out-migration is directed to a few common points, projection rates for the receiving communities is subject to the same judgmental decisions. Most enterprises in areas of out- and in-migration, both in the private and public sectors of the economy, are extremely reliant on the studies of sociologists for any realistic appraisal of the future. For example, the numerous migration studies on the Southern Appalachians have been utilized by schools, churches, and public agencies in northern cities such as Chicago, Detroit, and Cincinnati, as programs and policies are developed to deal with the adjustment problems of southern migrants.[24]

In the early 1940's the rural sociologists in the United States Department of Agriculture under the leadership of Carl C. Taylor were requested to assist in determining the "optimum" social and economic configuration for modern settlement, including arrangements of services, forms of holdings, and other variables. For years economists and sociologists had debated the advantages and disadvantages of Durkheimian mechanical vs. organic solidarity, or Toennies' *Gemeinschaft* vs. *Gesellschaft,* and had argued the efficacy and inefficacy of the "checkerboard system" of land division used generally in the United States since the passage of the bill establishing it in 1785. T. Lynn Smith calls it "one of the most vicious modes ever devised for dividing lands," [25] especially because it imposed distances which impeded neighboring. Other writers argued against the small trade center with too few people to provide adequate services. The problem was subjected to empirical testing when Nathan L. Whetten[26] studied settlement patterns in Saskatchewan, Canada. There the development of highways and modern communication had proceeded concomitantly with land settlement. He found a relatively large number of small centers developed to serve local families. Other studies by means of aerial photography[27] have been made of actual settlements in the western part of the United States where settlers were free to build homes where they wished, unimpeded by team-haul limitations. There, although the checkerboard system of land division had been imposed as in the Midwest, there was no evidence from the studies that people settled in the middle of their holdings, the place designated by many farm-management specialists as the most economically rational. Instead they typically built along the roads and within reasonable distance of neighbors. Also the studies revealed that even after the square units of the official surveys had been imposed, subsequent division tended to form longer rectangles (rather than squares) in the "string-along-the-road" or "line type" settlements. The application of such findings may be seen by visiting the Columbia River Basin settlement under the Grand Coulee Dam. The settlement pattern is the result of the Columbia Basin Joint Investigations contributed to by rural sociologists, accepted in large measure by action agencies and implemented on the basis of "140 years of westward movement and 40 years of reclamation settlement experience." [28]

Many rural sociologists and other professionals in the field of agriculture grew up on family-sized farms and tend to entertain a bias for that sized holding, as against the hacienda and the "factory farm." It is possible that many of the studies testing the relative merits of the two systems of settlement spring from a nostalgic commitment to the way of life nurtured by the family-sized farm. The use of such studies in resettlement and relocation seems to be solidly based, however, on the virtually uniform findings that the socioeconomic advantages accrue to the family-sized farm rather than to the larger holdings. Along with these studies are others which demonstrate the great cost, in terms of human suffering and maladjustment, of unplanned settlement.[29] Reclamation projects which occasioned the moving of families were guided in their resettlement work by such findings. Similarly, the settlement pattern used for the reservoir families under TVA who had to be transplanted elsewhere was under the direction of an action agency which gave prime consideration to the recommendations of rural sociologists such as Frank Alexander, with whom they worked closely during the entire process.

A related use occurred with frequency during the war years, when labor shortages on the farms and in industry were serious. Such shortages were relieved by relocation and recruitment of workers. Seasonal surplus farm labor was located largely by rural sociological studies, notably those of the Division of Farm Population and Rural Life. Their findings were used widely by Ford, Kaiser, and others for recruiting large numbers of persons to work in shipbuilding and in the automobile industry.[30]

The problems to which the rural ecologists turned their attention parallel very closely the problems which arose as fewer and fewer people were required on the nation's farms. Today there is a relatively new emphasis on nonagricultural development of the rural economy, based squarely on "the fact that probably only one farm boy out of every ten will have the opportunity to take over an adequate-sized commercial farm. . . . We have also made computations of the potential growth of the rural labor force in the 1960's in the absence of migration, which delimit the magnitude of the rural development problem." [31]

There could be no such exodus from farm to city, of course, without improved farm practices which enable one farmer now to produce the foods and fibers which twenty produced before. And technological knowledge in the hands of a few specialists is far from enough to motivate farmers to try new methods, to take risks in discarding the known ways, to learn to apply the up-to-date technique, and to make personal and family adjustments consequential to the new practice. A large body of rural sociological literature deals with adoption practices and the characteristics of those who adopt at differential rates.

Diffusion of Improved Practices and Technology[32]

Ecological considerations were given early attention by rural sociologists as they attempted to speed up the spread of improved practices, breeding stocks, and technology. Systems of influence and power were recognized as bearing a relation to the degree that social systems were *Gemeinschaft-like*, or neighborhood groupings, or *Gesellschaft-like*, or trade-center oriented. Influentials in these two situations were categorized as neighborhood, "grass roots," or popular leaders in contrast to county-wide or trade-center leaders.[33] These terms were gradually supplanted by those developed by Merton and Zimmerman:[34] the localites and cosmopolites. The various diffusion studies of such traits as the planting of hybrid corn and the use of weed killers, insecticides, and so on soon established that the localites tended more toward late adoption of practices than the cosmopolites, who tended to be the initiators. Also it was found that early adopters and innovators tended to rely on cosmopolite sources of information, such as mass media, coming in from outside the local neighborhoods, while late adopters relied more on local sources of information, especially friends and neighbors. One study demonstrated that each neighborhood may have its own "characteristic pace of diffusion" and that the "neighborhood educational level, and prevalence of favorable scientific farming attitudes generated a rank order of locality groups most closely approximating that of the average diffusion rate." [35] In the adoption process, cosmopolite influences are relatively great in the awareness stage, but in subsequent stages before adoption, localite influences are greater.[36] All these findings have been used by the Agricultural Extension Service both in planning and executing promotion campaigns. In fact, one of the most important changes which can be noted is the agricultural experts' knowledge of sociological and diffusion-study terminology. Thirty years ago few if any agriculturalists would have known the meaning of cosmopolite, localite, innovator, early and late adopter, and fewer still would have used these terms. Now the terms have fairly wide usage among nonsociological professional agricultural personnel throughout the United States. The terms are also diffusing in Europe and in developing countries where rural sociologists are working.

Perhaps for sociologists the most significant diffusion event in the history of the discipline is the spread of diffusion knowledge itself. By 1955, rural sociologists of the North Central states under assistance from the Farm Foundation had collected and published a report derived from the various diffusion studies. This report, *How Farm People Accept New Ideas*,[37] immediately came under such heavy demand that in the first four years over 80,000 were distributed, and translations had been made into several languages. In 1961 the same Sub-Committee on Diffusion decided to bring together and publish those studies on diffusion which would give more emphasis than the first bulletin did to the process through which individual adopters accept new ideas. This bulletin, called *Adopters of New Farm Ideas—Characteristics and Communications Behavior*,[38] like its predecessor, has met world-wide demand. In 1955 Beal and Bohlen, rural sociologists at Iowa State University, popularized and extended a visual presentation developed by Neil Raudabaugh, illustrating the diffusion of farm innovations. Eight years later they had given their presentation to 180 meetings, conferences, and other gatherings, to all types of change agents such as salesmen and dealers, advertising-agency personnel, extension workers, and industrial managers. Although many of the presentations were to church, education, and agricultural extension groups which did not pay a fee, it may be noted, for those who judge the success of a service by how much people are willing to pay, that some private firms paid handsomely for the demonstration and for subsequent consultations with its initiators.

Among the earliest and most famous of the rural sociology diffusion studies was that by Ryan and Gross.[39] This study, which focuses on the adoption of hybrid seed corn, found that the modal frequency of being aware of the new trait came seven years after the first farm operator had heard of it. The modal frequency of adoption came ten years after the trait was first adopted. The length of time between first awareness and general awareness, on the one hand, and first adoption and general adoption constitutes the essential data which have been used in a variety of ways. Ryan and Gross noted that the rate of diffusion approximated the S-shaped growth or learning curve, a form first recognized by Tarde and later applied by Chapin and Pemberton.[40] Of the two most widely distributed publications mentioned above on diffusion of farm practices, one states that "about 14 years elapsed between the introduction of hybrid seed corn and its adoption by most farmers. Soil testing, as a basis for fertilizer application, has been recommended for 20 years, yet, the majority of farmers have not adopted it." [41] Policies and procedures for reducing this time lag are based on the diffusion studies.

One use related to the above-mentioned characteristics of diffusion may be illustrated by Agricultural Extension practices involving the S-shaped rate-of-diffusion curve. The Director of Agricultural Extension in a Northern Plains state observed in his Ph.D. dissertation that the spread of artificial breeding of dairy cattle conformed to the S-shaped curve as expected. He went further and noted that after the success of the program was demonstrated and subsequent adoptions diminished in rate, there was an excessive wastage of time by the Extension staff who expended as much effort or more during the period of fall-off of adoptions as they had in the period of rapid rise of adoptions.[42] The surplus of effort after two or three years has been reduced considerably, at least in this investigator's own staff.

In the second of the two widely distributed diffusion reports, *Adopters of New Farm Ideas,* the following stages are specified: (1) Awareness, (2) Interest-information, (3) Evaluation-Application-Decision, (4) Trial, (5) Adoption. Although stages as employed by various investigators differ, stages comparable to these were validated by various investigators as the adoption of antibiotics was observed among farmers.[43] Likewise a set of stages which roughly parallels those specified above was validated for adoption of practices among Pennsylvania dairy farmers. Diffusion specialists themselves are dissatisfied with the conceptualization of stages and seek a reconceptualization which will show that "adoption of a farm practice is a bundle of related events flowing through time, not an instantaneous metamorphosis." [44] Nevertheless, the concept of stages has been generally diffused to change agents in agriculture and must be considered a use to which diffusion studies have been put.

A use of diffusion studies dependent on the specification of stages in the adoption of technology and ideas is the emphasis now placed on the trial or "dry-run" stage. Rogers observes that "most persons will not adopt an innovation without trying it first on a probationary basis." [45] Ryan and Gross found in their pioneering study that "however clearly the advantages of hybrid corn had been demonstrated by community experience, most farmers insisted upon personal experimentation before they would adopt the innovation completely." [46] The importance of the trial stage is further emphasized by the fact that innovators and early adopters move to it much faster than others, this being one of the chief features differentiating those who adopt early from those who adopt late. This, coupled with the research evidence suggesting that the adoption stage directly follows the trial, further increases the importance of the trial. For example, one study proves that a "free trial speeded up the adoption process for a weed spray as much as [an estimated] one year." [47] For a considerable time Agricultural Extension Services have known the importance of the trial period, as have business concerns selling such items as milk separators and vacuum cleaners.

In the last decades various sociological studies have shown that the effort expended in extending the various services to farmers and ranchers is disproportionately small toward the "lower or disadvantaged third." Often administrators have excused this lapse because they are relying on the "trickle-down" or "two-stage" models of diffusion. Two variations of these models are dominant: (1) that if change agents spend most of their time working with adoption leaders, these latter can be relied on to serve as models and disseminators of the new practice; and (2) that mass-media messages flow from radio and print to opinion leaders who in turn disseminate the ideas to those less liable to mass-media influence. Diffusion studies based on empirical reality have posed a question about the efficacy of such models and have belied the earlier belief that complete dissemination would occur by introducing the practice in question to the strata which are typically the early adopters. One Ohio study[48] found that only 2 per cent of the farmers were reached exclusively by indirect trickle-down effort expended by Agricultural Service workers, whereas 79 per cent had been reached by either direct contact with the agent or a combination of direct and indirect contact. As have many diffusion studies, Missouri investigations[49] found that influentials in the diffusion process were concentrated in the upper social ranks or strata, but their influence not only caused ideas and practices espoused by them to trickle down to farmers of lower rank but also spread the items to people of their own rank and upward to those of superior rank. The efficacy of the trickle-down model depends, of course, on the social structure and value orientation of the target system, and diffusion studies have emphasized this vital consideration.

A society with closed castes requires different strategy than an open-class society. In the latter, the innovators and early adopters may be higher in rank and class than others. Majority adopters, both those called "early" and "late," may constitute about 68 per cent of the population and have about average social rank. They may be influenced by the early adopters, but seldom by the innovators, as models. Laggards and late adopters have the lowest social rank. In terms of sources of information

> laggards and the late majority are most likely to depend upon friends and neighbors in the immediate locality as a source of new farm information than upon other sources. Innovators . . . [who get their ideas from agricultural scientists and others] cannot depend upon . . . others in the locality. . . . On the other hand, by the time the late majority and laggards consider adopting an idea, they are surrounded by other farmers who have information and opinions about it.[50]

The terms *traditional* vs. *modern,* and other parallel "ideal types" such as *Gemeinschaft*-like and *Gesellschaft*-like have been used to order actors, neighborhoods, communities, and other units in diffusion analysis.[51] To rural sociologists working in both the countries of the industrialized West and developing societies, the importance of a quality which has been called "economic rationality" seems obvious. The differences in motivation of farmers in the State of Washington in which "Gaines wheat . . . seed was released to seed growers one year and the next to the general public and . . . adopted by *over half* the wheat growers" [52] stands in contrast to village peasants of a developing country such as India. Various scales have been developed which are designed to reveal the rigidity of attitudes toward a whole complex of ideas: caste, superstition, the causes of misfortunes, and the most efficacious remedies. The placement of the individual actor on these scales (which roughly measure traditionalism-modernity in specific cultural settings) has been found to correlate highly with other scales measuring length of time required for adoption. As would be expected, the more modern, rational, or secular the actor's score on the one scale, the earlier his adoption rate tends to be. Also the modern, rational, secular, and *Gesellschaft*-like actor is found to place a high value on science and education, while those at the other end of the continuum display attitudes in which economic rationality is not of importance. Other scales constructed to measure social-psychological attributes, applied to actors in the United States, find a general willingness to be inquiring and flexible to correlate highly with the actual behavior of innovation and adoption—an attribute called "management orientation" as opposed to "traditional work orientation" made up of the opposite of such traits.[53] The use of such studies in the short run may be found in the different strategy used by action agencies working in target systems of the two different types. In the long run the importance of developing rationality through educational systems and other training centers becomes obvious. Innovators and early adopters are generally better educated, younger, possessed of more accurate self-images, less rigid and dogmatic, more specialized as agriculturalists, and more cosmopolitan than laggards and other later adopters.

Considerable attention has been given to the spread of ideas in interpersonal networks. One study[54] reports that the need for person-to-person information varies at different stages in the adoption process, beginning with only 37 per cent at the awareness stage and proceeding successively to 50, 63, and 50 per cent in subsequent stages. Personal influence from peers seems to be most necessary "when uncertainty prevails, [and the actor] . . . feels a need for reinforcement of his opinion through personal interaction." [55] In the early thirties rural sociologists began plotting social relations with sociometric techniques somewhat following the original work of Moreno. Always it was assumed that new traits and ideas would spread over the grapevine or network of relations.[56] The sociometric charts developed for neighborhoods and communities in various parts of the world were often used because they were relatively understandable. An administrator of a reclamation project or a resettlement colony, or a director of a state Agricultural Extension Service, who had little or no sociological training could understand the importance of interaction and relationships as symbolized on the charts and take these factors into account in his decisions. One such chart was used to explain why in two years 40 per cent of the colonists left the Dyess Colony in Arkansas.[57] Merely plotting relations of leavers compared with stayers proved that in the tension-fraught community whole sociometrically delineated groups left in defiance of the administration and later, after having made the break from the colony and separated from other defiant colleagues, evaluated the situation differently and asked to return. Such usage of sociometry has some aspects of the diffusion studies in which it has been employed recently by various diffusion specialists.[58] Sociometry then came to be used as a means of explaining adoption and diffusion. Models such as two-step communication and the trickle-down process could be studied and their limitations noted in relation to the stages of adoption, to the types of adopters, and to evaluative aspects of the social system in which the diffusion was taking place. Also such social factors as rank or stratification, extent of rationality or modernity in contrast to traditionalism, and cosmopolitanism vs. localism of actors in the network could be included. Many change agents, including Extension agents, made crude sociometric charts of the systems with which they worked. In their use many practices besides that of the spread of agricultural traits were studied by specialists in rural diffusion. Such qualities of interest to the community as leadership, group cleavage, and hidden power figures came under analysis.[59]

Nonagricultural traits of interest to rural sociologists have also been traced for their diffusion patterns. A pilot study which investigated the acceptance of Salk vaccine yielded enough information to be the basis for a state immunization campaign.[60] The relative effectiveness of the change agents has also been the subject of a diffusion study. For instance, one such study sought to determine the sources of information most used in new farmhouse construction in a particular county. So many farmers were building into their homes the suggestions which came from contractors and from lumber dealers that the Agricultural Extension Service, which had seen itself in the role of supplier of such information, decided to revamp its program. It shifted some of its work from the farmer to the lumber dealers and contractors in order to increase the diffusion of knowledge which needed imparting through these channels.

It has been found that some traits diffuse more rapidly than others. Dimensions which modify the adoption rate have been identified as: (1) cost, risk, and economic returns possible to the adopter, (2) complexity, (3) visibility, (4) divisibility, (5) compatibility with other social and cultural traits. Knowledge derived from research on these variables has been increasing.[61] One result in application of diffusion studies is the recognition that few traits can be adopted without occurrence of compensating changes in traits already in use. Action programs have occasionally planned for such modifications in the initial promotion of a diffusion program. The TVA, for example, promoted the "trial acre program"; that is, a "bundle" of improved practices developed by rural sociologists in Tennessee in order to help slow-to-adopt farmers to utilize available resources.[62] The "bundle" was constituted of interrelated items, so that given the initial change set in motion by the adoption of one item, the remainder of the bundle would complement the necessary adjustment. Such an approach had been previously stressed in the intensive experimental development programs of the Farm Security Administration.[63]

Economic enterprises in the United States were quick to see that commercial advertising and marketing could improve from studies which revealed the motives for adoption or nonadoption. Frequently mentioned uses of the diffusion studies are such activities as marketing, ad building, message formulation, and corporate public-image creation. One team which did much publicizing of diffusion studies reports presentations to at least twenty major corporations and long-term consultation with one of the largest petroleum companies in the nation on how to develop a working structure to market products from a new plant built in the Midwest.[64]

Major policy decisions within commercial companies dealing in such produce as fertilizer and agricultural chemicals have been made and modified in the light of information from the diffusion studies about the adoption policies of farmers. How and when a new product is introduced, what the selling and promotion strategy will be, the criteria by which dealers would be selected, and the methods by which they would be trained have been influenced by the studies. A few commercial companies, themselves caught up in the spirit of research, completed a three-year experiment of their own in which they attempted to construct and implement an experimental dealer-training program in which the objective was threefold: to improve the operation of local dealers, increase their profits, and secure more nearly optimum use of fertilizer and agricultural chemicals.[65]

A variable of the diffusion process has been found to reside in the recipient's evaluation of the communicator and the form and style of the communication. Consequently a related study of rural acceptance of radio and television caused what has been reported to be an almost immediate change in the programing and the advertising rates of both media. An allied use of rural sociological work, although not central to diffusion studies, came about as marketing information for consumers' programs was altered to be more attuned to different audience preferences as a result of evaluative studies of Agricultural Extension Service.[66]

Future Needs for Diffusion Research and Application

Rural sociologists trained in the industrialized West, in discussing patterns of diffusion, talk about the S-curve and frequently do not specify all the system conditions that attend the process of diffusion. Whether the diffusion is of improved practices or of disease, the findings which permit description of adoption following the S-curve usually ignore the importance of the element of authority, force, and power as related to the process. (In footnote 40 reference is made to this.) In Communist countries social change and diffusion have been speeded up through various means, including the application of force. Although Western studies have considered the "influential" and the "opinion-leader" types of actors who initiate, legitimize, and execute action in pluralities, not enough is known about the use of power and authoritarian procedures in speeding up change. Thus Lionberger found that once "influentials" had given their approval to an innovation, the rate of adoption increased markedly.[67] To the present authors it seems strange that although the S-curve describing adoption patterns is mentioned, no article on diffusion known to them mentions the J-curve so common in many sociological analyses. It seems that in power-centered systems the diffusion of orders might follow the J-curve rather than the S-curve. In any case, the means used by totalitarian systems in achieving adoption should be better understood by rural sociologists. Leaders in many still "free" developing countries are impatient with progress along lines of S-curve adoption.[68]

The criticism above of diffusion studies particularly as applied in underdeveloped countries indicates future possibilities.[69] For instance, from studies of social systems during time of disaster, it is entirely possible that we may apply much from the "halo effect" which is common at one phase of recovery from disasters brought on by bombardment, tornadoes, earthquakes, and panics. At this period of high emotive integration it might be possible to inculcate into the reshaping social system some diffusion items which would be ignored during ordinary times, when actors are at a less receptive pitch. Indeed, this receptivity to a new order after the old has been badly shaken seems to be at the base of planned disruption by Communist revolutionaries. Specialists in diffusion and social organization should be given the opportunity of exploring this possibility as a means of increasing the pace of social change during the strategic moment in a natural disaster sequence. Although much remains to be known about diffusion in the industrialized West—for example, why chlorination of water was so much more easily diffused than fluoridation of water—all too little is known about means for bringing rapid change with a minimum of suffering. Diffusion methods as they exist in a totalitarian society should be better understood, even though they would not be practiced. The "leapfrog" change wrought by totalitarian governments in the developing nations has too much appeal to the masses of people anxious for national progress to afford ignorance on the subject by the great democratic powers of the world. And incidentally such knowledge might help to explain differences in spread of such similar processes as water chlorination and fluoridation.

Legislative and Governmental Policy Formation Use of Rural Sociology

Despite the lack of agreement among sociologists and others concerning what is rural and what is urban and what constitutes the difference, there is virtually no disagreement concerning the utility of the census tabulation which separates the rural farm and the rural nonfarm population. The availability of the two separate tabulations may be traced directly to early rural sociological work and should be documented as a use. Galpin's early analysis of the 1920 census schedule, which the Bureau of the Census had tabulated by units no smaller than states, was done on eight selected counties. This tabulation, along with Brunner's study of 140 agricultural villages, resulted in the rural farm, rural nonfarm distinction made thereafter by the Bureau of the Census. The uses of the farm, nonfarm breakdowns as well as the rural, nonrural are manifold, some of the more important from the point of view of rural sociologists being the allocation of funds in accordance with legislation to the land-grant institutions for extension services, research in agricultural experiment stations, and the support of vocational agricultural education.

It is probably unnecessary to elaborate here the general uses of population material such as the important one of legislative representation, such items as distribution of state and federal aid, and market-research agencies' dependency on the demographer's figures. There is considerable evidence that no other lines of investigation and reporting are so much in demand by both public and private sectors of the economy and society as are population figures. Public utilities such as power and telephone companies and governmental services such as state departments of education plan their expansions, contractions, buildings, and location of equipment and resources in accordance with population projections by counties and minor civil divisions. One response concerning uses of rural sociology sums up a commonly expressed observation: where rural sociology is having difficulty in becoming established, or where it is first established in experiment stations, "I have been interested in noting how often the first bulletin to appear is a study of the population of the state with its various breakdowns—studies which apparently action programs and administrators, and even politicians, find to be useful." [70]

The excitement generated by a region's demography is conveyed in the following excerpts from an observer's account of the release of two population tables—nothing more—to local news media in a southern city. The demographer got amazing acclaim for telling people that what was happening was the opposite of what they wanted to happen. But he did it with figures, and that sounded so objective that they did not attack him. The newspapers soon realized that these population studies had news value. The newsmen started to study the tables on arrival and soon had the first of a series of feature stories ready for the next edition. Their analyses were not quite the kind that the demographer himself would have done, but they were not bad. Too many persons tended to forget the limitations of estimates. But the response! The letters fell into several categories:

1. "You cad! Our town has 10 per cent more telephones, etc., and you say we are losing population."
2. "Wonderful. Now, please tell us how many veterans and dependents of deceased veterans there are in the state?" (There were several of these demands for impossible things—things which could not be pulled out of a hat as the agencies seemed to expect.)
3. "Tell us more." Realistic requests for more information than the local small-town paper had printed, from architects, school boards, regional offices of the post office, and others. Our favorite sequence of such letters started with a request from a district bottling company for data on all counties in their area. A few days later a request from the southern headquarters office of the bottling company in a nearby state asked for estimates for all counties in the demographer's state. We had a good time guessing that the first man had been getting chewed out for his declining sales, but had

found his sales had slipped less than the population was estimated to have declined. We gathered that the headquarters office was impressed with the data when a few days later a manufacturer of glass bottles in a distant state wrote for the estimates.

4. The United States senator from the district called for copies, before his own newspaper in Washington could have carried the items. He later borrowed the stencils so that he could distribute copies to all the banks in the area.[71]

A uniquely specific use of demographic work by rural sociologists comes out of the State of Kentucky. The legislature of that state has designated that liquor licenses, granted on the basis of population, should be dispensed in intercensal years only in accordance with the intercensal population estimates as made by the Department of Rural Sociology at the University of Kentucky. Another southern state has through its rural sociology department provided nondemographers with a short method for rule-of-thumb projection of population by age from one decennial census to another.

In addition to the published census material, there are related unpublished materials and reports, emanating from rural sociologists and others in various divisions of the United States Department of Agriculture, which are significant for their utility. For example, the allocation of loan funds to the various states by the Farmers Home Administration has been based on such unpublished materials. Within the USDA itself, and within a number of other federal agencies, constant use is made of annual reports on the Hired Farm Working Force which are a source of information on earnings and employment of farm wage workers and occasional information on educational attainment, skill level, and occupational history of farm wage workers.[72]

There is general knowledge of the great movements represented in public policy whereby civil rights of a minority group are safeguarded, poverty is attacked in the Appalachians, or land is reclaimed through irrigation. And it is no surprise to anyone that basic research on the status of rural people in the affected areas has contributed to the formulation of the policy and the legislation concerning it. The work of rural sociologists on ethnic relations and integration has been sizable.[73] Its actual use is a bit difficult to document, although traditionalists often denounce the Supreme Court decision of 1951 which outlaws "separate but equal" educational facilities on the basis of its being a decision based on social science rather than on the law. There are other indications, somewhat negative, to be sure, which would indicate that rural sociological studies of race relations have been potent enough to be feared, and if possible suppressed, by supporters of the southern status quo. There is today restrictive legislation which prohibits "cultural studies" from being made with federal funds. In part this developed from an interracial study done in Mississippi by a rural sociologist some twenty years ago. Although the completed report was marked "confidential, for administrative use only," when it was submitted to its sponsoring agency, an administrative leakage to legislators (presumably to those most sensitive to any change in the status quo of the Negro) led to the legislation which ever since has been a barrier to free study of ethnic relations under the aegis of the government. Another important development, the so-called War on Poverty, has its genesis in the Southwestern Land Tenure Committee and other such committees composed largely of rural sociologists. These committees are often credited with being responsible for the Rural Development and Rural Areas Development programs[74] which were the forerunners of the War on Poverty in rural areas. For every one such Gargantuan project there are dozens and hundreds of others which depend for their inception or execution on the services of rural sociologists.

For example, rural sociological studies based on many kinds of investigations, besides the ecological type of study dealt with earlier in this chapter, are fundamental to changes in a wide array of educational institutions. Development of standards for school and university attainment,[75] curriculum planning at the state levels, realistic rural-area educational planning, and agricultural extension policy have shown a sensitivity to the findings of such studies as the correlation of the spread of curriculum changes and the cultural backgrounds of communities, the educational aspirations and the comparative educational achievement of rural youth, and the impact of mechanization on agricultural systems. Vocational education has been widely expanded to include manpower retraining. Rural industrialization studies have provided basic data for the planning of the content of retraining programs and for the location of retraining and development centers.[76] School dropouts constitute a general educational problem in both urban and rural communities. In one state the rural sociology department of the state university prepared an Experiment Station Bulletin devoted to the subject, which has become required reading for student teachers. The Extension Service in the same state has widely publicized the findings of the school dropout study, with the result that the author is engaged in a follow-up study specifically for rural youth dropouts.[77] An acceleration in research in a closely related field, *socialization and personality formation,* is evident among rural sociologists as it is among general sociologists. The importance of this work cannot be judged by the use to which it has been put. A few programs have been planned and initiated on state-wide bases, in which utilization is made of these studies of personality formation, socialization throughout life, and role taking. Initial work with the parent in order to reach the child is one such program. Specialties such as criminology, geriatrics, and the like take into account findings of researches on pertinent personality structures. Not essentially rural in nature, this work is being done by a group which includes many names identified with rural sociology.[78]

Policy formation in the field of conservation increasingly bears the mark of rural sociological studies. For example, after the broad policies of conservation were determined in the construction of Dalles Dam, there remained the unresolved financial settlement between the federal government and the Yakima Nation of Indians whose property had been used in the construction of the dam. At the request of the Indian Service of the United States Department of the Interior, an analysis of the socioeconomic status of the Yakimas was done by rural sociologists, and in large part on that basis the financial compensation was decided.[79]

Conservation of resources has been increasingly defined in terms of a man-land relationship, and for the "man" part of the duality, rural sociologists help to supply the information necessary for effective planning. Legislative programs and governmental policies on conservation of natural resources, leases, water rights, and subsurface minerals all reflect heavily the land-tenure studies of rural sociologists.[80] And who can say how important the many contributions of rural sociologists in the health field were in the formation of the Hill-Burton legislation on hospitals? Many believe that it was fundamental. What is the demand for outdoor recreation, and, once filled, how much is it used? How accessible can farm woodlots be to satisfy the reasonable demands of the public and the equally reasonable demands of the farmer-owner? What human and controllable factors can be linked to forest fires, and how can the control be exerted? There are rural sociologists on the Forest Services staffs of California, Ohio, Louisiana, and Colorado who help to interpret the human equation in federal and state practices for forest conservation and use.

Pennsylvania, Missouri, and Louisiana attempt to take into consideration the social factors and their implications as they assess accidents within the state. Rural sociologists contribute thus indirectly to the labor and traffic legislation as it is formulated in those states.

Various kinds of public welfare programs are based on research work originating among rural sociologists. A sizable amount of these concern problems of the aging. In one state rural sociologists undertook an interview study of a probability sample of persons sixty-five years of age and older, the study being financed by the State Department of Public Assistance. The information unearthed in the pilot county has, in the long run, been utilized for developing programs for older people in the state, especially by a state Council of Aging. Another state reports that its training programs in the Division of Public Health Education, as well as in the Regional Offices of the Department of Health Education and Welfare, use as teaching materials the systematic data from older persons within the state collected by rural sociologists. Also the Midwest Council for Social Research on Aging has applied in its recommendations various sociological studies of the aging and aged. Interestingly enough, the school of medicine uses the same materials in its teaching program.[81]

Studies of the aged and retired and their level of living, done in Kentucky, Connecticut, and Wisconsin, were exhibited at a House of Representatives hearing prior to the passage of social-security legislation. Studies from these same three states and from Texas were similarly presented to the United States Senate prior to the passage of social-security legislation in that chamber.[82]

Present-day uses of studies continue their day-to-day usefulness to government, but nothing in today's governmental scene equals in urgency the record set in the depression years of the 1930's for utilization of social science. A few studies stand out as signals which alerted a nation to the desperate plight of segments of the population. Carl Taylor and associates' *Disadvantaged Classes in American Agriculture*[83] and the monograph *Rich Land—Poor People*[84] might be cited. It can be claimed for the one that it provoked the top WPA administrators into a realization of the necessity for research in rural areas. It can be claimed for the other that it is typical of a host of such studies of the depression years which shocked, electrified, and moved to action the more complacent segments of the population. As the Franklin D. Roosevelt administration struggled with the depression, the major support for rural sociological research shifted to the Federal Emergency Relief Administration where Dwight Sanderson from Cornell, J. H. Kolb from the University of Wisconsin, and T. J. Woofter from the University of North Carolina served successively as co-ordinators of Rural Research in the Rural Section of the Division of Research and Statistics. The documentation of the impact of the great depression on rural America stands as one of the monuments built by rural sociologists.[85] Since they are depression publications, they focus on welfare and economic needs. A sampling of the subject matter (usually published by the United States Government Printing Office and dated sometime in the thirties) is suggested from some of the works here enumerated. *Landlord and Tenant on the Cotton Plantation*, by Thomas J. Woofter with the collaboration of Gordon Blackwell, Harold Hoffsommer, James G. Maddox, Jean M. Massell, B. C. Williams, and Waller Wynne, Jr., is one of the classics on the subject. A. R. Mangus' work *Rural Regions of the United States* opens with the statement: "The need for public assistance in the open country, villages, and small towns during the depression has followed definite geographic patterns." Outstanding among the dozens of monographs coming out of the period are, *The People of the Drought States*, by Conrad Taeuber and Carl C. Taylor, *Five Years of Rural Relief* by Waller Wynne, Jr., *Rural Families on Relief*, by Carle C. Zimmerman and Nathan L. Whetten, *Rural Youth on Relief*, by Bruce L. Melvin, and *Six Rural Problem Areas, Relief—Resources—Rehabilitation* by P. G. Beck and M. C. Forster. Some important publications of the time in the bureaucratic tradition, although presenting work of rural sociologists, did not bear their names. Such a monograph was *The Future of the Great Plains*, published by the United States Department of Agriculture in 1936.

For a generation of sociologists to whom the great depression is dusty history, it is fitting to catch the sense of purpose with which the hunger, misery, and frustration of large areas were revealed to those who could do something about it. Perhaps only the urgency of the civil-rights movement now matches what many rural sociologists saw then as their mission. One respondent writes:

I addressed a large crowd of Missouri Welfare persons at Rolla, in my first year at Missouri, giving facts about the way country people were living in the Missouri bootheel area, especially as to food. I told them of children who were starving right in the middle of excellent farm land. Local persons were at the meeting. Some were angry; others were astonished. It was part of the movement which was the beginning of living improvement in the Missouri bootheel. Eventually the Farm Security Administration took hold, physical examinations were given, and improvement was on its way.[86]

The proliferation of monographs was paralleled by a proliferation of federal action agencies, and both were a response to economic and social emergency. The times called for action—swift, ubiquitous, incisive—and, understandably, not always prudent and co-ordinated. The federal agencies of the time have been depicted as "barging into almost every local community, administering action programs that strongly affected local affairs, and dealing with things which were far from being non-controversial."[87] Strong local opposition to some of the administrative policies was common, and the contradictory goals and procedures of the differing agencies, or even of the same agencies at different times, caused confusion and resentment. Administrative districts of the several agencies seldom coincided with each other, or with local subdivisions of the county, or with natural communities or neighborhoods. Local representation very frequently ignored local informal leadership.

In order to co-ordinate these various programs, the agencies were reorganized in 1938, and the Division of State and Local Planning in the United States Department of Agriculture was set up to assist in establishing a more satisfactory linkage between the Secretary of Agriculture and the farmer at the grass roots. At the same time, to co-ordinate all these agencies at the local level, land-use planning committees at all levels of government were formed. The basic local unit was at the neighborhood and community level. Community and neighborhood delineation seemed to be of paramount importance, and dozens of rural sociologists in the Division of Farm Population and Rural Life of the Department of Agriculture and other federal agencies had assisted in such delineation in thirty-two states by 1941. Never have so many rural sociologists been employed in the government service. The satirical-minded might observe that the resulting improved linkage of the USDA to the farm groups of the nation was too successful. In a few years subsequent to the establishment of this mechanism for grass-roots state and federal planning, politicians and farmers' organizations had it abolished. The politicians feared its potential as a political weapon, and the farmers' organizations perceived that their almost monopolistic right to represent the farmers was in jeopardy.

Yet in the relatively few years of heavy government employment of rural sociologists, models for future types of studies were set, and linkages between theory and practice were accomplished which were landmarks for the discipline. So many programs came into being during this time that it proves to be a particularly propitious moment to observe the process of institutionalization. Most of the programs started off in a blaze of enthusiasm, and the early personnel were dedicated to a cause, much in the manner noted by Weber many years before. As formulated also by Weber, the programs became adjusted to less idealistic standards as increasing bureaucratization of the agencies took place. This tendency was scarcely observed by the agency itself, but was patently clear from the continuing results of a series of evaluation studies. One such study, for example, showed that the Farm Security Administration, in its loan and rehabilitation program, kept raising the floor of the minimum-income levels of the farm families it was reaching. In its earliest days of operation the poorer classes were being reached, but a combination of load of work, poor responses to repayments, bureaucratic pressures on the field workers to get increased productivity, and other factors caused the aid to flow increasingly to the "more productive" families. The poorer classes became progressively less represented in the program. As soon as this trend became publicized through the release of the various rural sociological studies, renewed attempts were made by the agency to develop programs which would more effectively reach the lower-income groups. The final institutional structure of this agency and many others was in part shaped in this manner by rural sociologists.

The group of studies of neighborhoods, cliques, and informal groupings has been one of the most-used by agencies interested in extension or education, settlement, resettlement, and other action programs. For example, the Soil Conservation Service has based its program consistently on what are called "neighbor groups." From five to fifteen families who are friends and informal acquaintances are the basic unit of organization.[88] Methods developed by rural sociologists have been used in the training of soil conservationists in delineating these neighbor groupings. Within a few years after organization, 33,000 of these groups had been located, including 284,000 farmers, and most of the groups remained active.[89]

An imaginative application of the social sciences together with the use of appropriate techniques for the development of agriculture, management, health, education, and other facets of social organization may be found in some of the programs in developing countries. The "basic democracies" which are being cultivated in Pakistan[90] and the credit organizations in Korea[91] might be cited as programs which have made differences in the lives of considerable numbers of people. But for boldness of range and magnitude of undertaking, we must turn to the Indian story. To be sure, the attempt to remold that huge nation by means consistent with its democratic tradition far exceeds the application of rural sociological principles. For present purposes, only a small part of the whole story whose end, of course, is nowhere in sight, will be recounted: the social change generated by the virtual partnership between the government of India and the Ford Foundation's Indian program, the latter under the administration of an American rural sociologist.[92]

The method chosen to move the country forward was that of government-led development programs intended to raise per-capita income and set growth in motion through a series of five-year plans applied under free democratic conditions.[93] A realistic catalogue of agricultural needs characterized the first two five-year plans, but their implementation proved to be somewhat too fragmented to achieve the desired results. Some of the projects undertaken during the first two planning periods were:

> Training centers for village workers, aid to extension departments for agricultural colleges, training centers in village crafts, training women for village extension work in home economics, organization and leadership of village youth activities, in-service training for village development personnel, strengthening the role of village school teachers in rural development, rural health service, research and training centers for village planning and rural housing, and scholarships to superior Gram Sevaks (Village Level Workers).[94]

These measures had varying degrees of lasting success, but evaluations of the total program attributed the increased agricultural yield in considerable measure to expanded crop acreage. Since there was little more land which could come into production, and since the combined projects left the food problem far from solved, new alternatives were sought in the Third Plan. The Intensive Agricultural District Program, or what is more commonly called the "package program," was then undertaken.

Unlike the earlier programs, which, although mutually reinforcing, were undertaken separately, the package program stressed improved practices which were to be used in combination—such practices as selection of improved seed; treatment of seed to prevent plant disease; improved tillage and equipment, fertilizer, and plant protection; improved harvesting, storage, and marketing. Also, unlike the earlier programs, the package programs were pilot programs, strategically located in respect to visibility and success probability and constituted so that whatever progress they might accomplish would virtually be a showcase demonstration of improved agricultural practices.

The objectives for the Stage I part of the long-term project are considered to have been accomplished in view of the following: yields have increased by 20 to 25 per cent among the million or more farmers in the pilot projects who have recovered two to three times as much money as they have invested in such inputs as fertilizer and insecticides; supporting organizations have been developed, such as are represented by the ten thousand agricultural officers at various governmental levels; warehouse organizations are now capable of making accessible to the farmer fertilizer and other supplies; effectiveness of co-operative societies is claimed to have increased. Diffusion practices and standard-of-living studies are discernible in the workings of the package program presently nearing completion of a phase as the third five-year plan draws to a close. This phase has been characterized by an approach new to India, by which the staff, through a district extension operation, is learning to understand, educate, and work with rank-and-file farmers in large numbers both in groups and as individuals. Stage II is presently emerging, the social targets of which are joint program planning between extension workers and village leaders, full program participation by all farmers, more complete farm planning, the simultaneous development of all farming enterprises using simple practices, better use of village resources in production, and joint efforts to make the co-operatives and other institutions more effective.

The concerted attack on underproduction of sufficient food for the nation is coupled with a similar emphasis on control of the stupendous swelling of the Indian population, this latter drive being timed to make the most of a technological break-through in cheap, easily used, efficient contraceptive devices in those parts of India where there is the greatest readiness. Practically all that is known about social organization, social rank, the use of power, effective communication systems, the diffusion process, ecological methods, the ends for which men strive, and the norms they employ in their striving has been applied and modified in this ongoing story of a great nation's first steps toward agricultural self-sufficiency.

Nonuses of Rural Sociology

Many eminent rural sociologists who have devoted major portions of their professional careers to particular lines of study will search in vain in these pages to find to what use their work has been put. This is regrettable, and it is excusable only in the light of the great difficulty which attends the documentation of use. It also probably reflects a society which does not use all of the available knowledge in its problem solving. Surely health investigations, in aspects other than the ecological, have unearthed information which should be useful to policy makers and administrators. Factors of health affected by or related to occupation, ethnicity, diet, sex, age, and the particular symptomatic conditions which might be clues to abnormalities are of importance equal to the ecological aspects of illness.[95] These are all underrepresented here because of the difficulty in demonstrating exactly how the data have been used. Other areas of long and painstaking research which seem almost neglected in the foregoing pages are stratification;[96] the small town; family studies; the rural-urban fringe; the impact of technology on rural life, co-operatives, and farmers' organizations;[97] and the impressive body of information concerning aspirations and career choices of rural youth.

Let us repeat here that the main body of this chapter represents a compilation of rural-sociology uses which was garnered from three successive waves of inquiry directed by the authors to a large cross section of rural sociologists of the United States. The many omissions in the presentation cannot in the least be attributed to them, but a great many inclusions would not appear here were it not for their thoughtful help. Also, the points of emphasis brought out in this chapter were reinforced by the emphases which were apparent in their hundreds of letters. Finally, the documentation of works referred to in the text is to a degree compiled in accordance with their suggestions. Textbooks have purposely been avoided as source material, the only two exceptions being two textbooks now out of print which were particularly rich in use documentation.

Almost half a century after the Purnell Act of 1924, which made federal funds available for rural-sociological research through the land-grant colleges and universities, only three out of four of the educational agencies entitled to the funds make use of them for their intended purposes. The truly strong rural-sociology departments or sections of departments are relatively few; perhaps they could be counted on the fingers of one hand. Certainly such a count would not require both hands. Thus any discussion of the nonuses of rural sociology must make reference to the lack of universal appreciation of its utility. Rural sociologists in Wyoming, Idaho, Arizona, or South Carolina would perhaps have fewer colleagues of their discipline with whom to compare notes than would rural sociologists now in many developing countries. However, for readers who are nonrural sociologists it is pointed out that generally in those states in which rural sociology is underrepresented the other social sciences, including general sociology, are likewise underrepresented. Generally it may be assumed that nonuse of rural sociology, because of its unavailability, does not differ essentially from nonuse of general sociology and other sociological specialties. There is still a discernible tendency among some college presidents, deans of agriculture, and directors of agricultural experiment stations and extension services to reflect the old school of thought in much the same way as some biologically oriented deans of colleges of medicine once considered that all the important problems of their units lay outside the social sciences. A few college presidents who could by no standard be branded anti-intellectual often prided themselves on their humanistic and literary backgrounds and believed sociology, including rural sociology, had less to offer than literature.

Notwithstanding the fact that only three out of four of the United States have rural-sociology departments or sections, the discipline is stronger and more used there than in other countries. In recent years Holland, West Germany, France, and other European countries have been fostering the discipline and putting it to use in much the same manner as it has been used in the United States. In fact, the relative recent growth of the discipline is greater in these old industrialized countries than it is here.

A nonuse of rural sociology which is perhaps most irritating to the rural sociologist frequently occurs on the state and federal level in the United States, as recognized leaders in the field of agriculture attempt to give the broad view of where we are going and whence we came. The lack of impact and the sense of injustice because of it is well shown in this excerpt from one of the respondents contributing to the present chapter.

> Last night . . . I skimmed Stewart Udall's *The Quiet Crisis*, and I found material from Thoreau, Major Powell, Gifford Pinchot, F. L. Olmstead, Walt Whitman, and other poetic and journalistic social thinkers. And also Lewis Mumford, some of it good stuff. . . . But the academic rural sociologists had no more place in it than they have in the Security Council of the United Nations. This is a book showing the need for conservation throughout the country. . . . If we do not even make an impression upon the Honorable Secretary of the Interior . . . we have not broken even the surface of the "fiberglass curtain" which surrounds the National Capital.[98]

It is difficult to say which is the worse of two evils: being ignored or being misrepresented. Another sociologist[99] recalls reading a report of a committee of agricultural administrators employed by one of the great foundations, on which his own dean, now retired, served. Policies for collaboration in agriculture with Latin American countries were specified. Those implemented by the nonsocial-science disciplines were openly emphasized because "sociologists were often socialistic."

Often thought of by their colleagues in general sociology to be of quite a conservative stripe (probably as farmers are reputed to be conservative on the national and state political scenes), rural sociology may have created a quite opposite impression by an incident at the American Association of Newspaper Editors in Washington, D.C., in April, 1959. Castro was addressing the group, and at one point he picked up a copy of rural Cuba by rural sociologist Lowry Nelson. "We are getting many ideas from this book by Professor Nelson of the University of Minnesota," declared the Cuban dictator.[100]

In any event it seems clear that neither have rural sociologists marketed their wares so that policy makers invariably think of their work when they face decisions nor have they apparently created an accurate image of themselves among potential users of their investigations.

What of the Future? [101]

The reader of this chapter will have noted that many uses of rural sociology grow out of localized research bases. Often there is no way to avoid what one respondent called the "patchwork" approach to research and its application. Another writes, "When rural sociologists were called on to help guide and formulate policy for broad national policies, we weren't able to deliver. Our research had been spotty, spasmodic, and concentrated on small local areas." [102] Some integration for state studies and their application has been supplied by the unit which earlier had the title Division of Farm Population and Rural Life and now is known as the Farm Population Branch of the Economic Research Service of the United States Department of Agriculture. Strategically placed rural sociologists in the various federal agencies help to provide a degree of integration, such as the sociologists in the research units of the USDA, in the Agricultural Research Service in the Federal Extension Service, and in the Bureau of the Census.

Occasionally efforts from many parts of the country are somehow integrated, as was the case when the rural sociologists of the State Experiment Stations and the Farm Population Branch of the USDA joined forces to supply to Congress the data required for the 1954 amendment to the Social Security Act which extended coverage to farmers and farm operators. If rural sociology is to provide the knowledge and experience necessary to bring the so-called "human element" adequately into agricultural policy and planning, more emphasis must be given to over-all general considerations in the nation and the world. There should be a national base for this integration. Since the United States has no national university as many countries do, the location of such a base will not be easily determined. For the short run, at least, it seems advisable to strengthen the Farm Population Branch by supplying it with more research funds which may be used in state-federal collaboration.

Changes in training and in job opportunities are already at hand by which rural sociologists of the future may expect that their work will be expanded in breadth and in depth. The theoretical and methodological training of rural sociologists is increasingly indistinguishable from that of the less applied specialties. The claim that rural sociology suffers from poverty of theory, if ever true, certainly is unfounded now, and in the field of methodology rural sociology often leads the way. The professional opportunities available in the extension service, in rural-urban planning as rural-urban interests merge in the great metropolitan areas, in the national poverty program, and in the developing nations of the world give a working latitude quite unknown to rural sociologists a generation ago. The very persistence in the developing nations (as well as in a nation as sophisticated in social organization as the USSR) of a "farm problem"—a comparative unresponsiveness of the agricultural sector of the economy to vigor and growth at the same rate as that experienced by other economic sectors—belies the widely held notion that, with the blurring of the rural-urban difference, rural sociology is little different from general sociology in the problems with which it deals. The recent resurgence and growth of rural sociology in Europe and in the more developed countries contradicts the thought that industrialization decreases the importance of rural sociology. Already the perspective of a sizable group of rural sociologists is considerably broadened as support for their work has increasingly come from private foundations of national and world scope, as well as from the Office of Education, the National Institutes of Health, and the Department of State. It is very likely that the rural sociologist of the future will continue occasionally to include among his research sites his immediately local and provincial surroundings. It is even more likely, however, that such parochial concerns will be given the advantage of comparative perspective by equally occasional inclusions of research sites of magnitude, "foreignness," and cultural complexity. All the omens are that "the best is yet to be."

REFERENCES

1. Elihu Katz, "Communication Research and the Image of Society: Convergence of Two Traditions," *American Journal of Sociology*, LXV (1960), 435–441.
2. Edmund deS. Brunner, *The Growth of a Science* (New York: Harper, 1957). Here (p. 144) see a listing of the presidential addresses before the Rural Sociological Society, many of which have dealt with the history of rural sociology. See also Charles J. Galpin, *My Drift into Rural Sociology* (Baton Rouge: Louisiana State University Press, 1938); and Walfred A. Anderson, *Bibliography of Researches in Rural Sociology* (Ithaca: New York Agricultural Experiment Station Rural Sociology Publication 52, 1957).
3. Brunner, *op. cit.*, pp. 3, 4.
4. *Ibid.*, p. 5.
5. Pitirim A. Sorokin, Carle C. Zimmerman, and Charles J. Galpin, *Systematic Source Book in Rural Sociology* (Minneapolis: University of Minnesota Press, Vol. I, 1930; Vol. II, 1931; Vol. III, 1932).
6. William H. Sewell, "Some Observations on Theory Testing," *Rural Sociology*, XXI (1956), 1.
7. Charles J. Galpin, *The Social Anatomy of an Agricultural Community* (Madison: Wisconsin AES Bulletin 34, 1915).
8. Bruce L. Melvin writes: "I heard [Robert E. Park] say at the meeting at Purdue

University in 1925 that [he] took his suggestions for city studies from C. J. Galpin." Personal correspondence.

9. *Op. cit.* Galpin's work was supplemented in time by many others who added refinements to delineation methods and adapted them to changing conditions. Among his early and best-known successors should be mentioned John H. Kolb, Dwight Sanderson, Carl C. Taylor, and Carle C. Zimmerman. For a more complete statement concerning both successors and forerunners, see Brunner, *op. cit.,* Chapter 2.

10. Edmund deS. Brunner writes that "the Galpin-Sanderson methods of determining community boundaries were used at first by New York State. . . . The N.Y. State Board would not approve a consolidation unless these procedures had been followed in determining the social community. . . . [They] also were used in a number of states in laying out communities, areas of representation on county committees in the Agricultural Planning Program." Personal correspondence. See Dwight Sanderson, *Locating the Rural Community* (Ithaca: Cornell University Extension Bulletin 413, 1939); John H. Kolb, *Rural Primary Groups* (Madison: Wisconsin AES, 1921); Carle C. Zimmerman and Carl C. Taylor, *Rural Organization: A Study of Primary Groups in Wake County* (Raleigh: North Carolina AES Bulletin, 1922); and Donald G. Hay and Robert A. Polson, *Rural Organizations in Oneida County* (Ithaca: New York AES Bulletin 871, 1951).

11. T. Lynn Smith was largely responsible for creating awareness of the importance of such factors as land division, settlement patterns, and the layout of roads. He did much of the basic research for this emphasis. See his article "The Social Effects of Land Division in Relationship to a Program of Land Utilization," *Journal of Farm Economics,* XVII (1935), 703–709. Sanders and Ensminger developed the "neighborhood cluster method" for delineation of communities and neighborhoods within communities. See Irwin T. Sanders and Douglas Ensminger, *Alabama Rural Communities: A Study of Chilton County* (Montevallo: Alabama College Bulletin 136, 1940).

12. In response to the authors' request for examples of uses of rural sociology, Walter C. McKain, Jr., writes that rural sociological research in "Connecticut, Pennsylvania, and Texas, to mention only three [states] . . . has helped . . . communities anticipate the opportunities and changes that are occasioned by highway programs, and by demonstrating how highways can be used to stimulate economic areas." See Walter C. McKain, *The Connecticut Turn Pike* (Stores: Connecticut AES Bulletin 387, 1965).

13. C. Horace Hamilton writes that the work done by rural sociologists in North Carolina "on community, and especially medical ecology, . . . was of great use to the Governor's Commission on Education Beyond the High School." Personal correspondence. See C. Horace Hamilton, *Community Colleges for North Carolina, a Study of Need, Location, and Service Areas* (Raleigh: North Carolina AES Bulletin, 1962); and John F. Thaden, *Equalizing Educational Opportunities through Community School Districts* (East Lansing: Michigan AES Special Bulletin 410, 1957).

14. Therel R. Black writes that in Utah Joseph A. Geddes' "Study on libraries . . . resulted directly in the passage of Utah legislation for the establishment of library districts and the providing of a state library system." Carl F. Kraenzel writes along the same line for the state of Montana, and Charles E. Lively notes that the Missouri State Library used sociological data on stratification and occupational subareas for the distribution of books. From personal correspondence.

15. James W. Longest, Frank D. Alexander, and Jean L. Harshaw, "The Function of the Neighborhood in the Farm and Home Management Program: A Case Study," *Rural Sociology,* XXVI (1961), 186–191. Of course, rural sociologists

have put to work groupings other than those featuring locality. "Work . . . done by James Longest and Frank Alexander in their Cornell AES Bulletin, *The Method Used for the Formation of Home Management Programs in a Town of Verona in Oneida County* resulted in letting leaders identified by local people in the community select their own members for . . . discussion groups," writes a Missouri informant. Allen Edwards writes along the same line for South Carolina. Personal correspondence.

16. C. Horace Hamilton, personal correspondence.
17. *Ibid.* See C. Horace Hamilton (collaborator), *Hospital Care in the United States* (New York: Commonwealth Fund, 1947).
18. John C. Belcher, *Medical Service Relationships in Harper County* (Stillwater: Oklahoma AES Bulletin, No. B-477, 1956). Belcher writes that "the principal finding [here] is that distance is not . . . [but] age, education, level of living and occupation are significantly associated with both use and health levels." Personal correspondence.
19. Edmund deS. Brunner, personal correspondence. C. Milton Coughenour in a letter broadens the concept of uses: "The most extensive use of information collected by rural sociologists in Kentucky has been made by welfare agencies, the Extension Service, churches, the community leaders in Eastern Kentucky and the Southern Appalachians. For years members of the Department have funneled information and provided counsel to groups of these kinds." In this work the following type of publication was much used: James Brown, *The Family Group in a Kentucky Farming Community* (Lexington, Ky.: AES Bulletin, 1952). See also Emory J. Brown, *Elements Associated with Activity and Inactivity in Rural Organizations* (State College, Penn.: AES Bulletin 574, 1954).
20. Otis Durant Duncan, personal correspondence. See also Margaret Jarman Hagood, *Farm Operator Family Level of Living Indexes for Counties of the United States*, 1940 and 1945 (Washington: Bureau of Agricultural Economics, 1947). This work and earlier indices by Charles E. Lively, Robert L. McNamara, and Raymond A. Mangus have been invaluable both as bases for sampling in surveys and for planning regions for administration.
21. Edmund deS. Brunner, personal correspondence.
22. See especially headings under Ensminger in Anderson, *op. cit.*
23. Charles E. Lively, personal correspondence.
24. See the sections, Migration and Mobility in Anderson, *op. cit.* B. H. Lubke writes: "Dr. Roscoe Giffin, sociologist at Berea . . . worked closely with some of these urban agencies in setting up programs and policies to deal with adjustment problems of southern migrants." Personal correspondence. A classic in rural sociology and important, as indicated below, in the development of Bureau of Census breakdowns is Edmund deS. Brunner *et al., American Agricultural Villages* (New York: Doran, 1927). For an insightful analysis of the relation of small towns to large cities, see Arthur J. Vidich and Joseph Bensman, *Small Town in Mass Society* (Princeton: Princeton University Press, 1958). This and the following were cited by rural sociologists in response to requests for suggestions on uses: Otto G. Hoiberg, *Exploring the Small Community* (Lincoln: University of Nebraska Press, 1955); and Irwin T. Sanders, *Making Good Communities Better* (Lexington: University of Kentucky Press, 1950).
25. T. Lynn Smith, *The Sociology of Rural Life* (New York: Harper, 1947), p. 267.
26. Nathan L. Whetten, The Social and Economic Structure of the Trade Centers in the Canadian Prairie Provinces with Social Reference to Its Changes, 1910–1930 (Cambridge: Harvard University unpublished Ph.D. Thesis, 1932).

27. Walter R. Goldschmidt, "Some Evidence on the Future Pattern of Rural Settlement," *Rural Sociology*, VIII (1943), 370–386. See also Irving A. Spaulding, "Perspective on Urbanization," *Rural Sociology*, XXVII (1962), 1–7.

28. Carl C. Taylor, "The Sociologists' Part in Planning the Columbia Basin," *American Sociological Review*, XI (1946), 321–330. Columbia Joint Investigations (Washington: USDA and Cooperating Agencies, 1944). For documentation, see Charles P. Loomis and J. Allan Beegle, *Rural Social Systems* (New York: Prentice-Hall, 1950), pp. 237 ff. See also Murray A. Straus, *Matching Farms and Families in the Columbia Basin Project* (Washington AES Bulletin 588, 1958).

29. For bibliographical and substantive findings on this subject, see especially Smith, *The Sociology of Rural Life*, Chapter 13. See also Walter R. Goldschmidt, *As You Sow* (Glencoe, Ill.: The Free Press, 1947); and Charles P. Loomis *et al.*, *Turrialba: Social Systems and the Introduction of Change* (Glencoe, Ill.: The Free Press, 1953). For the results of misguided settlement on the Great Plains, see Carl F. Kraenzel, *The Great Plains in Transition* (Norman: University of Oklahoma Press, 1955).

30. Paul J. Jehlik, personal correspondence. The opposite process also occurred, as the Farm Security Administration used these studies for recruiting workers "for dairy farms in such states as Ohio, Indiana and Illinois during the early World War II period of a critical shortage of farm workers." *Ibid.* There is some evidence indicating that rural sociological studies influenced policy in the United States treatment of large holdings in conquered countries after World War II.

31. Louis Ducoff, personal correspondence.

32. The two outstanding books on the subject are Herbert F. Lionberger, *Adoption of New Ideas and Practices* (Ames: Iowa State University Press, 1960); and Everett M. Rogers, *Diffusion of Innovations* (New York: The Free Press of Glencoe and Macmillan, 1962).

33. Charles P. Loomis and Douglas Ensminger, "Studies in Social Organization, Administration, Attitudes, and Opinions," in Charles P. Loomis, *Studies of Rural Social Organization* (Ann Arbor: Edwards Brothers, 1945), Chapter 5. See also Charles P. Loomis, *Social Systems: Essays on Their Persistence and Change* (Princeton: Van Nostrand, 1962), Essay 2.

34. Carle C. Zimmerman, *The Changing Community* (New York: Harper, 1938), pp. 5, 7. See also Robert K. Merton, *Social Theory and Social Structure* (Glencoe, Ill.: The Free Press, 1957), p. 393. Pitirim A. Sorokin was using the term *cosmopolitanism* in 1927. See his *Social Mobility* (New York: Harper, 1927), p. 541.

35. C. Milton Coughenour, "The Rate of Technological Diffusion among Locality Groups," *American Journal of Sociology*, LXIX (1964), 325–339. Quotations are from the manuscript of the paper before publication. Of course, pluralities other than neighborhoods are important in diffusion. See Eugene Wilkening, *Adoption of Improved Farm Practices as Related to Family Factors* (Madison: Wisconsin AES Research Bulletin 183, 1953).

36. George M. Beal and Everett M. Rogers, "Informational Sources in the Adoption Process of New Fabrics," *Journal of Home Economics*, XLIX (1957); and Bert L. Ellenbogen and G. Love, *Age, Status and the Diffusion of Preventive Health Practices* (Ithaca, N.Y.: AES Bulletin 64, 1964).

37. North Central Rural Sociology Subcommittee for the Study of Diffusion of Farm Practices, *How Farm People Accept New Ideas* (Ames: Iowa Agricultural Extension Service Special Report 15, 1955).

38. North Central Rural Sociology Subcommittee for the Study of Diffusion of Farm

Practices, *Adopters of New Farm Ideas: Characteristics and Communications Behavior* (East Lansing: Michigan AES Bulletin, 1961).

39. Bryce Ryan and Neal C. Gross, "Acceptance and Diffusion of Hybrid Corn Seed in Two Iowa Communities," *Rural Sociology*, VIII (1943), 15–24.
40. Gabriel Tarde, *The Laws of Imitation*, translated by Elsie C. Parsons (New York: Holt, Rinehart, and Winston, 1903); F. Stuart Chapin, *Cultural Change* (New York: Century, 1928); and H. Earl Pemberton, "The Curve of Culture Diffusion Rate," *American Journal of Sociology*, I (1936), 547–556. Sorokin has denied the validity of the S-shaped curve for cumulative distributions or the normal curve for noncumulative distributions in acceptance or spread of all ideas and traits. Rural sociologists have disagreed with him, but in the present authors' view Sorokin has the advantage of a broader vista than his critics. The inter-change illustrates the importance of adequate conceptualization in explanation and prediction. It is necessary that the "givens" or "other things equal" be specified. To maintain that the diffusion of an order to a well-trained army or to actors in other authoritarian situations follows the same pattern as the spread of hybrid seed corn in Iowa is absurd. It may be compared to the claim that such behavior as learning and growth under "voluntary" conditions which may ap-proximate the S-curve is the same as that of the "do or die" type which may more nearly fit the J-curve, so often used by sociologists to describe social phenomena.
41. North Central Rural Sociology Subcommittee for the Study of Diffusion of Farm Practices, *Adopters of New Farm Ideas*, p. 3.
42. John T. Stone, *How County Agricultural Agents Teach* (East Lansing: Michigan AES Service Mimeo. Bulletin).
43. George M. Beal, Everett M. Rogers, and Joe M. Bohlen, "Validity of the Concept of Stages in the Adoption Process," *Rural Sociology*, XXII (1957).
44. James H. Copp, Maurice L. Sill, and Emory J. Brown, "The Function of In-formation Sources in the Farm Practice Adoption Process," *Rural Sociology*, XXIII (1958), 146–158.
45. Rogers, *op. cit.*, pp. 84–85.
46. (As summarized in Rogers.) *Ibid.*, p. 85.
47. Gerald Klonglan *et al.*, "The Role of a Free Sample in the Adoption Process," paper presented at the Midwest Sociological Society, St. Louis, 1960. Of course it may be argued that the trial provides knowledge necessary for adoption. The cognitive aspect of adoption is crucial in adoption. See Leonard M. Sizer and Ward F. Porter, *The Relation of Knowledge to Adoption of Recommended Practices* (Morgantown: West Virginia AES Bulletin 446, 1960).
48. Everett M. Rogers and Harold R. Capener, *The Clientele of the County Exten-sion Agent* (Wooster: Ohio AES Research Bulletin 858, 1960).
49. Herbert F. Lionberger, "Community Prestige and the Choice of Sources of Farm Information," *Public Opinion Quarterly*, XXIII (1959), 110–118. See also Herbert F. Lionberger and C. Milton Coughenour, *Social Structure and Diffusion of Farm Information* (Columbia: Missouri AES Bulletin 631, 1957).
50. North Central Rural Sociology Subcommittee for the Study of Diffusion of Farm Practices, *Adopters of New Farm Ideas*, p. 8.
51. Rogers, *op. cit.*, Chapter 3. For special consideration of the family in relation to diffusion, see Wilkening, *op. cit.*
52. Ivan Nye, referring to a study in the state of Washington. Personal correspond-ence. See also Santi Priva Bose, "Characteristics of Farmers Who Adopt Agricul-tural Practices in Indian Villages," *Rural Sociology*, XXVI (1961), 138–146.
53. Daryl J. Hobbes, Factors Related to the Use of Agricultural Chemicals on Iowa

Farms (Ames: Iowa State University unpublished, M.S. Thesis, 1960) For a summary of various scales by the Italian rural sociologist, M. B. Venvenuti, Daniel Lerner, James H. Copp, and A. W. van den Ban see Rogers, *op. cit.*, pp. 62 ff. See also Denton E. Morrison, "Achievement Motivation of Farm Operators: A Measurement Study," *Rural Sociology*, XXIX (1964), 367–385.

54. George M. Beal and Everett M. Rogers, *The Adoption of Two Farm Practices in a Central Iowa Community* (Ames: Iowa Agricultural and Home Economics Experiment Station Special Report 26, 1960). In reference to the previous discussion of the trial it should be noted that 95 per cent of the respondents in this study stated that experience with the innovation gained then was reported as most important.

55. Rogers, *op. cit.*, p. 222.

56. Loomis and Beegle, *op. cit.*, Chapter 5.

57. *Ibid.*, pp. 140–142.

58. For a summary of the application of sociometry, see Rogers, *op. cit.*, pp. 228 ff.

59. Loomis *et al.*, *op. cit.* In this publication see the work in applied sociology of Roy A. Clifford, Eduardo Arze Loüriera, Antonio Arce, Norman W. Painter, Charles Proctor, Ralph H. Allee, Olen E. Leonard, and others.

60. John C. Belcher, from personal correspondence. See his article "Acceptance of the Salk Polio Vaccine," *Rural Sociology*, XXIII (1958), 158–171.

61. North Central Rural Sociology Subcommittee for the Study of Diffusion of Farm Practices, *Adopters of New Farm Ideas*, p. 4. See also F. C. Fliegel, "Differences among Improved Farm Practices as Related to Rates of Adoption," Pennsylvania AES Bulletin 691, 1962.

62. Charles L. Cleland, personal correspondence.

63. For the "package" or "flexible felt needs" approach as used in the Farm Security Administration, see Charles P. Loomis, *Studies of Rural Social Organization in the United States, Latin America and Germany op. cit.*, Chapter 19, "The New Mexican Experiment in Village Rehabilitation." For the package approach in India, see Douglas Ensminger, "The Original Fifteen Pilot Extension Projects," in Ministry of Community Development, Panchayati Raj and Cooperation, *Evolution of Community Development Programme in India* (Delhi: Government of India Press, 1963). See also Howard W. Beers and Douglas Ensminger, "The Development Block as a Social System?", *Indian Journal of Public Administration*, V (1959), 1–18.

64. Joe M. Bohlen and George M. Beal, personal correspondence. For a general treatment of action research, see Walter L. Slocum, "Sociological Research for Action Agencies—Some Guides and Hazards," *Rural Sociology*, XXI (1956), 196–199.

65. *Ibid.*

66. Alvin L. Bertrand, personal correspondence.

67. Herbert Lionberger, "Some Characteristics of Farm Operators Sought as Sources of Farm Information in a Missouri Community," *Rural Sociology*, XVIII (1953), 327–338. For steps in the direction advocated here, see the following excellent studies: Christopher Sower, John Holland, Kenneth Tiedke, and Walter Freeman, *Patterns of Community Involvement* (Glencoe, Ill.: The Free Press, 1957); Paul A. Miller, *Community Health Action* (East Lansing: Michigan State College Press, 1953); Christopher Sower and Walter Freeman, "Community Involvement in Community Development Programs," *Rural Sociology*, XXIII (1958), 25–33; George M. Beal, Paul Yarbrough, Gerald E. Klonglan, and Joe M. Bohlen, *Social Action in Civil Defense* (Ames: Iowa Agricultural and Home Economics Experiment Station, 1964); Joe M. Bohlen, George M. Beal, Gerald E. Klonglan,

and John L. Tait, *Community Power Structure and Civil Defense* (Ames: Iowa Agricultural and Home Economics Experiment Station, 1964); Edmund deS. Brunner, Irwin S. Sanders, and Douglas Ensminger, *Farmers of the World* (New York: Columbia University Press, 1945); Wade H. Andrews, *A Case Study of Rural Community Development and Leadership* (Wooster: Ohio AES Research Bulletin 808); Linwood Hodgdon, "Psychological and Sociological Factors in Rural Change," *Journal of the Indian Medical Association*, XL (March 16, 1963), 289–292; David E. Lindstrom, "Influence of Rural Institutions on Economic Development," *Illinois Agricultural Economics*, IV (1964); Selz C. Mayo "An Analysis of the Organizational Role of the Teacher of Vocational Agriculture," *Rural Sociology*, XXV (1960), 334–345; C. Paul Marsh and A. Lee Coleman, "Farmers' Practice-Adoption Rates in Relation to Adoption Rates of 'Leaders,'" *Rural Sociology*, XIX (1954), 180–181. Slocum, *op. cit.;* Afif I. Tannous, "Social Change in an Arab Village," *American Sociological Review*, VI (1941); Frank and Ruth Young, "Toward a Theory of Community Development," in *Science, Technology and Development: 7*, Social Problems of Development and Urbanization, United States Papers prepared for the United Nations Conference on the Application of Science and Technology for the Benefit of the Less Developed Areas, 1963; and William V. D'Antonio, William H. Form, Charles P. Loomis, and Eugene C. Erickson, "Institutional and Occupational Representations in Eleven Community Influence Systems," *American Sociological Review*, XXVI (1961), 440–447.

68. Howard W. Beers, "Application of Sociology in Development Programs," *Council on Economic and Cultural Affairs Paper* (January, 1963). See also Edward O. Moe, *New York Farmers' Opinions on Agricultural Programs* (Ithaca, N.Y.: AES Bulletin 498, 1952).

69. For reference to ideas sketched below, see the following by Charles P. Loomis: "Social Change and Social Systems," in Edward A. Tiryakian, ed., *Sociological Theory, Values and Socio-Cultural Change* (New York: The Free Press and Macmillan, 1963); "Tentative Types of Directed Social Change Involving Systemic Linkage," *Rural Sociology*, XXIV (1959), 383–390; and "Systemic Linkage of El Cerrito," *Rural Sociology*, XXIV (1959), 54–57.

70. Carl C. Taylor, personal correspondence. Among the most important of these many analyses are J. Allan Beegle (with Dale Hathaway and Keith Bryant), *Rural America 1960*, Census Monograph (forthcoming), and Douglas G. Marshall, *The Story of Price County, Wisconsin: Population Research in a Rural Development County* (Madison: Wisconsin AES Research Bulletin 220, 1960). See also Clinton L. Folse, *Illinois Rural and Urban Population* (Urbana, Ill.: AES Bulletin, 1952); and Ray E. Wakeley and Paul J. Jehlik, "Regional Research in Population Dynamics," *Rural Sociology*, XVIII (1953). Many bulletins by these and such other rural sociological demographers as J. Allan Beegle, Otis D. Duncan, C. Horace Hamilton, Clinton Jesser, George W. Hill, Conrad Taeuber, Selz C. Mayo, Lowry Nelson, Robert L. Skrabanek, J. F. Thaden, T. J. Woofter, and Margaret J. Hagood have been widely used. See the 253-item list of publications under Population in Anderson, *op. cit.*

71. Edna S. Pedersen in personal correspondence, describing incident from demographic work of Harald A. Pedersen.

72. Louis J. Ducoff, Chief of the Farm Population Branch, Economic and Statistical Analysis Division of the USDA, writes: "Census data on the farm and rural population by States are used in the allocation of funds to extension services, to agricultural experiment stations for research, and for the support of vocational agricultural education. Unpublished materials prepared by our office are used

by the Farmers Home Administration in the annual allocation of loan funds to the States. . . . Our annual reports on the Hired Farm Working Force . . . are widely used within the Department and by other Federal agencies and also supply information in connection with proposed legislation affecting farm wage workers." Personal correspondence.

73. See Robin M. Williams, Jr. "Concepts of Marginality in Rural Population Studies," *Rural Sociology*, V (1941), and also his *Strangers Next Door* (Englewood Cliffs, N.J.: Prentice-Hall, 1964). See also Vernon J. Parenton and R. J. Pellegrin, "Social Structure and the Leadership Factor in a Negro Community in South Louisiana," *Phylon* (1956); and T. Lynn Smith, "An Analysis of Rural Social Organization among the French-Speaking People of Southern Louisiana," *Journal of Farm Economics*, XVI (1934), 680–688.

74. Alvin L. Bertrand, personal correspondence. For a listing of sixty-one items on land tenure, including the well-known studies by Harold C. Hoffsommer, Edgar A. Schuler, Arthur F. Raper, Otis D. Duncan, Joseph Ackerman, and Robert T. McMillan, see Anderson, *op. cit.* See also Alvin L. Bertrand and Floyd L. Corty, eds., *Rural Land Tenure in the United States* (Baton Rouge: Louisiana State University Press, 1962).

75. Otis Durant Duncan and C. Arnold Anderson in personal correspondence. See also William H. Sewell, "Community of Residence and College Plans," *American Sociological Review*, XXIX (1964), 24–38; and Lowry Nelson, *The Education of the Farm Population in Minnesota* (St. Paul: Minnesota AES Bulletin 1944). Concerning this study, Nelson notes that it showed the low attendance level of the state, "next to Kentucky which was on the bottom as regards white males 16–17 years of age. [It] was a 'shocker' for the state. [The Farm Bureau became interested and so did other county groups interested in youth, so that the state] came up to 24 in 1950 . . . now I could never . . . say that the rise in rank was due to my work but. . . ." See also E. Grant Youmans, "Factors in Educational Attainment," *Rural Sociology*, XXIV (1959), 21–28.

76. Alvin L. Bertrand, personal correspondence.

77. E. Grant Youmans and C. Milton Coughenour, personal correspondence.

78. Lee G. Burchinal, Archibald O. Haller, and Marvin J. Taves, *Career Choices of Rural Youth in a Changing Society* (St. Paul: Minnesota AES Bulletin 458, 1962); William H. Sewell, "Infant Training and the Personality of the Child," *American Journal of Sociology*, LVIII (1952), 150–159; William H. Sewell and Archibald O. Haller, Jr., "Factors in the Relationship between Social Status and the Personality Adjustment of the Child," *American Sociological Review*, XXIV (1959), 511–520; James Cowhig, Jay Artis, J. Allan Beegle, and Harold Goldsmith, *Orientations toward Occupation and Residence: A Study of High School Seniors in Four Rural Counties of Michigan* (East Lansing: Michigan AES Special Bulletin 428, 1960). See these publications for a more complete listing of studies, including those of E. Grant Youmans and John R. Christiansen. A different kind of socialization is that of the Agricultural Extension agent. See Ivan F. Nye, *The Relationship of Certain Factors to County Agent Success* (Columbia: Missouri AES Research Bulletin 498, 1952). See also Eugene Wilkening, "Roles of Communicating Agents in Technological Change in Agriculture," *Social Forces*, XXXIV (1956), 361–367.

79. Prodipto Roy, personal correspondence.

80. For example, see George W. Hill, Walter Slocum, and Ruth O. Hill, *Man–Land Adjustment* (Madison: Wisconsin AES Bulletin 134, 1938); and George W. Hill, *Man in the "Cut-over"* (Madison: Wisconsin AES Bulletin 139, 1941).

81. A. H. Anderson and Walter L. Slocum, personal correspondence.

82. I. M. Baill, *The Farmers and Old Age Security* (Washington, D.C.: USDA AMS Bulletin 151, 1955). Here see references to the work by rural sociologists which went into a report by W. G. Adkins, Louis J. Ducoff, John R. Christiansen, Robert E. Galloway, Walter C. McKain, Jr., Roe R. Motheral, William H. Sewell, Robert L. Skrabanek, and others. See also *Hearings before the Committee on Ways and Means,* House of Representatives (83rd Congress, 2nd session), HR 7199 (Social Security Act Amendments of 1954), pp. 195–223.

83. Carl C. Taylor, Helen W. Wheeler, and E. L. Kirkpatrick, *Disadvantaged Classes in American Agriculture* (Washington, D.C.: Farm Security Administration and Bureau of Agricultural Economics, Social Research Report No. VII, 1938).

84. Max R. White, Douglas Ensminger, and Cecil L. Gregory, *Rich Land—Poor People* (Indianapolis: USDA, Farm Security Administration Research Report, 1, 1938).

85. Many of these publications are listed in Anderson, *op. cit.,* under the heading Relief and related headings.

86. Charles E. Lively, personal correspondence. See also the classical evaluation of the rural rehabilitation program: Olaf Larson, *Ten Years of Rural Rehabilitation in the United States* (Washington, D.C.: USDA, BAE, 1947).

87. Milton S. Eisenhower and Roy I. Kimmel, "Old and New in Agricultural Organization," *1940 Yearbook of Agriculture* (Washington, D.C.: U.S. Government Printing Office, 1940), p. 1130.

88. Selz C. Mayo and W. E. Barnett, "Neighbor Groups—An Informal System of Communication," *Rural Sociology,* XIX (1952), 271–273.

89. T. Wilson Longmore, "Special Agencies within the Department of Agriculture," in Charles P. Loomis *et al.,* eds., *Rural Social Systems and Adult Education* (East Lansing: Michigan State College Press, 1953), Chapter 7.

90. Harald A. Pedersen, personal correspondence. Edgar A. Schuler was also influential in this development. See his early contributions to the *Journal of Pakistan Academy of Village Development.*

91. Linwood L. Hodgdon, personal correspondence.

92. Douglas Ensminger has been the Ford Foundation's Representative in India since the inception of its program there in the early 1950's. The short presentation of its current agricultural program is based on *The Ford Foundation and Agricultural Development in India* (New Delhi: The Ford Foundation, March, 1965). See also Carl Taylor, Douglas Ensminger, Helen Wheeler Johnson, and Jean Joyce, *India's Roots of Democracy* (Bombay: Orient Longmans, 1965).

93. *Ibid.,* p. 9.

94. *Ibid.,* p. 12.

95. Thus Anderson, *op. cit.,* lists 228 items classified under Health. See Richard A. Kurtz, Donald E. Saathoff, and John N. Edwards, *Hospital Social Systems and Differential Perceptions* (Lincoln: University of Nebraska, HRP Report 2, 1961). The item most frequently mentioned by respondents in the present chapter is Charles R. Hoffer *et al., Health Needs and Health Care in Michigan* (East Lansing: Michigan AES Special Bulletin 365, 1950). The many rural sociological studies of farm accidents have been widely used. See William G. Mather and Prodipto Roy, *A Study of Accidents to Pennsylvania Farm People* (Harrisburg: Department of Public Instruction in Cooperation with Pennsylvania State University, 1957).

96. Harold Kaufman, *Prestige Classes in a New York Rural Community* (Ithaca: New York AES, 1944); Otis Dudley Duncan and Jay W. Artis, "Some Problems of Stratification Research," *Rural Sociology,* XVI (1951), 17–29; William H. Sewell, *The Construction and Standardization of a Scale for the Measurement*

of the Socio-Economic Status of Oklahoma Farm Families (Stillwater: Oklahoma AES Technical Bulletin 9, 1940). Also see Anderson, *op. cit.*

97. Carl C. Taylor, *The Farmers' Movement* (New York: American Book Co., 1953). See also Wayne C. Rohrer and Carl C. Taylor, "Adult Educational Programs or Activities of the General Farmers' Organizations and Cooperatives," in Loomis *et. al., Rural Social System and Adult Education,* Chapter 5. In this latter publication see the writings in applied sociology of Sheldon G. Lowry, Wayne C. Rohrer, T. Wilson Longmore, Frank C. Nall, Jack Preiss, Olen E. Leonard, and others.

98. Otis Durant Duncan, personal correspondence.

99. Charles P. Loomis.

100. Lowry Nelson, personal correspondence. A use of rural sociology highlighted here is the studies of Argentina, Bolivia, Cuba, Brazil, and Mexico done respectively by the rural sociologists Carl C. Taylor, Olen E. Leonard, Lowry Nelson, T. Lynn Smith, and Nathan L. Whetten. These books, produced during and shortly after World War II at the request of the United States Department of State and financed by that Department, furnish the best general available knowledge of rural life of the countries mentioned. See Carl C. Taylor, "Early Rural Sociological Research in Latin America," *Rural Sociology,* XXV (1960), 1–9. See *ibid.* for an excellent applied sociological contribution by Manuel Alers-Montalvo. For the rural sociologists' contribution in producing such strategic materials as cinchona bark (for quinine), rubber, rotenone, and fiber plants during World War II, see Loomis, *Studies in Rural Social Organization, op. cit.,* Chapter 14.

101. James H. Copp, ed., *Our Changing Rural Society: Perspectives and Trends* (Ames: Iowa State University Press, 1964). Among the other fine contributions in this monograph, see Thomas R. Ford and Willis A. Sutton, Jr., "The Impact of Change on Rural Communities and Fringe Areas—Review of a Decade's Research." An admirable investigation which might serve as a model in integration of disciplines which are in large measure the responsibility of William B. Baker is the following: fourteen reports of the Saskatchewan Royal Commission, beginning with *The Scope and Character of the Investigation* and ending with a *Program of Improvement* (Regina, Saskatchewan: Province of Saskatchewan Royal Commission on Agriculture and Rural Life from 1955 to 1957).

102. Walter C. McKain, personal correspondence.

Sociology in the Desegregation Process

Its Use and Disuse

THOMAS F. PETTIGREW

KURT W. BACK

chapter 25

Introduction

Pick up almost any prosegregationist tract or newspaper editorial and chances are high that there will be at least one hostile reference to sociologists and sociology. Witness the assertion of Wesley George in his tract *The Biology of the Race Problem:* "When the justices of the Supreme Court embraced the error of Myrdal without critical examination, they contributed to their own deception and deprived the people of the United States of their right to a firm foundation of truth for anything that purports to be the law of the land." [1] Or the charge of Virginius Dabney in an editorial in his newspaper the Richmond *Times-Dispatch* that "the violence at Little Rock . . . never would have happened if nine justices had not consulted sociologists and psychologists, instead of lawyers, in 1954, and attempted to legislate through judicial decrees." [2]

A naïve reader of such statements might understandably conclude that sociologists are dangerously powerful people and that sociology is making critically sinister contributions to the process of racial desegregation. The truth is, however, that sociologists have been neither dangerous nor powerful and sociological contributions to this key process of contemporary American society have been neither critical nor sinister. The *disuse*, rather than the use, of sociology is more apparent; the attacks of segregationists upon the field are perhaps flattering in their assumptions, but are simply not valid. To paraphrase Churchill, seldom have so many abused one profession for so little.

Segregationist critics have two specific phenomena in mind. They recall the influential sociological works of the *pre*desegregation era, like Myrdal's *An American Dilemma*, Drake and Cayton's *Black Metropolis*, and the numerous writings of Parks, Wirth, Odum, Charles Johnson, Guy Johnson, Frazier, and others. And they bristle over the quotation of some of these studies in the famous footnote 11, the social-science footnote to the Supreme Court's school desegregation opinion in 1954.[3] But the concern of this chapter is the use of sociology in American race relations since 1954. What is the promise of sociological theory in this area? What uses have been made of sociology and sociologists so far in the process? Why has the potential of sociology been barely tapped?

The Promise of Sociological Theory

From the perspective of the sociologist, the problem of segregation can be stated as follows: a set of physical characteristics, principally color of the skin, and a degree of ancestry with similar characteristics are used to make socially meaningful and invidious distinctions.[4] The sociologist as scientist investigates under what conditions these characteristics become salient, how the distinctions are maintained in socially patterned responses, and when these distinctions become socially relevant or irrelevant. Once structured in this fashion, problems of race and desegregation can be usefully approached from four different realms of contemporary theory: theories dealing with (1) the self, self-presentation, and symbolic interaction, (2) balance and equilibration, (3) stratification and structural-functional systems, and (4) social change.

THE SELF

The use of race as a measure of social distinction involves the inference of moral and social worth based on physical characteristics. The social import of bodily characteristics thus has consequences for both the definition and the limitation of the self as perceived by the victim of discrimination and for person perceptions between the victim and those with whom he interacts. Both of these consequences are dealt with in philosophy and social psychology. The philosophical question "Who am I?" goes back traditionally to Descartes. The definition of the self as a psychological problem harks back to William James in his classical chapter on the self in his *Principles of Psychology*. Likewise, the conditions of social and person perception have been traditional topics of psychology from the early theories of the recognition of emotions to the current theory of Fritz Heider and social experimentation on this topic. This work provides the raw material that sociologists must consider in determining the social patterns of interpersonal interaction. Cooley and Mead initiated such theorizing in sociology, leading today to Erving Goffman's treatment of behavior in social situations.

Goffman's notion of stigma appears particularly relevant.[5] He defines stigma as a physical characteristic from which moral and social worth can be derived. Prime examples of stigmas include physical deformities and deficiencies, such as illnesses, sensory or motor defects, or injuries. Some conspicuous social characteristics, such as race, sex, and age, can also become stigmas, if perceptions of them lead to socially invidious differentiations.[6] One practical outcome of this thinking is a new perspective on the definitions of racial integration and desegregation. Integration, in these terms, is achieved when the physical characteristics accompanying race are no longer a definition of the self. Desegregation, by comparison, occurs when society fully recognizes the stigma, but no longer assigns disabilities to those possessing the stigma. From this vantage point it becomes clear that desegregation can be accomplished by law as well as other social action, while integration requires different processes.

Extending these leads from self theory, sociology could make significant contributions to the present racial scene by concentrating empirical attention on the subtleties of Negro-white interactions. Up to this point little field data exist on this vital topic beyond the general descriptions of "racial etiquette" which are rapidly becoming outmoded. Interracial situations, such as children's summer camps, have been studied, but this work has had more success in measuring such gross aspects as preferences and the amount of interaction than in teasing out the more intricate aspects of conduct.[7] In other words, research so far has concentrated on the study of desegregation rather than integration. More pertinent approaches to the problem come from work on the bias introduced by the use of Negro and white interviewers in survey situations and from rigorous laboratory experimentation.[8]

BALANCE THEORIES

A second approach concerns the manner in which one's stigmatized characteristic is combined with other types of characteristics. Two general tendencies stand out. On the one hand, people try to obtain the highest possible "status score" through a summing up of characteristics; on the other hand, they evince a certain strain for consistency by minimizing the variability of their various characteristics. Both of these tendencies operate simultaneously and explain many of the strains and directions of the desegregation process.

The desire to define one's own status at as high a level as possible naturally causes the individual to select among his characteristics, rather than to add them all up. Thus, in maximizing his status, he has two choices. Either he can rely on the highest status he has accorded to any characteristic, or he can choose the highest ranked group to which he belongs. Reference-group theory has been developed to explain the consequences of choosing a particular group as a referent anchor, but little has been done to explain the choice of the specific reference group itself.

Some of the initial reference-group research highlights the practical importance of this body of theory for American race relations. In their classic World War II studies of *The American Soldier*, Samuel Stouffer and his associates compared the morale of Negro troops stationed in the South with that of Negro troops stationed in the North.[9] Surprisingly, they found morale roughly the same in the two regions, despite the South's severe restrictions on the Negro soldier's off-base activities. The key to understanding this result is provided by reference-group theory and its companion concept of relative deprivation. Racial characteristics provided the reference group for the Negro in the southern camp, for, as Stouffer wrote, "The psychological values of Army life to the Negro soldier in the South *relative to the southern Negro civilian* greatly exceeded the psychological values of Army life to the Negro soldier in the North *relative to the northern Negro civilian.*"[10] This is an instance where a reference group is chosen in which the individual has relatively high status, but the group itself has low status. Had the Negro soldiers chosen other soldiers as the relevant reference group, they would have felt considerably more deprived in the South. During World War II, however, racial characteristics continued to provide the strongest reference group.

The choice of the highest-status reference group leads to a different constellation. If the ascribed racial characteristics become less important to his self-image, a Negro of high achieved status should feel sharply deprived because of the discrimination the racial stigma continues to elicit. Such a person would make an effort to gain equality with people of the same educational and occupational levels—people to whom he now refers himself. Thus, the relaxation of racial barriers and improvement of the minority group in other statuses are precisely the conditions which should lead to greater relative deprivation and a more forceful push for equal rights. It should not be surprising, then, according to sociological theory, that a moderate amount of desegregation does not satisfy the minority group, but only whets the palate for more rapid and sweeping social change.

While reference-group behavior reflects consistency in the relation of the individual to his surrounding world, a similar striving for consistency occurs within the individual.[11] The concept of status consistency is the internal equivalent of reference-group behavior; and many of the theoretical and empirical uses of this concept parallel the race-relations perspectives gleaned from reference-group theory. Resolution of the stress generated by status inconsistency can result in neurotic symptoms or attempts to alter the environment.[12] Elton Jackson has shown that the type of resolution depends on the type of status inconsistency.[13] Those individuals of high ascribed status but low achieved status, such as white "Old Americans" with only a grammar-school education, seem especially disposed to psychoneurotic symptoms; while those of low ascribed status but high achieved status, such as college-educated Negro Americans, seem especially disposed to political liberalism and a willingness to change the social system.

At the practical level, these converging considerations provide insight into the nationwide Negro protest for change in the 1960's.[14] The actual gains of Negroes—in business, education, employment, health, housing, income, and voting—have been occurring faster since 1940 than during any other period of Negro American history. Yet these gains are relative to previous Negro conditions. When contrasted with the typical conditions of white Americans today, the position of Negro Americans assumes a desperately deprived character. The advances of past years have raised but not kept pace with Negro aspirations and expectations; the result is keen relative deprivation and a ringing demand for "all, here, now!" Furthermore, in Jackson's terms, the advances have led to higher achieved status for many Negroes, producing the low-ascribed, high-achieved inconsistent status pattern which often accompanies a willingness for change. Indeed, it was the best-educated Negro generation in the South's history that ignited the protest in 1960 with the southern college-led sit-in demonstrations against racial discrimination at lunch counters.[15]

SOCIAL-SYSTEM THEORY

The desire for consistency in status and belief is only one operating force in society. Sociological theory has always recognized a second principle: namely, structural and functional differentiation. Durkheim was one of the earliest theorists to categorize social organization according to whether it was dependent on balance or distinction, contrasting mechanical and organic solidarity.[16] Through this route, sociologists learned to distinguish certain characteristics of the social system, one of which is similarity and the other differentiation. In more recent theoretical work derived from balance theories, James Davis has shown the dividing point at which the principle of differentiation begins to operate.[17]

Social-system theory, and the principle of differentiation in particular, is invaluable in identifying and understanding the social supports and resistances in the desegregation process. Desegregation occurs not only because of the individual needs identified in balance theories but in accordance with the strains and instabilities which can be delineated in the social system. The "Black Belt" areas of the Deep South offer a case in point. These rural, traditional counties with relatively high Negro percentages in their populations form the hard core of segregationist resistance from the eastern shore of Maryland to east Texas. The question thus becomes: Why do these areas provide such stubborn barriers to racial change? The standard answers, of course, are true enough as far as they go. These are the areas where the deepest Negrophobia is harbored,[18] where the historical events of the past two centuries have left an imbedded legacy of white supremacy.[19]

But there are, in addition, basic social-system answers. The Black Belt is far less structurally differentiated than the rest of the South.[20] For example, there is considerably less differentiation between the "public" and "private" sectors of life. Hence, distinctions are not clearly drawn between, say, a lunch counter in a variety store and the dining-room table, or between the school as a public educational center and the school as a community social center. This lack of differentiation is also manifest in the ambivalence often shown public education in many Black Belt areas. Apart from racial considerations, schools can be seen as an unwelcome intrusion upon home instruction, as vehicles for implanting new and potentially dangerous ideas in both Negro and white youth; in short, as a threat to what is euphemistically called in these areas "the southern way of life." This factor is responsible in part for the readiness of many "dead-end" segregationists to abandon public education altogether, rather than to allow biracial public instruction. Indeed, one Black Belt county involved in the original 1954 Supreme Court ruling, Prince Edward County in Virginia, actually did close down all its public schools.

Here, too, Parsons' pattern variables can be usefully applied.[21] The Black Belt is still basically characterized by ascriptive, diffuse, particularistic, and affective orientations, though Morton Rubin has shown that change in these realms is under way.[22] In sharp contrast, racial desegregation and the absence of racial discrimination thrive in situations marked by precisely the opposite orientations: achievement, functionally specific, universalistic, and affectively neutral orientations. Thus, the interracial harmony of such groups as athletic teams and industrial unions—groups largely dominated by achievement, specific, universalistic, and affectively neutral orientations—tends to be dramatically superior to that of such counterpart groups as fraternities and craft unions—groups marked by orientations more approaching those of the Black Belt.[23]

The barriers to racial change erected by the Black Belt, then, go beyond such distinctly racial phenomena as anti-Negro attitudes and a prior history of plantation slavery. Social-system theory provides the insight that these rural-based barriers are also rooted in a less differentiated structure —a structure typified by orientations which run directly counter to those which most facilitate the desegregation process.

SOCIAL-CHANGE THEORY

Analyzing the alteration of social systems over time, sociologists have long sought a theory of social change. Here it is the scope of the theory that presents problems. It is often difficult to determine whether any particular change is an extremely long-term turn of history, a brief fluctuation, a part of a determined evolutionary trend, or some other manifestation of a radical change.

The desegregation movement can be analyzed within several frameworks. Evolutionary, equilibrium-strain, conflict, and social-movement models all offer useful perspectives. Thus, desegregation can be envisaged as a small part of a sweeping evolutionary process which is presently overturning nation-based cultures and civilizations,[24] or as an equilibrium reaction of American society to a long-term, festering strain,[25] or as the reaction to a rapidly escalating conflict between truly divergent interest groups,[26] or as the outcome of efforts by a series of loosely linked social movements.

Once again, these various theories are not mutually exclusive and often converge. This point is questioned, however, by a number of observers of the racial scene of the 1960's. Once the push for desegregation spread from the confines of the legislative and judicial halls to the streets, the usefulness of the Simmel-Coser conflict contentions became more readily apparent.[27] And some writers assume that these contentions are not only exclusively preferable but directly counter to theories, such as that of equilibrium-strain, which concentrate primarily on consensus and societal stability.[28] Louis Coser cogently answers such reasoning:

> Peace and the feud, conflict and order are correlative to each other. Both the cementing and the breaking of the cake of custom constitute part of the eternal dialectic of social life. One is hence ill-advised sharply to distinguish a sociology of order from a sociology of conflict, or a harmony model of society from a conflict model. Such attempts can only result in artificial

distinctions. The analysis of social conflicts brings to awareness aspects of social reality which may be obscured if analytical attention focuses too exclusively on phenomena of social order; but an exclusive attention to conflict phenomena may obscure the central importance of social order and needs to be corrected by a correlative concern with the ordered aspects of social life. We deal here not with distinct realities but only with differing aspects of the same reality, so that exclusive emphasis on one or the other is likely to lead the analyst astray.[29]

The theory of the development of social movements is also a part of the explanation of social change. This theory, of course, is especially valuable in analyzing some of the groups which have become organized and active in instituting or resisting racial change. Studies of the black Muslims and the Ku Klux Klan have been done within this framework;[30] but studies of other and more influential movements need to be undertaken as well—movements such as the Congress on Racial Equality (CORE), the National Association for the Advancement of Colored People (NAACP), the Student Non-Violent Coordinating Committee (SNCC), and the White Citizens' Councils (WCC). At this point, the direct links between the historical change of the large-scale system and the values and motivations of the individuals within change movements become obvious. The circle closes; social-movement considerations highlight the necessity and importance of all four types of theory discussed.

It is encouraging that in all four realms sufficient theories have developed for use in studying this process and that segregation, desegregation, and integration are areas which require the integration of these theories. It is a further sign of the maturity of the science of sociology that none of these theories has become an exclusive explanation. The promise of sociological theory for understanding desegregation, then, is a rich one, offering an attack which utilizes a variety of developed theoretical approaches.

Some Uses of Sociology in the Desegregation Process

If the promise of sociological theory is great, one can properly ask what use has been made of these ideas in the desegregation process to date. While the disuse is more immediately apparent than the use, sociology and sociologists have contributed to this salient issue in a number of ways and capacities. Three interrelated uses will be sampled here: sociologists as (1) trend predictors, (2) interpreters of specific events, and (3) desegregation consultants.

SOCIOLOGISTS AS TREND PREDICTORS

One of the potentials of sociology is the ability to make "educated" predictions of future and significant trends in American race relations. This potential can be illustrated by the broad qualitative predictions concerning desegregation made prior to the Supreme Court's 1954 decision and by the more specific quantitative predictions as to the county-by-county pattern of formal school desegregation within southern states.

Coleman has carefully examined the predictions about desegregation made by social scientists and published between 1950 and 1955.[31] His first finding was simply that few people had been willing to stick their necks out in this fashion in print. Finally, he located relevant predictions in ten articles and books by eight social scientists: Kenneth B. Clark, Guy Johnson, Charles S. Johnson, Herman Long, George Mitchell, Alwin W. Rose, Margaret Ryan, and Robin Williams. Most of these forecasts were shrewd projections from data collected on border-state desegregation that took place prior to the High Court's major ruling. How well did they do? One can judge for himself by comparing events of the process to date with the following composite version of their predictions, each point of which was generally advanced by a number, though not all, of the venturesome prognosticators:

Desegregation will occur. There will be a gradual and uneven acceptance of it both between and within communities; and it will come first in the Appalachians and the Upper South, last in the plantation and Black Belt areas. Acceptance and adjustment will be correlated inversely with the percentage of Negroes in the population and with the degree of prejudice in the area—but only loosely so, since other factors, especially firm leadership, will often be more crucial. For the most part, no mass mingling of the races in the public schools will result during the first few years. Violence and extreme tension will sometimes occur, but they will not inevitably or usually accompany desegregation. There will be, however, considerable evasion, litigation, confusion, and turmoil. A wide range of plans, solutions, and adjustments will be forthcoming. Where the authorities adopt a definite policy of desegregation, implement it without delay, and stand firm on the policy, there will be little trouble. Gradual plans will not necessarily be more effective than "immediate" change and may, in some instances, allow greater resistance to develop. Moreover, desegregation in one institution or area of life will not necessarily facilitate desegregation in other institutions or areas of life in the same community. But once desegregation does take place in a given school, official norms of equal treatment will soon develop. Nevertheless, equal status contacts between whites and Negroes will often remain rare, especially in social functions. Negroes will participate strongly in school activities where competence is determining (i.e., where universalistic standards apply, as in athletics).[32]

It appears that these early social-science predictions have proved amazingly accurate and could have been helpful if policy makers had given them more careful consideration.

Also possible are more detailed predictions as to the precise pattern in which desegregation unfolds. As previously noted, the desegregation process has been anything but random. When one reviews its history since 1954, clear ecological patterns emerge both between and within subregions and states. In fact, the same ecological patterns have emerged previously in research on a wide variety of southern social phenomena, ranging from the readiness to secede from the Union in 1860–1861 through lynching to current political behavior.[33] Generally speaking, desegregation has come first to the border and middle South, the cities, those areas with relatively small percentages of Negroes, and less traditional localities.

One ecological investigation set out to develop predictions for the intra-state patterns of racial change.[34] To forecast the county-by-county initiation of at least token school desegregation, three key census variables were employed: the percentages of urban dwellers, nonwhites, and white women in the labor force.[35] The prognostications derived from these border-state data can now be applied to three southern states—Florida, North Carolina, and Tennessee—which have sufficient educational desegregation to provide an adequate test.[36] As revealed in Table 25–1, significant relationships exist between the three-variable predictions and the unfolding patterns of racial change in these three states' educational systems. Particularly is this the case with Florida; while almost three out of four of the counties designated as the easiest to desegregate had biracial schools by 1963, none of those designated as most resistant had such schools. In other words, the earlier ecological pattern of educational desegregation noted in the border South continues to hold true for states farther South.

Such county-by-county predictions, once they achieve greater precision, would have considerable practical value. Consider, for example, the administration of the Civil Rights Acts of 1964 and 1965. All provisions of these Acts cannot be enforced simultaneously throughout the South; some selection of target areas is necessary. Reasonably accurate predictions as to the degree of segregationist resistance and integrationist insistence likely to be encountered in various areas would allow the planning of particular strategies, such as moving first in "compliant" areas so as to register early success, or tackling "resistant" areas first so as to demonstrate uncompromising intent, or employing some mixed strategy which combines these alternatives.

TABLE 25-1 *Predicted and Actual School Desegregation**

| State | PERCENTAGES OF DESEGREGATED COUNTIES BY FALL OF 1963 | | | | KENDALL RANK-ORDER CORRELATIONS BETWEEN PREDICTED AND ACTUAL DESEGREGATION | |
| | All Counties | Predicted Order of Desegregation | | | | |
		First Third	Middle Third	Last Third	Tau's	p
Florida	28.4 (19/67)	72.7 (16/22)	13.0 (3/23)	0.0 (0/22)	+.50	<.001
North Carolina	30.0 (30/100)	48.5 (16/33)	29.4 (10/34)	12.1 (4/33)	+.24	<.01
Tennessee	34.9 (29/83)	46.4 (13/28)	33.3 (9/27)	25.0 (7/28)	+.18	<.01

* Prediction formulas were originally presented in T. F. Pettigrew and M. R. Cramer, "The Demography of Desegregation," *Journal of Social Issues*, XV (Fall, 1959), 61–71. This table originally appeared in T. F. Pettigew, "Continuing Barriers to Desegregated Education in the South," *Sociology of Education*, XXXVIII (1965), 99–111.

SOCIOLOGISTS AS INTERPRETERS OF CURRENT EVENTS

Often sociologists can contribute to the understanding of the desegregation process by providing a "sociological perspective" in the interpretation of current situations. The 1964 political sorties of Alabama's Governor George Wallace into the North provide a pointed example of how this perspective can correct a myopic journalistic interpretation. Wallace, it will be recalled, entered the 1964 Democratic presidential primaries in Wisconsin, Indiana, and Maryland. To the surprise of many, he polled sizable minorities in each primary, ranging from roughly two-ninths in Wisconsin to three-sevenths in border-state Maryland. The immediate response of many mass-media analysts was to interpret these results as evidence of a white "backlash," a powerful reaction of white northerners to the insistent demands of Negro American protesters.

A more detached sociological view, free from the pressure of mass-media deadlines, questions such an interpretation. A backlash implies that many whites in the North, once at least mildly sympathetic to Negro aspirations, suddenly changed their minds and hardened their resistance to racial change. Other data, however, do not confirm this view. Thus, national public-opinion polls conducted by Louis Harris during this period revealed a steadily mounting majority in *favor* of the then-pending Civil Rights Act. While an estimated 63 per cent of adult Americans favored the bill in November of 1963, the figure rose to 68 per cent by February of 1964 and 70 per cent by May of 1964: a consistent gain of 7 per cent in six months.

Why, then, did Wallace do so well in three northern primaries? An array of well-established principles of political sociology suggests one of the critical, but overlooked, answers. Mass-media analysts emphasized the *percentage* of the votes won by Wallace, without thoroughly considering the size of the *total* vote. Especially in the Indiana and Maryland primaries, where the Alabamian did best, the number of votes cast was considerably larger than is typical of Democratic presidential primaries in these states. The so-called backlash, then, was apparently caused by the attraction to the polls of many people who do not normally vote in these primaries—people attracted by the issues of race and "states' rights" made salient by Wallace. Furthermore, the Alabama Governor's candidacy did not have to be regarded seriously, a factor of major importance in protest voting. Hadley Cantril has shown, for instance, how Frenchmen and Italians who vote for Communist candidates, although not members of the Party, find their electoral behavior a satisfying expression of protest, even though they would not care for the Communists to gain control of their government.[37] "Voting Communist can't hurt me," reasons one Frenchman. "It may help me. Nothing like putting a big scare into the *patron*."[38] In this American case, there was little chance that Wallace might actually become President of the United States, and so he made an ideal magnet for attracting protest voters of all varieties. Wallace's primary performances, then, in no way necessarily required or reflected any mass shifting of opinion or changing of minds. To reason that they did, as many journalists did, is to commit a blatant form of the ecological fallacy.

This sociological perspective receives support from analyses of other northern election results widely described as demonstrating the same racial backlash. In Boston school-committee elections, for example, a field of candidates ran for five positions in 1961, before the explosive *de facto* school segregation issue had erupted in the city, and a similar group ran again in 1963, after the issue had become focal. Among the candidates in both instances were a militant Negro and a white woman who between the two elections had distinguished herself as an outspoken defender of school segregation. In both elections the Negro candidate ran a strong, though losing, seventh, while the segregationist won a seat on both occasions. The mass media emphasized the segregationist's sharply higher percentage of the vote in 1963 than in 1961 and presented this as evidence of a white backlash. Yet, once again, an "out-from-under-the-rocks" phenomenon was probably operating. The number of Boston voters attracted to the polls in 1963 was approximately double that of 1961, and this increase was more than enough to account for the segregationist's better showing. Interesting, too, is the fact that the Negro candidate ran in 1963 as well or better in total votes in virtually every precinct.

The heralded white backlash, then, shifts its meaning when placed in full sociological perspective. Anti-Negro candidates for political office in the North, enhanced by the glare of television klieg lights, focus and make more salient the race issue; they draw upon the latent bigotry and realistic racial conflict which existed prior to their entrance upon the political stage; and they often succeed, at least for a time, in attracting to the polls many otherwise apathetic, alienated, authoritarian, or uninformed citizens who typically do not vote.[39] The backlash is more properly described as the familiar crisis phenomenon of polarization. Those who favored racial change before the crisis become more active; and those who opposed racial change before the crisis also become more active.

SOCIOLOGISTS AS DESEGREGATION CONSULTANTS

At the most practical level, sociologists can make their contributions as consultants. One member of the profession, for example, advised a public school board of a medium-sized, middle South city for two years prior to its initiation of desegregation. The board was especially anxious to avoid the strife and bad publicity engendered by school desegregation efforts in Little Rock, Charlotte, and New Orleans. The adviser pointed out that these cities had compounded social-class and racial conflicts. All three had limited their initial steps to one or two lower-status schools; thus, later disturbances were motivated not only by racial antipathy but also by a feeling that upper-status white leaders were selectively ignoring the interests of the less prosperous segments of the white community. The consultant urged his clients not to make the same mistake, but to begin the process in a large number of public schools which covered the social-class spectrum. His advice was followed and may have contributed to the calm acceptance of the event by the community.

Another consultation in a large southwestern city involved a social psychologist who helped to set up an elaborate mass-media campaign appealing for "law and order." The campaign was apparently successful. In a city renowned for its violence, public-school desegregation began without incident.

Consultations have also occurred in a number of key northern cities. In Chicago, a number of sociologists, including Robert Havighurst and Philip Hauser, have played highly publicized consulting roles on problems related to *de facto* school segregation in that city. Dan Dodson has often served in a similar way for communities throughout the New York metropolitan area. And the New York State Department of Education convened a social-science conference in April of 1964 on the subject of *de facto* school segregation, which was attended by race-relations specialists from throughout the country.

Applied surveys in key situations have proved to be an additional tool of value in sociological consulting on the desegregation process. Thus, J. K. Morland has on three occasions demonstrated the merit of such surveys for interested organizations. In 1955, he studied a student strike over desegregation in White Sulphur Springs, West Virginia, for the National Association for the Advancement of Colored People; in 1960, he studied the lunch-counter sit-in protests in Corpus Christi, Galveston, and San Antonio, Texas, for the Southern Regional Council; and in 1962, he surveyed the needs of southern educators for professional consultation on desegregation for the Potomac Institute.[40] In this third survey, incidentally, Morland discovered a surprising willingness and desire for professional help.

Kenneth Lenihan, at Columbia University's Bureau of Applied Social Research, is attempting to demonstrate the utility of survey data in reducing pluralistic ignorance.[41] Confirming previous research, he found that approximately two-thirds of his sample of white homeowners in suburban "Blissville" are not opposed to a Negro family living on the same street. Yet only one in five is willing to sell his home to a Negro, largely because he incorrectly perceives most of his neighbors to be against residential desegregation. Though only a third of the town actually opposes interracial living, 56 per cent believes a majority opposes it, with 20 per cent even thinking that 80 to 100 per cent of their fellow townsmen oppose it. Lenihan has discussed his findings with the mayor and town council of Blissville and publicized the results in the community. Follow-up surveys will test to see if pluralistic ignorance can in fact be reduced in this manner.

On other occasions, sociologists have voiced their opinions more directly. Some have served as expert witnesses in court cases dealing with desegregation and as consultants in the preparation of desegregation legal briefs.[42] And two sociologists who specialize in race relations even register their expert views on *de facto* segregation as elected public officials: Arnold Rose, of the University of Minnesota, is a state legislator, and Mel Ravitz, of Wayne State University, is a Detroit city councilman.[43]

These examples, unfortunately, mark the exceptions and not the rule. Sociologists have not often been called upon in consulting capacities. Remarks Lewis Killian, "Sociologists in the South have rarely had the opportunity to set foot inside state capitols—unless they were under investigation!"[44]

Why Has This Sociological Potential Not Been Fully Utilized?

There are, then, many potential uses of sociology in the desegregation process which have been concretely demonstrated through trend predictions, interpreting current situations, and consulting. The question thus becomes: Why has this sociological potential not been fully utilized? Three classes of interrelated factors can be advanced as a tentative answer: (1) the timidity of private foundations and governmental agencies about providing the funds for work in this "controversial" area; (2) an atmosphere of resistance to racial change by stern segregationists that acts to constrain both social-science research and its applications; and, finally, (3) a sociological bias in race relations toward studying the static and segregation-maintaining elements, rather than the dynamic and desegregation-impelling features. Each of these explanations warrants further discussion.

THE TIMIDITY OF FOUNDATIONS AND GOVERNMENTAL AGENCIES

The major private foundations and governmental research agencies have been extremely reluctant to support social research on the desegregation process.[45] Despite the obvious practical need for such work, the "controversial" nature of the subject makes it far easier to fund such "safe" areas as business education, the arts, and health research. Stuart Cook, in a 1957 paper on desegregation, first noted this funding timidity in print;[46] and only in the mid-1960's has this financial constraint on social-science contributions to the process begun to ease somewhat.

The effects of this situation on social research have been marked. Clearly indicated were large-scale interdisciplinary studies, employing longitudinal designs in a variety of carefully chosen communities. Only an empirical attack of such magnitude could have captured the emerging pattern of highly diverse accommodations to the racial change ordered by the Supreme Court in 1954. Compare the potential value of such a broad research effort with the limited case studies that have been possible so far.[47] Low-budget reports on only one community are the rule; many of them are theses or seminar projects, some remain on the descriptive level, all but a few sample only one time period, and there is almost no comparability of instruments and approach. Ironically, the first nationwide survey sampling of Negro American opinion, long sought by race-relations specialists, was finally executed in the summer of 1963 by a commercial concern financed by *Newsweek* magazine.[48] From the point of view of the lost opportunity to study intensively the beginnings of a unique process of social change, then, the results of funding timidity have been little short of tragic.

The reasons for this timidity are varied. One factor, as noted by Cook, involves segregationist southern congressmen. Some of these national legislators have angrily threatened to withdraw the valued tax-free status from private foundations and have menacingly reviewed governmental financing of social research. Another factor involves organized boycotts carried out by some segregationists against products identified with the foundations. Some of these boycotts were quite effective in the 1950's and apparently influenced foundation strategy.

A third factor is more subtle. No simple mechanical device or single research break-through is likely to provide simple solutions for the peculiarly complex problems of desegregation. In a topic similarly laden with controversy and conflict, birth control, it has proved possible to appropriate large amounts for the study of the purely technical aspects of reproduction and the development of pills which may aid in easing the population problem. No comparable hope for a pill or similar gadget has ever been suggested for desegregation, and so funding agencies are less able to avoid the emotionally charged aspects of the issue by focusing on such purely technical aspects.

A final factor is as much a product as a cause of the financial drought. Many competent sociologists, who until 1954 had specialized in race relations, chose to enter other areas when their desegregation research proposals were routinely refused support. In time, this has meant an ever decreasing number of researchers and proposals seeking money for work on desegregation. In other words, the expectation of funding rejection became self-fulfilling. The foundations and governmental agencies which have altered their policies now complain that they do not receive an adequate number of applications for competent social research on desegregation. Hopefully, as information about the policy changes of these funding agencies becomes more widely circulated, this situation will improve.

THE CONSTRAINING ATMOSPHERE OF SEGREGATIONIST RESISTANCE

By no means can all of the disuse of sociology be charged to financial restrictions. The constraining atmosphere created by segregationist resistance has directly influenced sociologists, as it has foundations and governmental agencies. While it is difficult to assess the limitations imposed by such an atmosphere, it is reasonable to infer that the number of direct institutional refusals to allow such research has actually been small, even in the South. More likely, the greatest deterrent has been created indirectly by the stifling climate which discourages sociologists from actually testing the limits of research opportunities. Interested as the researcher may be in the racial realm, he decides to work in a less controversial area. Or, if he persists in studying race relations, the perceived pressures severely narrow the range of specific problems he will tackle. Sociologists are, after all, only human, part of the society that they study. They are influenced by the same kind of social phenomena with which they deal. The possible detachment which training and investigation give may enable a researcher to identify these pressures and their effects, but he is still subject to them, just as a physician may better understand disease, but remains subject like other mortals to illness.

Aspects of this constraining phenomenon can be conveniently discussed under three categories: (1) values in social research; (2) the nonstructural bias; and (3) the nonactivist bias.

(1) Values in Social Research   Value issues are at least implicit in all realms of sociology; the field shares this feature with all other sciences, physical as well as social. Many of the implications of this fact are discussed in detail elsewhere in this volume. Yet this topic deserves special attention here because the value implications of any sociological work on desegregation are especially salient and, in some respects, unique due to the type of climate in which the work is performed.

There exists within the ranks of social science a real conflict around the role of values in social research. On one side of the issue, Nevitt Sanford argues that the role of social reformer should be a major one for the social scientist;[49] Redfield maintains that value deductions are actually drawn by social scientists from their science itself;[50] and Gouldner, in his now famous 1961 presidential address to the Society for the Study of Social Problems, dismissed the concept of a value-free sociology as a myth.[51]

On the other side, many agree with Conrad Arensberg that social scientists have no other end or purpose as scientists than devotion to science per se.[52] Bierstedt, for instance, believes that normative judgments lie entirely outside the realm of science; in the long run, he believes a sociologist contributes maximally to society through the development of sound knowledge about society.[53] The implications here, of course, are that a sound knowledge about society cannot be developed as long as values intrude and that *true* science must be value-free. Both of these implications can be challenged. It can be argued that only through the explicit recognition and use of the researcher's values can society be adequately understood. Moreover, nonsocial sciences do not appear deterred by the widespread holding of forthright values. Thus, biologists have distinct values about the pathogenic organisms they study, and few of them are neutral about cancer or polio. Likewise, physicists have definite values about the physical matter they study, and few of them are neutral about atomic and hydrogen bombs. Yet these value-laden biologists and physicists are not limited in the scope of their research, nor are they poorer scientists for their values. For social scientists to insist that this does not hold for them seems strange; it almost appears as if social scientists have given up the model of rational man for everybody but themselves.

In any event, the question of the relationship between values and science is a social problem in its own right. And of immediate importance is the fact that the debate on this issue offers a ready-made rationalization to the social scientist who wishes to avoid a controversial topic. Much as Little Rock's white liberal clergy avoided the thick of the fight by maintaining that controversy was unchristian,[54] social scientists can convince themselves that desegregation is simply too fraught with conflict and emotion to allow the type of dispassionate study which "true" science demands. The danger of such a position is obvious. It would eventuate in the research renunciation by sociology of all conflict situations in society when the societal lines of fracture are most clearly exposed—the very type of situations Samuel Stouffer argued would yield the most valuable insights.[55]

Two southern sociologists, Lewis Killian at Florida State University in Tallahassee and Kenneth Morland at Randolph-Macon Women's College in Lynchburg, Virginia, have candidly discussed the difficulties raised by their work on desegregation. Killian aided the Attorney-General of Florida in drafting a desegregation brief for the United States Supreme Court.[56] His research report dealt with opinions throughout the state as to the pace and manner in which the 1954 school desegregation ruling should be implemented. He faced two problems: one involved publicity, the other values. Killian found himself in the hot glare of constant mass-media attention and noted how such attention affected his political client, his respondents, and himself. The social scientist in such a role, he concludes, "is perforce a public relations man."

The second issue of values presented an even thornier problem. His client had previously argued for segregation before the United States Supreme Court and was preparing to argue for gradualism rather than immediate desegregation. Indeed, Killian's survey found that gradualism was in fact the much preferred alternative of most of the influential respondents questioned. On this matter of values Killian writes:

> There is little doubt that, in terms of his occupational ethos, the sociologist is expected to take a position in opposition to "gradualism" if that means simply delay or evasion. Even if he adopts a "gradualist" position, he still risks the charge of suffering from the conservative bias of the southern culture. On the other hand, even gradualism is considered radical by many southern politicians.[57]

In spite of these difficulties, Killian believes that sociologists should assume such a role when offered the opportunity. Government officials do not necessarily exploit social science, he argues, for their best interests frequently coincide with granting the social scientist as much independence as possible. More important, such a role gives the social scientist a chance to bring his theory and findings to bear directly on policy decisions. In the South, such a position may help shift the image of the sociologist from that of an "agitator" to one of an "expert." "He can never be sure that [his] theories will be accepted or how they will be used," warns Killian, "but he does gain an audience."

Morland has personally participated in prodesegregation organizations, conducted brief applied surveys and consulted for such organizations, and carried on extensive research on racial acceptance and preference among nursery-school children. In a paper given at the 1962 meetings of the American Sociological Association, he presented his rationale for playing these three roles of partisan, practitioner, and researcher:

> Whatever else he might do, it is the job of the sociologist to seek to increase the amount of valid and reliable knowledge about human groups. . . . The values held by the particular sociologist may lead him to engage in applied sociology or to reject opportunities to do so. Whatever his choice, however, it can be assumed to be based on non-scientific predilections, just as his decision to enter the field of sociology in the first place. In his role as consultant, the sociologist is required to help solve immediate and practical problems in line with the goals of the organization for which he is working. However, it is assumed that in so far as he acts as a sociological consultant, he suggests the means to particular ends, and cannot on a scientific basis propose the ends themselves. Of course, in choosing to act as a consultant for an organization, the sociologist can indirectly choose the ends for which he wishes to work. Fundamental in the author's assumptions about roles is that the sociological task of the development of systematic knowledge neither demands nor forbids that the sociologist apply his discipline to the area of practical problems. Furthermore, the roles of basic research and practical application have nothing directly to do with the sociologist's choice to take part in partisan activities. The decision to take an active citizen role in

race relations, or to refrain from doing so, is a non-rational, non-scientific, moral choice. With these assumptions as a basis of clarification, the author has found it possible to continue three lines of activity in a controversial area with the realization that there are separate and distinct role requirements in each activity.[58]

As with any multiple-role engagement, Morland has encountered role conflicts. Because of his partisan activities as a citizen, the public-school system in his community refused him research access to its kindergarten and elementary classes. In his practitioner role, he faces pressures for quick results and oversimplified interpretations. In his partisan role, he must resist the assumption of the group that the entire discipline of sociology is somehow in league with the organization because a sociologist is involved. And naturally the three roles make conflicting demands on his time and energy.

But Morland emphasizes that there are important compatibilities as well as conflicts between the three roles. He has found that consulting and applied surveys often offer excellent opportunities for the pragmatic testing of theory and measurement techniques. Likewise, his partisan activities have provided insights for sociological research; though emotionally involved, he has nevertheless gained new notions concerning prodesegregation leadership and segregationist opposition from these activities. Furthermore, his partisan participation has opened some doors, especially among the prodesegregationists, that might otherwise have remained closed. Morland concludes:

A warning of sociologists like Alfred McClung Lee and Alvin W. Gouldner is applicable here, namely that sociologists should guard against rigidity and professionalization. New insights are constantly required to further the discipline, and they can come from many directions. Engaging in the application of sociology and in citizen activities can loosen rigidity and provide stimulation—as long as the role requirement of each activity is kept clearly in mind, and if it is remembered that effectiveness in applied sociology and in citizen activity are dependent upon the development of sound theory of human groups.[59]

(2) *The Nonstructural Bias* An intensification of the problem of values in social research is by no means the only result of the constraining climate of the first decade of desegregation. This climate is also at least partly responsible for the recent failure of sociology to explore the structural and power bases underlying segregation and racial discrimination. Though the sociological works of previous years, from Dollard's *Caste and Class in a Southern Town* to Myrdal's *An American Dilemma*, brilliantly detailed these bases, the relationships between these structural roots and current racial change have been largely neglected.

A far more fashionable emphasis of recent years has been on attitude studies, particularly the attitudes of rank-and-file white segregationists. Interesting papers have also appeared on the Ku Klux Klan and other resistance groups.[60] But little work has focused on the sources of conservative power, such as the white southern "moderates." This has been true despite the fact that such racial crises as Little Rock and Birmingham offer clear indications of the vast importance of entrenched upper-status white resistance. A few examples suffice to make the point: many of the mob members in the Little Rock school riot were wage earners granted the day off in advance by two major employers in the city; school desegregation was delayed in Little Rock until an all-new, strategically located public high school could be completed to accommodate upper-class and upper middle-class children in all-white classrooms; and the head of the major industry in the Birmingham area openly supported extreme segregationist resistance in the city and state.

The sociological research which has been directed toward such structural and power aspects of the desegregation process further points up their importance. The Taeubers, for instance, have shown that residential segregation by race in the nation's standard metropolitan areas, certainly one of the most critical structural bulwarks against racial change, actually substantially increased between 1940 and 1950. Moreover, residential segregation continued to increase in the South, while only slightly moderating in the North, between 1950 and 1960.[61] And Richard Cramer has demonstrated that the relationship between attracting new industry and attitudes toward racial change among southern business leaders is far more complex and intricate than formerly supposed.[62]

Failure to exploit fully these peculiarly sociological insights concerning structure and power seems akin to the phenomenon documented by Paul Lazarsfeld and Wagner Thielens in *The Academic Mind*.[63] They studied the effects on 2,451 social scientists of "the difficult years" from 1946 to 1955, a period characterized in the nation at large by an intense interest in internal security and a concomitant concern with the political opinions and associations of college teachers. The chief effects were not gross. Those "permissive" social scientists who were most politically concerned maintained most of their previous associations and continued to subscribe to liberal journals. The actual changes wrought by academic apprehension were more subtle: some academicians toned down their writings; some were more careful in recommending reference material to their students lest it be criticized later as too controversial; others avoided researching potentially controversial problems. Much the same phenomena may well have operated in race-relations research during "the difficult years" of 1954–1963.

Gross changes have probably been rare. But more subtle changes have occurred, such as the avoidance of research on the influential sources of power which most effectively resist racial change and the failure to explore the basic structural changes that must take place in American society before the full inclusion of Negro Americans into the societal main stream is possible. This is not to imply that the scientist consciously makes this choice of topics in order to avoid alienating important interests. But it is to suggest that with limited time at his disposal the scientist will often select topics which seem most fruitful at the moment and can readily be performed in a restraining climate.

(3) *The Nonactivist Bias* The focus on low-status white segregationists has led not only to the research neglect of high-status white segregationists but of prodesegregation whites and Negroes as well. Values may intrude here, for, paradoxically, the sparseness of attention paid to prodesegregationists may partly reflect the sympathy which social scientists in general feel for desegregation. Such sympathy can lead to the investigation of immediate problems and obstacles, especially those raised by "the other side." Thus, the investigator can freely dissect the white supremacist, expose racist beliefs, and stress the changes necessary to counteract such resistance without feeling embarrassed about his "debunking." The situation becomes far more difficult if the weaknesses to be exposed relate to the side favored by the scientist. For example, work on conservative tendencies and even resistance to desegregation within the Negro community present a less inviting topic of research. Indeed, the scientist may feel that exposure of these conditions is itself a socially causative factor and may harm the desegregation movement.

Another result of directing so much attention toward lower-status segregationists, at least during the 1950's, has been the devaluation of prodesegregation activism. The apparent implicit assumption has been that social change would somehow come by itself if only the opposition of the racist extremists could be silenced. Frequently, of course, the social scientist is himself a member of the nonactive white group. In studying the motives and limitations of silent whites, the social scientist would be forced to perform a difficult feat of self-analysis. It is more conducive to one's self-esteem to study people who are different from oneself, such as racist extremists, and to emphasize the great power of the group attempting to uphold the status quo. This partial view of the picture makes it unnecessary to analyze one's own motivations. Further, unquestioned acceptance of a particular social structure has the dual function of indicating that any direct action is useless and of focusing on a static description of a monolithic system. Again one is reminded of the Little Rock clergy's rationalizations for their inactivity in the midst of racial crisis; many of the ministers emphasized that there was nothing they could do to counter the extremists and that none of the racist demonstrators were members of their congregations, thus avoiding the necessity of their actively supporting the prodesegregation forces.[64]

A recent sociological monograph on desegregation illustrates this rationalizing potential of the nonactivist bias.[65] White activists for desegregation in the South are portrayed as doomed to certain martyrdom; instead, it is argued, white liberals who play the "waiting role" are often far more effective. "They also serve," goes the rationalization, "who only stand and teach!" [66] But, the desegregationist might inquire, teach what? The "waiting role"?

These effects of the constraining atmosphere of the years since 1954—intensification of the issue of values in social research, the nonstructural bias, and the nonactivist bias—blend into the third and final reason for the relative disuse of sociology in the desegregation process so far.

A SOCIOLOGICAL BIAS TOWARD STATIC, SEGREGATION-MAINTAINING ANALYSES[67]

Many of the limitations of the sociological analysis of American race relations can by no means be attributed entirely to foundation timidity or resistance pressure. Rather, such limitations have been apparent in the sociological literature throughout this century. And the failure of sociology to foresee the present Negro protest, its form and growth, and its future direction is partly a function of this narrow approach.

Table 25–2 provides the relevant data, with a content breakdown of the 255 intergroup relations papers published from 1900 through 1958 in twenty of the most relevant sociological journals. Three classifications are made. The first distinction is between the personal and social systems. The second distinction divides the purely structural-static approach from the active approach which accepts far-reaching changes in the system. In individual perspective, this division separates attitudes from action; in social-system perspective, this division separates the static from considerations of social change. Finally, a third distinction is drawn according to the focus of the object. Does the paper deal principally with processes which favor integration, segregation, or both?

A glance at Table 25–2 reveals some susceptibility to the diverse problems and temper of each decade; yet there is also a general and pronounced trend toward static description and concern with segregation. Seventy-one per cent (180 of 255) of the papers focused on static aspects; 58 per cent (148 of 255) dealt solely with segregation processes; while only 30 per cent (76 of 255) dealt solely with integration processes.

Tracing the emphases over the years, the first decade of the century marked a special concentration on the static features of the social system which maintained segregation. This corresponded with a belief in the sta-

TABLE 25-2   Research in Intergroup Relations Reported in Major Sociological Journals*

| SYSTEM | INDIVIDUAL | | | | | | SOCIAL | | | | | |
| Topic | Attitudes | | | Action | | | Static | | | Change | | |
Focus on Factors Favoring / Time Period	Inte-gration	Segre-gation	Both	Inte-gration	Segre-gation	Both	Inte-gration	Segre-gation	Both	Inte-gration	Segre-gation	Both
1900–10	1											
1910–20								7				
1920–30	3	3	2		1	2	2	4		2	2	
1930–40	3	3		2	2	1	3	2	1	1	3	
1940–50	6	20	4	4	0		14	13	6	4	13	
1950–58	5	39	7	4	8	3	14	14	4	8	14	1
TOTAL	18	65	13	10	11	6	33	40	11	15	32	1

* Originally appeared in K. W. Back, "Sociology Encounters the Protest Movement for Desegregation," *Phylon*, XXIV (1963), 232–239.

bility of the society as it then existed and fitted with the popular separate-but-equal and stateways-cannot-change-folkways doctrines. The decade of change which followed evinced interest in the social system, static and changing, due to the recognition of the impact on society of World War I. During the 1920's and 1930's, attitude measurement introduced the opportunity of studying intergroup relations on an individual basis. And in the 1930's, the question of extremism in racial attitudes became especially prominent.

It was only after 1940, however, that many articles appeared on the relevance and development of negative outgroup attitudes. The breakthrough along these lines was the University of California study on the authoritarian personality.[68] This work presented a theory of intergroup relations on a purely individual level and provided a convenient set of scales that fathered a host of related studies. This advance accounts for the sudden imbalance of individual over social-system papers; while the personal system accounts for 48 per cent (123 of 255) of the total publications, it comprises almost two-thirds of the 1950–1958 production. Another major influence of the 1940's and 1950's was the publication of Myrdal's *An American Dilemma*, which in turn led to numerous descriptions of conditions which favored and opposed segregation. After 1954, studies on possible southern resistance to racial change reflected the Supreme Court ruling on school desegregation. But there continued to be a neglect of the forces which could hasten desegregation.

What is striking throughout is the lack of dynamic concerns that would have alerted sociology to the oncoming direct-action protests of the 1960's. Most of the papers which do treat Negro response deal merely with migration, an action within the social system having only an indirect, long-range effect. The next most frequent topic involved planned integration and interracial committees, not actions proposed by the minority group itself. Two less popular topics do touch on possible pressures toward social change. One analyzed Negro leadership types, and the other analyzed the types of persons predisposed to protest.

The great majority of sociological research publications on race relations, however, does not present a picture of individual responsibility and social change. These papers typically assume a constant, undefined pressure for integration in the discussion of the powerful personality factors and social institutions which oppose racial change. Criticism within social psychology in recent years has centered on the neglect of the positive resources of human beings: creativity, health, and self-fulfillment. An analogous criticism can be leveled at race-relations work in sociology, with its emphasis on restrictive static forces. Adoption of this static posture leads to a complete reliance on slow remedies, such as "education" or gradual institutional change. It omits, for example, the possible results of greatly enhanced pressure for integration.

To be sure, events in this sphere move so swiftly that sociology cannot be reproached for being unable to predict each event as it occurs. Yet this situation argues strongly for an application of the whole range of sociological theory to the study of the desegregation process. Many elements of sociological theory, such as relative deprivation considerations, heralded the racial crisis of the 1960's, but these fruitful leads were not fully exploited. A broader, bolder thrust in the sociological analysis of American race relations seems long overdue. No time has ever been more ripe for such a thrust than now.

A Recapitulation

In the desegregation process, the disuse of sociology is more apparent than its use. This situation has come about in spite of the rich promise of relevant sociological theory and the demonstrations of usefulness by individual sociologists. Four different theoretical emphases—centering upon the self, balance, the social system, and social change—all offer important leads for understanding desegregation. In addition, sociologists have in isolated instances proved their value as trend predictors, interpreters of specific events, and consultants.

Three interrelated reasons can be advanced to explain why the potential of sociology to contribute to the desegregation process has been barely tapped. First, the timidity of major foundations and granting agencies to support research in such a "controversial" realm caused a funding drought for most of the decade following 1954. Second, the pressures applied by stern segregationist resistance to racial change created a climate that was not conducive to broad-gauged scientific research. And, finally, a traditional overemphasis on static elements which bolster segregation in the sociological study of intergroup relations acted to deter the full exploitation of the sociological potential in this area.

All three of these barriers are now lowered. Funding sources are reevaluating their earlier positions; direct consultation services on desegregation problems are now explicitly offered by the federal government in the Civil Rights Act of 1964; and the sharp impact of the street protests of the 1960's has drawn sociological attention to the dynamic factors on the American scene which press toward rapid racial change. It can only be hoped that a great upsurge of research activity directed at desegregation will be forthcoming in the late 1960's and 1970's. At least three considerations make such an upsurge of interest imperative: (1) Desegregation is a now-or-never phenomenon; sociologists either start studying it immediately or the chance is lost completely. (2) Sociological insights and methods are needed to help in the practical solution of the many complex problems raised by such sweeping social changes. (3) And the process offers sociology a rare opportunity to test many of its theoretical formulations in the field on an issue of maximum salience.

REFERENCES

1. W. C. George, *The Biology of the Race Problem* (National Putnam Letters Committee, 1962), p. 56.
2. V. Dabney, "The Violence at Little Rock," Richmond *Times-Dispatch,* CV (September 24, 1957), 14.
3. The sociological works mentioned in Note 11 were E. Franklin Frazier's *The Negro in the United States* and Gunnar Myrdal's *An American Dilemma.*
4. Race in this context, then, is considered primarily as a social concept, rather than as a biological or psychological one. The definition and importance of racial concepts are dependent on social conditions, and racial distinctions are a function of social necessities. Thus, a division of the population into white and Negro sets the problem in a social context in the United States which contrasts sharply with that in other countries where either intermediate groups or a continuous degree of shading is recognized. It would be interesting to trace the progressive disuse of such terms as mulatto, quadroon, and octoroon in relation to changes in interracial relations (on the relation of color naming and the recognition of shades, see R. W. Brown and E. H. Lenneberg, "A Study in Language and Condition," *Journal of Abnormal and Social Psychology,* XLIX [1954], 454–462). In any event, the utility of treating race as a purely sociological concept is demonstrated by Thompson's observation that race as a stratification dimension tends to be most important in precisely those societies where a class system is not accepted as a normal way of life (see E. T. Thompson, "The South and the Second Emancipation," in A. P. Sindler, ed., *Change in the Contemporary South* [Durham, N.C.: Duke University Press, 1963], pp. 93–118).
5. E. Goffman, *Stigma* (Englewood Cliffs, N.J.: Prentice-Hall, 1963).
6. A similar view, based on existential philosophy, has been presented by Sartre (*Anti-Semite and Jew* [New York: Grove, 1960]). In his portrait of the anti-Semite, he discusses the problems of self-presentation of both the minority-group member and the aggressor. Both have the problem of being defamed by a few traits; but while the anti-Semite may welcome the definition of himself as a person who hates Jews, the problem for the Jew is more difficult. The minority-group member must strike a balance between asserting his existence beyond a prescribed set of traits and complete denial of these traits. This balance is what Sartre calls "authenticity," a concept which has already been applied to the description of Negro Americans (A. Booyard, "Portrait of the Inauthentic Negro," *Commentary,* X [1950], 56–64). The principal difference between Goffman and Sartre lies in the fact that Goffman, in the tradition of the symbolic interactionists, accepts the looking-glass self as a basic fact of social life, whereas Sartre considers it to be a possibly unavoidable tragedy.
7. For example, Marian R. Yarrow, ed., "Interpersonal Dynamics in a Desegregation Process," *Journal of Social Issues,* XXXVIII (Winter, 1958), 3–63.
8. A review of the race of interviewer bias literature is provided in T. F. Pettigrew, *A Profile of the Negro American* (Princeton, N.J.: Van Nostrand, 1964), pp. 49–51, 116–117. This work has focused on the bias encountered with Negro respondents; interesting research is called for on the differential responses of white respondents to Negro and white interviewers (a brief start in this direction

is reported in R. E. Rankin and D. T. Campbell, "Galvanic Skin Response to Negro and White Experimenters," *Journal of Abnormal and Social Psychology*, LI [1955], 30–33). Some of the most promising laboratory research in this realm has been summarized in I. Katz, "Review of Evidence Relating to Effects of Desegregation on the Intellectual Performance of Negroes," *American Psychologist*, XIX (1964), 381–399.

9. R. K. Merton and Alice S. Kitt, "Contributions to the Theory of Reference Group Behavior," in R. K. Merton and P. F. Lazarsfeld, eds., *Continuities in Social Research: Studies in the Scope and Method of "The American Soldier"* (Glencoe, Ill.: Free Press, 1950); and S. A. Stouffer, *Social Research to Test Ideas* (New York: Free Press, 1962), pp. 35–38.

10. *Ibid.*, p. 36.

11. Emile Benoit-Smullyan, "Status, Status Types and Status Interrelationships," *American Sociological Review*, IX (1944), 151–161; G. E. Lenski, "Status Crystallization: A Non-Vertical Dimension of Social Status," *American Sociological Review*, XIX (1954), 405–413; and J. C. Kimberly, "A Theory of Status Equilibration," in J. Berger, M. Zelditch, and B. Anderson, eds., *Sociological Theories in Progress* (Boston: Houghton Mifflin, 1964).

12. E. F. Jackson, "Status Consistency and Symptoms of Stress," *American Sociological Review*, XXVII (1962), 469–480; I. W. Goffman, "Status Consistency and Preference for Change in Power Distribution," *American Sociological Review*, XXII (1957), 275–281; and Lenski, *op. cit.*

13. Jackson, *op. cit.*

14. Documentation for this paragraph is provided in Pettigrew, *op. cit.*, Chapter 8.

15. Even among college Negroes, those from backgrounds of higher achieved status and who believed they were not mere pawns in an unchanging environment were more likely to participate in the protest demonstrations. See Pearl M. Gore and J. B. Rotter, "A Personality Correlate of Social Action," *Journal of Personality*, XXXI (1963), 58–64; and Ruth Searles and J. A. Williams, Jr., "Negro College Students' Participation in Sit-Ins," *Social Forces*, XL (1962), 215–220.

16. E. Durkheim, *The Division of Labor in Society* (New York: Macmillan, 1933).

17. J. A. S. Davis, "Structural Balance, Mechanical Solidarity, and Interpersonal Relations," *American Journal of Sociology*, LXVIII (1963), 444–462.

18. T. F. Pettigrew, "Regional Differences in Anti-Negro Prejudice," *Journal of Abnormal and Social Psychology*, LIX (1959), 28–36.

19. Price has demonstrated that this legacy remains even when the percentage of Negroes in a particular Black Belt county has sharply declined. See H. D. Price, *The Negro and Southern Politics* (New York: New York University Press, 1957), pp. 35–54.

20. Social symptoms of the restricted differentiation of rural America are not limited, of course, to race relations or to the South. For instance, thirteen different national surveys by Gallup, spanning the years from 1941 to 1961 and utilizing a variety of question wordings, have repeatedly shown farmers to harbor views concerning the rights of labor which sharply differ from those held by all other occupational groups, including business employers. Thus, farmers as a group are conspicuous in their disapproval of labor unions, minimum wage requirements, and four-day work weeks and in their support of the open shop and the reduction of pay with any reduction in the work week. Moreover, even union members who lived in communities of less than 2,500 persons voted significantly less in 1960 for the labor-backed Democratic Party than other union members. See Hazel Gaudet Erskine, "The Polls: Attitudes toward Organized Labor," *Public Opinion Quarterly*, XXVI (1962), 283–296.

21. T. Parsons, "Pattern Variables Revisited," *American Sociological Review*, XXV (1960), 467–482.
22. M. Rubin, "Land and Cultural Change in a Plantation Area," *Journal of Social Issues*, X (1954), 28–35.
23. These examples are taken from Ernest Works, "The Pattern Variables as a Framework for the Study of Negro-White Relations," unpublished manuscript.
24. K. W. Marek, *Yestermorrow: Notes on Man's Progress* (New York: Knopf, 1961). For sociological considerations of evolutionary aspects of social change, see articles by Parsons, Bellah, and Eisenstadt in *The American Sociological Review*, XXIX (1964), 339–386.
25. For a general discussion of the ability of functional theories to explain social change, see Francesca Cancian, "Functional Analysis of Change," *American Sociological Review*, XXV (1960), 818–827.
26. L. A. Coser, *The Functions of Social Conflict* (Glencoe, Ill.: Free Press, 1956); D. Henderson, "Minority Response and the Conflict Model," *Phylon*, XXV (1964), 18–26; and L. Killian and C. Grigg, *Racial Crisis in America* (Englewood Cliffs, N.J.: Prentice-Hall, 1964).
27. Coser, *op. cit.*
28. Henderson, *op. cit.*, and Killian and Grigg, *op. cit.*
29. L. A. Coser, "Conflict," *Encyclopedia of the Social Sciences*, in press.
30. E. U. Essien-Udom, *Black Nationalism* (Chicago: University of Chicago Press, 1962); C. E. Lincoln, *The Black Muslims in America* (Boston: Beacon, 1961); and J. W. Vander Zanden, "The Klan Revival," *American Journal of Sociology*, LXV (1960), 456–462.
31. A. L. Coleman, "Social Scientists' Predictions about Desegregation," *Social Forces*, XXXVIII (1960), 258–262.
32. Adapted from *ibid.*
33. A review of this work is provided in T. F. Pettigrew and M. R. Cramer, "The Demography of Desegregation," *Journal of Social Issues*, XV (1959), 61–71. For material specifically on the 1861 Tennessee vote to secede, see V. O. Key, *Southern Politics* (New York: Knopf, 1950), 75–78.
34. Pettigrew and Cramer, *op. cit.*
35. The percentage of white women in the labor force turned out to be a reasonably effective way to tap traditionalism; that is, a county with a relatively small percentage of white women in its recorded labor force was presumed to be more traditional than others.
36. Also reported in T. F. Pettigrew, "Continuing Barriers to Desegregated Education in the South," *Sociology of Education*, XXXVIII (1965), 99–111. Further work is now under way to construct more precise predictive formulas.
37. H. Cantril, *The Politics of Despair* (New York: Basic Books, 1958).
38. *Ibid.*, p. 71.
39. A large body of literature supports the proposition that people who generally do not vote are more apathetic, alienated, authoritarian, and uninformed than those who typically do vote. Relevant studies include G. M. Connelly and H. H. Field, "The Non-Voter, Who He Is, and What He Thinks," *Public Opinion Quarterly*, VIII (1944), 175–187; P. Hastings, "The Non-Voter in 1952: A Study of Pittsfield, Mass.," *Journal of Psychology*, XXXVIII (1954), 301–312; P. Hastings, "The Voter and the Non-Voter," *American Journal of Sociology*, LXII (1956), 302–307; H. Hyman and P. B. Sheatsley, "Some Reasons Why Information Campaigns Fail," *Public Opinion Quarterly*, XI (1947), 412–423; M. Janowitz and D. Marvick, "Authoritarianism and Political Behavior," *Public Opinion Quarterly*, XVII (1953), 185–201; S. M. Lipset, *Political Man* (New York:

Doubleday, 1960), pp. 79–103; F. H. Sanford, *Authoritarianism and Leadership* (Stevenson Brothers, 1950), p. 168; and S. A. Stouffer, *Communism, Conformity, and Civil Liberties* (New York: Doubleday, 1955). It should also be noted that this analysis was originally written in 1964. From 1964 to 1967 the journalistic term "backlash" gained even greater favor but its meaning subtly shifted to simple resistance to racial change in general. Thus, the 1966 elections of segregationist governors in Georgia and Florida was described as "backlash" examples, though these states were hardly political bastions of racial liberalism in previous years.

40. Two of these reports were published: J. K. Morland, "Lunch-Counter Desegregation in Corpus Christi, Galveston, and San Antonio, Texas," *Special Reports of the Southern Regional Council* (May, 1960); and J. K. Morland, *School Desegregation—Help Needed?* (Washington, D.C.: The Potomac Institute, 1962).

41. K. Lenihan, "Attitudes towards Negroes in a New Jersey Suburb," unpublished manuscript.

42. L. W. Killian, "The Social Scientist's Role in the Preparation of the Florida Desegregation Brief," *Social Problems*, III (1956), 211–214.

43. For examples of the views of these two men on *de facto* segregation, see Arnold Rose, *De Facto Segregation* (National Conference of Christians and Jews, 1964); and M. Ravitz, "Uneven School Progress in Detroit," in M. Weinberg, ed., *Learning Together* (Integrated Education Associates, 1964), pp. 61–67.

44. Killian, *op. cit.*, p. 214.

45. Smaller foundations which stand out as conspicuous exceptions to this trend include the Marshall Field Foundation, the New World Foundation, and the Taconic Foundation.

46. S. W. Cook, "Desegregation: A Psychological Analysis," *American Psychologist*, XII (1957), 1–13.

47. Examples of these limited case studies conducted since 1954 include E. Q. Campbell, *When A City Closes Its Schools* (Chapel Hill, N.C.: Institute for Research in the Social Sciences, 1960); E. Q. Campbell and T. F. Pettigrew, *Christians in Racial Crisis: A Study of the Little Rock Ministry* (Washington: Public Affairs Press, 1959); Killian and Grigg, *op. cit.;* D. C. Thompson, *The Negro Leadership Class* (Englewood Cliffs, N.J.: Prentice-Hall, 1963); and M. M. Tumin, *Desegregation: Resistance and Readiness* (Princeton: Princeton University Press, 1958). The far more extensive study by Robin Williams, Jr. (*Strangers Next Door* [Englewood Cliffs, N.J.: Prentice-Hall, 1964]), is a report of pre-1954 data.

48. W. Brink and L. Harris, *The Negro Revolution in America* (New York: Simon and Schuster, 1964).

49. R. N. Sanford, "Foreword," in *The Role of the Social Sciences in Desegregation* (Anti-Defamation League of B'nai B'rith, 1958).

50. R. Redfield, "Values in Action: A Comment," *Human Organization*, XVII (1958), 20–22.

51. A. Gouldner, "Anti-Minotaur: The Myth of a Value-Free Sociology," *Social Problems*, IX (1962), 199–213.

52. C. Arensberg, "Values in Action: A Comment," *Human Organization*, XVII (1958), 25–26.

53. R. Bierstedt, "Social Science and Public Service," paper given at meetings of the Society for the Study of Social Problems, St. Louis, 1961.

54. Campbell and Pettigrew, *op. cit.*

55. Stouffer, *Social Research to Test Ideas*, pp. 224, 231–238.

56. Killian, *op. cit.*

57. *Ibid.*, p. 214.

58. J. K. Morland, "Roles of Sociologist and Citizen in Race Relations in the South," paper given at meetings of the American Sociological Association, Washington, D.C., 1962.

59. *Ibid.*

60. Vander Zanden, *op. cit.*

61. K. E. Taeuber and Alma F. Taeuber, *Negroes in Cities* (Chicago: Aldine, 1965).

62. M. R. Cramer, "School Desegregation and New Industry: The Southern Community Leaders' Viewpoint," *Social Forces*, XLI (1963), 384–389.

63. P. F. Lazarsfeld and W. Thielens, Jr., *The Academic Mind* (Glencoe, Ill.: Free Press, 1958). See also a penetrating review of this volume: H. C. Kelman, "Apprehension and Academic Freedom," *Public Opinion Quarterly*, XXIII (1959), 181–188.

64. Campbell and Pettigrew, *op. cit.*

65. Killian and Grigg, *op. cit.*

66. *Ibid.*, p. 101.

67. This section is taken largely from K. W. Back, "Sociology Encounters the Protest Movement for Desegregation," *Phylon*, XXIV (1963), 232–239.

68. T. W. Adorno, Else Frenkel-Brunswik, D. J. Levinson, and N. Sanford, *The Authoritarian Personality* (New York: Harper, 1950).

Institutional

Problems in

Applied Sociology

PART **VI**

The Ethical

Problems of

Applied Sociology

ROBERT C. ANGELL

chapter 26

When a sociologist is acting in his scientific capacity, he is adding to, verifying, criticizing, or expounding a body of abstract knowledge. The problems he encounters are theoretical and methodological. The task that gives his efforts meaning is the extension of man's ability to comprehend the processes of social life. Sociology is then an end in itself. The sociologist's ethical responsibilities are to his colleagues in the quest, his students, his research assistants, and those affected by his research.

When sociology is not an end in itself, but becomes a means to some other end, it is applied sociology. The end may be to sell more automobiles, to improve the operation of a hospital, or to decide whether the school system or the police department should be given the task of driver education; in every case instrumental decisions have to be made, and sociology is called upon as a discipline that can help to make them. In this case there are ethical problems, too, many of them the same as in the "pure" case, but some quite different. Since the teaching function is not

725

characteristic of the role of applied sociologist, the ethical problems involving relations with teaching colleagues and with students become irrelevant. Most of the ethical questions stemming from research may still be apropos, but the role of applied sociologist entails in addition a wholly new set of ethical problems: those arising from the fact of employment by a principal whose major objective is not the furtherance of sociology as a scientific discipline.

There are three principal subroles that may be played by the applied sociologist: as consultant, as practitioner, and as researcher. The first two have mainly to do with the marshaling of existing knowledge, the third with the acquisition of new knowledge. The difference between the consultant and the practitioner is essentially that between the adviser and the doer.

The consultant is usually engaged by a going concern of some kind to bring to bear sociological knowledge on its ends and values, its resources of men and things. The sociologist is employed as an adjunct to the continuing staff to make his special contribution. His role is definitely ancillary, since he merely advises those who make decisions for the organization. In the course of his work he may find it necessary to make a reconnaissance of the situation, but he does not normally do systematic research.

Sociological practitioners are of two types: the "solo" professional and the organization man. Though having different degrees of independence, the two are alike in that their principal job is to apply sociology to the solution of group problems. An example of the solo professional is the marriage counselor. Here the group dealt with is small, the problems intimate, and the expertness of the clients limited. The analogy to the physician is very close. In this sense the role is one of trust far more than is the role of consultant. Like the consultant, however, he has to become thoroughly familiar with the particular case.

The practitioner as organization man can be illustrated by the sociologist employed as penologist in a prison system or as planner in a city government. This is a perfectly straightforward situation of a man with a kind of professional competence that is needed in the solution of practical problems. He has responsibility to carry out the authority delegated to him. This is a more active role than that of the consultant, whose responsibility is merely to give the best advice he can to those who are making policy.

In the research role the applied sociologist is usually in a contractual relationship with an organization like one to which he might be a consultant. But in this instance it is not the marshaling of existing knowledge that is in question, but the achievement of new knowledge. The contractor may desire this new knowledge for several reasons. In the simplest case he wants to make the wisest choice between alternative ways of performing the same function or reaching the same goal. Research will help to determine the most effective alternative. In a more complex case he wishes to evaluate the total operation of some department or program or possibly of the whole organization. This obviously requires study of the way broad objectives are split up into special tasks, of how personnel and resources are allocated to these tasks, and of the efficiency of performance. There are other possibilities, too: how, for instance, a body of trained personnel (who perhaps have been replaced by automation) can best be employed in other operations, or whether it would be desirable for the contracting organization to move one of its plants.

The Consultant

Of these three roles of the applied sociologist, that of the consultant involves the least worrisome ethical problems. Compared with the practitioner, he carries less responsibility. The clients of the practitioner are often completely dependent on him, but the organizations that employ consultants almost always have other means of marshaling relevant data and therefore need not take their advice.

One of the most basic of all ethical principles for professional men is that they do not misrepresent their own capabilities. The client is expecting expert service, and he has a right to receive it. In the first place, it would be grossly unethical for a rural sociologist to hold himself out as an expert on labor–management problems in large-scale industry. In professional relations the maxim *caveat emptor* does not apply. The buyer cannot beware because he does not know enough about what he is purchasing to tell whether he is getting the kind of service he is paying for. But let us suppose that the client has been mistakenly informed that the expert is an industrial sociologist and that the latter has in no way misrepresented his abilities prior to the first meeting of the two. What then? May he in good conscience remain silent and become a consultant? It would seem that he may not. The would-be client has a right to know that the sociologist does not possess the requisite knowledge and skill in the field of industrial sociology, and the sociologist is the one who can inform him. Of course if the client, after learning all the facts and having been told to look elsewhere, still wants to retain the sociologist as a consultant, the latter may ethically accept.

Sometimes the sociologist may enter upon a consulting relationship confident that he has the knowledge and interpretive skills that are necessary to render an adequate professional service to the client, but discovers after he has got into the work that he has not. In such instances, it is clear that he should explain the situation to the client and either suggest that his service be supplemented by those of someone who can contribute what he lacks or ask to be relieved of the role as consultant.

One of the problems that the sociologist as consultant frequently faces is that of every outside expert: the client has developed exaggerated expectations of what the professional has to offer toward the solution of his problems. At an early point in the relationship it behooves the sociologist to estimate how much help his advice may be to the client and to inform the latter frankly. The reputation of sociology will be quickly tarnished if its representatives foster expectations that cannot be fulfilled. It is better psychology and much better ethics to undersell the service being offered.

Most sociologists who take consulting work have an institutional base, usually a college or university. Such men have an ethical responsibility to their institutions not to allow a position as consultant to interfere with their academic duties, whether teaching, research, or administration. Although a very few institutions have tried to forbid consulting for remuneration by their full-time faculty, most of them allow such faculty to work as consultants on a minimum basis—perhaps up to 40 hours a month. Given the independence and lack of supervision that faculty men enjoy, these arrangements may tempt them to take the 40 hours out of the approximately 180 hours a month that academic men think of as normal for their positions. A man who does so does not lessen his effectiveness in any obvious way. He meets his classes, prepares his lectures, reads his student papers and examinations, attends committee meetings, and may even keep up his usual research pace. The difference will probably be in the amount of collateral reading he does and the amount of time he devotes to leisurely reflection. Unless consulting makes a contribution to the man's teaching and research sufficient to offset these changes, it will detract from his performance as a professor. It would therefore seem usually unethical to yield to the temptation to accomplish the work as consultant without lengthening the work week. And if he cannot lengthen the work week without tiring himself out and thus impairing his value as a faculty member, the ethical thing to do is either to refuse the invitation to become a consultant or to reduce his academic commitment through a part-time arrangement.

Usually the ostensible reason for employing a consultant is the real reason: to secure the benefit of the sociologist's knowledge and the advice springing therefrom. Occasionally, however, the ostensible reason is not the real reason. The policies of the head of an organization may be under attack by members of the board of directors or by a strong faction of his subordinates. He may wish to buttress his position by making it seem to have the support of social science. If the sociologist discovers in his exploratory discussions that this is indeed the fact, that the client is interested in his advice only if it conforms to the conclusions that the client has already reached, and that objective application of sociological knowledge to the problem in hand is indeed not desired, the ethical course is to refuse to become a consultant. And if the discovery is made only after consultation has started, the sociologist is ethically bound to break off the connection as promptly as the circumstances permit. It is perfectly proper to subordinate scientific knowledge to practical ends, but it is not proper to adulterate scientific knowledge in the process.

A much more difficult problem arises when the ends for which a client wishes to use sociological knowledge are not shared by all those connected with the organization. Suppose that a plant manager's only interest is to speed production and that he brings in a sociologist as consultant in order to advise him on the best way to utilize the informal groups of workers to achieve that end. The men in the shop would not agree, if they knew about the sociologist's employment, that the speeding up of production should be the sole end for which his knowledge should be employed. They might feel that advice on how to make the work more self-expressive to the workmen was of much greater importance. What is the ethical obligation of the sociologist under these conditions? Is he morally accountable for the ends of his client beyond being sure that they are not criminal? Must he decline to become a consultant because others will feel that these ends are inadequate or even pernicious? To say that he should is to impose an almost impossible burden upon him. He cannot be expected to find out what all the orientations of the various groups in the organization are. But there is perhaps a course he can take that will protect him from criticism. He can insist that no secret be made of why he was hired as a consultant and what the specific problems are on which he is working. Then if others in the organizations wish to protest or even urge that social scientists be employed as consultants on other problems, they may do so. The whole matter is in the open, and the issue can be aired.

A closely related but distinguishable problem springs from the contacts that a consultant may have with his client's subordinates. It frequently happens that in order to understand fully the questions on which he is being asked to give advice, he needs to talk with persons holding different roles in the organization. This is not a research undertaking in the ordinary sense, since it does not involve testing any hypothesis, but merely an attempt to grasp the problems to which his sociological knowledge is to be applied. These exploratory conversations may, however, appear to the client as a good way to obtain intelligence on the personal views of his subordinates. He may try to pump the sociologist with respect to matters having to do, not with efficiency of the system as such, but, for instance, with the loyalty of these subordinates. This poses a very difficult ethical problem. That a minor official has lost confidence in his superior may be pertinent information for the consultant, since it may suggest policies that need to be examined. In a general way, therefore, it is proper for such discontents to become part of the discussions between the sociologist and the client. But it would obviously not be professionally acceptable for the sociologist to name those that are discontented, even indirectly. The consultant is hired, not to spy for his employer, but to give his counsel on problems for which sociology offers help.

It is clear that the principal ethical problems of the consulting relation revolve around the fact that the applied sociologist has two masters: his profession and his client. This is not to say that the two are not frequently reinforcing. The sociologist has, for instance, a *professional* duty to bring to the service of his employer all the abilities he possesses. This includes the manner in which he writes up his report. The more objectively scientific his analysis is and the more firmly his conclusions and recommendations are based on this analysis, the better the service the client is receiving.

When there is no clear professional claim that is violated, the interests of the client must be protected. For instance, there is no reason why the consultations themselves should not be private. Nor is there any good reason why the sociologist's report should not be, too. There would be a question here if new scientific knowledge were being produced in the course of the consultation, but this is not the case. No interest of science is being violated, therefore, by confidentiality. In the case of business institutions, much of the value of the consultation to the client would be lost if his competitors were to share its results.

After the termination of the consulting relation, the rights of the client continue. Obviously the sociologist must not convey any of the information that he has learned to those who might use it to the detriment of the client. Further than that, the data the sociologist has secured are not public property, but belong to the client. The sociologist may not therefore ethically publish any of these data in a professional journal without the explicit permission of the client and may not even use them as material for teaching purposes without such permission.

The Practitioner

Since the practitioner usually devotes his full time to the role, he does not so often as the consultant face the ethical problem of being sure that other services that he is obligated to perform are not slighted. There is, however, the same problem of possible misrepresentation of his skills. This is more crucial for the solo practitioner than for the professional employed by an organization. In the latter case, the principle of *caveat emptor* can be applied effectively; the organization which hires a new staff man usually has ample opportunity to evaluate his qualifications. In the case of the individual practitioner, the client group may not know how to check his credentials; they have to take his skills on trust. Thus, the solo sociologist must be especially sure that he does not misrepresent his capabilities. He cannot promise to solve the client's problems, but he can at least make sure that he is competent to try.

Like the consultant, the practitioner has two masters: the profession of sociology and the person, group, or organization that has employed him. In the optimal case there is no clash between them. He draws on his knowledge of sociology to the best of his ability and puts it at the service of his client or the organization for which the practitioner works. But a number of contingencies may arise that pose difficult ethical problems.

First, consider the case of an expert on juvenile delinquency who is employed by a city government or a social agency to become the confidant of a vicious boys' gang (as in the experience of Dr. Yablonsky, who wrote *The Violent Gang*). This is a case where the sociologist is both an organization man—for his employer—and a solo practitioner—for his client, the gang. The employer cannot condone crime and therefore expects the sociologist to help enforce the law. The sociologist, on the other hand, knows that if he is to have any therapeutic role he must keep the boys' confidence in him as a friend. If he were to report their misdeeds, he would immediately lose all influence with them. What to do when he learns of some illegal escapade? Though no one has laid down an ethical canon for such cases, perhaps a reasonable principle would be for the sociologist to wink at minor infractions, while attempting as best he can to prevent them, but to tell the boys in advance that he will have to turn them in if they commit serious crimes, and in fact to do so. If crimes are committed, his usefulness with the gang may be at an end, but at least until they occur he will have served both masters successfully.

A different case is one in which the sociologist is asked by the employer or client to work toward ends which, though legal, he does not approve of. Thus a practitioner employed by a labor union, asked to help in a community-relations program that is ostensibly to reduce discrimination in employment, may discover that his main function is to make liaison with the more quiescent leaders of the Negro community and keep them from expressions of intense hostility toward organized labor. What are his ethical rights and duties in such a case? Probably many would avoid the issue by resigning the post and looking for a more congenial employer. But certainly one is not bound to do this. If he chooses to remain, he may ethically carry out the assignment, provided that he makes disclosure of his personal disagreement with what he has been asked to do. Thus the possibility that he will work less than enthusiastically on the project is made clear to the union leaders, so that they may turn to someone else if they prefer.

A third sort of situation is presented when the sociologist and the employer or client agree on ends, but disagree on means. Since presumably the practitioner has been employed precisely because he is an expert on instrumental matters, his duty to the discipline ot sociology is clear. He must follow the course of action that his scientific analysis of the situation calls for and must resist all efforts of the employer or the client to dictate his course. If he is a solo professional like the marriage counselor who is advising a wife on the restructuring of family relationships, this means that he must make the recommendation that seems to him most promising, even if it seems to favor the husband who has refused to talk with him, rather than the wife who is his client. In the case of the practitioner in an organization, it means that he must follow his sociological conscience, even if by so doing he loses his position.

The welfare of the client or organization for which the practitioner is working is, of course, of central concern. It follows that all data and information acquired in the role of practitioner are privileged and may not be used in any way that violates their confidentiality without express consent. On the other hand, the role of practitioner need not rule out the role of research scientist. The materials gathered over a period of time—in guided group work, marriage counseling, interethnic relations, or other fields of practice—provide a rich basis of general knowledge, valuable not only to other practitioners but to sociologists generally. It is perfectly proper, therefore, for the practitioner to use the materials gained from his practice as the basis of published research.

I have argued above that the relation of trust between the boys' gang and the social worker attached to it is essential for any therapeutic result. The case raises a broader question: the inherent right to privacy. The sociologist, like the physician and the clergyman, often comes to know intimate aspects of the lives of his clients. How far must absolute confidentiality be maintained? It would seem that no simple and absolute rule is possible, for there are times when the ethic of confidentiality is challenged by even higher principles, such as the preservation of life. It would be difficult to defend strict confidentiality of information given by a client when the foreseeable result is death or serious injury. Does the sociologist engaged in interracial work have the right to withhold from public agencies knowledge that instigation of a race riot is being planned? Is a prison sociologist warranted in hiding from prison authorities information of an impending outbreak of which he has learned in his professional capacity? Some questions of this kind are easily resolved, but others lie on the border line and may present perplexing problems of conscience.

The Researcher in a Practical Setting

As in the cases of the consultant and the practitioner, the researcher must not misrepresent his abilities. If he finds that the research that needs to be done for the client is not the sort that he is capable of doing well, he must make this clear to the client and either obtain the collaboration of someone better qualified or withdraw altogether.

The obligation of the applied sociologist to insure high quality in the research does not end with his own abilities. He must see to it that whatever assistance he employs is also well trained and capable. His responsibility is to take all the steps essential to reaching a thoroughly professional result.

A sociological investigator may be employed by a great variety of agencies to help further practical rather than scientific ends. These may be the ends of private business, of voluntary associations, of governmental organizations, of political parties, of churches. The motives may be selfish or unselfish, the findings important or trivial.

The fact that the sociological investigator is working for some person or organization that desires knowledge for ends other than the development of sociology does not mean that the research itself may not conform to the highest standards of scientific craftsmanship. It is true that the questions to which answers are sought will not be abstract and theoretical, but the interplay between empirical evidence and generalization remains the same. There is still need for good research design, objective analysis, and the drawing of valid inferences.

The most difficult ethical problems arise when the employer is not seeking a really objective analysis of a situation, but hopes, through research, to buttress claims for a product, or the need for a law, or the correctness of a policy. In other words, the employer wants the research to come out in a certain way and is going to be pleased with the investigator if it does. No reputable scientist would, of course, accept a commission to prove the truth of a hypothesis, but few employers would be so crude as to put the matter in those terms. Rather, it will become apparent that the employing group hopes that research will show them to have been on the right track. The sociologist is given to feel that a good member of the "team" could hardly find otherwise. This is a most insidious sort of influence, since it is so easy to design the research so that the results desired will be obtained. It usually takes only a slight distortion in the sampling procedure or in the phrasing of questions.

Yet any such distortion makes a travesty of the scientific method. The ease with which such manipulation can be hidden makes it all the more important that there be strong ethical commitments against the practice. A sociologist has an absolute obligation to make his research design as perfect as he knows how to make it and to carry it out to the letter. Sins of omission in not setting up adequate safeguards against bias are quite as serious as fudging data after they have been gathered. Suppose that a sociologist, for instance, has been asked by a taxpayers' league to investigate the adequacy of unemployment insurance in the hope that a proposed raise in the rate of weekly compensation will be proved unnecessary. Sensing how the wind blows, he is tempted to make his study cover only those who are receiving unemployment insurance for the first time. He might try to rationalize this by claiming that he will thus obtain cases that are "unspoiled," in the sense that they have not yet been influenced by labor-union spokesmen calling for higher benefits. But the convenient fact is that such "first timers" have not yet exhausted their savings and may therefore be able to get along on the insurance payments better than those who have suffered several episodes of unemployment. There are great opportunities for such self-delusion, and the only adequate protection against them is a determination on the part of the investigator to search for criticisms of the design he is proposing before he makes it definitive.

From the design stage on, the sociologist must be free of all client control in matters affecting the scientific merit of the research. He may have to alter his design for reasons of cost or of unsuitability to the client's need for particular sorts of knowledge, but he must not acquiesce in any modifications that impair scientific quality. On the other hand, he must carry out the assignment that has been agreed upon and must not try to change the character of the investigation just because his scientific interest has taken a new turn.

Although much research done for practical reasons is not published, if it is published there should be a clear statement of what the interests of the client were in having the research undertaken and how the skills and values of the sociologist were geared to it. It is particularly important that the public understand that sociologists cannot be hired to produce data to buttress a preconceived conclusion, but that their work is always done with full scientific objectivity.

Much of the research that sociologists do involves persons either as informants or as observed subjects. Since the welfare of such persons can be jeopardized in a number of ways, the investigator has a moral obligation to see to it that they are adequately protected.

Harm may come to subjects from the very procedures by which the data are gathered. Suppose, for instance, one of the armed services is interested in improving group co-operation under stress. In order to investigate alternative modes of communication and organization within the group, the sociologist may plan a series of simulated operations under conditions of stress. He is ethically bound to take every precaution both by testing the participants in advance and by carefully controlling the degree of stress so that none of them is subjected to injurious nervous strain. If the risk of such strain is inescapable, the sociologist should so inform the sponsor. Since practical problems are not usually crucial for the development of scientific theory, the sociologist may well feel there is no ethical justification for going ahead with such simulations. In a national emergency, however, and with the full support of a governmental agency and the consent of the participants, he may feel it ethically justifiable to proceed.

The same general principles obviously apply when the researcher becomes aware of potential harm to the participants during the course of the investigation—harm entirely unanticipated at the outset. He is then obligated to remove the source of possibly injurious effects if that can be done. If it cannot, he should inform the client of the situation. If the latter wishes to have the study go forward nevertheless, the investigator will have to consult his own conscience and decide whether the potential gains from the research can justify the risk. If he thinks that they do, he must still inform the subjects of the possibility of injury to them so that they may withdraw.

In pure research it is quite common to obtain informants or subjects by promising them a return of some sort, either partial credit in a college course, or the opportunity to learn research techniques by participating in a project, or a full statement of the research results, or a pecuniary reward. In applied research, the latter two inducements are those mainly offered. The applied sociologist must be careful not to promise more than he can deliver and must of course be scrupulous in carrying out the commitments he has made. Few things would bring the profession more quickly into public disrepute than for its practitioners to fail to keep their promises to those who have helped them in their research.

A subtle form of injury may be perpetrated by the investigator if he fails to honor the moral worth of an informant or subject by misleading him. Several kinds of deception have been frequently practiced by social scientists. For instance, in a field investigation a sociologist may become a participant observer, posing as a gardener, a truck driver, or a factory operative. In such a role he is able to get the confidence of others and to obtain valuable information from a set of persons under study—information that would not be available if he were known to be a researcher. In experimental studies an accomplice may be introduced into a group to play a role that has been carefully fixed by the investigator in order to have stimuli that are crucial to the experiment presented accurately. The other participants assume that the accomplice is one of them and react to him as if he were a free agent like the rest of them. A third practice is even more misleading, since it involves the giving of false information, rather than the withholding of true information. This may occur when a researcher wants to foster distrust among the members of a group for experimental reasons and does so by misreporting to one of the participants what others have actually done or said.

With reference to such practices, there is a clear line of ethical distinction between pure and applied research. For the purpose of obtaining important new scientific knowledge, deception of these kinds may sometimes be ethically tolerated, provided that this is the only way to reach the scientific goal and provided also that those who have been duped are later given a full explanation of what was done. The reasoning here is that any moral harm is temporary and is justified by the scientific gain. There does not appear to be any such ethical justification in the case of applied research. The ends are not scientific ones, but are the practical ones of the client. To make others unwitting means to his ends seems clearly unethical.

Informants and subjects may also be injured by divulging their identity. It is too often assumed that privacy needs to be protected only if results are to be published. This neglects the fact that communication of any kind may put information about a person in the hands of those whom he distrusts. Attitudes and opinions that he prefers to keep private may become known to the agency sponsoring the research. His intentions may be disclosed to those who wish to thwart them. If he is a public figure, his identification with certain positions may alienate his followers or give advantage to his opponents.

One might argue that if a person does not wish to have his privacy breached, he should not become a party to sociological investigations. But in a scientific culture such as that of the United States one is made to feel at the least unco-operative, at the most obstructionist, if one does not give information sought by a social scientist. It is for this reason that there has developed the practice of granting anonymity. Thus both the desire of the sociologist for data and the desire of the respondent for privacy are fulfilled.

But what of the situation when the research is being undertaken not in the service of pure science but for the practical ends of organization? Does this make any difference in the need for anonymity? It does not, and it does. One comes out with the same ethical conclusion, but for somewhat different reasons. Applied research is not so important as pure research. If this fact is appreciated by the potential informants and subjects—and it is the ethical responsibility of the researcher to make clear to them exactly what ends are being served by the investigation—then they need not feel under any social constraint to co-operate. This would make the granting of anonymity less urgent. On the other hand, the usual argument against granting anonymity—that it makes it harder for other social scientists to check the validity of the research—is much less compelling. The results are for private use and will probably not enter the scientific literature. Thus there is both less need for anonymity and less possible harm from granting it.

To refrain from using a person's name, however, is not necessarily to conceal identity. This is particularly true of prominent persons, whether in private or public life. Those who know them can identify them from the roles they occupy, from their style of conduct, and from the views they express. What is the ethical canon that should guide the sociologist in such cases?

It seems clear that the sociologist must consider very carefully what true anonymity requires in any particular case. In the extreme instance of information obtained from someone so obviously unique that it could have come only from him, it cannot be ethically disclosed at all in the absence of expressed permission. More commonly, the sociologist will have to disguise the circumstances surrounding the subject so as to make him unrecognizable. To do this is a manner that does not sacrifice information about causally relevant matters like social class or occupation requires great skill.

In the case of applied research it is clear that one cannot make the exception to absolute privacy that is sometimes made in pure research: that information may be shared in confidence with colleagues for strictly scientific purposes. Since the principal aim is not to add to the corpus of scientific knowledge, the breach of confidentiality cannot be justified.

There is another difficulty that sociologists need to be aware of. There are no legal safeguards backing up the guarantees proffered to informants. The sociologist may even be required under oath to disclose in court information that he has secured by promising anonymity. To our knowledge, this has not yet happened, and it is not likely to occur to informants as a possibility; but if they inquire about it, the research sociologist must make clear what the legal position is.

One further caution needs emphasis. Moral deviants are just as much entitled to the anonymity that has been promised as are moral conformers. Only at the bidding of a court of law may the sociologist divulge the identity of anyone against his will.

A related and very difficult ethical problem for the researcher is similar to one already discussed for the practitioner. This arises when the sociologist becomes a party to privileged information. In studying skid row for a committee on alcoholism, for instance, he may discover continued violation of the law. Does his duty as a citizen take priority over his duty as a research sociologist? It appears to be the consensus of the profession that, despite the fact that he is not afforded legal protection for privileged information, he must treat privileged information as confidential when he is fulfilling his research role. Disclosures of such information should be made only when failure to do so would involve clear and present danger to individuals or collectivities.

The privacy of an organization is not usually given protection equal to that afforded an individual or primary group. This is because formal collectivities are powerful forces in life, and citizens often believe that their activities should be open to public scrutiny. In pure sociological research there seem to be only two compelling reasons for the granting of anonymity to them: (1) the processes to be analyzed are closely connected with individual leaders whose privacy would be breached were anonymity not granted; and (2) the collectivity to be studied is of such a rare type that it might be spoiled as a research site by publicity. Since seldom would the leaders of one organization allow it to be studied for the benefit of another unless they had absolute confidence in the discretion of the leaders of the latter, the applied sociologist is only occasionally faced with the question of whether he should grant organizational anonymity. If he is faced with it, it would seem perfectly proper to grant it, since the function of exposing the organization to public scrutiny will probably not be served by applied research anyway.

The propriety of granting organizational anonymity is especially persuasive when the organization being studied is a subordinate part of the organization sponsoring the research. Thus a sociological investigator cannot become party to a study that might reveal to the administration of a company the particular working crews that are most critical of that administration. It is especially important in such cases to grant anonymity, because the persons approached may feel that they cannot with impunity refuse to participate in the study.

As in the case of persons, the sociologist must be sure that the identity of the organization is really disguised. All too often informal channels of communication operate to reveal that which is supposed to be secret. The main question for the sociologist becomes how far he must go in protecting the identity of collectivities.

Pure sociologists sometimes enter into consent agreements with representatives of organizations to study only certain aspects of these organizations in return for being permitted access to them. Such agreements are unlikely in the case of applied sociology, but must, of course, be honored if they have been entered into. Even if not mentioned in the agreement, confidential information must be respected.

The very difficult question whether pure sociologists may ethically penetrate organizations that bar all study of them is not faced by the applied researcher. Since he has not the high calling of developing abstract scientific knowledge, he has no claim to the special privileges that are sometimes enjoyed by those so engaged.

Another ethical problem that has been moot among pure sociologists is not likely to plague applied sociologists. This is the question of whether communities that are the objects of research have the right to anonymity. Obviously city governments or their departments may want to conceal the fact that they are making local studies, but, if known, there will be no doubt about what community they are studying. Perhaps occasionally a business firm will want to study a community where it may wish to locate a plant. In such case the argument against granting anonymity that is persuasive for the pure sociologist—that the public has a right to know the truth about communities—does not hold, since the results of the applied research will not be made generally available anyway. The obligation of the pure sociologist to make his results known is what raises the question of whether the identity of communities should be concealed.

Since the person or organization employing the applied sociologist has full property rights in the research results, the same principles with respect to communication and publication apply that were discussed for the consultant. The sociologist may, of course, make agreements in advance with the sponsor that will permit him to publish some or all of the results with or without the sponsor's later blessing. But if he has not obtained such permission in writing he cannot legitimately demand it at the end of the investigation.

Just as the sociologist has ethical obligations to the employer, the employer has ethical obligations not to distort the results of the research, especially in any published form. It is the part of prudence for a sociologist undertaking applied research to insist upon an agreement in advance that he shall be the sole judge of the scientific accuracy of any report of the findings and that no report will be published of which he has not first approved.

Conclusion

Throughout this discussion it has been apparent that the peculiar ethical problems of the applied sociologist stem mainly from the fact that he has two masters, his profession and his employer, whereas the pure sociologist has only his profession. (A university that employs a pure sociologist is assumed to want only that he be a worthy professional.) But it is clear that the profession as master is not concerned merely with technical skill and relations to one's co-workers and one's students. A profession is entrusted with societal functions, and its members must serve societal interests and be sensitive to societal values.

There are, then, three sets of people to whom the sociologist working in applied settings has obligations: his sociological confreres; those for whom he serves as consultant, practitioner, or researcher; and the general public. We have noted instances where the interests of the first two have to give way to the last. For example, even though it would be to the immediate advantage of sociology as a discipline, and to a business for which research is being done, for a sociologist secretly to try out various modes of influencing workers it is clearly unethical to do so. The dignity of men in a democratic society forbids treating them as unknowing guinea pigs.

When all is said and done, the ethical priorities for the applied sociologist are quite clear: Serve first the moral principles of your society, which include the universal decencies of mankind. Serve next the peculiar ethical standards that have been worked out by your sociological colleagues. Serve last the claims of any client or organization that has employed you.

NOTE: *I wish to express my deep indebtedness to the other members of the American Sociological Association's Committee on Professional Ethics, 1960–1964—Drs. Bernard Barber, Neal Gross, Robert A. Nisbet, and Albert J. Reiss, Jr.—for their willingness to let me draw upon the Draft Code of Ethics we jointly produced. Readers will understand that the prescriptive phrases used in this chapter stem not from any personal sense of moral authority but from the consensus reached in that committee.*

Evaluating Social Action Programs

HERBERT H. HYMAN

CHARLES R. WRIGHT

chapter **27**

Introduction

Ours is an age of planned social action directed to the solution of every conceivable type of problem. Programmatic or fragmentary attempts to solve current problems are found in such varied fields as business, labor, politics, law, health and welfare, education, the military, religion, and the family. Consider programs of training and rehabilitation of workers, supervisors, and executives; political campaigns; rehabilitation of criminals; public health campaigns; wars on poverty; military training; mass information campaigns; cultural exchange programs; reduction of intergroup conflict; reduction of prejudice; treatment of mental illness; treatment of alcoholism; programs to combat delinquency; and the adjustment of the aged.

Both governmental and private sponsors of action programs have come

741

to expect an accounting of a program's achievements. Critics must be answered, and usually their satisfaction requires more than subjective impressions by a program's administrators. Furthermore, the directors of a program often feel the need themselves for an assessment of its achievements and shortcomings. Evaluation has come to be accepted, even sought, as an accompaniment to rational action.

What more practical use of sociology could there be than to improve the methods of evaluation and to apply them in practice? The betterment of society has always inspired our field. We may work toward that end not only by scholarly analysis of problems or by direct effort at social action, but also in a scientific and yet active way as the evaluative service attached to the larger enterprise. In the process, all our skills as methodologists will be challenged, and, in the end, we will enlarge a whole branch of experimental design, enrich knowledge of social change, and hopefully accelerate its pace.

Evaluation means many things to different people, however, and as a consequence, the term *evaluation research* covers a wide range of activities in the assessment of social action. We shall limit our attention to those forms of evaluation which involve fact-finding about the results of planned social action. Even this limited definition requires further refinement; we restrict the term *evaluation research* to fact-finding methods that yield evidence that is objective, systematic, and comprehensive.[1] Our concern is with the methodology of evaluation research and the general contribution that a social-science orientation can make to the evaluation of social action programs.

It is neither possible nor necessary to review here a complete methodology of evaluation research. A few examples of books and monographs which describe the application of social research procedures to problems of evaluation may guide the reader.[2] Campbell and Stanley analyze the properties of a series of experimental designs and create some new ones which are appropriate to the design of evaluations. Hyman, Wright, and Hopkins develop certain basic principles of evaluation and illustrate their application to four studies of a program for training for citizenship. Hayes has prepared, under UNESCO auspices, "a manual for the use of field workers" concerned with evaluating development projects. A special issue of the UNESCO *International Social Science Bulletin* is devoted to discussions of evaluation techniques in a variety of fields such as intergroup relations, induced technological change, exchange of persons, fundamental education, mass-media campaigns, and adult education. Evaluation in mental health is the subject of an extensive review by a Subcommittee of the National Advisory Mental Health Council. Riecken discusses basic problems of program evaluation in his case study of the effects of volunteer summer work camps for young Americans. Powers and Witmer present a detailed evaluation of a community delinquency-prevention program.

Limitations of space demand that we be selective in our focus on methodological problems. The basic method of evaluation research, in our view, has five major aspects, each of which involves a body of methodological principles.[3] These are: (1) the conceptualization and measurement of the objectives of the action program and of unanticipated relevant outcomes; (2) the formulation of a research design and of the criteria for proof of the effectiveness of a program; (3) the research procedures themselves, including provisions for estimating and reducing errors in measurement; (4) problems of index construction and the proper evaluation of effectiveness; and (5) procedures for understanding the findings on effectiveness or ineffectiveness.

The basic principles of research design, the measurement procedures appropriate to evaluation, and the modes of analysis suited to appraising and understanding the effectiveness of programs of social action have all been treated thoroughly elsewhere. Here we shall set the problem in broader perspective and present a different kind of methodological discourse.

We shall first clarify and codify certain features of the independent variable in evaluation research, that is, "the program," and discuss the implications of these features for the conceptualization and execution of a project. Next we shall consider problems in the conceptualization of the dependent variable, that is, the program's intended and unintended effects, and elaborate some formerly neglected aspects of this phase of evaluation. Then we shall turn to broad questions of study design, considering first the need for comparative studies and second the value of research designs that allow for continuity, replication, and longitudinal research—designs that have been too rarely used in evaluation studies. Throughout the discussion we shall draw upon cases of research which not only illustrate the point at hand but also serve to demonstrate the variety of uses to which evaluation has been put. In a final section we shall view in detail an actual evaluation study, which will exemplify the principles and show the uses of sociology in action.

The Varieties of Evaluation: Concepts

Evaluation is the methodological accompaniment to planned social action. By playing the accompaniment, the sociologist replaces the little experiments of his own making by the great experiments in social change that are underway. He must appreciate the opportunity and grab it. By his own inventiveness he must graft onto the ongoing activity an appropriate and feasible experimental design that rigorously tests the effectiveness of the program. Let us assume that the right design can be invented and well executed despite the exigencies of the situation within which the evaluator must work. There are other real difficulties. The great social experiments are not neat and tidy. They are not created just to produce one little and temporary effect. Thus arise the difficulties of conceptualizing the dependent variables or effects of such an experiment. But big changes call for big measures. The independent variables must be powerful, many in number, and long in duration. Thus arises another major difficulty. What is it that has been put to the test? To this question we turn first.

CONCEPTUALIZING THE PROGRAM

"A Program"—A Most Deceptive Term Following the model of an experiment may mislead an evaluator; deceived by the term *"a program,"* he may pursue an illusion. All too often a program is simply a statement on paper of what the planners in an agency hoped to do that has never been fully translated into action by the field staff. Taking the word for the deed, an evaluator may try to observe the effects of a nonexistent treatment. By contrast, no experimenter could ever deceive himself so greatly as to make observations of the effects of a nonexistent stimulus, since he would know that he had not yet initiated the procedure.

Consider a government program which one of us was once called upon to evaluate during World War II. Posters containing various motivational appeals to the civilian population were to be widely distributed in many communities by members of a national voluntary organization. The process by which persuasive communication does or does not lead to mass action is a subtle matter and might have been invoked by an evaluator in designing the inquiry, but in this case such considerations were irrelevant. Although thousands of the posters had been printed and shipped all over the country, they simply sat in local depots for lack of any volunteers to distribute them. Where a program has no input, no output of effects can ensue, or any output observed must be attributed to some other factor.

The discrepancy between program as plan and program as reality is a matter of degree. Although a completely unrealized program like the one mentioned above may be rare, partially realized programs are common. Consider the findings from a survey of the rural health facilities in Egypt around 1950.[4] A program to meet the need for health facilities was to be developed on the basis of the survey, and an evaluation was then to be conducted. The survey revealed that a substantial program had already been established:

> There are at present 205 rural health centers in Egypt. Each unit is expected to have, under the present plan of operation, staff of one doctor, one nurse midwife, three assistant nurse midwives, one assistant nurse, one laboratory technician, one sanitarian, and one clerk. The unit is expected to serve 15,000 to 20,000 of population.[5]

The investigators might have moved directly to an evaluation of the existing program, but fortunately they conducted "a tabulation . . . of the personnel status and operating capacity of these health centers to determine what personnel deficiencies existed and to form a basis for planning training activities for the centers." [6] (See Table 27–1.)

TABLE 27–1. *Number of Rural Health Centers Lacking Personnel in the Indicated Category**

DATE OF ANALYSIS	DOC-TORS	SANI-TARIANS	LAB. TECH.	MID-WIVES	ASST. MID-WIVES	ASST. NURSES	CLERKS	UNITS HAVING NO PERSONNEL
Feb. 1951	58	90	37	180	90	127	91	53
Feb. 1952	30	78	7	179	69	173	97	3

* Weir *et al., op. cit.,* p. 97; adapted from Table 27.

Although the plan for the improvement of public health may have been fine, the program was not in actual operation in many instances, as the data in the table indicate. For example, 180 of the 204 rural health centers had no nurse midwives, and most lacked assistant nurses, while others lacked physicians or other medical personnel essential to the program.

The evaluator must incorporate into his design various measures of input. While logically these constitute measures of the independent variables or program, they may at times obviate the need for any measures of the dependent variables or effects, since a program with little or no input cannot, by definition, be producing results. They also clarify subsequent findings on change in the dependent variables and provide an index of the efficiency of a program, which might be defined as the effect per unit of expenditure. A program that produces a moderate effect for a small input may be better than a program that produces greater effects, but at a prohibitive cost.

Financial expenditures are one simple measure of input. For example, a community-development project in India established that the actual expenditures for one year of operation of the program were only 18 per cent of the planned budget.[7]

Units of input other than money may be used. In the Egyptian evaluation, man-hours actually worked were a highly informative measure. A tabulation made in one center "for a period of one month . . . indicated what each individual was doing each hour of the normal working day. Although all personnel were on duty from 8:30 A.M. to 2 P.M., it was found that on an average no category of personnel were pursuing useful work for over two and one-half hours per day." [8] Where materials are to be distributed as part of the program, the actual amounts reaching the target group are useful measures. In the Indian community-development program some 520 units of improved seed were to be distributed in a given year in a particular area, but in the first six months only 171 such units of seed were actually distributed.[9]

Although the manipulations by an experimenter may not always create in his subjects the intended social and psychological states, he at least does know in objective terms what the independent variables were. By contrast, the evaluator may be tracing the effects of an actual program which is very different in character from the one outlined on paper.

The discrepancy between original plan and operative program is understandable. Any plan is bound to suffer some modification as it is translated into a reality. It may have to be changed radically when circumstances dictate it. Also consider the scale of social action programs. They may last six weeks or six years—not the six hours or six days that is the life of an experiment. Time is bound to work its changes.

A program is often merely a sketch that has to be completed. The evaluator may have the sketch in hand, but to capture the total contents of the operative program in order to know what is causing the effects observed is very different from stating the nature of an experimental treatment. Consider a few of the independent variables employed in Cincinnati in a 1947 program to promote popular support for the United Nations: 12,868 people were reached through the Parent-Teachers Associations which devoted programs to the topic of world understanding; 14,000 children in the Weekday Church Schools held a World Community Day Program; 10,000 members of the Catholic Parent-Teacher Association were exhorted by their archbishop to support the United Nations; the radio stations broadcast facts about the United Nations, one of them scheduling spot programs 150 times a week; 225 meetings were served with literature and special speakers; in all, 59,588 pieces of literature were distributed and 2,800 clubs were reached by speakers; hundreds of documentary films were shown; and the slogan "Peace Begins with the United Nations—the United Nations Begins with You" was exhibited everywhere, in every imaginable form—on blotters, matchbooks, streetcar cards, and so on.[10]

It is ironic, but this massive campaign had very little effect. Suppose, however, that the campaign had been successful, but that the evaluators had not been foresighted enough to document in detail what had been described in capsule form as an "information campaign." Then it would have been impossible to identify the magic treatment which produced the effects.

Sometimes the fact that the treatment to be evaluated is extended in time makes the use of the singular term "*a program*," misleading. Other times, it is the extension of a program in *space* that leads to many treatments being labeled as a single program, with inevitable dangers of ambiguity in the conclusions. Take as an example of the latter the evaluation of a program intended to improve farm-management practices. The program lasted for six years and covered ten counties. Within each county, the major method involved varied forms of guidance by agricultural agents. Despite the fact that the leadership was fairly unbroken—after five years the agents who had initiated the program in seven counties were still involved—and despite the fact that the agents were given uniform training in a series of special training schools, there was considerable variability in the treatments administered to the farmers of the different counties. Table 27–2 presents some aspects of the operative program to show its multiform character and the variability between counties.

TABLE 27–2. *Variations in Execution of a Farm-Management Program in Ten Counties of New York State**

TOPICS IN EDUCATION PROGRAM	% OF COUNTIES IN WHICH ELEMENT OF PROGRAM REACHED A MAJORITY OF PARTICIPANTS
Analyzing farm records	100%
Soil testing	80
Principles of fertilization	70
Selection of seed	60
Culling of herd	50
Planning rotation	40
Partnership arrangements	20
Breeding programs	10
Recommendations for disease	0

* F. D. Alexander and J. W. Longest, *Evaluation of the Farm Management Phase of the Farm and Home Management Program in New York State.* (Ithaca: New York State Extension Service, State Colleges of Agriculture and Home Economics, 1962), adapted from pp. 15–17.

While the evaluation revealed that each of the topics in the educational program was at least mentioned in every one of the ten counties, the table shows that some topics were not discussed extensively enough to reach the majority of the target group in many of the counties. If we examine not merely the content of the educational program, but the teaching method the different agricultural agents employed, we observe even more dramatically that the program differed markedly between counties (see Table 27–3).

Still another index documents the variability in the operation of the program among the ten counties. For the four-year period 1956–1959, the amount of their total working time that the staff devoted to this program averaged 17 per cent, but the range over the ten counties was from 8 per cent to 28 per cent.[11]

Such findings illustrate the multiplicity of actual programs that operated

TABLE 27-3.

METHOD OF TEACHING	NUMBER OF COUNTIES IN WHICH EMPLOYED
Farm and home visits	10
College publications	9
Farm walks	5
Tours	3

under the rubric of one farm-management program because the program extended over ten counties. How much more variety one would find in a program of even greater scale! Consider the community-development program which was established in 1952 for all of India. In its first year it comprised 55 community-development projects, each of which contained three community-development blocks, for a total of 165 such blocks. Each block covered on the average 100 villages with a total population of 60,000 to 70,000 people and had a complement of about 38 field workers.

By 1959, 2,405 development blocks were functioning, covering some 303,000 villages and a population of 165 million people. Imagine the variability that might characterize the actual program and the performance of the staff in a given block, let alone the variety within a project or in the program for all of India.[12]

A large-scale program that is widely extended in space can be evaluated, however, by using proper sampling. For example, in an evaluation of the project in the Ghosi Community Development Block in India, which included 288 villages and a population of 120,000 people, the researchers stratified villages by size of population and then selected two villages from each of three strata, for a total sample of six villages. Within villages, households were stratified by various criteria, and a small number was drawn from each stratum for intensive study.[13]

The total or average effect demonstrated for all areas is perhaps the best single expression of a program's worth, since it measures the program as it operated under a wide variety of conditions. But what is *it* whose value has then been appraised? An average description based on all the different programs may at times be a meaningless abstraction. The evaluator is best advised to describe the various local programs that are operating and, depending on their variety, to make a decision that his inquiry is an evaluation of a single program, a series of replications, or a series of comparative evaluations. (The latter approaches will be reviewed in a later section of this chapter.)

A program that is extended in time or space has, at least, a unity despite its multiplicity. Some thread of identity and some common purpose runs throughout, if only because there are central directives emanating from one social agency. Therein lies the justification for the term, *a program*. By contrast, there is another type of operating situation into which an evaluator may blunder in which the notion of "a program" is extremely deceptive. The researcher may attempt a single evaluation of independent programs by different agencies with different goals because his powers of abstraction lead him to see them all as representative of some common category. Then he supplies a common yardstick by which to judge them all and evaluates them as a single program.

As a case in point, consider Philip E. Jacob's work: *Changing Values in College: An Exploratory Study of the Impact of College Teaching*, in which he concluded that basic values remained unchanged for most students at most American colleges. Our concern here is not with the accuracy of the finding, but rather to ask whether such an inquiry should be formulated as a single evaluation. Is it just or wise to test hundreds of separate private institutions with different goals against the common yardstick of some particular set of values, simply because they all deserve in some degree the name "college"? Admittedly, the federal government or a large foundation concerned with some overriding educational policy might call upon an evaluator for a grand study. Thus, in his excellent critique of the Jacob study, Barton takes the position that "evaluation research need not be limited to the practical purposes of administrators, . . . it may be undertaken to look into consequences which independent researchers or outside sponsors consider important." [14] However, one may entertain the alternative view that the common yardstick is arbitrary and the framework of the single evaluation inappropriate. In any case, it is clear that all sorts of problems follow on the decision to evaluate diverse colleges in terms of the value changes they produce.

For example, Jacob is forced to wrestle with problems he has created for himself: "What value or values . . . should *a college* appropriately seek? What is the relative significance of intellectual, aesthetic, moral, social, or religious values as outcomes of college experience?" [15] His quandary centers exclusively on which values should be used as a common yardstick, and not at all on the issue we pose: whether different colleges *should* be measured against a single yardstick. His very usage, *a* college, *the* teacher, ignores the variability of the programs and staffs subsumed under these abstract terms. In his Foreword to Barton's critique of the Jacob study, Lazarsfeld remarks on the controversies that the original work inspired and notes that one line of criticism has been "that it is not the task of *the* college to inculcate values." [16] Perhaps the easiest way for the evaluator to handle this criticism is to note that some colleges have accepted this task, while others have not, and to guide himself accordingly.

But even if one were to adopt change in values as the common yardstick appropriate for evaluating diverse colleges, one still does not have to regard such research as a single evaluation. It might be more illuminating to conceive of the research as a series of comparative evaluations for colleges with sharply contrasted programs, target groups, settings, and staffs and as replications of the same evaluation for the colleges with "identical" programs.

Cyclical Operations, Another Deceptive Feature of "a Program" A program that is compact in time and space, or under centralized control, may seem to create little ambiguity for conceptualization and subsequent evaluation. But what superficially appears to be one homogeneous program may in fact be many variations on a program that has been operated over a long period by a well-established action agency. The general description and specifications of the program may or may not correspond to the instance which the researcher evaluates, and the researcher should not confuse the general and the particular. Depending on which segment of the life history of the agency the researcher cuts out for study, he has a more or less arbitrary sampling of the run of subjects, staff, program, facilities or site, larger environment within which the program is imbedded, and the stage of efficiency which the whole operation has reached. In the examples discussed earlier, the evaluator is usually studying many different programs, but may mistakenly construe them as one. Here he is in the opposite, but still not enviable, position of studying one instance and construing it as typical of many.

The model is not so clear for programs which do not follow a regular cycle. Some established agencies operate their programs whenever the need or impulse dictates, intermittently whenever members of a target group present themselves, or continuously upon a never-ending flow of subjects, as in the case of hospitals or prisons. There are no sharp breaks in the pattern, but nevertheless there is change. The model, however, is very clear in cyclical programs such as college education, where at regular intervals new cohorts of subjects from some larger target population are exposed to the program, move through a full cycle, and depart. The intervals between cycles provide ample opportunity for radical changes and sharply delimit the specific program that has been evaluated. For example, some of the colleges which Jacob evaluated are very old institutions, and the actual evaluations represent a very small sample of the many cycles of program that have passed.[17]

The evaluator of a cycle of a well-established program should try to assess differences between the subjects, staff, program, site, larger environment, and stage of efficiency reached in his cycle and earlier cycles. Sometimes it helps simply to ask why he was called in on this cycle, since the answer may document the fact that some major turning point has occurred or suggest the suspicion that the cycle selected for evaluation was a hand-picked one.

Ideally, the researcher should conduct several evaluations of different cycles of the program in order to generalize his conclusions. Depending on the similarity of the situations, he might regard these either as a series of replications or as comparative studies. This may appear to be a formidable assignment, but studying a second cycle is not nearly so hard as doing a brand new evaluation. A good deal of the work has become routinized, and many of the difficult technical decisions have to be made only once. The replications can even be carried out in abbreviated form through the study of alumni or cohorts from earlier cycles. Such studies not only serve as approximations to the full-scale evaluation but also provide a way of studying the long-term persistence of effects, a problem of great importance in many evaluations. The gains from replications will be illustrated by the case study of the Encampment for Citizenship, to be reviewed later, wherein it was also established that the alumni design, despite its crudities, yields certain valid information.

Sometimes an evaluator is called in on the very first cycle of a program. It is certainly reasonable to assume that the program is not yet functioning at maximum efficiency, but it is also reasonable to believe that the early cycles of any program are peculiar. Enthusiasm fires the new enterprise. The staff has not yet become stale and tired. They are often bold and innovative and willing to risk their livelihood on something new, although there is also the possibility that they are castoffs who cannot find positions anywhere else. Where entry is voluntary, the first cohort of subjects may also be highly committed, since they are entering something new and unproved. Newcomb's classic study of Bennington, which in its structure, if not intent, was clearly an evaluation, conveys the feel of the first cycle of a program.[18] When Newcomb began his measurements in 1935, the senior class he studied was the very first cohort in the history of the institution, it having been founded upon their admission as freshmen in 1932.

There are, of course, occasional one-shot programs in which the first cycle is the only one. A special and critical situation may exist which, hopefully, is solved forever by the one-time application of the program, or an evaluation may demonstrate conclusively that the program should never be repeated. There are also occasional programs fraught with such great consequences that fortunately they are set in motion only once. The evaluation of strategic bombing in World War II, more particularly of the atom bombing of Japan, perhaps provides such an example.[19] But in most instances the evaluator of a first cycle has to face the question of the effectiveness of future cycles. Most action agencies initiating a new program hope that it will live forever and be repeated on every new target group in need of its attention.

Overlapping Cycles   Cyclical programs exhibit in sharpest form a feature of many continuing programs that is very important for the evaluator to consider, but difficult for him to handle. Consider the Encampment for

Citizenship, which operates a series of six-week summer cycles, each separated from the next by a ten-month interval. Since the program is small in magnitude and short in duration, each cohort is trained as a separate group and is insulated during training from earlier and later cohorts by the intervals between cycles. By contrast, higher education is characterized by overlapping cycles. Such programs are large in magnitude and years in duration; cohorts far along in their training have not left the program before new cohorts appear. Unless special methods are employed to insulate the cohorts, overlapping cycles provide a great deal of opportunity for those at different stages of training to make contact with each other and for the advanced to train the beginners. Training via interacting cohorts may even be facilitated by special methods. Thus the attending physician has already trained the resident who helps to train the intern, and the professor has trained the teaching assistant who helps to train the graduate student.

In continuing programs that do not have regular cycles, a similar situation prevails. In the mental hospital or prison, subjects in advanced stages of treatment or rehabilitation may be influencing the recent arrivals. It is also true of all noncontinuing programs which treat their subjects in batches or groups, rather than one at a time, that, unless prevented, there is much contact between subjects. But in contrast with the overlapping cycle, all the members of a noncontinuing program are equally naïve, and the training or socialization process is less potent, although still present in some degree.

Barton describes all these processes succinctly in his review of the Jacob study:

> One of the problems of which Jacob is most clearly aware is that the influence of "college" upon students is that of a complex institution, consisting not only of classroom instruction by a faculty but of other relationships to the faculty and of other people besides the faculty, notably class-mates and students of older age-grades. . . . At Bennington the juniors and seniors . . . had assimilated the very liberal attitudes of the faculty, and served as a powerful reinforcement to the faculty influence.[20]

Evaluations necessarily often include in the final score the effects of contacts between subjects and the training they render each other. Should the program receive the credit, and, if not, how shall the contribution of the other variables be extracted? Jacob's dilemma, as Barton notes, was that he

> originally focussed his study on "curricular, as distinct from 'extra-curricular' or 'co-curricular influences'" . . . but the influence of "the network of interlocking factors affecting students' values became increasingly apparent" so

that the notion of the "climate" of institutions was brought in, and especially the influence of the "prevailing sentiment of upperclassmen." [21]

We are presented with one more deceptive feature of the term *a program*. Interaction, socialization, and informal groups are the spice of life for the sociologist and social psychologist. Thus, they are prone to see such accompaniments to a program as integral features. But taking the role of an *evaluator* may call for a different perspective and some difficult judgments. Barton, sensitive to all the subtleties of these interaction processes, never once raises the evaluator's question as to whether Jacob *should* have tried to exclude these influences.

The interaction of cohorts certainly accompanies any program with overlapping cycles. Is it, however, an element of a program or simply accidental to its operation? Experimental designs and control groups are used by sophisticated evaluators in order to subtract from the final score of the program the contribution made by such extraneous factors as external events or growth caused by the passage of time. By the same token, why not subtract the training contribution of the older cohort in assessing the intrinsic worth of the program? Perhaps if a group of younger and older subjects were simply brought together without any program at all, the same effects would have occurred. In this light, evaluations which follow the classic control-group design may well commit an error if the control group is simply a number of equivalent individuals who have remained isolated from one another. The influence of sheer interaction will not have been subtracted by such a design.

Our formulation may at first appear eccentric. By a mere change in terminology, it may become more acceptable. Substitute for interaction the term "contamination" and the image of an older cohort "corrupting the young" rather than training them. Such is often the case in programs operating in prisons, military establishments, and even educational institutions.[22] Barton reminds us that at some of the colleges Jacob studied, "qualitative evidence suggests that the prestigeful student leaders and student institutions generally maintained values strongly opposed to those of the faculty in general, and succeeded in countering faculty influence to a great extent." [23] The professors at these colleges would hardly be inclined to regard such influences as part of their programs, and in their judgment the final score should not include such factors and thereby detract from their good evaluation.

How shall the evaluator reach a reasonable decision on when such influences—whatever their direction—are part of a program? A general answer to the question is not possible, but a rational decision can be made in each case simply by asking whether the agency intentionally designed its program so as to create or facilitate such interaction and training. If it did, the program should be given credit for the effects produced, since in such instances the interaction was not an accidental or unavoidable accompaniment, but rather an intended part of the program itself. Thus, the communal life of the Encampment for Citizenship is organized precisely to insure certain kinds of interaction and mutual training. Recruitment insures ethnic heterogeneity; housing arrangements further interracial contacts; workshops expose the individual to group influences. The Encampment even tries to bridge the interval between nonoverlapping cycles and to facilitate interaction between cohorts from different years. By meetings, visits, and correspondence throughout the year, interaction is encouraged, if only via the symbolic presence of others. Alumni are used to recruit new cohorts which may then be carried along by anticipatory socialization, even before they are exposed to the summer program.

In the instance of the Encampment, the evaluator's decision to regard interaction between subjects as a part of the program was easy, but the decision can be much more difficult. The safest course for the evaluator is to try to separate the contribution of processes like interaction so that any decision he makes is reversible. He can add these effects into the accounts or subtract them. Perhaps there are other components of a total program whose effects also must be isolated.

CONCEPTUALIZING ASPECTS OF A PROGRAM: THE
INDEPENDENT VARIABLES IN AN EVALUATION

In the attempt to conceptualize "a program," the evaluator may be led astray by the very term itself. He may think of the treatment and forget the context in which it is imbedded. Except in such rare instances as mass-media programs, the treatment is applied by a staff.[24] Perhaps it is the staff that is the potent force for change, rather than the program employed. With one turnover of personnel, the findings of an evaluation may no longer apply. Or perhaps a very good program, damaged by a poor staff, is curtailed because the evaluator has not distinguished between the two. To be sure, the staff is a part of any operative program, and its effect must be incorporated in any evaluation, but the evaluator must attempt to isolate its contribution. Where a program is cyclical, replication of an evaluation provides a way to do so, since turnover occurs in all organizations.[25] For noncyclical programs and one-time evaluations, a solution can only be approximate and inferential. By ingenious types of measurement and internal analysis, the evaluator must try to estimate the personal impact of the staff on the subjects who are treated.[26]

The staff and the program are contained within a site, and the ecology of sites often contributes to the effectiveness of programs and should be conceptualized by an evaluator. Many programs approach their target groups in their natural environment so that the site might more strictly be defined as a property of the subjects rather than of the program. For many other programs subjects are removed from their natural environment, taken for treatment to a specialized site whose character is carefully controlled, and then returned to their normal locations. The specialized site is in the strictest sense the property of the program. The process of removal, temporary residence, and return may be voluntary or forced, but in either case may account for the immediate effects and their subsequent transference.[27]

In estimating the contribution the site makes to the effectiveness of a program, the evaluator may often have to use inferential means. A more direct test is possible for cyclical programs, since minor rearrangements within the site occur frequently and even radical changes in site occur occasionally. Thus, the isolation which characterized the residential site of the Encampment for Citizenship appeared to be an important factor. It insulated the campers during training from undesirable influences from the larger society and increased interaction within the little community.[28] An opportunity to examine the influence of this factor arose in a later cycle of the program, when a second Encampment was established in a new site where the walls around the community were much more permeable.

Staff, site, and treatment are three elements of a program. The many examples already presented establish the fact that *the* treatment in most programs is anything but a unitary variable. The treatment is so lengthy, complex, and multiform that it demands analysis, but in its sprawl it often defies our powers of conceptualization. For sure, the distinction between the didactic element and the communal element of treatment should be made so as to evaluate the contribution of interaction between subjects and that of mutual training.

The programs that a researcher may be called upon to evaluate are so varied in content that no common guide to conceptualization is possible. But all treatments can be ordered along a few formal dimensions which are relevant to their effectiveness. The temporal dimension is an obvious example, and yet it is frequently neglected. We have in mind not only the duration of treatment but whether it is continuous or intermittent. If intermittent, is it regular in its phasing, or does it employ a system of "periodic reinforcement," which B. F. Skinner regards as a potent force for learning?

Conceptualizing a program in terms of staff, site, didactic and communal elements of treatment, and temporal pattern only provides a schema within which the evaluator can introduce further conceptual refinements. In our judgment, he should not push these refinements too far. He must certainly describe a program and its main elements, but sometimes that is where he should stop. Such description and basic conceptualization is quite different from endless dissection of a complex treatment which an agency regards as a functional unity.

Evaluation is action research first, scholarly inquiry only secondarily. To conceptualize a program variable whose influence cannot be put to any empirical test is a purely speculative exercise which has no implications for the current evaluation, although it may inspire a future evaluation.[29] Even to establish empirically the influence of a particular variable contained within the program which is beyond the powers of the action agency to modify is an academic finding. The evaluator should focus on the manipulable and the testable.

If our formulation appears too crude for the sociologist gifted in conceptual analysis, let him now turn his attention to the realm of effects. Here all his powers of conceptualization are demanded, since the refinement of dependent variables is essential.

CONCEPTUALIZING EFFECTS

Planned social action implies goals, and it may seem an obvious step for the evaluator to take such goals as given and to concentrate on other aspects of the research procedure. Nothing could be more wrong. Most social action programs have multiple objectives, some of which are very broad in nature, ambiguously stated, and possibly not shared by all persons who are responsible for the program. For example, it is reported that the basic aims of community development in India, under the First Five Year Plan, included, among other goals, the desire "to initiate and direct a process of integrated cultural change aimed at transforming the social and economic life of the villages."

"The aim of the movement was to create in the rural population a burning desire for a higher standard of living and the will to live better." [30]

How can the researcher hope to measure success in achieving so broad a goal as the transformation of "the social and economic life of the villages"? What constitutes "a burning desire"?

Basic concepts and goals are often elusive and vague. As Jahoda has observed about the evaluation of programs in the field of mental health: "there exists no psychologically meaningful and, from the point of view of research, operational description of what is commonly considered to constitute mental health." [31] Witmer and Tufts point to similar difficulties in conceptualization in the field of delinquency prevention:

> Despite the attractiveness of the idea, delinquency prevention is an elusive concept. What is to be prevented? Who is to be deterred? Are we talking about the numerous acts that most children commit that are "anti-social" in character; about the unconventional activities of "flaming" youth, "gone" youth, or youth otherwise disapproved of; about "official" delinquency, with emphasis on that which is of serious nature and likely to be continued unless something is done about it?
>
> Does prevention mean stopping misbehavior before it occurs, and, if so, what misbehavior? Does it mean keeping misbehavior from becoming pro-

gressively worse and more frequent? Or does prevention have a kind of public health connotation in that the emphasis is on underlying environmental conditions rather than on individual cases?

Each of these questions has been answered affirmatively by one or another proponent of delinquency prevention. And each has different implications for program planning and for likelihood of successful results.[32]

Even seemingly limited, concrete programs with specific aims pose difficulties. Riecken, for example, in evaluating a summer work camp program of the American Friends Service Committee reviewed a number of official documents describing the program and concluded that "we have been unable to discover in these writings a simple, clearly and comprehensively stated set of aims that will meet with the universal endorsement of the directors of the program."[33]

One consequence of such difficulties in conceptualization is that a great deal of the initial labor in evaluation research consists of attempts to formulate in a clear and measurable fashion a list of goals which can serve as the basis for determining the program's relative success. There is no codified set of principles to guide the researcher in the formulation of relevant, let alone critical, concepts and their accompanying operational indicators.[34] In this phase of evaluation there is no discounting the importance of an imaginative approach by the researcher. Although certain objectives can be readily measured—a program aimed at extending rural roads, for example, can be evaluated in part by counting the miles of new roads constructed—most objectives call for more sophisticated formulations. Furthermore, not all objectives are of equal importance, and many can be translated into a variety of alternative concepts.

Even though social science cannot provide the evaluator with hard and fast rules for formulating concepts and selecting among alternative formulations, it can at least encourage him to give systematic consideration to the conceptualization of the program's effects in terms of locus, time, and unanticipated consequences.

The Locus of Effects As we have noted elsewhere, a first principle in conceptualizing the objectives of an action program is "that some attempt must be made to analyze the kinds of formal entities that are involved, to locate the *regions* within which the concepts are set."[35] By "region" we mean initially whether the concepts pertain to an individual, an aggregate of individuals, a group, a total community or society, or a combination of these. To illustrate, a delinquency-prevention program might aim at "building the character" of individuals; at reducing the total number of delinquents in an area, or the proportion of delinquents in a particular social category; at changing the habits of juvenile gangs; at changing the community's ability to cope with potential delinquency through developing a more effective organizational structure for detecting and removing conditions which cause delinquency; or at some combination of such goals.[36]

The region of effects is important for determining both the kind of evidence of effectiveness to look for and the criteria of success. To continue the illustration, a program aimed at individual character development would look for evidence of changes within the individual or in his conduct. In this case, the degree of improvement in the individual is the gauge of success, and perhaps one "soul saved" is sufficient to consider the program successful. A program aimed at aggregates of individuals could, of course, simply add together the numbers of individuals who have improved, perhaps assessing effectiveness in terms of the difference between this sum and the number who might have improved without the program. An alternative which is common in practice is to collect evidence on net changes in individual attributes, again comparing such gains with what might have been achieved without the program. Thus, one could compare the proportion of boys who express certain antisocial attitudes before participating in a program with the proportion expressing such attitudes after the program. The net improvement could be compared with similar data from a control group. This focus on net gain or loss ignores the individual directions of change. Certain boys may have become more antisocial, while others became less, and others remained unchanged; it does not matter, for the evaluation is in terms of changes in the proportion of the boys having such attitudes. As another example, if a program aimed at changes in social groups, the evaluator might seek information about changes in such group characteristics as leadership, social norms, and organized activities. Finally, programs concerned with total communities or societies might require evidence on changes in the social environment that are believed to be related to delinquency (improving housing conditions, for example); or they might follow through in a second stage of evaluation to determine whether such changes in environment actually result in a reduction of delinquency in the community.

In addition to deciding which types of effect are central to the program's objectives, the evaluator must collect as evidence of effects the type of data that matches best with the region of effects as originally conceived. Evidence on net changes in attitudes in a group, for example, would be inappropriate for evaluating a program whose effectiveness was conceived in terms of individual case improvement; data from longitudinal case studies would match that region of effects better.

Once the major regions of programmatic objectives have been located, it is then necessary to specify and elaborate subregions of concepts within each major region selected. Here the evaluator is guided by the theoretical orientations of the relevant social disciplines. Psychology, for example, is rich in models of the individual, distinguishing the subregion of overt conduct from such inner states of the individual as his values, opinions, attitudes, motivations, interests, information, and skills. Sociology, social psychology, and anthropology provide guides to subregions concerning groups which would be salient to the evaluation of programs aiming at group change. Such group properties include the character of social norms, formal and informal organization, cohesiveness, and morale. A sociological orientation can also direct the evaluator to further specification of subregions of community change, such as social institutions, social stratification, and the normative system.

The final specification of regions and subregions of effects rests on the joint wisdom of the program director and the evaluator. Social science provides broad guidelines, and previous research has helped map the terrain. But most evaluations have focused on changes in individuals and aggregates; as a consequence almost any evaluation of programs aimed at changes on the group or total community level must begin at the frontiers of the application of theory to practice.

Once regions and subregions are specified, the specific variables that will be measured must be determined. The best working principle is that there is safety in numbers, and therefore the evaluator will do well to avoid reducing his evidence to single measures of a concept.

Temporal Aspects of Effects: Developmental Sequences and Social Chains
Cutting across the specification of goals in terms of their locus in individuals or larger units, and thereby further complicating the problem of conceptualization for the evaluator, is the dimension of time. Once the program's official objectives are specified, certain temporal considerations are readily apparent, although it is not always easy to provide for them in the study design. These are considerations of some particular effect at some point in time. If a program aims to change certain opinions held by individuals in the target audience, for example, one needs to know whether such changes are expected to occur immediately following exposure to the program, some relatively short time thereafter, or in some more distant time; further, are the changes expected to be temporary or to endure, and if the latter, for how long? For certain purposes immediate change is the proper measure of effects, but social psychological research in mass communications indicates the possibility of sleeper effects, that is, changes in opinions that do not occur until several weeks after exposure to a program. If a program aims at affecting the conduct of its audience, a long-range time perspective may be vital, since certain kinds of behavior may require a relatively long time span before the individuals involved have an opportunity to behave as expected. Thus, the effectiveness of a campaign aimed at increasing an individual's sense of civic responsibility and tendency to vote could not be determined until an election (or several elections) had passed. Problems of this nature, although many may seem self-evident,

often pose difficulties in study design. We shall postpone discussion of them, however, until a subsequent section on longitudinal designs.

A somewhat less obvious temporal problem is that of chains of effects. We distinguish three kinds of chain processes: the psychological developmental sequence, the social developmental sequence, and the social chain. In the first two the locus of effects is restricted to members of the original target audience who are the immediate subjects of the social-action program.

In the psychological developmental sequence, effects in a particular subregion (for example, cognitive changes) must occur in the target audience and then develop or change into effects in another subregion (for example, from cognitive change to attitudinal change to conduct). Usually such a "psychological movement" requires some time, and hence evaluation must be extended.

Take as an example the mass information campaign in Cincinnati. It was hoped that at some point in time individuals within the population would become more informed about the United Nations. Determining the point at which the cognitive changes were supposed to have occurred is problematic. If immediately, the evaluator might still raise the question whether they would persist. A subsequent measurement might establish that the information had all been forgotten. But even so, such a design might still have begged the real question. Perhaps implicit in the program was a model of a chain of effects, beginning with information leading to cognitive changes, which created new attitudes, which in turn disposed the individual to new forms of conduct.

An example of planned developmental sequences comes from the field of delinquency-prevention programs. Witmer and Tufts observe that certain delinquency programs seek to "prevent or reduce delinquency through educational or therapeutic measures applied in individual cases." [37] A complete evaluation of such programs, they argue, should first determine whether the immediate objectives of education or therapy were achieved; only then should success in terms of delinquency prevention be measured.

Such psychological chains of effects may often merely be implicit in the plans of the action agency. If the evaluator does not bring the model to light, and treats an intermediate link in the chain as the ultimate effect to be measured, there is danger that the agency—and perhaps the evaluator himself—will assume, without benefit of any empirical proof, that the chain process will go on to its desired end. Certainly, it is wise to evaluate effects all along the chain, but at what point in time do the transitions in the developmental sequence occur? There are no hard and fast rules, but fortunately for the evaluator chains of psychological effects can occur relatively quickly. For example, Hovland's sleeper effects, in which the reorganization of cognitive processes was followed by attitudinal changes, took only a few weeks.

By contrast, the evaluator has a much more tedious assignment when he deals with social developmental sequences in which the links that must be joined are changes in different societal sectors. Consider another example from the field of delinquency-prevention programs. Witmer and Tufts note that certain programs "would prevent or reduce delinquency through improving the environment . . . their aim is the removal or amelioration of certain conditions supposed to cause or foster delinquency, and the test of their effectiveness is whether delinquent acts become less frequent or less severe after the program is in full force." [38] But evaluating such programs is not simply a matter of measuring whether delinquent acts are reduced; suppose they are not. Clearly the program has failed; or has it? If a program aimed at delinquency reduction through improving housing conditions does not lead to a reduction in delinquency, then clearly it has failed in its ultimate objective. But this is a proper test of the effectiveness of such a program only if the program did in fact improve housing conditions. Witmer and Tufts argue that the evaluation should inquire about both issues: first, has the desired change in the environmental situation been brought about, and then, if it has, by how much has delinquency been reduced by the change? They suggest that the evaluation of the effectiveness of social developmental programs (as well as those based on psychological development) should be a two-step affair.

One can argue, of course, that the proper concern of the evaluator is with the ultimate effectiveness of any program, regardless of its degree of success or failure at intermediate stages. But he should still keep in mind the possibility that certain social-action programs are conceived in terms of intermediate and ultimate chains of effects and that evidence of success or failure at one link in the chain need not always imply success or failure at another. This matter is most serious when success at an early stage is taken as evidence of ultimate success. This point can be illustrated in connection with our third type of chain of effects—the social chain.

Ordinarily we conceive of a social-action program as directly affecting the persons, groups, or situation defined as its target. But there are important exceptions. Many social-action programs aim at changing an ultimate *target* population or society through influencing a smaller vehicle group of persons who are to act as the agents for social change. Programs may focus on opinion leaders, for example, in the hope that they in turn will affect large numbers of their followers. Programs aimed at the ultimate widespread diffusion of innovations may concentrate on key influentials in the community. Technical training programs which train foreign nationals provide another example. The ultimate aim of these programs is to assist the technological development of foreign areas; this is to be accomplished through the activities of the trained individuals when they return home. One link in the chain of effects is the success or failure of the program in training the individuals who attend the program. But success here may not mean success later. Some of the trainees may decide to remain in the host society or migrate to another nation rather than return home; others, on returning home, may find it impossible to apply their newly learned skills and attitudes. Indeed, such evaluations as exist in this area have made it clear how common these possibilities are. Hence it is important that the evaluator consider the relevant social chain of effects.

Unanticipated Consequences and Neglected Formal Aspects of Dependent Variables Evaluation aims to provide objective, systematic, and comprehensive evidence on the degree to which a program achieves its intended objectives *plus* the degree to which it produces unanticipated consequences which when recognized would also be regarded as relevant to the social-action agency.[39] Social-science literature is rich in examples of programs that produced totally unexpected side effects. Sometimes such effects have their locus in the target population. Riecken, for example, in evaluating the effects of a volunteer summer work camp for young persons, noted that although the program was successful in changing certain attitudes of the participants it also seemed to increase the degree to which some of them became alienated from the total society and developed something like an elite self-image—an outcome not in keeping with the program's intentions.[40] In other cases there are unanticipated but relevant consequences for persons outside the original target group. Carlson, for example, reports on a public-health mass information campaign which failed to increase the amount of information about venereal disease among certain publics or the rate at which they volunteered for treatment; nevertheless the campaign ultimately led to a reduction in the amount of untreated disease in the area because it boosted the morale of local health workers and stimulated them to more vigorous efforts on their job once the campaign had attracted public attention to their professional problem.[41]

How can the evaluator anticipate effects not foreseen by the action agency? Several procedures give him an advantage over the agency in anticipating such results: evidence of unexpected consequences from the records of previous cycles of an established program; speculation about the consequences if the intended effect reached an extreme value, such as would occur if an intended boost in the individual's self-confidence led to a false sense of eliteness; alertness to possible undesirable consequences which the agency once foresaw but believed it had avoided and therefore no longer thought about; and clues from the social-science literature. The importance of the literature cannot be overestimated. Familiarity with previous studies of similar action programs and general scientific knowledge about the area involved—whether delinquency, attitudinal change, or voting behavior—can unlock the door to many of the relevant conceptualizations of unexpected results.

Something more can be done at this phase of conceptualization, but rarely is, and we can only call attention to its possibilities here. Most evaluations are made in terms of dependent variables defined in a substantive manner; we have spoken, for example, of the subregions of attitudes, opinions, knowledge, conduct, and the contents contained within these regions. It would also be useful to conceive of a program's effects in terms of more formal aspects of the dependent variables. When dealing with attitudes and opinions, for example, an evaluation might consider the intensity, crystallization, congruence, consistency, linkage, and other formal aspects of an attitude structure, rather than the mere content of attitudes. A program might, for instance, intensify attitudes, even though it did not alter their contents, or it might activate an otherwise latent attitude. The utility of such a mode of conceptualization is implied by Barton in his critique of the Jacob study: "The notion that college should make people arrive at their values through conscious exploration gives us a directive as to what to measure—something like 'value-consciousness' or 'value-exploring activities.'" [42]

Conceptualization of formal variables often solves methodological problems and may also save the researcher from the embarrassment which can occur if he has to present negative findings to an action agency. Action agencies faced with negative findings are often skilled at inventing concepts of a formal nature. "Yes," they agree, "the program did not change any attitudes, but it did reinforce them"; or "It did not change the beliefs the group held but it clarified them."

Varieties of Evaluation: Study Designs

EXTENDING THE USEFULNESS OF EVALUATION BY COMPARATIVE DESIGNS

The evaluator too often sees a program in terms of the imagery of the neat, independent variable of an experiment and runs the many dangers we have previously described. He needs to enlarge his conception of a variable, but he must also enlarge his conception of the nature of an experiment. Too often he has been taught that the perfect design involves a comparison between an experimental group to which he gives a treatment and a control group to which he gives zero treatment and is thus regarded as receiving nothing. Elsewhere we have noted in detail, and we shall stress it again later, that the notion of a group receiving no treatment can be very misleading when applied to the evaluation of programs. During the long period when a program is operative, life cannot be suspended for a control group as is the case in a brief experiment, and, unknown to the evaluator, some other agency may be providing a different kind of treatment.

But let us suppose that there is no such ambiguity in interpretation, that the evaluator does overcome the many technical and practical difficulties and creates a beautiful but orthodox experimental design. Certainly it is useful to learn that an agency's program is better than doing nothing, but it may be more important for social policy to ask whether something still better could be done. The comparative design speaks to this important question. Instead of an experimental group and an untreated or control group, the evaluator compares groups exposed to different types of program or to different levels and combinations of treatment within a single program. It is a harsh standard for an evaluator to employ—to demand that a given program or treatment be better than another—but it is certainly realistic to ask what is the best way to allocate resources and whether a more economical and curtailed program would produce the same effect. The ambiguity in the notion of "zero treatment" is, of course, resolved in comparative evaluations. They may also be more feasible to apply than the orthodox design.[43] An agency may not want to deny all treatment to a group that needs help, or the group may not allow itself to be denied help from that or any other quarter. In programs that are concerned with the control and rehabilitation of dangerous forms of behavior, it is almost inconceivable that an agency would leave such individuals untreated simply to establish a conventional control group for the evaluator.

Comparisons between Factors within a Program The treatment employed within a program is generally complex in character. In the usual evaluation, the effects of the different component parts of the treatment cannot be separated. But, if an agency were to be sophisticated enough, or an evaluator persuasive enough, several equivalent groups could be exposed to different amounts and elements of the total treatment, and the component effects separated.

In the Egyptian rural health program mentioned above, a complex program of health and sanitary measures was applied to four equivalent villages in a kind of factorial design. Thus "The village of Aghour El Sughra was treated to Wells plus Fly Control. El Barada was treated to Wells, Latrines, and Refuse Disposal Service. Quaranfil to Wells, Latrines, Refuse Disposal, and Fly Control. Sindhbis to Wells, Latrines, Refuse Disposal, Fly Control, plus other preventive medical activities." As a result of this design, the evaluators were able to conclude that "the improvement . . . is due largely to the provision of water supply and latrines," since the gain in the two villages that received the more elaborate treatments was very little, but the village that received the most rudimentary treatment was far behind the other three.[44]

In this instance, the various factors produced different effects. But suppose they had all been proved equal. It might mean that all the treatments were equally good, but it could also mean that they were all equally bad—no better than nothing. We have resolved one kind of ambiguity with the comparative design, only to run the risk of another ambiguity. In principle, the solution is simple: merge the comparative design with the conventional design by adding an additional, pure control group which receives zero treatment. In practice it is not so simple. In the Egyptian study, there was, in fact, a fifth village, Aghour El Kubre, which was "to remain without improvements to provide basic vital statistics for comparison with the above villages." [45] Yet the ambiguity of the conventional control group and the difficulty of giving an equivalent group "nothing" are brought home when one notes that this fifth village, like the other four, was near "a recently developed health center that could serve as the base for the program." [46] Therefore all the villages had at least this minimal program. The point will become even clearer as we turn to another comparative evaluation, in which "the objective was to learn how much family planning could be achieved at how much cost in money, personnel and time."

Berelson and Freedman describe this large-scale program and evaluation involving the provincial Health Department of Taiwan, the support of the Population Council in the United States, and the research of the Population Studies centers in Taiwan and the University of Michigan. In Taichung, a city of about 300,000, small neighborhoods within each of three larger districts were exposed to four different treatments, designated "nothing," "mail," "everything (wives only)," and "everything (wives and husbands)." In the "everything" neighborhoods, communication and persuasion were administered via personal visits from field workers, whereas in the "mail" neighborhoods only a direct-mail or impersonal form of communication was used on two specific target groups, newlyweds and parents with two or more children. But what about the neighborhoods that acted as control groups, receiving, as the evaluators put it, "nothing"? "The city as a whole was exposed to only two aspects of the program: a general distribution of posters pointing out the advantages of family planning and a series of meetings with community leaders to inform them about the program, get their advice and enlist their support." [47]

"Nothing" is anything but nothing; apparently the various parties were either unwilling or unable to have a true zero treatment as a control. The point will become even stronger as we examine the total design of this particular comparative evaluation, which also wanted to examine the effect of word-of-mouth diffusion and therefore saturated the three larger districts with different concentrations of the everything treatment. Thus in fact twelve different combinations of treatment were evaluated, as schematically represented in Table 27–4. The combinations are ranked in order of their effectiveness, eleven months after the initiation of the program, in persuading the married women, aged twenty to twenty-nine, of that type of neighborhood to accept or purchase a contraceptive device.

TABLE 27-4. *Treatment Ranked According to Effectiveness**

| | AMOUNT OF SATURATION OF LARGER DISTRICT | | |
| | HEAVY | MEDIUM | LIGHT |
Treatment of the Neighborhood	*Half the neighborhoods*	*One-third the neighborhoods*	*One-fifth the neighborhoods*
Nothing	7.5 (tie)	11 (tie)	11 (tie)
Mail	7.5 (tie)	11 (tie)	9
Everything (wives)	2	3	5
Everything (wives and husbands)	1	6	4

* Adapted from Berelson and Freedman, *op. cit.*

The best treatment is ranked "first." Some of the "nothing" neighborhoods and families, in terms of what we earlier labeled social chains of effect, received rather substantial treatments, and, either directly or indirectly, none of these neighborhoods received nothing. By their comparative design, Berelson and Freedman were able to demonstrate that "the added effect of visiting husbands as well as wives was not worth the expense," that the indirect effects of programs via diffusion is indeed considerable, but "that the maximum return for minimum expenditure can be obtained with something less than the heavy . . . degree of concentration." [48]

In the Taiwan study, the everything treatment, a form administered to the neighborhoods by direct personal communication via a staff of eighteen field workers, was found to be the most effective. Neighborhoods receiving this treatment, even those within the least saturated districts, showed a higher percentage of women accepting birth-control measures than neighborhoods that received the mail treatment and were within heavily saturated districts. Even such a compelling finding, however, is subject to some ambiguity. Recall the principle that an evaluator must distinguish between the staff of a program and the treatment administered by that staff. In any comparative evaluation of treatments, one of which involves the use of staff and the other of which does not, there is a danger that the particular persons employed account for the apparent effectiveness of the personal form of treatment. Change the particular field workers used on the next cycle, and the advantage of direct home visits might evaporate.

In the instance of Taichung, the argument is perhaps unreasonable, since it is unlikely that all eighteen field workers would turn out to be extremely forceful personalities. However, a similar evaluation was made in Madras State, India, of three different methods to encourage BCG vaccination for tuberculosis. In some villages each household was approached individually. Other villages also received a mass-media approach, and still others received in addition a treatment involving group meetings organized through the local leadership. The gains from the various methods and combinations of method were quite clear, but one of the evaluators, Ranganathan, remarks:

> We did not have the time to *train persons* to use the methods and media in a uniform manner. We made use of the existing public health workers. . . . These people were all very well known and accepted by the people of the villages under study. They were also very good in community organization. Would it be correct to assume that the results of the study, especially the individual approach method, would have been different if the interviews were conducted by some other persons? [49]

Comparisons between Programs The enlightened self-interest of the agency and the virtuosity of the researcher create the comparative evaluation of factors within a program. The evaluator may have the intellectual power to conceptualize the important elements and to conceive the appropriate experimental test, but the agency has the power to arrange the test, if it sees fit. No matter how complex the total program may be and no matter how many subprograms it may contain, it is at least a unity in the practical sense that it is all within the jurisdiction of a single agency. Whatever the findings, the agency gains. The situation is completely different for the comparative evaluation of several programs operated by different agencies. In principle, the design has the same virtues: it provides a rigorous experimental test of a program and imposes the harsh, but legitimate, standard that a program be the best allocation of resources.[50] But one of the agencies is bound to lose in the invidious comparison. Whatever the persuasive powers of the evaluator, the likelihood of his arranging a simultaneous comparative evaluation of several programs having the same objectives but different sponsoring agencies seems small. In Jacob's study, the colleges were not parties to any plan for a comparative evaluation. They became innocent parties to the evaluation only because Jacob used findings from studies done at different times for other purposes. This is one reason for the crudities and technical imperfections of the study as a systematic comparative evaluation of programs, but this is also why it was feasible.

Lazarsfeld, contemplating some of the deficiencies in the Jacob inquiry and the complexity of the college program, calls for "systematically comparative research covering all the relevant interacting parts of the college as a social system. . . . It will require support from foundations . . . it will demand close collaboration between the educator and the social research technician." [51] But if this comparative research is to be explicitly evaluative, it may demand a kind of co-operation which is not likely to be given. In our discussion of continuities in evaluation research we shall present a design which has the feasibility of the secondary analysis and some of the systematic quality of the simultaneous comparative evaluation.

Comparisons between Programs in Different Settings In current usage, comparative research in sociology implies the study of a given problem in different societies. How different from our discussion of comparative evaluations of programs or factors within a program! But clearly there is a miniature equivalent to comparative sociology in the comparative evaluation of a program in two different sites. A major and perhaps neglected component of programs is the site in which they are conducted. If a site is changed on a subsequent cycle, or if the same program occurs in several sites simultaneously, an evaluator can make a comparative study of the effectiveness of this factor.

But there is a closer parallel to comparative sociology in the occasional comparative evaluation of a program that is operated in two different social environments. Here, the concern is not to reject one program (or factor) and endorse another, but to establish the generality of the effectiveness of a program. One can also combine the comparative study of programs or factors with the comparison of settings, since it may well be that the better method in one setting is the worse method in another setting. But generally one simply evaluates whether a single program is effective in more than one setting. For example, a pilot project in rural adult education was conducted in France in 1953–1954 under the auspices of UNESCO. Special television programs were broadcast to French villages which had organized "tele-clubs," and the influence of the programs as mediated through the clubs and their discussions was found to be considerable. In view of the success of the French program, UNESCO proposed a second such educational program, which was conducted in Japan in 1956.[52] Beginning in 1964, UNESCO has been sponsoring a comparative evaluation, conducted in India and Costa Rica, in which the relative effectiveness of several different types of programs in changing farm practices is being evaluated. In addition to control villages which are not receiving any special treatment, some villages in each country are being exposed to radio farm forums and other villages to printed matter then discussed in forums and preceded by literacy teaching.[53] Comparative evaluation of settings here assumes an almost global scale, but note that in this case the research was successive rather than simultaneous.

This is the mode of research that we call "continuities in evaluation." Perhaps by slow degrees and long continuity, comparative evaluators will begin to establish the utility of social-action programs in the very environments and societies most in need of social change: the developing countries. Then the uses of sociology will really be extended, and a more widely based theory of social change will result.

DESIGNS INVOLVING CONTINUITY, REPLICATION, AND
LONGITUDINAL STUDY: THEIR USE AND VALUE

Over a decade ago, the late Samuel Stouffer chided his fellow sociologists
and social psychologists for their failure to give more attention to replications of studies. "Experimental psychology," he observed, "which springs
more directly out of the natural science tradition, puts an emphasis on
replication which social psychologists and sociologists might well emulate." One reason for this failure, according to Stouffer, is the unfortunate
custom of applauding " 'originality' so highly that students acquire no
prestige out of 'just repeating what somebody else has done.' " He argued
that the safest check on the reliability, validity, and generalization of findings is the consistency of replications. Stouffer's comments were directed
specifically to studies based on survey techniques,[54] but they have a special
cogency for research that involves evaluation of social-action programs
and policy.

We shall distinguish three kinds of research operations that are subsumed under the label "replication."

1. There are studies that build upon, extend, and occasionally test
under varying circumstances the findings and hypotheses of previous research. For purposes of discussion here we shall call this practice "continuity in research" and note that it subsumes what we earlier called comparative evaluations.

2. Second, there are studies that attempt to duplicate, as closely as possible, the design, problem, hypotheses, and methods of earlier studies. We
call this practice "replication." It differs from continuity by attempting to
repeat all the relevant conditions of the earlier research.

3. Third, there is the attempt to conduct a study in several stages, extending it over a relatively long period of time in order to see what new
phenomena emerge. This practice we shall label "longitudinal," or long-
term, research. It is often regarded as the acid test of a program's effectiveness, but the emphasis on longitudinal research may at times be an evasive
tactic by which evaluation can be progressively postponed. For example,
the preface of a report on a program in India stated: "Since this was essentially an experimental program, considerable emphasis was put from the
very beginning on the need for evaluation and assessment." Yet a few sentences later the report continued:

When it is remembered that the program is to run over a period of five years
and that in most of the districts it is hardly two years old and that a large
part of this period has been taken up in making preliminary arrangements,
building up the requisite institutions and administrative and extension serv-

ices, it must be recognized that it is yet too early to pass judgment on the impact of the program on agricultural development. No attempt, therefore, has been made in this report to make an evaluation of the program.[55]

Where there is no postponement of intermediate stages of evaluation, the longitudinal study does add great power to an evaluation. A fine touch is added to Newcomb's original Bennington study by his twenty-five-year follow-up to determine whether his original subjects remained relatively nonconservative or regressed "to relatively conservative positions." [56]

In practice, the distinction between these three types of replicative research is not always clear cut. A single study, especially one that involves a large-scale, complex design, may encompass certain aspects of each type. But for purposes of discussion, it is useful to keep the three functions separate, for each has somewhat different consequences, implications, and values for evaluation research.

Lazarsfeld, in a preface to the second edition of *The People's Choice*, notes that there are at least three scientific gains from continuity.

1. Similar results corroborate earlier findings and thereby increase our confidence in them and in their generalizability.

2. Differences in results between two or more studies may be traced to differences in the specific test conditions and thereby enable us to specify the conditions under which relationships hold.

3. Differences in results may lead to the discovery of new explanatory factors that clarify the findings.[57]

Lazarsfeld's views, then, suggest that much is to be gained from continuity in research, even under circumstances that prohibit the strict replication of initial test conditions.

Sometimes continuity in evaluation yields benefits without any new data collection. Additional theoretical perspectives on the problem, derived from the growth of our science over the years, can lead to a reanalysis of the earlier data, new interpretations, and even the discovery of an otherwise buried finding. An example is provided by McCord and McCord's re-evaluation of the original Cambridge–Somerville Youth Study.[58] Before considering the re-evaluation, however, we shall give a brief history of the original project.

The Cambridge–Somerville Youth Study was an experiment in the prevention of delinquency which structured its original design to facilitate the eventual evaluation of the relative success or failure of the program, a rare and early instance of an action program that provided for its own evaluation from the start.

Two groups of 325 boys each, carefully matched, were formed out of a much larger number of referrals. Each group had the same number of "problem boys" judged by teachers and a team of experts to be "pre-delinquents." One group was to be let alone, thus serving as a "control" to the other, experimental or "treated" group. This latter group was to receive all the aid that a resourceful counselor, backed by the Study, the school, and community agencies, could possibly give.

The original plan called for a ten-year period of work with the T-boys. . . . At the conclusion of the ten-year treatment an evaluation of the conduct (and character) of the T-boys should be made in comparison with the conduct (and character) of their "twins," the C-boys.[59]

The assignment and treatment of boys began in late 1937. There were two interim evaluations, based on a variety of attitude scales and personality tests, in 1941–1942 and in 1943; but the major and final planned evaluation was based on the results achieved by the end of the treatment period, December, 1945. (The Study was terminated sooner than planned, because of the shortage of counselors and disruption of treatment caused by World War II.) The statistical comparison of records of delinquency between boys in the treatment group and those in the control group showed no significant differences in favor of the program; in these basic terms, then, the program failed to achieve its goals.[60] In 1955, ten years after the termination of the Youth Study, McCord and McCord undertook a long-term evaluation of the project.

The new evaluation of the Cambridge–Somerville Study was essentially a longitudinal one; the researchers searched for evidence of a long-term beneficial effect of the program in terms of differences in the court records of the criminal activities (convictions) of the treatment boys and the control boys from 1938 to 1955. There was no significant difference between the records of the two groups. Thus the longitudinal feature of the new study provided additional negative evidence of the program's effectiveness.

Thus far the new evaluation was an extension of the old. But a new approach was made possible by the continuity of interest in the problem. The experimental and control groups had been matched at the beginning of the program on a variety of factors, such as health, intelligence, emotional adjustment, home background, and "delinquency prognosis." Then a flip of a coin had determined which boys entered the experimental and which the control group. The procedure was perfect in design. But if the variables used for matching did not include certain factors critically related to delinquent or criminal tendencies and these factors had not distributed themselves randomly between the two groups, then the failure of the treatment group to behave "better" than the control group might simply reflect an initial imbalance of such causal factors. Knowledge about possible causes of crime and delinquency had expanded in the nearly two decades between the beginning of the project and the new evaluation. Obviously the composition of the treatment and control groups could not be changed, but the data could be reanalyzed, giving consideration to the newly suggested variables since there was sufficient information about them in the boys' files. The McCords present such a reanalysis: "By holding constant various factors in making a comparison between the treatment and the control groups, we could—in effect—correct errors in the initial matching.[61]

For example, parental discipline has been emphasized recently as a possible factor affecting delinquency and crime. Therefore the McCords searched the records of the social workers and counselors who had been in contact with the boys, to glean information about the parents' methods of disciplining them. The evaluators could then compare the amount of crime found among treatment boys and control boys who had experienced similar types of parental discipline. By this procedure the evaluators were able to take into account the possible influence on the dependent variable of a variety of factors which social-science theory now suggests were important but which had not been foreseen in the original experimental design. Obviously such an advantage from continuity in evaluation can be obtained only when it is possible to get the necessary facts about the new variables; it may be easier to obtain such facts about the experimental than the control group simply because the former has been the focus of attention during the action program.

Continuity has been distinguished from strict replication, that is, from studies that attempt to duplicate the conditions of previous research as much as possible. An example of a research design that explicitly involves the use of replication as a criterion for accepting or rejecting hypotheses is provided by studies on the socialization of medical students, by Merton and others, which implicitly are evaluative in character. Similar or equivalent surveys were conducted with several classes of medical students in different medical schools. In a methodological appendix to *The Student Physician*, the authors state that "results must be replicatively consistent if they are to be considered significant. That is, a finding in one group must also hold true in a second independent group, if the same general conditions prevail in both." [62] A case study of evaluation research involving several replications of the initial study is presented in Hyman, Wright, and Hopkins' work on the Encampment for Citizenship described below.[63]

Continuity in evaluational research may either be long-term or short-term, and while there is no precise definition of what is long, we reserve the term *longitudinal evaluations* for studies which cover a long time span. The new evaluation of the Cambridge–Somerville Youth Study certainly may be regarded as longitudinal; the evaluation explicitly tested the hypothesis that the treatment program would have a long-range influence on behavior despite its apparent failure to affect delinquency during the period of the program itself. One phase of the evaluation for the Encampment for Citizenship was a longitudinal follow-up on the campers four years after the initial evaluation.

A CASE STUDY INVOLVING CONTINUITY, REPLICATION, AND LONGITUDINAL EVALUATIONS

The discussion in this section draws chiefly on the experiences of the authors in a series of studies which not only were internally replicative but also provided continuity with similar research by others and included certain longitudinal features in the research design. These studies were evaluations of the effectiveness of the Encampment for Citizenship, an institution devoted to character development of a special sort: increasing the potential of youth for effective democratic citizenship.[64] Each summer the Encampment brings together from throughout the United States and abroad approximately 125 men and women, eighteen to twenty-four years old, of many races and diverse social backgrounds. They live together on a school campus for six weeks, during which time they are exposed to a program of lectures, workshops, discussions, and other educational experiences and social activities designed to "prepare young Americans for responsible citizenship and citizen leadership, to educate them in the meaning of democracy . . . and to train and equip them in the techniques of democratic action." [65]

The 1955 Encampment marked the tenth anniversary or cycle of the program, and the sponsors felt the need for a scientific evaluation of its effectiveness. The original basic design of the evaluation consisted of measurements taken on the 1955 campers at the beginning and end of the Encampment. These measurements covered various areas of potential change in the camper's character which were related to the goals of the program or which might have been unanticipated effects of the program. Seven basic regions of effects were included: basic values, orientation toward civic activity, cognition of social problems, salient social attitudes and opinions (such as attitudes toward civil rights and civil liberties), perceived relationships with the rest of society, certain skills and capacities, and conduct. (A variety of measurements were also made on relevant independent and intervening variables.)

The basic measurements before and after the six-week program demonstrated how much the cohort of campers changed, presumably because of the Encampment. Campers changed in many ways favorable to the program's goals and in very few ways, anticipated or not, regarded as unfavorable. As examples from the region of desired social attitudes and opinions, campers became more appreciative of traditional civil liberties, more tolerant of unpopular views, stronger in their defense of civil rights for minorities, and slightly less authoritarian in outlook; but they were not less likely to hold stereotyped views of various groups than when they started the program. By contrast, certain possible undesirable effects, unanticipated by the program, did not occur. For example, campers did not become more "radical" in their political ideology or more ethnocentric in their image of democracy. Results were obtained in other regions of desired effects. There was, for example, a slight reduction in political apathy; increased optimism (without exceeding the bounds of reality) about the ultimate solution of such social problems as race prejudice and unemployment; an unprejudicial selection of friends during the summer; and less susceptibility to prestigious political symbols. But there were very few changes in campers' basic values as indicated, for example, by the goals they considered worthy of personal sacrifice. This portion of the evaluation indicated that, on the whole, the program was effective.

Other evidence was necessary, of course, to help answer such important questions as whether similar changes would have occurred without the program; whether the changes were greater or less than those achieved by other programs; whether the effects were specific to the 1955 cohort or would occur in other cycles of the program; whether the effects were short-lived, being dissipated over the years following the Encampment; and whether new or additional effects would occur later, for example, in the region of conduct. Provisions for continuity, replication, and longitudinal research helped provide answers to such questions.

Information about changes which occur even without the Encampment program could in this case be provided by the study of control groups, following the classical experimental design, although this design is not always possible in evaluation research.[66] Evidence about "natural" changes was obtained from a mail survey of a sample of campers six weeks prior to their arrival at the Encampment.[67] Attitudes and opinions expressed in response to these questionnaires were compared with those expressed by campers six weeks later, when they started the program, thereby showing how much these attitudes ordinarily change. Changes in campers' opinions during this ordinary six-week period in their lives, reflecting the influence of nonprogrammatic sources of instability, were negligible. Against this standard, the changes brought about during the Encampment appeared substantial.

Questionnaires were again mailed to all campers six weeks after they left the Encampment, in order to measure the impact of the return to their home or college communities on their attitudes and conduct. These data showed, for example, that the program's apparent effects on attitudes toward civil liberties, tolerance, and civil rights did not vanish immediately after campers returned to their home towns, or even six weeks later.

Finally, an attempt was made to estimate the long-range persistence of Encampment-sponsored attitudes and conduct by conducting a simulated longitudinal study among ex-campers. A questionnaire was mailed to a random sample of alumni from each of the nine preceding cycles, 1946–1954, now one to nine years after their original exposure to the program.

The total initial research design is depicted in Table 27–5 as measurements A1 through A4, plus E.

In 1955 we were aware of only one other recent major study that had faced similar problems in evaluation: Riecken's study of summer work camps sponsored by the American Friends Service Committee.[68] We drew heavily upon Riecken's findings during this early phase of our own research, using certain of his questions and scales, and through this continuity a comparative evaluation was obtained. But this was only the first in a series of comparative evaluations produced by a chain of continuity. In 1958, when Dentler was called upon to evaluate several youth programs, in a research project conducted by the National Opinion Research Center, he designed his study to provide continuity with Riecken's research and with our 1955 study.[69] In certain respects, such comparative groups may be more realistic for evaluation research than the conventional untreated control group, a point discussed earlier in this chapter. As an example, recall that the Encampment had only a slight effect on campers' authoritarianism. Comparison with Riecken's findings and Dentler's findings showed that the Encampment's ineffectiveness in this matter was no greater than that of comparable institutions.

Other comparisons were made possible by using certain questions from national surveys of American youth. Data from these surveys provided standards against which the campers' opinions were compared; also changes in certain opinions held by campers were compared with the amount of change found in the national surveys during similar times, reflecting the effect of nonexperimental events.

Although we did not know it in 1955, unparalleled opportunities for replications of the original research arose in 1957 and 1958 when the Encampment requested additional research on its effectiveness. All told, there were three replications: two in New York in 1957 and 1958, and one at a new Encampment in California in 1958. By the extension of our studies into 1958, Dentler's evaluation then became available to us as a basis for a new comparative evaluation. (See Table 27–5.)

The two additional cycles studied in the New York Encampment clearly were replications. The California cycle may be conceived either as a replication or as a comparative study of the factor of site, which differed in certain important ways from the one in New York. The design of these three replications was essentially the same as the original study, except for an additional special concern with those campers who were college students, for whom control groups were obtained. The major findings about the effectiveness of the Encampment were consistently supported by the results of the three independent replications. For example, campers in all

TABLE 27–5. *Chronology and Design of Studies Evaluating the Encampment for Citizenship* *

GROUP UNDER STUDY	STAGES OF MEASUREMENT				
	1	2	3	4	5
	Pre-enrollment "self-control"; 6 weeks prior to Encampment (By mail)	Start of Encampment (In person)	End of Encampment (In person)	Short-term follow-up; 6 weeks after Encampment (By mail)	Long-term follow-up (By mail)
Initial Group (1955 Encampment)	A_1	A_2	A_3	A_4	A_5 (1959)
First replication (1957 Encampment)	B_1	B_2	B_3	B_4†	
Second replication (1958 New York Encampment)	C_1†	C_2	C_3	C_4†	
Third replication (1958 California Encampment)	D_1†	D_2	D_3	D_4†	
Alumni mail survey (1946–1954 Encampments)					E (1955)
Control groups (college)	B'_1 (1957) C'_1 (1958)			B'_4 C'_4	

Comparative "control" groups:
(1) H. Riecken's *Volunteer Work Camp* (Cambridge: Addison-Wesley, 1952).
(2) National opinion surveys (1955).
(3) R. Dentler's evaluation of summer interns (1958).

* Reprinted from C. R. Wright and H. H. Hyman, "The Evaluators," in Phillip Hammond, ed., *Sociologists at Work* (New York: Basic Books, 1964), Chapter 5.

† Note: Measurements B_4, C_1, C_4, D_1, and D_4 include college students only, among the Campers.

three new studies became more supportive of civil liberties and civil rights, more tolerant of unpopular views, and slightly less authoritarian—just as had been found in the original evaluation. This consistency in findings strengthened the evidence that the program was effective in these matters and reduced apprehensions that the success in 1955 was atypical. Changes that appeared constantly among the campers could not be dismissed as the product of extraneous events, since such events varied greatly during these three years.

The new studies also provided additional evidence on many of the interpretations about the dynamics of change set forth in the first evaluation. Once the first replication had supported many of the original findings on effectiveness, we could afford to give more attention to exploring causal factors. For example, one of the project's directors, Terence Hopkins, collected detailed evidence on small-group processes in terms of each camper's friendships and associations during the summer; these data were analyzed to shed light on the dynamics of attitude change.[70]

Then, in the spring of 1959 we received support for a truly longitudinal follow-up of the original 1955 group; through a mail questionnaire we measured the persistence of the Encampment's effects on attitudes and conduct some four years after the program. In addition to providing substantial evidence on the Encampment's long-range impact, and a methodological test of the value of the Alumni design, the new data permitted comparisons with findings from the six-week post-Encampment follow-up study mentioned above. As an example, certain changes produced during the 1955 Encampment, such as support for civil liberties, persisted in both the short-term and long-term period; but others, such as optimism about a rapid solution to race problems, were lost fairly abruptly upon return home; and still others, such as tolerance for unpopular views, were slowly altered to erode the Encampment gains (but not completely). No single pattern of post-Encampment changes prevailed; consequently, findings from the short-term follow-up study could not be generalized to the long run. The genuine longitudinal study proved invaluable to the evaluation.

Concluding Note

Throughout this chapter the emphasis has been on the usefulness of a social-science approach to the evaluation of social-action programs. In closing, we must at least note that there is another benefit from the application of social science to evaluation—the contributions evaluation research can make to basic social science, and especially to theories of social change. What opportunities for advancing our knowledge evaluation affords! It provides excellent and ready-made opportunities to examine individuals, groups, and societies in the grip of major forces for change. In its application it contributes not only to a science of social planning and a more rationally planned society but also to the perfection of a realistically tested social theory.

REFERENCES

NOTE: *We are pleased to express our thanks to Gerda Lorenz and Muriel Cantor for their research and library assistance and to Eleanor Singer for her valuable editorial suggestions.*

1. See Otto Klineberg, "The Problem of Evaluation Research," *International Social Science Bulletin*, VII, No. 3 (1955), 348.
2. See Donald Campbell and Julian Stanley, "Experimental and Quasi-Experimental Designs for Research on Teaching," in N. L. Gage, ed., *Handbook of Research on Teaching* (Chicago: Rand McNally, 1963), Chapter 5; Herbert H. Hyman, Charles R. Wright, and Terence K. Hopkins, *Applications of Methods of Evaluation: Four Studies of the Encampment for Citizenship*, University of California Publications in Culture and Society (Berkeley: University of California Press, 1962); Samuel Hayes, *Measuring the Results of Development Projects* (Paris: UNESCO, 1959); *International Social Science Bulletin*, VII, No. 3 (1955); Subcommittee of the National Advisory Mental Health Council, *Evaluation in Mental Health* (U.S. Department of Health, Education and Welfare, 1955); Henry W. Riecken, *The Volunteer Work Camp: A Psychological Evaluation* (Cambridge, Massachusetts: Addison-Wesley, 1952); Edwin Powers and Helen Witmer, *An Experiment in the Prevention of Juvenile Delinquency: The Cambridge-Somerville Youth Study* (New York: Columbia University Press, 1951).
3. See Hyman, Wright, and Hopkins, *op. cit.*, pp. 3–86.
4. John M. Weir *et al.*, "An Evaluation of Health and Sanitation in Egyptian Villages," *Journal of the Egyptian Public Health Association*, XXVII, No. 3 (1952), 55–114.
5. *Ibid.*, p. 96.
6. *Ibid.*, p. 97.
7. Louis Moss, "The Evaluation of Fundamental Education," *International Social Science Bulletin*, VII, No. 3 (1955), 402.
8. Weir *et al.*, p. 98.
9. Quoted in Hayes, *op. cit.*, p. 35.
10. Shirley A. Star and Helen MacGill Hughes, "Report on an Educational Campaign: The Cincinnati Plan for the United Nations," *American Journal of Sociology*, LV, No. 4 (January, 1950), 390.
11. Alexander and Longest, *op. cit.*, p. 18.
12. *Community Development and Economic Development, Part IIA: A Case Study of the Ghosi Community Development Block Uttar Pradesh, India* (Bangkok: Economic Commission for Asia and the Far East, United Nations, 1960), pp. 2–4.
13. *Ibid.*, pp. 5–7.
14. Allen H. Barton, *Studying the Effects of College Education, A Methodological Examination of "Changing Values in College"* (New Haven: The Hazen Foundation, 1959), p. 13.

15. Philip E. Jacob, *Changing Values in College: An Exploratory Study of the Impact of College Teaching* (New York: Harper, 1957), p. ix; italics supplied.
16. Barton, *op. cit.*, p. 5; italics supplied.
17. Jacob's evaluation used the method of secondary analysis, exploiting studies that already had been conducted for other purposes. While this places the investigator at the mercy of other people's designs, it does have the advantage that the sampling of cycles, although not systematic, is much more extended in time.
18. Theodore M. Newcomb, *Personality and Social Change* (New York: Holt, Rinehart, and Winston, 1943).
19. D. Krech and E. Ballachey, *A Case Study of a Social Survey*, Japanese Survey, United States Bombing Survey, University of California Syllabus Series, Syllabus T G (Berkeley: University of California Press, 1948).
20. Barton, *op. cit.*, p. 60.
21. *Ibid.*
22. It has been argued that in a mental hospital "one of the causes of regression is residence in a regressed ward; that being completely surrounded by regressed patients is a regressing factor: that it is better for the chronic patients to be mixed." *Mental Hospitals Join the Community, Milbank Memorial Fund Quarterly*, XLII, No. 3 (July, 1964), Part 2, p. 38.
23. Barton, *op. cit.*, p. 60.
24. Communications research makes the argument even more compelling. The influence of the mass-media message is often a function of the credibility of the communicator. See, for example, Carl I. Hovland and W. Weiss, "The Influence of Source Credibility on Communication Effectiveness," *Public Opinion Quarterly*, XV (1951), 635–650.
25. An excellent illustration is provided in an evaluation of a program of group therapy for delinquents, where it was reasonable to expect that the peculiar genius of the first therapist was being evaluated, rather than the formal treatment itself. Unfortunately he left the program, but fortunately the replication of the evaluation established that the program also worked for his successor. See H. Ashley Weeks, *Youthful Offenders at Highfields* (Ann Arbor: University of Michigan Press, 1958).
26. See, for example, our Encampment study where we asked the youth questions on their perceptions and reactions to the staff. Hyman, Wright, and Hopkins, *op. cit.*
27. See our discussion of "The Return Home" in the Encampment monograph, *ibid.*, Chapter 6.
28. Insulation may sometimes work against the goals of a program. The residential islands of foreign students on large American campuses reduce both interaction between foreign and American students and informal training, although they may provide necessary psychological comfort and support for the stranger.
29. Our advice would be quite different if replications on subsequent cycles, continuities in research, or comparative studies are a realistic prospect. Under such conditions, speculations are no longer idle, but are guidelines to the future design of evaluation studies which may provide the empirical tests. See our discussion of these types of designs below.
30. S. C. Dube, *India's Changing Villages*, as quoted in Peter Du Sautoy, *The Organization of a Community Development Programme* (London: Oxford University Press, 1962), p. 126.
31. Marie Jahoda, as quoted in *Evaluation in Mental Health* (Washington, D.C.: U.S. Department of Health, Education and Welfare, 1955), p. 6.

32. Helen L. Witmer and Edith Tufts, "The Effectiveness of Delinquency Prevention Programs" (U.S. Department of Health, Education and Welfare, Social Security Administration—Children's Bureau, Publication Number 350, 1954), pp. 1–2.
33. Riecken, *op. cit.*, p. 27.
34. For an instructive general treatment of problems in the construction of concepts and indicators in social research, see Lazarsfeld and Rosenberg, eds., *The Language of Social Research* (Glencoe, Ill.: The Free Press, 1955).
35. Hyman, Wright, and Hopkins, *op. cit.*, p. 9.
36. There are many different ways in which agencies may combine goals. Some goals may, in turn, be instrumental for other goals being conceived in sequential terms. For a discussion of such unusual combinations, see our later discussion of "chains of effects."
37. *Op. cit.*, p. 5.
38. *Ibid.*
39. Hyman, Wright, and Hopkins, *op. cit.*, pp. 5–6.
40. *Op. cit.*
41. Robert O. Carlson, "The Influence of the Community and the Primary Group on the Reactions of Southern Negroes to Syphilis," unpublished Ph.D. dissertation, Columbia University, 1952.
42. Barton, *op. cit.*, p. 24.
43. The comparison group serves the same analytical functions as the conventional control group. Any differences between the several groups cannot be attributed to such extraneous factors as external events, growth, or practice from repeated testing since these influences are present in all the groups. The inherent limitation of the conventional design which Solomon described—that the sensitization to the treatment created by pretesting is not measurable—is also solved by the comparative design since all the groups are sensitized to whichever treatment they are subsequently given. The comparative design resolves another ambiguity as well, namely, whether the effects are attributable to the program or merely represent the salutary effects of giving a neglected group some attention—a kind of "Hawthorne phenomenon."
44. Weir *et al., op. cit.*, p. 75. The finding refers to one class of effects. On some dependent variables, other factors were effective.
45. *Ibid.*, p. 56.
46. *Ibid.*
47. Bernard Berelson and Ronald Freedman, "A Study in Fertility Control," *Scientific American*, CCX (May, 1964), 6.
48. *Ibid.*, p. 10.
49. K. Srinivasan and K. Ranganathan, "Three Educational Procedures Compared," in *Studies and Research in Health Education*, Vol. 5, International Conference on Health and Health Education, n.d., p. 594 (published by the *International Journal of Health Education*).
50. In any comparison of total programs, the findings may be a function of any of the components—staff, site, or treatment. In his attempt to unravel the explanation, the evaluator may neglect the obvious component mentioned earlier: the relative duration and temporal features of the several programs.
51. P. F. Lazarsfeld, Foreword to Barton, *op. cit.*, p. 10.
52. J. Dumazedier, *Television and Rural Adult Education* (Paris: UNESCO, 1956); *Rural Television in Japan, A Report on an Experiment in Adult Education* (Paris: UNESCO, Series on Press, Film and Radio in the World Today, 1960), Chapter 4, p. 67. For a related study, see J. C. Mathur and P. Neurath, *An Indian Experi-*

ment in Farm Radio Forums (Paris: UNESCO, 1959), in which a radio farm program in India was evaluated. Apropos our earlier remark that agencies do not like to deny the benefits of treatment to needy subjects, in the Japanese study the program and clubs should have been organized within a limited area to make the evaluations comparable. Strong opposition to this plan developed in Japan on the grounds that such an educational opportunity should not be denied to many villages. A compromise solution was finally achieved.

53. Personal communication, UNESCO, Division of Applied Social Sciences. A third treatment is introduced into the design *asymmetrically* in India, but not Costa Rica, involving what is known as *animation*. Villagers are given special training and then act as "animateurs" or stimulators of social change in their home communities.

54. Samuel A. Stouffer *et al., The American Soldier: Adjustment during Army Life* (Princeton: Princeton University Press, 1949), p. 46.

55. Report (1961–1963), "Intensive Agricultural District Programme" by the Expert Committee on Assessment and Evaluation, Ministry of Food and Agriculture, Department of Agriculture, India.

56. T. M. Newcomb, "Persistency and Regression of Changed Attitudes: Long Range Studies," *Journal of Social Issues*, XIX, No. 4 (October, 1963), p. 6. Some of the special difficulties that arise in such extended longitudinal inquiries are well illustrated by Newcomb, and some ingenious methodological solutions are advanced.

57. Paul F. Lazarsfeld, Bernard Berelson, and Hazel Gaudet, *The People's Choice*, 2nd ed. (New York: Columbia University Press, 1948), pp. xiv–xix.

58. William and Joan McCord (with Irving K. Zola), *Origins of Crime: A New Evaluation of the Cambridge–Somerville Youth Study* (New York: Columbia University Press, 1959).

59. Powers and Witmer, *op. cit.*, p. vii.

60. Reminiscent of our earlier distinction between a program as planned and as actually realized, however, questions have been raised whether the actual treatment of the boys approximated that which was planned closely enough to constitute a fair trial of the original plan; also, other criteria of success have been applied, such as ratings of adjustment of boys in both groups and individual case analyses.

61. McCord and McCord, *op. cit.*, p. 24.

62. Robert K. Merton, George G. Reader, and Patricia L. Kendall, eds., *The Student Physician* (Cambridge: Harvard University Press, 1957), p. 304. The way in which the replications and also longitudinal studies improved certain of these evaluations is presented in Patricia Kendall, "Evaluating an Experimental Program in Medical Education," in M. Miles, ed., *Innovation in Education* (New York: Columbia University, Teachers' College Bureau of Publications, 1964), Chapter 15.

63. *Op. cit.*

64. *Ibid.*

65. *Ibid.*, p. 8.

66. For a fuller discussion of the problems of controlled experiments in evaluation, see *ibid.*, pp. 17–53.

67. For a discussion of this specialized design, see the extended treatment in the original monograph, *ibid.*, pp. 42–49.

68. *Op. cit.*

69. R. A. Dentler, *The Young Volunteers: An Evaluation of Three Programs of the*

American Friends Service Committee (Chicago: National Opinion Research Center, 1959).

70. Terence K. Hopkins (with the assistance of Sanci Michael), *Group Structure and Opinion Change: An Analysis of the Encampment for Citizenship* (New York: Bureau of Applied Social Research, Columbia University, mimeographed, 1962).

Resistance to

Sociological Data:

A Case Study

JUDITH R. KRAMER

chapter 28

Although there are always sociological gadflies to goad us to take up the burden of social responsibility, there is seldom sufficient suggestion of the nature of the beast or the burden. Unfortunately, neither eloquence of sociological advocacy nor urgency of social cause can substitute for specific guideposts in the responsible use of knowledge. The exercise of such responsibility presupposes an understanding of both its social requirements and its sociological limits. If we examine the expectations sociologists encounter in the minority community, we may increase our grasp of the difficulties involved in meeting the social demands made upon sociology generally.

The sociologist entering the minority community to get information is also asked to give it. In the reciprocity of the field, the community grants the observer an inside view of its social life in exchange for an outside view of its social structure. Although a number of field observers have recognized the psychic satisfactions the interview affords the respondent,[1] few have noted the cognitive functions of the findings. The detachment of an observer who is in but not of the community provides a perspective as crucial to social action as to scientific method. In order to pursue their interests effectively, the members of a minority community, for example, require objective knowledge about the position of their community in the larger society and their own position in the minority community.

A sociological analysis of social structure requires data on internal differentiation. Therein lies the dilemma. The minority community, like any community, is stratified; it encompasses a variety of attitudes and behavior. Its ideology, however, insists upon a "united front" that denies differences lest they appear as cleavages. Research that is officially sanctioned and subsidized by defense agencies is more likely to focus on the attitudes and behavior of the dominant group than on those of the minority group. By implication, the findings attribute the minority situation to the prejudice and discrimination of the dominant group, absolving the minority group from any responsibility for its social disadvantages; community research thus serves to support the communal ideology.

Such ideology-bound research, however, does not provide the leaders of the minority group with data enabling them to adapt the organizational structure of the community to the changing interests of its members, and organizations that fail to take cognizance of social change risk the loss of support and subsidy. With the survival of a minority way of life at stake, community leaders seek sociological knowledge to convert into social strategies safeguarding the community from loss of members and the members from loss of identity. Thus the official representatives of the community are unofficially interested in its internal differentiation. They must know the facts (and consequences) of social stratification in order to maintain the minority community and/or to transform the minority situation.

When we proposed a study of stratification and generation in the Minneapolis Jewish community,[2] for example, every defense and education agency in the city was interested in its outcome, but none in its subsidy. They preferred to sponsor studies of Gentile attitudes toward Jews (on the assumption that anti-Semitism among Gentiles was the root of all social evil) or of Jewish attitudes toward Judaism (on the assumption that philo-Semitism among Jews was the source of American social survival). Our situation with the Jewish agencies was not unlike that of a sociological red hen; everyone wanted a piece of the bread, but no one wanted to help bake it.

The study proceeded without benefit of subsidy. Free of financial support, we were also free to study the problems of stratification and generation as conceptualized by sociological theory, rather than as conceived by ideological issues. One agency, however, did ask us to find out what we could about local interest in Jewish organizations as an unpaid postscript to the interview. Other agencies later wanted to discuss the implications of our findings for organizational programming; they were particularly eager to engage the active interest of the younger generation in order to be assured of the support of the sons and heirs of the second-generation businessmen who were their present mainstay.[3]

The leaders of a minority community represent the vested interests in its survival; their interest in sociology is a strategic one. The sociological knowledge needed in social action, however, involves in-group information rarely and reluctantly given to an outsider. The shared secrets of communal life are considered the special prerogative of the socially committed. Any sociological challenge to their ideological monopoly challenges the very structure of the minority community. Since the strength of the minority community lies in a solidarity as much simulated as real, it is discomforted by the discovery and disclosure of internal differences that might invite divisive tactics.

Insofar as the public disclosure of its private life increases the vulnerability of the minority group to the power of the dominant group, the publication of communal data is regarded as an act of social betrayal akin to the violation of sociological confidence. Not the anonymity of an individual identity, but the status of a minority community is threatened by public access to its social secrets. As a result, the minority community fights findings that are not kept within its fold, attacking both the validity of the research and the competence of the researcher.

The publication of *Children of the Gilded Ghetto* was greeted with the customary charges of heresy; the reception in the Jewish press was similar to the one Negroes gave E. Franklin Frazier's *Black Bourgeoisie*.[4] Leaders of the Jewish community were united in their condemnation of a book written by "outsiders"; the sociological results of social detachment, however sympathetic, were considered the unqualified and unfounded criticism of angry young authors washing Jewish linen in public.[5]

Analogous to the potential of sociology for changing the structure of the community is its potential for maintaining or transforming the situation of the individual. An individual dissatisfied with his status quo must know the opportunities for changing his way of life before he can avail himself of them. Once aware of alternatives, he must know the means of achieving them in order for his motivation to have social consequence. Just as knowledge of the prerequisites of behavior and attitudes makes possible the social mobility of an individual, so knowledge of its consequences makes possible an evaluation of its personal worth to him. The individual who is able to translate sociological hindsight into social foresight is equipped to assess the means of transforming his situation in terms of their relative costs and rewards.

Sociological knowledge has particular importance for the minority-group member, who is likely to know more about the alternatives that are closed to him than those that are open to him. The cultural heritage of a minority group bequeaths to each generation an acute awareness of its social deprivations, but the experience of the past may not constitute an adequate basis for effective behavior in the present. Although the limits of the minority situation change from one generation to the next, the awareness of social change rarely keeps pace. Inappropriate historical projection may prevent minority-group members from testing the limits of a new social reality.

The difficulties of ascertaining and assessing social alternatives are compounded by the characteristic confusion of class and ethnic identity among minority-group members. When a particular class situation is closely associated with the minority situation, it is likely to be incorporated into the self-image of the minority group as well as into the stereotypes of the dominant group. When certain occupations appear to constitute the only basis for membership in the minority community, the consideration of alternatives is not only clouded by invalid information but fraught with personal ambivalence. There are, therefore, minority-group members who prefer to believe in extensive discrimination than to examine their own hesitation to integrate. The psychological consequences of the minority situation thus contribute to its social perpetuation by controlling the aspirations for existing opportunities.

The demand for sociological knowledge derives from the desire to know what is socially possible and promising. The individual in search of autonomy needs all the knowledge he can acquire; the areas of uncertainty are sufficient to guarantee errors and unanticipated consequences in the calculus of social action without further deprivation of sociological information. Insofar as sociologists fail to make their knowledge available and accessible, they contribute to social irrationality. Without relinquishing ethical neutrality, sociologists can specify alternatives that permit the individual a more realistic evaluation of his situation and a more rational decision. C. Wright Mills points out "that the individual can understand his experience and gauge his own fate only by becoming aware of those of all individuals in his circumstances." [6]

A sociological understanding of the social condition eases the individual's sense of isolation. "No one quite knows what the other is like, and all compare their private selves with the public appearance of others." [7] The apparent disparities exacerbate social and psychological tensions and impede their resolution. Without knowing what their peers are, in fact, doing and how, individuals are shut off from social support and shared ways of coping with reality.

The third generation is more than curious about life outside the gilded ghetto; it is concerned. The comforts of the enclosed community are no longer adequate compensation for its constraints; young Jews are seeking other ways to live. There is, however, no institutionalized source of social knowledge. Jewish agencies foster such insulation. They are more concerned with social exclusion than self-exclusion, and therefore they concentrate more on the opinions of Gentiles than on the opportunities generated by Gentiles.[8] In failing to specify available alternatives, agencies delimit rather than delineate social opportunities.

Both the virtue and the defect of the sociologist's "trained incapacity" is his relative knowledge of the social resources of the community and his relative ignorance of the personal capacities of the individual. He is therefore in no position to judge (as he is often asked to do) the outcome of a decision to utilize the structure of social opportunities. The responsibility for the pursuit of social values remains the individual's; the responsibility for spelling out the social ways and means for implementing values falls to the sociologist. Organizations oriented more to opportunity than to opinion could serve as intermediaries between the individual and the sociologist, if such a function did not conflict with their ideology. By making available alternatives known, agencies would be making possible changes in individual situations. To educate the minority community instead of the dominant community, however, might transform its structure and thus threaten its survival.

Robert Lynd has urged that "the variables in the social scientist's equation must include not only the given set of structured institutions, but also *what the present human carriers of those institutions are groping to become.*" [9] But the social agencies of the Jewish community find that message distasteful; their vested interest lies in established institutions rather than aspiring individuals. To maintain the status quo of the gilded ghetto they must maintain the social identity of the inhabitants as it is, rather than risk what it might become.

Like the minority community, the academic profession has its own ideological responses to socially relevant sociological research. The abdication of social responsibility for the power that inheres in sociological knowledge is most often excused by professional expediency, that is, by the psychic income derived from pure research addressed to appreciative peers and by the material income derived from applied research in behalf of special interests. There is little professional concern or private subsidy for the study of the minority community. Most research to date has been instigated by social agencies and formulated in terms of parochial needs. The results add more heat to the polemics of the minority situation than they shed light on its determining forces. Research informed by sociological theory rather than formed by social ideology is rare.

To attack the problems of minority groups is to incur the risk of double jeopardy: the charge of betrayal by the community whose confidence has been violated and the charge of popularization by the profession whose monopoly has been challenged. The sharing of sociological knowledge with those studied does not so much dilute its substance as diminish its scarcity value, further attenuating the already tenuous status of the sociologist. As long as sociologists talk only to each other, they incur little social risk; the price of their professional security, however, is the failure to fulfill the social promise of the sociological imagination.

REFERENCES

1. See, for example, David Riesman, "A Field Report: Some Observations on the Interviewing," in Paul F. Lazarsfeld and Wagner Thielens, Jr., *The Academic Mind* (Glencoe, Ill.: The Free Press, 1958), pp. 266–370; and Kaspar D. Naegele, "Some Problems in the Study of Hostility and Aggression in Middle-Class American Families," in Norman W. Bell and Ezra F. Vogel, eds., *A Modern Introduction to the Family* (Glencoe, Ill.: The Free Press, 1960), pp. 417–428.

2. The study was jointly undertaken by Judith R. Kramer and Seymour Leventman and published as *Children of the Gilded Ghetto* in 1962 by Yale University Press.

3. The effectiveness of some of the strategies suggested by our data surprised sociologist and social actionist alike. The usual round of luncheons and card parties planned by Jewish organizations had little appeal for college-educated sons seeking an appropriate style of life. Activities that transcended the social boundaries of the community, transforming parochialism into cosmopolitanism, were more attuned to their status aspirations. The first such socially oriented occasion was a great success, in spite of its organizational support! It was a cocktail party in honor of a newly published book paying tribute to the assistance given to Jews during Hitler's holocaust by European non-Jews. Among those invited were members of local embassies and their social peers in the dominant community. The third generation turned out in large numbers, if only to seek status in the company of cosmopolites.

4. Glencoe, Ill.: The Free Press, 1957. For claiming that the Negro middle class had status without substance, Frazier was accused of disloyalty to his race. This charge against him became so common that even his obituary in *The New York Times* commented on it.

5. The reviews carried by Minneapolis newspapers and Jewish periodicals revealed more of the response of the community than of the content of the book. The local reviewers were less concerned with the facts of the study than the fact of its publication. After summarizing the findings (often without comment and occasionally with affirmation), they proceeded to defend the community by attacking the authors. The sociological portrayal of the community that aroused its social paranoia was most often attributed to the self-hatred of the eastern-born and university-trained authors, who were themselves a shameful reflection on the third generation.

6. C. Wright Mills, *The Sociological Imagination*, Evergreen ed. (New York: Grove Press, 1961), p. 5.

7. Naegele, *op. cit.*, p. 426.

8. Hughes observed the irony of the situation some time ago. "In fact, Jews spend millions to reform Christians; the reform wanted is that the Christians should think better of the Jews." Everett C. and Helen M. Hughes, *Where Peoples Meet* (Glencoe, Ill.: The Free Press, 1952), p. 107.

9. Robert S. Lynd, *Knowledge for What?* (Princeton: Princeton University Press, 1946), p. 180.

The Sociologist in the Nonacademic Setting

JOHN W. RILEY, JR.

chapter 29

Recent studies indicate that approximately one sociologist in four is now employed in the nonacademic setting. But this figure does not even hint at the true story of the widespread involvement of sociologists in the world of affairs; for among the sociologists whose primary affiliations are academic, the majority are also engaged in various nonacademic enterprises.[1]

What follows is an organizational analysis of the roles and status of sociologists in nonacademic settings as these are taking shape in contemporary society. In contrast to academic sociologists, over 85 per cent of whom hold appointments within college or university departments of sociology, nonacademic sociologists follow no single typical career pattern. They are to be found in positions at various levels in government agencies, in nonprofit organizations, in business and industry, in self-employment; and within each of these employment areas, their roles are highly diversified. Furthermore, any particular nonacademic position typically involves a greater number of functions than the usual academic position, often in-

789

cluding a wide array of varied research, training, consultative, administrative, and managerial tasks.

Despite the wide variation in these nonacademic sociological roles, the process of adjustment to them seems to have followed a fairly consistent pattern. This chapter will consider certain common aspects of these career lines as they seem to be evolving under the impact of increasing demand for sociological services. There is no systematic body of relevant information. But a review of the literature, examination of new materials provided by many nonacademic sociologists, and some application of sociological theory allow us to begin to suggest the nature of the process by which the sociologists may move from the traditional academic setting to a new nonacademic environment.

Nonacademic sociologists, in their own writings, frequently concentrate on their problems and difficulties. Such negative reports often suggest the lines along which positive solutions are being worked out. In a 1959 survey of social scientists working outside the university, for example, the Russell Sage Foundation found that their problems fell into three major categories: (1) lack of clarity about the expectations of them that make up their roles, (2) differences between organizational and professional goals, and (3) uncertainty over the social scientist's status in the organization.[2] Although this survey does not reflect some of the most recent developments in the career patterns of nonacademic sociologists, these general problem areas remain largely the same.

We shall deal here with developments along three lines: clarity of role definitions, professional identity, and status. These considerations will be thought of as "elements" in a crude model which begins to predict solutions to the problems typically encountered by nonacademic sociologists. Reduced to its simplest "evolutionary" form, this model suggests that clarity of role definitions supports a sense of professional identity and that a combination of clear expectations of functions and behavior and identity maintenance tends to maximize the opportunities for high status. Or, in the still relatively rare instance where sociologists have been assigned initially to high-status positions in nonacademic settings, the model suggests that high status, in turn, will minimize conflicts and ambiguities in roles within the organization. At the same time, it will reduce the sociologist's personal anxieties about maintaining his professional identity.

New Roles for Sociologists

Irrespective of the particular setting, nonacademic sociologists have found themselves in awkward organizational relationships to the practitioners and men of action who not only maintain different values but are committed to entirely different ways of coping with problems. The consequent strains have often been severe. Yet the difficulties have tended to disappear once a clear distinction has been made, on both sides, between *organizational* conflict, which may be inevitable in the early stages, and feelings of *personal* inadequacy, which may be quite illegitimate.

LEGITIMATION AND RESOLUTION OF ROLE CONFLICT

The sociologist in a nonacademic position, like any incumbent of a new role, usually steps into a relatively unstructured and ambiguous situation. The institutional supports which strengthen the academic sociologist's position have not yet been established; not even the asset of a popular stereotype is present to pattern expectations of his behavior. As Whitman has put it, the nonacademic sociologist often "finds himself in a situation where role definitions are not precise and where the expectations are not consistent." [3] Thus issues arise around the "academic" freedom to choose research topics, attendance at professional meetings, publication rights, and a myriad of mundane matters which are typically taken for granted by university scholars.

In the military establishment, for example, where sociologists have been subsidized to investigate fundamental problems, the support has been sporadic and often based on misconceptions of the potentials. The explanation for this, according to Janowitz, lies in the "liberal" tradition of the social sciences. Thus a tension has developed between the professional soldier and the sociologist. "The professional soldier often sees the social scientist as naïve, even though he must defer to him because of professional courtesy. The social scientist sees the professional soldier as dogmatic." [4] The result is that the sociologist, responding to these basic differences in values, has often begun his task by using a cautious, segmental, and technical method, rather than a comprehensive and widely ranging approach to the military establishment.

A similar set of problems is faced by the sociologist in business organizations. "The businessman and the social scientist represent two occupational groups with divergent values and goals." [5] One particularly acute problem is the difference in the time perspectives of the two. The businessman is oriented, at least in a major part of his role, to making decisions and taking action on a daily basis. Though he may recognize the importance of long-range studies, he is usually under pressure to cope with short-term situations. Another difference in values frequently comes to light in the assumed motivation of the on-the-job sociologist. As Carlson has pointed out:

There lingers in the minds of some businessmen a vague uneasiness that sociologists have a predilection for social reform which might be disruptive of the smooth operation of their firms. [Similarly] the sociologist may view the relationship with uneasiness. The prospect of employment in industry may be regarded as an invitation to join forces in a great conspiracy to manipulate and mislead workers, consumers and the general public.[6]

These differences in value orientation, until they are recognized on both sides as inevitable and legitimate, create strain and mistrust.

Another difference—this one having to do as much with social organization as with values—is even more frequently cited as a cause of initial difficulties. When the nonacademic colleagues of the nonacademic sociologist are members of the practicing professions (doctors, lawyers, architects, preachers, social workers), their relationship to people is quite different from the scholar's. Whereas the sociologist as scholar typically *studies* the behavior of people, the physician or social worker is committed to *helping* the patient or client. Consequently, when the sociologist's subjects and the doctor's patients or social worker's clients are one and the same, the potential for conflict of emphasis is obvious.[7] A recently published symposium, *Sociologists at Work*, underscores the common notion that whenever sociologists are asked questions, their typical answer is "We'll have to do some research." [8] The practicing professional man, of course, takes quite a different stance. It is rare in medical practice, for example, for the research question to be raised at all. The sociologist, on the other hand, is often stereotyped as merely asking and answering questions. Sometimes, indeed, he appears to be quite unconcerned about any practical application of his work.[9]

It seems clear, then, that there is a necessary initial period of mutual conflict and adjustment. However, this by no means precludes a later resolution in which the sociologist and his new colleagues develop effective and congruent perceptions of each other.[10] Leichter's realistic comment on her experience as a sociologist in a social-welfare agency illustrates the process:

> The role of the sociologist is a product of the interaction between those with differing professional subcultures, languages, styles of thought, and habits of work. In such a situation discrepancies in role expectations are inevitable. . . . Since role definitions were relatively unstructured, shifts constantly occurred, and the process of definition was slow. A good deal of time and energy inevitably goes into working out role definitions in a situation of this sort.[11]

The ultimate solution seems to lie in a mutual understanding, and ways and means are available for achieving this result. First, as the collaboration progresses there should be provision for continuing reviews and redefinitions. Second, there must be a clear recognition that such collaborative efforts are necessarily carried out within a framework of differences. Finally, it must be recognized that *both* basic and applied research can be carried out in *both* academic and nonacademic settings. Only in rare and special cases, where a well-thought-out and systematic definition of the situation has been made in the beginning phases, are such efforts unnecessary.[12]

SELECTIVE ROLE PLAYING

Another important dimension in the role-adjustment process of the non-academic sociologist has to do with the variety of new role partners—the heterogeneous role set[13]—with whom he must interact. His problem is to integrate the differing expectations of the multiple role partners. By contrast, the academic sociologist in a liberal arts college finds that his role as sociologist relates to role partners whose main reference is, like his own, to the academic system: students, departmental colleagues, and administrators. These relationships tend to be highly structured and well articulated. The sources of conflict are to a large extent anticipated, and available means of conflict resolution defined. The academic system, furthermore, provides a normative framework for relationships between its members and persons outside academia. The kinds of academic role which the professor plays in his day-to-day activities thus tend to be appropriate, regardless of which role partner is involved.

In comparison, the role set typically encountered by the nonacademic sociologist is characterized by a more heterogeneous array of role partners functioning at more widely separated points in the social structure: a situation described by Merton as a basic source of potential disturbance.[14] The medical sociologist in a hospital provides a good illustration. In the usual hospital setting, his role partners might include all or many of the following: the hospital director, administrators, physicians, surgeons, psychiatrists, psychologists, social workers, nurses, interns, various medical technicians, aides, orderlies, volunteers, clerical personnel, patients, and patients' relatives. Not all of these relationships will be equally important, to be sure. There will be some shifting in the patterning of relationships, so that some are central at one time, peripheral at other times. Nevertheless, the medical sociologist's role set includes at any time at least some of the occupants of all these positions within the hospital system. Yet his full complement of role partners also includes sociological colleagues who are outside the hospital system entirely. It is thus obvious that the nonacademic sociologist can function effectively only if he finds means of reconciling the differing expectations of these various members of his role set.

Although little systematic knowledge is available, our informal survey of the experience to date suggests that selective role playing is clearly one answer. At the outset of a new assignment the sociologist often fails to make such selections. Thus, he sometimes assumes that all his role partners in the nonacademic setting know nothing about his field, and consequently he feels called upon to act as a missionary or propagandist. Sometimes, at the other extreme, he may overestimate their knowledge of his discipline and speak too technically, thus acquiring a reputation for jargon and esoteric views. Or he may lose his identity as a sociologist, proceeding to function as though he were himself a practitioner and thus losing his essential utility as a sociologist. As the nonacademic assignment progresses, however, it becomes obvious to the sociologist that he must be *at times* a missionary, *at times* a technical expert, *at times* a practitioner. He learns that he can accomplish such selection because he need not be uniformly visible to *all* members of his role set at *all* times. As Merton has put it more generally, "Some insulation of some role activities from observability by some members of the role set will reduce conflict; uniform observability of all role activities by all members of the role set is bound to increase conflict." [15] Recent experience of industrial sociologists serves to underscore the importance of selective role playing as a solution to such problems.[16]

A New Sense of Professional Identity

Let us turn next to the second "element" in our model: the mechanisms which are available to the nonacademic sociologist for the maintenance of his professional identity.

Throughout his academic training, the sociologist acquires skills, aspirations, and self-conceptions which are oriented toward the image of the "pure" scientist. He learns to place high value on his freedom to choose the problems to be studied, to develop theories, and to select methods for testing evolving hypotheses. His education has usually devoted but little time to the practical applications of research. It is not surprising, then, that many sociologists have doubts and anxieties about entering careers in applied fields or working in nonacademic settings. Negative reactions of their academic colleagues, either actual or anticipated, may add to their hesitation and reluctance. They hear much advice against a career outside the mainstream of the discipline. They are told that "captive" scientists lose their freedom to select problems. They encounter questions about the dubious motives and the commitment of the professional who chooses applied work. They read allegations that scientists who go into applied work have little competence and less creative capacity. And they are warned about the loss of professional status.[17] As Ferguson has recently reported:

There has been and still is a feeling among *some* social scientists . . . that those who work in industry are not of the elite . . . because only the university setting is attractive to the most competent. In the physical sciences, however, the level of scientific contribution from industrial laboratories has almost dispelled this prejudice, and this feeling is also rapidly becoming common among social scientists.[18]

Once on the job in a new setting, moreover, the nonacademic sociologist seems to be faced repeatedly with the possible loss of his professional identity. He solves only part of his dilemma by realistically recognizing the legitimacy and inevitability of role conflict. Nor can selective role playing necessarily guarantee the viability of his relationships to academic—as well as to his nonacademic—peers. He typically receives little support from his occupational role set. What he often misses most is "the informal day-to-day contacts and a sense of having recognized membership in an informal and relatively intimate group of colleagues." [19] He suffers from what might be called a "role deficit." He comes to realize that if he is to function successfully qua sociologist in the nonacademic setting, he must, above all else, find means of maintaining identification with his profession.

Although isolation from his profession is thus a very real threat to the applied sociologist, there are steps he can take to maintain contact. He can keep up to date with the literature, visit university departments, teach a course in the local college or university, or consult with sociological colleagues about research problems. Sociologists who combine nonacademic work with teaching, or who work with others from their own or a closely related discipline, do not appear to suffer from role deficit. The trend toward a shifting back and forth between academic and nonacademic positions which Sibley has noted [20] may, consequently, prove to have long-term relevance. Moreover, this practice gives academic sociologists a greater appreciation of the roles played by their colleagues in nonacademic assignments.

CONTRIBUTIONS TO THE DISCIPLINE

Mutual tolerance and understanding are only part of the relationship between the academic and nonacademic sociologist. Far more significant is the growing recognition among both groups of the basic contributions to sociological knowledge, theory, and method. So it is important in assessing the work of the nonacademic sociologist to emphasize, specifically, the potential benefits of his efforts to the discipline itself. The relatively limited scope of experimentation in sociology for the verification of hypotheses and findings makes applied research in practical situations particularly important. In this process, gaps in knowledge are identified, new fields of study are discovered, and vast stores of data are provided.[21] Moreover, nonacademic sociologists have abundant opportunity to investigate problems of basic methodological or theoretical concern, which may eventually lead to contributions to method or reformulations of theory.[22]

Indeed, the work of the nonacademic sociologist is stimulated by certain demands placed on him which the academic sociologist need not face. The applied sociologist cannot, for example, put aside a problem merely because it does not lend itself to conventional sociological analysis. Instead, freed from the necessity of conforming to prevailing sociological orthodoxy, he is frequently under pressure to innovate and must therefore improvise.[23] Many nonacademic sociologists, consequently, are clearly challenged by the new perspectives they are afforded and by the new problems they are constantly required to meet. In the process, they are not only developing a new respect for their own discipline but also earning the regard and esteem of their academically based colleagues.

SOCIOLOGY AND THE COMMUNITY

Another important bulwark to the professional identity of the nonacademic sociologist is the perspective which he necessarily gains on "the obligation placed by society on sociology, as on all sciences, to pay its own way by contributions to knowledge of recognized social utility." [24]

Sociology, from its earliest beginnings as an academic discipline in this country, has taken the position that social problems could be analyzed from the vantage point of social structure. Crime as a social problem offers a good example. For many years sociologists have investigated the varying incidence of crime through comparative studies of crime rates in different societies and through ecological studies of the distribution of crime in urban areas. They have also studied correlates of crime and have interested themselves in such special problems as prostitution, professional crime, and racketeering.[25] Since these problem areas have also been the concern of social workers, this led to the early development of a relationship between the academic discipline of sociology and the practicing profession of social work.

Shortly after the turn of the century, however, sociology showed signs of a temporary withdrawal from such "applied" relationships, beginning to concentrate on the building of a basic science. Several decades of productive scholarship followed. But the depression had the effect of re-establishing some of sociology's traditional concern with social problems; and the effort to mobilize social-science resources during World War II marked the return, as Parsons has noted, "to applied interests over a far broader front than before." [26] In both military and industrial establishments, sociologists became active in the national effort. In the military, sociologists were concerned, for the most part, with problems of morale and the management of personnel. A few served in intelligence research and psychological-warfare operations, and larger numbers worked on such problems as political warfare, social aspects of small-unit efficiency, patterns of leadership and control, and structural and cultural aspects of the military.[27] Similarly, the relationship between industry and sociology began to take shape in earnest during World War II. In particular, developments in such fields as industrial sociology and survey research procedures—especially as these were applied to marketing problems and to the specific social and political issues created by wartime shortages—gave added impetus to the applied function. The collaboration was mutually beneficial: business and industry needed answers which the sociologists could provide, and the sociologists needed research sites in which to develop useful findings.[28]

Since the war, there has been a gradual but steady rapprochement between the academic world of sociological ideas and the practical world of human affairs. An especially important area for the nonacademic sociologist has been the practicing professions. In 1955, Donald Young, as President of the American Sociological Society, stimulated this development by emphasizing that sociologists had not yet taken advantage of the many opportunities offered:

> Leaders in the practicing professions where an understanding of human behavior is clearly of crucial major importance, as in the health services and social work, are becoming increasingly dissatisfied with [the] traditional and uncertain approach to the problems of social behavior encountered in their specialties. They know that there are thousands of social scientists at work on related if not identical problems, and are impatient that the results of this work have been of so little practical importance.[29]

Consequently a new pattern has emerged in which sociologists and other specialists participate in research and training for a number of applied professions.[30] The historical affiliation between sociology and social work has recently been renewed, primarily through the participation of sociologists in the training of social-work students and in social-work research. Perhaps the most dramatic example of this new pattern has occurred in the general field of health. Of all positions outside traditional departments of sociology, the largest number open to sociologists are reported to be in schools of medicine, nursing, and public health.[31] Social research is thus becoming an important aspect of the research programs in schools of public health and is beginning to contribute to research in medical-school programs. Indeed, a new trend may be in the making which will include sociology in the basic sciences that underlie the practice of medicine.

Similarly, impressive tasks and opportunities lie ahead for the sociologists who are being called to responsible positions in other professional schools or institutes: business, engineering, law, education, and theology. Furthermore, the enhanced recognition of the relevance of sociological concepts and insights to urban planning and architecture, legal procedures, educational systems,[32] church affairs—and many more—provides an increasingly important identification between the nonacademic sociologists and their university-based colleagues.

Although sociologists have no equivalent concept for "justice," "health," or "wealth"—the working criteria for law, medicine, and economics[33]— they are now confronted with increasing opportunities to contribute to the great decisions of our time. Their essential position of "value neutrality" may, in short, turn out to be an asset rather than a handicap. In business and industry such central problems as the resolution of intergroup conflict, or the isolation and analysis of factors in the planning and administering of change, are increasingly being seen as essentially sociological in nature.[34] In the federal government the range of relevant problems—civil rights, poverty, foreign aid, mental health, just to name a few—is perhaps even more awesome. Even in connection with the all-important issues of war and peace, despite the severe limitations imposed by security considerations, the role of sociologists seems destined to be played out in one form or another. As long as the military focus was on nuclear war, officially stimulated research dealt with the social and psychological aspects of disaster. As concepts of limited warfare have emerged, however, the perspective on the social consequences of military operations has changed. As Janowitz has pointed out:

> The analysis of the sociological consequences of limited warfare cannot be understood within the categories used by the American military establishment. . . . An understanding of how American social structure has influenced the development of our military institutions and how military organizations adapt to and resist change is at the root of the matter.[35]

Clearly, the notion that the university is the only proper operating base for the sociologist, together with the belief that the only reputable form of sociological inquiry is "pure" research, is diminishing. And with these changes, the invidious distinction which has frequently separated the academic from the nonacademic sociologist will also lose its divisive force. Thus it becomes more and more possible for the sociologist to work outside of academic, while still retaining his professional identity.

The New Status of the Nonacademic Sociologist

We have been assuming that a satisfactory resolution of the role problems and the identity problems of nonacademic sociologists will, in the long run, tend to eliminate the ambiguity and relative inferiority which has typically been characteristic of their status. Although the specifics of such a process are still far from clear, a number of empirical clues, together with some related theoretical insights, suggest two points. First, the ambiguity which has frequently marked the occupational status of the nonacademic sociologist is gradually being resolved as more realistic definitions develop. And second, the opportunities for nonacademic sociologists in influential positions of relatively high status appear to be increasingly plentiful. A brief discussion of these two points should provide additional though still incomplete understanding of the transition of the sociologist from an academic to a nonacademic setting.

THE DEVELOPMENT OF AN UNAMBIGUOUS POSITION

As with the problem of his roles, the nonacademic sociologist has often found himself assigned to a new organizational status which is unclear and ambiguous. In the business world, for example, Carlson notes that "management is often puzzled by how to classify and assign a sociologist within the corporate structure. It may wonder if he is not too specialized and hence limited in the career development which can be held out for him." [36] Consequently, the representative of a relatively new science such as sociology often finds it necessary to demonstrate its relevance in "a rather rigid bureaucratic, authoritarian, status conscious, institutional situation." [37]

So far as sociologists in the federal government are concerned, a recent study shows that frequently they must meet qualifications set up, not for the sociologist, but for the statistician, psychologist, public-health analyst, education-research specialist, and program specialist. This inappropriate definition of their status restricts the employment opportunities for sociologists in the federal government and thus works against the development called for by many leaders of the profession; namely, the wider use of sociological knowledge for the practical concerns of society.[38]

Such status ambiguities manifest themselves in the misconception held by that person in the organization to whom the sociologist reports. In the typical case there is an unrealistic understanding of sociological skills and capabilities. A panacea may be expected which sociology is not able to provide. Or skepticism may so color the enterprise that there is no serious expectation of any beneficial results at all. The sociologist is then in the unhappy position of having to convince his superiors that a sociologist can make any worthwhile contribution whatsoever.

In attempting to work out this status problem in the organization, the sociologist has occasionally made the mistake of giving his status the narrow and safe definition of technician. Indeed, in some cases sociologists appear to have been trained to be inconspicuous. Many of them have been so successful in this status that they have made no impact on the organization at all, and findings of their studies simply have never been implemented. This tendency has been noted in the practicing professions and also in business, where Carlson has found that sociologists frequently accept a narrow definition of their status. Unwilling or unable to expand the scope of their positions, they tend to function only as "research experts." Consequently, management takes over the responsibility for defining research problems, initiating projects, and determining guidelines. Sociologists then find themselves confined to the activities of collecting and analyzing data.

Another "resolution" to the status problem occurs in situations where the practitioner grows overly dependent on the sociologist. The businessman or the doctor, for example, becomes so involved with sociological expertise that he loses sight of his own philosophy of management or practice. Conversely, the sociologist himself may become so dependent on the new organization in which he finds himself that he fails to communicate new knowledge effectively to others in the organization.[39]

These instances of the general failure to establish a clear position for the sociologist in a nonacademic setting all reflect, in one way or another, the underlying differences we have noted between the professional goals of the sociologist and the organizational goals of the person to whom he reports.[40] Although there is no simple solution to the problem created by this difference in perceived goals, a recent study by Glaser suggests that the status ambiguity of scientists in industry can be reduced if the scientific and the organizational goals are brought into some degree of congruence. Many past studies of nonacademically based scientists have concluded that their orientations tend to be either "cosmopolitan" (with primary allegiance to the discipline) or "local" (with primary allegiance to the organization). Glaser's study, in contrast, points out that a "local-cosmopolitan" orientation has emerged whenever "a congruence of goals" has been attained and that this new orientation "reduces in considerable measure, if not completely, the strains between organizational and professional requirements . . ."[41]

In this connection, three recommendations, drawn from a survey of industrial cases in which social-science knowledge had been effectively utilized, take on broader meaning:

1. The sociologist must understand the practitioner's problems, and the practitioner must know what the application of the sociological knowledge entails. "Social science is not a commodity that can be purchased at the local appliance store and then installed like a television set or a refrigerator."[42]

2. The sociologist must let the practitioner know which aspects of his discipline may be useful and also make him aware of the limitations of current knowledge. Each must acquire realistic expectations of the other; otherwise the sociologist will find himself confronted either with a level of expectation that is beyond realization or with an unrealistic skepticism.

3. If the sociologist is to produce new knowledge which stands any chance of yielding concrete results for the organization with which he is working, the knowledge itself must be translated (or easily translatable) into specific courses of alternative action.[43] Here the sociologist himself

needs orientation; he must realize that, in an applied setting, he will be called upon to demonstrate the potential relevance of his research for the field in which he is working.

Where such efforts have been made successfully, the problem of status ambiguity, at least in the business setting, seems to have been largely dispelled. At this juncture, however, there is too little experience on which to base any general principles as to how this outcome may be guaranteed.

POSITIONS OF HIGH STATUS AND INFLUENCE

On one point, however, we can be quite certain. The experience to date strongly suggests a correlation between ambiguity of status *definition* and a low *rank* in the organizational hierarchy. We turn, consequently, to an issue typically confronted by all nonacademic sociologists; that is, the status level at which they should be asked to function.

Experience has produced abundant illustrations of the variety of relatively low-level positions in which the nonacademic sociologist has found himself. Thus in the field of mental health he may turn up as a trouble shooter, a consultant, a sampling expert, but only occasionally as an administrator or research director. Similarly, in the area of corrections and penology, he may be classified as a counselor, a case-history interviewer, an actuary, a report writer, a probation officer—only sometimes as a criminologist or prison administrator.

The sociologist in such a low or nondescript status thus frequently finds himself severely handicapped. He may, for example, be in a "special project office," isolated from the main concerns of the practicing profession or from other departments which might otherwise find his discipline useful. He may be relegated to a "safe" place in the structure, where he cannot do much harm. Or he may be placed in a "safe" position under supervisors who are in a position to control his activities, even though they may have little knowledge of his specialized field.[44] In many law schools, for example, it is simply assumed that the sociologist should have his research and teaching directed by a lawyer. Or the sociologist's work may be evaluated by a person trained in another field. In social work, for example, "a high value is placed on adequate supervision and much responsibility rests with the supervisor. But the techniques for such supervision are limited, since the supervisor is not technically trained in the discipline of sociology. This makes it difficult to distinguish the competence of the field as a whole from that of the individual sociologist." [45]

The question of differences in rank is also raised in relation to specific professional distinctions. The sociologist is sometimes in a difficult position, for example, when he is working in the professions of medicine and law. Thus Sibley found that advanced degrees in sociology had not yet gained unequivocal acceptance as credentials of professional status in the nonacademic world. The Ph.D. carries none of the specific prerogatives of the M.D. or even the LL.B.[46]

So much for the rather dismal record of the past. But if we are correct in estimating positive trends in role clarification and identity maintenance, we should begin to see important changes in the status of nonacademic sociologists. Not only should sociologists reach increasingly high levels (as other problems are resolved), but increasing numbers of high-entry positions should become available to them as the worth and value of the discipline itself is more widely demonstrated. And this, of course, is precisely what seems to be happening.

Siegel and Robbins, for example, are at some pains to emphasize the importance of this point in their case study of a social-science program in a hospital. Precisely because the sociologist must relate to doctors, nurses, social workers, psychologists, and therapists, it was recognized that he could not "function as a representative of his own discipline" if he were to become enmeshed in the bureaucracy. Hence he was attached directly to the medical director, and in this status he was able to carry out his mission of contributing to the development of a therapeutic environment. Indeed, it was only "by making the sociologist a key person" that the hospital was able to provide a human laboratory "and to proceed to test the validity and utility of social science data." [47]

The challenge today lies in the tendency for more high-level positions to develop in nonacademic settings than there are competent sociologists available and willing to fill them. The problem, of course, is one of an appropriate fit between status level and the individual competence of the particular sociologist. There are many sociologists, but we do not argue that all of them automatically deserve high nonacademic status.

The emerging details of these nonacademic career lines remain somewhat obscure; but the current trend suggests that sociologists and offices of social research are increasingly being attached to high-ranking officers in the sponsoring organizations. This clearly reflects an enhanced estimate of the field and a recognition that sociologists, as well as scientists from other fields, require autonomy and opportunity to demonstrate their potential.

Concluding Note

The history of science tells us in unmistakable terms that in any discipline a trend toward nonacademic activities and concerns is irreversible, but there is no precedent to assure us that the opportunities currently open to sociology will be met. Sociologists may take considerable satisfaction in the knowledge that their services are sought after by the community, but this will be of small consequence if a discrepancy is allowed to develop between social expectations and sociological performance. Sociology is thus at a critical point in its development.

The nonacademic sociologist may be buffeted on one side by demands and expectations in the field in which he is active and, on the other, by the necessity to maintain his standing in the eyes of his sociological colleagues, some of whom vigorously oppose his work. However, it is not necessary for him to capitulate by taking on the protective coloring of the organization he serves. Nor is he required to make up his role deficit by becoming compulsively involved in sociological activities, neglecting his obligation to the organization which employs him.

He must recognize his responsibility to work in areas useful to his organization, and at the same time he must insist on freedom to delve into sociological problems not immediately relevant to the organization. Sociologists, both academic and nonacademic, seem generally to agree that the sociologist is most effective only when maintaining primary identification with the field of sociology. In the last analysis the successful utilization of sociology will depend on continuing efforts to formulate and test ideas and hypotheses in the basic science itself.

REFERENCES

NOTE: *Grateful acknowledgment is made to Rosalie Goldwater and Marguerite F. Levy for their effective assistance in the collection and organization of some of the materials on which this chapter is based and to Matilda White Riley, Robert K. Merton, Henry W. Riecken, and Orville G. Brim, Jr., for their generous contribution of ideas and critical comment.*

1. For detailed information on the occupational distribution of sociologists, see Matilda White Riley, "Membership of the American Sociological Association, 1950–59," *American Sociological Review*, XXV (1960), 914–926; Elbridge Sibley, *The Education of Sociologists in the United States* (New York: Russell Sage Foundation, 1963); and Abbott L. Ferriss, "Sociological Manpower," *American Sociological Review*, XXIX, No. 1 (February, 1964), 103–114. Elbridge Sibley, "The Sociologist as a Staff Member in Organized Social Science" (Paper presented at the Annual Meeting of the American Sociological Association, Washington, D.C., August 30, 1962).
2. Russell Sage Foundation, *Annual Report, 1958–1959* (New York: Russell Sage Foundation, 1959), p. 13.
3. Lauris B. Whitman, "The Sociologist in Organized Religion" (Paper presented at the Annual Meeting of the American Sociological Association, Washington, D.C., August 30, 1962), p. 1.
4. Morris Janowitz, *Sociology and the Military Establishment* (New York: Russell Sage Foundation, 1959), p. 15.
5. Ruth Leeds and Thomasina Smith, *Using Social Science Knowledge in Business and Industry: Report of a Seminar* (Homewood, Ill.: Irwin, 1963), p. 5. See also Joseph W. Newman, "Working with Behavioral Scientists," *Harvard Business Review*, July–August, 1958, p. 71.

6. Robert O. Carlson, "The Sociologist in Business and Industry" (Paper presented at the Annual Meeting of the American Sociological Association, Washington, D.C., August 30, 1962), p. 12.
7. Donald Young, "Sociology and the Practicing Professions," *American Sociological Review*, XX (1955), 647.
8. Phillip E. Hammond, ed., *Sociologists at Work* (New York: Basic Books, 1964).
9. Leeds and Smith, *op. cit.*, pp. 11–12.
10. Russell Sage Foundation, *Annual Report, 1959–1960* (New York: Russell Sage Foundation, 1960), p. 13.
11. Hope J. Leichter, "The Sociologist as Staff Member in Welfare and Community Service" (Paper presented at the Annual Meeting of the American Sociological Association, Washington, D.C., August 30, 1962), p. 4.
12. Russell Sage Foundation, *Annual Report, 1959–1960*, p. 9.
13. Robert K. Merton, *Social Theory and Social Structure* (Glencoe, Ill.: The Free Press, 1957), p. 369.
14. *Ibid.*, p. 370.
15. Personal communication.
16. Lawrence L. Ferguson, "Social Scientists in the Plant," *Harvard Business Review*, May–June, 1964, p. 138.
17. Russell Sage Foundation, *Annual Report, 1960–1961* (New York: Russell Sage Foundation, 1961), p. 8.
18. Ferguson, *op. cit.*, p. 139.
19. Russell Sage Foundation, *Annual Report, 1960–1961*, p. 13.
20. Sibley, *op. cit.*, p. 51.
21. Young, *op. cit.*, p. 642.
22. See, for example, John W. Riley, Jr., ed., "Social Research and Life Insurance," *American Behavioral Scientist*, VI (1963).
23. Sibley, *op. cit.*, p. 177.
24. Young, *op. cit.*, pp. 641–642.
25. Lloyd E. Ohlin, *Sociology and the Field of Corrections* (New York: Russell Sage Foundation, 1956), p. 7.
26. Talcott Parsons, "Problems of Sociology as a Profession," *American Sociological Review*, XXIV (1959), 555.
27. Janowitz, *op. cit.*, p. 5.
28. Leeds and Smith, *op. cit.*, p. 2. See also Robert A. Dahl, Mason Haire, and Paul Lazarsfeld, eds., *Social Science Research on Business: Product and Potential* (New York: Columbia University Press, 1959).
29. Young, *op. cit.*, p. 642.
30. See especially the series of publications on "Sociology and the Professions" prepared for the American Sociological Association by Russell Sage Foundation. Bulletins have been published on public health, the military establishment, education, mental health, and corrections; additional titles in preparation will be concerned with the police, social work, law, and religion.
31. Sibley, *op. cit.*, p. 50.
32. For a detailed discussion of sociological research in education, see Orville Brim, Jr., *Sociology and the Field of Education* (New York: Russell Sage Foundation, 1958).
33. Henry W. Riecken in a personal communication.
34. See John W. Riley, Jr., "Solving Social Problems through the Private Sector," in *Broadening the Dimensions of Public Affairs* (New York: National Industrial Conference Board, 1965), pp. 25–40.
35. Janowitz, *op. cit.*, p. 105.

36. Carlson, *op. cit.*, p. 12

37. Russell Sage Foundation, *Annual Report, 1958–1959*, p. 10.

38. Nahum Z. Medalia and Ward S. Mason, "Position and Prospects of Sociologists in Federal Employment," *American Sociological Review*, XXVIII (1963), 285.

39. Leeds and Smith, *op. cit.*, pp. 16–18.

40. See, for example, Simon Marcson, "Motivation and Productivity in Industry," in *Behavioral Science Research in Industrial Relations*, Industrial Relations Monograph No. 21 (New York: Industrial Relations Counselors, 1962).

41. Barny G. Glaser, "The Local-Cosmopolitan Scientist," *American Journal of Sociology*, LXIX, No. 3 (November, 1963), 250.

42. Leeds and Smith, *op. cit.*, p. 2.

43. *Ibid.*, p. 3.

44. Russell Sage Foundation, *Annual Report, 1958–1959*, pp. 11–12.

45. Leichter, *op. cit.*, p. 6.

46. Sibley, *op. cit.*, p. 177.

47. N. H. Siegel and L. L. Robbins, "The Sociologist in Health and Medicine" (Paper presented at the Annual Meeting of the American Sociological Association, Washington, D.C., August 30, 1962), p. 6.

Nonconventional Uses of Sociology as Illustrated by Peace Research

AMITAI ETZIONI

chapter 30

Introduction

Sociologists who study disarmament are at a double disadvantage: both the contributions of sociology as a discipline and the investment of the society as a whole in this field are so small that the study of disarmament is a prime "underdeveloped" area. In the early 1960's the United States government spent about $7 billion a year on defense research and development, but only about $6 million a year on disarmament and arms control research. Senators openly questioned the need for such research.[1] The exact amount of money spent by private foundations and universities on disarmament research is unknown, but the best estimates suggest that in proportion to their total expenditures it is even lower than government

806

spending. Still, the United States seems to spend more on disarmament research than any other country. The United States is also one of the few nations that have a special government agency (the Arms Control and Disarmament Agency), privately endowed foundations (for example, the Carnegie Endowment for International Peace, the Institute for International Order), and academic research institutes (such as the Center for Conflict Resolution at the University of Michigan, the Center for Conflict and Integration at Stanford University, and the Institute of War and Peace Studies at Columbia University) devoted to these problems.

Sociological contributions to this field, though growing, are still minor. There are probably not more than twenty sociologists who regularly devote part of their research time to the study of disarmament and arms control (hereafter referred to simply as "disarmament"). Only a very few sociology departments conduct classes or seminars in this field or otherwise provide training for future sociologists who wish to specialize in this area. It was only in the early sixties that a section devoted to disarmament began to appear with some regularity at the annual meetings of the American Sociological Association and at some regional meetings. Considerably more sociological work is conducted in areas closely related to disarmament, especially international relations; but this, too, is a new and developing field. To survey the use of sociology in this field is therefore to study pioneering efforts, new beginnings, infantile diseases, and the potential value of contributions as yet unmade.

Sociological contributions take four basic forms: *facts, theorems, methods,* and *perspectives.* Differences among the four reflect the substance of the sociology applied, rather than the sociological context in which it operates. Although no data are available, we have the impression that the four approaches are not employed equally in the study of disarmament. Few facts are available; theorems may be used somewhat more often, but still inadequately; methods are more popular; and perspectives probably receive more attention and have more impact than the other three categories combined. Each of the four kinds of sociological contributions creates some special problems. We shall present some illustrations for each of the categories and briefly review the questions raised by its use. No attempt will be made here to survey the field. Unless otherwise specified, statements refer to the United States.

Sociological Facts

Every discipline commands a store of facts with which its practitioners are familiar and which are potentially useful to members of other disciplines as well as to decision makers. There are difficult methodological problems involved in the definition of sociological facts, their independence from a theoretical framework that defines concepts, and the difference between sociological and historical or psychological facts. Without going into these questions here, we observe that there is a body of information with which sociologists are more likely to be familiar than members of other disciplines, and some of these facts have a bearing on questions of disarmament.

Like most international problems, disarmament is closely related to domestic dynamics. Changes in international relations are affected by changes in foreign policy, and these, in turn, are affected by intrasocietal processes. This is true for all countries, but particularly for mass democracies. In this context a sociologist might mention the fact that there is a secular trend in the United States, even in peacetime, for a growing proportion of voters to consider foreign policy more important than domestic concerns in deciding how to vote. Survey data show that when asked about the most important issues facing the American people, the percentage of those who answered that foreign policy, world affairs, and defense are most important has grown significantly larger over the years, despite temporary reversals. In the period between November, 1935, and January, 1939, this figure ranged between 11 and 26 per cent, with the highest percentage obtaining at the outbreak of the Spanish Civil War. In the period between February, 1948, and October, 1959, those who felt that such issues were most important never fell below 30 per cent, and in all but one survey (October, 1949) were at least 40 per cent of those polled. Fluctuations can be seen in the figures presented in Table 30–1, but most of them can be linked to a specific world event, and each such event seems to contribute to a growth in foreign policy concern.[2]

When decision makers—for example, the President of the United States and his advisers—consider a change in foreign policy that would be conducive to peace, such as the one initiated by President Kennedy in his "Strategy for Peace" speech on June 10, 1963, the adaptability of public opinion is a major question. While the President can act without public support, or even against it, such acts have a political price. United States recognition of Communist China, for instance, was considered too costly by most politicians in the fifties. It was not a simple task for Roosevelt to prepare the American public for his declaration of war. Thus, a decision maker seeks to know, before he launches a major change in the course of foreign policy, how easy it will be to convince the public that the change is needed and how rigidly the public will adhere to earlier policies—in short, how great the political cost is likely to be. If the cost is expected to be high and the change is not vital, it is likely that it will not be carried out at all.

The sociological storeroom includes some relevant facts for such decisions. For instance, a sociologist might point out that the public generally accepted the Eisenhower space policy with little resistance. In 1957, the

TABLE 30-1.

YEAR	PERCENTAGE NAMING FOREIGN PROBLEMS MOST VITAL
November, 1935	11%
December, 1936	26%
December, 1937	23%
January, 1939	14%
February, 1948	33%
April, 1948	73%
June, 1948	50%
October, 1949	34%
May, 1950	46%
1951	Foreign policy was most salient issue
1953	Korean Policy was most salient issue
June, 1954	52%
September, 1956	46%
September, 1957	43%
March, 1958	64%
September, 1958	44%
February, 1959	40%
May, 1959	44%
October, 1959	51%

majority of the American people did not know what a satellite was,[3] considered the Soviet Union backward in general and in scientific and technological matters in particular, and was hence unprepared for the launching of a Soviet Sputnik on October 5, 1957.[4] Though much pressure from Congress followed, demanding that we match the Soviet deed, and the Democrats threatened to make a campaign issue out of the "neglect" of space, President Eisenhower preferred not to enter a space race with the USSR for a number of reasons, especially his devotion to balancing the budget. He belittled the Soviet achievements by referring to the satellite as "this small ball," which, he said, was no cause for alarm since it was "certainly not going to drop on their [the public's] heads." Sherman Adams, Special Assistant to the President, referred to the orbiting of satellites as an "international basketball game." [5] Samuel Lubell, who studied public reaction to the space problem in the following weeks, found that by and large it accepted both the President's explanation and his policy; people often even used the very same phrases Eisenhower did to account for their position.[6]

Space, it might be argued, was a new, undefined, "unspecified" issue in 1957, so that whoever first "imprinted" it faced little resistance. The President was first, and thus won public approval. But one might question if such ready followship could be gained on matters about which the public had already formed a definite opinion. How readily can one change an imprint once made, and at what cost?

Here a sociologist can cite several facts. In 1961, when President Kennedy decided to transform the space race into a major issue, in sharp contrast to Eisenhower, he encountered little difficulty in recruiting public support. In a major speech he defined putting an American on the moon as the "most important decision we can make as a nation." [7] After this speech and several similar ones, the public mood shifted considerably. An even more dramatic shift was achieved on a policy question that had been imprinted much more than the space race, namely, the nuclear test-ban treaty.

Public opinion played a more significant role in shaping the test-ban treaty than is common in foreign policy issues. The treaty was negotiated after mid-1963, as the country approached an election year, a period during which political leaders traditionally approach controversial issues with more uneasiness than usual. Moreover, a ban of thermonuclear tests, Kennedy had promised, was to be in the form of a treaty, which required ratification by the Senate. But Senate support for the treaty was lacking. Kennedy and his staff were concerned about the international and domestic costs that would be incurred by signing a treaty the Senate refused to ratify. Favorable public opinion had to be generated to gain the support of wavering senators. If this could not be done, the *signing* of the treaty might have to be avoided.

Initially, public opinion was not very favorable. The negotiations between the United States and the USSR began barely seven months after the Cuban missile crisis and after the USSR had arbitrarily and abruptly resumed testing in 1961, thus ending a three-year moratorium on testing that had been observed by both sides. Suspicions of the Soviets' offer to ban tests in 1963 were high; *The New York Times*, for instance, wondered if this was not a "Soviet trap." [8] But, when the Senate convened to ratify the treaty, public-opinion polls showed that 81 per cent of those polled gave "unqualified" support to the treaty, as compared to 52 per cent two months earlier.[9] Kennedy succeeded in gaining public support.

Many other such facts about trends and shifts in public opinion are valuable to a decision maker who wants to support disarmament measures actively and thereby comes into conflict with the policy that prevailed in earlier periods. The exact lesson to be drawn from such facts is much more difficult to spell out. There are the usual problems of secondary analysis: the data on the reception of Kennedy's space policy are not exactly parallel to those collected in the Eisenhower era; Lubell's data are mainly qualitative. Moreover, interpretation of the facts is hazardous. While it seems obvious that an ultrarigid image of public opinion is not justified, the speed with which one can move on various issues is a more difficult question. What range of policies is the President free to follow within the limit of a given political cost? How rapidly can he shift courses without losing, let us say, more than a quarter of the public? How much explaining must he do before or after the fact? How important is bipartisan support? And the support of mass media?

Two questions remain largely unanswered after a tour of the existing store of facts—questions which are almost unresearched: first, what are the dynamics involved in changing the *Gestalt* of a foreign policy, rather than a specific item of policy? Kennedy represented the test-ban treaty largely as a measure that would improve United States security and even its military might, while he played down its role as a step toward disarmament.[10] That is, he put a *new* policy *measure* into an *old*, accepted *Gestalt*, the cold-war perspective. He introduced in a similar fashion the sale of American wheat to the USSR, to which conservatives objected. This raises the following question: Could he have introduced other tension-reducing and disarmament measures, increased commitments to the United Nations, and so on, within the old frame of reference? At what point, if any, would the contradiction between a strategy for peace and the cold-war framework become evident?[11] Would a backlash be triggered? And under what conditions, at what cost, could a new frame of reference be successfully introduced?

Second, is it true—and one has the unsubstantiated impression that it is—that the public can more easily be moved up on a hate-the-enemy scale than down, even—perhaps especially—when the public is already "high" on such a scale and one would normally expect a "ceiling" effect to set in? It was apparently much easier for Kennedy to elicit support in his 1961 "call to the flag" speech (following a Berlin crisis) than in his 1963 call for a "strategy for peace." The Soviet Union, an estranged ally during World War II, became an archenemy in the few short months between late 1946 and early 1947. How long did it take France to accept Germany as an ally after World War II and for Roosevelt to alter American feelings about Germany in the pre-World War II years? If the sociological store included more facts on these questions, they would be of use for a President and staff faced with the need for a broad change of foreign policy, especially changes of the magnitude of effective pursuit of disarmament.

Besides being relevant to national policy-making processes, sociological facts are also valuable for international research and its consumers, from the United World Federalists to Peace Corps consultants. One of the propositions most widely espoused in the literature of international relations by the designers of the International Cooperation Years and by supporters of joint American-Soviet scientific efforts, of student and leader exchanges, and so forth, is that more contacts between members of different societies lead to greater understanding and affinity between them.[12] As on many other issues, the case in favor of this proposition can be argued on common-sense grounds as potently as the case against it.

Two studies provide some facts that have a direct bearing on this question. Daniel Lerner reports that French businessmen are more likely to favor increased contact with other Europeans, in the form of a close alliance, if they have had some exposure to foreigners than if they have been isolated. He measured this exposure first by using the amount of export business as an indicator; he then found that this was highly correlated with travel to foreign countries, the reading of foreign publications, and familiarity with European culture.

Lerner made this finding after having tried to differentiate between those who favored increased contact and those who favored less contact on the basis of more traditional sociological variables such as age, birthplace, domicile, and size of firm. When correlated with attitudes toward increased contact, none of these variables accounted for a significant variation in the sample's attitudes, which favored increased contact by a ratio of 2.8 to 1. However, when previous exposure was considered, those with the least such exposure favored contact by a ratio of only 2 to 1, while those with the most exposure favored contact by a ratio of 6 to 1.[13]

Sociologists played a comparatively important role in correcting one major misconception about the effects of nuclear war. The central question considered was whether or not a society could survive such a war. Assumptions about the postattack state are one important factor affecting not only the decision makers who contemplate triggering a nuclear war and evaluate tactics that might lead to war (such as the initiation of limited warfare) but also those who deal with other considerations, such as the relative investment in peace efforts, civil defense, and the like.

As with most estimates, some normative factors enter these deliberations (such as how much one values 100,000 lives or one's commitment to a small ally). Next, it is extremely difficult to obtain all the relevant and valid information. The addition of any relevant fact can alter the picture. Early studies of the recovery period tended to be highly statistical in their approach, in that they counted the number of dead as compared to survivors and the number of GNP units lost versus those remaining.[14] These calculations almost completely ignored, among other considerations, the structure of society; that is, the loss of people in strategic roles and key facilities would have a much greater retarding effect on recovery than the loss of others. Sociologists showed, by using facts from their storeroom, that such crucial people and facilities were more likely to be lost than less vital elements of the society, given the attack conditions assumed by the initial studies.

These studies assumed attacks to be concentrated on cities. Dentler and Cutright considered the affects of a comparatively small (2,000 megaton) nuclear attack on seventy urban areas. These areas are almost exactly the same locations chosen by the Office of Civil and Defense Mobilization in 1959 as the most likely targets in a nuclear war. They used census figures on the percentages of urban populations employed in key occupations and arrived at the following results: while 46 per cent of the total population would be lost in the projected nuclear attack, this would include 73 per cent of all accountants and architects, 62 per cent of all physicians, 79 per cent of all salaried managers in the transportation equipment industry, 71 per cent of all foremen in the metals industry, and 76 per cent of all tool-and-die makers.

Dentler and Cutright also projected a composite picture of the United States Congress after such a nuclear attack on urban areas. Based on the elections of 1956 and 1958, they predicted the loss of almost half the 435 existing congressional districts. Because of population densities in certain areas of the United States, notably the industrial Northeast, they projected a Congress (if elections could be held) that would be dominated by Republicans and southern Democrats.[15]

The problems raised by these facts are not peculiar to sociological contributions in this field, although they may be somewhat more accentuated. First, there are not enough facts; almost each fact we have now immediately raises additional factual questions we must have answered before we can use the original fact responsibly. Second, the facts we *do* have are not necessarily available when needed. There is no "storeroom" of the type we have alluded to metaphorically; facts exist in discrete, dispersed units. As a rule we rely on the memory of one man with a small, high-turnover staff to provide facts. Of course, there are various indices, catalogues, and abstracts, but generally those which serve the peace researcher are less well codified, developed, and systematized than those in most other fields.[16]

Finally, giving advice on the basis of "facts" without any theoretical analysis raises further problems. As long as the underlying dynamics are unknown, it is impossible to know the conditions under which a "fact"—for example, a statistical regularity—will hold true. Suppose that a sociologist had predicted in 1950, on the basis of past and present knowledge, that at least one-third of all patients entering mental hospitals would remain hospitalized until their death. (If discharged, they would have to be readmitted after a short period of time.) Then, rather suddenly, tranquilizers were introduced and, in addition, many senile patients were transferred to homes for the aged. The readmission figure would be drastically reduced. This sort of problem is particularly severe in the study of international relations, because our knowledge of the "emergent" properties involved is limited and their effects are particularly difficult either to discount or to include.[17]

A professional often warns his client that the facts on which he is basing his advice or prediction are expected to "hold" only "if all other conditions are equal." These conditions he cannot specify, as a rule, when facts are used, partly because they are unknown. He is thus exposed to a backlash of disappointment when the advice fails to work. His early warning is almost always disregarded.[18] While this is true in general, it particularly haunts the sociologist who studies disarmament, because the number of variables involved is especially large, information is, in part, classified, cross-cultural data are often of poor quality, and the stakes are the highest.

Theorems

Some of the problems involved in using "naked" facts are reduced, while other problems emerge, when theorems are employed. A *theorem* is a statement about the relationship between two or more variables which is supported by some data. (A *proposition* is an unsupported theorem.) The distinction between sociological and nonsociological theorems is much easier to draw than that between sociological and nonsociological facts. Only statements dealing with the relations between sociological concepts as independent and dependent variables (although intervening variables need not be sociological) concern us.

Theorems are transferable from one body of data to another and therefore can be "used" for the interpretation of data other than those with which they were initially tested and applied in a situation other than the one in which they were first "found" or supported. One routinely transfers theorems between bodies of data with similar configurations of relevant variables. "Transferring" a statement about the effect of informal communication on the acceptance of formal communication—for instance, from reports on readers of bus advertisements to an examination of those who watch television programs—is an example. (It is always possible that a new variable will be triggered by such a transfer; for example, the emotional involvement in television watching might be smaller, and hence willingness to accept formal communication without informal backing greater. But the more generally similar the two bodies of data are, the less likely this is to happen.)

Second, theorems can be transferred from one subfield to another, using quite different data. This requires considerable reinterpretation of indicators, but involves the same basic variables. Let us take, for instance, the transfer of a theorem from the field of industrial relations to the study of the military establishment. The process involves first abstraction and then respecification. To save space, let us be content with a trivial example. We find that to the extent that workers view their foreman as a father-figure, they are likely to view the profit making of the factory they work in as just. We abstract this and state that the stronger the identification of low-ranking members of a complex organization with those higher in rank, the more likely they are to view the organization's goals as legitimate. We then respecify and apply this proposition to the army, for instance, and state that we expect that the more soldiers view their officers as father-figures, the more likely they are to view the war effort as just.

Finally, the most difficult task is that of moving theorems from one level of abstraction to another. In addition to abstraction and respecification, which involve a reformulation of the indicators, new variables must be added—the emergent properties of the system to which the theorem is extended. For example, statements about the effects of interaction on conflict, when transferred from intrasocietal studies to international ones, must be revised to take into account that the most important regulatory machinery for intrasocietal conflict—the state—is absent on the international level. On both levels there are processes of escalation due to incremental growth of hostilities (A responds with increased aggression to a random increase in B's aggression, to which B responds with an additional increase in aggression, and so on). But on the societal level, this tends to bring to the activation "third party" mechanisms (for example, the police and the courts), which limit the conflict and return it to a lower level of aggression. On the international level, by and large, regulation must be self-imposed. (An interesting exception occurs when a Big Power acts as a policeman, as in the Middle East during the Sinai campaign.)

On all levels, but particularly on this one, the transfer of a theorem weakens it; it must be retested in the new context. But it should not be ignored that such transfers are regularly made and that we tend to give more credence to statements thus transferred than to those that have no systematic support at all, even though neither statement has been confirmed. The art of theoretical extrapolation is in urgent need of study and improvement; it is futile to expect that professionals can convince their client not to use the theorems transferred until their validity is reconfirmed and thus until the extent of their applicability in a new context is determined.

Many theorems are loosely transferred, as when one personifies a nation and expects it to act on the basis of guilt, defensiveness, and so on, in essence forecasting reactions on the basis of an implicit anthropomorphism. Osgood used an interpersonal image to build his theory on ways and means to reduce international tensions. "John and Ivan—who stand facing each other, near the middle but on opposite sides, of a long, rigid, neatly balanced seesaw . . . John and Ivan gradually work their ways back to safety by a series of self-initiated, but reciprocated, steps—very much as they had originally moved out against each other." [19] Such applications tend to ignore the shift from one context to another, the special characteristics of each context, and the procedures for systematically taking such differences into account. But several applications have been more carefully carried out and successfully completed, as the following examples illustrate.

Sociologists studying consumer behavior and voting patterns have shown that mass media have much less direct effect on the voter or the consumer than has often been claimed. For example, among those who reported a change of brand when they last bought food, Katz and Lazarsfeld report that 37.6 per cent of those who changed brands mentioned personal influence, 30.3 per cent radio advertising, 30 per cent newspaper advertising, 24.8 per cent magazine advertising, and 20.9 per cent salespeople (these figures add up to more than 100 per cent because of multiple answers, but within each group the salience of the factors was found to decrease in the same order).[20] To transfer this finding abstractly, we might say that choices between political and economic alternatives are affected more by primary-group contacts (and psychological predispositions) than by impersonal, formal communication.

The theorem was respecified to apply to attitudes toward the United Nations. During the late forties, a civic group in Cincinnati decided to mount a campaign to increase support for the UN. The group sponsored traditional advertising in newspapers and on the radio, as well as discussions, debates, lectures, and so forth, conceiving of their job as informational, not motivational. Two sociologists who were interested in the problem of the effect of adult education on attitudes toward international issues studied this campaign. They carried out a "before and after" survey, which enabled them to discover that many people were "reached" by the program (12,868 through the P.T.A., all school children, and 14,000 Weekday Church School children; 59,588 pieces of literature were distributed, 2,800 clubs were supplied with speakers, and so on). After the second survey wave, the authors wrote:

> It is the interested, rather than the informed, who are more accessible. And, at each level of information, the interested are more likely to hold the desired attitudes of internationalism and belief in the United Nations. In a sense, then, interest is prior for an informational campaign. . . . The conclusion is that the people reached by the campaign were those least in need of it, and that the people missed by it were the new audience the plan hoped to gain.[21]

The extent of application is small in these cases; attitudes toward the United Nations seem, on the relevant variables, to be not analytically much different from those previously studied. More "interesting," in terms of theoretical pay-off, is the application of sociological theorems concerning interpersonal relations at the interstate level. One such theorem—one that seems to be valid—is the theorem of homophyly. As developed by Lazarsfeld and Merton, the theorem states that people whose sociological characteristics are similar are more likely to become friends than those whose characteristics differ.[22] Since many nonsociologists consider this statement obvious and therefore trivial, it should be pointed out that the contrary statement, "opposites attract," is just as "obvious." Although "opposites attract" is true for magnets in an electric field and perhaps for some psychological characteristics of people, similarities in economic status, level of education, religion, and the like seem to be more conducive than differences to friendship, mating, and formation of cohesive groups.

The same is possibly true on the international level. That is, if one sets out to join nations into communities, those that are similar to each other, on certain structural variables, will be more cohesive than those that are different, all other things being equal. In terms of economic status, the federations, common markets, and similar forms of interstate unions that have been initiated in the last decades have, so far, encompassed countries that were either developed or underdeveloped, but not both. There is a Central American common market, one evolving in South America, some in Africa, and one in western Europe, but none was initiated as a mixture of "developed" and "underdeveloped" countries. This, one might feel, could be due to geographical proximity, rather than sociological similarity. But Mexico joined the South American Free Trade Area, rather than one in North America; North African countries, despite their greater proximity to Europe than to many of their African affiliates, have entered African customs unions, not the European Economic Community (EEC).

Of greater interest is the development of the European Economic Community itself. There have been at least a half-dozen different efforts to form European regional organizations since World War II, including the Western European Union, the Organization of European Economic Cooperation, and the North Atlantic Treaty Organization. Though all these organizations tried to provide a basis for European integration that extended into the social, political, and economic spheres, not one of them was able to do so. These organizations differ from the more successful EEC primarily in the degree of their heterogeneity. First, their membership is at least twice as large as that of the EEC. They have between fourteen and twenty-two members, while the EEC has only six. This is consonant with research which shows that groups are more cohesive if they include fewer, rather than more, people.[23]

More important is the fact that EEC membership is much more homogeneous than that of the other organizations. Whereas the latter include countries with social-democratic governments, such as Norway, there is no such member of the EEC. Whereas they include authoritarian countries like Portugal, the European Economic Community does not. Whereas many of the unsuccessful European organizations included both neutralist and NATO members, the EEC was initiated by only NATO members.

Whereas other European organizations have both countries that are largely Protestant and countries that are largely Catholic, the EEC has no predominantly Protestant members.[24]

It is important to emphasize that homogeneity in itself is not a *sufficient condition* for the successful initiation of an international community. The Arab countries, for instance, are highly similar to one another, but despite this all efforts have so far failed to form a common market, an international bloc, or any other form of international community. Note also that the six western European countries were highly "similar" to one another long before they initiated a community in 1958.

Nor is homogeneity a *necessary condition*. Many nation-states, the United States, for example, are communities despite a high degree of internal differentiation, both among the founding units and the present member-states. This, of course, does and did exact a price in terms of social solidarity—a price that in the case of the United States included a civil war—but it did not prevent the ultimate evolution of one community. Homogeneity is thus a predisposing or auxiliary condition, but it is neither necessary nor sufficient. But this does not invalidate the transfer of the proposition; on the contrary, homophyly among persons has the same status. Not every two people who are similar in background form a friendship, even if they come to know each other. But they are more likely to become friends than people whose backgrounds are dissimilar in the ways discussed above for nations.

What can be learned from the theorem of homophyly about the possibility of a world-wide community? Does it not suggest that it will be impossible to form one, since lack of homogeneity is most manifest on this level? In part, the answer is affected by one's estimate of the pace of processes that alter global homogeneity. While the degree of homogeneity is a given at any point in time, it changes over time. Several processes contributing to homogeneity are at work, including the development of the underdeveloped nations (though, so far, the gap between the "have" and the "have not" countries has increased rather than decreased),[25] the development of world-wide communication systems (though the effect of these has often been exaggerated), and finally the evolution of regional communities.

The evolution of regional communities is of special interest because it illustrates both the merits of transferring sociological propositions from intrasocietal to intersocietal analysis and the possibility of "stringing" together theorems derived from various sources to form a set of propositions pertaining to international systems. (The relevance of this to disarmament is that many authorities believe disarmament cannot be achieved and that, if achieved, it could not be maintained unless some form of world authority were established; such an authority requires, as a basis of policy formation, the evolution of an international community.)

To create a world community, some agreement must exist among the countries involved. The formation of a world government in one step is an unrealistic goal because of the lack of world consensus. By looking at the ways in which consensus is obtained within a society and then transferring the abstracted model to the international level, we may make some suggestions about more realistic roads to international community.

Since, as we have noted, smaller groups are more likely to be homogeneous than larger ones, one process that often occurs within nations is the formation of subgroups, which are able to reach consensus more easily than larger, more diverse groups. Within the United States, the process of political decision making proceeds from state primaries to national party conventions to interaction between parties within Congress. In a multiparty system, the process includes factional decisions within a party and party decisions within a coalition. Described abstractly, the process can be seen as operating on two levels: first, subgroups which are relatively homogeneous and can reach consensus relatively easily; then these groups send representatives to the next level, where consensus can now be reached because diversity has been reduced on a lower level.

At the international level we can see similar examples of this process. Within the Organization of American States two smaller economic groupings are emerging: South American and Central American. Within the United Nations, there are several voting blocs, each representing a certain regional group. Given our understanding of consensus formation within national societies, this process of regional group formation tends to be, though it is not necessarily, a useful step on the road to a world community.[26]

Another transfer of levels of analysis is seen in the work of Galtung. Working with a theory of aggression that can be relevant at both the individual and national levels, he suggests that

Aggression is most likely to arise in social positions in rank-disequilibrium. In a system of individuals it may take the form of a crime, in a system of groups the form of revolutions, and in a system of nations the form of war. But these extreme forms of aggression are unlikely to occur unless 1) other means of equilibration towards a complete topdog configuration have been tried, and 2) the culture has some practice in violent aggression.[27]

Sociological Methods

There are no methods that are intrinsically sociological, but sociologists have developed and used research techniques about which they are frequently consulted by practitioners of other disciplines as well as nonacademic consumers. One such technique is the survey, by which we systematically explore what other people think, know, feel, or believe. One early use of this method is of much interest here. It was developed in England when the urban, industrial middle class wanted to know what the working class thought.[28] Similar surveys have served as a communication device for corporations, churches, armies, societies—and now international organizations—to channel "upward" what lower units or subunits see and feel.

The lay person is inclined, when acting without reflection, to assume that since all men are similar, he can use his knowledge of himself and of his acquaintances to understand the motivation and behavior of others. But one's knowledge of one's mind and body is rather fragmented and is distorted by emotions and stereotypes. And, because of culture-bound socialization, most persons uninitiated in the social sciences are *unable* to empathize with members of other classes, nations, or cultures. The device of "interviewing" taxi drivers or cleaning women compares poorly with survey methods as a source of information about "what people think." Diplomatic reports, often based on impressions gained at a cocktail party or a local pub, are much inferior to cross-cultural surveys, despite all the latter's shortcomings.

One such survey, carried out among a representative sample in the United States, probed the dimensions of the cold war, as the "man in the street" sees it. The report of this study suggests that:

> The Cold War might be seen in the perspective of polarities—Communism versus capitalism, democracy versus totalitarianism, a Russian world versus an American world—but virtually no one sees the Cold War in these dimensions!
>
> Russia is seen either as simply making a power play for extended and perhaps global control *or* she is seen as trying to spread Communism. In "opposition" to this, the United States is seen, most broadly, as trying to keep the peace.
>
> Only one American in five sees the United States as trying to spread democracy as a national purpose in our relations with Russia. Virtually nobody mentions capitalism. The contest is usually posed as Russian expansion *versus* U.S. maintaining the peace, or the spread of Russian Communism *versus* the U.S. keeping the peace. The majority of the American public, therefore, sees the Cold War as a threat of force, with the threat of war as the ultimate possibility.
>
> But Americans do not necessarily see global war or a nuclear exchange between the great powers as the inevitable outcome. The population is about evenly split (one-third to one-third) in estimating that a big war is likely or unlikely. This balance is apparently slowly tipping toward those who think it will not happen. . . .
>
> Although few people volunteered a policy of disarmament, when the broad spectrum of possible policies including arms control, test bans, progressive reduction in arms, disarmament, etc., was raised, more than half the popu-

lation thought that such steps should certainly be tried and continued. Between one-fourth and one-third thought that such steps would be worthwhile, and one-fourth, although skeptical over their worth, still thought that the U.S. should continue a strong policy of interest in these measures. . . .

To probe further into the broad perspective under which the Cold War might be seen by the U.S. public, five ways of looking at U.S.–U.S.S.R. relations were posed. These five are by no means exhaustive of perspectives but they do range over the scale of viewpoints and they provide a check on the more spontaneously expressed opinions already reported and encountered early in the interview. The five in the order of their acceptance are as follows:

"The cold war with Russia is a fight between two very different ways of life with different values and ideas." 89 per cent agree.

"Our problems with Russia are just like having trouble with a 'bad guy' or a delinquent who won't behave." 63 per cent agree.

"We have a Cold War with Russia because the United States and Russia are each trying to do what they want and their interests interfere with each other." 55 per cent agree.

"Our troubles with Russia are just a question of which country is going to survive as a powerful nation." 49 per cent agree.

"We have a Cold War with Russia because the United States and Russia don't really try to work together and understand one another." 29 per cent agree.[29]

On the other hand, the findings of surveys have often been used to show how uninformed people are. A survey carried out by the Survey Research Center in 1964 indicated that 28 per cent of the sample interviewed did not know that there was a Communist government in China. Thirty-nine per cent had never heard of the Nationalist Chinese government, and an astonishing 25 per cent answered "No" when asked, "Have you happened to hear anything about the fighting in Viet Nam?"[30] These findings are used to demand greater investment in education, including adult education, and more sharing of information with the public, ranging from demands for more presidential press conferences to demands for more public information programs on TV.

The United States is constantly taking surveys of what people in other countries think about this country, the U.S.S.R., China, and so on in general terms as well as with regard to specific policies. For instance, when asked in 1958 about their willingness to allow NATO missile bases with American equipment in their countries, parliamentarians were found to favor the idea in Great Britain, Italy, and France (by margins of 73, 28, and 22 per cent, respectively) but to oppose the idea in Germany and Japan (by 12 per cent and 75 per cent—in the latter case NATO was, of course, not mentioned).[31]

Almond reported small changes in western European public-opinion support for the United States after the launching of Sputnik. Some people expressed sentiments of neutrality after Sputnik, although they had previously favored a strongly pro-United States position by their respective countries. For example, the percentage claiming that Great Britain should side with the West declined from 53 per cent in May, 1957, to 49 per cent in October, 1958, while those favoring neutralism increased from 29 to 38 per cent during the same period.[32] These results call into question the widely held belief that the effect of Sputnik was dramatic. Shifts for all countries studied are below 10 per cent, many considerably smaller.

Although excessive concern with our "image" and crude efforts to manipulate it are correctly criticized, one might note that these surveys provide one of the few avenues for the United States to systematically learn what other nations think about it. Such surveys serve to counteract some of the influence of domestic public-opinion polls. In this sense, they make United States foreign policy somewhat less nationalistic. The units of international action in the nuclear age are often blocs of nations, not individual states. Each bloc has one or more elite states or superpowers. As there are neither bloc parliaments nor international elections, public-opinion polls conducted in other countries by the superpower help to increase the responsiveness of the elite state to other members of its world.

The impact is obviously small, since foreign policy is affected by many more salient factors than public opinion. Moreover, most of the influence attributed to public opinion is conceded to the domestic public opinion of the superpower itself. Yet "foreign" public opinion does play a role. When the United States employed nonlethal gas in Vietnam early in 1965, there was a strong public reaction. To explain the President's carefully worded statement on this issue, a staff writer for the Washington *Post* said that "officials favoring the promotion of the gases appear to view these same statements as a diplomatic retreat in the face of the sharp public reaction around the world."[33]

During the Cuban crisis of October, 1962, the influence of foreign public opinion was recognized by Attorney-General Robert Kennedy, who argued against a bombing of the Soviet missile sites. He reminded the group of Pearl Harbor. "For the United States to attack a small country like Cuba without warning," he said, "would irreparably hurt our reputation in the world—and our own conscience."[34] A leading news service described the ending of the United States airlift operation in the Congo, during November, 1964, as a step taken in part as a response to adverse foreign opinion, especially among African, Asian, and Latin American countries.[35]

It is relevant to point out here why public opinion in third countries surveyed by sociological techniques and interpreted by persons with sociological training tends to have a moderating effect on the foreign policy of the superpower. This is not always the case; West Germany has often demanded and achieved a "tougher" line against the USSR, and so have the Nationalistic Chinese against the mainland government. But by and large, the effect tends to be moderating. One reason is that the United

States has multifaceted involvements on many fronts. When it faces an escalation of tensions in one theater, its allies and friends in the others are likely to be less engaged and less concerned than the United States. Thus, for instance, the European allies tended to counsel moderation during the Cuban missile crisis of 1962 and favor negotiations in Vietnam in 1965. Allies in the Far East and South Asia were urging restraint during various Berlin crises. The net result, since confrontations tend to be limited to one front at a time, has been a generalized pressure toward moderation.

A study of the general effect of voting by nonaligned countries in the General Assembly of the United Nations indicates similar findings for bloc behavior there. The study covered eighty of the most important roll-call votes in the Fifteenth and Sixteenth General Assemblies. Included are key votes in both plenary and committee sessions. In those instances where the United States and the Soviet Union voted differently, 26.1 per cent of the votes cast by the fifty nonaligned countries coincided with those of the United States, and 29.2 per cent with those of the Soviet Union. The author then isolates seven countries which have consistently voted more frequently with the United States than with the Soviet Union (Austria, Finland, Ireland, Sweden, Yugoslavia, Cyprus, and Israel). This is balanced by eleven Arab countries, which have voted more frequently with the Soviet Union than with the United States at a ratio very similar to that of the seven countries which tended to vote with the United States.[36]

Sociologists have used survey methods to show that people in many countries are more favorable to world government than is often claimed. A public-opinion survey in the United States, Great Britain, France, India, West Germany, and Japan asked respondents: "Would you favor or oppose setting up a world-wide organization which would make sure—by *regular inspection*—that *no* nation, including Russia and the United States, makes atom bombs, hydrogen bombs, and missiles?" The respondents in each country favored such an organization by at least 70 per cent, with West Germany and Japan having 92 and 91 per cent in favor, respectively. When each respondent was asked if he would personally report any knowledge of illegal weapons manufacture to such an organization, those in all but one nation (Great Britain) answered affirmatively by more than 63 per cent.[37] In Great Britain, 50 per cent agreed.

In a similar vein, the European Coordination Centre for Research and Documentation in Social Sciences carried out a survey in Norway, Poland, and France during January, 1965. The study, sociopsychological in nature, attempted to discover what conceptions of a disarmed world were held by persons living in societies with different social structures. The answers are not used to draw a picture of such a world, but to explore the factors relevant to the formation of such concepts.[38]

The use of these methods raises several technical as well as ethical questions.[39] Technically, multinational surveys are likely to be less accurate

than national ones because the ambiguity present in any survey questionnaire is multiplied not only by several different contexts but by several
languages as well. The reliability of the data will also vary from country to
country, depending on the sophistication of the collectors in each. Until
linguistics is developed as a science, the parallel phrasing of questions to
elicit the same response, both cognitively and normatively, is a doubtful
art.[40]

Ethically, government by public-opinion polls is similar to government
by referendum; it involves direct interaction between a national elite and
the citizenry, with little blending of diverse interests and viewpoints
through the representative-democratic process. Sentiments often have no
chance to be dissipated, compromises no chance to be worked out. But as
long as the importance of public-opinion polls is not exaggerated, so that
they serve as one additional channel of public expression and do not replace others, they are desirable additions to the democratic process, making governments more responsive without making them excessively responsive.[41] In the international community, where few other channels
exist, public-opinion polls supply one of the few mechanisms that provide
some responsiveness, often substandard, rarely excessive, of a superpower
to the peoples of other countries.

Sociological Perspectives

Probably the most important contribution sociology has made so far to the
study of war and peace, and the one most difficult for its clients to acknowledge, is the addition of a special perspective on questions of international relations. When attending various meetings of sociologists with policy makers, I have found again and again that the main virtue of
specific sociological recommendations was the expression of a viewpoint, a way of looking at things, that would otherwise have been neglected. As Shils has said of sociology,

> Its rigorously scientifically established general truths are still very few, and
> they are not at the center of sociological thought. The achievements of so-
> ciology in concrete descriptive research are, likewise, more important for the
> general orientation which they exemplify in increasingly nuanced form, than
> for the particular details that convey it, which are themselves often only of
> transient interest. The general orientation is not the goal of sociological the-
> ory; but it is its most important by-product and precondition.[42]

Together with other social scientists, particularly psychologists, sociologists have pointed out the need for a margin of safety in international
systems to act as a safeguard against the dangers of unintentional and
irrational behavior.

Military command and communications systems that control the use of nuclear weapons are designed by engineers who are experts in operations analysis and systems development. They tend to worry about problems such as the transmission of powerful signals, the prevention of decoding by enemy agents, and the speed of communication. Being preoccupied with perfecting the technical aspects of communications systems, they tend to have a "trained incapacity" to deal with others. Social scientists, in the late fifties and early sixties, focused attention on the special dangers posed by the human components in these systems. They warned that a nuclear force might be triggered by unauthorized action, by misunderstood communications, by misinterpretation of the acts of the enemy, by psychological distortion under the pressures of a crisis.[43] These criticisms were followed by some corrections in the system, such as the introduction of electronic locks on missiles that can be opened only from a command position, the introduction of double-key systems on other missiles, and tougher psychological screening of personnel with access to command positions.

An example of this interaction might be found in the following letter the author sent to *The New York Times:*

> The events of the last few days make the question of the reliability of the "fail-safe" system all too vital. The *Times* Oct. 21 report states that Pentagon officials feel that accidental nuclear war is most unlikely to occur because of a mechanical failure, as suggested in the novel by Burdick and Wheeler, since the Strategic Air Command bombers wait in their alert positions for a positive signal to go ahead. A mechanical failure could produce garbled communication or fail to provide any, but is quite unlikely inadvertently to produce the specific code signal required. . . .
>
> There is no way to select the personnel who have access to nuclear triggers or communication commands, or who feed information to the decision-makers in a way that will prevent a mentally disturbed individual from initiating a nuclear war sooner or later. As the number of triggers grows, the probability that one such person will be found also grows. As the international tension grows, the potentially mentally disturbed are more likely to act out.
>
> The military, which has invested millions in preventing mechanical accidents, has done less toward preventing a human failure.[44]

A month later, following a letter from the White House to the author of *The New York Times*'s letter, and surely many other developments, the following item appeared in the same newspaper:

> The Defense Department is ordering precautions in all the military services against the possibility that emotionally unstable persons may somehow get near nuclear weapons and set them off. . . .
>
> These regulations will require strict screening of military personnel who

may be assigned to positions of control and handling of nuclear weapons or nuclear devices.

The regulations also will provide for screening of persons who merely have access to the weapons.[45]

Another danger to which sociologists and anthropologists have called attention is the possible lack of communication *between* the sides rather than between "broadcasters" and "recipients" on one side or the other owing to cultural differences. Thus, it has been pointed out that "the Russian word *mir* means peace; however, it does not carry over the full English connotation. Peace in English means both the absence of war and the existence of a condition of 'tranquility.' The condition of tranquility is not included in the concept *mir*. The word 'compromise' has no equivalent in Russian, to cite another example." [46]

These considerations point to dangers from within, but sociologists have also raised severe questions about the rationality of the whole strategy called the "balance of terror." The concept most often used, either explicitly or implicitly, is Weber's "irrational rationality." [47] Weber suggested that the perfection of means can lead simultaneously to the undermining of goals, until a formidable combination of means stands like a pyramid without a king to glorify. He analyzed Puritan asceticism, whose denial of gratification lost its rationale, once secularism had abolished belief in God. Similarly, the asceticism of capitalism loses its meaning, once saving is no longer necessary to provide the basis for the development of the means of production. More broadly, he saw the same ritualization in the adherence to bureaucratic rules (the means) even when this endangers the service offered to the client (the goal). Still more generally, he showed that the rational approach to life, which is necessary to the age of capitalism, bureaucracy, and science, undermines nonrational commitments to moral goals and normative limitations on the selection of means. Sociologists have applied these general observations to the continual increase in the potency of modern armaments.

The construction of the vast, complex, intricate military apparatus which deterrence requires demands high-speed computers to calculate its moves, teams of experts and electronic brains to think through its tactics, and hundreds of millions of dollars per year to keep it going. The machinery of deterrence is rational; that is, the parts are all interdependent, and each one is "justified" by the others. If one has bombers, for example, they are useless unless runways are supplied; if there are runways, they must be protected from bombs; both the bombers and their defenses need someone to command them, hence the need to protect the headquarters and maintain "jam-free" communications networks at all times. Thus, each item "makes sense" because of its contribution to the others.

The proponents of deterrence point out that the whole deterrence machine breaks down unless every one of its parts is present and functioning. There is simply no getting away with partial measures. In fact, half-deterrence is more dangerous than full deterrence, because it gives illusory strength and security. One becomes aggressive or complacent while actually being highly vulnerable. Once the enemy discovers his opponent's weak spot, he can paralyze him.

The crucial question, then, is not whether one or another item on the deterrence list is necessary; for given the deterrence strategy, they are all necessary, and there is little point in asking, "Could we do without a nuclear bomber? Do we really need more Polaris subs?" The question is: Assuming that we spend the many hundreds of millions of dollars each year that this machinery requires; assuming we build all the weapons, weapons systems, flying commands, underwater bombs, antimissile missiles, radiation counters, and what not—what will it give us? If this enormous, ultracomplex system, this investment of resources, of human energy, and of ingenuity, would yield a relatively assured peace—or at least a substitute for nuclear warfare—many of us might seriously consider buying it. In the bargain we might have to give up a large part of our income and reduce our investment in schools, medical research, and economic development, not to mention private consumption. We might even have to turn our society into something resembling an immense fortress, live in concrete-walled bunkers, put our sons into trenches, subordinate many of our basic freedoms to security regulations. Again, if this state would keep us from nuclear war, it might be worth the price.

But like any supercomplex mechanism, in this apparatus of automats and explosives, human commanders and computers, electronic beams and buck privates, something—something basic—might go wrong. It is impossible to have any assurance that such a system will function reliably. Let us suppose that the Russians invent a device to neutralize the American radar system ("fooling" the radar with decoys has been suggested) or develop a drug that neutralizes fallout the way a base neutralizes an acid; for that matter, let us imagine any other Russian technological break-through of the magnitude of their invention of high-thrust missiles, or a major security leak that reveals to the Russians our main defense gap. What is there in the strategy of deterrence to stop them from exploiting their advantage to the hilt?

One can cite numerous cases—from France's Maginot Line against Germany to the greatly feared poison gas deployed in World War I, from the American defense installations at Pearl Harbor to Hitler's "ultimate" weapon, the V-2 rocket—when all human calculations and preparations failed. Too many times the "safe" defense provides no safety; the "ultimate" weapons are lost along with those who relied on them. In earlier wars, in which the means of destruction were primitive by comparison, such failures were rarely decisive. But now a gap may cost some sixty million deaths beyond the sixty millions or so provided for in the neat calculations of military strategists.

Those who place their confidence in deterrence seem unaware that in a nuclear war one flaw may prove fatal. They are handicapped in realizing such facts by traditional American overconfidence, based on many past victories, no major defeats, long security, and 150 years of hegemony in the Western Hemisphere. There is the implication that the United States, if it desires, can build a force to maintain American security while continuing to realize domestic national objectives. But if this vast apparatus cannot yield such security, especially if, as we shall see immediately, its very construction enhances the likelihood of nuclear war, then this machine is not only not a rational system; it is systematic madness. There is no more safety in a stockpile of bombs, missiles, and guns than there is in one powder keg. And the larger and more complex the stockpile, the more likely this Pandora's box will be to spring open of its own accord—and the more awesome will be its contents.

There were sociologists among those social scientists who, through private meetings with the President, his aides, members of Congress, the press, statements on television, in paid advertisements, and in letters to the editor, kept pressing similar perspectives. David Riesman recounts:

In July, 1961, Dr. Erich Fromm and I went to Washington to discuss the Berlin crisis in the context of the internal politics of both the Soviet Union and the United States with some officials in the government and a few Senators. In the case of the latter, what impressed me was their openness toward and appreciation for people like ourselves, in whose disinterestedness they had confidence and who could discuss with them the significance of events already pre-interpreted for them by the mass media or by official briefings. For example, we could suggest the possibility that the Soviet Union's by no means monolithic and fanatical support of the Ulbricht regime was not part of an attempt to take over West Berlin, and that a settlement of the crisis was conceivable.

One perspective which I have often found helpful whether with public officials or college students or professional people is that of pluralistic ignorance. Many Senators themselves suffer from lack of reciprocal communication; thus one can find those who believe that their misgivings about a particular policy are perhaps shared only by another Senator and their two legislative assistants, and I think here especially of senators who are not on the Foreign Relations Committee or the Armed Services Committee, and who have not considered themselves experts. Any doubts they might express at a briefing could readily be overridden by men from the State Department or the Pentagon, who might not in every case either tell or know the full story behind a particular policy. To encourage a mindless opposition to the "whiz kids" of the Pentagon or the government intellectuals of the State Department would be the last thing I would ever want to do; to raise questions about styles of rationality in different social strata or national culture might help inoculate the Senators against excessive humility and deference toward experts in the Executive Branch.[48]

In sum, sociologists have suggested several perspectives:

1. They provided an institutionalized reminder of considerations ignored because of the pressures of crises and the blind spots of "trained incapacities" even though they are known abstractly in more reflective, less action-oriented situations.

2. They stressed the role of cultural, social, and psychological factors in systems in which attention had been focused on those of mechanical and electrical engineering.

3. They acted as representatives of the humanist perspective, to which social science tends to be more sensitizing than either natural science or political experience.

"Interaction" among the Four Categories

The four categories by which sociological knowledge has been structured have so far been treated as independent units. However, they also appear in various combinations and thus affect each other. But this "interaction" is more complicated than that suggested by the textbook model, where a theoretical statement is confronted with facts and revised according to the discrepancies uncovered.[49] Not only are facts often collected first and theoretical statements formulated later; the accumulation of findings to test a theorem is still a rare phenomenon, and theorems that are tested by facts and found inadequate are rarely discarded; but also much of the interaction that takes place is between perspectives and theorems and between perspectives and facts, not between theorems and facts.

Studies of the role of military institutions in democratic societies illustrate this point. Few, if any, of the studies conducted by sociologists in this area are normatively neutral. Some of the authors may not have deliberately planned to conduct a study which demonstrates that the military is (or is not) distorting democratic control; some may not even be aware that their study has a direct bearing on this question. Most readers, however, will be affected both cognitively and expressively. Cognitively, they will find new evidence for or against their fear of domination by the "military-industrial" complex. Expressively, the tone, the terms, the slant, and sometimes the findings of such a study affect their evaluation of the military and its threat to democracy.

Probably the most widely read sociological work on this subject is basically an expression of a perspective. It makes few theoretical statements in the technical sense used here and does not build its case on the presentation of a body of sociological data. C. Wright Mills, in *The Power Elite*,[50] sees a fairly monolithic power elite in the United States, at the core of which is a military-industrial complex. This complex combines varied interests and powerful elements of society with an ideology, a state of mind. The military establishment and the "military mind" are presented as a direct threat to the American democratic process. In terms of our classification, *The Power Elite* provides a perspective on American society, but scarcely considers other categories of sociological knowledge.

But our profession has contributed more than this one book to the study on an issue of this magnitude. Although there are no studies that *directly* submit the perspective put forward in *The Power Elite* to an empirical test —it may well be too generalized, abstract, and normative to be susceptible to such verification[51]—there are several studies that have a bearing on one or more aspects of this perspective. A study by Morris Janowitz, *The Professional Soldier*, is one of the best in this category.[52] He examines the nature of the training system of the United States military in detail and shows that it works to *reduce* the "military" orientation of the officers, thus weakening Mills's thesis. He explores the effects of changing needs of the military—from "heroic leaders" to "military managers"—which in turn weaken some of the sociological bases for the concept of the "military mind" and reduce the distance between it and the civilian mentality. As Lyons comments in reviewing the Janowitz work, the military managers have become highly "civilianized." [53]

Another study with such characteristics is one by Lyons and Masland, which shows that the increasing demand for officers forces the military to rely increasingly on civilian institutions for their training.[54] (A rapidly growing body of research on the role of the military in developing societies reveals similar characteristics.[55])

An example of the interaction between theory and perspective, without the direct benefit of any data, can be seen in the effect sociological theory has had on students of world government. There is a growing belief that the world will not be safe from nuclear destruction until some form of world government is established. Hans Morgenthau, known for his *Realpolitik* approach to international problems, has stated, "Total disarmament requires as its corollary the existence of a supranational authority capable of committing organized force to the defense of the legal order and the political status quo." [56]

For a while, ideas of how such a government might be created were largely influenced by legal thought. Various writers argued that a world constitutional assembly should be convened, a world constitution drafted and submitted for ratification to all the national governments, and thus a world government established.[57] It was suggested that this effort be accompanied by an educational campaign that would organize grand debates, in each nation and in the United Nations, to illuminate the virtues of such a plan.[58] Other authors focused attention on the legal details of a world constitution and government, rather than on their genesis.[59]

Sociologists have introduced important correctives to this view by stressing the links sociological theory has articulated between legal institutions and their social bases. They have suggested that if a government is to be formed and remain viable, consensus is required on both its form and its policy. This consensus is found only when differences among the various social groups that make up the unit to be governed collectively are limited or declining and when basic values as well as procedural ones are shared.[60] However, the world community is at present lacking in these qualities, and they can be built up only gradually.[61] The effect of such sociological statements has been to create a slow and far from complete revision of expectations concerning the time at which a world government will be feasible and the pace at which it will proceed.[62]

Sociologists and Peace Action

While individual sociologists have played prominent roles in the peace movement, the large majority of sociologists have not been involved.[63] The American Sociological Association has studiously avoided taking a position on this question, as it has on other matters of social action. One member has referred to the Association's "long-standing policy" of apoliticism.[64] When attempts were made to circumvent this situation, numerous voices were raised to stress and re-emphasize the notion of the ASA as a "scientific society" and hence to object strenuously against any implication of social action. However, other social-science associations have tended to take a more flexible view. For example, the American Psychological Association adopted a statement on social and political action which says, "The Association should speak for the psychological profession on social and political issues only when psychologists have a professional expertise which is clearly relevant to the issues involved, and when there is a substantial convergence of judgment among psychologists on the nature and implications of relevant scientific data." While couched in cautious language, this statement opens the door for a responsible role for psychologists as a group in American society. A president of the American Psychological Association, Charles E. Osgood, published a popular book outlining a policy leading toward peace in the year of his election[65] and used his office to interact with decision makers in Washington, including Senator Hubert Humphrey and members of the United States Information Agency, the Department of Defense, and the Senate Arms Control and Disarmament Agency, among many others, to bring attention to a view that he and many other, though by no means all or even most, psychologists are known to share.

Several issues are involved. One is a fear complex regarding macroanalysis, which the application of sociology to international problems entails. A hardly novel historical approach to sociology serves to emphasize this point. We started with grand social theories, formulated in emotion-laden terms (such as progress), covering no more and no less than all of history and all of mankind; we began by flying so high on the verbal trapeze that most of our propositions could not be pinned down, and those that could be often did not withstand empirical tests. The grand designs collapsed.[66] Then we chose to advance step by step.[67] Research tools were developed by studying the radio listening of housewives, and concepts were sharpened by analyzing small groups of college sophomores. Such a concentration was essential for a transitional period; but work that is quite suitable for a transitional stage is inadequate, even inhibiting, if it remains the prevailing focus. Sociological theory is to be further extended and methods of collecting and analyzing data improved, but sociology is now ready for the study of macro-units.

Another reason sociology, as a profession, has shied away from macroanalysis is the fear of value judgments, which seem to be more rampant in macro- than in microanalysis. Weber's bequest is the separation of understanding from criticism, which is the basis of all rational, and hence scientific, analysis. But Weber carefully distinguished between a *wert-frei* and a *wert-los* approach (between one free of values and one without values, or literally valueless). A *wert-frei* sociologist holds his values in abeyance while he follows the guidelines his data reveal, allowing them to speak, rather than imposing on the data the findings he prefers. Thus, he is "free" from values while engaging in the procedural act of science. But this is not to imply that the work of the very same sociologist needs to be *wert-los*, either in his professional or his citizen role.

In his professional role, the sociologist, like any other scientist, must choose his research topic by nonscientific, normative criteria. "Must"—because there are no intrinsically scientific criteria for this selection. One might say one ought to fill in the lacunae of sociological theory. But as there are more unknown than known spots, how is one to tell, on what scientific consideration, which to fill first? Moreover, since so much of our theoretical work is tentative, rechecking the known is as important as exploring the unknown. Hence, the list of topics a sociologist can legitimately choose from for his study is inexhaustive. Selection is thus invariably determined by intellectual curiosity, aesthetic values, fads, career interests, availability of funds, leadership of senior colleagues, and so on. But there is nothing intrinsic in sociology as a discipline that makes the study of macroscopic units less respectable than the study of microscopic ones, now that it is equipped with the basic skills and tools necessary to study both kinds of units.

Finally, sociological scientism is revealed in the research attitude toward social action of many members of the profession. This is a severe case of the inroads that the professional role of the sociologist has made into his role as a member of the community's educated elite. This is a question not just of being a poor citizen but of not living up to a special social obligation that we have as persons who know society expertly. To indicate more clearly what I have in mind, let me point to a term that is helpful for social as well as sociological analysis: *role pairs.* Role pairs are roles that frequently appear together in a society, in the sense that they are played by the same actor. The importance of such combinations is that they provide the most effective means of communication known between two roles: personal union. They also allow economy of resources, such as that found in the housewife-mother, watchman–elevator-boy, teacher-researcher, doctor–medical professor.

The role pair of sociologist-intellectual is a particularly effective one. Not that all sociologists have ever been intellectuals, or all intellectuals sociologists, but there seems to have been a much higher degree of overlap in earlier generations. The growing tendency to disassociate the two roles is particularly dysfunctional because the effectiveness of such a role combination is greater now than it was in the days when it was more common, for now sociology commands a body of theory and methodology as well as a store of validated knowledge about man in society which can provide a much-needed background for speculation about society.[68] The social analysis of Daniel Bell, Lewis Coser, Nathan Glazer, David Riesman, Denis Wrong, and other contemporary sociologists who fulfill this role pair is much more hardheaded, soundly based, and politically sophisticated than that provided by earlier generations of social analysts or that of their former college mates who majored in English literature and still interpret the American scene in the light of moods revealed in *Moby Dick* or "understand" the Soviet Union because they have suffered with Dostoevsky and Pasternak.

As a discipline, sociology does not encourage, or at least does not train for, the sociologist-intellectual pairing of roles. In earlier days the clergy and radical movements provided the sparks that fused sociological training with policy concern. Today, in the age of specialization, more and more sociologists feel that what is proper behavior in their role as scientists is proper behavior in their community role as well; the only way they face a policy problem is through the lenses of theory and methodology. Civil defense, for example, becomes a subject for a study of attitudes ("people who fear war more are also more in favor of fallout shelters") or an occasion to try out a new computer program in mass dynamics. The sociologist's scientific role is pre-empting time, energy, and resources that belong to his role as intellectual, as one who is committed to the study of policy. Thus not only is he against nuclear war; he applies his knowledge of society to understand why nations become inflexible in the face of such a danger, "freezing" rather than acting, and he shares his analysis with those who seek to reduce the danger by political action, but lack the benefits of the sociologist's training and expertise.

Most of these considerations would apply to social action in other matters, let us say civil rights, just as much as to questions of peace and disarmament. However, there is one special consideration. Many of us who work in this area have a sense of urgency, of crisis. While such a sense is common among those committed to most action courses—civil-rights leaders, for instance, feel that now is the time for all men to speak up and work for realization of the American dream—the emergency created by the threat to the very survival of civilization seems more total, immediate, and definitive than any other; the danger of nuclear war seems at least as imminent as Nazi rule in Germany did in the late twenties. Is this not the kind of occasion when special dispensation has to be given from norms of professional purism that seem absolute in less extreme situations? Jews are sometimes entitled not to fast on the Day of Atonement, Catholics to eat meat on Friday in an emergency. Could not the ASA's official stand against social action be more loosely interpreted, given the circumstances? Would members who hold these norms as standards to judge their more action-oriented colleagues not do better to be more tolerant in this situation? Whatever the answer, it will have much bearing on the usefulness of sociology for the advancement of peace and disarmament.

REFERENCES

NOTE: *This chapter is the outgrowth of the author's work at the Institute of War and Peace Studies at Columbia University. The methodological discussion of the non-conventional applications of sociological findings benefited from Project DA-DSS-W-49-083-66-01 of the Advance Research Projects Agency, Department of Defense, in progress. I am indebted to Patricia Nash, Ruth Leeds, and William Vickrey for comments on an earlier version of this article.*

1. Hearing before U.S. Senate Committee on Foreign Relations, February 23, 1965.
2. The data were collected by the American Institute of Public Opinion. I am grateful to Mrs. Leiba Brown for providing them.
3. Donald N. Michael, in "The Beginning of the Space Age and American Public Opinion," *Public Opinion Quarterly*, XXIV, No. 4 (Winter, 1960), 573–582, stated that 54 per cent of the American public had never heard of a space satellite six months before the Sputnik was launched. Only 20 per cent of the population had any real idea of the nature and purpose of such a satellite. (He obtained the data from the Survey Research Center at the University of Michigan.)
4. The Opinion Research Corporation, in "America's Reaction to the New Soviet Challenge" (Princeton: February, 1958), p. A8, reported that almost half the respondents were shocked by the launching of Sputnik.
5. Quoted in Donald W. Cox, *The Space Race* (Philadelphia: Chilton, 1962), pp. 17, 28.

6. Samuel Lubell, "Sputnik and American Public Opinion," *Columbia University Forum*, I, No. 1 (Winter, 1957), 18.
7. *The New York Times*, May 26, 1961, p. 12.
8. *Ibid.*, July 7, 1963, p. 1E.
9. Washington *Post*, September 16, 1963.
10. United States Senate, Committee of Foreign Relations, *Nuclear Test Ban Treaty: Hearings on Executive M*, 88th Congress, 1st Session, August 12–17 (Washington, D.C.: Government Printing Office, 1963), pp. 97–109. For additional documentation and discussion of the Kennedy experiment see the author's "A Gradualist Strategy at Work," in his *Studies in Social Change* (New York: Holt, Rinehart and Winston, 1966), pp. 57–78.
11. An indication of what such a challenge would be like can be seen in General Thomas S. Power's book *Design for Survival* (New York: Coward-McCann, 1965). He argues that one cannot arm and disarm at the same time.
12. Kenneth Holland, President of the Institute for International Education, has said that educational exchange programs have "become a major instrument of United States foreign policy in disseminating aid and knowledge and promoting mutual understanding throughout the world." "For Understanding and Knowledge," *Bulletin of the Atomic Scientists*, XXI, No. 4 (April, 1965), 45.
13. Daniel Lerner, "French Businessmen Look at the E.D.C.," *Public Opinion Quarterly*, XX, No. 1 (Spring, 1956), 212–221. Lerner provides figures only in the form of ratios.
14. See Herman Kahn, *On Thermonuclear War* (Princeton: Princeton University Press, 1960), especially Chapter 2, pp. 76, 82, 83. "Will the Survivors Envy the Dead?"
15. Robert A. Dentler and Phillips Cutright, *Hostage America* (Boston: Beacon, 1963), pp. 16–19.
16. Among the more useful journals, see *International Political Science Abstract* (Oxford: Blackwell); *Journal of Conflict Resolution* (Ann Arbor: University of Michigan); *Journal of Peace Research* (Oslo: Universitetsforlaget); *Peace Research Abstracts Journal* (Clarkson, Ontario: Canadian Peace Research Institute). Other bibliographical sources include U.S. Arms Control and Disarmament Agency, *A Basic Bibliography: Disarmament, Arms Control and National Security* (Washington, D.C.: U.S. Disarmament Administration, Department of State); Margaret Mead, ed., *Cultural Patterns and Technical Change* (UNESCO: Tensions and Technology Series, Holland, 1953.)
17. Emergent variables are those elements inherent in a system which are qualitatively different from those in less complex systems. See Talcott Parsons, *The Structure of Social Action* (Glencoe, Ill.: The Free Press, 1949), p. 35, fn. In the field of international relations, the institutionalized use of force in interunit relations would be an example.
18. Max F. Millikan, "Inquiry and Policy: The Relation of Knowledge to Action," in Daniel Lerner, ed., *The Human Meaning of the Social Sciences* (New York: Meridian, 1959), pp. 158–180.
19. Charles E. Osgood, *An Alternative to War and Surrender* (Urbana: University of Illinois Press, 1962), pp. 86–87.
20. Elihu Katz and Paul F. Lazarsfeld, *Personal Influence* (Glencoe, Ill.: The Free Press, 1955), pp. 176–177.
21. Shirley A. Star and Helen MacGill Hughes, "Report on an Educational Campaign: The Cincinnati Plan for the United Nations," *American Journal of Sociology*, LV, No. 4 (January, 1950), 397–398.

22. Robert K. Merton, "Patterns of Social Life: Explorations in the Sociology and Social Psychology of Housing," unpublished manuscript.
23. Bernard Berelson and Gary A. Steiner, *Human Behavior: An Inventory of Scientific Findings* (New York: Harcourt, Brace & World, 1964), p. 358.
24. For details of the evidence, see the author's *Political Unification: A Comparative Study of Leaders and Forces* (New York: Holt, Rinehart, and Winston, 1965).
25. In 1953, the per capita Gross Domestic Product averaged for the United States, the United Kingdom, and Western Germany was 19.8 times higher than the averaged GDP for Kenya, Upper Volta, and India. In 1962, although the increase in each of the three underdeveloped countries was greater than 10 per cent, the difference between the two groups still favored the developed countries, by an even higher rate of 28.3 to 1. Figures derived from the UN Department of Economics and Social Affairs, *Yearbook of National Account Statistics* (New York: United Nations, 1964).
26. See the author's "Atlantic Union, the Southern Continents, and the United Nations," in Roger Fisher, ed., *International Conflict and Behavioral Science* (New York: Basic Books, 1964), pp. 179–207. See also "The Dialectics of Supranational Unification," *American Political Science Review*, LVI (December, 1962), 927–935.
27. Johan Galtung, "Structural Theory of Aggression," *Journal of Peace Research*, No. 2 (1964), 95–119. Quoted from pp. 98–99.
28. Nathan Glazer, "The Rise of Social Research in Europe," in Lerner, *op. cit.*, pp. 59–60.
29. Stephen B. Withey, "Public Opinion on War and Shelters," *New University Thought*, II, No. 3 (Spring, 1962), 6–19. The study is based on interviews with a national (48 states) probability sample (1,474 individuals) of adults (twenty-one years or over) who are living in dwelling units that are not institutions or transient quarters such as hotels. Such a sample, in its size and more importantly in its manner of selection, is accurate in representing the national picture within a standard error of about 1.5 per cent. Twice this margin of possible error comes close to a guaranty of the range within which the true national figure would fall.
30. Survey Research Center data, reported in *American Behavioral Scientist*, VIII (March, 1965), 34.
31. Lloyd A. Free, *Six Allies and a Neutral* (Glencoe, Ill.: The Free Press, 1959), p. 181.
32. Gabriel A. Almond, "Public Opinion and the Development of Space Technology," in Joseph M. Goldsen, chairman, *International Political Implications of Activities in Outer Space* (Santa Monica, Calif.: RAND, 1960), p. 118.
33. Washington *Post*, April 4, 1965, p. A34.
34. "Cuban Crisis: A Step-by-Step Review," *The New York Times*, November 3, 1962, p. 6.
35. *Facts on File*, 1964, p. 423.
36. Francis O. Wilcox, "The Nonaligned States and the UN," in Lawrence W. Martin, ed., *Neutralism and Nonalignment* (New York: Praeger, 1962), pp. 127–130.
37. William M. Evan, "An International Public Opinion Poll on Disarmament and 'Inspection by the People': A Study of Attitudes toward Supranationalism," in Seymour Melman, ed., *Inspection for Disarmament* (New York: Columbia University Press, 1958), pp. 231–250.
38. *Information Bulletin* of the European Coordination Center for Research and Documentation in Social Sciences (Vienna: February, 1965), p. 3.
39. For a discussion of these problems in greater detail, see: Stein Rokkan, "Introduction: The Use of Sample Surveys in Comparative Research," *International*

Social Science Journal, XVI, No. 1 (1964), 7–18; and E. Jacobson, "Methods Used for Producing Comparable Data in the OCSR Seven-Nation Attitude Survey," *Journal of Social Issues,* X, No. 4 (1954), 40–51.

40. For further comments on this last point, see the author's *A Comparative Analysis of Complex Organizations* (New York: The Free Press of Glencoe, 1961), pp. 298 ff.

41. The problem of the proper measure of responsiveness is explored in the author's *Political Unification, passim.*

42. Edward M. Shils, "The Calling of Sociology," in T. Parsons *et al.,* eds., *Theories of Society,* II (New York: The Free Press of Glencoe, 1961), p. 1411.

43. See the author's *The Hard Way to Peace* (New York: Collier, 1962), especially pp. 45–53. See also his *Winning without War* (Garden City, N.Y.: Doubleday-Anchor, 1965), pp. 159–169.

44. Amitai Etzioni, "'Fail-Safe' Questioned" (Letter to the Editor), New York *Times,* October 26, 1962.

45. Jack Raymond, "U.S. Tightens Screening Rules for Handlers of Atomic Bombs," *The New York Times,* November 24, 1962.

46. Edwin H. Fedder, "Communication and American–Soviet Negotiating Behavior," *Background,* VIII, No. 2 (August, 1964), p. 109. See also Stuart Chase, *Power of Words* (New York: Harcourt, Brace, 1954), pp. 4–5.

47. Max Weber, *The Theory of Social and Economic Organization,* translated by A. M. Henderson and Talcott Parsons (Glencoe, Ill.: The Free Press, 1947), pp. 214–215. See also his *The Protestant Ethic and the Spirit of Capitalism,* translated by Talcott Parsons (New York: Scribner, 1958), pp. 155–184.

48. Personal communication with the author.

49. On this model and its limitations, see Matilda White Riley, "Sources and Types of Sociological Data," in Roger E. L. Faris, ed., *Handbook of Modern Sociology* (Chicago: Rand McNally, 1964), pp. 978–1026.

50. C. Wright Mills, *The Power Elite* (New York: Oxford University Press, 1959). See also Fred Cook, *The Warfare State* (New York: Macmillan, 1962).

51. For a critique of the conceptual apparatus of the "power elite," see Daniel Bell, "The Power Elite Reconsidered," *American Journal of Sociology,* LXIV, No. 3 (November, 1958), 238–250.

52. Morris Janowitz, *The Professional Soldier* (Glencoe, Ill.: The Free Press, 1960).

53. Gene M. Lyons, "The Military Mind," *Bulletin of the Atomic Scientists,* XIX, No. 9 (November, 1963), p. 20.

54. Gene M. Lyons and John W. Masland, *Education and Military Leadership* (Princeton: Princeton University Press, 1959).

55. See Moshe Lissak, "Selected Literature on Revolutions and Coups d'États in Developing Nations," in Morris Janowitz, ed., *The New Military* (New York: Russell Sage Foundation, 1964), pp. 339–362. See also Morris Janowitz, *The Military in the Political Development of New Nations* (Chicago: University of Chicago Press, 1964). Of general interest is the work of John J. Johnson, who uses a large variety of data, including novels and poetry, to support his viewpoint. See his *The Military and Society in Latin America* (Stanford: Stanford University Press, 1964).

56. Hans J. Morgenthau, "The Political Conditions for an International Police Force," *International Organization,* XVII, No. 2 (Spring, 1963), 403.

57. Among the better-known proposals for the establishment of a world government are those by Cord Meyer, Jr., in *Peace or Anarchy* (Boston: Little, Brown, 1947), and Werner Levi, in *Fundamentals of World Organization* (Minneapolis: University of Minnesota Press, 1950).

58. Norman Cousins, *In Place of Folly* (New York: Harper, 1961).
59. Grenville Clark and Louis Sohn, *World Peace through World Law* (Cambridge: Harvard University Press, 1958).
60. Talcott Parsons, "A Functional Theory of Change," in Eva and Amitai Etzioni, eds., *Social Change* (New York: Basic Books, 1964), pp. 83–97.
61. Amitai Etzioni, *The Hard Way to Peace*, pp. 173–202.
62. Philip Green, "Alternatives to Overkill: Dream and Reality," *Bulletin of the Atomic Scientists*, XIX, No. 9 (November, 1963), pp. 23–26.
63. Among the thirty-eight members of the American Faculty Council for the Gradualist Way to Peace, a national organization, were five sociologists, including Alex Inkeles, Talcott Parsons, Seymour M. Lipset, Paul F. Lazarsfeld, and Amitai Etzioni. On the thirty-four-member national board of SANE (Committee for a Sane Nuclear Policy), there is one sociologist, David Riesman.
64. Edwin M. Lemert, "The A.S.A. and Public Policy" (Letter to the Editor), *American Sociological Review*, XXX, No. 1 (February, 1965), 131.
65. Charles E. Osgood, *op. cit.*
66. This point was previously made in the author's "Social Analysis as a Sociological Vocation," *American Journal of Sociology*, LXX, No. 5 (March, 1965), 613–622. Compare to Ralf Dahrendorf, "Toward a Theory of Social Conflict," *Journal of Conflict Resolution*, II, No. 2 (June, 1958), 170–183.
67. Lewis Anthony Dexter, "A Note on Selective Inattention in Social Science," *Social Problems*, VI (Fall, 1958), 176–182.
68. For a discussion, from various perspectives, of how the role pair of sociologist and social analyst operates or fails to operate, see Alvin W. Gouldner, "The Myth of a Value-free Sociology," *Social Problems*, IX (Winter, 1962), 199–213; and Alfred R. Lindesmith, "Social Problems and Sociological Theory," *Social Problems*, VIII (Fall, 1960), 98–101. For discussion of how the two roles inform each other, see Robert K. Merton, "Social Problems and Sociological Theory," in Merton and Robert A. Nisbet, eds., *Contemporary Social Problems* (New York: Harcourt, Brace, and World, 1961), pp. 697–737; and Robert K. Merton, *Mass Persuasion* (New York: Harper, 1946), pp. 185–189.

Social Accounting

PHILIP M. HAUSER

chapter **31**

Historical Perspective

Although accounting is a well-understood practice in respect to business operations and more recently in respect to the economy as a whole, the title of this chapter, "Social Accounting," is essentially a neologism. There are no social accounts corresponding to business accounts or national accounts which provide a social, as distinguished from an economic, balance sheet or profit-and-loss statement. There has, however, been a proliferation of statistics relating to the "social" as distinguished from the "economic," and the growing corpus of social statistics may in a broad sense be interpreted, if not as a set of social accounts, at least as prolegomena to what may well become a social accounting system.

Some historical and sociological perspectives on the emergence of accounting practices and the factors associated with them are appropriate as a preliminary to the consideration of the present state of social accounting and the contribution of sociology to its development. Accounting first was a set of principles and practices for collecting, collating, and reporting information relating to the activities of an organization, so that they could be evaluated in relation to the organization's objectives. In contemporary language, accounting broadly considered is an information-control system designed to serve the needs of administrators of an organization or a program. Although such information can relate to any aspect of an organization's activities, in practice, accounting has focused on financial and

839

economic affairs. Without question the most important products of accounting systems are the balance sheet for individual firms and the national
accounts for nations.

Records and summary reports have accompanied the distribution or exchange of goods and services from the earliest times. Systems of recording
—writing and numerical notation—as by-products of permanent human
settlement and the emergence of towns and cities can be traced back to
Mesopotamia, the Indus Valley, Egypt, and Central America.[1] The emergence of paper and pen in Egypt in the fifth century B.C., the development
of government records in ancient Rome, and the preparation of tax and
expenditure statements, including perhaps the drafting of the first budget
(attributed to Emperor Augustus in A.D. 5), represent important mile-
stones in the development of accounting procedures and practices. The
church and government both contributed to advances in accounting during the medieval period.

The utilization of accounting methods for private business is associated
with the rise of Italian commerce during the thirteenth century. Double-
entry records and summary reports characterized the activities of business
ventures and provided both creditors and investors and merchants and
customers with information about their positions. Public accounting became a recognized profession performing auditing functions for business
enterprises. Public accountants were at first part-time and itinerant functionaries whose activities included the practice of law or teaching, but, by
the second half of the seventeenth century, full-time public accountants
were practicing their profession in England.

The continued development of systems of writing and of numerical notation and their use in the keeping of records and the writing of summary
reports in "accounting" and auditing are associated, of course, with the
increased size and density of population.[2] Urban living produced increased division of labor, specialization, interdependence, and vulnerability. These necessitated the development of mechanisms of co-ordination,
integration, and control which generated and stimulated the elaboration
of records and accounting procedures.

Paralleling the emergence of financial and economic records and accountants was the early evolution of statistics and statisticians. The practical maturing of this field, however, is much more recent.[3] There are
isolated instances of the compiling of quantitative information by governments on matters other than finances and data of military concern, but
governments did not embark on the systematic collection of statistics until
toward the end of the eighteenth and the beginning of the nineteenth
centuries. The United States provided for a decennial census in the Constitution (Article I, Section II). The French Constituent Assembly called
for the publication of a statistical account of the resources of France and
required a census to be taken in 1791. A number of nations were engaged

in the systematic collection and publication of statistics in the nineteenth century. Statistics more than accounting was a function of the national government. The term *statistics* referred to "matters of state," reflecting the relationship between record keeping and the performances of state function. The term *statist* was in fact sometimes used for statisticians during the nineteenth century.[4]

The emergence of mass society and urbanization as a way of life has inexorably been accompanied by the expansion of government functions with the increasing need for co-ordination, integration, and the resolution of conflicts propagated by diverse and conflicting interests. The proliferation of government functions led to more and more record keeping in the expansion of both accounting and statistics as guides to policy and action. The systematic collection of information about the state of finances and the economy, public and private, was followed by the systematic collection of information about the social order—about noneconomic matters. The expansion and elaboration of social statistics, if not entirely the result of, is at least closely allied in time with, the emergence and development of sociology. In any case, sociology contributed greatly to the progress of social statistics and, in turn, was profoundly affected by its development. This is well illustrated in the case of the United States.

In the early history of this country there was relatively little in the way of statistical information, particularly in respect to the social as distinguished from the economic, and of course there were few personnel dealing with statistics. Nevertheless, by the time the federal government was established in 1789, statistics had become an important tool in the conduct of government.[5]

Inherited from colonial times were some statistics on population which became available from 1610; on the slave trade from 1619; on the daily wages of workmen from 1621; on weekly basic diets in 1622; on exports and imports in 1697; on bills of credit and Treasury notes in 1703. Indices of wholesale prices can be calculated beginning in 1720 and tax collections from 1765. Private insurance statistics were available from 1759. These data, although they had social implications, were mainly economic in character, and they were collected primarily by reason of interest in economic matters.

Similarly, federal government statistics were first related to such matters as government finances, foreign trade, water transport, balance of international payments, postal services, and patents. Early in the life of the federal government, statistical series included data on hay, cotton, and cottonseed acreage production and prices from 1790; on gold and silver production in 1792; on iron-ore and pig-iron production from 1799; on currency stock and currency in circulation from 1800; on public land sales from 1800; on banking from 1811. It is noteworthy, however, that although the major bodies of data were financial and economic in character, some information was of a social nature. From the very beginning, for example, some statistics were gathered on military personnel, on elections, and on membership in religious bodies. Moreover, among the early series of data established by the new federal government were statistics on medical schools and dentists from 1810 and immigration from 1820. It may be observed that the noneconomic included both the political and social, a differentiation which was not to emerge, in general, until the latter part of the nineteenth century.[6]

The expansion of federal statistics in the United States, as in the world as a whole, may be viewed and traced as a function of social change—the product of the increased complexity and interdependence of the social order. This is exemplified in the history of the Decennial Census of the United States. In the first census in 1790, for example, inquiries were restricted to a few population items, the schedule calling only for the names of heads of families and the age, sex, color, and free or slave status of members of the household.[7] By 1800, the number of inquiries had doubled, although they were still limited to the same topics: age, sex, color, and free or slave status. By 1820, the census inquiries included a number of new topics, both economic and social, testimony to the new problems engaging the attention of Congress in the emergent more complex order. For the first time, the schedule included questions relating to workers engaged in agriculture, commerce, and manufacture and—also for the first time—naturalization. Within a decade, by 1830, the census schedule required the reporting of the number of deaf and dumb and blind. In the census of 1840, information relating to work activity was expanded, seven categories of work being specified. Information was also required on pensions for "revolutionary and military services." This census, incidentally, was the first on which the newly formed American Statistical Association (1839) attempted to exert influence, as was indicated in its memorial to Congress.[8]

In 1850, there was a major expansion in census inquiries. The portion of urban population in the nation had tripled since the first census sixty years previously, rising from 5 to over 15 per cent. Economic and social change were accelerating, and the problems confronting the federal government were, in consequence, increasing. For the census of 1850, Congress required six schedules. Schedule No. 1 relating to free inhabitants was a greatly elaborated population schedule. It contained inquiries calling for detailed occupational returns for all males over fifteen years of age, by reason of the growing interest in the work force and the increasingly minute division of labor. New items included a question on the value of real estate owned, a question possessing both economic and social significance. There were a number of social inquiries concerning place of birth, whether married within the year, school attendance, literacy, and physical disabilities.

Schedule No. 2 related to slave inhabitants. It required information on the name of slaveowners, the number of slaves, and their characteristics. Schedule No. 3 called for information on mortality, including descriptions of all persons who had died during the previous year. Schedules 4 and 5 were primarily economic in character, the former relating to agriculture and the latter to manufacturing, mining, fisheries, and all kinds of "mercantile commercial or trading business."

Of especial significance in the development of social statistics was schedule No. 6. It called for "social statistics" for each political subdivision, including such items as valuation of estates; annual taxes; colleges, academies, and schools; seasons and crops; libraries; newspapers and periodicals; religion; pauperism; crime; and wages. Although some of these items were also economic in character, it is significant that they were labeled as "social" and interpreted as indications of social differentiation. The census of 1850 may well be regarded as the first United States census attuned to the statistical needs of the emerging mass society and providing data for at least a crude form of "social accounting."

The censuses of 1860 and 1870 in general followed the pattern of the census of 1850. Some important modifications, however, were introduced in 1870 by Francis A. Walker, who served as Superintendent of the Census. Five new questions were added to the population schedule: two on place of birth of foreign parents; two on "constitutional relations," following the Fourteenth Amendment of the Constitution (the right to vote and its abridgment); and one on month of birth for persons born during the year.

In the census of 1880 five schedules were also used, as in the preceding census, relating to population, agriculture, manufacturing, mortality, and social statistics. There were new population questions, mainly social in character, relating to relationship to head of household, marital status, illness as well as disability, and unemployment (months unemployed during the census year). Although the statistics on unemployment naturally had economic significance, there can be little doubt that there was much interest also in their social implications.

Subsequent censuses, as conditions changed, continued to add new questions as well as to drop old ones. Some of the more important additions were questions on ability to speak English, immigration, tenure of home, and veteran status in the census of 1890. The questions relating to English and immigration obviously reflected growing concern with the problems of acculturation of large numbers of European immigrants. The questions relating to home tenure reflected the growing interest in problems of tenancy. That relating to veteran status was obviously in response to the increasing claims of veterans. The census of 1900 included new questions relating to farm residence, duration of marriage, and fertility. Rapid urbanization was draining people from the farms in the nation, creating problems in rural as well as in urban areas. Decreasing birth rates and differential fertility were also beginning to attract national attention.

In 1910, a question was added on mother tongue to provide information on ethnic origin. In 1930, questions were added on rent or value of home owned and whether the household had a radio set.[9] The question on rent or value of home owned was an effort to get at the social and economic status of families, which was becoming recognized as an important variable prerequisite to an understanding of various types of social differences. The question relating to radio was, of course, an effort to measure the diffusion of this new medium of mass communication. The severe problems generated by the almost full decade of depression in the 1930's was followed by a battery of new social questions in the census of 1940. These included questions relating to internal migration, years of school completed, and the labor force, including employment status, income, usual occupation, and social-security number. The drastic change in internal migratory flows produced by the depression led to a focus of interest on internal migration as contrasted with the previous interest in immigration. In fact, to make room for this question, inquiries relating to immigration were decreased. The new question on years of school completed was in response to the need for better measurements of educational level. The old question on illiteracy had become virtually meaningless because almost all the population had become literate to some extent. The high level of unemployment and the pressure for obtaining information on the number and characteristics of the unemployed during the depression led to a series of developments culminating in the adoption of the new "labor force" concept and the abandonment of the old "gainful worker" concept. It also led to the beginning of a new series of current as well as decennial census data relating to employment and unemployment. The question on social-security number was a logical sequel to the enactment of social-security legislation during the 1930's. In general, the elaboration of inquiries relating to workers reflected an increasing national concern with the problems of employment, unemployment, and welfare.

In the census of 1950, questions relating to income were elaborated and extended to larger proportions of the population. New questions also appeared relating to mobility. In the census of 1960, in response to the growing problems of transportation, decentralization, suburbanization, and the increasing mobility of the population, questions were introduced relating to place of work, means of transportation to work, and length of residence in the same dwelling unit.

Furthermore, apart from these developments in the Census of Population, new censuses were established, reflecting new and growing needs. The early inquiries and schedules relating to industry, agriculture, and commerce were precursors to the Census of Manufacturers initiated in 1904, the quinquennial Census of Agriculture in 1925, and the Census of

Distribution in 1930. The Census of Religious Bodies was provided for in 1906. The newer censuses include, in response to chronic problems of urban housing, the Census of Housing first taken in 1940; and in response to the chronic problems of urban transport, the Census of Transportation in 1963. Finally, it may be observed in respect to the Census Bureau that the new problems of the depression and developments during World War II and its postwar aftermath generated new and still expanding programs of current statistics to supplement the decennial census program. The emergence of current statistics may be taken as an indication of the increasing recognition of the role of statistics as a form of knowledge for current use, rather than for the historical record.

The elaboration of census statistics was, of course, not entirely an additive matter. The social statistics collected in the censuses of 1880 and 1890, for example, have not since been equaled by the census, although some of the types of data collected then are now available from other sources.

The development of the census program through the years in response to new needs generated by social change and, more specifically, by the increasing urbanization of life was paralleled by the elaboration of statistical activities throughout the federal government, all of whose divisions conduct statistical activities of some sort. Major statistical agencies emerged in the Departments of Agriculture and Labor and in the United States Public Health Service. As has been indicated, the proliferation and elaboration of statistics was a response to emergent problems. But they also created new problems: the harassment of respondents, duplication and overlap in the work of federal agencies, considerations of cost and efficiency. The need to control, co-ordinate, and integrate federal statistics led to the establishment of the Committee on Government Statistics in 1933 and, eventually, to the Federal Reports Act in 1941 and the creation of the Office of Statistical Standards in the Bureau of the Budget in the Executive Office of the President of the United States. It is the function of this office to serve as the central co-ordinating agency of the statistical system of the federal government.

The increase in statistics and their utilization was not restricted to the federal government alone. Similar developments occurred in state and local governments and in the private sector. The proliferation of statistics in the private sector—in business, labor, and civic organizations—matched that in government and for essentially similar reasons. Important private statistical data-collecting and publishing efforts include those of the National Industrial Conference Board, the National Bureau of Economic Research, the Dodge Corporation, Standard and Poor, Dun and Bradstreet, and McGraw-Hill. They include also the activities of Gallup, Roper, and Harris survey organizations and such units as Audit and Surveys, National Analysts, the University of Michigan Survey Research Center, and the University of Chicago National Opinion Research Center.

Finally, it should be observed that the evolution of social statistics in the United States in response to the emergent needs of the changing social order was, of course, paralleled on the world scene. A drive for internationally systematic and comparable statistics was initiated during the nineteenth century.[10] Great impetus has been given to this project in the post-World War II activities of the United Nations and the Specialized Agencies. In fact, it may be observed that just as national statistics were developed in response to the need for sound facts in a more complex and interdependent mass society, the evolution of international statistics reflected the growing need for comparable data in the shrinking and ever more interdependent world. The United Nations' Statistical Yearbook and Demographic Yearbook, and its many other annual and current publications, as well as the statistical publications of the Specialized Agencies, are contributing basic data for international social, as well as financial and economic, accounting and may be taken as indications of the evolving of a world order.

The Contribution of Sociology to Social Accounting

The brief overview presented above of the emergence of systematic information about the "social" in the form of social statistics is, in one sense, an illustration of the use of sociology. That is, it utilizes a sociological framework for interpreting and better understanding the development of social statistics and their function as, at least, prolegomena to social accounting. The contribution of sociologists to the development of social statistics is both direct and indirect, and it is significant. Among the early sociologists, both Durkheim and Weber provided a framework for the utilization of statistics in sociological research; and Durkheim certainly made use of social statistics, especially in respect of suicide, for sociological analysis.[11] The emergence of the "social survey," to which sociologists contributed, not only provided social statistics but also gave impetus to the collection of new types of data.[12]

In the twentieth century, the influence of sociology in the development of statistics and in their utilization both in sociological analysis and in social engineering became increasingly manifest. It is not possible here to trace individual contributions or to list all the persons involved. But individually and collectively they exerted great influence on the development of social statistics, pioneered in their analysis, and paved the way for utilization of the data in policy formation and administration.

The uses of sociology in respect to social accounting may be considered in two categories: first, the uses of sociology in the actual development of social data; and second, the uses of social data in policy and action pro-grams.

USES OF SOCIOLOGY IN THE DEVELOPMENT OF SOCIAL DATA

Sociologists have been prominent in influencing the Bureau of the Census to introduce new concepts, new types of tabulations, and new analytical procedures which greatly increased the potential of the census data, on the one hand, for social-science analysis, and, on the other hand, for use in policy formation and action programs. Being the largest general-purpose statistical agency in the federal government, the Bureau and its developments have had a major impact on social statistics. Since the census data serve as bench marks for many purposes, census concepts, procedures, and tabulations exert tremendous influence on the collection and compilation of statistics throughout the nation. Some sociologists have made their careers largely inside the Bureau and are among its highest officials.[13] Moreover, sociologists exerted considerable influence on the census by means of the activities over the years of various committees of the American Sociological Association and through membership on committees of other professional organizations such as the American Statistical Association and the Population Association of America.[14] The influence of sociology on census activities may be considered under a number of headings.[15]

Areal Differentiation Early developments in empirical sociology led to emphasis on the difference between "natural" and "political" units. It was recognized that political boundaries were the result of historical development and processes which often had little, if any, usefulness for the delineation and analysis of functional entities—economic, ecological, and demographic—and were scarcely functional with respect to specific criteria such as the consumer market, the labor market, commuting, newspaper circulation, and so on. This consideration, together with the influence of the sociological literature dating back to the nineteenth century on the difference between rural and urban patterns of life, were undoubtedly among the forces which led to increasing use of nonpolitical distinctions for purposes of census tabulation and analysis.

Among these were the urban-rural dichotomy, including the differentiation between "rural farm" and "rural nonfarm." The elaboration of this classification first centered on the "urban-rural continuum," based on classification by city size and extending to the rural-farm and rural-nonfarm areas, and led eventually to the melding of the metropolitan and nonmetropolitan areas classification with the urban-rural continuum.

The same influences led to the emergence of the "metropolitan district" concept, which developed into "metropolitan areas" and then into the present "standard metropolitan statistical areas" and "standard consolidated areas." The metropolitan-area concept was an effort to measure the functional entity which developed around the political city; and its usefulness was enhanced by introducing subdivisions of the metropolitan area, such as that represented by the "central city" and the "metropolitan ring," the "urbanized area," the "urban fringe," and the subclassification of rural elements in the metropolitan area. Work on the delineation of metropolitan and urban-rural classifications is by no means completed. Even now, further consideration is being given to the matter by a committee of the Social Science Research Council, to the work of which sociologists are contributing.

The subdivision of the nation into significant regional groupings also contributed both to the research and social-engineering uses of social data. The census classification of the nation into nine "geographic divisions" was for a number of purposes condensed into three or four regional groupings (namely, the North, South, and West or the Northeast, North Central, South, and West). The limitations of this regional classification, based on state units, led through a series of steps to the system of over 500 "state economic areas," including the metropolitan economic areas, and the identification of some 121 "economic subregions" and 13 "economic regions." [16] This system of areal units enables the analyst, whether interested in research or in action programs, to deal more efficiently with the subdivisions of the United States than is possible with information for over 3,000 counties and to combine the state economic-area building blocks into more realistic functional areas to delineate subregions and regions than is possible through combinations of political units.

Finally, another important areal development to which sociologists have contributed significantly is that leading to the delineation of census tracts, first for cities and then for entire metropolitan areas.[17] The census-tract grid had its origin in the desire to trace changes from census to census within the city or metropolitan area, especially, at the outset, with respect to health and welfare matters. Such an analysis was impossible without subdividing the political or functional unit into relatively small area components whose boundaries would remain fixed from census to census. The census-tract grid system, from a modest beginning in 1910, picked up momentum and has greatly enriched opportunities for research, for planning, and for action programs within cities and metropolitan areas.

Nativity, Race, and Ethnic Classification Given the heterogeneous population comprising the United States, it was natural for the census early to include classifications by race, nativity, and ethnicity. Sociological interest in problems of acculturation and assimilation greatly influenced the character and detail of tabulations containing these classifications and stimulated a number of racial and ethnic studies. The population is differentiated by "white" and "nonwhite" groupings, with nonwhites subclassified into components of which the Negroes are, of course, the largest. The census nativity classification distinguishes not only native and foreign-born but also native of foreign-born or of mixed parentage. A distinction is also made between foreign-born and foreign stock, the latter including both the first and second generations. Ethnic classification is based largely on place of birth of the person or of his parents. Helpful in the differentiation of ethnic groupings has also been the question of mother tongue.

The Household and Family From the beginning of census taking in the United States, the "household" was the unit of enumeration. "Household" and "family" were, in fact, synonymous terms in census usage through 1930. Needless to say, statistics based on this practice were frustrating to sociologists concerned with analysis of the family—that is, two or more persons related by blood, marriage, or adoption—as distinguished from the household, which included other persons such as lodgers, servants, hired men, and the like, as well as multiple families (two or more nuclear family units). In consequence, under the leadership of sociologists in the Bureau of the Census, the family was differentiated from the household for purposes of tabulation beginning with the census of 1940, and statistics relating to families were greatly expanded. Moreover, a classification system for families was developed which has greatly extended the analytical and use potential of the data.

With more detailed family statistics, it became possible to develop the "family cycle" concept, which has greatly illuminated the changes occurring in the family from its formation to its eventual dissolution and has pointed up the differential characteristics of the family in its various stages of development.[18]

Socioeconomic Differentiation Sociological interest in problems of social class, social stratification, and social mobility also generated pressures on the census to provide more useful data. The occupational information collected in the census was utilized over the years in various ways by investigators seeking some index of socioeconomic status.[19] The division of labor in our society, however, and the overlapping and conflict of criteria of status represented by occupational classification systems as such, left much to be desired in efforts to measure socioeconomic level. The introduction of the question on tenure—that is, whether the home was owned or rented —and questions on the rent paid and value of home owned provided a much more effective measure of status than had previously been available. The introduction in 1940 of the questions on years of school completed and income constituted a major milestone in providing a basis for an index of socioeconomic status; and this was followed in subsequent censuses by more comprehensive inquiries on income. These developments permitted the construction of more sophisticated indices of status.[20]

The Census of Housing also collected items useful for analysis of socioeconomic status, including data on quality of housing, facilities, and the like.

Demographic Tabulations: Fertility and Internal Migration The development of demography as a subfield of sociology as well as an interdisciplinary field also set forces in motion which greatly influenced the census. Growing interest in fertility as a result of fluctuating birth rates and in internal migration by reason of significant changes in migratory streams led to important developments in concepts and tabulations relating to these items. Information was obtained on children ever born, age at and duration of marriage, and multiple marriages; and tabulations were developed for the analysis of own children in households and the calculation of fertility ratios, that is, the ratio of children under five to women of childbearing age. These innovations in census data made possible comprehensive studies of fertility differentials and changes and contributed to the development of "cohort analysis" as well as to the interrelating of census and vital registration information.[21]

Similarly, the demographic interest in internal migration led to the evolving of census data so as to permit not only indirect but also direct measurements of internal migratory movements. The latter were based on the question on "place of residence" in the year or five years preceding the census. The answer to this question can be compared with the place of enumeration to determine the migrant and place of origin as well as destination. Tabulations were developed also on place of birth in relation to place of residence to provide data on longer-term movements.[22]

Finally, it may be noted that demographic interest per se, supplemented by the interest of human ecologists and sociologists, led also to measurement of other forms of population mobility. This was made possible by the question on "length of residence" in the dwelling unit and the reporting of "place of work," which would be related to place of residence.[23]

Labor Force Information on "gainful workers" based on the reporting of "gainful occupation" was collected in reasonably comparable form from the census of 1870 to that of 1930. As indicated above, the data for gainful workers became woefully inadequate for the analytical, planning, and action needs in respect of unemployment during the depression of the 1930's. A number of sociologists, in collaboration with economists and statisticians, contributed to acceptance of the labor-force concept, as distinguished from that of the gainful worker. This modification not only has provided better data on employment and unemployment on a current, as well as on a decennial, basis but also has permitted a functional classification of the entire population of working age. It is also significant that application of the labor-force concept and the methods of measuring the labor force represent one of the best-documented case histories of improvements in the methodology of the social survey, including sampling, questionnaire design, tabulation, and publication procedures.[24]

Other Population Differentiation Sociological interest in various types of social grouping also led to new and elaborated kinds of tabulation and analysis. For example, growing interest in gerontology resulted in special tabulations and analyses of the aged. Concern with the problems of juvenile delinquency and other problems of youth led to special tabulations relating to the young. Interest in the changing role of women in our rapidly urbanizing society led to special tabulations and analyses of data by sex. As special attention was focused on various population groups, census data have been custom-made to meet the new needs.

Housing Information relating to housing in the United States, as has been indicated above, was first incorporated into the decennial population censuses in the form of questions calling for tenure and eventually rent of tenant-occupied, and value of owner-occupied, homes. Social problems as well as the physical problems of the slum became matters of national, as well as local, concern. They were among the forces which led to the first Census of Housing in the United States, taken in 1940. In 1949 provision was made by law for a decennial census of housing. The Census of Housing of 1940 and 1950 provided basic information about physical, occupancy, and quality aspects of housing. Inquiries included types of structure, year built, tenure, color of occupants, number of rooms, persons per room, condition, rent or value, and facilities—water, toilet, bath, kitchen sink, refrigeration, and heating.

Continued national attention to the social and economic aspects of housing, and its increasing political importance, led to a national housing inventory taken by the Bureau of the Census in 1956. In addition to including items for comparability with the census returns, new data were collected on components of change in the housing inventory, including the number of units added through construction, conversion, and change from residential to nonresidential use and units lost through demolition, merger, and change from residential to nonresidential use.

The 1960 Census of Housing included a number of innovations. It incorporated the gross changes in data used in the 1956 inventory; it expanded coverage of private living accommodations; it included inquiries on such things as number of bedrooms, number of bathrooms, elevators in the structure, duration of vacancy, year the occupancy started, hot water, heating fuel, source of the water supply, and sewage disposal; and it called also for number of automobiles and certain items relating to equipment, namely, air conditioning, home food freezers, clothes-washing machines, clothes-drying machines, and telephones. The increased utilization of sampling procedures made feasible the increase in information obtained.[25]

Current Statistics   National concern with the problem of unemployment during the depression of the 1930's led not only to the basic changes in concept and methods of measurement for estimating the size of the labor force and its components—employment and unemployment—but also to greatly increasing resources for the conduct of statistics on a current basis for current use. *The Monthly Report on the Labor Force* which was originated in the Works Progress Administration was transferred to the Bureau of the Census when the depression-born agency was terminated in 1941. This monthly labor-force survey became a vehicle for collecting general demographic information and has, for some years now, been published as the *Current Population Report.* In effect, a sample survey of population of the United States is taken every month to provide not only current information about the labor force but also, on a rotating basis, information on various population characteristics, including the subjects of the decennial census and more. Thus, current information is available on such subjects as marital status, school enrollment, household characteristics, internal migration, fertility, individual and family income, and the like. With increasing pressure for current data for current use, the current statistical program was expanded to include current estimates on the size of population, now estimated for the United States, the states, and major metropolitan areas; occasional population projections for the United States; and estimates of farm population (issued jointly with the Economic Research Service of the United States Department of Agriculture). Results of special censuses taken at the expense of local governments are also issued on a continuing basis.

Pressures continue to mount for increasing the scope of current statistics, including more geographical information. These have taken the form of proposals for a quinquennial census of population, an annual sample census of population, and a greatly expanded sampling program that would permit, on a rotating basis, the collection, compilation, and publication of statistics for major areas of the United States, including individual metropolitan areas. It is safe to predict that the program of current statistics will continue to grow.[26]

Methodology   Although attention is focused above primarily on the substantive data which have been developed by reason of sociological interest, it must not be overlooked that sociologists also had a hand in important methodological developments which affected not only the census but social-survey procedures in general. These developments related to virtually every facet of census and social-survey procedures, including sampling, schedule design, pretesting, postenumerative checks, quality-control methods, tabulation procedures, matching studies, classification systems, cross tabulations, and indices of various types. Moreover, in the absence of adequate data, techniques were devised for indirect analysis. These included, for example, the imputing of the characteristics of census-tract populations to its residents to study differential fertility and mortality; regression analyses; and indirect standardization.[27]

Monographs   Finally, it should be indicated that sociologists had a prominent hand in the development and writing of census monographs and numerous studies based on the census. In 1920, monographs produced by the Census Bureau included: Niles Carpenter, *Immigrants and Their Children* (1927); Frank Alexander Ross, *School Attendance in 1920* (1924); Leon E. Truesdell, *Farm Population of the United States* (1926).[28]

In connection with the 1950 census, with the co-operation of the Social Science Research Council, a series of census monographs were published, including the following written by sociologists: Paul C. Glick, *American Families* (1957); Otis Dudley Duncan and Albert J. Reiss, Jr., *Social Characteristics of Urban and Rural Communities, 1950* (1956); E. P. Hutchinson, *Immigrants and Their Children, 1850–1950* (1956); Eleanor H. Bernert, *America's Children* (1958); Henry D. Sheldon, *The Older Population of the United States* (1958); Conrad and Irene B. Taeuber, *The Changing Population of the United States* (1958);[29] W. G. Grabill, C. V. Riser, and P. K. Whelpton, *The Fertility of American Women* (1958).

A similar program is under way, based on the 1960 census, which includes the following monographs by sociologists, some with members of other disciplines: Dale E. Hathaway and Allan Beegle, *Rural America;* John K. Folger and Charles B. Nam, *Education of the American Population;* Patricia Hodge and Philip M. Hauser, *The Metropolitan Community;* Daniel O. Price, *Negroes in the United States;* Alice M. Rivlin and John C. Beresford, *The American Family;* and Conrad and Irene B. Taeuber, *The Population of the United States in the Twentieth Century.*

THE IMPACT OF SOCIOLOGY ON OTHER GOVERNMENT STATISTICS

The impact of sociologists on social statistics has not been confined, of course, to the census. As in the case of the census, sociologists have exerted influence from the outside as well as the inside of government agencies. It is not possible to trace all the influences which sociologists have exerted on noncensus data, but some major impacts might well be noted.

Vital and Health Statistics Although vital registration systems were first established in the United States in 1880 for mortality and 1915 for fertility, it was a long time before the birth and death data derived therefrom became satisfactory for research and action purposes. The registration systems, in fact, did not encompass the entire nation until 1933. In this development, a number of sociologists contributed in important ways. Apart from persistent efforts to improve the completeness of registration, influence was exerted to produce tabulations based on "place of residence," as distinguished from "place of occurrence." This was particularly important because it permitted the relating of the vital event—that is, the birth or the death—to the characteristics of the community in the context of which the event could be better understood, rather than to the place of occurrence, which increasingly became the hospital, frequently located in a political entity other than that of the place of residence. Pressure was exerted over the years, also, for the improvement in the reporting of cause of death and for the development of tabulations that permitted ever more intensive analyses such as those represented by parity and order of birth, by census-type area classifications, and by such personal, social, and economic characteristics as could be placed on the birth and death certificates. Stress has been laid on standardization and uniform registration certificates and procedures. Moreover, the scope of studies of natality and mortality in relation to socioeconomic characteristics has been considerably broadened and promises to contribute greatly to policy and action programs as well as to sociological and medical knowledge. More recently sociologists have influenced the establishment of a marriage registration system in January, 1957, and a divorce registration area in January, 1958.

Also greatly influenced by sociological interest in morbidity and its consequences has been the design and conduct of surveys relating to health statistics. These efforts, sparked by the United States National Committee on Vital and Health Statistics, culminated in the introduction of the National Health Survey in 1957, providing a continuous series of reports based on a sample of the population of the United States. Even more recently established was the Health Records Survey, which will produce health statistics based on information provided by the establishments that give hospital, medical, nursing, or personal care.

Responsibility for the vital and health statistical activities outlined above, and for some others, rests with the National Center for Health Statistics in the Public Health Service, Department of Health, Education, and Welfare.[30]

Education Statistics The Office of Education of the Department of Health, Education, and Welfare has over the years developed statistical activities which provide national information about education. Schools in the United States are, of course, administered largely by local government. The compilation of national educational statistics is, therefore, largely a task of assembling the data resulting from independent school systems in the fifty states, including some 30,000 school districts and 2,000 institutions of higher education. In addition to assembling the school data from these sources, the Office of Education also conducts a number of statistical surveys and special studies. By these means, information is obtained on such subjects as school enrollment, teachers, graduates, degrees granted, and finances. Limited information is also on hand for parochial and private schools and various federal programs concerned with education.

It should be observed that educational statistics—specifically, information on years of school completed—are also made available by the Bureau of the Census through its decennial Census of Population and current surveys. Other agencies provide various types of specialized educational information. For example, the Public Health Service publishes reports on medical and dental training, the National Science Foundation on the development of scientific manpower, and the Department of Labor on school dropouts and other educational matters related to the development of labor-force skills.[31]

Social-Security Programs The creation of the social-security system during the depression expanded welfare programs and also propagated new forms of social statistics. A number of programs were designed to maintain income flow disrupted by disability, old age, or death of the breadwinner. The most comprehensive of these is the Old Age Survivors and Disability Insurance established by the Social Security Act of 1935. Information about these programs is available through the Social Security Administration in the Department of Health, Education, and Welfare on a monthly and annual basis and embraces number and amount of insurance benefits by type of benefit, the status of Old Age and Survivors Insurance and Disability Insurance trust funds, contributions and taxes collected, and data on applicants for account numbers, family benefits, number of insured workers, and their wages in covered employment. More detailed information is shown in special sample tabulations; there are also annual and trend data. Statistics are also compiled on quarterly reports received from employers, showing the number of employees, specified pay periods, employees who worked any time during the quarter, taxable wages for the quarter, and characteristics of the establishment, such as size, employment, taxable wages, and so forth. Information is given on self-employed persons and many farm wage workers.

Statistical information is also made available for other programs, such as that conducted under the Railroad Retirement Act of 1935. The Civil Service Commission supplies data on separate federal retirement systems for such groups as military personnel, judges, and the like. Similarly, comparable information is provided by the Veterans Administration and also by a number of state and local governments with programs covering their employees.[32]

Welfare Services The Social Security Act of 1935 and subsequent amendments provided for federal grants to state welfare programs for aid to the blind, dependent children, and the totally disabled; medical programs for the aged; and the like. Statistics are on file for the number of recipients and payments under these public-assistance programs. Similarly, statistics are compiled relating to the maternal and child-welfare programs administered through the Children's Bureau. Included in this program are grants to states to assist in the expansion and improvement of services to mothers and children. In addition to these programs administered by the Department of Health, Education, and Welfare are others for the support of vocational-rehabilitation services for the physically and mentally handicapped and for training rehabilitation personnel for research and demonstration projects in the field of vocational rehabilitation. These programs also generate statistics which are released periodically.[33]

Manpower, Employment, and Labor Statistics It has been observed that the census makes available basic labor-force statistics in the decennial census and, in co-operation with the Bureau of Labor Statistics, in a series of current reports. Many other types of data relating to manpower and employment are to be had through the Department of Labor. These include estimates of employment, hours, and earnings in nonagricultural establishments prepared under a joint federal-state program. These data are supplemented by figures for specific industries available through other federal agencies such as the Interstate Commerce Commission and the Civil Service Commission. The Bureau of Labor Statistics also conducts an annual survey of the number of scientists, engineers, and technicians on industry payrolls, reported by type of scientist and function. Estimates of agricultural employment are made available through the Department of Agriculture in its Statistical Reporting Service.

Some 1,800 local employment offices operated by state employment security agencies affiliated with the Bureau of Employment Security in the Department of Labor are also sources of basic information about the labor force. These offices provide continuous information on local labor-market conditions. Area labor-market reports contain information on employment and anticipated labor requirements and labor turnover by industry; estimates of unemployment, including insured unemployment; and some information on labor demand and supply.

A wide range of additional types of information relating to manpower is made available through the Department of Labor, including data on industrial training, productivity estimates, labor turnover, industrial injuries, work stoppages, collective bargaining, and foreign labor.

Finally, it may be observed that important types of information are provided through the Bureau of Employment Security on unemployment insurance, also established under the Social Security Act of 1935. The data include total amount of employment insurance claims by state for some 145 major and local areas on a weekly basis. Monthly data are also compiled, giving state figures on initial claims, weeks of unemployment claims, weeks compensated, benefits paid, average weekly members insured, disqualifications, allowances to dependents, and similar data.[34]

Much of the information relating to labor force and manpower, of course, is economic rather than social in character. Many of these series of data, however, have important social implications and utility in relation to sociological analysis as well as action programs. In any case, sociologists have also participated in the development of these programs and helped to make them available in a form to maximize their utility.

Immigration and Naturalization The basic information on immigrants and naturalization has been made available, over the years, through the Immigration and Naturalization Services, Department of Justice. Statistics are compiled and presented on admissions of both immigrants and nonimmigrants (tourists, students, visitors for business, foreign officials, and so on). Statistics are shown on country or region of birth; last permanent residence; basis of admission under the immigration laws; sex, age, occupation; marital status of immigrants; and the like. Alien population is shown by nationality and state of residence. Data are presented on characteristics of persons naturalized as United States citizens, along with information on country of former allegiance.[35]

Criminal and Judicial Statistics The administration of criminal justice in the United States is performed largely through state and local governments. In consequence, there is no single source of comprehensive information on crime, criminals, and the administration of criminal justice for the nation as a whole. Some data are available, however, in the establishment and elaboration of which sociologists have made important contributions. The Federal Bureau of Investigation publishes *Crime in the United States—Uniform Crime Reports*. These reports give statistics on seven classes of offenses known to police for the United States and for standard metropolitan statistical areas. The data include information on arrests by offense, on age, sex, and race of the offenders. Statistics are based on reports from local police departments and are still plagued with problems of definition and comparability.

The administrative office of the United States Courts issues annual and quarterly reports on activity of the courts including data on criminal cases as well as civil cases, the former including information on type of offense, number of defendants, disposition of the case, and probation. Civil court statistics are also collected and published.

The Children's Bureau in the Department of Health, Education, and Welfare collects and annually publishes juvenile court statistics. The data show the number of juvenile cases by type of court, by sex, and on a sample basis. Supplementary information from courts in large cities is also obtained on the offense and type of disposition. Interestingly enough, at the present time there are no nationwide data on state courts handling adult offenders. Such a series was begun by the Bureau of the Census in 1932, but was discontinued in 1946.

The Bureau of Prisons in the Department of Justice issues statistics on prisoners in state and federal correctional institutions for adult offenders. This program includes detailed reports on admissions and releases and annual reports on executions and personnel employed in state and federal institutions. It also provides data relating to federal prisoners and parollees.

Although sociologists have over the years exerted pressures for the improvement in statistics relating to offenders, juvenile and adult, as well as data on the administration of criminal justice, much remains to be done to obtain comprehensive and comparable information.[36]

Other Social Data   Many other types of statistics are collected by the federal government, most of them needed for economic and financial analysis, which nevertheless have important social implications. In consequence, these statistics have also been subject to the influences exerted by sociologists. Among them are the statistics related to consumer income, expenditures, and savings which are provided in various forms by the Bureau of the Census, the Bureau of Labor Statistics, and the Economic Research Service in the Department of Agriculture; distribution statistics— data relating to wholesale, retail, and the service trades—obtained largely through the Bureau of the Census; production statistics, through the Bureau of the Census and the Department of Agriculture and other agencies; statistics relating to transportation, public utilities, and communication to which many agencies contribute, including the Bureau of the Census in the new Census of Transportation initiated in 1963. The National Science Foundation is providing increasing information about resources for research and development, including material on social-science research activities. Also, of more than tangential interest, to complete the picture of social statistics which can be utilized for social accounting, are the growing bodies of data relating to public lands, parks, recreation, and elections.[37]

USES OF SOCIAL DATA IN POLICY AND ADMINISTRATION

It is not always possible to attribute the uses of social data in policy and action directly to the influence of sociology. It has been indicated that many different forces have contributed to the emergence and evolution of the social statistics, and similarly many disciplines, including sociology, have had a part in the application of social statistics to problem solution. Nevertheless, it cannot be denied that sociology can well claim some credit, not only for the development of social data but also for their application and use.

A very important general contribution of sociology, and the social sciences in general in respect to the use of social data, lies in the acceleration they have effected in their quantification. In addition, sociologists and other social scientists have pressed for the use of such data in the solution of social problems. For example, Professor Richmond Mayo-Smith, writing in 1910, observed, "We are surrounded by sociological or social problems which urgently demand solution. We cannot wait for the completed science; we must seek to understand the conditions affecting the particular problem before us. This may be called practical sociology. Everywhere in this domain we find statistics a useful instrument of investigation." [38]

The quantification of social data has become ever more feasible as sociologists and others have contributed to the development of better methods of measurement and to the improvement of general statistical methodology, including more efficient sampling of human population, better design of schedules, the introduction of pretesting and postenumeration surveys, the development of various methods of evaluating the quality of the data obtained, and the general analysis of error and its sources. Sociology in general and many individual sociologists have contributed greatly to the proliferation of sample surveys as an instrument for obtaining data for policy formation and action programs in many fields. [39]

The Federal Government　It has been indicated that social statistics were generated largely by social-engineering needs and especially needs felt by the federal government. It follows, then, that social statistics have been so widely used by the government in planning and in administration that examples are legion. Only a few of the more important can be cited here.

A relatively early major example is to be found in the activities of the President's Research Committee on Social Trends. The committee was chaired by an economist, Dr. Wesley C. Mitchell, but the Director of Research was a sociologist, William F. Ogburn. In his foreword to the two-volume report, President Herbert Hoover stated, "It should serve to help all of us to see where the social stresses are occurring and where the major efforts should be undertaken to deal with them constructively." The two large summary volumes published by the committee were supplemented by thirteen monographs, about half of them written by sociologists.[40] It is impossible to trace the full impact of these studies on policy and administration, but the authoritative intelligence they contributed on a wide range of problems undoubtedly had great influence in many directions, public and private, in the decades which followed their publication.

A more specific major use of social statistics is to be found in the establishment of the social-security system in the 1930's. The President's Committee on Economic Security, which conducted the basic social research and prepared the estimates which paved the way for the drafting of the social-security legislation, although chaired by an economist, Professor Edwin C. Witte, nevertheless employed sociologists in the conduct of its activities. The staff of the committee analyzed social data, using projective and estimation techniques that indicated the number and characteristics of potential beneficiaries under the various social-security programs, including both the insurance programs and the assistance programs. Thus social scientists, including sociologists employing social statistics, not only played a prominent part in establishing the framework for the social-security system but also continued to play a role in the evaluation of the program and in its various amendments over the years.[41]

Social scientists, including sociologists, also contributed materially to the conduct of World War II. Census and other types of data were utilized in the initial establishment and operation of the selective-service system, including the setting of draft quotas, and in estimating the supply of manpower for military as well as civilian purposes. The sample social survey became a powerful instrument in the hands of the Research Branch of the Information and Education Division of the United States Army. The data it collected on the attitudes of the American soldier during the war provided knowledge underlying many decisions affecting recruitment, training, utilization, and eventual discharge of the armed forces. Particularly important was the employment of social statistics as a basis for facilitating the adjustment of the American soldier to army life.[42]

Social statistics collected, analyzed, or applied by sociologists, among others, contributed materially to other aspects of national security. Wartime rationing programs were to a considerable extent planned and administered on the basis of census and other forms of social statistics. Programs for civilian defense, during and subsequent to the war, were similarly designed to a considerable extent on the basis of the social statistics which were available. Programs relating to agriculture were benefited by the flow of social-survey statistics which were greatly extended.

Widespread use of social statistics, also involving sociologists, can be found in the planning and conduct of public-health programs at the federal, state, and local levels. Basic census and vital statistics have been supplemented, over the years, by special surveys including morbidity surveys, as indicated above, culminating in the National Health Survey which provides a continuous flow of information for the planning and administration of health programs, public and private.

Public-housing and urban-renewal programs, similarly, are heavy consumers of social statistics. The Census of Housing and current housing statistics played a prominent role in the planning, administration, and evaluation of federal, state, and local programs. Especially useful to the housing and urban-renewal agencies have been the small-area statistics collected by the census, including not only the census-tract data but also the tabulations by individual city blocks.

One of the more recent utilizations of social statistics for long-range planning is afforded by the work of the Outdoor Resources Recreation Review Commission, charged by Congress with the task of reviewing the present and prospective needs of the American people for outdoor recreation resources. In some twenty-seven volumes, to which sociologists have materially contributed, it has published eloquent testimony on present and future outdoor recreational needs.[43]

Another very significant area in which the utilization of social statistics has played a prominent role is that relating to civil rights and equality of opportunity. Social statistics have been effectively utilized in measuring the differences in opportunity and achievement for our diverse ethnic and racial stocks. More specifically, they have been drawn upon in an important way in the civil-rights program. Their significance is illustrated by an experience in which the writer was involved some years ago in an executive session of a committee of the United States House of Representatives. Bitter opposition was voiced to the inclusion of the question on years of school completed and income in the census of 1940 by a southern member of this committee, who explicitly stated that the data were sure to be used "to help make the Niggers dissatisfied." It is perhaps pertinent to observe that his forebodings in 1939 were well founded, as revealed by subsequent developments.

Great impetus was given, of course, to the cause of the Negro in his quest for equal opportunity and full civil rights by the magnum opus *The American Dilemma*. Although the author was Gunnar Myrdal, more an economist than a sociologist, sociologists played prominent roles in the research and consultation, including the collection and analysis of social statistics, on which the work was based.[44]

Finally, it may be noted in view of the current interest in school desegregation that the census and other statistics, available by census tracts and other small areas within the city, have provided a basis for planning school integration throughout the United States.

Still another example of the utilization of social statistics in a significant way is afforded in the developing antipoverty program. In this field, an explicit form of social accounting is practiced in differentiating those afflicted with poverty from the affluent. Moreover, social statistics permit a reasonably detailed analysis of the characteristics of the poor to provide a basis for organizing programs to deal with the basic causes of poverty. The data reveal such factors as lack of education, lack of skills, and excessive family size, on the one hand, and on the other, the depletion of area resources and the erosion of economic base. A very important element in the antipoverty program, the provision for increasing federal aid to education, will be greatly dependent on the availability of social statistics to delineate the population which is eligible for the aid, to allocate the funds available, and to measure the impact of the program as it develops.

Finally, in concluding the consideration of uses of social data by the federal government and the public it serves, reference should be made to the use of population statistics as a basis for the allocation of funds, including grants-in-aid. In the United States Department of Health, Education, and Welfare alone, programs which use population figures as an element in the distribution of grants-in-aid or financial assistance include the following: (1) in the Office of the Secretary, educational television construction, surplus property; (2) in the Public Health Service, research on cancer, chronic illness, the aged, general health, and heart disorders; construction of hospitals and medical facilities; work in mental health and radiological health; control of tuberculosis and water pollution; (3) in the Office of Education, acquisition of laboratory and other special equipment; supervisory and related services; guidance, counseling, and testing; state programs; vocational and technical education; land-grant colleges; library services and construction; adult basic education; work-study program; (4) in the Vocational Rehabilitation Administration, extension and improvement of vocational-rehabilitation services; (5) in the Welfare Administration, maternal and child-health services; crippled children's services; child-welfare services.[45]

The new antipoverty and educational programs also employ population data as a factor in the allocation of funds. Programs in other federal agencies similarly use population data for allocation of funds and services.

State and Local Areas Many of the federal government's uses of social statistics are, of course, paralleled by comparable uses by state and local governments. This is particularly true in respect to such programs as public health and welfare, public housing, urban renewal, and public roads. A major and increasing use of social statistics at the state and local levels is to be found in such activities as city, metropolitan area, and regional planning. In connection with these functions, the small-area data, including those by census tract and city blocks, are particularly useful.

Other local governmental uses of social statistics include planning for educational needs, including school plants and their location, teachers, and other educational facilities; and the design of special programs to meet special needs such as those represented by integration programs, adult education, vocational education, and programs for the socially disadvantaged or culturally deprived. The use of social statistics also figures prominently in programs designed to deal with juvenile delinquency and crime, recreation, transportation, traffic control, sewage, water supply, and so on. Furthermore, in many states population data serve to set government personnel schedules, salary rates, local government powers, and the like.

A specific example of the uses of social statistics and sociology at the local government level is afforded by the programs of the Chicago Community Inventory and the Population Research and Training Center at the University of Chicago. The Chicago Community Inventory was established at the University of Chicago in 1946 to serve as a focal point for statistics and studies focused on the city and metropolitan area of Chicago. The idea for the project was initiated by Ernest W. Burgess and Louis Wirth, who believed that an "inventory" of the facts about the area, maintained on a current basis, would be useful for local policy and administrative purposes and also serve as a basis for significant sociological research. Since 1946 this organization has performed a number of services, including (1) the collection of new data, as in the sample census of Chicago in 1949; (2) analysis of census and other data for local agencies, including public agencies such as the Department of City Planning, the Community Renewal Program, the Board of Education, and the Department of Health, and private agencies, including the Welfare Council of Metropolitan Chicago, the Metropolitan Planning and Housing Council, the Chicago Association of Commerce and Industry, the Federation of Jewish Agencies, among others; (3) the preparation of current population estimates and projections; (4) serving as liaison between local public and private agencies and the Bureau of the Census, as in the design of census tracts and planning of census-tract tabulations; (5) conducting basic research into urban and metropolitan problems, as exemplified in such publications as Otis Dudley Duncan and Beverly Duncan, *The Negro in Chicago*, Beverly Duncan and Philip M. Hauser, *Housing a Metropolis—Chicago*, and Karl and Alma Taeuber, *Negroes in Cities*.[46]

The same organization became also the Population Research and Training Center to provide a better umbrella for national and international studies conducted by the Center. By no means incidental in the performance of these various functions are the opportunities provided to graduate students to obtain research and operating experience as well as income.[47]

As an outgrowth of the research and statistical services performed by the Chicago Community Inventory and the Population Research and Training Center the writer, as Director, has also served as a consultant to various agencies, including the Department of City Planning, the Urban Renewal Program, the Department of Health, and the Board of Education, among other public and private bodies. In the consultant activities social statistics and sociology in general are brought to bear in the formation of policy and programs vitally affecting the city. Good examples of this type are contained in the recent report on integration of public schools by a panel on which the writer served as chairman and a report on policies for the comprehensive plan of Chicago prepared by the Department of City Planning, to which the writer served as a consultant.[48] Other local programs to which the Chicago Community Inventory has made important contributions over the years include various aspects of city planning in Chicago, urban-renewal planning and projects, public-school planning, the determination of public-school attendance areas, and the development of a program for dealing with "skid row." Moreover, the *Local Community Fact Book* published decennially since 1940 provides Chicago area agencies, public and private, with basic information about each of the city's seventy-five community areas and, beginning in 1960, with similar information for the entire Standard Metropolitan Statistical Area.

At the University of Chicago other centers also play a role in providing social statistics for local as well as national uses. These include the Community and Family Study Center and the National Opinion Research Center. Similar centers exist in other cities, although no systematic compilation of them is available. Comparable activities, however, are to be found in at least Cleveland, Detroit, Kansas City, and Seattle.

Political Parties An increasingly important use of social statistics is also evident in the functioning of political parties, which, in recent years, have become important consumers of the sample social survey designed to get at attitudes, preferences, leanings, and characteristics of the population for planning and measuring the impact of political campaigns. Although it is fashionable for many politicians to take the position that public opinion and the election polls are untrustworthy, there are few who do not resort to their use for their own planning and action purposes. Moreover, there is evidence that the public-opinion poll is playing an increasingly prominent part in the deliberation of legislative bodies at the local, state, and federal level and the policy postures of public officials.

General Public Uses of Social Data The use of social statistics for policy and administration is, of course, not restricted to government. There are very few sectors of American society, if any, that do not increasingly draw heavily on social statistics for program purposes.

In the business world, for example, various types of research organization have proliferated in recent years, including research aimed at the social, attitudinal, and behavioral characteristics of the consumer. Marketing surveys of all types have greatly increased. Census and other types of social statistics are utilized for delineating sales territories and fixing sales quotas. The data are also used in connection with locating plants, warehouses, and wholesale, retail, and service establishments. Similarly, social statistics are increasingly used in the determination of personnel policy and programs involving recruitment, training, retention, promotion, and retirement of workers. Social statistics are used as guidelines in industrial relations in general, including collective bargaining.

As labor has become more organized and unions have grown and become more solidly established, labor research organizations have also emerged. Labor is, therefore, also using social statistics in dealing with such problems as employment and unemployment, labor education, collective bargaining, and participation in the political process.

Many other types of organizations systematically use social statistics for their programing and administrative purposes. These include civic, welfare, and church organizations. Civic organizations are increasingly using social statistics for the analysis of local problems with which the community at large or the specific organizations are concerned. Private welfare organizations, as well as public, use census and other social data to obtain background information on specific neighborhoods and areas within cities or other political units and are particularly heavy consumers of census-tract information. Churches of virtually all denominations have been making increasing use of census and other social statistics for a variety of purposes, including church and seminary location and relocation, and the development of current programs of special interest to their parishioners.

Examples of specific uses of the social data could be multiplied almost indefinitely. The Bureau of the Census, alone, which has been making an effort to track the use of its statistics, can literally point to tens of thousands of requests for data for a wide range of uses. One recent tabulation of requests by type of application led to the following categorization of uses: marketing and sales planning; research planning; store and plant location; sales potential; advertising; business promotion; publication, news or magazine article, radio or television program; talk or speech; regulatory or law requirement. The same tabulation listed who requested the information: (1) public—local organizations, city governments, county governments, state governments, federal government, other governmental units, state organizations, individuals, students, universities and colleges, religious organizations, national organizations; (2) private—newspapers and magazines, utilities, communications media, advertising agencies, business services, radio and television operators, general consumer's trade associations, manufacturers, real estate interests, insurance companies, consultants, engineers, banks, savings and loan companies, mortgage companies.

A relatively new use of basic social data has recently been pioneered by the Bureau of the Census in making available to consumers decks of sample punched cards or computer magnetic tape for a 1/1,000 and 1/10,000 sample drawn from the 1960 Census of Population.[49] An analysis of the purchasers of these samples for their own tabulation purposes discloses a wide spectrum of organizations: other federal agencies, universities and colleges, foundations, business corporations, state agencies, research organizations, advertising and marketing organizations, and various types of foreign organizations. The availability of these basic sources of statistics will undoubtedly add greatly to the list of specific uses of social data. Needless to say, these examples provided by the Bureau of the Census could be enlarged enormously by the similar requests to other federal agencies.

Finally, practitioners of various types, including sociologists, representing the newly emergent social-engineering professions are also avid consumers of social statistics. These include social workers, marriage and family counselors, probation officers, vocational counselors, lay analysts, and the like.

In these and many other ways, the data to whose development sociologists have contributed are employed by the American public. What is obscured is, of course, the extent to which sociologists are also among the requesters and actual users of the data, but that many sociologists are so involved is certain.

International   Finally, it must be mentioned that paralleling the increasing emphasis on comparable international statistics, various international agencies and organizations are making greater use of social data for program purposes. Prominent among these are, of course, the United Nations and its Specialized Agencies. These agencies also make contributions to the production of social statistics.[50] Sociologists, among others, have been prominent in the United Nations and the Specialized Agencies, especially in UNESCO, FAO, and WHO, both in the production and programmatic use of social statistics.

Sociologists, among others, have pointed to the importance of social statistics for planning economic development and dealing with concomitant social changes. For example, Nathan Keyfitz and the writer, in separate missions, helped the Burmese government to plan and conduct census operations for economic and social planning purposes. The writer also served as a United Nations Statistical Advisor to the governments of the Union of Burma and of Thailand, respectively, in the establishment of central statistical systems to meet planning needs.[51] In Burma, this task involved legislation and administrative organization to create a central statistical system; the development of statistical programs on a wide front, including population labor force, industry, cottage-industry, agriculture, foreign-trade, and various other types of data including Gross National Product; the organization of a civil-service cadre of statisticians; and the design of a pattern of statistical publications. The social statistics which were collected and published under the programs initiated were extensively utilized by the Burmese planning and administrative bodies.

Other sociologists have performed similar functions in other areas. One central agency which has been particularly important, however, in the improvement of social statistics in developing areas is administered by a sociologist in the Census Bureau. Specifically, the International Statistical Programs Office has played a prominent role in the training of social statisticians and in providing consultant and advisory services to developing areas throughout the world.

It is not possible here to compile an exhaustive list of all the sociologists who have had a significant impact on the advancement of social statistics and their use in developing areas. Many have had widespread influence through international agencies, conferences, and seminars. The reports of these organizations and meetings contain the names of many sociologists who participated and who contributed in important ways to better social data in the developing areas.[52]

In general, the contribution that sociologists, among others, have made not only provided for the collection of basic data on population, labor force, vital statistics, education, delinquency and crime, law enforcement, welfare services, communication, and so on but also for the analysis of the data, for the conduct of the research, and for the utilization of the data in program planning, administrative control, and program evaluation.

The widespread awareness in the international, as well as the national, sphere of the fact and implications of explosive population growth must be reckoned among the more significant contributions of sociologists to public policy and practice. For a number of reasons, demography in the United States has virtually become a subdiscipline of sociology,[53] and the preponderant proportion of American demographers, at least, are sociologists. Demographers in general and many general sociologists have played prominent roles in disseminating the facts about population growth and pointing up their implications for policy and action.[54]

The spread of knowledge about excessive population growth and its consequences has had a phenomenal sequel over the past several decades. The threat of overcrowding has become so much a matter of international, national, and local concern that anxiety has been translated into policy and policy into action programs. Thus it is possible to trace the impact of population statistics directly into the formation of national policies to dampen rates of growth as in India, Mainland China, Pakistan, Tunisia, Korea, and Egypt and into experiments designed to measure and evaluate fertility-control programs.[55] Experimentation in fertility control is still in its infancy, and its continued development will undoubtedly fill out one of the most important case studies of "the use" of sociology.

Finally, it should be noted that the training of demographers for action programs as well as for teaching and research is done largely in departments of sociology, as, for example, in this country, at the Office of Population Research at Princeton; the Population Research and Training Center at the University of Chicago; the Population Studies Center at the University of Michigan; the Population Studies Center at the University of Pennsylvania; and more recently the International Population Program at Cornell University and the center for Demography and Ecology at the University of Wisconsin. At the University of California (Berkeley), training in demography has recently (1965) become an interdisciplinary program including sociology, public health, and economics. At these centers not only are American students trained as demographers but also, with extensive fellowship and other forms of assistance, increasingly large numbers of students from abroad, and especially from developing areas, receive their training in conjunction with center activities and largely through departments of sociology.[56]

As the world continues to shrink in size through improved means of communication, and as increased world interdependence ushers in new needs requiring new programs, it may be anticipated that new forms of international social data will emerge and greater uses will be made of them. Sociologists will undoubtedly continue to play important roles both in data development and in their application.

NEEDED FUTURE DEVELOPMENTS

Although social statistics and their utilization have proliferated, especially during the past several decades, much remains to be done to perfect "social accounting."

In the developing regions of the world in Asia, Latin America, and Africa, statistics, at best, are in rudimentary form. In fact, one of the indications of their underdeveloped economies is their statistical deficiency. As recently as mid-century about one-fifth of the world's population had not yet been covered by a census, and vital statistics were not available for almost half of the world's population.[57] For a considerable proportion of the population for which census data and vital statistics are available, the material is badly defective. For other types of social data deficiencies are even greater. In the developing regions of the world, there is still a great need for the development of census and vital registration statistics and for the organization of statistical systems that will provide the economic and social intelligence required for sound planning and administration.

The pressures for more and better data in such areas will undoubtedly mount because of the necessarily greater mix of central economic and social planning which characterizes them, as compared with the presently economically advanced areas in comparable stages. In the experience of the latter, the operation of the free market, entailing greatly decentralized decision making, produced economic development and urbanization even while the processes involved were not well understood. In the developing nations, where decision making is much more centralized, there is a great premium on having adequate knowledge as a basis for planning and administration. It may be anticipated, therefore, that statistical enterprises of all kinds, including social statistics, will be stimulated and encouraged in the near future. Great advances have already been achieved in recent years, mainly with the technical assistance of the United Nations, the Specialized Agencies, the bilateral programs of the economically advanced areas, and the great foundations.

In general, however, the key task in the developing nations, for some time to come, will consist (1) in the initiation and organization of statistical systems—including the design of statistical programs—censuses, vital statistics, current sample surveys, and a wide variety of administrative statistics; (2) in the training of cadres of statistical personnel; (3) in the procuring of tabulation equipment; and (4) in the effectuation of efficient administration of statistical programs.

In the economically developed areas, statistical collection, tabulation, publication, dissemination, and administration are, of course, in much more advanced stages. But, despite the great progress made in the availability of social statistics and their utilization, "social accounting" is still a distant, if ever attainable, goal. Moreover, great gaps still exist even in the availability of basic data for many purposes. For example, in the United States statistics are still very deficient in such social areas as marriage and divorce, delinquency and crime, law enforcement, education, religion, current population for local areas, consumer expenditure and savings, current housing, recreation, and elections. There is still considerable misunderstanding of the role of statistics in the contemporary world and resistance to their development in significant places.[58]

It may be expected, however, that the inexorable demands for more and better data will grow as our economic and social orders continue to become even more urbanized and therefore increasingly interdependent and vulnerable to friction and dislocation. The need for co-ordination and integration will result in increased centralization of decision making in all sectors of the economy and society and will be manifest in business, labor, education, religion, and other private sectors, as well as in government.

The availability of the computer may be counted on to hasten the trend toward centralized decision making and therefore to augment the demand for more and better social data. Moreover, the capacity, speed, and precision of the computer may conceivably permit the collection and co-ordination of social data in an unprecedented way. For example, with the centralized records now available about a large and increasing portion of the total population of the United States in the Social Security Administration and in the Vital Registration system, the computer may bring about a linkage in records that would revolutionize both cross-section and longitudinal statistics.[59] In effect, a national registration system may be achieved through record linkage that would represent a major break-through and produce a knowledge explosion in the realm of social, as well as economic, aggregative information. It would also provide a central record of, and for, the individual with great implications on many fronts that could permit uses both inimical to, and favorable to, the interests of the person. An example of the former would be the possible use of a centralized record in a national registration system for police purposes. An example of the latter would be the use by a physician of a centralized and complete medical record of a person or a family.

The prospect of record linkage through the technology of the computer opens up new vistas of specific types of social statistics for research, planning, and administrative purposes. Conceivably it could bring about a system of "social accounting" that in some respects, at least, might approximate the developments in economic accounting. But enthusiasm for and about the computer must also be tempered by sobering consideration of its limitations.[60] In our democratic and free society we may anticipate great resistance to record linkages resulting in a completely centralized record system; and it must always be borne in mind that the computer is the only device ever created that can make 250,000 mistakes per millesecond.

Concluding Observations

It would be manifestly inaccurate to claim that sociologists are primarily responsible for the development of social statistics. It is clear, however, that the development of the discipline of sociology, in general, as well as a number of individual sociologists, has contributed materially both to the development of statistics and to their application in dealing with a wide range of contemporary problems.

The development and utilization of social statistics parallels, in many respects, the development of financial and economic statistics and their use in accounting procedures. But at this date "social accounting" is by no means so well structured and formalized a procedure as financial and economic accounting. Nothing has yet been conceived on the social statistical front that has the definitive power and elegance of a financial balance sheet or a set of national accounts. This should not be surprising, because many of the cost-benefit types of consideration in the realm of the social cannot be stated in monetary terms, as is possible in a corporate balance sheet or in the national accounts.

Nevertheless, it must be remembered that the national accounts are of relatively recent origin and that they are still undergoing considerable refinement and development. It will admittedly be much more difficult to devise a framework comparable to the national accounts into which most social statistics can be fitted. It is possible, however, that continuing developments will suggest multiple, if not single, frameworks to permit better synthesis and summarization of social statistics. Moreover, it may become increasingly possible to simulate, if not fully to achieve, cost-benefit types of analysis in the realm of the social. The potential of the computer in permitting record linkage may conceivably result in significant breakthroughs in the synchronization of both cross-section and longitudinal social statistics. In any case, the continued evolution of social statistics will undoubtedly take the direction of making possible ever more comprehensive and precise social accounting to parallel the accounting now possible in the realm of the financial and the economic.

REFERENCES

NOTE: *Acknowledgment is made of the counsel of Dr. Conrad Taeuber, Assistant Director, Bureau of the Census, in the preparation of this chapter.*

1. See "Accounting," *Encyclopaedia Britannica* (1965), I, 78 ff.; for greater detail see N. A. H. Stacey, *English Accountancy: A Study in Social and Economic History, 1800–1954* (Gee, 1954); A. C. Littleton and B. S. Yamey, eds., *Studies in the History of Accounting* (Homewood, Ill.: Irwin, 1956).
2. Philip M. Hauser, "Statistics and Society" (Presidential address), *Journal of the American Statistical Association*, LVIII (March, 1963), 1–12.
3. *Ibid.* See also Nathan Keyfitz, "Government Statistics," in *Encyclopedia for the Social Sciences* (Crowell-Collier), forthcoming. For greater detail see John Koren, ed., *The History of Statistics* (New York: Macmillan, 1918).
4. James William Nixon, *A History of the International Statistical Institute* (International Statistical Institute, 1960), p. 5.
5. Hauser, *op. cit.*, pp. 6 ff.
6. Albion W. Small, *Origins of Sociology* (Chicago: University of Chicago Press, 1924), pp. 315 ff.
7. Historical data drawn from Carroll D. Wright, *The History and Growth of the United States Census* (Washington, D.C.: Government Printing Office, 1900), and U.S. Bureau of the Census, *Historical Statistics of the United States, Colonial Times to 1957* (Washington, D.C.: Government Printing Office, 1960).
8. Paul J. Fitzpatrick, "Statistical Societies in the United States in the Nineteenth Century," *American Statistician*, XI (December, 1957), 13–21.
9. Hauser, *op. cit.*
10. Nixon, *op. cit.*
11. For Weber's position see Talcott Parsons, *The Structure of Social Action* (Glencoe, Ill.: The Free Press, 1949), pp. 610 ff; Emile Durkheim, *The Rules of Sociological Method* (Glencoe, Ill.: The Free Press, 1938), pp. 125 ff. Also his *Suicide* (Glencoe, Ill.: The Free Press, 1950).
12. Allen Eaton and Shelby Millard Harrison, *A Bibliography of Social Surveys* (New York: Russell Sage Foundation, 1930).
13. U.S. Bureau of the Census, *Procedural Report on the 1960 Censuses of Popula-*

tion and Housing, Working Paper No. 16 (Washington, D.C.: U.S. Government Printing Office, 1963), pp. 224 ff.

14. *Ibid.*, pp. 217 ff.

15. See introductory sections of decennial census reports for definitions of census concepts to which reference is made.

16. Donald J. Bogue and Calvin L. Beale, *Economic Areas of the United States* (Glencoe, Ill.: The Free Press, 1961).

17. U.S. Bureau of the Census, *U.S. Census of Population and Housing: 1960. Census Tracts*. Final Report PHC (1) (Washington, D.C.: U.S. Government Printing Office, 1962).

18. See Paul C. Glick, *American Families* (New York: Wiley, 1957).

19. Alba M. Edwards, *Comparative Occupation Statistics for the United States, 1870 to 1940* (Washington, D.C.: U.S. Government Printing Office, 1943), pp. 175 ff; Albert J. Reiss, Jr., *et al.*, *Occupations and Social Status* (Glencoe, Ill.: The Free Press, 1961).

20. For example, U.S. Bureau of the Census, "Socio-economic Characteristics of the Population: 1960," *Current Population Reports*—Technical Series P-23, No. 12 (July 31, 1964).

21. See Census of Population, 1960, Vol. II, *Subject Reports* for reports relating to fertility (Reports 3A, 4A, 4B). See also Wilson H. Grabill, Clyde V. Kiser, and P. K. Whelpton, *The Fertility of American Women* (New York: Wiley, 1958); P. K. Whelpton, *Cohort Fertility* (Princeton: Princeton University Press, 1954); U.S. Public Health Service, National Center for Health Statistics, *Vital Statistics of the United States* (annual).

22. See Census of Population, 1960, Vol. II, *Subject Reports* for reports relating to internal migration (Reports 2A, 2B, 2C, 2D). For a major migration study, see also *Population Redistribution and Economic Growth, United States, 1870–1950*, Vol. I, Everett S. Lee *et al.*, Vol. II, Simon Kuznets *et al.*, Vol. III, Hope Eldridge and Dorothy S. Thomas, *American Philosophical Society*, Vol. I, 1957; Vol. II, 1960; Vol. III, 1964.

23. See Census of Population, 1960, Vol. II, *Subject Reports* for reports relating to "mobility" and "journey to work" (Reports 2B, 2C, 6B).

24. See A. J. Jaffe and Charles D. Stewart, *Manpower Resources and Utilization* (New York: Wiley, 1951); Louis J. Ducoff and Margaret J. Hagood, *Labor Force Definition and Measurement* (Social Science Research Council, Bulletin 56, 1947); U.S. President's Committee to Appraise Employment and Unemployment Statistics, *Measuring Employment and Unemployment* (Washington, D.C.: U.S. Government Printing Office, 1962); Philip M. Hauser, "The Labor Force and Gainful Workers—Concept, Measurement and Comparability," *American Journal of Sociology*, Vol. LIV, No. 4 (January, 1949); Philip M. Hauser, "Labor Force," in Robert E. L. Faris, ed., *Handbook of Modern Sociology* (Chicago: Rand McNally, 1964), Chapter 5, pp. 161–190.

25. See 1960 Census of Housing—Vol. I to VII; and "Current Housing Reports" as listed in Bureau of the Census, *Catalogue* (quarterly and annual).

26. The Bureau of the Census has prepared plans for expansion of current census statistics, as has also the Office of Statistical Standards of the Bureau of the Budget for federal statistics as a whole. For most recent plans contact the agencies.

27. For example, see Census series of "Working Papers" and "Technical Papers." List available from the Bureau of the Census.

28. Census Monographs of 1920 published by U.S. Government Printing Office. Complete list available from Census.

29. Census Monographs of 1950, published by John Wiley and Sons. Complete list available from Census. The complete list of the proposed 1960 Census Monographs is available from the Bureau of the Census or Social Science Research Council.

30. For principal publications, see U.S. Bureau of the Budget, Office of Statistical Standards, *Statistical Services of the United States Government* (Washington, D.C.: U.S. Government Printing Office, 1963), pp. 105 ff.

31. *Ibid.*, pp. 103–104.

32. *Ibid.*, pp. 104–105.

33. *Ibid.*, p. 108.

34. *Ibid.*, pp. 114 ff.

35. *Ibid.*, p. 112.

36. *Ibid.*, pp. 112–113. See also Harry Manuel Shulman, "The Reporting of Criminal Statistics in the United States," a report to the U.S. Bureau of the Budget, Office of Statistical Standards (draft—unpublished).

37. U.S. Bureau of the Budget, Office of Statistical Standards, *op. cit.*, see Part III, pp. 85–136.

38. Richmond Mayo-Smith, *Statistics and Sociology* (New York: Columbia University Press, 1910), p. 16.

39. For example, Samuel A. Stouffer, *Social Research to Test Ideas* (Glencoe, Ill.: The Free Press, 1962); Samuel A. Stouffer *et al.*, *The American Soldier* (Princeton: Princeton University Press, 1949), Vols. I, II; Pauline V. Young, *Scientific Social Surveys and Research* (New York: Prentice-Hall, 1942); William J. Goode and Paul K. Hatt, *Methods in Social Research* (New York: McGraw-Hill, 1952); Paul F. Lazarsfeld and Morris Rosenberg, *The Language of Social Research* (Glencoe, Ill.: The Free Press, 1955); Herbert Hyman, *Survey Design and Analysis* (Glencoe, Ill.: The Free Press, 1955); Robert K. Merton, Marjorie Fiske, and Patricia L. Kendall, *The Focused Interview* (Glencoe, Ill.: The Free Press, 1956); Frederick F. Stephan and Philip J. McCarthy, *Sampling Opinions—An Analysis of Survey Procedures* (New York: Wiley, 1958).

40. President's Research Committee on Social Trends, *Recent Social Trends* (New York: McGraw-Hill, 1933). List of monographs facing title page.

41. Edwin E. Witte, *The Development of the Social Security Act* (Madison: University of Wisconsin Press, 1963).

42. Stouffer *et al.*, *op. cit.*

43. U.S. Outdoor Recreation Resources Review Commission, *Outdoor Recreation for America* (Washington, D.C.: U.S. Government Printing Office, 1962). For complete list of publications see Appendix C, pp. 199–203.

44. Gunnar Myrdal, *An American Dilemma* (New York: Harper, 1944). For complete list of contributors see "Author's Preface," pp. ix–xx.

45. U.S. Department of Health, Education, and Welfare, *Grants in Aid and Other Financial Assistance Programs Administered by the U.S. Department of Health, Education, and Welfare* (Washington, D.C.: U.S. Government Printing Office, 1964–65 edition).

46. For fuller detail of program and bibliography see University of Chicago, Population Research and Training Center and Chicago Community Inventory, *Summary Report, 1947–63* (January, 1964).

47. See University of Chicago, Population Research and Training Center, *Statement of Program 1964–65–66* (1964).

48. Advisory Panel on Integration of the Public Schools, *Report to the Board of Education, City of Chicago*, March 31, 1964; Department of City Planning, City of Chicago, *Basic Policies for the Comprehensive Plan of Chicago*, August, 1964.

49. U.S. Bureau of the Census, *Catalogue*, 1964, pp. 135 ff.

50. *United Nations Publications, A Reference Catalogue* (annual and also accumulated form from 1945 to current year). Publication list of Specialized Agencies may be obtained through headquarters offices of the Agencies.
51. Philip M. Hauser, *Review of the Statistical Situation in Thailand* (United Nations, 1956) (restricted); also Philip M. Hauser and Evelyn M. Kitagawa, "Demographic Glimpses into Burma, 1952," *The Interrelations of Demographic, Economic and Social Problems, in Selected Underdeveloped Areas*, Proceedings of the 1953 Annual Conference (Milbank Memorial Fund, 1954), pp. 103–129.
52. For example, see United Nations, *Asia and the Far East Seminar on Population*, Bandung, November 21 to December 3, 1955 (United Nations, 1957), pp. 55–61; *United Nations, Seminar on Regional Planning*, Tokyo, July 28 to August 8, 1958 (United Nations, 1958), pp. 36–45; Philip M. Hauser, ed., *Urbanization in Asia and the Far East* (Calcutta: UNESCO, 1957), pp. 271–276; Philip M. Hauser, ed., *Urbanization in Latin America* (Paris: UNESCO, 1961), pp. 325–327; Bert F. Hoselitz and Wilbert E. Moore, *Industrialization and Society* (UNESCO, 1963), see "Table of Contents." See also *Science, Technology and Development*, United States Papers Prepared for the United Nations Conference on the Application of Science and Technology for the Benefit of the Less De-developed Areas, especially Vol. VII, *Social Problems of Development and Urbanization*, and Vol. XI, *Human Resources—Training of Scientific and Technical Personnel.*
53. Philip M. Hauser and Otis Dudley Duncan, *The Study of Population: An Inventory and Appraisal* (Chicago: University of Chicago Press, 1959), Chapter 5, pp. 106 ff.
54. For example, see Edward Alsworth Ross, *Standing Room Only?* (New York: Century, 1927); Warren S. Thompson, *Population Problems* (New York: McGraw-Hill, 1930); Frank Lorimer and Frederick Osborne, *Dynamics of Population* (New York: Macmillan, 1934); E. B. Reuter, *Population Problems* (Philadelphia: Lippincott, 1937); Paul H. Landis, *Population Problems* (New York: American Book Co., 1943); Thomas Lynn Smith, *Population Analysis* (New York: McGraw-Hill, 1948); Philip M. Hauser, ed., *Population and World Politics* (Glencoe, Ill.: The Free Press, 1958); Philip M. Hauser, *Population Perspectives* (New Brunswick, N.J.: Rutgers University Press, 1960); William Petersen, *Population* (New York: Macmillan, 1961); Philip M. Hauser, ed., *The Population Dilemma* (Englewood Cliffs, N.J.: Prentice-Hall, 1963); Ralph Thomlinson, *Population Dynamics* (New York: Random House, 1965).
55. Ronald Freedman, "Sample Surveys for Family Planning Research in Taiwan," *Public Opinion Quarterly*, XXVIII, 373–382; Ronald Freedman and B. Berelson, "A Study of Fertility Control," *Scientific American*, CCX, 29–37; Ronald Freedman *et al.*, "Fertility Trends in Taiwan: Tradition and Change," *Population Studies*, XVI, 219–236; Reuben Hill, J. Mayone Stycos, and Kurt W. Back, *The Family and Population Control—A Puerto Rico Experiment in Social Control* (Chapel Hill: University of North Carolina Press, 1959); J. Mayone Stycos and Kurt W. Back, *The Control of Human Fertility in Jamaica* (Ithaca, N.Y.: Cornell University Press, 1964); Donald J. Bogue has experimental family planning and evaluation studies under way in Chicago and other parts of the United States.
56. The Population Council, New York, has been a major factor in making demographic training available to students from abroad and especially from the developing areas. See their annual reports.
57. Forrest Linder, "World Demographic Data," in Hauser and Duncan, *op. cit.*, pp. 321–360.
58. Committee on Post Office and Civil Service, House of Representatives, *The*

Federal Paperwork Jungle (Washington, D.C.: U.S. Government Printing Office, 1965) (89th Congress, 1st Session, House Report No. 52).

59. For example, see H. B. Newcombe and J. M. Kennedy, "Record Linkage," *A.C.M. Communications,* V (1962), 563; H. B. Newcombe, J. M. Kennedy, S. J. Axford, and A. P. James, "Automatic Linkage of Vital Records," *Science,* CXXX (1959), 954.

60. For example, see Oliver C. Selfridge, "Social Responsibility and Computers," in James M. Beshers, ed., *Computer Methods in the Analysis of Large Scale Social Systems* (Cambridge, Mass.: Joint Center for Urban Studies of the Massachusetts Institute of Technology and Harvard University, 1964), pp. 126–180; also discussion of this paper by Joseph Weizenbaum, pp. 181–182.

Name Index

Subject Index